Lecture Notes in Computer Science 11362

Commenced Publication in 1973
Founding and Former Series Editors:
Gerhard Goos, Juris Hartmanis, and Jan van Leeuwen

Editorial Board Members

David Hutchison
Lancaster University, Lancaster, UK

Takeo Kanade
Carnegie Mellon University, Pittsburgh, PA, USA

Josef Kittler
University of Surrey, Guildford, UK

Jon M. Kleinberg
Cornell University, Ithaca, NY, USA

Friedemann Mattern
ETH Zurich, Zurich, Switzerland

John C. Mitchell
Stanford University, Stanford, CA, USA

Moni Naor
Weizmann Institute of Science, Rehovot, Israel

C. Pandu Rangan
Indian Institute of Technology Madras, Chennai, India

Bernhard Steffen
TU Dortmund University, Dortmund, Germany

Demetri Terzopoulos
University of California, Los Angeles, CA, USA

Doug Tygar
University of California, Berkeley, CA, USA

More information about this series at http://www.springer.com/series/7412

C. V. Jawahar · Hongdong Li ·
Greg Mori · Konrad Schindler (Eds.)

Computer Vision – ACCV 2018

14th Asian Conference on Computer Vision
Perth, Australia, December 2–6, 2018
Revised Selected Papers, Part II

Springer

Editors
C. V. Jawahar
IIIT Hyderabad
Hyderabad, India

Greg Mori
Simon Fraser University
Burnaby, BC, Canada

Hongdong Li
ANU
Canberra, ACT, Australia

Konrad Schindler ⓘⒹ
ETH Zurich
Zurich, Zürich, Switzerland

ISSN 0302-9743 ISSN 1611-3349 (electronic)
Lecture Notes in Computer Science
ISBN 978-3-030-20889-9 ISBN 978-3-030-20890-5 (eBook)
https://doi.org/10.1007/978-3-030-20890-5

LNCS Sublibrary: SL6 – Image Processing, Computer Vision, Pattern Recognition, and Graphics

This Springer imprint is published by the registered company Springer Nature Switzerland AG
The registered company address is: Gewerbestrasse 11, 6330 Cham, Switzerland

Preface

The Asian Conference on Computer Vision (ACCV) 2018 took place in Perth, Australia, during December 2–6, 2018. The conference featured novel research contributions from almost all sub-areas of computer vision.

This year we received a record number of conference submissions. After removing the desk rejects, 979 valid, complete manuscripts were submitted for review. A pool of 34 area chairs and 1,063 reviewers was recruited to conduct paper reviews. Like previous editions of ACCV, we adopted a double-blind review process to determine which of these papers to accept. Identities of authors were not visible to reviewers and area chairs; nor were the identities of the assigned reviewers and area chairs visible to authors. The program chairs did not submit papers to the conference.

Each paper was reviewed by at least three reviewers. Authors were permitted to respond to the initial reviews during a rebuttal period. After this, the area chairs led discussions among reviewers. Finally, a physical area chairs was held in Singapore, during which panels of three area chairs deliberated to decide on acceptance decisions for each paper. At the end of this process, 274 papers were accepted for publication in the ACCV 2018 conference proceedings, of which five were later withdrawn by their authors.

In addition to the main conference, ACCV 2018 featured 11 workshops and six tutorials.

We would like to thank all the organizers, sponsors, area chairs, reviewers, and authors. Special thanks go to Prof. Guosheng Lin from Nanyang Technological University, Singapore, for hosting the area chair meeting. We acknowledge the support of Microsoft's Conference Management Toolkit (CMT) team for providing the software used to manage the review process.

We greatly appreciate the efforts of all those who contributed to making the conference a success.

December 2018

C. V. Jawahar
Hongdong Li
Greg Mori
Konrad Schindler

Organization

General Chairs

Kyoung-mu Lee   Seoul National University, South Korea
Ajmal Mian   University of Western Australia, Australia
Ian Reid   University of Adelaide, Australia
Yoichi Sato   University of Tokyo, Japan

Program Chairs

C. V. Jawahar   IIIT Hyderabad, India
Hongdong Li   Australian National University, Australia
Greg Mori   Simon Fraser University and Borealis AI, Canada
Konrad Schindler   ETH Zurich, Switzerland

Advisor

Richard Hartley   Australian National University, Australia

Publication Chair

Hamid Rezatofighi   University of Adelaide, Australia

Local Arrangements Chairs

Guosheng Lin   Nanyang Technological University, Singapore
Ajmal Mian   University of Western Australia, Australia

Area Chairs

Lourdes Agapito   University College London, UK
Xiang Bai   Huazhong University of Science and Technology,
             China
Vineeth N.   IIT Hyderabad, India
 Balasubramanian
Gustavo Carneiro   University of Adelaide, Australia
Tat-Jun Chin   University of Adelaide, Australia
Minsu Cho   POSTECH, South Korea
Bohyung Han   Seoul National University, South Korea
Junwei Han   Northwestern Polytechnical University, China
Mehrtash Harandi   Monash University, Australia
Gang Hua   Microsoft Research, Asia

Rei Kawakami	University of Tokyo, Japan
Tae-Kyun Kim	Imperial College London, UK
Junseok Kwon	Chung-Ang University, South Korea
Florent Lafarge	Inria, France
Laura Leal-Taixé	TU Munich, Germany
Zhouchen Lin	Peking University, China
Yanxi Liu	Penn State University, USA
Oisin Mac Aodha	Caltech, USA
Anurag Mittal	IIT Madras, India
Vinay Namboodiri	IIT Kanpur, India
P. J. Narayanan	IIIT Hyderabad, India
Carl Olsson	Lund University, Sweden
Imari Sato	National Institute of Informatics
Shiguang Shan	Chinese Academy of Sciences, China
Chunhua Shen	University of Adelaide, Australia
Boxin Shi	Peking University, China
Terence Sim	National University of Singapore, Singapore
Yusuke Sugano	Osaka University, Japan
Min Sun	National Tsing Hua University, Taiwan
Robby Tan	Yale-NUS College, USA
Siyu Tang	MPI for Intelligent Systems
Radu Timofte	ETH Zurich, Switzerland
Jingyi Yu	University of Delaware, USA
Junsong Yuan	State University of New York at Buffalo, USA

Additional Reviewers

Ehsan Abbasnejad
Akash Abdu Jyothi
Abrar Abdulnabi
Nagesh Adluru
Antonio Agudo
Unaiza Ahsan
Hai-zhou Ai
Alexandre Alahi
Xavier Alameda-Pineda
Andrea Albarelli
Mohsen Ali
Saad Ali
Mitsuru Ambai
Cosmin Ancuti
Vijay Rengarajan Angarai
    Pichaikuppan
Michel Antunes
Djamila Aouada

Ognjen Arandjelovic
Anil Armagan
Chetan Arora
Mathieu Aubry
Hossein Azizpour
Seung-Hwan Baek
Aijun Bai
Peter Bajcsy
Amr Bakry
Vassileios Balntas
Yutong Ban
Arunava Banerjee
Monami Banerjee
Atsuhiko Banno
Aayush Bansal
Dániel Baráth
Lorenzo Baraldi
Adrian Barbu

Nick Barnes
Peter Barnum
Joe Bartels
Paul Beardsley
Sima Behpour
Vasileios Belagiannis
Boulbaba Ben Amor
Archith Bency
Ryad Benosman
Gedas Bertasius
Ross Beveridge
Binod Bhattarai
Arnav Bhavsar
Simone Bianco
Oliver Bimber
Tolga Birdal
Horst Bischof
Arijit Biswas

Soma Biswas
Henryk Blasinski
Vishnu Boddeti
Federica Bogo
Tolga Bolukbasi
Terrance Boult
Thierry Bouwmans
Abdesselam Bouzerdoum
Ernesto Brau
Mathieu Bredif
Stefan Breuers
Marcus Brubaker
Anders Buch
Shyamal Buch
Pradeep Buddharaju
Adrian Bulat
Darius Burschka
Andrei Bursuc
Zoya Bylinskii
Weidong Cai
Necati Cihan Camgoz
Shaun Canavan
Joao Carreira
Dan Casas
M. Emre Celebi
Hakan Cevikalp
François Chadebecq
Menglei Chai
Rudrasis Chakraborty
Tat-Jen Cham
Kwok-Ping Chan
Sharat Chandran
Chehan Chang
Hyun Sung Chang
Yi Chang
Wei-Lun Chao
Visesh Chari
Gaurav Chaurasia
Rama Chellappa
Chen Chen
Chu-Song Chen
Dongdong Chen
Guangyong Chen
Hsin-I Chen
Huaijin Chen
Hwann-Tzong Chen

Jiacheng Chen
Jianhui Chen
Jiansheng Chen
Jiaxin Chen
Jie Chen
Kan Chen
Longbin Chen
Ting Chen
Tseng-Hung Chen
Wei Chen
Xi'ai Chen
Xiaozhi Chen
Xilin Chen
Xinlei Chen
Yunjin Chen
Erkang Cheng
Hong Cheng
Hui Cheng
Jingchun Cheng
Ming-Ming Cheng
Wen-Huang Cheng
Yuan Cheng
Zhi-Qi Cheng
Loong Fah Cheong
Anoop Cherian
Liang-Tien Chia
Chao-Kai Chiang
Shao-Yi Chien
Han-Pang Chiu
Wei-Chen Chiu
Donghyeon Cho
Nam Ik Cho
Sunghyun Cho
Yeong-Jun Cho
Gyeongmin Choe
Chiho Choi
Jonghyun Choi
Jongmoo Choi
Jongwon Choi
Hisham Cholakkal
Biswarup Choudhury
Xiao Chu
Yung-Yu Chuang
Andrea Cohen
Toby Collins
Marco Cristani

James Crowley
Jinshi Cui
Zhaopeng Cui
Bo Dai
Hang Dai
Xiyang Dai
Yuchao Dai
Carlo Dal Mutto
Zachary Daniels
Mohamed Daoudi
Abir Das
Raoul De Charette
Teofilo Decampos
Koichiro Deguchi
Stefanie Demirci
Girum Demisse
Patrick Dendorfer
Zhiwei Deng
Joachim Denzler
Aditya Deshpande
Frédéric Devernay
Abhinav Dhall
Anthony Dick
Zhengming Ding
Cosimo Distante
Ajay Divakaran
Mandar Dixit
Thanh-Toan Do
Jose Dolz
Bo Dong
Chao Dong
Jingming Dong
Ming Dong
Weisheng Dong
Simon Donne
Gianfranco Doretto
Bruce Draper
Bertram Drost
Liang Du
Shichuan Du
Jean-Luc Dugelay
Enrique Dunn
Thibaut Durand
Zoran Duric
Ionut Cosmin Duta
Samyak Dutta

Pinar Duygulu
Ady Ecker
Hazim Ekenel
Sabu Emmanuel
Ian Endres
Ertunc Erdil
Hugo Jair Escalante
Sergio Escalera
Francisco Escolano Ruiz
Bin Fan
Shaojing Fan
Yi Fang
Aly Farag
Giovanni Farinella
Rafael Felix
Michele Fenzi
Bob Fisher
David Fofi
Gian Luca Foresti
Victor Fragoso
Bernd Freisleben
Jason Fritts
Cheng-Yang Fu
Chi-Wing Fu
Huazhu Fu
Jianlong Fu
Xueyang Fu
Ying Fu
Yun Fu
Olac Fuentes
Jan Funke
Ryo Furukawa
Yasutaka Furukawa
Manuel Günther
Raghudeep Gadde
Matheus Gadelha
Jürgen Gall
Silvano Galliani
Chuang Gan
Zhe Gan
Vineet Gandhi
Arvind Ganesh
Bin-Bin Gao
Jin Gao
Jiyang Gao
Junbin Gao

Ravi Garg
Jochen Gast
Utkarsh Gaur
Xin Geng
David Geronimno
Michael Gharbi
Amir Ghodrati
Behnam Gholami
Andrew Gilbert
Rohit Girdhar
Ioannis Gkioulekas
Guy Godin
Nuno Goncalves
Yu Gong
Stephen Gould
Venu Govindu
Oleg Grinchuk
Jiuxiang Gu
Shuhang Gu
Paul Guerrero
Anupam Guha
Guodong Guo
Yanwen Guo
Ankit Gupta
Mithun Gupta
Saurabh Gupta
Hossein Hajimirsadeghi
Maciej Halber
Xiaoguang Han
Yahong Han
Zhi Han
Kenji Hara
Tatsuya Harada
Ali Harakeh
Adam Harley
Ben Harwood
Mahmudul Hasan
Kenji Hata
Michal Havlena
Munawar Hayat
Zeeshan Hayder
Jiawei He
Kun He
Lei He
Lifang He
Pan He

Yang He
Zhenliang He
Zhihai He
Felix Heide
Samitha Herath
Luis Herranz
Anders Heyden
Je Hyeong Hong
Seunghoon Hong
Wei Hong
Le Hou
Chiou-Ting Hsu
Kuang-Jui Hsu
Di Hu
Hexiang Hu
Ping Hu
Xu Hu
Yinlin Hu
Zhiting Hu
De-An Huang
Gao Huang
Gary Huang
Haibin Huang
Haifei Huang
Haozhi Huang
Jia-Bin Huang
Shaoli Huang
Sheng Huang
Xinyu Huang
Xun Huang
Yan Huang
Yawen Huang
Yinghao Huang
Yizhen Huang
Wei-Chih Hung
Junhwa Hur
Mohamed Hussein
Jyh-Jing Hwang
Ichiro Ide
Satoshi Ikehata
Radu Tudor Ionescu
Go Irie
Ahmet Iscen
Vamsi Ithapu
Daisuke Iwai
Won-Dong Jang

Dinesh Jayaraman
Sadeep Jayasumana
Suren Jayasuriya
Hueihan Jhuang
Dinghuang Ji
Mengqi Ji
Hongjun Jia
Jiayan Jiang
Qing-Yuan Jiang
Tingting Jiang
Xiaoyi Jiang
Zhuolin Jiang
Zequn Jie
Xiaojie Jin
Younghyun Jo
Ole Johannsen
Hanbyul Joo
Jungseock Joo
Kyungdon Joo
Shantanu Joshi
Amin Jourabloo
Deunsol Jung
Anis Kacem
Ioannis Kakadiaris
Zdenek Kalal
Nima Kalantari
Mahdi Kalayeh
Sinan Kalkan
Vicky Kalogeiton
Joni-Kristian Kamarainen
Martin Kampel
Meina Kan
Kenichi Kanatani
Atsushi Kanehira
Takuhiro Kaneko
Zhuoliang Kang
Mohan Kankanhalli
Vadim Kantorov
Nikolaos Karianakis
Leonid Karlinsky
Zoltan Kato
Hiroshi Kawasaki
Wei Ke
Wadim Kehl
Sameh Khamis
Naeemullah Khan

Salman Khan
Rawal Khirodkar
Mehran Khodabandeh
Anna Khoreva
Parmeshwar Khurd
Hadi Kiapour
Joe Kileel
Edward Kim
Gunhee Kim
Hansung Kim
Hyunwoo Kim
Junsik Kim
Seon Joo Kim
Vladimir Kim
Akisato Kimura
Ravi Kiran
Roman Klokov
Takumi Kobayashi
Amir Kolaman
Naejin Kong
Piotr Koniusz
Hyung Il Koo
Dimitrios Kosmopoulos
Gregory Kramida
Praveen Krishnan
Ravi Krishnan
Hiroyuki Kubo
Hilde Kuehne
Jason Kuen
Arjan Kuijper
Kuldeep Kulkarni
Shiro Kumano
Avinash Kumar
Soumava Roy Kumar
Kaustav Kundu
Sebastian Kurtek
Yevhen Kuznietsov
Heeseung Kwon
Alexander Ladikos
Kevin Lai
Wei-Sheng Lai
Shang-Hong Lai
Michael Lam
Zhenzhong Lan
Dong Lao
Katrin Lasinger

Yasir Latif
Huu Le
Herve Le Borgne
Chun-Yi Lee
Gim Hee Lee
Seungyong Lee
Teng-Yok Lee
Seungkyu Lee
Andreas Lehrmann
Na Lei
Spyridon Leonardos
Marius Leordeanu
Matt Leotta
Gil Levi
Evgeny Levinkov
Jose Lezama
Ang Li
Chen Li
Chunyuan Li
Dangwei Li
Dingzeyu Li
Dong Li
Hai Li
Jianguo Li
Stan Li
Wanqing Li
Wei Li
Xi Li
Xirong Li
Xiu Li
Xuelong Li
Yanghao Li
Yin Li
Yingwei Li
Yongjie Li
Yu Li
Yuncheng Li
Zechao Li
Zhengqi Li
Zhengqin Li
Zhuwen Li
Zhouhui Lian
Jie Liang
Zicheng Liao
Jongwoo Lim
Ser-Nam Lim

Kaimo Lin
Shih-Yao Lin
Tsung-Yi Lin
Weiyao Lin
Yuewei Lin
Venice Liong
Giuseppe Lisanti
Roee Litman
Jim Little
Anan Liu
Chao Liu
Chen Liu
Eryun Liu
Fayao Liu
Huaping Liu
Jingen Liu
Lingqiao Liu
Miaomiao Liu
Qingshan Liu
Risheng Liu
Sifei Liu
Tyng-Luh Liu
Weiyang Liu
Xialei Liu
Xianglong Liu
Xiao Liu
Yebin Liu
Yi Liu
Yu Liu
Yun Liu
Ziwei Liu
Stephan Liwicki
Liliana Lo Presti
Fotios Logothetis
Javier Lorenzo
Manolis Lourakis
Brian Lovell
Chen Change Loy
Chaochao Lu
Feng Lu
Huchuan Lu
Jiajun Lu
Kaiyue Lu
Xin Lu
Yijuan Lu
Yongxi Lu

Fujun Luan
Jian-Hao Luo
Jiebo Luo
Weixin Luo
Khoa Luu
Chao Ma
Huimin Ma
Kede Ma
Lin Ma
Shugao Ma
Wei-Chiu Ma
Will Maddern
Ludovic Magerand
Luca Magri
Behrooz Mahasseni
Tahmida Mahmud
Robert Maier
Subhransu Maji
Yasushi Makihara
Clement Mallet
Abed Malti
Devraj Mandal
Fabian Manhardt
Gian Luca Marcialis
Julio Marco
Diego Marcos
Ricardo Martin
Tanya Marwah
Marc Masana
Jonathan Masci
Takeshi Masuda
Yusuke Matsui
Tetsu Matsukawa
Gellert Mattyus
Thomas Mauthner
Bruce Maxwell
Steve Maybank
Amir Mazaheri
Scott Mccloskey
Mason Mcgill
Nazanin Mehrasa
Ishit Mehta
Xue Mei
Heydi Mendez-Vazquez
Gaofeng Meng
Bjoern Menze

Domingo Mery
Pascal Mettes
Jan Hendrik Metzen
Gregor Miller
Cai Minjie
Ikuhisa Mitsugami
Daisuke Miyazaki
Davide Modolo
Pritish Mohapatra
Pascal Monasse
Sandino Morales
Pietro Morerio
Saeid Motiian
Arsalan Mousavian
Mikhail Mozerov
Yasuhiro Mukaigawa
Yusuke Mukuta
Mario Munich
Srikanth Muralidharan
Ana Murillo
Vittorio Murino
Armin Mustafa
Hajime Nagahara
Shruti Nagpal
Mahyar Najibi
Katsuyuki Nakamura
Seonghyeon Nam
Loris Nanni
Manjunath Narayana
Lakshmanan Nataraj
Neda Nategh
Lukáš Neumann
Shawn Newsam
Joe Yue-Hei Ng
Thuyen Ngo
David Nilsson
Ji-feng Ning
Mark Nixon
Shohei Nobuhara
Hyeonwoo Noh
Mehdi Noroozi
Erfan Noury
Eyal Ofek
Seong Joon Oh
Seoung Wug Oh
Katsunori Ohnishi

Iason Oikonomidis
Takeshi Oishi
Takahiro Okabe
Takayuki Okatani
Gustavo Olague
Kyle Olszewski
Mohamed Omran
Roy Or-El
Ivan Oseledets
Martin R. Oswald
Tomas Pajdla
Dipan Pal
Kalman Palagyi
Manohar Paluri
Gang Pan
Jinshan Pan
Yannis Panagakis
Rameswar Panda
Hsing-Kuo Pao
Dim Papadopoulos
Konstantinos Papoutsakis
Shaifali Parashar
Hyun Soo Park
Jinsun Park
Taesung Park
Wonpyo Park
Alvaro Parra Bustos
Geoffrey Pascoe
Ioannis Patras
Genevieve Patterson
Georgios Pavlakos
Ioannis Pavlidis
Nick Pears
Pieter Peers
Selen Pehlivan
Xi Peng
Xingchao Peng
Janez Perš
Talita Perciano
Adrian Peter
Lars Petersson
Stavros Petridis
Patrick Peursum
Trung Pham
Sang Phan
Marco Piccirilli

Sudeep Pillai
Wong Ya Ping
Lerrel Pinto
Fiora Pirri
Matteo Poggi
Georg Poier
Marius Popescu
Ronald Poppe
Dilip Prasad
Andrea Prati
Maria Priisalu
Véronique Prinet
Victor Prisacariu
Hugo Proenca
Jan Prokaj
Daniel Prusa
Yunchen Pu
Guo-Jun Qi
Xiaojuan Qi
Zhen Qian
Yu Qiao
Jie Qin
Lei Qin
Chao Qu
Faisal Qureshi
Petia Radeva
Venkatesh Babu
  Radhakrishnan
Ilija Radosavovic
Bogdan Raducanu
Hossein Rahmani
Swaminathan Rahul
Ajit Rajwade
Kandan Ramakrishnan
Visvanathan Ramesh
Yongming Rao
Sathya Ravi
Michael Reale
Adria Recasens
Konstantinos Rematas
Haibing Ren
Jimmy Ren
Wenqi Ren
Zhile Ren
Edel Garcia Reyes
Hamid Rezatofighi

Hamed Rezazadegan
  Tavakoli
Rafael Rezende
Helge Rhodin
Alexander Richard
Stephan Richter
Gernot Riegler
Christian Riess
Ergys Ristani
Tobias Ritschel
Mariano Rivera
Antonio Robles-Kelly
Emanuele Rodola
Andres Rodriguez
Mikel Rodriguez
Matteo Ruggero Ronchi
Xuejian Rong
Bodo Rosenhahn
Arun Ross
Peter Roth
Michel Roux
Ryusuke Sagawa
Hideo Saito
Shunsuke Saito
Parikshit Sakurikar
Albert Ali Salah
Jorge Sanchez
Conrad Sanderson
Aswin Sankaranarayanan
Swami Sankaranarayanan
Archana Sapkota
Michele Sasdelli
Jun Sato
Shin'ichi Satoh
Torsten Sattler
Manolis Savva
Tanner Schmidt
Dirk Schnieders
Samuel Schulter
Rajvi Shah
Shishir Shah
Sohil Shah
Moein Shakeri
Nataliya Shapovalova
Aidean Sharghi
Gaurav Sharma

Pramod Sharma
Li Shen
Shuhan Shen
Wei Shen
Xiaoyong Shen
Zhiqiang Shen
Lu Sheng
Baoguang Shi
Guangming Shi
Miaojing Shi
Zhiyuan Shi
Takashi Shibata
Huang-Chia Shih
Meng-Li Shih
Sheng-Wen Shih
Atsushi Shimada
Nobutaka Shimada
Daeyun Shin
Young Min Shin
Koichi Shinoda
Tianmin Shu
Zhixin Shu
Bing Shuai
Karan Sikka
Jack Sim
Marcel Simon
Tomas Simon
Vishwanath Sindagi
Gurkirt Singh
Maneet Singh
Praveer Singh
Ayan Sinha
Sudipta Sinha
Vladimir Smutny
Francesco Solera
Amir Arsalan Soltani
Eric Sommerlade
Andy Song
Shiyu Song
Yibing Song
Humberto Sossa
Concetto Spampinato
Filip Šroubek
Ioannis Stamos
Jan Stuehmer
Jingyong Su

Jong-Chyi Su
Shuochen Su
Yu-Chuan Su
Zhixun Su
Ramanathan Subramanian
Akihiro Sugimoto
Waqas Sultani
Jiande Sun
Jin Sun
Ju Sun
Lin Sun
Min Sun
Yao Sun
Zhaohui Sun
David Suter
Tanveer Syeda-Mahmood
Yuichi Taguchi
Jun Takamatsu
Takafumi Taketomi
Hugues Talbot
Youssef Tamaazousti
Toru Tamak
Robert Tamburo
Chaowei Tan
David Joseph Tan
Ping Tan
Xiaoyang Tan
Kenichiro Tanaka
Masayuki Tanaka
Jinhui Tang
Meng Tang
Peng Tang
Wei Tang
Yuxing Tang
Junli Tao
Xin Tao
Makarand Tapaswi
Jean-Philippe Tarel
Keisuke Tateno
Joao Tavares
Bugra Tekin
Mariano Tepper
Ali Thabet
Spiros Thermos
Shangxuan Tian
Yingli Tian

Kinh Tieu
Massimo Tistarelli
Henning Tjaden
Matthew Toews
Chetan Tonde
Akihiko Torii
Andrea Torsello
Toan Tran
Leonardo Trujillo
Tomasz Trzcinski
Sam Tsai
Yi-Hsuan Tsai
Ivor Tsang
Vagia Tsiminaki
Aggeliki Tsoli
Wei-Chih Tu
Shubham Tulsiani
Sergey Tulyakov
Tony Tung
Matt Turek
Seiichi Uchida
Oytun Ulutan
Martin Urschler
Mikhail Usvyatsov
Alexander Vakhitov
Julien Valentin
Ernest Valveny
Ian Van Der Linde
Kiran Varanasi
Gul Varol
Francisco Vasconcelos
Pascal Vasseur
Javier Vazquez-Corral
Ashok Veeraraghavan
Andreas Velten
Raviteja Vemulapalli
Jonathan Ventura
Subhashini Venugopalan
Yashaswi Verma
Matthias Vestner
Minh Vo
Jayakorn Vongkulbhisal
Toshikazu Wada
Chengde Wan
Jun Wan
Renjie Wan

Baoyuan Wang
Chaohui Wang
Chaoyang Wang
Chunyu Wang
De Wang
Dong Wang
Fang Wang
Faqiang Wang
Hongsong Wang
Hongxing Wang
Hua Wang
Jialei Wang
Jianyu Wang
Jinglu Wang
Jinqiao Wang
Keze Wang
Le Wang
Lei Wang
Lezi Wang
Lijun Wang
Limin Wang
Linwei Wang
Pichao Wang
Qi Wang
Qian Wang
Qilong Wang
Qing Wang
Ruiping Wang
Shangfei Wang
Shuhui Wang
Song Wang
Tao Wang
Tsun-Hsuang Wang
Weiyue Wang
Wenguan Wang
Xiaoyu Wang
Xinchao Wang
Xinggang Wang
Yang Wang
Yin Wang
Yu-Chiang Frank Wang
Yufei Wang
Yunhong Wang
Zhangyang Wang
Zilei Wang
Jan Dirk Wegner

Ping Wei
Shih-En Wei
Wei Wei
Xiu-Shen Wei
Zijun Wei
Bihan Wen
Longyin Wen
Xinshuo Weng
Tom Whelan
Patrick Wieschollek
Maggie Wigness
Jerome Williams
Kwan-Yee Wong
Chao-Yuan Wu
Chunpeng Wu
Dijia Wu
Jiajun Wu
Jianxin Wu
Xiao Wu
Xiaohe Wu
Xiaomeng Wu
Xinxiao Wu
Yi Wu
Ying Nian Wu
Yue Wu
Zheng Wu
Zhirong Wu
Jonas Wulff
Yin Xia
Yongqin Xian
Yu Xiang
Fanyi Xiao
Yang Xiao
Dan Xie
Jianwen Xie
Jin Xie
Fuyong Xing
Jun Xing
Junliang Xing
Xuehan Xiong
Yuanjun Xiong
Changsheng Xu
Chenliang Xu
Haotian Xu
Huazhe Xu
Huijuan Xu

Jun Xu
Ning Xu
Tao Xu
Weipeng Xu
Xiangmin Xu
Xiangyu Xu
Yong Xu
Yuanlu Xu
Jia Xue
Xiangyang Xue
Toshihiko Yamasaki
Junchi Yan
Luxin Yan
Wang Yan
Keiji Yanai
Bin Yang
Chih-Yuan Yang
Dong Yang
Herb Yang
Jianwei Yang
Jie Yang
Jin-feng Yang
Jufeng Yang
Meng Yang
Ming Yang
Ming-Hsuan Yang
Tien-Ju Yang
Wei Yang
Wenhan Yang
Yanchao Yang
Yingzhen Yang
Yongxin Yang
Zhenheng Yang
Angela Yao
Bangpeng Yao
Cong Yao
Jian Yao
Jiawen Yao
Yasushi Yagi
Mang Ye
Mao Ye
Qixiang Ye
Mei-Chen Yeh
Sai-Kit Yeung
Kwang Moo Yi
Alper Yilmaz

Xi Yin
Zhaozheng Yin
Xianghua Ying
Ryo Yonetani
Donghyun Yoo
Jae Shin Yoon
Ryota Yoshihashi
Gang Yu
Hongkai Yu
Ruichi Yu
Shiqi Yu
Xiang Yu
Yang Yu
Youngjae Yu
Chunfeng Yuan
Jing Yuan
Junsong Yuan
Shanxin Yuan
Zejian Yuan
Xenophon Zabulis
Mihai Zanfir
Pablo Zegers
Jiabei Zeng
Kuo-Hao Zeng
Baochang Zhang
Cha Zhang
Chao Zhang
Dingwen Zhang
Dong Zhang
Guofeng Zhang
Hanwang Zhang
He Zhang
Hong Zhang
Honggang Zhang
Hua Zhang
Jian Zhang

Jiawei Zhang
Jing Zhang
Kaipeng Zhang
Ke Zhang
Liang Zhang
Linguang Zhang
Liqing Zhang
Peng Zhang
Pingping Zhang
Quanshi Zhang
Runze Zhang
Shanghang Zhang
Shu Zhang
Tianzhu Zhang
Tong Zhang
Wen Zhang
Xiaofan Zhang
Xiaoqin Zhang
Xikang Zhang
Xu Zhang
Ya Zhang
Yinda Zhang
Yongqiang Zhang
Zhang Zhang
Zhen Zhang
Zhoutong Zhang
Ziyu Zhang
Bin Zhao
Bo Zhao
Chen Zhao
Hengshuang Zhao
Qijun Zhao
Rui Zhao
Heliang Zheng
Shuai Zheng
Stephan Zheng

Yinqiang Zheng
Yuanjie Zheng
Zhonglong Zheng
Guangyu Zhong
Huiyu Zhou
Jiahuan Zhou
Jun Zhou
Luping Zhou
Mo Zhou
Pan Zhou
Yang Zhou
Zihan Zhou
Fan Zhu
Guangming Zhu
Hao Zhu
Hongyuan Zhu
Lei Zhu
Menglong Zhu
Pengfei Zhu
Shizhan Zhu
Siyu Zhu
Xiangxin Zhu
Yi Zhu
Yizhe Zhu
Yuke Zhu
Zhigang Zhu
Bohan Zhuang
Liansheng Zhuang
Karel Zimmermann
Maria Zontak
Danping Zou
Qi Zou
Wangmeng Zuo
Xinxin Zuo

Contents – Part II

Oral Session O2: Object Tracking and Segmentation

Poster Session P1

Embedded Polarizing Filters to Separate Diffuse and Specular Reflection

Laurent Valentin Jospin(iD), Gilles Baechler(✉)(iD), and Adam Scholefield(iD)

School of Computer and Communication Sciences, Audiovisual Communications
Laboratory, Ecole Polytechnique Fédérale de Lausanne, Lausanne, Switzerland
laurent.jospin@alumni.epfl.ch, gilles.baechler@gmail.com

Abstract. Polarizing filters provide a powerful way to separate diffuse
and specular reflection; however, traditional methods rely on several captures and require proper alignment of the filters. Recently, camera man-
ufacturers have proposed to embed polarizing micro-filters in front of
the sensor, creating a mosaic of pixels with different polarizations. In
this paper, we investigate the advantages of such camera designs. In particular, we consider different design patterns for the filter arrays and
propose an algorithm to demosaic an image generated by such cameras.
This essentially allows us to separate the diffuse and specular components
using a single image. The performance of our algorithm is compared with
a color-based method using synthetic and real data. Finally, we demonstrate how we can recover the normals of a scene using the diffuse images
estimated by our method.

Keywords: Polarizing micro-filter · Diffuse and specular separation ·
Photometric stereo

1 Introduction

The light reflected from a scene can be broadly classified into *diffuse* and *specular*
terms. While the diffuse term is slowly varying for different pairs of viewing and
lighting angles, specularities take the form of strong highlights that can vary
quickly as either angle changes. Separating these two components is useful in
many different imaging applications. For example, photometric stereo [1] estimates surface normals from images taken under different illuminations; however,
like many algorithms, the process assumes that the scene is Lambertian, i.e the
reflection is purely diffuse.

As a second example, consider the problem of estimating spatially-varying
bidirectional reflectance distribution functions (SVBRDFs). The knowledge of
the complete SVBRDF enables the reproduction of objects from any viewing
direction and under variable lighting conditions. Typically, one fits a parametric model to samples obtained by capturing images with different viewing and
lighting directions. Although for very simple materials the specular and diffuse
components of the model can be fit from only the shape of the SVBRDF, often

© Springer Nature Switzerland AG 2019
C. V. Jawahar et al. (Eds.): ACCV 2018, LNCS 11362, pp. 3–18, 2019.
https://doi.org/10.1007/978-3-030-20890-5_1

this process can be done much more accurately if the two components are separated prior to model fitting. Other applications that benefit from this separation include tracking, object recognition and image segmentation.

1.1 Related Work

There are a number of approaches to perform this separation, using either a single or multiple images [2]. Most single-image approaches are color-based: this process was pioneered by Shafer [3], with the so-called *dichromatic reflection model*. A key observation is that, for dielectrics, the spectrum of the specularity is similar to the spectrum of the light source, whereas the diffuse spectrum also encompasses information about the color of the surface: this results in a T-shaped space [4] whose limbs represent the diffuse and specular components in the dichromatic reflection model. Approaches based on this model [5,6] assume that the scene has been segmented into different parts with a uniform diffuse distribution, which make them unpractical for highly textured scenes. More recent work alleviates the need for segmentation by integrating spatio-temporal information [7]. Similar approaches with different color spaces such as HSI [8], rotated RGB [9], or custom spaces [10–12] have also been proposed. As well as color-based techniques, the so-called *neighborhood analysis* methods [13–15] leverage the information from neighboring pixels to infer the reflective component at a given point.

Multi-image approaches use strategies as varied as structured illumination [16–18], different viewing angles [19,20], or light-field imaging [21,22]. Another multiple image approach makes use of polarizing filters. With a single filter in front of the lens, Nayar et al. [23] recast the separation problem as a linear system using multiple captures under different polarizations. Building on their work, a number of methods propose to combine color information with polarizing filters to separate the reflective components [17,24–26].

Ma et al. [17] and Debevec et al. [27] suggest the use of filters *both* in front of the camera and the light sources, which leads to a slightly different model for the recorded intensity.

Recently, cameras have been proposed with an array of polarizing micro-filters placed just in front of the image sensor [28–31]. Analogously to a Bayer filter, the micro-filter of each pixel is oriented in one of a finite number of possible directions (see Fig. 1). Potentially, this can enable the separation of the diffuse and specular components from a single image with the accuracy and robustness of multi-image polarization methods.

1.2 Proposed Approach

In this paper, we investigate the feasibility of using these types of cameras for the separation of specularities by proposing an algorithm to demosaic images generated with polarizing micro-filter arrays. As well as regular patterns, we also study random arrangements with varying numbers of orientations and show that these arrangements offer advantages over regular patterns.

Fig. 1. Illustration of the concept of a filter array with different polarization orientations. The micro-filters are represented with disks and the arrow indicates the direction of polarization.

In addition to demosaicing, we demonstrate the usefulness of micro-filter arrays for photometric stereo. Using a light dome with several light sources having different polarizing orientations, we show that the separation of the diffuse and specular components using our design can significantly improve the estimation of the surface normals of objects. This approach is essentially the dual of [32], where a camera with micro-polarizers is combined with a multi-view approach to infer the shape of objects.

The code and data required to reproduce all the results presented in this paper will be made available online with the camera-ready version.

2   Problem Statement

Polarization is a physical property of light that characterizes the orientation of electromagnetic transverse waves in space. A wave is said to be *polarized* when its orientation follows a regular pattern in space: for example, when the wave oscillates in a fixed direction it is called *linearly polarized*. In contrast, *unpolarized light* is composed of a mixture of electromagnetic waves with different orientations. A *linear polarizing filter* (or polarizer) is a physical device that only lets through light with a given polarization. Given a light wave polarized in direction ϕ with initial intensity I_0, the polarizing filter will project it onto its orientation θ. This is summarized by *Malus' law*, which quantifies the light intensity I after it goes through the filter: $I = I_0 \cos^2(\phi - \theta)$. Unpolarized light can be thought of as containing all orientations equally, hence the resulting intensity is simply $I_0/2$, which is the mean value of $I_0 \cos^2(\phi - \theta)$ over all orientations.

Polarization is of interest here because the diffuse and specular reflections affect polarization differently. Specular reflections are caused by direct reflection of the incoming light at an object's surface. Therefore, this type of reflection preserves the polarization of the incoming light. Diffusion is slightly more complex. The diffusion created by the surface reflections can be thought of as the combination of several specular reflections in all orientations due to the rough nature of most materials at the microscopic level. The polarization of the light reflected by this microfacet model is not preserved. On the other hand, some of the light is also scattered inside the medium; the polarization of such light is retained. We can leverage this observation to separate diffuse and specular reflection. In fact, we separate polarized and unpolarized light, which we can associate to the specular and diffuse components as long as the subsurface scattering is relatively weak.

In particular, suppose we have a scene illuminated by a single light source polarized with an angle ϕ; this can be achieved by placing a linear polarizer in front of it. For now, assume that ϕ is known; later, we show that this is unnecessary as it can be easily estimated. Furthermore, suppose we have a digital camera with a filter array of linear polarizers with K different orientations in front of its sensor. We describe the image formation process as follows. Let $\mathbf{X}_k \in \mathbb{R}^{N \times N}$, $k = 1, 2, ..., K$, be a collection of K images, each filtered with a distinct orientation θ_k. From Malus' law, we can express each individual image as the sum of a constant diffuse term and a specular term that is modulated according to the polarization of the filters:

$$\mathbf{X}_k = \frac{1}{2}\mathbf{Z}_d + \mathbf{Z}_s \cos^2(\phi - \theta_k), \tag{1}$$

where $\mathbf{Z}_d$ and $\mathbf{Z}_s$ are the diffuse and specular components, respectively. Equivalently, we can rewrite (1) by flattening $\mathbf{X}_k$ into a vector $\mathbf{x}_k = \text{vec}(\mathbf{X}_k)^1$:

$$\mathbf{x}_k = \underbrace{\left[\frac{1}{2}\mathbf{I} \ \cos^2(\phi - \theta_k)\mathbf{I}\right]}_{\mathbf{C}_k} \begin{bmatrix} \mathbf{z}_d \\ \mathbf{z}_s \end{bmatrix}. \tag{2}$$

Here, $\mathbf{z}_d = \text{vec}(\mathbf{Z}_d) \in \mathbb{R}^{N^2}$, $\mathbf{z}_s = \text{vec}(\mathbf{Z}_s) \in \mathbb{R}^{N^2}$ and $\mathbf{C}_k \in \mathbb{R}^{N^2 \times 2N^2}$ is the matrix that modulates the specularity with the correct attenuation and combines the diffuse and specular terms.

To model a camera with a micro-array of polarizing filters, we need to select only one polarization orientation for each pixel. To model this, let $\mathbf{y}_k = \mathbf{A}_k \mathbf{x}_k$, where $\mathbf{A}_k \in \mathbb{R}^{N^2 \times N^2}$ is a mask that zeroes the measurements that we do not have access to; it has the form of a diagonal matrix with a 1 where the pixel is selected and a 0 otherwise. Note that, since we have one polarizing filter per pixel, $\sum_{k=1}^{K} \mathbf{A}_k = \mathbf{I}$. At this stage, we make no assumption about the filter orientations: they can be regularly or irregularly structured over the array. Finally, the measured image is given by

$$\mathbf{y} = \sum_{k=1}^{K} \mathbf{y}_k = \mathbf{AC} \begin{bmatrix} \mathbf{z}_d \\ \mathbf{z}_s \end{bmatrix}, \tag{3}$$

---

[1] Note that we use bold uppercase letters for matrix notation and the same letter in lowercase for its flattened version. Throughout this chapter, we interchangeably use both notations to denote the same object.

where

$$A = [A_1, A_2, \ldots, A_K] \in \mathbb{R}^{N^2 \times KN^2},$$
$$C = [C_1, C_2, \ldots, C_K]^\top \in \mathbb{R}^{KN^2 \times 2N^2}.$$

Using this formulation, our aim is to estimate z_d and z_s given the measurements y and the downsampling matrix $S = AC$. To simplify notation we write the "superimage" with both diffuse and specular components as $z = [z_d, z_s]^\top$.

3   Algorithms

We propose a general approach to separate the diffuse and specular components. Finding both components using only a single image is an under-constrained problem, which we propose to regularize using the TV norm:

$$\hat{z} = \arg \min_x \|y - Sz\|_2^2 + T(z), \tag{4}$$

where $T(z) = \gamma_d \|Z_d\|_{TV} + \gamma_s \|Z_s\|_{TV}$ is the regularization term. Here γ_d, γ_s are regularization parameters and $\| \cdot \|_{TV}$ is the total variation (TV) norm[2]. Typically, the TV norm is defined as the ℓ^1 norm of the first order differential operator, although some authors also consider the ℓ^2 norm of the same differential operator. A compromise between the two approaches is the *Huber norm* or *Huber loss*, defined as $L(z) = \sum L(x_i)$, where

$$L(x) = \begin{cases} \frac{1}{2}x^2 & \text{for } |x| < 1 \\ |x| - \frac{1}{2} & \text{otherwise.} \end{cases} \tag{5}$$

We show below how to solve (4) with these different variations of the TV norm. The advantage of the ℓ^1 approach is that, since it favors solutions that have a sparse first order derivative, it maintains edges in the image. In contrast, the ℓ^2 approach can blur edges but performs well on other parts of the image. The ℓ^2 formulation can also lead to faster algorithms.

3.1   Minimizing the ℓ^2 TV Norm

Although general optimization packages can be used to solve (4), the sampling matrix S is very large and therefore these techniques are limited to relatively small-sized images. In order to overcome this, we observe that (4) can be expressed as a sparse linear system. To see this, note that $T(\cdot)$, in the case of the ℓ^2 TV norm, can be written as

$$T(z) = z^\top D^\top W Dz, \tag{6}$$

---

[2] Technically, the TV norm is only a semi-norm.

where $\mathbf{D}$ is the 2D discrete differential operator matrix and $\mathbf{W}$ encapsulates the effect of γ_d and γ_s. Finally, setting the derivative of (4) to zero yields the following sparse linear system:

$$(\mathbf{S}^\top \mathbf{S} + \mathbf{D}^\top \mathbf{W} \mathbf{D}) \hat{\mathbf{z}} = \mathbf{S}^\top \mathbf{y}. \tag{7}$$

Although this system is very large, the matrix $\mathbf{S}^\top \mathbf{S} + \mathbf{D}^\top \mathbf{W} \mathbf{D}$ is sparse, symmetric and positive definite, and thus can be efficiently solved using approaches such as the conjugate gradient method. This leads to an algorithm that has linear complexity in the number of pixels.

3.2   Minimizing the ℓ^1 TV Norm

Unfortunately, unlike the ℓ^2 case, we cannot find a closed form solution with the ℓ^1 norm. Instead, we propose to use the split Bregmann method [33] to solve (4) iteratively. In particular, (4) can be written as

$$\hat{\mathbf{z}} = \arg\min_{\mathbf{z}, \mathbf{d}} \| \mathbf{y} - \mathbf{Sz} \|_2^2 + \gamma_d \| \mathbf{d_d} \|_1 + \gamma_s \| \mathbf{d_s} \|_1 \quad \text{s.t.} \quad \begin{bmatrix} \mathbf{d_d} \\ \mathbf{d_s} \end{bmatrix} = \mathbf{D} \begin{bmatrix} \mathbf{z_d} \\ \mathbf{z_s} \end{bmatrix}, \tag{8}$$

so that each step of the Bregmann iteration algorithm consists of solving

$$(\mathbf{z}^{k+1}, \mathbf{d}^{k+1}) = \arg\min_{\mathbf{z}, \mathbf{d}} \| \mathbf{y} - \mathbf{Sz} \|_2^2 + \gamma_d \| \mathbf{d_d} \|_1 + \gamma_s \| \mathbf{d_s} \|_1 + \lambda \| \mathbf{d} - \mathbf{Dz} - \mathbf{b}^k \|_2^2, \tag{9}$$

where $\mathbf{b}^{k+1} = \mathbf{b}^k + (\mathbf{Dz}^{k+1} - \mathbf{d}^{k+1})$. To solve (9), we can alternate between minimizing over $\mathbf{z}$ and $\mathbf{d}$:

$$\mathbf{z}^{k+1} = \arg\min_{\mathbf{z}} \| \mathbf{y} - \mathbf{Sz} \|_2^2 + \lambda \| \mathbf{d}^k - \mathbf{Dz} - \mathbf{b}^k \|_2^2, \tag{10}$$

$$\mathbf{d}^{k+1} = \arg\min_{\mathbf{d}} \gamma_d \| \mathbf{d_d} \|_1 + \gamma_s \| \mathbf{d_s} \|_1 + \lambda \| \mathbf{d} - \mathbf{Dz}^{k+1} - \mathbf{b}^k \|_2^2. \tag{11}$$

The main advantage of this approach is that (11) is now decoupled over space, and thus has a closed form solution. Additionally, (10) is now an ℓ^2 minimization, which again has a closed form solution. In practice, only a few iterations of the split Bregmann algorithm are needed to converge so the method is acceptably fast and has linear complexity in the number of pixels in the image.

3.3   Minimizing the Huber TV Norm

When using the Huber norm regularization, the minimization problem (4) becomes

$$\hat{\mathbf{z}} = \arg\min_{\mathbf{z}, \mathbf{d}} \| \mathbf{y} - \mathbf{Sz} \|_2^2 + \gamma_d L (\mathbf{D_s z_d}) + \gamma_s L (\mathbf{D_s z_s}). \tag{12}$$

Setting the derivative to 0, we obtain

$$2\mathbf{S}^\top \mathbf{Sz} - 2\mathbf{S}^\top \mathbf{y} + \gamma_d \mathbf{D_d}^\top L' (\mathbf{D_s z_d}) + \gamma_s \mathbf{D_s}^\top L' (\mathbf{D_s z_s}) = \mathbf{0}. \tag{13}$$

As $L(\mathbf{z})$ is twice differentiable, (13) is easy to solve using, for example, Newton's method. To initialize the iteration, we propose to use the solution of the ℓ^2 TV norm.

3.4   Unknown Light Polarization

In the above description, we assumed that the polarization angle ϕ of the incoming light was known. Although it can be directly measured in controlled experiments, this is not necessary since it can be accurately estimated using the following procedure. First, for each image $\mathbf{z}_k$, we estimate its mean from the available pixels:

$$\mu_k = \sum_{n=1}^{N^2} [\mathbf{y}_k]_n / \sum_{n=1}^{N^2} [\mathbf{A}_k]_{nn}. \tag{14}$$

Using the linearity of the mean, we have

$$\begin{bmatrix} \mu_1 \\ \mu_2 \\ \vdots \\ \mu_K \end{bmatrix} = \mu_d + \begin{bmatrix} \cos(\phi - \theta_1)^2 \\ \cos(\phi - \theta_2)^2 \\ \vdots \\ \cos(\phi - \theta_K)^2 \end{bmatrix} \mu_s, \tag{15}$$

where μ_d and μ_s are the mean values of $\mathbf{z}_d$ and $\mathbf{z}_s$. For $K > 3$, this set of non-linear equations is overdetermined, and finding ϕ, μ_d and μ_s corresponds to solving the following minimization problem:

$$\begin{bmatrix} \hat{\phi} \\ \hat{\mu}_d \\ \hat{\mu}_s \end{bmatrix} = \arg\min_{\phi, \mu_d, \mu_s} \sum_{k=1}^{K} \left(\mu_k - \mu_d - \mu_s \cos(\phi - \theta_k)^2 \right)^2. \tag{16}$$

4   Practical Considerations

Before evaluating and comparing our proposed approach to existing methods, we discuss below a few algorithmic and design choices.

4.1   One-Step vs. Two-Step Algorithm

Our proposed algorithm separates the components and interpolates the images in a single step. One might wonder how much we gain by performing this estimation in a single step as opposed to a two-stage approach where we first demosaic every individual image $\mathbf{X}_k$ and then fit a cosine to the interpolated images to identify the specular and diffuse components.

Figure 2 shows a comparison between our direct reconstruction algorithm and the two-stage approach. Here, the same ℓ^2 TV norm regularization is used for both the direct approach and the interpolation step of the two-stage approach.

Even though the two approaches are close in performance when the number of orientations is 4, the two-stage approach performance clearly worsens when the number of orientations increases. Also, the two-stage approach peaks at 39.7 dB, whereas the direct reconstruction continues to increase to 40.95 dB. While the observed performance gain is not huge, it is significant for many applications. The versatility of our algorithm over the two-stage approach is also an advantage

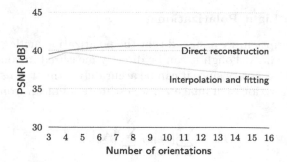

Fig. 2. Influence of the number of orientations with a random filter design: comparison of our proposed algorithm, which performs the separation in one shot, with a two stage approach, which first interpolates the different channels and then extracts the specularity by fitting a cosine. Both methods use the ℓ^2 TV-norm as regularizer.

when investigating different filter design patterns. In this regard, we observe that the direct reconstruction saturates at around 8–10 orientations, suggesting that existing camera designs based on 4 orientations are not optimal. In the rest of this paper, we exclusively use the single-step approach.

4.2 Comparison of the Different Regularizers

As stated earlier, the TV norm is typically defined in terms of the ℓ^1 norm, which leads to sharper edges, while the ℓ^2 norm formulation is faster and can perform better on certain regions of the image. Finally, the Huber norm provides a tradeoff between the ℓ^1 and ℓ^2 variants. To quantify these differences, we ran a comparison of the results obtained with the three proposed norms. The results are given for one image in Fig. 4. As we can see, there is not much difference in terms of PSNR, particularly between the ℓ^2 and Huber norm regularization. We also observe that the ℓ^1 regularized image is a bit sharper but also slightly noisier. In terms of performance, the ℓ^2 and Huber norm algorithms are 5.7x and 3.3x faster than the ℓ^1 algorithm, respectively. Based on these observations and computational speed, we choose to favor the ℓ^2 norm for the rest of the experiments.

4.3 Filter Design Patterns and Number of Orientations

There are a number of ways to design the micro-filter array, including (pseudo) random patterns and regular grids. Examples of images acquired with these designs are depicted in Fig. 3c and d. To obtain these images, we use Blender with the raytracing engine Cycles [34] and create ground truth diffuse and specular images from different render passes. We then simulate the effect of the filters by appropriately weighting and mixing the diffuse and specular components. The corresponding estimated diffuse components are shown in Fig. 3e and f. Additionally, in Fig. 5, we compare the average performance of these two designs for a selection of synthetic images. Overall, we observe that the filter design does not

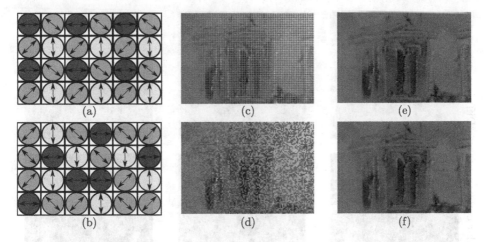

Fig. 3. Filter designs with 4 different orientations: example of (a) a regular grid vs. (b) a random grid design. Simulated image acquisitions using (c) a regular grid and (d) a random grid filter design. The last column illustrates the estimation of the diffuse component using our algorithm.

significantly influence the peak signal-to-noise ratio (PSNR). Nevertheless, as shown in Fig. 3e and f, random patterns lead to a slightly better qualitative estimation and, more importantly, the reconstruction artifacts induced by random patterns are more pleasing to the eye.

4.4 Cost of Introducing the Filter Array

Finally, it is also interesting to investigate how much is lost by using a polarizing micro-filter, compared to a traditional camera, when one does not wish to separate the diffuse and specular components. In Fig. 6, we see that the sum of our diffuse and specular estimations is very close to the original image, suggesting that, even if the separation fails, the sum is almost indistinguishable from the output of a traditional camera.

5 Experiments

We test our ℓ^2 TV norm-based algorithm in three different scenarios: rendered images, real images with simulated polarizing filters, and real images with real polarizers. Simulated data is again generated with Blender Cycles raytracing engine [34]. The second scenario consists of real images captured by Shen and Zheng [11]: the ground truth of the diffuse components is provided along with the original images. We also provide our own captured images, taken under fixed polarized light sources, using a Nikon D810 DSLR camera with a polarizer in front of its lens. Note that even though the polarizing filter is not placed directly in front of the sensor, we neglect the effect that the lens might have on the light

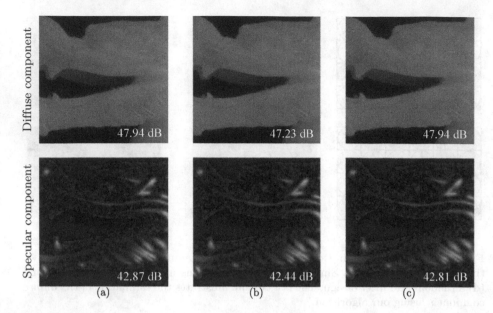

Fig. 4. Reconstructed diffuse and specular parts with (a) ℓ^2, (b) ℓ^1 and (c) Huber norms.

polarization. In practice, it may slightly change the polarization phase, but this would be accounted for in the device calibration. To obtain a diffuse ground truth, we capture one image with the polarizing filter oriented orthogonal to the light's polarization. For all setups, we first generate all complete images $\mathbf{X}_k$ for $k = 1, 2, \ldots, K$ and then apply the downsampling operator $\mathbf{A}$ to simulate the effect of the polarized filter array.

5.1 Single Image Diffuse and Specular Separation

Given the results from Fig. 5, we focus on a random filter array design and 16 orientations for our algorithm. For all experiments, we set $\gamma_d = 0.01$ and

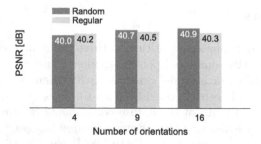

Fig. 5. Comparison of the reconstruction error on the diffuse component with regular versus random grid designs.

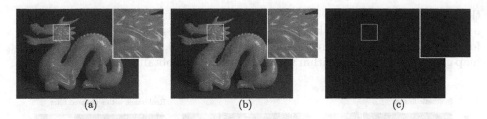

Fig. 6. Comparison of (a) the ground truth image to (b) the sum of our diffuse and specular estimations (PSNR = 43.8 dB). The difference (c) is almost zero suggesting that very little is lost by introducing a polarizing micro-filter.

$\gamma_s = 0.002$. It is possible to obtain slightly improved results with parameter tuning, but we avoided it.

To provide context, we compare our approach with the single image color-based technique proposed by Shen and Zheng in [11]. We should emphasize that their method takes as input a standard image while ours takes an image captured with the proposed filter array. Rather than being a fair comparison between algorithms, this experiment allows us to quantify the performance improvement offered by the proposed setup.

Performing this comparison raises a number of challenges in terms of color management. In particular, our algorithm operates in a linear color space, whereas [11] uses the sRGB space. To deal with this, we run our algorithm in the linear space and convert our estimated images to sRGB for comparison. Additionally, the images provided by [11] are in sRGB format and we convert them to a linear color space to apply our algorithm.

Figures 7 and 8 depict the results for two images from each of the three different scenarios previously mentioned. For all images, our custom setup significantly outperforms [11]. This is particularly true for images with complex surfaces such as Figs. 7b and 8b.

5.2   Photometric Stereo

Photometric stereo [1] infers surface normals from multiple images under different lighting by assuming that the surface of the objects are Lambertian materials. Unfortunately, this assumption is rarely satisfied as scenes often contain specular components and occlusions. In this section, we use our algorithm to first obtain a solid approximation of the diffuse part of the scene and then use it to recover the surface normals.

For this experiment, we use a *light dome* that is composed of 58 lamps spread on a hemisphere surrounding the object of interest. A digital camera is placed at the zenith of the hemisphere. We install linear polarizing filters with unknown orientation in front of each light source as well as in front of the camera. We capture several images, one under each illumination of the fixed lights for four different polarization orientations of the filter positioned in front of the camera;

these four orientations are used to create mosaiced images on which we apply our algorithm to estimate the diffuse component. These diffuse images are then fed to the photometric stereo algorithm [1]. In Fig. 9, we compare the normal map generated by our algorithm with the normal map obtained from unprocessed

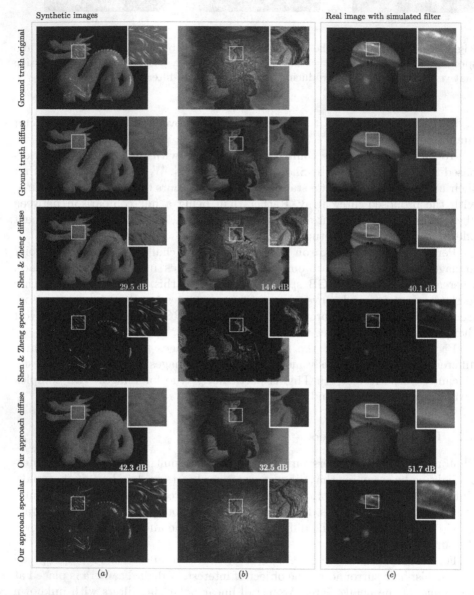

Fig. 7. Performance evaluation on two synthetic images and one real image with a simulated polarizer: (a) the Stanford dragon [35], (b) a digital painting with a computer-generated normal map, and (c) the fruits image from [11].

Fig. 8. Performance evaluation on three real images, one with a simulated polarizer and two with real polarizers: (a) the animals image from [11], (b) a jade dragon, and (c) a painting.

images (i.e. with no separation of the diffuse component) as well as from Shen and Zheng's algorithm [11]. Note that the ground truth normal maps are computed using the non-mosaiced images. In all scenes, the gain of using our algorithm is clearly noticeable.

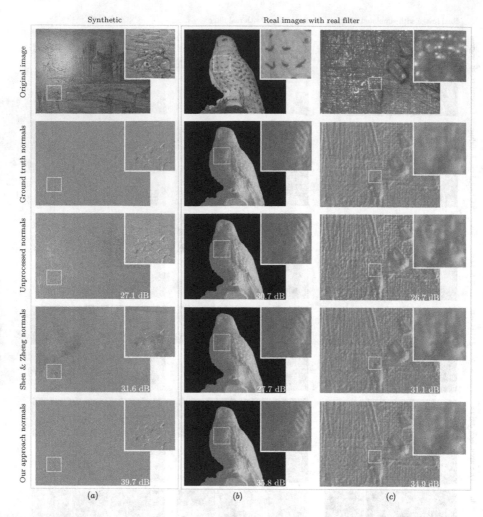

Fig. 9. Estimation of the normal map of three different scenes: (a) a rendered painting, (b) an owl figurine, and (c) a close-up of a real painting. From top to bottom, we show the original image, the ground truth normals, the normal estimation using the original image, the normal estimation using the proposed diffuse estimate and the normal estimation using the diffuse estimate from [11].

6   Conclusion

We have studied the benefits of using a camera equipped with polarizing micro-filters for the separation of diffuse and specular terms. We presented a simple algorithm to demosaic images produced by such cameras and extract the diffuse term. Regarding the diffuse extraction, we have shown that our relatively simple algorithm can significantly outperform other single-image based techniques. A more accurate knowledge of the diffuse term can then be leveraged in other imaging applications such as photometric stereo; we demonstrate that our technique improves the estimation of the normal maps on various scenes. For future work, we believe that including more elaborate priors based on, for example some of the existing color-based techniques, will improve the estimation.

References

1. Woodham, R.J.: Photometric method for determining surface orientation from multiple images. Opt. Eng. **19**, 191139 (1980)
2. Artusi, A., Banterle, F., Chetverikov, D.: A survey of specularity removal methods. Comput. Graph. Forum **30**, 2208–2230 (2011)
3. Shafer, S.A.: Using color to separate reflection components. Color Res. Appl. **10**, 210–218 (1985)
4. Klinker, G.J., Shafer, S.A., Kanade, T.: The measurement of highlights in color images. Int. J. Comput. Vis. **2**, 7–32 (1988)
5. Gershon, R.: The use of color in computational vision. Technical report, Department of Computer Science, University of Toronto (1987)
6. Klinker, G.J., Shafer, S.A., Kanade, T.: A physical approach to color image understanding. Int. J. Comput. Vis. **4**, 7–38 (1990)
7. Mallick, S.P., Zickler, T., Belhumeur, P.N., Kriegman, D.J.: Specularity removal in images and videos: a PDE approach. In: Leonardis, A., Bischof, H., Pinz, A. (eds.) ECCV 2006. LNCS, vol. 3951, pp. 550–563. Springer, Heidelberg (2006). https://doi.org/10.1007/11744023_43
8. Yang, J., Liu, L., Li, S.Z.: Separating specular and diffuse reflection components in the HSI color space. In: IEEE International Conference on Computer Vision Workshops, pp. 891–898 (2013)
9. Mallick, S.P., Zickler, T.E., Kriegman, D.J., Belhumeur, P.N.: Beyond lambert: reconstructing specular surfaces using color. In: IEEE Computer Society Conference on Computer Vision and Pattern Recognition, vol. 2, pp. 619–626. IEEE (2005)
10. Bajcsy, R., Lee, S.W., Leonardis, A.: Detection of diffuse and specular interface reflections and inter-reflections by color image segmentation. Int. J. Comput. Vis. **17**, 241–272 (1996)
11. Shen, H.L., Zheng, Z.H.: Real-time highlight removal using intensity ratio. Appl. Opt. **52**, 4483–4493 (2013)
12. Tan, R.T., Nishino, K., Ikeuchi, K.: Separating reflection components based on chromaticity and noise analysis. IEEE Trans. Pattern Anal. Mach. Intell. **26**, 1373–1379 (2004)
13. Mallick, S.P., Zickler, T., Belhumeur, P., Kriegman, D.: Dichromatic separation: specularity removal and editing. In: ACM SIGGRAPH 2006 Sketches, p. 166. ACM (2006)
14. Tan, R.T., Ikeuchi, K.: Separating reflection components of textured surfaces using a single image. IEEE Trans. Pattern Anal. Mach. Intell. **27**, 178–193 (2005)
15. Yoon, K.J., Choi, Y., Kweon, I.S.: Fast separation of reflection components using a specularity-invariant image representation. In: IEEE International Conference on Image Processing, pp. 973–976. IEEE (2006)
16. Lamond, B., Peers, P., Ghosh, A., Debevec, P.: Image-based separation of diffuse and specular reflections using environmental structured illumination. In: IEEE Computational Photography (2009)

17. Ma, W.C., Hawkins, T., Peers, P., Chabert, C.F., Weiss, M., Debevec, P.: Rapid acquisition of specular and diffuse normal maps from polarized spherical gradient illumination. In: Eurographics Symposium on Rendering, pp. 183–194. Eurographics Association (2007)
18. Nayar, S.K., Krishnan, G., Grossberg, M.D., Raskar, R.: Fast separation of direct and global components of a scene using high frequency illumination. ACM Trans. Graph. **25**, 935–944 (2006)
19. Jaklič, A., Solina, F.: Separating diffuse and specular component of image irradiance by translating a camera. In: Chetverikov, D., Kropatsch, W.G. (eds.) CAIP 1993. LNCS, vol. 719, pp. 428–435. Springer, Heidelberg (1993). https://doi.org/10.1007/3-540-57233-3_56
20. Lin, S., Li, Y., Kang, S.B., Tong, X., Shum, H.Y.: Diffuse-specular separation and depth recovery from image sequences. In: Heyden, A., Sparr, G., Nielsen, M., Johansen, P. (eds.) ECCV 2002. LNCS, vol. 2352, pp. 210–224. Springer, Heidelberg (2002). https://doi.org/10.1007/3-540-47977-5_14
21. Meng, L., Lu, L., Bedard, N., Berkner, K.: Single-shot specular surface reconstruction with gonio-plenoptic imaging. In: Proceedings of the IEEE International Conference on Computer Vision, pp. 3433–3441 (2015)
22. Wang, H., Xu, C., Wang, X., Zhang, Y., Peng, B.: Light field imaging based accurate image specular highlight removal. PLOS ONE **11**, e0156173 (2016)
23. Nayar, S.K., Fang, X.S., Boult, T.: Removal of specularities using color and polarization. In: IEEE Computer Society Conference on Computer Vision and Pattern Recognition, pp. 583–590 (1993)
24. Kim, D.W., Lin, S., Hong, K.S., Shum, H.Y.: Variational specular separation using color and polarization. In: MVA, pp. 176–179 (2002)
25. Nayar, S.K., Fang, X.S., Boult, T.: Separation of reflection components using color and polarization. Int. J. Comput. Vis. **21**, 163–186 (1997)
26. Umeyama, S., Godin, G.: Separation of diffuse and specular components of surface reflection by use of polarization and statistical analysis of images. IEEE Trans. Pattern Anal. Mach. Intell. **26**, 639–647 (2004)
27. Debevec, P., Hawkins, T., Tchou, C., Duiker, H.P., Sarokin, W., Sagar, M.: Acquiring the reflectance field of a human face. In: SIGGRAPH, pp. 145–156 (2000)
28. 4D Technologies: Polarization camera for image enhancement. https://www.4dtechnology.com/products/polarimeters/polarcam
29. FluxData: Polarization imaging camera FD-1665P. http://www.fluxdata.com/products/fd-1665p
30. Photonic Lattice: Polarization imaging camera PI-110. https://www.photonic-lattice.com/en/products/polarization_camera/pi-110/
31. Ricoh Imaging Company Ltd.: Polarization camera. https://www.ricoh.com/technology/tech/051_polarization.html
32. Cui, Z., Gu, J., Shi, B., Tan, P., Kautz, J.: Polarimetric multi-view stereo. In: Proceedings of the IEEE Conference on Computer Vision and Pattern Recognition, pp. 1558–1567 (2017)
33. Goldstein, T., Osher, S.: The split bregman method for l1-regularized problems. SIAM J. Img. Sci. **2**, 323–343 (2009)
34. Blender Online Community: Blender - A 3D modelling and rendering package. Blender Foundation, Blender Institute, Amsterdam (2017)
35. Stanford Graphics Lab: The Stanford 3D Scanning Repository. http://graphics.stanford.edu/data/3Dscanrep/

SCPNet: Spatial-Channel Parallelism Network for Joint Holistic and Partial Person Re-identification

Xing Fan[1,2], Hao Luo[1,2], Xuan Zhang[2], Lingxiao He[3], Chi Zhang[2], and Wei Jiang[1(✉)]

[1] Zhejiang University, Hangzhou, China
{xfanplus,haoluocsc,jiangwei_zju}@zju.edu.cn
[2] Megvii Inc. (Face++), Beijing, China
{zhangxuan,zhangchi}@megvii.com
[3] Institute of Automation, Chinese Academy of Sciences, Beijing, China
lingxiao.he@nlpr.ia.ac.cn

Abstract. Holistic person re-identification (ReID) has received extensive study in the past few years and achieves impressive progress. However, persons are often occluded by obstacles or other persons in practical scenarios, which makes partial person re-identification non-trivial. In this paper, we propose a spatial-channel parallelism network (SCPNet) in which each channel in the ReID feature pays attention to a given spatial part of the body. The spatial-channel corresponding relationship supervises the network to learn discriminative feature for both holistic and partial person re-identification. The single model trained on four holistic ReID datasets achieves competitive accuracy on these four datasets, as well as outperforms the state-of-the-art methods on two partial ReID datasets without training.

Keywords: Person re-identification · Deep learning ·
Spatial-channel parallelism

1 Introduction

Person re-identification (ReID) is a popular research problem in computer vision. However, existing works always focus on the holistic person images, which cover a full glance of one person. There are some holistic person images shown in Fig. 1(c). In the realistic scenario, the person may be occluded by some moving or static obstacles (e.g. cars, walls, other persons), as shown as in Fig. 1(a) and (b). Therefore, partial person ReID is an important issue for real-world ReID applications and has gradually attracted researchers' attention. The occlusions will change the feature of person appearance, which presents a big challenge to identify a person across views. There are few studies focusing on partial person ReID, while most current holistic person based approaches can not well solve the partial person images. From this perspective, studying partial person ReID,

© Springer Nature Switzerland AG 2019
C. V. Jawahar et al. (Eds.): ACCV 2018, LNCS 11362, pp. 19–34, 2019.
https://doi.org/10.1007/978-3-030-20890-5_2

Fig. 1. Samples of holistic person and partial person images.

especially jointing holistic person ReID, is necessary and crucial both for academic research and practical ReID applications.

Most of current ReID studies use representation learning [18,39] or metric learning [4,6,14,20,29] to learn a global feature, which is sensitive to the occlusions changing the person appearance. Some works, which use part or pose guided alignment [25,28,32,35–37] to learn local features, can boost the performance of holistic person ReID, but may fail to get good alignment information when the person images are non-holistic. To overcome the above problems, several partial ReID methods have been proposed in recent years. Sliding Window Matching (SWM) [41] introduces an alternative solution for partial ReID by setting up a sliding window of the same size as the probe image and using it to search for the most similar region within each gallery person. However, for SWM, the size of probe person is smaller than the size of the gallery person. Some part-to-part matching (PPM) based methods divide the image into many parts of the same size and use local part-level features to solve partial ReID. The searching process of SWM and PPM based methods is time-consuming. Hence [13] proposed Deep Spatial feature Reconstruction (DSR), which exploits the reconstruction error of two images of different sizes to leverage Fully Convolution Network (FCN). Replacing part-based searching with direct reconstruction, DSR accelerates the process of ReID. However, DSR needs partial ReID data to train a good partial ReID model.

In this paper, we propose an end-to-end model named spatial-channel parallelism network (SCPNet), which is only trained on holistic ReID datasets but performs well on both holistic and partial person ReID datasets. In the proposed framework, SCPNet includes a global branch and a local branch. As same as most of traditional methods, the global branch uses the global average pooling (GAP) to extract the global feature. To acquire the local feature, we divide feature maps into several equal parts from top to down and then apply the horizontal pooling to get local features of each part. Inspired by the motivation that we expect the global feature can store certain local information, we design a loss to leverage global branch through the local feature, which is the output of the local branch. Due to this design, SCPNet can learn how to do partial ReID and keep working in holistic person ReID at the same time without partial ReID training data.

In previous research works, combing the global feature with the local feature is a common solution to boost the performance. However, the dimension of the feature vector determines the speed of retrieval process. SCPNet can only use the output features of the global branch to halve the dimension and speed up retrieval, because the features contain the local information. In the following, we overview the main contents of our method and summarize the contributions:

- We propose a novel approach named Spatial-Channel Parallelism Network (SCPNet) for both holistic and partial person ReID, which effectively use the local features to leverage the global features in the training phase.
- Besides, our SCPNet can perform better on partial ReID with only being trained on holistic ReID datasets, which let it more suitable for the practical ReID scene.
- Experimental results demonstrate that the proposed model achieves state-of-the-art results on four holistic ReID datasets. And our unsupervised cross-domain results of partial ReID beat the supervised state-of-the-art results by a large margin on Partial REID [41] and Partial-iLIDS [40] datasets.

2   Related Works

Since the proposed approach joints holistic and partial person ReID using deep convolutional networks, we briefly introduce some related deep learning based works in this section.

Representation Learning. Deep representation learning which regards ReID as a classification task such as verification or identification problem, is a commonly supervised learning method in person ReID [8,18,39]. In [39], Zheng *et al.* make the comparison between verification baseline and identification baseline: (1) For the former, a pair of input person images is judged whether they belong to the same person by a deep model. (2) For the latter, the method treats each identity as a category, and then minimizes the softmax loss. In some improved works [18], person attributes loss is combined with verification or identification loss to learn a better feature description.

Metric Learning. In deep metric learning, the deep model can directly learn the similarity of two images according to the L2 distance of their feature vectors in the embedding space. The typical metric loss includes contrastive loss, triplet loss and quadruplet loss in terms of the training pairs. Usually, two images of the same person are defined as a positive pair, whereas two images of different persons are a negative pair. Contrastive loss minimizes the features distance of the positive pairs while maximizing the features distance of the negative pairs. However, triplet loss [20] is motivated by the margin enforced between positive and negative pairs. A triplet only has two identities, and quadruplet adds an extra identity to get a new negative pair. In addition, selecting suitable samples for the training model through hard mining has been shown to be effective [14,29]. Combining softmax loss with metric learning loss to speed up the convergence is also a popular method [10].

Part-Based Methods. Part-based methods are commonly used to extract local features in holistic person ReID. This kind of methods has very great inspiration for occlusion problem in partial person ReID. In details, human pose estimation and landmark detection having achieved impressive progress, several recent works in ReID employ these tools to acquire aligned subregion of person images [28,34,35,37]. Then, using a deep model extract the spatial local features of each part is an effective way to boost the performance of global features. Another common solution is to divide images into several parts without an alignment [25,32,36] and concatenate the features of each part. However, when occlusion happened, the above methods are usually inefficient because of the incomplete pose points or disturbed local features. In addition, they usually concatenate the global and local features to avoid losing the global information, which means they need extra extracted global features. The SCPNet is inspired by using the local features to leverage the global features, and is suitable for both holistic and partial person ReID.

Partial Person ReID. Solving the occlusion problem in person ReID is important for the ReID applications. However, there have been few methods which consider how to learn a better feature to match an arbitrary patch of a person image. In some other tasks, some works [7,11] easily wrap an arbitrary patch of an image to a fixed-size image, and then extract the fixed-length feature vector for matching. In [41], Zheng *et al.* improved it into a global-to-local matching model named Sliding Window Matching (SWM) that can capture the spatial layout information of local patches, and also introduced a local patch-level matching model called Ambiguity-sensitive Matching Classifier (AMC) that was based on a sparse representation classification formulation with explicit patch ambiguity modeling. However, the computation cost of AMC-SWM is expensive because it extracts feature using much time without sharing computation. He *et al.* proposed a method [13] that leveraged Fully convolutional Network (FCN) to generated certain-sized spatial feature maps such that pixel-level features are consistent. Then, it used Deep Spatial feature Reconstruction (DSR) to match a pair of person images of different sizes. DSR need to solve an optimization problem to calculate the similarity of two feature maps of different size, which increases the time consumption in application. To this end, we propose a model called SCPNet which can output a fixed-length feature vector to solve both holistic and partial ReID.

3   Our Proposed Approach

In this section, we present our spatial-channel parallelism network (SCPNet) as in Fig. 2.

In SCPNet, a single global feature is generated for the input image, and the L2 distance of such features are used as similarity in the inference stage. However, the global feature is learned jointly with local features in the learning stage.

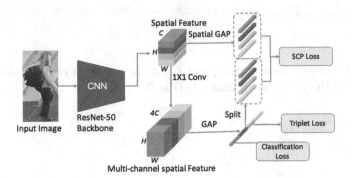

Fig. 2. Structure of our SCPNet model. We feed input images forward into the ResNet-50 [12] backbone network and extract output $C \times H \times W$ feature maps of last convolutional layer. Then we divide a feature map into four spatial horizontal stripes and apply global average pooling (GAP) for each stripe producing local features. We also apply an 1×1 convolutional layer on the feature map to produce multi-channel spatial feature representation, and then we use GAP to obtain the compact feature. The compact feature is split into four feature vector parts by the channel. Finally, three losses are computed.

For each image, we use a CNN, such as ResNet50 [12], to extract a feature map as the original appearance representation, which is the output of the last convolution layer ($C \times H \times W$, where C is the channel number and $H \times W$ is the spatial size. On the other hand, an 1×1 convolutional layer is applied to the feature map to extend the channel number from C to RC, where R is the number of body region ($R = 4$ in Fig. 2), then a global pooling is applied to extract the global feature (a RC-d vector). On the other hand, the feature map is uniformly divided into R parts in vertical direction, and a global pooling is applied for each of them to extract R local features (C-d vectors).

Intuitively, the global feature represents the whole person, while R local features represent different body regions. However, both of these features have drawbacks if trained independently. For the global feature, it often focuses on certain part and ignores other local details. For the local features, as demonstrated in [21], an effective receptive field only occupies a fraction of the full theoretical receptive field and a lot of local information is still preserved after many convolution layers. Since their effective receptive fields are small, they lack enough context information to well represent the corresponding body region. Moreover, because of misalignment, such as pose variation and inaccurate detection boxes, a local feature may not correspond to the body regions accurately.

To alleviate the drawbacks, we propose a spatial-channel parallelism method. After obtaining the global feature and local features, each local feature is mapped to a part of the global feature (with the same color as in Fig. 2). In more details, the r-th local feature, which is a C-dimensional vector, should be closer to the continuously C channels from the rC-th to the $(r + 1)C$-th in the global feature. We use the local features to let each part of the global feature focus on certain body regions by introducing a spatial-channel parallelism loss as follows:

$$L_{SCP} = \sum_{r=1}^{R} \|f_{s,r} - f_{c,r}\|_2^2 \tag{1}$$

where $f_{s,r}$ is the r-th local feature, and $f_{c,r}$ is the r-th part of the global feature (the rC-th to the $(r+1)C$-th channel) (Fig. 3).

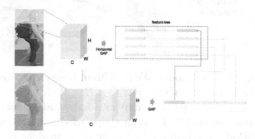

Fig. 3. The example of spatial-channel parallelism. The feature map of the global branch is produced from the entire original feature map of the local branch. Each channel part of the global branch has global receptive filed (blue region) and contains global information of the whole input image, while the first part of the local branch maps to the orange region in the image. (Color figure online)

The two types of features should be close, because it is actually a re-learning process which enforces every channel part to learn the corresponding local spatial feature, but from the entire feature map, see Fig. 4(b). The misalignment can be handled because the corresponding part is extracted automatically from whole input even when the relevant part appears in other position of the input image. Thus the resulting re-learned feature is a more robust representation.

In this way, with the supervision of local features, each part of the global feature is forced to learn local representation of the corresponding part of the input. Hence each region of the body is focused by certain channels in the global feature, which makes the global feature hold more local details and more discriminative. Moreover, different from local features, each part of the global feature has a global receptive field, which leads to better representation of the corresponding local region. It also has no rigid spatial segmentation, thus the global feature is more robust to pose variation and inaccurate bounding boxes.

In the learning stage, the loss is comprised of three losses: the metric learning loss L_{metric}, the classification loss L_{class} and the spatial-channel parallelism loss L_{SCP}. For the metric learning loss, the similarity between two images is defined by the L2 distance of their global features, and the TriHard loss proposed by [14] is chosen, where for each sample, the most dissimilar one with the same identity and the most similar one with a different identity is chosen to obtain a triplet. For the classification loss, a softmax is applied for each image with the identity. The spatial-channel parallelism loss is given in Eq. (1), which requires local features to compute. And the final loss is the sum of above three loss as following:

$$L = L_{class} + L_{metric} + \lambda L_{SCP} \qquad (2)$$

where λ is the weight of spatial-channel parallelism loss.

In the inference stage, only the global feature is needed. For a holistic person, its ReID feature is represented by the whole global feature, while for a partial person, its ReID feature is represented by part of the global feature. Hence, the similarity of two person images is computed as the L2 distance of the shared part of their global features. For both holistic and partial ReID, we use the same feature vector and let SCPNet to learn to determine which part of feature should be extracted automatically.

4 Experiments

4.1 Datasets

We train a single model end-to-end on four challenging holistic ReID datasets, including Market-1501 [38], DukeMTMC-reID [22], CUHK03 [15] amd CUHK-SYSU [30], and then test on these four datasets. Furthermore, we also directly test the trained model on two partial ReID datasets including Partial REID [41] and Partial-iLIDS [40] without training.

Market-1501 consists of 32,668 bounding box images from 1,501 person identities captured by six cameras in front of a supermarket. The provided pedestrian bounding boxes are detected by Deformable Part Model (DPM) [9]. The training set consists of 12,936 images from 751 identities and testing set contains the other 19,732 images from 750 identities.

DukeMTMC-reID consists of 36,411 images from 1,812 person identities captured by 8 high-resolution cameras. There are 1,404 identities appear in more than two cameras and the other 408 identities are regarded as distractors. Training set consists of 702 identities and testing set contains the rest 702 identities.

CUHK03 consists of 14,096 images from 1,467 person identities captured by six cameras in the CUHK campus. Both manually labeled pedestrian bounding boxes and automatically detected bounding boxes are provided. In this paper, we use the manually labeled version.

CUHK-SYSU contains 18,184 full images and 99,809 bounding boxes from 8,432 person identities are provided. The dataset is divided into training set containing 11,206 images of 5,532 identities and testing set containing the other 6,978 images of 2,900 identities.

Partial REID contains 600 images of 60 people, with 5 full-body images and 5 partial images per person. The images were collected at an university campus with different viewpoints, background and different types of severe occlusions.

Partial-iLIDS is a simulated partial person datasets based on i-LIDS [40]. There are 119 people with total 476 person images captured by multiple non-overlapping cameras. Some images occlusion, sometimes rather severe, caused by people and luggage.

4.2 Implementation Details

We implement our propose SCPNet model using the PyTorch framework. The backbone network is the ResNet-50 [12] model pre-trained on ImageNet. In training phase, the input image is resized to 288×144 then randomly cropped to 256×128 with random horizontal flip. The mini-batch size is set to 64, in which each identity has 4 images. Before feeding the input image into the network, we subtract the mean value and then divide it by the standard deviation as same as the normalization procedure of the ResNet-50 [12] trained on ImageNet.

We use the Adam optimizer with the default hyper-parameters ($\epsilon = 10^{-8}$, $\beta_1 = 0.9$, $\beta_2 = 0.999$) to minimize the network loss. The initial learning rate is 10^{-3}, and we lower the learning rate twice at epoch 80 and 180 to 10^{-4} and 10^{-5} respectively. The total training takes 300 epochs. Weight decay is set to 10^{-5} and never changes. We also add a dropout layer for classification and the dropout ratio is set to 0.75 in all our experiments.

We will release the code and trained weights of our SCPNet model after publication and more details can be found in the code.

4.3 Results

In this section, we focus on five aspects: (1) The Ablation study on spatial-channel parallelism. (2) The influence of number of parts. (3) The influence of SCP loss weight. (4) State-of-the-arts results of holistic ReID. (5) State-of-the-arts results of partial ReID.

For partial ReID datasets, similar to Market-1501 [38], we provide top-k accuracy by finding the most similar correct match in the top k candidates.

Ablation Study. To evaluate the benefits of the proposed SCPNet, we compare it with a baseline network. The baseline network is the same as SCPNet, but without the SCP loss in the learning stage. For the baseline network, there are three features can be extracted as the ReID feature in the experiments: (1) the global feature, which is the output of the global branch, (2) the local feature, which is the concatenation of all features in the local branch, (3) and the concat feature, which is the concatenation of the previous two features. For SCPNet, we set $R = 4$ and $\lambda = 10$ in the experiments.

As Table 1 shown, we report the rank-1 accuracy of four experiments on totally six ReID datasets mentioned. For the baseline network, we report the results when the global/local/concatenate feature is used as the ReID features. It is easy to see that the concatenate feature is superior to both the global and the local feature in the baseline network. However, the SCPNet always outperforms the baseline network with the concat feature on the ReID datasets. It is shown that let the global feature and the local feature learn each other by spatial-channel parallelism is better than simply concatenating them. Moreover, the channel number used as ReID feature in SCPNet is only half of that in the baseline using the concat feature.

Table 1. Influence of different features. When SCP loss is not used, we apply softmax and triplet loss on spatial feature branch, channel feature branch or both branches respectively. When SCP loss is used, we use structure shown in Fig. 2 and extract different output as final representation.

Settings		Results (r = 1), $R = 4, \lambda = 10$					
Model	Branch	Market-1501	DukeMTMC-reID	CUHK03	CUHK-SYSU	Partial ReID	Partial-iLIDs
Baseline	Local	90.7	77.5	90.3	94.5	61.0	83.2
	Global	92.0	80.2	89.6	93.1	60.0	78.2
	Concate	92.8	81.7	92.7	93.6	61.0	**84.9**
SCPNet		**94.1**	**84.8**	**93.3**	**94.6**	**68.3**	**84.9**

On the partial ReID task, the local branch performs better than the global branch on Partial REID and Partial-iLIDS datasets, which indicates that local features are more important for partial ReID. And our SCPNet exceeds the global branch of *Baseline* by more than 6.0% rank-1 accuracy (1.3%–4.6% rank-1 accuracy for holistic ReID). It can be learned that our proposed SCPNet improves much more performance in partial ReID than holistic ReID. In addition, the SCPNet is not inferior to the concatenate branch, which includes local and global features. In other words, the local information is transferred from the local branch to the global branch. The results of ablation study show the effectiveness of our proposed approach.

Influence of Number of Parts. Because the size of the output feature map of the SCPNet is 8×4 in our experiments, we can divide the feature map into $1, 2, 4, 8$ parts respectively. As shown as Table 2, when $R = 1$, two branches are both global branches and the SCPNet achieves worst performance on all six datasets. When we set $R > 1$, the SCPNets perform better than the SCPNet ($R = 1$) on all datasets, which shows that the local features are beneficial to ReID.

SCPNet with few strips will become a common global feature model, which cannot fully utilize the spatial-channel parallelism with more local feature. SCPNet with more strips cannot preserve semantic information of person components, which influences the performance. e.g., Fig. 4(a) ($R = 8$), more strips would divide the head and bag into two parts. The experimental result suggests

Table 2. Influence of different number of parts (rank-1 accuracies, $\lambda = 1$).

R	Market-1501	DukeMTMC-reID	CUHK03	CUHK-SYSU	Partial ReID	Partial-iLIDS
1	92.0	80.8	89.9	93.8	61.3	82.4
2	93.3	**82.9**	**90.9**	**94.2**	65.3	**85.7**
4	**93.4**	82.0	90.3	93.9	**67.0**	84.9
8	93.2	82.6	90.9	94.1	65.0	84.0

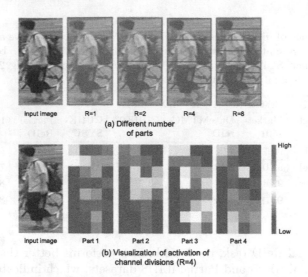

(a) Different number of parts

(b) Visualization of activation of channel divisions (R=4)

Fig. 4. Strip horizontal division. SCPNet with few strips cannot use local information well. SCPNet with more strips cannot preserve the semantic information well (e.g., a "half head" when $R = 8$). (b) Spatial-channel parallelism. For every position, we calculate the maximum of all channels belong to this part of the global feature. It shows that each part focuses mainly on the corresponding spatial part.

that SCPNet with 4 strips can make full use of local information, and preserve more semantic information. Figure 4(a) illustrates the different strip horizontal division.

We choose $R = 4$ to do the subsequent experiments in this paper.

Influence of SCP Loss Weight. We fix $R = 4$ and use different weights (λ) of SCP loss to do the experiments. As shown as Table 3, when $\lambda = 0$, the model (*Baseline* mentioned previously) gets the lowest rank-1 accuracy on all datasets. In overall, the performance of the SCPNet is gradually improving when λ increases from 0.5 to 10, which demonstrates the effectiveness of the spatial-channel parallelism again. If we continue to increase λ, the SCPNet will not improve performance again on five datasets except Partial-iLIDS. When $R = 4$ and λ is around 10, the proposed SCPNet achieves the best performance.

Comparison with Single-Dataset Setting. Unlike many existing methods, we train a single model on all four datasets. For a fair comparison, without any extra modification or hyperparameter searching, we also train our SCPNet on each dataset alone using exactly the same setting. As shown in Table 4, SCPNet-s is inferior to SCPNet-a, but it still outperforms the baseline by a large margin.

With adjustments especially for single-dataset setting, our SCPNet-s can acquire even better performance. For example, SCPNet-s can achieve 91.7% by changing mini-batch size from 64 to 48 on Market-1501 (Fig. 5).

Table 3. Influence of SCP loss weight (rank-1 accuracies, $R = 4$).

λ	Market-1501	DukeMTMC-reID	CUHK03	CUHK-SYSU	Partial ReID	Partial-iLIDS
0	92.0	80.2	89.6	93.1	60.0	78.2
0.5	93.2	81.7	90.0	94.0	63.3	83.2
1	93.4	82.0	90.3	93.9	67.0	84.9
2	93.6	82.6	91.2	94.2	65.3	84.9
4	93.8	83.6	92.2	94.4	66.0	84.0
6	**94.1**	83.9	92.3	94.3	64.7	84.9
8	93.8	83.8	92.4	94.3	68.0	84.0
10	**94.1**	**84.8**	**93.3**	**94.6**	**68.3**	84.9
12	93.9	83.3	92.2	94.6	64.0	**86.6**
16	93.5	83.6	92.5	94.6	67.3	82.3

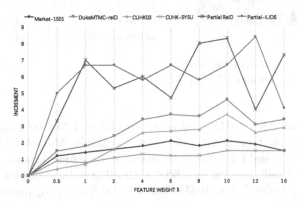

Fig. 5. The increments of rank-1 accuracy on six datasets. We use the results of SCPNet ($\lambda = 0$) as the baseline and compute the increment of SCPNet results with different λ.

The proposed SCP loss can enforce the model to learn more discriminative features. When some region is occluded, feature in other regions is still available. As shown in Table 5, when trained on CUHK-SYSU then tested on Market-1501 and DukeMTMC-reID, SCPNet outperforms baseline significantly (only 1.2% gap on CHUK-SYSU, but 12.1% and 15.0% gap on Market-1501 and DukeMTMC-reID respectively), which implies it has learned to extract richer feature and is more robust to occlusions and appearance variation. Furthermore, SCPNet can focus on human body rather than occlusions. As shown in Fig. 6, when the upper or bottom part is occluded, the activation of distractor parts is suppressed, which makes SCPNet suitable for partial ReID task. Misalignment is also handled because we extract each part of feature from whole regions rather than rigid local pooling regions. SCP loss cannot well deal with the occlusion in the vertical direction. We admit that this is a disadvantage, and may introduce vertical stripes into SCP loss in the future.

Table 4. Comparison of single model and dataset-specific model. We just report rank-1 accuracies. A method with "-s" means that the model is trained with corresponding single dataset, while "-a" means the model is trained with all four datasets. Baseline is the global branch without SCP loss.

Method	Market-1501	DukeMTMC-reID	CUHK03	CUHK-SYSU
Baseline-s	88.1	77.6	89.5	90.7
SCPNet-s	91.2	80.3	90.7	91.9
SCPNet-a	94.1	84.8	93.3	94.6

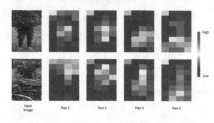

Table 5. Trained on CUHK-SYSU then tested on Market-1501 and DukeMTMC-reID directly.

Method	Market-1501	DukeMTMC-reID
Baseline-s	56.0	26.6
SCPNet-s	68.1	41.6

Fig. 6. Occlusion visualization of activation of channel divisions (R = 4)

Results on Holistic ReID. We compare our SCPNet to existing state-of-the-art methods on four holistic datasets, including Market-1501, CUHK03, DukeMTMC-ReID, and CUHK-SYSU. Because these four datasets are not overlapping, we train only one single model with all training samples. For Market-1501, CUHK03, DukeMTMC-ReID, and CUHK-SYSU, we mainly report the mAP and CMC accuracy as same as the standard evaluation. For CUHK03, because we train one single model for all benchmarks, it is slightly different from the standard procedure in [15], which splits the dataset randomly 20 times, and the gallery for testing has 100 identities each time. We only randomly split the dataset once for training and testing. In addition, we mainly report CMC accuracy and did not consider mAP because of the different gallery size.

The results are shown in Tables 6, 7, 8 and 9. For the SCPNet, we choose the results of the experiment with $\lambda = 10$ and $R = 4$. Overall, our proposed SCPNet achieves the best performance on Market-1501, CUHK-SYSU and CUHK03, and lags behind the best results with a slight gap on DukeMTMC-ReID. It is worth mentioning that DSR also reported its results on Market1501, which our SCPNet outperforms by 10.5% rank-1 accuracy and 17.5% mAP. In conclusion, the SCPNet can perform well on the holistic person ReID task.

Results on Partial ReID. We compare the proposed SCPNet to the state-of-the-art methods, including AMC, SWM, AMC+SWM, DSR and Resizing model, on the Partial REID and Partial-iLIDS datasets. There are $p = 60$ and $p = 119$ individuals in each of the test sets for Partial REID and Partial-iLIDS datasets

Table 6. Experimental results on the Market-1501 with single query

Method	mAP	r = 1	r = 5
LDNS [33]	35.7	61.0	-
Gated S-CNN [26]	39.6	65.9	-
IDNet+VeriNet [5]	45.5	71.8	-
Re-ranking [43]	63.6	77.1	-
PIE [37]	56.0	79.3	94.4
XQDA+SSM [2]	68.8	82.2	-
TriHard [14]	69.1	84.9	-
Spindle [35]	-	76.9	91.5
CamStyle [44]	68.7	88.7	-
GLAD [28]	73.9	89.9	-
HA-CNN [16]	75.5	91.2	-
DSR [13]	64.3	83.6	-
SCPNet-s	75.2	91.2	97.0
SCPNet-a	**81.8**	**94.1**	**97.7**

Table 7. Experimental results on the CUHK03 with detected dataset

Methods	r = 1	r = 5	r = 10
LOMO+XQDA [17]	44.6	-	-
LDNS [33]	62.6	90.0	94.8
Gated S-CNN [26]	61.8	-	-
LSTM Simaese [27]	57.3	80.1	88.3
Re-ranking [43]	64.0	-	-
PIE [37]	67.1	92.2	96.6
TriHard [14]	75.5	95.2	99.2
OIM [31]	77.5	-	-
Deep [10]	84.1	-	-
SOMAnet [3]	72.4	95.2	95.8
IDNet+VeriNet [42]	83.4	97.1	98.7
GLAD [28]	85.0	97.9	99.1
Spindle [35]	88.5	97.8	98.6
SCPNet-s	90.7	98.0	99.0
SCPNet-a	**93.3**	**98.7**	**99.2**

Table 8. Experimental results on the DukeMTMC-reID

Method	mAP	r = 1	r = 5
BoW+KISSME [38]	12.2	25.1	-
IDNet [39]	45.0	65.2	-
TriHard [14]	53.5	72.4	-
SVDNet [24]	56.8	76.7	86.4
CamStyle [44]	57.6	78.3	-
HA-CNN [16]	63.8	80.5	-
GP-reID [1]	**72.8**	**85.2**	**93.9**
SCPNet-s	62.6	80.3	89.6
SCPNet-a	68.5	84.8	91.9

Table 9. Experimental results on the CUHK-SYSU

Methods	mAP	r = 1	r = 5
VGG16+RSS [30]	55.7	62.7	-
DLDP [23]	74.0	76.7	-
NPSM [19]	77.9	81.2	-
SCPNet-s	90.0	91.9	96.9
SCPNet-a	**93.1**	**94.6**	**98.0**

respectively. The state-of-the-art results are taken from [13] and more details can be found in it. For the SCPNet, λ is set to 10 and R is 4. Note that the state-of-the-art results are achieved by supervised learning, while our SCPNet has not been trained on the Partial REID and Partial-iLIDS datasets. As Table 10 shown, our SCPNet finally achieves 68.3% and 84.9% rank-1 accuracy on Partial REID and Partial-iLIDS respectively. These unsupervised cross-domain results beat existing supervised learning methods by a large margin (25.3% and 30.3% rank-1 accuracy on Partial REID and Partial-iLIDS respectively). However, the

Baseline ($R = 4, \lambda = 0$) also performs better than existing methods. This surprising result gives us an inspiration. We can use the holistic person images to train a partial ReID model, because holistic person images are more easily collected than partial person images. And with our proposed spatial-channel parallelism, the ReID model can be more suitable for partial person images without extra computational cost in the inference stage.

Table 10. Experimental results on Partial REID Datasets with single query ($N = 1$)

Method	Type	Partial REID, $p = 60$			Partial-iLIDS, $p = 119$		
		r = 1	r = 5	r = 10	r = 1	r = 5	r = 10
Resizing model	Supervised	19.3	40.0	51.3	21.9	43.7	55.5
SWM [41]	Supervised	24.4	52.3	61.3	33.6	53.8	63.3
AMC [41]	Supervised	33.3	52.0	62.0	46.8	69.6	81.9
AMC+SWM [41]	Supervised	36.0	60.0	70.7	49.6	72.7	84.7
DSR (Multi-scale) [13]	Supervised	43.0	75.0	76.7	54.6	73.1	85.7
Baseline	Unsupervised	60.0	78.3	83.7	78.2	89.1	92.4
SCPNet-a[a]	Unsupervised	56.3	73.3	80.5	69.8	89.9	**95.0**
SCPNet-a	Unsupervised	**68.3**	**80.7**	**88.3**	**84.9**	**92.4**	94.1

[a]After the initial version of this paper, [13] releases a new evaluation protocol, and we also provide scores under the new protocol here.

5   Conclusions

In this paper, we propose a two-branch deep CNN network called Spatial-Channel Parallelism Network (SCPNet) with a local feature branch and a global feature branch. The local feature branch output local features without a global view, while the global feature branch output global features with heavily coupling and redundancy. With spatial-channel parallelism, the channel feature branch can learn local spatial feature through the guidance of local feature branch, and the re-learned local features are more discriminative with a global view, achieving a balance between global and local representation. In this way, the network can also extract local features automatically from the whole image which makes it also more suitable for partial ReID. A single SCPNet model is trained end-to-end on four holistic ReID datasets and achieves the state-of-the-art results on all four datasets. Furthermore, the trained model also outperforms the state-of-the-art results on two partial ReID datasets by a large margin without training.

References

1. Almazan, J., Gajic, B., Murray, N., Larlus, D.: Re-id done right: towards good practices for person re-identification. arXiv preprint arXiv:1801.05339 (2018)
2. Bai, S., Bai, X., Tian, Q.: Scalable person re-identification on supervised smoothed manifold. In: CVPR (2017)

3. Barbosa, I.B., Cristani, M., Caputo, B., Rognhaugen, A., Theoharis, T.: Looking beyond appearances: synthetic training data for deep CNNs in re-identification. Comput. Vis. Image Underst. **167**, 50–62 (2018)
4. Chen, W., Chen, X., Zhang, J., Huang, K.: Beyond triplet loss: a deep quadruplet network for person re-identification. In: CVPR (2017)
5. Chen, Y.C., Zhu, X., Zheng, W.S., Lai, J.H.: Person re-identification by camera correlation aware feature augmentation. IEEE Trans. Pattern Anal. Mach. Intell. **40**(2), 392–408 (2018)
6. Cheng, D., Gong, Y., Zhou, S., Wang, J., Zheng, N.: Person re-identification by multi-channel parts-based CNN with improved triplet loss function. In: CVPR (2016)
7. Donahue, J., et al.: Decaf: a deep convolutional activation feature for generic visual recognition. In: ICML (2014)
8. Fan, X., Jiang, W., Luo, H., Fei, M.: SphereReID: Deep Hypersphere Manifold Embedding for Person Re-Identification. arXiv preprint arXiv: 1807.00537 (2018)
9. Felzenszwalb, P.F., Girshick, R.B., McAllester, D., Ramanan, D.: Object detection with discriminatively trained part-based models. IEEE Trans. Pattern Anal. Mach. Intell. **32**(9), 1627–1645 (2010)
10. Geng, M., Wang, Y., Xiang, T., Tian, Y.: Deep transfer learning for person re-identification. arXiv preprint arXiv:1611.05244 (2016)
11. Girshick, R., Donahue, J., Darrell, T., Malik, J.: Rich feature hierarchies for accurate object detection and semantic segmentation. In: CVPR (2014)
12. He, K., Zhang, X., Ren, S., Sun, J.: Deep residual learning for image recognition. In: CVPR (2016)
13. He, L., Liang, J., Li, H., Sun, Z.: Deep spatial feature reconstruction for partial person re-identification: Alignment-free approach. arXiv preprint arXiv:1801.00881 (2018)
14. Hermans, A., Beyer, L., Leibe, B.: In defense of the triplet loss for person re-identification. arXiv preprint arXiv:1703.07737 (2017)
15. Li, W., Zhao, R., Xiao, T., Wang, X.: Deepreid: deep filter pairing neural network for person re-identification. In: CVPR (2014)
16. Li, W., Zhu, X., Gong, S.: Harmonious attention network for person re-identification. arXiv preprint arXiv:1802.08122 (2018)
17. Liao, S., Hu, Y., Zhu, X., Li, S.Z.: Person re-identification by local maximal occurrence representation and metric learning. In: CVPR (2015)
18. Lin, Y., Zheng, L., Zheng, Z., Wu, Y., Yang, Y.: Improving person re-identification by attribute and identity learning. arXiv preprint arXiv:1703.07220 (2017)
19. Liu, H., et al.: Neural person search machines. In: ICCV (2017)
20. Liu, H., Feng, J., Qi, M., Jiang, J., Yan, S.: End-to-end comparative attention networks for person re-identification. IEEE Trans. Image Process. **26**, 3492–3506 (2017)
21. Luo, W., Li, Y., Urtasun, R., Zemel, R.: Understanding the effective receptive field in deep convolutional neural networks. In: NIPS (2016)
22. Ristani, E., Solera, F., Zou, R., Cucchiara, R., Tomasi, C.: Performance measures and a data set for multi-target, multi-camera tracking. In: Hua, G., Jégou, H. (eds.) ECCV 2016. LNCS, vol. 9914, pp. 17–35. Springer, Cham (2016). https://doi.org/10.1007/978-3-319-48881-3_2
23. Schumann, A., Gong, S., Schuchert, T.: Deep learning prototype domains for person re-identification. arXiv preprint arXiv:1610.05047 (2016)
24. Sun, Y., Zheng, L., Deng, W., Wang, S.: SVDNet for pedestrian retrieval. In: ICCV (2017)

25. Sun, Y., Zheng, L., Yang, Y., Tian, Q., Wang, S.: Beyond part models: person retrieval with refined part pooling. arXiv preprint arXiv:1711.09349 (2017)
26. Varior, R.R., Haloi, M., Wang, G.: Gated siamese convolutional neural network architecture for human re-identification. In: Leibe, B., Matas, J., Sebe, N., Welling, M. (eds.) ECCV 2016. LNCS, vol. 9912, pp. 791–808. Springer, Cham (2016). https://doi.org/10.1007/978-3-319-46484-8_48
27. Varior, R.R., Shuai, B., Lu, J., Xu, D., Wang, G.: A Siamese long short-term memory architecture for human re-identification. In: Leibe, B., Matas, J., Sebe, N., Welling, M. (eds.) ECCV 2016. LNCS, vol. 9911, pp. 135–153. Springer, Cham (2016). https://doi.org/10.1007/978-3-319-46478-7_9
28. Wei, L., Zhang, S., Yao, H., Gao, W., Tian, Q.: GLAD: Global-local-alignment descriptor for pedestrian retrieval. In: ACM Multimedia (2017)
29. Xiao, Q., Luo, H., Zhang, C.: Margin sample mining loss: a deep learning based method for person re-identification. arXiv preprint arXiv:1710.00478 (2017)
30. Xiao, T., Li, S., Wang, B., Lin, L., Wang, X.: End-to-end deep learning for person search. arXiv preprint arXiv:1604.01850 (2016)
31. Xiao, T., Li, S., Wang, B., Lin, L., Wang, X.: Joint detection and identification feature learning for person search. In: CVPR (2017)
32. Yao, H., Zhang, S., Zhang, Y., Li, J., Tian, Q.: Deep representation learning with part loss for person re-identification. arXiv preprint arXiv:1707.00798 (2017)
33. Zhang, L., Xiang, T., Gong, S.: Learning a discriminative null space for person re-identification. In: CVPR (2016)
34. Zhang, X., et al.: AlignedReID: surpassing human-level performance in person re-identification. arXiv preprint arXiv: 1711.08184 (2017)
35. Zhao, H., et al.: Spindle net: person re-identification with human body region guided feature decomposition and fusion. In: CVPR (2017)
36. Zhao, L., Li, X., Zhuang, Y., Wang, J.: Deeply-learned part-aligned representations for person re-identification. In: ICCV (2017)
37. Zheng, L., Huang, Y., Lu, H., Yang, Y.: Pose invariant embedding for deep person re-identification. arXiv preprint arXiv:1701.07732 (2017)
38. Zheng, L., Shen, L., Tian, L., Wang, S., Wang, J., Tian, Q.: Scalable person re-identification: a benchmark. In: ICCV (2015)
39. Zheng, L., Yang, Y., Hauptmann, A.G.: Person re-identification: past, present and future. arXiv preprint arXiv:1610.02984 (2016)
40. Zheng, W.S., Gong, S., Xiang, T.: Person re-identification by probabilistic relative distance comparison. In: CVPR (2011)
41. Zheng, W.S., Li, X., Xiang, T., Liao, S., Lai, J., Gong, S.: Partial person re-identification. In: ICCV (2015)
42. Zheng, Z., Zheng, L., Yang, Y.: A discriminatively learned CNN embedding for person re-identification. arXiv preprint arXiv:1611.05666 (2016)
43. Zhong, Z., Zheng, L., Cao, D., Li, S.: Re-ranking person re-identification with k-reciprocal encoding. In: CVPR (2017)
44. Zhong, Z., Zheng, L., Zheng, Z., Li, S., Yang, Y.: Camera style adaptation for person re-identification. arXiv preprint arXiv:1711.10295 (2017)

GhostVLAD for Set-Based Face Recognition

Yujie Zhong[1]([✉]), Relja Arandjelović[2]([✉]), and Andrew Zisserman[1,2]([✉])

[1] VGG, Department of Engineering Science, University of Oxford, Oxford, UK
{yujie,az}@robots.ox.ac.uk
[2] DeepMind, London, UK
relja@google.com

Abstract. The objective of this paper is to learn a compact representation of image sets for template-based face recognition. We make the following contributions: first, we propose a network architecture which aggregates and embeds the face descriptors produced by deep convolutional neural networks into a compact fixed-length representation. This compact representation requires minimal memory storage and enables efficient similarity computation. Second, we propose a novel GhostVLAD layer that includes *ghost clusters*, that do not contribute to the aggregation. We show that a quality weighting on the input faces emerges automatically such that informative images contribute more than those with low quality, and that the ghost clusters enhance the network's ability to deal with poor quality images. Third, we explore how input feature dimension, number of clusters and different training techniques affect the recognition performance. Given this analysis, we train a network that far exceeds the state-of-the-art on the IJB-B face recognition dataset. This is currently one of the most challenging public benchmarks, and we surpass the state-of-the-art on both the identification and verification protocols.

1 Introduction

While most research on face recognition has focused on recognition from a single-image, *template* based face recognition, where a set of faces of the same subject is available, is now gaining attention. In the unconstrained scenario considered here, this can be a challenging task as face images may have various poses, expression, illumination, and may also be of quite varying quality.

A straightforward method to tackle multiple images per subject is to store per-image descriptors extracted from each face image (or frame in a video), and compare every pair of images between sets at query time [25,26]. However, this type of approach can be memory-consuming and prohibitively slow, especially for searching tasks in large-scale datasets. Therefore, an aggregation method that can produce a compact template representation is desired. Furthermore, this representation should support efficient computation of similarity and require minimal memory storage.

C. V. Jawahar et al. (Eds.): ACCV 2018, LNCS 11362, pp. 35–50, 2019.
https://doi.org/10.1007/978-3-030-20890-5_3

More importantly, the representation obtained from image sets should be discriminative *i.e.* template descriptors of the same subject should be close to each other in the descriptor space, whereas those of different subjects should be far apart. Although common aggregation strategies, such as average pooling and max-pooling, are able to aggregate face descriptors to produce a compact template representation [4,22] and currently achieves the state-of-the-art results [4], we seek a better solution in this paper.

As revealed by [15], image retrieval encoding methods like Fisher Vector encoding and T-embedding increase the separation between descriptors extracted from related and unrelated image patches. We therefore expect a similar encoding to be beneficial for face recognition, including both verification and identification tasks. This insight inspires us to include a similar encoding, NetVLAD [2], in the design of our network.

In this paper, we propose a convolutional neural network (Fig. 1) that satisfies all the desired properties mentioned above: it can take any number of input faces and produce a compact fixed-length descriptor to represent the image set. Moreover, this network embeds face descriptors such that the resultant template-descriptors are more discriminative than the original descriptors. The representation is efficient in both memory and query speed aspects, *i.e.* it only stores one compact descriptor per template, regardless of the number of face images in a template, and the similarity between two templates is simply measured as the scalar product (*i.e.* cosine similarity) of two template descriptors.

However, one of the key problems in unconstrained real-world situations is that some faces in a template may be of low quality – for example, low resolution, or blurred, or partially occluded. These low-quality images are distractors and are likely to hurt the performance of the face recognition system if given equal weight as the other (good quality) faces. Therefore, a sophisticated network should be able to reduce the impact of such distracting images and focus on the informative ones.

To this end, we extend the NetVLAD architecture to include *ghost clusters*. These are clusters that face descriptors can be soft assigned to, but are excluded from the aggregation. They provide a mechanism for the network to handle low quality faces, by mainly assigning them to the ghost clusters. Interestingly, although we do not explicitly learn any importance weightings between faces in each template, such property emerges automatically from our network. Specifically, low quality faces generally contribute less to the final template representation than the high-quality ones.

The networks are trained in an end-to-end fashion with only identity-level labels. They outperform state-of-the-art methods by a large margin on the public IJB-A [18] and IJB-B [30] face recognition benchmarks. These datasets are currently the most challenging in the community, and we evaluate on these in this paper.

This paper is organized as following: Sect. 2 reviews some related work on face recognition based on image sets or videos; the proposed network and implementation details are introduced in Sect. 3, followed by experimental results reported in Sect. 4. Finally a conclusion is drawn in Sect. 5.

2   Related Work

Early face recognition approaches which make use of sets of face examples (extracted from different images or video frames) aim to represent image sets as manifolds [1,12,17,19], convex hulls [5], Gaussian Mixture Models [28], or set covariance matrices [29], and measure the dissimilarity between image sets as distance between these spaces.

Later methods represent face sets more efficiently using a single fixed-length descriptor. For example, [21] aggregates local descriptors (RootSIFT [3]) extracted from face crops using Fisher Vector [23] (FV) encoding to obtain a single descriptor per face track. Since the success of deep learning in image-based face recognition [22,25,26,35], simple strategies for face descriptor aggregation prevailed, such as average-[22] and max-pooling. However, none of these strategies are trained end-to-end for face recognition as typically only the face descriptors are learnt, while aggregation is performed post hoc.

A few methods go beyond simple pooling by computing a weighted average of face descriptors based on some measure of per-face example importance. For example, [7] train a module to predict human judgement on how memorable a face is, and use this memorability score as the weight. In [33], an attention mechanism is used to compute face example weights, so that the contribution of low quality images to the final set representation is down-weighted. However, these methods rely on pretrained face descriptors and do not learn them jointly with the weighting functions, unlike our method where the entire system is trained end-to-end for face recognition.

Two other recent papers are quite related in that they explicitly take account of image quality: [9] first bins face images of similar quality and pose before aggregation; whilst [20] introduces a fully end-to-end trainable method which automatically learns to down-weight low quality images. As will be seen in the sequel, we achieve similar functionality implicitly due to the network architecture, and also exceed the performance of both these methods (see Sect. 4.4). As an interesting yet different method which can also filter low-quality images, [24] learns to aggregate the raw face images and then computes a descriptor.

Our aggregation approach is inspired by the image retrieval literature on aggregating local descriptors [2,15]. Namely, Jégou and Zisserman [15] find that, compared to simple average-pooling, Fisher Vector encoding and T-embedding increase the contrast between the similarity scores of matching and mismatching local descriptors. Motivated by this fact, we make use of a trainable aggregation layer, NetVLAD [2], and improve it for the face recognition task.

3   Set-Based Face Recognition

We aim to learn a compact representation of a face. Namely, we train a network which digests a set of example face images of a person, and produces a fixed-length template representation useful for face recognition. The network should satisfy the following properties:

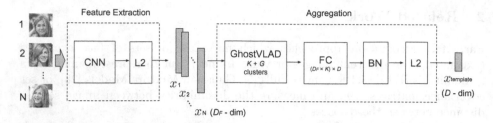

Fig. 1. Network architecture. Input images in each template are first passed through a convolutional neural network (*e.g.* ResNet-50 or SENet-50 with an additional FC layer and L2-normalization) to produce a face descriptor per image. The descriptors are aggregated into a single fixed-length vector using the GhostVLAD layer. The final D-dimensional template descriptor is obtained by reducing dimensionality using a fully-connected layer, followed by batch normalization (BN) and L2-normalization.

(1) Take any number of images as input, and output a fixed-length template descriptor to represent the input image set. (2) The output template descriptor should be compact (*i.e.* low-dimensional) in order to require little memory and facilitate fast template comparisons. (3) The output template descriptor should be discriminative, such that the similarity of templates of the same subject is much larger than that of different subjects.

We propose a convolutional neural network that fulfills all three objectives. (1) is achieved by aggregating face descriptors using a modified NetVLAD [2] layer, GhostVLAD. Compact template descriptors (2) are produced by a trained layer which performs dimensionality reduction. Discriminative representations (3) emerge because the entire network is trained end-to-end for face recognition, and since our GhostVLAD layer is able to down-weight the contribution of low-quality images, which is important for good performance [7,9,33].

The network architecture and the new GhostVLAD layer are described in Sects. 3.1 and 3.2, respectively, followed by the network training procedure (Sect. 3.3) and implementation details (Sect. 3.4).

3.1 Network Architecture

As shown in Fig. 1, the network consists of two parts: feature extraction, which computes a face descriptor for each input face image, and aggregation, which aggregates all face descriptors into a single compact template representation of the input image set.

Feature Extraction. A neural network is used to extract a face descriptor for each input face image. Any network can be used in our learning framework, but in this paper we opt for ResNet-50 [10] or SENet-50 [11]. Both networks are cropped after the global average pooling layer, and an extra FC layer is added to reduce the output dimension to D_F. We typically pick D_F to be low-dimensional (*e.g.* 128 or 256), and do not see a significant drop in face recognition performance compared to using the original 2048-D descriptors. Finally, the individual face descriptors are L2 normalized.

Aggregation. The second part uses GhostVLAD (Sect. 3.2) to aggregate multiple face descriptors into a single $D_F \times K$ vector (where K is a parameter of the method). To keep computational and memory requirements low, dimensionality reduction is performed via an FC layer, where we pick the output dimensionality D to be 128. The compact D-dimensional descriptor is then passed to a batch-normalization layer [13] and L2-normalized to form the final template representation $x_{template}$.

3.2   GhostVLAD: NetVLAD with Ghost Clusters

The key component of the aggregation block is our *GhostVLAD* trainable aggregation layer, which given N D_F-dimensional face descriptors computes a single $D_F \times K$ dimensional output. It is based on the NetVLAD [2] layer which implements an encoding similar to VLAD encoding [14], while being differentiable and thus fully-trainable. NetVLAD has been shown to outperform average and max pooling for the same vector dimensionality, which makes it perfectly suited for our task. Here we provide a brief overview of NetVLAD (for full details please refer to [2]), followed by our improvement, GhostVLAD.

NetVLAD. For N D_F-dimensional input descriptors $\{x_i\}$ and a chosen number of clusters K, NetVLAD pooling produces a single $D_F \times K$ vector V (for convenience written as a $D_F \times K$ matrix) according to the following equation:

$$V(j, k) = \sum_{i=1}^{N} \frac{e^{a_k^T x_i + b_k}}{\sum_{k'=1}^{K} e^{a_{k'}^T x_i + b_{k'}}} (x_i(j) - c_k(j)) \tag{1}$$

where $\{a_k\}$, $\{b_k\}$ and $\{c_k\}$ are trainable parameters, with $k \in [1, 2, \ldots, K]$. The first term corresponds to the soft-assignment weight of the input vector x_i for cluster k, while the second term computes the residual between the vector and the cluster centre. The final output is obtained by performing L2 normalization.

GhostVLAD. We extend NetVLAD with "ghost" clusters to form *GhostVLAD*, as shown in Fig. 2. Namely, we add further G "ghost" clusters which contribute to the soft assignments in the same manner as the original K clusters, but residuals between input vectors and the ghost cluster centres are ignored and do not contribute to the final output. In other words, the summation in the denominator of Eq. 1 instead of to K goes to $K + G$, while the output is still $D_F \times K$ dimensional; this means $\{a_k\}$ and $\{b_k\}$ have $K + G$ elements each, while $\{c_k\}$ still has K. Another view is that we are computing NetVLAD with $K + G$ clusters, followed by removing the elements that correspond to the G ghost clusters. Note that GhostVLAD is a generalization of NetVLAD as with $G = 0$ the two are equivalent. As with NetVLAD, GhostVLAD can be implemented efficiently using standard convolutional neural network building blocks, *e.g.* the soft-assignment can be done by stacking input descriptors and applying a convolution operation, followed by a convolutional soft-max; for details see [2].

The intuition behind the incorporation of ghost clusters is to make it easier for the network to adjust the contribution of each face example to the template

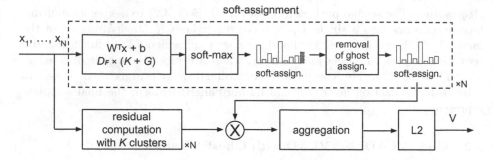

Fig. 2. GhostVLAD. For each input descriptor, NetVLAD performs soft-assignment into K cluster centres, computed as a linear transformation followed by a soft-max. It then, for each cluster centre, aggregates all residuals between input descriptors and the cluster centre, weighted with the soft-assignment values. The final vector is produced as a concatenation of the per-cluster aggregated residuals; for more details see Eq. 1 and [2]. We introduce G "ghost" clusters in the soft-assignment stage, where the "ghost" assignment weight is illustrated with a dotted red bar (here we show only $G = 1$ ghost cluster). The ghost assignments are then eliminated and residual aggregation proceeds as with NetVLAD. This mechanism enables the network to assign uninformative descriptors to ghost clusters thus decreasing their soft-assignment weights for non-ghost clusters, and therefore reducing their contribution to the final template representation. (Color figure online)

representation by assigning examples to be ignored to the ghost clusters. For example, in an ideal case, a highly blurry face image would be strongly assigned to a ghost cluster, making the assignment weights to non-ghost clusters close to zero, thus causing its contribution to the template representation to be negligible; in Sect. 4.5 we qualitatively validate this intuition. However, note that we do not explicitly force low-quality images to get assigned to ghost clusters, but instead let the network discover the optimal behaviour through end-to-end training for face recognition.

3.3 Network Training

In this section we describe how to train the network for face recognition, but note that GhostVLAD is a general layer which can also be used for other tasks.

Training Loss. Just for training purposes, we append the network with a fully-connected "classification" layer of size $D \times T$, where D is the size of the template representation and T is the number of identities available in the training set. We use the one-versus-all logistic regression loss as empirically we found that it converges faster and outperforms cross-entropy loss. The classification layer is discarded after training and the trained network is used to extract a single fixed-length template representation for the input face images.

Training with Degraded Images. For unconstrained face recognition, it is important to be able to handle images of varying quality that typically occur in the wild. The motivation behind our network architecture, namely the GhostVLAD layer, is to enable it to down-weight the influence of these images on the template representation. However, since our training dataset only contains good quality images, it is necessary to perform data augmentation in the form of image degradation, such as blurring or compression (see Sect. 3.4 for details), in order to more closely match the varying image quality encountered at test time.

3.4   Implementation Details

This section discusses full details of the training process, including training data, data augmentation, network initialization, *etc.*

Training Data. We use face images from the training set of the VGGFace2 dataset [4] to train the network. It consists of around 3 million images, covering 8631 identities. For each identity, there are on average 360 face images across different ages and poses. To perform set-based training, we form image sets on-the-fly by repeatedly sampling a fixed number of images belonging to the same identity.

Data Augmentation. Training images are resized such that the smallest dimension is 256 and random crops of size 224×224 are used as inputs to the network. Further augmentations include random horizontal flipping and a random rotation of no greater than $10°$.

We adopt four methods to degrade images for training: isotropic blur, motion blur, decreased resolution and JPEG compression. Each degradation method has a probability of 0.1 to be applied to a training image, where, to prevent over-degradation, a maximum of two transformations per image is allowed. Isotropic blur is implemented using a Gaussian filter where the standard deviation is uniformly sampled between 6 and 16. For motion blur, the angle of motion is uniformly sampled between 0 and $359°$, and the motion length is fixed to 11. Resolution decrease is simulated by downscaling the image by a factor of 10 and scaling it back up to the original size. Finally, we add JPEG compression artefacts by randomly compressing the images to one of three compression ratios: 0.01, 0.05 and 0.09.

Training Procedure. The network can be trained end-to-end in one go, but, to make the training faster and more stable, we divide it into three stages; all stages only use the VGGFace2 [4] dataset. In the first two stages, parts of the network are trained for single-image face classification (*i.e.* the input image set consists of a single image), and image degradation is not performed. Firstly, the feature extractor network is pre-trained for single-image face classification by temporarily (just for this stage) appending a classification FC layer on top of it, and training the network with the cross-entropy loss. Secondly, we train the whole network end-to-end for single-image classification with one-versus-all logistic regression loss, but exclude the ghost clusters from GhostVLAD because training images are not degraded in this stage. Finally, we add ghost clusters and enable image degradation, and train the whole network using image sets with one-versus-all logistic regression loss.

Parameter Initialization. The non-ghost clusters of GhostVLAD are initialized as in NetVLAD [2] by clustering its input features with k-means into K clusters, where only non-degraded images are used. The G ghost clusters are initialized similarly, but using degraded images for the clustering; note that for $G = 1$ (a setting we often use) k-means simplifies to computing the mean over the features. The FC following GhostVLAD which performs dimensionality reduction is then initialized using the PCA transformation matrix computed on the GhostVLAD output features.

Training Details. The network is trained using stochastic gradient descend with momentum, implemented in MatConvNet [27]. The mini-batch consists of 84 face images, *i.e.* if we train with image sets of size two, a batch contains 42 image sets, one per identity. When one-versus-all logistic regression loss is used, for each image set, we update the network weights based on the positive class and only 20 negative classes (instead of 8631) that obtain the highest classification scores. The initial learning rate of 0.0001 is used for all parameters apart from GhostVLAD's assignment parameters and the classification FC weights, for which we use 0.1 and 1, respectively. The learning rates are divided by 10 when validation error stagnates, while weight decay and momentum are fixed to 0.0005 and 0.9, respectively.

4   Experiments

In this section, we describe the experimental setup, investigate the impact of our design choices, and compare results with the state-of-the-art.

4.1   Benchmark Datasets and Evaluation Protocol

Standard and most challenging public face recognition datasets IJB-A [18] and IJB-B [30] are used for evaluation. In contrast to single-image based face datasets such as [4,8,16,22], IJB-A and IJB-B are intended for template-based face recognition, which is exactly the task we consider in this work. The IJB-A dataset contains 5,712 images and 2,085 videos, covering 500 subjects. The IJB-B dataset is an extension of IJB-A with a total of 11,754 images and 7,011 videos from 1,845 subjects, as well as 10,044 non-face images. There is no overlap between subjects in VGGFace2, which we use for training, and the test datasets. Faces are detected from images and all video frames using MTCNN [34], the face crops are then resized such that the smallest dimension is 224 and the central 224×224 crop is used as the face example.

Evaluation Protocol. We follow the standard benchmark procedure for IJB-A and IJB-B, and evaluate on "1:1 face verification" and "1:N face identification". The goal of *1:1 verification* is to make a decision whether two templates belong to the same person, done by thresholding the similarity between the templates. Verification performance is assessed via the receiver operating characteristic (ROC) curve, *i.e.* by measuring the trade-off between the true accept rates (TAR) *vs* false accept rates (FAR). For *1:N identification*, templates from the probe set are used to rank all templates in a given gallery. The performance is measured using the true positive identification rate (TPIR) *vs* false positive identification rate (FPIR) (*i.e.* the decision error trade-off (DET) curve) and *vs* Rank-N (*i.e.* the cumulative match characteristic (CMC) curve). Evaluation protocols are the same for both benchmark datasets. For IJB-A and for IJB-B identification, we report, as per standard, the mean and standard deviation of the performance measures.

4.2   Networks, Deployment and Baselines

Our Networks. As explained earlier in Sect. 3.1, we use two different architectures as backbone feature extractors: ResNet-50 [10] and SENet-50 [11]. They are cropped after global average-pooling which produces a $D_F = 2048$ dimensional face descriptor, while we also experiment with reducing the dimensionality via an additional FC, down to $D_F = 256$ or $D_F = 128$.

To disambiguate various network configurations, we name the networks as *Ext*-GV-*S*(-g*G*), where *Ext* is the feature extractor network (*Res* for ResNet-50 or *SE* for SENet-50), *S* is the size of image sets used during training, and *G* is the number of ghost clusters (if zero, the suffix is dropped). For example, *SE-GV-3-g2* denotes a network which uses the SENet-50 as the feature extractor, training image sets of size 3, and 2 ghost clusters.

Network Deployment. In the IJB-A and IJB-B datasets, there are images and videos available for each subject. Here we follow the established approach of [4,6] to balance the contributions of face examples from different sources, as otherwise a single very long video could completely dominate the representation. In more detail, face examples are extracted from all video frames, and their additive contributions to the GhostVLAD representation are down-weighed by the number of frames in the video.

The similarity between two templates is measured as the scalar product between the template representations; recall that they have unit norm (Fig. 1).

Baselines. Our network is compared with several average-pooling baselines. The baseline architecture consists of a feature extractor network which produces a face descriptor for each input example, and the template representation is performed by average-pooling the face descriptors (with source balancing), followed by L2 normalization. The same feature extractor networks are used as for our method, ResNet-50 or SENet-50, abbreviated as *Res* and *SE*, respectively, with an optionally added FC layer to perform dimensionality reduction down to 128-D or 256-D. These networks are trained for single-image face classification, which is equivalent to stage 1 of our training procedure from Sect. 3.4, and also corresponds to the current state-of-the-art approach [4] (albeit with more training data – see Sect. 4.4 for details and comparisons). No image degradation is performed as it decreases performance when combined with single-image classification training.

Table 1. Verification performance on the IJB-B dataset. A higher value of TAR is better. D_F is the face descriptor dimension before aggregation. D is the dimensionality of the final template representation. K and G are the number of non-ghost and ghost clusters in GhostVLAD, respectively. 'No. faces' is the number of faces per set used during training. 'Deg.' indicates whether the training images are degraded. All training is done using the VGGFace2 dataset.

Row id	Network	D_F	D	K	G	No. faces	Deg.	1:1 Verification TAR (FAR=)			
								$1E-5$	$1E-4$	$1E-3$	$1E-2$
1	Res [4]	2014	2048	-	-	1	✗	0.647	0.784	0.878	0.938
2	Res	128	128	-	-	1	✗	0.646	0.785	0.890	0.954
3	SE	128	128	-	-	1	✗	0.670	0.803	0.896	0.954
4	SE	256	256	-	-	1	✗	0.677	0.807	0.892	0.955
5	SE-2	256	256	-	-	2	✓	0.679	0.810	0.902	0.958
6	Res-GV-2	128	128	8	0	2	✓	0.715	0.835	0.916	0.963
7	SE-GV-2	128	128	8	0	2	✓	0.721	0.835	0.916	0.963
8	SE-GV-2	256	128	8	0	2	✗	0.685	0.823	0.925	0.963
9	SE-GV-2	256	128	8	0	2	✓	0.738	0.850	0.923	0.964
10	SE-GV-2	256	128	4	0	2	✓	0.729	0.841	0.914	0.957
11	SE-GV-2	256	128	16	0	2	✓	0.722	0.848	0.921	0.964
12	SE-GV-3	256	128	8	0	3	✓	0.741	0.853	0.925	0.963
13	SE-GV-4	256	128	8	0	4	✓	0.747	0.852	0.922	0.961
14	SE-GV-3-g1	256	128	8	1	3	✓	0.753	0.861	**0.926**	0.963
15	SE-GV-4-g1	256	128	8	1	4	✓	**0.762**	**0.863**	**0.926**	0.963
16	SE-GV-3-g2	256	128	8	2	3	✓	0.754	0.861	0.926	**0.964**
17	SE-GV-4	256	256	8	0	4	✓	0.713	0.838	0.919	0.963
18	SE-GV-4-g1	256	256	8	1	4	✓	0.739	0.853	0.924	0.963

In addition, we train the baseline architecture SENet-50 with average-pooling using our training procedure (Sect. 3.3), *i.e.* with image sets of size 2 and degraded images, and refer to it as *SE-2*.

4.3   Ablation Studies on IJB-B

Here we evaluate various design choices of our architecture and compare it to baselines on the IJB-B dataset, as it is larger and more challenging than IJB-A; results on verification and identification are shown in Tables 1 and 2, respectively.

Feature Extractor and Dimensionality Reduction. Comparing rows 1 *vs* 2 of the two tables shows that reducing the dimensionality of the face features from 2048-D to 128-D does not affect the performance much, and in fact sometimes improves it due to added parameters in the form of the dimensionality reduction FC. As the feature extractor backbone, SENet-50 consistently beats ResNet-50, as summarized in rows 2 *vs* 3.

Table 2. Identification performance on the IJB-B dataset. A higher value of TPIR is better. See caption of Table 1 for the explanations of column titles. Note, for readability standard deviations are not included here, but are included in Table 3.

Row id	Network	D_F	D	K	G	No. faces	Deg.	1:N Identification TPIR				
								FPIR = 0.01	FPIR = 0.1	Rank-1	Rank-5	Rank-10
1	Res [4]	2048	2048	-	-	1	✗	0.701	0.824	0.886	0.936	0.953
2	Res	128	128	-	-	1	✗	0.688	0.833	0.901	0.950	0.963
3	SE	128	128	-	-	1	✗	0.712	0.849	0.908	0.949	0.963
4	SE	256	256	-	-	1	✗	0.718	0.854	0.908	0.948	0.962
5	SE-2	256	256	-	-	2	✓	0.717	0.857	0.909	0.949	0.962
6	Res-GV-2	128	128	8	0	2	✓	0.762	0.872	0.917	0.953	0.964
7	SE-GV-2	128	128	8	0	2	✓	0.753	0.880	0.917	0.953	0.964
8	SE-GV-2	256	128	8	0	2	✗	0.751	0.884	0.912	0.952	0.962
9	SE-GV-2	256	128	8	0	2	✓	0.760	0.879	0.918	0.955	0.964
10	SE-GV-2	256	128	4	0	2	✓	0.749	0.868	0.914	0.953	0.963
11	SE-GV-2	256	128	16	0	2	✓	0.759	0.879	0.918	0.954	**0.965**
12	SE-GV-3	256	128	8	0	3	✓	0.764	0.885	0.921	0.955	0.962
13	SE-GV-4	256	128	8	0	4	✓	0.752	0.878	0.914	0.952	0.960
14	SE-GV-3-g1	256	128	8	1	3	✓	0.770	**0.888**	**0.923**	0.956	**0.965**
15	SE-GV-4-g1	256	128	8	1	4	✓	**0.776**	**0.888**	0.921	**0.957**	0.964
16	SE-GV-3-g2	256	128	8	2	3	✓	0.772	0.886	0.922	**0.957**	0.964
17	SE-GV-4	256	256	8	0	4	✓	0.732	0.870	0.912	0.952	0.963
18	SE-GV-4-g1	256	256	8	1	4	✓	**0.776**	0.883	0.921	**0.957**	**0.965**

Training for Set-Based Face Recognition. The currently adopted set-based face recognition approach of training with single-image examples and performing aggregation post hoc (*SE*, row 4) is clearly inferior to our training procedure which is aware of image sets (*SE-2*, row 5).

Learnt GhostVLAD Aggregation. Using the GhostVLAD aggregation layer (with $G = 0$ *i.e.* equivalent to NetVLAD) together with our set-based training framework strongly outperforms the standard average-pooling approach, regardless of whether training is done with non-degraded images (*SE-GV-2*, row 8 *vs SE*, rows 3 and 4), degraded images (*SE-GV-2*, row 9 *vs SE-2*, row 5), or if a different feature extractor architecture (ResNet-50) is used (*Res-GV-2*, row 6 *vs Res*, row 2). Using 256-D *vs* 128-D face descriptors as inputs to GhostVLAD, while keeping the same dimensionality of the final template representation (128-D), achieves better results (rows 9 *vs* 7), so we use 256-D in all latter experiments.

Training with Degraded Images. When using our set-based training procedure, training with degraded images brings a consistent boost, as shown in rows 9 *vs* 8, since it better matches the test-time scenario which contains images of varying quality.

Number of Clusters K. GhostVLAD (and NetVLAD) have a hyperparameter K – the number of non-ghost clusters – which we vary between 4 and 16 (rows 9 to 11) to study its effect on face recognition performance. It is expected that K shouldn't be too small so that underfitting is avoided (*e.g.* $K = 1$ is similar to average-pooling) nor too large in order to prevent over-quantization and

Table 3. Comparison with state-of-the-art for *verification* and *identification* on the IJB-B dataset. A higher value of TAR and TPIR is better. D is the dimension of the template representation. The training datasets abbreviations are VGGFace2 [4] (VF2) and MS-Celeb-1M [8] (MS). Our best network, SE-GV-4-g1, sets the state-of-the-art by a significant margin on both verification and identification on the challenging IJB-B dataset (except for concurrent work [31]).

Network	Training dataset	D	1:1 Verification TAR				
			$FAR = 1E - 5$	$FAR = 1E - 4$	$FAR = 1E - 3$	$FAR = 1E - 2$	
SE [4]	VF2	2048	0.671	0.800	0.888	0.949	
SE [4]	MS+VF2	2048	0.705	0.831	0.908	0.956	
MN-vc [32]	VF2	2048	0.708	0.831	0.909	0.958	
SE+DCN [31]	VF2	-	0.730	0.849	**0.937**	**0.975**	
SE-GV-3	VF2	128	0.741	0.853	0.925	0.963	
SE-GV-4-g1	VF2	128	**0.762**	**0.863**	0.926	0.963	
			1:N Identification TPIR				
			$FPIR = 0.01$	$FPIR = 0.1$	Rank-1	Rank-5	Rank-10
SE [4]	VF2	2048	0.706±0.047	0.839±0.035	0.901±0.030	0.945±0.016	0.958 ± 0.010
SE [4]	MS+VF2	2048	0.743±0.037	0.863±0.032	0.902±0.036	0.946±0.022	0.959 ± 0.015
SE-GV-3	VF2	128	0.764±0.041	0.885±0.032	0.921±0.023	0.955±0.013	0.962 ± 0.010
SE-GV-4-g1	VF2	128	**0.776 ± 0.030**	**0.888 ± 0.029**	**0.921 ± 0.020**	**0.956 ± 0.013**	**0.964 ± 0.010**

overfitting. As in traditional image retrieval [14], we find that a wide range of K achieves good performance, with $K = 8$ being the best.

Ghost Clusters. Introducing a single ghost cluster ($G = 1$) brings significant improvement over the vanilla NetVLAD, as shown by comparing *SE-GV-3-g1 vs SE-GV-3* (rows 14 *vs* 12) and *SE-GV-4-g1 vs SE-GV-4* (rows 15 *vs* 13). Using one ghost cluster is sufficient as increasing the number of ghost clusters to two does not result in significant differences (row 16 *vs* row 14). Ghost clusters enable the system to automatically down-weight the contribution of low quality images, as will be shown in Sect. 4.5, which improves the template representations and benefits face recognition.

Set Size Used During Training. To perform set-based training, as described in Sect. 3.4, image sets are created by sampling a fixed number of faces for a subject; the number of sampled faces is another parameter of the method. Increasing the set size from 2 to 3 consistently improves results (rows 9 *vs* 12), while there is no clear winner between using 3 or 4 face examples (worse for $G = 0$, rows 12 *vs* 13, better for $G = 1$, rows 15 *vs* 14).

Output Dimensionality. Comparisons are also made between networks with 128-D output features and those with 256-D (*i.e.* row 13 *vs* 17 and row 15 *vs* 18), and we can see that networks with 128-D output achieve better performance while being more memory-efficient.

4.4   Comparison with State-of-the-Art

In this section, our best networks, *SE-GV-3* and *SE-GV-4-g1*, are compared against the state-of-the-art on the IJB-B dataset. For results on IJB-A refer to the extended version of this paper [36]. The currently best performing method [4] is the same as our *SE* baseline (*i.e.* average-pooling of SENet-50 features trained for single-image classification) but trained on a much larger training set, MS-Celeb-1M dataset [8], and then fine-tuned on VGGFace2.

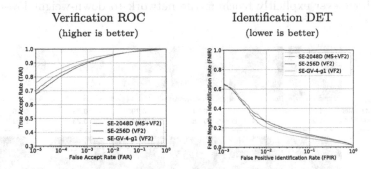

Fig. 3. Results on the IJB-B dataset. Our *SE-GV-4-g1* network which produces 128-D templates, beats the best baseline (*SE* with 256-D templates) and the state-of-the-art trained on a much larger dataset (*SE* with 2048-D templates) trained on VGGFace2 and MS-Celeb-1M).

From Table 3 and Fig. 3, it is clear that the GhostVLAD network (*SE-GV-4-g1*) convincingly outperforms previous methods and sets a new state-of-the-art for both identification and verification on the IJB-B dataset. The network achieves the best TAR at $FAR = 1E - 5$ and $FAR = 1E - 4$, and is only lower than a concurrent work [31] at $FAR = 1E - 3$ and $FAR = 1E - 2$. Furthermore, our networks produce much smaller template descriptors than previous state-of-the-art networks (128-D *vs* 2048-D), making them more useful in real-world applications due to smaller memory requirements and faster template comparisons.

The results are especially impressive as we only train using VGGFace2 [4] and beat methods which train with much more data, such as [4] which combine VGGFace2 and MS-Celeb-1M [8], *e.g.* TAR at $FAR = 1E - 5$ of 0.762 *vs* 0.705 for verification on IJB-B, and TPIR at $FPIR = 0.01$ of 0.776 *vs* 0.743 for identification on IJB-B. When considering only methods trained on the same data (VGGFace2), our improvement over the state-of-the-art is even larger: TAR at $FAR = 1E - 5$ of 0.762 *vs* 0.671 for verification on IJB-B, and TPIR at $FPIR = 0.01$ of 0.776 *vs* 0.706 for verification on IJB-B.

4.5   Analysis of Ghost Clusters

Addition of ghost clusters was motivated by the intuition that it enables our network to learn to ignore uninformative low-quality images by assigning them to the discarded ghost clusters. Here we evaluate this hypothesis qualitatively.

Recall that GhostVLAD computes a template representation by aggregating residual vectors of input descriptors, where a residual vector is a concatenation of per non-ghost cluster residuals weighted by their non-ghost assignment weights (Sect. 3.2). Therefore, the contribution of a specific example image towards the template representation can be measured as the norm of the residual.

Figure 4 show that our intuition is correct – the network automatically learns to dramatically down-weight blurry and low-resolution images, thus improving the signal-to-noise ratio. Note that this behaviour emerges completely automatically without ever explicitly teaching the network to down-weight low-quality images.

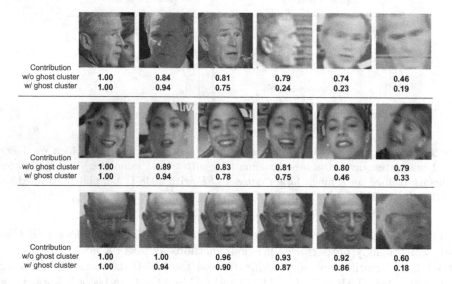

Fig. 4. **Effect of ghost clusters.** Each row shows shows 6 images from a template in the IJB-B dataset. The contribution (relative to the max) of each image to the final template representation is shown (see Sect. 4.5 for details), for the cases of no ghost clusters ($G = 0$, network SE-GV-3) and one ghost cluster ($G = 1$, network SE-GV-4-$g1$) in GhostVLAD. Introduction of a single ghost cluster dramatically reduces the contribution of low-quality images to the template, improving the signal-to-noise ratio.

5   Conclusions

We introduced a neural network architecture and training procedure for learning compact representations of image sets for template-based face recognition. Due to the novel GhostVLAD layer, the network is able to automatically learn to weight face descriptors depending on their information content. Our template representations outperform the state-of-the-art on the challenging IJB-A and IJB-B benchmarks by a large margin.

The network architecture proposed here could also be applied to other image-set tasks such as person re-identification, and set-based retrieval. More generally, the idea of having a 'null' vector available for assignments could have applicability in many situations where it is advantageous to have a mechanism to remove noisy or corrupted data.

Acknowledgements. We thank Weidi Xie for his useful advice, and we thank Li Shen for providing pre-trained networks. This work was funded by an EPSRC studentship and EPSRC Programme Grant Seebibyte EP/M013774/1.

References

1. Arandjelović, O., Cipolla, R.: An information-theoretic approach to face recognition from face motion manifolds. Image Vis. Comput. **24**(6), 639–647 (2006)
2. Arandjelović, R., Gronat, P., Torii, A., Pajdla, T., Sivic, J.: NetVLAD: CNN architecture for weakly supervised place recognition. In: Proceedings of the CVPR (2016)
3. Arandjelović, R., Zisserman, A.: Three things everyone should know to improve object retrieval. In: Proceedings of the CVPR (2012)
4. Cao, Q., Shen, L., Xie, W., Parkhi, O.M., Zisserman, A.: VGGFace2: a dataset for recognising faces across pose and age. In: Proceedings of the International Conference on Automatic Face & Gesture Recognition (2018)
5. Cevikalp, H., Triggs, B.: Face recognition based on image sets. In: Proceedings of the CVPR (2010)
6. Crosswhite, N., Byrne, J., Stauffer, C., Parkhi, O.M., Cao, Q., Zisserman, A.: Template adaptation for face verification and identification. In: Proceedings of the International Conference on Automatic Face & Gesture Recognition (2017)
7. Goswami, G., Bhardwaj, R., Singh, R., Vatsa, M.: MDLFace: memorability augmented deep learning for video face recognition. In: 2014 IEEE International Joint Conference on Biometrics (IJCB), pp. 1–7. IEEE (2014)
8. Guo, Y., Zhang, L., Hu, Y., He, X., Gao, J.: MS-celeb-1M: a dataset and benchmark for large-scale face recognition. In: Leibe, B., Matas, J., Sebe, N., Welling, M. (eds.) ECCV 2016. LNCS, vol. 9907, pp. 87–102. Springer, Cham (2016). https://doi.org/10.1007/978-3-319-46487-9_6
9. Hassner, T., et al.: Pooling faces: template based face recognition with pooled face images. In: CVPR Workshops, pp. 59–67 (2016)
10. He, K., Zhang, X., Ren, S., Sun, J.: Deep residual learning for image recognition. In: Proceedings of the CVPR (2016)
11. Hu, J., Shen, L., Sun, G.: Squeeze-and-excitation networks. In: Proceedings of the CVPR (2018)
12. Huang, Z., Wang, R., Shan, S., Chen, X.: Projection metric learning on Grassmann manifold with application to video based face recognition. In: Proceedings of the CVPR, pp. 140–149 (2015)
13. Ioffe, S., Szegedy, C.: Batch normalization: accelerating deep network training by reducing internal covariate shift. In: Proceedings of the ICML (2015)
14. Jégou, H., Douze, M., Schmid, C., Pérez, P.: Aggregating local descriptors into a compact image representation. In: Proceedings of the CVPR (2010)
15. Jégou, H., Zisserman, A.: Triangulation embedding and democratic aggregation for image search. In: Proceedings of the CVPR (2014)
16. Kemelmacher-Shlizerman, I., Seitz, S., Miller, D., Brossard, E.: The megaface benchmark: 1 million faces for recognition at scale. In: Proceedings of the CVPR, June 2016

17. Kim, T., Arandjelović, O., Cipolla, R.: Boosted manifold principal angles for image set-based recognition. Pattern Recognit. **40**(9), 2475–2484 (2007)
18. Klare, B., et al.: Pushing the frontiers of unconstrained face detection and recognition: IARPA Janus benchmark-A. In: Proceedings of the CVPR, pp. 1931–1939 (2015)
19. Lee, K., Ho, J., Yang, M., Kriegman, D.: Video-based face recognition using probabilistic appearance manifolds. In: Proceedings of the CVPR (2003)
20. Liu, Y., Yan, J., Ouyang, W.: Quality aware network for set to set recognition. In: Proceedings of the CVPR, pp. 5790–5799 (2017)
21. Parkhi, O.M., Simonyan, K., Vedaldi, A., Zisserman, A.: A compact and discriminative face track descriptor. In: Proceedings of the CVPR. IEEE (2014)
22. Parkhi, O.M., Vedaldi, A., Zisserman, A.: Deep face recognition. In: Proceedings of the BMVC (2015)
23. Perronnin, F., Liu, Y., Sánchez, J., Poirier, H.: Large-scale image retrieval with compressed fisher vectors. In: Proceedings of the CVPR (2010)
24. Rao, Y., Lin, J., Lu, J., Zhou, J.: Learning discriminative aggregation network for video-based face recognition. In: Proceedings of the ICCV, pp. 3781–3790 (2017)
25. Schroff, F., Kalenichenko, D., Philbin, J.: FaceNet: a unified embedding for face recognition and clustering. In: Proceedings of the CVPR (2015)
26. Taigman, Y., Yang, M., Ranzato, M., Wolf, L.: Deep-face: closing the gap to human-level performance in face verification. In: IEEE CVPR (2014)
27. Vedaldi, A., Lenc, K.: MatConvNet: convolutional neural networks for Matlab. In: Proceedings of the ACMM (2015)
28. Wang, W., Wang, R., Huang, Z., Shan, S., Chen, X.: Discriminant analysis on Riemannian manifold of Gaussian distributions for face recognition with image sets. In: Proceedings of the CVPR, pp. 2048–2057 (2015)
29. Wang, W., Wang, R., Shan, S., Chen, X.: Discriminative covariance oriented representation learning for face recognition with image sets. In: Proceedings of the CVPR, pp. 5599–5608 (2017)
30. Whitelam, C., et al.: IARPA Janus benchmark-B face dataset. In: CVPR Workshop on Biometrics (2017)
31. Xie, W., Shen, L., Zisserman, A.: Comparator networks. In: Ferrari, V., Hebert, M., Sminchisescu, C., Weiss, Y. (eds.) ECCV 2018. LNCS, vol. 11215, pp. 811–826. Springer, Cham (2018). https://doi.org/10.1007/978-3-030-01252-6_48
32. Xie, W., Zisserman, A.: Multicolumn networks for face recognition. In: Proceedings of the BMVC (2018)
33. Yang, J., Ren, P., Chen, D., Wen, F., Li, H., Hua, G.: Neural aggregation network for video face recognition. In: Proceedings of the CVPR, pp. 4362–4371 (2017)
34. Zhang, R., Isola, P., Efros, A.A.: Colorful image colorization. In: Leibe, B., Matas, J., Sebe, N., Welling, M. (eds.) ECCV 2016. LNCS, vol. 9907, pp. 649–666. Springer, Cham (2016). https://doi.org/10.1007/978-3-319-46487-9_40
35. Zheng, Y., Pal, D., Savvides, M.: Ring loss: convex feature normalization for face recognition. In: Proceedings of the CVPR, pp. 5089–5097 (2018)
36. Zhong, Y., Arandjelović, R., Zisserman, A.: GhostVLAD for set-based face recognition. arXiv preprint arXiv:1810.09951 (2018)

Learning Image-to-Image Translation Using Paired and Unpaired Training Samples

Soumya Tripathy[1(✉)], Juho Kannala[2], and Esa Rahtu[1]

[1] Tampere University of Technology, Tampere, Finland
{soumya.tripathy,esa.rahtu}@tut.fi
[2] Aalto University of Technology, Helsinki, Finland
juho.kannala@aalto.fi

Abstract. Image-to-image translation is a general name for a task where an image from one domain is converted to a corresponding image in another domain, given sufficient training data. Traditionally different approaches have been proposed depending on whether aligned image pairs or two sets of (unaligned) examples from both domains are available for training. While paired training samples might be difficult to obtain, the unpaired setup leads to a highly under-constrained problem and inferior results. In this paper, we propose a new general purpose image-to-image translation model that is able to utilize both paired and unpaired training data simultaneously. We compare our method with two strong baselines and obtain both qualitatively and quantitatively improved results. Our model outperforms the baselines also in the case of purely paired and unpaired training data. To our knowledge, this is the first work to consider such hybrid setup in image-to-image translation.

1 Introduction

Many vision and graphics problems such as converting grayscale to colour images [1], satellite images to maps [2], sketches to line drawings [3], and paintings to photographs [4] can be seen as image-to-image translation tasks. Traditionally, each problem has been tackled with specific architectures and loss functions that do not generalize well to other tasks. Recently, Generative Adversarial Networks (GANs) [5] have provided an alternative approach, where the loss function is learned from the data instead of defining it manually. Impressive results have been demonstrated in several areas such as image inpainting [6], style transfer [4], super-resolution [7] and image colorisation [1]. Still, only a few papers consider a general purpose solution. One such work is [2] that proposes a conditional GAN architecture applicable to a wide range of translations tasks. Unfortunately, the system requires a large set of input-output image pairs for

Electronic supplementary material The online version of this chapter (https://doi.org/10.1007/978-3-030-20890-5_4) contains supplementary material, which is available to authorized users.

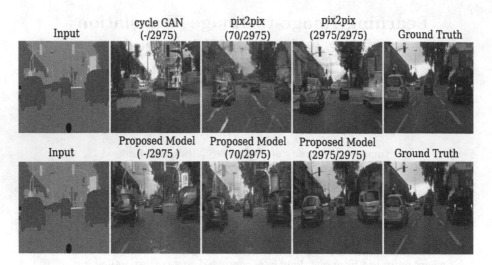

Fig. 1. An example result for label map to photograph translation task. From left to right (columnwise): input label map, cycleGAN [4] vs proposed model (only unpaired training examples), pix2pix [2] vs proposed model (70 paired data out of 2975 training samples), pix2pix [2] vs proposed model (2975 paired training samples) and the ground truth. Our hybrid model provides a clear benefit over the baseline methods.

training. While such data might be easy to obtain for certain tasks (e.g. image colorization), it poses a major restriction in general.

To overcome this limitation, several works [4,8–13] have proposed models that learn the mapping using only a set of (unpaired) examples from both domains (e.g. a set of photographs and another set of paintings). Although suitable data is substantially easier to obtain, the problem becomes highly underconstrained. This clearly hampers the performance compared to models using paired training samples. For example, Fig. 1 shows semantic label to photograph translation results for [4]. It is quite evident that [4] gets confused between the labels as it produces buildings in the place of trees. This problem of label switching is very common in such models and it arises due to the lack of supervision.

In practice, it would be beneficial to study a hybrid solution that is able to take advantage of both types training data. In many real-world applications, one can afford to produce a small set of paired training samples (e.g. 30) providing strong constraints for the task. The additional unpaired samples facilitate the learning of further details and improve the quality of the outputs. As shown in the Fig. 1, our hybrid approach produces better quality results than the models using either paired or unpaired type of data during the training. Moreover, since there exists already a few datasets with paired training examples (e.g. semantic segmentation [14], image colorization [1], super-resolution [15], and time hallucination [16]) it would make sense to leverage this information to slightly different but related problems.

State of the art methods such as [4,8] and [2,17] are carefully designed to deal with unpaired and paired data respectively. For example, [2] utilizes conditional

GAN framework [18] to take advantage of the paired training samples and [4] uses a cyclic structure with unconditional GANs to handle the unpaired examples during training. In practice, we found it difficult to use the existing models to take advantage of both types of training examples simultaneously.

In this paper, we propose a new general purpose image-to-image translation approach that is able to utilize both paired and unpaired training examples. To our knowledge, this is the first work to study such hybrid problem. The additional contributions of our paper are (1) a new adversarial cycle consistency loss that improves the translation results also in purely unpaired setup, (2) a combination of structural and adversarial loss improving learning with paired training samples and (3) we demonstrate that it is possible to improve translation results by using training samples from related external dataset.

2   Related Work

2.1   Generative Adversarial Network (GAN)

The original GAN [5] consists of two competing network architectures called generator and discriminator. The generator network produces output samples which should ideally be indistinguishable from the training distribution. Since it is infeasible to engineer a proper loss function, the assessment is done by the discriminator network. Both networks are differentiable, which allows to train them jointly. Originally, GANs were mainly used to generate images from random inputs [7]. However, recent works also consider cases where generation is guided by an additional input such as semantic label map [18], text [19,20], or attributes [21]. These kinds of models are generally known as conditional GANs [18].

2.2   Image-to-Image Translation Using Paired Training Data

Conditional GAN architectures have been widely applied in image-to-image translation tasks where sufficient amount of paired training examples are available [2,17,22,23]. In particular, [2] proposed a general purpose image to image translator "pix2pix" for various applications such as semantic maps to real image, edges to shoe images, and gray to color images. This work was later extended in [17] to produce high-resolution outputs. In addition, some recent work have obtained excellent results without adversarial learning [24]. However, it would be difficult to generalize them to unpaired training samples.

2.3   Image-to-Image Translation Using Unpaired Training Data

Three concurrent works "cycleGAN" [4], "DiscoGAN" [8] and "DualGAN" [9] propose architectures consisting of two generator-discriminator pairs. The first pair learns a forward mapping from source to target domain, while the second pair learns the inverse of it. Both pairs are trained simultaneously using adversarial losses and an additional loss that encourages cascaded mapping to reproduce the original input image (referred as cycle consistency loss in [4]).

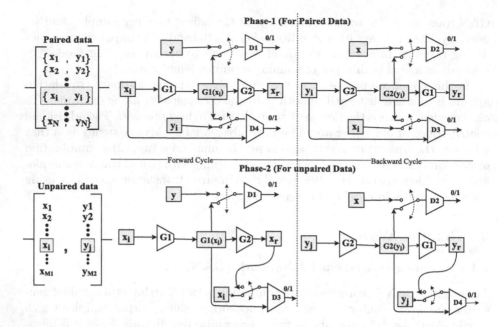

Fig. 2. The overall architecture of the proposed model for paired and unpaired training inputs. The two generators provide the forward and backward mappings $G1 : X \rightarrow Y$ and $G2 : Y \rightarrow X$. The discriminators $D1$ and $D2$ implement an adversarial loss encouraging the generators to produce outputs indistinguishable from the corresponding training distributions. The conditional discriminators $D3$ and $D4$ work in dual role by encouraging the translated images to be similar to ground truth for paired training samples and implementing an adversarial cycle consistency loss for unpaired training samples.

Recently, "CoGAN" [10] proposed a weight sharing strategy to learn a common representation across domains. This work was later extended in [11] by combining GANs and variational autoencoders [25]. "XGAN" [12] proposed a semantic consistency loss to preserve the semantic content of the image during the transfer. Few recent works [26,27] are also proposed to scale domain transfer from two domains to multiple domains. Finally, unpaired domain translation is studied without using adversarial loss [13]. Despite the recent progress, the results are still clearly inferior compared to methods using paired data (e.g. see Fig. 1).

3   Method

3.1   Task Definition

The overall task is to obtain a mapping from a source domain X to a target domain Y. Figure 1 illustrates an example case where X and Y correspond to semantic label maps and streetview photographs, respectively. The mapping is learned using a given training data, which in our case may consist of both aligned image pairs $\{x_i, y_i\}_{i=1}^N$ and (unaligned) image samples $\{x_i\}_{i=1}^{M_X}$ and $\{y_j\}_{j=1}^{M_Y}$. Here $x_i \in X$, $y_j \in Y$, N is the number of aligned samples, and M_X, M_Y are the number of unpaired samples from each domain. Two interesting special cases occur if $N = 0$ (fully unpaired setup) or $M_X = M_Y = 0$ (fully paired setup).

3.2 Basic Architecture

The overall architecture of our solution is illustrated in Fig. 2. The system contains two generator networks $G1$ and $G2$. The generator $G1$ provides a mapping from domain X to domain Y denoted as $G1 : X \to Y$ (e.g. semantic map to photograph), whereas the second generator learns the inverse of this mapping denoted as $G2 : Y \to X$ (e.g. photograph to semantic map). Generator networks are trained using adversarial loss [5] that is implemented by two discriminator networks $D1$ and $D2$. $D1$ aims to distinguish between transformation results $G1(x)$ and given training samples $y \in Y$. $D2$ works similarly for $G2(y)$ and $x \in X$. These loss functions will guide the generators to produce samples that are indistinguishable from the training image distributions $x \sim p_{data}(x)$ and $y \sim p_{data}(y)$ in corresponding domains. Following [5], the exact formulation with respect to $G1$ and $D1$ is

$$\mathcal{L}_{GAN}(G1(X), D1(Y)) = \mathbb{E}_y\left[logD1(y)\right] + \mathbb{E}_x\left[log(1 - D1(G1(x_i)))\right] \quad (1)$$

where x and y are from data distribution $p_{data}(x)$ and $p_{data}(y)$ respectively. The corresponding objective $\mathcal{L}_{GAN}(G2(Y), D2(X))$ for $G2$ and $D2$ is obtained similarly. Note that Eq. (1) does not depend on the pairing of the training samples. Therefore, this part of the loss function can be applied to all training samples in the same way.

3.3 Cycle Consistency

Given only the discriminators $D1$ and $D2$, the learning problem remains poorly constrained and would not converge to a meaningful solution. Following [4], we circumvent the problem by adding a cycle consistency loss that encourages the cascaded mapping to reproduce the original input. Mathematically, $G2(G1(x)) \approx x$ and $G1(G2(y)) \approx y$, where $x \in X$ and $y \in Y$. The intuition behind the cycle consistency is that if we translate from one domain to another and then back again we should arrive where we started (e.g. translating a sentence from one language to another and then back again).

In [4], the cycle consistency loss was defined as $L1$ difference between the reconstruction $G2(G1(x))$ and the input x (similarly for y). Such loss would only be able to measure pixel level agreement between the images, although we might actually be more interested in semantic similarity (e.g. if you translate a sentence to another language and then back, the result might have the exact same meaning but expressed with different words). To this end, we propose a new adversarial cycle consistency loss implemented by two conditional discriminator networks $D3$ and $D4$ [18]. The dual input conditional discriminator D3 aims to make x_r as realistic as x_i. More formally:

$$\mathcal{L}_{cGAN}(G2(G1(X)), D3(G1(X), X)) = \mathbb{E}_x\left[log D3(G1(x_i), x_i)\right] \qquad (2)$$
$$+ \mathbb{E}_x\left[log(1 - D3(G1(x_i), x_r))\right]$$

This formulation encourages x_i and x_r to be similar in terms of image content. Similar expression can be written for $\mathcal{L}_{cGAN}(G1(G2(Y)), D4(G2(Y), Y))$ in backward cycle.

3.4   Conditional Adversarial Loss for Aligned Training Samples

In principle, the formulation (3) would be applicable to both unpaired and paired training data. However, for paired training samples (x_i, y_i) we can actually obtain much tighter constraint by enforcing the similarly between transformation result $G1(x_i)$ and the corresponding ground truth y_i. Now recall that the objective of the conditional discriminator $D4$ was to distinguish between real and reconstructed samples in domain Y. Therefore, the same network can be reused to discriminate between real (y_i) and generated image $(G1(x_i))$ in domain Y given the input x_i. The corresponding loss function would be

$$\mathcal{L}_{cGAN}(G1(X), D4(X, Y)) = \mathbb{E}_{x,y}\left[log D4(x_i, y_i)\right] + \mathbb{E}_x\left[log(1 - D4(x_i, G1(x_i)))\right] \quad (3)$$

By utilising $D3$ and $D4$ in a dual role, we can obtain more compact architecture and efficient learning. Figure 2 illustrates how our architecture works in the case of paired and unpaired image samples.

3.5   Complete Learning Objective

The complete learning objective would be a composition of the presented loss functions. In order to further stabilise the learning process, we add weighted versions of the L1 cycle consistency loss and an identity loss [4] to our full objective. These are defined as follows:

$$\mathcal{L}_{cyc\ell_1}(G1, G2) = \mathbb{E}_x\left[\|\ x_r - x_i\ \|_1\right] + \mathbb{E}_y\left[\|\ y_r - y_i\ \|_1\right] \qquad (4)$$
$$\mathcal{L}_{idt}(G1, G2) = \mathbb{E}_y\left[\|\ G1(y_i) - y_i\ \|_1\right] + \mathbb{E}_x\left[\|\ G2(x_i) - x_i\ \|_1\right] \qquad (5)$$

The complete loss function for paired training samples $\{x_i, y_i\}_{i=1}^N$ and for the unpaired training samples $\{x_i\}_{i=1}^{M_X}$ and $\{y_j\}_{j=1}^{M_Y}$ are given in (6) and (7) respectively.

$$\mathcal{L}(G1, G2, D1, D2, D3, D4) = \mathcal{L}_{GAN}(G1(X), D1(Y)) + \mathcal{L}_{GAN}(G2(Y), D2(X)) \quad (6)$$
$$+ \mathcal{L}_{cGAN}(G1(X), D4(X, Y)) + \mathcal{L}_{cGAN}(G2(Y), D3(X, Y))$$
$$+ \lambda_1 \mathcal{L}_{cyc\ell_1}(G1, G2) + \lambda_2 \mathcal{L}_{idt}(G1, G2)$$

$$\mathcal{L}(G1, G2, D1, D2, D3, D4) = \mathcal{L}_{GAN}(G1(X), D1(Y)) + \mathcal{L}_{GAN}(G2(Y), D2(X)) \quad (7)$$
$$+ \mathcal{L}_{cGAN}(G2(G1(X)), D3(G1(X), X)) + \mathcal{L}_{cGAN}(G1(G2(Y)), D4(G2(Y), Y))$$
$$+ \lambda_1 \mathcal{L}_{idt}(G1, G2) + \lambda_2 \mathcal{L}_{cyc\ell_1}(G1, G2)$$

λ_1 and λ_2 denote the corresponding weights for $\mathcal{L}_{idt}$ and $\mathcal{L}_{cyc\ell_1}$. Moreover, for paired data case we have experimented with perceptual loss using VGG19 pre-trained network [28] as used in [17].

The major difference to previous literature (e.g. [2] and [4]) is the proposed four discriminator construction that work together with two generators to facilitate both paired and unpaired data simultaneously. The added structure enables new use cases, but also improves the performance in the case of only paired or unpaired data. We experimentally validate our model in the subsequent sections.

4   Network Architectures

The architecture of $G1$ and $G2$ are same and contain 9-residual blocks [29], pair of convolution block with stride - 2 and another pair of fractionally strided convolution block with stride 1/2. The architecture of $D1$, $D2$, $D3$ and $D4$ are similar to PatchGAN [2,4]. However, $D3$ and $D4$ have provision to take the extra conditional information as their input channels. In our case for all the four discriminators, the size of the patch is 70×70. More details are given in the supplementary material.

4.1   Training Details

Initially, all the datasets are resized to $256 \times 256 \times 3$. During training, they are upscaled to $286 \times 286 \times 3$ and random crops of size $256 \times 256 \times 3$ are used as input to the model. First the paired data are applied to our model for 50 epochs and then unpaired data are applied for the rest from total epochs of 200. For the calculation of $\mathcal{L}_{cGAN}$ and $\mathcal{L}_{GAN}$, we have used least square loss [30] instead of log likelihood loss. Moreover, the discriminators are updated from a pool of 50 generated images instead of the most recent generated one. Similar strategies are used in [4,31] to stabilize the training of GANs. For all the experiments, λ_1 and λ_2 in the loss function are 10 and 5 respectively. Our model is optimized with an Adam optimizer [32] and batch size is kept constant with 1. The starting learning rate for $G1, G2$ and $D1, D2$ is kept at 0.0002 whereas for $D3, D4$ is kept at 0.0001. For $D3, D4$, the learning rate is fixed for all the epochs whereas the learning rate of others are kept at 0.0002 for 100 epochs and linearly decayed to zero in the remaining epochs.

5   Experiments

In this section, we validate our method in several image-to-image translation setups using three different datasets: Cityscapes [33], maps vs aerial images [2,4], and Mapillary Vistas [34]. The obtained results are qualitatively and quantitatively compared against two recent baseline methods: cycleGAN [4] and pix2pix [2] which utilise unpaired and paired training data respectively. These baselines were selected since they are the most relevant previous works with

Fig. 3. Qualitative results for label map to photograph (first to fifth row) and photograph to label map (sixth to eighth row) translation tasks. The method corresponding to the results in each column is indicated above. The information in parenthesis denote the number of paired training examples and the total number of training data. We recommend the reader to zoom-in for observing the differences better.

respect to our architecture and since they were shown to outperform many previous state-of-the-art methods in the corresponding publications. In the following sections we will explain the exact experiments and results for each dataset
separately.

5.1   Translation Between Semantic Label Maps and RGB Images

Cityscapes [33] dataset consists of 3475 road scene images recorded in several
locations in Germany. For urban scene understanding, these images are provided
with the corresponding pixel level semantic annotations as shown in Figs. 1 and 3
as input and ground truth pair. The dataset is further split into training and validation parts containing 2975 and 500 samples respectively. We utilise Cityscapes
to perform two types of translation tasks: (1) from semantic maps to RGB photographs and (2) from RGB photographs to semantic labels. Furthermore, we
will modify the number of training samples for which the alignment between
RGB images and label maps are utilised. This is done in order to assess how
the number of paired vs. unpaired samples affect the results. We are particularly
interested in cases where there are relatively few paired samples (e.g. 50) and a
large number of unpaired data.

5.2   Qualitative Comparison

Figures 3 and 4 show the qualitative results of our model and the baseline methods [2,4]. The information in parenthesis denote the number of paired training
samples and the total number of training samples. Note that since pix2pix [2]
is not able to use unpaired training data, the corresponding total number of
training samples is always equal to the number of paired samples. Similarly
CycleGAN [4] uses only unpaired data.

One may notice from the results that CycleGAN gets confused between tree
and building labels. We observed that this kind of behaviour is very common
throughout the dataset. Unfortunately, CycleGAN does not provide any easy
way to include additional supervision to prevent such phenomenon. In contrast,
our method can utilise supervision from aligned image pairs and we observed that
already a small set of such pairs (e.g. 30) prevents this type of label switching
problems.

When comparing to pix2pix results, one can observe a clear benefit from the
additional unpaired samples used in our method. Moreover, the visual quality of
our results using pairing information for only 30 samples seems to be comparable
to those obtained by pix2pix using pairing information for all 2975 training
examples. One can find further example results from the supplementary material.

5.3   Quantitative Comparison

In addition to the qualitative results, we also assess the methods quantitatively.
To this end, we will follow the approach presented in [14]. For the first transformation task (labels to RGB), we apply a pretrained segmentation network [35]

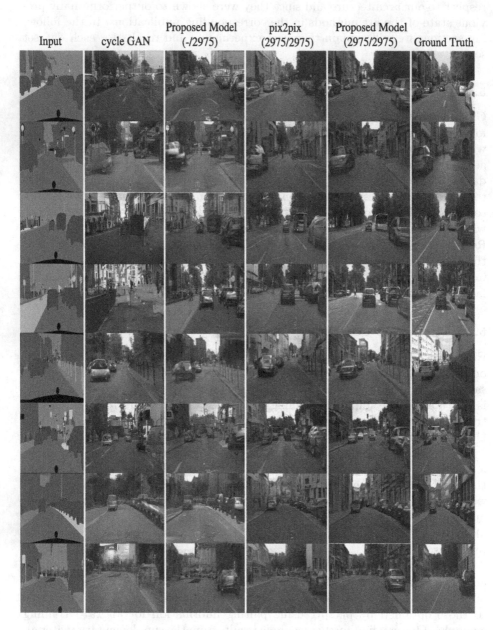

Fig. 4. Qualitative results for label map to photograph translation tasks. The results correspond to direct comparison of proposed method in a complete paired and unpaired setup. The information in parenthesis denote the number of paired training examples and the total number of training data. We recommend the reader to zoom-in for observing the differences better.

to the generated RGB images and compare the obtained label maps against the ground truth semantic segmentation maps. Following [14], we compute pixel accuracy, mean accuracy and mean Intersection over Union (IU). In the case of RGB to label map translation, we compute the same metrics directly between our outputs and the corresponding ground truth maps. Note that the generated output label maps must be quantised before calculating the results. Table 1 contains the obtained results for different methods and training setups.

In particular, our method seems to outperform the CycleGAN even if there are no paired training samples available. The key to this improvement is the proposed new adversarial cycle consistency loss. Furthermore, there is a clear additional improvement in the results when even a small set of paired training samples are added. We also note that our method obtains similar results as pix2pix when pairing is provided for all training samples. We can observe the improvement over pix2pix when including a perceptual loss (VGG loss [17]) in our model. Finally, we observed the training time per one epoch (3000 samples) for the pix2pix, cyclegan and proposed method as 5.97 min, 18.15 min and 19.65 min respectively. Increase in the training time is due to the additional structure in the network whereas the test time remains the same.

Table 1. Quantitative results for semantic label to photograph and photograph to semantic label translation tasks obtained using Cityscapes [33] dataset.

Models	$\frac{paired}{total}$	label → photo			photo → label		
		Pixel Acc.	Mean Acc.	IU	Pixel Acc.	Mean Acc.	IU
Cycle GAN [4]	-/2975	0.47	0.12	0.08	0.47	0.12	0.09
Our Model	-/2975	**0.56**	**0.16**	**0.12**	**0.53**	**0.17**	**0.12**
pix2pix [2]	30/30	0.58	0.18	0.12	0.65	0.20	0.15
Our Model	30/2975	**0.66**	**0.19**	**0.14**	**0.66**	0.20	0.15
pix2pix [2]	50/50	0.60	0.17	0.12	**0.68**	**0.22**	**0.16**
Our Model	50/2975	**0.65**	**0.19**	**0.13**	0.67	0.20	0.15
pix2pix [2]	70/70	0.62	0.18	0.13	**0.70**	0.21	**0.17**
Our Model	70/2975	**0.67**	**0.19**	**0.14**	0.68	0.21	0.16
pix2pix [2]	2975/2975	0.68	0.21	0.15	0.75	0.28	0.21
Proposed	2975/2975	0.68	0.21	0.15	0.74	0.29	0.22
Proposed (VGG)	2975/2975	**0.70**	0.21	**0.16**	**0.76**	**0.32**	**0.24**

5.4 Translation Between Aerial Photographs and Maps

Aerial photograph and maps dataset proposed in [2,4] consists of 1096 image pairs of aerial photographs and maps. As in the previous section, we use this dataset to learn transformations from photographs to maps and vice versa. Figure 5 shows a few illustrative example results for our method and the baselines. In this experiment, we show our results obtained using only 50 paired data out of 1096 training samples. However, other similar training setups lead to

Input   cycle GAN   pix2pix 50/1096   Proposed Model 50/1096   pix2pix 1096/1096   Ground Truth

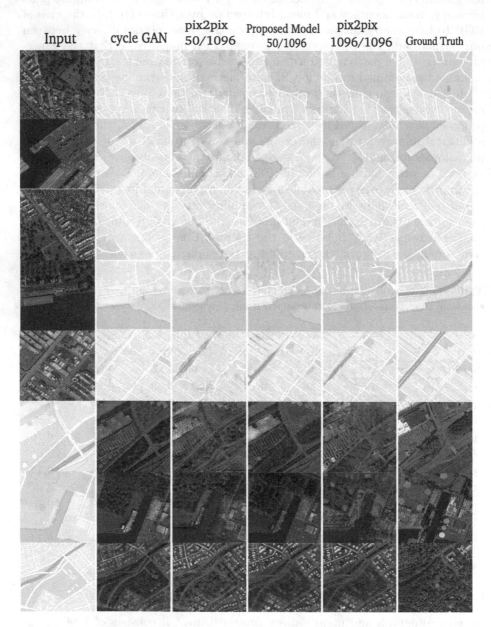

Fig. 5. Translation from aerial images to maps (first to fifth row) and vice versa (sixth to eighth row).

Input   Cycle Gan   pix2pix   Our Model (W/O unpaired data)   Our Model (W unpaired data)   Ground Truth

Fig. 6. Translation results from semantic label maps to RGB images on Mapillary Vistas dataset [34]. The method corresponding to the results in each column is indicated above. The last row shows a zoom-up corresponding to the red rectangle on the row above. (Color figure online)

comparable results. The obtained results indicate similar improvements over the baselines as in the case of label map to RGB image transformation. Our model successfully learns mappings for areas such as vegetation which are completely ignored by cycle GAN [4] (see Fig. 5). The other baseline, pix2pix, is not able to compete when only a small set of paired samples are available.

5.5   Translation Using Supervision Across Datasets

In addition to the previous experiments where train and test images originate from a single dataset, we assess the ability of our model to transfer knowledge from one dataset to another. For this purpose, we take all 2975 aligned training pairs from the Cityscapes dataset [33] and an additional 100 unaligned example images[1] from the Mapillary Vistas dataset presented in [34].

Mapillary Vistas contain similar road scene images and semantic label maps as Cityscapes. However, the Mapillary Vistas images are recorded from a much wider set of geographical locations around the world and therefore the images have substantially greater variability compared to Cityscapes. For instance, the road scenes in an African city may look quite different from those in Germany. Our task is to learn a translation model from semantic label maps to Mapillary Vistas style road scene images. Since we do not use any pairing information from Mapillary Vistas, the pix2pix model can be trained using only the Cityscape examples. On the other hand, CycleGAN can be trained using examples from both dataset. However, the results were clearly better if the model was trained using only Mapillary data as presented in Fig. 6.

For our method, we provide the results in two setups: (1) using only paired training samples from Cityscapes (same as pix2pix) and (2) using paired samples from Cityscapes and unpaired samples from Mapillary Vistas. The example results are provided in Fig. 6. Our model seems to be better in terms of producing realistic textures and overall structure compared to the baselines. Furthermore, we observe a clear improvement from the additional unpaired Mapillary Vistas data indicating that it is possible leverage the supervision from similar dataset to improve the image-to-image translation results.

6   Conclusions

We proposed a new general purpose method for learning image-to-image translation models from both aligned and unaligned training samples. Our architecture consists of two generators and four discriminators out of which two operate in dual role depending on type of the training instance. The advantage of this construction is that our model can utilise all training data irrespective of its type. We assessed the proposed method against two strong baselines presented recently. The results indicated both qualitative and quantitative improvements,

---

[1] It is not necessary to use the maps from the Mapillary Vistas since the Cityscapes maps can be used with Mapillary vistas RGB images as (unpaired) training examples.

even in the case where training data solely consists of paired or unpaired samples. To our knowledge, this is the first work to consider such hybrid setup in image-to-image translation.

References

1. Zhang, R., et al.: Real-time user-guided image colorization with learned deep priors (2017). arXiv preprint: arXiv:1705.02999
2. Isola, P., Zhu, J.Y., Zhou, T., Efros, A.A.: Image-to-image translation with conditional adversarial networks. In: 2017 IEEE Conference on Computer Vision and Pattern Recognition (CVPR), pp. 5967–5976 (2017)
3. Simo-Serra, E., Iizuka, S., Ishikawa, H.: Mastering sketching: adversarial augmentation for structured prediction. ACM Trans. Graph. **37**, 11:1–11:13 (2018)
4. Zhu, J.Y., Park, T., Isola, P., Efros, A.A.: Unpaired image-to-image translation using cycle-consistent adversarial networks. In: 2017 IEEE International Conference on Computer Vision (ICCV), pp. 2242–2251 (2017)
5. Goodfellow, I., et al.: Generative adversarial nets. In: Advances in Neural Information Processing Systems, pp. 2672–2680 (2014)
6. Pathak, D., Krahenbuhl, P., Donahue, J., Darrell, T., Efros, A.A.: Context encoders: feature learning by inpainting. In: Proceedings of the IEEE Conference on Computer Vision and Pattern Recognition, pp. 2536–2544 (2016)
7. Ledig, C., et al.: Photo-realistic single image super-resolution using a generative adversarial network (2016). arXiv preprint
8. Kim, T., Cha, M., Kim, H., Lee, J., Kim, J.: Learning to discover cross-domain relations with generative adversarial networks (2017). arXiv preprint: arXiv:1703.05192
9. Yi, Z., Zhang, H., Tan, P., Gong, M.: DualGAN: unsupervised dual learning for image-to-image translation (2017). arXiv preprint
10. Liu, M.Y., Tuzel, O.: Coupled generative adversarial networks. In: Advances in Neural Information Processing Systems, pp. 469–477 (2016)
11. Liu, M.Y., Breuel, T., Kautz, J.: Unsupervised image-to-image translation networks. In: Advances in Neural Information Processing Systems, pp. 700–708 (2017)
12. Royer, A., et al.: XGAN: unsupervised image-to-image translation for many-to-many mappings (2017). arXiv preprint: arXiv:1711.05139
13. Hoshen, Y., Wolf, L.: Nam-unsupervised cross-domain image mapping without cycles or GANs (2018)
14. Long, J., Shelhamer, E., Darrell, T.: Fully convolutional networks for semantic segmentation. In: Proceedings of the IEEE Conference on Computer Vision and Pattern Recognition, pp. 3431–3440 (2015)
15. Johnson, J., Alahi, A., Fei-Fei, L.: Perceptual losses for real-time style transfer and super-resolution. In: Leibe, B., Matas, J., Sebe, N., Welling, M. (eds.) ECCV 2016, Part II. LNCS, vol. 9906, pp. 694–711. Springer, Cham (2016). https://doi.org/10.1007/978-3-319-46475-6_43
16. Shih, Y., Paris, S., Durand, F., Freeman, W.T.: Data-driven hallucination of different times of day from a single outdoor photo. ACM Trans. Graph. (TOG) **32**, 200 (2013)
17. Wang, T.C., Liu, M.Y., Zhu, J.Y., Tao, A., Kautz, J., Catanzaro, B.: High-resolution image synthesis and semantic manipulation with conditional GANs. In: Proceedings of the IEEE Conference on Computer Vision and Pattern Recognition (2018)

18. Mirza, M., Osindero, S.: Conditional generative adversarial nets (2014). arXiv preprint: arXiv:1411.1784
19. Zhang, H., et al.: StackGAN: text to photo-realistic image synthesis with stacked generative adversarial networks. In: IEEE International Conference on Computer Vision (ICCV), pp. 5907–5915 (2017)
20. Hong, S., Yang, D., Choi, J., Lee, H.: Inferring semantic layout for hierarchical text-to-image synthesis (2018). arXiv preprint: arXiv:1801.05091
21. Yan, X., Yang, J., Sohn, K., Lee, H.: Attribute2Image: conditional image generation from visual attributes. In: Leibe, B., Matas, J., Sebe, N., Welling, M. (eds.) ECCV 2016, Part IV. LNCS, vol. 9908, pp. 776–791. Springer, Cham (2016). https://doi.org/10.1007/978-3-319-46493-0_47
22. Lin, J., Xia, Y., Qin, T., Chen, Z., Liu, T.Y.: Conditional image-to-image translation. In: Proceedings of the IEEE Conference on Computer Vision and Pattern Recognition (CVPR) (2018)
23. Wang, C., Xu, C., Wang, C., Tao, D.: Perceptual adversarial networks for image-to-image transformation. IEEE Trans. Image Process. 27, 4066–4079 (2018)
24. Chen, Q., Koltun, V.: Photographic image synthesis with cascaded refinement networks. In: 2017 IEEE International Conference on Computer Vision (ICCV), pp. 1520–1529 (2017)
25. Doersch, C.: Tutorial on variational autoencoders (2016). arXiv preprint: arXiv:1606.05908
26. Choi, Y., Choi, M., Kim, M., Ha, J.W., Kim, S., Choo, J.: StarGAN: unified generative adversarial networks for multi-domain image-to-image translation. In: The IEEE Conference on Computer Vision and Pattern Recognition (CVPR) (2018)
27. Anoosheh, A., Agustsson, E., Timofte, R., Van Gool, L.: ComboGAN: unrestrained scalability for image domain translation (2017). arXiv preprint: arXiv:1712.06909
28. Simonyan, K., Zisserman, A.: Very deep convolutional networks for large-scale image recognition (2014). arXiv preprint: arXiv:1409.1556
29. He, K., Zhang, X., Ren, S., Sun, J.: Deep residual learning for image recognition. In: Proceedings of the IEEE Conference on Computer Vision and Pattern Recognition, pp. 770–778 (2016)
30. Mao, X., Li, Q., Xie, H., Lau, R.Y., Wang, Z.: Multi-class generative adversarial networks with the L2 loss function. CoRR, abs/1611.04076 2 (2016)
31. Shrivastava, A., Pfister, T., Tuzel, O., Susskind, J., Wang, W., Webb, R.: Learning from simulated and unsupervised images through adversarial training. In: The IEEE Conference on Computer Vision and Pattern Recognition (CVPR), vol. 3, p. 6 (2017)
32. Kingma, D.P., Ba, J.: Adam: a method for stochastic optimization (2014). arXiv preprint: arXiv:1412.6980
33. Cordts, M., et al.: The cityscapes dataset for semantic urban scene understanding. In: Proceedings of the IEEE Conference on Computer Vision and Pattern Recognition, pp. 3213–3223 (2016)
34. Neuhold, G., Ollmann, T., Bulò, S.R., Kontschieder, P.: The mapillary vistas dataset for semantic understanding of street scenes. In: 2017 IEEE International Conference on Computer Vision (ICCV), pp. 5000–5009 (2017)
35. Yu, F., Koltun, V.: Multi-scale context aggregation by dilated convolutions (2015). arXiv preprint: arXiv:1511.07122

BitNet: Learning-Based Bit-Depth Expansion

Junyoung Byun, Kyujin Shim, and Changick Kim[✉]

School of Electrical Engineering, KAIST, Daejeon, Republic of Korea
{bjyoung,kjshim1028,changick}@kaist.ac.kr

Abstract. Bit-depth is the number of bits for each color channel of a pixel in an image. Although many modern displays support unprecedented higher bit-depth to show more realistic and natural colors with a high dynamic range, most media sources are still in bit-depth of 8 or lower. Since insufficient bit-depth may generate annoying false contours or lose detailed visual appearance, bit-depth expansion (BDE) from low bit-depth (LBD) images to high bit-depth (HBD) images becomes more and more important. In this paper, we adopt a learning-based approach for BDE and propose a novel CNN-based bit-depth expansion network (BitNet) that can effectively remove false contours and restore visual details at the same time. We have carefully designed our BitNet based on an encoder-decoder architecture with dilated convolutions and a novel multi-scale feature integration. We have performed various experiments with four different datasets including MIT-Adobe FiveK, Kodak, ESPL v2, and TESTIMAGES, and our proposed BitNet has achieved state-of-the-art performance in terms of PSNR and SSIM among other existing BDE methods and famous CNN-based image processing networks. Unlike previous methods that separately process each color channel, we treat all RGB channels at once and have greatly improved color restoration. In addition, our network has shown the fastest computational speed in near real-time.

Keywords: Bit-depth expansion · De-quantization · False contours

1 Introduction

The human visual system can perceive a wide range of luminance up to 12~14 orders in magnitude [22]. Therefore modern displays have been evolved to support high dynamic range (HDR), which is a wide scope of expressible luminance, to show more natural appearance to the human eyes. Accordingly, they also have

---

J. Byun and K. Shim—Contributed equally, listed alphabetically.

Electronic supplementary material The online version of this chapter (https://doi.org/10.1007/978-3-030-20890-5_5) contains supplementary material, which is available to authorized users.

© Springer Nature Switzerland AG 2019
C. V. Jawahar et al. (Eds.): ACCV 2018, LNCS 11362, pp. 67–82, 2019.
https://doi.org/10.1007/978-3-030-20890-5_5

(a) 8-bit image   (b) 3-bit image   (c) 3-bit to 8-bit result

Fig. 1. An example of bit-depth expansion (BDE). In (b), false contour artifacts have occurred, and details are lost due to the insufficient bit-depth. In (c), our proposed BitNet removes false contour artifacts and restores disappeared details effectively

been improved to support the high bit-depth (HBD) which is essential for the HDR [25] so that they can express more realistic and accurate colors. The bit-depth is the number of bits for each channel of a pixel and determines the total number of describable colors. Although many TVs and mobile devices such as Galaxy S9 and iPhone X already support bit-depth of 10 to satisfy HDR standards [12], most media sources are still at bit-depth of 8 or lower, thus the displays cannot take full advantage regardless of their ability. Hence, bit-depth expansion (BDE), which converts low bit-depth (LBD) images to HBD images, has recently drawn much attention.

BDE is also useful in many other applications. It can be used as postprocessing in remote control systems because they optionally reduce the bit-depth of screen data to decrease the amount of transmission for real-time operation. Additionally, it can be used as pre-processing for the professional image adjustment to prevent unwanted artifacts [13].

As shown in Fig. 1, there are two main challenges in BDE: removing false contour artifacts and restoring disappeared visual information such as color and texture. Most existing methods [5,7,18,19,23,24,27,28] only focus on eliminating false contours and are nearly unable to restore original colors. Furthermore, it is almost impossible to use them in practice because of their exceedingly long iterative operations.

To tackle these problems, we propose a carefully designed bit-depth expansion network (BitNet) based on a convolutional neural network (CNN). To the best of our knowledge, CNN-based approaches for BDE have hardly been developed. Specifically, our BitNet can precisely detect and selectively remove false contour artifacts while maintaining original edges. Furthermore, it can capture the contextual information and recover visual appearance effectively. To show this, we have demonstrated various experiments, and our network has outperformed recent BDE methods [19,27,28] and other famous image processing networks [4,20] which are newly trained for BDE.

Our contributions are summarized as follows:

(1) We have carefully designed a network for BDE with various experiments on the effect of dilated convolutions and a novel multi-scale feature integration. Our algorithm learns inherent characteristics of natural images and eliminates false contours and restores visual details at the same time, whereas other existing methods [5,7,18,19,23,24,27,28] only focus on false contour removal. As a result, we have achieved the best performance in terms of PSNR and SSIM [29] against other existing algorithms and newly trained famous CNN-based image processing networks.
(2) We have dramatically increased the processing speed to enable practical application of BDE. While traditional methods take more than 20 s per image, our BitNet can process 768×512 images at a real-time speed over 25fps.
(3) Unlike previous methods separately process each color channel, we treat all RGB channels at once. For a more detailed investigation, we have compared our network with a channel-wise version of BitNet (BitNet-Chan) and found that treating all RGB channels together makes an important improvement for accurate color restoration.
(4) We have verified that our BitNet is universally well-suited for various images with different sizes, bit-depth, and domain by using four different test datasets while it is trained with only one dataset.

This paper is organized as follows. In Sect. 2, we review various previous methods related to BDE. Section 3 describes the structure of our proposed network in detail. In Sect. 4, we describe our experiments and results. In Sect. 5, we examine the performance of each different structural design of our network. Section 6 concludes our paper and suggests possible future work.

2 Related Work

Since bit-depth expansion (BDE) became increasingly important, various methods have been proposed. The zero padding (ZP) algorithm, which is the simplest method, appends '0's after the least significant bit (LSB) of a low bit-depth (LBD) pixel. The multiplication by ideal gain (MIG) algorithm matches the scope of the current LBD space to the scope of the target high bit-depth (HBD) space by naive multiplication. The bit replication (BR) [26] repeatedly copies and appends current LBD bit values after LSB. Although they are fast and straightforward, they do not consider any spatial characteristics of the image. Therefore, they lose local consistency and generate strong false contour artifacts.

To deal with those problems, filter-based BDE methods have been suggested. The adaptive bit-depth expansion (ABDE) method [18] expands the bit-depth with ZP and segments false contour regions. Then it reduces false contours with low pass filtering (LPF). On the other hand, Park et al. [24] have proposed a method that detects false contours with directional contrast features and smooths them with a 3-layer fully connected network and bi-directional smoothing. However, they usually suffer from inaccurate smoothing which may also blur the true edges even with the segmentation or detection process.

At the same time, optimization-based methods have also appeared. Akira et al. [23] have formulated the prior of target HBD values and the likelihood of noisy LBD values, and they have solved the BDE problem as a maximum a posteriori (MAP) estimation. The more advanced, ACDC algorithm [28] has adopted graph signal processing scheme and has formulated the BDE problem as a minimum mean squared error (MMSE) and a MAP estimation via convex optimization. It estimates HBD images from the AC signal after MAP and the DC signal after MMSE with the estimated AC signal. However, these methods are based on heuristic models and unable to account for various natural images. On the contrary, we allow the network to learn various inherent characteristics from numerous natural images, and it shows outperforming results.

One of the other major approaches is the interpolation-based methods. The contour region reconstruction (CRR) method [5] estimates an HBD image by linear interpolation based on an up-distance map and a down-distance map from the upward contour edges and downward contour edges, respectively. However, it cannot be applied to the regions with local extrema. Therefore, the content adaptive (CA) algorithm [27] creates inner skeletons in these problematic areas and performs additional bilateral filtering for these skeleton pixels to reduce the reconstruction error.

Different from the above methods, a novel intensity potential-based BDE algorithm has been proposed recently [19]. It has introduced a scalar potential field to model the complex relationship among pixels in an LBD image. It first clusters connected pixels with the same intensity in each channel and finds their effective boundaries. Then an HBD image is estimated through non-linear mapping functions from the LBD image and the potential field whose field sources are the effective boundaries.

Almost all existing BDE methods are only focusing on how to remove the false contours without blurring other original contours. Also, they usually treat false contour detection and false contour removal separately. However, our BitNet deals with both detection and removal at once as well as the visual restoration with end-to-end training. On the other hand, many deep learning-based methods have been suggested for compression artifacts removal [8,11], denoising [17,30], and various image processing [4,20]. However, to the best of our knowledge, CNN-based approaches for BDE have hardly been developed.

3   Methodology

Our BitNet is based on an encoder-decoder structure to reduce the computational cost and carefully designed with novel architectural components. We first generate a coarse HBD image by zero padding (ZP) from an input LBD image and produce a refined HBD image through our BitNet. We illustrate the detailed network architecture in Fig. 2.

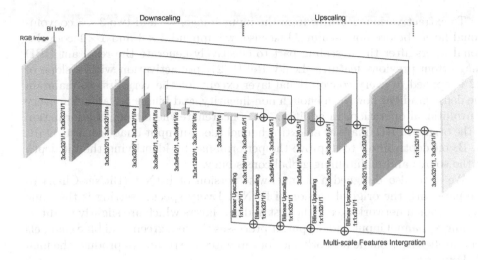

Fig. 2. An illustration of our BitNet. Each block represents a feature map except for an input and a final output. The input is a concatenation of an original image and its bit-depth information. We denote the kernel size × output channel/stride/dilation rate of each convolution beside the connection lines. Both r_d and r_u are set to two in our BitNet. Plus signs indicate the summation of corresponding feature maps.

Our network can be divided into two parts: downscaling and upscaling. In the downscaling part, features are summarized through gradual spatial reduction. We use 3×3 convolutions of stride two instead of pooling layers for a wider receptive field. In the upscaling part, we use 3×3 fractionally strided convolutions [9] of stride 0.5 to constantly expand the spatial size of the features until the original size. After each strided convolution for downscaling, a 3×3 convolution with the dilation rate of r_d is applied, while a 3×3 convolution with the dilation rate of r_u is performed before each strided convolution for upscaling. In our BitNet, both r_d and r_u are set to two for a broader receptive field which is important to handle high-resolution images.

We assume that the network would recover original colors during the downscaling and rebuild the visual appearance during the upscaling. Therefore, we add each intermediate feature from the downscaling part to each corresponding upscaled feature, as shown in Fig. 2, for better visual reconstruction. Also, because the receptive field is large enough, small kernels are sufficient to remove false contours and recover accurate and consistent colors even across wide and soft areas such as a cloud, lake, and wall.

We also assume that every intermediate feature would encode a resultant image with different attributes. Hence, we have designed a novel multi-scale feature integration module which merges previous features of various scales at the end of the upscaling. Specifically, we enlarge the features through bilinear interpolation to match the spatial size and employ 1×1 convolutions to select appropriate features and match the number of channels. It also facilitates better gradient flow to the entire network.

To extract various features from the input image, we add two 3×3 convolutional layers before downscaling. Likewise, we append 3×3 and 1×1 convolutional layers after the upscaling part to effectively generate the resultant HBD image from previous features. Leaky ReLU [21] pre-activation with a slope of 0.2 is applied in every convolutional layer except for the very first to maintain the dense gradient flow with enough non-linearity, and biases are added in every convolutional operation. In addition, we concatenate the bit-depth information of the original LBD image as an extra channel (i.e., an input image consists of [R, G, B, bit-depth info]) to improve the performance by identifying the bit-depth of the source and maintaining global consistency.

We have also designed a channel-wise version of BitNet (BitNet-Chan) to compare with the original version of BitNet. Every specific setting is the same as the original network except the first and last layers which are slightly modified for single-channel input and output. It processes the red, green, and blue channels separately with a single network and concatenates the results to produce the final HBD image.

4   Experimental Results

4.1   Datasets

We use MIT-Adobe FiveK dataset [3] to train and test our network. The dataset consists of 5,000 16-bit images taken by several photographers from a broad range of light conditions, scenes, and subjects. The dataset provides 5 sets of enhancement settings for all images made by 5 specialists. We use the photographs enhanced by expert E. Since the sizes of the images vary from 2.5 megapixels to 24.4 megapixels, the longer side of all images is scaled down to 1280 pixels by bilinear interpolation. We use the first 4,000 images (i.e., from a0001 to a4000) as training images and the remaining 1,000 images as test images.

Additionally, we adopt ESPL v2 dataset [16], Kodak dataset [15], and TESTIMAGES dataset [2] to test the generalization ability of our network. The ESPL v2 dataset contains 25 1920×1080 synthetic images with bit-depth of 8, and the Kodak dataset consists of 24 768×512 natural images also with bit-depth of 8. Finally, the TESTIMAGES dataset includes 40 800×800 images with bit-depth of 16. In the ESPL v2 dataset, we adopt only the pristine images without distortion. Besides, in the TESTIMAGES dataset, we use the photographs with the shifting indicator 'B01C00'.

4.2   Training

To generate training pairs for the network, we first quantize HBD images from a training set of the MIT-Adobe FiveK dataset into LBD images. Then the network is trained to minimize l_1 loss which is defined as

$$l_1(I^{q_i}, I) = \frac{1}{B} \sum_i \frac{1}{N_i} \|f(ZP(I_i^{q_i})) - I_i\|_1, \tag{1}$$

where $f(.)$ represents our BitNet, B is batch size, $ZP(.)$ is a zero padding function, $I_i^{q_i}$ represents a quantized q_i-bit LBD image from an ith original HBD image I_i, and N_i is the number of pixels in I_i. This l_1 loss minimizes difference between the resultant HBD images from BitNet and the original HBD images.

All the 3×3 convolutional kernels in our BitNet are initialized by filling the center with 1 and the rest with 0 to help stable training. For the 1×1 convolution layers, Xavier initialization [10] is applied to give sufficient variability on features aggregation. We train the network with a batch size of 1 for 100 epochs with Adam-optimizer [14]. Learning rate is set to 1e-4 for the first 75 epochs and 1e-5 for the remaining 25 epochs. Besides, we adopt three kinds of data augmentation: random horizontal flipping, random scaling from 0.5× to 1×, and random bit-depth from 3 to 6. The random seed is fixed at 10,000 for every training.

To compare with other deep learning-based methods, we also train two well-known image processing networks including CAN32+AN [4] and LRNN [20]. We used the official implementation[1] for CAN32+AN and ported LRNN into the Tensorflow framework based on the Keras [6] implementation[2]. Both methods equally follow our training scheme including the additional bit-depth information channel, but LRNN has been trained with five 288×288 randomly cropped images similar to the [20], while three data augmentations are equally applied. Unless we do so, it takes too long to train with full-sized images. We use the cascade integration scheme for LRNN which is more appropriate for smoothing false contours. We implemented networks using Tensorflow framework [1]. We also compare with other existing methods including CA [27], ACDC [28], and IPAD [19], which are implemented[3] in MATLAB by the author of [19].

4.3 Experiments

We compared our BitNet with IPAD, CAN32+AN, and LRNN on the MIT-Adobe FiveK dataset. We also tested on ESPL v2, Kodak, and TESTIMAGES dataset without any additional training to compare the generalization ability. In this case, five methods including ACDC, CA, IPAD, LRNN, and CAN32+AN are compared to our BitNet in terms of average BDE quality and execution time. We performed experiments in the following system environment: Intel i7-8700k CPU, 16GB RAM, and single NVIDIA GeForce GTX 1080 Ti GPU.

In addition to the figures in the paper, more results can be seen in the supplementary material. Note that all images in the paper and the supplementary material are set as bit-depth of 8 for display. Also, we recommend viewing the images in a proper electronic form for their clear appearance & recognition.

4.4 Qualitative Results

Figure 3 shows the test results of expansion from 3-bits to 8-bits using IPAD and four different deep networks on the MIT-Adobe FiveK dataset [3]. The first image

---

[1] https://github.com/CQFIO/FastImageProcessing.
[2] https://github.com/silverneko/Linear-RNN.
[3] https://sites.google.com/site/jingliu198810/publication.

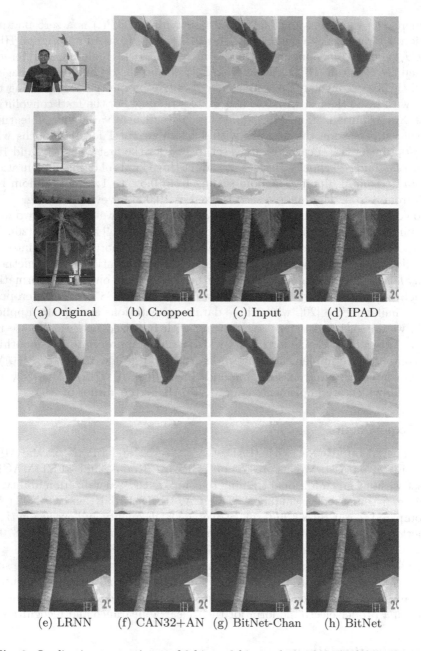

(a) Original   (b) Cropped   (c) Input   (d) IPAD

(e) LRNN   (f) CAN32+AN   (g) BitNet-Chan   (h) BitNet

Fig. 3. Qualitative comparisons of 3-bit to 8-bit results with MIT-Adobe FiveK

of Fig. 3(h) clearly shows that BitNet well restores underwater structural details. In the second image which includes the clouds, BitNet effectively removes false contours and also reverts the erroneous colors to natural colors. On the contrary, IPAD and BitNet-Chan have difficulties in restoring natural color tone. They

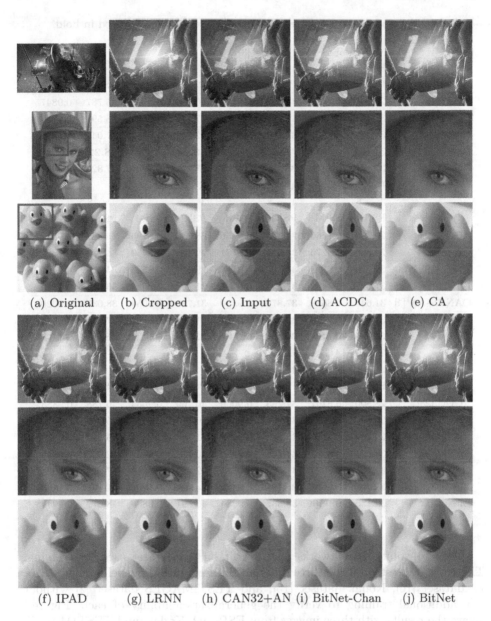

(a) Original   (b) Cropped   (c) Input   (d) ACDC   (e) CA

(f) IPAD   (g) LRNN   (h) CAN32+AN (i) BitNet-Chan   (j) BitNet

Fig. 4. Qualitative comparisons of 3-bit to 8-bit results. From the top, three images are from ESPL v2, Kodak, and TESTIMAGES dataset, respectively

handle each RGB channel separately, so they do not have enough information to effectively restore the colors. However, the third image with the night sky shows that Bit-Chan removes false contours much better. This means the smoothing ability of BitNet sharply drops on unseen color patterns, while Bit-Chan well removes false contours regardless of the colors.

Table 1. Average evaluation results. The best result is highlighted in bold.

| | MIT-Adobe FiveK dataset [3] | | | | | | | |
| | 3 → 16 | | 4 → 16 | | 5 → 16 | | 6 → 16 | |
	PSNR	SSIM	PSNR	SSIM	PSNR	SSIM	PSNR	SSIM
IPAD [19]	29.283	0.8425	34.990	0.9201	40.404	0.9628	45.787	0.9847
LRNN [20]	31.422	0.8884	35.876	0.9454	37.679	0.9691	38.598	0.9787
CAN32+AN [4]	32.277	0.8964	37.781	0.9537	42.642	0.9809	47.042	0.9926
BitNet-Chan	33.162	0.8993	38.581	0.9565	**43.424**	0.9825	**48.225**	**0.9935**
BitNet	**33.426**	**0.9086**	**38.634**	**0.9587**	43.291	**0.9826**	47.826	0.9933

| | ESPL v2 dataset [16] | | | | Kodak dataset [15] | | | |
| | 3 → 8 | | 4 → 8 | | 3 → 8 | | 4 → 8 | |
	PSNR	SSIM	PSNR	SSIM	PSNR	SSIM	PSNR	SSIM
ACDC [28]	28.594	0.7766	34.329	0.8756	28.656	0.8196	34.682	0.9132
CA [27]	29.375	0.8270	35.511	0.9171	29.145	0.8439	34.738	0.9312
IPAD [19]	29.776	0.8381	35.762	0.9186	29.201	0.8536	34.908	0.9340
LRNN [20]	31.377	0.8480	37.094	0.9200	31.368	0.8984	36.615	0.9559
CAN32+AN [4]	31.645	0.8633	37.870	0.9320	31.778	0.9054	38.037	0.9620
BitNet-Chan	31.975	0.8469	38.401	0.9381	31.594	0.8886	37.479	0.9547
BitNet	**32.876**	**0.8802**	**38.968**	**0.9459**	**32.683**	**0.9181**	**38.482**	**0.9657**

| | TESTIMAGES dataset [2] | | | | | | | |
| | 3 → 16 | | 4 → 16 | | 5 → 16 | | 6 → 16 | |
	PSNR	SSIM	PSNR	SSIM	PSNR	SSIM	PSNR	SSIM
ACDC [28]	28.800	0.8207	34.763	0.9069	40.769	0.9634	46.788	0.9883
CA [27]	28.886	0.8655	34.821	0.9343	40.173	0.9722	45.010	0.9906
IPAD [19]	29.494	0.8770	35.573	0.9414	41.188	0.9738	46.610	0.9895
LRNN [20]	31.321	0.8912	37.108	0.9484	40.153	0.9743	42.604	0.9865
CAN32+AN [4]	31.215	0.8929	37.584	0.9525	42.945	0.9810	47.543	0.9924
BitNet-Chan	**32.598**	0.9064	**38.956**	**0.9630**	**44.481**	**0.9857**	**49.404**	**0.9948**
BitNet	32.136	**0.9069**	38.337	0.9584	43.791	0.9836	48.672	0.9941

Deep convolutional networks may overfit on the dataset used for training. Therefore, we tested on the three different datasets including well-known ESPL v2 dataset [16], Kodak dataset [15], and TESTIMAGES dataset [2] without any additional training to verify the generalization ability of each. Figure 4 shows the results with three images from ESPL v2, Kodak, and TESTIMAGES dataset, respectively. BitNet demonstrates its outstanding ability for false contour removal and color restoration. In the first image, BitNet better restores the original color of the heavy armor and express the light source more naturally. In addition, BitNet well eliminates the false contours in the second photograph while maintaining the details of the eyelashes and the hair. On the other hand, BitNet-Chan has demonstrated remarkable smoothing capabilities in the duck image while CA [27] and ACDC [28] yield glow artifacts.

Table 2. Average execution time per image. ESPL v2 contains 1920×1080 images, Kodak consists of 768×512 images, and TESTIMAGES includes 800×800 images. Unit is second for all. The best result is highlighted in bold.

	ESPL v2 dataset [16]				Kodak dataset [15]			
	$3 \to 8$		$4 \to 8$		$3 \to 8$		$4 \to 8$	
	GPU	CPU	GPU	CPU	GPU	CPU	GPU	CPU
ACDC [28]	-	5203.395	-	5382.344	-	934.351	-	924.973
CA [27]	-	737.851	-	520.057	-	147.869	-	142.835
IPAD [19]	-	339.107	-	280.251	-	33.833	-	22.908
LRNN [20]	0.874	4.882	0.875	4.871	0.312	0.952	0.312	0.943
CAN32+AN [4]	0.367	7.140	0.366	7.161	0.071	1.361	0.071	1.348
BitNet-Chan	0.585	8.944	0.586	8.938	0.113	1.719	0.113	1.667
BitNet	**0.198**	**2.976**	**0.198**	**2.957**	**0.038**	**0.561**	**0.038**	**0.554**
	TESTIMAGES dataset [2]							
	$3 \to 16$		$4 \to 16$		$5 \to 16$		$6 \to 16$	
	GPU	CPU	GPU	CPU	GPU	CPU	GPU	CPU
ACDC [28]	-	1560.481	-	1541.790	-	1442.176	-	1407.948
CA [27]	-	177.715	-	133.238	-	96.041	-	63.278
IPAD [19]	-	32.156	-	33.427	-	40.452	-	52.538
LRNN [20]	0.386	1.513	0.390	1.509	0.390	1.507	0.395	1.508
CAN32+AN [4]	0.115	2.207	0.115	2.193	0.115	2.180	0.115	2.177
BitNet-Chan	0.182	2.702	0.161	2.697	0.182	2.693	0.182	2.689
BitNet	**0.062**	**0.898**	**0.062**	**0.895**	**0.062**	**0.893**	**0.062**	**0.897**

4.5 Quantitative Results

For quantitative evaluation, we measured the peak signal to noise ratio (PSNR) and the structural similarity (SSIM) [29] between the original HBD image and the resultant HBD image, following the previous work [19,27].

Table 1 includes the average evaluation results with the MIT-Adobe FiveK dataset. Our proposed networks outperform other existing methods in every case. Compared to IPAD, which is an existing state-of-the-art method for BDE, our method shows a significant improvement in both PSNR and SSIM. In particular, for the BDE from 3-bits to 16-bits with the MIT-Adobe FiveK dataset, the PSNR and SSIM gains are 4.143 and 0.0661, respectively. Note that BitNet shows better performance than BitNet-Chan for 3-bit and 4-bit input, whereas BitNet-Chan shows a higher PSNR for 6-bit input. However, in the case of BDE from 6-bits to 16-bits, the visual differences are very minor among the results.

The results from the other three datasets are also shown in Table 1. Compared to others, our method shows much higher performances in all cases. In the ESPL v2 dataset and the Kodak dataset, BitNet outperforms than BitNet-Chan. However, for the TESTIMAGES dataset, BitNet-Chan shows better results than BitNet. It is because BDE on the TESTIMAGES dataset mainly requires false

Table 3. Performance comparison to investigate the effect of the bit-depth information channel and dilation rates. The numbers inside the brackets denote $\langle r_d, r_u \rangle$, which are the rates of convolution layers in downscaling and upscaling part, respectively. The best result is highlighted in bold.

	MIT-Adobe FiveK dataset [3]							
	$3 \rightarrow 16$		$4 \rightarrow 16$		$5 \rightarrow 16$		$6 \rightarrow 16$	
	PSNR	SSIM	PSNR	SSIM	PSNR	SSIM	PSNR	SSIM
$\langle 1, 1 \rangle$ w/o bit info	33.064	0.9043	38.408	0.9572	43.133	0.9822	47.665	0.9931
$\langle 1, 2 \rangle$ w/o bit info	32.934	0.9027	38.262	0.9564	42.868	0.9817	47.463	0.9929
$\langle 2, 1 \rangle$ w/o bit info	32.966	0.9041	38.321	0.9572	42.948	0.9821	47.332	0.9930
$\langle 2, 2 \rangle$ w/o bit info	33.018	0.9044	38.271	0.9569	43.012	0.9819	47.410	0.9929
$\langle 1, 1 \rangle$ w/ bit info	33.323	0.9079	38.632	0.9585	**43.372**	**0.9827**	**47.973**	**0.9934**
$\langle 1, 2 \rangle$ w/ bit info	33.333	0.9066	38.627	0.9585	43.369	**0.9827**	47.946	**0.9934**
$\langle 2, 1 \rangle$ w/ bit info	33.361	0.9076	38.624	0.9581	43.358	0.9825	48.024	0.9933
$\langle 2, 2 \rangle$ w/ bit info	**33.426**	**0.9086**	**38.634**	**0.9587**	43.291	0.9826	47.826	0.9933

contour removal, not color restoration, and BitNet-Chan has better smoothing capabilities than BitNet.

4.6 Execution Time

Table 2 shows the average processing time per image on the three datasets. ACDC, CA, and IPAD show different execution times depending on both image sizes and the number of bit-depth, while execution times of CNN-based methods mainly depend on the image resolution. While ACDC, CA, and IPAD take more than 20 s per image, BitNet shows real-time speeds of 25fps or higher for 768×512 images with a single GPU. Note that our BitNet is at least 500 times faster than IPAD with a GPU, and compared to LRNN and CAN, BitNet is about 2 to 8 times faster, even with better performance. Meanwhile, BitNet-Chan is about three times slower than BitNet because it has to infer each color channel separately due to memory limitations of the GPU.

5   Discussion

5.1   Bit-Depth Information Channel

To see the effectiveness of the bit-depth information channel, we trained the network without the additional channel to the RGB input. Table 3 shows the results with the MIT-Adobe FiveK dataset. The bit-depth information channel identifies the bit-depth of the input to the network and improves the performance in all cases.

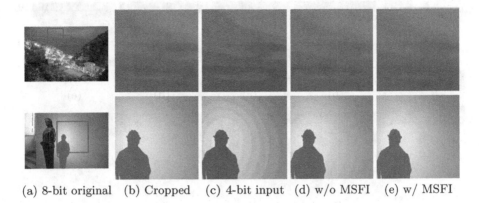

(a) 8-bit original   (b) Cropped   (c) 4-bit input   (d) w/o MSFI   (e) w/ MSFI

Fig. 5. Comparison of 4-bit to 8-bit results w/ and w/o multi-scale feature integration

Table 4. Performance comparison w/ and w/o multi-scale feature integration on the MIT-Adobe FiveK Dataset. The best result is highlighted in bold.

	MIT-Adobe FiveK dataset [3]							
	$3 \rightarrow 16$		$4 \rightarrow 16$		$5 \rightarrow 16$		$6 \rightarrow 16$	
	PSNR	SSIM	PSNR	SSIM	PSNR	SSIM	PSNR	SSIM
2, 2 w/o integration	33.208	0.9072	38.262	0.9582	**43.294**	0.9826	**47.974**	**0.9934**
2, 2 w/ integration	**33.426**	**0.9086**	**38.634**	**0.9587**	43.291	0.9826	47.826	0.9933

5.2 Dilation Rates

To investigate the effect of the dilation rates, we trained and tested the networks of various rates with the MIT-Adobe FiveK dataset. The dilation rates of convolution layers in downscaling and upscaling part, which are denoted as r_d and r_u in Fig. 2, were equally set in each part. We compared four different combinations (i.e $\langle 1, 1 \rangle$, $\langle 2, 2 \rangle$, $\langle 2, 1 \rangle$ and $\langle 2, 2 \rangle$) of r_d and r_u, and Table 3 shows the results. Without the bit-depth information channel, the dilation rates do not affect the performance much. However, when the bit-depth information is adopted, the $\langle 2, 2 \rangle$ combination shows better performance for the input with bit-depth of 3 or 4. Although its performance is slightly degraded when the input is bit-depth of 5 or 6, PSNR is already over 43, and the difference of SSIM is minuscule at 1e-4, so the visual differences are very little among the results. Therefore, we set both r_d and r_u as two in our BitNet, because it works better for more difficult cases and has a wider receptive field which is important to handle high-resolution images.

5.3 Multi-scale Feature Integration

Our novel multi-scale feature integration (MSFI) module in BitNet enlarges and integrates the previous features at the end of the upscaling. To evaluate how much MSFI improves the performance, we trained the network with and without MSFI and compared their performance. Figure 5 and Table 4 show the

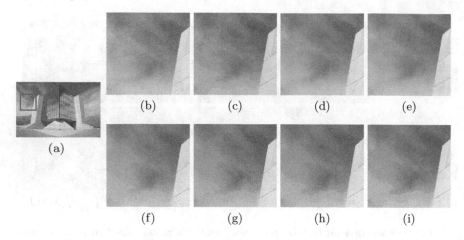

Fig. 6. Comparison of BDE results with different number of integrated multi-scale features. (a) Original 8-bit image (b) Cropped 8-bit image (c) Input 3-bit image (d) 3-bit to 8-bit result of BitNet (e)~(i) Results from the single trained BitNet which additive connections are gradually removed from the smallest feature

test results with the MIT-Abode FiveK dataset. Figure 5(e) shows that BitNet with MSFI eliminates the false contours more effectively. In Table 4, MSFI shows a noticeable performance improvement for 3 and 4-bit to 16-bit BDE. When bit-depth of the input is 5 or 6, the performance is slightly degraded, but the visual differences are minimal among the results. Additionally, we investigated the effect of MSFI by gradually discarding additive connections in MSFI from the smallest feature in our single trained BitNet and visualized each BDE result. As shown in Fig. 6, more disconnections lead to worse false contour removal. Therefore, using enlarged features from small features is important for removing false contour artifacts.

6   Conclusion

In this paper, we use a learning-based approach for bit-depth expansion. We have carefully designed our BitNet with a novel multi-scale feature integration for effective false contour removal and investigated the impact of various combinations of the dilation rates. We have also found that, unlike traditional ways which separately handle each channel, it is better to treat all the color channels together for effective color restoration. Compared to other existing methods, our network estimates more accurate HBD images at a much faster speed. However, BitNet tends to depend on learned color patterns. This can be improved by combining a channel-wise version of BitNet or adopting random hue and contrast augmentations. In addition, the performance can be increased by using a well-designed loss function [31].

Acknowledgement. This work was supported by MCST (Ministry of Culture, Sports & Tourism)/KOCCA (KoreaCreativeContentAgency) (R2016030044 - Development of

Centext-Based Sports Video Analysis, Summarization, and Retrieval Technologies). The authors would like to thank Jing Liu [19] for releasing source codes for various BDE methods.

References

1. Abadi, M., et al.: TensorFlow: large-scale machine learning on heterogeneous systems (2015). https://www.tensorflow.org/. Software available from tensorflow.org
2. Asuni, N., Giachetti, A.: TESTIMAGES: a large-scale archive for testing visual devices and basic image processing algorithms. In: STAG - Smart Tools & Apps for Graphics Conference (2014). https://doi.org/10.2312/stag.20141242
3. Bychkovsky, V., Paris, S., Chan, E., Durand, F.: Learning photographic global tonal adjustment with a database of input/output image pairs. In: The IEEE Conference on Computer Vision and Pattern Recognition (CVPR), June 2011
4. Chen, Q., Xu, J., Koltun, V.: Fast image processing with fully-convolutional networks. In: The IEEE International Conference on Computer Vision (ICCV), October 2017
5. Cheng, C.H., Au, O.C., Liu, C.H., Yip, K.Y.: Bit-depth expansion by contour region reconstruction. In: The IEEE International Symposium on Circuits and Systems, pp. 944–947, May 2009
6. Chollet, F., et al.: Keras (2015). https://keras.io
7. Daly, S., Feng, X.: Decontouring: Prevention and removal of false contour artifacts. In: The International Society for Optical Engineering (SPIE). vol. 5292, pp. 130–149 (2004)
8. Dong, C., Deng, Y., Loy, C.C., Tang, X.: Compression artifacts reduction by a deep convolutional network. In: The IEEE International Conference on Computer Vision (ICCV), pp. 576–584, December 2015
9. Dumoulin, V., Visin, F.: A guide to convolution arithmetic for deep learning (2016), arXiv preprint arXiv:1603.07285
10. Glorot, X., Bengio, Y.: Understanding the difficulty of training deep feedforward neural networks. In: Teh, Y.W., Titterington, M. (eds.) Proceedings of the Thirteenth International Conference on Artificial Intelligence and Statistics, Proceedings of Machine Learning Research, vol. 9, pp. 249–256. PMLR, May 2010
11. Guo, J., Chao, H.: One-to-many network for visually pleasing compression artifacts reduction. In: The IEEE Conference on Computer Vision and Pattern Recognition (CVPR), pp. 4867–4876, July 2017
12. Hall, C., Lowe, M.: Mobile HDR: Dolby vision, HDR10 and mobile HDR premium explained (2018). https://www.pocket-lint.com/phones/news/dolby/138387-mobile-hdr-dolby-vision-hdr10-and-mobile-hdr-premium-explained. Accessed 23 June 2018
13. Keysers, D., Lampert, C.H., Breuel, T.M.: Color image dequantization by constrained diffusion. In: The International Society for Optical Engineering (SPIE), vol. 6058, p. 6058-1–6058-10, January 2006
14. Kingma, D., Ba, J.: Adam: a method for stochastic optimization. In: International Conference on Learning Representations (ICLR), May 2015
15. Kodak: Kodak lossless true color image suite (1999). http://r0k.us/graphics/kodak/. Accessed 23 June 2018
16. Kundu, D., Evans, B.L.: Full-reference visual quality assessment for synthetic images: a subjective study. In: The IEEE International Conference on Image Processing (ICIP), pp. 2374–2378, September 2015

17. Lefkimmiatis, S.: Universal denoising networks: a novel CNN architecture for image denoising. In: The IEEE Conference on Computer Vision and Pattern Recognition (CVPR), June 2018
18. Liu, C.H., Au, O.C., Wong, P.H.W., Kung, M.C., Chao, S.C.: Bit-depth expansion by adaptive filter. In: IEEE International Symposium on Circuits and Systems, pp. 496–499, May 2008
19. Liu, J., Zhai, G., Yang, X., Chen, C.W.: IPAD: intensity potential for adaptive de-quantization. IEEE Trans. Image Process. (2018)
20. Liu, S., Pan, J., Yang, M.-H.: Learning recursive filters for low-level vision via a hybrid neural network. In: Leibe, B., Matas, J., Sebe, N., Welling, M. (eds.) ECCV 2016. LNCS, vol. 9908, pp. 560–576. Springer, Cham (2016). https://doi.org/10. 1007/978-3-319-46493-0_34
21. Maas, A.L., Hannun, A.Y., Ng, A.Y.: Rectifier nonlinearities improve neural network acoustic models. In: ICML Workshop on Deep Learning for Audio, Speech and Language Processing (2013)
22. Mantiuk, R., Krawczyk, G., Myszkowski, K., Seidel, H.P.: Perception-motivated high dynamic range video encoding. Special Issue ACM Transa. Graph. (SIG-GRAPH) **23**, 733–741 (2004)
23. Mizuno, A., Ikebe, M.: Bit-depth expansion for noisy contour reduction in natural images. In: The IEEE International Conference on Acoustics, Speech and Signal Processing (ICASSP), pp. 1671–1675, March 2016
24. Park, M.H., Lee, J.W., Park, R.H., Kim, J.S.: False contour reduction using neural networks and adaptive bi-directional smoothing. IEEE Trans. Consum. Electron. **56**(2), 870–878 (2010)
25. Seetzen, H., et al.: High dynamic range display systems. Special Issue ACM Trans. Graph. (SIGGRAPH), 760–768 (2004)
26. Ulichney, R.A., Cheung, S.: Pixel bit-depth increase by bit replication. In: The International Society for Optical Engineering (SPIE), vol. 3300, pp. 3300-1–3300-10, January 1998
27. Wan, P., Au, O.C., Tang, K., Guo, Y., Fang, L.: From 2D extrapolation to 1D interpolation: content adaptive image bit-depth expansion. In: The IEEE International Conference on Multimedia and Expo (ICME), pp. 170–175, July 2012
28. Wan, P., Cheung, G., Florencio, D., Zhang, C., Au, O.C.: Image bit-depth enhancement via maximum a posteriori estimation of AC signal. IEEE Trans. Image Process. **25**(6), 2896–2909 (2016)
29. Wang, Z., Bovik, A.C., Sheikh, H.R., Simoncelli, E.P.: Image quality assessment: from error visibility to structural similarity. IEEE Trans. Image Process. **13**(4), 600–612 (2004)
30. Zhang, K., Zuo, W., Zhang, L.: FFDNET: toward a fast and flexible solution for cnn-based image denoising. IEEE Trans. Image Process. **27**(9), 4608–4622 (2018)
31. Zhao, H., Gallo, O., Frosio, I., Kautz, J.: Loss functions for image restoration with neural networks. IEEE Trans. Comput. Imaging **3**(1), 47–57 (2017)

Attributes Consistent Faces Generation Under Arbitrary Poses

Fengyi Song[1,2]([envelope]), Jinhui Tang[1], Ming Yang[2], Weiling Cai[2], and Wanqi Yang[2]

[1] School of Computer Science and Engineering,
Nanjing University of Science and Technology, Nanjing, China
jinhuitang@mail.njust.edu.cn
[2] School of Computer Science and Technology,
Nanjing Normal University, Nanjing, China
{f.song,myang,caiwl,yangwq}@njnu.edu.cn

Abstract. Generating visual images automatically given semantic attributes description helps building friendly human-machine interface as criminal suspects depicting and customer-oriented product design. However, this is a hard task since there exist great semantic and structure gaps between attributes description and visual images, which further cause great inference uncertainty in transforming from attribute description to vivid visual images. We aim to reduce the posterior distribute complexity given attributes ($P(I|A)$) by exploring face structure knowledge and imposing semantic consistency constraint in an end-to-end learning fashion. Our contributions are three-fold: (1) we address the semantic and structure consistent problem in attribute-conditioned image generation; (2) the proposed method can generate attribute consistent face images with high quality in both detailed texture and also clear structure; (3) we provide an interface for generating attribute consistent images with diverse poses.

Keywords: Visual attributes · Face generation ·
Structure and semantic gaps

1 Introduction

As a semantic mid-level feature representation, attributes shows advantages to low-level features in semantic interpretable, feature coding efficiency, and good generability in depicting kinds of visual objects. Attribute learning has received extensive attention for its potential application in image retrieval [29], object detection and recognition [7], scene understanding [25], action recognition [35], zero-shot learning [17,24], etc. Most of these tasks address the attributes extraction, i.e., estimate the attributes response of a given image. In some real scenarios, it is urged to obtain visual images according to some semantic attributes description. For example, generating face images of the criminal according to the given description by the witness; generating the prototype image of shoes

© Springer Nature Switzerland AG 2019
C. V. Jawahar et al. (Eds.): ACCV 2018, LNCS 11362, pp. 83–97, 2019.
https://doi.org/10.1007/978-3-030-20890-5_6

Fig. 1. Illustration of challenging pose variation greatly degrading attribute conditioned image generation. The left part shows faces with challenging pose, while the right part shows faces in frontal pose. The target images are shown in the first line, and the corresponding sampled images by decoder of CVAE with MSE loss and semantic loss (refer to the Sect. 3.3) are shown in the following two lines respectively.

or clothes according to the description given by the customers, etc. We call this *attribute-conditioned image generation*.

Attribute-conditioned image generation is a non-trivial task. The challenges origin from the intrinsic limitation of attribute representation, which lead to ambiguous appearance and structure of the generated image especially for objects with large pose variation (see Fig. 1). Firstly, semantic interpretable makes attribute a good human-computer interface, but also leads to great semantic gap between attributes and images pixels. Secondly, high visual information abstraction makes attribute quiet efficient in feature coding, but also provides limited detailed visual information for generating vivid visual images. Thirdly, most attributes depicting local features, which brings good generalizability across categories, but also provides little information about the whole structure of objects, further leads to confused structure of generated images. For a short, there are great semantic and structure gaps between attributes and images, which should not be neglected in attribute-conditioned image generation.

Attribute-conditioned image generation is beyond traditional feature visualization [4,22,32] and is also distinct from image-conditioned image generation [12,14,37]. Although feature visualization also addressing image generation given the features representation, there is much direct spatial and textual correspondence between feature representation and images. These strong correspondences can be explored for better visualization. For example, these enriched correspondences are explored for visualizing LBP [4], HOG [32], etc. For image-conditioned image generation, there is enriched closely related visual information can be explored for better image generation. For example, transform line-drawn sketch image to detailed visual image [21], change the styles of images while preserving the main content [12,14], and rectify the deteriorated images caused by rainy, fog, and haze [37].

Compared to feature visualization and image-conditioned image generation [12,14,37], attributes provide less direct spatial and textual information for image generation. Consequently, there is great flexibility and uncertainty in image generation process. As illustrated in the Fig. 2, given some attribute

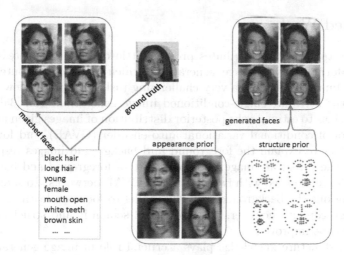

Fig. 2. Illustration of great confusion for image generation only given attribute description. Given the attributes description of an image, there may a set of possible faces (see the top-left images) with varying appearance and structure layout, and it is hard to generate the unique ground-truth image (see the top-middle image). It is necessary to explore structure and appearance knowledge for generating images with improved quality w.r.t clean appearance and clear pose (see the top-right images).

description like *'a smiling young lady with long black hair and brown skin'*, there will be a set of possible face image satisfying this description (as show in the top-left of Fig. 2), and it is hard to teach the model to generate the unique ground-truth image (see the top-middle face image in Fig. 2). Considering the great structure and appearance gaps between attributes and images, we consider the following strategies for generating attribute consistent images with improved quality in fidelity and right posture (see the top-right faces in Fig. 2): (1) the structure information is weakly or implicitly covered in attribute description, it is necessary to provide structure prior for better image generation; (2) semantic consistence should be added as the criterion for learning the transformation from attribute to images; (3) If we have a pre-image coarsely consistent with the given attribute description, the image generation model can put emphasis on learning the residual visual information between the pre-image and target image.

We implement these ideas with the typical generation model of conditional variational auto-encoder (CVAE) [15], and evaluate the proposed method on the unconstrained face datasets named Labeled Face in the Wild (LFW) [18]. However, to the best of our knowledge, there is no quantity analysis measurement for estimating the quality of the generated images. Consequently, we propose three measurements for estimating the reconstruction accuracy w.r.t the texture, shape, and semantic consistence respectively. We empirically demonstrate that the proposed method can generate attribute-consistent face images with improved quality in texture, shape, and semantic consistence under the resolution of 128 × 128 (we do not try larger size, since the raw resolution image on the LFW is nearly 128 × 128).

2   Related Work

As we have stated above, attributes provide little detailed visual texture and structure information for image generation, which lead to attributes single-conditioned image generation a very challenging task. There are a few of works devoted to the attribute single-conditioned image generation. Yan [34] tried to treat this task as to estimate the posterior distribution of images given attributes with the tool of conditional variational auto-encoder (CVAE), and forcing the latent variables to explain the foreground and background images respectively. Specifically, they treat an image as a composite of foreground and background layers, which are modeled with two interactive CVAE networks. To some extent, disentangling out the background help the model to focus on learning the foreground image content, however, the problem of semantic and structure consistence still not be improved.

Actually, structure knowledge plays a crucial role in image generation process. Reed et al. [26] proposed that the image generation model should not only cares about what to draw but also where to draw, and they explored objects box and location of key parts to improve the text description conditioned bird image generation. Dosovitskiy et al. [6] explored a set of graphics codes indicating shape, position and lighting for generating 3D chair. What is more, line-drawn images provide strong structure information together with attributes for generating reality images [9,21]. However, to the best of our knowledge, there is no work addressing structure consistency for attribute conditioned face image generation yet.

Semantic consistence is also important in attribute-conditioned image generation, and to the best of our knowledge, there are few works giving quantity analysis about this index for the attribute-conditioned image generation. However, semantic consistence has received attentions from researches in style transfer [14], super-resolution [19], and also image-conditioned image generation [5,11]. It is necessary to incorporate semantic consistence consideration for attribute-conditioned image generation.

Technically, attribute-conditioned image generation is also related to general conditioned image generation including labels, sketches, source images, etc. Conditioned image generation has benefited from the great advances in deep network learning with large model capacity and proper optimization techniques. Typical generation models are variational auto-encoder (VAE) [15,28] and generative adversarial network (GAN) [8]. With these two typical models, kinds of methods addressing various real applications are proposed. These methods are miscellaneous with different further consideration including condition exploration strategy [9,12,20,26,27], model structure design [1,2,34,36], and also suitable loss estimation [5,14]. Zhang [36] proposed stack-GAN for generating high resolution image in two stage way, i.e., firstly using stage-I GAN to generate a low resolution image and feeding this image to the generator of the stage-II GAN. Cai [2] similarly proposed coarse-to-fine image generation with multi-stage VAE, for which the capacity of the decoder is enhanced by concatenate a residual block network. Besides the above improvements on model architecture, suitable loss function are also explored, such as the perception loss [5,11,14,37] and L_1 loss, and multi-type loss combination is also considered [37].

Compared to image-conditioned image generation [12,37], attribute-conditioned image generation has little direct appearance and structure information to utilize. The purpose of this work is to bridge the semantic and structure gaps between attributes and visual images for improved attribute conditioned face generation, and propose an approach to incorporate structure knowledge and imposing semantic consistence in an end-to-end learning fashion. On the other hand, considering no source image can be used for guiding image generation, we propose to cascade the output of a pre-trained attribute-conditioned model as the appearance prior to further improve the generated images, which motivated by strategy of coarse-to-fine and residual learning [2,36].

3   Attributes Consistent Faces Generation Under Arbitrary Poses

In this section, we will first introduce the formulation of attribute conditioned image generation by conditional variational auto-encoder, and then describe the proposed several strategies for achieving attribute-consistent face generation with improved appearance and structure quality.

3.1   The Formulation of Attribute-Conditioned Image Generation

The key of automatic image generation is to estimate the distribution of visual object x, i.e., $p_\theta(x)$. However, this is a challenging task due to its unknown complex distribution caused by great variation in appearance and structure. It is assumed that there exist some factors z explaining the distribution of visual objects, i.e., $p_\theta(x|z)$. Variational auto-encoder (VAE) [15,28] provides a flexible formulation of this idea with the latent variable probabilistic model, where the latent variables are responsible for explaining image distribution and need not to have specific meaning. With the Bayesian inference and distribution approximation technique, the objective of VAE is to compute the maximum log-likelihood with the formulation as follows:

$$\log p(x) = \mathbb{E}_{z \sim q_\phi(z|x)} p_\theta(x|z) + KL(q_\phi(z|x), p_\theta(z|x)) \\ - KL(q_\phi(z|x), p(z)) \quad (1)$$

where, $q_\phi(z|x)$ is the encoder, and $p_\theta(x|z)$ is the decoder, and $p(z)$ is the prior of distribution of latent variables and commonly assumed as a standard normal distribution. Further, the objective is transformed to optimize its lower bounds.

$$\log p(x)_{LB} = \mathbb{E}_{z \sim q_\phi(z|x)} p_\theta(x|z) - KL(q_\phi(z|x), p(z)) \quad (2)$$

With the help of reparameterization trick, Eq. (2) can be optimized through gradient back-propagation. Using the deep network as the implementation of both the encoder and decoder further enhanced the model capacity of VAE.

While VAE provides a theoretical ensured tool for image generation from a noise vector sampled from $p(z)$, however, a noise vector provides nearly no clear understandable information, resulting the generated images as only the randomly samples of posterior $p_\theta(x|z)$.

In real applications, generating expected images according to the specific condition is much desired. For example, generating face images consistent with some visual semantic description, formed as a set of attributes values a. Consequently, conditional variational auto-encoder (CVAE) [31,33] is to compute the posterior $p(x|a)$. The objective of CVAE can be easily induced from VAE by incorporating the attributes description a, and is formulated as:

$$\log p(x|a)_{LB} = \mathbb{E}_{z \sim q_\phi(z|x,a)} p_\theta(x|z,a) - KL(q_\phi(z|x,a), p(z|a)) \tag{3}$$

Given attributes description a, the target images to be generated are more concrete compared to images sampled randomly from VAE. This seems lead a shrunk searching space for the generation algorithm, however, we should noticed that the attribute consistence criterion put great desire for learning high accurate mapping from the given attributes description to the corresponding images. What is more, there are relatively less training samples as the evidence for learning this mapping.

3.2 Generating Faces with Clear Posture

The intrinsic drawback of attributes representation is that there is insufficient structure information available for conducting the image generation, which leads to ambiguous structure of the generated image under large pose (see Fig. 1). Alternatively, we consider incorporating explicit structure knowledge. Actually, landmarks locations can give a suitable description of structure of object. For example, there are nearly several dozen landmarks defined on the facial parts for face alignment [13]. Choosing landmarks locations as the structure knowledge owns several advantages: (1) efficient and sufficient to depict the structure information of object, such as pose; (2) can be obtained automatically by the pre-trained localization model at the training phase of image generation model, and friendly specified by interactive user at the testing phase (e.g., chosen from a candidate shape sets clustered on the training samples).

Next, it is crucial to explore the structure knowledge for improved image generation. Conditional variational auto-encoder as a typical image generation model provides a flexible way for incorporating structure knowledge. With the additional structure knowledge s, much information is provided for the decoder, i.e., $p_\theta(x|z,a,s)$. At the training phase, the structure knowledge s also induce the encoder $q_\phi(z|x,a,s)$ forcing the latent variable z to explain both the appearance and structure variations. It is naturally to formulate the augmented conditional variational auto-encoder as follows:

$$\log p(x|a,s)_{LB} = \mathbb{E}_{z \sim q_\phi(z|x,a,s)} p_\theta(x|z,a,s)$$
$$- KL(q_\phi(z|x,a,s), p(z|a,s)) \tag{4}$$

For attribute-conditioned face image generation, we obtained the facial land-marks locations with the off-the-shelf facial landmark localizer [13].

3.3 Generating Faces with Consistent Appearance

Actually, it is hard to bridging the semantic gap between attributes and images directly on representation level. While the hidden layers demonstrate semantic explainable meanings in deep network used for representation learning, we consider implementing the above formulated conditional variational auto-encoder for attribute-conditioned image generation by deep network, and forcing its hidden layers also owns semantic meanings. Consequently, it is expected that the semantic connection between attributes and images can be embedded into the projection to be learned from attributes to images.

The shortcoming of CVAE is that the generated images are blur, and the reason lies on the used pixel-to-pixel reconstruction loss in $\mathbb{E}_{z \sim q_\phi(z|x,a,s)} p_\theta(x|z,a,s)$. Motivated by the perceptual loss used in image style transform and super-resolution [14], it is necessary to introduce such loss into conditional variational auto-encoder for generating images with better semantic consistence as the attribute description. Similarly, the newly introduced reconstruction loss is defined on the hidden layers representation. For example, we choose a set of hidden layers $S_l = \{l_i, l_j, l_k\}$ to measure the semantic consistence between the generated image $\hat{x}$ and the target image x, the loss are defined as follows: $\sum_{i \in S} \frac{1}{C_i H_i W_i} \|\phi_i(\hat{x}) - \phi_i(x)\|^2$, where the mapping $\phi_i(\cdot)$ represent the response of layer i in the pre-trained feature representation model, and C_i, H_i, W_i indicate the channel number and the size of hidden layer i respectively. It is reasonable to choose the frontal hidden layers for shareable semantic consistence, and choose the higher hidden layers for typical semantic consistence.

3.4 Appearance Facilitated Image Generation

Attribute-conditioned image generation is very difficult than image-to-image transformation, since there is no appearance image available for conducting image generation directly. The generation model may get stuck in straight-forward learning the projection from attribute to images. Motivated by residual networks [10] and coarse-to-fine stacked image generation [36], we consider exploring the generated image of a pre-trained general attribute-conditioned CVAE. Specifically, the pre-trained general CVAE is a vanilla attribute-conditioned image generation model. Then, we feed the generated image x' to another conditional variational auto-encoder as the appearance prior. With the contribution of the pre-trained CVAE, the latter CVAE can work hard on modeling the residual appearance between x' and the ground-truth image x.

3.5 Model Architecture

The architecture of the proposed method is shown in Fig. 3. The encoder of CVAE is mainly built by a deep network containing five modules, while each module stacks a convolutional layer (conv) with the kernel size of 4×4 and the stride of 2, a batch normalization layer (BN), and a LeakyRelu nonlinear activation layer. The inputs of the encoder $(q_\phi(z|x, x', a, s))$ are the ground-truth image x, the attributes a, the structure information s, and the coarsely predicted consistent image x'. The decoder has the similar inputs by replacing the ground-truth image with the latent vector (at the testing phase, the latent vector is sampled from a standard normal distribution). The main part of the decoder is built with the symmetric structure as the encoder using the convolutional layer with the kernel size of 3×3 and the stride of 1, and an up-sampling layer with the scale of 2.

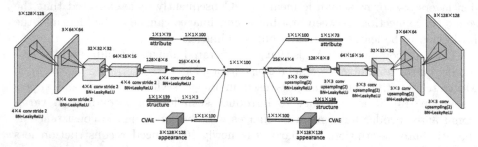

Fig. 3. Illustration of the architecture of the proposed approach. The CVAE is the pre-trained model for predicting the coarsely consistent image as the appearance prior conducing further image generation process.

We empirically find that the dimension of the latent variable vector affects the model performance greatly; the reason may be attributed to the distinct explanation ability of different number of latent variables. We also give the statistical analysis of the model performance under different setting of latent variable dimension in the Experiments section.

4 Experiments

We first introduce the used datasets and the experimental settings including the performance measurements and the comparison methods. Then we report the detailed performance and comparison with other closely related methods. Next, we discuss the affection of the dimension of the latent variables in the conditional variational auto-encoder. Finally, we illustrate the flexibility of the proposed method in generating attribute consistent face images under arbitrary poses.

4.1 Datasets and Experimental Settings

Datasets. The Labeled Face in the Wild (LFW) [18] is a typical unconstrained face dataset containing more than 13,000 images of 5,749 different individuals. Kumar [16] enriched LFW datasets with 73 semantic attributes for describing facial characteristics. We investigate the performance of the proposed attribute-conditioned face generation on LFW following the standard experimental protocol (there is no individual overlap between the training-and-testing data). Each face is aligned and central cropped. Specifically, we use the method [13] to perform 68 landmark points localization, and then use the eye position for face alignment, then central facial region is cropped with less background but covering most head region (with width as 2 times of eyes distance, and height as 2.5 times of heights of 68 landmarks). Finally all the faces are scaled to 128×128. Much high resolution is not considered, since the average resolution of faces on LFW is nearly 128×128. The structure information is represented as the localized coordinates of the 68 landmark points and degree of three pose states including yaw, roll, and pitch. For disCVAE as the comparison method, we used the published image with 64×64 resolution [34].

Comparison Methods. We choose two methods as the comparison methods.

- *Baseline Method.* We take the attribute-single-conditioned variational auto-encoder (CVAE) as the baseline, which is implemented with the semantic loss defined on the hidden layers (Relu1_1,Relu3_1,Relu3_1) of pre-trained 19-layer VGGNet [30].
- *Comparison Method.* We choose the disentangling CVAE [34] as the state-of-the-art approaches addressing attribute-conditioned face generation.

We do not compare with conditional GAN approach, since there is no work addressing attribute-conditioned face generation, and we empirically find that conditional GAN can perfectly reconstruct training images even for background, but for testing data, the generated images show very bad visual fidelity for illustration.

Image Quality Measurements. To the best of our knowledge, most published image generation methods do not give quantity analysis of the quality of generated images while directly illustrate the generated images. Besides image illustration, we propose three measures for measuring the quality of generated images. With the assumption that two similar images should have similar feature representation, we propose to measure the quality of the generated image *(sampled image from decoder with random noise vector)* by estimating the texture, geometric, and semantic similarity to the ground-truth image in some specified feature spaces. We name these corresponding reconstruction losses as texture loss, shape loss, and semantic loss respectively, and summarized as follows:

- *Texture Loss.* Compute the Chi-square distance of two images in the Local Binary Pattern (LBP) [23] feature space. We set the cell size as 16×16 for extracting LBP feature on 128×128 images.
- *Shape Loss.* Compute the L2 distance of two images in the Histogram of Oriented Gradients (HOG) [3] feature space. We set the cell size as 8×8 for extracting LBP feature on 128×128 images.
- *Semantic Loss.* Compute the L2 distance of two images in the hidden layers (Relu1_1, Relu3_1, Relu3_1) of pre-trained 19-layer VGGNet [30].

In order to compare the performance with disCVAE method with the same quantity scale, we rescaled the image size of 64×64 (used in disCVAE [34]) to 128×128.

4.2 Results

Effectiveness of the Proposed Method. Figure 4 illustrates the generated faces of the proposed method and the other comparison methods. Compared with other methods, our method shows advantage in generating faces with improved quality in clear pose, detailed appearance, and also high image resolution. To be noticed that, although the faces contain large variations in posture, expression, and also facial occlusion, the proposed method can generate faces recovering the semantic consistent appearance, persevering right posture, and also smoothing out the noisy background even with the facial occlusion.

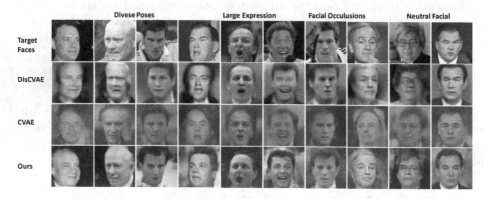

Fig. 4. Illustration of the generated faces of several comparison methods. These faces contain large variations in posture, expression, and also facial occlusion. All the faces have the resolution of 128×128 except the images used in disCVAE [34] with the resolution of 64×64.

Table 1 gives quantitative evaluation on three reconstruction loss introduced in previous sections, estimating the reconstruction quality on characteristics of semantic, shape, and texture. We can see that the proposed method outperforms other methods on all the three measurements.

Flexibility in Generating Faces Under Arbitrary Posture. With the augmented structure prior, we can generate faces with diverse poses by concatenate the attribute with typical structure prior (see Fig. 5). Here, we use k-means for clustering typical face structure on the training data and choose 3 typical face structure. From Fig. 5, we can see that with the same attribute condition but with different structure prior, the generated faces show similar appearance to the ground-truth image but with diverse posture.

Table 1. Comparative performances of the proposed method and other comparison methods. The reconstruction loss in texture, shape, and semantic are computed between the ground-truth image and generated image *(sampled from the decoder by feeding with a random gaussian noise vector)* on three kinds of feature space including LBP, HOG, and hidden layers feature in VGG-19 model.

Methods	Reconstruction loss		
	Semantic	Shape	Texture
disCVAE [34]	61331.30	14.03	15225.70
CVAE [31]	39791.70	12.83	12898.34
Ours	**38272.50**	**12.36**	**12242.93**

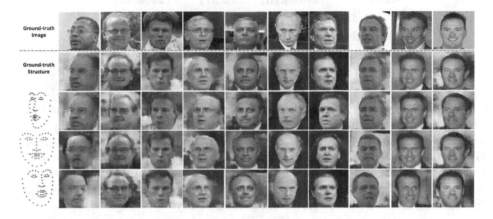

Fig. 5. Illustration of the flexibility in generating faces with diverse poses but constrained to the same attributes description. Three typical face structures are chosen for illustrating the performance of the proposed method w.r.t the attribute consistency and pose diversity. These three typical face structures are clustered on the training data. Actually, such kind of face structure can also be given manually with great flexibility as the user expected.

Contribution of the Individual Strategies. To illustrate the effectiveness of the proposed strategies for tackling attribute consistent face generation, we investigate the contribution of each strategy individually, i.e., the contribution of the structure exploration strategy ('-StructExplor') and appearance facilitation strategy ('-AppearFacili'). Since these two strategies can also apply to other variants of conditional variational auto-encoder, we conduct the experiments on both vanilla CVAE and disentangling CVAE [34]. The detailed investigation of their effects can be seen in Table 2. We can see that the both strategies nearly always promote the quality of generated faces w.r.t. the proposed three quality measurements, while makes these reconstruction losses greatly decreased. Although the structure exploration strategy increased the texture loss a little for disCVAE, further combining with appearance facilitation strategy also greatly improved the reconstruction ability.

Table 2. Contribution of the individual strategies. We test the effectiveness of the appearance facilitation strategy ('-AppearFacili'), structure exploration strategy ('-StructExplor'), and also combine both of them (Both) to the vanilla CVAE and also its variants disCVAE. The down arrow ↓ indicates the decreased reconstruction loss, and the up arrow ↑ means the versus.

Methods	Reconstruction loss		
	Semantic loss	Shape loss	Texture loss
disCVAE [34]	61331.30	14.03	15225.70
-AppearFacili	56091.00↓	13.55↓	13298.76↓
-StructExplor	60464.30↓	14.01↓	15619.36↑
-Both	**47468.70↓**	**12.97↓**	**12903.23↓**
CVAE [31]	39791.70	12.83	12898.34
-AppearFacili	39065.80↓	12.52↓	12895.42↓
-StructExplor	38915.90↓	12.45↓	12263.01↓
-Both	**38272.50↓**	**12.36↓**	**12242.93↓**

In addition, we can also see that structure exploration strategy demonstrate great advantage in reducing the reconstruction loss than appearance facilitation strategy on advanced CVAE, but does not show improved results for the relatively weak model of disCVAE [34]. This may indicate that structure exploration can further enhance the quality of generated image for advanced learning model, while the appearance facilitation may enhance the quality of generated image for learning model with relative weak learning ability.

Effects of Different Dimensions of the Latent Variable. Figure 6 shows the effects of the latent variable with dimensions of 100, 256, 512, 768, and 1024. There is a tendency that image generation model with large dimension of the

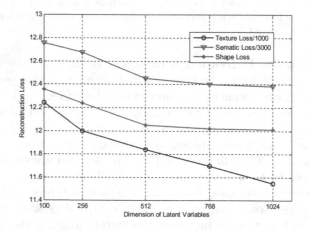

Fig. 6. Illustrating the affection of different dimensions of latent variables. We choose typical dimension as 100, 256, 512, 768, and 1024 for latent variables. For better illustration, we scaled the texture loss and the semantic loss with 1000 and 3000 respectively.

latent variable generate high quality faces w.r.t the proposed three reconstruction losses measurements. This may attribute to the enriched information contained in the large dimension latent variable for image generation.

5 Conclusion

In this paper, we address the attribute consistent face generation under arbitrary poses. For improved quality of generated images with clear structure and consistent semantic with the attribute description, we propose several strategies including incorporating structure knowledge, imposing semantic consistence constrain in the end-to-end learning fashion, and explore appearance image to facilitate further image generation in the stacked way. Experiments on the wild face generation demonstrate the effectiveness of the proposed approaches. Consequently, the generated faces show clear pose and clean appearance with high image resolution. In addition, the proposed explicit structure knowledge exploration approach also provide a flexible way for generating faces with diverse poses but constrained to the same attribute description.

Acknowledgement. The authors are grateful to the editors and anonymous reviewers for helpful comments and suggestions. The authors also thank Hui Song for helpful discussion. This work was supported in part by China Postdoctoral Science Foundation (Grant No. 2017M621749), National Key Research and Development Program of China (Grant No. 2016YFB1001001), National Natural Science Foundation of China (Grant No. 61432008, 61603193, 61876087), Natural Science Foundation of Jiangsu Province (Grant No. BK20171479, BK20161020, BK20161560), and Program of Natural Science Research of Jiangsu Higher Education Institutions (Grant No. 15KJB520023).

References

1. Bao, J., Chen, D., Wen, F., Li, H., Hua, G.: CVAE-GAN: fine-grained image generation through asymmetric training. In: ICCV, pp. 2764–2773 (2017)
2. Cai, L., Gao, H., Ji, S.: Multi-stage variational auto-encoders for coarse-to-fine image generation. arXiv:1705.07202 (2017)
3. Dalal, N., Triggs, B.: Histograms of oriented gradients for human detection. In: CVPR, pp. 886–893 (2005)
4. Dangelo, E., Jacques, L., Alahi, A., Vandergheynst, P.: From bits to images: inversion of local binary descriptors. TPAMI **36**(5), 874–887 (2014)
5. Dosovitskiy, A., Brox, T.: Generating images with perceptual similarity metrics based on deep networks. In: NIPS, pp. 658–666 (2016)
6. Dosovitskiy, A., Springenberg, J.T., Brox, T.: Learning to generate chairs with convolutional neural networks. In: CVPR, pp. 1538–1546 (2015)
7. Farhadi, A., Endres, I., Hoiem, D., Forsyth, D.: Describing objects by their attributes. In: CVPR, pp. 1778–1785 (2009)
8. Goodfellow, I., et al.: Generative adversarial nets. In: Advances in Neural Information Processing Systems, vol. 27, pp. 2672–2680 (2014)
9. Guo, Q., Zhu, C., Xia, Z., Wang, Z., Liu, Y.: Attribute-controlled face photo synthesis from simple line drawing. In: ICIP, pp. 2946–2950 (2017)

10. He, K., Zhang, X., Ren, S., Sun, J.: Deep residual learning for image recognition. In: CVPR, pp. 770–778 (2016)
11. Hou, X., Shen, L., Sun, K., Qiu, G.: Deep feature consistent variational autoencoder. In: Workshop on Applications of Computer Vision, pp. 1133–1141 (2017)
12. Isola, P., Zhu, J., Zhou, T., Efros, A.A.: Image-to-image translation with conditional adversarial networks. In: CVPR, pp. 5967–5976 (2017)
13. Jin, X., Tan, X.: Face alignment by robust discriminative Hough voting. Pattern Recogn. **60**, 318–333 (2016)
14. Johnson, J., Alahi, A., Fei-Fei, L.: Perceptual losses for real-time style transfer and super-resolution. In: Leibe, B., Matas, J., Sebe, N., Welling, M. (eds.) ECCV 2016. LNCS, vol. 9906, pp. 694–711. Springer, Cham (2016). https://doi.org/10.1007/978-3-319-46475-6_43
15. Kingma, D.P., Welling, M.: Auto-encoding variational bayes. In: ICLR (2014)
16. Kumar, N., Berg, A.C., Belhumeur, P.N., Nayar, S.K.: Describable visual attributes for face verification and image search. TPAMI **33**(10), 1962–1977 (2011)
17. Lampert, C.H., Nickisch, H., Harmeling, S.: Attribute-based classification for zero-shot visual object categorization. TPAMI **36**(3), 453–465 (2014)
18. Learned-Miller, E., Huang, G.B., RoyChowdhury, A., Li, H., Hua, G.: Labeled faces in the wild: a survey. In: Kawulok, M., Celebi, M.E., Smolka, B. (eds.) Advances in Face Detection and Facial Image Analysis, pp. 189–248. Springer, Cham (2016). https://doi.org/10.1007/978-3-319-25958-1_8
19. Ledig, C., et al.: Photo-realistic single image super-resolution using a generative adversarial network. In: CVPR, pp. 4681–4690 (2016)
20. Li, M., Zuo, W., Zhang, D.: Convolutional network for attribute-driven and identity-preserving human face generation. arXiv preprint arXiv:1608.06434 (2016)
21. Liang, Y., Song, M., Xie, L., Bu, J.: Face sketch-to-photo synthesis from simple line drawing. In: Signal & Information Processing Association Summit and Conference, pp. 1–5 (2012)
22. Mahendran, A., Vedaldi, A.: Understanding deep image representations by inverting them. In: CVPR, pp. 5188–5196 (2015)
23. Ojala, T., Pietikainen, M., Maenpaa, T.: Multiresolution gray-scale and rotation invariant texture classification with local binary patterns. TPAMI **24**(7), 971–987 (2002)
24. Palatucci, M., Pomerleau, D., Hinton, G.E., Mitchell, T.M.: Zero-shot learning with semantic output codes. In: NIPS, pp. 1410–1418 (2009)
25. Patterson, G., Hays, J.: Sun attribute database: discovering, annotating, and recognizing scene attributes. In: CVPR, pp. 2751–2758 (2012)
26. Reed, S.E., Akata, Z., Mohan, S., Tenka, S., Schiele, B., Lee, H.: Learning what and where to draw. In: NIPS, pp. 217–225 (2016)
27. Reed, S.E., Akata, Z., Yan, X., Logeswaran, L., Schiele, B., Lee, H.: Generative adversarial text to image synthesis. In: ICML, pp. 1060–1069 (2016)
28. Rezende, D.J., Mohamed, S., Wierstra, D.: Stochastic backpropagation and approximate inference in deep generative models. In: ICML, pp. 1278–1286 (2014)
29. Siddiquie, B., Feris, R.S., Davis, L.S.: Image ranking and retrieval based on multi-attribute queries. In: CVPR, pp. 801–808 (2011)
30. Simonyan, K., Zisserman, A.: Very deep convolutional networks for large-scale image recognition. In: ICLR (2015)
31. Sohn, K., Yan, X., Lee, H.: Learning structured output representation using deep conditional generative models. In: NIPS, pp. 3483–3491 (2015)
32. Vondrick, C., Khosla, A., Malisiewicz, T., Torralba, A.: HOGgles: visualizing object detection features. In: ICCV, pp. 1–8 (2014)

33. Walker, J., Doersch, C., Gupta, A., Hebert, M.: An uncertain future: forecasting from static images using variational autoencoders. In: Leibe, B., Matas, J., Sebe, N., Welling, M. (eds.) ECCV 2016. LNCS, vol. 9911, pp. 835–851. Springer, Cham (2016). https://doi.org/10.1007/978-3-319-46478-7_51

34. Yan, X., Yang, J., Sohn, K., Lee, H.: Attribute2Image: conditional image generation from visual attributes. In: Leibe, B., Matas, J., Sebe, N., Welling, M. (eds.) ECCV 2016. LNCS, vol. 9908, pp. 776–791. Springer, Cham (2016). https://doi.org/10.1007/978-3-319-46493-0_47

35. Yao, B., Jiang, X., Khosla, A., Lin, A., Guibas, L.J., Feifei, L.: Human action recognition by learning bases of action attributes and parts. In: ICCV, pp. 1331–1338 (2011)

36. Zhang, H., et al.: StackGAN: text to photo-realistic image synthesis with stacked generative adversarial networks. In: ICCV, pp. 5907–5915 (2017)

37. Zhang, H., Sindagi, V., Patel, V.M.: Image de-raining using a conditional generative adversarial network. arXiv preprint arXiv:1701.05957 (2017)

Cooperative Adversarial Network
for Accurate Super Resolution

Zhong-Qiu Zhao$^{(\boxtimes)}$, Jian Hu, Weidong Tian, and Ning Ling

School of Computer Science and Information Engineering,
HeFei University of Technology, Hefei, Anhui, China
{z.zhao,wdtian}@hfut.edu.cn, hoojame@mail.hfut.edu.cn, 523975233@qq.com

Abstract. Convolutional neural networks for super-resolution (SR) have recently improved global pixel similarity. To estimate visually pleasing SR images, general SR methods focus on optimizing a network by minimizing the feature loss provided by a pre-trained classification network. These estimated SR images are usually enriched with high-frequency texture details, but accompanied with large global pixel error. In this paper, we design a cooperative adversarial network (CAN) for SR, which consists of two sub-networks: chaser and enhancer. The chaser estimates visually pleasing SR images by optimizing feature loss provided by the enhancer, and the enhancer promotes the SR images of the chaser with less global pixel error. In addition, the enhancer fuses multiple residual features from different layers to reserve different level details for the SR images. In order to merge the two sub-networks into a unified network, we define an equilibrium ratio of the pixel-wise loss of chaser to enhancer for controlling alternate process of three training units. Compared to existing multi-network models, our CAN shows competitive performance with less parameters.

Keywords: Convolutional neural networks · Super-resolution · Adversarial network

1 Introduction

The problem of single image super-resolution (SISR) is to estimate a super-resolved image (I^{SR}) with a low-resolution image (I^{LR}) input, where I^{LR} is a low-resolution counterpart of a high-resolution image (I^{HR}). The SISR is widely used in various computer vision fields, where many image details are required, such as security, surveillance imaging, and medical imaging.

There have been many reconstruction methods solving the ill-posed SISR problem (information contained in a small patch is not sufficient for detail recovery) directly, such as interpolation-based methods (bicubic, Lanczos [33]), edge-based methods [34], statistical methods [35,36], patch-based methods [37–39].

Supported by the National Natural Science Foundation of China (No. 61672203) and Anhui Natural Science Funds for Distinguished Young Scholar (No. 170808J08).

C. V. Jawahar et al. (Eds.): ACCV 2018, LNCS 11362, pp. 98–114, 2019.
https://doi.org/10.1007/978-3-030-20890-5_7

In recent years, the example-based SISR methods have improved the state-of-the-art performance constantly by learning a mapping from LR to HR image with large image databases. As deep learning owns powerful modeling capability, the convolution neural network for SR (SRCNN [1]) successfully made a start of applying deep learning methods for SR without any engineered features.

Lately, the transposed convolution [2,3] and the efficient sub-pixel convolution [4] were respectively adopted to replace the bicubic interpolation for upsampling. However, these networks are too shallow to reconstruct SR images using large receptive field. Then, a very deep network (VDSR [5]) using skip-connection to extract residual features showed fast training convergence and good reconstruction performance. Nevertheless, all networks mentioned above are optimized with mean square error of per-pixel (pixel-wise loss), which inevitably generate blurry reconstructions.

To recover texture details and avoid smooth reconstruction, Johnson et al. [6] used the pre-trained network as perceptual loss function to train a SR network. In much the same way, a SR generative adversarial network (SRGAN) [7] employs a deep skip-connection residual network as generator (SR network), which is optimized with a perceptual loss calculated on feature maps of classification network. These perceptual loss SR networks [6,8] perform better on reconstructing texture details and sharp edges than these networks of pixel-wise loss, but the recovered HR images are usually with lower global average pixel similarity. In addition, the hard-trained and time-consuming perceptual loss network or discriminator is useless in reconstruction process.

To mitigate these issues, we propose a cooperative adversarial network (CAN), which consists of two sub-networks: one is named as chaser, the other is named as enhancer. The chaser is optimized by a perceptual loss, and generates SR images. Different from SRGAN, the enhancer fuses multi-residual to provide efficient feature loss and enhances quality of the SR images generated by the chaser rather than distinguishing the SR images from real images. In a word, our contributions of this paper can be concluded in three aspects: (1) Compared to existing two-network models, the proposed CAN can reconstruct SR images of competitive performance with less parameters. (2) We propose an alternately iterative training method of three training units to alternately train the two sub-networks, which helps to merge two cooperative but adversarial SR networks into a unified SR network. (3) We concatenate residual features of different level residual blocks to build a multi-residual fusion network, which reconstructs SR image containing different level details.

2   Related Work

2.1   Residual Convolutional Network

Very Deep Convolutional Network (VDSR) [5] predicts residual details rather than actual high frequency information of an image, and makes the deep network of 20 convolution layers with faster convergence speed and higher accuracy than non-residual networks. In fact, He et al. [9] firstly proposed residual blocks by combining the input features with the output residual features. Learning residual details prevents network from the vanishing/exploding gradients problem [10], and makes it possible to design deeper convolutional neural networks for SR. With deeper networks, more complex function can be modeled and a larger receptive field (*i.e.*, more context) can be used to predict image details. According to the visualization researches [30], features in shallow layers respond to corners or edges, and deep layers show abstract features of entire objects. A complex SR mapping of residual dense network [11] was learned by using the features of different level convolution layers.

However, the VDSR only adopts residual features of the last convolution layer. Furthermore, the VDSR is trained with a big image set containing multiple factor scales so that it can deal with images of various factor scales. While, the images of different factor scales are processed with a fixed receipt field (41×41). Therefore, we propose a multi-residual fusion network by combining the residual features from different layers of residual blocks. Obviously, the multi-residual network can utilize the image details of multi-scale receipt fields, so it becomes more feasible to train it with the big dataset containing several factor scales. In our CAN, the chaser has the same structure as the VDSR (*i.e.*, baseline), and the multi-residual fusion network is taken as the enhancer.

2.2 Perceptual Loss Network

Perceptual loss network can measure perceptual and semantic differences between images. Justin Johnson *et al.* [6,7] use a pre-trained classification network as the perceptual loss network to train a SR network, which can reconstruct more visually pleasing SR image. In fact, the key factor of making perceptual loss network work is that the pre-trained classification network can output similar feature representations of I^{SR} to these of I^{HR}. The similarity of convolutional feature maps between I^{SR} and I^{HR} can better explain the similarity of I^{SR} and I^{HR} in the local structure, feature distribution and main content.

However, the perceptual loss network trained on classification image set is unable to extract efficient and precise features of SR image set when images in SR database differ much from the images in classification database. In addition, the pre-trained loss network is useless in the reconstruction process. So we propose a multi-residual SR network, which is more efficient to extract and concatenate multi-scale features than VGG-based classification network [19], as the perceptual loss network to play an enhancer role in final reconstruction process.

2.3 Adversarial Network

Adversarial network is firstly proposed in GANs [12], and has been widely used in the field of image-to-image translation [13,14]. The adversarial process of two neural networks is that the generator G tries to generate fake images while the discriminator D tries to estimate the probability with which an image comes from the ground truth data rather than from G. The G and the D are alternately trained by optimizing an adversarial min-max problem. The information entropy of the probability is the key to alternatively update G and D, and it achieves a balance when the discriminator cannot tell the difference between the real and the generated images. In our CAN, we define an equilibrium value using the ratio of the pixel-wise loss of the chaser to the enhancer in order to min-maximize the feature loss that is computed from the chaser and the enhancer.

3   Cooperative Adversarial Network

Different from existing multi-network models [6,7,15], our CAN consists of two cooperative but adversarial networks (see as Fig. 1): chaser network and enhancer network. On cooperative side, the enhancer reconstructs an enhanced SR image (I_E^{SR}) from the SR image reconstructed by the chaser (I_C^{SR}) and provides feature maps to compute feature loss $\ell^{fea}(I_C^{SR}, I^{HR})$ between I_C^{SR} and the corresponding ground truth high-resolution image I^{HR} for training the chaser. On adversarial side, the chaser updates itself to minimize the perceptual loss $\ell^C(I_C^{SR}, I^{HR})$ between I_C^{SR} and I^{HR}, while the enhancer updates itself to minimize the pixel-wise loss $\ell(I_E^{SR}, I^{HR})$ between I_E^{SR} and I^{HR} but maximize the feature loss $\ell^{fea}(I_C^{SR}, I^{HR})$. We set strides to be 1 and pad zeros before convolutions in order to keep the sizes of all feature maps the same as input image. Network architecture is detailed in Subsect. 3.1. Loss functions are introduced in Subsect. 3.2. The alternately iterative training method is described in Subsect. 3.3.

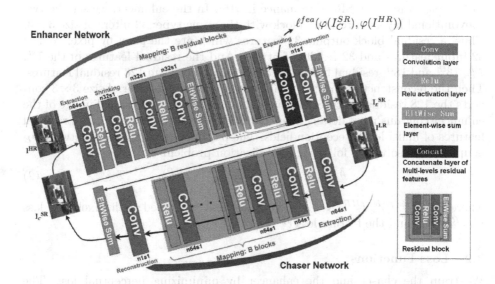

Fig. 1. Overview of cooperative adversarial network. The chaser estimates a SR image I_C^{SR} with an interpolated low-resolution image I^{LR}. The enhancer reconstructs an enhanced SR image I_E^{SR} from I_C^{SR}. In mapping parts, the chaser has B convolution layers with corresponding number filters (n) and stride (s), while the enhancer has B residual blocks with skip connection.

3.1   Network Architectures

Chaser Network has the same framework of skip connection as the VDSR [5], which consists of three kinds of convolutional layers: 1 extraction layer, 18 mapping layers, and 1 reconstruction layer. The extraction layer extracts 64 feature maps from the input image with 64 filters of size 3×3. Each mapping layer has the same filters: 64 filters of size 3×3. The reconstruction layer reconstructs a residual image with a single convolutional filter of size 3×3. Finally, the reconstructed image I_C^{SR} is obtained pixel by pixel by the sum of input image I^{LR} and the residual image. The chaser updates parameters θ_C to solve the following minimization problem:

$$\hat{\theta}_C = \arg \min_{\theta_C} \ell^C(I_C^{SR}, I^{HR}) \tag{1}$$

where $\ell^C(I_C^{SR}, I^{HR})$ is the perceptual loss weighted combined with pixel-wise loss $\ell(I_C^{SR}, I^{HR})$ and the feature loss $\ell^{fea}(I_C^{SR}, I^{HR})$, which are further discussed in Subsect. 3.2.

Enhancer Network is a multi-residual fusion network consisting of 1 extraction layer, 1 shrinking layer, 18 mapping layers, 1 expanding layer, and 1 reconstruction layer. The extraction layer and reconstruction layer are the same as those in the chaser. The shrinking layer reduces the dimension of feature maps from 64 to 32 with 32 filters of size 3×3. A mapping layer is made up of a residual block, and the residual block of two convolutional layers has been proved to be able to improve SR performance in [16]. In the enhancer, we set the two convolutional layers of residual block with the same type: 32 filters of size 3×3. Thus, a residual block outputs 32 features which are the pixel by pixel sum of 32 input features and 32 residual features. And the residual features of the 1st, 7th, 13th and 18th residual blocks are concatenated to form 128 residual features. Then the reconstruction layer with a single convolutional filter of size 3×3 converts the 128 residual features into a residual image. So the residual image of the enhancer contains more details than that of the chaser by merging more residual features of multi-levels reception fields. The parameters of enhancer network θ_E is updated to solve the following minimization problem:

$$\hat{\theta}_E = \arg \min_{\theta_E} \ell^E(I_E^{SR}, I_C^{SR}, I^{HR}) \tag{2}$$

where $\ell^E(I_E^{SR}, I_C^{SR}, I^{HR})$ is the perceptual loss combined with pixel-wise loss $\ell(I_E^{SR}, I^{HR})$ and the feature loss $\ell^{fea}(I_C^{SR}, I^{HR})$.

3.2   Loss Functions

We train the chaser and the enhancer by minimizing perceptual loss. The cooperative and adversarial relationship between the chaser and the enhancer is reflected in the min-maximum of the feature loss, which is similar to the segAN (Image Segmentation Adversarial Network) [17]. Different from the segAN [17], the two sub-networks in our CAN are trained with the different perceptual losses that are weighted combined feature loss and pixel-wise loss.

Feature Loss is the pixel-wise error on the feature representations between predicted image and ground truth. Because convolutional features of an image reflect the characteristics of local structure, feature distribution and main content, some existing methods [6,14,18] adopt convolutional feature representations of the pre-trained classification network VGG [19] to measure the feature similarity between I^{SR} and I^{HR}. In our CAN, the multi-residual representations concatenated from different layers in the enhancer are adopted to measure the feature similarity between I_C^{SR} and I^{HR}. We formulate the feature loss as:

$$\ell^{fea}(I_C^{SR}, I^{HR}) = \frac{1}{n} \sum_{i=1}^{n} \ell(\varphi_i(I_C^{SR}), \varphi_i(I^{HR})) \tag{3}$$

where $\varphi_i(x)$ indicates the ith feature representation output from the expanding layer (concatenate n residual feature maps) when the enhancer is fed with the image x. $\ell(x, y)$ represents the pixel-wise error of 1-norm between image x and y, which is formulated as following:

$$\ell(x, y) = \frac{1}{WH} \sum_{w=1}^{W} \sum_{h=1}^{H} \|x_{w,h} - y_{w,h}\|_1 \tag{4}$$

Perceptual Loss should reflect not only the perceptual similarity but also the global pixel similarity between I^{SR} and I^{HR}. Similar to the definition in [6], we define the perceptual loss of the chaser $\ell^C(I_C^{SR}, I^{HR})$, which combines the pixel-wise loss and the feature loss as the following formula:

$$\ell^C(I_C^{SR}, I^{HR}) = \rho \cdot (\omega \cdot \ell^{fea}(I_C^{SR}, I^{HR}) + (1 - \omega) \cdot \ell(I_C^{SR}, I^{HR})) \tag{5}$$

where coefficient $\omega(0 \leq \omega \leq 1)$ denotes the influence of $\ell^{fea}(I_C^{SR}, I^{HR})$. The experimental setting of ω is introduced in Subsect. 4.2. ρ is the balance weight to avoid the negative effects of the feature loss being much higher or lower than the pixel-wise loss. So we define ρ as following:

$$\rho = \sqrt{|\log_{10}(\frac{\ell^{fea}(I_C^{SR}, I^{HR})}{\ell(I_C^{SR}, I^{HR})})|} \tag{6}$$

In fact, the image I_C^{SR} is so more similar with I^{HR} on the characteristics of main content and objects distribution that general convolutional features can not sensibly represent the differences between them. So the enhancer provides the multi-residual convolutional features to compute $\ell^{fea}(I_C^{SR}, I^{HR})$, and updates parameters by maximizing the feature loss and minimizing the pixel-wise loss $\ell(I_E^{SR}, I^{HR})$. We give the perceptual loss of the enhancer $\ell^E(I_E^{SR}, I_C^{SR}, I^{HR})$ as the following formula:

$$\ell^E(I_E^{SR}, I_C^{SR}, I^{HR}) = \ell(I_E^{SR}, I^{HR}) + \frac{\ell(I_E^{SR}, I^{HR})}{\ell(I_E^{SR}, I^{HR}) + \ell^{fea}(I_C^{SR}, I^{HR})} \tag{7}$$

On the whole, the training process of our CAN is min-maximum process of feature loss:

$$\min_{\theta_C} \max_{\theta_E} \ell^{fea}(I_C^{SR}, I^{HR}) \tag{8}$$

When the feature loss finally converges to a balance, the chaser and the enhancer are merged into a unified SR network. An alternative training of two steps is proved to be stable and convergent in SegAN [17]. Considering the consistency of cooperation between chaser and enhancer on SR task, we propose an alternative training method of three training units to reconcile these two independent SR-task networks with each other.

3.3   Training Method

The challenge of merging two cooperative but adversarial networks into a unified network is how to train the chaser and the enhancer cooperatively so that feature loss can fast converge to an equilibrium value. We present an alternately iterative method to train the CAN.

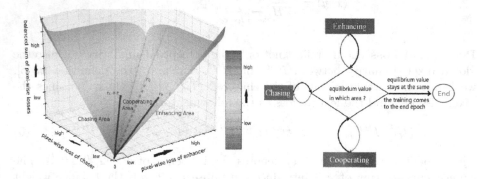

Fig. 2. Outline of alternately iterative training. equilibrium value r falls into three training areas $(0, r_0-\varepsilon]$, $(r_0-\varepsilon, r_0+\varepsilon)$ and $[r_0+\varepsilon, +\infty)$ according to the empirical value r_0 and the tolerance value ε. The corresponding training unit is adopted to run for e epochs when r falls in any one training area. The alternately iterative training does not stop until r stays at the same or the training comes to the end epoch. Referring to the Eq. (5) for calculation of the balanced sum.

Alternately Iterative Training is an iterative procedure of alternately choosing one from three training units: chasing (only the chaser updates parameters), enhancing (only the enhancer updates weights of layers) and cooperating (both the chaser and the enhancer update their parameters). To separate training procedure into three units, We define an equilibrium value R according to the pixel-wise loss of chaser and that of enhancer, which is formulated as follows:

$$R = \frac{\ell(I_C^{SR}, I^{HR})}{\ell(I_E^{SR}, I^{HR})} \tag{9}$$

The equilibrium value R can reflect a gap between I_C^{SR} and I_E^{SR}, and the chaser tries to narrow the gap while the enhancer tries to widen it. What's more, the final equilibrium value R is empirically more than 1.0, which is easily evaluated. Thus, we suppose an empirical equilibrium value r_0, and equilibrium value r finally converges to the neighborhood $(r_0 - \varepsilon, r_0 + \varepsilon)$. So the equilibrium value r of every forward propagation step must be at 3 specific areas: $(0, r_0 - \varepsilon]$, $(r_0 - \varepsilon, r_0 + \varepsilon)$ and $[r_0 + \varepsilon, +\infty)$. As illustrated in Fig. 2, different areas correspond to different training units. When the equilibrium value r belongs to an area, a corresponding training unit is selected to run for e epochs. The empirical value r_0 and ε can be dynamically adjusted. For example, we increase r_0 a little when the chasing unit is continuously selected for more than three times, while decrease ε a little when the cooperating unit is continuously performed for more than three times.

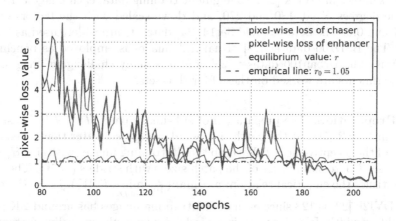

Fig. 3. Convergence curves of alternately iterative training. CAN is trained with SGD algorithm [20]. The green line of equilibrium value r reveals the alternate and iterative training process. (<80 epochs: pre-training; >80 epochs: alternately iterative training)

Who Trains First is a key point to start the alternately iterative training procedure. In fact, the chaser can not update parameters until the enhancer provides an accurate feature loss. Besides, it is the precondition to fine-tune parameters of the enhancer that the chaser achieves convergence. So the enhancer updates itself first with training image pairs (I^{LR}, I^{HR}). Then the chaser adjusts parameters to minimize perceptual loss, which means that the chasing unit starts running. And the alternately iterative training procedure starts. Finally, two cooperative but adversarial networks are trained as a unified network when the equilibrium value falls in the cooperating area. Figure 3 shows an example of the convergence curves of alternately iterative training, which indicates that adopting three training units not only makes full use of adversarial relationship of the chaser and the enhancer, but also efficiently reconciles these two independent SR-task networks with each other. It is clear that only adopting two training units ($\varepsilon = 0$: chasing unit and enhancing unit) is hard to merge these two independent networks into a unified network, and only adopting the cooperating unit ($\varepsilon = 1$) can not ensure the efficiency of fine-tuning the chaser with a relatively stable feature loss.

4   Experiments and Discussions

4.1   Implementation Details

Training and Testing Datasets. Different training sets are used in various learning-based SR methods. For example, ImageNet dataset [21] is adopted by SRCNN [1] and SRGAN [7], 91-image dataset [36] and General-100 dataset are employed in FSRCNN [3], and DVI2K dataset [22] has high diversity in semantic contents and high resolution. In this paper, we train our network with 800 training samples in DVI2k [22]. To augment training data, each image is rotated with the degrees of 90, 180 and 270, and down-scaled with the factors of 0.9, 0.8, 0.7 and 0.6. The Set5 [23] and Set14 [24] datasets are widely used as benchmarks. The BSD100 dataset [25] of natural images is employed as benchmark for VDSR. The Urban100 dataset [26] contains many challenging images. Our test experiments are worked on these four datasets.

Data Preparation. The preparation of sub-image pairs (I^{LR}, I^{HR}) is similar to that in VDSR [5], but the patch size of sub-image is greater than or equal to the size of the receptive field f. We crop the ith training image (with size $H_i \times W_i$) of a dataset D into sub-images of the patch size p with stride s ($= \frac{4p}{5}$). The patch size p satisfies the empirical relation: $p = \max(\frac{1}{10} \cdot \min_{\forall i \in D}(H_i, W_i), f)$. So the patch size of DVI2k [22] is 128 since each of 800 training images has around 2 K pixels on height or width. In order to train a model for multiple up-scaling factors and boost reconstruction performance for large scales, we prepare training dataset with the scale augmentation [5]. Thereby, a batch of 32 sub-images are obtained for the training image with multiple different scale factors ($\times 2$, $\times 3$, $\times 4$).

Training Details. To provide accurate feature loss for the chaser, we firstly train the enhancer for 80 epochs only with the pixel-wise loss (Enhancer(pix)). The learning rate is initially set to be 0.1 and then reduced by half every 10 epochs. We compare the Enhancer(pix) network with other methods in Subsect. 4.2.

Then, the chaser updates parameters to minimize the perceptual loss with the patches of DVI2k dataset. That is, the chasing unit of the alternately iterative training starts. We set the empirical equilibrium value r_0 to be 1.05 and the tolerance value ε to be 0.02. The alternately iterative training is performed for 120 epochs on DVI2k dataset. Every activated training unit continuously runs for 4 epochs. The initial learning rates of the chaser and the enhancer are set to be 0.01 and decreased by half every 12 epochs. All the weights of convolution layers are initialized with the same method in [27], and the momentum is set to be 0.9. Our models are performed with the Python API of Caffe [28].

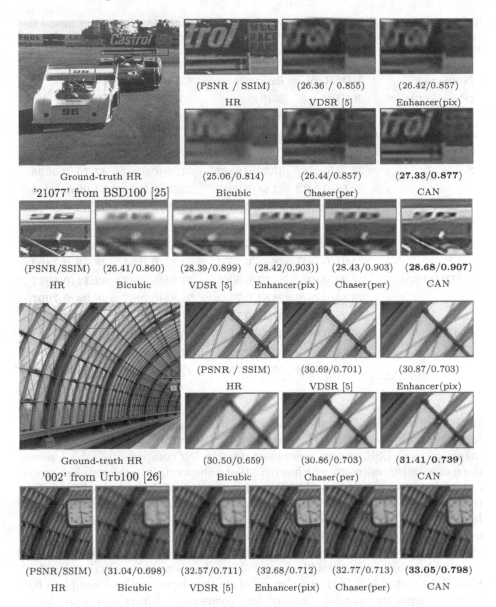

Fig. 4. Visual comparison of SR results among our models. The SR images in blue (or red) box are reconstructed with an scale factor 3 (or 4). The hightest PSNR/SSIM are in **bold**. (Color figure online)

4.2 Model Analysis

Multi-residual Fusion Network, designed as our enhancer, concatenates multiple residual features from different residual blocks to reconstruct a

Table 1. The quantitative contrasts for model analysis. ♯Parameter means the parameter of convolution layers, which is in charge of dominant computational cost. Bold text indicates the best and blue text indicates the second best performance.

Networks		VDSR [5]	Enhancer(pix)	Chaser(per)	CAN
♯Parameter		664704	351936	664704	1016640
Loss function		pixel-wise loss	pixel-wise loss	perceptual loss	perceptual loss
Residuals fusion		–	√	–	√
Results (up-scales)		PSNR/SSIM	PSNR/SSIM	PSNR/SSIM	PSNR/SSIM
Set5 [23]	×2	37.53/0.9587	37.54/0.9587	37.59/0.9590	**37.76/0.9598**
	×3	33.66/0.9213	33.68/0.9217	33.75/0.9231	**34.09/0.9288**
	×4	31.35/0.8838	31.38/0.8845	31.49/0.8862	**32.02/0.8914**
Set14 [24]	×2	33.03/0.9124	33.04/0.9126	33.12/0.9128	**33.44/0.9137**
	×3	29.77/0.8314	29.76/0.8314	29.78/0.8317	**29.97/0.8369**
	×4	28.01/0.7647	28.03/0.7651	28.12/0.7664	**28.49/0.7803**
BSD100 [25]	×2	31.90/0.8960	31.97/0.8966	31.91/0.8962	**32.14/0.8977**
	×3	28.82/0.7976	28.84/0.7983	28.83/0.7983	**28.94/0.7997**
	×4	27.29/0.7251	27.32/0.7267	27.36/0.7272	**27.54/0.7342**
Urb100 [26]	×2	30.76/0.9140	30.78/0.9145	30.82/0.9147	**30.98/0.9193**
	×3	27.14/0.8279	27.20/0.8285	27.34/0.8291	**27.73/0.8366**
	×4	25.18/0.7524	25.27/0.7531	25.36/0.7547	**26.09/0.7847**

super-resolved image. Visual comparison in Fig. 4 shows that our multi-residual fusion network, viz. Enhancer(pix) reconstructs SR images with the same performance as the VDSR or even more clear-cut. For fair comparison, Table 1 shows the quantitative contrasts, which reveals that enhancer(pix) achieves close scores of peak signal-to-noise ratios (PSNR) and structural similarity index [29] (SSIM) to the VDSR. However, the enhancer(pix) has less parameters than the VDSR. In our opinion, this effect is caused by the advantages of the multi-residual fusion over residual blocks. Firstly, the enhancer can provide efficient representations of multiple receipt fields, so that reconstruction image reserves both fine details preserved in shallow residual blocks and sharp shapes contained in deep residual blocks. As stated in [30], feature maps of shallow layers contain complete fine details of input image, while those of deep layers retain blurry and coarse information of main shapes. The residual feature maps of different layers shown in Fig. 5 support this conclusion. Secondly, it is more feasible to train our enhancer with big SR image set containing several factor scales. Further, the enhancer is deeper and thinner than the VDSR with obvious decrease of parameters. A high resolution pixel of reconstruction image is estimated better by multi-scale larger patches of the input image. For example, the enhancer utilizes 4 patches with the size of $((2k - 1) \cdot (i + 1) - 1)^2$ (filter size $k = 3$, the index of residual block $i = 1, 7, 13, 18$) to estimate a pixel.

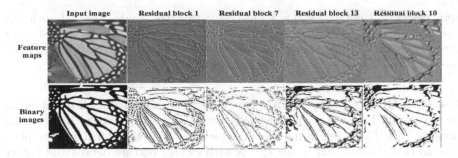

Fig. 5. The concatenated feature maps from the multiple layers in the enhancer and their binary images, which shows that residual features of the deeper convolutional layers reserve more blurry and coarse information of main shapes.

Trained with the Perceptual Loss. To define a perceptual loss with empirical influence value ω in Eq. (5). Figure 6 shows the performance curves using different ω, from which we can see that models trained with the perceptual loss ($\omega = 0.5$) attain the highest SSIM scores and PSNR scores. Thus, the combined perceptual loss helps a lot to improve SR image quality. And both the SSIM and PSNR score are increased a little when models trained with only the pixel-wise loss ($\omega = 0$), which reflects that the enhancer improves image quality of I_C^{SR} a little. The models trained with only the feature loss ($\omega = 1$) attain the lowest scores of PSNR and SSIM, but gain more SSIM score than PSNR, because the feature loss measures image similarity of local structure rather than that of global pixel. Thereby, we set ω to be 0.5 for a trade-off between lower global pixel error and

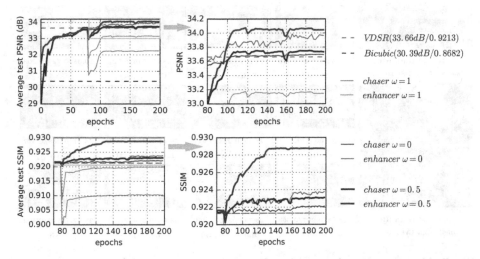

Fig. 6. Test curves of different perceptual losses. (tested on Set5 [23] with up-sample 3, <80 epochs: pre-training; >80 epochs: alternately iterative training). For clarity, the average SSIMs after the 75th epoch are shown. $\rho = 1$ when $\omega = 0, 1$.

more perceptual details. Figure 4 illustrates that the chaser trained with the perceptual loss (chaser(per)) reconstructs more distinct textures and sharper edges than VDSR. Table 1 shows the chaser(per) obtains higher SSIM and PSNR sores than the VDSR on all the test datasets.

One Plus One Is More Than Two. The chaser updates itself to minimize the perceptual loss and reconstructs SR image I_C^{SR} with more pleasing visual contents, then I_C^{SR} is fed to the enhancer for decreasing the global average pixel error so that the final SR image I_E^{SR} is with clearer texture details and higher global pixel-wise similarity. The results illustrated in Figs. 4 and 7 show that

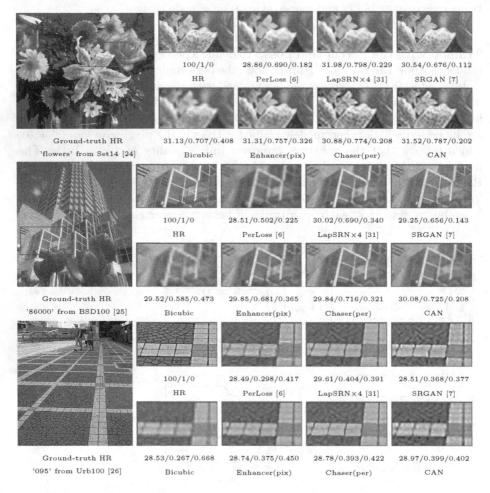

Fig. 7. Visual comparison of 4× SR results among multi-network models. The best PSNR/SSIM/LPIPS are in red, and the second best are in blue. (Color figure online)

the CAN estimates superior SR image with more distinct edge details than the Enhancer(pix). As shown by the quantitative contrast in Table 1, the CAN attains higher scores of PSNR and SSIM than the chaser(per). In the Fig. 6, compared to the chaser and enhancer trained with only the pixel-wise loss ($\omega =$ 0), the models trained with the perceptual loss ($\omega = 0.5$) attain higher SSIM scores with a little increase of PSNR scores. So our CAN of min-maximizing the feature loss attains better reconstruction results than the model of cascading chaser and enhancer only with the pixel-wise loss.

4.3 Comparisons and Discussions

The proposed Chaser(per) and CAN are compared with state-of-the-arts multi-network models (the PerLoss [6], the SRGAN [7], and the LapSRN [31]). To be fair, all LR images are down-sampled using the same bicubic kernel, and all measures are calculated on the y-channel of center-cropped with removal of a 4-pixel wide strip from each border. In order to provide quantitative contrast of perceptual similarity, the Learned Perceptual Image Patch Similarity [32] (LPIPS) metric is adopted, which is more correlated with human perception.

Compared with Multi-network Models, our chaser(per) and CAN attain competitive performance with less parameters. Figure 7 shows that chaser(per) obtains more sharp textures than the LapSRN [31]. While the LapSRN shows competitive performance with less parameters in Table 2 because of sharing different level residual feature maps. However, the scale factor of LapSRN is limited by cascading multiple networks. Compared to the PerLoss [6], chaser(per) reconstructs SR images of higher structure similarity and the global pixel similarity because our perceptual loss is combined with pixel-wise loss and feature loss. Table 2 summarizes model specifications and SR results, which indicates that our CAN yields higher scores of PSNR and SSIM with **72%** less parameters than SRGAN [7]. What's more, the LPIPS metric of our CAN is smaller than that of the pixel-wise loss networks (SRResNet [7]).

Artificial Contrast Pixels. Although our CAN gains larger LPIPS metric than SRGAN, it retains clearer edge lines and more smooth texture details than SRGAN (see the SR image '86000' in Fig. 7). In addition, SRGAN reconstructs SR images of visually pleasing details with artificial high-contrast pixels, while the CAN reconstructs visually pleasing SR images with smooth contrast pixels (see the red dots on petals of the 'flowers' in Fig. 7). We speculate that the artificial contrast pixels are caused by the feature loss. Different from SRGAN, the perceptual loss network in our CAN is also a SR network (*i.e.,* enhancer), which minimizes the pixel-wise loss to decrease global pixel error so that the contrast pixels are smooth. Thus, our CAN reconstructs SR images of high global pixel similarity and structure similarity. To some extent, although the CAN is a multi-scale model like the VDSR, the bicubic interpolation limits its performance and computation. To speed up the CAN, the chaser can be replaced by transposed convolution based network, like the SRResNet [7], in future work.

Table 2. The quantitative contrasts of $4\times$ **SR results among multi-network models.** ♯Lay means the number of convolutional layers in SR sub-network. ♯Par means the million parameters of convolution layers and transposed convolution layers. *Fea-loss* means the network which used for computing feature loss. The best PSNR/SSIM/LPIPS are in red, and the second best are in blue.

Methods	♯Lay	♯Par	Fea-loss	Set5 [23]	Set14 [24]	BSD100 [25]	Urb100 [26]
Bicubic	–	–	–	28.42/0.8104/0.341	26.00/0.7019/0.440	25.96/0.6675/0.526	23.14/0.6577/0.462
PerLoss [6]	12	0.25	VGG16	27.09/0.7680/0.154	24.99/0.6731/0.261	24.95/0.6317/0.280	23.02/0.6247/0.251
LapSRN [31]	11+11	0.60	–	31.54/0.8853/0.181	28.19/0.7721/0.297	27.32/0.7281/0.398	25.21/0.7562/0.268
SRResNet [7]	39	3.73	–	32.05/0.8910/0.177	28.53/0.7804/0.285	27.57/0.7354/0.374	26.07/0.7839/0.266
SRGAN [7]	39	3.73	VGG54	29.40/0.8472/0.090	26.02/0.7397/0.162	25.16/0.6688/0.200	24.32/0.6643/0.175
Chaser(per)	20	0.66	Enhancer	31.49/0.8862/0.202	28.12/0.7664/0.279	27.36/0.7272/0.396	25.36/0.7547/0.268
CAN	20+39	1.02	Enhancer	32.02/0.8914/0.141	28.49/0.7803/0.234	27.54/0.7342/0.346	26.09/0.7847/0.222

5   Conclusions

In this work, we propose a cooperative adversarial network (CAN), which reconstructs SR image not only with perceptual details but also with high global pixel similarity. Our CAN consists of two cooperative but adversarial sub-networks: a chaser and an enhancer. The chaser network reconstructs SR image from LR image, while the enhancer network further enhances the SR image quality. We design a multi-residual network as the enhancer to compute the feature loss and the perceptual loss which measures both perceptual error and global pixel error. Correspondingly, we also define an equilibrium value to control the alternately iterative training of the chaser and the enhancer so that the two sub-networks are merged into a unified network. Compared to existing methods, our CAN obtains competitive global pixel similarity and visual improvements. Further, our CAN can be a multi-task solution to other computer vision problems such as simultaneous SR+denoising and SR+semantic segmentation.

References

1. Dong, C., Loy, C.C., He, K., Tang, X.: Image super-resolution using deep convolutional networks. IEEE Trans. Pattern Anal. Mach. Intell. **38**, 295–307 (2016)
2. Zeiler, M.D., et al.: Deconvolutional networks. In: 2010 IEEE Computer Society Conference on Computer Vision and Pattern Recognition, pp. 2528–2535 (2010)
3. Dong, C., Loy, C.C., Tang, X.: Accelerating the super-resolution convolutional neural network. In: Leibe, B., Matas, J., Sebe, N., Welling, M. (eds.) ECCV 2016. LNCS, vol. 9906, pp. 391–407. Springer, Cham (2016). https://doi.org/10.1007/978-3-319-46475-6_25
4. Shi, W., et al.: Real-time single image and video super-resolution using an efficient sub-pixel convolutional neural network. In: 2016 IEEE Conference on Computer Vision and Pattern Recognition (CVPR), pp. 1874–1883 (2016)

5. Kim, J., Lee, J.K., Lee, K.M.: Accurate image super-resolution using very deep convolutional networks. In: 2016 IEEE Conference on Computer Vision and Pattern Recognition (CVPR), pp. 1646–1654 (2016)
6. Johnson, J., Alahi, A., Fei-Fei, L.: Perceptual losses for real-time style transfer and super-resolution. In: Leibe, B., Matas, J., Sebe, N., Welling, M. (eds.) ECCV 2016. LNCS, vol. 9906, pp. 694–711. Springer, Cham (2016). https://doi.org/10.1007/978-3-319-46475-6_43
7. Ledig, C., et al.: Photo-realistic single image super-resolution using a generative adversarial network. In: 2017 IEEE Conference on Computer Vision and Pattern Recognition (CVPR), pp. 105–114 (2017)
8. Sajjadi, M.S.M., Schölkopf, B., Hirsch, M.: Enhancenet: single image super-resolution through automated texture synthesis. In: 2017 IEEE International Conference on Computer Vision (ICCV), pp. 4501–4510 (2017)
9. He, K., Zhang, X., Ren, S., Sun, J.: Deep residual learning for image recognition. In: 2016 IEEE Conference on Computer Vision and Pattern Recognition (CVPR), pp. 770–778 (2016)
10. Bengio, Y., Simard, P.Y., Frasconi, P.: Learning long-term dependencies with gradient descent is difficult. IEEE Trans. Neural Networks 5(2), 157–66 (1994)
11. Zhang, Y., Tian, Y., Kong, Y., Zhong, B., Fu, Y.: Residual dense network for image super-resolution. CoRR abs/1802.08797 (2018)
12. Goodfellow, I.J., et al.: Generative adversarial nets. In: NIPS (2014)
13. Liu, Y., Qin, Z., Luo, Z., Wang, H.: Auto-painter: cartoon image generation from sketch by using conditional generative adversarial networks. CoRR abs/1705.01908 (2017)
14. Zhu, J.Y., Park, T., Isola, P., Efros, A.A.: Unpaired image-to-image translation using cycle-consistent adversarial networks. In: 2017 IEEE International Conference on Computer Vision (ICCV), pp. 2242–2251 (2017)
15. Wang, Y., Wang, L., Wang, H., Li, P.: RAN: resolution-aware network for image super-resolution. IEEE Trans. Circuits Syst. Video Technol. **PP**, 1 (2018)
16. Lim, B., et al.: Enhanced deep residual networks for single image super-resolution. In: 2017 IEEE Conference on Computer Vision and Pattern Recognition Workshops (CVPRW), pp. 1132–1140 (2017)
17. Xue, Y., et al.: SegAN: adversarial network with multi-scale l_1 loss for medical image segmentation. Neuroinformatics **16**, 383–392 (2018)
18. Mahendran, A., Vedaldi, A.: Understanding deep image representations by inverting them. In: 2015 IEEE Conference on Computer Vision and Pattern Recognition (CVPR), pp. 5188–5196 (2015)
19. Simonyan, K., Zisserman, A.: Very deep convolutional networks for large-scale image recognition. CoRR abs/1409.1556 (2014)
20. LeCun, Y.: Gradient-based learning applied to document recognition. Proc. IEEE **86**, 2278–2324 (1998)
21. Russakovsky, O., et al.: Imagenet large scale visual recognition challenge. Int. J. Comput. Vis. **115**, 211–252 (2015)
22. Timofte, R., et al.: Ntire 2017 challenge on single image super-resolution: methods and results. In: 2017 IEEE Conference on Computer Vision and Pattern Recognition Workshops (CVPRW), pp. 1110–1121 (2017)
23. Bevilacqua, M., Roumy, A., Guillemot, C., Alberi-Morel, M.L.: Low-complexity single-image super-resolution based on nonnegative neighbor embedding. In: BMVC (2012)
24. Zeyde, R., Elad, M., Protter, M.: On single image scale-up using sparse-representations. In: Curves and Surfaces (2010)

25. Timofte, R., De Smet, V., Van Gool, L.: A+: adjusted anchored neighborhood regression for fast super-resolution. In: Cremers, D., Reid, I., Saito, H., Yang, M.-H. (eds.) ACCV 2014. LNCS, vol. 9006, pp. 111–126. Springer, Cham (2015). https://doi.org/10.1007/978-3-319-16817-3_8

26. Huang, J.B., Singh, A., Ahuja, N.: Single image super-resolution from transformed self-exemplars. In: 2015 IEEE Conference on Computer Vision and Pattern Recognition (CVPR), pp. 5197–5206 (2015)

27. He, K., Zhang, X., Ren, S., Sun, J.: Delving deep into rectifiers: surpassing human-level performance on imagenet classification. In: 2015 IEEE International Conference on Computer Vision (ICCV), pp. 1026–1034 (2015)

28. Jia, Y., Shelhamer, E., et al.: Caffe: convolutional architecture for fast feature embedding. In: ACM Multimedia (2014)

29. Wang, Z., Bovik, A.C., Sheikh, H.R., Simoncelli, E.P.: Image quality assessment: from error visibility to structural similarity. IEEE Trans. Image Process. 13, 600–612 (2004)

30. Dosovitskiy, A., Brox, T.: Inverting visual representations with convolutional networks. In: 2016 IEEE Conference on Computer Vision and Pattern Recognition (CVPR), pp. 4829–4837 (2016)

31. Lai, W.S., Huang, J.B., Ahuja, N., Yang, M.H.: Deep Laplacian pyramid networks for fast and accurate super-resolution. In: 2017 IEEE Conference on Computer Vision and Pattern Recognition (CVPR), pp. 5835–5843 (2017)

32. Zhang, R., Isola, P., Efros, A.A., Shechtman, E., Wang, O.: The unreasonable effectiveness of deep features as a perceptual metric. CVPR (2018)

33. Irani, M., Peleg, S.: Improving resolution by image registration. CVGIP: Graph. Model Image Process. 53, 231–239 (1991)

34. Sun, J., Xu, Z., Shum, H.: Image super-resolution using gradient profile prior. In: 2008 IEEE Conference on Computer Vision and Pattern Recognition, pp. 1–8 (2008)

35. Xiong, Z., Sun, X., Wu, F.: Robust web image/video super-resolution. IEEE Trans. Image Process. 19, 2017–2028 (2010)

36. Yang, J., Wright, J., Huang, T.S., Ma, Y.: Image super-resolution via sparse representation. IEEE Trans. Image Process. 19, 2861–2873 (2010)

37. Freedman, G., Fattal, R.: Image and video up scaling from local self-examples. ACM Trans. Graph. 30, 12:1–12:11 (2011)

38. Yang, J., Lin, Z.L., Cohen, S.: Fast image super-resolution based on in-place example regression. In: 2013 IEEE Conference on Computer Vision and Pattern Recognition, pp. 1059–1066 (2013)

39. Wang, Y., Wang, L., Wang, H., Li, P.: Information-compensated downsampling for image super-resolution. IEEE Signal Process. Lett. 25, 685–689 (2018)

Cross-Spectral Image Patch Matching by Learning Features of the Spatially Connected Patches in a Shared Space

Dou Quan[iD], Shuai Fang[iD], Xuefeng Liang[iD], Shuang Wang[(✉)][iD], and Licheng Jiao[iD]

Intelligent Perception and Image Understanding of Ministry of Education, School of Artificial Intelligence, Xidian University, Xian 710071, Shaanxi, China
shwang@mail.xidian.edu.cn

Abstract. Cross-spectral image patch matching is a challenging problem due to the significant difference between two images caused by different imaging mechanisms. We consider cross-spectral image patches can be matched because there exists a shared semantic feature space among them, in which the semantic features from different spectral images will be more independent of the spectral domains. To learn this shared feature space, we propose a progressive comparison of spatially connected feature metric learning with a feature discrimination constrain (SCFDM). The progressive comparison of spatially connected feature network keeps the property of each spectral domain in its corresponding low-level feature space, and interacts the cross-spectral features in a high-level feature space. The feature discrimination constrain enforces the framework to refine the shared semantic space for feature extraction. Extensive experiments shows that SCFDM outperforms the state-of-the-art methods on the cross-spectral dataset in terms of FPR95 and the training convergence. Meanwhile, it also demonstrates a better generalizability on a single spectral dataset.

1 Introduction

Due to the complexity and diversity of imaging conditions, capturing an image with rich and sharp information through a single sensor is not ensured. Fortunately, different spectral images could alleviate this limitation because they provide complementary information [12,21]. For example, the visible spectrum images (VIS) have rich color and texture, but the quality depends on the illumination condition. Instead, the near-infrared images (NIR) keep the high texture quality even in a low-light environment, but lack the color information [10]. It is analogous for the depth images, MRI images, ultrasound images, just to name a few. To effectively take the complementary advantages from them, we

Electronic supplementary material The online version of this chapter (https://doi.org/10.1007/978-3-030-20890-5_8) contains supplementary material, which is available to authorized users.

(a)   (b)   (c)

Fig. 1. The non-linear appearance differences between visible spectrum (VIS) and near-infrared (NIR) images. First row is the VIS images; second row is the corresponding NIR images

must register these images or calibrate the corresponding sensors first. Therefore, the cross-spectral image patch matching becomes crucial but very challenging because of the non-linear appearance differences between the corresponding points in different spectral images, as shown in Fig. 1.

The traditional matching methods are based on the handcraft local feature descriptors [4, 8, 18, 22], and perform well on the single spectral images [5, 19, 27]. In recent years, the deep learning-based methods have shown a considerable advantage in local feature learning [1–3, 9, 11, 13, 15, 23–26, 28]. Hence, to tackle the image patch matching problem, the direct idea uses deep learning methods to learn the patch feature descriptor. Many studies have reported that such descriptors learning methods had a better generalizability than the handcraft descriptors [2, 3, 25]. However, their performances heavily relies on certain engineering works, e.g. the feature distance selection, loss function design, and the strategy of training sample mining. Another solution, namely metric learning, transforms the patch matching task into a binary classification task by adding a classifier network after feature extraction [1, 11, 23]. Thus, the whole framework is optimized by the cross-entropy loss. This idea wisely avoids the engineering works in descriptor learning and implemented by two ways. One metric learning borrows the two-branch architecture from descriptor learning to extract features (see Fig. 2(a)), and then the classifier network compares their similarity at a feature space [11]. Another proposes a 2-channel network that compares the image patches from pixel-level [23], as shown in Fig. 2(b), in which the learning process is more compact. Experiments demonstrated that 2-channel network achieved a faster training convergence and a better performance. However, it was initially designed for the single spectral image patch matching instead of cross-spectral images.

The challenge of this work is the significant difference between cross-spectral images at pixel-level due to the varied imaging mechanisms. Therefore, the low level features of one type of spectral images have their private space, which is distinct from other types. We consider cross-spectral image patches can be matched because there exists a shared semantic feature space among them, in which the low-level characteristic in each private space is removed and only semantic feature is kept for comparison. Therefore, we aim at enforcing the network to extract patch features from the shared space. This idea can improve the generalizability of a framework, like descriptor learning. Meanwhile, we also want to borrow the advantage of the metric learning. To this end, we propose a progressive comparison of spatially connected feature metric learning with a feature discrimination constrain (SCFDM), as shown in Fig. 3. Specifically, cross-spectral patches are spatially connected, rather than in the channel, as the input of a single branch metric learning network. As the receptive field is small in the first few convolution layers, the extracted features are relatively independent and keep their own properties of corresponding private spaces. When going deeper into the network, the receptive field becomes bigger, the features of cross-spectral patches are progressively compared more at semantic level. In order to learn the shared semantic space, the feature network is constrained by a contrastive loss, which penalizes the non-matched patch-pairs with a small distance and the matched patch-pairs with a larger distance. The cross-entropy loss function of metric learning network optimizes the whole framework, which makes the predicted matching labels more consistent with the ground truth.

Therefore, the main contribution of this work is threefold:

- We propose a progressive comparison of spatially connected feature metric learning for cross-spectral image patch matching problem, which considers not only the difference at pixel-level but also the similarity at semantic level.
- We propose a feature discrimination constrain using a contrastive loss function, which enforces the feature network to learn the shared semantic feature space of cross-spectral images.
- Experiments on the public cross-spectral VIS-NIR dataset and the single-spectral multi-view stereo dataset demonstrate that our proposal outperforms six state-of-the-art deep learning-based methods on accuracy, meanwhile, speeds up the training convergence and improves the generalizability.

2   Related Work

The traditional image patch matching methods are based on the handcraft local feature descriptors, such as, SIFT [18], SURF [4], shape context [5], ORB [22], DAISY [27], binary feature descriptors BRIEF [8], and frequency features [19]. Although, the handcraft feature descriptors had achieved great success in many specific domains, they commonly have less generalizability. Recently, deep learning methods have shown significant advantages in feature learning, as well as in image patch matching. They are more effective than traditional methods, and have a wider range of applications [24]. Basically, the existing deep image patch matching methods can be divided into two categories: *descriptor learning* and *metric learning*.

2.1   Descriptor Learning

The descriptor learning uses the convolutional networks to extract the discriminative features, and then measure their similarity to determine if they are matched.

Simoserra et al. [25] applied the Siamese network to extract features whose architecture is shown in Fig. 2(a), and optimized the network by the hinge embedding
loss function that requires the distance of matched patch-pairs as close to zero and
the distance of non-matched patch-pairs to be greater than a threshold. Balntas et
al. [3] proposed a positive-negative network (PN-Net) to learn feature descriptors
from the triplets of patch-pairs, in which there are one matched patch-pair and
two non-matched patch-pairs. With the optimization using softPN loss, PN-Net
can achieve a better matching performance and a faster convergence. Later, Aguilera et al. [2] brought the idea of PN-Net into cross-spectral image patch matching,
and proposed a Quadruplet network (Q-Net) that extracted features through the
same four convolution networks. Tian et al. [26] proposed a deep convolution network to learn a high performance descriptor in Euclidean space, namely L2-Net.
It emphasizes on the distance between matched pair is relatively smaller than that
of non-matched pair, rather than an absolute value. This strategy alleviates the
overfitting problem by constraining the feature vectors and feature maps, and further improves the matching performance.

Descriptor learning usually has a better generalizability than the handcraft
feature descriptors. However, its performance relies on the descriptors distance
selection, the loss function design and the strategy of training sample mining.

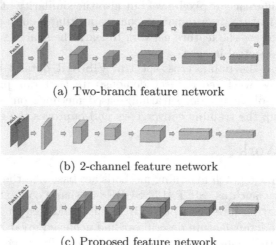

(a) Two-branch feature network

(b) 2-channel feature network

(c) Proposed feature network

Fig. 2. The different architectures of feature network to extract features. (a) Two-
branch feature network (siamese network and pseudo-siamese), which connects the
patches in the last feature layer. (b) 2-channel feature network, which compares the
patch-pair from pixel-level. (c) Our proposed feature network, which progressively compares the spatially connected patch-pair

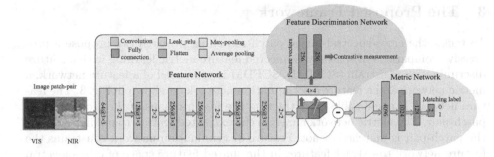

Fig. 3. The proposed framework of progressive comparison of spatially connected feature metric learning with a feature discrimination constrain (SCFDM). It has three components: *feature network*, *metric network*, and *feature discrimination network*. The feature network is for extracting the feature of image patch-pairs, the metric network is for measuring the feature similarity, and the feature discrimination constrains the feature network to learn the shared semantic feature space of cross-spectral images. The entire framework is jointly optimized by the contrastive loss and the cross-entropy loss

2.2   Metric Learning

To avoid the limitation of descriptor learning, metric learning transforms the image patch matching into a binary classification task that predicts whether the input patch-pair is matched or not. Inspired by siamese network, the method [11] extracts features of two patches through a two-branch convolutional network that shares the weights. The extracted feature vectors are then connected together as the input of a fully connected layer network to predict the matching label. Thanks to the shared weights, the number of parameters to be optimized are greatly reduced. Zagoruyko and Komodakis [23] discussed varied network architectures for image patch matching problem including siamese network, pseudo-siamese, central-surround two stream, and 2-channel network. Pseudo-siamese network is similar to siamese network, but does not share the weights of two convolutional branches. Hence, it is more flexible to learn the mapping function from the image patches to their matching labels, but has a higher possibility of falling into the overfitting. Central-surround two-stream network pays attention not only on the whole patch but also on its center for feature extraction. The 2-channel network puts two image patches together in channel as a tensor, see Fig. 2(b), and input the tensor into a single-branch convolutional network to compare the patch-pair at pixel-level. This design makes the learning process more compact and then speeds up the convergence of training. Aguilera et al. [1] have shown that the 2-channel network achieved a better performance. However, the cross-spectral images are considerably different at pixel-level, it would be better to compare them at semantic level rather than pixel-level.

3   The Proposed Framework

To tackle the cross-spectral image patch matching problem, we propose a progressive comparison of spatially connected feature metric learning with a feature discrimination constrain (SCFDM). SCFDM is composed of a feature network, a metric network and a feature discrimination network, as shown in Fig. 3. The feature network is responsible for extracting the feature maps of the cross-spectral patch-pair. The metric network analyzes the extracted feature to predict whether the patch-pair is matched or not. Feature discrimination network constrains the feature network to extract features in the shared feature space of cross-spectral images. The details are given in below.

3.1   Feature Network

Since cross-spectral images are formed by different imaging mechanisms, the pixel information and low-level features of different spectral images are distinct and in their corresponding private spaces. Therefore, cross-spectral image patches should not be compared directly at pixel-level. We consider there exists a shared semantic feature space where the high-level features of cross-spectral images could be more robustly compared. To learn this shared space, we design a single branch convolutional network based on VGG net [24], which has less parameters to be optimized than multi-branch networks. In order to effectively utilize this architecture, we spatially connect two patches as the input, as shown in Fig. 2(c). This setting brings an advantage of progressive comparison on spatially connected cross-spectral features. Specifically, the extracted low-level features of connected patch-pair are mostly independent with respected to the spectral domain because of the small size of the convolution kernel in the first few layers, i.e. smaller receptive field. After several convolution and pooling operations, the deeper layers have larger receptive field and progressively interact the features of cross-spectral patches at semantic level. Thus, the feature network learns the semantic feature map and keeps certain characteristics of each patch at the corresponding side. We then treat the left half of the feature map as the feature of the left patch, and same for the right half.

3.2   Metric Network

Our feature network plays a similar role as descriptor learning. To reach an advanced performance, descriptor learning heavily relies on the hard training sample mining [25]. It results in a lower training efficiency compared to metric learning. As a consequence, we would like to use metric learning to improve the efficiency by predicting if two patches are matched or not. The metric network consists of three fully connected layers and a softmax layer. To avoid overfitting, the first two fully connected layers are followed by a dropout operation with a deactivation rate of 0.25.

Consistent with most metric learning methods, we use the cross-entropy loss function to optimize the framework as well

$$E_1 = -\frac{1}{N} \sum_{i=1}^{N} \left(y^i log\left(\hat{y}^i\right) + \left(1 - y^i\right) log\left(1 - \hat{y}^i\right)\right), \qquad (1)$$

where N denotes the number of input samples per batch (two patches make up one sample), y^i and $\hat{y}^i$ are the ground truth label and predicted label of i_{th} sample, respectively. If the i_{th} sample is matched, then $y^i = 1$, otherwise, $y^i = 0$.

Many metric learning methods [11,23] concatenate patch features to a vector as input. Instead, we compute the absolute differences of the left and right feature maps of patch-pairs obtained by the feature network, which is named as a residual map as shown in the middle of Fig. 3. This operation can directly measure the similarity between two feature maps. In practice, we apply an instance normalization on the residual map to avoid the vanishing gradient problem caused by a large number of 0 after the subtraction. Afterwards, the residual map is vectorized as the input of fully connected layer.

3.3   Feature Discrimination Network

Only the metric network cannot ensure the feature network to extract features of cross-spectral patches from the shared space, in which the semantic features of matched patches are similar but those of non-matched patches are distinct. Hence, metric learning usually has less generalizability than descriptor learning. To borrow the merit of descriptor learning, we design a feature discrimination network that constrains the feature network learning by a contrastive loss function. Unlike the hinge embedding loss in [25], the contrastive loss is a convex function and will not lead to the vanishing gradient problem [9]. In this work, it is defined for N samples per batch as below

$$E_2 = \frac{1}{N} \sum_{i=1}^{N} y^i \frac{2}{Q} \left(D\left(X_1^i, X_2^i\right)\right)^2 + 2\left(1 - y^i\right) Q e^{\frac{-2.77}{Q} D\left(X_1^i, X_2^i\right)}, \qquad (2)$$

where X_1, X_2 are a pair of cross-spectral image patches, and y denotes the label of the patch-pair. Q is a penalty parameter. The larger Q is, the greater penalty negative samples have, and vice versa. $D\left(X_1^i, X_2^i\right)$ represents the average Euclidean distance of the eigenvector of the i_{th} sample, which is calculated as follows:

$$D\left(X_1, X_2\right) = \frac{1}{m} ||G(X_1) - G(X_2)||_2, \qquad (3)$$

where $G(X_1)$, $G(X_2)$ denote the feature vectors of X_1 and X_2, respectively. m is the number of dimension of $G(X)$.

In order to adapt to our problem, we specifically tailor two operations in the feature discrimination network. First, we apply the global average pooling to vectorize the feature map instead of the fully connection. The reason is that the global average pooling can greatly reduce the number of parameters and prevent overfitting [17]. Second, unlike the method [9] using L_1 norm for the contrastive loss, we employ the average Euclidean distance, Eq. 3, because it has demonstrated a superior performance in numerous studies [20,25].

4   Experiment

To demonstrate the efficiency and effectiveness of SCFDM, we train it on a cross-spectral dataset, VIS-NIR patch dataset, and compare it with six state-of-the-arts including 2-channel network [1], siamese network [1], pseudo-siamese network [1], PN-Net [3], Q-Net [2], and L2-Net [26]. Although SCFDM is designed for cross-spectral image patch matching, we also evaluate it on a benchmark of single spectral dataset, namely Multi-view stereo correspondence dataset, to illustrate a better generalizability. The details are given in below.

4.1   Datasets

VIS-NIR patch dataset has been used as a benchmark cross-spectral image patch dataset in [1,2] for evaluating the metric learning and descriptor learning methods, which were collected from the public VIS-NIR scene dataset by Aguilera [1,7]. It has nine categories including over 1.6 million VIS-NIR patch-pairs in total, in which each patch has a size of 64×64. The patches were cropped around the SIFT points in VIS image, the half of VIS image patches and their corresponding NIR image patches form the matched pairs, the other half VIS image patches and the random NIR image patches compose the non-matched pairs. The number of patch-pairs per category is listed in Table 1. Figure 4 shows four samples of patch-pairs from the dataset. Similar to the studies [1,2], our framework is also trained on the country category and test on the remaining categories.

Table 1. The nine categories of VIS-NIR patch dataset for the experiment

Category	Country	Field	Forest	Indoor	Mountain	Oldbuilding	Street	Urban	Water
Number of Patch-Pairs	277504	240896	376832	60672	151296	101376	164608	147712	143104

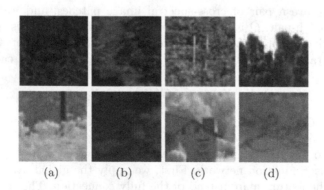

(a)   (b)   (c)   (d)

Fig. 4. Four image patch samples from training set. The first row is the VIS images and the second row is the NIR images, which are converted into the grayscale images. (a) and (b) are matched pairs, (c) and (d) are non-matched pairs

Multi-view stereo correspondence dataset is a single spectral image dataset, it consists of corresponding patches sampled from 3D reconstructions [6]. It has three subsets: Liberty, Notredame and Yosemite. Each subset contains 100k, 200k, and 500k patch-pairs. Each patch was cropped around an interest point, Difference of Gaussian (DOG), with a size of 64×64. Half of these pairs are matched, which have the same 3D points ID, and the corresponding interest points are within 5 pixels in position, 0.25 octaves of scale, and $\frac{\pi}{8}$ radians in angle. The other half are non-matched pairs that have different 3DpointID, and correspond to interest points lying outside 10 pixels in position, 0.5 octaves of scale, and $\frac{\pi}{4}$ radians in angle. Between patches in a pair, there exist notable changes in illumination, rotation, translation and perspective. Previous studies [6,11,23,26] have treated it as the standard evaluation dataset. Therefore, we follow the study [6] to train our framework on one subset and test on other two.

4.2 Training

All training and test were implemented on NVIDIA GTX 1080 GPU. The framework was jointly optimized for the entire loss $E = E_1 + E_2$ by using mini-batch SGD with a batch size of 128, and applying the Adam solver [14], with learning rate 0.0002 and momentum parameters $\beta_1 = 0.5$, $\beta_2 = 0.999$. All samples were normalized to $[0, 1]$. For more details about the parameters of feature network and metric network, please refer to the section 1 of supplementary document. Consistent with the state-of-the-arts methods, we used the false positive rate at 95% recall (FPR95) as the evaluation metric during the test. The smaller FPR95 is, the better performance the method achieves.

4.3 Test

Ablation Study. Since there are two loss functions for framework optimization and a penalty parameter Q to adjust the contrastive loss, we would like to see the contributions of these components in the framework. The evaluation is carried on VIS-NIR patch dataset. Firstly, the framework without the feature discrimination constrain, SCFM, is evaluated as the baseline. Then, the entire framework SCFDM, spatially connected feature metric learning with the feature discrimination constrain is evaluated by varying Q value. The FPR95 results and their mean and standard deviation (STD) on eight test categories in VIS-NIR patch dataset are listed in Table 2.

The Mean and STD show that SCFDM reaches a better FPR95 than SCFM on average. This indicates the feature discrimination constrain does enforce the feature network to extract the features of cross-spectral patches from the shared semantic space, and further helps the metric network to result in a lower FPR95. Moreover, we can see the penalty parameter Q plays a crucial rule of adjusting the feature learning procedure. A smaller Q makes the matched samples have more penalty, reversely, a greater Q makes the non-matched samples have more penalty. So, an appropriate Q can assist the feature network to learn the best share feature space. Table 2 shows the best Q is 2. Thus, we will use this setting in later experiments. For more detailed evaluation, please refer to the ROC curves of SCFM and SCFDM in the section 2 of supplementary document.

In addition, to intuitively illustrate the effectiveness of the shared feature space, we visualized the differences of the extracted features of cross-spectral image patches at each convolutional layer. Ideally, the features of matched patches should gradually become similar when going to the deeper layers, and this should not appear for non-matched patches. To this end, we cut the feature map after each convolutional layer into the left half and the right half, which are corresponding to each spectral image patch, and calculated their residual map. Subsequently, the residual map was globally averaged to form a vector. We then tiled the vector to a square or rectangle shape for the visualization. Figure 5 demonstrates the visualization of three non-matched and three matched pairs. The brightness represents the difference of two patch features. The brighter the map appears, the more different two features are, and vice versa. Figure 5(a) shows that the difference between features of non-matched pairs in each layer is gradually increasing. Figure 5(b) shows that the difference of matched pairs are gradually decreasing. One can see these two trends are rather obvious. Moreover, we tested the framework without the feature discrimination constrain (SCFM) as well, and show the visualization in Fig. 5(c). Very interesting, there is no obvious change of feature difference through each of six convolutional layers. To have a statistic analysis, we randomly selected 250 matched and 250 non-matched patch-pairs, and computed the average Euclidean distance of feature vectors after the last convolutional layer in SCFDM and SCFM. Table 3 shows that the feature difference of matched pairs is significantly smaller than non-matched pairs in SCFDM. However, the results of SCFM are very similar. All above confirms that the feature discrimination network enforces the feature network to learn the shared semantic feature space. The extracted features of cross-spectral image patches are more robust for comparison and help the metric network to improve the matching performance.

Table 2. The evaluations of SCFM and SCFDM with varied Q values in terms of FPR95 on VIS-NIR patch dataset

Models	Field	Forest	Indoor	Mountain	Oldbuilding	Street	Urban	Water	Mean	STD
SCFM	11.64	1.58	4.40	7.09	3.09	5.15	1.02	6.50	5.06	3.20
SCFDM($Q = \frac{1}{2}$)	9.41	4.29	6.66	9.39	3.72	4.99	1.52	5.91	5.73	2.55
SCFDM($Q = 1$)	8.68	1.18	4.95	6.86	3.80	4.09	0.94	6.29	4.59	2.51
SCFDM($Q = 2$)	8.35	1.09	5.63	6.06	2.95	3.96	0.90	5.84	4.34	2.43
SCFDM($Q = 3$)	10.03	2.58	6.27	7.66	3.20	4.57	0.95	4.95	5.02	2.73

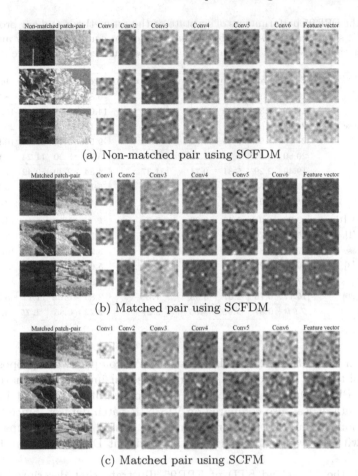

(a) Non-matched pair using SCFDM

(b) Matched pair using SCFDM

(c) Matched pair using SCFM

Fig. 5. The visualization of feature differences of cross-spectral patch-pairs at each convolutional layer in feature network. Dark represents smaller difference, reversely, bright indicates larger difference. (a) The feature differences of non-matched patch-pairs that are obtained by SCFDM. (b) The feature differences of matched patch-pairs that are obtained by SCFDM. (c) The feature differences of matched patch-pairs that are obtained by SCFM

Table 3. The average Euclidean distance of feature vectors for matched and non-matched patch-pair in SCFDM and SCFM

SCFDM		SCFM	
Matched	Non-matched	Matched	Non-matched
0.62	1.73	0.47	0.58

Table 4. The FPR95 performances of six state-of-the-art methods and our proposal on the VIS-NIR scene dataset. All methods were trained on country category and tested in the other eight categories. The italic font indicates the best performance

Models	Field	Forest	Indoor	Mountain	Oldbuilding	Street	Urban	Water	Mean	STD
2-channel [1]	16.95	*0.49*	4.54	17.01	5.72	6.82	1.44	15.56	8.56	6.46
siamese [1]	19.09	17.34	24.09	17.03	11.51	14.06	10.03	16.42	16.19	4.14
pseudo-siamese [1]	24.08	19.62	21.46	24.02	16.79	19.16	14.35	23.12	20.32	3.29
PN-Net [3]	24.56	3.91	6.56	15.99	6.84	9.51	4.40	15.62	10.92	6.73
Q-Net [2]	20.80	3.12	6.11	12.32	5.42	6.57	3.30	11.24	8.61	5.57
L2-Net [26]	19.49	2.29	5.81	9.71	4.37	4.84	2.39	9.42	7.29	5.30
SCFM	11.64	1.58	*4.40*	7.09	3.09	5.15	1.02	6.50	5.06	3.20
SCFDM	*8.35*	1.09	5.63	*6.06*	*2.95*	*3.96*	0.90	*5.84*	*4.34*	*2.43*
2-channel DA [1]	9.96	*0.12*	4.4	8.89	2.3	*2.18*	1.58	6.4	4.47	3.36
siamese DA [1]	15.79	10.76	11.60	11.15	5.27	7.51	4.60	10.21	9.61	3.43
pseudo-siamese DA [1]	17.01	9.82	11.17	11.86	6.75	8.25	5.65	12.04	10.31	3.35
PN-Net DA [3]	20.09	3.27	6.36	11.53	5.19	5.62	3.31	10.72	8.26	5.31
Q-Net DA [2]	17.01	2.70	6.16	9.61	4.61	3.99	2.83	8.44	6.91	4.47
L2-Net DA [26]	16.77	0.76	2.07	5.98	*1.89*	2.83	*0.62*	11.11	5.25	5.43
SCFDM DA	*7.91*	0.87	*3.93*	*5.07*	2.27	2.22	0.85	*4.75*	*3.48*	*2.25*

Evaluation on VIS-NIR Patch Dataset. We compared our proposal with the state-of-the-art methods [1–3] for cross-spectral image patch matching in terms of FPR95. Due to the excellent performance of L2-Net [26] in visible spectrum data, it was also compared on VIS-NIR patch dataset. Since the data augmentation can improve the performance, we carried out two groups of comparisons: with data augmentation (DA) and without DA. Results are listed in Table 4.

Overall, the Mean and STD of FPR95 illustrate that descriptor learning methods (PN-Net [3], Q-Net [2] and L2-Net [26]) perform better than metric learning methods (siamese and pseudo-siamese) when the data augmentation is not applied, especially on forest, indoor, oldbuilding, street and urban. However, the performances of metric learning methods are greatly improved after applying the data augmentation, which does not appear on the descriptor learning methods. Specifically, the performances of 2-channel, siamese and pseudo-siamese are improved 47.78%, 40.64% and 49.26%, respectively. Instead, PN-Net, Q-Net, and L2-Net are just improved 24.36%, 19.74%, and 27.98%. Our analysis shows that the descriptor learning methods already involve some sample mining strategies, which can create more training samples. Thus, they are not benefited much from the data augmentation.

Among these state-of-the-arts, 2-channel model shows an impressive performance due to its 2-channel patch fusion. By contrast, we can see our SCFM demonstrates a better accuracy because it compares features of cross-spectral patches more in the high-level feature space rather than the pixel-level. Although 2-channel model achieves the best accuracy on Forest category, the higher Mean

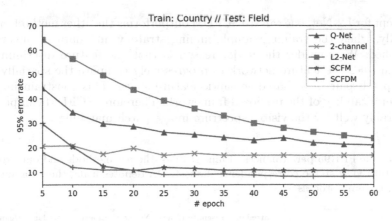

Fig. 6. The proposed model compared with other models in *the efficiency of the training*, which trained on the country sequence and tested on the field sequence. The significant performance improvement of our model, leads to lower error rates and faster convergence

and STD show it has fallen into the overfitting. The reason is that the training category (country) appears very similar like Forest. More importantly, our SCFDM outperforms all other methods in terms of the average accuracy (Mean) and the robustness (STD), even if the data augmentation is not applied. Compared with 2-channel DA, the Mean of FPR95 is improved 22.15% in SCFDM DA, specifically for Field, Indoor, Mountain, Oldbuilding, Street, Urban, Water are improved 20.58%, 10.68%, 42.97%, 1.30%, 1.83%, 46.20%, 25.78%, respectively.

Training Efficiency on VIS-NIR Scene Dataset. Beyond the FPR95, the convergence rate is another key factor to evaluate a method. We then select top five methods including our proposals, and train them on the Country category and test on the Field category. Figure 6 plots the 95% error rate against the number of training epochs.

One can see that the convergence rate of metric learning (2-channel and SCFM) is much faster than the descriptor learning (Q-Net and L2-Net). Our SCFDM achieves the fastest convergence, only requires 15 epochs. This is because SCFDM consists of a metric learning component, but its optimization process is ruled by the feature discrimination constrain. This constrain helps the framework to quickly learn the shared feature space and further avoids the overfitting.

Evaluation on Multi-view Stereo Correspondence Dataset. To demonstrate the generalizability of our proposal, we also compare SCFDM with state-of-the-art methods on the single spectral image dataset, i.e. multi-view stereo correspondence dataset [29]. We used 500K samples of one subset in the dataset for method training, and chose 100K samples of the other two subsets for test, which is consistent with the research [29]. The results of each method are listed in Table 5.

Except for L2-Net, one can see SCFDM outperforms the other methods again, especially, when the training sample mining strategy and data augmentation are applied. We consider the major reason is that the feature discrimination constrain rules the feature network to progressively compare the spatially connected patch pair in a shared semantic feature space. This constrain improve the generalizability of the proposed framework. Therefore, SCFDM can perform considerably well for the visible spectrum image patch matching.

Table 5. The FPR95 performances of nine state-of-the-art methods and our proposal on the Multi-view stereo correspondence dataset. DA denotes using the data augmentation in training process

Training	Notredame	Yosemite	Liberty	Yosemite	Liberty	Notredame	Mean	STD
Test	Liberty		Notredame		Yosemite			
TNet-TGLoss DA [16]	9.91	13.45	3.91	5.43	10.65	9.47	8.8	3.21
TNet-TLoss DA [16]	10.77	13.90	4.47	5.58	11.82	10.96	9.58	3.39
PN-Net [3]	8.13	9.65	3.71	4.23	8.99	7.21	6.98	2.26
Q-Net DA [2]	7.64	10.22	4.07	3.76	9.34	7.69	7.12	2.44
DeepDesc [25]	10.9		4.40		5.69		6.99	2.80
L2-Net [26]	3.64	5.29	1.15	1.62	4.43	3.30	3.23	1.45
L2-Net DA [26]	2.36	4.7	*0.72*	*1.29*	*2.57*	*1.71*	*2.22*	*1.26*
MatchNet [11]	6.90	10.77	3.87	5.67	10.88	8.39	7.44	2.56
DeepCompare 2ch-2stream DA [23]	4.85	7.20	1.90	2.11	5.00	4.10	4.19	1.81
DeepCompare 2ch-deep DA [23]	4.55	7.40	2.01	2.52	4.75	4.38	4.26	1.74
SNet-Gloss DA [16]	6.39	8.43	1.84	2.83	6.61	5.57	5.27	2.26
SCFDM	4.57	6.67	1.95	2.51	5.89	6.37	4.66	1.84
SCFDM DA	*1.47*	*4.54*	1.29	1.96	2.91	5.20	2.89	1.50

5   Conclusions

In this paper, we proposed a progressive comparison of spatially connected feature metric learning with a feature discrimination constrain (SCFDM) to tackle the cross-spectral image patch matching problem. Both experiments on the cross-spectral dataset and the single spectral dataset demonstrate that SCFDM outperforms state-of-the-art methods. We consider its superiority comes from two aspects. One is the progressive comparison of spatially connected features of cross-spectral image patches. This strategy makes the low-level features be independent and keep their own properties of corresponding spectral domains, meanwhile, interact the high-level features to learn the shared properties. Another is the feature discriminant network, which is designed for constraining the feature network to extract features in the shared semantic feature space. Thanks to this constrain, SCFDM achieves not only a better overall accuracy and generalizability, but also a faster training convergence. In the future work, we are going to investigate the data fusion methods that is more suitable for cross-spectral image patch matching.

References

1. Aguilera, C.A., Aguilera, F.J., Sappa, A.D., Aguilera, C., Toledo, R.: Learning cross-spectral similarity measures with deep convolutional neural networks. In: CVPR, pp. 1–9 (2016)
2. Aguilera, C.A., Sappa, A.D., Aguilera, C., Toledo, R.: Cross-spectral local descriptors via quadruplet network. Sensors **17**(4), 873 (2017)
3. Balntas, V., Johns, E., Tang, L., Mikolajczyk, K.: PN-Net: conjoined triple deep network for learning local image descriptors. Preprint arXiv:1601.05030 (2016)
4. Bay, H., Ess, A., Tuytelaars, T., Gool, L.V.: Speeded-up robust features (SURF). Comput. Vis. Image Underst. **110**(3), 346–359 (2008)
5. Belongie, S., Malik, J., Puzicha, J.: Shape matching and object recognition using shape contexts. IEEE TPAMI **24**(4), 509–522 (2002)
6. Brown, M., Hua, G., Winder, S.: Discriminative learning of local image descriptors. IEEE TPAMI **33**(1), 43–57 (2011)
7. Brown, M., Susstrunk, S.: Multi-spectral sift for scene category recognition. In: CVPR, pp. 177–184 (2011)
8. Calonder, M., Lepetit, V., Strecha, C., Fua, P.: BRIEF: binary robust independent elementary features. In: Daniilidis, K., Maragos, P., Paragios, N. (eds.) ECCV 2010. LNCS, vol. 6314, pp. 778–792. Springer, Heidelberg (2010). https://doi.org/10.1007/978-3-642-15561-1_56
9. Chopra, S., Hadsell, R., Lecun, Y.: Learning a similarity metric discriminatively, with application to face verification. In: CVPR, pp. 539–546 (2005)
10. Firmenichy, D., Brown, M., Ssstrunk, S.: Multispectral interest points for RGB-NIR image registration. In: ICIP, pp. 181–184 (2011)
11. Han, X., Leung, T., Jia, Y., Sukthankar, R., Berg, A.C.: MatchNet: unifying feature and metric learning for patch-based matching. In: CVPR, pp. 3279–3286 (2015)
12. Juefeixu, F., Pal, D.K., Savvides, M.: NIR-VIS heterogeneous face recognition via cross-spectral joint dictionary learning and reconstruction. In: CVPR, pp. 141–150 (2015)
13. Kim, J., Lee, J.K., Lee, K.M.: Accurate image super-resolution using very deep convolutional networks. In: CVPR, pp. 1646–1654 (2016)
14. Kingma, D., Ba, J.: Adam: a method for stochastic optimization. Computer Science (2014)
15. Krizhevsky, A., Sutskever, I., Hinton, G.E.: ImageNet classification with deep convolutional neural networks. In: NIPS, pp. 1097–1105 (2012)
16. Kumar, B.G., Carneiro, G., Reid, I.: Learning local image descriptors with deep siamese and triplet convolutional networks by minimising global loss functions. In: CVPR, pp. 5385–5394 (2016)
17. Lin, M., Chen, Q., Yan, S.C.: Network in network. Preprint arXiv:1312.4400 (2013)
18. Lowe, D.G.: Distinctive image features from scale-invariant keypoints. IJCV **60**(2), 91–110 (2004)
19. Mikolajczyk, K., Schmid, C.: A performance evaluation of local descriptors. IEEE TPAMI **27**(10), 1615–1630 (2005)
20. Nie, F., Huang, H., Cai, X., Ding, C.H.: Efficient and robust feature selection via joint $\ell 2$, 1-norms minimization. In: Advances in Neural Information Processing Systems, pp. 1813–1821 (2010)
21. Pinggera, P., Breckon, T., Bischof, H.: On cross-spectral stereo matching using dense gradient features. In: CVPR (2012)

22. Rublee, E., Rabaud, V., Konolige, K., Bradski, G.: ORB: an efficient alternative to SIFT or SURF. In: ICCV, pp. 2564–2571 (2012)
23. Zagoruyko, S., Komodakis, N.: Learning to compare image patches via convolutional neural networks. In: CVPR, pp. 4353–4361 (2015)
24. Simonyan, K., Zisserman, A.: Very deep convolutional networks for large-scale image recognition. preprint arXiv:1409.1556 (2014)
25. Simoserra, E., Trulls, E., Ferraz, L., Kokkinos, I., Fua, P., Morenonoguer, F.: Discriminative learning of deep convolutional feature point descriptors. In: ICCV, pp. 118–126 (2015)
26. Tian, Y., Fan, B., Wu, F.: L2-Net: deep learning of discriminative patch descriptor in Euclidean space. In: CVPR (2017)
27. Tola, E., Lepetit, V., Fua, P.: Daisy: an efficient dense descriptor applied to wide-baseline stereo. IEEE TPAMI **32**(5), 815–830 (2010)
28. Wang, S., Quan, D., Liang, X., Ning, M., Guo, Y., Jiao, L.: A deep learning framework for remote sensing image registration. ISPRS J. Photogrammetry Remote Sens. **145**, 148 (2018)
29. Winder, S., Hua, G., Brown, M.: Picking the best daisy. In: CVPR, pp. 178–185 (2009)

Semantic Segmentation Refinement by Monte Carlo Region Growing of High Confidence Detections

Philipe Ambrozio Dias$^{(\boxtimes)}$ (iD) and Henry Medeiros$^{(\boxtimes)}$ (iD)

Marquette University, Milwaukee, WI 53233, USA
{philipe.ambroziodias,henry.medeiros}@marquette.edu

Abstract. The semantic segmentation produced by most state-of-the-art methods does not show satisfactory adherence to object boundaries. Methods such as fully-connected conditional random fields (CRFs) can significantly refine segmentation predictions. However, they rely on supervised parameter optimization that depends upon specific datasets and predictor modules. We propose an unsupervised method for semantic segmentation refinement that takes as input the confidence scores generated by a segmentation network and re-labels pixels with low confidence levels. More specifically, a region growing mechanism aggregates these pixels to neighboring areas with high confidence scores and similar appearance. To minimize the impact of high-confidence prediction errors, our algorithm performs multiple growing steps by Monte Carlo sampling initial seeds in high-confidence regions. Our method provides both running time and segmentation improvements comparable to state-of-the-art refinement approaches for semantic segmentation, as demonstrated by evaluations on multiple publicly available benchmark datasets.

Keywords: Segmentation refinement ·
Instance semantic segmentation · Unsupervised post-processing

1 Introduction

The identification of the objects present in an image is a primary goal of computer vision. Such a determination can be carried out at different levels of granularity, which correspond to four well-known subproblems: image classification, object detection, semantic segmentation, and instance segmentation. These subproblems aim to achieve increasingly complex goals and have therefore been addressed with different levels of success.

We acknowledge the support of USDA ARS agreement #584080-5-020, and of NVIDIA Corporation with the donation of the GPU used for this research.

Electronic supplementary material The online version of this chapter (https://doi.org/10.1007/978-3-030-20890-5_9) contains supplementary material, which is available to authorized users.

© Springer Nature Switzerland AG 2019
C. V. Jawahar et al. (Eds.): ACCV 2018, LNCS 11362, pp. 131–146, 2019.
https://doi.org/10.1007/978-3-030-20890-5_9

In recent years, the combination of deep Convolutional Neural Networks (CNN) and increasingly larger publicly available datasets has led to substantial improvements to the state of the art in image classification [1,2]. For segmentation tasks, however, the performance of conventional CNN architectures is limited by the typical downsampling (pooling) intrinsic to such networks. Downsampling is employed to learn hierarchical features, but it ultimately leads to imprecise, coarse segmentation in scenarios that require pixel-wise predictions. Strategies including *atrous* convolutions [3] and upsampling [4–6] have been proposed to address this limitation, but the segmentation they produce still tend not to be finely aligned with the boundaries of the objects. Post-processing approaches such as conditional random fields (CRFs) [3,7] have been successful in segmentation refinement, but their performance depends on proper optimization of parameters for each specific dataset and predictor module being used.

In this paper, we propose the *Region Growing Refinement (RGR)* algorithm, an unsupervised and easily generalizable post-processing module that performs appearance-based region growing to refine the predictions generated by a CNN for semantic segmentation. Based on the classification scores available from the detector, our method first divides the image into three regions: high confidence background, high confidence object, and uncertainty region. The pixels within the uncertainty region, which are the ones that tend to be misclassified by CNN-based methods, are then labeled by means of region growing. We apply Monte Carlo sampling to select initial seeds from the high confidence regions, which are then grown according to a distance metric computed in the 5-D space of spatial and color coordinates. Our model has the advantage of not requiring any dataset-specific parameter optimization, working in a fully unsupervised manner.

We report experiments using different CNNs, datasets and baselines. We first employ the Fully Convolutional Instance-aware Semantic Segmentation (FCIS) algorithm [8] as a predictor module as well as the baseline for our performance evaluation. Since the ground truth annotations composing the MS COCO dataset contain non-negligible inaccuracies in terms of boundary adherence, we also assess RGR efficacy on the PASCAL VOC 2012 [9] validation set an on selected sequences from the DAVIS dataset [10]. Compared to the first two datasets, annotations provided for the DAVIS dataset are more fine-grained, with tighter boundary adherence. As a result, in addition to relatively small increases in segmentation accuracy for the MS COCO (+1.5% in AP) and the PASCAL datasets (+0.5% in $mAP\%$), we report significantly better results for the DAVIS sequences (+3.2% in $\mathcal{J}(IoU)\%$), which more realistically reflect the segmentation improvement observed through qualitative (visual) inspection.

We also compare the RGR algorithm against the state-of-the-art but supervised methods dense CRF [7] and DT-EdgeNet [11], for refinement of Deeplab [3] predictions. RGR provides both running time and segmentation refinement performance comparable to the optimized versions of both supervised methods, but without requiring neither dataset- nor model-specific fine-tuning.

2 Related Work

The relatively recent development of CNNs trained on large publicly available datasets represented an inflection point in image understanding research. Compared to the period when models based on hand-engineered features (e.g. HOG [12], SIFT [13]) were the norm, currently the state of the art in object recognition tasks is being improved at a dramatically faster pace [2].

However, traditional CNN-based methods that are effective for image classification and object detection present limitations for segmentation tasks. The combination of max-pooling and *striding* operations constitute a standard strategy for learning hierarchical features, which are a determining factor in the success of deep learning models. They explore the transition invariance favored by image-level labeling tasks, i.e., the fact that only the presence of an object matters, not its location. Such premise, however, does not hold for pixel-dense classification tasks, which require precise object localization. As pointed out by Chen et al. in [3], such spatial insensitivity and image downsampling inherent to conventional CNNs are two major hindering factors for their performance in image segmentation. An especially noticeable effect is that these methods generate coarse segmentation masks with limited boundary adherence.

One particularly successful strategy for segmentation tasks is the concept of fully convolutional networks (FCNs) [4]. In FCNs, the traditionally fully connected layers at the end of conventional CNNs are replaced by convolutional layers, which upsample the feature maps to generate a pixel-dense prediction. Different upsampling or *decoding* approaches have been proposed, including the use of deconvolution layers [4,14], and encoder-decoder architectures with skip-layer connections [5,6,15,16]. Other methods focus on reducing the downsampling rate. The Deeplab architecture [3] is one such method in which the concept of dilated (or *atrous*) convolutions is successfully employed to reduce the downsampling rate from 1/32 to 1/8.

A variation of the semantic segmentation problem is instance segmentation, which requires detecting and segmenting individual object instances. Coarse segmentations significantly hamper this type of task, since neighboring instances of objects of the same class are frequently merged into a single segmentation. Dai et al. in [17] introduced the concept of instance-sensitive FCNs, in which a FCN is designed to compute score maps that determine the likelihood that a pixel belongs to a relative position (e.g. right-upper corner) of an object instance. FCIS [8] is an extension of that approach, which achieved the state-of-the-art performance and won the COCO 2016 segmentation competition.

In addition to adjustments in CNN architectures, multiple works have investigated the use of low-level information strategies to construct models for object detection and semantic segmentation. Girschick et al. in [18] introduced the model known as RCNN that performs object detection by evaluating multiple region proposals. In RCNN, the region proposals are generated using Selective Search [19], which consists of merging a set of small regions [20] based on different similarity measures, an approach closely related to the concept of superpixels.

Superpixels are perceptually meaningful clusters of pixels, which are grouped based on color similarity and other low-level properties. Stutz et al. [21] provide a review of state-of-the-art superpixel approaches. One of the most widely-used methods is the Simple Linear Iterative Clustering (SLIC) algorithm [22], a *k-means*-based method that groups pixels into clusters according to their proximity in both spatial and color spaces. Semantic segmentation models using superpixels traditionally employ them as a pre-processing step. The image is first divided into superpixels, followed by a prediction step in which each element is individually evaluated using engineered hierarchical features [23] or CNNs [24,25].

In addition to the generation of region proposals or pre-segmentation elements, local-appearance information has been also employed in post-processing steps to improve segmentations obtained with deep CNN models. One possible approach consists of adapting the GrabCut model [26], which is a well-known method for interactive segmentation based on the minimization of an energy function that models the background and foreground as Gaussian mixture models (GMM). Another such post-processing approach is to model the problem as a CRF defined over neighboring pixels or small patches. Krähenbühl et al. in [7] introduced an efficient algorithm for fully connected CRFs containing pairwise potentials that associate all pairs of pixels in an image. This algorithm is successfully exploited by the Deeplab model [3] to produce fine-grained segmentations.

Chen et al. introduced the DT-EdgeNet in [11], which is a computationally cheaper alternative that replaces the dense CRF with a domain-transform approach that refines the segmentation using a modern edge-preserving filtering method. Both approaches, however, have to be optimized in a supervised manner when applied to different datasets or combined with different predictors.

3   Proposed Approach

The method we propose for refinement of segmentation boundaries is a generic **unsupervised** post-processing module that can be coupled to the output of any CNN or similar model for semantic segmentation. Our RGR algorithm consists of four main steps: (1) identification of low and high confidence classification regions; (2) Monte Carlo sampling of initial seeds; (3) region growing; and (4) majority voting and final classification. The operations that comprise these steps are described in detail below. In our description, we make reference to Fig. 1 and Algorithm 1, which list the operations performed by our method for each proposed detection in an image. If detections for multiple classes are present, the algorithm is executed on the score maps associated with each class, and the final classification is defined by computing the maximum likelihood across classes.

(1) Step 1 - Thresholding the Image into Three Regions: Conventional models typically infer a final classification by pixel-wise thresholding the scores obtained for each class. Instead of relying on intermediate threshold values, our refinement module directly exploits the available classification scores to differentiate between three regions: (a) high confidence foreground (or object) R_F; (b) high

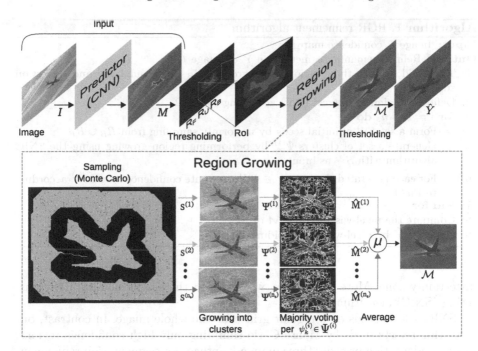

Fig. 1. Best viewed in color. Diagram illustrating the sequence of tasks performed by the proposed RGR model for segmentation refinement. Each task and its corresponding output (shown below the arrows) are described in Algorithm 1. (Color figure online)

confidence background R_B; and (c) uncertainty region R_U. As defined in Eq. 1, these regions are identified using two high confidence thresholds τ_F and τ_B

$$R_F = \{p_j | M(p_j) \geq \tau_F\},$$
$$R_U = \{p_j | \tau_B < M(p_j) < \tau_F\}, \tag{1}$$
$$R_B = \{p_j | M(p_j) \leq \tau_B\},$$

where p_j is the j-th pixel in the input image I, and $M(p_j)$ is its corresponding score in the detection confidence map M computed by the original predictor (usually a CNN). High confidence regions correspond to areas where pixels present scores near the extremes of the likelihood range. For normalized score maps, values lower than a threshold $\tau_B \sim 0.0$ identify pixels in the high confidence background, while values larger than $\tau_F \sim 1.0$ indicate high confidence foreground elements. To recover possible false negatives, morphological shrinking is performed on the background R_B boundaries. The fourth leftmost image in Fig. 1 illustrates the division of the image into the three regions R_F, R_U, and R_B.

(2) Step 2 - Monte Carlo Sampling of Initial Seeds: Inspired by the notion of pixel affinity employed by many algorithms for superpixel segmentation, our method applies a region growing approach to classify pixels within the

---

Algorithm 1. RGR refinement algorithm

Input: Image I, confidence map M
Output: Refined semantic segmentation $\hat{Y}$ of image I
1: Threshold M into three regions: background R_B, foreground R_F and uncertain zone R_U
2: Define a Region of Interest (RoI) according to Eq. 2
3: **for** i = 1 to n_s **do**
4:     Form a set $S^{(i)}$ of initial seeds by uniformly sampling from $R_B \cup R_F$
5:     Generate a set of clusters $\Psi^{(i)}$ by performing region growing using the SNIC algorithm with $S^{(i)}$ as input
6:     For each generated cluster $\psi_k^{(i)} \in \Psi^{(i)}$, compute confidence map $\hat{M}^{(i)}$ according to Eq. 4
7: **end for**
8: Compute the pixel-wise average $\mathcal{M}$ of $\hat{M}^{(i)}$, $i = 1, \ldots, n$
9: Generate $\hat{Y}$ by pixel-wise thresholding $\mathcal{M}$

---

uncertainty zone. More specifically, we build on the simple non-iterative clustering (SNIC) algorithm [27].

SNIC selects seeds on a regular grid over the whole image. In contrast, our algorithm selects seeds by Monte Carlo sampling only high confidence regions. Such an adaptation provides three main advantages for segmentation refinement. First, our random selection of seeds allows clusters of flexible size. This is beneficial for: (i) growing into larger regions that were missed by the predictor, and (ii) forming smaller clusters, rather than *leaking* into nearby pixels. Second, it enforces the classification of unlabeled pixels to derive from high confidence information. And third, at each Monte Carlo iteration, clusters are grown from different sets of randomly selected seeds. Combined with majority voting per cluster and pixel-wise averaging across iterations (detailed in Step 3), this procedure acts as a filter against false positives detected with high confidence by the predictor.

Our Monte Carlo approach consists of n_s iterations. At each iteration i, a set $S^{(i)}$ of initial seeds is defined by uniformly sampling the high-confidence area $R_H = R_B \cup R_F$. Let p_h represent pixels within the region R_H, where the index $h = 1, \ldots, |R_H|$. Uniform sampling of seeds can thus be performed index-wise according to $h \sim U(1, |R_H|)$. We determine the number of seeds to be sampled $|S^{(i)}|$ based on the sampling domain area (i.e. $|R_H|$) and the desired average spacing between samples σ, i.e., $|S^{(i)}| = |R_H|/\sigma$. The spacing between seeds ensures the availability of paths through which all the initial centroids can propagate throughout the uncertainty region.

(3) Step 3 - Region Growing: The dashed block at the bottom of Fig. 1 illustrates the sequence of operations performed by RGR for region growing. To reduce the computation time, we restrict the region growing to a Region of Interest (RoI) around the uncertain zone R_U. Based on the spatial distance to R_U, the background R_B can be split into two regions: far background R_{fB} and near background R_{nB}. Since the far background is unlikely to influence the clustering

of the uncertain region, R_{fB} can be ignored during region growing. Hence, we define the RoI for region growing as

$$RoI = R_{nB} \cup R_F \cup R_U. \tag{2}$$

Initial centroids are then grown according to an adaptation of the SNIC algorithm. As in SNIC, we measure the similarity between a pixel and a centroid as their distance in a five-dimensional space of color and spatial coordinates. Let the spatial position of a pixel be represented by a vector $\mathbf{x} = [x\ y]^T$, while its color is expressed in the CIELAB color-space by $\mathbf{c} = [l\ a\ b]^T$. The distance $d_{j,k}$ between a pixel j and a centroid k is given by Eq. 3, where θ_s and θ_m are normalizing factors for spatial and color distances, respectively

$$d_{j,k} = \sqrt{\frac{\|\mathbf{x}_j - \mathbf{x}_k\|_2^2}{\theta_s} + \frac{\|\mathbf{c}_j - \mathbf{c}_k\|_2^2}{\theta_m}}. \tag{3}$$

Also as in SNIC, our region growing implementation relies on a priority queue, which is constantly populated with nodes that correspond to unlabeled pixels 4- or 8-connected to a region being grown. This queue is sorted according to the similarity between the candidate pixel and the average (centroid) of the growing region, given by Eq. 3. While the queue is not empty, each iteration consists of: (1) popping the first element of the queue, which corresponds to the unlabeled pixel that is most similar to a neighboring centroid k; (2) annexing this pixel to the respective cluster $\psi_k^{(i)}$; (3) updating the region centroid; and (4) populating the queue with neighbors of this pixel that are still unlabeled.

We add a constraint to the original SNIC algorithm in order to reduce the incidence of false detections. A node is only pushed into the queue if its distance to the corresponding centroid is smaller than a certain value d_{Max}. This strategy ensures that an unlabeled pixel within R_U will only inherit information from high confidence pixels that are sufficiently similar to it. This creates the possibility of "orphan" elements, i.e., pixels for which no node is ever created. Such pixels are therefore classified as background. For each set of initial seeds $S^{(i)}$, the region growing process generates a cluster map $\Psi^{(i)}$ that associates each pixel to a respective cluster $\psi_k^{(i)}$.

(4) Step 4 - Majority Voting and Final Classification: Following the region growing process, RGR conducts a majority voting procedure to ultimately classify each generated cluster into foreground or background. As expressed in Eq. 4, a pixel p_j contributes a positive vote for foreground classification if its original prediction score $M(p_j)$ is larger than a threshold τ_0. We compute the ratio of positive votes across all pixels $p_j \in \psi_k^{(i)}$ to generate a refined likelihood map $\hat{M}^{(i)}$ for each set of clusters according to

$$Y_k^{(i)} = \left\{ p_j \in \psi_k^{(i)} | M(p_j) > \tau_0 \right\}, \tag{4}$$

$$\hat{M}^{(i)}(p_j) = \frac{|Y_k^{(i)}|}{|\psi_k^{(i)}|}. \tag{5}$$

The likelihood maps $\hat{M}^{(i)}$ obtained from the n_s Monte Carlo samplings are averaged to generate a final pixel dense score map $\mathcal{M} = \frac{1}{n_s} \sum_{i=1}^{n_s} \hat{M}^{(i)}$. Finally, each pixel is classified into foreground if more than 50% of its average votes are positive. Otherwise, the region is labeled as background, that is,

$$\hat{Y}(p_j) = \mathbb{1}_{\mathcal{M}(p_j) > 0.5}, \tag{6}$$

where $\hat{Y}(p_j)$ is the final binary classification map and $\mathbb{1}$ is an indicator variable that assumes the value 1 when the corresponding condition is satisfied.

4   Experiments

To the best of our knowledge, the COCO dataset is the largest publicly available dataset for semantic/instance segmentation, with a total of 2.5 million labeled instances in $328,000$ images [6]. However, as discussed in Sect. 4.1, COCO's ground truth annotations contain imprecisions intrinsic from its labeling procedure. To minimize the influence of dataset-specific errors, we assess the performance of our algorithm on: (i) the COCO 2016 validation set; (ii) the PASCAL VOC 2012 dataset; and (iii) selected video sequences of the DAVIS dataset.

Since RGR is an unsupervised post-processing refinement module, it can be coupled to any semantic segmentation network. In Sect. 4.1, we evaluate its performance in comparison to SNIC superpixels for refinement of FCIS predictions. In Sect. 4.2, RGR, CRF, DT-EdgeNet and GrabCut are compared for refinement of Deeplab predictions.

4.1   Comparison Against Superpixel Refinement

We denote the combination of the publicly available FCIS model and the refinement module RGR as FCIS+RGR. Since RGR works in a region growing manner that is inspired by the concept of superpixel segmentation, our performance analysis also includes FCIS+SNIC, a naive refinement method that consists of performing majority voting within superpixels generated with SNIC.

Following a grid-search executed on the PASCAL VOC dataset, for all our experiments FCIS+SNIC employs SNIC with $\theta_m = 0.1$ and superpixel size of $100\,\mathrm{px}$. RGR thresholds were defined as follows. First, τ_0 corresponds to the original detector optimal threshold. For FCIS this value is 0.4, as reported in [8]. To identify the high confidence foreground, we empirically selected a high confidence threshold τ_F corresponding to $1.5 \times \tau_0$, hence 0.6. As for the background detection, we set the high confidence lower threshold to $\tau_B = 0.0$.

COCO 2016 Segmentation Dataset. Based on the COCO official guidelines, we evaluate the performance obtained by FCIS, FCIS+SNIC, and FCIS+RGR on the validation set composed of $40k$ images. Table 1 summarizes the performance of the three methods according to the standard COCO metrics, including average precision (AP) averaged over 0.5:0.95 intersection over union (IoU) thresholds and at different scales. While increasing the number of true positive

Table 1. Comparison between results obtained by FCIS, FCIS+SNIC and FCIS+RGR on the COCO 2016 (val), the PASCAL VOC 2012 (val), and the DAVIS datasets.

	COCO 2016						VOC 2012	DAVIS	
	AP (%)	AP_{50} (%)	AP_{75} (%)	AP_S (%)	AP_M (%)	AP_L (%)	mAP (%)	$\mathcal{J}(IoU)$ (%)	$\mathcal{F}$ (%)
FCIS	35.1	60.1	36.5	9.8	38.4	59.8	70.6	71.2	69.9
FCIS+SNIC	34.9	59.0	36.4	9.3	38.2	59.6	70.6	72.8	70.4
FCIS+RGR	**36.9**	**60.6**	**39.3**	**11.4**	**40.7**	**60.5**	**71.1**	**74.4**	**72.7**

detections (+0.3% in AR) for all the scenarios, the naive FCIS+SNIC approach also decreases the AP by introducing a larger number of false positives.

Our refinement model, RGR, on the other hand, increases the baseline FCIS overall performance by 1.8%. Compared to the improvement of 0.5% in AP_{50}, the increase of 2.8% in AP_{75} demonstrates that RGR is particularly successful for cases where the detections obtained from the input CNN are accurately located.

Figure 2 presents the average precision obtained for each of the 80 COCO categories. Since its region growing is based on local affinity characteristics, it is natural that the RGR refinement is especially effective for objects with more uniform appearance (e.g. airplane, frisbee). Nevertheless, these results also demonstrate the robustness of the refinement provided by RGR, since no object category shows a noticeable decrease in average precision.

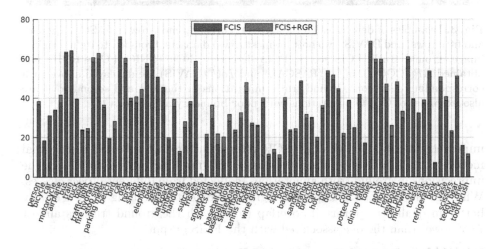

Fig. 2. AP obtained by FCIS and FCIS+RGR for each of the 80 COCO categories.

A closer visual inspection of the output labels also shows that the metrics obtained might be misleading. Despite the extensive efforts described in [8] to create such a massive dataset, for some instances, the ground truth segmentation annotations lack accurate adherence to real object boundaries. As a consequence,

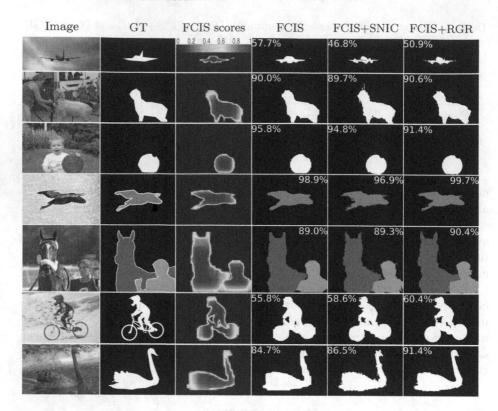

Fig. 3. Examples of detections on the COCO (three top-most rows), PASCAL (fourth and fifth rows) and DAVIS (two bottom-most rows) datasets. From left to right: original image, ground truth, FCIS scores, FCIS detection, FCIS+SNIC, FCIS+RGR. The obtained AP (COCO), mAP (PASCAL) and IoU (DAVIS) are displayed above each corresponding detection. Ground truth annotations in the first and second rows are also examples of COCO annotations with poor boundary adherence.

improvements obtained through RGR refinement are not reflected in the final metrics for a significant number of images. Figure 3 provides examples of the imprecisions in ground truth annotations, collected from different object classes. While for the *airplane* example the segmentation obtained using RGR is clearly better in qualitative terms, its overlap (IoU) with the ground truth is almost 7.0% lower than the one associated with the FCIS output.

PASCAL VOC 2012 Segmentation Dataset. Table 1 also contains a summary of the results obtained by FCIS, FCIS+SNIC and our method FCIS+RGR on the PASCAL VOC 2012 validation set. The segmentation refinement generated using RGR provides a final mAP slightly better (+0.5%) than both FCIS and the refined version using naive superpixel-wise majority voting.

Since boundaries constitute a small fraction of the total image pixels, such a small difference in performance does not properly reflect the higher boundary adherence provided by RGR refinement. Thus, we follow the strategy presented in [28] and also evaluate segmentation accuracy on a narrow region closer to the boundaries to better quantify the improvements obtained by RGR. Figure 5 shows the mean IoU obtained according to the width of the evaluated region around boundaries. RGR outperforms FCIS+SNIC by +2.0% in terms of mean IoU in regions 10-pixels near the boundaries, which better reflects the more detailed segmentation provided by RGR that is clear in the qualitative examples such as in Fig. 3.

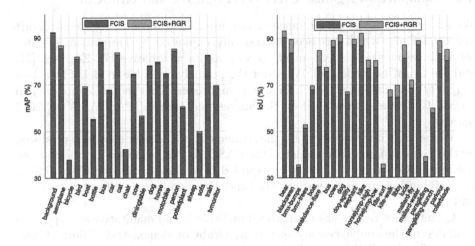

Fig. 4. Results obtained obtained by FCIS and FCIS+RGR on transfer learning experiments. *Left:* Mean average precision (mAP) for each of the PASCAL VOC 2012 classes (val). *Right:* Mean IoU obtained for each of the selected DAVIS video sequences.

DAVIS 2016 Selected Video Sequences. Given the aforementioned inaccuracies in the annotations available for the COCO and PASCAL datasets, we additionally report quantitative results on selected video sequences of the DAVIS dataset. The DAVIS dataset for Video Object Segmentation is composed of high quality video sequences [10], with pixel-accurate ground truth segmentation for each frame. From its 50 original video sequences, we selected a total of 24 sequences that contain target objects whose corresponding classes are contained within the 80 objects categories composing the COCO dataset. These sequences encompass 13 different COCO classes, including classes for which FCIS+RGR did not provide significant performance improvements on the COCO evaluation (e.g. *person, bicycle, boat* and *bear*).

As summarized in Table 1, segmentations obtained using FCIS+RGR have an average $\mathcal{J}(IoU)$ 3.2% higher than those generated by FCIS, and 1.6% better than the results obtained using a naive superpixel-wise majority voting for refinement. The official metrics for performance evaluation on DAVIS also include a contour accuracy metric $\mathcal{F}$, which corresponds to a F-measure computed based on the contour precision and recall. Segmentations refined using RGR yielded an increase of 2.8% in $\mathcal{F}$, confirming its ability to improve boundary adherence. Figure 4 presents the results obtained for each video sequence, with FCIS+RGR providing improvements in the range between 1.1% and 6.9% depending on the sequence. The fact that larger quantitative improvements are obtained for the DAVIS sequences corroborates our argument that the annotations available for the COCO and PASCAL datasets provide limited information regarding boundary accuracy/adherence of segmentation methods.

4.2 Comparison Against CRF, DT-EdgeNet and GrabCut

We also compare the performance of our method against the state-of-the-art dense CRF [7], which has been successfully exploited by Deeplab models for semantic segmentation refinement, as well as its alternative DT-EdgeNet [11] and the GrabCut model [26]. We adopt the publicly available model of Deeplab-LargeFOV as the base model for our comparison. This model is pre-trained on MS COCO and fine-tuned on the augmented *trainval* PASCAL VOC 2012 dataset.

We perform our evaluation for the refinement of the segmentations produced by the Deeplab-LargeFOV model on the PASCAL validation set. In this case, we configure RGR to use a different τ_F sampled from the distribution $U(0.5, 0.9)$ in each MC region growing iteration. The other thresholds remain fixed at $\tau_B = 0.0$ and $\tau_0 = 0.5$.

Quantitative results are summarized in Table 2, and qualitative examples are available in the supplementary materials. GrabCut demonstrated limited ability to refine the CNN predictions, which is expected since: (i) it assumes that all pixels initialized as background/foreground are correct, and (ii) the formulation using GMMs shows limited performance when the background/foreground appearance varies significantly. In contrast, by growing from a much higher number of seeds, RGR forms multiple clusters that significantly differ in terms of appearance but can share the same semantic labels.

The combination of an optimized CRF with Deeplab-LargeFOV culminates in a mAP of 80.1%, while the alternative using optimal DT-EdgeNet provides 78.9%. Our fully unsupervised RGR algorithm yields 79.2% mAP on this same scenario, being hence competitive with both optimized supervised models but with the advantage of not requiring any dataset-specific fine-tuning.

The higher generalization capability of our method is highlighted by transfer learning experiments. We compared RGR and CRF for the refinement of FCIS detections in the scenario described in Sect. 4.1, i.e., on the same selected sequences of the DAVIS dataset but without performing any dataset-specific fine-tuning for any method. While RGR again improves segmentation quality by 3.2%, in this scenario CRF provides only 2.7%. This demonstrates the advantage of our unsupervised approach, which can be employed on different datasets without the need for fine-tuning. Albeit providing significant improvements in segmentation performance, the dense CRF is strongly dependent on supervised optimization of hyper-parameters for specific datasets and predictor models.

Table 2. Comparison between different refinement methods for different networks.

	VOC 2012		DAVIS
	mAP (%)		IoU (%)
Deeplab	76.1	FCIS	71.2
Deeplab+GrabCut	77.9 (+1.8)	FCIS+GrabCut	71.2 (+0.0)
Deeplab+DT	78.9 (+2.8)	FCIS+DT	NA*
Deeplab+CRF	80.1 (+3.9)	FCIS+CRF	73.9 (+2.7)
Deeplab+RGR	79.2 (+3.1)	FCIS+RGR	74.4 (+3.2)

*implementation public available only for the Deeplab model.

4.3 Inference Time

Finally, we evaluate the inference time of RGR in comparison to dense CRF. As explained above, our algorithm consists of four main steps: (1) thresholding, (2) Monte Carlo sampling of seeds, (3) region growing, and (4) majority voting. Steps 1, 2 and 4 are currently implemented in MATLAB (R2017a), while the region growing step is implemented in C++ based on the SNIC algorithm. Runtime assessment was performed on an Intel Xeon^{TM}CPU E5-2620 v3 @ 2.40 GHz (62 GB). The average runtime per image in the PASCAL VOC dataset is ∼0.5 s with 3 Monte Carlo iterations. This is lower than the 0.8 s average inference time of CRF's publicly available implementation, as reported in [11].

A breakdown of the runtime analysis shows that the region growing step requires only ∼0.2 s per Monte Carlo (MC) iteration, which is comparable to the 0.18 s required by the CPU-based implementation of the domain transform method described in [11]. We highlight that the multiple MC iterations are easily parallelizable. As summarized in Fig. 5, using MATLAB's Parallel Pool the runtime obtained for 10 MC iterations is less than 0.1 s higher than the 0.5 s/image obtained for 3 MC iterations, which corresponds to a performance improvement of 0.1% in the scenario described in Sect. 4.1.

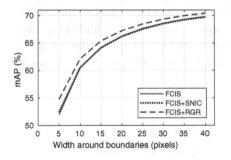 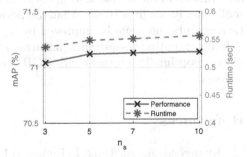

Fig. 5. *Left:* Mean average precision (*mAP*) on PASCAL on regions near object boundaries. *Right:* Runtime (orange) and performance (blue) of RGR according to the number of MC iterations (n_s) in the scenario described in Sect. 4.1. (Color figure online)

4.4   Failure Cases

As demonstrated by the experimental results, the quality of the refinement obtained using RGR depends on the accuracy of the detector model used as input, especially in terms of localization. Although Monte Carlo sampling improves the robustness against high confidence false positives, errors might be propagated if the score maps collected from the detector module (CNN) contain regions with high concentrations of false positives. An example of such case is found in Fig. 3. Given the high confidence of the false positives generated by the FCIS model for internal parts of the bicycle wheels, RGR is unable to correct these mistakes and hence these regions remain incorrectly segmented.

5   Conclusion

We have presented RGR, an effective unsupervised post-processing algorithm for segmentation refinement. Traditionally, the final classification step of existing methods for semantic segmentation consists of thresholding score maps obtained from CNNs. Based on the concepts of Monte Carlo sampling and region growing, our algorithm achieves an adaptive thresholding by exploiting high confidence detections and low-level image information. Our results demonstrate the efficacy of RGR refinement, showing increased precision on three different segmentation datasets. Our algorithm provides segmentation improvements competitive with existing state-of-the-art refinement methods, but with the advantage of not requiring any dataset- or model-specific optimization of parameters.

Moreover, we highlight limitations of existing datasets in terms of boundary adherence of available ground truth annotations. This is an intrinsic limitation of annotations procedures that rely on approximating segmentations as polygons. In such cases, the quality of the segmentation is proportional to the number of vertices selected by the user, but hand selecting more points increases the labeling time per object. As future work, we consider exploiting RGR for improving annotations available for existing datasets or designing an alternative annotation tool. Finally, we hypothesize that the performance of existing CNNs for semantic segmentation could be improved by training with RGR as an additional step before computing losses. Such an arrangement could lead to a detector module that optimally interacts with RGR, identifying keypoints for the refinement process.

References

1. Krizhevsky, A., Sutskever, I., Hinton, G.E.: ImageNet classification with deep convolutional neural networks. In: Advances in Neural Information Processing Systems, pp. 1–9 (2012)
2. He, K., Zhang, X., Ren, S., Sun, J.: Deep residual learning for image recognition. In: IEEE Conference on Computer Vision and Pattern Recognition (CVPR), pp. 770–778 (2016)

3. Chen, L.C., Papandreou, G., Kokkinos, I., Murphy, K., Yuille, A.L.: DeepLab: semantic image segmentation with deep convolutional nets, atrous convolution, and fully connected CRFs. IEEE Trans. Pattern Anal. Mach. Intell. **40**, 834–848 (2018)
4. Long, J., Shelhamer, E., Darrell, T.: Fully convolutional networks for semantic segmentation. In: IEEE Conference on Computer Vision and Pattern Recognition (CVPR), 7–12 June, pp. 3431–3440 (2015)
5. Ronneberger, O., Fischer, P., Brox, T.: U-Net: convolutional networks for biomedical image segmentation. In: Navab, N., Hornegger, J., Wells, W.M., Frangi, A.F. (eds.) MICCAI 2015, Part III. LNCS, vol. 9351, pp. 234–241. Springer, Cham (2015). https://doi.org/10.1007/978-3-319-24574-4_28
6. Lin, G., Milan, A., Shen, C., Reid, I.: RefineNet: multi-path refinement networks for high-resolution semantic segmentation. In: IEEE Conference on Computer Vision and Pattern Recognition (CVPR) (2017)
7. Krähenbühl, P., Koltun, V.: Efficient inference in fully connected CRFs with Gaussian edge potentials. In: Advances in Neural Information Processing Systems, pp. 109–117 (2011)
8. Li, Y., Qi, H., Dai, J., Ji, X., Wei, Y.: Fully convolutional instance-aware semantic segmentation. In: IEEE Conference on Computer Vision and Pattern Recognition (CVPR), pp. 2359–2367 (2017)
9. Everingham, M., Van Gool, L., Williams, C.K.I., Winn, J., Zisserman, A.: The PASCAL Visual Object Classes Challenge 2012 (VOC 2012) Results. http://www.pascal-network.org/challenges/VOC/voc2012/workshop/index.html
10. Perazzi, F., Pont-Tuset, J., McWilliams, B., Gool, L.V., Gross, M., Sorkine-Hornung, A.: A benchmark dataset and evaluation methodology for video object segmentation. In: IEEE Conference on Computer Vision and Pattern Recognition (CVPR), pp. 724–732 (2016)
11. Chen, L.C., Barron, J.T., Papandreou, G., Murphy, K., Yuille, A.L.: Semantic image segmentation with task-specific edge detection using CNNs and a discriminatively trained domain transform. In: IEEE Conference on Computer Vision and Pattern Recognition (CVPR), pp. 4545–4554 (2016)
12. Dalal, N., Triggs, B.: Histograms of oriented gradients for human detection. In: IEEE Conference on Computer Vision and Pattern Recognition (CVPR), vol. 1, pp. 886–893. IEEE (2005)
13. Lowe, D.G.: Distinctive image features from scale-invariant keypoints. Int. J. Comput. Vis. **60**, 91–110 (2004)
14. Noh, H., Hong, S., Han, B.: Learning deconvolution network for semantic segmentation. In: IEEE International Conference on Computer Vision (ICCV 2015), pp. 1520–1528 (2015)
15. Badrinarayanan, V., Kendall, A., Cipolla, R.: SegNet: a deep convolutional encoder-decoder architecture for image segmentation. IEEE Trans. Pattern Anal. Mach. Intell. **39**, 2481–2495 (2017)
16. Hariharan, B., Arbeláez, P., Girshick, R., Malik, J.: Hypercolumns for object segmentation and fine-grained localization. In: IEEE Conference on Computer Vision and Pattern Recognition (CVPR), 7–12 June, pp. 447–456 (2015)
17. Dai, J., He, K., Li, Y., Ren, S., Sun, J.: Instance-sensitive fully convolutional networks. In: Leibe, B., Matas, J., Sebe, N., Welling, M. (eds.) ECCV 2016, Part VI. LNCS, vol. 9910, pp. 534–549. Springer, Cham (2016). https://doi.org/10.1007/978-3-319-46466-4_32

18. Girshick, R., Donahue, J., Darrell, T., Malik, J.: Rich feature hierarchies for accurate object detection and semantic segmentation. In: IEEE Conference on Computer Vision and Pattern Recognition (CVPR), pp. 580–587 (2014)
19. Uijlings, J.R.R., Van De Sande, K.E.A., Gevers, T., Smeulders, A.W.M.: Selective search for object recognition. Int. J. Comput. Vis. **104**, 154–171 (2013)
20. Felzenszwalb, P.F., Huttenlocher, D.P.: Efficient graph-based image segmentation. Int. J. Comput. Vis. **59**, 167–181 (2004)
21. Stutz, D., Hermans, A., Leibe, B.: Superpixels: an evaluation of the state-of-the-art. Comput. Vis. Image Underst. **166**, 1–27 (2017)
22. Achanta, R., Shaji, A., Smith, K., Lucchi, A., Fua, P., Süsstrunk, S.: SLIC superpixels compared to state-of-the-art superpixel methods. IEEE Trans. Pattern Anal. Mach. Intell. **34**, 2274–2281 (2012)
23. Gould, S., Rodgers, J., Cohen, D., Elidan, G., Koller, D.: Multi-class segmentation with relative location prior. Int. J. Comput. Vis. **80**, 300–316 (2008)
24. Farabet, C., Couprie, C., Najman, L., LeCun, Y.: Learning hierarchical features for scene labeling. IEEE Trans. Pattern Anal. Mach. Intell. **35**, 1915–1929 (2013)
25. Mostajabi, M., Yadollahpour, P., Shakhnarovich, G.: Feedforward semantic segmentation with zoom-out features. In: IEEE Conference on Computer Vision and Pattern Recognition (CVPR), pp. 3376–3385 (2015)
26. Rother, C., Kolmogorov, V., Blake, A.: Grabcut: interactive foreground extraction using iterated graph cuts. ACM Trans. Graph. (TOG) **23**, 309–314 (2004)
27. Achanta, R., Sabine, S.: Superpixels and polygons using simple non-iterative clustering. In: IEEE Conference on Computer Vision and Pattern Recognition (CVPR), pp. 4651–4660 (2017)
28. Ghiasi, G., Fowlkes, C.C.: Laplacian pyramid reconstruction and refinement for semantic segmentation. In: Leibe, B., Matas, J., Sebe, N., Welling, M. (eds.) ECCV 2016, Part III. LNCS, vol. 9907, pp. 519–534. Springer, Cham (2016). https://doi.org/10.1007/978-3-319-46487-9_32

A Deep Blind Image Quality Assessment with Visual Importance Based Patch Score

Zhengyi Lv, Xiaochuan Wang, Kai Wang, and Xiaohui Liang^(✉)

State Key Laboratory of Virtual Reality Technology and Systems,
Beihang University, Beijing, China
Liang_xiaohui@buaa.edu.cn

Abstract. Convolutional neural networks (CNNs)-based no-reference image quality assessment (NR-IQA) suffers from insufficient training data. The conventional solution is splitting the training image into patches, assigning each patch the quality score, while the assignment of patch score is not consistent with the human visual system (HVS) well. To address the problem, we propose a patch quality assignment strategy, introducing the weighting map to describe the degree of visual importance of each distorted pixel, integrating the weighting map and the feature map to pool the quality score of each patch. With the patch quality, a CNNs-based NR-IQA model is trained. Experimental results demonstrate that proposed method, named as blind image quality metric with improved patch score (BIQIPS), improves the performance on most of the distortion types, especially on the types of local distortions, and achieves state-of-the-art prediction accuracy among the NR-IQA metrics.

Keywords: Image quality assessment · Patch score ·
Convolutional neural networks · Visual importance

1 Introduction

Perception quality of images is a fundamental metric in image-related system. Particularly, it is dominant in the verification and optimization of image encoding [1], transmission [2] and enhancement [3]. Depending on whether the reference image is available or not, objective image quality assessment (IQA) methods fall into three categories: Full-reference IQA (FR-IQA), Reduced-reference IQA (RR-IQA) and No-reference IQA (NR-IQA). FR-IQA directly uses the difference between the distorted and reference images, achieving the most related predict quality toward subjective evaluation. RR-IQA uses part information of reference image, which is widely used in transmission systems. As a challenge, NR-IQA predicts the quality of distorted image without its reference image. Noting that the reference image is hardly available in most applications, NR-IQA methods are thereby preferable.

Supported by National Nature Science Foundation of China (No. 61572058) and National Key R&D Program of China (No. 2017YFB1002702).

C. V. Jawahar et al. (Eds.): ACCV 2018, LNCS 11362, pp. 147–162, 2019.
https://doi.org/10.1007/978-3-030-20890-5_10

Previous NR-IQA methods predict the quality of distorted image with natural scene statistics (NSS) prior. It firstly extracts NSS features from distorted image, and then pools the features with a supported vector regression (SVR). The SVR can efficiently prevent the quality prediction from over-fitting provided that training samples are insufficient. However, the design of NSS features is coarse and time-consuming. Recently, CNNs is introduced into NR-IQA, where the CNNs model is trained as a feature extractor. Compared with previous work, CNNs-based methods directly predict image quality without handcraft features, thus is adequate for real-world applications. However, the prediction accuracy is heavily relied on the training data. Current subjective IQA datasets are far away from being sufficient.

With the aim to maintain the prediction accuracy and generalization of trained IQA model, current CNNs-based NR-IQA methods split the training image into patches for solving the problem of insufficient training data [4], assigning each patch the same quality as the training image for solving the problem of absence of "ground-truth" quality of patches. The patch score assignment strategy, however, is against HVS that local quality of patch does not equal the quality of the training image due to the masking effect of HVS. To solve the problem, [5] firstly proposed an image patch model, measuring the local quality of image patch with FR-IQA metrics. Particularly, a polynomial curve presenting the fitting of local quality against the entire image's subjective score is trained with SSIM and MSE. By fitting the patch local quality with the subjective score of the entire training image, it achieved significant improvement on public IQA datasets. However, the prediction accuracy on images with local distortions is still inadequate.

To address the problem, we propose a novel CNNs-based blind image quality metric with improved patch score (BIQIPS). Firstly, we establish a mapping between the "ground-truth" quality score of patches and the subjective quality score of the entire image. Particularly, we pool the "ground-truth" quality score of patches with both structure features and visual importance information of each pixel. With the image patches and its associated quality score, we train a NR-IQA CNN model with an end-to-end optimization. Experimental results show that our proposed metric achieves state-of-the-art prediction accuracy. Specially, our model works well on local distortions, e.g., quantization noise, non-eccentricity pattern noise, and local block-wise distortions of different intensity. Our contribution can be concluded as:

- A novel strategy to estimate a quality score for each image patch is proposed to incorporate the visual importance of each pixel into Patch-Score Pooling process to enhance the accuracy of the proxy quality score.
- A NR-IQA CNNs model with "ground-truth" image patch score is proposed to overcome the ill-posed problems and significantly improves the prediction and robustness.

2   Related Work

No-reference IQA methods began with distortion-specific quality assessment [6] such as common image blurring and noise, then a large number of studies aimed at eliminating the interference of different types of distortions and finding a unified mechanism similar to human visual system (HVS), gradually transitioned to non-distortion-specific assessment [7] which extracted the relevant features via deep learning or extracted by NSS [8]. In our research, we focus on non-distortion-specific assessment studies.

In earlier studies of NSS-based methods, features were extracted in transformation domains. Moorthy and Bovik extracted features in the wavelet domain [7]. Then Mittal et al. captured NSS features from mean subtracted normalized images [9]. BRISQUE [9] extracted features from the spatial domain, which leads to a significant reduction in computation.

Different from NSS based methods, CORNIA [10] is one of the first purely data-driven NR-IQA methods which directly established the mapping relationship between codebook and image quality by means of k-means clustering. The algorithm used raw-image-patches as local descriptors and soft-assignment coding for encoding, and regressed using SVR for estimating image quality. Similarly to CORNIA, QAF [11] constructs a codebook using spare filter based on image log-Gabor responses.

Recently, with the successful application of convolutional neural networks (CNN) in the field of computer vision and image processing. CNNs-based methods are introduced to the NR-IQA framework by regressing images on the subjective scores without any hand-crafted features. Kang et al. [4] first applied a CNNs model to NR-IQA to train an end-to-end model and achieved performance leaps than classic methods. Wang et al. [12] proposed a CNNs based NR-IQA method which fuses the image quality score from the image patches with the aid of recognized distorted type. Liang et al. [13] proposed an IQA method using dual-path convolutional neural network.

As mentioned in section one, although CNNs-based NR-IQA methods achieved outstanding performances, the problems it brings can't be ignored. A lot of work has been done. Kim et al. [14] proposed a two-stage shared deep model for CNNs-based NR-IQA: First, the model is trained with respect to each patch. The divided image patches are regressed onto the target local metric scores, which are derived from a conventional FR-IQA metric; Second, mean values and the standard deviations of the extracted representative features from patches are regressed to an image quality employing a perception strategy. Bosse et al. [15] proposed a deep neural networks for FR-IQA and NR-IQA which comprises ten convolutional layers and five pooling layers for feature extraction, and two fully connected layers for regression.

3   Framework of BIQIPS

In this section, we introduce our approach for NR-IQA. An overview of our framework is illustrated in Fig. 1. The model contains two steps, i.e., feature extraction and Patch-Score pooling (step 1), CNNs model for NR-IQA (step 2). Step 1: BIQIPS inputs a distorted image and its corresponding reference image, generates the feature map and the weighting map, and then gets the "ground-truth" quality score (Patch-Score) for distorted image patches with the linear function. Step 2: BIQIPS puts distorted image patches into the CNNs model, after processing with CNNs model, features are regressed onto Patch-Score obtained in step 1. Throughout, let I_r be a reference image, I_d be the distorted image, and S_d be the subjective quality score of the distorted image.

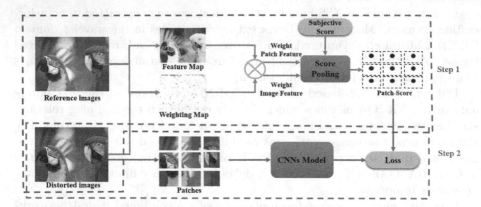

Fig. 1. Overall training process of the BIQIPS.

3.1   Feature Extraction

The relationship between visual saliency (VS) and IQA has been investigated and it is widely accepted that incorporating VS information appropriately can benefit IQA metrics in previous studies. VS has already been used as a weighting function for quality score pooling in [16]. Toward this end, we adopt a improved visual sensitivity map [17] as the weighting function.

Feature Map. The FR-IQA method SSIM [18] is adopted to extract the feature map I_f of the distorted image. SSIM takes full advantage of the reference image and distorted image information, and can reflect the characteristics of distortions.

Weighting Map. Instead of directly using the visual sensitivity map in [17], we makes improvements to it to better fit our model. It achieved low performance on non-structural distortions in [17], where color change is an essential cue of distortion. Hence the distorted images I_d and its corresponding reference images I_r are directly fed into the CNNs without image normalization, the objective error maps are calculated using the raw distorted images and reference images in our framework. This improvement can keep more structure and color information to enhance the accuracy of the proxy quality score for each image patch and stabilize the quality regression process in step 2. Assume the visual sensitivity map has been retrained and regenerated, we use bilinear interpolation to resize it to the size of the original image called weighting map I_v which can reflect the visual importance of each pixel. It is worth noting that despite the difference in preprocessing, the two map are essentially the same, all reflecting the visual importance of distortion.

Feature Fusion. We fuse the feature map and weighting map in the Patch-Score Pooling stage. To be specific, the weighting map can be used as a sort of the importance of the feature I_f of the distorted image pixels and explores implicit ranking relationship within feature map to as a guidance to enhance the accuracy of the proxy quality score in an adaptive manner. We evaluate above discussion in Sect. 4.5. Figure 2 shows examples of feature maps and the corresponding weighting maps.

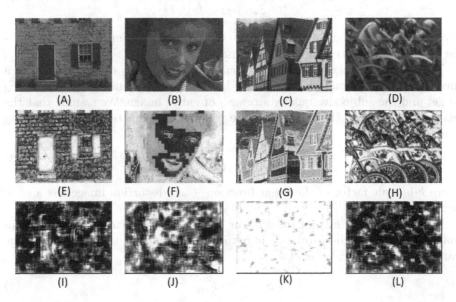

Fig. 2. Examples of the feature maps and weighting maps for each distortion type: (A), (B), (C), and (D) are distorted images with four different distortion types (JP2K, JPEG, WN, GB) in TID2008; (E), (F), (G), and (H) are feature maps generated by SSIM; (I), (G), (K), and (L) are weighting maps.

3.2   Patch-Score Pooling

With the feature map I_f of the distorted image and the corresponding the weighting maps I_v, our goal is to estimate the Patch-Score $\{S_{p1}, .., S_{pN}\}$ for patches $\{P_{d1}, .., P_{dN}\}$ of I_d, where N is the number of patches non-overlapping sampled form one image. S_{pn} is the nth Patch-Score. P_{dn} is the nth patch. All the patches have the same size.

We get the weighted image feature of the entire distorted image adopted the pooling strategy in our methods shares a form as:

$$F_d = \frac{\sum_{(i,j)\in I_r} I_v(i,j) \times I_f(i,j)}{\sum_{(i,j)\in I_r} I_v(i,j)} \tag{1}$$

where F_d is the weighted image feature of the entire image. (i, j) is the pixel coordinates on the image.

Meanwhile, the weighted patch feature of the distorted image patch is derived shares a form as:

$$F_{pn} = \frac{\sum_{(i,j)\in P_{dn}} I_v(i,j) \times I_f(i,j)}{\sum_{(i,j)\in P_{dn}} I_v(i,j)} \tag{2}$$

where F_{pn} is the weighted patch feature of the distorted image patch. (i, j) is the pixel coordinates on the distorted image patch P_{dn}.

The weighted image feature can reflect the image quality directly, so we use a linear function f to map the consistency between the weighted image feature F_d we get and the subjective quality score S_d of entire image. We assume that the relationship between the two is a simple proportional function in the following form,

$$f(F_d) = k \cdot F_d$$
$$s.t.\ f(F_d) = S_d \tag{3}$$

where k is scale factor of the linear function, each distortion image has a scale factor.

Finally, with the help of scale factor k, the "ground-truth" image score of image patches (Patch-Score) S_{pn} is obtained to multiply the weighted image feature F_{pn} by the scale factor k:

$$S_{pn} = k \cdot F_{pn} \tag{4}$$

Noting that the perceptive quality of all patches sampled from one image is different for HVS, so the Patch-Score of distorted image patches are distributed around the subjective quality score of the corresponding distorted image as shown in Fig. 3.

3.3   CNNs Model for NR-IQA

We present deep CNNs model for our BIQIPS. For an input distorted image, we split it up to N patches without overlaps. In the training stage, the patches are put into the CNNs model, after processing with CNNs model, features are regressed onto Patch-Score obtained in step 1; In the testing stage, the CNNs model predicts quality score for each small patch, the final quality score of the input image is the average sum of the quality score of small patches. The architecture of our proposed CNNs model is illustrated in Fig. 4. Our model is comprised

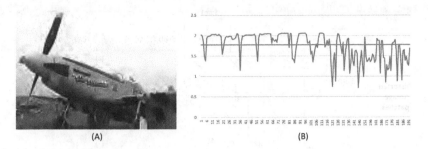

(A)   (B)

Fig. 3. (A) is a distorted image with JPEG2000 compression. (B) is the "ground-truth" quality score distribution map of distorted image patches, where the orange line represent the subjective quality score of (A), the blue line represent the "ground-truth" quality score of patches sampled from (A). (Color figure online)

of four convolutional layers which all adopt a rectified linear unit (Relu) [19], a sum layer, a max pooling layer and then followed by two fully connected layers.

(1) **Architecture:** First, convolutional networks with filter size of 5×5 and 3×3 are used to continuously extract different receptive field local features inspired by the recent work [20]. Each convolutional layer takes ReLU as a activation function instead of traditional sigmoid or tanh activation function. In order to optimize the back propagation better and effective converge, we mimic the deep residual network [21], including a sum layer which adds the outputs of the *Conv2* and *Conv3* convolutional layers. The padding of *Conv3* is set to 1 to ensure that the dimensions of the output feature maps remain unchanged. Then the feature maps processed by the sum layer are sent to the pooling layer. Combining with max-pooling layer, we can effectively reduce feature maps into manageable size while maintaining the features rotation, translation, scaling invariance. At the end of the model, two fully connected layers are used to regress features onto the subjective score of patches: Patch-Score. Relu is used for the first fully-connected layer. Meanwhile, we apply the dropout to reduce the time consumption and prevent overfitting in training stage which are applied to the fully-connected layer *FC1*.

Finally, the objective function which aims at minimizing the Euclidean loss is defined as

$$\min_{\theta} \| (f(P_{dn}, \theta) - S_{pn} \|^2 \tag{5}$$

where P_{dn} and S_{pn} denote the input distorted image patch and Patch-Score respectively. $f(P_{dn}, \theta)$ is the predicted score of P_{dn} with CNN model weights θ.

(2) **Preprocessing:** Although luminance and contrast change can be considered distortions in some applications, we think they belong to the category of data enhancement, not considered in the type of image distortion. So similar to [4], we employ a simple local contrast normalization method in which mean subtraction and divisive normalization are processed before the image patches are fed to the CNN model. It helps optimization reach the global minima much

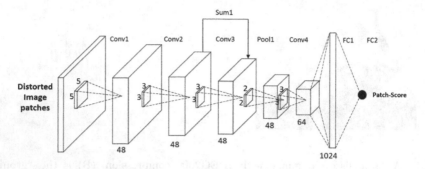

Fig. 4. The CNN network architecture of BIQIPS in step 2.

faster. Suppose the intensity value of a pixel at location (i,j) is $I(i,j)$, the normalized value $\bar{I}(i,j)$ is derived as follows:

$$\bar{I}(i,j) = \frac{I(x,y) - u(x,y)}{\sigma(x,y) + \epsilon}$$

$$u(x,y) = \sum_{a=\frac{-W}{2}}^{a=\frac{W}{2}} \sum_{b=\frac{-H}{2}}^{b=\frac{H}{2}} (I(x+a,y+b))$$

$$\sigma(x,y) = \sqrt{\sum_{a=\frac{-W}{2}}^{a=\frac{W}{2}} \sum_{b=\frac{-H}{2}}^{b=\frac{H}{2}} (I(x+a,y+b) - u(x,y))^2}$$

(6)

where ϵ is a small positive constant that prevents dividing by zero. W and H are the normalization window sizes.

(3) **Training and Testing:** The stochastic gradient decent (SGD) with the standard backpropagation is used in Eq. (5) to minimize the loss between predicted score and Patch-Score. The learning rate is initially set to 0.01. Then it is changed to 1/10 of the previous one every ten epochs. After reaches 0.00001, it becomes a fixed value. Momentum factor and weight decay are fixed in 0.9 and 0.0005 respectively in CNNs model training. We perform SGD until convergence when training and save the model parameters that generate the highest performance on the testing set.

4 Experiment and Analysis

In this section, we report a series of experiments to validate the effectiveness of the proposed model. We apply the deep learning toolbox Caffe [22] to build the CNNs model for step 2 of BIQIPS. The experiment results are demonstrated in the following subsections.

4.1 Datasets

Dataset used for experiments are two:

LIVE Database [23]: A total of 779 distorted images with five different distortions: JP2k compression (JP2K), JPEG compression (JPEG), White Noise (WN), Gaussian blur (BLUR) and Fast Fading (FF) at 7–8 degradation levels derived from 29 reference images. The differential Mean Opinion Score (DMOS) for each distorted image is provided. The DMOS ranges from [0, 100] where higher values indicate lower quality.

TID2008 Database [24]: 25 reference images and 1700 distorted images with 17 different distortions at four degradation levels. Each image is associated with a Mean Opinion Score (MOS) in the range [0, 9]. Higher MOS indicates higher quality. In our experiment, the last two distortion types (Mean shift (intensity shift), Contrast change) are not included because of data preprocessing in step 2 and being part of the data enhancement.

In order to ensure the consistency and rigidity of the experiment, we rescale the ground-truth subjective score to the range [0, 1].

4.2 Evaluation Settings

To evaluate the performances of the proposed IQA metric, two correlation criterions are applied in our experiment, i.e., Spearman's rank order correlation coefficient (SROCC) and Pearson's linear correlation coefficient (PLCC). SROCC measures how well one quantity can be described as a monotonic function of another quantity, and PLCC measures the linear dependence between two quantities.

Table 1. SROCC comparison on the LIVE IQA database

	Metrics	JP2K	JPEG	WN	BLUR	FF	**ALL**
FR-IQA	PSNR	0.895	0.881	0.985	0.782	0.891	0.876
	SSIM [18]	0.961	0.972	0.969	0.952	0.956	0.948
	FSIM [25]	0.970	0.981	0.967	0.972	0.949	0.964
NR-IQA	BRISQUE [9]	0.914	0.965	0.979	0.951	0.877	0.940
	NIQE [26]	0.917	0.938	0.967	0.934	0.859	0.914
	CNN [4]	0.952	0.977	0.978	0.962	0.908	0.956
	BIECON [14]	0.952	0.974	0.980	0.956	0.923	0.961
	H-IQA [27]	**0.983**	0.961	**0.984**	**0.983**	**0.989**	**0.982**
	Ours	0.960	**0.981**	0.975	0.951	0.943	<u>0.973</u>

4.3   Performances

To validate our approach, we conduct extensive evaluations, where three state-of-the art FR-IQA methods and eight state-of-the-art NR-IQA methods are compared. Experiment conditions may be different from other NR-IQA methods since the proportion of training data is different. Because they iterate train-test process up to many times, the experiment results are convincing. It is fair to compare our method with other no-reference IQA methods. What's more, we randomly divide the reference images into two subsets (80% for training, 20% for testing), and their corresponding distorted images are separated in the same way so that there is no overlap between the two subsets. The CNNs model is trained in a non-distortion-specific way which means all the distortion types are used at the same time. In order to choose the best model, the model with the lowest validation error is chosen over 80 epochs. To eliminate the bias due to division of the data, the correlation coefficients are averaged after the process was repeated 20 trials. We trained our network on non-overlapping patches at stride 32 in step 2. For each trial, the image datasets are randomly selected as described above. The top model for each evaluation criterion is shown in boldface. In addition, BIQIPS are conducted through the two steps, as described in Sect. 3.

Table 2. PLCC comparison on the LIVE IQA database

	Metrics	JP2K	JPEG	WN	BLUR	FF	ALL
FR-IQA	PSNR	0.876	0.903	0.917	0.780	0.880	0.856
	SSIM [18]	0.941	0.946	0.982	0.900	0.951	0.906
	FSIM	0.910	0.985	0.976	0.978	0.912	0.960
NR-IQA	BRISQUE [9]	0.922	0.973	0.985	0.951	0.903	0.942
	NIQE [26]	0.937	0.956	0.977	0.952	0.913	0.915
	CNN [4]	0.953	0.981	0.984	0.953	0.933	0.953
	BIECON [14]	0.965	0.987	0.970	0.945	0.931	0.962
	H-IQA [27]	**0.977**	0.984	**0.993**	**0.990**	**0.960**	**0.982**
	Ours	0.966	**0.988**	0.977	0.951	0.945	<u>0.969</u>

Evaluation on LIVE. The SROCC and PLCC of NR-IQA metrics on the LIVE IQA dataset are compared according to the distortion type in Tables 1 and 2. Our method outperforms previous state-of-the-art FR-IQA methods and achieves about 1% better than BIECON, and the accuracy is slightly lower than the accuracy of H-IQA [27]. This does not mean that our method performance is poor. In fact as the accuracy of the prediction gets higher and even approaches 100%, the performance improvement has no practical significance, but it faces the risk of over-fitting. In Sect. 4.2, the cross dataset test fully demonstrates that our model has excellent practice generalization ability. Thus, our method still achieves well performances.

Evaluation on TID2008. Table 3 shows the SROCC on the TID2008 database which takes more distortion types into account. Among all IQA metrics, our method significantly outperforms previous methods by a large margin and improves the performance on most of the distortion types, especially on the types of local distortions. Specifically, the significant improvements on distortion types like #14 (non-eccentricity pattern noise) and #15 (local block-wise distortions of different intensity) quantitatively demonstrate the effectiveness of our Patch-Score pooling mechanism. Our method achieves 2% improvements than CNN-IPM, 10% SROCC improvements than RankIQA, and 15% SROCC improvements than HOSA. These observation demonstrate that our method significantly improves the prediction and robustness.

Table 3. SROCC comparison on the TID2008 IQA database

Methods	#1	#2	#3	#4	#5	#6	#7	#8	#9
BRISQUE [9]	0.886	**0.887**	0.819	0.794	0.932	**0.931**	0.799	0.783	0.677
CNN [4]	0.79	0.744	0.767	0.851	0.882	0.827	0.7	0.899	**0.919**
CNN-IPM [5]	0.908	0.876	0.915	**0.867**	0.928	0.89	0.842	0.945	0.867
RankIQA [28]	0.891	0.785	0.914	0.63	0.851	0.88	**0.91**	0.835	0.894
HOSA [29]	0.854	0.63	0.792	0.356	0.908	0.765	0.834	0.882	0.86
Ours	**0.914**	0.883	**0.92**	0.865	**0.931**	0.912	0.901	**0.953**	0.89
Methods	#10	#11	#12	#13	#14	#15	ALL		
BRISQUE [9]	0.842	0.832	0.44	0.827	−0.003	0.4565	0.618		
CNN [4]	0.908	0.93	0.839	0.808	0.513	0.718	0.621		
CNN-IPM [5]	**0.939**	0.92	0.837	0.805	0.736	0.752	<u>0.861</u>		
RankIQA [28]	0.826	0.898	0.704	0.81	0.532	0.612	0.785		
HOSA [29]	0.893	0.942	0.747	0.701	0.199	0.327	0.743		
Ours	0.938	**0.948**	**0.84**	**0.834**	**0.807**	**0.812**	**0.886**		

4.4   Predicted Local Score Visualization

To show the result of the BIQIPS visually, we test the ability to predict local quality of the proposed method. With the trained model, BIQIPS can predict the local quality score without using reference images. We predicted the local quality score map for patches which sampled in the size 32×32 at a stride 16, and normalize the predicted scores into the range [0, 255] to form a quality score map for visualization. In Fig. 5, the darker the block is, the worse the quality is. Each col shows each distortion type, i.e., JP2K, JPEG, WN, GB, which is the most serious degree of distortion in TID2008.

As we can see from the picture, the prediction of local quality score can accurately reflect the distorted position of the image and the results generally conform the HVS.

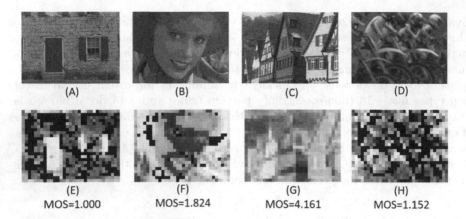

Fig. 5. Examples of predicted local quality score maps for each distortion type: (A), (B), (C), and (D) are distorted images with four different distortion types (JP2K, JPEG, WN, GB) in TID2008; (E), (F), (G), and (H) are predicted local quality score maps obtained by BIQIPS.

4.5 Effect of Visual Importance

To illustrate the important role of weighting in our method, the validation experiment is conducted. Table 4 shows the results about the performance on the three local distortions (QN, NEPN, LBD) and the overall with four Patch-Score pooling options. BIQIPS (without SSIM and weight) means that each patch is assigned a quality score as its source image's ground truth score, BIQIPS (with SSIM) don't apply the weighting map as the weight function, BIQIPS (with SSIM and sensitivity) directly apply the visual sensitivity map [17] as the weight function, BIQIPS (with SSIM and weight) is the method we described in Sect. 3, and then patches with Patch-Score obtained by the four options are sent to the CNNs model for training respectively.

It can be see from the table that the weighting map has a significant improvement on the performance gain. It shows that NEON ($\langle$gain$\rangle = 19.5\%$) profits most from adding feature maps and visual importance information, followed by QN ($\langle$gain$\rangle = 17\%$), and LBS ($\langle$gain$\rangle = 10.3\%$). This also proves that the weighting map is more suitable for our model than the sensitivity map.

Table 4. SROCC comparison with four Patch-Score pooling options on the TID2008 IQA database

Metrics	QN	NEPN	LBD	Overall
BIQIPS (without SSIM and weight)	0.731	0.612	0.709	0.753
BIQIPS (with SSIM)	0.840	0.730	0.748	0.855
BIQIPS (with SSIM and sensitivity)	0.850	0.745	0.762	0.860
BIQIPS (with SSIM and weight)	**0.901**	**0.807**	**0.812**	**0.885**

To have a visual understanding, Fig. 6 shows the predicted local quality visualization for two types of distortions (QN and NEPN). As we can see from the picture, the FR-IQA method SSIM focuses on the structural distortion mainly, while QN, NEPN, and LBD belong to the non-structural distortion. When SSIM is applied to extract the feature between the reference and distorted images, it just detects the pixel domain differences. Adding visual importance happens to circumvent such confusion by reducing the feature importance of non-interested area, and such improve the overall prediction performance of the BIQIPS.

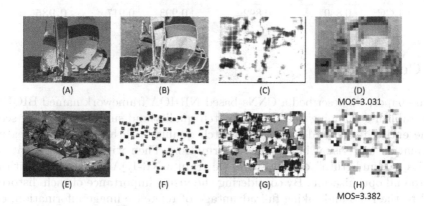

Fig. 6. Examples of predicted local quality score maps for two types of local distortions: (A) and (E)are distorted images with QN and NEPN in TID 2008; (B) and (F) are feature maps generated by SSIM; (C) and (G) are weighting maps; (D) and (H) are predicted local quality score maps obtained by BIQIPS;

4.6   Cross Dataset Test

To evaluate the generalization ability of BIQIPS, we trained the BIQIPS using the LIVE IQA datasets, and tested on the TID2008 datasets. Since the TID2008 datasets contains more distortion types, only the four types distortions, i.e., JPEG, JPEG2000 compression, WN, and BLUR that are shared by LIVE and TID2008 datasets are experimented. The DMOS scores in LIVE range from 0 to 100, while the MOS scores in TID2008 fall in the range 0 and 9. In order to ensure the consistency of the experiment, we perform a nonlinear mapping on the predicted scores produced by the model trained on LIVE. A nonlinear mapping based on a logistic regression is used to match the predicted DMOS and MOS to evaluate SROCC. We randomly divide the TID2008 into two parts of 80% and 20% 100 times in the same way as the method [4]. Each time 80% of data is used for estimating parameters of the logistic function and 20% is used for testing.

The results of the cross-dataset test are shown in Table 5. We compare performance of our method with four state-of-the-art no-reference IQA methods, where H-IQA [27] takes advantage of adversarial learning. As we can see, although the accuracy of H-IQA [27] on the LIVE database is higher than our method, our method achieves the best generalization ability. This also reflects the accuracy of our method from another aspect.

Table 5. SROCC and PLCC comparison of the models trained using LIVE IQA datasets and tested on the TID2008 datasets

Metrics	CORNIA [10]	BRISQUE [9]	CNN [4]	H-IQA [27]	Ours
SROCC	0.890	0.882	0.920	0.934	**0.951**
LCC	0.880	0.892	0.903	0.917	**0.935**

5   Conclusions

In this paper, we described a CNNs-based NR-IQA framework named BIQIPS. We establish a mapping between the patch quality and subjective quality score of the entire image, and present the patch quality with both structure feature information and visual importance information. Then with the image patches and its "ground-truth" quality score, we train a NR-IQA CNN model with an end-to-end optimization. By considering the visual importance of each distorted pixel to the HVS and taking full advantage of reference image information, our algorithm predicts image quality well correlated with human perception, and achieves state-of-the-art performance and demonstrates the best generalization ability on NR-IQA.

References

1. Wu, H.R., Rao, K.R.: Digital Video Image Quality and Perceptual Coding. CRC Press, Boca Raton (2017)
2. Ahmad, R., Halsall, F., Zhang, J.S.: The transmission of compressed video over ATM networks. In: Teletraffic Symposium, 11th Performance Engineering in Telecommunications Networks, pp. 1–20. IEE Eleventh UK, IET (1994)
3. Nakayama, Y., et al.: Abdominal CT with low tube voltage: preliminary observations about radiation dose, contrast enhancement, image quality, and noise. Radiology **237**, 945–951 (2005)
4. Kang, L., Ye, P., Li, Y., Doermann, D.: Convolutional neural networks for no-reference image quality assessment. In: Proceedings of the IEEE Conference on Computer Vision and Pattern Recognition, pp. 1733–1740 (2014)
5. Heng, W., Jiang, T.: From image quality to patch quality: an image-patch model for no-reference image quality assessment. In: 2017 IEEE International Conference on Acoustics, Speech and Signal Processing (ICASSP), pp. 1238–1242. IEEE (2017)
6. Narvekar, N.D., Karam, L.J.: A no-reference perceptual image sharpness metric based on a cumulative probability of blur detection. In: 2009 International Workshop on Quality of Multimedia Experience, QoMEx 2009, pp. 87–91. IEEE (2009)
7. Moorthy, A.K., Bovik, A.C.: A two-step framework for constructing blind image quality indices. IEEE Signal Process. Lett. **17**, 513–516 (2010)

8. Chandler, D.M.: Seven challenges in image quality assessment: past, present, and future research. ISRN Signal Process. **2013**, 53 (2013)
9. Mittal, A., Moorthy, A.K., Bovik, A.C.: No-reference image quality assessment in the spatial domain. IEEE Trans. Image Process. **21**, 4695–4708 (2012)
10. Ye, P., Kumar, J., Kang, L., Doermann, D.: Unsupervised feature learning framework for no-reference image quality assessment. In: 2012 IEEE Conference on Computer Vision and Pattern Recognition (CVPR), pp. 1098–1105. IEEE (2012)
11. Zhang, L., Gu, Z., Liu, X., Li, H., Lu, J.: Training quality-aware filters for no-reference image quality assessment. IEEE Multimedia **21**, 67–75 (2014)
12. Wang, H., Zuo, L., Fu, J.: Distortion recognition for image quality assessment with convolutional neural network. In: 2016 IEEE International Conference on Multimedia and Expo (ICME), pp. 1–6. IEEE (2016)
13. Liang, Y., Wang, J., Wan, X., Gong, Y., Zheng, N.: Image quality assessment using similar scene as reference. In: Leibe, B., Matas, J., Sebe, N., Welling, M. (eds.) ECCV 2016. LNCS, vol. 9909, pp. 3–18. Springer, Cham (2016). https://doi.org/10.1007/978-3-319-46454-1_1
14. Kim, J., Lee, S.: Fully deep blind image quality predictor. IEEE J. Sel. Top. Signal Process. **11**, 206–220 (2017)
15. Bosse, S., Maniry, D., Müller, K.R., Wiegand, T., Samek, W.: Deep neural networks for no-reference and full-reference image quality assessment. IEEE Trans. Image Process. **27**, 206–219 (2018)
16. Zhang, L., Shen, Y., Li, H.: VSI: a visual saliency-induced index for perceptual image quality assessment. IEEE Trans. Image Process. **23**, 4270–4281 (2014)
17. Kim, J., Lee, S.: Deep learning of human visual sensitivity in image quality assessment framework. In: Proceedings of the IEEE Conference on Computer Vision and Pattern Recognition (CVPR) (2017)
18. Wang, Z., Bovik, A.C., Sheikh, H.R., Simoncelli, E.P.: Image quality assessment: from error visibility to structural similarity. IEEE Trans. Image Process. **13**, 600–612 (2004)
19. Nair, V., Hinton, G.E.: Rectified linear units improve restricted Boltzmann machines. In: Proceedings of the 27th International Conference on Machine Learning (ICML 2010), pp. 807–814 (2010)
20. Simonyan, K., Zisserman, A.: Very deep convolutional networks for large-scale image recognition. arXiv preprint arXiv:1409.1556 (2014)
21. He, K., Zhang, X., Ren, S., Sun, J.: Deep residual learning for image recognition. In: Proceedings of the IEEE Conference on Computer Vision and Pattern Recognition, pp. 770–778 (2016)
22. Jia, Y., et al.: Caffe: convolutional architecture for fast feature embedding. In: Proceedings of the 22nd ACM international conference on Multimedia, pp. 675–678. ACM (2014)
23. Sheikh, H.R., Wang, Z., Cormack, L., Bovik, A.C.: Live image quality assessment database release 2 (2005, 2016)
24. Ponomarenko, N., Lukin, V., Zelensky, A., Egiazarian, K., Carli, M., Battisti, F.: Tid 2008-a database for evaluation of full-reference visual quality assessment metrics. Adv. Mod. Radioelectron. **10**, 30–45 (2009)
25. Zhang, L., Zhang, L., Mou, X., Zhang, D.: Fsim: A feature similarity index for image quality assessment. IEEE Trans. Image Process. **20**, 2378–2386 (2011)
26. Mittal, A., Soundararajan, R., Bovik, A.C.: Making a completely blind image quality analyzer. IEEE Signal Process. Lett. **20**, 209–212 (2013)

27. Lin, K.Y., Wang, G.: Hallucinated-IQA: no-reference image quality assessment via adversarial learning. In: Proceedings of the IEEE Conference on Computer Vision and Pattern Recognition, pp. 732–741 (2018)
28. Liu, X., van de Weijer, J., Bagdanov, A.D.: RankIQA: learning from rankings for no-reference image quality assessment. Computer Vision and Pattern Recognition, https://arxiv.org/abs/1707.08347v1 (2017)
29. Xu, J., Ye, P., Li, Q., Du, H., Liu, Y., Doermann, D.: Blind image quality assessment based on high order statistics aggregation. IEEE Trans. Image Process. **25**, 4444–4457 (2016)

Robust Video Background Identification
by Dominant Rigid Motion Estimation

Kaimo Lin[1(✉)], Nianjuan Jiang[2], Loong Fah Cheong[1], Jiangbo Lu[2],
and Xun Xu[1]

[1] National University of Singapore, Singapore, Singapore
linkaimo1990@gmail.com, eleclf@nus.edu.sg, alex.xun.xu@gmail.com
[2] Shenzhen Cloudream Technology, Dalian, China
{jiangnj,jiangbo}@cloudream.com

Abstract. The ability to identify the static background in videos captured by a moving camera is an important pre-requisite for many video applications (e.g. video stabilization, stitching, and segmentation). Existing methods usually face difficulties when the foreground objects occupy a larger area than the background in the image. Many methods also cannot scale up to handle densely sampled feature trajectories. In this paper, we propose an efficient local-to-global method to identify background, based on the assumption that as long as there is sufficient camera motion, the cumulative background features will have the largest amount of trajectories. Our motion model at the two-frame level is based on the epipolar geometry so that there will be no over-segmentation problem, another issue that plagues the 2D motion segmentation approach. Foreground objects erroneously labelled due to intermittent motions are also taken care of by checking their global consistency with the final estimated background motion. Lastly, by virtue of its efficiency, our method can deal with densely sampled trajectories. It outperforms several state-of-the-art motion segmentation methods on public datasets, both quantitatively and qualitatively.

1 Introduction

Identifying background features from an image sequence is an important vision task, subserving many other applications such as video stabilization, 3D scene reconstruction, background color model estimation for video segmentation, etc. When the camera is stationary, this task is considerably simplified. In this paper, we focus on the difficult scenarios when the camera is moving and that the foreground might occupy an image area larger than the background. Our objective is to identify those static parts of the background (hence forth to be called just background, unless otherwise specified) even though they may only occupy a small part of the scene in some frames.

This work was supported by the Singapore PSF grant 1521200082, and partly done when Kaimo, Nianjuan and Jiangbo were with Advanced Digital Sciences Center (ADSC), Singapore.

RANSAC is the prevailing method for finding background features across two frames, when the assumption that the vast majority of the feature matches belong to that of the background is true. For videos with large moving foreground, it is evident that this simple strategy will fail [13,14]. A recent method [3] utilizes segmentation from the previous frames to help resolve difficulties experienced in subsequent parts of the video. This propagation strategy may relieve but not remove the aforementioned problems entirely. For instance, it depends on the quality of the previous segmentation: foreground motions that are intermittent, i.e., stationary at irregular intervals, may be accidentally labelled as background, and this wrong label is in turn erroneously propagated to later frames. Trajectory-based motion segmentation methods consider the entire trajectories across all the frames, and generally do not suffer from this kind of error propagation. Among this class of approaches, the 3D motion segmentation methods [12,15,28] are usually computationally too expensive to process densely sampled feature trajectories. 2D motion segmentation methods [9,18] may be fast but produce over-segmented results when the background features exhibit large depth variation.

In this paper, we address the background identification problem based on two observations that we believe to be true most of the times. Firstly, the background should be visible in every frame, even though it may not occupy the largest area in these frames. Secondly, as long as there is enough camera motion such that there is enough turnover of the background features, i.e., enough new background features enter into the field of view, collecting all these background features together will usually make them the group with the largest number of feature trajectories. Therefore, the background identification problem becomes that of linking the new features into their proper groups as they enter into view. This is done via some features that are visible in both the old and the new frames, but of the details, more later. While there might also be turnover of the foreground objects, they usually cannot be linked together as one group.

Since we assume that there is enough camera motion, most trajectories will not be visible throughout the entire duration. Thus we divide the video into multiple short overlapping clips (Fig. 1(a)) and from the many potential background motion groups identified from the short clips (Fig. 1(b)), we attempt to link these groups and then identify the linked group that is globally the most dominant, i.e., largest. For the linking step, we construct a directed graph with the local motion candidates being the nodes, and two nodes from neighboring video clips are connected by an edge if they share common trajectories, with the weight of the edge being related to the size of the groups involved. Then we search through all the possible motion paths (Fig. 1(c)) that traverse from the first video clip to the last one. The optimal motion path is the one that covers the largest amount of feature trajectories, and thus corresponds to the desired background motion. Finally, to deal with foreground objects with intermittent motions and thus being labelled wrongly as background during the frames when they are not moving, we enforce global consistency in the trajectory labeling to rectify the errors (Fig. 1(d)).

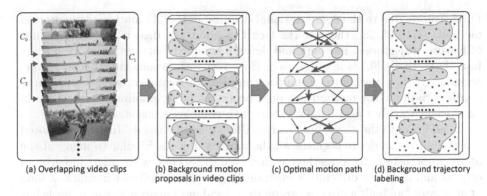

(a) Overlapping video clips   (b) Background motion proposals in video clips   (c) Optimal motion path   (d) Background trajectory labeling

Fig. 1. Pipeline of our background feature identification method. (a) Divide sequence into multiple overlapping clips $\{C_i\}$ Red points in (b) and (d) are feature trajectories in video clips. Red arrows in (c) is the global dominant rigid motion that contains the largest amount of feature trajectories. (Color figure online)

To describe the motions in the local clips, we use a set of epipolar geometries (**EG**) computed from neighboring video frames. Therefore, our method can effectively handle videos with large depth variation. Our method is much simpler compared to the existing motion segmentation techniques, since we are only concerned with the background motion and treat all other motions as foreground motions. Our motion estimation method is very fast, and the whole pipeline can run very efficiently even with densely sampled trajectories.

2   Related Work

While the aim of video object segmentation is to segment out the foreground objects from a video sequence, this approach can indeed be used to perform background extraction. However, many of these works require some degree of human intervention, such as the semi-supervised methods [1,8,16,21,22,26] which require a small amount of manual annotation, and the fully-supervised methods [2,6,31] which require repeating result correction by the user. Our work is completely autonomous, like the unsupervised methods of video object segmentation [5,10,11,19,24,27,29]. However, the underlying assumption of our work is less brittle compared to those subscribed to by these works. For instance, [10,29] rely on the ability of object proposals to detect the foreground objects; this might fail to work when the foreground objects have complex non-compact shapes. [19,27] detect foreground objects by analysing the 2D motion field based on a simple assumption that they usually move differently from their surroundings. However, the 2D motions of some background objects may also have this property if the background has large depth variation.

Trajectory-based motion segmentation methods usually produce multiple independent motion groups; however, they usually stop short of actually identifying the background motion, or just use a simple background metric such as size.

Furthermore, due to the computational demand of the 3D motion segmentation methods [4,12,25,28], these works lack the ability to deal with large amount of feature trajectories. For long and densely sampled feature trajectories, some fast 2D methods [9,18] may be used. However, their results may become over-segmented when the figure-ground is complex, for instance, scenes with large depth variation. Our method not only processes large amount of trajectory in an efficient way, but also handle videos with complex scene structures.

In addition to the above approaches, Bideau and Learned-Miller [3] proposed a probabilistic model to segment all the moving objects. Similar to many of the above approaches, their method cannot handle scenes with large foreground objects and may face difficulties when dealing with intermittent motions. Zhang *et al.*'s work [30] built a directed graph from local motion groups; this approach is closely related to ours. Our method is different from theirs in two aspects. Most importantly, we identify the background motion as the one with the largest amount of feature trajectories in the aggregate, while their method is based on the conjecture that the background trajectory matrix should exhibit a lower rank. This assumption is a serious qualification: it will not work if the foreground motions are also rigid. Another difference is that our method tries to find as many rigid motions as possible in each video clip, instead of committing to a clean segmentation for all the feature trajectories based on traditional motion segmentation methods. This allows us to recover from errors that might arise at the local clip levels.

3   Algorithm Overview

Given a dynamic video with large foreground objects, we first extract feature trajectories $\{T_0, ..., T_i\}$ using the method [23]. We followed the instruction from [23] and used the author's codes to generate the feature trajectories. Trajectories are extracted at a fixed interval in both horizontal and vertical directions. Our algorithm takes these trajectories as input and outputs those belong to the static background by estimating the dominant rigid motion in the video. The system pipeline is shown in Fig. 1.

The system first divides the input video into many short overlapping video clips of variable lengths, i.e., $\{C_0, ..., C_i\}$ (Fig. 1(a)). Inside each video clip C_i, we propose multiple motion candidates $\{M_i^0, ..., M_i^m\}$, which contain different sizes of trajectory groups (Fig. 1(b)). Each M_i^m represents a rigid motion inside C_i. The global background motion for the entire video is a collection of the background motions in these video clips, i.e., select one M_i^m for each C_i.

Since the background motions inside the video clips may not always be the majority one with the presence of large foreground objects, we identify it using a graph search method in a global manner (Fig. 1(c)). Specifically, we construct a directed graph with M_i^m in each C_i as graph nodes. Directed edges are only created from nodes in C_i to those in C_{i+1} with shared trajectories. Among all the possible motion paths that start from the very first clip to the last one, we select the one that contains the largest amount of feature trajectories as our global background motion.

For objects with intermittent motions, i.e. they may be static in some video clips, their motions in those clips may be wrongly labeled as background. Therefore, we further perform a temporal consistency check and background motion refinement to rectify those wrongly labeled trajectories (Fig. 1(d)).

4   Motion Estimation in Video Clips

Given a clip C with time window W, we divide the feature trajectories into three categories, i.e., $\{T_i^t\}_W$. The indicator t is set according to the following rules.

$$t = \begin{cases} 1, & T_i \text{ is always visible within } W \text{ (e.g., } T_5 \text{ and } T_{13} \text{ in Fig. 2)} \\ 0, & T_i \text{ is partially visible within } W \text{ (e.g., } T_{25} \text{ in Fig. 2)} \\ -1, & T_i \text{ is invisible within } W \end{cases} \tag{1}$$

The indicator t of a trajectory T_i is set to 1 if the trajectory lives throughout the entire time window (we call them full-length trajectories inside the time window), otherwise, it is set to 0 or -1. This labeling of feature trajectories will be used to facilitate dividing the input video into overlapping video clips.

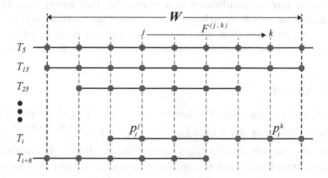

Fig. 2. Motion model defined by a set of feature trajectories inside a clip C with time window W. Red points are tracked features on each trajectory. (Color figure online)

4.1   Video Clips Generation

Starting from the first video frame, we keep adding new frames to expand the time window W_0 of the first video clip C_0 as long as the number of the full-length feature trajectories inside C_0, i.e. $\{T_i^t\}_{C_0}^{t=1}$, is more than 80% of all the visible trajectories inside it, as define below,

$$\frac{|\{T_i^t\}_{C_0}^{t=1}|}{|\{T_i^t\}_{C_0}^{t=1}| + |\{T_i^t\}_{C_0}^{t=0}|} \geq 0.8 \tag{2}$$

The next video clip C_1 starts from the middle frame of C_0 and expands in the same way. We repeat this process until the end of the video sequence is reached.

We experimentally set the 80% ratio here to achieve a balance between enough camera movement within a clip and adequate trajectory overlap with the next video clip. As a result, long video clips will be generated when the camera movement is small. This ensures that even under small camera movement, there will always be enough motion cues within a particular clip for robust motion estimation.

Fig. 3. Examples of motion candidates in a video clip. Full-length trajectories inside the green rectangles are used to estimate the best-fitting motion models. Red points represent feature trajectories that are labeled as members of the motion candidates, while blue points are non-member feature trajectories. (Color figure online)

4.2   Motion Model

In our method, a rigid motion M defined by a set of trajectories $\{T_i^t\}_C^{t=0,1}$ is represented by a series of fundamental matrices $\{F^{(j,k)}\}_C^{0<|j-k|\le r}$, where j, k are the video frame indices inside clip C (see Fig. 2). Here, r is empirically set to five as the feature tracking error is usually acceptable within this range for good fundamental matrix estimation. We estimate the fundamental matrix $F^{(j,k)}$ by applying the 8-point algorithm [7] on the feature matches extracted from these trajectories that are both visible at frames j and k.

To decide if a trajectory T_i belongs to a known rigid motion $\left\{F^{(j,k)}\right\}_C^{0<|j-k|\le r}$, we compute its geometric errors based on the point-to-epipolar-line distance. Specifically, for each $F^{(j,k)}$, if T_i is both visible at frames j and k, we extract a feature match (p_i^j, p_i^k) from it (see Fig. 2) and compute its geometric error with respect to $F^{(j,k)}$ as follows:

$$g(p_i^j, p_i^k, F^{(j,k)}) = d(p_i^k, F^{(j,k)} p_i^j), \tag{3}$$

where p_i^j and p_i^k are all homogeneous coordinates and d denotes the Euclidean point-to-line distance. If the error is smaller than a threshold ε_f ($\varepsilon_f = 1.5$ in our implementation), we mark this feature match as a positive match. If more than 90% of the tested feature matches from T_i are marked as positive, we label T_i as a member of the rigid motion.

4.3   Motion Estimation in Video Clips

Knowing that the background features may not constitute the majority in a video clip, we cannot hypothesize the background motion in the regular RANSAC fashion, i.e. randomly select eight full-length trajectories in RANSAC iterations. Instead, we adopt a local scanning scheme to effectively detect multiple motion candidates inside each clip.

For each video clip C_i, we first divide the starting frame of C_i into overlapping cells, e.g. 30% overlap with a uniform size $L \times L$. For each cell, we collect the full-length trajectories inside it, and estimate a best-fitting motion in the regular RANSAC fashion. Specifically, in each RANSAC iteration, we randomly select eight full-length trajectories to compute a motion as described in Sect. 4.2. Then, we label the rest of the full-length trajectories inside the cell and count the inliers. If the inliers of the final best-fitting motion exceeds 80% of all the full-length trajectories within that cell, we regard the estimated motion M_i^m as a plausible background motion candidate for C_i. Otherwise, it is discard. Note that we only use full-length trajectories here to ensure that we can compute a motion with a minimum eight trajectories.

After the RANSAC model fitting for all the single cells, we obtain a set of motion candidates $\{M_i^m\}$. Since the background region may consist of several discrete parts across the image domain due to the large dynamic foreground motions and the estimated motions from single cells can be locally biased, we also perform the model fitting process on combinations of the single cells that yield $\{M_i^m\}$. In our experiments, we find that combinations of up to three single cells are usually sufficient for robust background motion estimation. Eventually, successful motions from these combined cells together with those from the single cells form the final motion candidate set for C_i.

These motion candidates are estimated using full-length trajectories inside local cells. We still need to decide the membership of other trajectories inside the clip with respect to each of motion candidates. Figure 3 shows some labeling results of the motion candidates. As we can see, unlike traditional motion segmentation methods that perform a clean segmentation of the trajectories and assign a unique label to each T_i, our method usually generates multiple overlapping motion groups. Most importantly, since the motion candidates are estimated from densely overlapping cells, there is a high chance that the background will be the majority in at least one of these cells, and thus the true background motion can be estimated.

5   Dominant Motion Path Estimation

Once we obtain the motion candidates in each video clip, we construct a directed graph with these motion candidates as graph nodes (see Fig. 1(c)). For two neighboring video clips C_i and C_{i+1}, we create a directed edge between two motion candidates if there exist some common trajectories between them, e.g. M_i^j and M_i^n in C_i are both connected to M_{i+1}^k in C_{i+1}.

5.1 Graph Edge Weight

Among the multiple motion paths that traverse from the first video clip to the last, we now seek the optimal one that has the largest sum of trajectories along its path, i.e. the dominant rigid motion. A feature trajectory T_i may live through multiple video clips and it may not always be the member of the motions along the path. For better trajectory counting along a motion path, we divide each T_i into N sub-trajectories, where N is the number of video clips it spans. We then assign each sub-trajectory with a value of $v = \frac{1}{N}$. With this simple normalization, we are now ready to count the number of trajectories in the following manner.

For an edge between M_i^j and M_{i+1}^k, an edge weight is defined as

$$e_{i,i+1}^{j,k} = \sum_c G(T_c, M_{i+1}^k) \cdot v_c + \sum_n G(T_n, M_{i+1}^k) \cdot v_n, \tag{4}$$

where v_c are the values of sub-trajectories common to both M_i^j and M_{i+1}^k, and v_n are the values of those in M_{i+1}^k that have newly appeared in C_{i+1}. Therefore, we favor those strong connections, e.g. edge between M_i^n and M_{i+1}^k in Fig. 4 that have larger number of shared trajectories, because a consistent background motion path should have maximum overlapping trajectory groups.

$G(T_i, M)$ is a weighting term that reflects the geometric error of a sub-trajectory under a certain motion candidate. It is defined as:

$$G(T_i, M) = exp\left(-\frac{g_M^i \cdot g_M^i}{2\sigma^2}\right), \tag{5}$$

where $\sigma = 0.15$, and g_M^i is the average geometric error of trajectory T_i under motion M (see Eq. (3)). When a motion candidate is connected to multiple motions with similar number of shared trajectories, it will favor the connection with lower fitting error.

5.2 Optimal Path Search

Given a starting motion candidate M_0^j in the first video clip and an ending one M_q^k in C_q, we estimate the optimal motion path from M_0^j to M_q^k that contains the largest number of trajectories by defining an objective function that maximizes the edge weights:

$$P(M_0^j, M_q^k) = \max_{(n,k)\in\Phi} \left\{P(M_0^j, M_{q-1}^n) + e_{q-1,q}^{n,k}\right\}, \tag{6}$$

where Φ is the set of connected edges from all motion candidates in C_{q-1} to M_q^k. When $q = 1$, we have $P(M_0^j, M_1^k) = e_{0,1}^{j,k} + \Omega(M_0^j)$, where $\Omega(M_0^j)$ is the sum of the sub-trajectories' values inside M_0^j, weighted by their corresponding geometric errors as in Eq. (4).

This optimal motion path searching problem between a motion candidate M_0^m in C_0 to any other candidate M_i^m in C_i can be easily solved by dynamic programming. Finally, the global optimal motion path, starting from the first video clip to the last one, is selected by the following:

$$P_{dom} = \max_{j,k} \left\{ P(M_0^j, M_{S-1}^k) \right\}, \tag{7}$$

where S is the total number of the video clips.

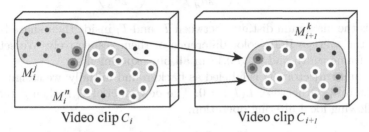

Fig. 4. Trajectory counting between two connected motions. Green circles: shared trajectories between M_i^j and M_{i+1}^k. White circles: shared trajectories between M_i^n and M_{i+1}^k. Yellow circles: newly appeared trajectories in C_{i+1} that belong to M_{i+1}^k. (Color figure online)

6 Background Trajectory Labeling

After obtaining the optimal motion path P_{dom}, i.e. background motion group, we label the sub-trajectories inside the selected motion candidates as background. Since a feature trajectory usually lives through multiple clips, and the optimal motion path may give its sub-trajectories different labels due to reasons like intermittent motion of the foreground objects or motion estimation errors, we need to perform a temporal consistency check for all the trajectories and use only reliable ones to compute the motion model of the global background motion.

Specifically, given the background motion path, we first identify reliable background feature trajectories that are entirely covered by the path, i.e. those whose all sub-trajectories are labelled as background. Then, we compute the global background motion model M_{back}, using those reliable background trajectories as described in Sect. 4.2. Note that the time window of M_{back} covers the entire video. Finally, we use M_{back} to label all the feature trajectories in the video. And the labelled background trajectories will be the initial output of our algorithm.

6.1 Local Trajectory Label Filtering

Due to tracking errors, some background feature trajectories, especially those close to object boundaries, may be wrongly labeled as non-background trajectories, while most of its neighbors are correctly labeled. To obtain spatially-smooth but edge-preserving labeling results, we apply a local filtering process on the labeled trajectories based on their color similarity and spatial-temporal connectivity. Specifically, we regard two trajectories T_i and T_j as neighbors in the spatial-temporal domain if they have at least one shared video frame and their minimum distance inside these shared frames is less than a threshold (5% of the frame width in our implementation). For each pair of such trajectory neighbors, we assign a weight $w_{i,j}$ to them, defined as follows:

$$w_{i,j} = exp\left(-\frac{d_s^2}{2\sigma_d^2}\right) \cdot exp\left(-\frac{d_c^2}{2\sigma_c^2}\right), \tag{8}$$

where d_s is the maximum distance between T_i and T_j inside their shared frames and d_c is the average RGB color difference of them respectively. We set σ_d to 2% of the frame width and $\sigma_c = 0.18$ in all our experiments.

If a feature trajectory T_i is labeled as background initially, we assign a value $L(T_i) = 1.0$ to it. Otherwise, $L(T_i) = 0$. The new label of T_i is then determined by the following local filtering operation:

$$L(T_i)^* = \sum_{j \in Ne(i)} w_{i,j} \cdot L(T_j), \tag{9}$$

where $Ne(i)$ is the set of trajectory neighbors of T_i. If $L(T_i)^* > 0.5$, we set the new label of T_i as background. Otherwise, it is labeled as non-background trajectory. The filtering step produces the final results for background segmentation.

7   Experiments

We compare our method with several most recent state-of-the-art motion segmentation and background identification methods, which include the motion trajectory segmentation method [9], dense binary motion segmentation method [3], and the robust background identification method by Zhang et al. [30]. These methods represent different approaches for background identification tasks. The experiments are conducted with several well-known public datasets, where high quality ground truth foreground masks are provided. Specifically, we include **FBMS-59** [18] (55 videos used), **DAVIS** [20] (32 videos used), Complex Background Data Set [17] (**CBDS**), Camouflaged Animals Data Set [3] (**CADS**), and the videos used in [30] for our analysis. These datasets contain various types of dynamic video (e.g. freely-moving camera, large depth variation, small foreground movement, highly dynamic scenes). Note that we discard some videos from **FBMS-59** [18] and **DAVIS** [20] that violate the following criteria: (1) Available foreground mask should cover all the moving objects in the scenes. (2) The static background, regardless of its size, should always be visible. (3) No severe lens distortion in the video.

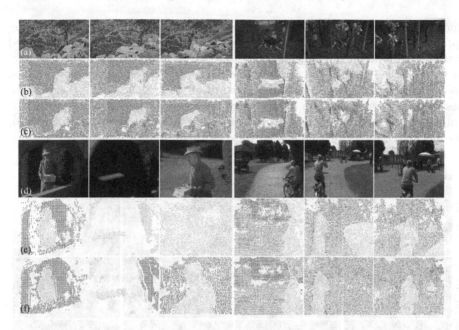

Fig. 5. Visual comparison with Keuper *et al.* [9]. Rows (b) and (e) are results from [9]. Rows (c) and (f) are our results. The background features are shown in red and the non-background features are in green. (Color figure online)

Table 1. Comparison of precision and recall on datasets **FBMS** and **DAVIS** with Keuper *et al.* [9].

Method	Precision (%)		Recall (%)		F-score	
	FBMS	DAVIS	FBMS	DAVIS	FBMS	DAVIS
Keuper	95.5	99.5	89.9	91.8	91.8	95.4
Ours	95.0	99.0	98.3	98.3	96.4	98.6

7.1 Comparison with Keuper *et al.* [9]

Keuper *et al.*'s method [9] is currently the state-of-the-art 2D motion segmentation method. To compare with their method, we test both methods on datasets **FBMS-59** [18] and **DAVIS** [20]. The input feature trajectories are extracted by [23] for both methods. Since the output of [9] are multiple groups of feature trajectories, we select the one that contains the largest amount of trajectories and label the features inside as background. The comparison of average precision and recall for background features identification is shown in Table 1. As we can see from the table, our method achieves similar high accuracy as Keuper *et al.*'s method, while the recall of our method is significantly better. Figure 5 shows some typical cases that may fail Keuper *et al.*'s method. Firstly, their method may not work well on scenes with large depth variation (top two cases in Fig. 5), which is a typical limitation of 2D motion segmentation methods without using a projective motion model. Secondly, when the background is severely occluded by the foreground moving objects (bottom left case in Fig. 5), their method may fail to track the background motion, and instead, creates new motion groups. Finally, since their method utilizes color information along with other motion cues in their energy function, it may over-segment the background region if it contains components with large color difference (bottom right case in Fig. 5). Our method, on the other hand, can very well handle such difficult cases.

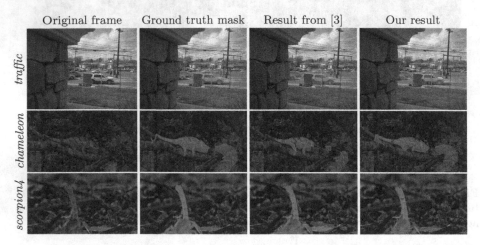

Fig. 6. Visual comparison with Bideau and Learned-Miller's method [3].

7.2   Comparison with Bideau and Learned-Miller's Method [3]

We also compare our method with Bideau and Learned-Miller's method [3], which is a recent foreground object segmentation method. The datasets we use in this experiment are the Complex Background Data Set from [17] and the Camouflaged Animals Data Set from their own work. Since the main purpose of their method is segmenting foreground objects and the objects in these datasets are relatively small, we compute the precision and recall of pixels/features that locate on the foreground moving objects instead of background this time. The results are reported in Table 2. As we can see, in most cases, our method achieves better precision and recall. In general, our method produces more accurate and complete segmentation of the foreground objects, see examples in Fig. 6. The method proposed by [3], on the other hand, has difficulty dealing with foreground intermittent motions ('*chameleon*' sequence in Fig. 6), which are explicitly handled in our method by utilizing global motion cues.

7.3   Comparison with Zhang *et al.* [30]

To evaluate the performance of our method on videos with large foreground objects, we compare our method with Zhang *et al.*'s method [30] on the highly dynamic videos used in their work. Some segmentation results are shown in Fig. 7. As we can see, our method can also produce very good segmentation results on these videos. Since we use projective motion model in our motion estimation step, the estimated background motion usually covers the entire background region. The motion segmentation method by Zhang *et al.* may produce over-segmented results as reported in their paper (yellow and green points on the background wall in Fig. 7(a)). Therefore, it requires further post-processing to merge these background motion groups. Also, the background metric used in their method may be violated if the foreground motions are also rigid motions or nearly rigid motions (Fig. 7(e)). Our background metric is based on the total number of feature trajectories a rigid motion contains in the entire video, which is proved to be more robust according to our experiment results.

Table 2. Comparison of precision and recall on datasets **CBDS** and **CADS** with Bideau [3].

Sequence		Bideau [3]		Ours	
		preci.	recall	preci.	recall
CBDS [17]	*'drive'*	0.36	**0.90**	**0.72**	0.63
	'forest'	**0.81**	0.77	0.79	**0.82**
	'parking'	0.897	0.89	**0.902**	**0.92**
	'store'	0.91	0.78	**0.94**	**0.84**
	'traffic'	0.73	0.83	**0.83**	**0.85**
CADS [3]	*'chameleon'*	**0.96**	0.53	0.94	**0.66**
	'frog'	0.49	0.38	**0.50**	**0.40**
	'glowwormbeetle'	0.84	0.88	**0.92**	**0.94**
	'scorpion1'	**0.46**	0.08	0.24	**0.22**
	'scorpion2'	0.58	0.48	**0.66**	**0.56**
	'scorpion3'	0.83	**0.41**	**0.84**	0.31
	'scorpion4'	0.66	**0.76**	**0.79**	0.74
	'snail'	0.95	**0.90**	**0.98**	0.86
	'stickinsect'	0.06	0.17	**0.20**	**0.31**

7.4   Limitations and Discussions

Our method may not work well in some special cases. Firstly, for videos with many short feature trajectories (only 2–3 feature points on a trajectory) extracted from non-rigid objects like river and sea, where the features on these subtle dynamically moving objects may not violate the epipolar constraint during their short lifetime. Therefore, they may be wrongly labeled as background. Secondly, for videos captured by camera that hardly moves, if the foreground motion is also rigid and occupies the majority of the scene all the time (e.g. a video recorded by a standing person with a close-up view of a running train

Fig. 7. Comparison with Zhang *et al.* [30]. Row (a), (c), and (e) are results from [30]. Row (b), (d), and (f) are our results. (Color figure online)

in front), our method may also fail to identify the correct background features. Computational wise, our method usually takes less than five minutes to process a video of around 100 frames and 50,000 trajectories on a PC with 2.4 GHz CPU.

8   Conclusion

In this work, we propose a robust background feature identification method that can handle moving foreground objects that are large or exhibit intermittent motions. Our method is designed based on the assumption that the background motion will contain the largest amount of feature trajectories when the local background trajectories are aggregated over the entire sequence. Accordingly, we develop a local-to-global dominant motion group identification pipeline. Since the motions are characterized using fundamental matrices, there is no issue with over-segmentation, problem that plagues the 2D motion segmentation approach. With careful design, our motion estimation method can efficiently handle large amount of trajectories and robustly propose potential rigid motions in video clips. The comprehensive experiment results show that our method outperforms several most recent state-of-the-art motion segmentation methods both quantitatively and qualitatively.

References

1. Badrinarayanan, V., Galasso, F., Cipolla, R.: Label propagation in video sequences. In: Proceedings of CVPR, June 2010
2. Bai, X., Wang, J., Simons, D., Sapiro, G.: Video snapcut: robust video object cutout using localized classifiers. ACM Trans. Graph. (2009)
3. Bideau, P., Learned-Miller, E.: It's moving! a probabilistic model for causal motion segmentation in moving camera videos. In: Leibe, B., Matas, J., Sebe, N., Welling, M. (eds.) ECCV 2016. LNCS, vol. 9912, pp. 433–449. Springer, Cham (2016). https://doi.org/10.1007/978-3-319-46484-8_26
4. Elhamifar, E., Vidal, R.: Sparse subspace clustering. In: Proceedings of CVPR, pp. 2790–2797 (2009)
5. Faktor, A., Irani, M.: Video segmentation by non-local consensus voting. In: BMVC (2014)
6. Fan, Q., Zhong, F., Lischinski, D., Cohen-Or, D., Chen, B.: JumpCut: non-successive mask transfer and interpolation for video cutout. ACM Trans. Graph. **34**, 195 (2015)
7. Hartley, R.I., Zisserman, A.: Multiple View Geometry in Computer Vision, 2nd edn. Cambridge University Press, Cambridge (2004)
8. Jain, S.D., Grauman, K.: Supervoxel-consistent foreground propagation in video. In: Fleet, D., Pajdla, T., Schiele, B., Tuytelaars, T. (eds.) ECCV 2014. LNCS, vol. 8692, pp. 656–671. Springer, Cham (2014). https://doi.org/10.1007/978-3-319-10593-2_43
9. Keuper, M., Andres, B., Brox, T.: Motion trajectory segmentation via minimum cost multicuts. In: Proceedings of ICCV (2015). http://lmb.informatik.uni-freiburg.de//Publications/2015/KB15b
10. Lee, Y.J., Kim, J., Grauman, K.: Key-segments for video object segmentation. In: Proceedings of ICCV (2011)
11. Li, F., Kim, T., Humayun, A., Tsai, D., Rehg, J.M.: Video segmentation by tracking many figure-ground segments. In: Proceedings of ICCV (2013)
12. Li, Z., Guo, J., Cheong, L.F., Zhiying Zhou, S.: Perspective motion segmentation via collaborative clustering. In: Proceedings of ICCV, December 2013
13. Liu, S., Tan, P., Yuan, L., Sun, J., Zeng, B.: MeshFlow: minimum latency online video stabilization. In: Leibe, B., Matas, J., Sebe, N., Welling, M. (eds.) ECCV 2016. LNCS, vol. 9910, pp. 800–815. Springer, Cham (2016). https://doi.org/10.1007/978-3-319-46466-4_48
14. Liu, S., Yuan, L., Tan, P., Sun, J.: Bundled camera paths for video stabilization. ACM Trans. Graph. **32**(4), 78:1–78:10 (2013)
15. Ma, Y., Derksen, H., Hong, W., Wright, J.: Segmentation of multivariate mixed data via lossy data coding and compression. IEEE Trans. Pattern Anal. Mach. Intell. **29**(9), 1546–1562 (2007)
16. Maerki, N., Perazzi, F., Wang, O., Sorkine-Hornung, A.: Bilateral space video segmentation. In: Proceedings of CVPR (2016)
17. Narayana, M., Hanson, A., Learned-Miller, E.: Coherent motion segmentation in moving camera videos using optical flow orientations. In: Proceedings of ICCV, pp. 1577–1584 (2013)

18. Ochs, P., Malik, J., Brox, T.: Segmentation of moving objects by long term video analysis. IEEE Trans. Pattern Anal. Mach. Intell. **36**, 1187–1200 (2014)
19. Papazoglou, A., Ferrari, V.: Fast object segmentation in unconstrained video. In: Proceedings of ICCV, December 2013
20. Perazzi, F., Pont-Tuset, J., McWilliams, B., Gool, L.V., Gross, M., Sorkine-Hornung, A.: A benchmark dataset and evaluation methodology for video object segmentation. In: CVPR (2016)
21. Perazzi, F., Wang, O., Gross, M., Sorkine-Hornung, A.: Fully connected object proposals for video segmentation. In: Proceedings of ICCV, December 2015
22. Ramakanth, S.A., Babu, R.V.: SeamSeg: video object segmentation using patch seams. In: Proceedings of CVPR (2014)
23. Sundaram, N., Brox, T., Keutzer, K.: Dense point trajectories by GPU-accelerated large displacement optical flow. In: Daniilidis, K., Maragos, P., Paragios, N. (eds.) ECCV 2010. LNCS, vol. 6311, pp. 438–451. Springer, Heidelberg (2010). https://doi.org/10.1007/978-3-642-15549-9_32
24. Taylor, B., Karasev, V., Scoatto, S.: Causal video object segmentation from persistence of occlusions. In: Proceedings of CVPR (2015)
25. Vidal, R., Tron, R., Hartley, R.: Multiframe motion segmentation with missing data using powerfactorization and GPCA. Int. J. Comput. Vis. **79**, 85–105 (2008)
26. Vijayanarasimhan, S., Grauman, K.: Active frame selection for label propagation in videos. In: Fitzgibbon, A., Lazebnik, S., Perona, P., Sato, Y., Schmid, C. (eds.) ECCV 2012. LNCS, vol. 7576, pp. 496–509. Springer, Heidelberg (2012). https://doi.org/10.1007/978-3-642-33715-4_36
27. Wang, W., Shen, J., Porikli, F.: Saliency-aware geodesic video object segmentation. In: Proceedings of CVPR (2015)
28. Xu, X., Cheong, L.F., Li, Z.: Motion segmentation by exploiting complementary geometric models. In: Proceedings of CVPR (2018)
29. Zhang, D., Javed, O., Shah, M.: Video object segmentation through spatially accurate and temporally dense extraction of primary object regions. In: Proceedings of CVPR (2013)
30. Zhang, F.L., Wu, X., Zhang, H.T., Wang, J., Hu, S.M.: Robust background identification for dynamic video editing. ACM Trans. Graph. **35**, 197 (2016)
31. Zhong, F., Qin, X., Peng, Q., Meng, X.: Discontinuity-aware video object cutout. ACM Trans. Graph. **31**, 175 (2012)

SMC: Single-Stage Multi-location Convolutional Network for Temporal Action Detection

Zhikang Liu[1,2], Zilei Wang[1(✉)], Yan Zhao[1], and Ye Tian[1]

[1] Department of Automation,
University of Science and Technology of China, Hefei, China
[2] Megvii Inc. (Face++), Beijing, China
{lzk,zy10113,yeah}@mail.ustc.edu.cn, zlwang@ustc.edu.cn

Abstract. Temporal action detection in untrimmed videos is an important and challenging visual task. State-of-the-art works always adopt a multi-stage pipeline, i.e., a class-agnostic segment proposal followed by a multi-label action classification. This pipeline is computationally slow and hard to optimize as each stage need be trained separately. Moreover, a desirable method should go beyond segment-level localization and make dense predictions with precise boundaries. We introduce a novel detection model in this paper, Single-stage Multi-location Convolutional Network (SMC), which completely eliminates the proposal generation and spatio-temporal feature resampling, and predicts frame-level action locations with class probabilities in a unified end-to-end network. Specifically, we associate a set of multi-scale default locations with each feature map cell in multiple layers, then predict the location offsets to the default locations, as well as action categories. SMC in practice is faster than the existing methods (753 FPS on a Titan X Maxwell GPU) and achieves state-of-the-art performance on THUMOS'14 and MEXaction2.

Keywords: Temporal action detection · End-to-end · Multi-scale · SMC

1 Introduction

Temporal action detection has attracted increasing attention recently, owning to its applications in various areas such as video analysis and surveillance. This visual task aims to detect action instances from untrimmed long videos. It is challenging since not only predicting action categories but also precisely localizing where the actions of interest take place is required. State-of-the-art methods always address this issue in a multi-stage manner [1–3]: the temporal action proposal stage produces high-recall temporal window candidates(e.g., sliding windows), and then these candidates are passed through the following classifier to predict the category with an optional refinement of the temporal bounds [4,5]. These approaches may suffer from one or more of the following drawbacks.

© Springer Nature Switzerland AG 2019
C. V. Jawahar et al. (Eds.): ACCV 2018, LNCS 11362, pp. 179–195, 2019.
https://doi.org/10.1007/978-3-030-20890-5_12

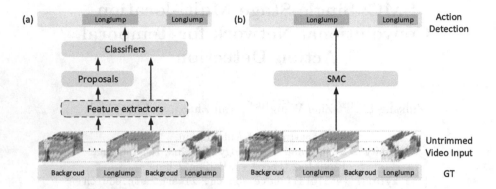

Fig. 1. A comparison between multi-stage temporal action detection framework and SMC. (a) Multi-stage temporal action detection framework: proposal generation followed by a separate classification over the proposals. Additional feature extraction is also in need in some works. (b) Our temporal action detection framework: a new end-to-end model (SMC) is introduced, which outputs action detections directly from a single-stage network over the input video

(1) The proposal generator and the classifier are separate and thus independently trained, which can be suboptimal. (2) The external proposal generation or exhaustive sliding window methods require additional calculation, and the test data need to be passed through for multiple times, leading to low computational efficiency. (3) The segment-level action proposals are always approximate and the sliding windows are pre-determined. Thus they are not able to precisely predict flexible action boundaries.

In this paper, we propose a novel model Single-stage Multi-location Convolutional (SMC) Network for temporal action detection, which can addresses all of the issues above. SMC is end-to-end trainable and completely eliminates the proposal generation and additional feature extraction by encapsulating all the computations into a single network. Unlike the proposal and sliding-window techniques which always take pre-determined short video segments as input, SMC network uses full 3D convolution along the temporal dimension which enables SMC to encode as many frames as the GPU memory allows. Thus, SMC can see more contextual information about the human actions and appearance in untrimmed videos. In addition, inspired by the single shot object detection models like YOLO [6,7] and SSD [8], our SMC network associates the anchor action instances of multiple locations with the feature maps at different scales, making the network flexible to handle action instances of various lengths. Our model processes input video in a single pass, and directly outputs the frame-level temporal boundaries and action categories.

A comparison between the multi-stage temporal action detection framework and our SMC model is illustrated in Fig. 1. We can see that our single-stage approach is much simpler than multi-stage approaches. Beyond high-quality detection, our single-stage framework also provides a high processing speed at 753

FPS on a single Titan X Maxwell GPU. Our model is one of the first temporal action detection method that conducts detection totally in a single-stage from raw video frames, and significantly outperforms earlier methods in both accuracy and efficiency.

In summary, this paper makes three main contributions:

(1) We propose one of the first single-stage end-to-end trainable temporal action detection model, which detects human actions from raw video frames using multi scale anchor locations.
(2) As we do the entire task in a single stage, our method is much faster than the previous state-of-the-art methods.
(3) Extensive experiments on two challenging benchmark datasets demonstrate that our model significantly boosts the accuracy of temporal action detection over a wide range of IoU thresholds.

2   Related Work

Action Recognition. Action recognition on short video clips is a well-studied problem [9]. The task is to take trimmed video clips of a single human action and predict the action class present in the video [10–13]. Traditional methods are mainly based on hand-crafted features [10], such as STIP-3D [14] and HOG3D [15]. In the past several years, there have also been attempts to apply deep learning to action recognition [11,12,16]. Here we only review the brief action recognition methods that are also useful in temporal action detection. Frame-level Convolutional Neural Network (CNN) is introduced into this task in [17]. Then, two-stream architectures [11,18] capture both appearance and motion information by applying 2D CNN such as VGG [19] and ResNet [20] on single frame images and optical flow fields respectively. 3D CNN architecture (C3D [16]) adopts short video clips as input to encode spatio-temporal features. In these frame-level and clip-level methods, video-level predictions are always simply generated by max pooling or average pooling on top of the CNNs. They have not taken long range temporal structure into account. To exploit temporal structure, some works resort to the recurrent architecture [12,21,22]. Recurrent Neural Network (RNN) is placed on top of deep ConvNets, with each time step taking a single frame or a short clip as input. Such methods are designed for human actions in video clips with relatively short duration.

Temporal Action Detection. Temporal action detection is to detect action instances in untrimmed videos where the categories and temporal boundaries of action instances both need be predicted. Traditional method for temporal action detection involves multiple stages: independent feature extraction or sliding window based action proposal generation, and a separate sophisticated classification over the features or proposals [23–25]. Shou *et al.* [2] proposes a segment based convolutional neural network (S-CNN) which fine-tunes multi-stage 3D ConvNets for binary proposal and uses an additional 3D ConvNets for classification.

In the same spirit, CDC [26] and TCN [27] employ the proposal generation mechanisms to boost accuracy via a localization 3D ConvNets at test time. CBR [28] adopts a two-stage temporal action detection pipeline which uses the cascaded boundary regression to refine the temporal boundaries of the sliding window proposals. TURN [29] uses the unit-level coordinate regression to refine the proposals' boundary. Such multi-stage approaches treat the feature extraction or proposal generation and the classification as two independent processing stages, which inhibits collaboration between them and results in repeated computation within two stages. Our SMC network differs from these methods mainly in that we encapsulate all the computations in a single stage.

Recently, RNN and specifically Long Short-Term Memory (LSTM) have been employed by some approaches to detect actions with arbitrary lengths [5,30,31]. These methods bypass the need for sliding window search or proposal mechanism by predicting an action label at each time step of the recurrent structure. However, it is difficult for RNN to keep long time memory in practice [32] and the inherent frame-level smoothing produced by the RNN framework is harmful to the task of precise action localization [31]. An alternative choice is to use 3D convolution. For instance, R-C3D [33] encodes a large video buffer with a fully-convolutional 3D ConvNet, and uses 3D pooling to extract features at arbitrary length. We also adopt 3D convolutional and pooling layers, which enable our SMC network to handle action instances of arbitrary temporal length.

There are also some attempts to detect actions in a single stream. Zhu *et al.* [34] proposes a multi-task learning framework for action detection which simultaneously perform proposal, classification and regression. But the input video clips to their network are short (16 frames) with limited contextual information. SSAD [35] proposes a single shot classifier for temporal action detection. Actually, the method in [35] is a two-stage method, which adopts an independent feature extractors and an independent SSAD classifier. Their feature extractors and SSAD classifier are separately trained. In our method, we get rid of the time-consuming optical flow and tightly integrate all the components into a single network, which results in a more efficient and effective architecture for unified temporal action detection. Moreover, owing to temporal dimension reduction in 3D conv and smaller feature extractor (SSAD extracts two-stream VGG16 features and C3D features), SMC has much fewer per frame FLOPs compared to SSAD, with about 1GFLOPs and 30GFLOPs respectively.

SS-TAD [36] propose a single-stream temporal action detection method, which integrates joint action detection with its semantic sub-tasks in a single framework. But SS-TAD is built in a recurrent architecture, which limits its efficiency and accuracy. The fully convolutional based SMC is faster than SS-TAD (753FPS vs 701FPS), and outperforms SS-TAD at all IoU thretheds on THUMOS-14 as reported in the experiments.

Object Detection. Action detection in untrimmed continuous videos is intrinsically relative to object detection in images. Initial deep learning based object detection approaches adopt object proposal generation as a distinct preprocessing stage. R-CNN [37] uses deep convolutional networks to efficiently classify

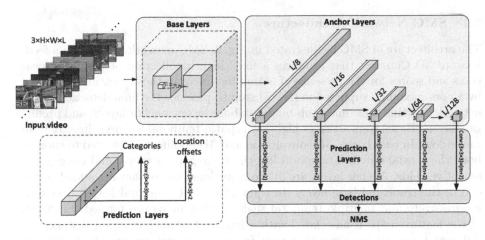

Fig. 2. SMC network architecture. SMC network contains three main sub-modules: base layers, anchor layers and prediction layers. Anchor layers are added to the end of base layers. The prediction layers predict the location offsets to anchor instances and class confidence scores. Non-maximum suppression (NMS) is used to produce the final detection

multiple region proposals independently generated by a separate selective search. Fast R-CNN [38] makes convolutional feature maps be shared among the object proposals to improve training and test speed. Faster R-CNN [39] introduces a Region Proposal Network (RPN) that shares full-image convolutional features with the detection network, thus enabling nearly cost-free region proposals.

Another subsequent generation of object detectors is single shot detectors, such as YOLO [6,7] and SSD [8], which provides a unified end-to-end framework for simultaneously outputting object anchor positions alongside their predicted category confidence scores and location offsets. Inspired by these single shot developments, we propose a framework that tightly integrates all the computation into a single pass to achieve effective temporal action localization and classification.

3   Singe-Stage Multi-location Convolutional Network

In this section, we describe the Singe-stage Multi-location Convolutional Network (SMC) in details. SMC takes advantage of three main characteristics of single shot object detection models such as YOLO [6,7] and SSD [8]: (1) the spatio-temporal features are directly learned from raw videos, and no additional feature extractor is in need; (2) we adopt the temporal pooling and use the feature maps from different 3D convolutional layers for prediction, making SMC naturally be able to handle action instances of various lengths; (3) unlike the multi-stage frameworks, SMC directly predicts action categories and temporal boundaries in untrimmed video using 3D convolutional prediction layers, which enables the end-to-end training.

3.1 SMC Network Architecture

The architecture of SMC is illustrated in Fig. 2. SMC network is based on a feed-forward 3D ConvNet that produces a fixed-length collection of temporal locations and scores for the presence of action instances in those locations, followed by a non-maximum suppression (NMS) step to produce the final detection. SMC network contains three main sub-modules: base layers, anchor layers, and prediction layers. Base layers abstract high-level spatio-temporal features directly from raw videos. In base layers, 3D convolution and 3D pooling are adopted to shorten both the spatial size and temporal length of the feature maps, and enlarge the receptive fields. Anchor layers are 3D convolutional layers that are added to the end of the truncated base layers. In these layers the temporal length decreases progressively and multiple temporal scale feature maps are formed. Each cell of the feature maps is associated with a fixed set of anchor action instances of different temporal locations. For each feature map cell, we use the prediction layers to get the location offsets and the category confidence scores relative to associated anchor instances in this cell.

Base Layers. The input to the base layers is a sequence of RGB video frames with the dimension of $\mathbb{R}^{3 \times L \times H \times W}$, where L, H, W are the length, height, and width of the input sequence. Note that we reshape the size of input frames to 96×96 as the GPU memory is limited, *i.e.*, $H = W = 96$ in this work. 3D ConvNets have shown to be effective at learning spatio-temporal features in video volume data analysis problems. The base layers are based on the 3D ConvNets model C3D described in [16]. The base layers consist of five 3D convolution layers and five 3D max-pooling layers. All 3D convolution filters are $3 \times 3 \times 3$ with stride 1. The number of filters are 64, 128, 256 respectively in the first three 3D convolutional layers and 512 in the remaining 3D convolutional layers. Rectified Linear Units (ReLU) [40] activation function is applied to the output of each 3D convolutional layer. The kernel size is set to $2 \times 2 \times 2$ for the first three 3D max-pooling layers and $1 \times 2 \times 2$ for the remaining pooling layers. All the pooling stride is set to 1. After the max-pooling5, the height and width of feature maps are reduced to 3 and the temporal size is decreased to $L/8$.

Anchor Layers. Anchor layers decrease the temporal dimension progressively and remain the height and width dimensions same, which allows SMC get action predictions from multiple scale feature maps. We stack four anchor convolutional layers (Conv6, Conv7, Conv8, Conv9) at the end of the base layers. In all of these anchor layers, the convolutional kernel is set to $3 \times 3 \times 3$, the temporal stride remains as 2, the spatial stride remains as 1, and the number of filters are 256. Thus, the output of the feature maps of anchor layers are F_6, F_7, F_8, F_9 with the sizes of $(256 \times (L/16) \times 3 \times 3)$, $(256 \times (L/32) \times 3 \times 3)$, $(256 \times (L/64) \times 3 \times 3)$, $(256 \times (L/128) \times 3 \times 3)$, respectively. All of the convolutional layers are followed by Rectified Linear Units (ReLU) [40] activation function. We do not use the pooling technique in these layers. The output of 3D max-pool5 layer, which we name as $F5$, with size $(512 \times (L/8) \times 3 \times 3)$ is used as anchor feature map as well.

As the feature maps from different levels within a network have different receptive field sizes [41], we use lower anchor layers to detect short actions as they have relatively small receptive fields, and the upper anchor layers to detect long actions. For the feature maps of each anchor layers, we associate a set of default anchor action instances with each feature map cell. The size of each cell is set to $C \times 3 \times 3 \times 3$, where C is the number of channels. For each anchor instance, we predict the relative location offsets to the default location, as well as action categories in a convolutional manner, which will be detailed in the introduction of prediction layers. Suppose we use n anchor layers ($n = 5$ in this work). The base scale for each anchor layer is computed as:

$$s_k = s_{\min} + \frac{s_{\max} - s_{\min}}{n - 1}(k - 1), k \in [1, n] \tag{1}$$

where $s_{\min}$ is 0.1 and $s_{\max}$ is set to 0.9, which means that the lowest layer has a base scale of 0.1 and the highest layer has a base scale of 0.9. Thus all the layers are in a regular space. For each anchor layer, we define a set of scale rations $r_k = \{r_d\}_{d=1}^{D_k}$, where D_k is the number of the scale rations. We set $r_k = \{0.8, 1, 1.5\}$ for F_5, F_6, F_7 and F_8, and $\{0.7, 0.85, 1\}$ for F_9. For each of the anchor instance, we compute $l_d = s_k \cdot r_d$, $d \in [1, D_k]$ as the default length. For an anchor layer F_k with length of N_k, we set the center of each anchor instance to $c_i = \frac{i+0.5}{N_k}$, $i \in [0, N_k]$, and we truncate the coordinates of the anchor instances such that they are within [0,1]. In this way, there are D_k anchor instances with the length l_d at each center location c_i. For an anchor feature map F_k with the length N_k and D_k scale rations, the number of the associated anchor instances for this layer is $N_k \cdot D_k$.

Prediction Layers. We use 3D convolutional filters to predict the location offsets relative to the anchor instance coordinates and action categories. For an anchor layer F_k with length of N_k and D_k scale rations, we use $(D_k \cdot (m + 2))$ temporal convolutional filters with kernel size $3 \times 3 \times 3$ to compute m category confidence scores and 2 location offsets at each cell in the feature map. Thus the output size of the corresponding prediction layer is $(N_k \times (D_k \cdot (m + 2)))$. We reshape the output to $((N_k \times D_k) \cdot (m + 2))$, and each anchor instance gets a prediction score vector $(p_{class}, \delta\hat{c}, \delta\hat{l})$, where p_{class} is the category confidence score vector with the length m and $\delta\hat{c}, \delta\hat{l}$ are the location offsets. The adjusted action location can be computed as:

$$\hat{c} = c_i + \alpha_1 \cdot l_d \cdot \delta\hat{c}$$
$$\hat{l} = l_d \cdot \exp(\alpha_2 \cdot \delta\hat{l}) \tag{2}$$

where $\hat{c}$ and $\hat{l}$ are the center location and length of the predicted action instance. c_i and l_d are the center location and length for the relative anchor instance, respectively. Both α_1 and α_2 are set to 0.1 to control the effect of the location offsets in order to make the training more efficient.

3.2   Training of SMC Network

Training Data Preparation. As the Graphics Processing Unit (GPU) memory is limited, we cannot sent the whole video sequence into the GPU at a time. So we break the video sequence into segments, and feed as many frames as the GPU memory can contain at a time. Each input segment contains L continuous frames. We set $L = 192$ frames in practical. For training data augmentation, we fetch the segments with 75% overlap from the untrimmed videos. Then, we only keep the segments containing at least one ground truth instance. All of the input frames are then resized to 96×96. We randomly shuffle the segments' order in the training set to make the network converge faster.

Matching Strategy. At training time, we need to establish the correspondence between the anchor action instances and the ground truth instances. In the training videos, we calculate the IoU overlap of each anchor instance with each ground truth instance. If the highest IoU overlap is higher than a threshold (0.5), we regard it as positive, otherwise negative. In this way, a ground truth instance can match multiple anchor instances, which allows the SMC network to predict high confidences for multiple anchor instances rather than only the one with the maximum overlap. Similar matching strategy is widely adopted by state-of-the-art object detection methods, such as Faster R-CNN [39] and SSD [8].

Hard Negative Mining. After the matching step, only a small group of anchor instances match the ground truth instances, causing a significant imbalance between the positive and negative examples. Therefore, we use the hard negative mining to reduce the number of negative examples. We sort all the negative examples using the highest confidence score for each anchor instance and pick the top ones to ensure that the ratio between positives and negatives keeps $3 : 1$. This ratio is determined by empirical validation.

Training Objective. The training objective of SMC network is a multi-task loss function. We design the loss function L to jointly train classification and location regression.

$$L = \frac{1}{N_{cls}} \sum_i L_{cls}(\boldsymbol{p}_i, p_i^g) + \alpha \frac{1}{N_{pos}} \sum_i L_{loc}(\boldsymbol{t}_i, \boldsymbol{t}_i^g) + \beta L_2(\Theta) \tag{3}$$

where N_{cls} and N_{pos} stand for the number of the training instances and the number of positive instances. L_{cls} is the loss for classification. L_{loc} is the Smooth $L1$ loss [38] for the location offsets. $\boldsymbol{p}_i = \{p_i^j\}_{j=1}^m$ is the predicted category probability vector of the i-th anchor instances while p_i^g is the corresponding ground truth label. $\boldsymbol{t}_i = \{\delta \hat{c}_i, \delta \hat{l}_i\}$ denotes the predicted location offsets to anchor instance. $\boldsymbol{t}_i^g = \{\delta c_i, \delta l_i\}$ denotes the coordinate transformation of the ground truth location to the anchor instances. Here the coordinate transformation are computed as follows:

$$\delta c_i = [(c_i^* - c_i)/l_d]/\alpha_1$$
$$\delta l_i = [\log(l_i^*/l_d)]/\alpha_2 \tag{4}$$

where c_i and l_d are the center location and length of the relative anchor instance while c_i^* and l_i^* denote them for the ground truth. Both α_1 and α_2 are set to 0.1 as well. Our classification loss is the softmax loss over multiple categories:

$$L_{cls} = L_{soft\max} = -\log(\frac{\exp(p_i^g)}{\sum_j \exp(p_i^j)}) \tag{5}$$

$L_2(\Theta)$ is the $L2$ regularization loss where Θ stands for all the parameters of the SMC network. α and β are the loss trade-off parameters, which is set to 1 and 0.0005 respectively through cross validation.

3.3 Prediction

At prediction time, we follow the data preparation method mentioned in the training procedure to produce the test segments with the following two changes: (1) we fetch the test segments from untrimmed videos with 25% overlap; (2) we keep all the segments and feed them into the SMC network. The location predictions are in the form of relative displacement of length and center point of anchor action instances. Equation (2) is adopted to get the real locations of the predicted actions. The locations are then post-precessed by non-maximum suppression (NMS) at a threshold (*e.g.* 0.2) lower than mAP evaluation threshold to get the final location predictions.

4 Experiments

We evaluate the effectiveness of the proposed SMC network on two large-scale temporal action detection benchmark datasets: THUMOS'14 [42] and MEXaction2 [43]. We first introduce these two datasets and implementation details, then we compare the performance of SMC network with other state-of-the-art methods.

4.1 Datesets and Setup

THUMOS'14 [42]. The temporal action detection subset of THUMOS'14 dataset is challenging and widely used. This subset contains more than 22 h of video from 20 different sport activities. The validation set which is conventionally used as the training set for action detection contains 200 untrimmed videos, and the test set contains 213 untrimmed videos. These untrimmed videos are annotated with the temporal intervals that depict human actions. The validation set totally contains 3007 action instances while the test set contains 3358 action instances. Each untrimmed video contains multiple action instances.

MEXaction2 [43]. This dataset consists of two action classes: "HorseRiding" and "BullChargeCape". This dataset contains three subsets: UCF101 Horse Riding clips, INA videos, and YouTube clips. UCF101 Horse Riding clips and

Table 1. Temporal action detection performance (mAP %) comparison at different temporal IoU thresholds on THUMOS'14 dataset.

IoU thresholds	0.3	0.4	0.5	0.6	0.7
Wang et al. [47]	14.6	12.1	8.5	4.7	1.5
Oneata et al. [4]	28.8	21.8	15.0	8.5	3.2
Yeung et al. [31]	36.0	26.4	17.1	-	-
Shou et al. [2]	36.3	28.7	19.0	10.3	5.3
Yuan et al. [5]	33.6	26.1	18.8	-	-
Buch et al. [48]	37.8	-	23.0	-	-
Shou et al. [26]	40.1	29.4	23.3	13.1	7.9
Lin et al. [35]	43.0	35.0	24.6	-	-
Dai et al. [27]	-	33.3	25.6	15.9	9.0
Xu et al. [33]	44.8	35.6	28.9	-	-
Buch et al. [36]	45.7	-	29.2	-	9.6
No BR SMC	45.0	36.2	32.4	24.8	17.0
Separate opt SMC	35.0	31.3	28.3	23.2	16.2
SMC (Ours)	**45.8**	**37.2**	**33.4**	**28.5**	**20.3**

YouTube clips are trimmed and used for training, whereas INA videos are untrimmed with approximately 77 h in total, and divided into the training, test, and validation sets. With regard to annotated action instances for temporal action detection, there are 1336 action instances for training, 329 action instances for testing, and 310 action instances for validation.

Evaluation Metrics. For both datasets, we compare our model against other action detection methods according to Mean Average Precision (mAP). The mAP is computed by the official toolkit provided by THUMOS'14 [42]. A predicted action instance is considered correct when it has the correct action category and its temporal IoU with the ground truth is larger than the threshold. Various IoU thresholds are used to evaluate the performance. Redundant detections for the same ground truth are not allowed.

4.2   Implementation Details

We adopt the Stochastic Gradient Descent (SGD) update rule [44] with the aforementioned multi-task loss function to optimize the parameters of our SMC network. The base layers of SMC network are based on the C3D [16]. Therefore, we initialize the 3D ConvNet part of SMC with the C3D weights trained on the UCF101 dataset [45]. Since the GPU memory is limited, the input segment length L is set to 192 frames at 10 frames per second which covers approximately 19.2 s of video. Our choice is based on the fact that 99.2% of all the action instances' duration are less than 19.2 s in the benchmark datasets. All the frames are resized to 96×96. We implement SMC network based on Caffe [46] and C3D [16].

Table 2. The performances of different combinations of the anchor layers on THU-MOS'14

Anchor layers in use	mAP @IoU 0.3	mAP @IoU 0.5	mAP @IoU 0.7
F5	36.8	24.4	15.1
F5,F6	44.6	31.9	19.0
F5,F6,F7	45.6	33.1	20.2
F5,F6,F7,F8	45.8	33.3	20.3
F5,F6,F7,F8,F9	45.8	33.4	20.3

4.3   Experiments on THUMOS'14

For the training of SMC network, all the 200 annotated untrimmed videos from the validation set are used. The final results are reported on 213 videos in the test set. All the layers of SMC are trained with a fixed learning rate of 0.0001.

We summarize the results of applying our model to the task of temporal action detection on THUMOS'14 in Table 1. We can observe that our SMC model achieves state-of-the-art performance for this task for different overlap thresholds. When the IoU threshold in evaluation is set to 0.5, SMC comprehensively outperforms the current state-of-the-art methods by a large mAP margin (*e.g.* 33.4% compared to 24.6% as reported in [35]). The newly proposed R-C3D framework [33] has reported 28.9% mAP at the IoU threshold 0.5 for the THUMOS'14 dataset. Our model still performs better than this very recent method. We outperforms the newly proposed end-to-end method [36] at all IoU threthods on THUMOS-14 (45.8% vs 45.7%, 33.4% vs 29.2%, and particularly 20.4% vs 9.6% at IoU threthods 0.3, 0.5, 0.7, respectively). Our model shows significant improvement especially when the IoU threshold is high. We think the main reason is that we avoid the segment-level proposal stage, and the frame-level coordinates provided by boundary regression in SMC are more precise than segment-level coordinates. We tested SMC without boundary regression (No BR SMC) on THUMOS'14 at different IoU thresholds. The mAP results are summarized in Table 1. The boundary regression becomes increasingly important when the IoU threshold increases.

In order to verifying the improvement of jointly tuning both feature extraction and prediction stages, we evaluated the performance of separately optimizing each stage of SMC (Separate opt SMC). We use trimmed videos in training set to train the base layers. Then, we let the parameters of base layers freezed and train the other layers on the untrimmed videos in training set. The results are summarized in Table 1.

The performances of different combinations of the anchor layers on THUMOS-14 are summarized in Table 2. It can be seen that all the anchor layers make contribution to the final results. We tested on the inputs of $96 \times 96 \times 128$ and $128 \times 128 \times 128$ (hight × width × length) to prove the robustness of your proposed approach. The results are summarized in Table 3. The performance decreases when reducing the length of input frames.

Table 3. The performances on different inputs on THUMOS'14

IoU thresholds	0.3	0.4	0.5	0.6	0.7
SMC ($96 \times 96 \times 128$)	42.5	34.4	31.4	26.3	18.8
SMC ($128 \times 128 \times 128$)	45.2	36.0	33.1	27.2	20.0

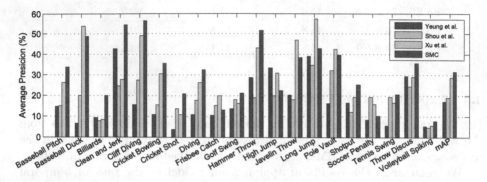

Fig. 3. Detection average precision comparison over different action categories with the overlap threshold 0.5 on THUMOS'14 (best viewed in color) (Color figure online)

The Average Precision (AP) results of each action category in THUMOS'14 at the IoU threshold 0.5 are illustrated in Fig. 3. The SMC network outperforms the other state-of-the-art methods for 11 out of 20 action categories. For some action categories, our model is second best by a small margin (*e.g.*, Golf Swing, Pole Vault and Throw Discus). Figure 4(a) shows some qualitative results from two videos in the THUMOS'14 dataset.

4.4   Experiments on MEXaction2

We use all of the 38 untrimmed video in the MEXaction2 training set to train our model. As the distribution of the length of action instances in MEXaction2 is similar to the THUMOS'14, we keep the length of the input buffer to be 192 frames, and sample frames at 10 FPS as well. The learning rate is kept at 0.0001 for the first 20 epochs and then decreases to 0.00001 for 10 further epochs. We augment the data by horizontal flipping of the frames. We finetune the THUMOS'14 pretrained model on the MEXaction2 dataset.

Table 4 lists a comparative evaluation of the proposed SMC network with state-of-the-art methods. Following the standard practice [43], we evaluate our method in terms of mAP at 0.5 IoU threshold and compare with dense trajectory (DTF) based method [43], S-CNN [2] and SSAD [35]. Our method significantly outperforms other methods for all action categories in MEXaction2, and the average performance is improved from 11.0% to 20.2%. The performance improvement over the standard methods on BullChargeCape is up to 18.1%. The improvement on HorseRiding is not that high. This is mainly because that

Table 4. Average precision on MEXaction2. The temporal IoU threshold is set to 0.5 during evaluation.

AP(%)	BullChargeCape	HorseRiding	mAP
DTF [43]	0.3	3.1	1.7
S-CNN [2]	11.6	3.1	7.4
SSAD [35]	16.5	5.5	11.0
SMC	**34.6**	**5.8**	**20.2**

Table 5. Activity detection speed at test time. The speed of SMC model is measured with the batch size of 4. SMC is the fastest activity detector on record.

	FPS
S-CNN [2]	60
CDC [26]	500
DAP [3]	134.1
R-C3D [33] (on Titan X Maxwell)	569
R-C3D [33] (on Titan X Pascal)	1030
SS-TAD [36] (on Titan X Maxwell)	701
SMC (ours on Titan X Maxwell)	**753**
SMC (ours on Titan X Pascal)	**1401**

a moment is considered as positive only when the horse is running. Negative moments that a man sits on horseback and the horse is standing or walks slowly are very confusing. We visually show the prediction results for the MEXaction2 test samples in Fig. 4(b).

4.5   Activity Detection Speed

Our model is very efficient since it has only a single stream. As illustrated in Table 5, we compare our model with four other models in terms of detection speed. As we can see, SMC is the fastest activity detector on record. S-CNN [2] is bottlenecked by the time-consuming sliding window proposal strategy and has a speed of 60 FPS. DAP [3] incorporates a proposal prediction step on the top of LSTM and possesses a speed of 134.1 FPS. The LSTM recurrent architecture does not enable parallelization over the elements of a sequence which seriously harms the efficiency of model. R-C3D [33] uses extra prediction layers for temporal proposals and requires feature resampling. Our SMC network completely eliminates the proposal generation and additional feature extraction. We adopt the fully convolutional manner, thus the computation can be parallelized over time. In this way, SMC offers a significant boost in the processing speed, and it operates at 753 FPS on a single GeForce GTX Titan X (Maxwell) GPU.

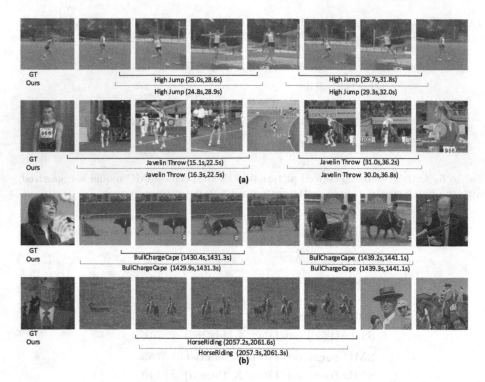

Fig. 4. Qualitative visualization of the predicted actions by SMC network (best viewed in color). Figure (a) and (b) show detection results for two videos in THUMOS'14 and MEXaction2. We show the key frames of the video with detections and ground truth segments along the time axis below the images. Ground truth action segments are marked in black and predicted action segments are marked in green. Predicted segments with IoU more than 0.5 is considered as correct (Color figure online)

5   Conclusions

We propose SMC, a single-stage end-to-end trainable convolutional neural network for temporal action detection. Our SMC network drops the proposal generation and external feature extraction, and can directly predict action instances in untrimmed videos. We evaluate our method on two larger-scale action detection datasets with diverse characteristics. The results demonstrate that our SMC can produce more reliable action detections with much higher speed than the existing state-of-the-art methods. In future work, we plan to leverage this model as a base component for more complex video understanding tasks, such as dense video captioning and activity understanding.

Acknowledgement. This work is supported by the National Natural Science Foundation of China under Grant 61673362 and 61836008, Youth Innovation Promotion Association CAS (2017496), and the Fundamental Research Funds for the Central Universities.

References

1. Caba Heilbron, F., Carlos Niebles, J., Ghanem, B.: Fast temporal activity proposals for efficient detection of human actions in untrimmed videos. In: CVPR (2016)
2. Shou, Z., Wang, D., Chang, S.F.: Temporal action localization in untrimmed videos via multi-stage CNNs. In: CVPR (2016)
3. Escorcia, V., Caba Heilbron, F., Niebles, J.C., Ghanem, B.: DAPs: deep action proposals for action understanding. In: Leibe, B., Matas, J., Sebe, N., Welling, M. (eds.) ECCV 2016. LNCS, vol. 9907, pp. 768–784. Springer, Cham (2016). https:// doi.org/10.1007/978-3-319-46487-9_47
4. Oneata, D., Verbeek, J., Schmid, C.: The LEAR submission at Thumos 2014 (2014)
5. Yuan, J., Ni, B., Yang, X., Kassim, A.A.: Temporal action localization with pyramid of score distribution features. In: CVPR (2016)
6. Redmon, J., Divvala, S., Girshick, R., Farhadi, A.: You only look once: unified, real-time object detection. In: CVPR (2016)
7. Redmon, J., Farhadi, A.: Yolo9000: better, faster, stronger. In: CVPR (2017)
8. Liu, W., et al.: SSD: single shot MultiBox detector. In: Leibe, B., Matas, J., Sebe, N., Welling, M. (eds.) ECCV 2016. LNCS, vol. 9905, pp. 21–37. Springer, Cham (2016). https://doi.org/10.1007/978-3-319-46448-0_2
9. Herath, S., Harandi, M., Porikli, F.: Going deeper into action recognition: a survey. Image Vis. Comput. (2017)
10. Ji, S., Xu, W., Yang, M., Yu, K.: 3D convolutional neural networks for human action recognition. PAMI (2013)
11. Simonyan, K., Zisserman, A.: Two-stream convolutional networks for action recognition in videos. In: NIPS (2014)
12. Yue-Hei Ng, J., Hausknecht, M., Vijayanarasimhan, S., Vinyals, O., Monga, R., Toderici, G.: Beyond short snippets: deep networks for video classification. In: CVPR (2015)
13. Zhu, Y., Long, Y., Guan, Y., Newsam, S., Shao, L.: Towards universal representation for unseen action recognition. In: CVPR (2018)
14. Laptev, I.: On space-time interest points. IJCV (2005)
15. Klaser, A., Marszałek, M., Schmid, C.: A spatio-temporal descriptor based on 3D-gradients. In: BMVC(2008)
16. Tran, D., Bourdev, L., Fergus, R., Torresani, L., Paluri, M.: Learning spatiotemporal features with 3D convolutional networks. In: CVPR (2015)
17. Karpathy, A., Toderici, G., Shetty, S., Leung, T., Sukthankar, R., Fei-Fei, L.: Large-scale video classification with convolutional neural networks. In: CVPR (2014)
18. Feichtenhofer, C., Pinz, A., Wildes, R.: Spatiotemporal residual networks for video action recognition. In: NIPS (2016)
19. Simonyan, K., Zisserman, A.: Very deep convolutional networks for large-scale image recognition. In: ICLR (2014)
20. He, K., Zhang, X., Ren, S., Sun, J.: Deep residual learning for image recognition. In: CVPR (2016)
21. Baccouche, M., Mamalet, F., Wolf, C., Garcia, C., Baskurt, A.: Sequential deep learning for human action recognition. In: Salah, A.A., Lepri, B. (eds.) HBU 2011. LNCS, vol. 7065, pp. 29–39. Springer, Heidelberg (2011). https://doi.org/10.1007/978-3-642-25446-8_4
22. Donahue, J., et al.: Long-term recurrent convolutional networks for visual recognition and description. In: CVPR (2015)

23. Gaidon, A., Harchaoui, Z., Schmid, C.: Actom sequence models for efficient action detection. In: CVPR (2011)
24. Jain, M., van Gemert, J.C., Snoek, C.G.: What do 15,000 object categories tell us about classifying and localizing actions? In: CVPR (2015)
25. Oneata, D., Verbeek, J., Schmid, C.: Efficient action localization with approximately normalized fisher vectors. In: CVPR (2014)
26. Shou, Z., Chan, J., Zareian, A., Miyazawa, K., Chang, S.F.: CDC: convolutional-de-convolutional networks for precise temporal action localization in untrimmed videos. In: CVPR (2017)
27. Dai, X., Singh, B., Zhang, G., Davis, L.S., Chen, Y.Q.: Temporal context network for activity localization in videos. In: ICCV (2017)
28. Gao, J., Yang, Z., Nevatia, R.: Cascaded boundary regression for temporal action detection. In: BMVC (2017)
29. Gao, J., Yang, Z., Sun, C., Chen, K., Nevatia, R.: TURN TAP: temporal unit regression network for temporal action proposals. In: ICCV (2017)
30. Yeung, S., Russakovsky, O., Jin, N., Andriluka, M., Mori, G., Fei-Fei, L.: Every moment counts: dense detailed labeling of actions in complex videos. IJCV (2015)
31. Yeung, S., Russakovsky, O., Mori, G., Fei-Fei, L.: End-to-end learning of action detection from frame glimpses in videos. In: CVPR (2016)
32. Singh, B., Marks, T.K., Jones, M., Tuzel, O., Shao, M.: A multi-stream bi-directional recurrent neural network for fine-grained action detection. In: CVPR (2016)
33. Xu, H., Das, A., Saenko, K.: R-C3D: region convolutional 3D network for temporal activity detection. In: ICCV (2017)
34. Zhu, Y., Newsam, S.: Efficient action detection in untrimmed videos via multi-task learning. In: WACV (2017)
35. Lin, T., Zhao, X., Shou, Z.: Single shot temporal action detection. In: ACMMM (2017)
36. Buch, S., Escorcia, V., Ghanem, B., Fei-Fei, L., Niebles, J.C.: End-to-end, single-stream temporal action detection in untrimmed videos. In: BMVC (2017)
37. Girshick, R., Donahue, J., Darrell, T., Malik, J.: Rich feature hierarchies for accurate object detection and semantic segmentation. In: CVPR (2014)
38. Girshick, R.: Fast R-CNN. In: ICCV (2015)
39. Ren, S., He, K., Girshick, R., Sun, J.: Faster R-CNN: towards real-time object detection with region proposal networks. In: NIPS (2015)
40. Glorot, X., Bordes, A., Bengio, Y.: Deep sparse rectifier neural networks. In: ICAIS (2011)
41. Zhou, B., Khosla, A., Lapedriza, A., Oliva, A., Torralba, A.: Object detectors emerge in deep scene CNNs. In: ICLR (2015)
42. Jiang, Y., et al.: THUMOS challenge: action recognition with a large number of classes (2014). http://crcv.ucf.edu/THUMOS14/
43. MEXaction2 (2015). http://mexculture.cnam.fr/xwiki/bin/view/Datasets/Mex+action+dataset
44. Bottou, L.: Large-scale machine learning with stochastic gradient descent. In: Lechevallier, Y., Saporta, G. (eds.) COMPSTAT 2010, pp. 177–186. Springer, Heidelberg (2010). https://doi.org/10.1007/978-3-7908-2604-3_16
45. Soomro, K., Zamir, A.R., Shah, M.: UCF101: a dataset of 101 human actions classes from videos in the wild. CRCV-TR-12-01 (2012)
46. Jia, Y., et al.: Caffe: convolutional architecture for fast feature embedding. In: ACMMM (2014)

47. Wang, L., Qiao, Y., Tang, X.: Action recognition and detection by combining motion and appearance features. In: THUMOS14 Action Recognition Challenge (2014)
48. Buch, S., Escorcia, V., Shen, C., Ghanem, B., Niebles, J.C.: SST: single-stream temporal action proposals. In: CVPR (2017)

SAFE: Scale Aware Feature Encoder for Scene Text Recognition

Wei Liu[(✉)], Chaofeng Chen, and Kwan-Yee K. Wong

Department of Computer Science, The University of Hong Kong,
Pokfulam, Hong Kong
{wliu,cfchen,kykwong}@cs.hku.hk

Abstract. In this paper, we address the problem of having characters with different scales in scene text recognition. We propose a novel scale aware feature encoder (SAFE) that is designed specifically for encoding characters with different scales. SAFE is composed of a multi-scale convolutional encoder and a scale attention network. The multi-scale convolutional encoder targets at extracting character features under multiple scales, and the scale attention network is responsible for selecting features from the most relevant scale(s). SAFE has two main advantages over the traditional single-CNN encoder used in current state-of-the-art text recognizers. First, it explicitly tackles the scale problem by extracting scale-invariant features from the characters. This allows the recognizer to put more effort in handling other challenges in scene text recognition, like those caused by view distortion and poor image quality. Second, it can transfer the learning of feature encoding across different character scales. This is particularly important when the training set has a very unbalanced distribution of character scales, as training with such a dataset will make the encoder biased towards extracting features from the predominant scale. To evaluate the effectiveness of SAFE, we design a simple text recognizer named scale-spatial attention network (S-SAN) that employs SAFE as its feature encoder, and carry out experiments on six public benchmarks. Experimental results demonstrate that S-SAN can achieve state-of-the-art (or, in some cases, extremely competitive) performance without any post-processing.

Keywords: Scene text recognition · Scale aware feature encoder

1 Introduction

Scene text recognition refers to recognizing a sequence of characters that appear in a natural image. Inspired by the success [2] in neural machine translation, many of the recently proposed scene text recognizers [6,7,20,21,29] adopt an encoder-decoder framework with an attention mechanism. Despite the remarkable results reported by them, very few of them have addressed the problem of having characters with different scales in the image. This problem often prevents existing text recognizers from achieving better performance.

© Springer Nature Switzerland AG 2019
C. V. Jawahar et al. (Eds.): ACCV 2018, LNCS 11362, pp. 196–211, 2019.
https://doi.org/10.1007/978-3-030-20890-5_13

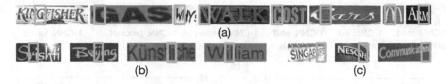

Fig. 1. Examples of text images having characters with different scales. The green rectangles represent the effective receptive field of a single-CNN encoder. (a) The character scale may vary greatly because of font style, font size, text arrangements, *etc.* (b) For characters in the same image with the same font style and font size, their scales may still vary depending on which characters they are. For instance, lower case letters 'l' and 'i' are usually much 'narrower' than other characters. (c) The distortion of text can also result in different character scales within the same image. (Color figure online)

In a natural image, the scale of a character can vary greatly depending on which character it is (for instance, 'M' and 'W' are in general wider than 'i' and 'l'), font style, font size, text arrangement, viewpoint, *etc.* Figure 1 shows some examples of text images containing characters with different scales. Existing text recognizers [6,7,20–22,28,29] employ only one single CNN for feature encoding, and often perform poorly for such text images. Note that a single-CNN encoder with a fixed receptive field[1] (refer to the green rectangles in Fig. 1) can only effectively encode characters which fall within a particular scale range. For characters outside this range, the encoder captures either only partial context information of a character or distracting information from the cluttered background and neighboring characters. In either case, the encoder cannot extract discriminative features from the corresponding characters effectively, and the recognizer will have great difficulties in recognizing such characters.

In this paper, we address the problem of having characters with different scales by proposing a simple but efficient scale aware feature encoder (SAFE). SAFE is designed specifically for encoding characters with different scales. It is composed of (i) a multi-scale convolutional encoder for extracting character features under multiple scales, and (ii) a scale attention network for automatically selecting features from the most relevant scale(s). SAFE has two main advantages over the traditional single-CNN encoder used in current state-of-the-art text recognizers. First, it explicitly tackles the scale problem by extracting scale-invariant features from the characters. This allows the recognizer to put more effort in handling other challenges in scene text recognition, like those caused by character distortion and poor image quality (see Fig. 2a). Second, it can transfer the learning of feature encoding across different character scales. This is particularly important when the training set has a very unbalanced distribution of character scales. For instance, the most widely adopted SynthR dataset [12] has only a small number of images containing a single character (see Fig. 2b). In order to keep the training and testing procedures simple and efficient, most of the previous methods [6,7,20,22,29] resized an input image to

---

[1] Although the receptive field of a CNN is large, its effective region [24] responsible for calculating each feature representation only occupies a small fraction.

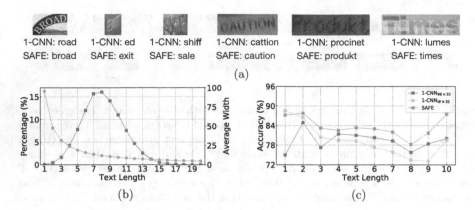

(a)

(b)   (c)

Fig. 2. Advantages of SAFE over the single-CNN encoder (1-CNN). (a) SAFE performs better than 1-CNN in handling distorted or low-quality text images. (b) The distribution of text lengths in SynthR [12] and the average character width in text images of different lengths after being resized to 96 × 32. (c) Detailed performance of recognizers with 1-CNN and with SAFE on recognizing text of different lengths. All the models are trained using SynthR. 1-CNN$_{96\times32}$ is trained by resizing the images to 96 × 32, whereas 1-CNN$_{W\times32}$ is trained by only rescaling images to a fixed height while keeping their aspect ratios unchanged.

a fixed resolution before feeding it to the text recognizer. This resizing operation will therefore result in very few training images containing large characters. Obviously, a text recognizer with a single-CNN encoder cannot learn to extract discriminative features from large characters due to limited training examples. This leads to a poor performance on recognizing text images with a single character (see Fig. 2c). Alternatively, [28,34] resized the training images to a fixed height while keeping their aspect ratios unchanged. This, however, can only partially solve the scale problem as character scales may still vary because of font style, text arrangement, distortion, *etc.* Hence, it is still unlikely to have a well-balanced distribution of character scales in the training set. Training with such a dataset will definitely make the encoder biased towards extracting features from the predominant scale and not able to generalize well to characters of different scales. Unlike the single-CNN encoder, SAFE can share the knowledge of feature encoding across different character scales and effectively extract discriminative features from characters of different scales. This enables the text recognizer to have a much more robust performance (see Fig. 2c).

To evaluate the effectiveness of SAFE, we design a simple text recognizer named scale-spatial attention network (S-SAN) that employs SAFE as its feature encoder. Following [21,34], S-SAN employs a spatial attention network in its LSTM-based decoder to handle a certain degree of text distortion. Experiments are carried out on six public benchmarks, and experimental results demonstrate that S-SAN can achieve state-of-the-art (or, in some cases, extremely competitive) performance without any post-processing.

2   Related Work

Many methods have been proposed for scene text recognition in recent years. According to their strategies of recognizing words in text images, previous text recognizers can be roughly classified into bottom-up and top-down approaches.

Recognizers based on the bottom-up approach first perform individual character detection and recognition using character-level classifiers, and then they integrate the results across the whole text image to get the final word recognition. In [26,31,32,35], hand-crafted features (e.g., HOG) were employed to train classifiers for detecting and recognizing characters in the text image. With the recent success of deep learning, many methods [4,13,16,33] used deep networks to train character classifiers. In [33], Wang et al. used a CNN to extract features from the text image for character recognition. [4] first over-segmented the whole text image into multiple character regions before using a fully-connected neural network for character recognition. Unlike [4,33] which used a single character classifier, [16] combined a binary text/no-text classifier, a character classifier and a bi-gram classifier to compute scores for candidate words in a fixed lexicon. To recognize text without a lexicon, a structured output loss was used in their extended work [13] to optimize the individual character and N-gram predictors.

The above bottom-up methods require the segmentation of each character, which is a highly non-trivial task due to the complex background and different font size of text in the image. Recognizers [6,7,10,12,14,20,22,28,29,34] which are based on the top-down approach directly recognize the entire word in the image. In [12] and [14], Jaderberg et al. extracted CNN features from the entire image, and performed a 90k-way classification (90k being the size of a pre-defined dictionary). Instead of using only CNNs, [10,22,28] also employed recurrent neural networks to encode features of word images. All these three models were optimized by the connectionist temporal classification [8], which does not require an alignment between the sequential features and the ground truth labelling.

Following the success of the attention mechanism [2] in neural machine translation, recent text recognizers [6,7,20,21,29,34] introduced a learnable attention network in their decoders to automatically select the most relevant features for recognizing individual characters. In order to handle distorted scene text, [22,29] employed a spatial transformer network (STN) [15] to rectify the distortion of the entire text image before recognition. As it is difficult to successfully train a STN from scratch, [7] proposed to encode the text image from multiple directions and used a filter gate to generate the final features for decoding. Unlike [7,22,29] which rectified the distortion of the entire image, a hierarchical attention mechanism was used in [21] to rectify the distortion of individual characters.

Different from [7,21,22,29] which focused on recognizing severely distorted text images, we address the problem of having characters with different scales. This is a common problem that exists in both distorted and undistorted text recognition. The scale-spatial attention network (S-SAN) proposed in this paper belongs to the family of attention-based encoder-decoder neural networks. Unlike previous methods [6,7,20–22,28,29] which employed only a single CNN as their feature encoder, we introduce a scale aware feature encoder (SAFE) to extract scale-invariant features from characters with different scales. This guarantees a much more robust feature extraction for the text recognizer. Although a similar idea has been proposed for semantic segmentation [5] to merge segmentation maps from different scales, it is the first time that the scale problem has been identified and efficiently handled for text recognition using an attention-based encoder-decoder framework. Better still, SAFE can also be easily deployed in other text recognizers to further boost their performance.

3   Scale Aware Feature Encoder

The scale aware feature encoder (SAFE) is conceptually simple: in order to extract discriminative features from characters with different scales, feature encoding of the text image should first be carried out under different scales, and features from the most relevant scale(s) are then selected at each spatial location to form the final feature map for the later decoding. SAFE is thus a natural and intuitive idea. As illustrated in Fig. 3, SAFE is composed of a multi-scale convolutional encoder and a scale-attention network. Throughout this paper, we omit the bias terms for improved readability.

Multi-scale Convolutional Encoder. The multi-scale convolutional encoder is responsible for encoding the original text images under multiple scales. The basic component of the multi-scale convolutional encoder takes the form of a backbone convolutional neural network. Given a single gray image $\mathbf{I}$ as input, a multi-scale pyramid of images $\{\mathbf{X}_s\}_{s=1}^N$ is first generated. $\mathbf{X}_s$ here denotes the image at scale s having a dimension of $W_s \times H_s$ (width × height), and $\mathbf{X}_1$ is the image at the finest scale. In order to encode each image in the pyramid, N backbone CNNs which share the same set of parameters are employed in the multi-scale convolutional encoder (see Fig. 3). The output of our multi-scale convolutional encoder is a set of N spatial feature maps

$$\{\mathbf{F}_1, \mathbf{F}_2, \cdots, \mathbf{F}_N\} = \{\mathrm{CNN}_1(\mathbf{X}_1), \mathrm{CNN}_2(\mathbf{X}_2), \cdots, \mathrm{CNN}_N(\mathbf{X}_N)\}, \qquad (1)$$

where CNN_s and $\mathbf{F}_s$ denote the backbone CNN and the output feature map at scale $s \in \{1, 2, \cdots, N\}$ respectively. $\mathbf{F}_s$ has a dimension of $W_s' \times H_s' \times C'$ (width × height × #channels).

Unlike dominant backbone CNNs adopted by [6,7,22,28,29] which compress information along the image height dimension and generate unit-height feature maps, each of our backbone CNNs keeps the spatial resolution of its feature map $\mathbf{F}_s$ close to that of the corresponding input image $\mathbf{X}_s$. Features from both text and non-text regions, as well as from different characters, therefore remain distinguishable in both the width and height dimensions in each feature map. In order to preserve the spatial resolution, we only apply two 2×2 down-sampling layers (see Fig. 3) in each of our backbone CNNs. Each feature map $\mathbf{F}_s$ is therefore sub-sampled only four times in both width and height (i.e., $W_s' = W_s/4$ and $H_s' = H_s/4$). More implementation details related to our backbone CNNs can be found in Sect. 5.2.

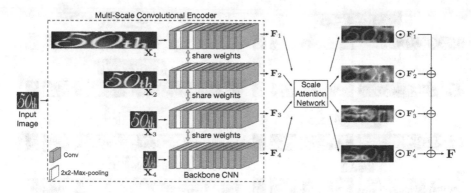

Fig. 3. The architecture of SAFE ($N = 4$). As most of the text images contain only a single word, the scale problem along the height dimension is not as severe as that along the width dimension. In our implementation, we resize the input images to 4 different resolutions, namely 192×32, 96×32, 48×32 and 24×32 respectively. The saliency maps in the scale attention network represent the scale attention for the feature maps extracted under 4 different resolutions. $\odot$ and $\oplus$ denote element-wise multiplication and summation respectively.

Scale Attention Network. The scale attention network is responsible for automatically selecting features from the most relevant scale(s) at each spatial location to generate the final scale-invariant feature map $\mathbf{F}$. In the proposed scale attention network, the N convolutional feature maps outputted from the multi-scale convolutional encoder are first up-sampled to the same resolution $\{\mathbf{F}'_1, \mathbf{F}'_2, \cdots, \mathbf{F}'_N\} = \{u(\mathbf{F}_1), u(\mathbf{F}_2), \cdots, u(\mathbf{F}_N)\}$, where $u(\cdot)$ is an up-sampling function, and $\mathbf{F}'_s$ is the up-sampled feature map with a dimension of $W' \times H' \times C'$ (width $\times$ height $\times$ #channels). Through extensive experiments, we find that the performances of different up-sampling functions (*e.g.*, bilinear interpolation, nearest interpolation, *etc.*) are quite similar. We therefore simply use bilinear interpolation in our implementation.

After obtaining the up-sampled feature maps, our scale attention network utilizes an attention mechanism to learn to weight features from different scales. Since the size of the characters may not be constant within a text image (see Fig. 3), the computation of attention towards features from different scales takes place at each spatial location. In order to select the features from the most relevant scale(s) at the spatial location (i, j), N scores are first computed for evaluating the importance of features from the N different scales

$$
\begin{bmatrix} f_1(i,j) \\ f_2(i,j) \\ \vdots \\ f_N(i,j) \end{bmatrix} = \mathbf{W} \begin{bmatrix} \mathbf{F}'_1(i,j) \\ \mathbf{F}'_2(i,j) \\ \vdots \\ \mathbf{F}'_N(i,j) \end{bmatrix} \tag{2}
$$

where $f_s(i, j)$ is the score of the C'-dimensional feature vector $\mathbf{F}'_s(i, j)$ at location (i, j) of the corresponding feature map $\mathbf{F}'_s$ at scale s, and $\mathbf{W}$ is the parameter

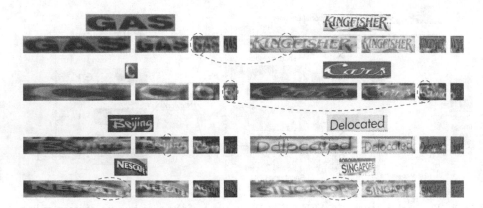

Fig. 4. Visualization of scale attention in the proposed SAFE. The saliency maps of the scale attention are superimposed on the images of the corresponding scales.

matrix. The proposed scale attention network then defines the scale attention at location (i, j) as

$$\omega_s(i, j) = \frac{\exp(f_s(i, j))}{\sum_{s'=1}^{N} \exp(f_{s'}(i, j))}, \tag{3}$$

where $\omega_s(i, j)$ is the attention weight for the feature vector $\mathbf{F}'_s(i, j)$. Finally, the scale-invariant feature map $\mathbf{F}$ can be computed as

$$\mathbf{F}(i, j) = \sum_{s=1}^{N} \omega_s(i, j) \mathbf{F}'_s(i, j). \tag{4}$$

The final feature map $\mathbf{F}$ has the same dimension as each up-sampled feature map $\mathbf{F}'_s$. Note that the scale attention network together with the multi-scale convolutional encoder are optimized in an end-to-end manner using only the recognition loss. As illustrated in Fig. 4, although we do not have the ground truth to supervise the feature selection across different scales, the scale attention network can automatically learn to attend on the features from the most relevant scale(s) for generating the final feature map $\mathbf{F}$.

4   Scale-Spatial Attention Network

To demonstrate the effectiveness of SAFE proposed in Sect. 3, we design a scale-spatial attention network (S-SAN) for scene text recognition. S-SAN uses SAFE as its feature encoder, and employs a character aware decoder composed of a spatial attention network and a LSTM-based decoder. Figure 5 shows the overall architecture of S-SAN.

4.1   SAFE

To extract scale-invariant features for recognizing characters with different scales, S-SAN first employs SAFE proposed in Sect. 3 to encode the original text

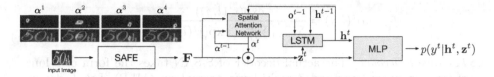

Fig. 5. The architecture of S-SAN. The saliency maps represent the spatial attention at different decoding steps. ⊙ denotes element-wise multiplication.

image. By imposing weight sharing across backbone CNNs of different scales, SAFE keeps its number of parameters to a minimum. Comparing with previous encoders adopted by [3,6,7,20–22,28,29] for text recognition, SAFE not only keeps its structure as simple as possible (see Table 1), but also effectively handles characters with different scales. This enables S-SAN to achieve a much better performance on recognizing text in natural images (see Tables 3 and 4).

4.2 Character Aware Decoder

The character aware decoder of S-SAN is responsible for recurrently translating the scale-invariant feature map $\mathbf{F}$ into the corresponding ground truth labelling $\mathbf{y} = \{y^1, y^2, ..., y^T, y^{T+1}\}$. Here, T denotes the length of the text and y^{T+1} is the end-of-string (eos) token representing the end of the labelling. In this section, we refer to the process of predicting each character y^t as one time/decoding step.

Spatial Attention Network. The function of the spatial attention network is to generate a sequence of context vectors from the scale-invariant feature map $\mathbf{F}$ for recognizing individual characters. Following [21,34], our spatial attention network extends the standard 1D attention mechanism [6,7,20,29] to the 2D spatial domain. This allows the decoder to focus on features at the most relevant spatial locations for recognizing individual characters, and handle a certain degree of text distortion in natural images. At a particular decoding step t, we compute the context vector $\mathbf{z}^t$ as a weighted sum of all feature vectors in $\mathbf{F}$, i.e., $\mathbf{z}^t = \sum_{i=1}^{W'} \sum_{j=1}^{H'} \alpha^t(i,j)\mathbf{F}(i,j)$, where $\alpha^t(i,j)$ is the weight applied to $\mathbf{F}(i,j)$ as determined by the spatial attention network. For the recognition of a single character at decoding step t, the context vector $\mathbf{z}^t$ should only focus on features at the most relevant spatial locations (i.e., those corresponding to the single character being recognized). To compute $\alpha^t(i,j)$ at the current decoding step t, we first exploit a simple CNN to encode the previous attention map $\boldsymbol{\alpha}^{t-1}$ into

$$\mathbf{A}^{t-1} = \text{CNN}_{\text{spatial}}(\boldsymbol{\alpha}^{t-1}). \tag{5}$$

We then evaluate a relevancy score at each spatial location as

$$r^t(i,j) = \mathbf{w}^{\mathrm{T}}\tanh[\mathbf{M}\mathbf{h}^{t-1} + \mathbf{U}\mathbf{A}^{t-1}(i,j) + \mathbf{V}\mathbf{F}(i,j)], \tag{6}$$

where $\mathbf{h}^{t-1}$ is the previous hidden state of the decoder (explained later), $\mathbf{M}$, $\mathbf{U}$ and $\mathbf{V}$ are the parameter matrices, and $\mathbf{w}$ is a parameter vector. Finally, we normalize the scores to obtain the attention weight

$$\alpha^t(i,j) = \frac{\exp(r^t(i,j))}{\sum_{i'=1}^{W'} \sum_{j'=1}^{H'} \exp(r^t(i',j'))}. \tag{7}$$

LSTM-Based Decoder. The actual decoder of S-SAN takes the form of a long short-term memory layer and a multi-layer perceptron (MLP). Let L denote the set of 37-class (26 letters + 10 digits + eos) case-insensitive characters in our task. At the decoding step t, the LSTM-based decoder defines a probability distribution over L as

$$\mathbf{h}^t = \text{LSTM}(\mathbf{h}^{t-1}, \mathbf{o}^{t-1}, \mathbf{z}^t) \tag{8}$$

$$p(y^t|\mathbf{h}^t, \mathbf{z}^t) = \text{SoftMax}(\mathbf{W}_y \begin{bmatrix} \mathbf{h}^t \\ \tanh(\mathbf{W}_z \mathbf{z}^t) \end{bmatrix}), \tag{9}$$

where $\mathbf{h}^{t-1}$ and $\mathbf{h}^t$ denote the previous and current hidden states respectively, $\mathbf{o}^{t-1}$ is the one-hot encoding of the previous character y^{t-1}, $\mathbf{W}_y$ and $\mathbf{W}_z$ are the parameters of two linear layers in the MLP, and SoftMax denotes the final layer of the MLP for outputting the probability. The probability of the sequential labelling is then given by the product of the probability of each label, i.e.,

$$p(\mathbf{y}|\mathbf{I}) = \prod_{t=1}^{T+1} p(y^t|\mathbf{h}^t, \mathbf{z}^t). \tag{10}$$

5   Datasets and Implementation Details

5.1   Datasets

Following [13,14,20–22,29], S-SAN is trained using the most commonly adopted dataset released by Jaderberg *et al.* [12] (referred to as SynthR). This dataset contains 8-million synthetic text images together with their corresponding word labels. The distribution of text lengths in SynthR is shown in Fig. 2b. The evaluation of S-SAN is carried out on the following six public benchmarks.

- **IIIT5K** [25] contains 3,000 word test images collected from the Internet. Each image is associated to a 50-word lexicon and a 1K-word lexicon.
- **Street View Text (SVT)** [31] contains 647 test word images which are collected from Google Street View. Each word image has a 50-word lexicon.
- **ICDAR-2003 (IC03)** [23] contains 860 text images for testing. Each image has a 50-word lexicon defined by Wang *et al.* [31]. A full lexicon is constructed by merging all 50-word lexicons. Following [31], we recognize the images having only alphanumeric words (0-9 and A-Z) with at least three characters.
- **ICDAR-2013 (IC13)** [18] is derived from ICDAR-2003, and contains 1,015 cropped word test images without any pre-defined lexicon. Previous methods [20,21,29] recognize images containing only alphanumeric words with at least three characters, which results in 857 images left for evaluation. In Sect. 6, we refer to IC13 with 1,015 images as **IC13-L** and that with 857 images as **IC13-S**, where 'L' and 'S' stand for large and small respectively.

- **Street View Text Perspective (SVT-P)** [27] contains 639 test images which are specially picked from the side-view angles in Google Street View. Most of them suffer from a large perspective distortion.
- **ICDAR Incidental Scene Text (ICIST)** [17] contains 2,077 text images for testing. Many of them are severely distorted and blurry. To make a fair comparison with [3,6], we also discard the images with non-alphanumeric characters in ICIST, which results in 1,811 images for testing. Like IC13, we refer to ICIST with 2,077 images as **ICIST-L** and that with 1,811 images as **ICIST-S** in Sect. 6.

5.2   Network Architecture

Scale Aware Feature Encoder. The detailed architecture of the backbone CNN in SAFE is illustrated in Table 1. The basic backbone CNN consists of nine convolutional layers. The stride and padding size of each convolutional layer both equal 1. All the convolutional layers use ReLU as the activation function. Batch normalization [11] is used after every convolutional layer. In our implementation, the multi-scale pyramid of images used in the multi-scale convolutional encoder has 4 scales, with images having a dimension of 192×32, 96×32, 48×32 and 24×32 respectively. The dimensions of the corresponding feature maps $\{\mathbf{F}_s\}_{s=1}^4$ are $48 \times 8 \times 512$, $24 \times 8 \times 512$, $12 \times 8 \times 512$ and $6 \times 8 \times 512$ respectively. In our scale attention network, the spatial resolutions of the up-sampled[2] feature maps $\{\mathbf{F}'_s\}_{s=1}^4$ are all 24×8 (i.e., same as that of $\mathbf{F}_2$ which is extracted from $\mathbf{X}_2$ with a dimension of 96×32).

Character Aware Decoder. The character aware decoder employs a LSTM layer with 256 hidden states. In the spatial attention network, $\text{CNN}_{\text{spatial}}(\cdot)$ is one 7×7 convolutional layer with 32 channels. In Eq. (6), $\mathbf{h}^{t-1}$, $\mathbf{A}(i,j)$ and $\mathbf{F}(i,j)$ are vectors with a dimension of 256, 32 and 512 respectively, and $\mathbf{w}$ is a parameter vector of 256 dimensions. Consequently, the dimensions of $\mathbf{M}$, $\mathbf{U}$ and $\mathbf{V}$ are 256×256, 256×32 and 256×512 respectively. The initial spatial attention map is set to zero at each position.

5.3   Model Training and Testing

Adadelta [36] is used to optimize the parameters of S-SAN. During training, we use a batch size of 64. The proposed model is implemented using Torch7 and trained on a single NVIDIA Titan X GPU. It can process about 150 samples per second and converge in five days after about eight epochs over the training dataset. S-SAN is trained in an end-to-end manner only under the supervision of the recognition loss (i.e., the negative log-likelihood of Eq. (10)). During testing, for unconstrained text recognition, we directly pick the label with the highest probability in Eq. (9) as the output of each decoding step. For constrained recognition with lexicons of different sizes, we calculate the edit distances between the

---

[2] We obtain $\mathbf{F}'_1$ by actually down-sampling $\mathbf{F}_1$.

Table 1. Comparison of encoders among different text recognizers. 'STN', 'BLSTM' and 'SCAN' denote the spatial transformer network [15], the bi-directional LSTM and our scale attention network respectively. The configurations of the convolutional layers follow the format of [$kernel\ size, number\ of\ channels$] × $number\ of\ layers$. Cells with a gray background indicate convolutional blocks with residue connections. For the max-pooling layers, the kernel size and strides in both width and height dimensions follow the format of ($kernel_w, kernel_h, stride_w, stride_h$).

Model	STN	Backbone CNN					BLSTM	SCAN	Encoder Size
		Unit 1	Unit 2	Unit 3	Unit 4	Unit 5			
CRNN [28]	0	[3, 64]×1	[3, 128]×1	[3, 256]×2	[3, 512]×2	[2, 512]×1	2	0	8.3M
RARE [29]	1	(2,2,2,2)	(2,2,2,2)	(2,2,1,2)	(2,2,1,2)				16.5M
STAR-Net [22]	1	[3, 64]×5 / (2,2,2,2)	[3, 128]×4 / (2,2,2,2)	[3, 256]×4 / (1,2,1,2)	[3, 512]×4 / (1,2,1,2)	[3, 512]×1	1	0	14.6M
Char-Net [21]	1	[3, 64]×3 / (2,2,2,2)	[3, 128]×2 / (2,2,2,2)	[3, 256]×6	[3, 256]×4	[3, 512]×3	0	0	12.8M
FAN [6] Bai et al. [3]	0	[3, 32]×1 [3, 64]×1 / (2,2,2,2)	[3, 128]×3 / (2,2,2,2)	[3, 256]×5 / (2,2,1,2)	[3, 512]×11	[3, 512]×6 [2, 512]×2	1	0	45.8M
1-CNN	0	[3, 64]×1 / (2,2,2,2)	[3, 128]×1 / (2,2,2,2)	[3, 256]×3	[3, 512]×3	[3, 512]×1	0	0	9.03M
SAFE								1	9.04M
SAFE$_{res}$	0	[3, 64]×2 / (2,2,2,2)	[3, 128]×3 / (2,2,2,2)	[3, 256]×5	[3, 512]×9	[3, 512]×7	0	1	38.9M

prediction of the unconstrained text recognition and all words in the lexicon, and take the one with the smallest edit distance and highest recognition probability as our final prediction. In Tables 3 and 4, 'None' indicates unconstrained scene text recognition (*i.e.*, without imposing any lexicon). '50', '1K' and 'Full' denote each scene text recognized with a 50-word lexicon, a 1,000-word lexicon and a full lexicon respectively.

6   Experiments

Experiments are carried out on the six public benchmarks. Ablation study is first conducted in Sect. 6.1 to illustrate the effectiveness of SAFE. Comparison on the performance of S-SAN and other methods is then reported in Sect. 6.2, which demonstrates that S-SAN can achieve state-of-the-art performance on standard benchmarks for text recognition.

6.1   Ablation Study

In this section, we conduct an ablation study to demonstrate the effectiveness of SAFE. Note that all the models in the ablation study are trained using the commonly adopted SynthR dataset, and we only use the accuracies of unconstrained text recognition for comparison.

To demonstrate the advantages of SAFE over the single-CNN encoder (1-CNN), we first train five versions of text recognizers which employ single backbone CNN for feature encoding. The architecture of the backbone CNNs and

Table 2. Ablation study of the proposed SAFE.

Model	Image size	IIIT5K	SVT	IC03	IC13-S	IC13-L	SVT-P	ICIST-S	ICIST-L
1-CNN$_{24\times32}$	24 × 32	71.0	70.9	82.8	80.2	79.3	54.6	56.1	51.0
1-CNN$_{48\times32}$	48 × 32	81.3	81.8	90.5	87.6	86.2	68.8	66.3	60.3
1-CNN$_{96\times32}$	96 × 32	82.6	83.2	91.0	89.7	87.7	69.9	67.1	61.7
1-CNN$_{192\times32}$	192 × 32	82.1	83.2	90.6	89.5	87.2	68.5	65.1	59.5
1-CNN$_{W\times32}$	W × 32	83.6	82.2	91.3	90.1	89.4	63.3	62.4	57.4
	48 × 32, 96 × 32	84.2	84.7	92.3	89.7	88.3	71.6	70.5	64.4
	96 × 32, 192 × 32	83.7	84.9	92.4	**91.1**	88.9	72.1	68.8	62.9
S-SAN	24 × 32, 48 × 32, 96 × 32	85.0	84.4	92.0	90.7	89.8	72.9	70.7	64.7
	48 × 32, 96 × 32, 192 × 32	85.0	84.5	91.9	90.7	89.7	71.8	70.3	64.4
	24 × 32, 48 × 32, 96 × 32, 192 × 32	**85.2**	**85.5**	**92.9**	91.1	**90.3**	**74.4**	**71.8**	**65.7**

the decoders in the single-scale recognizers are identical to those in S-SAN. As illustrated in Table 2, we train the recognizers with the single-CNN encoder under different experimental settings, which resize the input text image to different resolutions. For simplicity, we directly use the encoder with the resolution of the training images to denote the corresponding recognizer. For example, 1-CNN$_{24\times32}$ stands for the single-CNN recognizer trained with images having a resolution of 24 × 32. As resizing images to a fixed resolution during training and testing would result in the training dataset having very few images containing large characters (see Fig. 2b), we also train a version of the single-CNN recognizer by resizing the image to a fixed height while keeping its aspect ratio unchanged (denoted as 1-CNN$_{W\times32}$ in Table 2). In order to train the recognizer with a batch size larger than 1, we normalize all the images to have a resolution of 192 × 32. For an image whose width is smaller than 192 after being resized to a height of 32, we pad it with the mean value to make its width equal to 192. Otherwise, we directly resize the image to 192 × 32 (there are very few text images with a width larger than 192). From the recognition results reported in Table 2, we see that S-SAN with SAFE outperforms the other recognizers with a single-CNN encoder by a large margin.

We also evaluate the scale selection of SAFE by using different combinations of rescaled images in the pyramid. As shown in Table 2, S-SAN with four scales (192 × 32, 96 × 32, 48 × 32 and 24 × 32) in the pyramid has the best performance on all the six public benchmarks.

6.2 Comparison with Other Methods

The recognition accuracies of S-SAN are reported in Table 3. Compared with the recent deep-learning based methods [13,14,20–22,28,29], S-SAN can achieve state-of-the-art (or, in some cases, extremely comparative) performance on both constrained and unconstrained text recognition.

In particular, we compare S-SAN against RARE [29], STAR-Net [22] and Char-Net [21], which are specifically designed for recognizing distorted text. In order to handle the distortion of text, RARE, STAR-Net and Char-Net all employ spatial transformer networks (STNs) [15] in their feature encoders. From

Table 3. Text recognition accuracies (%) on six pubic benchmarks. *[14] is not strictly unconstrained text recognition as its outputs are all constrained to a pre-defined 90K dictionary.

Method	IIIT5K			SVT		IC03			IC13-S	IC13-L	SVT-P	ICIST-L
	50	1K	None	50	None	50	Full	None	None	None	None	None
ABBYY [31]	24.3	-	-	35.0	-	56.0	55.0	-	-	-	-	-
Wang et al. [31]	-	-	-	57.0	-	76.0	62.0	-	-	-	-	-
Mishra et al. [25]	64.1	57.5	-	73.2	-	81.8	67.8	-	-	-	-	-
Wang et al. [33]	-	-	-	70.0	-	90.0	84.0	-	-	-	-	-
PhotoOCR [4]	-	-	-	90.4	78.0	-	-	-	-	87.6	-	-
Phan et al. [27]	-	-	-	73.7	-	82.2	-	-	-	-	-	-
Almazán et al. [1]	91.2	82.1	-	89.2	-	-	-	-	-	-	-	-
Lee et al. [19]	-	-	-	80.0	-	88.0	76.0	-	-	-	-	-
Yao et al. [35]	80.2	69.3	-	75.9	-	88.5	80.3	-	-	-	-	-
Jaderberg et al. [16]	-	-	-	86.1	-	96.2	91.5	-	-	-	-	-
Su et al. [30]	-	-	-	83.0	-	92.0	82.0	-	-	-	-	-
Jaderberg et al. [13]	95.5	89.6	-	93.2	71.7	97.8	97.0	89.6	-	81.8	-	-
Jaderberg et al. [14]	97.1	92.7	-	95.4	80.7*	**98.7**	**98.6**	93.1*	-	**90.8***	-	-
R²AM [20]	96.8	94.4	78.4	96.3	80.7	97.9	97.0	88.7	90.0	-	-	-
CRNN [28]	97.8	95.0	81.2	**97.5**	82.7	98.7	98.0	91.9	-	89.6	66.8	-
SRN [29]	96.5	92.8	79.7	96.1	81.5	97.8	96.4	88.7	87.5	-	-	-
RARE [29]	96.2	93.8	81.9	95.5	81.9	98.3	96.2	90.1	88.6	-	71.8	-
STAR-Net [22]	97.7	94.5	83.3	95.5	83.6	96.9	95.3	89.9	-	89.1	73.5	-
Char-Net [21]	-	-	83.6	-	84.4	-	-	91.5	90.8	-	73.5	60
S-SAN	**98.4**	**96.1**	**85.2**	97.1	**85.5**	98.5	97.7	92.9	**91.1**	90.3	**74.4**	**65.7**

the recognition results in Table 3, we find S-SAN outperforms all the three models by a large magain on almost every public benchmark. Even for the datasets IIIT5K and SVT-P that contain distorted text images, S-SAN without using any spatial transformer network can still achieve either extremely competitive or better performance. In order to explore the advantages of S-SAN comprehensively, we further report the complexity of these three models. In our implementation, S-SAN has 10.6 million parameters in total, while the encoders of RARE, STAR-Net and Char-Net already have about 16.5 million, 14.8 million and 12.8 million parameters respectively, as reported in Table 1.

By comparing with RARE, STAR-Net and Char-Net, we can see that S-SAN is much simpler but can still achieve much better performance on recognizing distorted text. This is mainly because SAFE can effectively handle the problem of encoding characters with varying scales. On one hand, with the multiscale convolutional encoder encoding the text images under multiple scales and the scale attention network automatically selecting features from the most relevant scale(s), SAFE can extract scale-invariant features from characters whose scales are affected by the distortion of the image. On the other hand, by explicitly tackling the scale problem, SAFE can put more attention on extracting

Table 4. Text recognition accuracies (%) of models using more training data.

Method	IIIT5K			SVT		IC03			IC13-L	SVT-P	ICIST-S	ICIST-L
	50	1K	None	50	None	50	Full	None	None	None		None
AON [7]	**99.6**	98.1	87.0	96.0	82.8	98.5	97.1	91.5	-	73.0	-	68.2
FAN [6]	99.3	97.5	87.4	97.1	85.9	**99.2**	97.3	94.2	93.3	-	70.6	66.2
Bai et al. [3]	99.5	97.9	88.3	96.6	87.5	98.7	97.9	94.6	**94.4**	-	73.9	-
S-SAN	99.0	97.9	90.5	97.1	87.0	98.5	97.6	93.7	91.9	77.1	76.9	70.7
S-SAN$_{res}$	99.3	**98.3**	**91.5**	**98.6**	**89.6**	99.1	**98.0**	**94.9**	93.8	**81.6**	**80.0**	**73.4**

discriminative features from distorted characters, which enables S-SAN a more robust performance when handling distortion of text images.

Note that the previous state-of-the-art methods [3,6] employ a 30-layer residual CNN with one BLSTM network in their encoders. We also train a deep version of our text recognizer (denoted as S-SAN$_{res}$), which employs a deep backbone CNN (denoted as SAFE$_{res}$ in Table 1). Besides, [6] and [3] were both trained using a 12-million dataset, which consists of 8-million images from SynthR and 4-million pixel-wise labeled images from [9]. Following [3,6], we also train S-SAN$_{res}$ using the 12-million dataset. The results of S-SAN$_{res}$ are reported in Table 4. As we can see from the table, S-SAN$_{res}$ achieves better results than [3,6] on almost every benchmark. In particular, S-SAN$_{res}$ significantly outperforms [3,6] on the most challenging dataset ICIST. Besides, unlike [6] which requires extra pixel-wise labeling of characters for training, S-SAN can be easily optimized using only the text images and their corresponding labels.

7 Conclusion

In this paper, we present a novel scale aware feature encoder (SAFE) to tackle the problem of having characters with different scales in the text images. SAFE is composed of a multi-scale convolutional encoder and a scale attention network. It can automatically extract scale-invariant features from characters with different scales. By explicitly handling the scale problem, SAFE can put more effort on handling other challenges in text recognition. Moreover, SAFE can transfer the learning of feature encoding across different character scales. This is particularly important for text recognizers to achieve a much more robust performance as it is nearly impossible to precisely control the scale distribution of characters in a training dataset. To demonstrate the effectiveness of SAFE, we design a simple but efficient scale-spatial attention network (S-SAN) for scene text recognition. Experiments on six public benchmarks illustrate that S-SAN can achieve state-of-the-art performance without any post-processing.

Acknowledgments. We gratefully acknowledge the support of NVIDIA Corporation with the donation of the Titan X Pascal GPU used for this research.

References

1. Almazán, J., Gordo, A., Fornés, A., Valveny, E.: Word spotting and recognition with embedded attributes. IEEE Trans. Pattern Anal. Mach. Intell. **36**(12), 2552–2566 (2014)
2. Bahdanau, D., Cho, K., Bengio, Y.: Neural machine translation by jointly learning to align and translate (2014). arXiv preprint: arXiv:1409.0473
3. Bai, F., Cheng, Z., Niu, Y., Pu, S., Zhou, S.: Edit probability for scene text recognition (2018). arXiv preprint: arXiv:1805.03384
4. Bissacco, A., Cummins, M., Netzer, Y., Neven, H.: PhotoOCR: reading text in uncontrolled conditions. In: IEEE International Conference on Computer Vision (2013)
5. Chen, L.C., Yang, Y., Wang, J., Xu, W., Yuille, A.L.: Attention to scale: scale-aware semantic image segmentation. In: IEEE Conference on Computer Vision and Pattern Recognition (2016)
6. Cheng, Z., Bai, F., Xu, Y., Zheng, G., Pu, S., Zhou, S.: Focusing attention: towards accurate text recognition in natural images (2017). arXiv preprint: arXiv:1709.02054v3
7. Cheng, Z., Liu, X., Bai, F., Niu, Y., Pu, S., Zhou, S.: Arbitrarily-oriented text recognition (2017). arXiv preprint: arXiv:1711.04226
8. Graves, A., Fernández, S., Gomez, F., Schmidhuber, J.: Connectionist temporal classification: labelling unsegmented sequence data with recurrent neural networks. In: International Conference on Machine Learning (2006)
9. Gupta, A., Vedaldi, A., Zisserman, A.: Synthetic data for text localisation in natural images. In: IEEE Conference on Computer Vision and Pattern Recognition (2016)
10. He, P., Huang, W., Qiao, Y., Loy, C.C., Tang, X.: Reading scene text in deep convolutional sequences. In: AAAI Conference on Artificial Intelligence (2016)
11. Ioffe, S., Szegedy, C.: Batch normalization: accelerating deep network training by reducing internal covariate shift. In: International Conference on Machine Learning (2015)
12. Jaderberg, M., Simonyan, K., Vedaldi, A., Zisserman, A.: Synthetic data and artificial neural networks for natural scene text recognition. In: Workshop on Deep Learning, Advances in Neural Information Processing Systems (2014)
13. Jaderberg, M., Simonyan, K., Vedaldi, A., Zisserman, A.: Deep structured output learning for unconstrained text recognition. In: International Conference on Learning Representations (2015)
14. Jaderberg, M., Simonyan, K., Vedaldi, A., Zisserman, A.: Reading text in the wild with convolutional neural networks. Int. J. Comput. Vis. **116**(1), 1–20 (2016)
15. Jaderberg, M., Simonyan, K., Zisserman, A., Kavukcuoglu, K.: Spatial transformer networks. In: Advances in Neural Information Processing Systems (2015)
16. Jaderberg, M., Vedaldi, A., Zisserman, A.: Deep features for text spotting. In: Fleet, D., Pajdla, T., Schiele, B., Tuytelaars, T. (eds.) ECCV 2014, Part IV. LNCS, vol. 8692, pp. 512–528. Springer, Cham (2014). https://doi.org/10.1007/978-3-319-10593-2_34
17. Karatzas, D., et al.: ICDAR 2015 competition on robust reading. In: IEEE International Conference on Document Analysis and Recognition (2015)
18. Karatzas, D., et al.: ICDAR 2013 robust reading competition. In: IEEE International Conference on Document Analysis and Recognition (2013)

19. Lee, C.Y., Bhardwaj, A., Di, W., Jagadeesh, V., Piramuthu, R.: Region-based discriminative feature pooling for scene text recognition. In: IEEE Conference on Computer Vision and Pattern Recognition (2014)
20. Lee, C.Y., Osindero, S.: Recursive recurrent nets with attention modeling for OCR in the wild. In: IEEE Conference on Computer Vision and Pattern Recognition (2016)
21. Liu, W., Chen, C., Wong, K.Y.K.: Char-Net: a character-aware neural network for distorted scene text recognition. In: AAAI Conference on Artificial Intelligence (2018)
22. Liu, W., Chen, C., Wong, K.K., Su, Z., Han, J.: STAR-Net: a spatial attention residue network for scene text recognition. In: British Machine Vision Conference (2016)
23. Lucas, S.M., et al.: ICDAR 2003 robust reading competitions: entries, results, and future directions. Int. J. Doc. Anal. Recognit. 7(2–3), 105–122 (2005)
24. Luo, W., Li, Y., Urtasun, R., Zemel, R.: Understanding the effective receptive field in deep convolutional neural networks. In: Advances in Neural Information Processing Systems (2016)
25. Mishra, A., Alahari, K., Jawahar, C.: Scene text recognition using higher order language priors. In: British Machine Vision Conference (2012)
26. Neumann, L., Matas, J.: Real-time scene text localization and recognition. In: IEEE Conference on Computer Vision and Pattern Recognition (2012)
27. Phan, T., Shivakumara, P., Tian, S., Tan, C.: Recognizing text with perspective distortion in natural scenes. In: IEEE International Conference on Computer Vision (2013)
28. Shi, B., Bai, X., Yao, C.: An end-to-end trainable neural network for image-based sequence recognition and its application to scene text recognition. IEEE Trans. Pattern Anal. Mach. Intell. 39, 2298–2304 (2016)
29. Shi, B., Wang, X., Lyu, P., Yao, C., Bai, X.: Robust scene text recognition with automatic rectification. In: IEEE Conference on Computer Vision and Pattern Recognition (2016)
30. Su, B., Lu, S.: Accurate scene text recognition based on recurrent neural network. In: Cremers, D., Reid, I., Saito, H., Yang, M.-H. (eds.) ACCV 2014, Part I. LNCS, vol. 9003, pp. 35–48. Springer, Cham (2015). https://doi.org/10.1007/978-3-319-16865-4_3
31. Wang, K., Babenko, B., Belongie, S.: End-to-end scene text recognition. In: IEEE International Conference on Computer Vision (2011)
32. Wang, K., Belongie, S.: Word spotting in the wild. In: Daniilidis, K., Maragos, P., Paragios, N. (eds.) ECCV 2010, Part I. LNCS, vol. 6311, pp. 591–604. Springer, Heidelberg (2010). https://doi.org/10.1007/978-3-642-15549-9_43
33. Wang, T., Wu, D.J., Coates, A., Ng, A.Y.: End-to-end text recognition with convolutional neural networks. In: IEEE International Conference on Pattern Recognition (2012)
34. Yang, X., He, D., Zhou, Z., Kifer, D., Giles, C.L.: Learning to read irregular text with attention mechanisms. In: Twenty-Sixth International Joint Conference on Artificial Intelligence, IJCAI 2017 (2017)
35. Yao, C., Bai, X., Shi, B., Liu, W.: Strokelets: a learned multi-scale representation for scene text recognition. In: IEEE Conference on Computer Vision and Pattern Recognition (2014)
36. Zeiler, M.D.: ADADELTA: an adaptive learning rate method (2012). arXiv preprint: arXiv:1212.5701

Neural Abstract Style Transfer
for Chinese Traditional Painting

Bo Li[1][(✉)], Caiming Xiong[2], Tianfu Wu[3], Yu Zhou[4], Lun Zhang[1],
and Rufeng Chu[5]

[1] Alibaba Group, Beijing, China
{shize.lb,lunzhangl}@alibaba-inc.com
[2] Salesforce Research, San Francisco, CA, USA
cxiong@salesforce.com
[3] Department of ECE, NC State University, Raleigh, NC, USA
tianfu_wu@ncsu.edu
[4] Beijing University of Posts and Telecommunications, Beijing, China
yuzhou@bupt.edu.cn
[5] Beijing Winsense Technology Co. Ltd., Beijing, China
rfchu@winsense.ai

Abstract. Chinese traditional painting is one of the most historical artworks in the world. It is very popular in Eastern and Southeast Asia due to being aesthetically appealing. Compared with western artistic painting, it is usually more visually abstract and textureless. Recently, neural network based style transfer methods have shown promising and appealing results which are mainly focused on western painting. It remains a challenging problem to preserve abstraction in neural style transfer. In this paper, we present a Neural Abstract Style Transfer method for Chinese traditional painting. It learns to preserve abstraction and other style jointly end-to-end via a novel MXDoG-guided filter (Modified version of the eXtended Difference-of-Gaussians) and three fully differentiable loss terms. To the best of our knowledge, there is little work study on neural style transfer of Chinese traditional painting. To promote research on this direction, we collect a new dataset with diverse photo-realistic images and Chinese traditional paintings (The dataset will be released at https://github.com/lbsswu/Chinese_style_transfer.). In experiments, the proposed method shows more appealing stylized results in transferring the style of Chinese traditional painting than state-of-the-art neural style transfer methods.

Keywords: Neural style transfer · Chinese traditional painting

1 Introduction

Chinese traditional painting is an ancient art form, in which natural objects are painted with sparse, yet expressive, brush strokes. It consists of diverse styles (e.g, claborate-style painting, Chinese landscape painting, and ink and wash)

© Springer Nature Switzerland AG 2019
C. V. Jawahar et al. (Eds.): ACCV 2018, LNCS 11362, pp. 212–227, 2019.
https://doi.org/10.1007/978-3-030-20890-5_14

and has influenced many countries and nations in Eastern and Southeast Asia. It's now a typical symbol of Chinese culture and an important part of the artistic world.

Recently, convolutional neural network (CNN) [10] based style transfer methods have shown successful applications in transferring the style of a certain type of artistic painting, e.g, Vincent van Gogh's "The Starry Night", to a real world photograph, e.g., an image taken by iPhone. Since the seminal work of Gatys et al. [4], it has attracted a lot of attentions from both academia [5,7,12,20,21,25,28] and industry [1,3,8,23]. Although the work of neural style transfer has shown promising progress on transferring artistic images with rich textures and colors, e.g., the oil paintings, we observe that it is less effective in transferring Chinese traditional painting.

Unlike western oil paintings which are often concrete and realistic, Chinese traditional freehand painting reveals an artistic results of a likeness in spirit rather than in appearance. As a result, different styles of sparse brush strokes are widely utilized to depict different kinds of objects. Thus they are more abstract, textureless and less colorful. And this "abstract style" is not captured well by current neural style transfer methods due to lack of corresponding constraints.

Style & Content Images   Fast-Neural-Style   Ours

Fig. 1. Stylized examples of neural style transfer [4] and our method for Chinese traditional painting. The left column shows the input content image and style image. The middle column shows the transferred result of the neural style transfer method [4]. The right column shows the stylized result of our proposed method. From which we can see, the result generated by our method is more sparse and the style is more like the style image. (Color figure online)

Figure 1 shows an example. The left figure shows an input real image superposed with a Chinese traditional painting as target style. The middle figure shows the stylized result of neural style transfer [4,7] which does not capture the abstract style as concise and clean as the target style image. For instance, trees (solid rectangle) and mountains (dashed rectangle) are not transferred very well, as there are still many redundant edges or stokes on them, which should be abstracted out w.r.t. the style image. Besides, strokes in the stylized results do not align with those in the style image. For example, the style of strokes in the dark area (solid rectangle in the middle figure) stylized by Fast-Neural-Style [7] is still quite different as the one (solid rectangle in the left figure) in the style image, making these areas looks trivial and non-smooth. These comparisons make it clear that we need to learn to "abstract" and keep a smooth and natural transfer that consistent with the style of Chinese traditional painting. This issue has not been addressed in existing methods.

In this paper, we focus on the specific and important problem of style transfer of Chinese traditional painting. Then, to address above issues of current neural style transfer methods, we propose a modified extended difference-of-Gaussians (MXDoG) based style transfer approach for Chinese traditional painting, where a MXDoG filter is utilized to abstract an image. Based on the MXDoG, we formulate three new terms in the loss function for neural style transfer beside the conventional content loss and style loss.

The first loss term is a MXDoG content loss, which penalizes the discrepancy of appearance between the stylized image and the MXDoG filtered image. We suppose the representation of the **abstract content** of an image is also separable along with the **content** and the **style** of the same image, and this loss term will impose a new constraint that requires the stylized image to have a "balanced content" that accommodating to both the "content" and the "MXDoG abstracted content" of an image. The second loss term penalizes the dissimilarity between the MXDoG filtered image of the stylized image and the content image. It is inspired by the work of [14] which uses the Laplacian operator. The third loss term focuses on style, which encourages that the MXDoG filtered image of the stylized image and the style image to have similar styles. The second and third terms are mainly used to penalize large noisy edges in stylized images to make the result more natural. These three loss terms are fully differentiable, thus our style transfer network can be trained end-to-end by stochastic gradient descent method.

An example of our stylized image is shown in Fig. 1(c). Overall, our model shows more appealing style which respects the target style image than neural style transfer methods. For example, our model produces less strokes for the mountain peak in the dashed rectangle than Fast-Neural-Style [7]. This is more in accord with Chinese traditional painting in terms of sparse strokes. In addition, for the dark area (solid rectangle) in the content image, our stylized result is more in accord with the dark area in the style image.

It's worth noted that our method is not necessarily only applicable to Chinese traditional painting. The proposed three new loss terms are used for handling the abstractness and textureless in style transfer, since artworks (e.g., ukiyoe, cartoon, oil painting) have different extents of abstraction, it can work for general art styles by adapting the hyper-parameters of these loss terms. Automatically learning the hyper-parameters is very attractive, we leave it as an interesting future work and focus our efforts on transferring Chinese traditional painting.

To the best of our knowledge, there is no publicly available dataset for evaluating Chinese traditional painting style transfer, thus we collect a new dataset that contains a variety of natural scenes and Chinese traditional paintings. The dataset will be released to facilitate further research on this direction.

In experiments, we compare our method with the neural style methods [4,7,12] on transferring the style of Chinese tradition paintings, and show that our method performs better on transferring image textures, abstract contents, and colors. In addition, the stylized images are "clean", natural and have strong layers of graphics.

We make the following contributions to the community of image style transfer:

- We reintroduce the problem of style transfer of Chinese traditional painting, which poses new challenges and largely omitted by current research.
- We propose a MXDoG filter to abstract the content of an image, and utilize it to transfer the style of Chinese traditional painting.
- We propose three MXDoG based loss terms to guide the neural networks to learn how to "abstract", and demonstrate its effects on test images under different conditions. In this way, we also verify the representations of "abstract content", "content" and "style" of an image can be separated by the neural networks.
- We collect a new Chinese traditional painting dataset to promote the research on style transfer of Chinese traditional painting.

2   Related Works

We briefly review related works of neural style transfer and style transfer of Chinese traditional painting below.

Neural Style Transfer. Gatys et al. [4] first propose the neural network based style transfer method, in which they synthesizing images that have the style of one image and the content of another. In their method, the style is represented by the Gram matrix, and the content is represented by high-level convolutional feature maps. Here, the Gram matrix is the global statistics of the image based on outputs from convolutional layers. Gatys's work has received lot of attentions and triggered a whole line of research on deep learning based style transfer. [20,21] investigate several variants of Gatys' method for illumination and season transfer. Li et al. [12] utilize the patch-based Markov random field method to represent the style of the image with neural networks. Luan et al. [18] propose a method for photo to photo style transfer, which shows high quality in photo-realistic.

Recently, Li et al. [14] introduce a Laplacian loss term to preserve detailed content image structures. The key difference between our work and [14] is XDoG vs LoG, rather than DoG vs LoG. DoG (Difference-of-Gaussians) is a fast approximation of the LoG (Laplacian of Gaussians), while XDoG is built on DoG/LoG which detects edges by thresholding DoG responses, rather than searching for the zero crossings in the second derivative (see Eq. (6)). XDoG is more aesthetically appealing than DoG/LoG due to its effects on **edge enhancement**. Edge enhancement focuses more appropriately on the weight (thickness) and structure (shape) of edges, thus providing better results for stylistic and artistic applications [31].

Fast Neural Style Transfer. Above neural style transfer methods utilize optimization for image style transfer, usually, it takes more than 40 s to process an image. Johnson et al. [7] utilize the perceptual loss to train feed-forward neural networks, which can be running in real time on GPU. Almost at the same time, Ulyanov et al. [28] propose an unsupervised real time method, but a multi-scale neural network is used. Li and Wand [13] also propose a feed-forward method to accelerate their patch-based Markov method [12]. Recently, Ulyanov et al. [29] further propose an instance normalization method which significantly improves the quality of fast neural style transfer.

Style Transfer with GAN. Recently, several work [13,17,34,35] try to use or incorporate generative adversarial networks (GAN) for image style transfer. Specifically, the Cycle-GAN method [35] produces amazing results in transferring an image with a painter's style, e.g., Vincent van Gogh, Monet. However, this method is not stable, needs much more time and requires large number of unpaired content and style images for training. What's more, the style of a painting maybe quite different from another even they are painted by the same artist, thus it may be not desirable when we just want to transfer the style of a specific artwork.

Style Transfer for Chinese Traditional Painting. Before deep neural network is prevalent, many researchers [2,11,27,30,32,33] focus on simulation of the interaction of water, ink, paper and brushes to render Chinese tradition painting. Recently, [15] propose to transfer Chinese painting using multi-scale neural network, however, their method is not end-to-end, and requires sketches or edges for input. Overall, there is little work specifically for style transfer of Chinese traditional painting, thus challenges of style transfer of Chinese traditional painting are largely omitted by our community. In this paper, we make an preliminary analysis of these challenges, and hope more researchers will join and promote the research on this direction.

3   Method

We first briefly review the neural style transfer method, then we introduce the modified extended difference-of-Gaussians (MXDoG) filter, which produces a novel representation for image abstraction in our framework. Based on MXDoG, we further introduce the structure and loss functions of our neural network architecture.

3.1   Neural Style Transfer

Given a content image I_c and a style image I_s, the goal of image style transfer is to generate an image I showing the content of I_c in the style of I_s. Gatys et al. [4] formulate the image style transfer as an energy minimization problem which consisting of a content loss and a style loss. Both losses are computed with an ImageNet pretrained object classification network (i.e. VGG-19 [26]).

Inputing an image I_c to the pre-trained network, we can get the l-th feature map $F_l(I) = \phi^l(I)$ which corresponds to the response of the l-th layer. The dimension of $F_l(I)$ is $N_l \times M_l(I)$, where N_l is the number of filters (channels) in the l-th layer, and $M_l(I) = H_l(I) \times W_l(I)$ is the spatial dimension of the l-th feature map, i.e. the product of its height and width.

With above notations, the objective of neural style transfer method can be represented as follows:

$$L_T(I, I_c, I_s) = \alpha * L_C(I, I_c) + \beta * L_S(I, I_s) \tag{1}$$

where α and β are the weighting factors showing the relative importance of the two components, the content loss is the mean-squared distance between the feature map of I_c and I at a specified layer l:

$$L_C(I, I_c) = \frac{1}{N_l M_l(I_c)} \sum_{ij} (F_l(I) - F_l(I_c))_{ij})^2 \tag{2}$$

and the style loss is the mean-squared distance between the correlations of the filter responses (i.e., Gram matrices) of I_s and I at several appointed layers:

$$L_S(I, I_s) = \sum_l \frac{\sum_{ij}(G_{ij}^l(I) - G_{ij}^l(I_s))^2}{N_l^2} \tag{3}$$

where $G_{ij}^l(I) = \frac{1}{M_l(I)} \sum_{k=1}^{M_l(I)} \phi_{ik}^l(I)\phi_{jk}^l(I)$ is the Gram matrix of $F_l(I)$. The stylized image is generated by iteratively minimizing Eq. (1).

Instead of solving an optimization problem, Johnson et al. [7] propose a much faster feed-forward network to directly mapping an input image to the stylized one, this method is called Fast-Neural-Style transfer. Denote the parameters of the feed-forward network as w, the training objective is as follows:

$$w^* = argmin_w E_I[L_T(I, I_c, I_s)] \tag{4}$$

where E is the expectation.

3.2 Modified Extended Difference-of-Gaussians

The extended difference-of-Gaussians (XDoG) operators have been shown to yield a range of subtle artistic effects, such as ghosting, speed-lines, negative edges, indication, and abstraction etc [31]. Chinese traditional painting share some similar characters with above artistic paintings, e.g, abstraction, texture-less, emphasis of edges. Thus XDoG filters are attractive for us in improving the quality of style transfer for Chinese traditional painting.

(a) Source Image　　　(b) XDoG　　　(c) Thresholded XDoG　　　(d) MXDoG

Fig. 2. Filtered results of XDoG, Thresholded XDoG, and MXDoG.

Given an image I, traditional XDoG filter can be formulated as:

$$I^{xd} = \mathcal{T}_{\varepsilon,\varphi}(\mathcal{D}_{\sigma,k,\tau}(I)) \tag{5}$$

where $\mathcal{T}$ is the XDoG filter and $\mathcal{D}$ is a variant of the difference-of-Gaussians filter in [31]. $\mathcal{T}$ can be formulated by a thresholding function with a continuous ramp:

$$\mathcal{T}_{\varepsilon,\varphi}(u) = \begin{cases} 1 & u \geq \varepsilon \\ 1 + tanh(\varphi \cdot (u - \varepsilon)) & \text{otherwise.} \end{cases} \tag{6}$$

where φ and ε are the related thresholding parameters. And $\mathcal{D}$ can be formulated as

$$D_{\sigma,k,\tau}(x) = g_\sigma(x) - \tau \cdot g_{k\sigma}(x) \tag{7}$$

where $g_\sigma(x) = \frac{1}{2\pi\sigma^2}exp(-\frac{\|x\|^2}{2\sigma^2})$ is the Gaussian smoothing filter, k represents a trade-off parameter balancing accurate approximation and adequate sensitivity [19], σ is the standard deviation and τ is the control parameter.

Traditional XDoG is aesthetically appealing and can abstract an image to some extent (see Fig. 2(b)). However, it's still not enough for general natural images, as there are many small pieces in the image (which is still too detailed). In addition, the XDoG processed image is generally too "white" and is not very compatible with the style of Chinese traditional painting (as the contrast of black and white colors in Chinese traditional painting is generally striking). To this end, we propose a novel modified XDoG (MXDoG) that is a thresholded version of XDoG, and incorporate morphology operations to filter out the small pieces in an image. Our MXDoG is formulated as:

$$I^{md} = morph\_filter(I^{td}) \tag{8}$$

where $morph\_filter$ is the morphology operation which filtering out image regions with their areas smaller than a predefined minimum size A_{min}, and I^{td} (Fig. 2(c)) is the thresholded XDoG which is formulated as:

$$I^{td}(x) = \begin{cases} 0 & I^{xd}(x) \leq \mu \\ 1, & \text{otherwise.} \end{cases} \tag{9}$$

where μ is the mean of I^{xd}.

For a color image, we compute MXDoG for each channel separately. The final result of our MXDoG operator on a sampled image is shown in Fig. 2(d).

3.3　Network Architecture

Our style transfer system consists of two components: a *generative network* and a *loss network*, as illustrated in Fig. 3. The generative network is responsible for transforming a user-provided image I_c (**as a common practice, we use the**

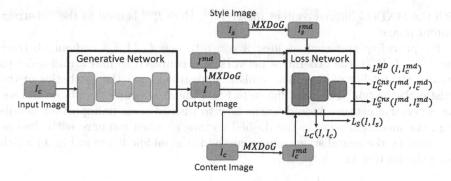

Fig. 3. Network architecture including a generative network and a loss network. As a common practice, we use the content image I_c as the input image to do style transfer.

content image I_c as the input image) to a corresponding stylized image. It is a deep residual convolutional neural network with similar network structure as [6]. The loss network is an ImageNet [24] pretrained object classification network, and is fixed during the training of the generative network. Throughout this paper, we use the 16-layer VGG network [26] as the loss network. Besides the content loss and style loss used in [4] and [7], we introduce three new MXDoG-based losses. The generative network is trained using stochastic gradient descent to minimize the following overall loss function:

$$L(I, I_c, I_s, I^{md}, I_c^{md}, I_s^{md}) = \lambda_1 L_C(I, I_c) + \lambda_2 L_C^{MD}(I, I_c^{md})$$
$$+ \lambda_3 L_S(I, I_s) + \lambda_4 L_C^{Cns}(I^{md}, I_c^{md}) + \lambda_5 L_S^{Cns}(I^{md}, I_s^{md}) \qquad (10)$$

Here λ_i is the weighting factors to combine various loss components. The content loss L_C is computed as Eq. (2). It is worth noted that although the content loss provides some extent of "abstraction", it is still not enough (see Fig. 1). The style loss L_S is computed as Eq. (3). As the styles of traditional Chinese artworks are often textueless and lack of color information, we strengthen the effects of style transfer by using more low-level and high-level layers for style reconstruction than [7]. The implementation details will be exposed in our experiment. Details of our proposed three new loss terms (i.e., L_C^{MD}, L_C^{Cns}, and L_S^{Cns}) are as follows:

MXDoG Content Loss. Given content image I_c, we utilize the MXDoG filter to produce the abstract content image I_c^{md}. Then I_c^{md} is used as the input to the loss network to extract high-level features of VGG-16 net. Similar to the content loss, we compute mean-squared Euclidean distance between feature representations $F_l(I)$ and $F_l(I_c^{md})$ as: $L_C^{MD}(I, I_c^{md}) = L_C(I, I_c^{md})$, In the experiments, we use the same mid-level layer, i.e., *relu3_3*, for both the content loss and XDoG content loss.

L_C^{MD} penalizes the output image I when it deviates in content from the target I_c^{md}. In other words, L_C^{MD} asks the output image I to have similar appearances with the MXDoG filtered content image I_c^{md}. Here I_c^{md} is used as the "abstract content image".

By providing two content loss: a concrete one $L_C(I, I_c)$ and an abstract one $L_C^{MD}(I, I_c^{md})$, the generative network is encouraged to find a mid-point to balance the fidelity of the photorealistic appearance and the aesthetics of the artistic abstraction. The right figure in Fig. 1 shows a sample result, we can see the generative network indeed learns how to discard some unimportant details (e.g., the mountain peak in the dashed rectangle) when compare with the one produced by the neural style transfer method (the middle figure in Fig. 1) which using the content loss only.

MXDoG Content Constraint Loss. In the stylized image, there are often some noisy edges or distorted artifacts which is inconsistent with the content image. Inspired by [14], we introduce a new loss that constrain I^{md} to have similar appearances to I_c^{md}. This loss is defined as the mean-squared distance between I^{md} and I_c^{md}, which drives the stylized image to have similar detail structures as the content image. This loss is dubbed as MXDoG content constraint loss as: $L_C^{Cns}(I^{md}, I_c^{md}) = L_C(I^{md}, I_c^{md})$, where I_c^{md} and I^{md} are computed by Eq. (8). We use the layer *relu3_3* of VGG16 [26] to get the mid-level patterns and impose the MXDoG content constraint on it.

As MXDoG extracts the "abstract content" of an image, this loss only penalizes the deviation of relatively larger edges or patterns instead of very detail fine structures. This is different from the Laplacian loss used in [14].

MXDoG Style Constraint Loss. In addition to the MXDoG content constraint, we also add a new loss that constrain I^{md} to have similar styles as I_s^{md}. The motivation is if the styles of two images are similar, then the styles of their MXDoG filtered images are also similar. As similar to the style loss L_S, we compute the mean-squared error between the Gram matrices of I^{md} and I_s^{md}: $L_S^{Cns}(I^{md}, I_s^{md}) = L_S(I^{md}, I_s^{md})$, where I_s^{md} is also computed by Eq. (8). This loss further constrains the style consistence of the stylized image and the style image.

4   Results

4.1   Implementation Details

Our model builds upon the fast neural style transfer framework of [7], which using the perceptual loss to train feed-forward neural networks to make the stylization achieving real time performance. We only introduces some computational burden on computing the MXDoG loss terms during offline training, and it doesn't adding any extra cost on online testing. The model is trained on the Microsoft COCO database [16], which has around $80k$ training images. We resize these images to 256×256 and train our model using a batch size of 4 for 2 epochs. We adopt Adam [9] for training with a learning rate of 1×10^{-3}. Equation (10) is

Fig. 4. Sampled style and content images from the Chinese traditional painting dataset.

utilized as the loss function with the balancing weights $\lambda_1 = 1.0$, $\lambda_2 = 0.1 \sim 0.3$, $\lambda_3 = 5.0$, $\lambda_4 = 2 \times 10^2$ and $\lambda_5 = 1 \times 10^3$. For the computation of our MXDoG, we set $\tau = 0.94$, $\sigma = 1.0$, $k = 1.6$, $\varphi = 50$, $\varepsilon = -0.1$ and $A_{min} = 10$. We compute the content loss at layer $relu3\_3$ and style reconstruction loss at layers $relu1\_2$, $relu2\_1$, $relu2\_2$, $relu3\_1$, $relu3\_3$, $relu4\_1$ and $relu4\_3$ of the VGG-16 loss network. All the parameters are chosen based on the MS-COCO 2014 validation set. We implement our method using PyTorch [22] with CUDA 7.5 and cuDNN 5.0. It takes about 8 h to train a model with a single NVIDIA Tesla K40 GPU. After training, our generative network can accept arbitrary input image size, and we resize the input image with the longer edge as 768 before style transfer.

4.2   Chinese Traditional Painting Dataset

To the best of our knowledge, there is little work study on neural network based Chinese traditional painting style transfer. Thus we collect one with 1000 content images that accommodate to the extent of Chinese traditional painting. These images are collected by web search engines, e.g., Google, Baidu and Bing. They are mostly the photorealistic scenes of mountain, lake, river, bridge, and buildings in regions south of the Yangtze River. It includes not only the scenes of China, but also beautiful pictures of Rhine, Alps, Yellow Stone, Grand Canyon, etc. These images are only used for testing. Besides, we also collect 100 traditional Chinese artworks. These artworks are used as the style images in this paper, which are the typical freehand brush works of China. Some typical style and content images of this dataset are presented in Fig. 4. The whole dataset including all the content and style images will be released to public for further research.

4.3 Baselines

To verify the capability of our model, we compare our method with state-of-the-art methods, i.e., Neural-Style Transfer by Gatys et al. [4], Fast-Neural-Style Transfer by Johnson et al. [7], and CNN-MRF by Li and Wand [12]. As they all released their packages, we train their models by using the Chinese traditional painting as style images for comparison. Details will be described in the following.

4.4 Qualitative Results

We compare our method with state-of-the-art methods for a variety of style and content images on Chinese traditional painting dataset. On the left column of Fig. 5, we stylising a photograph with the same artwork for Neural-Style, CNN-MRF and our method. Result of each method is displayed on the right. To analyse the effect of style transfer, we also select two patches and enlarged them for better visualization. From the whole image of the stylized results (the first figure of each method), we can see the Neural-Style method fails to stylize the water. The whole image is a little dark, which may because the optimization-based method fail to find a good solution to balance the photorealistic content image and the textureless style image. The CNN-MRF method fails to stylize a smooth result, which may because that method requires a good correspondence between content image and style image. For the mountain peak (i.e., the second patch with blue border), we can see the result of our method is most similar to the one (i.e., blue bounding box) in the style image. On the right column of Fig. 5, we compare our method with [7]. From the patches of tree and water, we can see our method presents styles more like ones in the style image.

Fig. 5. Left: Comparisons of our method and state-of-the-art Neural-Style [4] and CNN-MRF [12]. Right: Comparisons of our method and Fast-Neural-Style [7]. (Color figure online)

Besides, we can see the stylized results generated by our method is sparser and have a high contrast, which are more similar to the style image. These results verify the superiority of our method.

4.5   Ablation Study

Figure 6 shows an illustration of effects of our three newly introduced losses, i.e., the MXDoG content loss L_C^{MD}, the MXDoG content constraint loss L_C^{Cns} and the MXDoG style constraint loss L_S^{Cns} (*we use a high style weight* $\lambda_3 = 100.0$ *for verification*). Figure 6(a) shows the style and content images, Fig. 6(b) shows the result generated by *our base model* that training with only style and content losses (L_S and L_C), this similar to the Neural Style Transfer method [4]. The second column of Fig. 6 shows the stylized results produced by different variants of our model. Specifically, Fig. 6(c) corresponds to the model that trained with only L_C, L_S, and L_C^{MD}, Fig. 6(d) corresponds to the model that trained with L_C, L_S, L_C^{MD}, and L_C^{Cns}, Fig. 6(e) corresponds our model with full losses. Compare with Fig. 6(b) and (c), we can see, with loss term L_C^{MD}, the stylized result is more natural and has a higher image contrast (e.g., the building in the dashed ellipse in Fig. 6(b) and (c)), but also introduce some artifacts. By adding loss functions of L_C^{Cns} and L_S^{Cns} sequentially, the result is more and more cleaned (refer to the solid ellipses in Fig. 6(c) (d) (e)).

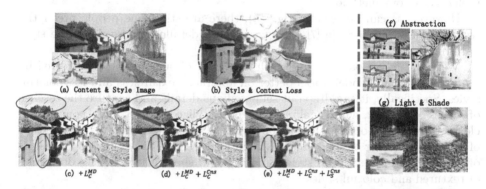

Fig. 6. Left: Illustration of effects of our newly introduced losses. (a) style & content images, (b) stylized result of *our base model* that training with only content and style losses as Neural Style [4], (c, d, e) are the results generated by different variants of our model that trained with different MXDoG losses. Right: Two typical failure examples of our method. See text for details.

4.6   User Study

We carry out a user study to quantitatively evaluate the proposed method. We first randomly select 10 styles of typical Chinese traditional painting, then randomly select 10 stylized images for each style. We invite 60 people, aged from 21 to 45, with diverse educational backgrounds, to participate in our study, each person is asked to cope with 30 randomly selected stylized images, resulting a total of 1,800 trials. In this user study, we compare with the Fast-Neural-Style [7] which can be seen as the fast version of [4]. In each trial, a user is showed with the original image, the style image, and results of [7] and our model. The order of

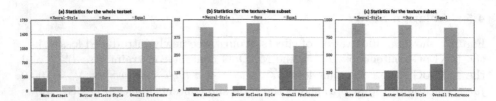

Fig. 7. Results of user study. For each group, the blue bar shows the votes received by Fast-Neural-Style, the green bar shows the votes of our method, and the yellow bar shows the votes of "Equally good or undecided". (Color figure online)

the stylized results is randomized to avoid participants' laziness. For each person, we ask three questions: "Which of the two stylized results is more abstract?", "Which of the two stylized results better reflects the style of the painting?", and "Overall, which of the two stylized results do you prefer?". Participants have to select either one of the stylized results or "Equally good or undecided". Overall results of the user study are showed in Fig. 7(a), which indicating a clear preference of our method.

However, as can be seen in Fig. 7(a), there are still some people prefer the result of Fast-Neural-Style [7], thus we make a detailed study about the style patterns.

We first analyse patterns for which the result of our method is preferred by users. We find our model works better on abstract, textureless and less colorful styles. Specifically, it can drop out some tedious details and capture the essence of scenes or objects, which making the whole stylized images looks concise and clean. To verify our observation, we further split the stylized results by the extent of texture and color of style images[1]. Figure 7(b) shows the statistics on results of less textured and colorful styles, and Fig. 7(c) shows the statistics on results of textured and colorful styles.

For votes on "More Abstract" and "Better Reflects Style", we can see stylized results of our method are more preferred on transferring less textured and colorful styles. We think this is because more details in the photo are expected to be discarded to match the style of the style image.

However, the preponderance of our method on "Overall Preference" is shrunk, which indicates that although some people think our stylized results are more abstract and closer to the style image, they still like the more concrete images generated by the Fast-Neural-Style. This reflects some inconsistence of "abstraction" and "aesthetical-appealing", and also more powerful method is needed for abstraction, as we can see, the leaves and tree branches on the right of Fig. 5 is still not good enough as the style image.

---

[1] For instance, figures in the first row of Fig. 4 represent typical examples of textured and colorful style images, while figures in the second row of Fig. 4 stand for the texture-less and less colorful styles.

4.7 Failure Examples

Although our method works well with the general Chinese traditional painting style transfer, we find it still could not achieve the result of a trained human artist in case of "abstraction" and handling the "light and shade". Figure 6(f) shows our model fails to find the correct correspondence of roof between the content image and the style image. Besides, the roofs in the stylized result should have black colors and curving shapes as the one in the style image, instead of rigid shapes chequered with black and white colors. We think the deep reason is that the neural network is still lack of the human-level "abstraction" capability. Some research [31] show "abstraction" may have strong relevance with the semantic correspondence, thus we believe training a good loss network that can recognize objects and scenes in both photorealistic and artistic images will be a good promising direction. Figure 6(g) shows our method also fails to stylize images with alternating light and shade. Experiments indicate this is a common failure for all the neural style transfer methods and we leave it as an interesting future work.

5   Discussion and Conclusion

Chinese traditional painting is very popular in Eastern Asia, the style of which is often abstract and textureless. This is very different from Western Oil painting, and is not well transferred by current neural style transfer methods [4,7,12]. To tackle this problem, we propose a novel neural style transfer method for Chinese traditional painting. We first introduce a MXDoG filter, then incorporate the MXDoG function with three new loss terms for network training. The effects of our method are verified on test images with diverse conditions. To further promote this research direction, we introduce the Chinese traditional painting dataset which containing diverse content and style images to the public.

Although our method shows superiorities on "abstraction" and in accordance with Chinese traditional painting over current neural style methods, it should be pointed out that the abstraction and aesthetics produced by our model has limitations and does not compete to the one produced by a trained artist. For example, The tree branches stylized by our model in Fig. 5 is still not comparable with ones in the style image. However, as *abstraction* remains some of the fundamentally unsolved problems in non-photorealistic rendering (NPR) [31], this arguably good results still help a lot for our neural style model to get a freehand painting and might steer deeper research into the artistic neural style transfer community.

Acknowledgement. T. Wu is supported by ARO award W911NF1810295, ARO DURIP award W911NF1810209 and NSF IIS 1822477.

References

1. Artisto (2016). http://artisto.my.com/
2. Baxter, B.: Dab: interactive haptic painting with 3D virtual brushes. In: ACM SIGGRAPH 2001 Video Review on Animation Theater Program, p. 10 (2001)
3. Becattini, F., Ferracani, A., Landucci, L., Pezzatini, D., Uricchio, T., Del Bimbo, A.: Imaging Novecento. A mobile app for automatic recognition of artworks and transfer of artistic styles (2016)
4. Gatys, L.A., Ecker, A.S., Bethge, M.: Image style transfer using convolutional neural networks. In: Proceedings of the IEEE Conference on Computer Vision and Pattern Recognition (2016)
5. Gatys, L.A., Ecker, A.S., Bethge, M., Hertzmann, A., Shechtman, E.: Controlling perceptual factors in neural style transfer. In: Proceedings of the IEEE Conference on Computer Vision and Pattern Recognition, July 2017
6. Huang, H., et al.: Real-time neural style transfer for videos. In: CVPR (2017)
7. Johnson, J., Alahi, A., Fei-Fei, L.: Perceptual losses for real-time style transfer and super-resolution. In: Leibe, B., Matas, J., Sebe, N., Welling, M. (eds.) ECCV 2016, Part II. LNCS, vol. 9906, pp. 694–711. Springer, Cham (2016). https://doi.org/10. 1007/978-3-319-46475-6_43
8. Joshi, B.J., Stewart, K., Shapiro, D.: Bringing impressionism to life with neural style transfer in come swim. CoRR abs/1701.04928 (2017)
9. Kingma, D.P., Ba, J.: Adam: a method for stochastic optimization. CoRR abs/1412.6980 (2014)
10. Lecun, Y., Bottou, L., Bengio, Y., Haffner, P.: Gradient-based learning applied to document recognition. Proc. IEEE **86**, 2278–2324 (1998)
11. Lee, J.: Simulating oriental black-ink painting. IEEE Comput. Graph. Appl. **19**(3), 74–81 (1999)
12. Li, C., Wand, M.: Combining Markov random fields and convolutional neural networks for image synthesis. CoRR abs/1601.04589 (2016)
13. Li, C., Wand, M.: Precomputed real-time texture synthesis with Markovian generative adversarial networks. CoRR abs/1604.04382 (2016)
14. Li, S., Xu, X., Nie, L., Chua, T.S.: Laplacian-steered neural style transfer. In: Proceedings of the ACM Multimedia Conference (MM) (2017)
15. Lin, D., Wang, Y., Xu, G., Li, J., Fu, K.: Transform a simple sketch to a Chinese painting by a multiscale deep neural network. Algorithms **11**(1), 4 (2018)
16. Lin, T., et al.: Microsoft COCO: common objects in context. CoRR abs/1405.0312 (2014)
17. Liu, Y., Qin, Z., Luo, Z., Wang, H.: Auto-painter: cartoon image generation from sketch by using conditional generative adversarial networks. CoRR abs/1705.01908 (2017)
18. Luan, F., Paris, S., Shechtman, E., Bala, K.: Deep photo style transfer (2017). arXiv preprint: arXiv:1703.07511
19. Marr, D., Hildreth, E.: Theory of edge detection. Proc. R. Soc. Lond. Ser. B **207**, 187–217 (1980)
20. Nikulin, Y., Novak, R.: Exploring the neural algorithm of artistic style. CoRR abs/1602.07188 (2016)
21. Novak, R., Nikulin, Y.: Improving the neural algorithm of artistic style. CoRR abs/1605.04603 (2016)
22. Paszke, A., et al.: Automatic differentiation in PyTorch (2017)
23. Prisma (2016). http://prisma-ai.com/

24. Russakovsky, O., et al.: ImageNet large scale visual recognition challenge. Int. J. Comput. Vis. (IJCV) **115**(3), 211–252 (2015)
25. Selim, A., Elgharib, M., Doyle, L.: Painting style transfer for head portraits using convolutional neural networks. ACM Trans. Graph. **35**(4), 129:1–129:18 (2016)
26. Simonyan, K., Zisserman, A.: Very deep convolutional networks for large-scale image recognition. CoRR abs/1409.1556 (2014)
27. Strassmann, S.: Hairy brushes. In: Conference on Computer Graphics and Interactive Techniques, pp. 225–232 (1986)
28. Ulyanov, D., Lebedev, V., Vedaldi, A., Lempitsky, V.S.: Texture networks: Feedforward synthesis of textures and stylized images. CoRR abs/1603.03417 (2016)
29. Ulyanov, D., Vedaldi, A., Lempitsky, V.S.: Instance normalization: the missing ingredient for fast stylization. CoRR abs/1607.08022 (2016)
30. Way, D.L., Lin, Y.R., Shih, Z.C.: The synthesis of trees in Chinese landscape painting using silhouette and texture strokes. J. WSCG **10**, 499–506 (2002)
31. Winnemöller, H., Kyprianidis, J.E., Olsen, S.C.: XDoG: an extended differenceof-Gaussians compendium including advanced image stylization. Comput. Graph. **36**(6), 740–753 (2012)
32. Xu, S., Xu, Y., Kang, S.B., Salesin, D.H., Pan, Y., Shum, H.Y.: Animating Chinese paintings through stroke-based decomposition. ACM Trans. Graph. **25**(2), 239–267 (2006)
33. Zhang, S.H., Chen, T., Zhang, Y.F., Hu, S.M., Martin, R.: Video-based running water animation in Chinese painting style. Sci. China Inf. Sci. **52**(2), 162–171 (2009)
34. Zhao, H., Li, H., Cheng, L.: Synthesizing filamentary structured images with GANs. CoRR abs/1706.02185 (2017)
35. Zhu, J.Y., Park, T., Isola, P., Efros, A.A.: Unpaired image-to-image translation using cycle-consistent adversarial networks (2017). arXiv preprint: arXiv:1703.10593

Detector-in-Detector: Multi-level Analysis for Human-Parts

Xiaojie Li[1], Lu Yang[2], Qing Song[2], and Fuqiang Zhou[1][(✉)]

[1] Beihang University, Beijing 100191, China
{xiaojieli,zfq}@buaa.edu.cn
[2] Beijing University of Posts and Telecommunications, Beijing 100876, China
{soeaver,songqing512}@bupt.edu.cn

Abstract. Vision-based person, hand or face detection approaches have achieved incredible success in recent years with the development of deep convolutional neural network (CNN). In this paper, we take the inherent correlation between the body and body parts into account and propose a new framework to boost up the detection performance of the multi-level objects. In particular, we adopt region-based object detection structure with two carefully designed detectors to separately pay attention to the human body and body parts in a coarse-to-fine manner, which we call Detector-in-Detector network (DID-Net). The first detector is designed to detect human body, hand and face. The second detector, based on the body detection results of the first detector, mainly focus on detection of small hand and face inside each body. The framework is trained in an end-to-end way by optimizing a multi-task loss. Due to the lack of human body, face and hand detection dataset, we have collected and labeled a new large dataset named *Human-Parts* with 14,962 images and 106,879 annotations. Experiments show that our method can achieve excellent performance on *Human-Parts*.

Keywords: Convolutional neural network · Detector in Detector · Human parts

1 Introduction

Robust detection of human body, face and hand in the wild are canonical sub-problems of general object detection. They are prerequisite for various person-based tasks such as pedestrian detection [1], person re-identification [2,3], facial landmarking [4] and driver behavior monitoring [5]. The problems of human parts detection in the wild have been intensely studied for decades and significant progress have been made in recent detection algorithms due to the advancement of deep Convolutional Neural Networks (CNN) such as [1,6] in person detection, [7,8] in face detection and [9–11] in hand detection.

Human parts are multi-level objects [12], where face and hand are sub-objects of body. There are many other multi-level objects in our daily life such as laptop

© Springer Nature Switzerland AG 2019
C. V. Jawahar et al. (Eds.): ACCV 2018, LNCS 11362, pp. 228–240, 2019.
https://doi.org/10.1007/978-3-030-20890-5_15

and keyboard, lung and lung-nodule or bus and wheel, which are shown in Fig. 1. However, most detection frameworks ignore the inherent correlation between multi-level objects and coarsely treat these **sub-objects** and **objects** as normal objects when they solve this multi-level objects detection problem. In this paper, we perform the person, face and hand detection tasks together to explore the more efficient detection methods for the multi-level objects.

When doing this multi-level objects task using general detection algorithm, detection performance for large objects, such as the human body, is relatively straightforward. The crucial challenges in real-world applications mainly come from training detectors for small objects such as face and hand due to large pose variations and serious occlusions, which make them still far from achieving the same detection capabilities as a human. Due to the large scale variance between the body (objects) and small body parts (sub-objects), the whole image is mainly occupied by the big objects like human body. Small hand and face usually occupy a relatively smaller area in practice. Thus, there are more background information than the small objects during training, which results in a serious disturbance when doing small objects detection. To cope with the problems, inspired by the top-down pose estimation approaches that first locate and crop all persons from image and then solve the single person pose estimation problem in the cropped person patches [2,3], we proposed a region-based convolutional neural network, named Detector-in-Detector Network (**DID-Net**), which allows the network to see the body in the pictures first and then look inside these bodies to find the tiny faces and hands. Our network contains two region-based detectors: *BodyDetector* and *PartsDetector*. The *BodyDetector* adopt the traditional Faster R-CNN implementation to predict a set of human body bounding boxes. Then the feature maps of the detected bodies are wrapped and sent to the second region-based *PartsDetector* to predict the bounding boxes of hand and face. In *PartsDetector*, many background regions that are useless for training are cut down. Thus there is less disturbance inside the cropped body features, which is beneficial to the detection of small parts. The whole network is trained in an end-to-end way.

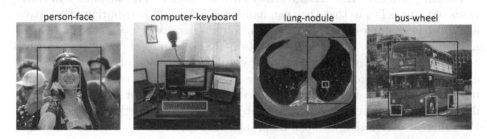

person-face   computer-keyboard   lung-nodule   bus-wheel

Fig. 1. Examples of multi-level objects. Boxes in green are sub-objects of boxes in blue. (Color figure online)

In order to demonstrate the proposed method in more practical scenes, we construct a new *Human-Parts* dataset, which contains 14,962 well-labeled images for human body, face and hand in realistic unconstrained conditions. To the best of our knowledge, it is the first detection dataset that combines three important parts of human. The dataset as well as the source code is available at https:// github.com/xiaojie1017/Human-Parts.

2   Related Work

2.1   Object Detection Methods

CNN-based object detection algorithms fall into two categories. The first category is built upon a two-stage pipeline [14,20,40], where the first stage proposes candidate object bounding boxes and the second stage extracts features using RoIPool from each candidate box and performs classification and bounding-box regression. The second category divides the image into a grid, then simultaneously makes prediction for each square or rectangle in the grid, and finally figures out the bounding boxes of targeting objects based on the predictions of the squares or rectangle, such as [15–17]. That design will achieve relatively faster computational speed. However, the one-stage methods can not achieve comparable accuracy with two-stage approaches. In this regard, most of the existing human parts detection methods employ the two-stage pipeline such as [8,18,19].

2.2   Human-Parts Detection Methods

Faster R-CNN [20] trains the object proposal and classifier at the same time on the same base network. Region Proposal Networks (RPN) in the Faster R-CNN [20] are successful in eliminating the need for a precomputed object proposals [8,18,19], as well as our work are all the frameworks extended from Faster R-CNN framework. Other object-proposal-free detectors for human parts such as [21,22], perform detection in a fully convolutional manner as RPN does for proposing bounding boxes. Cascaded stages design algorithms are widely used in human parts detection tasks recently such as [23,24]. The advantage of these cascaded stages lies in that they can handle unbalanced distribution of negative and positive samples. In the low-resolution stages, weak classifiers can reject most false positives. In the high-resolution stages, stronger classifiers can save computation with fewer proposals. [23] employs a cascade of classifiers to efficiently reject backgrounds. In [24] three stages of carefully designed CNNs are used to predict face and landmark in a coarse-to-fine manner. However, most of detection methods perform multi-level objects detection together without taking the inherent correlation between them into account.

2.3   Top-Down Pose Estimation Methods

Top-down human pose estimation algorithms perform pose estimation task using two separated networks: one person detection network and one single person pose estimation network. Persons are first detected in an image with the detector.

Then the detected person will be cropped from the image and the single person pose estimation network is used to predict the keypoints of each person. A number of top-down algorithms achieve excellent performance on COCO [25] keypoint benchmark such as [2,3]. By sharing features efficiently, Mask-RCNN [26] can do this task in an end-to-end approach. It first generates proposals of person. Then it predict K masks for each proposal, one for each of K keypoint types, which is a Pose-estimator-in-Detector structure.

As a consequence, instead of conducting traditional cascaded stages detection methods that refine predictions step by step, we deal with the multi-level objects detection task using a Detector-in-Detector network. That approach perform parts detection inside each person proposal inspired by the top-down pose estimation methods. Details will be discussed in Sect. 3.

3   Detector-in-Detector Network

The architecture of the proposed Detector-in-Detector network (DID-Net) is illustrated in Fig. 2. We extended Faster RCNN structure by appending another light-weight parts detector after it, which is a Detertor-in-Detector structure. The framework contains two detectors: (1) *BodyDetector* is designed for human body, hand and face detection. (2) *PartsDetector* is appended for hand and face detection inside the selected body bounding boxes, which are detected by *BodyDetector*.

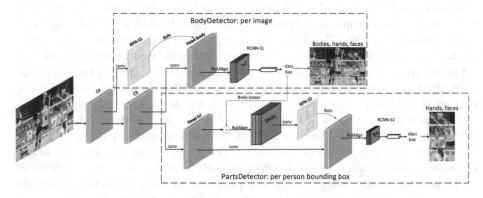

Fig. 2. The pipeline of the proposed DID-Net framework. (1) *BodyDetector*, which contains RPN-S1 and RCNN-S1, is used to detect body, hand and face. (2) *BodyDetector*, which contains RPN-S2 and RCNN-S2, is used to predict hand and face inside the body bounding boxes detected by *BodyDetector*.

3.1   BodyDetector

BodyDetector uses the same structure with Faster RCNN. Our backbone network is Resnet-50 [13], which is pre-trainied on ImageNet [27]. First, the backbone network generates a series of convolutional feature maps at several scales.

We denote these feature maps as (C2, C3, C4, C5) which is extracted from last layer of each scale stage. To increase the resolution of the C5 feature maps, we reduce the effective stride from 32 pixels to 16 pixels as done in [28]. Consequently, their corresponding strides of each layer are (4, 8, 16, 16) pixels with respect to the input image. C4 features are used to predict a set of proposals using the region proposal network, which we named it RPN-S1. Then features of each proposal are cropped from Head-body and pooled into a fixed-size feature vector using RoI Align (We use 7×7 size as [20] does). The features are then fed into RCNN-S1 to do per-proposal classification operation and box refinement of body, hand and face. For model compactness, Head-body is generated after a 1×1 convolutional layer with 256 kernels over the top features of C5 to reduce the dimension. The RoI Align layer is added on the top of the feature maps of Head-body. Two new fully connected (fc) layers of dimension 1024 are applied on the RoI Align features, followed by the bounding box regression and classification branches.

3.2 PartsDetector

PartsDetector shares the same convolutional features of the first stage by simply adding the **Head-hf** to C5 in parallel with **Head-body**, which contains 256 channels features as the same as **Head-body**. The predicted body bounding boxes of the first stage with high classification scores will be chosen. Non-maximum suppression (NMS) [29] is performed on the chosen proposals to eliminate highly overlapped detection bounding boxes. After box regression, the features of person proposals will be wrapped from Head-hf with RoI Align and pooled into size 24×24. RPN-S2 is applied on the wrapped body features to generate RoIs of hand and face. Then the features of RoIs will be extracted from another set of features, which are 256 channels features outputted by adding two 3×3 convolutional layers over Head-hf. Two fully connected layers are appended after the extracted RoI features for further classification and box regression using RCNN-S2. In this stage, we use size 24×24 for the RoI Align size of body and use size 5×5 for the cropped features of hand or face due to the scale variance between them.

During training, we select the top 16 body detections within each image considering the dataset we used, which usually contains a maximum number of 11 persons in one image. While the positions of body bounding boxes are generated during training and are uncertain before. To handle this, we generate the ground truth annotations inside the predicted human body in an online way. When the original face and hand ground truth lie inside or partly inside the detected body bounding boxes, They will be regarded as the ground truth annotations of that body. After transferring the coordinate of these hand and face boxes from the original image to the body bounding boxes, a new batch of training data for hand and face inside each body can be sent to the *PartsDetector* for parts detection. In this detector, we treat every detected human body as one input image in the first detector when writing the implementation code. NMS is applied to eliminate highly overlapped detection bounding boxes during inference and training.

3.3   Loss Function

Our network is trained to minimize a multi-task loss, which is composed of classification and bounding-box regression losses of RPN and RCNN modules from the two detectors. We use softmax cross-entropy loss for classification and smooth *L1* loss [20] for bounding-box regression. For the RPN stage in two detectors, the classification loss is softmax cross-entropy loss over background/foreground classes. The loss can be formulated as Eq. 1. Here, $\mathcal{L}_{rpn}^{s1}$ and $\mathcal{L}_{cls}^{s1}$ denote the losses of RPN-S1 and RCNN-S1 in *BodyDetector*, and $\mathcal{L}_{rpn}^{s2}$ and $\mathcal{L}_{cls}^{s2}$ denote losses of RPN-S1 and RCNN-S2 in *PartsDetector*.

$$\mathcal{L} = \mathcal{L}_{rpn}^{s1} + \mathcal{L}_{cls}^{s1} + \mathcal{L}_{rpn}^{s2} + \mathcal{L}_{cls}^{s2} \tag{1}$$

4   Experiments

4.1   Human-Parts Datasets

In this paper, we collected and labeled a detection dataset named *Human-Parts* which contains annotations of three categories, including person, hand and face. The proposed dataset contains high-resolution images which are randomly selected from AI-challenger [35] dataset. Person category has already been labeled in this dataset. However, the small human whose body parts are hard to distinguish or the vague ones whose body contours are hard to recognize are missed-labeled in this dataset. We added the missed person body annotations and labeled hand and face additionally in each image. The number of persons in each image range from 1 to 11. In total, our dataset consists of 14,962 images (we use 12,000 for train, 2,962 for testing) with 10,6879 annotations (35,306 persons, 27,821 faces and 43,752 hands). Our dataset followed the same standard annotation principles as Wider Face [34] and VGG Hand dataset [11]. We have labeled every visible person, hand or face with xmin, ymin, xmax and ymax coordinates and ensured that annotations cover the entire objects including the blocked parts but without extra background. The annotation format follows PASCAL VOC [36]. The representative images and annotations are shown in Fig. 3. More details about this dataset and comparisons with other human parts datasets can be seen in Table 1.

Fig. 3. Samples of annotated images in *Human-Parts* dataset.

Table 1. Comparison of different human parts detection datasets

DataSet	Images	Person	Hand	Face	Total instance
Caltech [30]	42,782	✓	-	-	13,674
CityPersons [31]	2,975	✓	-	-	19,238
EgoHands [32]	4,800	-	✓	-	15,053
VGG Hand [11]	11,194	-	✓	-	13,050
FDDB [33]	2,854	-	-	✓	5,171
Wider Face [34]	32,203	-	-	✓	393,703
Human Parts	14,962	✓	✓	✓	106,879

4.2   Implementation Details

We perform all experiments on *Human-Parts* dataset. Training and evaluation are performed on the 12,000 images in the *train* set and the 2,962 images on the *test* set. For evaluation, we use the standard average precision (AP) and mean average precision (mAP). We report AP and mAP scores using the intersection over union (IoU) [36] threshold at 0.5. All networks are fine-tuned from a pre-trained ImageNet classification network ResNet-50. Our system is implemented in Pytorch and source code will be made publicly available.

For anchor generation, we use scales $(64^2, 128^2, 256^2, 512^2)$ in the *BodyDetector* stage and $(32^2, 64^2, 128^2, 256^2)$ in the *PartsDetector* stage considering the scale variance of body and body parts. All anchors have the aspect ratio of (0.5, 1, 2) due to the large variations of hand and face in the wild. During training, the mini-batch size of 512 is employed for the RCNN-S1 stage of *BodyDetector*, and 32 is employed for each person RoI in the RCNN-S2 stage of *PartsDetector*. Multi-scale training strategy is adopted to be robust to different scale objects. In our method, the shorter side is resized to (416, 480, 576, 688, 864, 1024) pixels. We only use horizontal image flipping augmentation. In the testing phase, the shorter side of each image is resized to 800 pixels and tested independently. For other settings, we follows the work [20].

During training, we adopt an end-to-end learning procedure using stochastic gradient descent (SGD). The whole network is trained for 30,000 iterations with initial learning rate of 0.01. We decay the learning rate by 0.1 at 20,000 iterations. A momentum of 0.9 and a weight decay of 0.0005 are used. During inference, *BodyDetector* module outputs 300 best scoring anchors as detections. While in the *PartsDetector* module, we only select 30 best scoring anchors on account of limited parts inside each body region. The results of hand and face in *BodyDetector* and *PartsDetector* are fused together and NMS with a threshold of 0.45 is performed on the outputs due to the existence of large overlap objects in the wild such as Fig. 3.

4.3   Main Results

In Table 2, we perform studies of traditional Faster RCNN training with different data and our DID-Net. *Separate Network* adopts only one category detection task in one ResNet-50 Faster R-CNN network. *Union Network* performs three categories detection together in the same Network as *Single Network*. From Table 2 we can see that:

Table 2. Basic results of Faster RCNN and our DID-Net. **P** denotes person, **H** denotes hand and **F** denote face. The bold values are the best performance in each column

	Train data	Detector	Person AP	Face AP	Hand AP	mAP
Separate network	P	ResNet-50-Faster	88.1	-	-	90.2
	F		-	95.9	-	
	H		-	-	86.7	
Union network	P + H + F	ResNet-50 -Faster	89.3	93.0	82.3	88.2
Our network	P + H + F	ResNet-50-DID	**89.6**	**96.1**	**87.5**	**91.1**

- **Person AP.** The AP performance of person is increased from 88.1 to 89.6 after conducting multi-objects detection task together in a single network, from which we can infer that the saliency of hand and face will contribute to the detection performance of the person. Works of [37,38] also show that the facial contributes based supervision can effectively enhance the capability of a face detection network.
- **Small Parts AP.** The AP values of small parts in *Union Nework* decrease compared with the *Separate Network*. The reasons mainly come from the scale variance between human body and body parts. In practice, the whole image is mainly occupied by the big objects like human body. Small hand and face usually occupy a relatively smaller area. Given a fixed anchor scales and anchor ratios, there will be less small anchors generated by RPN, which lead to the poor performance of small parts detection.

Compared with *Single Network* and *Union Network*, DID-Net conducts another RPN inside each body, where less disturbance from other objects or background exist. The network can learn more spacial region relationship between body parts. In addition, when extracting features of the person proposals, we pooled these wrapped features to size 24 × 24, which will be larger than the original person feature maps mostly. That operation will zoom out the features of the small parts and result in a high resolution of feature maps for further detection. Results show that our DID-Net outperforms the *Separate Network* and *Union Network*, which demonstrate the efficiency of our framework.

4.4   Ablation Study

In Table 3, we evaluate how different components affect the detection performance of *PartsDetector*. For fair comparison, we fixed the parameters of the backbone network and *BodyDetector*. Thus the person AP in Table 3 is constant.

Table 3. Experiment results about how structure design and the number of training bodies affect the detection performance of *PartsDetector*

PartsDetector	Person RoI	Person AP	Face AP	Hand AP	mAP
RPN-S2 + RCNN-S2	16	89.6	**96.1**	**87.5**	**91.1**
RPN-S2	16	89.6	93.5	83.3	88.8
RPN-S2 + RCNN-S2	8	89.6	95.4	86.0	90.3

- **Architecture.** There are two designs of *PartsDetector*: (1) *RPN-S2 + RCNN-S2* design: It follows the structure we described in Sect. 3. Two RoI Align operations are adopted as shown in Fig. 2. (2) *RPN-S2* is changed to output the classification and box regression of each RoI directly as SSD did. There is only one RoI Align operation. Table 3 shows that two-stage design of *PartsDetector* can achieve a higher accuracy on small parts detection.
- **Person RoI.** Person RoI represents that how many person bodies after NMS operation are selected from the *BodyDetector* during training. We use a different number of 8 and 16 for this number and conduct experiments. Larger number is not used considering the computation efficiency. Results show that, if the selected bodies are less than the bodies the image really contains during training, the features of Head-hf will not contain enough response to unselected bodies. And that incomplete training will lead to a performance drop of the *PartsDetector*.

4.5   Comparisons with the State-of-Arts

We compare the proposed DID-Net to the state-of-the-art methods performed on *Human-Parts* dataset in Table 4, which includes SSD (training image size are 512×512), Faster R-CNN, RFCN [28] with online hard example mining(OHEM) [39] and FPN [40]. SSD is conducted using original settings of paper. For those region-based detectors, multi-scale training (described in Sect. 4.2), anchor scales of $(64^2, 128^2, 256^2, 512^2)$, anchor ratios of $(0.5, 1, 2)$ and RoI Align are adopted in all models during training. All the models are trained for 30,000 iterations with a initial learning rate of 0.01, a weight decay of 0.0005 and a momentum of 0.9.

Results show that our DID-Net achieves the highest accuracy on person and hand category. Region-based two-stage detection models (Faster R-CNN, RFCN, FPN) outperform single-stage detectors (SSD), which demonstrates the ability of two-stage detectors. FPN achieves better performance on hand and face detection performance than Faster R-CNN owing to the efficient fusion of features with

Table 4. Table of Average Precision on validation set of Human parts. Our DID-Net outperforms SSD [15], Faster R-CNN [20], RFCN [28] with OHEM [39] and FPN [40] on person and face detection. Comparable results are achieved on face detection ability compared with FPN

	Backbone	Multi scale	RoI Align	AP_{person}	AP_{face}	AP_{hand}	mAP
SSD	VGG16	-	-	84.3	90.4	77.4	84.0
Faster R-CNN	ResNet-50	✓	✓	89.2	93.0	82.3	88.1
RFCN + ohem	ResNet-50	✓	✓	88.9	93.2	84.5	88.9
FPN	ResNet-50	✓	✓	87.9	**96.5**	85.4	89.9
DID-Net	ResNet-50	✓	✓	**89.6**	96.1	**87.5**	**91.1**

different scales. While the performance of person dropped slightly than Faster R-CNN due to the scale variance between human body and body parts. After adding the *PartsDetector* to the basic *BodyDetector*, the detection performance of face and hand in our architecture have a large promotion.

4.6 Qualitative Results

We show some qualitative human parts detection results on sample images in Fig. 4. From the Faster RCNN results in the first row, we observe that there still exists some small hands or faces (in yellow boxes), which can not be detected. While in the results of DID-Net, those hard parts can be found. Results can be seen in the second row of Fig. 4.

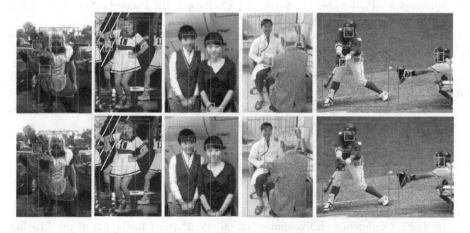

Fig. 4. Some example results of Faster RCNN (Top) and the proposed DID-Net (Bottom). Green boxes are the detected persons. Red boxes are the detected hands. Purple boxes are the detected faces. Yellow boxes in the first row are the missed objects of Faster-RCNN. (Color figure online)

5   Conclusion

In this paper, we propose a Detector-in-Detector network (DID-Net) for the multi-level objects by simply appending a light-weight *PartsDetector* after Faster RCNN structure to perform parts detection inside each body. We implement our methods on *Human-Parts* dataset and experiments show that our methods can achieve an excellent performance, especially for small hands and faces. The novel framework we constructed can also be performed on other multi-level objects. In addition, we have also build a dataset named *Human-Parts*, which aims to the human body, hand, and face in many realistic environments. Others can also use our dataset for related tasks and applications.

References

1. Ribeiro, D., Mateus, A., Nascimento, J.C., Miraldo, P.: A real-time pedestrian detector using deep learning for human-aware navigation (2016)
2. Chen, Y., Wang, Z., Peng, Y., Zhang, Z., Yu, G., Sun, J.: Cascaded pyramid network for multi-person pose estimation (2017)
3. Papandreou, G., et al.: Towards accurate multi-person pose estimation in the wild, pp. 3711–3719 (2017)
4. Xiao, S., et al.: Recurrent 3D–2D dual learning for large-pose facial landmark detection. In: IEEE International Conference on Computer Vision, pp. 1642–1651 (2017)
5. Dhawan, A., Honrao, V.: Implementation of hand detection based techniques for human computer interaction. Comput. Sci. **72**, 6–13 (2013)
6. Ghorban, F., Marín, J., Yu, S., Colombo, A., Kummert, A.: Aggregated channels network for real-time pedestrian detection (2018)
7. Samangouei, P., Najibi, M., Davis, L., Chellappa, R.: Face-MagNet: magnifying feature maps to detect small faces (2018)
8. Zhu, C., Zheng, Y., Luu, K., Savvides, M.: CMS-RCNN: contextual multi-scale region-based CNN for unconstrained face detection (2017)
9. Deng, X., et al.: Joint hand detection and rotation estimation by using CNN. IEEE Trans. Image Process. **27** (2016)
10. Le, T.H.N., Quach, K.G., Zhu, C., Chi, N.D., Luu, K., Savvides, M.: Robust hand detection and classification in vehicles and in the wild. In: Computer Vision and Pattern Recognition Workshops, pp. 1203–1210 (2017)
11. Mittal, A., Zisserman, A., Torr, P.: Hand detection using multiple proposals. In: British Machine Vision Conference, pp. 75.1–75.11 (2011)
12. Zhao, K., Zhang, W., Jiang, Y.: Semantic interactions in multi-level objects segmentation. In: International Conference on Computational and Information Sciences, pp. 665–668 (2010)
13. He, K., Zhang, X., Ren, S., Sun, J.: Deep residual learning for image recognition. In: IEEE Conference on Computer Vision and Pattern Recognition, pp. 770–778 (2016)
14. Girshick, R.: Fast R-CNN. Comput. Sci. (2015)
15. Liu, W., et al.: SSD: single shot multibox detector, pp. 21–37 (2015)
16. Li, Z., Zhou, F.: FSSD: feature fusion single shot multibox detector (2017)

17. Redmon, J., Divvala, S., Girshick, R., Farhadi, A.: You only look once: unified, real-time object detection, pp. 779–788 (2015)
18. Jiang, H., Learnedmiller, E.: Face detection with the faster R-CNN, pp. 650–657 (2016)
19. He, K., Fu, Y., Xue, X.: A jointly learned deep architecture for facial attribute analysis and face detection in the wild (2017)
20. Ren, S., He, K., Girshick, R., Sun, J.: Faster R-CNN: towards real-time object detection with region proposal networks. In: International Conference on Neural Information Processing Systems, pp. 91–99 (2015)
21. Hu, P., Ramanan, D.: Finding tiny faces (2016)
22. Najibi, M., Samangouei, P., Chellappa, R., Davis, L.S.: SSH: single stage headless face detector, pp. 4885–4894 (2017)
23. Li, H., Lin, Z., Shen, X., Brandt, J., Hua, G.: A convolutional neural network cascade for face detection. In: Computer Vision and Pattern Recognition, pp. 5325–5334 (2015)
24. Zhang, K., Zhang, Z., Li, Z., Qiao, Y.: Joint face detection and alignment using multitask cascaded convolutional networks. IEEE Sign. Process. Lett. **23**, 1499–1503 (2016)
25. Lin, T.-Y., et al.: Microsoft COCO: common objects in context. In: Fleet, D., Pajdla, T., Schiele, B., Tuytelaars, T. (eds.) ECCV 2014. LNCS, vol. 8693, pp. 740–755. Springer, Cham (2014). https://doi.org/10.1007/978-3-319-10602-1_48
26. He, K., Gkioxari, G., Dollár, P., Girshick, R.: Mask R-CNN (2017)
27. Deng, J., Dong, W., Socher, R., Li, L.J., Li, K., Li, F.F.: ImageNet: a large-scale hierarchical image database. In: IEEE Conference on Computer Vision and Pattern Recognition, CVPR 2009, pp. 248–255 (2009)
28. Dai, J., Li, Y., He, K., Sun, J.: R-FCN: object detection via region-based fully convolutional networks (2016)
29. Girshick, R., Iandola, F., Darrell, T., Malik, J.: Deformable part models are convolutional neural networks, pp. 437–446 (2014)
30. Dollar, P., Wojek, C., Schiele, B., Perona, P.: Pedestrian detection: a benchmark. In: Proceedings Conference on Computer Vision Pattern Recognition, pp. 304–311 (2009)
31. Zhang, S., Benenson, R., Schiele, B.: CityPersons: a diverse dataset for pedestrian detection (2017)
32. Bambach, S., Lee, S., Crandall, D.J., Yu, C.: Lending a hand: detecting hands and recognizing activities in complex egocentric interactions. In: IEEE International Conference on Computer Vision (2016)
33. Jain, V., Learned-Miller, E.: FDDB: a benchmark for face detection in unconstrained settings (2010)
34. Yang, S., Luo, P., Chen, C.L., Tang, X.: WIDER FACE: a face detection benchmark. In: IEEE Conference on Computer Vision and Pattern Recognition, pp. 5525–5533 (2016)
35. Wu, J., et al.: AI challenger: a large-scale dataset for going deeper in image understanding (2017)
36. Everingham, M., Gool, L., Williams, C.K., Winn, J., Zisserman, A.: The pascal visual object classes (VOC) challenge. Int. J. Comput. Vis. **88**, 303–338 (2010)
37. Qin, H., Yan, J., Li, X., Hu, X.: Joint training of cascaded CNN for face detection. In: IEEE Conference on Computer Vision and Pattern Recognition, pp. 3456–3465 (2016)
38. Yang, S., Luo, P., Loy, C.C., Tang, X.: Faceness-Net: face detection through deep facial part responses. IEEE Trans. Pattern Anal. Mach. Intell. **PP**, 1 (2017)

39. Shrivastava, A., Gupta, A., Girshick, R.: Training region-based object detectors with online hard example mining, pp. 761–769 (2016)
40. Lin, T.Y., Dollar, P., Girshick, R., He, K., Hariharan, B., Belongie, S.: Feature pyramid networks for object detection, pp. 936–944 (2016)

Aligning Salient Objects to Queries: A Multi-modal and Multi-object Image Retrieval Framework

Sounak Dey[1] , Anjan Dutta[1(✉)] , Suman K. Ghosh[1] , Ernest Valveny[1] ,
Josep Lladós[1] , and Umapada Pal[2]

[1] Computer Vision Center, Autonomous University of Barcelona, Barcelona, Spain
{sdey,adutta,sghosh,josep,ernest}@cvc.uab.es
[2] CVPR Unit, Indian Statistical Institute, Kolkata, India
umapada@isical.ac.in

Abstract. In this paper we propose an approach for multi-modal image retrieval in multi-labelled images. A multi-modal deep network architecture is formulated to jointly model sketches and text as input query modalities into a common embedding space, which is then further aligned with the image feature space. Our architecture also relies on a salient object detection through a supervised LSTM-based visual attention model learned from convolutional features. Both the alignment between the queries and the image and the supervision of the attention on the images are obtained by generalizing the Hungarian Algorithm using different loss functions. This permits encoding the object-based features and its alignment with the query irrespective of the availability of the co-occurrence of different objects in the training set. We validate the performance of our approach on standard single/multi-object datasets, showing state-of-the art performance in every dataset.

1 Introduction

Content Based Image Retrieval (CBIR) has been for decades one of the prevalent topics in Computer Vision. Rapidly the field has evolved towards a more human-centered view. Thus, cross-media image retrieval systems emerged, allowing users to express the queries in a more natural way using different input modalities, such as text, speech, or sketches.

Text-based image retrieval (TBIR) is the most widely established modality, due to the simplicity of matching text queries with manually assigned keywords describing the image content. Human annotation of large databases of images is time consuming and may lack completeness. Thus, current trends explore TBIR systems that could bridge the semantic gap with queries based on natural language descriptions of the image content. Despite its wider expressiveness there can still be circumstances where text cannot be adequate to portray the query and it can be difficult to establish the link between text and image contents.

C. V. Jawahar et al. (Eds.): ACCV 2018, LNCS 11362, pp. 241–255, 2019.
https://doi.org/10.1007/978-3-030-20890-5_16

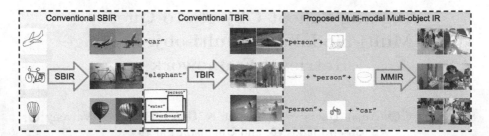

Fig. 1. In conventional SBIR and TBIR, during the training phase, respectively a sketch and a text representation is mapped to the image representation of corresponding class. Querying images with multiple labels has been explored within the TBIR domain [18] (as shown in the last row of Conventional TBIR column). Querying images with multiple objects using multi-modal queries provides convenience in searching, but it is an extremely challenging task and has not been addressed yet.

With the advent of touch screen and pen input devices, sketches have emerged as an alternative mode to provide the query that can deal with the limitations of text and images. Sketches are a natural way to conceptualize visual objects in terms of simplified shapes and their pose, however they have a few constraints. Sketching needs some idea and ability in drawing shapes that can make some users uncomfortable with this modality. Thus a SBIR (Sketch Based Image Retrieval) framework can not replace conventional text based retrieval which has its own benefits (e.g. utilization of keyboard versus stylus). Thus both modalities can complement each other. Although numerous methodologies for SBIR have been proposed, none of them allow to utilize text as an extra or complementary query modality. Thus, the first motivation for the work presented in this paper is to propose a multi-modal image retrieval approach where the query can be either sketch or text or both. To make the different modalities compatible, a common semantic embedding space is defined.

Another noteworthy constraint of most existing image retrieval pipelines is that they can only manage situations where just a single salient object is significant – see Fig. 1. This motivates the second challenge of the present work, i.e. allowing to express queries that can refer to multiple objects. In this way, the proposed model provides more expressiveness to the search language since users can construct queries consisting of different concepts that are aligned to the salient objects of the target images. To the best of our understanding, none of the SBIR techniques can deal with multi-object scenarios. Although some of the strategies [7] based on textual queries can recover relevant images containing multiple objects.

Consequently, we propose a unified multi-modal and multi-object image retrieval (MMIR) framework, which permits to retrieve images containing multiple objects, expressing the query using text, sketches or a combination of both. The framework is based on a deep network architecture in which multi-modality is addressed by projecting word2vec representations of sketches and text into a common semantic space aligned with the image feature space. To deal with multi-object search we integrate an LSTM-based visual attention model that learns to discover relevant zones of the image. To match the set of attention glimpses with the set of queries we propose a Hungarian loss that finds the best correspondence between both sets. The Hungarian loss is also used to introduce supervision while training the visual attention model by guiding the result of the attention towards object bounding boxes.

The main contributions of this work are: (1) The proposal of a common semantic space among text and sketches, obtained through word2vec representation of both input modalities, and aligned with the image feature space; (2) A visual attention model that automatically detects salient objects from an image, that is trained in a supervised way in order to minimize the assignment cost between attention output and object bounding boxes.

The rest of the paper is organized as follows: in Sect. 2, we review the relevant state-of-the-art. Sect. 3 describes in detail our proposed cross-modal/multi-object image retrieval framework. In Sect. 4, we describe the experimental framework and present the results of the experiments. Finally, Sect. 5 draws the conclusions and outlines the future directions.

2   Related Work

In this section we review image retrieval using text – text based image retrieval (TBIR) – and sketches – sketch based image retrieval (SBIR). Subsequently, as our method detects object as part of multi-object image retrieval by means of an attention procedure, we also discuss about the state of the art on attention models.

Advances in feature learning have recently provided effective feature representations for different modalities such as text [4,20], images [6,22], and hand-drawn sketches [29,43] which have been shown to greatly improve the retrieval performance. A common approach when dealing with multi-modal data is to learn a joint embedding to map all modalities into a common latent space [25]. However, in multi-modal image retrieval [35], the complementary use of text and sketch to express the queries has not been much explored [2].

TBIR, dating back to the late 1970s, has evolved from just a keyword-based task to a more challenging task based on natural language descriptions (e.g., sentences and paragraphs) [10]. Queries in the form of sentences rather than keywords refer not only to object categorical information but also interactions, such as spatial relationships between objects [12,39]. In our work we keep text in the simple form of keywords, but we permit to express objects relationships as combination of several text or sketch based queries. Recently, projecting text into the word2vec space has been shown to achieve a high level of accuracy in TBIR [5]. Thus, we also rely on wor2vec to represent text queries, but we also extend this idea to obtain a semantic embedding of sketches into the word2vec space.

SBIR is one of the alternative ways of searching and overcoming the limitations imposed by TBIR systems. Apart from images, sketches have been successfully used for 3D shape retrieval purpose as well [38,44]. Since sketch is more close to the semantic representation, it tends to help retrieving target results in the user mind from a semantic perspective [37]. Here, the main challenge is to bridge the domain gap between sketches and natural images. In literature, methods addressing this issue can be grouped into two categories: (1) hand-crafted methods, (2) deep learning-based methods. The hand-crafted features (e.g. SIFT [16]), gradient field HOG (GF-HOG [9]) are extracted from both the sketches and edge maps of natural images and further clustered using 'Bag-of-Words' (BoW), histogram of edge local orientations (S-HELO) [27] or Learned Key Shapes (LKS) [28]). One of the major limitations for such methods is the difficulty to match the edge maps to non-aligned sketches with large variations and ambiguity. To address the domain shift issue, convolutional neural networks (CNNs) methods [11] have recently been used to learn domain-transformable features from sketches and images with an end-to-end framework [29,43]. In our work, we address these semantic gap by directly projecting sketches to a semantic space using word2vec, that is further aligned with the image space.

The current deep SBIR methods tend to perform well only in a single object scenario with a simple contour shape on a clean background [15,29,43]. Recently, there have been attempts to apply deep learning to multi-label image recognition task [34,36,41]. Razavian *et al.* [24] applies off-the-shelf features extracted from a deep network pre-trained on ImageNet [26] for multi-label image classification. Wang *et al.* [34] utilize RNNs to learn a joint image-label embedding to characterize the semantic label dependency as well as the image-label relevance. Some works exploit object proposals to only focus on the informative regions, which effectively eliminate the influences of the non-object areas and thus demonstrate significant improvement in multi-label image recognition task [36,41]. More specifically, Wei *et al.* [36] propose a Hypotheses-CNN-Pooling framework to aggregate the label scores of each specific object hypotheses to achieve the final multi-label predictions. Yang *et al.* [41], formulate the multi-label image recognition problem as a multi-class multi-instance learning problem to incorporate local information and enhance the discriminative ability of the features by encoding the label view information. As an alternative we propose to use an attention model to discover image regions relevant to each of the objects.

Visual attention model has gained a lot of interest recently. In image captioning [40] visual attention assists the generation of descriptive captions. [42] targeted attention on a set of concepts extracted from the image to generate captions. In visual question answering [31,45] several models have been proposed which attend to image regions or questions when generating an answer. Concurrently, [1] analyzed the consistency between human and deep network attention in visual question answering. Our goal differs in that we are interested in how attention on salient objects can be aligned with the queried object. We use the attention correction proposed in [14] to create a supervised attention for salient object detection. A Hungarian Loss [32] function is proposed to match the salient objects with the queries projected to a semantic embedding space.

3   Multi-modal and Multi-object Image Retrieval

In this section we describe the proposed methodology (see the architecture in Fig. 2). The query (text and sketch) is embedded into a common semantic space. For each image in the image database, an LSTM based attention map generator finds several attention maps (one at every time step of LSTM) based on a CNN feature map and the previous attention map. These attention maps are trained in a supervised way and can be thought of as the relative importance of the different areas of the image in order to get the feature representation of the different salient objects in the image. For every attention map, the CNN features are weighted and averaged to get the final feature representation at every step. Thus, we obtain a set of features corresponding to different salient objects in the image. On the other hand, we allow for multiple queries each of them embedded in the semantic space. Consequently we have a set of query features and a set of image features that have to be matched and aligned. To compute a distance between these two sets, we use a Hungarian loss that gives the minimum cost assignment between them. Cosine distance between query features and object features is used to compute the individual cost between each pair query/object. In the following sections we introduce the details of each of the components of this global architecture.

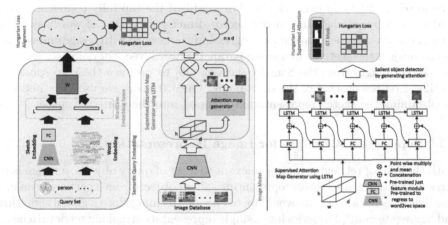

Fig. 2. Architecture of the proposed unified MMIR framework. The semantic query network (in purple) and the image model (in orange) are aligned using the Hungarian loss (in blue). Right side of the figure elaborates supervised attention map generator (in green). The Hungarian loss for attention (in blue) computes the assignments in test time and computes the assignments and loss during training. (Color figure online)

3.1   Semantic Query Embedding

For successful retrieval of images given text or sketch as query, a proper embedding space must be defined, where both text and sketch can be directly compared to the image with a distance measure. In the case of sketches this has been achieved by learning a global feature using triplet loss [29] or similarity loss [23]. For text, either one hot vector encoding based on a fixed vocabulary or some semantic embedding mapping words into a continuous vector space can be used. In our case, we chose to use a semantic embedding as it gives the opportunity to use generic words as query and the model is not restricted to a certain vocabulary of words. For the combination of sketch and text, in [2] two different subspaces were proposed, one between text and image another between sketch and image. However, end to end training of different subspaces is difficult and unstable.

We argue that a better option is to find a subspace where all three modalities can be compared. Therefore, we propose a semantic space to embed the queries, capturing the common properties of text and sketch. In particular, we use word2vec [19] representation to obtain this semantic space. For the text we use directly the word2vec embedding of the words. Sketch images are regressed to the word2vec space by using a CNN based regressor. In the following we provide the details of each embedding.

For word encoding, we have used the standard word2vec [19] representation, which is pre-trained on the set of words from the English Wikipedia[1]. This word representation produces a feature vector of 1000 dimensions.

For the regression of sketch images into semantic space, we adopt a modified version of the VGG-16 network [30]. We modified the top fully connected layer module to accommodate the output vector dimension to that of word2vec. The entire network was then trained as a regression framework with cosine embedding loss to project the sketches in a space parallel to word2vec. For doing so, we used the sketch images from the Sketchy dataset [29] to produce the corresponding word2vec representation of the class name. Once trained, we used the network for obtaining the sketch representation mapped into the word2vec space.

3.2   Supervised Attention for Image Representation

With the goal of retrieving images relevant to a set of query objects, our aim is to extract a set of feature vectors representing salient objects from a particular image. Another possible alternative would be to encode the image into a global signature and aggregate multiple queries into a single representation making retrieval a nearest neighbour problem in this feature space. However we argue that this approach has severe limitations. Firstly, to find a suitable global image representation that can encode the presence of multiple objects we should train with a well curated dataset containing possible combination of different objects. Such a dataset would be huge and training would be complex and take a lot of time. Secondly, although aggregation of queries could be solved in various ways, there is not an easy way to encode their relative position, which can be crucial to match with that of image. In [18] this problem is dealt with by using a spatial query box and then learning the

---

[1] https://www.wikipedia.org/.

relative position by using a conventional CNN. However, the position has to be provided by user which can limit the usability of the query interface. Another possibility would be to use a state-of-the-art object detector to detect object and compute the corresponding feature vectors for each object. However, most object detection pipelines assume rectangular objects and do not consider the image context around them. In addition, such an approach would eventually make the pipeline hard to train end-to-end due to different loss functions.

With all this in mind, we propose a different alternative by using a more flexible method based on an LSTM together with an attention model to detect multiple objects (in the form of mask) one at every step. The input to the attention model is a set of features extracted with a conventional CNN corresponding to a spatial grid in which every point represents an area in the image (through its receptive field). In a nutshell, our LSTM based object detector is trained to output one attention map at every step which depends on the previous attention map and the CNN features. The LSTM remembers the attended regions through the hidden vector, which prohibits it to attend the same object multiple times.

The soft attention mechanism was first used in computer vision by [40] where the attention model is not supervised in a sense that there is no loss calculated directly on the attention weights. Thus, the attention mechanism is free to attend anywhere, being only guided by the final output, which is calculated from the result of the attended features. However this model can be extended by applying a direct supervision i.e by directing the model "where to attend" [14]. In this work we used a similar framework but we did the following changes. Firstly, we changed the cross entropy loss between the target and the generated attention map and the softmax over the grid locations by a sigmoid cross entropy loss and a sigmoid activation function to generate a binary map over the grid. This follows from the hypothesis that every grid location is independent and can be a potential region to attend. Secondly, in our case the order in which the different targets (corresponding to objects) are attended is not relevant. Thus, we need a way to match the unordered set of targets with the unordered set of generated attention maps. We solve this by finding minimum cost between the two sets by using a generalized Hungarian loss. We outline the details of the formulation for this matching later.

More formally, the attention model computes n different attention maps and corresponding image representations for a single image using an LSTM network. The input to the LSTM is a set of features extracted from a pre-trained CNN-based feature extractor resulting in L vectors, $\{\mathbf{a}_1, ..., \mathbf{a}_L\}, \mathbf{a}_i \in \mathbb{R}^d$ that correspond to L spatial locations of an image. The LSTM generates n attention maps, $\{\alpha_t \in [0,1]^L, t = 1, ..., n\}$ and their corresponding image representations: $\{\mathbf{x}_t \in \mathbb{R}^d, t = 1, ..., n\}$. Our LSTM model can be visualized in Fig. 2. At every step, the input the LSTM takes as intput the hidden representation $\hat{h}$, the local features given by $\{\mathbf{a}_1, ..., \mathbf{a}_L\}$ and the attention map generated at previous time step. To generate the attention map the hidden vector is passed through an MLP layer followed by sigmoid activation, which provides attention maps that can be interpreted as the importance of every spatial location for the detection/retrieval of a certain object. Considering α_{i_l}, for $l = 1, 2, ..., L$ to be the weights on the L spatial grids for the ith step, the final image representation for i^{th} attention map is the weighted average of image features over all spatial locations, $\mathbf{x}_i = \sum_{l=1}^{L} \alpha_{i_l} \mathbf{a}_l$.

3.3 Hungarian Loss

In our framework we have to match two unordered sets of elements keeping two constraints. On one hand, we have m queries (represented as points in the regressed word2vec space) and n (where $n > m$) different image representations of every single image corresponding to the different attention computed through the LSTM. For retrieval we have to find the best matching between these two sets. On the other hand, in order to train in a supervised way the attention model we have to align the set of bounding boxes of the salient objects with the result of the n steps of the LSTM.

We have solved both problems using the same framework formulating them as a bi-partite graph matching problem, and using a variation of the Hungarian loss introduced in [32]. In this way, we compute the loss as the minimum cost assignment between every pair of elements in both sets. Given a cost matrix between every pair of elements, the computation of the minimum cost assignment is done by the Hungarian algorithm [21] in polynomial time.

We use two different cost functions for each of the two problems. The cost between the query features q and the computed image features x is given by the cosine dissimilarity between the query and the feature.

$$C_{\text{sim}}(\mathbf{q}_i, \mathbf{x}_j) = 1 - \cos(\mathbf{q}_i, \mathbf{x}_j)$$

For supervising the attention model, we have used the binary cross entropy as a cost function between each of the ground truth masks β and each of the generated attention maps α.

$$C_{\text{attn}}(\alpha_i, \beta_j) = -(\alpha_i \log(\beta_j) + (1 - \alpha_i) \log(1 - \beta_j))$$

4   Experimental Results

4.1   Implementation Details

We have implemented our method on PyTorch framework. For all experiments, the image features are extracted using the feature module of the pre-trained VGG-16 network model. This feature representation is particularly appropriate for our task as it can effectively capture high-level semantic information from the images and at the same time it naturally retains most spatial information. For sketches, we used the same VGG-16 model but replacing the last layer in the classifier module with a specific layer to accommodate the regression of the features extracted from the sketch to the word2vec space. The output is a feature vector of 1000 dimensions, which is then mapped to a common joint neural embedding space. Its jointly trained by freezing the feature extraction part on both the query and the image side. The salient object detector based on supervised attention model was implemented using the mask generated from the bounding boxes of the objects in MS-COCO images. In case of the Sketchy database, we used the bounding box of the sketches in the image mask. This was possible because the dataset was designed for fine grained SBIR. We first compare the proposed method with several previous SBIR methods for single object, including hand-crafted features: GF-HOG [8], S-HELO [27], LSK [28]; and deep learning based: Siamese CNN [23], Sketch-a-Net (SaN) [43], GN Triplet [29], 3D shape [33], DSH [15] as shown in the Table 2. For all the methods mentioned above we follow the same protocol and evaluation metrics as in [15]. In the case of [15] we used the trained model for 128-bits provided in the author's github repository.

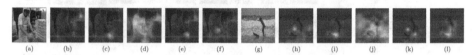

(a)   (b)   (c)   (d)   (e)   (f)   (g)   (h)   (i)   (j)   (k)   (l)

Fig. 3. Images of (a) person with pizza and (g) person with surfboard; (b)–(f) and (h)–(l) are respective n ($n = 5$) attention maps for image (a) and (b) obtained by our LSTM-based image model.

4.2   Datasets

Sketchy Dataset [29]: This is a large collection of sketch-photo pairs. The dataset consists of images belonging to 125 different classes, each having 100 images. After having these total $125 \times 100 = 12,500$ images, crowed workers were employed for sketching the objects that appear in these 12,500 images, which resulted in 75,471 sketches.

TU-Berlin Dataset [3]: The TU-Berlin dataset contains 250 categories with a total of 20,000 sketches. We also utilize the extended set provided in [15], with natural images corresponding to the sketch classes with a total size of 204,489.

MS-COCO Dataset [13]: Originally it is a large scale object detection, segmentation, and captioning dataset. We use the MS.COCO dataset for constructing a database of images containing multiple objects. As the label number for each image also varies considerably, rendering MS-COCO is even more challenging. We use the class names of the Sketchy dataset and take all possible combinations by taking two, three, four, five class names. Afterwards, we download the images belonging to these combined classes, and use them for training and retrieval. Few combined classes having less than 10 images are eliminated, leaving 125 number of combined classes for the experiment with at least 900 images.

4.3   Ablation Analysis

In this subsection, we perform some experiments to carefully analyze the contribution of the critical components of our proposed model. For this study we used

rabbit

person

chair   book

person   hand bag

bowl   table

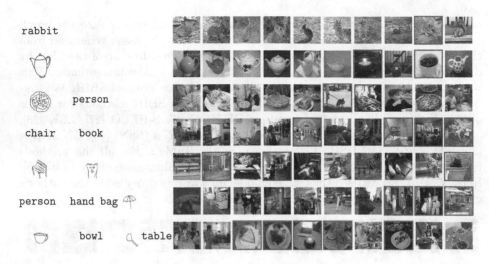

Fig. 4. Qualitative results obtained by our proposed method: eight example queries consisting texts as well as sketches with their top-10 retrieval results on the Sketchy, TU-Berlin and MS-COCO dataset. Red boxes indicates false positives. (Best viewed in pdf)

single object retrieval from the Sketchy [29] using sketch as a query modality. In an effort to evaluate each of our contributions, we trained every variation of the system with exactly the same training data.

In the first row of Table 1 we show the results that we obtain if we replace the VGG-16 network that regresses the wor2vec representation of sketches by another VGG-16 network that just outputs a one-hot encoding representation of the word that represents the class of the sketch. The sketch features obtained from the one-hot encoding produce reasonable retrieval performances, but the figures are still clearly lower than our original design in the last row of the table (12% less in mAP). We speculate this is because hidden representations and knowledge within the trained neural network is able to store more information by correlating the data points that are semantically close.

We also introduce two other variations by replacing the supervised attention module with a global average pooling of image features (second row of Table 1) and a standard attention model without mask level supervision (third row) in order to show the impact of the supervised attention model in detecting salient objects. The comparison reveals the fact that supervised attended regions have a relevant impact on the results and therefore, are capable of discovering the discriminating regions, which facilitates the task of multi-label image classification. The global pooling basically provides no segregated object information and fails to generalize knowledge from the seen objects together to the unseen ones. The general attention is also suboptimal in exploring the object features individually (Fig. 3).

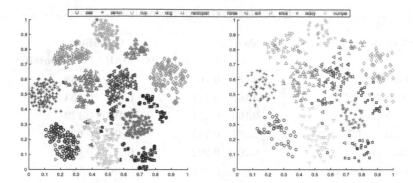

Fig. 5. *t-SNE* visualization of our image and sketch embeddings of 10 representative categories from the Sketchy dataset. After embedding the images as well as the sketches to the common space by our model, natural images and sketch queries from most of the categories are almost scattered into the same clusters. (Best viewed in pdf)

Table 1. Ablation analysis

Description	Sketchy
Regressed vector → one hot vector	0.688
Supervised attention → global pooling	0.726
Supervised attention → general attention	0.754
Full model	**0.809**

Finally, in (Fig. 5), we elucidate t-SNE [17] visualization of the image features and sketch features corresponding to 10 different categories. We can see that the distributions of the features in both domains are very similar reflecting that the network is capable to align features among both modalities.

4.4   Results and Discussions

Single Object: In Table 2, we report the comparison of mAP and precision@200 over all SBIR methods on two datasets. Generally, deep learning-based methods can achieve much better performance than handcrafted methods and the results on Sketchy are higher than those on TU-Berlin since the data in Sketchy is relatively simpler with fewer categories. The corresponding precision-recall (P-R) curves for both the datasets are illustrated in Fig. 6(a) and (b). Our method leads with significant improvements over the best-performing comparison methods on the two datasets, respectively in both mAP and precision@200. We argue that this is because our architecture is specifically designed to handle visual alignment of the query to the images using the Hungarian Loss.

Multiple Objects: For retrieving images with multiple objects, we have considered the MS-COCO dataset as mentioned above. Two existing methods are

Table 2. Image retrieval performance

Methods	Sketchy		TU-Berlin	
	mAP	Precision@200	mAP	Precision@200
GF-HOG [8]	0.135	0.167	0.114	0.158
S-HELO [27]	0.161	0.181	0.121	0.153
LKS [28]	0.193	0.231	0.151	0.172
Siamese CNN [23]	0.587	0.745	0.489	0.623
SaN [43]	0.208	0.292	0.178	0.182
GN Triplet [29]	0.651	0.797	0.597	0.782
3D shape [33]	0.161	0.181	0.123	0.147
DSH [15]	0.620	0.694	0.556	0.743
Proposed (Sketch)	**0.809**	**0.886**	**0.653**	**0.796**
Proposed (Text)	**0.802**	**0.881**	**0.641**	**0.727**
Proposed (Sketch + Text)	**0.803**	**0.882**	**0.645**	**0.735**

considered for comparison: SSCC [18] and UA [2]. However, it is worth mentioning that none of the above two methods works with multi-modal queries; as they
allow retrieving images with multiple queries, we slightly modified these methods to accept multi-modal queries. The multi-modal multi-object image retrieval
mean average precision (mAP@all) of our proposed method and the two baselines are reported in Table 3 and the corresponding precision-recall (P-R) curves
are shown in Fig. 6(c). The performance margins between our proposed method
and the selected state-of-the-art methods are significant, suggesting the existing
cross-modal image retrieval methods fail to handle the multi-modal multi-object
image retrieval task. SSCC [18] attains relatively better results. A possible reason
for this is allowance of multiple queries and a relatively simple model for query

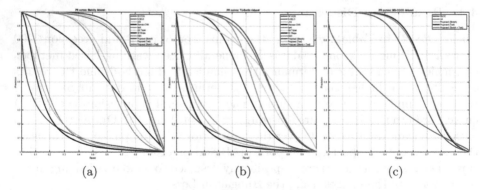

(a)   (b)   (c)

Fig. 6. Precision-recall curves obtained by different methods on (a) Sketchy, (b) TU-
Berlin, (c) MS-COCO datasets. (Best viewed in pdf)

processing. However, this method is designed only for text modality and also deals with semantic constraints, which can be a reason of the worse performance than our proposed system. Some qualitative results of retrieving images using multi-modal and multi-object queries are Fig. 4. It can be seen that our proposed method is able to produce acceptable retrieval results. Albeit some false alarms are produced, they mostly have some visual similarity with the actual retrieval.

Table 3. Multiple objects

Methods	MS-COCO	
	mAP	Precision@200
SSCC [18]	0.623	0.667
UA [2]	0.354	0.413
Proposed (Sketch)	0.697	0.753
Proposed (Text)	0.696	0.751
Proposed (Sketch + Text)	**0.693**	**0.749**

5 Conclusions and Future Work

In this paper, we have proposed a common neural network model for sketch as well as text based image retrieval. One of the most important advantages of our framework is that it allows to retrieve images queried by terms of multiple modalities (text and sketch). We have designed an image attention mechanism based on LSTM that allows to put attention on the specific zones of the images depending on the inter related objects which usually co-occur in nature. This has been learned by our model from the images in the training set. We have tested our proposed framework on the challenging Sketchy dataset for single object retrieval and on a collection of images from the COCO dataset for multiple object retrieval. Furthermore, we have compared our experimental results with three state-of-the-art methods. We have found that our method performs satisfactorily better than the considered state-of-the-art methods on all the two datasets with some cases of failure with justifiable reasons. For the future we plan to investigate on more efficient training strategies, as few shot learning approaches that learn from a small amount of training data in human-centered scenarios that allow users to search in their own databases in a more efficient and effortless manner.

Acknowledgement. This work has been partially supported by the European Union's Marie Skłodows-ka Curie grant agreement No. 665919 (H2020-MSCA-COFUND-2014:665919:CV-PR:01), the Spanish projects TIN2015-70924-C2-2-R, TIN2014-52072-P, and the CERCA Program of Generalitat de Catalunya.

References

1. Das, A., Agrawal, H., Zitnick, L., Parikh, D., Batra, D.: Human attention in visual question answering: do humans and deep networks look at the same regions? CVIU **163**, 90–100 (2017)
2. Dey, S., Dutta, A., Ghosh, S.K., Valveny, E., Lladós, J., Pal, U.: Learning cross-modal deep embeddings for multi-object image retrieval using text and sketch. In: ICPR, pp. 916–921 (2018)
3. Eitz, M., Hildebrand, K., Boubekeur, T., Alexa, M.: Sketch-based image retrieval: benchmark and bag-of-features descriptors. IEEE TVCG **17**(11), 1624–1636 (2011)
4. Frome, A., et al.: DeViSE: a deep visual-semantic embedding model. In: NIPS, pp. 2121–2129 (2013)
5. Gordo, A., Almazán, J., Murray, N., Perronin, F.: LEWIS: latent embeddings for word images and their semantics. In: ICCV, pp. 1242–1250 (2015)
6. Gordo, A., Almazán, J., Revaud, J., Larlus, D.: Deep image retrieval: learning global representations for image search. In: Leibe, B., Matas, J., Sebe, N., Welling, M. (eds.) ECCV 2016. LNCS, vol. 9910, pp. 241–257. Springer, Cham (2016). https://doi.org/10.1007/978-3-319-46466-4_15
7. Gordo, A., Larlus, D.: Beyond instance-level image retrieval: leveraging captions to learn a global visual representation for semantic retrieval. In: CVPR, pp. 5272–5281 (2017)
8. Hu, R., Barnard, M., Collomosse, J.: Gradient field descriptor for sketch based retrieval and localization. In: ICIP, pp. 1025–1028 (2010)
9. Hu, R., Collomosse, J.: A performance evaluation of gradient field hog descriptor for sketch based image retrieval. CVIU **117**(7), 790–806 (2013)
10. Krishna, R., et al.: Visual genome: connecting language and vision using crowd-sourced dense image annotations. IJCV **123**, 32–73 (2017)
11. Krizhevsky, A., Sutskever, I., Hinton, G.E.: ImageNet classification with deep convolutional neural networks. In: NIPS, pp. 1097–1105 (2012)
12. Lan, T., Yang, W., Wang, Y., Mori, G.: Image retrieval with structured object queries using latent ranking SVM. In: Fitzgibbon, A., Lazebnik, S., Perona, P., Sato, Y., Schmid, C. (eds.) ECCV 2012. LNCS, vol. 7577, pp. 129–142. Springer, Heidelberg (2012). https://doi.org/10.1007/978-3-642-33783-3_10
13. Lin, T.-Y., et al.: Microsoft COCO: common objects in context. In: Fleet, D., Pajdla, T., Schiele, B., Tuytelaars, T. (eds.) ECCV 2014. LNCS, vol. 8693, pp. 740–755. Springer, Cham (2014). https://doi.org/10.1007/978-3-319-10602-1_48
14. Liu, C., Mao, J., Sha, F., Yuille, A.L.: Attention correctness in neural image captioning. In: AAAI, pp. 4176–4182 (2017)
15. Liu, L., Shen, F., Shen, Y., Liu, X., Shao, L.: Deep sketch hashing: fast free-hand sketch-based image retrieval. In: CVPR, pp. 2862–2871 (2017)
16. Lowe, D.G.: Object recognition from local scale-invariant features. In: ICCV, pp. 1150–1157 (1999)
17. van der Maaten, L., Hinton, G.: Visualizing data using t-SNE. JMLR, 2579–2605 (2008)
18. Mai, L., Jin, H., Lin, Z., Fang, C., Brandt, J., Liu, F.: Spatial-semantic image search by visual feature synthesis. In: CVPR, pp. 1121–1130 (2017)
19. Mikolov, T., Chen, K., Corrado, G., Dean, J.: Efficient estimation of word representations in vector space. In: ICLR (2013)
20. Mikolov, T., Sutskever, I., Chen, K., Corrado, G.S., Dean, J.: Distributed representations of words and phrases and their compositionality. In: NIPS, pp. 3111–3119 (2013)

21. Munkres, J.: Algorithms for the assignment and transportation problems. JSIAM **5**(1), 32–38 (1957)
22. Paulin, M., Mairal, J., Douze, M., Harchaoui, Z., Perronnin, F., Schmid, C.: Convolutional patch representations for image retrieval: an unsupervised approach. IJCV **121**, 149–168 (2017)
23. Qi, Y., Song, Y.Z., Zhang, H., Liu, J.: Sketch-based image retrieval via siamese convolutional neural network. In: ICIP, pp. 2460–2464 (2016)
24. Razavian, A.S., Azizpour, H., Sullivan, J., Carlsson, S.: CNN features off-the-shelf: an astounding baseline for recognition. In: CVPRW, pp. 512–519 (2014)
25. Reed, S., Akata, Z., Lee, H., Schiele, B.: Learning deep representations of fine-grained visual descriptions. In: CVPR, pp. 49–58 (2016)
26. Russakovsky, O., et al.: ImageNet large scale visual recognition challenge. IJCV, 211–252 (2015)
27. Saavedra, J.M.: Sketch based image retrieval using a soft computation of the histogram of edge local orientations (S-HELO). In: ICIP, pp. 2998–3002 (2014)
28. Saavedra, J.M., Barrios, J.M., Orand, S.: Sketch based image retrieval using learned keyshapes (LKS). BMVC **1**, 1–10 (2015)
29. Sangkloy, P., Burnell, N., Ham, C., Hays, J.: The sketchy database: learning to retrieve badly drawn bunnies. ACM SIGGRAPH (2016)
30. Simonyan, K., Zisserman, A.: Very deep convolutional networks for large-scale image recognition. arXiv abs/1409.1556 (2014)
31. Singh, S., Hoiem, D., Forsyth, D.: Learning to localize little landmarks. In: CVPR, pp. 260–269 (2016)
32. Stewart, R., Andriluka, M., Ng, A.Y.: End-to-end people detection in crowded scenes. In: CVPR, pp. 2325–2333 (2016)
33. Wang, F., Kang, L., Li, Y.: Sketch-based 3D shape retrieval using convolutional neural networks. In: CVPR, pp. 1875–1883 (2015)
34. Wang, J., Yang, Y., Mao, J., Huang, Z., Huang, C., Xu, W.: CNN-RNN: a unified framework for multi-label image classification. In: CVPR, pp. 2285–2294 (2016)
35. Wang, K., Yin, Q., Wang, W., Wu, S., Wang, L.: A comprehensive survey on cross-modal retrieval. arXiv 1607.06215 (2016)
36. Wei, Y., et al.: HCP: a flexible CNN framework for multi-label image classification. In: PAMI, pp. 1901–1907 (2016)
37. Xiao, C., Wang, C., Zhang, L., Zhang, L.: Sketch-based image retrieval via shape words. In: ACM ICMR, pp. 571–574 (2015)
38. Xie, J., Dai, G., Zhu, F., Fang, Y.: Learning barycentric representations of 3D shapes for sketch-based 3D shape retrieval. In: CVPR, pp. 3615–3623 (2017)
39. Xu, H., Wang, J., Hua, X.S., Li, S.: Interactive image search by 2D semantic map. In: ACM ICWWW, pp. 1321–1324 (2010)
40. Xu, K., et al.: Show, attend and tell: neural image caption generation with visual attention. In: ICML (2015)
41. Yang, H., Tianyi Zhou, J., Zhang, Y., Gao, B.B., Wu, J., Cai, J.: Exploit bounding box annotations for multi-label object recognition. In: CVPR, pp. 280–288 (2016)
42. You, Q., Jin, H., Wang, Z., Fang, C., Luo, J.: Image captioning with semantic attention. In: CVPR, pp. 4651–4659 (2016)
43. Yu, Q., Liu, F., Song, Y.Z., Xiang, T., Hospedales, T.M., Loy, C.C.: Sketch me that shoe. In: CVPR, pp. 799–807 (2016)
44. Zhu, F., Xie, J., Fang, Y.: Learning cross-domain neural networks for sketch-based 3D shape retrieval. In: AAAI, pp. 3683–3689 (2016)
45. Zhu, Y., Groth, O., Bernstein, M., Fei-Fei, L.: Visual7w: grounded question answering in images. In: CVPR, pp. 4995–5004 (2016)

Fast Light Field Disparity Estimation via a Parallel Filtered Cost Volume Approach

Adam Stacey[1](✉), Will Maddern[2], and Surya Singh[1]

[1] The University of Queensland, Brisbane, Australia
adam.stacey@uq.net.au, spns@uq.edu.au
[2] University of Oxford, Oxford, UK
wm@robots.ox.ac.uk

Abstract. The Guided Light Field Cost Volume (GLFCV) is a light field disparity estimation algorithm designed for (GPU) parallelization by refactoring the process, such that costly optimizations that combine and refine depth maps are simplified. The algorithm involves shearing the light field over a range of disparities and computing a cost volume for each sheared sub-aperture image. A guided filter is then run on the computed cost for each disparity. For the final disparity estimate, each pixel is assigned disparity associated with the lowest filtered cost. Execution time and accuracy were evaluated on Lytro Illum imagery and also on synthetic light fields from the HCI 4D light field benchmark. The approach presented executes in four seconds (on an NVIDIA Titan XP), with only 10% of pixels in the disparity estimate deviating from ground truth. This compares favourably to existing accurate approaches, whose execution time is in the order of minutes.

1 Introduction

Disparity estimation is, in part, what gives light fields or plenoptic images more generally, depth and dimensional significance. Compared to conventional imaging, light field sensors capture a richer and more general representation of a scene, thus affording a more accurate estimation of the environment and overcoming the fundamental depth flattening of traditional cameras. However, translating the extra data into usable information requires more computation, generating an interest in parallelized approaches.

Disparity estimation algorithms often focus on accuracy. However, approximate disparity estimation presents opportunities, especially in the robotics community where computational time and efficiency are paramount. While not mutually exclusive, there is a tradeoff between speed and accuracy, with each application requiring tuning to get the "best" performance for that application.

While disparity estimation for a light field can be treated as an extension to traditional stereo techniques, its unique four-dimensional data representation also allows for an approach tailored to it directly. One of the least computationally expensive methods is a technique by Dansereau and Bruton [3], where

© Springer Nature Switzerland AG 2019
C. V. Jawahar et al. (Eds.): ACCV 2018, LNCS 11362, pp. 256–268, 2019.
https://doi.org/10.1007/978-3-030-20890-5_17

depth information is estimated by applying 2D gradient operators to slices of the light field in s, x and t, y dimensions[1]. By calculating the orientation of the plane passing through each light field sample, the depth of the point is estimated. Slices of the light field in the s, x and t, y dimensions are Epipolar Plane Images (EPI) [21]. As well as the many other algorithms that make use of gradient information in the EPI [10,24,25], there are a host of algorithms that use traditional stereo matching between sets of subaperture images [7,20] or compute disparity from defocus cues by building a focal stack from a sheared light field [14,21,22]. Part of the development of Guided Light Field Cost Volume (GLFCV) draws on the more parallelizable aspects of these approaches and combines them into a final disparity estimate.

As with most image manipulation algorithms, there are many linearly independent calculations that lend themselves to parallelization (i.e., they are of an "embarrassingly parallel" class). However, many of the aforementioned algorithms rely on optimisation functions to either merge disparity estimates of two techniques or correct errors. These optimisation functions are a costly part of the algorithm and are not inherently parallelizable. Some CPU implementations of depth estimation, such as work by Jeon *et al.* [7] and Lowney *et al.* [16], make limited use of multiple CPU cores in parallel, but not in a data parallel manner applicable to GPU architectures. Algorithms developed in this way perform the same operation on different subsets of the same data synchronously across multiple cores. The core idea with approximate disparity estimation in GLFCV is to use the parallelizable guided filter [4], to combine disparity estimates and simplify this "expensive" optimization step. The guided filter is an edge preserving smoothing operator similar to a bilateral filter, but with the addition of using a guide image.

The key contribution of this work is in maintaining state of the art accuracy, while excluding any algorithmic steps that do not parallelize. This is done by incorporating the *Truncated Absolute Difference of Color and Gradient* (TAD C+G) and guided filtering intermediate results before combining for the final disparity map, where other techniques require regularisations. Throughout the algorithm, it has been structured for parallel data flow and it is easily tunable for either speed or accuracy. No training is required for the algorithm, which eliminates the reliance on training data and time, and allows it to be relatively camera-agnostic. These characteristics are what separates this work from implementing existing algorithms for GPU architecture.

It is noted that the regularization step of conventional approaches, such as OBER variants or SC_GC [18] or Tao *et al.* [21], involve a global minimization across all disparity indications, using a confidence metric or energy function to smooth the estimation. This hinders parallelization and would result in limited speed up on a GPU if implemented directly.

---

[1] Four dimensional light field data can be parameterised as $L(x, y, s, t)$ [9], which is a pair of planar coordinates where for every fixed pair of (s, t), varying the (x, y) coordinates gives a different pinhole view (or sub-aperture image) of the scene. This parameterisation is used throughout.

The method and dataflow for the GLFCV approach are described in Sect. 2. Its run-time efficiency and disparity estimates are compared with published state of the art routines in Sect. 3.

2   Algorithm Design

The goal of the algorithm is to be data parallel, so as to support GPU implementation. This involves avoiding complex optimisation functions to combine disparity estimates. Instead, a guided filter is used to progressively integrate estimates from cost volumes computed on 4D shears of the light field.

2.1   Cost Volume

Cost Volume is calculated between 4D shears of the light field over a range of disparity values. Computing these shears is akin to computing the focal stack. This is shown in Eqs. 1 and 2, where the image sheared by disparity d is $\overline{L}_d(x, y)$. For GLFCV, the shearing of sub-aperture views is done using bilinear interpolation, as per Tao $et\ al.$ [21].

$$L_d(x, y, s, t) \;=\; L(x + sd, y + td, s, t) \tag{1}$$

$$\overline{L}_d(x, y) \;=\; \frac{1}{N} \sum_s \sum_t L_d(x, y, s, t) \tag{2}$$

The TAD C+G cost volume metric [6] was chosen over defocus cues and traditional stereo correspondence, as it has been shown to be more accurate [19]. Equation 3 shows the stereo form of the TAD C+G cost volume, where $M(p, d)$ and $G(p, d)$ match pixel p at disparity d for intensity and gradient respectively, and β, τ_c and τ_g are tunable parameters. This equation was adapted for the 4D light field (Eq. 4), where L_{ref} is the central sub-aperture image. These equations are repeated for the R, G and B channels for use on a colour image.

$$
\begin{aligned}
M(p, d) &\;=\; |I_{left}(p) - I_{right}(p - d)| \\
G(p, d) &\;=\; |\nabla_x(I_{left}(p)) - \nabla_x(I_{right}(p - d))| \\
C(p, d) &\;=\; \beta \cdot min(\tau_c, M(p, d)) + \\
&\quad\; (1 - \beta) \cdot min(\tau_g, G(p, d))
\end{aligned}
\tag{3}
$$

$$
C_d = \frac{1}{N} \sum_s \sum_t \Big(\beta \cdot min\big(\tau_c, abs(L_d(x, y, s, t) - L_{ref})\big) \\
+ \; (1 - \beta) \cdot min\big(\tau_g, abs(\nabla L_d(x, y, s, t) - \nabla L_{ref})\big) \Big)
\tag{4}
$$

The gradient of L_{ref} can be precomputed as it remains constant for every alpha and value of s, t. The summation and normalisation over the sub-aperture images ((s, t) dimension) can be done over a smaller subset of (s, t) to trade accuracy for a faster execution time.

2.2   Filtering

The cost volume, as computed by Eq. 4, is inherently noisy. Thus some level of filtering helps; Jeon *et al.* [7] use a bilateral edge-preserving filter [12] on each cost slice to combat noise in the cost volume prior to their other refinement techniques. The guided filter, an edge-preserving filter by He *et al.* [4], has better performance around edges than the bilateral filter and is a non-approximate linear time algorithm. Zhang *et al.* [25] use it as an intermediate step in their spinning parallelogram operator method. They observe that, for their method, the guided filter alone is only sufficient for synthetic light fields without the aliasing and noise present in light fields from lenslet-based plenoptic cameras. Given that the guided filter is not sufficient when only used as a smoothing operator over a final disparity map, it is included in the algorithm to smooth each C_d, using the central sub-aperture image as the guide image. Because the guide image remains constant, the variances of each local patch in the guide image can be precomputed and used for each input image [4].

The final disparity estimate is calculated by an *argmin* of the cost volume over all alpha values in the disparity range. A final guided filter is then run over the disparity map for smoothing (see also an overview in Fig. 1 and description in Algorithm 1).

Algorithm 1. GLFCV disparity estimation

Input: LF: 2-D array of sub-aperture images
  $shifts$: Array of values over disparity range
Output: D: Disparity estimate

1 $L_{ref} = LF[\frac{S}{2}, \frac{T}{2}]$ // Central sub-aperture image
2 Compute ∇L_{ref}
3 Compute local patch variances within L_{ref}
4 **foreach** $d \in shifts$ **do**
5 $\quad$ $C_d \leftarrow 0$
6 $\quad$ **foreach** $(s, t) \in LF$ **do**
7 $\quad\quad$ Compute $L_d(x, y, s, t)$ (1)
8 $\quad\quad$ $C_d = C_d +$ TAD-C+G contribution (4)
9 $\quad$ **end**
$\quad$ // Divide by number of sub-aperture images
10 $\quad$ $C_d = \frac{C_d}{ST}$
11 $\quad$ GuidedFilter(C_d)
12 **end**
13 $D = \underset{d}{\mathrm{argmin}}(C_d)$
14 GuidedFilter(D)
15 **return** D

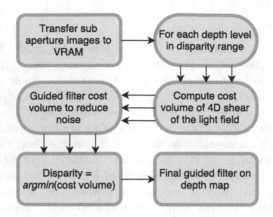

Fig. 1. GLFCV data flow: Multiple arrows between blocks indicate GPU parallelization.

2.3 Computational Complexity

The computational complexity of this algorithm is $\Theta(DNP)$, where D, N, P are defined as follows:

- D: depth resolution
- N: number of sub-aperture images in the light field
- P: number of pixels in each sub-aperture image

All setup and finalisation code (calculating alpha step sizes etc.) is constant time except for computing the gradient of the reference image, precomputing the variances for the guided filter, and performing the final guided filter, all three of which have $\Theta(P)$ complexity. Calculating the gradient of an image with the Sobel operator is convolutional, and therefore linear in the number of pixels. The guided filter is also linear in the number of pixels, regardless of window size [4].

For each of D alpha values, every sub-aperture image must be remapped (for the shearing), and have gradient and contribution to cost volume computed. Each of these three operations are $\Theta(P)$. Still for each alpha value, the guided filter must be applied to cost volume and the *argmin* calculated. Therefore, for each alpha value, $\Theta(NP)$ operations must be completed.

As lenslets are round, the number of sub-aperture images is usually a square number, which may be thought of as a quadratic in u or v sub-aperture dimensions. A trade-off can be made by using a lower depth resolution, computing cost from fewer sub-aperture views, downsampling each sub-aperture image, or a combination of all three.

3   Evaluation

The parallel data flow design of GLFCV provides the user a mechanism to trade-off accuracy and speed by adjusting the number of sub-aperture views and the resolution of light field to use. For the purposes of this evaluation, a halfway balancing point has been used that demonstrates that the method is equally fast and accurate without emphasizing a particular design constraint. It is also the case that different algorithms have a limit to their accuracy, even given infinite computation time, upper-bounded by the quality (resolution and the number of sub-aperture images) of the original light field. For example, GLFCV run on a single channel (grayscale) version of the light field images resulted in the algorithm running three times as fast, but with approximately double the average error. It is worth noting that the relationship with accuracy is different depending on which dimension the input is reduced in.

3.1 GPU Implementation

Using a combination of custom CUDA [15] kernels and OpenCV [2] CUDA APIs, average compute utilization on an NVIDIA Titan XP was 76% and custom kernels achieved 92%. Improvements can be made by further combining kernels or rearranging block/thread allocations so as to allow concurrent execution of multiple kernels, such as computing cost volume between two pairs simultaneously.

3.2 Execution Time

Depth map generation times for different light fields with three different classes of computer are shown in Table 1. Because the CUDA kernels themselves are different sizes for different light fields, there is some non-linearity in runtime comparison. This because the resource requirements that result in some dimensions of light field fitting perfectly on specific hardware, but light fields that are marginally bigger or smaller do not fit as well and result in lower GPU utilization. It is expected that implementing improvements, as suggested in Subsect. 3.1, would smooth this non-linearity. Grayscale calculations always execute approximately three times faster, as the algorithm processes the color channels individually.

Performance gains of GLFCV with respect to other algorithms is shown in Table 1. The HCI 4D light field benchmark [5] also provides timing comparisons, but does not take into account the hardware the submitted times were run on. Table 1 provides a baseline against algorithms that are also on the benchmark and confirms that GLFCV execution time is approximately proportional to the advertised FLOPS of the GPU hardware. This shows that GPU utilization does not fluctuate hugely for different hardware.

3.3 Accuracy

The HCI 4D light field benchmark [5] uses a dataset of synthetic light fields rendered from Blender [1] with ground truth disparity maps. Ground truth disparity is released for all but the four test scenes. An algorithm can only be evaluated against the ground truth of the test scenes by submitting disparity maps and runtimes to the authors of the benchmark. The GLFCV algorithm has been submitted to the benchmark and results published online[2].

Table 1. Runtime comparisons and scaling: Times are in seconds. The N/A indicates the code would not compile or run on that system. Profiling indicated that for GPUs with less than 4GB VRAM, the compute utilization was hindered by a memory bottleneck, but not enough to significantly deviate from scaling with advertised GFLOPS. There is also a memory bandwidth bottleneck in transferring the light field to the GPU, which could be mitigated by staggered transfers.

Computer	Light Field Dimension and Algorithm (time in seconds)					
	$7 \times 7 \times 328 \times 328 \times 3$		$7 \times 7 \times 311 \times 362 \times 3$		$14 \times 14 \times 376 \times 541 \times 3$	
	Hae Gon Jeon [7]	GLFCV	Tao and Hadap [21]	GLFCV	Lowney et al. [16]	GLFCV
Laptop i7-4850GQ — GT750M (VRAM: 2GB, GFLOPS: 743)	N/A	14.6	79.1	15.4	524.1	82.3
Desktop i7-6700K — GTX980Ti (VRAM: 6GB, GFLOPS: 6054)	236.9	2.1	N/A	2.7	374.4	10.4
Workstation Xeon E5-1650 v4 — TitanX (Pascal) (VRAM: 12 GB, GFLOPS: 10974)	223.6	1.9	N/A	1.9	462.4	7.2

Synthetic Light Fields. Figure 2 shows the accuracy performance of the algorithm against ground truth for a variety of scenes. Nearly all of the error is concentrated on edges because, although the guided filter is an edge-preserving filter, it also performs a smoothing operation and thickens edges in the disparity map. A weakness of the algorithm is apparent in the third light field (boxes) of Fig. 2 in the fine occlusions presented by the lattice side on the box. One of the characteristics of the algorithm is to fatten all depth regions slightly. As a result, regions such as the side of the box are prone to large errors in the calculated disparity map.

Speed and accuracy comparisons can be drawn from the scatter plot in Fig. 3. It shows that (at the time of writing) there are no algorithms that are both faster and more accurate than the one presented. By making tradeoffs between speed and accuracy, it is easy to move parallel to the lines in the figure. From this, there is also no clear best method, as most related techniques have results scattered throughout the region. The only methods that outperform our approach in terms of runtime while approaching our accuracy are the very recent CNN (Convolutional Neural Network) based approaches [17] (published at the time of ACCV submission). However, these require training on large-scale augmented datasets for extended periods of time: Shin *et al.* [17] reports training times of 5 to 6 days on a GTX 1080Ti. In addition, their CNN training is performed on only synthetic data since ground truth is not available for real-world light field images. Our method does not require any training and only a few parameters are required to generalize to different input datasets or cameras.

---

[2] Available at: http://hci-lightfield.iwr.uni-heidelberg.de.

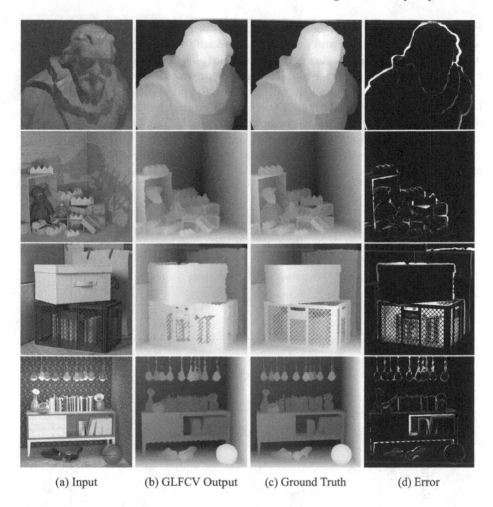

(a) Input   (b) GLFCV Output   (c) Ground Truth   (d) Error

Fig. 2. Disparity estimates on images in the training set of the HCI benchmark

Included in the HCI benchmark [5], are complex and contrived scenes. In the above analysis these scenes are combined with results from other scenes. Approaches that perform best on complex scenes in the HCI benchmark are CNNs or involve regularisations that do not lend themselves to parallel computing architectures such as OBER-cross+ANP. A comparison between OBER-cross+ANP and GLFCV is shown in Fig. 4. This scene draws attention to one of the main limitations of GLFCV, in that by employing a series of filters, some high frequency (sharp edge) information can be lost. This particular region is highlighted in Fig. 5. Another important property of GLFCV is that computation time is completely independent of the scene content and source of the light field as it does not require any training.

Physical Scenes. Although the synthetic benchmark scenes assess many aspects of the algorithm, and provide comparison to other available algorithms, it is important to assess the performance on physical light fields. Such non-ideal light fields contain noise and aliasing not present in the benchmark scenes. Figure 6 shows the computed depth maps for five light fields captured with a Lytro plenoptic camera. Although there is no ground truth available for these scenes, it provides a qualitative comparison against Tao *et al.* [21] and other state of the art methods which use this dataset. The extra noise, compared to synthetic scenes, is evident in the results, but does not break the algorithm in any significant way.

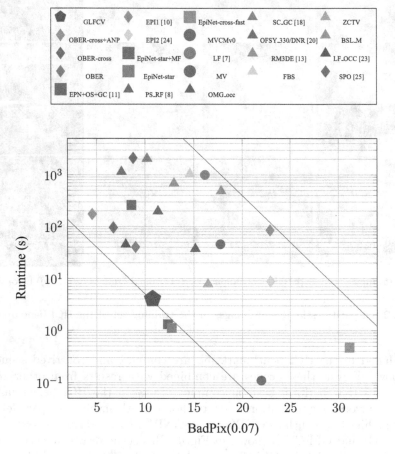

Fig. 3. Algorithm accuracy against runtime using the bad pixel metric from the HCI benchmark: Diamond indicates use of EPI (Epipolar Plane Images), square indicates CNN, circle indicates stereo matching, triangle indicates other methods. The parallel lines are a guide to indicate the region in which most current algorithms can move within by making various trade offs. The exact curve for trading speed and accuracy is different for each approach.

Figure 7 shows depth maps computed on light fields from the Lytro Illum plenoptic camera and a comparison to the depth map computed by the Lytro software. Runtime of the depth calculation in the Lytro software is hard to gauge, as a large portion of the computation is done when importing from a camera; a process which takes approximately 25 s (on the workstation class hardware in Table 1). Further, it might be expected that the Lytro software would perform well on images from Lytro's own hardware. Results generated by the algorithm have approximation (and thus may be said to contain some errors), but are bounded representations of the depth in the scene.

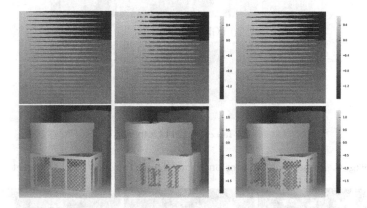

Fig. 4. Comparison with best performing algorithm on a complex scene. The most accurate algorithm for complex scenes on HCI (OBER-cross+ANP) is on the right, GLFCV is in the middle and ground truth on the left.

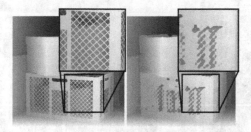

Fig. 5. The worst performing type of region for GLFCV. Ground truth (left) and GLFCV output (right) on a scene with a region of fine occlusions.

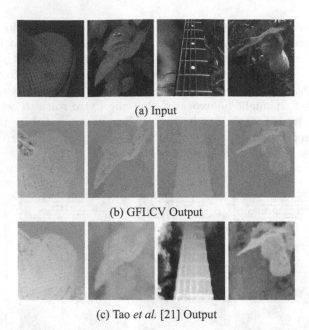

(a) Input

(b) GFLCV Output

(c) Tao *et al.* [21] Output

Fig. 6. Disparity estimates on scenes from Tao *et al.* [21] Dataset

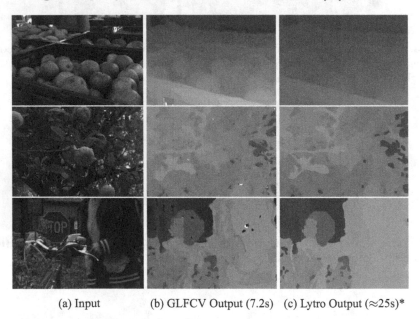

(a) Input   (b) GLFCV Output (7.2s)   (c) Lytro Output (≈25s)*

Fig. 7. Results on scenes from the Stanford Lytro Light Field Archive [16]
Note: Runtime of the depth calculation in the Lytro software is hard to estimate, as
a portion of the computation is done when importing from a camera; a process which
takes approximately 25 s (lower bound) on the same hardware as our method.

4   Conclusion

The light field disparity estimation algorithm presented in this paper was designed primarily for parallel data flow, allowing for efficient implementations on parallel computing architectures. This was done by replacing regularisations and other linearly dependent techniques with cost volume and filtering. By taking this approach as opposed to a CNN based approach, there is no reliance on training data or training time and the algorithm can perform well on light fields from different sources. A consequence of the techniques chosen to avoid regularisation is poor accuracy in regions with fine occlusions.

GLFCV adapts the TAD C+G cost volume metric for use with sheared 4D light fields to produce state of the art disparity maps. Cost contributions are refined with a guided filter at each iteration of the algorithm. The algorithm was designed for parallelization and a CUDA based implementation has shown it to be one of the fastest algorithms with similar accuracy, providing a $5-100+$ times speed-up over reference methods (e.g., 2 s compared to 224 s [as shown in Table 1]). This approach was evaluated on reference datasets, Lytro Illum imagery, and also on synthetic light fields from the HCI 4D light field benchmark. It is also amenable to other plenoptic sensors.

References

1. Blender Online Community: Blender - a 3D modelling and rendering package. Blender Foundation, Blender Institute, Amsterdam (2017). http://www.blender.org
2. Bradski, G.: The OpenCV library. Dr. Dobb's Journal of Software Tools (2000)
3. Dansereau, D., Bruton, L.: Gradient-based depth estimation from 4D light fields. In: Proceedings of the 2004 International Symposium on Circuits and Systems, ISCAS 2004, vol. 3, pp. III-549. IEEE (2004)
4. He, K., Sun, J.: Fast guided filter. CoRR abs/1505.00996 (2015). http://arxiv.org/abs/1505.00996
5. Honauer, K., Johannsen, O., Kondermann, D., Goldluecke, B.: A dataset and evaluation methodology for depth estimation on 4D light fields. In: Lai, S.-H., Lepetit, V., Nishino, K., Sato, Y. (eds.) ACCV 2016. LNCS, vol. 10113, pp. 19–34. Springer, Cham (2017). https://doi.org/10.1007/978-3-319-54187-7_2
6. Hosni, A., Bleyer, M., Gelautz, M.: Secrets of adaptive support weight techniques for local stereo matching. Comput. Vis. Image Underst. **117**(6), 620–632 (2013). https://doi.org/10.1016/j.cviu.2013.01.007
7. Jeon, H.G., et al.: Accurate depth map estimation from a lenslet light field camera. In: 2015 IEEE Conference on Computer Vision and Pattern Recognition (CVPR), pp. 1547–1555. IEEE (2015)
8. Jeon, H.G., et al.: Depth from a light field image with learning-based matching costs. IEEE Trans. Pattern Anal. Mach. Intell. **PP**(99), 1–14 (2017)
9. Johannsen, O., et al.: A taxonomy and evaluation of dense light field depth estimation algorithms. In: 2nd Workshop on Light Fields for Computer Vision at CVPR (2017)
10. Johannsen, O., Sulc, A., Goldluecke, B.: What sparse light field coding reveals about scene structure. In: Proceedings of the IEEE Conference on Computer Vision and Pattern Recognition, pp. 3262–3270 (2016)

11. Luo, Y., Zhou, W., Fang, J., Liang, L., Zhang, H., Dai, G.: EPI-patch based convolutional neural network for depth estimation on 4D light field. In: Liu, D., Xie, S., Li, Y., Zhao, D., El-Alfy, E.S. (eds.) ICONIP 2017. LNCS, vol. 10636, pp. 642–652. Springer, Cham (2017). https://doi.org/10.1007/978-3-319-70090-8_65

12. Ma, Z., He, K., Wei, Y., Sun, J., Wu, E.: Constant time weighted median filtering for stereo matching and beyond. In: Proceedings of the IEEE International Conference on Computer Vision, pp. 49–56 (2013)

13. Neri, A., Carli, M., Battisti, F.: A multi-resolution approach to depth field estimation in dense image arrays. In: 2015 IEEE International Conference on Image Processing (ICIP), pp. 3358–3362, September 2015. https://doi.org/10.1109/ICIP.2015.7351426

14. Ng, R., Levoy, M., Brédif, M., Duval, G., Horowitz, M., Hanrahan, P.: Light field photography with a hand-held plenoptic camera. Comput. Sci. Techn. Rep. CSTR **2**(11), 1–11 (2005)

15. NVIDIA Corporation: CUDA parallel computing platform (2016). http://www.nvidia.com/object/cuda_home_new.html

16. Raj, A.S., Lowney, M., Shah, R.: Light-field database creation and depth estimation (2016). https://stanford.edu/class/ee367/Winter2016/Lowney_Shah_Sunder_Raj_Report.pdf, computational Imaging and Display Report (Winter 2016)

17. Shin, C., Jeon, H.G., Yoon, Y., Kweon, I.S., Kim, S.J.: Epinet: a fully-convolutional neural network using epipolar geometry for depth from light field images. CoRR abs/1804.02379 (2018)

18. Si, L., Wang, Q.: Dense depth-map estimation and geometry inference from light fields via global optimization. In: Lai, S.-H., Lepetit, V., Nishino, K., Sato, Y. (eds.) ACCV 2016. LNCS, vol. 10113, pp. 83–98. Springer, Cham (2017). https://doi.org/10.1007/978-3-319-54187-7_6

19. Stacey, A.: GPU Acceleration of Light Field Depth Estimation. Bachelor thesis, The University of Queensland, June 2017

20. Strecke, M., Alperovich, A., Goldluecke, B.: Accurate depth and normal maps from occlusion-aware focal stack symmetry. In: IEEE Conference on Computer Vision and Pattern Recognition (CVPR) (2017)

21. Tao, M.W., Hadap, S., Malik, J., Ramamoorthi, R.: Depth from combining defocus and correspondence using light-field cameras. In: The IEEE International Conference on Computer Vision (ICCV), October 2013

22. Tao, M.W., Srinivasan, P.P., Malik, J., Rusinkiewicz, S., Ramamoorthi, R.: Depth from shading, defocus, and correspondence using light-field angular coherence. In: Proceedings of the IEEE Conference on Computer Vision and Pattern Recognition, pp. 1940–1948 (2015)

23. Wang, T.C., Efros, A.A., Ramamoorthi, R.: Occlusion-aware depth estimation using light-field cameras. In: Proceedings of the IEEE International Conference on Computer Vision, pp. 3487–3495 (2015)

24. Wanner, S., Goldluecke, B.: Globally consistent depth labeling of 4D light fields. In: 2012 IEEE Conference on Computer Vision and Pattern Recognition (CVPR), pp. 41–48. IEEE (2012)

25. Zhang, S., Sheng, H., Li, C., Zhang, J., Xiong, Z.: Robust depth estimation for light field via spinning parallelogram operator. Comput. Vis. Image Underst. **145**, 148–159 (2016)

Perceptual Conditional Generative Adversarial Networks for End-to-End Image Colourization

Shirsendu Sukanta Halder, Kanjar De$^{(\boxtimes)}$, and Partha Pratim Roy

Indian Institute of Technology Roorkee, Roorkee 247667, India
shalder@cs.iitr.ac.in,{kanjar.cspdf2017,proy.fcs}@iitr.ac.in

Abstract. Colours are everywhere. They embody a significant part of human visual perception. In this paper, we explore the paradigm of hallucinating colours from a given gray-scale image. The problem of colourization has been dealt in previous literature but mostly in a supervised manner involving user-interference. With the emergence of Deep Learning methods numerous tasks related to computer vision and pattern recognition have been automatized and carried in an end-to-end fashion due to the availability of large data-sets and high-power computing systems. We investigate and build upon the recent success of Conditional Generative Adversarial Networks (cGANs) for Image-to-Image translations. In addition to using the training scheme in the basic cGAN, we propose an encoder-decoder generator network which utilizes the class-specific cross-entropy loss as well as the perceptual loss in addition to the original objective function of cGAN. We train our model on a large-scale dataset and present illustrative qualitative and quantitative analysis of our results. Our results vividly display the versatility and the proficiency of our methods through life-like colourization outcomes.

Keywords: Colourization · Generative Adversarial Networks · Image Reconstruction

1 Introduction

Colours enhance the information as well as the expressiveness of an image. Colour images contain more visual information than a gray-scale image and is useful for extracting information for high-level tasks. Humans have the ability to manually fill gray-scale images with colours taking into consideration the contextual cues. This clearly indicates that black-and-white images contain some latent information sufficient for the task of colourization. The modelling of this latent information to generate chrominance values of pixels of a target gray-scale image is called colourization. Image colourization is a daunting problem because a colour image consists of multi-dimensional data according to defined colour-spaces whereas a gray-scale image is just single-dimensional. The main obstacle is that different colour compositions can lead to a single gray level but the reverse is not true.

© Springer Nature Switzerland AG 2019
C. V. Jawahar et al. (Eds.): ACCV 2018, LNCS 11362, pp. 269–283, 2019.
https://doi.org/10.1007/978-3-030-20890-5_18

For example, multiple shades of blue are possible for the sky, leaves of trees attain colours according to seasons, different colours of a pocket billiards (pool) ball. The aim of the colourization process is not to hallucinate the exact colour of an object (See Fig. 1), but to transfer colours plausible enough to fool the human mind. Image colourization is a widely used technique in commercial applications and a hot researched topic in the academia world due to its application in heritage preservation, image stylization and image processing.

In the last few years, Convolutional Neural Networks (CNNs) have emerged as compelling new state-of-the-art learning frameworks for Computer Vision and Pattern Recognition [1,6] applications. With the recent advent of Generative Adversarial Networks (GANs) [4], the problem of transferring colours have also been explored in the context of GANs using Deep Convolutional Neural Networks [8,13]. The proposed method involves utilizing conditional Generative Adversarial Networks (cGANs) modelled as an image-to-image translation framework.

The main contribution of this paper is proposing a variant of Conditional-GANs which tries to learn a functional mapping from input grayscale image to output colourized image by minimizing the adversarial loss, per pixel loss, classification loss and the high-level perceptual loss. The proposed model is validated using an elaborate qualitative and quantitative comparison with existing methods. A detailed ablation study which demonstrates the efficiency and potential of our model over baselines is also presented.

The rest of this paper is arranged as Sect. 2 describes previous works described in literature. Section 3 describes our proposed Perceptual-cGAN. Section 4 demonstrates a detailed qualitative and quantitative analysis of images colourized by our proposed system along with ablation studies of different objective functions. The final Sect. 5 consists of concluding remarks.

Fig. 1. The process of image colourization focuses on hallucinating realistic colours.

2 Related Work

The problem of colourization has been studied extensively by numerous researchers due to its importance in real-world applications. Methods involving user-assisted scribble inputs were the primary methods explored for the daunting problem of assigning colours to a one-dimensional gray-scale image. Levin et al. [10] used user-based scribble annotations for video-colourization which propagated colours in the spatial and temporal dimensions ensuring consistency to produce colourized films. This method relied on neighbouring smoothness by optimization through a quadratic cost function. Shapiro [17] proposed a framework where the geometry and the structure of the luminance input was considered on top of user-assisted information for colourization by solving a partial differential equation. Noda et al. [14] formulates the colourization problem into a maximum a posteriori (MAP) framework using Markov Random Field (MRF) as a prior.

User-involved methods achieve satisfying results but they are severely time-consuming, needs manual labour and the efficacy is dependent on the accuracy of the user interaction. In order to alleviate these problems, researchers resorted to example-based or reference-based image colourization. Example-based methods require a reference image from the user for the transfer of colours from a source image to a target gray-scale image. Reinhard et al. [15] used simple statistical analysis to establish mapping functions that impose a source image's colour characteristics onto a target image. Welsh et al. [23] proposed to transfer only chrominance values to a target image from a source by matching the luminance and textural information. The luminance values of the target image are kept intact. The success of example-based methods rely heavily on the selection of an appropriate user-determined reference image. Hence it faces a limitation as there is no standard criterion for choosing an example image and hence depends on the user skill. Also the reference image may have different illumination conditions resulting in anomalous colour transfer.

In recent years, the use of Deep Learning methods have emerged as prominent methods for the task of Pattern Recognition, even outperforming human ability [5]. They have shown promising results in colourization by directly mapping gray-scale target images to output colors by learning to combine low level features and high-level cues. Cheng et al. [2] proposed the first deep learning framework using low-level features from patch, intermediate DAISY features [20] and a high-level semantic features as output to a neural network ensemble. Zhang et al. [25] proposed an automatic colourization process by posing it as a multinomial classification task for ab values. They observed that in natural images the distribution of ab values were desaturated and used class re-balancing for obtaining accurate chromatic components. A joint end-to-end method using two parallel CNNs and incorporation of local and global priors was proposed by Iizuka [7]. The potential of GANs in learning expressive features trained under an unsupervised scheme propelled researchers to use GANs for the task of colourization. Isola et al. [8] explored the idea of Conditional-GANs in an image-to-image framework by learning a loss function for mapping input to output images.

3   Proposed Method

In this section, we describe our proposed algorithm along with the architecture of the Convolutional Neural Networks employed for our method. We explore the situation of GANs in a conditional setting [8,13] where the objective function of the generator is constrained on the conditional information and consequentially generates the output. The addition of this conditional variables enhanced the stability of the original GAN frame-work proposed by Goodfellow *et al.* [4]. Our proposed method builds upon the cGAN by incorporating adjunct losses. In addition to the adversarial loss and the per-pixel constraint, we add the perceptual loss and the classification loss in our objective function. We explain in detail about the loss functions and the networks used.

3.1 Loss Function

Conditional-GANs [8] try to learn a mapping from the input image I to output J. In this case, the generator not only aspires to win the mini-max game by fooling the discriminator but also has to be as close as possible with the ground truth. The per-pixel loss is utilized for this constraint. While the discriminator network of the cGAN remains the same when compared to the original GAN, the objective function of the Generator networks are different. The objective function of cGAN [8] is

$$\mathcal{L}_{cGAN} = min_G max_D \, \mathbb{E}_{\mathbb{I}}[\log(1 - D(G(I)))] + \mathbb{E}_{\mathbb{I},\mathbb{J}}[\log D(J)] \qquad (1)$$

Here I represents the input image, J represents the coloured image, G represents the Generator and D represents the Discriminator. Isola *et al.* [8] established through their work that $\mathcal{L}_1$ is better due to their less blurring effect and also helps in reducing artifacts that are introduced by using only cGAN. Our proposed model Colourization using Perceptual Generator Adversarial Network (CuPGAN), builds up on this cGAN with incorporated additive perceptual loss and classification loss. Traditional loss functions that operate at per-pixel level are found to be limited in their attempt to capture the contextual and the perceptual features. Recent researches have demonstrated the competence of loss functions based on the difference of high-level feature in generating compelling visual performance [9]. However, in many cases they fail to preserve the low-level colour and texture information [24]. Therefore, we incorporate both the perceptual loss and the per-pixel loss for preservation of both the high-level and the low-level features. The high-level features are extracted from VGGNet model [19] trained on the ImageNet dataset [3]. Like [7], we add an additional classification loss that helps our model to guide the training of the high-level features.

For input gray-scale image I and colourized image J, the perceptual loss between I and J in this case is defined as:

$$\mathcal{L}_{per} = \frac{1}{C, H, W} \sum_{c=1}^{C} \sum_{w=1}^{W} \sum_{h=1}^{H} \|V_i(G(I^{c,w,h})) - V_i(J^{c,w,h})\|_2 \qquad (2)$$

where V_i represents a non-linear transformation by the ith layer of the VGGNet, G represents the transformation function of the generator and (C, W, H) are the channels, width and height respectively. The $\mathcal{L}_{L1}$ loss between I and J is defined as:

$$\mathcal{L}_{L1} = \sum_{c=1}^{C} \sum_{w=1}^{W} \sum_{h=1}^{H} \|G(I) - \tilde{J}\| \tag{3}$$

Here, $\tilde{J}$ represents J in CIELAB color space. The difference between $G(I)$ and J is fundamentally the difference of their ab values.

The final objective function of the proposed generator network is

$$\mathcal{L}_{CuPGAN} = \mathcal{L}_{adv} + \lambda_1 \mathcal{L}_{L1} + \lambda_2 \mathcal{L}_{class} + \lambda_3 \mathcal{L}_{per} \tag{4}$$

Here $\mathcal{L}_{adv}$ is the adversarial loss, $\mathcal{L}_{L1}$ is the content-based per-pixel loss, $\mathcal{L}_{class}$ is the classification loss and $\mathcal{L}_{per}$ is the perceptual loss and $\lambda_1, \lambda_2, \lambda_3$ are positive constants.

3.2 Generator Network

The generator network in the proposed architecture follows a similar architecture like U-Net [16]. The U-Net was originally proposed for bio-medical image segmentation. The architecture of U-Net consists of a contracting path which acts as an encoder and expanding path which acts as a decoder. The skip connections are present to avoid any information and content loss due to convolutions. The success of U-Net propelled the utilization of U-Net architecture in many works [8]. The elaborate generator network along with the feature map dimensions and the convolutional kernel sizes is shown in Fig. 2. In the encoding process, the input feature map is reduced in height and width by a factor of 2 at every level. In the decoding process, the feature maps are enlarged in height and width by a factor of 2. At every decoding level, there is a step of feature-fusion from the opposite contracting path. The final transposed convolutional layer obtained are the ab values which when concatenated with the L (luminance) channel, gives us a colourized version of the input gray-scale image. The feature vector at the point of deflection of the encoding and the decoding path is processed through two fully-connected layers to obtain the vector for the classification loss. All the layers use the ReLU activation function except for the last transpose convolutional layer which uses the hyperbolic tangent (tanh) function.

3.3 Discriminator Network

The discriminator network used for the proposed method consists of four convolutional layers with kernel size 5×5 and stride length 2×2 followed by 2 fully-connected (FC) layers. The final FC-layer uses a Sigmoid activation to classify the image as real or fake. Figure 3 shows the architecture of the discriminator network used for the proposed CuPGAN.

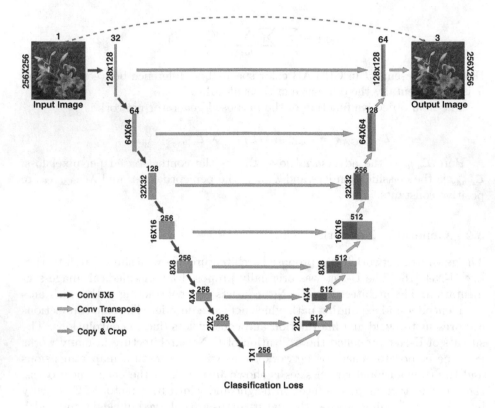

Fig. 2. Network architecture of the proposed Generator network.

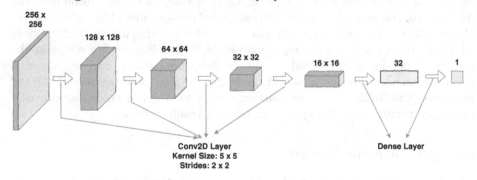

Fig. 3. Network architecture of our Discriminator Network

4 Experimental Results

4.1 Experimental Settings

All the training images are converted from RGB into the CIELAB colour space. Only the L channel of images are fed into the network and the network tries to estimate the chromatic components ab. The values of the luminance and the chrominance components are normalized between $[-1,1]$. The training images are re-sized to 256×256 in all cases. Every convolutional transpose layer in the decoder part of the generator network has a dropout with probability 0.5. Each layer in both the discriminator and the generator is followed by a batch-normalization layer. We use the Places365-Standard dataset [26] which contains about 1.8 million images. We filter the images that are grayscale and also those that have negligible colour variations which reduces our training dataset to 1.6 million images. For our experiments, we empirically set $\lambda_1 = 100$, $\lambda_2 = 10$ and $\lambda_3 = 1$ as the weights of the per-pixel, classification and perceptual loss respectively. We use the *relu1_2* layer of the VGGNet for computing the perceptual loss. The proposed system is implemented in Tensorflow. We train our network using the Adagrad optimizer with a learning rate of 10^{-4} and a batch-size of 16. Under these settings, the model is trained for 20 epochs on a system with NVIDIA TitanX Graphics Processing unit (GPU).

4.2   Quantitative Evaluations

We evaluate our proposed algorithm on different metrics and compare it with the existing state-of-the art colourization methods [7,25]. The metrics used for comparison are Peak Signal to Noise Ratio (PSNR) [12], Structural Similarity Index Measure (SSIM) [21], Mean Squared Error (MSE), Universal Quality Index (UQI) [22] and Visual Information Fidelity (VIF) [18]. We carry out our quantitative comparison on the test dataset of Places365. It contains multiple images of the 365 different classes used in the training dataset. The quantitative evaluations are shown in Table 1. The proposed method CuPGAN performs better in all metrics except for the VIF and UQI where it shows competitive performance on the Places365 test dataset [26].

Table 1. Comparative evaluation of PSNR, SSIM, MSE, UQI and VIF on Places365 dataset [26]

Method	Zhang [25]	Iizuka [7]	CuPGAN
PSNR	25.44	27.14	*28.41*
SSIM	0.95	0.95	*0.96*
MSE	262.08	135.89	*107.93*
UQI	0.56	*0.60*	0.58
VIF	0.886	*0.905*	0.896

4.3   Qualitative Evaluations

We demonstrate and compare our results in a qualitative manner against the existing methods [7,25]. Figure 4 displays the comparative qualitative results. We observe that in the first image Zhang *et al.* [25] hallucinates bluish colour for the grass while Iizuka *et al.* [7] produces a less saturated image compared

Grayscale   Zhang [25]   Iizuka [7]   CuPGAN   Ground Truth

Fig. 4. Qualitative comparison on the test partition of Places365 dataset [26]. The results display the robustness and versatility of our proposed method for colourizing both indoor and outdoor images (Color figure online)

to ours and the ground-truth. In the second image, both methods [7,25] tend to over-saturate the colour of the structure while our result is closest to the ground-truth. In the third image of the indoor scene, Zhang *et al.* [25] tends to impart yellowish colour to the indoors contrasting our and Iizuka's [25] result and also the ground-truth. In the fourth and the last image, both methods [7,25] tend to distort colours in the grass and the road respectively. Our method does not demonstrate any such colour distortions. In the fifth image, our method tends to over-estimate the grass regions near the foothills of the mountain but displays more vibrancy as compared to [7,25]. The results of the sixth and the seventh images are satisfactory for all methods. From what we observed, Zhang *et al.* tends to over-saturate the colours of the image. The qualitative comparison ensures that not only does our method produce images of crisp quality and of adequate saturation, but it also tends to produce less colour distortions and colour anomalies.

4.4   Real World Images

In order to establish the efficiency of our model we collect some images from the internet randomly and colourize these images using all the competing methods used in the quantitative evaluations as discussed in Sect. 4.2. Figure 5 shows the colourization on real world images. We can observe that Zhang *et al.* [25] tends to over-saturate the colour components as visible from the first and the third image. Also, [25] produces some colour anomalies visible from the zebras (fourth image) and the road (fifth image). Iizuka *et al.* [7] tends to under-saturate the images as visible from the third and fourth image. The colourization from our proposed method produces more visually-appealing and sharp results comparatively.

4.5   Ablation Studies

For demonstrating the effectiveness of our loss function, we train our model using a subset of the Places365 data-set [26]. We created the subset by randomly selecting 30 different classes from the complete data-set. We train our proposed model using three different component loss functions: (1) using only $\mathcal{L}_{L1}$ loss, (2) using only $\mathcal{L}_{per}$ and (3) using both $\mathcal{L}_{L1}$ and $\mathcal{L}_{per}$ (*ours*). The use of the first loss function corresponds directly to the objective function used in the *cGAN* model proposed by Isola *et al.* [8]. We provide both qualitative and quantitative comparisons for validating our point. The qualitative results are displayed in Fig. 6. The results display the effectiveness of using both $\mathcal{L}_{L1}$ and $\mathcal{L}_{per}$ loss together over using them discretely. Table 2 displays the quantitative comparison of using the mentioned loss functions. We can infer both qualitatively and quantitatively that our objective function performs better than using only $\mathcal{L}_{L1}$ or only only $\mathcal{L}_{per}$.

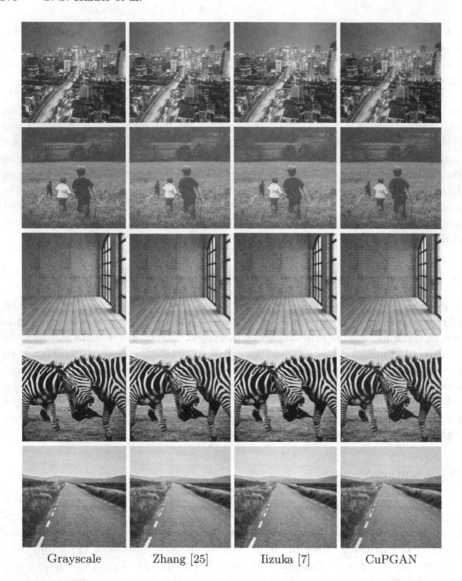

Grayscale   Zhang [25]   Iizuka [7]   CuPGAN

Fig. 5. Qualitative comparison on the random images from the internet

Table 2. Evaluation of PSNR, SSIM, MSE, UQI and VIF on subset test data-set from Places365 [26]

Method	$\mathcal{L}_{L1}$	$\mathcal{L}_{per}$	Ours
PSNR	22.00	17.40	*23.19*
SSIM	0.88	0.63	*0.91*
MSE	552.42	1341.66	*529.53*
UQI	*0.50*	0.20	0.49
VIF	0.85	0.53	*0.86*

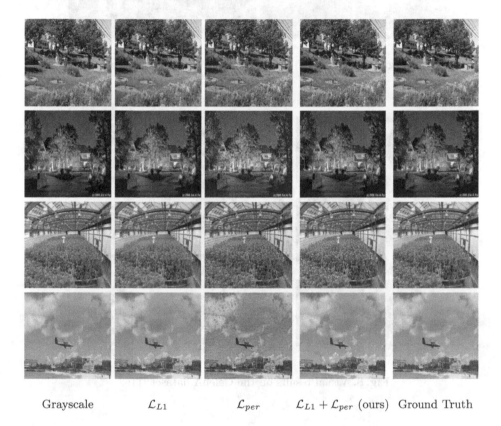

| Grayscale | $\mathcal{L}_{L1}$ | $\mathcal{L}_{per}$ | $\mathcal{L}_{L1} + \mathcal{L}_{per}$ (ours) | Ground Truth |

Fig. 6. Ablation: Qualitative comparison on the subset-test partition of Places365 dataset [26]

4.6   Historic Black and White Images

We also test our model on 20th century black and white images. Due to the type of films and cameras used in the past, we can never be perfectly sure about the type of colours and shades that was originally there. The images used have significant artifacts and have irregular borders which makes it an ill-posed task to reckon colours. In spite of all these issues, our model is able to colourize these images producing satisfactory results. In Fig. 7 we show some examples of colourization of these historic images and we observe visually pleasing results.

Fig. 7. Colourization of historic black and white images

Fig. 8. Visual results on the CelebA dataset [11]

4.7   Adaptability

In order to establish the adaptability of our proposed method, we train our model on a very different dataset than the Places365 dataset [26]. We use the large-scale CelebFaces Attributes or the CelebA dataset [11] for training. CelebA is a large-scale dataset which contains more than 200K images with 40 attributes. The classification loss of the generator objective is calculated using the cross-entropy loss of the attributes. We provide a visual analysis and quantitative evaluation of our method on this dataset as well. We use the metrics described in Sect. 4.2. Table 3 shows the evaluation of our model on the CelebA dataset. The

Table 3. Quantitative evaluations on the CelebA dataset [11]

Metrics	CuPGAN
PSNR	**25.9**
SSIM	**0.89**
UQI	**0.70**
VQI	**0.78**

quantitative evaluations assure that our model can be employed easily to another dataset for the process of colourization. Figure 8 demonstrates the visual results on the CelebA dataset [11] supplements our claim of adaptability to versatile datasets.

5 Conclusion

In this paper, we develop on the Conditional Generative Adversarial Networks (cGANs) framework to deal with the task of image colourization by incorporating the recently flourished perceptual loss and cross-entropy classification loss. We train our proposed model CuPGAN in an end-to-end fashion. Quantitative and qualitative evaluations establish the significant enhancing effects of adding the perceptual and classification loss as compared to the vanilla Conditional-GANs. Also, experiments conducted on standard data-sets show promising results when compared to the standard exclusive state-of-the art image colourization methods evaluated using five standard image quality measures like PSNR, SSIM, MSE, UIQ and VIF. Our proposed method performs appreciably well producing clear and crisp quality colourized pictures even in cases of images picked from the internet and historic black and white images.

Acknowledgements. We would like to thank Mr. Ayan Kumar Bhunia for his guidance and help regarding implementation and development of the model. We would also like to thank Mr. Ayush Daruka and Mr. Prashant Kumar for their valuable discussions.

References

1. Bengio, Y.: Learning deep architectures for AI. Found. Trends Mach. Learn. **2**, 1–55 (2009)
2. Cheng, Z., Yang, Q., Sheng, B.: Deep colorization. In: Proceedings of the IEEE International Conference on Computer Vision, pp. 415–423 (2015)
3. Deng, J., Dong, W., Socher, R., Li, L.J., Li, K., Fei-Fei, L.: ImageNet: a large-scale hierarchical image database. In: IEEE Conference on Computer Vision and Pattern Recognition, CVPR 2009, pp. 248–255. IEEE (2009)
4. Goodfellow, I., et al.: Generative adversarial nets. In: Advances in Neural Information Processing Systems, pp. 2672–2680 (2014)

5. He, K., Zhang, X., Ren, S., Sun, J.: Delving deep into rectifiers: surpassing human-level performance on ImageNet classification. In: 2015 IEEE International Conference on Computer Vision (ICCV), pp. 1026–1034 (2015). https://doi.org/10.1109/ICCV.2015.123

6. He, K., Zhang, X., Ren, S., Sun, J.: Identity mappings in deep residual networks. In: Leibe, B., Matas, J., Sebe, N., Welling, M. (eds.) ECCV 2016. LNCS, vol. 9908, pp. 630–645. Springer, Cham (2016). https://doi.org/10.1007/978-3-319-46493-0_38

7. Iizuka, S., Simo-Serra, E., Ishikawa, H.: Let there be Color! Joint end-to-end learning of global and local image priors for automatic image colorization with simultaneous classification. ACM Trans. Graph. **35**(4), Article: 110, 110:1–110:11 (2016). (Proc. of SIGGRAPH 2016)

8. Isola, P., Zhu, J.Y., Zhou, T., Efros, A.A.: Image-to-image translation with conditional adversarial networks. arXiv preprint (2017)

9. Johnson, J., Alahi, A., Li, F.: Perceptual losses for real-time style transfer and super-resolution. CoRR abs/1603.08155 (2016). http://arxiv.org/abs/1603.08155

10. Levin, A., Lischinski, D., Weiss, Y.: Colorization using optimization. In: ACM SIGGRAPH 2004 Papers, SIGGRAPH 2004, pp. 689–694. ACM, New York (2004). https://doi.org/10.1145/1186562.1015780. http://doi.acm.org/10.1145/1186562.1015780

11. Liu, Z., Luo, P., Wang, X., Tang, X.: Deep learning face attributes in the wild. In: Proceedings of International Conference on Computer Vision (ICCV) (2015)

12. Mannos, J., Sakrison, D.: The effects of a visual fidelity criterion of the encoding of images. IEEE Trans. Inf. Theor. **20**(4), 525–536 (2006). https://doi.org/10.1109/TIT.1974.1055250

13. Nazeri, K., Ng, E., Ebrahimi, M.: Image colorization using generative adversarial networks. In: Perales, F.J., Kittler, J. (eds.) AMDO 2018. LNCS, vol. 10945, pp. 85–94. Springer, Cham (2018). https://doi.org/10.1007/978-3-319-94544-6_9

14. Noda, H., Niimi, M., Korekuni, J.: Simple and efficient colorization in YCbCr color space. In: 18th International Conference on Pattern Recognition (ICPR 2006), vol. 3, pp. 685–688 (2006). https://doi.org/10.1109/ICPR.2006.1053

15. Reinhard, E., Adhikhmin, M., Gooch, B., Shirley, P.: Color transfer between images. IEEE Comput. Graph. Appl. **21**(5), 34–41 (2001). https://doi.org/10.1109/38.946629

16. Ronneberger, O., Fischer, P., Brox, T.: U-net: convolutional networks for biomedical image segmentation. CoRR abs/1505.04597 (2015). http://arxiv.org/abs/1505.04597

17. Sapiro, G.: Inpainting the colors. In: IEEE International Conference on Image Processing 2005, vol. 2, pp. II-698–701 (2005). https://doi.org/10.1109/ICIP.2005.1530151

18. Sheikh, H.R., Bovik, A.C.: Image information and visual quality. IEEE Trans. Image Process. **15**(2), 430–444 (2006). https://doi.org/10.1109/TIP.2005.859378

19. Simonyan, K., Zisserman, A.: Very deep convolutional networks for large-scale image recognition. CoRR abs/1409.1556 (2014)

20. Tola, E., Lepetit, V., Fua, P.: Daisy: an efficient dense descriptor applied to wide-baseline stereo. IEEE Trans. Pattern Anal. Mach. Intell. **32**(5), 815–830 (2010)

21. Wang, Z., Bovik, A.C., Sheikh, H.R., Simoncelli, E.P.: Image quality assessment: from error visibility to structural similarity. IEEE Trans. Image Process. **13**(4), 600–612 (2004). https://doi.org/10.1109/TIP.2003.819861

22. Wang, Z., Bovik, A.: A universal image quality index. IEEE Signal Process. Lett. **9**(3), 81–84 (2002). https://doi.org/10.1109/97.995823

23. Welsh, T., Ashikhmin, M., Mueller, K.: Transferring color to greyscale images. In: Proceedings of the 29th Annual Conference on Computer Graphics and Interactive Techniques, SIGGRAPH 2002, pp. 277–280. ACM, New York (2002). https://doi.org/10.1145/566570.566576. http://doi.acm.org/10.1145/566570.566576

24. Zhang, H., Sindagi, V., Patel, V.M.: Image de-raining using a conditional generative adversarial network. arXiv preprint arXiv:1701.05957 (2017)

25. Zhang, R., Isola, P., Efros, A.A.: Colorful image colorization. In: Leibe, B., Matas, J., Sebe, N., Welling, M. (eds.) ECCV 2016. LNCS, vol. 9907, pp. 649–666. Springer, Cham (2016). https://doi.org/10.1007/978-3-319-46487-9_40

26. Zhou, B., Lapedriza, A., Khosla, A., Oliva, A., Torralba, A.: Places: a 10 million image database for scene recognition. IEEE Trans. Pattern Anal. Mach. Intell. **40**(6), 1452–1464 (2018)

Self-Referenced Deep Learning

Xu Lan[1]([✉]), Xiatian Zhu[2], and Shaogang Gong[1]

[1] Queen Mary University of London, London, UK
{x.lan,s.gong}@qmul.ac.uk
[2] Vision Semantics Ltd., London, UK
eddy@visionsemantics.com

Abstract. Knowledge distillation is an effective approach to transferring knowledge from a teacher neural network to a student target network for satisfying the low-memory and fast running requirements in practice use. Whilst being able to create stronger target networks compared to the vanilla non-teacher based learning strategy, this scheme needs to train *additionally* a large teacher model with expensive computational cost. In this work, we present a Self-Referenced Deep Learning (SRDL) strategy. Unlike both vanilla optimisation and existing knowledge distillation, SRDL distils the knowledge discovered by the in-training target model *back* to itself to regularise the subsequent learning procedure therefore eliminating the need for training a large teacher model. SRDL improves the model generalisation performance compared to vanilla learning and conventional knowledge distillation approaches with *negligible* extra computational cost. Extensive evaluations show that a variety of deep networks benefit from SRDL resulting in enhanced deployment performance on both coarse-grained object categorisation tasks (CIFAR10, CIFAR100, Tiny ImageNet, and ImageNet) and fine-grained person instance identification tasks (Market-1501).

1 Introduction

Deep neural networks have been shown to be effective for solving many computer vision tasks [12,22,24,31,39,42]. However, they are often computationally expensive due to having very deep and/or wide architectures with millions of parameters [12,39,49]. This leads to slow execution and the need for large storage, reducing their deployability to situations with low memory and limited computing budget, e.g. mobile phones. This has given rise to efforts in developing more compact models, such as parameter binarisation [35], filter pruning [29], model compression [11], and knowledge distillation [15].

Among these existing techniques, knowledge distillation [15] is a generic approach suitable to a wide variety of networks and applications. It is based on the observation that compared to large networks, small networks often have similar representation capacities but are harder to define and train the parameters of a target function [1,3]. As a solution to this challenge, knowledge distillation first trains a deeper and/or wider "teacher" network (or an ensemble model),

ⓒ Springer Nature Switzerland AG 2019
C. V. Jawahar et al. (Eds.): ACCV 2018, LNCS 11362, pp. 284–300, 2019.
https://doi.org/10.1007/978-3-030-20890-5_19

then learns a smaller "student" network to imitate the teacher's classification probabilities [15] and/or feature representations [1,36] (Fig. 1(b)). This imposes additional information beyond conventional supervised learning signals (Fig. 1(a)), leading to a more discriminative student model than learning the target model without the teacher's knowledge. However, this generalisation improvement comes with significant extra computational cost and model training time of the teacher model.

In contrast to knowledge distillation, fast model optimisation aims to reduce the cost of training a target model. While it is relatively fast to train a model on small datasets such as CIFAR10 [23] in a few hours, model training on larger datasets like the ILSVRC dataset [37] requires a few weeks. Hence, fast optimisation in deep model training has increasingly become an important problem to be addressed. There are several different approaches to fast optimisation, such as model initialisation [8,34] and learning rate optimisation [7,20,50].

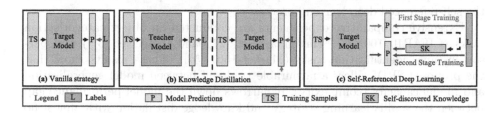

Fig. 1. Illustration of three different deep network learning methods. (a) The vanilla training: Optimise the target model from the supervision of training label for M epochs in one stage. (b) The Knowledge Distillation training: Firstly learn a teacher model in a *computationally intensive* manner; Then extract the learned knowledge from the teacher model; Lastly optimise the target model by leveraging both the label data and the teacher's knowledge for M epochs. (c) The proposed SRDL training: In the first stage, learn the target model by the label supervision for half $(M/2)$ epochs (similar to (a) but with a different learning rate strategy), and extract intermediate knowledge from the thus-far trained model (similar to (b) but without a heavy teacher model to train); In the second stage, continuously optimise the target model from the joint supervision of the labelled training data and the self-discovered knowledge for another half $(M/2)$ epochs.

In this work, we aim to jointly solve both knowledge distillation for model compression and fast optimisation in model learning using a unified deep learning strategy. To that end, we propose a **Self-Referenced Deep Learning** (SRDL) strategy that integrates the knowledge distillation concept into a vanilla network learning procedure (Fig. 1(c)). Compared to knowledge distillation, SRDL exploits different and *available* knowledge without the need for additionally training an expensive teacher by self-discovering knowledge with the target model itself during training. Specifically, SRDL begins with training the target network by a conventional supervised learning objective as a vanilla strategy, then extracts self-discovered knowledge (inter-class correlations) during model train-ing, and continuously trains the model until convergence by satisfying two losses concurrently: a conventional supervised learning loss, and an *imitation loss* that regulates the classification probability predicted by the current (thus-far) model with the self-discovered knowledge. By doing so, the network learns significantly better than learning from a conventional supervised learning objective alone, as we will show in the experiments.

Our **contributions** are: **(I)** We investigate for the first time the prob-lems of knowledge distillation based model compression and fast optimisation in model training using a unified deep learning approach, an under-studied problem although both problems have been studied independently in the literature. **(II)** We present a stage-complete learning rate decay schedule in order to maximise the quality of intermediate self-discovered knowledge and therefore avoid the negative guidance to the subsequent second-stage model optimisation. **(III)** We further introduce a random model restart scheme for the second-stage training with the purpose of breaking the optimisation search space constraints tied to the self-referenced deep learning process.

Extensive comparative experiments are conducted on object categorisation tasks (CIFAR10/100 [23], Tiny ImageNet [27], and ImageNet [37]) and per-son instance identification tasks (Market-1501 [52]). These results show that the proposed SRDL offers a favourable trade-off between model generalisation and model capacity (complexity). It narrows down the model performance gap between the vanilla learning strategy and knowledge distillation with almost no extra computational cost. In some cases, SRDL even surpasses the performance of conventional knowledge distillation whilst maintaining the model learning effi-ciency advantage.

2   Related Work

Knowledge Distillation. Model compression by knowledge distillation was firstly studied in [2] and recently re-popularised by Hinton et al. [15]. The ratio-nale behind distillation is the introduction of extra supervision from a teacher model in training the target model in addition to a conventional supervised learning objective such as the cross-entropy loss subject to the labelled training data. The extra supervision were typically obtained from a pre-trained powerful teacher model in the form of classification probabilities [15], feature representa-tion [1,36], or inter-layer flow (the inner product of feature maps) [48]. Knowl-edge distillation has been exploited to distil easy-to-train large networks into harder-to-train small networks [36], or transfer high-level semantics to earlier layers [26], or simultaneously enhance and transfer knowledge on-the-fly [25].

Recently, some theoretical analysis have been provided to relate distillation to information learning theory for which a teacher provides privileged information (e.g. sample explanation) to a student in order to facilitate fast learning [33,43]. Zhang et al. [51] exploited this idea for video based action recognition by con-sidering the computationally expensive optic flow as privileged information to enhance the learning of a less discriminative motion vector model. This avoids the high cost of computing optic flow in model deployment whilst computing cheaper motion vectors enables real-time performance.

In contrast to all the above existing works, we aim to eliminate the extra teacher model training all together. To this end, we uniquely explore self-discovered knowledge in target model training by *self-distillation*, therefore more cost-effective. Concurrent with our work, Furlanello et al. [9] independently proposes training the networks in generations, in which the next generation is jointly guided by the standard one-hot classification labels and the knowledge learned in the previous generation. However, the training budget of each generation is almost the same as the vanilla strategy, leading to the total cost of this method several times more expensive than vanilla training.

Fast Optimisation. Fast optimisation of deep neural networks has gained increasing attention for reducing the long model training time by rapid model learning convergence [21,38]. A simple approach is by Gaussian initialisation with zero mean and unit variance, and Xavier initialisation [10]. But these are not scalable to very deep networks. More recent alternatives have emerged [13]. The rational is that good model initialisation facilitates model learning to rapidly reach the global optimum with minimal vanishing and/or exploding gradients. Additional options include improved optimisation algorithms to mitigate the slow convergence of SGD by sidestepping saddle points in the loss function surface [18], and learning rate refinement that exploits a cycle rate to train a neural network in the context of ensembling multiple models [16]. However, model ensemble multiplies the deployment cost by times.

In the spirit of fast model optimisation, our method aims to achieve more generalisable model learning without extra computational cost for learning an independent teacher model. By self-distillation, the proposed method can improve the performance of both small and large networks, so it is generally applicable.

3   Self-Referenced Deep Training

3.1   Problem Statement

For supervised model learning, we assume n labelled training samples $\mathcal{D} = \{(I_i, y_i)\}_i^n$. Each sample belongs to one of C classes $y_i \in \mathcal{Y} = [1, 2, \cdots, C]$, with the ground-truth label typically represented as a one-hot vector. The objective is to learn a classification deep CNN model generalisable to unseen test data through a cost-effective training process.

In this work, we formulate a novel deep learning approach that improves the model generalisation capability through employing self-discovered knowledge as additional supervision signal with marginal extra computational cost and hence not hurting the computing scalability. We call this strategy **Self-Referenced Deep Learning** (SRDL). We begin with revisiting the vanilla deep model training method (Fig. 1(a)) before elaborating the proposed SRDL approach.

3.2 Vanilla Deep Model Training

For training a classification deep model, the softmax cross-entropy loss function is usually adopted. Specifically, we predict the posterior probability of a labelled sample I over any class c via the softmax criterion:

$$p(c|\boldsymbol{x}, \boldsymbol{\theta}) = \frac{\exp(z_c)}{\sum_{j=1}^{C} \exp(z_j)}, \quad z_j = \boldsymbol{W}_j^\top \boldsymbol{x}, \quad c \in \mathcal{Y} \tag{1}$$

where $\boldsymbol{x}$ refers to the embedded feature vector of I, $\boldsymbol{W}_j$ the j-th class prediction function parameter, and $\boldsymbol{\theta}$ the neural network model parameters. We then compute the cross-entropy loss on a labelled sample $\boldsymbol{x}$ (in a mini-batch) as:

$$\mathcal{L}_{\text{ce}} = \log\left(p(y|\boldsymbol{x})\right) \tag{2}$$

where y specifies the ground-truth label class of $\boldsymbol{x}$.

Discussion. For a model subject to the vanilla training (Fig. 1(a)), the cross-entropy loss is utilised to supervise the model parameters (e.g. by the stochastic gradient descent algorithm) iteratively in a *one-stage* procedure. This training method relies *only* on the supervision of per-sample label, but *ignores* the discriminative knowledge incrementally discovered by the in-training model itself. It may lead to sub-optimal optimisation. We overcome this problem by introducing a mechanism to exploit self-discovered intermediate knowledge in a computationally economic manner.

3.3 Self-Referenced Deep Learning

SRDL Overview. The proposed SRDL approach is a knowledge referenced end-to-end deep model training strategy. The overview of our SRDL approach is depicted in Fig. 2. This is realised through reformulating the vanilla training process into two equal-sized stages:

1. In the first stage (Fig. 2(i)), SRDL learns the target model as a vanilla algorithm with a conventional supervised learning objective, while tries to induce reliable knowledge.
2. In the second stage (Fig. 2(ii)), SRDL continues to train the model by a conventional supervised loss and a self-discovered knowledge guided imitation loss concurrently.

For model training, SRDL consumes the same number of epochs as the vanilla counterpart. The extra marginal cost is due to self-discovered knowledge extraction (see **Evaluation Metrics** in Sect. 4). Consequently, SRDL allows to benefit model generalisation as knowledge distillation at faster optimisation speed. Once the target model is trained, it is deployed to the test data same as the vanilla method.

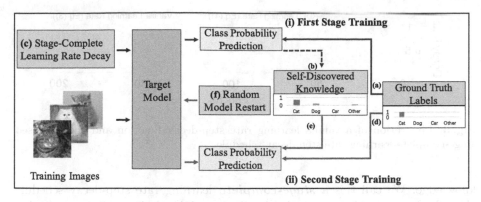

Fig. 2. Overview of the proposed Self-Referenced Deep Learning (SRDL). The SRDL strategy consists of two stages training: **First stage:** We train the target model by a cross-entropy loss (Eq. (2)) with **(a)** the available label supervision for half epochs, whilst learning to **(b)** extract discriminative intermediate knowledge concurrently (Eq. (5)). To maximise the quality of self-discovered knowledge, we introduce **(c)** a pass-complete learning rate decay schedule (Eq. (4)). **Second stage:** we continuously optimise the target model for the other half epochs by the joint supervision (Eq. (7)) of both **(d)** the label data and **(e)** self-discovered intermediate knowledge in an end-to-end manner. We **(f)** randomly restart the model for the second stage to break the optimisation search space constraint from self-referenced deep learning mechanism.

(I) First Stage Learning. In the first stage of SRDL, we train the deep model θ by the cross-entropy loss Eq. (2). Model training is often guided by a learning rate decay schedule such as the step-decay function [12,17]:

$$\epsilon_t = \epsilon_0 \times f_{\text{step}}(t, M), \quad t \in [1, \cdots, M] \tag{3}$$

where ϵ_t denotes the learning rate at the t-th epoch (initialised as ϵ_0, in total M epochs), and $f_{\text{step}}(t, M)$ the step-decay function. The learning rate decay aims to encourage the model to converge to a satisfactory local minimum without random oscillation in loss reduction during model training. However, if applying the conventional step-decay scheme throughout the optimisation process, SRDL may result in premature knowledge during training. This is because, the model still resides in an unstable local minimum due to that the learning rate drop is not sufficiently quick [47].

To overcome this problem, we propose to deploy an *individual* and *complete* step-decay schedule for both first and second stages of SRDL (Fig. 2(c)), subject to the condition of remaining the same training epochs (cost). Formally, this schedule is expressed as:

$$\epsilon_t = \epsilon_0 \times f_{\text{step}}(t, 0.5M) \tag{4}$$

The intuition is that, the in-training model can be *temporarily* pushed towards a reasonably stable local minimum within the same number of (e.g. $0.5M$) epochs to achieve a more-ready state therefore help ensure the quality of self-discovered

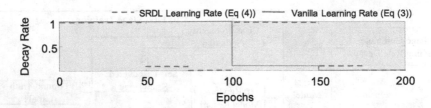

Fig. 3. Illustration of a vanilla learning rate step-decay function and the proposed stage-complete learning rate step-decay schedule.

knowledge. We call this a ***stage-complete*** learning rate step-decay schedule (Fig. 3). Our evaluations verify the significance of this design while guaranteeing the goodness of the self-referenced knowledge (see Table 4).

At the end of the first stage of SRDL with a "half-trained" model (denoted as $\boldsymbol{\theta}^*$), we extract the self-discovered knowledge in the form of per-sample class probability prediction (Fig. 2(b)). Formally, we compute the class probability for each training sample $\boldsymbol{x}$ by a *softened* softmax operation as:

$$\tilde{p}(c|\boldsymbol{x}, \boldsymbol{\theta}^*) = \frac{\exp(z_c/T)}{\sum_{j=1}^C \exp(z_j/T)}, \quad z_j = \boldsymbol{W}_j^\top \boldsymbol{x}, \ c \in \mathcal{Y} \tag{5}$$

where the temperature parameter T controls the softening degree, with higher values meaning more softened predictions. We set $T = 3$ in our experiments as suggested in [15].

(II) Second Stage Learning. To improve the generalisation performance of the model, we use the self-discovered knowledge to provide training experience at second stage model learning in SRDL. We quantify the imitation of the current model to the knowledge $\tilde{p}(j|\boldsymbol{x}, \boldsymbol{\theta}^*)$ with Kullback Leibler (KL) divergence (Fig. 2(e)), formulated as:

$$R_{\mathrm{kl}} = \sum_{j=1}^C \tilde{p}(j|\boldsymbol{x}, \boldsymbol{\theta}^*) \log \frac{\tilde{p}(j|\boldsymbol{x}, \boldsymbol{\theta}^*)}{\tilde{p}(j|\boldsymbol{x}, \boldsymbol{\theta})}. \tag{6}$$

where $\tilde{p}(j|\boldsymbol{x}, \boldsymbol{\theta})$ is the class probability prediction of the up-to-date model $\boldsymbol{\theta}$ computed by Eq. (5). The overall loss function for the second stage in SRDL is:

$$\mathcal{L} = \mathcal{L}_{\mathrm{ce}} + T^2 * R_{\mathrm{kl}} \tag{7}$$

with the squared softening-temperature (Eq. (5)) as the balance weight. The gradient magnitudes produced by the soft targets $\tilde{p}$ are scaled by $\frac{1}{T^2}$, so we multiply the distillation loss term by a factor T^2 to ensure that the relative contributions of ground-truth and teacher probability distributions remains. In doing so, the network model learns to both predict the correct class label (cross-entropy loss $\mathcal{L}_{\mathrm{ce}}$) and align the class probability of previous training experience (imitation loss R_{kl}) concurrently.

Random Model Restart. A key difference between SRDL and knowledge distillation is that SRDL enables a model to learn from its own (previously revealed) knowledge through training experience rather than from an independent teacher's knowledge. This self-discovered knowledge is represented in the "half-trained" model parameters θ^*. If we further train the model at the second stage from θ^* by Eq. (7), the learning may become less explorable for better local or global minimum due to the stacking effect of the imitation loss and the model parameter status. Therefore, we start the second stage training with *randomly* initialised model parameters.

This scheme is based on three considerations: (1) A large proportion of the knowledge learned in the first stage has been extracted and used in the second stage. (2) The same training data will be used. (3) Random initialisation offers another opportunity for the model to converge to a better local minimum. Our experiment validates the effectiveness of this *random restart* scheme (see Table 5 in Sect. 4.5).

SRDL model training is summarised in Algorithm 1. In our experiments, a SRDL trained model is tested against both the vanilla model training strategy and the knowledge distillation method.

Algorithm 1. Self-Referenced Deep Learning

1: **Input**: Labelled training data $\mathcal{D}$; Training epochs M;
2: **Output**: Trained CNN model θ;
3: **(I) First stage learning**
4: **Initialisation**: t=1; Random model θ initialisation;
5: **while** $t \leq 0.5 * M$ **do**
6:      (i) Update the learning rate ϵ_t (Eq (4));
7:      (ii) Update θ by cross-entropy loss (Eq (2));
8: **end**
9: **Knowledge Extraction** Induce per-sample class probability predictions (Eq (5));
10: **(II) Second stage learning**
11: **Initialisation**: t=1; Random model θ restart;
12: **while** $t \leq 0.5 * M$ **do**
13:      (i) Update the learning rate ϵ_t (Eq (4));
14:      (ii) Update θ by soft-feedback referenced loss (Eq (7));
15: **end**

---

4 Experiments

4.1 Experimental Setup

Datasets. For experimental evaluations, we use four benchmarking datasets including both coarse-grained object classification and fine-grained person instance identification Specifically, the ***CIFAR*10** and ***CIFAR*100** [23] datasets contain 32×32 sized natural images from 10 and 100 object classes.

Both adopt a 50,000/10,000 train/test image split. The **Tiny ImageNet** [27] consists of 110,000 64 × 64 images from 200 object classes. We adopt the standard 100,000/1,000 train/val setting. The **ImageNet** [22] is a large scale 1,000-class object image classification benchmark, providing 1.2 million images for training, and 50,000 images for validation. The **Market-1501** [52] is a person re-identification dataset. Different from image classification as tested in the above four datasets, person re-identification is a more fine-grained recognition problem of matching person instance across non-overlapping camera views. It is a more challenging task due to the inherent zero-shot learning knowledge transfer from seen classes (identities) to unseen classes in deployments, i.e. no overlap between training and test classes. Market-1501 has 32,668 images of 1,501 different identities (ID) captured by six outdoor cameras. We use the standard 751/750 train/test ID split. Following [30,41], we train the network by the cross-entropy loss (Eq. (2)) and use the feature layer's output as the representation of person bounding box images for test by the Euclidean distance metric.

Performance Metrics. For performance measurement, we adopt the top-1 classification accuracy for image classification, the standard Cumulative Matching Characteristic (CMC) accuracy (Rank-n rates) and mean Average Precision (mAP) for person instance recognition (re-id). The CMC is computed for each individual rank k as the cumulative percentage of the truth matches for probes returned at ranks $\leq k$. And the Rank-1 rate is often considered as the most important performance indicator of an algorithm's efficacy. The mAP is to measure the recall of multiple truth matches, computed by first computing the area under the Precision-Recall curve for each probe, then calculating the mean of Average Precision over all probes. We measure the model optimisation complexity with the FLoating-point OPerations (FLOPs): `Forward-FLOPs` * `Epochs` * `Training-Set-Size`.

Neural Networks. We use 7 networks in our experiments: one typical student net, ResNet-32 [12]; two typical teacher nets, ResNet-110 [12] and Wide ResNet WRN-28-10 [49]; and four varying sized nets, ResNet-50, DenseNet-121, DenseNet-201 and DenseNet-BC ($L = 190$, $k = 40$) [17].

Implementation Details. For all three image classification datasets, we use SGD with Nesterov momentum and set the mini-batch size to 128, the initial learning rate to 0.1, the weight decay to 0.0002, and the momentum to 0.9. For Market-1501, we use the same SGD but with the mini-batch size of 32. We assign sufficient epochs to all models to ensure convergence. On CIFAR datasets, the training budget is 300 epochs for DenseNet, and 200 epochs for ResNet and Wide ResNet models, same as [16]. We set 150/120 epochs on Tiny ImageNet/Market-1501 for all models. All model optimisation methods take the same epochs to train the target networks. We adopt a common learning rate decay schedule [16]: the learning rate drops by 0.1 at the 50% and 75% epochs. The data augmentation includes horizontal flipping and randomly cropping from images padded by 4 pixels on each side with missing pixels filled by original

Table 1. Comparison between SRDL and the vanilla learning strategy on image classification. Metric: Accuracy (Acc) Rate (%). "Gain": the performance gain by SRDL over vanilla. TrCost: Model training cost in unit of 10^{16} FLOPs, **lower is better**. M: Million. The first/second best results are in red/blue.

Dataset	# Param	CIFAR10		CIFAR100		Tiny ImageNet	
Metrics		Acc	TrCost	Acc	TrCost	Acc	TrCost
ResNet-32+vanilla	0.5M	92.53	0.08	69.02	0.08	53.33	0.32
ResNet-32+**SRDL**		**93.12**	0.08	**71.63**	0.08	**55.53**	0.32
Gain (SRDL-vanilla)		+0.59	0	+2.61	0	+2.20	0
WRN-28-10+vanilla	36.5M	94.98	12.62	78.32	12.62	58.38	50.48
WRN-28-10+**SRDL**		**95.41**	12.62	**79.38**	12.62	**60.80**	50.48
Gain (SRDL-vanilla)		+0.43	0	+1.06	0	+2.42	0
DenseNet-BC+vanilla	25.6M	**96.68**	10.24	**82.83**	10.24	**62.88**	40.96
DenseNet-BC+**SRDL**		96.87	10.24	83.59	10.24	64.19	40.96
Gain (SRDL-vanilla)		+0.19	0	+0.76	0	+1.31	0

image reflections [12]. We report the average performance of 5 independent runs for each experiment.

4.2 Comparison with the Vanilla Learning Strategy

We compared the image classification performance between SRDL and the vanilla optimisation strategy. We make the following observations from Table 1:

1. All three networks ResNet-32, WRN-28-10, and DenseNet-BC improve the classification performance when trained by the proposed SRDL. For example, ResNet-32 achieves an accuracy gain of 0.59% on CIFAR10, of 2.61% on CIFAR100, and of 2.20% on Tiny ImageNet. This suggests the applicability of SRDL to standard varying-capacity network architectures.
2. SRDL achieves superior model generalisation performance with nearly zero extra model training cost[1].
3. Smaller network (ResNet-32) with fewer parameters generally benefits more from SRDL in model generalisation performance, making our method more attractive to resource-limited applications. Hence, our SRDL addresses the notorious hard-to-train problem in small networks to some degree [1].

Results on ImageNet. We test the large scale ImageNet with DenseNet201 and obtain the Top-1/5 rates 77.20%/94.57% by the vanilla vs 77.72%/94.89% by our SRDL. This suggests that SRDL generalises to large scale object classification settings.

---

[1] The computational cost of knowledge extraction required by both SRDL and Knowledge Distillation [15] is marginal (less than 0.67% model training cost) and hence omitted for analysis convenience.

4.3 Comparison with Knowledge Distillation

We compared our SRDL with the closely related Knowledge Distillation (KD) method [15]. With KD, we take ResNet-32 as the target model, WRN-28-10 and ResNet-110 as the pre-trained teacher models to produce the per-sample class probability targets (i.e. the teacher's knowledge) for the student. From Table 2 we draw these observations:

Table 2. Comparison between SRDL and Knowledge Distillation (KD) on image classification. Metric: Accuracy (Acc) Rate (%). TrCost: Model training cost in unit of 10^{16} FLOPs, **lower is better**. Number in bracket: model parameter size. The first/second best results are in red/**blue**.

Target Net	Method	Teacher Net	CIFAR10		CIFAR100		Tiny ImageNet	
			Acc	TrCost	Acc	TrCost	Acc	TrCost
ResNet-32	Vanilla	N/A	92.53	0.08	69.02	0.08	53.33	0.32
(0.5M)	KD	WRN-28-10 (36.5M)	**92.83**	12.70	72.58	12.70	56.80	50.80
		ResNet-110 (1.7M)	92.75	0.30	71.17	0.30	55.06	1.20
	SRDL	N/A	93.12	0.08	**71.63**	0.08	**55.53**	0.32

1. KD is indeed effective to improve small model generalisation compared to the vanilla optimisation, particularly when using a more powerful teacher (WRN-28-10). However, this is at the price of extra 157× (12.70/0.08-1 or 50.80/0.32-1) model training cost. When using ResNet-110 as the teacher in KD, the performance gain is less significant.
2. SRDL approaches the performance of KD(WRN-28-10) on CIFAR100 and Tiny ImageNet, whilst surpasses it on CIFAR10. This implies that while small model is inferior to KD in self-discovering knowledge among a large number of classes, it seems to be superior for small scale tasks with fewer classes.
3. SRDL consistently outperforms KD(ResNet-110) in both model performance and training cost, indicating that KD is not necessarily superior than SRDL in enhancing small model generalisation (teacher dependent). This may be partly due to the overfitting of a stronger teacher model (e.g. ResNet-110) which leads to less extra supervision information. To test this, we calculated the average cross entropy loss of the final epoch. We observed 0.0087 (ResNet-110) vs 0.1637 (ResNet-32), which is consistent with our hypothesis.

4.4 Evaluation on Person Instance Recognition

In person re-identification (re-id) experiment, we compared SRDL with the vanilla model learning strategy using the same CNN nets, and also compared with ten recent the state-of-the-art re-id methods. Two different networks are tested: ResNet-50 (25.1M parameters) and DenseNet-121 (7.7M parameters). Table 3 shows that:

Table 3. Evaluation of person re-id (instance recognition) on Market-1501. The first/ second best results are in red/blue.

Query type	Single-query		Multi-query	
Metrics (%)	Rank-1	mAP	Rank-1	mAP
SCS [5]	51.9	26.3	-	-
G-SCNN [44]	65.8	39.5	76.0	48.4
HPN [32]	76.9	-	-	-
MSCAN [28]	80.3	57.5	86.8	66.7
JLML [30]	85.1	65.5	89.7	74.5
SVDNet [41]	82.3	62.1	-	-
PDC [40]	84.1	63.4	-	-
TriNet [14]	84.9	69.1	90.5	76.4
IDEAL [24]	86.7	67.5	91.3	76.2
DPFL [6]	88.6	72.6	92.2	80.4
BraidNet-CS+SRL [46]	83.7	69.5	-	-
DaRe [45]	86.4	69.3	-	-
MLFN [4]	90.0	**74.3**	92.3	**82.4**
ResNet-50+vanilla	87.5	69.9	91.4	78.5
ResNet-50+**SRDL**	**89.3**	73.5	**93.1**	81.5
Gain (SRDL-vanilla)	+1.8	+3.6	+1.7	+3.0
DenseNet-121+vanilla	**90.1**	74.0	**93.6**	81.7
DenseNet-121+**SRDL**	91.7	76.8	94.2	83.5
Gain (SRDL-vanilla)	+1.6	+2.8	+0.6	+1.8

1. All CNN models benefit from SRDL on the person re-id task, boosting the re-id performance for both single-query and multi-query settings.
2. SRDL trained CNNs show superior re-id performance over most state-of-the-art methods. In particular, SRDL trained DenseNet-121 achieves the best re-id matching rates among all the competitors.

Note that, this performance gain is obtained from a general-purpose network without applying any specialised person re-id model training "bells and whistles". This is in strong contrast to existing deep re-id methods [28,32,40,44] where specially designed network architectures with complex training process are required in order to achieve the reported results.

4.5 Component Analysis and Discussion

We further conducted SRDL component analysis using ResNet-32 on CIFAR100.

Stage-Complete Schedule. Table 4 compares our stage-complete learning rate decay schedule with the conventional *stage-incomplete* counterpart. It is evident that without the proposed schedule, self-referenced learning can be highly misleading due to unreliable knowledge extracted from the "half-trained" model. This validates the aforementioned model optimisation behaviour consideration (see the discussion underneath Eq. (4)).

Table 4. Stage-complete schedule.

Decay strategy	Accuracy (%)
Stage-incomplete	58.11
Stage-complete	**71.63**

Random Model Restart. Table 5 shows that model random restart for the second stage training in SRDL brings 1.90% (71.63%–69.73%) accuracy gain. This verifies our design motivation that the discriminative knowledge is well preserved in the training data and self-discovered correlation; Hence, random model initialisation for the second stage training of SRDL enables to break the optimisation search space constraint without losing the available information, and eventually improving the model generalisation capability.

Table 5. Random model restart.

Random restart	Accuracy (%)
✗	69.73
✓	**71.63**

Model Ensemble. Table 6 shows that the ensemble of "half-trained" and final models can further boost the performance by 0.70% (72.33%–71.63%) with more (double) deployment cost. This suggests that the two models induced sequentially during training are partially complementary, which gives rise to model ensembling diversity and results in model performance boost. Besides, we also tested an ensemble of two randomly initialised networks each trained by the vanilla learning strategy for $M/2$ epochs, obtaining the Top-1 rate 72.02% vs 72.33% by SRDL. This shows that our SRDL ensemble outperforms the vanilla counterpart.

Table 6. Model ensemble.

Model ensemble	Accuracy (%)
✗	71.63
✓	**72.33**

Model Generalisation Analysis. As shown in [19], model generalisation is concerned with the width of a local optimum. We thus examined the solutions θ_v and θ_s discovered by the vanilla and SRDL training algorithms, respectively. We added small perturbations as $\theta_*(d, v) = \theta_* + d \cdot v$, $* \in \{v, s\}$ where v is a uniform distributed direction vector with a unit length, and $d \in [0, 5]$ controls the change magnitude. The loss is quantified by the cross-entropy measurement between the predicted and ground-truth labels. Figure 4 shows the robustness of each solution against the parameter perturbation, indicating the width of local optima as $\theta_v < \theta_s$. This suggests that our SRDL finds a wider local minimum than the vanilla therefore more likely to generalise better.

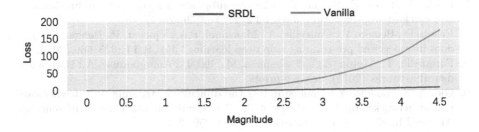

Fig. 4. The width analysis of solution local optima.

5   Conclusion

In this work, we presented a novel Self-Referenced Deep Learning (SRDL) strategy for improving deep network model learning by exploiting self-discovered knowledge in a two-stage training procedure. SRDL can train more discriminative small and large networks with little extra computational cost. This differs from conventional knowledge distillation which requires a separate pre-trained large teacher model with huge extra computational and model training time cost. Conceptually, SRDL is a principled combination of vanilla model optimisation and existing knowledge distillation, with an attractive trade-off between model generalisation and model training complexity. Extensive experiments show that a variety of standard deep networks can all benefit from SRDL on both coarse-grained object categorisation tasks (image classification) and fine-grained person instance identification tasks (person re-identification). Significantly, smaller networks benefit from more performance gains, making SRDL specially good for low-memory and fast execution applications. Further component analysis gives insights to the SRDL's model design considerations.

Acknowledgements. This work was partly supported by the China Scholarship Council, Vision Semantics Limited, the Royal Society Newton Advanced Fellowship Programme (NA150459), and Innovate UK Industrial Challenge Project on Developing and Commercialising Intelligent Video Analytics Solutions for Public Safety (98111-571149).

References

1. Ba, J., Caruana, R.: Do deep nets really need to be deep? In: NIPS (2014)
2. Bucilua, C., et al.: Model compression. In: SIGKDD. ACM (2006)
3. Bucilua, C., Caruana, R., Niculescu-Mizil, A.: Model compression. In: SIGKDD (2006)
4. Chang, X., Hospedales, T.M., Xiang, T.: Multi-level factorisation net for person re-identification. In: CVPR (2018)
5. Chen, D., Yuan, Z., Chen, B., Zheng, N.: Similarity learning with spatial constraints for person re-identification. In: CVPR (2016)
6. Chen, Y., Zhu, X., Gong, S., et al.: Person re-identification by deep learning multi-scale representations. In: ICCV Workshop (2017)
7. Duchi, J., Hazan, E., Singer, Y.: Adaptive subgradient methods for online learning and stochastic optimization. JMLR **12**, 2121–2159 (2011)
8. Erhan, D., Bengio, Y., Courville, A., Manzagol, P.A., Vincent, P., Bengio, S.: Why does unsupervised pre-training help deep learning? JMLR **11**, 625–660 (2010)
9. Furlanello, T., Lipton, Z.C., Tschannen, M., Itti, L., Anandkumar, A.: Born again neural networks (2018). arXiv e-prints
10. Glorot, X., Bengio, Y.: Understanding the difficulty of training deep feedforward neural networks. In: Proceedings of the Thirteenth International Conference on Artificial Intelligence and Statistics, pp. 249–256 (2010)
11. Han, S., Mao, H., Dally, W.J.: Deep compression: compressing deep neural networks with pruning, trained quantization and Huffman coding. In: ICLR (2016)
12. He, K., et al.: Deep residual learning for image recognition. In: CVPR (2016)
13. He, K., Zhang, X., Ren, S., Sun, J.: Delving deep into rectifiers: surpassing human-level performance on ImageNet classification. In: ICCV (2015)
14. Hermans, A., Beyer, L., Leibe, B.: In defense of the triplet loss for person re-identification (2017). arXiv e-prints
15. Hinton, G., Vinyals, O., Dean, J.: Distilling the knowledge in a neural network (2015). arXiv e-prints
16. Huang, G., Li, Y., Pleiss, G., Liu, Z., Hopcroft, J.E., Weinberger, K.Q.: Snapshot ensembles: train 1, get M for free. In: ICLR (2017)
17. Huang, G., Liu, Z., Weinberger, K.Q., van der Maaten, L.: Densely connected convolutional networks. In: CVPR (2017)
18. Johnson, R., Zhang, T.: Accelerating stochastic gradient descent using predictive variance reduction. In: NIPS (2013)
19. Keskar, N.S., et al.: On large-batch training for deep learning: generalization gap and sharp minima (2016). arXiv e-prints
20. Kingma, D., Ba, J.: Adam: a method for stochastic optimization (2014). arXiv e-prints
21. Krähenbühl, P., Doersch, C., Donahue, J., Darrell, T.: Data-dependent initializations of convolutional neural networks. In: ICLR (2016)
22. Krizhevsky, A., et al.: ImageNet classification with deep convolutional neural networks. In: NIPS (2012)
23. Krizhevsky, A., Hinton, G.: Learning multiple layers of features from tiny images (2009)
24. Lan, X., Wang, H., Gong, S., Zhu, X.: Deep reinforcement learning attention selection for person re-identification (2017). arXiv e-prints
25. Lan, X., Zhu, X., Gong, S.: Knowledge distillation by on-the-fly native ensemble (2018). arXiv preprint: arXiv:1806.04606

26. Lan, X., Zhu, X., Gong, S.: Person search by multi-scale matching. In: Ferrari, V., Hebert, M., Sminchisescu, C., Weiss, Y. (eds.) ECCV 2018, Part I. LNCS, vol. 11205, pp. 553–569. Springer, Cham (2018). https://doi.org/10.1007/978-3-030-01246-5_33

27. Le, Y., Yang, X.: Tiny ImageNet visual recognition challenge. CS 231N (2015)

28. Li, D., Chen, X., Zhang, Z., Huang, K.: Learning deep context-aware features over body and latent parts for person re-identification. In: CVPR (2017)

29. Li, H., Kadav, A., Durdanovic, I., Samet, H., Graf, H.P.: Pruning filters for efficient ConvNets. In: ICLR (2017)

30. Li, W., Zhu, X., Gong, S.: Person re-identification by deep joint learning of multi-loss classification. In: IJCAI (2017)

31. Li, W., Zhu, X., Gong, S.: Harmonious attention network for person re-identification. In: CVPR (2018)

32. Liu, X., et al.: HydraPlus-Net: attentive deep features for pedestrian analysis. In: ICCV (2017)

33. Lopez-Paz, D., Bottou, L., Schölkopf, B., Vapnik, V.: Unifying distillation and privileged information (2015). arXiv e-prints

34. Mishkin, D., Matas, J.: All you need is a good init. In: ICLR (2015)

35. Rastegari, M., Ordonez, V., Redmon, J., Farhadi, A.: XNOR-Net: ImageNet classification using binary convolutional neural networks. In: Leibe, B., Matas, J., Sebe, N., Welling, M. (eds.) ECCV 2016, Part IV. LNCS, vol. 9908, pp. 525–542. Springer, Cham (2016). https://doi.org/10.1007/978-3-319-46493-0_32

36. Romero, A., Ballas, N., Kahou, S.E., Chassang, A., Gatta, C., Bengio, Y.: FitNets: hints for thin deep nets (2014). arXiv e-prints

37. Russakovsky, O., Deng, J., et al.: ImageNet large scale visual recognition challenge. IJCV 115(3), 211–252 (2015)

38. Saxe, A.M., McClelland, J.L., Ganguli, S.: Exact solutions to the nonlinear dynamics of learning in deep linear neural networks (2013). arXiv e-prints

39. Simonyan, K., Zisserman, A.: Very deep convolutional networks for large-scale image recognition (2015). arXiv e-prints

40. Su, C., Li, J., Zhang, S., Xing, J., Gao, W., Tian, Q.: Pose-driven deep convolutional model for person re-identification. In: ICCV (2017)

41. Sun, Y., Zheng, L., Deng, W., Wang, S.: SVDNet for pedestrian retrieval (2017). arXiv preprint

42. Szegedy, C., Liu, W., Jia, Y., Sermanet, P., Reed, S., et al.: Going deeper with convolutions. In: CVPR (2015)

43. Vapnik, V., Izmailov, R.: Learning using privileged information: similarity control and knowledge transfer. JMLR 16(20232049), 55 (2015)

44. Varior, R.R., Haloi, M., Wang, G.: Gated siamese convolutional neural network architecture for human re-identification. In: Leibe, B., Matas, J., Sebe, N., Welling, M. (eds.) ECCV 2016, Part VIII. LNCS, vol. 9912, pp. 791–808. Springer, Cham (2016). https://doi.org/10.1007/978-3-319-46484-8_48

45. Wang, Y., et al.: Resource aware person re-identification across multiple resolutions. In: CVPR (2018)

46. Wang, Y., Chen, Z., Wu, F., Wang, G.: Person re-identification with cascaded pairwise convolutions (2018)

47. Welling, M., Teh, Y.W.: Bayesian learning via stochastic gradient Langevin dynamics. In: ICML (2011)

48. Yim, J., Joo, D., Bae, J., Kim, J.: A gift from knowledge distillation: fast optimization, network minimization and transfer learning. In: CVPR (2017)

49. Zagoruyko, S., Komodakis, N.: Wide residual networks (2016). arXiv e-prints
50. Zeiler, M.D.: ADADELTA: an adaptive learning rate method (2012). arXiv e-prints
51. Zhang, B., Wang, L., Wang, Z., Qiao, Y., Wang, H.: Real-time action recognition with enhanced motion vector CNNs. In: CVPR (2016)
52. Zheng, L., Shen, L., Tian, L., Wang, S., Wang, J., Tian, Q.: Scalable person re-identification: a benchmark. In: ICCV (2015)

Hybrid Diffusion: Spectral-Temporal Graph Filtering for Manifold Ranking

Ahmet Iscen[1]([✉]), Yannis Avrithis[2], Giorgos Tolias[1], Teddy Furon[2], and Ondřej Chum[1]

[1] VRG, FEE, CTU in Prague, Prague, Czech Republic
ahmet.iscen@cmp.felk.cvut.cz
[2] Univ Rennes, Inria, CNRS, IRISA, Rennes, France

Abstract. State of the art image retrieval performance is achieved with CNN features and manifold ranking using a k-NN similarity graph that is pre-computed off-line. The two most successful existing approaches are *temporal filtering*, where manifold ranking amounts to solving a sparse linear system online, and *spectral filtering*, where eigen-decomposition of the adjacency matrix is performed off-line and then manifold ranking amounts to dot-product search online. The former suffers from expensive queries and the latter from significant space overhead. Here we introduce a novel, theoretically well-founded *hybrid filtering* approach allowing full control of the space-time trade-off between these two extremes. Experimentally, we verify that our hybrid method delivers results on par with the state of the art, with lower memory demands compared to spectral filtering approaches and faster compared to temporal filtering.

1 Introduction

Most image retrieval methods obtain their initial ranking of the database images by computing similarity between the query descriptor and descriptors of the database images. Descriptors based on local features [16,22] have been largely replaced by more efficient CNN-based image descriptors [9,20]. Regardless of the initial ranking, the retrieval performance is commonly boosted by considering the manifold structure of the database descriptors, rather than just independent distances of query to database images. Examples are query expansion [1,5] and diffusion [8,11,12]. *Query expansion* uses the results of initial ranking to issue a novel, enriched, query [5] on-line only. *Diffusion* on the other hand, is based on the k-NN graph of the dataset that is constructed off-line, so that, assuming novel queries are part of the dataset, their results are essentially pre-computed. Diffusion can then be seen as infinite-order query expansion [12].

The significance of the performance boost achieved by diffusion has been recently demonstrated at the "Large-Scale Landmark Recognition"[1] challenge in conjunction with CVPR 2018. The vast majority of top-ranked teams have used query expansion or diffusion as the last step of their method.

---

[1] https://landmarkscvprw18.github.io/.

© Springer Nature Switzerland AG 2019
C. V. Jawahar et al. (Eds.): ACCV 2018, LNCS 11362, pp. 301–316, 2019.
https://doi.org/10.1007/978-3-030-20890-5_20

Recently, efficient diffusion methods have been introduced to the image retrieval community. Iscen *et al.* [12] apply diffusion to obtain the final ranking, in particular by solving a large and sparse system of linear equations. Even though an efficient *conjugate gradient* (CG) [10] solver is used, query times on large-scale datasets are in a range of several seconds. A significant speed-up is achieved by *truncating* the system of linear equations. Such an approximation, however, brings a slight degradation in the retrieval performance. Their method can be interpreted as graph filtering in the *temporal* domain.

In the recent work of Iscen *et al.* [11], more computation is shifted to the off-line phase to accelerate the query. The solution of the linear system is estimated by low-rank approximation of the k-NN graph Laplacian. Since the eigenvectors of the Laplacian represent a Fourier basis of the graph, this is interpreted as graph filtering in the *spectral* domain. The price to pay is increased space complexity to store the embeddings of the database descriptors. For comparable performance, a 5k–10k dimensional vector is needed per image.

In this paper, we introduce a *hybrid* method that combines spectral filtering [11] and temporal filtering [12]. This hybrid method offers a trade-off between speed (*i.e.*, the number of iterations of CG) and the additional memory required (*i.e.*, the dimensionality of the embedding). The two approaches [11,12] are extreme cases of our hybrid method. We show that the proposed method pairs or outperforms the previous methods while either requiring less memory or being significantly faster – only three to five iterations of CG are necessary for embeddings of 100 to 500 dimensions.

While both temporal and spectral filtering approaches were known in other scientific fields before being successfully applied to image retrieval, to our knowledge the proposed method is novel and can be applied to other domains.

The rest of the paper is organized as follows. Related work is reviewed in Sect. 2. Previous work on temporal and spectral filtering is detailed in Sects. 3.1 and 3.2 respectively, since the paper builds on this work. The proposed method is described in Sect. 4 and its behavior is analyzed in Sect. 5. Experimental results are provided in Sect. 6. Conclusions are drawn in Sect. 7.

2   Related Work

Query expansion (QE) has been a standard way to improve recall of image retrieval since the work of Chum *et al.* [5]. A variety of approaches exploit local feature matching and perform various types of verification. Such matching ranges from selective kernel matching [23] to geometric consensus [4,5,14] with RANSAC-like techniques. The verified images are then used to refine the global or local image representation of a novel query.

Another family of QE methods are more generic and simply assume a global image descriptor [1,7,8,13,18,21,27]. A simple and popular one is average-QE [5], recently extended to α-QE [20]. At some small extra cost, recall is significantly boosted. This additional cost is restricted to the on-line query phase. This is in contrast to another family of approaches that considers an off-line pre-processing of the database. Given the nearest neighbors list for database images,

QE is performed by adapting the local similarity measure [13], using reciprocity constraints [7,18] or graph-based similarity propagation [8,12,27]. The graph-based approaches, also known as diffusion, are shown to achieve great performance [12] and to be a good way for feature fusion [27]. Such on-line re-ranking is typically orders of magnitude more costly than simple average-QE.

The advent of CNN-based features, especially global image descriptors, made QE even more attractive. Average-QE or α-QE are easily applicable and very effective with a variety of CNN-based descriptors [9,15,20,24]. State-of-the-art performance is achieved with diffusion on global or regional descriptors [12]. The latter is possible due to the small number of regions that are adequate to represent small objects, in contrast to thousands in the case of local features.

Diffusion based on tensor products can be attractive in terms of performance [2,3]. However, in this work, we focus on the page-rank like diffusion [12,28] due to its reasonable query times. An iterative on-line solution was commonly preferred [8] until the work of Iscen et al. [12], who solve a linear system to speed up the process. Additional off-line pre-processing and the construction and storage of additional embeddings reduce diffusion to inner product search in the spectral ranking of Iscen et al. [11]. This work lies exactly in between these two worlds and offers a trade-off exchanging memory for speed and vice versa.

Fast random walk with restart [25] is very relevant in the sense that it follows the same diffusion model as [12,28] and is a hybrid method like ours. It first disconnects the graph into distinct components through clustering and then obtains a low-rank spectral approximation of the residual error. Apart from the additional complexity, parameters etc. of the off-line clustering process and the storage of both eigenvectors and a large inverse matrix, its online phase is also complex, involving the Woodbury matrix identity and several dense matrix-vector multiplications. Compared to that, we first obtain a very low-rank spectral approximation of the original graph, and then solve a sparse linear system of the residual error. Thanks to orthogonality properties, the online phase is nearly as simple as the original one and significantly faster.

3   Problem Formulation and Background

The methods we consider are based on a nearest neighbor graph of a dataset of n items, represented by $n \times n$ adjacency matrix W. The graph is undirected and weighted according to similarity: W is sparse, symmetric, nonnegative and zero-diagonal. We symmetrically normalize W as $\mathcal{W} := D^{-1/2}WD^{-1/2}$, where $D := \mathrm{diag}(W\mathbf{1})$ is the diagonal degree matrix, containing the row-wise sum of W on its diagonal. The eigenvalues of $\mathcal{W}$ lie in $[-1, 1]$ [6].

At query time, we are given a sparse $n \times 1$ observation vector $\mathbf{y}$, which is constructed by searching for the nearest neighbors of a query item in the dataset and setting its nonzero entries to the corresponding similarities. The problem is to obtain an $n \times 1$ ranking vector $\mathbf{x}$ such that retrieved items of the dataset are ranked by decreasing order of the elements of $\mathbf{x}$. Vector $\mathbf{x}$ should be close to $\mathbf{y}$

but at the same time similar items are encouraged to have similar ranks in $\mathbf{x}$, essentially by exploring the graph to retrieve more items.

3.1 Temporal Filtering

Given a parameter $\alpha \in [0, 1)$, define the $n \times n$ *regularized Laplacian* function by

$$\mathcal{L}_\alpha(A) := (I_n - \alpha A)/(1 - \alpha) \tag{1}$$

for $n \times n$ real symmetric matrix A, where I_n is the $n \times n$ identity matrix. Iscen *et al.* [12] then define $\mathbf{x}$ as the unique solution of the linear system

$$\mathcal{L}_\alpha(\mathcal{W})\mathbf{x} = \mathbf{y}, \tag{2}$$

which they obtain approximately in practice by a few iterations of the *conjugate gradient* (CG) method, since $\mathcal{L}_\alpha(\mathcal{W})$ is positive-definite. At large scale, they truncate $\mathcal{W}$ by keeping only the rows and columns corresponding to a fixed number of neighbors of the query, and re-normalize. Then, (2) only performs re-ranking within this neighbor set.

We call this method *temporal*[2] *filtering* because if $\mathbf{x}, \mathbf{y}$ are seen as signals, then $\mathbf{x}$ is the result of applying a linear graph filter on $\mathbf{y}$, and CG iteratively applies a set of recurrence relations that determine the filter. While $\mathcal{W}$ is computed and stored off-line, (2) is solved online (at query time), and this is expensive.

3.2 Spectral Filtering

Linear system (2) can be written as $\mathbf{x} = h_\alpha(\mathcal{W})\mathbf{y}$, where the *transfer function* h_α is defined by

$$h_\alpha(A) := \mathcal{L}_\alpha(A)^{-1} = (1 - \alpha)(I_n - \alpha A)^{-1} \tag{3}$$

for $n \times n$ real symmetric matrix A. Given the eigenvalue decomposition $\mathcal{W} = U\Lambda U^\top$ of the symmetric matrix $\mathcal{W}$, Iscen *et al.* [11] observe that $h_\alpha(\mathcal{W}) = Uh_\alpha(\Lambda)U^\top$, so that (2) can be written as

$$\mathbf{x} = Uh_\alpha(\Lambda)U^\top \mathbf{y}, \tag{4}$$

which they approximate by keeping only the largest r eigenvalues and the corresponding eigenvectors of $\mathcal{W}$. This defines a low-rank approximation $h_\alpha(\mathcal{W}) \approx U_1 h_\alpha(\Lambda_1)U_1^\top$ instead. This method is referred to as *fast spectral ranking* (FSR) in [11]. Crucially, Λ is a diagonal matrix, hence h_α applies element-wise, as a scalar function $h_\alpha(x) := (1 - \alpha)/(1 - \alpha x)$ for $x \in [-1, 1]$.

At the expense of off-line computing and storing the $n \times r$ matrix U_1 and the r eigenvalues in Λ_1, filtering is now computed as a sequence of low-rank

---

[2] "Temporal" stems from conventional signal processing where signals are functions of "time"; while "spectral" is standardized also in graph signal processing.

matrix-vector multiplications, and the query is accelerated by orders of magnitude compared to [12]. However, the space overhead is significant. To deal with approximation errors when r is small, a heuristic is introduced that gradually falls back to the similarity in the original space for items that are poorly represented, referred to as FSRw [11].

We call this method *spectral filtering* because U represents the Fourier basis of the graph and the sequence of matrix-vector multiplications from right to left in the right-hand side of (4) represents the Fourier transform of $\mathbf{y}$ by $U^\top$, filtering in the frequency domain by $h_\alpha(\Lambda)$, and finally the inverse Fourier transform to obtain $\mathbf{x}$ in the time domain by U.

4   Hybrid Spectral-Temporal Filtering

Temporal filtering (2) is performed once for every new query represented by $\mathbf{y}$, but $\mathcal{W}$ represents the dataset and is fixed. Could CG be accelerated if we had some very limited additional information on $\mathcal{W}$?

On the other extreme, spectral filtering (4) needs a large number of eigenvectors and eigenvalues of $\mathcal{W}$ to provide a high quality approximation, but always leaves some error. Could we reduce this space requirement by allocating some additional query time to recover the approximation error?

The answer is positive to both questions and in fact these are the two extreme cases of *hybrid spectral-temporal filtering*, which we formulate next.

4.1   Derivation

We begin with the eigenvalue decomposition $\mathcal{W} = U \Lambda U^\top$, which we partition as $\Lambda = \operatorname{diag}(\Lambda_1, \Lambda_2)$ and $U = (U_1\ U_2)$. Matrices Λ_1 and Λ_2 are diagonal $r \times r$ and $(n-r) \times (n-r)$, respectively. Matrices U_1 and U_2 are $n \times r$ and $n \times (n-r)$, respectively, and have the following orthogonality properties, all due to the orthogonality of U itself:

$$U_1^\top U_1 = I_r, \quad U_2^\top U_2 = I_{n-r}, \quad U_1^\top U_2 = \mathbf{O}, \quad U_1 U_1^\top + U_2 U_2^\top = I_n. \tag{5}$$

Then, $\mathcal{W}$ is decomposed as

$$\mathcal{W} = U_1 \Lambda_1 U_1^\top + U_2 \Lambda_2 U_2^\top. \tag{6}$$

Similarly, $h_\alpha(\mathcal{W})$ is decomposed as

$$h_\alpha(\mathcal{W}) = U h_\alpha(\Lambda) U^\top \tag{7}$$

$$= U_1 h_\alpha(\Lambda_1) U_1^\top + U_2 h_\alpha(\Lambda_2) U_2^\top, \tag{8}$$

which is due to the fact that diagonal matrix $h_\alpha(\Lambda)$ is obtained element-wise, hence decomposed as $h_\alpha(\Lambda) = \operatorname{diag}(h_\alpha(\Lambda_1), h_\alpha(\Lambda_2))$. Here the first term is exactly the low-rank approximation that is used by spectral filtering, and the second is the approximation error

$$e_\alpha(\mathcal{W}) := U_2 h_\alpha(\Lambda_2) U_2^\top \tag{9}$$

$$= (1 - \alpha)\left(U_2(I_{n-r} - \alpha\Lambda_2)^{-1}U_2^\top + U_1 U_1^\top - U_1 U_1^\top\right) \tag{10}$$

$$= (1 - \alpha)\left(\left(U_2(I_{n-r} - \alpha\Lambda_2)U_2^\top + U_1 U_1^\top\right)^{-1} - U_1 U_1^\top\right) \tag{11}$$

$$= (1 - \alpha)\left(\left(I_n - \alpha U_2\Lambda_2 U_2^\top\right)^{-1} - U_1 U_1^\top\right) \tag{12}$$

$$= h_\alpha(U_2\Lambda_2 U_2^\top) - (1 - \alpha)U_1 U_1^\top. \tag{13}$$

We have used the definition (3) of h_α in (10) and (13). Equation (12) is due to the orthogonality properties (5). Equation (11) follows from the fact that for any invertible matrices A, B of conformable sizes,

$$(U_1 A U_1 + U_2 B U_2)^{-1} = U_1 A^{-1} U_1 + U_2 B^{-1} U_2, \tag{14}$$

which can be verified by direct multiplication, and is also due to orthogonality.

Now, combining (8), (13) and (6), we have proved the following.

Theorem 1. *Assuming the definition (3) of transfer function h_α and the eigenvalue decomposition (6) of the symmetrically normalized adjacency matrix $\mathcal{W}$, $h_\alpha(\mathcal{W})$ is decomposed as*

$$h_\alpha(\mathcal{W}) = U_1 g_\alpha(\Lambda_1) U_1^\top + h_\alpha(\mathcal{W} - U_1\Lambda_1 U_1^\top), \tag{15}$$

where

$$g_\alpha(A) := h_\alpha(A) - h_\alpha(\mathbf{O}) = (1 - \alpha)\left((I_n - \alpha A)^{-1} - I_n\right) \tag{16}$$

for $n \times n$ real symmetric matrix A. For $x \in [-1, 1]$ in particular, $g_\alpha(x) := h_\alpha(x) - h_\alpha(0) = (1 - \alpha)\alpha x/(1 - \alpha x)$.

Observe that Λ_2, U_2 do not appear in (15) and indeed it is only the largest r eigenvalues Λ_1 and corresponding eigenvectors U_1 of $\mathcal{W}$ that we need to compute. The above derivation is generalized from h_α to a much larger class of functions in Appendix A.

4.2 Algorithm

Why is decomposition (15) of $h_\alpha(\mathcal{W})$ important? Because given an observation vector $\mathbf{y}$ at query time, we can express the ranking vector $\mathbf{x}$ as

$$\mathbf{x} = \mathbf{x}^s + \mathbf{x}^t, \tag{17}$$

where the first, *spectral*, term $\mathbf{x}^s$ is obtained by spectral filtering

$$\mathbf{x}^s = U_1 g_\alpha(\Lambda_1) U_1^\top \mathbf{y}, \tag{18}$$

as in [11], where g_α applies element-wise, while the second, *temporal*, term $\mathbf{x}^t$ is obtained by temporal filtering, that is, solving the linear system

$$\mathcal{L}_\alpha(\mathcal{W} - U_1\Lambda_1 U_1^\top)\mathbf{x}^t = \mathbf{y}, \tag{19}$$

which we do by a few iterations of CG as in [12]. The latter is possible because $\mathcal{L}_\alpha(\mathcal{W} - U_1 \Lambda_1 U_1^\top)$ is still positive-definite, like $\mathcal{L}_\alpha(\mathcal{W})$. It's also possible without an explicit dense representation of $U_1 \Lambda_1 U_1^\top$ because CG, like all Krylov subspace methods, only needs *black-box* access to the matrix A of the linear system, that is, a mapping $\mathbf{z} \mapsto A\mathbf{z}$ for $\mathbf{z} \in \mathbb{R}^n$. For system (19) in particular, according to the definition (1) of $\mathcal{L}_\alpha$, we use the mapping

$$\mathbf{z} \mapsto \left(\mathbf{z} - \alpha \left(\mathcal{W}\mathbf{z} - U_1 \Lambda_1 U_1^\top \mathbf{z}\right)\right) / (1 - \alpha), \tag{20}$$

where product $\mathcal{W}\mathbf{z}$ is efficient because $\mathcal{W}$ is sparse as in [12], while $U_1 \Lambda_1 U_1^\top \mathbf{z}$ is efficient if computed right-to-left because U_1 is an $n \times r$ matrix with $r \ll n$ and Λ_1 is diagonal as in [11].

4.3 Discussion

What is there to gain from spectral-temporal decomposition (17) of $\mathbf{x}$?

First, since the temporal term (19) can recover the spectral approximation error, the rank r of U_1, Λ_1 in the spectral term (18) can be chosen as small as we like. In the extreme case $r = 0$, the spectral term vanishes and we recover temporal filtering [12]. This allows efficient computation of only a few eigenvectors/values, even with the Lanczos algorithm rather than the approximate method of [11]. Most importantly, it reduces significantly the space complexity, at the expense of query time. Like spectral filtering, it is possible to *sparsify* U_1 to compress the dataset embeddings and accelerate the queries online. In fact, we show in Sect. 6 that sparsification is much more efficient in our case.

Second, the matrix $\mathcal{W} - U_1 \Lambda_1 U_1^\top$ is effectively like $\mathcal{W}$ with the r largest eigenvalues removed. This improves significantly the condition number of matrix $\mathcal{L}_\alpha(\mathcal{W} - U_1 \Lambda_1 U_1^\top)$ in the temporal term (19) compared to $\mathcal{L}_\alpha(\mathcal{W})$ in the linear system (2) of temporal filtering [12], on which the convergence rate depends. In the extreme case $r = n$, the temporal term vanishes and we recover spectral filtering [11]. In turn, even with small r, this reduces significantly the number of iterations needed for a given accuracy, at the expense of computing and storing U_1, Λ_1 off-line as in [11]. The improvement is a function of α and the spectrum of $\mathcal{W}$, and is quantified in Sect. 5.

In summary, for a given desired accuracy, we can choose the rank r of the spectral term and a corresponding number of iterations of the temporal term, determining a trade-off between the space needed for the eigenvectors (and the off-line cost to obtain them) and the (online) query time. Such choice is not possible with either spectral or temporal filtering alone: at large scale, the former may need too much space and the latter may be too slow.

5 Analysis

How "easier" for CG is $\mathcal{W} - U_1 \Lambda_1 U_1^\top$ in (19) compared to $\mathcal{W}$ in (2)?

In solving a linear system $A\mathbf{x} = \mathbf{b}$ where A is an $n \times n$ symmetric positive-definite matrix, CG generates a unique sequence of iterates $\mathbf{x}_i$, $i = 0, 1, \dots$, such that the A-norm $\|\mathbf{e}_i\|_A$ of the error $\mathbf{e}_i := \mathbf{x}^* - \mathbf{x}_i$ is minimized over the Krylov subspace $\mathcal{K}_i := \langle \mathbf{b}, A\mathbf{b}, \dots, A^i\mathbf{b} \rangle$ at each iteration i, where $\mathbf{x}^* := A^{-1}\mathbf{b}$ is the exact solution and the A-norm is defined by $\|\mathbf{x}\|_A := \sqrt{\mathbf{x}^\top A \mathbf{x}}$ for $\mathbf{x} \in \mathbb{R}^n$.

A well-known result on the rate of convergence of CG that assumes minimal knowledge of the eigenvalues of A states that the A-norm of the error at iteration i, relative to the A-norm of the initial error $\mathbf{e}_0 := \mathbf{x}^*$, is upper-bounded by [26]

$$\frac{\|\mathbf{e}_i\|_A}{\|\mathbf{e}_0\|_A} \le \phi_i(A) := 2\left(\frac{\sqrt{\kappa(A)} - 1}{\sqrt{\kappa(A)} + 1}\right)^i, \tag{21}$$

where $\kappa(A) := \|A\| \, \|A^{-1}\| = \lambda_1(A)/\lambda_n(A)$ is the 2-norm *condition number* of A, and $\lambda_j(A)$ for $j = 1, \dots, n$ are the eigenvalues of A in descending order.

In our case, matrix $\mathcal{L}_\alpha(\mathcal{W})$ of linear system (2) has condition number

$$\kappa(\mathcal{L}_\alpha(\mathcal{W})) = \frac{1 - \alpha\lambda_n(\mathcal{W})}{1 - \alpha\lambda_1(\mathcal{W})} = \frac{1 - \alpha\lambda_n(\mathcal{W})}{1 - \alpha}. \tag{22}$$

The first equality holds because for each eigenvalue λ of $\mathcal{W}$ there is a corresponding eigenvalue $(1 - \alpha\lambda)/(1 - \alpha)$ of $\mathcal{L}_\alpha(\mathcal{W})$, which is a decreasing function. The second holds because $\lambda_1(\mathcal{W}) = 1$ [6].

Now, let $\mathcal{W}_r := \mathcal{W} - U_1 \Lambda_1 U_1^\top$ for $r = 0, 1, \dots, n - 1$, where Λ_1, U_1 represent the largest r eigenvalues and the corresponding eigenvectors of $\mathcal{W}$ respectively. Clearly, $\mathcal{W}_r$ has the same eigenvalues as $\mathcal{W}$ except for the largest r, which are replaced by zero. That is, $\lambda_1(\mathcal{W}_r) = \lambda_{r+1}(\mathcal{W})$ and $\lambda_n(\mathcal{W}_r) = \lambda_n(\mathcal{W})$. The latter is due to the fact that $\lambda_n(\mathcal{W}) \le -1/(n-1) \le 0$ [6], so the new zero eigenvalues do not affect the smallest one. Then,

$$\kappa(\mathcal{L}_\alpha(\mathcal{W}_r)) = \frac{1 - \alpha\lambda_n(\mathcal{W})}{1 - \alpha\lambda_{r+1}(\mathcal{W})} \le \kappa(\mathcal{L}_\alpha(\mathcal{W})). \tag{23}$$

This last expression generalizes (22). Indeed, $\mathcal{W} = \mathcal{W}_0$. Then, our hybrid spectral-temporal filtering involves CG on $\mathcal{L}_\alpha(\mathcal{W}_r)$ for $r \ge 0$, compared to the baseline temporal filtering for $r = 0$. The inequality in (23) is due to the fact that $|\lambda_j(\mathcal{W})| \le 1$ for $j = 1, \dots, n$ [6]. Removing the largest r eigenvalues of $\mathcal{W}$ clearly improves (decreases) the condition number of $\mathcal{L}_\alpha(\mathcal{W}_r)$ relative to $\mathcal{L}_\alpha(\mathcal{W})$. The improvement is dramatic given that α is close to 1 in practice. For $\alpha = 0.99$ and $\lambda_{r+1}(\mathcal{W}) = 0.7$ for instance, $\kappa(\mathcal{L}_\alpha(\mathcal{W}_r))/\kappa(\mathcal{L}_\alpha(\mathcal{W})) = 0.0326$.

More generally, given the eigenvalues $\lambda_{r+1}(\mathcal{W})$ and $\lambda_n(\mathcal{W})$, the improvement can be estimated by measuring the upper bound $\phi_i(\mathcal{L}_\alpha(\mathcal{W}_r))$ for different i and r. A concrete example is shown in Fig. 1, where we measure the eigenvalues of the adjacency matrix $\mathcal{W}$ of a real dataset, remove the largest r for $0 \le r \le 300$ and plot the upper bound $\phi_i(\mathcal{L}_\alpha(\mathcal{W}_r))$ of the relative error as a function of rank r and iteration i given by (21) and (23). Clearly, as more eigenvalues are removed, less CG iterations are needed to achieve the same relative error; the approximation error represented by the temporal term decreases and at the same time the linear system becomes easier to solve. Of course, iterations become more expensive as r increases; precise timings are given in Sect. 6.

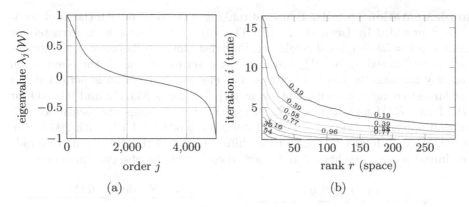

Fig. 1. (a) In descending order, eigenvalues of adjacency matrix $\mathcal{W}$ of Oxford5k dataset of $n = 5,063$ images with global GeM features by ResNet101 and $k = 50$ neighbors per point (see Sect. 6). Eigenvalues on the left of vertical red line at $j = 300$ are the largest 300 ones, candidate for removal. (b) Contour plot of upper bound $\phi_i(\mathcal{L}_\alpha(\mathcal{W}_r))$ of CG's relative error as a function of rank r and iteration i for $\alpha = 0.99$, illustrating the space(r)-time(i) trade-off for constant relative error. (Color figure online)

6 Experiments

In this section we evaluate our hybrid method on popular image retrieval benchmarks. We provide comparisons to baseline methods, analyze the trade-off between runtime complexity, memory footprint and search accuracy, and compare with the state of the art.

6.1 Experimental Setup

Datasets. We use the revisited retrieval benchmark [19] of the popular Oxford buildings [16] and Paris [17] datasets, referred to as $\mathcal{R}$Oxford and $\mathcal{R}$Paris, respectively. Unless otherwise specified, we evaluate using the *Medium* setup and always report mean Average Precision (mAP). Large-scale experiments are conducted on $\mathcal{R}$Oxford $+\mathcal{R}$1M and $\mathcal{R}$Paris $+\mathcal{R}$1M by adding the new 1M challenging distractor set [19].

Image Representation. We use GeM descriptors [20] to represent images. We extract GeM at 3 different image scales, aggregate the 3 descriptors, and perform whitening, exactly as in [20]. Finally, each image is represented by a single vector with $d = 2048$ dimensions, since ResNet-101 architecture is used.

Baseline Methods. We consider the two baseline methods described in Sect. 3, namely temporal and spectral filtering. *Temporal filtering* corresponds to solving a linear system with CG [12] and is evaluated for different numbers of CG iterations. It is used with truncation at large scale to speed up the search [12] and is denoted by *Temporal†*. *Spectral filtering* corresponds to FSR and its FSRw variant [11]. Both FSR variants are parametrized by the rank r of the approximation, which is equal to the dimensionality of the spectral embedding.

Implementation Details. Temporal ranking is performed with the implementation[3] provided by Iscen *et al.* [12]. The adjacency matrix is constructed by using top $k = 50$ reciprocal neighbors. Pairwise similarity between descriptors $\mathbf{v}$ and $\mathbf{z}$ is estimated by $(\mathbf{v}^\top \mathbf{z})_+^3$. Parameter α is set to 0.99, while the observation vector $\mathbf{y}$ includes the top 5 neighbors. The eigendecomposition is performed on the largest connected component, as in [11]. Its size is 933,412 and 934,809 for $\mathcal{R}$Oxford $+\mathcal{R}$1M and $\mathcal{R}$Paris $+\mathcal{R}$1M, respectively. Timings are measured with Matlab implementation on a 4-core Intel Xeon 2.60 GHz CPU with 200 GB of RAM. We only report timings for the diffusion part of the ranking and exclude the initial nearest neighbor search used to construct the observation vector.

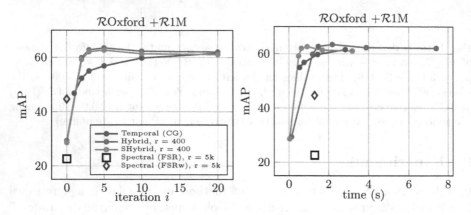

Fig. 2. mAP *vs.* CG iteration i and mAP *vs.* time for temporal, spectral, and hybrid filtering. Sparsified hybrid is used with sparsity 99%.

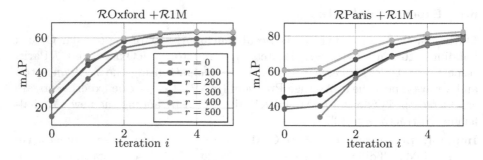

Fig. 3. mAP *vs.* CG iteration i for different rank r for our hybrid method, where $r = 0$ means temporal only.

6.2   Comparisons

Comparison with Baseline Methods. We first compare performance, query time and required memory for temporal, spectral, and hybrid ranking.

---
[3] https://github.com/ahmetius/diffusion-retrieval/.

With respect to the memory, all methods store the initial descriptors, *i.e.* one 2048-dimensional vector per image. Temporal ranking additionally stores the sparse regularized Laplacian. Spectral ranking stores for each vector an additional embedding of dimensionality equal to rank r, which is a parameter of the method. Our hybrid method stores both the Laplacian and the embedding, but with significantly lower rank r.

We evaluate on $\mathcal{R}$Oxford $+\mathcal{R}$1M and $\mathcal{R}$Paris $+\mathcal{R}$1M with global image descriptors, which is a challenging large scale problem, *i.e.* large adjacency matrix, where prior methods fail or have serious drawbacks. Results are shown in Fig. 2. Temporal ranking with CG is reaching saturation near 20 iterations as in [12]. Spectral ranking is evaluated for a decomposition of rank r whose computation and required memory are reasonable and feasible on a single machine. Finally, the proposed hybrid method is evaluated for rank $r = 400$, which is a good compromise of speed and memory, as shown below.

Spectral ranking variants (FSR, FSRw) are not performing well despite requiring about 250% additional memory compared to nearest neighbor search in the original space. Compared to hybrid, more than one order of magnitude higher rank r is required for problems of this scale. Temporal ranking achieves good performance but at much more iterations and higher query times. Our hybrid solution provides a very reasonable space-time trade-off.

Runtime and Memory Trade-Off. We report the trade-off between number of iterations and rank r, representing additional memory, in more detail in Fig. 3. It is shown that the number of iterations to achieve the top mAP decreases as the rank increases. We achieve the optimal trade-off at $r = 400$ where we only need 5 or less iterations. Note that, the rank not only affects the memory and the query time of the spectral part in a linear manner, but the query time of the temporal part too (20).

Sparsification of spectral embeddings is exploited in prior work [11]. We sparsify the embeddings of our hybrid method by setting the smallest values of U_1 to zero until a desired level of sparsity is reached. We denote this method by *SHybrid*. This sparse variant provides memory savings and an additional speedup due to the computations with sparse matrices. Figure 4 shows that performance loss remains small even for extreme sparsity *e.g.* 99%, while the results in Fig. 2 show that it offers a significant speedup in the global descriptor setup.

Performance-Memory-Speed Comparison with the baselines is shown in Table 1. Our hybrid approach enjoys query times lower than those of temporal with truncation or spectral with FSRw, while at the same time achieves higher performance and requires less memory than the spectral-only approach.

We summarize our achievement in terms of mAP, required memory, and query time in Fig. 5. Temporal ranking achieves high performance at the cost of high query time and its truncated counterpart saves query time but sacrifices performance. Spectral ranking is not effective at this scale, while our hybrid solution achieves high performance at low query times.

Comparison with the State of the Art. We present an extensive comparison with existing methods in the literature for global descriptors at small and large

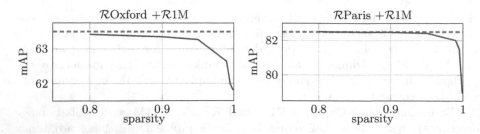

Fig. 4. mAP *vs.* level of sparsification on our hybrid method for $r = 400$. Dashed horizontal line indicates no sparsification.

Table 1. Performance, memory and query time comparison on $\mathcal{R}$Oxford $+\mathcal{R}$1M with GeM descriptors for temporal (20 iterations), truncated temporal (20 iterations, 75k images in shortlist), spectral ($r = 5k$), and hybrid ranking ($r = 400$, 5 iterations). Hybrid ranking is sparsified by setting the 99% smallest values to 0. Reported memory excludes the initial descriptors requiring 8.2 GB. U_1 is stored with double precision.

	Temporal [12]	Temporal† [12]	Spectral (FSRw) [11]	SHybrid
mAP	61.6	59.0	42.1	62.6
Time (s)	2.8	1.0	1.3	0.9
Memory (MB)	205	205	35,606	264

Table 2. mAP comparison with existing methods in the literature on small and large scale datasets, using Medium and Hard setup of the revisited benchmark.

	$\mathcal{R}$Oxford		$\mathcal{R}$Oxf $+\mathcal{R}$1M		$\mathcal{R}$Paris		$\mathcal{R}$Paris $+\mathcal{R}$1M	
	Medium	Hard	Medium	Hard	Medium	Hard	Medium	Hard
NN-search	64.7	38.5	45.2	19.9	77.2	56.3	52.3	24.7
α-QE [19]	67.2	40.8	49.0	24.2	80.7	61.8	58.0	31.0
Temporal [12]	69.9	40.4	61.6	33.2	88.9	78.5	85.0	71.6
Temporal† [12]	-	-	59.0	31.4	-	-	79.7	65.2
FSR [11]	70.4	42.0	22.6	5.8	88.6	77.9	66.6	40.2
FSRw [11]	70.7	42.2	42.1	18.8	88.7	78.0	77.4	59.7
SHybrid (ours)	70.5	40.3	62.6	34.4	88.7	78.1	82.0	66.8

scale (1M distractors). We choose $r = 400$ and 5 iterations for our hybrid method, 20 iterations for temporal ranking, $r = 2k$ and $r = 5k$ for spectral ranking at small and large scale, respectively. Temporal ranking is also performed with truncation on a shortlist size of $75k$ images at large scale. The comparison is presented in Table 2. Our hybrid approach performs the best or second best right after the temporal one, while providing much smaller query times at a small amount of additional required memory.

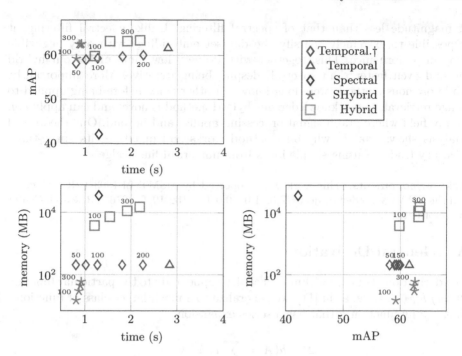

Fig. 5. Time (s) - memory (MB) - performance (mAP) for different methods. We show mAP *vs.* time, memory *vs.* time, and memory *vs.* mAP on $\mathcal{R}$Oxford $+\mathcal{R}$1M. Methods in the comparison: temporal for 20 iterations, truncated temporal for 20 iterations and shortlist of size 50k, 75k, 100k, 200k and 300k, spectral (FSRw) with $r = 5k$, hybrid with $r \in \{100, 200, 300, 400\}$ and 5 iterations, sparse hybrid with 99% sparsity, $r \in \{100, 200, 300, 400\}$ and 5 iterations. Text labels indicate the shortlist size (in thousands) for truncated temporal and rank for hybrid. Observe that the two plots on the left are aligned horizontally with respect to time, while the two at the bottom vertically with respect to memory.

7   Conclusions

In this work we have tested the two most successful manifold ranking methods of temporal filtering [12] and spectral filtering [11] on the very challenging new benchmark of Oxford and Paris datasets [19]. It is the first time that such methods are evaluated at the scale of one million images. *Spectral filtering*, with both its FSR and FSRw variants, fails at this scale, despite the significant space required for additional vector embeddings. It is possible that a higher rank would work, but it wouldn't be practical in terms of space. In terms of query time, *temporal filtering* is only practical with its truncated variant at this scale. It works pretty well in terms of performance, but the query time is still high.

Our new *hybrid filtering* method allows for the first time to strike a reasonable balance between the two extremes. Without truncation, it outperforms temporal filtering while being significantly faster, and its memory overhead is one order of magnitude less than that of spectral filtering. Unlike spectral filtering, it is possible to extremely sparsify the dataset embeddings with only negligible drop in performance. This, together with its very low rank, makes our hybrid method even faster than spectral, despite being iterative. More importantly, while previous methods were long known in other fields before being applied to image retrieval, to our knowledge our hybrid method is novel and can apply *e.g.* to any field where graph signal processing applies and beyond. Our theoretical analysis shows exactly why our method works and quantifies its space-time-accuracy trade-off using simple ideas from numerical linear algebra.

Acknowledgements. This work was supported by MSMT LL1303 ERC-CZ grant and the OP VVV funded project CZ.02.1.01/0.0/0.0/16_019/0000765 "Research Center for Informatics".

A   General Derivation

The derivation of our algorithm in Sect. 4.1 applies only to the particular function (filter) h_α (3). Here, as in [11], we generalize to a much larger class of functions, that is, any function h that has a series expansion

$$h(A) = \sum_{i=0}^{\infty} c_i A^i. \tag{24}$$

We begin with the same eigenvalue decomposition (6) of $\mathcal{W}$ and, assuming that $h(\mathcal{W})$ converges absolutely, its corresponding decomposition

$$h(\mathcal{W}) = U_1 h(\Lambda_1) U_1^\top + U_2 h(\Lambda_2) U_2^\top, \tag{25}$$

similar to (8), where U_1, U_2 have the same orthogonality properties (5).

Again, the first term is exactly the low-rank approximation that is used by spectral filtering, and the second is the approximation error

$$e_\alpha(\mathcal{W}) := U_2 h(\Lambda_2) U_2^\top \tag{26}$$

$$= \sum_{i=0}^{\infty} c_i U_2 \Lambda_2^i U_2^\top \tag{27}$$

$$= \sum_{i=0}^{\infty} c_i \left(U_2 \Lambda_2 U_2^\top\right)^i - c_0 U_1 U_1^\top \tag{28}$$

$$= h(U_2 \Lambda_2 U_2^\top) - h(0) U_1 U_1^\top. \tag{29}$$

Again, we have used the series expansion (24) of h in (27) and (29). Now, Eq. (28) is due to the fact that

$$(U_2 \Lambda_2 U_2^\top)^i = U_2 \Lambda_2^i U_2^\top \tag{30}$$

for $i \geq 1$, as can be verified by induction, while for $i = 0$,

$$U_2 \Lambda_2^0 U_2^\top = U_2 U_2^\top = I_n - U_1 U_1^\top = (U_2 \Lambda_2 U_2^\top)^0 - U_1 U_1^\top. \tag{31}$$

In both (30) and (31) we have used the orthogonality properties (5).

Finally, combining (25), (29) and (6), we have proved the following.

Theorem 2. *Assuming the series expansion (24) of transfer function h and the eigenvalue decomposition (6) of the symmetrically normalized adjacency matrix $\mathcal{W}$, and given that $h(\mathcal{W})$ converges absolutely, it is decomposed as*

$$h(\mathcal{W}) = U_1 g(\Lambda_1) U_1^\top + h(\mathcal{W} - U_1 \Lambda_1 U_1^\top), \tag{32}$$

where

$$g(A) := h(A) - h(\mathbf{O}) \tag{33}$$

for $n \times n$ real symmetric matrix A. For $h = h_\alpha$ and for $x \in [-1, 1]$ in particular, $g_\alpha(x) := h_\alpha(x) - h_\alpha(0) = (1 - \alpha)\alpha x / (1 - \alpha x)$.

This general derivation explains where the general definition of function g (33) is coming from in (16) corresponding to our treatment of h_α in Sect. 4.1.

References

1. Arandjelovic, R., Zisserman, A.: Three things everyone should know to improve object retrieval. In: CVPR, June 2012
2. Bai, S., Bai, X., Tian, Q., Latecki, L.J.: Regularized diffusion process on bidirectional context for object retrieval. IEEE Trans. PAMI (2018)
3. Bai, S., Zhou, Z., Wang, J., Bai, X., Jan Latecki, L., Tian, Q.: Ensemble diffusion for retrieval. In: ICCV (2017)
4. Chum, O., Mikulik, A., Perdoch, M., Matas, J.: Total recall II: query expansion revisited. In: CVPR, June 2011
5. Chum, O., Philbin, J., Sivic, J., Isard, M., Zisserman, A.: Total recall: automatic query expansion with a generative feature model for object retrieval. In: ICCV, October 2007
6. Chung, F.R.: Spectral Graph Theory, vol. 92. American Mathematical Society (1997)
7. Delvinioti, A., Jégou, H., Amsaleg, L., Houle, M.: Image retrieval with reciprocal and shared nearest neighbors. In: VISAPP, January 2014
8. Donoser, M., Bischof, H.: Diffusion processes for retrieval revisited. In: CVPR (2013)
9. Gordo, A., Almazan, J., Revaud, J., Larlus, D.: End-to-end learning of deep visual representations for image retrieval. IJCV **124**(2) (2017)
10. Hackbusch, W.: Iterative Solution of Large Sparse Systems of Equations. Springer, New York (1994). https://doi.org/10.1007/978-1-4612-4288-8
11. Iscen, A., Avrithis, Y., Tolias, G., Furon, T., Chum, O.: Fast spectral ranking for similarity search. In: CVPR (2018)
12. Iscen, A., Tolias, G., Avrithis, Y., Furon, T., Chum, O.: Efficient diffusion on region manifolds: recovering small objects with compact CNN representations. In: CVPR (2017)
13. Jégou, H., Harzallah, H., Schmid, C.: A contextual dissimilarity measure for accurate and efficient image search. In: CVPR, June 2007
14. Joly, A., Buisson, O.: Logo retrieval with a contrario visual query expansion. In: ACM Multimedia, October 2009

15. Kalantidis, Y., Mellina, C., Osindero, S.: Cross-dimensional weighting for aggregated deep convolutional features. arXiv preprint arXiv:1512.04065 (2015)
16. Philbin, J., Chum, O., Isard, M., Sivic, J., Zisserman, A.: Object retrieval with large vocabularies and fast spatial matching. In: CVPR, June 2007
17. Philbin, J., Chum, O., Isard, M., Sivic, J., Zisserman, A.: Lost in quantization: improving particular object retrieval in large scale image databases. In: CVPR, June 2008
18. Qin, D., Gammeter, S., Bossard, L., Quack, T., Van Gool, L.: Hello neighbor: accurate object retrieval with k-reciprocal nearest neighbors. In: CVPR (2011)
19. Radenović, F., Iscen, A., Tolias, G., Avrithis, Y., Chum, O.: Revisiting Oxford and Paris: large-scale image retrieval benchmarking. In: CVPR (2018)
20. Radenović, F., Tolias, G., Chum, O.: Fine-tuning CNN image retrieval with no human annotation. IEEE Trans. PAMI (2018)
21. Shen, X., Lin, Z., Brandt, J., Wu, Y.: Spatially-constrained similarity measure for large-scale object retrieval. IEEE Trans. PAMI **36**(6), 1229–1241 (2014)
22. Sivic, J., Zisserman, A.: Video Google: a text retrieval approach to object matching in videos. In: ICCV (2003)
23. Tolias, G., Jégou, H.: Visual query expansion with or without geometry: refining local descriptors by feature aggregation. Pattern Recogn. **47**(10), 3466–3476 (2014)
24. Tolias, G., Sicre, R., Jégou, H.: Particular object retrieval with integral max-pooling of CNN activations. ICLR (2016)
25. Tong, H., Faloutsos, C., Pan, J.Y.: Fast random walk with restart and its applications. In: Proceedings of the IEEE International Conference on Data Mining, pp. 613–622 (2006)
26. Trefethen, L.N., Bau III, D.: Numerical Linear Algebra. SIAM (1997)
27. Zhang, S., Yang, M., Cour, T., Yu, K., Metaxas, D.N.: Query specific fusion for image retrieval. In: Fitzgibbon, A., Lazebnik, S., Perona, P., Sato, Y., Schmid, C. (eds.) ECCV 2012. LNCS, pp. 660–673. Springer, Heidelberg (2012). https://doi.org/10.1007/978-3-642-33709-3_47
28. Zhou, D., Weston, J., Gretton, A., Bousquet, O., Schölkopf, B.: Ranking on data manifolds. In: NIPS (2003)

Learning Free-Form Deformations for 3D Object Reconstruction

Dominic Jack[✉], Jhony K. Pontes, Sridha Sridharan, Clinton Fookes,
Sareh Shirazi, Frederic Maire, and Anders Eriksson

Queensland University of Technology, Brisbane, QLD 4000, Australia
{d1.jack,s.sridharan,c.fookes,s.shirazi,
f.maire,anders.ariksson}@qut.edu.au, j.kaesemodel@hdr.qut.edu.au

Abstract. Representing 3D shape in deep learning frameworks in an accurate, efficient and compact manner still remains an open challenge. Most existing work addresses this issue by employing voxel-based representations. While these approaches benefit greatly from advances in computer vision by generalizing 2D convolutions to the 3D setting, they also have several considerable drawbacks. The computational complexity of voxel-encodings grows cubically with the resolution thus limiting such representations to low-resolution 3D reconstruction. In an attempt to solve this problem, point cloud representations have been proposed. Although point clouds are more efficient than voxel representations as they only cover surfaces rather than volumes, they do not encode detailed geometric information about relationships between points. In this paper we propose a method to learn free-form deformations (FFD) for the task of 3D reconstruction from a single image. By learning to deform points sampled from a high-quality mesh, our trained model can be used to produce arbitrarily dense point clouds or meshes with fine-grained geometry. We evaluate our proposed framework on synthetic data and achieve state-of-the-art results on surface and volumetric metrics. We make our implementation publicly available (Tensorflow implementation available at github.com/jackd/template_ffd.).

1 Introduction

Imagine one wants to interact with objects from the real world, say a chair, but in an augmented reality (AR) environment. The 3D reconstruction from the seen images should appear as realistic as possible so that one may not even perceive the chair as being virtual. The future of highly immersive AR and virtual reality (VR) applications highly depends on the representation and reconstruction of high-quality 3D models. This is obviously challenging and the computer vision and graphics communities have been working hard on such problems [1–3].

This research was supported by the Australian Research Council through the grant ARC FT170100072. Computational resources used in this work were provided by the HPC and Research Support Group, QUT.

© Springer Nature Switzerland AG 2019
C. V. Jawahar et al. (Eds.): ACCV 2018, LNCS 11362, pp. 317–333, 2019.
https://doi.org/10.1007/978-3-030-20890-5_21

The impact that recent developments in deep learning approaches have had on computer vision has been immense. In the 2D domain, convolutional neural networks (CNNs) have achieved state-of-the-art results in a wide range of applications [4–6]. Motivated by this, researchers have been applying the same techniques to represent and reconstruct 3D data. Most of them rely on volumetric shape representation so one can perform 3D convolutions on the structured voxel grid [7–12]. A drawback is that convolutions on the 3D space are computationally expensive and grow cubically with resolution, thus typically limiting the 3D reconstruction to exceedingly coarse representations.

A recent shape representation that has been investigated to make the learning more efficient is point clouds [13–16]. However, such representations still lack the ability of describing finely detailed structures. Applying surfaces, texture and lighting to unstructured point clouds are also challenging, specially in the case of noisy, incomplete and sparse data.

The most extensively used shape representation in computer graphics is that of polygon meshes, in particular using triangular faces. This parameterisation has largely been unexplored in the machine learning domain for the 3D reconstruction task. This is in part a consequence of most machine learning algorithms requiring regular representation of input and output data such as voxels and point clouds. Meshes are highly unstructured and their topological structure usually differs from one to another which makes their 3D reconstruction from 2D images using neural networks challenging.

In this paper, we tackle this problem by exploring the well-known free-form deformation (FFD) technique [17] widely used for 3D mesh modelling. FFD allows us to deform any 3D mesh by repositioning a few predefined control points while keeping its topological aspects. We propose an approach to perform 3D mesh reconstruction from single images by simultaneously learning to select and deform template meshes. Our method uses a lightweight CNN to infer the low-dimensional FFD parameters for multiple templates and it learns to apply large deformations to topologically different templates to produce inferred meshes with similar surfaces. We extensively demonstrate relatively small CNNs can learn these deformations well, and achieve compelling mesh reconstructions. An overview of the proposed method is illustrated in Fig. 1.

Our Contributions Are Summarized as Follows:

- We propose a novel learning framework to reconstruct continuous 3D meshes from single images;
- we quantitatively and qualitatively demonstrate that relatively small neural networks require minimal adaptation to learn to simultaneously select appropriate models from a number of templates and deform these templates to perform 3D mesh reconstruction; and
- we extensively investigate simple changes to training and loss functions to promote variation in template selection.

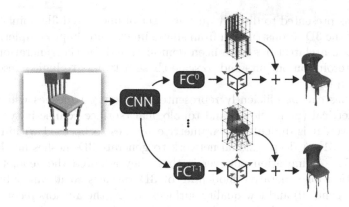

Fig. 1. Given a single image, our method uses a CNN to infer FFD parameters ΔP (red arrows) for multiple templates T (middle meshes). The ΔP parameters are then used to deform the template vertices to infer a 3D mesh for each template (right meshes). Trained only with surface-sampled point-clouds, the model learns to apply large deformations to topologically different templates to produce inferred meshes with similar surfaces. Likelihood weightings γ are also inferred by the network but not shown. FC stands for fully connected layer. (Color figure online)

2 Related Work

Interest in analysing 3D models has increased tremendously in recent years. This development has been driven in part by a rapid growth of the amount of readily available 3D data, the astounding progress made in the field of machine learning as well as a substantial rise in the number of potential application areas, *i.e.* Virtual and Augmented Reality.

To address 3D vision problems with deep learning techniques a good shape representation should be found. Volumetric representation has been the most widely used for 3D learning [7–12, 18–22]. Convolutions, pooling, and other techniques that have been successfully applied to the 2D domain can be naturally applied to the 3D case for the learning process. Volumetric autoencoders [21,23] and generative adversarial networks (GANs) have been introduced [24–26] to learn probabilistic latent space of 3D objects for object completion, classification and 3D reconstruction. Volumetric representation however grows cubically in terms of memory and computational complexity as the voxel grid resolution increases, thus limiting it to low-quality 3D reconstructions.

To overcome these limitations, octree-based neural networks have been presented [27–30], where the volumetric grid is split recursively by dividing it into octants. Octrees reduce the computational complexity of the 3D convolution since the computations are focused only on regions where most of the object's geometry information is located. They allow for higher resolution 3D reconstructions and a more efficient training, however, the outputs still lack of fine-scaled geometry. A more efficient 3D representation using point clouds was recently proposed to address some of these drawbacks [13–16]. In [13] a generative neural network was presented to directly output a set of unordered 3D points that can be used for the 3D reconstruction from single image and shape completion tasks. By now, such architectures have been demonstrated for the generation of relatively low-resolution outputs and to scale these networks to higher resolution is yet to be explored.

3D shapes can be efficiently represented by polygon meshes which encode both geometrical (point cloud) and topological (surface connectivity) information. However, it is difficult to parametrize meshes to be used within learning frameworks [31]. A deep residual network to generate 3D meshes has been proposed in [32]. A limitation however is that they adopted the geometry image representation for generative modelling of 3D surfaces so it can only manage simple (*i.e.* genus-0) and low-quality surfaces. In [2], the authors reconstruct 3D mesh objects from single images by jointly analysing a collection of images of different objects along with a smaller collection of existing 3D models. While the method yields impressive results, it suffers from scalability issues and is sensitive to semantic segmentation of the image and dense correspondences.

FFD has also been explored for 3D mesh representation where one can intrinsically represent an object by a set of polynomial basis functions and a small number of coefficients known as control points used for cage-like deformation. A 3D mesh editing tool proposed in [33] uses a volumetric generative network to infer per-voxel deformation flows using FFD. Their method takes a volumetric representation of a 3D mesh as input and a high-level deformation intention label (*e.g.* sporty car, fighter jet, etc.) to learn the FFD displacements to be applied to the original mesh. In [34,35] a method for 3D mesh reconstruction from a single image was proposed based on a low-dimensional parametrization using FFD and sparse linear combinations given the image silhouette and class-specific landmarks. Recently, the DeformNet was proposed in [36] where they employed FFD as a differentiable layer in their 3D reconstruction framework. The method builds upon two networks, one 2D CNN for 3D shape retrieval and one 3D CNN to infer FFD parameters to deform the 3D point cloud of the shape retrieved. In contrast, our proposed method reconstructs 3D *meshes* using a single lightweight CNN with *no* 3D convolutions involved to infer a 3D mesh template and its deformation flow in one shot.

3   Problem Statement

We focus on the problem of inferring a 3D mesh from a single image. We represent a 3D mesh c by a list of vertex coordinates $\mathbf{V} \in \mathbb{R}^{n_v \times 3}$ and a set of triangular faces $\mathbf{F} \in \mathbb{Z}^{n_f \times 3}$, $0 \leq F_{ij} < n_v$ defined such that $\mathbf{f}_i = [p, q, r]$ indicates there is a face connecting the vertices $\mathbf{v}_p$, $\mathbf{v}_q$ and $\mathbf{v}_r$, *i.e.* $c = \{\mathbf{V}, \mathbf{F}\}$.

Given a query image, the task is to infer a 3D mesh $\tilde{c}$ which is close by some measure to the actual mesh c of the object in the image. We employ the FFD technique to deform the 3D mesh to best fit the image.

3.1   Comparing 3D Meshes

There are a number of metrics which can be used to compare 3D meshes. We consider three: Chamfer distance and earth mover distance between point clouds, and the intersection-over-union (IoU) of their voxelized representations.

Chamfer Distance. The Chamfer distance λ_c between two point clouds A and B is defined as

$$\lambda_c(A, B) = \sum_{a \in A} \min_{b \in B} \|a - b\|^2 + \sum_{b \in B} \min_{a \in A} \|b - a\|^2. \tag{1}$$

Earth Mover Distance. The earth mover [37] distance λ_{em} between two point clouds of the same size is the sum of distances between a point in one cloud and a corresponding partner in the other minimized over all possible 1-to-1 correspondences. More formally,

$$\lambda_{em} = \min_{\phi : A \to B} \sum_{a \in A} \|a - \phi(a)\|, \tag{2}$$

where ϕ is a bijective mapping.

Point cloud metrics evaluated on vertices of 3D meshes can give misleading results, since large planar regions will have very few vertices, and hence contribute little. Instead, we evaluate these metrics using a point cloud sampled uniformly from the surface of each 3D mesh.

Intersection Over Union. As the name suggests, the intersection-over-union of volumetric representations IoU is defined by the ratio of the volumes of the intersection over their union,

$$\text{IoU}(A, B) = \frac{|A \cap B|}{|A \cup B|}. \tag{3}$$

3.2   Deforming 3D Meshes

We deform a 3D object by freely manipulating some control points using the FFD technique. FFD creates a grid of control points and its axes are defined by the orthogonal vectors $\mathbf{s}, \mathbf{t}$ and $\mathbf{u}$ [17]. The control points are then defined by l, m and n which divides the grid in $l+1, m+1, n+1$ planes in the $\mathbf{s}, \mathbf{t}, \mathbf{u}$ directions, respectively. A local coordinate for each object's vertex is then imposed.

In this work, we deform an object through a trivariate Bernstein tensor – a weighted sum of the control points – as in Sederberg and Parry [17]. The deformed position of any arbitrary point is given by

$$\mathbf{s}(s, t, u) = \sum_{i=0}^{l} \sum_{j=0}^{m} \sum_{k=0}^{n} B_{il}(s) B_{jm}(t) B_{kn}(u) \mathbf{p}_{ijk}, \tag{4}$$

where $\mathbf{s}$ contains the coordinates of the displaced point, $B._N(x)$ is the Bernstein polynomial of degree N which sets the influence of each control point on every vertex, and $\mathbf{p}_{ijk}$ is the i, j, k-th control point. This can be expressed in matrix form as

$$\mathbf{S} = \mathbf{BP}, \tag{5}$$

where the rows of $\mathbf{P} \in \mathbb{R}^{M \times 3}$ and $\mathbf{S} \in \mathbb{R}^{N \times 3}$ are coordinates of the M control points and N displaced points respectively and $\mathbf{B} \in \mathbb{R}^{N \times M}$ is the deformation matrix.

4   Learning Free-Form Deformations

Our method involves applying deformations encoded with a parameter $\Delta \mathbf{P}^{(t)}$ to T different template models $c^{(t)}$ with $0 \leq t < T$. We begin by calculating the Bernstein decomposition of the face-sample point cloud of each template model, $\mathbf{S}^{(t)} = \mathbf{B}^{(t)} \mathbf{P}^{(t)}$. We use a CNN to map a rendered image to a set of shared high level image features. These features are then mapped to a grid deformation $\Delta \tilde{\mathbf{P}}^{(qt)}$ for each template and example independently to produce a perturbed set of surface points for each template/example,

$$\tilde{\mathbf{S}}^{(qt)} = \mathbf{B}^{(t)} \left(\mathbf{P}^{(t)} + \Delta \tilde{\mathbf{P}}^{(qt)} \right). \tag{6}$$

We also infer a weighting value $\gamma^{(qt)}$ for each template from the shared image features, and train the network using a weighted Chamfer loss,

$$\lambda_0 = \sum_{q, t} f \left(\gamma^{(qt)} \right) \lambda_c \left(s^{(q)}, \tilde{s}^{(qt)} \right), \tag{7}$$

where f is some positive monotonically increasing scalar function.

In this way, the network learns to assign high weights to templates which it has learned to deform well based on the input image, while the sub-networks for each template are not highly penalized for examples which are better suited to other templates. We enforce a minimum weight by using

$$\gamma^{(qt)} = (1 - \epsilon_\gamma) \gamma_0^{(qt)} + \frac{1}{T} \epsilon_\gamma, \tag{8}$$

where $\gamma_0^{(qt)}$ is the result of a softmax function where summation is over the template index t and ϵ_γ is a small constant threshold, $0 < \epsilon_\gamma \ll 1$.

For inference and evaluation, we use the template with the highest weight,

$$t^* = \arg \max_t \gamma^{(qt)}, \tag{9}$$

$$\tilde{c}^{(q)} = \{\tilde{\mathbf{S}}^{(qt^*)}, \mathbf{F}^{(t^*)}\}. \tag{10}$$

Previous work using learned FFD [36] infers deformations based on learned embeddings of voxelized templates. By learning distinct sub-networks for each template we forgo the need to learn this embedding explicitly, and our sub-networks are able to attain a much more intimate knowledge of their associated template without losing information via voxelization.

Key advantages of the architecture are as follows:

- no 3D convolutions are involved, meaning the network scales well with increased resolution;
- no discretization occurs, allowing higher precision than voxel-based methods;
- the output $\Delta\tilde{\mathbf{P}}$ can be used to generate an arbitrarily dense point cloud – not necessarily the same density as that used during training; and
- a mesh can be inferred by applying the deformation to the Bernstein decomposition of the *vertices* while maintaining the same face connections.

Drawbacks include,

- the network size scales linearly with the number of templates considered; and
- there is at this time no mechanism to explicitly encourage topological or semantic similarity.

4.1   Diversity in Model Selection

Preliminary experiments showed training using standard optimizers with an identity weighting function f resulted in a small number of templates being selected frequently. This is at least partially due to a positive feedback loop caused by the interaction between the weighting sub-network and the deformation sub-networks. If a particular template deformation sub-network performs particularly well initially, the weighting sub-network learns to assign increased weight to this template. This in turn affects the gradients which flow through the deformation sub-network, resulting in faster learning, improved performance and hence higher weight in subsequent batches. We experimented with a number of network modifications to reduce this.

Non-linear Weighting. One problem with the identity weighting scheme $(f(\gamma) = \gamma)$ is that there is no penalty for over-confidence. A well-trained network with a slight preference for one template over all the rest will be inclined to put all weight into that template. By using an f with positive curvature, we discourage the network from making overly confident inferences. We experimented with an entropy-inspired weighting $f(\gamma) = -\log(1 - \gamma)$.

Explicit Entropy Penalty. Another approach is to penalize the lack of diversity directly by introducing an explicit entropy loss term,

$$\lambda_e = \sum_t \bar{\gamma}^{(t)} \log\left(\bar{\gamma}^{(t)}\right), \tag{11}$$

where $\bar{\gamma}^{(t)}$ is the weight value of template t averaged over the batch. This encourages an even distribution over the batch but still allows confident estimates for the individual inferences. For these experiments, the network was trained with a linear combination of weighted Chamfer loss λ_0 and the entropy penalty,

$$\lambda_e' = \lambda_0 + \kappa_e \lambda_e. \tag{12}$$

While a large entropy error term encourages all templates to be assigned weight and hence all subnetworks to learn, it also forces all subnetworks to try and learn all possible deformations. This works against the idea of specialization, where each subnetwork should learn to deform their template to match query models close to their template. To alleviate this, we anneal the entropy over time

$$\kappa_e = e^{-b/b_0} \kappa_{e0}, \tag{13}$$

where κ_{e0} is the initial weighting, b is the batch index and b_0 is some scaling factor.

Deformation Regularization. In order to encourage the network to select a template requiring minimal deformation, we introduce a deformation regularization term,

$$\lambda_r = \sum_{q,t} \gamma^{(qt)} |\Delta \tilde{\mathbf{P}}^{(qt)}|^2, \tag{14}$$

where $|\cdot|^2$ is the squared 2-norm of the vectorized input.

Large regularization encourages a network to select the closest matching template, though punishes subnetworks for deforming their template a lot, even if the result is a better match to the query mesh. We combine this regularization term with the standard loss in a similar way to the entropy loss term,

$$\lambda_r' = \lambda_0 + \kappa_r \lambda_r, \tag{15}$$

where κ_r is an exponentially annealed weighting with initial value κ_{r0}.

4.2 Deformed Mesh Inference

For the algorithm to result in high-quality 3D reconstructions, it is important that the vertex density of each template mesh is approximately equivalent to (or higher than) the point cloud density used during training. To ensure this is the case, we subdivide edges in the template mesh such that no edge length is greater than some threshold ϵ_e. Example cases where this is particularly important are illustrated in Fig. 2.

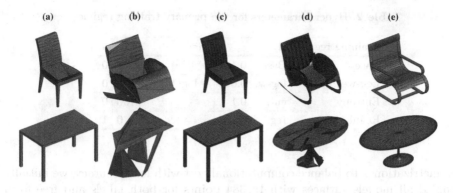

Fig. 2. Two examples of poor mesh model output (chair and table) as a result of low vertex density. (a) Original low vertex-density mesh. (b) Original mesh deformed according to inferred FFD. (c) Subdivided mesh. (d) Subdivided mesh deformed according to same FFD. (e) Ground truth.

4.3 Implementation Details

We employed a MobileNet architecture that uses depthwise separable convolutions to build light weight deep neural networks for mobile and embedded vision applications [38] without the final fully connected layers and with width $\alpha = 0.25$. Weights were initialized from the convolutional layers of a network trained on the 192×192 ImageNet dataset [39]. To reduce dimensionality, we add a single 1×1 convolution after the final MobileNet convolution layer. After flattening the result, we have one shared fully connected layer with 512 nodes followed by a fully connected layer for each template. A summary of layers and output dimensions is given in Table 1.

Table 1. Output size of network layers. Each template fully connected (FC) layer output is interpreted as $3 \times 4^3 = 192$ values for $\Delta \tilde{\mathbf{P}}^{(qt)}$ and a single $\gamma^{(qt)}$ value.

Layer	Output size
Input image	$192 \times 256 \times 3$
MobileNet CNN	$6 \times 8 \times 256$
1×1 convolution	$6 \times 8 \times 64$
Flattened	$3,072$
Shared FC	512
Template FC$^{(t)}$	$192 + 1$

We used a subset of the ShapeNet Core dataset [40] over a number of categories, using an 80/20 train/evaluation split. All experiments were conducted using 4 control points in each dimension $(l = m = n = 3)$ for the free form

Table 2. Hyper parameters for the primary training regimes.

Training regime	ID	ϵ_γ	$f(\gamma)$	κ_{e0}	κ_{r0}
Base	Base	0.1	γ	0	0
Log-weighted	log-w.	0.001	$-\log(1-\gamma)$	0	0
Entropy	ent.	0.1	γ	100	0
Regularized	reg.	0.1	γ	0	1

parametrizations. To balance computational cost with loss accuracy, we initially sampled all models surfaces with $16,384$ points for both labels and free form decomposition. At each step of training, we sub-sampled a different $1,024$ points for use in the Chamfer loss.

All input images were $192 \times 256 \times 3$ and were the result of rendering each textured mesh from the same view from $30°$ above the horizontal, $45°$ away from front-on and well-lit by a light above and on each side of the model. We trained a different network with 30 templates for each category. Templates were selected manually to ensure good variety. Models were trained using a standard Adam optimizer with learning rate 10^{-3}, $\beta_1 = 0.9$, $\beta_2 = 0.999$ and $\epsilon = 10^{-8}$. Mini-batches of 32 were used, and training was run for $100,000$ steps. Exponential annealing used $b_0 = 10,000$.

For each training regime, a different model was trained for each category. Hyper-parameters for specific training regimes are given in Table 2. To produce meshes and subsequent voxelizations and IoU scores, template meshes had edges subdivided to a maximum length of $\epsilon_e = 0.02$. We voxelize on a 32^3 grid by initially assigning any voxel containing part of the mesh as occupied, and subsequently filling in any unoccupied voxels with no free path to the outside.

5   Experimental Results

Qualitatively, we observe the networks preference in applying relatively large deformations to geometrically simple templates, and do not shy away from merging separate features of template models. For example, models frequently select the bi-plane template and merge the wings together to match single-wing aircraft, or warp standard 4-legged chairs and tables into structurally different objects as shown in Fig. 3.

5.1   Quantitative Comparison

For point cloud comparison, we compare against the works of Kuryenkov $et\ al.$ [36] (DN) and Fan $et\ al.$ [13] (PSGN) for 5 categories. We use the results for the improved PSGN model reported in [36]. We use the same scaling as in these papers, finding transformation parameters that transform the ground-truth meshes to a minimal bounding hemisphere $z \geq 0$ of radius 3.2 and applying this

Table 3. $1000 \times (\lambda_c/\lambda_{em}/1 - \text{IoU})$ for our different training regimes, compared against state-of-the-art models DN [36] and PSGN [13]. Lower is better. λ_c and λ_{em} values for PSGN are from the latest version as reported by Kuryenkov *et al.* [36], while IoU values are from the original paper. mean$_5$ is the mean value across the plane, bench, car, chair and sofa categories, while mean$_{13}$ is the average across all 13.

	Training regime				Other methods	
	Base	log-w.	ent.	reg.	DN	PSGN
Plane	31/306/292	31/310/297	31/300/289	33/304/307	100/560/-	140/115/399
Bench	42/280/431	39/280/425	40/284/418	45/275/445	100/550/-	210/980/450
Car	58/328/210	60/333/219	58/325/207	59/324/216	90/520/-	110/380/169
Chair	36/280/407	35/275/393	35/277/392	37/277/401	130/510/-	330/770/456
Sofa	64/329/275	63/320/275	64/324/271	65/319/276	210/770/-	230/600/292
Mean$_5$	**46**/305/323	**46**/304/322	**46**/300/**315**	48/**292**/329	130/580/-	200/780/353
Cabinet	37/249/282	37/250/282	36/251/264	37/246/279	-	-/-/229
Monitor	38/253/369	37/250/367	37/255/367	43/255/380	-	-/-/448
Lamp	52/402/514	49/393/480	44/384/473	55/425/520	-	-/-/538
Speaker	72/312/301	68/309/304	71/313/301	73/308/315	-	-/-/263
Firearm	39/312/332	30/279/281	32/288/326	39/301/345	-	-/-/396
Table	47/352/447	46/331/432	46/342/420	49/319/450	-	-/-/394
Cellphone	16/159/241	15/150/224	15/154/192	15/154/222	-	-/-/251
Watercraft	83/408/493	48/296/340	49/304/361	53/317/367	-	-/-/389
Mean$_{13}$	47/305/353	**43**/**290**/332	**43**/292/**329**	46/294/348	-	250/800/360

transformation to the inferred clouds. We also compare IoU values with PSGN [13] on an additional 8 categories for voxelized inputs on a 32^3 grid. Results for all 13 categories with each different training regime are given in Table 3. All our training regimes out-perform the others by a significant margin on all categories for point-cloud metrics (λ_c and λ_{em}). We also outperform PSGN on IoU for most categories and on average. The categories for which the method performs worst in terms of IoU – tables and chairs – typically feature large, flat surfaces and thin structures. Poor IoU scores can largely be attributed to poor width or depth inference (a difficult problem given the single view provided) and small, consistent offsets that do not induce large Chamfer losses. An example is shown in Fig. 4. We acknowledge this experimental setup gives us a slight advantage over DN and PSGN. Most notably, these approaches used renderings from different angles, compared to our uniform viewing angles. In practice, we found using varied viewing angles had a small negative effect on our results, though this regression could be partially offset by a higher capacity image network.

DN and PSGN also only trained a single model, where as we trained a new model for each category (though DN used category information at evaluation time). For a more fair comparison, we trained a single network using two templates from each of the 13 categories investigated on a dataset of all 13 categories. Again we note a regression in performance, though we still significantly outperform the other methods. We present this approach purely for simple, fair

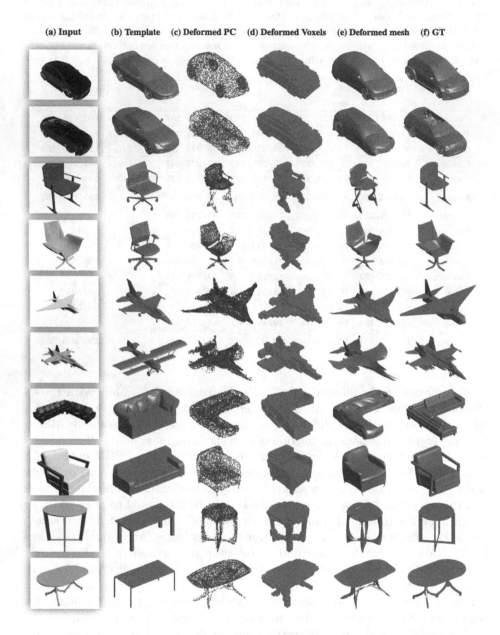

Fig. 3. Representative results for different categories. Column (a) shows the input image. Column (b) shows the selected template model. Column (c) shows the deformed point cloud by FFD. The deformed voxelized model is shown in column (d). Column (e) shows our final 3D mesh reconstruction, and the ground truth is shown in column (f).

(a)   (b)   (c)   (d)

Fig. 4. An example of a qualitatively accurate inference with a low IoU score, $\lambda_{IoU} =$ 0.33. Small errors in depth/width inference correspond to small Chamfer losses. For comparison, black voxels are true positives (intersection), red voxels are false negatives and green voxels are false positives. (Color figure online)

comparison with PSGN – we do not suggest it is the most optimal approach to extending our model to multiple categories, though leave further investigation to future work.

Chamfer losses for varied views and multiple categories are given in Table 4.

Table 4. $1000 \times \lambda_c$. ent.: same as original paper. 8-view: same as ent. but trained on a random view of 8. 8-view-full: same as 8-view but uses a full-features MobileNet architecture. 13c: same as 8-view, but a single model for all 13 categories, 2 templates per category. 13c-long: same as 13c but trained for twice as long.

	ent.	8-view	8-view-full	DN [36]	13c	13c-long	PSGN [13]
Plane	31	38	37	100	54	53	140
Bench	40	50	43	100	53	52	210
Car	58	61	59	90	71	68	110
Chair	35	44	42	130	48	46	330
Sofa	64	72	71	210	79	77	230
Mean$_5$	46	53	50	130	61	59	204
Mean$_{13}$	43	52	50	-	67	62	250

5.2 Template Selection

We begin our analysis by investigating the number of times each template was selected across the different training regimes, and the quality of the match of the undeformed template to the query model. Results for the sofa and table categories are given in Fig. 5. We illustrate the typical behaviour of our framework with the sofa and table categories, since these are categories with topologically similar models and topologically different models respectively. In both cases, the base training regime resulted in a model with template selection dominated by a small number of templates, while additional loss terms in the form of deformation regularization and entropy succeeded in smearing out this distribution to some extent. The behaviour of the non-linear weighting regime is starkly different across the two categories however, reinforcing template dominance for the category with less topological differences across the dataset, and encouraging variety for the table category.

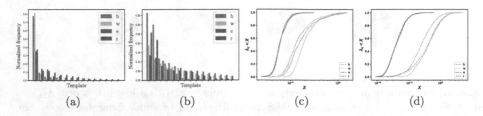

(a)   (b)   (c)   (d)

Fig. 5. Normalized count of the number of times each template was selected, sorted descending (a, b), and cumulative Chamfer error (c, d) for the deformed models (dashed) and undeformed template models (dotted) for the sofa category (a, c) and table category (b, d). b, w, e, r legend entries correspond to base, log-weighted, entropy and regularized training regimes respectively.

In terms of the Chamfer loss, all training regimes produced deformed models with virtually equivalent results. The difference is apparent when inspecting the undeformed models. Unsurprisingly, penalizing large deformation via regularization results in the best results for the undeformed template, while the other two non-base methods selected templates slightly better than the base regime.

To further investigate the effect of template selection on the model, we trained a base model with a single template ($T = 1$), and entropy models with $T \in \{2, 4, 8, 16\}$ templates for the sofa dataset. In each case, the top N templates selected by the 30-template regularized model were used. Cumulative Chamfer losses and IoU scores are shown in Fig. 6.

Surprisingly, the deformation networks manage to achieve almost identical results on these metrics regardless of the number of templates available. Additional templates do improve accuracy of the undeformed model up to a point, suggesting the template selection mechanism is not fundamentally broken.

5.3   Semantic Label Transfer

While no aspect of the training related to semantic information, applying the inferred deformations to a semantically labelled point cloud allows us to infer another semantically labelled point cloud. Some examples are shown in Fig. 7. For cases where the template is semantically similar to the query object, the additional semantic information is retained in the inferred cloud. However, some templates either do not have points of all segmentation types, or have points of segmentation types that are not present in the query object. In these cases, while the inferred point cloud matches the surface relatively well, the semantic information is unreliable.

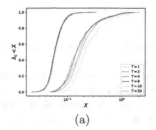
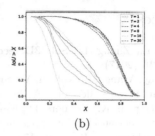

(a)   (b)

Fig. 6. Cumulative Chamfer loss (left) and IoU results (right) for models with limited templates. All models with $T > 1$ trained under the entropy regime (e) on the sofa category. $T = 1$ model was trained with the base training regime. Dotted: undeformed selected template values, dashed: deformed model values.

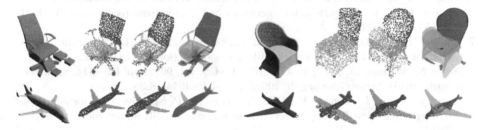

Fig. 7. Good (left block) and bad (right block) examples from the chair and plane categories. For each block, left to right: Input image; selected template's semantically segmented cloud; deformed segmented cloud; deformed mesh. Models trained with additional entropy loss term (ent.).

6 Conclusion

We have presented a simple framework for combining modern CNN approaches with detailed, unstructured meshes by using FFD as a fixed sized intermediary and learning to select and deform template point clouds based on minimally adjusted off-the-shelf image processing networks. We out-perform state-of-the-art methods with respect to point cloud generation, and perform at-or-above state-of-the-art on the volumetric IoU metric, despite our network not being optimized for it. We present various mechanisms by which the diversity of templates selected can be increased and demonstrate these result in modest improvements.

We demonstrate the main component of the low metric scores is the ability of the network to learn deformations tailored to specific templates, rather than the precise selection of these templates. Models with only a single template to select from achieve comparable results to those with a greater selection at their disposal. This indicates the choice of template – and hence any semantic of topological information – makes little difference to the resulting point cloud, diminishing the trustworthiness of topological or semantic information.

References

1. Penner, E., Zhang, L.: Soft 3D reconstruction for view synthesis. ACM Trans. Graph. **36** (2017)
2. Huang, Q., Wang, H., Koltun, V.: Single-view reconstruction via joint analysis of image and shape collections. ACM Trans. Graph. **34** (2015)
3. Maier, R., Kim, K., Cremers, D., Kautz, J., Nießner, M.: Intrinsic3D: high-quality 3D reconstruction by joint appearance and geometry optimization with spatially-varying lighting. In: ICCV (2017)
4. Krizhevsky, A., Sutskever, I., Hinton, G.E.: ImageNet classification with deep convolutional neural networks. In: NIPS, pp. 1097–1105 (2012)
5. Farabet, C., Couprie, C., Najman, L., LeCun, Y.: Learning hierarchical features for scene labeling. TPAMI **35**, 1915–1929 (2013)
6. Graves, A., Liwicki, M., Fernández, S., Bertolami, R., Bunke, H., Schmidhuber, J.: A novel connectionist system for unconstrained handwriting recognition. TPAMI **31**, 855–868 (2009)
7. Choy, C.B., Xu, D., Gwak, J.Y., Chen, K., Savarese, S.: 3D-R2N2: a unified approach for single and multi-view 3D object reconstruction. In: Leibe, B., Matas, J., Sebe, N., Welling, M. (eds.) ECCV 2016. LNCS, vol. 9912, pp. 628–644. Springer, Cham (2016). https://doi.org/10.1007/978-3-319-46484-8_38
8. Yan, X., Yang, J., Yumer, E., Guo, Y., Lee, H.: Perspective transformer nets: learning single-view 3D object reconstruction without 3D supervision. In: NIPS (2016)
9. Qi, C.R., Su, H., Nießner, M., Dai, A., Yan, M., Guibas, L.J.: Volumetric and multi-view CNNs for object classification on 3D data. In: CVPR (2016)
10. Kar, A., Häne, C., Malik, J.: Learning a multi-view stereo machine. In: NIPS (2017)
11. Zhu, R., Galoogahi, H.K., Wang, C., Lucey, S.: Rethinking reprojection: closing the loop for pose-aware shape reconstruction from a single image. In: NIPS (2017)
12. Wu, J., Wang, Y., Xue, T., Sun, X., Freeman, W.T., Tenenbaum, J.B.: MarrNet: 3D shape reconstruction via 2.5D sketches. In: NIPS (2017)
13. Fan, H., Su, H., Guibas, L.J.: A point set generation network for 3D object reconstruction from a single image. In: CVPR (2017)
14. Qi, C.R., Su, H., Mo, K., Guibas, L.J.: PointNet: deep learning on point sets for 3D classification and segmentation. In: CVPR (2017)
15. Qi, C.R., Yi, L., Su, H., Guibas, L.J.: PointNet++: deep hierarchical feature learning on point sets in a metric space. In: NIPS (2017)
16. Lin, C.H., Kong, C., Lucey, S.: Learning efficient point cloud generation for dense 3D object reconstruction. In: AAAI (2018)
17. Sederberg, T., Parry, S.: Free-form deformation of solid geometric models. In: SIGGRAPH (1986)
18. Ulusoy, A.O., Geiger, A., Black, M.J.: Towards probabilistic volumetric reconstruction using ray potential. In: 3DV (2015)
19. Wu, Z., Song, S., Khosla, A., Tang, X., Xiao, J.: 3D ShapeNets: a deep representation for volumetric shapes. In: CVPR (2015)
20. Cherabier, I., Häne, C., Oswald, M.R., Pollefeys, M.: Multi-label semantic 3D reconstruction using voxel blocks. In: 3DV (2016)
21. Sharma, A., Grau, O., Fritz, M.: VConv-DAE: deep volumetric shape learning without object labels. In: Hua, G., Jégou, H. (eds.) ECCV 2016. LNCS, vol. 9915, pp. 236–250. Springer, Cham (2016). https://doi.org/10.1007/978-3-319-49409-8_20

22. Rezende, D.J., Eslami, S.M.A., Mohamed, S., Battaglia, P., Jaderberg, M., Heess, N.: Unsupervised learning of 3D structure from images. In: NIPS (2016)
23. Girdhar, R., Fouhey, D.F., Rodriguez, M., Gupta, A.: Learning a predictable and generative vector representation for objects. In: Leibe, B., Matas, J., Sebe, N., Welling, M. (eds.) ECCV 2016. LNCS, vol. 9910, pp. 484–499. Springer, Cham (2016). https://doi.org/10.1007/978-3-319-46466-4_29
24. Wu, J., Zhang, C., Xue, T., Freeman, W.T., Tenenbaum, J.B.: Learning a probabilistic latent space of object shapes via 3D generative-adversarial modeling. In: NIPS (2016)
25. Liu, J., Yu, F., Funkhouser, T.A.: Interactive 3D modeling with a generative adversarial network. In: 3DV (2017)
26. Gwak, J., Choy, C.B., Garg, A., Chandraker, M., Savarese, S.: Weakly supervised generative adversarial networks for 3D reconstruction. In: 3DV (2017)
27. Riegler, G., Ulusoy, A.O., Geiger, A.: OctNet: learning deep 3D representations at high resolutions. In: CVPR (2017)
28. Wang, P.S., Liu, Y., Guo, Y.X., Sun, C.Y., Tong, X.: O-CNN: octree-based convolutional neural networks for 3D shape analysis. In: SIGGRAPH (2017)
29. Häne, C., Tulsiani, S., Malik, J.: Hierarchical surface prediction for 3D object reconstruction. In: 3DV (2017)
30. Tatarchenko, M., Dosovitskiy, A., Brox, T.: Octree generating networks: efficient convolutional architectures for high-resolution 3D outputs. In: ICCV (2017)
31. Lun, Z., Gadelha, M., Kalogerakis, E., Maji, S., Wang, R.: 3D shape reconstruction from sketches via multi-view convolutional networks. In: 3DV (2017)
32. Sinha, A., Unmesh, A., Huang, Q., Ramani, K.: SurfNet: generating 3D shape surfaces using deep residual network. In: CVPR (2017)
33. Yumer, M.E., Mitra, N.J.: Learning semantic deformation flows with 3D convolutional networks. In: Leibe, B., Matas, J., Sebe, N., Welling, M. (eds.) ECCV 2016. LNCS, vol. 9910, pp. 294–311. Springer, Cham (2016). https://doi.org/10.1007/978-3-319-46466-4_18
34. Kong, C., Lin, C.H., Lucey, S.: Using locally corresponding CAD models for dense 3D reconstructions from a single image. In: CVPR (2017)
35. Pontes, J.K., Kong, C., Eriksson, A., Fookes, C., Sridharan, S., Lucey, S.: Compact model representation for 3D reconstruction. In: 3DV (2017)
36. Kurenkov, A., et al.: DeformNet: free-form deformation network for 3D shape reconstruction from a single image. Volume abs/1708.04672 (2017)
37. Rubner, Y., Tomasi, C., Guibas, L.J.: The earth mover's distance as a metric for image retrieval. Int. J. Comput. Vis. **40**, 99–121 (2000)
38. Howard, A.G., et al.: Mobilenets: efficient convolutional neural networks for mobile vision applications. arXiv preprint arXiv:1704.04861 (2017)
39. Deng, J., Dong, W., Socher, R., Li, L.J., Li, K., Fei-Fei, L.: ImageNet: a large-scale hierarchical image database. In: CVPR, pp. 248–255 (2009)
40. Chang, A.X., et al.: ShapeNet: an Information-Rich 3D Model Repository. Technical report arXiv:1512.03012 [cs.GR] (2015)

CalliGAN: Unpaired Mutli-chirography Chinese Calligraphy Image Translation

Yiming Gao and Jiangqin Wu[✉]

Zhejiang University, College of Computer Science, Hangzhou, China
{gor_yatming,wujq}@zju.edu.cn

Abstract. The style translation of Chinese calligraphy image is a challenging problem: changing the style and layout of strokes while retaining the content attributes like overall structure and combination of radicals. The existing calligraphy character generation methods, such as brush modeling, skeleton rendering, strokes extracting and assembling, *etc.*, are ineffective and difficult to apply to multi-chirography styles and numerous data. The recent neural style transfer methods for general image-to-image style translation tasks can not apply to our problem due to the different meanings of the "style". The GAN-based methods demonstrating good results require image-pairs for training, which is hard to collect in our task. Therefore, in this paper we propose a novel GAN-based model, called CalliGAN, for the mutli-chirography Chinese calligraphy image translation. In CalliGAN, We present a joint optimization method which only requires unpaired multiple chirography sets for training. In our experiment, we build a chirography style dataset called Chiro-4 and then compare our method with various general translation methods. The experiment results demonstrate the validity of our method on calligraphy style translation task.

1   Introduction

Chinese calligraphy is an ancient and complicated visual art which is a valuable treasure of Chinese culture. Calligraphy lovers are fond of appreciating and imitating famous works because of their aesthetic qualities. But traditional calligraphy works easily lost or destroyed in the long history of Chinese calligraphy. And imitating a realistic and graceful calligraphy work requires a lot of time to learn and train repeatedly. In order to create calligraphy characters in specific style while preserving the content of original ones(see Fig. 1), in this paper we propose a mutli-chirography Chinese calligraphy image translation method.

A large number of methods are proposed in the field of calligraphy character generation, but the synthesized results are unsatisfying. Existing methods mainly include three directions. (1) Brush model based generation methods

Supported by the National Nature Science Foundation of China (No. 61379073), the Fundamental Research Funds for the Central Universities (2018FZA5012), and China Academic Digital Associative Library (CADAL).

C. V. Jawahar et al. (Eds.): ACCV 2018, LNCS 11362, pp. 334–348, 2019.
https://doi.org/10.1007/978-3-030-20890-5_22

[22,27] construct a virtual brush model or simulate a realistic writing environment to generate the calligraphy character, but can not generate the character in specific style. (2) The rendering manuscript methods [30] synthesize corresponding calligraphy character by rendering stroke texture of specific style on the given skeleton which are slow and unable to generate numerous characters at the same time. (3) Image-based calligraphy generation methods [28] first extract radicals and strokes from existing calligraphy characters, then assemble and deform corresponding components to synthesize target characters. However, it fails to extract automatically and effectively when strokes are complicated.

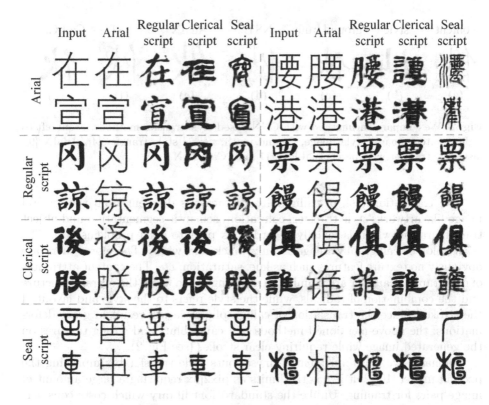

Fig. 1. Mutli-chirography Chinese calligraphy image translation on the Chiro-4 dataset. First to fourth rows are the results of CalliGAN on Arial font, regular script, clerical script and seal script, respectively. The first and sixth columns are listed as the source calligraphy images, followed by four target styles.

It's a complex task for human to recognize differences between chirography styles and design style features artificially, but a easy job for convolutional neural networks (CNNs). In recent years, CNNs have great performance in image understanding tasks such as classification [8,14,23], detection [5], and segmentation [17], thus, proving that CNNs have a good ability to capture the semantic representations of images.

Gatys *et al.* [4] uses pre-trained CNNs to extract the content and style representations of two images respectively and combine them by minimizing the content loss and Gram loss. After that various CNN-based style transfer methods [9,11,15] are also proposed which employ different loss functions to represent style. Recently, a variety of Generative Adversarial Networks (GANs) [6,19,20] are used for generating realistic images by the adversarial training between generator and discriminator. WGAN [1] and WGAN-GP [7] improve the stability of learning and gets rid of problems like mode collapse, so we leverage its gradient penalty term in our approach.

content   style   ground truth   NST   AdaIN   FST   CalliGAN

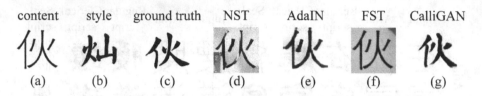

(a)   (b)   (c)   (d)   (e)   (f)   (g)

Fig. 2. We compare our method with CNN-based style transfer methods. From left to right: content image, style image, ground truth, neural style transfer [4], AdaIN [9], fast style transfer with perceptual loss [11] and CalliGAN.

The translation task of calligraphy character is different from the general image like artworks style transfer, coloration, semantic segmentation and object transfiguration which is usually regarded as pixel-to-pixel problems [10]. The pixel color of calligraphy image is only black and white. Therefore, there are obviously no texture features such as hue, saturation, *etc.* The content attributes of calligraphy character are mainly the meaning of the word, the overall structure and the combination of radicals, while the style refers to the style and layout of the strokes. Since the translation of calligraphy style will result in great deformations, the above-mentioned methods will cause blurs and wrong textures on the generated image while requiring clear strokes (see Fig. 2).

Kaonashi-tyc [25] implement Chinese fonts style transfer by improving the pix2pix model [10], but it has the limits as pix2pix requiring a large amount of image-pairs for training. Unlike the standard font library which costs considerable effort to create manually, enough image-pairs of calligraphy are difficult and expensive to collect due to the damage and loss of works in the long history. So supervised image-to-image translation methods do not suit to our task.

In order to solve problems caused by image-pairs, various unsupervised methods are proposed. DTN [24] constrains the content in a pre-trained feature space. But Chinese calligraphy has about one hundred thousand classes and only few samples for each class, thus, it is not feasible to pretrain a content classification network. SimGAN [21] preserves content by self-regularization loss and transfers style by adversarial loss. UNIT [16] combines variational autoencoders (VAEs) [13] and GANs. But both SimGAN and UNIT have the bad performance when deformation between source and target style is great. CycleGAN [31] proposes a cycle consistency loss to constrain the content between the input and the translated image. However, it needs one GAN model for one mapping which contains numerous parameters and is inefficient to train with multifarious types of chirography. Therefore, we extend the domain classification loss in StarGAN [2] to achieve mutli-chirography translation using only one GAN which uses auxiliary classifier to control multiple domains. Although these methods perform well in general image stylization, the results are not satisfactory for calligraphy image when the deformation is great.

In this paper, we propose CalliGAN, a novel model for multi-chirography Chinese calligraphy image translation without image-pairs training. The CalliGAN generates calligraphy characters with source content and target chirography style according to the label information. For different translations, there is only one generator. The model learns the mappings between all the chirography styles, as well as the general attributes. The main contributions of our paper are:

(1) Unlike the general cGAN [2,19], we propose a novel conditional GAN-based model which consists of encoder-decoder generator G, chirography style label generator H, and discriminator D, to achieve calligraphy image translation. In our model, we use encoder g of G to compress and extract the content representations $g(x)$ of the source image x, H to encode label c to the more meaningful feature maps $H(c)$, and decoder f of G to decode the embedding of $g(x)$ and $H(c)$ into a specific style character. In addition, we also use self-attention modules [29] in G to capture the correlation of distant radicals.

(2) We propose a joint optimization method based on WGAN-GP to train the networks with unpaired chirography style sets. We use the cycle consistency loss to constrain the content attributes and the chirography classification loss to control the chirography style. In G, we introduce an encoded loss defined as a L1 sparse regularization in the output of g to enforce g extract the content of character. Our experiment shows that the deep encoder g has the ability to extract the semantic of characters, as the high-level representations for the same word in different style are similar. In D, we propose a history adversarial loss to keep strokes clear which is proved to be effective in our experiment.

(3) We build a chirography dataset called Chiro-4, containing Arial font, regular script, clerical script and seal script. We compare CalliGAN with some baseline methods on this dataset to prove the effectiveness of our method.

2   CalliGAN

Our main goal is to learn the mapping between different chirography styles. We define the data of different chirography styles as X_i, i = 1, 2..., N (N is the types of chirography style sets C. We denote the data distribution of specific chirography style as $x \sim p_{data}(X_i)$. Our model based on conditional GANs includes the mapping $G : \{X_i, c\} \rightarrow X_c$ from observed image x to output image $y \equiv G(x, c)$ in specific style according to chirography style label c, while $x \in X_i$, $c \in C$ and

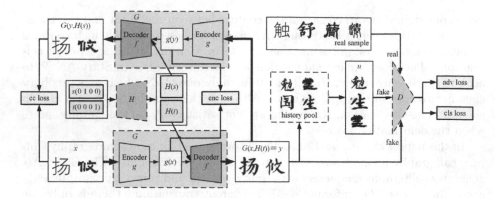

Fig. 3. Overview of CalliGAN. CalliGAN consists of encoder-decoder generator G, chirography style label generator H, discriminator D and history pool.

expecting $y \sim p_{data}(X_c)$. We can regard G as a combination of three mapping, including content mapping g, label mapping h and style mapping f. The content mapping maps observed images into content feature space, $g : X_i \rightarrow F_{content}$. The label mapping transfers label vectors to label feature maps, $h : C \rightarrow F_{label}$. And the style mapping maps content features to output image according to the label feature maps, $f : \{F_{content}, h(c)\} \rightarrow X_c$. The discriminator D in our model aims to distinguish between input x and output $G(x, c)$ and recognize the type of x or $G(x, c)$ by adding auxiliary classifier, $D : X \rightarrow \{D_{adv}(X), D_{cls}(X)\}$, which pushes the generator to create calligraphy character images that are indistinguishable from real images with correct category. See Fig. 3 for an overview.

2.1 Network Architecture

Encoder-Decoder Generator. The generator network G in CalliGAN is used to transfer the chirography styles of calligraphy character images. We improve the generative networks from [11] which perform well in general neural style transfer. We divide G into encoder g and decoder f, the encoder g is responsible for extracting content features of input, and the decoder f is in charge of reconstructing content features to stylized output according to label information.

Unlike common cGANs [2,19] which concatenate the label information and the input image directly, we combine the labels with the content features. The reason is that we wish g to have the ability of extracting the same content features from two same calligraphys in different styles. So if there are two mappings in our case by using the methods in cGANs, including $g : \{X_i, h(c)\} \rightarrow F_{content}$ and $f : F_{content} \rightarrow X_c$, G will generate the same outputs for same words no matter what the labels are, because the content features captured by g will be finally same and make f output the same.

The encoder contains a stride-1 ConvBlock (Convolution-InstanceNorm [26]-ReLU) layer with 7×7 kernels, two stride-2 ConvBlocks with 4×4 kernels, a SelfAttn (self-attention module), several ResBlocks (residual block [8]) and another SelfAttn. Local features like strokes can be captured by ConvBlocks. And we use SelfAttn to make the encoder focus on the global feature like the structure. ResBlock is used to further capture content attributes. The decoder consists of several ResBlocks which reconstruct the features based on labels, a SelfAttn, two fractionally-strided ConvBlocks with stride 1/2 and a convolution layer with 7 × 7 kernels. See top of Fig. 4 for details.

Chirography Style Label Generator. The input vector and the label vector are simply concatenated in cGAN [19] which transfer a 1D noise vector to an image. But in many cases, a 2D to 2D transformation is required, thus the simplest solution is to extend each channel of a 1D label vector to a 2D feature with the same size as the input feature like [2]. This approach utilizes very few features to represent label informations, and we think it is not enough to represent style information. Therefore, we map the feature label vector to the feature map of more channels, and we learn this mapping through neural networks. Therefore, we map the label vectors to more meaningful feature maps with more channels. It's difficult to design this mapping artificially, but is easy for the CNNs which we call chirography style label generator H.

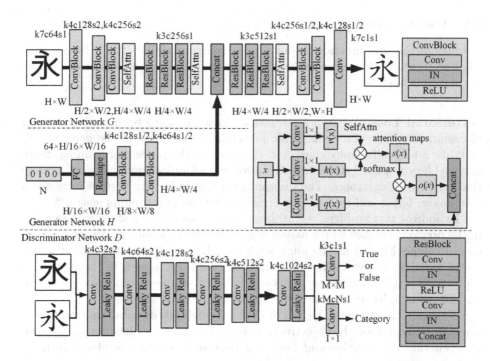

Fig. 4. Network Architecture of the generator and discriminator in CalliGAN. We define k as the kernel size, n as the number of channels and s as the stride in each convolutional layer (Conv). IN means instance normalization.

Generator H first utilizes a full connection layer to extend the information of the label vector, and then reshapes outputs into 2D feature maps. The extended labels are input to two fractionally-strided ConvBlocks with stride $1/2$ for generating the more stylized features as well as adapting the label size to the content features. Finally, we concatenate the label and content feature maps as the input of decoder f. See middle of Fig. 4 for details.

Discriminator. To guide the training of the generator, the discriminator is required to judge whether the input image is a real calligraphy image or not and recognize its chirography style category. We use PatchGANs [10,31] as the discriminator D to classify whether the local image patches are real or fake at patch-level, which have fewer parameters than a full-image discriminator. The discriminator leverages several stride-2 convolution layers with 4×4 kernels to compress and extract the high-level features of images (see bottom of Fig. 4). Each convolutional layer is followed by Leaky ReLU [18] with $\alpha = 0.2$. In order to recognize the category of the global image, an auxiliary classifier should be added to the last layer of D. We also add a convolution layer without the sigmoid to the last layer of D like [20] which is used to calculate the losses of WGAN.

2.2 Loss Function

We denote the loss function, input image, source style label and target style label as $\mathcal{L}$, x, s and t respectively. The definitions of the symbols in our model are shown in Sect. 2.

Adversarial Loss. We apply adversarial losses $\mathcal{L}_{adv}$ to both generators and discriminator. $\mathcal{L}_{adv}$ plays a key role in making the output of the generator G look like a real calligraphy character. However, in the process of training, there may be blurs or absurd stains, which is intolerable for black and white calligraphy that requires clear strokes. The discriminator will judge the blurred image as a fake image, but it will forget these errors as the training time increases.

To address this problem, we utilize a history pool [21] to store fake samples in the previous batches which may contain the blurred samples. We set S as the size of the pool and b as the mini-batch size. In each iteration of the discriminator training, we first store the currently generated images in the pool with a probability p. And then, we randomly select b samples from the pool as the unclear calligraphy image set U. We denote the unclear sample as $u \in U$.

We regard the outputs $D_{adv}(x)$ of D as a probability distribution over inputs given by D. Therefore, the objective of D is to maximize the distribution distance between the real samples and both the fake and unclear samples, which we express as:

$$\mathcal{L}_{adv}(D) = \mathbb{E}_{x,t}[D_{adv}(G(x, H(t)))] + \mathbb{E}_u[D_{adv}(u)] - \alpha \mathbb{E}_x[D_{adv}(x)]$$
$$+ \lambda_{gp} \cdot \mathbb{E}_{\hat{x}}[(\| \nabla_{\hat{x}} D_{adv}(\hat{x}) \|_2 - 1)^2], \tag{1}$$

while the gradient penalty [7] term is used for more stable training and higher quality of WGAN and the λ_{gp} represents its weight. The $\hat{x}$ is sampled uniformly along straight lines between a pair of a real and a generated images. And we set $\alpha = (M + N)/L$, while M, N and L are the number of unclear, fake and real samples, respectively. In practice, we make $M = N = L$.

The objective of G and H is to make the distribution of the generated image approximate to the real image. Thus, the objective of G and H is defined as:

$$\mathcal{L}_{adv}(G, H) = -\mathbb{E}_{x,t}[D_{adv}(G(x, H(t)))]. \tag{2}$$

Chirography Style Classification Loss. Our goal is to translate the input image from source chirography style to target style based on the style label, which can be properly classified to the target style. For this purpose, We use real images to train the auxiliary classifier of D, and input the generated image of G into the classifier to optimize G and H. Therefore, there are two terms in objective,

$$\mathcal{L}_{cls}(D) = \mathbb{E}_{x,s}[-\log D_{cls}(s \mid x)] \tag{3}$$

where $D_{cls}(s \mid x)$ represents a probability distribution over chirography style labels computed by D and

$$\mathcal{L}_{cls}(G, H) = \mathbb{E}_{x,t}[-\log D_{cls}(t \mid G(x, H(t)))]. \tag{4}$$

Cycle Consistency Loss. Although the adversarial and classification loss enforce G to generate realistic and well-classified calligraphy character images, these losses have no way to preserve the content attributes while changing the style. Thus, we leverage cycle consistency loss to constrain the consistency of content attributes between input image and translated image by using the L1 sparse regularization between input image and reconstructed image. We define the objective as:

$$\mathcal{L}_{cc}(G, H) = \mathbb{E}_{x,t,s}[\| x - G(G(x, H(t)), H(s)) \|], \tag{5}$$

where $G(G(x, H(t)), H(s))$ is the translated image of $G(x, H(t))$ called reconstructed image. By minimizing the loss, reconstructed image will approximate to input image, $G(G(x, H(t)), H(s)) \approx x$.

Content Encoded Loss. For calligraphy imags, the same calligraphy character should have the same meaning, structural skeleton and radical combination. So we utilize the encoder g of G to extract the high-level content features of input before we reconstruct the stylized image according to the label. We propose the content encoded loss to further constrain the similarity of $g(x)$ and $g(G(x, H(t))$ on the basis of the cycle consistency loss. We assume that content attributes of $g(x)$ and $g(G(x, H(t))$ have high proximity due to $\mathcal{L}_{cc}(G, H)$, so the high-level representations gived by g ought to be similar. We define the objective as:

$$\mathcal{L}_{enc}(G, H) = \mathbb{E}_{x,t}[\| g(x) - g(G(x, H(t))) \|]. \tag{6}$$

Full Objective. Our full objective of generators and discriminator are defined respectively as:

$$\mathcal{L}(D) = \lambda_{adv} \cdot \mathcal{L}_{adv}(D) + \lambda_{cls} \cdot \mathcal{L}_{cls}(D), \tag{7}$$

$$\mathcal{L}(G,H) = \lambda_{adv} \cdot \mathcal{L}_{adv}(G,H) + \lambda_{cls} \cdot \mathcal{L}_{cls}(G,H)$$
$$+ \lambda_{cc} \cdot \mathcal{L}_{cc}(G,H) + \lambda_{enc} \cdot \mathcal{L}_{enc}(G,H), \tag{8}$$

where λ_{adv}, λ_{cls}, λ_{cc} and λ_{enc} are hyper-parameters that respectively represent the importance of the adversarial loss, chirography style classification loss, the cycle consistency loss and the content encoded loss.

3   Experiment

3.1   Dataset

We build a chirography dataset with four styles, including Arial font, regular script, clerical script and seal script, which we call Chiro-4. The reason for choosing these four fonts is that there are manifest differences between them in style. The Chiro-4 contains totally 40,000 images, 10,000 for each style. We randomly select 9,600 images from each style as a training set, and the rest as a validation set. There is no overlap between the training set and the validation set.

We collect calligraph images from CADAL[1] [3], which digitizes more than 4,000 famous ancient calligrapher's works like Yan Zhenqing, Ou Yangxun and so on. The regular script is mostly similar to printed fonts of which shape is square and strokes are straight and neat. The glyph of official script is generally wide and flat of which horizontal strokes are long while the vertical strokes are short. The seal script is slender with dense upper and sparse lower of which lines are well-proportioned. Because the works of seal script are fewer than others in history, we augment the data by shifting. Finally, we use Arial as standard fonts which looks simple and neat on the ground that it completely abandons the style and leaves only the skeleton. We generate and augment Arial images of nearly 2,000 high frequency Chinese words.

3.2   Implementation Details

We set the hyper-parameters $\lambda_{adv} = 1$, $\lambda_{cls} = 1$, $\lambda_{cc} = 10$, $\lambda_{enc} = 0.5$ and $\lambda_{gp} = 10$ for all experiments. Since the color of calligraphy image is only black and white, we use the 128 grayscale with 1 channel as the input of the experiments. The model is trained setting the learning rate to 0.0001 and using Adam [12] with $\beta_1 = 0.5$ and $\beta_2 = 0.999$. We update the generators after updating the discriminator five times as WGAN-GP [7]. The size of the history pool S is set to 500, and the probability of storage p is set to 0.5. We train all models for 500 epochs with batch size b of 32. We spent nearly 6 days training the model on a NVIDIA TITAN Xp GPU.

---

[1] www.cadal.zju.edu.cn.

3.3 Qualitative Evaluation

Comparison with CNN-Based Methods. We test several CNN-based methods in our chirography style translation experiment, including the NST [4] (Fig. 2d), AdaIN [9] (Fig. 2e) and FST [11] (Fig. 2f). Figure 2 shows that these methods keep the staple of the content (black part in Fig. 2a) and add the wrong texture to the background (white part in Fig. 2a). Our method (the results shown in Fig. 2g) translates only the stroke style and overall layout of Fig. 2a into b without changing the content as the ground truth Fig. 2c. Therefore, the general artwork style is different from chirography style, while the former focuses more on texture.

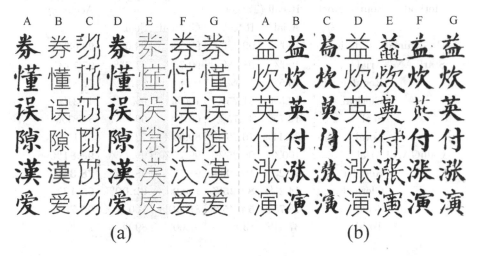

(a)   (b)

Fig. 5. We compare CalliGAN with GAN-based methods in Arial-Regular script translation task, while (a) is from Arial to Regular script and (b) is the opposite. The symbols A, B, C, D, E, F and G represent the input image, ground truth in standard fonts library, UNIT [16], SimGAN [21], CycleGAN [31], zi2zi [25] and CalliGAN, respectively.

Comparison with GAN-Based Methods. We compare some GAN-based methods with ours as shown in the Fig. 5. For non-multi domain translation methods, we test on a Arial and regular script due to their standardized and neat strokes. For the supervised training of zi2zi [25], We collect nearly 5,500 Arial-Regular pairs and augment the data to 10,000. Zi2zi achieves the translation which is close to ground truth by learning the mapping of image-pairs. SimGAN [21] utilizes self-regularization to constrain content and only adversarial training to transfer style, resulting in almost unchanged output as input. UNIT [16] and CycleGAN [31] preserve the content attributes and learn the style, but the results are unrealistic. Obviously, CalliGAN achieves the same performance as zi2zi without image-pairs, and the results generated are realistic and perceptually plausible. In our opinion, the good performance of CalliGAN owes to the commonness of calligraphy characters learned from mutli-chirography.

Comparison with Multi-domain Methods. We compare our method to multi-domain translation methods StarGAN [2] (see Fig. 6a, b, c). In comparison, CalliGAN produces more stylized results than StarGAN especially on clerical script and seal script. Our method generates high-quality calligraphy character images with clearer strokes and better retention of content. However, StarGAN fails to keep the balance between content and style for the task with great deformation, leading to the blurry results.

Table 1. The accuracy and recall rate of StarGAN [2] and CalliGAN on the pre-trained Inception-V3 network.

Method	Source label	Recall (Target)				Accuracy
		Arial	Regular	Clerical	Seal	
Pre-trained validation set		100%	99.7%	99.2%	99.6%	99.63%
StarGAN	Arial	100%	93.5%	99.75%	97.75%	97.75%
	Regular	16.5%	100%	90%	84.75%	72.81%
	Clerical	12.5%	51.75%	100%	9%	43.31%
	Seal	12.75%	37.75%	69%	99.75%	54.81%
	Total	35.44%	70.75%	89.69%	72.81%	67.17%
CalliGAN	Arial	100%	96.25%	99.75%	99.25%	**98.81%**
	Regular	16.25%	100.00%	98.75%	98.25%	**78.31%**
	Clerical	14.25%	**84.25%**	100.00%	**62.00%**	**65.13%**
	Seal	18.75%	**54.75%**	**89.50%**	100.00%	**65.75%**
	Total	37.31%	83.81%	97.00%	89.88%	77.00%

3.4 Quantitative Evaluation

In addition to human perception judgment, we also design a automatic quantitative evaluation measure. We randomly select 9,000 images of each style on Chiro-4 as the training set, and pretrain a Inception-V3 classification network. The network achieves 99.7% accuracy in the validation set consisting of the remaining images. For quantitative evaluation, we only compare with StarGAN which is most effective unpaired method in qualitative evaluation due to difficulty in collecting multi-chirography image-pairs.

As shown in Table 1, it's easier to translate the Arial and regular script to other styles. One reason is that strokes of clerical and seal script are relatively complex. The other is that each calligrapher's clerical and seal script works are few, making the dataset contain many calligraphers' works and styles be not unified. Through comparison, it can be seen that CalliGAN's results have better classification effect than StarGAN's, indicating that CalliGAN can produce more stylized results.

3.5   The Role of Each Component

We study the role of each component (see Fig. 3) in CalliGAN. The following results demonstrate that each component plays an important role in CalliGAN. As shown in Fig. 6d, without H, the translation of overall style and layout performs well, but poor for some strokes. Figure 6e shows that the results without the history pool and history adversarial loss are blurry and contain artifacts. Cycle consistency loss $\mathcal{L}_{cc}$ and content encoded loss $\mathcal{L}_{enc}$ complement each other, while playing the key roles in preserving content attributes. Without one of them, it's difficult to keep the consistent of content while changing the style (see Fig. 6f, g).

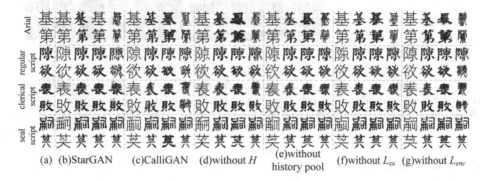

(a)   (b)StarGAN   (c)CalliGAN   (d)without H (e)without history pool   (f)without L_{cc} (g)without L_{enc}

Fig. 6. Results of StarGAN [2] and CalliGAN with/without some components. From left to right: ground truth, StarGAN, CalliGAN, without H, without history pool, without $\mathcal{L}_{cc}$, without $\mathcal{L}_{enc}$. The four columns of each grid are the results of target style, including Arial, regular script, clerical script and seal script, as the rows from top to bottom.

3.6   Visualization of Results

Analysis of Content Encoded Loss. We perform the experiment to analyze $\mathcal{L}_{enc}$ and study whether the output of encoder has the ability to represent the content. We choose 50 relevant Arial-Regular pairs and 50 random image-pairs from Chiro-4 to analyze the distance correlation between the original images and the encoded features. Figure 7a shows that the L2 distance between input images is positively correlated with the L2 distance between the encoded features. Images with the same content (blue) are less distant and vice versa (green). The results show that g is able to extract the semantic of characters.

Label Feature Maps From H. Figure 7b shows that the output feature maps of H contain more features than the simple extension of label vectors. For each location of the feature maps, there are 256-dimensional style labels which are more appropriate than a few identical labels due to the diversity of chirography styles. Each stroke of the character usually has different styles.

Self-attention Module. We visualize the attention maps of the three self-attention modules in G. Figure 7c shows that the module pays more attention to the strokes and structure of calligraphy characters at the lower level. As the network deepens (see Fig. 7d, e), more and more attention is paid to fewer radicals and strokes. Self-attention can better capture the relevance of distant strokes.

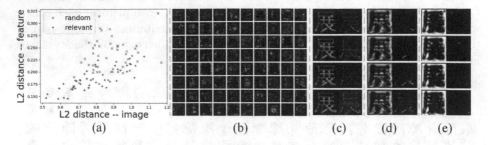

(a)   (b)   (c)   (d)   (e)

Fig. 7. Visualization of our experiments. (a) shows the distance correlation between the images and encoded features. (b) shows part of the label feature maps. (c)–(e) shows the attention maps (right) of some locations (left). (Color figure online)

4   Conclusions

In this paper, we propose CalliGAN, a GAN to perform mutli-chirography Chinese calligraphy image translation using a single model with unpaired training. We propose a chirography style label generator to map the label vectors to the label feature maps and combine it with an encoder-decoder generator. Aiming at training CalliGAN to generate realistic calligraphy images without image-pairs, we propose (1) a content encoded loss to assist cycle consistency loss to constrain the content, (2) a history pool to assist adversarial loss to make strokes clear, and we use a chirography style classification loss to learn the style. Our method is able to generate realistic and stylized calligraphy images and outperforms the existing unsupervised style translation methods. In the future, we will further study the common content space between the calligraphy character images and more complex chirography style translation.

References

1. Arjovsky, M., Chintala, S., Bottou, L.: Wasserstein GAN. arXiv preprint arXiv:1701.07875 (2017)
2. Choi, Y., Choi, M., Kim, M., Ha, J., Kim, S., Choo, J.: StarGAN: unified generative adversarial networks for multi-domain image-to-image translation. CoRR abs/1711.09020 (2017). http://arxiv.org/abs/1711.09020
3. Gao, P., Wu, J., Xia, Y., Lin, Y.: CADAL digital calligraphy system. In: Proceedings of the 12th ACM/IEEE-CS Joint Conference on Digital Libraries, JCDL 2012, pp. 357–358. ACM, New York (2012)

4. Gatys, L.A., Ecker, A.S., Bethge, M.: A neural algorithm of artistic style. Comput. Sci. (2015)
5. Girshick, R., Donahue, J., Darrell, T., Malik, J.: Rich feature hierarchies for accurate object detection and semantic segmentation. In: Proceedings of the IEEE Conference on Computer Vision and Pattern Recognition, pp. 580–587 (2014)
6. Goodfellow, I., et al.: Generative adversarial nets. In: Advances in Neural Information Processing Systems, pp. 2672–2680 (2014)
7. Gulrajani, I., Ahmed, F., Arjovsky, M., Dumoulin, V., Courville, A.C.: Improved training of wasserstein GANs. In: Advances in Neural Information Processing Systems, pp. 5769–5779 (2017)
8. He, K., Zhang, X., Ren, S., Sun, J.: Deep residual learning for image recognition. In: Proceedings of the IEEE Conference on Computer Vision and Pattern Recognition, pp. 770–778 (2016)
9. Huang, X., Belongie, S.: Arbitrary style transfer in real-time with adaptive instance normalization. CoRR, abs/1703.06868 (2017)
10. Isola, P., Zhu, J.Y., Zhou, T., Efros, A.A.: Image-to-image translation with conditional adversarial networks. In: 2017 IEEE Conference on Computer Vision and Pattern Recognition (CVPR), pp. 5967–5976. IEEE (2017)
11. Johnson, J., Alahi, A., Fei-Fei, L.: Perceptual losses for real-time style transfer and super-resolution. In: Leibe, B., Matas, J., Sebe, N., Welling, M. (eds.) ECCV 2016. LNCS, vol. 9906, pp. 694–711. Springer, Cham (2016). https://doi.org/10.1007/978-3-319-46475-6_43
12. Kingma, D., Ba, J.: Adam: a method for stochastic optimization. Comput. Sci. (2014)
13. Kingma, D.P., Welling, M.: Auto-encoding variational bayes. Statistics **1050**, 10 (2014)
14. Krizhevsky, A., Sutskever, I., Hinton, G.E.: Imagenet classification with deep convolutional neural networks. In: Advances in Neural Information Processing Systems, pp. 1097–1105 (2012)
15. Li, C., Wand, M.: Combining Markov random fields and convolutional neural networks for image synthesis. In: Proceedings of the IEEE Conference on Computer Vision and Pattern Recognition, pp. 2479–2486 (2016)
16. Liu, M.Y., Breuel, T., Kautz, J.: Unsupervised image-to-image translation networks. In: Advances in Neural Information Processing Systems, pp. 700–708 (2017)
17. Long, J., Shelhamer, E., Darrell, T.: Fully convolutional networks for semantic segmentation. In: Proceedings of the IEEE Conference on Computer Vision and Pattern Recognition, pp. 3431–3440 (2015)
18. Maas, A.L., Hannun, A.Y., Ng, A.Y.: Rectifier nonlinearities improve neural network acoustic models. In: Proceedings ICML, vol. 30, p. 3 (2013)
19. Mirza, M., Osindero, S.: Conditional generative adversarial nets. Comput. Sci., 2672–2680 (2014)
20. Radford, A., Metz, L., Chintala, S.: Unsupervised representation learning with deep convolutional generative adversarial networks. Comput. Sci. (2015)
21. Shrivastava, A., Pfister, T., Tuzel, O., Susskind, J., Wang, W., Webb, R.: Learning from simulated and unsupervised images through adversarial training. In: The IEEE Conference on Computer Vision and Pattern Recognition (CVPR). vol. 3, p. 6 (2017)
22. Strassmann, S.: Hairy brushes. ACM SIGGRAPH Comput. Graph. **20**, 225–232 (1986)

23. Szegedy, C., Vanhoucke, V., Ioffe, S., Shlens, J., Wojna, Z.: Rethinking the inception architecture for computer vision. In: Proceedings of the IEEE Conference on Computer Vision and Pattern Recognition, pp. 2818–2826 (2016)
24. Taigman, Y., Polyak, A., Wolf, L.: Unsupervised cross-domain image generation. CoRR abs/1611.02200 (2016). http://arxiv.org/abs/1611.02200
25. kaonashi tyc: zi2zi: Master chinese calligraphy with conditional adversarial networks. Website (2017). http://github.com/kaonashi-tyc/zi2zi
26. Ulyanov, D., Vedaldi, A., Lempitsky, V.S.: Instance normalization: the missing ingredient for fast stylization. CoRR abs/1607.08022 (2016). http://arxiv.org/abs/1607.08022
27. Wong, H.T., Ip, H.H.: Virtual brush: a model-based synthesis of Chinese calligraphy. Comput. Graph. **24**(1), 99–113 (2000)
28. Xia, Y., Wu, J., Gao, P., Lin, Y., Mao, T.: Ontology-based model for Chinese calligraphy synthesis. Comput. Graph. Forum **32**, 11–20 (2013)
29. Zhang, H., Goodfellow, I., Metaxas, D., Odena, A.: Self-attention generative adversarial networks. arXiv preprint arXiv:1805.08318 (2018)
30. Zhang, Z., Wu, J., Yu, K.: Chinese calligraphy specific style rendering system. In: Proceedings of the 10th Annual Joint Conference on Digital Libraries, pp. 99–108. ACM (2010)
31. Zhu, J.Y., Park, T., Isola, P., Efros, A.A.: Unpaired image-to-image translation using cycle-consistent adversarial networks. In: 2017 IEEE International Conference on Computer Vision (ICCV), pp. 2242–2251. IEEE (2017)

End-to-End Detection and Re-identification Integrated Net for Person Search

Zhenwei He(ID) and Lei Zhang(✉)(ID)

School of Microelectronics and Communication Engineering, Chongqing University,
No. 174 Shazheng Street, Shapingba District, Chongqing 400044, China
{hzw,leizhang}@cqu.edu.cn

Abstract. This paper proposes a pedestrian detection and re-identification (re-id) integrated net (I-Net) in an end-to-end learning framework. The I-Net is used in real-world video surveillance scenarios, where the target person needs to be searched in the whole scene videos, and the annotations of pedestrian bounding boxes are unavailable. Comparing to the successful OIM method [31] for joint detection and re-id, we have three distinct contributions. First, we implement a Siamese architecture instead of one stream for an end-to-end training strategy. Second, a novel on-line pairing loss (OLP) with a feature dictionary restricts the positive pairs. Third, hard example priority softmax loss (HEP) with little computation cast is proposed to deal with the online hard example mining. We show our results on CUHK-SYSU and PRW datasets. Our method narrows the gap between detection and re-identification, and achieves a superior performance.

Keywords: Person search · Deep learning

1 Introduction

Real-world video surveillance tasks such as criminals search [29], multi-camera tracking [26] need to search the target person from different scenes. In other words, the algorithms for real-world person search tasks are asked to find the target person from a whole image. Therefore, this problem is generally issued by two separate steps: person detection from single image and person re-identification (re-id). These two problems are challenging due to the influences of poses, viewpoints, lighting, occlusion, resolution, background *etc.* Therefore, they have been paid too much attention in recent research [2,3,21,27].

Although numerous endeavor on person detection and re-identification has been made, most of them handle these two problems independently. The traditional methods divide the person search task into two sub-problems. First, a

This work is supported by National Natural Science Fund of China (Grant 61771079) and Chongqing Science and Technology Project (cstc2017zdcy-zdzxX0002).

C. V. Jawahar et al. (Eds.): ACCV 2018, LNCS 11362, pp. 349–364, 2019.
https://doi.org/10.1007/978-3-030-20890-5_23

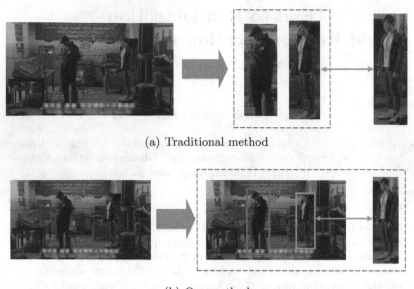

(a) Traditional method

(b) Our method

Fig. 1. Comparison of the traditional method and our method. In the (a), Traditional method need detect all persons in the picture and cropped them for the further re-id model. Our new method (I-Net) in (b) can find the target person from a whole image directly.

detector is implemented to predict the bounding boxes of the persons from the images. Second, the detected persons are cropped based on the bounding boxes for the further re-identification task. Actually, most advanced re-identification method are modeled on the manually cropped pedestrian images [3,14,15], and the manually cropped pedestrian samples are much better than the specially trained detector because of inevitable false detection. Additionally, person search task should be a joint work of detection and re-id, which requires the close cooperation of both two parts. Therefore, in this paper, we propose a new model to jointly train these two parts in a unified deep framework end-to-end, which aims to search the target person from whole image scene.

Specifically, to reduce the gap between traditional algorithms and practical applications, we propose an Integrated Net (I-Net) to simultaneously learn the detector and re-identifier by an end-to-end manner. Figure 1 shows the difference between traditional scheme and the proposed I-Net in application scenario. Different from the traditional re-id method, which got a separated two steps (detection and re-identification) for the person search task, our I-Net can predict the location (bounding box) of the target person from a whole image. The joint learning of the detector and re-identifier in I-Net for person search brings lots of benefits: On one hand, the co-learning of the detector and re-identifier helps the re-id part to handle the misalignments of bounding boxes and the false positives provided by the detector, such that the re-id part can be more robust than independent training. On the other hand, the detection and re-id reuse the same features which can accelerate the search speed.

Triplet loss [24] is a loss function for the verification problems, it's widely used for the re-id tasks [6,7,19]. Triplet loss sometimes encounters the stagnate problem during the training phase because the condition of the loss function can be easily satisfied. Further, in order to remit the stagnate problem and achieve the purpose of co-learning of person detection and re-id, an on-line pairing loss (OLP loss) and a hard example priority softmax loss (HEP loss) are proposed in I-Net. By storing the features of different persons in a dynamic dictionary, a positive pair and lots of negative pairs can be captured for every iterations. Such that, the positive pairs is restricted by more negative pairs than the Triplet loss [24], which is helpful to remit the stagnate problem. HEP Loss is an auxiliary loss based on softmax, which considers the hard example priority strategy. This loss function drops some easily distinguished samples to reduces computation cast and achieves a better results than traditional softmax. Besides, comparing to the OIM loss [31] which generates positive and negative pairs with out of date features, our model based on the Siamese architecture generates real-time positive pairs during the training phase. We achieved an advanced performance on the person search task with our special designed loss function for joint training. The contribution and novelty of this paper are summarized in three folds:

- We propose a Siamese structure based Integrated Net (I-Net) for an end-to-end learning strategy. Based on the special net structure, our I-Net can generate a better real-time positive pairs than OIM [31], which leads to a better performance.
- On-line pairing (OLP) loss with an online feature dictionary is proposed to strictly restrict the positive pair. Since that, it's more helpful to remit the stagnate problem in the training phase.
- A hard example priority strategy is implemented in Hard example priority (HEP) loss which focus on the online hard example mining. Benefit from the results of OLP, we achieve a better performance than traditional softmax but with less computation cast.

2   Related Work

In recent years, lots of researches on person detection and re-identification were conducted independently. In this section, we will introduce some closely related works for a better presentation of our paper.

Person Re-identification. Most re-id work focus on two aspects: feature representation [1,5,38] and similarity metric [16,17,23]. All of these methods achieved great success in the past few years, Chen et al. [5], jointly optimized the two tasks simultaneously for re-id, Cheng et al. [6] presented a novel multi-channel parts-based model with triplet loss. Additionally, in order to remit the influence of stagnate problem of triplet loss, Chen et al. [4] enlarged the three-steam network to quadruplet network such that one more negative pair can be obtained to strength the condition. For our special designed OLP loss function, we generate amounts of negative samples to remit the stagnate problem during the training phase and a better results for the person search task is achieved.

Pedestrian Detection. Traditional pedestrian detection methods are based on hand-crafted features and Adaboost classifiers, such as ACF [8], LDCF [20], Checkerboards [34] and Integral Channels Features (ICF) [9]. These methods dominated the detection field for years due to their effectiveness. Recently, convolutional neural network (CNN) based deep learning methods have achieved significant progress in pedestrian detection. Tian *et al.* [28] jointly optimized the pedestrian detection with semantic tasks, including pedestrian attributes and scene attributes. Song *et al.* [27] combined multiple deep networks with one fully-connected layer to improve the detection accuracy. In [33], CNN features extracted by RPN [22] are fed into the random forest for pedestrian detection. In our work, we implemented our detection module based on the Faster-RCNN [22], which is used to generate proposals for our further re-identification part.

End-to-End Person Search. Recently, some works were proposed to address the person search task. ID-discriminative Embedding (IDE) and Confidence Weighted Similarity (CWS) were proposed by Zheng *et al.* [37]. While NPSM [18] based on LSTM was used to reduce the region containing the target automatically. Xiao *et al.* [31] jointly trained both two tasks with OIM loss, which updated features of a labeled identity every hundreds of iterations. As a result, the out-of-date features stored by OIM can't properly compute the loss function. Benefiting from the Siamese structure, our I-Net can generate a real-time positive pairs during the training phase and lead to a better performance.

3   The Proposed I-Net

We propose a new I-Net framework that jointly handles the pedestrian detection and person re-id into an end-to-end Siamese network. The architecture is shown in Fig. 2. Given a pair of images with the persons with same identity, two pedestrian proposal networks (PPN) with shared parameters are learnt to predict the proposals of pedestrians from the two images. The feature maps pooled by region of interest (ROI) pooling layer are then fed into the fully-connected (fc) layers to extract 256-D L2-normalized features for the re-id task. After that, these features are stored in an on-line dynamic feature dictionary, in order to generate one positive pair and lots of negative pairs for OLP loss and HEP loss.

3.1   Deep Model Structure

The basic model of I-Net is the VGG16 architecture [25]. Which has 5 stacks of convolutional part, including 2, 2, 3, 3, 3 convolutional layers for each stack. 4 max-pooling layer are followed on the first 4 stacks. On the top of *conv5_3* layer, we generate feature maps with 512 channels which are used to predict pedestrian proposals. A $512 \times 3 \times 3$ convolutional layer is first added to get the

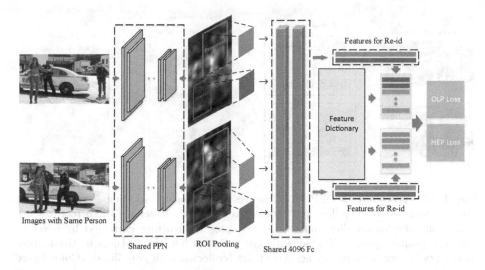

Fig. 2. The net structure of our I-Net. A pair of images including the person with same identity are fed into the two PPNs of the I-Net respectively. Two PPNs shared same parameters generate proposals for pedestrians. These proposals are then fed into the further fc layers to get the corresponding features. The input features and the feature dictionary are then used to form positive and negative pairs, which participate the computation of OLP loss and HEP loss for joint training.

features for pedestrian proposals. Similar to faster RCNN [22], we then associate 9 anchors at each feature map, and a softmax classifier (cls.) is used to predict whether the anchor is a pedestrian or not. A SmoothL1Loss (reg.) is used for bounding box regression. Finally, 128 proposals for each image after the non-maximum suppression (NMS) are obtained. In fact, the two branches of the PPN are shared same parameters during the training phase.

A ROI pooling layer [11] is integrated into I-Net to pool the generated proposals from both two PPNs. The pooled features from both two branches are then fed into the two fc layers of 4096 neurons. In order to remove the false positives of proposals, a two class softmax layer (person vs. non-person) is trained to classify them. Then a 256-D L2-normalized features generated by an extra fc layer which are then fed into the OLP loss and HEP loss for guiding the whole training phase. With the SoomthL1loss which is used to correct the bounding boxes of proposals, the proposed I-Net can be jointly trained for simultaneous person detection and re-identification in an end-to-end architecture. The whole network structure is shown in the Fig. 2.

3.2 On-Line Pairing Loss (OLP)

128 proposals per image are learned by PPNs are then fed into the re-identification part. For person re-id, the proposal features can be divided into 3 types, including background (B), persons with identity information (p-w-id)

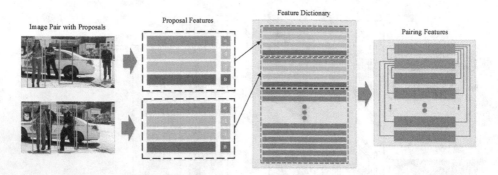

Fig. 3. The procedure of OLP. The features of proposals including B (red), p-w-id (green), and p-w/o-id (yellow and labeled as −1) are extracted. These features are stored into the feature dictionary. OLP loss uses the features extracted by I-Net to compose positive pairs (collected with green line) while the features in the feature dictionary is used to construct negative pairs (collected with gray lines). (Color figure online)

and persons without identity information (p-w/o-id). The division depends on the IOU between the proposals and the ground truth. As shown in Fig. 3, the B, p-w-id and p-w/o-id are represented by red, green, and yellow bounding box, respectively. In the OLP loss, an on-line feature dictionary is designed where the features of p-w-id, p-w/o-id, and a part of B are stored with corresponding labels. Note that, the number of the stored features depends on the number of proposals per PPN. Specifically, we use 40 times number of proposals per PPN in our experiment. Notably, once the number of features in the dictionary reaches the maximum number, the out-of-date feature will be replaced.

In order to minimize the discrepancy of the features from the same id, while maximizing the discrepancy of different, we use the person proposals from the two stream of I-Net and the stored feature dictionary to establish positive and negative pairs. Suppose that the proposal group for loss computation is $(\mathbf{p}_1, \mathbf{p}_2, \mathbf{n}_1, \mathbf{n}_2..., \mathbf{n}_k)$, where $(\mathbf{p}_1, \mathbf{p}_2)$ stands for proposals from the same identity person generated by I-Net in forward propagation and $(\mathbf{n}_1, \mathbf{n}_2..., \mathbf{n}_k)$ are the features stored in the dictionary. For each proposal group, we tend to formulate two symmetrical subgroups by taking $\mathbf{p}_1$ and $\mathbf{p}_2$ as anchor, alternatively. For example, when $\mathbf{p}_1$ is regarded as anchor, the $(\mathbf{p}_1, \mathbf{p}_2)$ is the positive pair. $(\mathbf{p}_1, \mathbf{n}_1)$, $(\mathbf{p}_1, \mathbf{n}_2)$, ... , $(\mathbf{p}_1, \mathbf{n}_k)$ are negative pairs. Alternatively, when $\mathbf{p}_2$ is regarded as anchor, $(\mathbf{p}_2, \mathbf{p}_1)$ is the positive pair. $(\mathbf{p}_2, \mathbf{n}_1)$, $(\mathbf{p}_2, \mathbf{n}_2)$, ... , $(\mathbf{p}_2, \mathbf{n}_k)$ are negative pairs. Considering the large amount of negative samples, the OLP loss is established based on softmax function. Suppose we get m subgroups in one iteration, and $\mathbf{x}_A^i$, $\mathbf{x}_p^i$, $(\mathbf{x}_{n_1}^i, \mathbf{x}_{n_2}^i..., \mathbf{x}_{n_k}^i)$ stand for the anchor, positive and negative features of ith subgroup, respectively. The OLP loss function is represented as follows.

$$L_{OLP} = -\frac{1}{m} \sum_{i=1}^{m} log \frac{e^{d(\mathbf{x}_A^i, \mathbf{x}_p^i)}}{e^{d(\mathbf{x}_A^i, \mathbf{x}_p^i)} + \sum_{j=1}^{k} e^{d(\mathbf{x}_A^i, \mathbf{x}_{n_j}^i)}} \tag{1}$$

where the function $d(\cdot)$ stands for the cosine distance of two features. Because these features are L2-normalized, the cosine distance can be directly computed by the inner product. In gradient computation, we only calculate the deviation from the anchor feature.

Then, the deviation of the OLP loss function with respect to $\mathbf{x}_A^i$ for the ith subgroup can be calculated as:

$$\frac{\partial L_{OLP}}{\partial \mathbf{x}_A^i} = (q^i - 1)\mathbf{x}_P^i + \sum_{l=1}^{k}(\hat{q}_l^i \mathbf{x}_{n_l}^i) \tag{2}$$

where q^i and $\hat{q}_l^i$ are expressed in Eqs. (3) and (4).

$$q^i = \frac{e^{d(\mathbf{x}_A^i, \mathbf{x}_p^i)}}{e^{d(\mathbf{x}_A^i, \mathbf{x}_p^i)} + \sum_{j=1}^{k} e^{d(\mathbf{x}_A^i, \mathbf{x}_{n_j}^i)}} \tag{3}$$

$$\hat{q}_l^i = \frac{e^{d(\mathbf{x}_A^i, \mathbf{x}_{n_l}^i)}}{e^{d(\mathbf{x}_A^i, \mathbf{x}_p^i)} + \sum_{j=1}^{k} e^{d(\mathbf{x}_A^i, \mathbf{x}_{n_j}^i)}}, l = 1, ..., k \tag{4}$$

Following the standard BP optimization in CNN, stochastic gradient descent (SGD) is adopted in the training phase of I-Net.

From the OLP loss (1), we can see that a large number of negative features can be processed at one time by utilizing the cosine distance guided softmax function. In terms of the softmax character, the cosine distance between anchor and positive samples tends to be maximized which improves the performance.

3.3 Hard Example Priority Softmax Loss (HEP)

The OLP loss function aims to restrict the cosine distance of positive pairs to be larger than negative pairs. However, the identity information is not fully exploited. Therefore, we propose a HEP softmax loss function for person identity classification. Different from the traditional softmax loss, we propose a hard example priority strategy, which focuses on the classes of hard negative pairs.

Suppose that there are C identities in the dataset. The HEP loss function aims to classify all proposals (except p-w/o-id) into $C + 1$ classes (C classes plus B). In order to calculate the HEP loss, we annotate the proposals based on IOU between the proposal and the ground truth. To this end, when the cosine distances among the positive pair and negative pairs are computed by the OLP loss as described in Sect. 3.2, we can find out the top 20 maximum distances of the negative pairs, and record their corresponding labels as priority classes. In order to keep the fixed total number of the priority classes, we also randomly choose an uncertain number of classes from the remaining classes, such that totally $M(M << C + 1)$ classes are selected to compute the final loss. Finally, the HEP softmax loss function is represented as:

$$L_{HEP} = -\frac{1}{n} \sum_{i=1}^{n} \sum_{j=1}^{M} \mathbf{1}(label = j) log \frac{e^{x_j^i}}{\sum_{k=1}^{M} e^{x_k^i}} \tag{5}$$

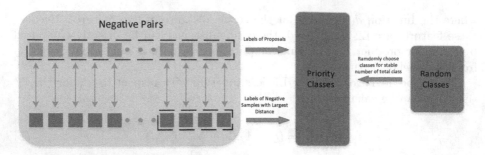

Fig. 4. The protocol for choosing the priority class for the HEP loss function, First, the labels of PPN generated proposals during the forward propagation were selected as priority class. Second, labels of negative samples from negative pairs which got the largest consine distances were selected. At last, same random classes were chosen to make sure the total number of priority class fixed.

where x^i_j stands for the i-th proposal's score from the classifier and j stands for the j-th class. Suppose that **L** stands for the pool of priority classes. The protocol for choosing the M classes with hard example priority strategy is summarized as below, which can be recognized in Fig. 4.

1. The label indexes of generated proposals from the input image pair in the forward propagation are first stored in the priority classes pool **L** to ensure the ground truth class.
2. For each subgroup (described in Sect. 3.1), the label indexes of negative samples from the top 20 negative pairs with the maximum distances are stored in the priority classes pool **L**. This step makes sure the hard classes are priority considered.
3. If the size of pool **L** is still smaller than M (a preset value), then we randomly generate the classes indexes without repetition and store them in the chosen priority pool **L**.

This strategy ensures that the classes of hard samples are priority selected. That is, if a person with identity is hard to distinguish from others, then the proposals of the corresponding identity must participate the HEP softmax loss computation in Eq. (5). Additionally, the loss function has little computation cast because the cosine distances are pre-computed by OLP.

4   Experiments

To evaluate the effectiveness of our approach, we conduct a number of experiments on the CUHK-SYSU dataset [30] and PRW dataset [37]. We first compare our results to state-of-the-art methods on both two datasets in Sects. 4.2 and 4.3. Then the discussion of our model is presented in Sect. 4.3.

4.1   Experimental Setup

Implementation Details. Our I-Net is implemented on Caffe [13] and py-faster-rcnn [22] platform. VGG16 [25] is the basic network of I-Net and the trained model in [30] was used for network initialization. The first two stacks of convolutional layers are frozen while training our net. The two streams of the I-Net shared the same parameters for both initialization and training. The pedestrian proposal network (PPN) at each branch generates 128 proposals. We randomly choose 5 background proposals per image to store in the feature dictionary. In I-Net, all loss functions are imposed the same loss weight. The learning rate is initialized to 0.001, and drops to 0.0001 in 50k iterations. Totally, 60k iterations are set to insure convergence.

CUHK-SYSU Dataset. The CUHK-SYSU dataset [30] is a large person search dataset containing 18184 images from the hand-held cameras and movie snapshots, which has a large variations in viewpoint, lighting, resolution, *etc.* It annotated 8432 different persons and 96143 bounding boxes. Each labeled person has at least two images from different viewpoints. The dataset provided 11206 images with 5532 identities as the training set, and 6978 images with 2900 identities for test. Our experiments follow the protocols provided by the dataset.

PRW Dataset. The PRW dataset [37] is extracted from 10-hour video captured by 6 cameras, which 5 are 1080×1920 HD and 1 is 576×720 SD. Totally 11816 frames are manually annotated, which contains 43110 pedestrian bounding boxes, among which 34304 pedestrians are annotated with 932 IDs. The PRW dataset provides 5134 frames with 482 labeled identities as training set while 6112 frames with 450 labeled identities are used as testing set. The PRW dataset ask the model to search the target person from the whole testing set, which is challenging.

4.2   Experiments on CUHK-SYSU

In this section, we perform several experiments on the CUHK-SYSU datasets to investigate the effectiveness of our I-Net. For baseline comparisons, we select three pedestrian detection methods and five person re-id approaches, which then results in 15 baselines. The three detection methods, CCF [32], Faster-RCNN [22] with resnet50 [12] and ACF [8], are used for detecting pedestrians. Besides, we also use the detection ground truth of the test set as the perfect detector. For the re-identification problem, we evaluate several famous re-id feature representation methods including DenseSIFT-ColorHist (DSIFT) [35], Bag of Words (BoW) [36], Local Maximal Occurrence (LOMO) [17] and ID-Net (The re-identification part of OIM [31]) to extract features for re-identification, while Euclidean, Cosine similarity, KISSME [23], and XQDA [17] are used as metric method for them. We combine these detection methods and re-identification methods as the examples of traditional person search model.

Further, we implement the OIM loss model [31], the End-to-End model (initialized model) [30] and NPSM [18] as the competitor, which addressed the

Table 1. Comparisons between our framework and other methods on CUHK-SYSU

Detector	Re-id method	mAP (%)	Top-1 (%)
ACF	DSIFT [35]+Euclidean	21.7	25.9
	DISFT [35]+KISSME [23]	32.3	38.1
	BOW [36]+KISSME [23]	42.4	48.4
	LOMO [17]+XQDA [17]	55.5	63.1
	IDNet [31]	56.5	63.0
CCF	DSIFT [35]+Euclidean	11.3	11.7
	DISFT [35]+KISSME [23]	13.4	13.9
	BOW [36]+KISSME [23]	26.9	29.3
	LOMO [17]+XQDA [17]	41.2	46.4
	IDNet [31]	50.9	57.1
CNN	DSIFT [35]+Euclidean	34.5	39.4
	DISFT [35]+KISSME [23]	47.8	53.6
	BOW [36]+KISSME [23]	56.9	62.3
	LOMO [17]+XQDA [17]	68.9	74.1
	IDNet [31]	68.6	74.8
GT	DSIFT [35]+Euclidean	41.1	45.9
	DISFT [35]+KISSME [23]	56.2	61.9
	BOW [36]+KISSME [23]	62.5	67.2
	LOMO [17]+XQDA [17]	72.4	76.7
	IDNet [31]	73.1	78.3
End-to-End (Initialized model) [30]		55.7	62.7
OIM [31]		75.5	78.7
NPSM [18]		77.9	81.2
I-Net (ours)		**79.5**	**81.5**

same person search problem. All our experiments are following the protocol of the CUHK-SYSU dataset, and we test the models on the gallery size of 100.

In experiment, the top-1 accuracy and the mAP (mean average precision) are used for evaluating the person re-identification performance. Specifically, the re-identification results are shown in Table 1, from which we can see that the proposed I-Net achieves a top-1 accuracy of 81.5% and mAP of 79.5%, which beats all compared methods. From Table 1, we can observe that the state-of-the-art end-to-end person search methods (OIM, NPSM, I-Net) always outperform the traditional person search methods (detection+person re-id). It is noteworthy that even the perfect detector (ground truth) with re-id methods had a inferior results compared to the end-to-end method, which demonstrates that it is important and necessary to integrate detection and re-id together for joint modeling. Benefited from siamese architecture, our model generated a real-time positive and negative pairs which leads to 4% higher in mAP than our baseline OIM. Additionally, our method also outperforms NPSM by 1.6% in mAP with lower computation cast.

4.3   Experiments on PRW Dataset

We also conduct some experiments on PRW [37] dataset by using I-Net, OIM (baseline) [31] and some state-of-the-art detection and re-id methods. For the detection, the DPM [10], ACF [8] and their related RCNN methods and LDCF [20] are implemented, and the LOMO [17]+XQDA [17], bag of words vector [36], IDE_{det}, CWS [37] are used for re-identification. At last, we get 14 kinds of methods by combining these detector and re-identification methods. For the RCNN, AlexNet is implemented as the base network according to [37]. On the other hand, OIM was also implemented on the dataset as an end-to-end person search method. The results are shown in Table 2, from which we can see that our method achieves the best results. It's noteworthy that our method also outperforms OIM by 2.6% in mAP and 2.0% in top-1.

Table 2. Results of PRW datasets

Methods	mAP (%)	Top-1 (%)
DPM [10]+BOW [36]	9.7	31.1
DPM [10]+IDE_{det} [37]	18.8	45.9
DPM-Alex+LOMO+XQDA [17]	13.0	34.1
DPM-Alex+IDE_{det} [37]	20.3	47.4
DPM-Alex+$IDE_{det} + CWS$ [37]	20.5	48.3
ACF [8]+LOMO+XQDA [17]	10.5	30.9
ACF [8]+IDE_{det} [37]	17.5	43.8
ACF-Alex+LOMO+XQDA [17]	10.3	30.6
ACF-Alex+$IDE_{det} + CWS$ [37]	17.8	45.2
LDCF [20]+BOW [36]	9.1	29.8
LDCF [20]+LOMO+XQDA [17]	11.0	31.1
LDCF [20]+IDE_{det} [37]	18.3	44.6
LDCF [20]+$IDE_{det} + CWS$ [37]	18.3	45.5
OIM (baseline) [31]	23.0	46.7
I-Net (ours)	**25.6**	**48.7**

4.4   Model Discussion

In this section, we discuss the effectiveness of Joint Loss and the influence of feature dictionary size. All results in this section are tested on CUHK-SYSU dataset.

Analysis of Joint Loss. Our HEP loss can be recognized as a variation of softmax which treats the task as a classification problem. While the traditional softmax loss function have to compute all classes of the dataset every iteration, our HEP loss function gets the priority classes based on the cosine distances of negative pairs. This strategy makes our loss function achieves better performance and reduces the computation cast. Otherwise, as an auxiliary loss function of OLP, it can promote the effectiveness of the OLP loss function. In order to take an insight of the joint training between OLP loss, softmax and HEP loss, three different cases: OLP only, OLP with softmax loss, and OLP with HEP are discussed, respectively. The OIM which is our baseline is also shown.

Table 3. Comparisons among different loss types.

Loss type	mAP (%)	Top-1 (%)
OLP only	73.6	76.2
OIM	75.5	78.7
OLP with softmax	78.7	80.9
OLP with HEP	79.5	81.5

The results with four types of loss functions are shown in Table 3. We can see that a single OLP loss without joint training achieves a inferior result. By adding the softmax loss in our framework for the joint training, both of the mAP and top-1 exceed the OIM loss function by 3.2% and 2.5%, respectively. Such that, the effectiveness of joint loss is demonstrated. Further, the joint training of OLP and HEP outperforms the traditional softmax by 0.8% in mAP and 0.6% in top-1, which shows that the drop of some easily distinguished samples helped the model improve its effectiveness and reduce the computation cast.

Table 4. Influence of the number of features stored in OLP.

	Number of features		
mAP (%)	20×128	40×128	80×128
OLP only	73.2	74.3	72.9
OLP+HEP	78.4	**79.5**	79.1
Top-1 (%)	20×128	40×128	80×128
OLP only	76.0	77.5	75.6
OLP+HEP	80.7	**81.5**	81.1

Influence of Stored Features. The number of features from the proposals stored in the dictionary is a major parameter which influences our model. This parameter is set as 40 times number of proposals generated by each PPN.

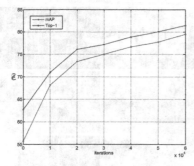 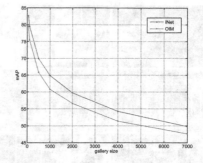

(a) Accuracy during the training phase   (b) Accuracy changed with gallery size

Fig. 5. Experiment results. Figure (a) is the trend of mAP and top-1, which was changed during the training phase. Figure (b) is the mAP from different gallery size.

Such that $40 \times 128 = 5120$ features will be stored. To explore the influence of the feature dictionary, OLP only and the joint training of OLP and HEP with different number of stored features have been tested. The results are shown in Table 4.

The experiments show that 40 times proposal number achieves the best result. Both 20 times and 80 times the proposal number get a inferior results. This kind of phenomenon may expose the two problems mentioned before. A large feature dictionary size may make the stored feature stored out of date, which may influence the quality of negative pairs. On the contrary, a small feature dictionary size means a smaller number of negative pairs, which can't fully restrict the positive pair, such that the training phase may stagnated.

Accuracy During the Training Phase. Our I-Net is training for 60k iterations. The variation trend of during the training phase is shown in Fig. 5(a), which shows that both mAP and top-1 index are increasing during the whole training phase. Both mAP and top-1 are increasing sharply during the training phase, and the learning rate is changed at 50k iterations. The model is convergence for 60k iterations.

Gallery Size. Person search problem should be more challenging when the gallery size is growing up. Therefore, we evaluate our method on different gallery size from 50 to 6978 (full set) on the CUHK-SYSU. All test images are covered even in a small gallery size according to the dataset testing protocol. The result is shown in Fig. 5(b). As the gallery size increased, the model suffer a significantly descend in both mAP and top-1. It's noteworthy that our I-Net still beats the OIM methods on all gallery sizes. More hard samples are chosen as distracter while the gallery size extends, which increases the difficulty to find the target person. The person search task based on the large gallery size is a challenging task, which may be our future mission.

Fig. 6. Visualization of some person search results on the CUHK-SYSU dataset. Every row of the figure is a result of a query. The cyan bounding boxes from the pictures of first column are target persons. The last three columns are matched samples. The red bounding boxes are false alarms, and green bounding boxes are successful matches. (Color figure online)

Visualization of Person Search Results. The Fig. 6 presents some person search results of our I-Net on the CUHK-SYSU dataset. Rows 1, 2 are successful matched samples which find the target person from other images, and row 3 gets a false alarm because of the similar clothes. The row 4 is a failure case, which may caused by the dusky light condition of the query person.

5   Conclusions

In this paper, we introduce a novel end-to-end learning framework for large-scale person search. By jointly modeling pedestrian detection and re-identification, an integrated convolutional neural network (I-Net) is proposed. Specifically, a novel on-line pairing loss (OLP) and hard example priority based softmax (HEP) are proposed for supervising the joint training. For OLP loss, we propose to design a feature dictionary which is used to store a large amounts of features, such that more negative pairs can be obtained to improve the training effect. Besides that, we propose a hard example priority strategy based HEP loss, which has improved the effectiveness as well as the efficiency. By testing the I-Net on the CUHK-SYSU [30] and PRW [37] dataset, the effectiveness of our I-Net is validated.

References

1. Ahmed, E., Jones, M., Marks, T.K.: An improved deep learning architecture for person re-identification. In: Computer Vision and Pattern Recognition, pp. 3908–3916 (2015)
2. Cao, C., Wang, Y., Kato, J., Zhang, G., Mase, K.: Solving occlusion problem in pedestrian detection by constructing discriminative part layers. In: Applications of Computer Vision, pp. 91–99 (2017)
3. Chen, S.Z., Guo, C.C., Lai, J.H.: Deep ranking for person re-identification via joint representation learning. IEEE Trans. Image Process. **25**(5), 2353–2367 (2016)
4. Chen, W., Chen, X., Zhang, J., Huang, K.: Beyond triplet loss: a deep quadruplet network for person re-identification (2017)
5. Chen, W., Chen, X., Zhang, J., Huang, K.: A multi-task deep network for person re-identification (2017)
6. Cheng, D., Gong, Y., Zhou, S., Wang, J., Zheng, N.: Person re-identification by multi-channel parts-based CNN with improved triplet loss function. In: Computer Vision and Pattern Recognition, pp. 1335–1344 (2016)
7. Ding, S., Lin, L., Wang, G., Chao, H.: Deep feature learning with relative distance comparison for person re-identification. Pattern Recognit. **48**(10), 2993–3003 (2015)
8. Dollar, P., Belongie, S., Perona, P.: Fast feature pyramids for object detection. IEEE Trans. Pattern Anal. Mach. Intell. **36**(8), 1532 (2014)
9. Dollar, P., Tu, Z., Perona, P., Belongie, S.: Integral channel features. In: British Machine Vision Conference, BMVC 2009, London, UK, 7–10 September 2009, Proceedings (2009)
10. Felzenszwalb, P.F., Girshick, R.B., Mcallester, D., Ramanan, D.: Object detection with discriminatively trained part-based models. IEEE Trans. Pattern Anal. Mach. Intell. **32**(9), 1627–1645 (2010)
11. Girshick, R.: Fast R-CNN. Computer Science (2015)
12. He, K., Zhang, X., Ren, S., Sun, J.: Deep residual learning for image recognition. In: Computer Vision and Pattern Recognition, pp. 770–778 (2016)
13. Jia, Y., et al.: Caffe: convolutional architecture for fast feature embedding. In: ACM International Conference on Multimedia, pp. 675–678 (2014)
14. Li, W., Wang, X.: Locally aligned feature transforms across views. In: Computer Vision and Pattern Recognition, pp. 3594–3601 (2013)
15. Li, W., Zhao, R., Wang, X.: Human reidentification with transferred metric learning. In: Lee, K.M., Matsushita, Y., Rehg, J.M., Hu, Z. (eds.) ACCV 2012. LNCS, vol. 7724, pp. 31–44. Springer, Heidelberg (2013). https://doi.org/10.1007/978-3-642-37331-2_3
16. Li, X., Zheng, W.S., Wang, X., Xiang, T.: Multi-scale learning for low-resolution person re-identification. In: IEEE International Conference on Computer Vision, pp. 3765–3773 (2015)
17. Liao, S., Hu, Y., Zhu, X., Li, S.Z.: Person re-identification by local maximal occurrence representation and metric learning. In: Computer Vision and Pattern Recognition, pp. 2197–2206 (2015)
18. Liu, H., et al.: Neural person search machines (2017)
19. Liu, J., et al.: Multi-scale triplet CNN for person re-identification. In: ACM on Multimedia Conference, pp. 192–196 (2016)
20. Nam, W., Dollar, P., Han, J.H.: Local decorrelation for improved pedestrian detection. In: NIPS, pp. 1–9 (2014)

21. Ouyang, W., Zeng, X., Wang, X.: Modeling mutual visibility relationship in pedestrian detection. In: Computer Vision and Pattern Recognition, pp. 3222–3229 (2013)
22. Ren, S., He, K., Girshick, R., Sun, J.: Faster R-CNN: towards real-time object detection with region proposal networks. IEEE Trans. Pattern Anal. Mach. Intell. **39**(6), 1137–1149 (2017)
23. Roth, P.M., Wohlhart, P., Hirzer, M., Kostinger, M., Bischof, H.: Large scale metric learning from equivalence constraints. In: IEEE Conference on Computer Vision and Pattern Recognition, pp. 2288–2295 (2012)
24. Schroff, F., Kalenichenko, D., Philbin, J.: FaceNet: a unified embedding for face recognition and clustering, pp. 815–823 (2015)
25. Simonyan, K., Zisserman, A.: Very deep convolutional networks for large-scale image recognition. Computer Science (2014)
26. Song, B., Kamal, A.T., Soto, C., Ding, C., Farrell, J.A., Roychowdhury, A.K.: Tracking and activity recognition through consensus in distributed camera networks. IEEE Trans. Image Process. **19**(10), 2564–2579 (2010)
27. Song, H., Wang, W., Wang, J., Wang, R.: Collaborative deep networks for pedestrian detection. In: IEEE Third International Conference on Multimedia Big Data, pp. 146–153 (2017)
28. Tian, Y., Luo, P., Wang, X., Tang, X.: Pedestrian detection aided by deep learning semantic tasks, pp. 5079–5087 (2014)
29. Wang, X.: Intelligent multi-camera video surveillance: a review. Pattern Recognit. Lett. **34**, 3–19 (2013)
30. Xiao, T., Li, S., Wang, B., Lin, L., Wang, X.: End-to-end deep learning for person search (2016)
31. Xiao, T., Li, S., Wang, B., Lin, L., Wang, X.: Joint detection and identification feature learning for person search. In: The IEEE Conference on Computer Vision and Pattern Recognition (CVPR), July 2017
32. Yang, B., Yan, J., Lei, Z., Li, S.Z.: Convolutional channel features. In: IEEE International Conference on Computer Vision, pp. 82–90 (2015)
33. Zhang, L., Lin, L., Liang, X., He, K.: Is faster R-CNN doing well for pedestrian detection? In: Leibe, B., Matas, J., Sebe, N., Welling, M. (eds.) ECCV 2016. LNCS, vol. 9906, pp. 443–457. Springer, Cham (2016). https://doi.org/10.1007/978-3-319-46475-6_28
34. Zhang, S., Benenson, R., Schiele, B.: Filtered channel features for pedestrian detection, pp. 1751–1760 (2015)
35. Zhao, R., Ouyang, W., Wang, X.: Unsupervised salience learning for person re-identification. In: IEEE Conference on Computer Vision and Pattern Recognition, pp. 3586–3593 (2013)
36. Zheng, L., Shen, L., Tian, L., Wang, S., Wang, J., Tian, Q.: Scalable person re-identification: a benchmark. In: IEEE International Conference on Computer Vision, pp. 1116–1124 (2015)
37. Zheng, L., Zhang, H., Sun, S., Chandraker, M., Yang, Y., Tian, Q.: Person re-identification in the wild, pp. 3346–3355 (2016)
38. Zheng, Z., Zheng, L., Yang, Y.: A discriminatively learned CNN embedding for person re-identification (2016)

A CNN-Based Depth Estimation Approach with Multi-scale Sub-pixel Convolutions and a Smoothness Constraint

Shiyu Zhao[1], Lin Zhang[1]($\boxtimes$) (iD), Ying Shen[1], and Yongning Zhu[2]

[1] School of Software Engineering, Tongji University, Shanghai 201804, China
{1731558,cslinzhang,yingshen}@tongji.edu.cn
[2] College of Arts and Media, Tongji University, Shanghai 201804, China
yzhu@tongji.edu.cn

Abstract. Depth estimation from a single image is of paramount importance in various vision tasks, such as obstacle detection, robot navigation, 3D reconstruction, *etc.* However, how to get an accurate depth map with clear details and a fine resolution remains an unresolved issue. As an attempt to solve this problem, we propose a novel CNN-based approach, namely $MSCN_{NS}$, which involves multi-scale sub-pixel convolutions and a neighborhood smoothness constraint. Specifically, $MSCN_{NS}$ makes use of sub-pixel convolutions which fuse multi-scale features from different branches of the network to retrieve a high resolution depth map with fine details of the scene. Furthermore, $MSCN_{NS}$ incorporates a neighborhood smoothness regularization term to make sure that spatially closer pixels with similar features would have close depth values. The effectiveness and efficiency of $MSCN_{NS}$ have been corroborated through extensive experiments conducted on benchmark datasets.

Keywords: Monocular depth estimation · Multi-scale feature fusion · Sub-pixel convolution · Neighborhood smoothness

1 Introduction

Accurate depth information is vital to many computer vision tasks, such as scene understanding [3,5,20], 3D reconstruction [33], obstacle detection [28], *etc.* However, collecting depth is expensive or even impossible in some scenarios and in those cases, depth estimation is required. Generally, stereo vision approaches [7,24,32] are good solutions for this task. However, they require binocular images from two cameras and are very time consuming to get an accurate disparity map. Therefore, for data consisting of only monocular images, how to predict depth from a single still image becomes profoundly important. However, it is a very challenging task since one captured image may correspond to numerous real world scenes [2] and there are no reliable depth cues available, *e.g.* stereo correspondences or motions [16].

© Springer Nature Switzerland AG 2019
C. V. Jawahar et al. (Eds.): ACCV 2018, LNCS 11362, pp. 365–380, 2019.
https://doi.org/10.1007/978-3-030-20890-5_24

To handle such a problem, various solutions have been proposed in the literature. Primary methods [15,22,23] in this field usually formulated depth estimation as a markov random field (MRF) learning problem and resorted to hand-crafted features, such as SIFT, GIST, PHOG, *etc.* Later, data-driven approaches [9,11] were explored. Those approaches made use of hand-crafted features to retrieve the most similar candidates in the training set for a given query image. And then, the corresponding depth candidates were warped and fused to produce the final prediction. However, all these methods were usually designed for specific conditions and thus could only achieve reluctantly acceptable results.

With the emergence and popularity of CNNs (Convolutional Neural Networks), recently, researchers have begun exploring CNNs in the context of depth estimation and preliminary better results in terms of both the efficiency and the accuracy have been achieved. Inspired by the great success already achieved along this direction, in this paper, we focus on how to further explore deep models for solving the depth estimation problem and propose a CNN-based approach with multi-scale sub-pixel convolutions and a neighborhood smoothness constraint, namely $MSCN_{NS}$ (Multi-scale Sub-pixel Convolutional Network with a Neighborhood Smoothness constraint). In our approach, we use multi-scale features from different branches of our network to get fine details in the prediction and further improve our model with the neighborhood smoothness constraint as a regularization term during the training phase.

The remainder of this paper is organized as follows. We first introduce the related work and our contributions in Sect. 2 and then present the proposed method $MSCN_{NS}$ in Sect. 3. After that, the experimental results and analysis are elaborated in Sect. 4. Finally, we conclude the paper in Sect. 5.

2 Related Work and Our Contributions

2.1 Related Work

In this paper, we focus on how to better explore deep models for solving the problem of depth estimation from monocular images. Some representative methods closely related to our study are briefly reviewed here.

The first depth estimation model exploiting CNN was proposed by Eigen *et al.* [2]. In Eigen *et al.*'s model, there were two paths, the coarse-scale one and the fine-scale one, mapping the input image to the target prediction. The coarse-scale path outputted a coarse depth map and the fine-scale path refined the output with more details of the scene. In their later work [1], Eigen and Fergus extended their model [2] using more paths to solve multiple tasks, including depth estimation, semantic segmentation and surface normal prediction. In [19], inspired by Eigen *et al.*'s work [1,2], Mousavian *et al.* followed such a multi-path network to predict the semantic label and the depth value of each pixel jointly with shared representations. In Li *et al.*'s work [14], authors considered local details in the predictions and proposed a two-streamed CNN that could simultaneously predict depth and depth gradients, which were then fused together into an accurate and detailed depth map.

Different from Eigen *et al.*'s work [1, 2], other methods added more spices into CNNs for depth estimation. Liu *et al.* [16] assumed that pixels in one super-pixel own the same depth value and inferred the pixel-level depth through a conditional random field (CRF) whose unary and pairwise potentials were learned by a CNN. Later, they improved their model by introducing a super-pixel pooling operation [17] to remove redundant convolutions and reduce computation costs. Similarly, Li *et al.* [13] and Wang *et al.* [27] involved super-pixel-level predictions and then refined them to the pixel-level predictions via CRFs. Moreover, Roy *et al.* [21] combined CNNs with a regression forest, using shallow architectures at each tree node, to avoid the request of large datasets.

More recently, deeper networks for this task have been exploited. Laina *et al.* [12] leveraged the residual learning from ResNet [6] and proposed a fully convolutional architecture with a novel up-sampling method called up-projection, while Xu *et al.* [30, 31] proposed two kinds of sequential deep networks, the cascade one and the unified graphical one, which fused complementary information derived from multiple side outputs of ResNet by the means of CRFs.

2.2 Our Motivations and Contributions

Having investigated the literature, we find that in the field of depth estimation based on CNNs there is still large room for further improvement. First, since CNN is usually to reduce feature maps' dimensions, many CNN-based works [1,2,12] can only generate low resolution outputs and adopt bilinear interpolation to restore the resolution, which leads to blur in the predictions. Second, even though multi-scale features are involved, there are still many details missing in current methods [1,2,19].

In this work, we attempt to solve the aforementioned problems to some extent by proposing a CNN-based approach with multi-scale sub-pixel convolutions and a neighborhood smoothness constraint, namely $MSCN_{NS}$. The advantages and novelties of $MSCN_{NS}$ are highlighted as follows:

(1) We formulate depth estimation problem as a super-resolution problem on depth and take a novel multi-scale target learning method which benefits large network training. And our model, $MSCN_{NS}$, is able to achieve the state-of-the-art results on popular datasets for monocular depth estimation, as well as running much faster than existing methods.

(2) For a fine prediction, $MSCN_{NS}$ makes a good use of multi-scale sub-pixel convolutions, which fuse multi-scale features derived from different branches of the network. Such structures are quite novel as well as reasonable. First, recovering the resolution of depth map can be naturally formulated as a super-resolution problem on depths and the sub-pixel convolution originally proposed by Shi *et al.* [25] is an efficient method to deal with RGB image super-resolution problem. Thus, the sub-pixel convolution is very likely to be effective on depth estimation. Second, many previous studies *e.g.* [1, 2, 19, 29] have shown that, for depth estimation as well as for other pixel-level classification or regression problems, more accurate predictions can be

obtained by combining information from multiple scales. Based on those considerations, we propose the multi-scale sub-pixel convolution as a first attempt to explore super-resolution techniques on depth estimation. More details concerning the sub-pixel convolution will be described in Sect. 3.3.

(3) Considering that adjacent pixels with similar features in an image should have close depth values, we have proposed a neighborhood smoothness constraint as a regularization term to train $MSCN_{NS}$. When constructing such a constraint, we adopt features learned from CNN automatically instead of traditional hand-crafted features to evaluate the similarity of adjacent pixels in order that it can be integrated with other parts of our model seamlessly. Additionally, our neighborhood smoothness constraint is highly explainable by regarding it as a pixel level conditional random field (CRF).

3 $MSCN_{NS}$: The Proposed Method

In this section, we present details of the proposed depth estimation approach $MSCN_{NS}$, including the problem formulation, the network architecture, the multi-scale sub-pixel convolution and the neighborhood smoothness constraint. Figure 1 gives the outline of the model, which will be described later.

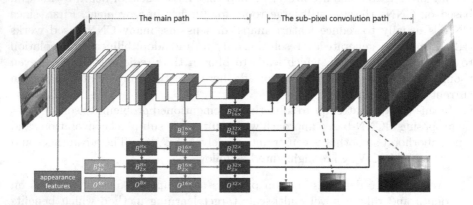

Fig. 1. The outline of our model. The blue objects represent the smoothness branch and other coloured objects connecting to the main path with vertical arrows are scale branches. Note that scale branches have no interaction with each other and the horizontal arrows just mean the features from a scale branch will be fused into the corresponding sub-pixel convolution. (Color figure online)

3.1   Problem Formulation and Overiew

Following previous works, we formulate the task of depth estimation from monocular RGB images as the problem of learning a non-linear mapping $F : \mathcal{I} \to \mathcal{D}$, which maps the image space $\mathcal{I}$ to the depth space $\mathcal{D}$. We denote the training set as $\mathcal{T} = (X_i, Y_i), i \in \mathbb{N}$, where $X_i \in \mathcal{I}$ and $Y_i \in \mathcal{D}$ representing the corresponding depth map of X_i, and denote the test set by $\mathcal{Q}$. Our goal is to construct an

F which (a) minimizes the distance of $F(X_j)$ and Y_j, (b) ensures that the resolution of $F(X_j)$ is the same as Y_j's and (c) preserves fine details of the scene in $F(X_j)$ for a given input $X_j \in \mathcal{Q}$.

For (a) and (b), we consider making use of CNN with a low resolution output and taking advantage of the sub-pixel convolution to recover the resolution. And for (c), we introduce multi-scale features into the sub-pixel convolution. Therefore, our method can be defined as,

$$P_{final} = F_1(X_j)$$

$$F_n(X_j) = SP_n(F_{2n}(X_j), \varphi_{2n}(X_j), \varphi_{2^2 n}(X_j), ..., \varphi_{2^k n}(X_j)) \qquad (1)$$

where $n, k \in \mathbb{N}$, P_{final} refers to our final prediction, n and $2^k n$ refer to the downscaling factors, SP_n refers to a sub-pixel convolution which recovers the resolution to $1/n$ of the original input resolution and $\varphi_{2^t n}(\cdot)$ ($t = 1, 2, ..., k$) refers to an function to get feature maps related to a downscaling factor of $2^t n$.

3.2   Network Architecture

We now describe the details of our model. As shown in Fig. 1, our network contains a main path, a sub-pixel convolution path, a smoothness branch and several scale branches. The main path follows the design of DenseNet [8] without the global pooling and the fully connection. We denote the features at a certain scale from the main path by $M_{n\times}$ where n is the downscaling factor of the features whose dimensions are $1/n$ the size of the input. Note that $n \in \{4, 8, 16, 32\}$ which we call the scale set and denote by $\mathcal{S}$.

Each scale branch uses $M_{n\times}$ with a certain n, generates features of larger scales via a cascade of transposed convolutions and finally outputs a predicted depth map. We denote the scale branch using $M_{n\times}$ by $B^{n\times}$ and the prediction of $B^{n\times}$ by $O^{n\times}$. Note that $O^{n\times}$ has the same resolution as input's and n in $B^{n\times}$ means that features with a downscaling factor of n (i.e., $M_{n\times}$) from the main path are used. As for features at different scales generated by transposed convolutions of the branch, we denote them by $B^{n\times}_{m\times}$, respectively, where m is the downscaling factor of the features and $m = \{x \mid x \in \{2, 4, 8, 16\}, x < n\}$. The smoothness branch takes $M_{2\times}$ (features coming from the main path with a downscaling factor of 2) as input and tries to learn features to measure the similarity of neighboring pixels.

The sub-pixel convolution path contains four multi-scale sub-pixel convolutions. Each sub-pixel convolution fuses $B^{n\times}_{m\times}$ ($\forall n \in \mathcal{S} \wedge n > m$) with a certain m and the output of the previous sub-pixel convolution and then generates a higher resolution depth map with a downscaling factor of t ($t = m/2$). We call this sub-pixel convolution $SP_{t\times}$ and denote its output by $P_{t\times}$. For illustration, $P_{4\times}$ can be presented as,

$$P_{4\times} = SP_{4\times}(P_{8\times}, B^{16\times}_{8\times}, B^{32\times}_{8\times}). \qquad (2)$$

During the training phase of our approach, we adopt a multi-scale target learning method to train the sub-pixel convolutions. That is, for a given sample $(X_i, Y_i) \in \mathcal{T}$ we minimize the l_2 distance between Y_i and each of $1\times$ scale predictions which contain $P_{1\times}$ and $O^{n\times}$ ($n = 4, 8, 16, 32$, respectively). And then, we down-sample Y_i to Y_i^t where t is the downscaling factor and minimize the l_2 distance of Y_i^t and the corresponding $P_{t\times}$ to make sure that details of the scene are preserved. Moreover, we fuse $1\times$ scale predictions via weighted average and minimize the l_2 distance between Y_i and the averaged prediction. Thus, our loss function can be defined as a sum of several l_2 distances,

$$L_2 = l_2(Y_i, P_{1\times}) + l_2(Y_i, \tilde{Y}_{fs}) + \lambda_1 \sum_{n \in \mathcal{S}} l_2(Y_i, O^{n\times}) + \sum_{t \in \{2,4,8\}} \lambda_2^t l_2(Y_i^t, P_{t\times}) \quad (3)$$

where $l_2(\cdot)$ refers to the l_2 distance, λ_1 and λ_2^t are given constants, $\mathcal{S}$ is the scale set and $\tilde{Y}_{fs}$ refers to the weighted average prediction defined as,

$$\tilde{Y}_{fs} = w_0 P_{1\times} + \sum_{i \in \mathcal{S}} w_i O^{i\times} \quad (4)$$

where w_0 and w_i are weights for fusing $1\times$ scale predictions and those weights are learned automatically via CNN.

Additionally, we formulate the neighborhood smoothness constraint as a regularization term, L_{smooth}, for training our model, which will be described concretely in Sect. 3.4. Finally, our final loss function can be defined as,

$$L = L_2 + L_{smooth} . \quad (5)$$

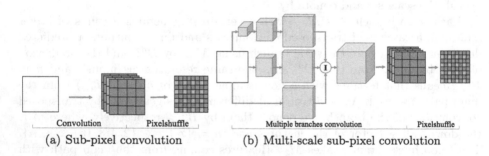

(a) Sub-pixel convolution   (b) Multi-scale sub-pixel convolution

Fig. 2. (a) illustrates the original sub-pixel convolution proposed by [25]. (b) outlines our multi-scale sub-pixel convolution, which fuses more features from different scale branches. The circle with I in it means concatenating features from different branches. And the number of branches before concatenation may be less or more than 3, depending on the output scale of the multi-scale sub-pixel convolution.

3.3   Multi-scale Sub-pixel Convolution

Sub-pixel convolution is first proposed by Shi et $al.$ [25] as an efficient up-sampling method for RGB image super-resolution problem. It is originally defined as,

$$I^{SR} = f^L(I^{LR}) = PS(W_L * f^{L-1}(I^{LR}) + b_L) \quad (6)$$

where I^{LR} refers to a low resolution RGB image, I^{SR} refers to the high resolution RGB image to be recovered, f^{L-1} refers to a neural network with $L-1$ layers, W_L and b_L are parameters of Layer L and $PS(\cdot)$ is a shuffling operator that rearranges the elements of an $H \times W \times C \cdot r^2$ tensor to a tensor of the shape $rH \times rW \times C$ where r is the upscaling factor.

Inspired by this, we formulate predicting depth map of a fine resolution as a multi-stage super-resolution problem on depths. In each stage, the predicted depth map is up-sampled by the factor of 2. Therefore, different scale targets should be considered during training and our multi-scale target learning strategy is born. Furthermore, considering that features from early layers of a CNN carry more detail information of the input image and the information is very likely to benefit preserving more details of the scene in the prediction, we construct several branches called scale branches in our network and fuse features of different scales from those branches into the sub-pixel convolution. Finally, suppose that the resolution of the original input image is $H \times W$ and our multi-scale sub-pixel convolution can be defined as,

$$P_{n\times} = PS(H([P_{2n\times}, B_{2n\times}^{2^2 n\times}, B_{2n\times}^{2^3 n\times}, ..., B_{2n\times}^{32\times}])), n \in \{1, 2, 4, 8\} \tag{7}$$

where $[\cdot]$ refers to the concatenation of input feature maps, $H(\cdot)$ refers to a series of convolutional layers which output a tensor with the shape of $H/(2n) \times W/(2n) \times 1 \cdot 4$ and $PS(\cdot)$ represents a pixelshuffle operation which shuffles the output of $H(\cdot)$ to a predicted depth map of resolution $H/n \times W/n$. Note that the aforementioned notation $SP_n(\cdot)$ in (1) is equivalent to $PS(H(\cdot))$ in (7). Figure 2 gives illustrations of the original sub-pixel convolution and our multi-scale sub-pixel convolution.

3.4 Neighborhood Smoothness

The neighborhood smoothness constraint is based on the prior that neighboring pixels with similar appearances in an image are likely to correspond to close depth values. In Liu et al.'s work [16], it is presumed that pixels within a superpixel have the same depth value and superpixels with similar appearances have closer depth values. And they make use of hand-crafted features to measure the similarity of adjacent superpixels. Different from them, we use features learned by CNN to measure the similarity of neighboring pixels and the features of each pixel are extracted in a patch whose center is this pixel. And then, we use the weighted average of features of a pixel to represent the appearance of the pixel and define a constraint term in the loss function, L_{smooth}, as,

$$L_{smooth} = \frac{\lambda_3}{2} \sum_{j-i=1} (y_i - y_j)^2 e^{-t(r_i - r_j)^2} \tag{8}$$

where λ_3 and t are positive constants, i and j are the location of two adjacent pixels in a row or a column, r_i and r_j refer to appearances of the two pixels, and y_i and y_j refer to predicted depth values. For better comprehensibility, we will explain why we choose such a formulation and how we implement it, together with why it should work in the following.

As (8) shows, there are two parts, namely, L_2 and the weight part. L_2 is used to make the predictions of adjacent pixels closer. However, not all adjacent pixels should own close depth. So weights are introduced for such situations. Adjacent pixels which look "different" should own a smaller weight whereas similar pixels should own a larger weight. Therefore, we choose e^x as weights and x should be related to the similarity. We expect to use low level features to formulate the similarity and the first several layers of the CNN are able to learn various low level features. Therefore, we feed $2\times$ feature maps ($M_{2\times}$, blue one in Fig. 1) from the main path to one DenseBlock with 128 output channels. A convolution layer with a kernel size of 5×5 follows this DenseBlock and generates 4 channel output. The 4 channel output is then shuffled into one channel to up-sample its dimension to the original input's. Finally, each value in the output is regarded as the feature of the pixel in the same location (e.g. r_i or r_j in (8)).

Actually, our neighborhood smoothness constraint can be explained as a conditional random field (CRF) with pairwise potentials defined as,

$$\varphi(y_i, y_j, r_i, r_j) = \mu\left(y_i, y_j\right) k\left(r_i, r_j\right) \tag{9}$$
$$\mu\left(y_i, y_j\right) = \frac{1}{2}(y_i - y_j)^2 \ , \ k\left(r_i, r_j\right) = \lambda e^{-t(r_i - r_j)^2}$$

where $\mu(y_i, y_j)$ represents the compatibility function between pixel i and j and $k(r_i, r_j)$ represents a self-defined weight kernel.

4   Experiments

4.1   Experimental Protocol

We evaluate our method on two popular datasets which are publicly available and widely used in the area of depth estimation, Make3D Range Image Dataset [23] and NYU Depth Dataset V2 [26]. The same as prior works, four criteria were considered for quantitative evaluation.

- Average relative error (rel): $\frac{1}{T} \sum_i \frac{|y_i - y_i^*|}{y_i^*}$.
- Root mean squared error (rms): $\sqrt{\frac{1}{T} \sum_i (y_i - y_i^*)^2}$.
- Average log10 error (log10): $\frac{1}{T} \sum_i |log_{10}y_i^* - log_{10}y_i|$.
- Accuracy with threshold (thr): percentage (%) of y_i
  $s.t. : \max\left(\frac{y_i}{y_i^*}, \frac{y_i^*}{y_i}\right) = \delta < thr$.

where y_i and y_i^* are the predicted depth and the ground-truth depth of the pixel i, respectively, and T is the total number of pixels in the evaluated image.

To clearly validate the effectiveness of the multi-scale target learning, the multi-scale sub-pixel convolution and the neighborhood smoothness constraint, we considered the following four baselines:

- **DenseNet-TC** (DenseNet with Transposed Convolution): We trained a DenseNet without the global pooling and the fully connection for depth estimation and used transposed convolution to get a fine resolution of the predicted depth map.
- **DenseNet-MT** (DenseNet with Multi-scale Targets): We trained a network similar as DenseNet-TC and added the multi-scale target learning to it. Specially, each transposed convolution was followed with an extra convolution layer to get an output of a certain scale.
- **DenseNet-SC** (DenseNet with Sub-pixel Convolution): We replaced the transposed convolution in DenseNet-MT with the original sub-pixel convolution in [25].
- **MSCN** (multi-scale sub-pixel convolution network): The proposed approach without the neighborhood smoothness constraint.

4.2 Implementation Details

We implement our method on the popular CNN platform, PyTorch[1]. Training is done on Ubuntu 16.04 with an NVIDIA Titan X Pascal GPU. We choose DenseNet-121 as the main path. We reference the implementation of DenseNet-121 in the vision project[2] and use the pre-trained model to initialize parameters of the four denseblocks. Other layers of the network are initialized by the mean of xavier [4]. We use Adam strategy with $weight\_decay = 0.0005$ and set $\lambda_1 = 0.5$, $\lambda_2^i = 1/i, (i = 2, 4, 8)$, $\lambda_3 = 0.01$ and $t = 2$. The batch size is set to 16 due to the memory limitation. The learning rate is set to 0.001 at the very beginning and reduced 70% every M epochs. The value of M depends on the size of the dataset. Generally, we set it to 6~10 for NYU Depth v2 and 20~60 for Make3D.

For data augmentation, we follow the strategies proposed in [2] and the parameters are described here. The scaling factor $s \in \{1, 1.2, 1.5\}$, the rotation factor $r \in [-5, 5]$, and the color scaling factor $c \in [0.85, 1.15]$. Moreover, translation and flipping are conducted over all image pairs.

4.3 Ablation Study on Components

We compare the proposed method $MSCN_{NS}$ with several aforementioned baselines to validate the effectiveness of the multi-scale target learning, the multi-scale sub-pixel convolution and the neighborhood smoothness constraint, respectively. The results are shown in Table 1, from which we could have the following findings. First, all approaches with the multi-scale target learning perform better than DenseNet-TC, indicating that our multi-scale target learning is very effective for depth estimation. Second, DenseNet-SC outperforms DenseNet-MT and MSCN outperforms both DenseNet-SC and DenseNet-MT with a great increase on performance. Such a result clearly demonstrates that sub-pixel convolution is more suitable than the widely used transposed convolution for this task and the

---

[1] http://pytorch.org/.
[2] https://github.com/pytorch/vision.

Table 1. Baseline comparison on NYU Depth v2. DenseNet-TC and DenseNet-MT verify multi-scale target learning. DenseNet-SC and MSCN verify the multi-scale sub-pixel convolution. MSCN and $MSCN_{NS}$ verify the neighborhood smoothness constraint.

Method	Error (lower is better)			Accuracy (higher is better)		
	rel	log10	rms	$\delta < 1.25$	$\delta < 1.25^2$	$\delta < 1.25^3$
DenseNet-TC	0.248	0.101	0.786	0.585	0.870	0.962
DenseNet-MT	0.240	0.097	0.761	0.601	0.879	0.965
DenseNet-SC	0.227	0.094	0.720	0.613	0.885	0.969
MSCN	0.154	0.068	0.569	0.755	0.941	0.986
$MSCN_{NS}$	**0.128**	**0.059**	**0.523**	**0.813**	**0.964**	**0.992**

Table 2. Intermediate output comparison on NYU Depth v2. $O^{4\times} \sim O^{32\times}$ are outputs of corresponding scale branches. $P_{8\times} \sim P_{1\times}$ are outputs of corresponding sub-pixel convolutions. Note that $P_{1\times}$ is the final output of our method.

Output	Error (lower is better)			Accuracy (higher is better)		
	rel	log10	rms	$\delta < 1.25$	$\delta < 1.25^2$	$\delta < 1.25^3$
$O^{4\times}$	0.289	0.136	1.049	0.426	0.742	0.911
$O^{8\times}$	0.203	0.098	0.772	0.596	0.870	0.966
$O^{16\times}$	0.156	0.076	0.634	0.719	0.914	0.978
$O^{32\times}$	0.154	0.075	0.635	0.726	0.915	0.978
$P_{8\times}$	0.174	0.087	0.748	0.656	0.902	0.974
$P_{4\times}$	0.154	0.075	0.663	0.723	0.932	0.982
$P_{2\times}$	0.137	0.064	0.573	0.781	0.954	0.990
$P_{1\times}$	**0.128**	**0.059**	**0.523**	**0.813**	**0.964**	**0.992**

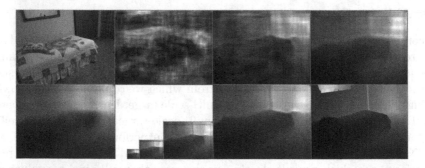

Fig. 3. One test sample in NYU Depth V2. The first row (from left to right) is the RGB image, $O^{4\times}$, $O^{8\times}$ and $O^{16\times}$ and the second row (from left to right) is $O^{32\times}$, $P_{8\times}$, $P_{4\times}$, $P_{2\times}$, $P_{1\times}$ (the final prediction) and the ground-truth depth map.

Table 3. Performance evaluation of different methods on NYU Depth v2.

Method	Error (lower is better)			Accuracy (higher is better)		
	rel	log10	rms	$\delta < 1.25$	$\delta < 1.25^2$	$\delta < 1.25^3$
Saxena *et al.* [23]	0.349	-	1.214	0.447	0.745	0.897
Karsch *et al.* [10]	0.350	0.131	1.2	-	-	-
Liu *et al.* [18]	0.335	0.127	1.06	-	-	-
Eigen *et al.* [2]	0.215	-	0.907	0.611	0.887	0.971
Liu *et al.* [17]	0.234	0.095	0.842	0.604	0.885	0.973
Mousavian *et al.* [19]	0.200	-	0.816	0.568	0.856	0.956
Roy and Todorovic [21]	0.187	0.078	0.744	-	-	-
Eigen and Fergus [1]	0.158	-	0.641	0.769	0.950	0.988
Li *et al.* [14]	0.143	0.063	0.635	0.788	0.958	0.991
Laina *et al.* (l_2) [12]	0.138	0.060	0.592	0.785	0.952	0.980
$MSCN_{NS}$ (Ours)	**0.128**	**0.059**	**0.523**	**0.813**	**0.964**	**0.992**

Table 4. Time evaluation on NYU Depth v2. All methods are evaluated using the same computer with an NVIDIA Titan X (Pascal) GPU.

Method	Time
Karsch *et al.* [10]	60 s
Eigen *et al.* [2]	2.091 s
Eigen and Fergus [1]	5.622 s
Liu *et al.* [17]	1.291 s
Laina *et al.* [12]	0.257 s
$MSCN_{NS}$ (Ours)	**0.019 s**

Table 5. Performance evaluation of different methods on Make3D.

Method	C1 error (lower is better)			C2 error (lower is better)		
	rel	log10	rms	rel	log10	rms
Saxena *et al.* [23]	-	-	-	0.370	0.187	-
Karsch *et al.* [10]	0.355	0.127	9.20	0.361	0.148	15.10
Liu *et al.* [18]	0.335	0.137	9.49	0.338	0.134	12.60
Liu *et al.* [16]	0.314	0.119	8.60	0.307	0.125	12.89
Zhang *et al.* [34]	0.374	0.127	9.18	0.364	0.141	14.11
Liu *et al.* [17]	0.312	0.113	9.10	0.305	0.120	13.24
Roy and Todorovic [21]	-	-	-	0.260	0.119	12.40
Li *et al.* [13]	0.278	0.092	7.19	0.279	0.102	10.67
$MSCN_{NS}$ (Ours)	**0.254**	**0.080**	**6.92**	**0.249**	**0.088**	**10.47**

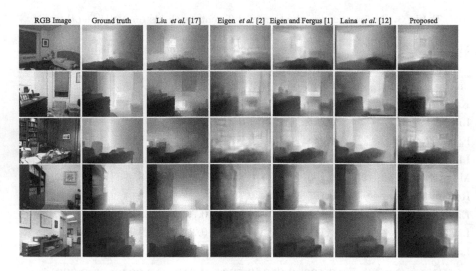

Fig. 4. Qualitative evaluations on NYU Depth v2. Note that the output resolution of the proposed method is the same as input's, whereas Eigen et al.'s [2] is 1/4 of the input's, Eigen and Fergus's [1] is 1/2 of the input's and Laina et al.'s [12] is 1/2 of the input's.

Fig. 5. Qualitative evaluations of our approach on Make3D. Fine boundaries of objects in different environments are provided in our predictions.

proposed multi-scale sub-pixel convolution is very powerful for improving the predictions. This result is quite reasonable, since multi-scale information benefits keeping details of the scene in the prediction. Third, compared with MSCN, $MSCN_{NS}$ gains obvious performance increases on all criteria. Considering that the only difference between them is that the former is trained with the neighborhood smoothness regularization term, we can conclude that our neighborhood smoothness constraint further improve the results.

Since there are multiple outputs ($O^{4\times} \sim O^{32\times}$ and $P_{8\times} \sim P_{1\times}$) in our network, we display the qualitative results of them in Fig. 3 and present the quantitative comparisons in Table 2, from which several interesting conclusions can be drawn. First, the performances from $O^{4\times}$ to $O^{32\times}$ increase sequentially whereas the figures become less sharp. Such a phenomenon clearly illustrates that the early layers of the network provide more information about the contour of the object and deeper layers provide more useful information for depth values. Thus, there is a trade-off between sharpness and accuracy using single scale features. Second, $P_{8\times} \sim P_{1\times}$ are nearly the same irrespective of the resolution, which indicates that our multi-scale sub-pixel convolution overcomes this trade-off and is able to provide a sharp and accurate prediction.

4.4   Evaluation on NYU Depth Dataset V2

The NYU Depth Dataset V2 [26] is an indoor scene RGB-D dataset. Following Laina *et al.*'s work [12], we sample frames with a fixed step out of each training sequence and acquire approximately 12k images. After the offline data augmentation, we finally get around 72k samples for training. For test, we use the standard test set, which contains 694 images with filled-in depth values, to compare with previous works. During our experiment, all images with the corresponding depth maps are down-sampled to 320 × 240.

To show the superiority of $MSCN_{NS}$, we compare it with the state-of-the-art methods in terms of the prediction accuracy and the inference speed. The results are listed in Tables 3 and 4. It can be seen that our method outperforms other methods on all criteria. And it runs much faster and only consumes 1/13 the time of the runner-up, meaning that it can meet the requirement of real-time application. Moreover, our training set with 72K images is smaller than Laina *et al.*'s [12] with 95K images, as well as Eigen and Fergus's [1] with 120K images. Besides, the size of our model is approximately 100 M, which is 40% that of Laina *et al.*'s and 1/8 that of Eigen and Fergus's. For further comparison, we provide qualitative results of several methods in Fig. 4.

4.5   Evaluation on Make3D

The Make3D dataset [23] is an outdoor scene RGB-D dataset, containing 534 images with the resolution of 1704 × 2272. Officially, images of this dataset are split into 400 images for training and 134 images for test. We get 9.6K images via offline data augmentation and resize all images to 345 × 460. Following Laina *et al.*'s work [12], we further reduce the resolution of the images by half as the input of our network. Following previous works, we report our results using two kinds of criteria, C1 error and C2 error, as previous works used. C1 errors are calculated only in the regions with the ground-truth less than 70 meters while C2 errors are calculated over the entire images.

We evaluate our method using the official test set with 134 images and list the comparison results with several state-of-the-art approaches in Table 5. It can be observed that our method outperforms all competitors on all criteria. Moreover, it should be noted that Make3D is an outdoor depth dataset. And thus the range of its depth values is much larger than that of indoor dataset like NYU Depth v2, which brings more challenges for the prediction. Nevertheless, our method makes a great improvement on the metric log10 which refers to an absolute error on logarithm. Therefore, it can be concluded that our method is superior to predict relatively accurate depth value in spite of a large range of ground truth value.

We also provide the qualitative evaluations on Make3D, which are presented in Fig. 5. Since the depth range is large, we provide the reverse depth map for better visualization. As is shown, our method provides fine boundaries of objects even in complex environments involving buildings, shrubs and trees.

5   Conclusion

In this paper, we have presented a CNN-based approach for depth estimation from a single monocular image. In our model, there is a main path, a sub-pixel convolution path, a smoothness branch and four scale branches. The main path and scale branches generate features of different scales. And the sub-pixel convolution path leverages the multi-scale sub-pixel convolutions to get an accurate depth map. During training, a novel multi-scale target learning strategy is adopted to train the sub-pixel convolutions. Moreover, we have proposed a novel neighborhood smoothness constraint that makes use of features from the smoothness branch to further improve the performance. Our approach is able to achieve the state-of-the-art results, as well as running much faster. Additionally, it can provide more details of the scene and high resolution depth maps.

Acknowledgement. This work was supported in part by the Natural Science Foundation of China under Grant 61672380, in part by the Fundamental Research Funds for the Central Universities under Grant 2100219068, and in part by the Shanghai Automotive Industry Science and Technology Development Foundation under Grant 1712.

References

1. Eigen, D., Fergus, R.: Predicting depth, surface normals and semantic labels with a common multi-scale convolutional architecture. In: ICCV, pp. 2650–2658. IEEE (2015)
2. Eigen, D., Puhrsch, C., Fergus, R.: Depth map prediction from a single image using a multi-scale deep network. In: NIPS, pp. 2366–2374. MIT Press (2014)

3. Eitel, A., Springenberg, J.T., Spinello, L., Riedmiller, M., Burgard, W.: Multimodal deep learning for robust RGB-D object recognition. In: IROS, pp. 681–687. IEEE (2015)
4. Glorot, X., Bengio, Y.: Understanding the difficulty of training deep feedforward neural networks. JMLR **9**, 249–256 (2010)
5. Gupta, S., Arbeláez, P., Girshick, R., Malik, J.: Indoor scene understanding with RGB-D images: bottom-up segmentation, object detection and semantic segmentation. IJCV **112**, 133–149 (2015)
6. He, K., Zhang, X., Ren, S., Sun, J.: Deep residual learning for image recognition. In: CVPR, pp. 770–778. IEEE (2016)
7. Hirschmuller, H.: Accurate and efficient stereo processing by semi-global matching and mutual information. In: CVPR, pp. 807–814. IEEE (2005)
8. Huang, G., Liu, Z., Maaten, L.V.D., Weinberger, K.Q.: Densely connected convolutional networks. In: CVPR, pp. 2261–2269. IEEE (2017)
9. Karsch, K., Liu, C., Kang, S.B.: Depth extraction from video using non-parametric sampling. In: Fitzgibbon, A., Lazebnik, S., Perona, P., Sato, Y., Schmid, C. (eds.) ECCV 2012, Part V. LNCS, vol. 7576, pp. 775–788. Springer, Heidelberg (2012). https://doi.org/10.1007/978-3-642-33715-4_56
10. Karsch, K., Liu, C., Kang, S.B.: Depth transfer: depth extraction from video using non-parametric sampling. IEEE Trans. PAMI **36**, 2144–2158 (2014)
11. Konrad, J., Wang, M., Ishwar, P.: 2D-to-3D image conversion by learning depth from examples. In: CVPRW, pp. 16–22. IEEE (2012)
12. Laina, I., Rupprecht, C., Belagiannis, V., Tombari, F., Navab, N.: Deeper depth prediction with fully convolutional residual networks. In: 3DV, pp. 239–248. IEEE (2016)
13. Li, B., Shen, C., Dai, Y., van den Hengel, A., He, M.: Depth and surface normal estimation from monocular images using regression on deep features and hierarchical CRFs. In: CVPR, pp. 1119–1127. IEEE (2015)
14. Li, J., Klein, R., Yao, A.: A two-streamed network for estimating fine-scaled depth maps from single RGB images. In: CVPR, pp. 3372–3380. IEEE (2017)
15. Liu, B., Gould, S., Koller, D.: Single image depth estimation from predicted semantic labels. In: CVPR, pp. 1253–1260. IEEE (2010)
16. Liu, F., Shen, C., Lin, G.: Deep convolutional neural fields for depth estimation from a single image. In: CVPR, pp. 5162–5170. IEEE (2015)
17. Liu, F., Shen, C., Lin, G., Reid, I.: Learning depth from single monocular images using deep convolutional neural fields. IEEE Trans. PAMI **38**, 2024–2039 (2016)
18. Liu, M., Salzmann, M., He, X.: Discrete-continuous depth estimation from a single image. In: CVPR, pp. 716–723. IEEE (2014)
19. Mousavian, A., Pirsiavash, H., Košecká, J.: Joint semantic segmentation and depth estimation with deep convolutional networks. In: 3DV, pp. 611–619. IEEE (2016)
20. Ren, X., Bo, L., Fox, D.: RGB-(D) scene labeling: features and algorithms. In: CVPR, pp. 2759–2766. IEEE (2012)
21. Roy, A., Todorovic, S.: Monocular depth estimation using neural regression forest. In: CVPR, pp. 5506–5514. IEEE (2016)
22. Saxena, A., Chung, S.H., Ng, A.Y.: Learning depth from single monocular images. In: NIPS, pp. 1161–1168. MIT Press (2006)
23. Saxena, A., Sun, M., Ng, A.Y.: Make3D: learning 3D scene structure from a single still image. IEEE Trans. PAMI **31**, 824–840 (2009)
24. Seki, A., Pollefeys, M.: SGM-Nets: semi-global matching with neural networks. In: CVPRW, pp. 21–26. IEEE (2017)

25. Shi, W., et al.: Real-time single image and video super-resolution using an efficient sub-pixel convolutional neural network. In: CVPR, pp. 1874–1883. IEEE (2016)
26. Silberman, N., Hoiem, D., Kohli, P., Fergus, R.: Indoor segmentation and support inference from RGBD images. In: Fitzgibbon, A., Lazebnik, S., Perona, P., Sato, Y., Schmid, C. (eds.) ECCV 2012, Part V. LNCS, vol. 7576, pp. 746–760. Springer, Heidelberg (2012). https://doi.org/10.1007/978-3-642-33715-4_54
27. Wang, P., Shen, X., Lin, Z., Cohen, S., Price, B., Yuille, A.L.: Towards unified depth and semantic prediction from a single image. In: CVPR, pp. 2800–2809. IEEE (2015)
28. Wang, Z., Liu, H., Wang, X., Qian, Y.: Segment and label indoor scene based on RGB-D for the visually impaired. In: Gurrin, C., Hopfgartner, F., Hurst, W., Johansen, H., Lee, H., O'Connor, N. (eds.) MMM 2014, Part I. LNCS, vol. 8325, pp. 449–460. Springer, Cham (2014). https://doi.org/10.1007/978-3-319-04114-8_38
29. Xie, S., Tu, Z.: Holistically-nested edge detection. In: ICCV, pp. 1395–1403. IEEE (2015)
30. Xu, D., Ricci, E., Ouyang, W., Wang, X., Sebe, N.: Multi-scale continuous CRFs as sequential deep networks for monocular depth estimation. In: CVPR, pp. 161–169. IEEE (2017)
31. Xu, D., Ricci, E., Ouyang, W., Wang, X., Sebe, N.: Monocular depth estimation using multi-scale continuous CRFs as sequential deep networks. IEEE Trans. PAMI 41, 1426–1440 (2018). (Early Access)
32. Zbontar, J., LeCun, Y.: Stereo matching by training a convolutional neural network to compare image patches. JMLR, 2287–2318 (2016)
33. Zeng, A., Song, S., Nießner, M., Fisher, M., Xiao, J., Funkhouser, T.: 3DMatch: learning local geometric descriptors from RGB-D reconstructions. In: CVPR, pp. 199–208. IEEE (2017)
34. Zhang, Y., et al.: Search-based depth estimation via coupled dictionary learning with large-margin structure inference. In: Leibe, B., Matas, J., Sebe, N., Welling, M. (eds.) ECCV 2016, Part V. LNCS, vol. 9909, pp. 858–874. Springer, Cham (2016). https://doi.org/10.1007/978-3-319-46454-1_52

Ranking Loss: A Novel Metric Learning Method for Person Re-identification

Min Cao[1,3], Chen Chen[1,3(✉)], Xiyuan Hu[1,3], and Silong Peng[1,2,3]

[1] Institute of Automation Chinese Academy of Sciences, Beijing, China
{caomin2014,chen.chen}@ia.ac.cn
[2] Beijing Visytem Co., Ltd., Beijing, China
[3] University of Chinese Academy of Sciences, Beijing, China

Abstract. Person re-identification is the problem of matching pedestrians under different camera views. The goal of person re-identification is to make the truly matched pedestrian pair rank as the first place among all pairs, with the direct translation in math language, which equals that the distance of matched pedestrian pair is the minimum value of the distances of all pairs. In this paper, we propose a novel metric learning method for person re-identification to learn such an optimal feature mapping function, which minimizes the difference between the distance of matched pair and the minimum distance of all pairs, namely *Ranking Loss*. Furthermore, we develop an improved version of ranking loss by using p-norm as a smooth approximation of minimum function, with the advantage of manipulating parameter p to control the distance margin between matched pair and unmatched pair to benefit the re-identification accuracy. We also present an efficient solver using only a small portion of pairs in computation, achieving almost the same performance as using all. Compared with other loss function, the proposed ranking loss optimizes the ultimate ranking goal in the most direct and intuitional way, and it directly acts on the whole gallery set efficiently instead of comparatively measuring in small subset. The detailed theoretical discussion and experimental comparisons with other loss functions are provided, illustrating the advantages of the proposed ranking loss. Extensive experiments on two datasets also show the effectiveness of the proposed method compared to state-of-the-art methods.

1 Introduction

Person re-identification (re-id), which addresses the problem of identifying the same person captured from different non-overlapping cameras, is a valuable research subject for building the intelligent video monitoring system. It is also a challenging research subject due to the significant intra-class variations on visual appearance caused by the change in illumination, occlusion and person pose across different views. Nevertheless, person re-id has made great progress in recent years thanks to the continuous efforts of the researchers.

Most existing person re-id studies focus on metric learning in the supervised setting [1–4]. The training set with labelled matching pairs for each pair of

© Springer Nature Switzerland AG 2019
C. V. Jawahar et al. (Eds.): ACCV 2018, LNCS 11362, pp. 381–397, 2019.
https://doi.org/10.1007/978-3-030-20890-5_25

camera views is fully utilized to learn an optimal mapping function from the original feature space to the new feature space, so that positive pair (i.e. a pair of people from different views sharing the same identity) has a smaller distance than negative pair (i.e. a pair of people from different views sharing the different identity) in the new feature space.

Towards this end, the most direct way is to learn a mapping function, with which the distance of positive pair equals the minimum value of distances of all pairs with the given query person. Based on this, we propose a novel loss function for person re-id, minimizing the difference between the distance of positive pair and the minimum value of distances of all pairs. Other loss functions for person re-id are modeled with different format of setting constraints on distances, such as, the distance of positive pair is lower than a given threshold and the distance of negative pair is greater than the threshold [5,6], or the distance of positive pair is lower than the distance of negative pair with a margin [1,2,7]. Although these loss functions ultimately optimize towards the same goal as the proposed loss function, i.e. positive pair has a smaller distance than negative pair, they still achieve the ranking goal in a relatively indirect way, for instance, measuring comparative similarity in a huge number of small subset (e.g. triplet loss or quadruplet loss) or setting a insufficiently necessary hard threshold (e.g. binary classification loss). The proposed loss function works toward the ranking goal directly to push the positive pair rank as the first place among all, and can obtain better performance in person re-id than other loss functions. In addition, since the proposed loss function acts directly on the whole set efficiently, the sample imbalance problem occurred in implementing other loss functions does not exist in the context of the proposed method.

To achieve better model optimization, considering the properties of non-smooth and non-differentiable at some points for the minimum function in the proposed loss function, p-norm, an analytic function, with great differentiable property, is utilized as a smooth approximation of minimum function ($p < 0$). The introduced parameter p is set by theoretic analysis rather than choosing carefully like the other loss functions. And it is worth mentioning that, the relatively larger value for the parameter p (i.e. $p \to 0$) results in a strong constraint on a larger margin between the distances of positive pairs and negative pairs, that is, further enlarging inter-class variations and reducing the intra-class variations, which is effective for improving the accuracy of model in person re-id. Furthermore, we also develop an efficient solver for the model where only a small part of pairs are used in the computation. It can obtain almost the same performance on the testing set compared to the normal solver by using all negative pairs.

In summary, we make three contributions in this paper as follows:

(1) We propose a novel ranking loss function for metric learning based person re-id, which optimizes the ultimate re-id ranking in the most direct way.
(2) We utilize p-norm to develop a smooth and continuously differentiable version of the proposed ranking loss function, with the advantage of controlling the distance margin by manipulating parameter p to achieve better generalization ability.

(3) We propose an efficient optimization algorithm by using a small portion of pedestrian pairs instead of using all pairs in computation.

2   Related Work

In general, person re-id problem is solved by three crucial steps: feature extraction [8–10], metric learning [1,3,5–7,11] and re-ranking [12–14]. Extensive methods have been proposed focusing on one or more of the steps. For a detailed review of person re-id, the interested readers can refer to [15]. In this section, we only briefly review some representative metric learning based methods that are related to our work.

We can divide metric learning based person re-id methods into two broad categories: closed-form solution based and iterative-learning based. The closed-form solution based methods [9,11,16] are usually related to Linear Discriminative Analysis technology and the optimal solution can be obtained by the generalized eigenvalue decomposition. However, because the number of samples is generally lower than the dimension of samples' feature vector in person re-id, there is usually the singular problem in this kind of methods. In the iterative-learning based methods [1,3,5–7], an objective function is usually constructed and solved by iterative optimization algorithms to satisfy the constraints on samples of the training set. According to the objective function, the iterative-learning methods can be summarized as three main types: the binary classification loss based [5,6], the triplet loss based [1,7] and the quadruplet loss based [2]. In PCCA [5], the objective function is optimized so that the distances of positive pairs are lower than a given threshold and the distances of negative pairs are greater than the threshold. Compared with the binary classification loss with a fixed threshold, a generalized similarity metric for person re-id was proposed with an adaptive threshold [6]. Ding et al. [7] proposed a deep neural network where the relative distances between positive pairs and negative ones are maximized. Zhou et al. [4] presented a novel set to set (S2S) loss layer in deep learning framework that focuses on maximizing the margin between the intra-class set and inter-class set, while preserving the compactness of intra-class samples. In addition to the triplet loss based methods, some methods have been proposed to combine and jointly optimize the binary classification loss and the triplet loss for pursuing better performance [17,18]. Recently, Chen et al. [2] proposed a quadruplet deep network by introducing a quadruplet ranking loss to achieve a smaller intra-class variation and a larger inter-class variation.

3   Ranking Loss Function for Person Re-identification

3.1   Problem Description

Given a query person q from one camera view and a candidate set with N people $\mathcal{G} = \{g_i \,|\, i = 1, 2, \ldots, N \}$ from another camera view. The distance between q and g_i is measured by

$$d_L(q, g_i) = \|L(\boldsymbol{x_q} - \boldsymbol{x_{g_i}})\|^2, \tag{1}$$

where $\boldsymbol{x_q}$ and $\boldsymbol{x_{g_i}}$ are the feature vector of the person q and g_i obtained by the feature extraction step. L is a feature transformation matrix.

A ranking list $\mathcal{L}(q, \mathcal{G}) = \{g_1^r, g_2^r, \ldots, g_N^r\}$ can be obtained by the distances between the query person and the candidates in ascending order, i.e. $d(q, g_1^r) < d(q, g_2^r) < \ldots < d(q, g_N^r)$. For person re-id, we hope that the candidate having the same identity with the query person q (also known as the positive sample) is closer to the top of the ranking list. Certainly, it will be perfect in the case where the positive sample ranks first. To do this, we develop a model to learn an optimal feature transformation L by the training set.

3.2 Modeling

Without loss of generality, we introduce our method in this subsection based on the assumption that there is the case of single-shot, i.e one query person shares the same identity with only one gallery person in the candidate.

For each query person q_i ($i = 1, \ldots, M$), in the candidate set $\mathcal{G}$, there are always one person denoted by g^{i+} having the same identity with q_i, and all the rest of people having the different identity with q_i denoted by g_j^{i-} ($j = 1, 2, \ldots, N - 1$). With the goal of prioritizing the positive sample g^{i+} on the ranking list, we find an optimal feature transformation L by which the distance between feature vectors of q_i and positive sample g^{i+} is the minimum value of distances between feature vectors of q_i and each sample in the set $\mathcal{G}$. So, the objective function is deduced:

$$\min_L f^*(L) = \sum_{i=1}^{M} [d_L(q_i, g^{i+}) - \min_{g_n \in \mathcal{G}} d_L(q_i, g_n)]. \tag{2}$$

For the convenience of expression, we simplify the notation $d_L(q_i, g^{i+})$ as $d_{q_i,g^{i+}}$ and the simplifications of all other $d_L(\cdot, \cdot)$ are similar to this below.

When $\min_{g_n \in \mathcal{G}} d_{q_i,g_n} = d_{q_i,g^{i+}}$ for each term in $f^*(L)$, that is, all positive samples rank first in the corresponding ranking list, the objective function reaches its the lower bound value of zero. However, the minimum function in Eq. 2 is non-smooth and non-differentiable at some points. As a result, it is an intractable problem to solve the model in Eq. 2. For this, we use p-norm as a smooth approximation of the minimum function:

$$\left(\sum_{g_n \in \mathcal{G}} (d_{q_i,g_n})^p\right)^{\frac{1}{p}} \approx \min_{g_n \in \mathcal{G}} d_{q_i,g_n}. \tag{3}$$

Then, the new objective function is given:

$$\min_L f(L) = \sum_{i=1}^{M} [d_{q_i,g^{i+}} - \left(\sum_{g_n \in \mathcal{G}} (d_{q_i,g_n})^p\right)^{\frac{1}{p}}]. \tag{4}$$

This model in Eq. 4 not only inherits the advantage of the one in Eq. 2, i.e. learning the transformation L by a direct way with request of the positive pair being in the top rank, but also is favorable for solving the optimal transformation L. In addition, the introduced parameter p controls the degree of margin between distances of positive pair and negative pair, resulting in more flexibility for model to obtain a better performance.

Now, we elaborate on why the model in Eq. 4 has these advantages. For this, we reformulate p-norm in Eq. 3 as:

$$\left(\sum_{g_n \in \mathcal{G}} (d_{q_i,g_n})^p\right)^{\frac{1}{p}} = [(d_{q_i,g^{i+}})^p + (d_{q_i,g_1^{i-}})^p + \ldots + (d_{q_i,g_{N-1}^{i-}})^p]^{\frac{1}{p}}$$
$$= [(d_{q_i,g^{i+}})^p(1 + (\frac{d_{q_i,g_1^{i-}}}{d_{q_i,g^{i+}}})^p + \ldots + (\frac{d_{q_i,g_{N-1}^{i-}}}{d_{q_i,g^{i+}}})^p]^{\frac{1}{p}}. \tag{5}$$

Substituting Eq. 5 into Eq. 4, we can find that the minimum value of the objective function $f(L)$ is reached if and only if $(\frac{d_{q_i,g_t^{i-}}}{d_{q_i,g^{i+}}})^p = 0$ $(\forall t = 1, \ldots, N-1)$ for each person q_i. Since we want to achieve $d_{q_i,g^{i+}} < d_{q_i,g_t^{i-}}$ $(\forall t = 1, \ldots, N-1)$ for each person q_i, meaning $\frac{d_{q_i,g_t^{i-}}}{d_{q_i,g^{i+}}} > 1$ for all terms, it is possible to satisfy $(\frac{d_{q_i,g_t^{i-}}}{d_{q_i,g^{i+}}})^p = 0$ only if $p < 0$. It follows that the model in Eq. 4 with a smooth and continuously differentiable loss function can achieve same functionality as the one in Eq. 2, as long as we choose an appropriate parameter of p.

Based on the basic constraint of $p < 0$, there are two cases where $(\frac{d_{q_i,g_t^{i-}}}{d_{q_i,g^{i+}}})^p = 0$ is satisfied as follows:

(1) when $p \to -\infty$, the value of $\frac{d_{q_i,g_t^{i-}}}{d_{q_i,g^{i+}}}$ just need to be slightly larger than 1. It means that the margin between distances of positive pairs and negative pairs is very small;

(2) when $p \to 0$, the value of $\frac{d_{q_i,g_t^{i-}}}{d_{q_i,g^{i+}}}$ need to be much larger than 1. It means that the margin between distances of positive pairs and negative pairs is big.

It is obvious that when we optimize the objective function and search its minimum solution in Eq. 4, the value of p controls the degree of margin between distances of positive pairs and negative pairs. We have the flexibility of choosing p based on the demand for the margin.

We argue that the performance of model on the testing set can be improved by further enlarging the inter-class variations and reducing the intra-class variations [19]. Therefore, it is beneficial to set p as a relative large value (i.e. set $p \to 0$) in the experiments. However, it is imperative to note here that, with p getting closer and closer to zero, the correspondingly learnt transformation L results in $\frac{d_{q_i,g_t^{i-}}}{d_{q_i,g^{i+}}} \to \infty$ for satisfying $(\frac{d_{q_i,g_t^{i-}}}{d_{q_i,g^{i+}}})^p = 0$, which means the denominator $d_{q_i,g^{i+}} \to 0$ and the constraint on the value of the numerator $d_{q_i,g_t^{i-}}$ is weaken in the process of optimization. To avoid two undesirable consequences: (1) the model overfitting, (2) lose the control of the margin between distances of positive pairs and negative pairs, we propose a safer choice to set $p \to 0$ but not getting closer to the value of zero. In the experiments, we set $p = -5$ and provide a detailed validation for the performance of the proposed method with different value of p, to justify our analysis above.

3.3   Optimization

It is worth noting that we improve the model from Eq. 2 to Eq. 4 with a smooth and continuously differentiable objective function at the cost of increased computational complexity. Specifically, all corresponding negative pairs for each positive pair are need to be traversed for optimizing the model in Eq. 4. On the contrary, only one negative pair for each positive pair involves in the computation for optimizing the model in Eq. 2.

Therefore, in the process of optimizing the model in Eq. 4, we simplify the computation and only the first k sample pairs with smallest distances for each positive pair are used in the computation. We use the gradient descent scheme with line search to solve the model and the simplified objective function at t-th iteration is formulated as:

$$f_t(L) = \sum_{i=1}^{M} [d_{q_i,g^{i+}} - (\sum_{g_n \in \Omega_t^{i,j,k}} (d_{q_i,g_n})^p)^{\frac{1}{p}}], \tag{6}$$

where $\Omega_t^{i,j,k} \subseteq \mathcal{G}$ includes first k sample pairs with smallest distances obtained by the feature transformation L_{t-1}. If $k = N$, we have $\Omega_t^{i,j,k} = \mathcal{G}$ with which the optimization process is equivalent to the one in Eq. 4; if $k = 1$, the model reverts to the one in Eq. 2.

The corresponding gradient at t-th iteration is derived as follows:

$$\frac{\partial f_t(L)}{\partial L} = \sum_{i=1}^{M} [\pi_L(q_i, g^{i+}) - \rho(q_i, g^{i+}) \sum_{g_n \in \Omega_t^{i,j,k}} (d_{q_i,g_n})^{p-1} \pi_L(q_i, g_n)], \tag{7}$$

where $\pi_L(\cdot, *)$ is the derivative of distance measurement d_L with respect to L:

$$\pi_L(\cdot, *) = 2L(\boldsymbol{x}_. - \boldsymbol{x}_*)(\boldsymbol{x}_. - \boldsymbol{x}_*)^T, \tag{8}$$

and $\rho(q_i, g^{i+})$ is a constant:

$$\rho(q_i, g^{i+}) = (\sum_{g_n \in \Omega_t^{i,j,k}} (d_{q_i,g_n})^p)^{\frac{1}{p}-1}. \tag{9}$$

With each iteration to approximate the optimal solution, the positive pair (q_i, g^{i+}) is constantly pushed into the first rank with a minimum distance among the distances of all sample pairs (q_i, g_n), where $n \in \mathcal{G}$. It follows that although we discard some sample pairs in the process of optimization, it's still equivalent to solving the model with all sample pairs. In experiments, we set $k = 2$, and the related comparison experiments are carried out and prove that the proposed method with $k = 2$ can achieve almost the same performance and shorter running time compared to the one with $k = N$.

For convenience, we name the proposed method as R-Loss below. The overall optimization process of R-Loss is shown in Algorithm 1.

3.4   Model Extension

In this section, we extend our method to the general case: multi-shot, i.e for a query person, there are more than one positive sample in the candidate set.

We formally express this case. For each query person q_i ($i = 1, \ldots, M$), there are several positive samples denoted by $\mathcal{G}^{i+} = \{g_j^{i+} \in \mathcal{G} \mid j = 1, 2, \ldots, N^{i+}\}$, and a majority of negative samples denoted by $\mathcal{G}^{i-} = \{g_j^{i-} \in \mathcal{G} \mid j = 1, 2, \ldots, N^{i-}\}$, where $N^{i+} + N^{i-} = N$.

For the case of single-shot, we hope that the positive sample can rank first in the ranking list for the test set, so the distance of positive pair is the minimum of the distances of all pairs is our objective in the training process. Similarly, for the case of multi-shot, we certainly hope that one of the positive samples can rank first for the test set. For obtain a better performance in the test set, we propose a stronger constraint on the training set that is all positive sample pairs be in the front of the ranking list. For this, we learn the optimal transformation L, so that the distance of each positive pair is the minimum of the distances of this positive pair and all negative pairs with the same query person. Therefore, the objective function is deduced:

$$\min_L f_{ex}(L) = \sum_{i=1}^{M} \sum_{g_j^{i+} \in \mathcal{G}^{i+}} [d_{q_i, g_j^{i+}} - (\sum_{g_n \in \{g_j^{i+}\} \cup \mathcal{G}^{i-}} (d_{q_i, g_n})^p)^{\frac{1}{p}}]. \quad (10)$$

Algorithm 1. The R-Loss gradient descent algorithm

Input:

    The query set $\mathcal{Q}$ from one camera and the candidate set $\mathcal{G}$ from another camera, with label information.

    Initialize $L_0 = I$ (unit matrix), $\eta = 10^{-4}$ and $t = 1$.

Output:

    The optimal transformation matrix L.

1: Compute $f_0(L_0)$ and $\frac{\partial f_0(L)}{\partial L} |_{L=L_0}$ according to Eq.6 and Eq.7, respectively.
2: **do**
3:     Update $L_t = L_{t-1} - \eta \frac{\partial f_{t-1}(L)}{\partial L} |_{L=L_{t-1}}$.
4:     Compute $f_t(L_t)$ according to Eq.6.
5:     if $f_t(L_t) \geq f_{t-1}(L_{t-1})$
6:         $\eta \leftarrow 0.9\eta$.
7:         if $\eta < 10^{-20}$
8:             $L = L_t$.
9:             break.
10:       end
11:       Return the 3-th step.
12:     else
13:       $\eta \leftarrow 1.1\eta$.
14:     end
15:     if $f_{t-1}(L_{t-1}) - f_t(L_t) < 10^{-5}$
16:       $L = L_t$.
17:       break.
18:     end
19:     Compute $\frac{\partial f_t(L)}{\partial L} |_{L=L_t}$ according to Eq.7.
20:     Update $t \leftarrow t + 1$.
21: **end**
22: **return** The learnt optimal transformation L.

When $N^{i+} = 1$, the model in Eq. 10 reverts to the one in Eq. 4. We use the gradient descent scheme to solve the model in Eq. 10. The solving process is similar to Algorithm 1 and is not be repeated here.

4   Discussion About Different Loss Functions

In this section, we present a detailed discussion about the differences between the proposed ranking loss function and the existing three classical loss functions: the binary classification loss, the triplet loss and the quadruplet loss. Figure 1 illustrates how the relationships of distances between positive pairs and negative pairs are constrained for these loss functions.

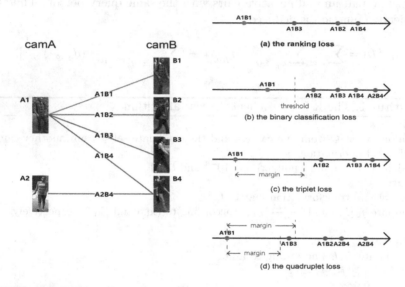

Fig. 1. The relationships between positive pairs' distances and negative pairs' distances for loss functions. The blue line and point represent the positive pair and the red ones represent the negative pair. Better viewed in colour. (Color figure online)

First of all, we formalize the three loss function with the general case of multi-shot as follows:

(1) the binary classification loss function,

$$\min_{L} f^*_{binary}(L) = \sum_{i=1}^{M} \sum_{j=1}^{N} \max(0, y_{ij}(d_{q_i,g_j} - c)), \qquad (11)$$

where $y_{ij} = \begin{cases} 1 & g_j \in \mathcal{G}^{i+} \\ -1 & g_j \in \mathcal{G}^{i-} \end{cases}$ is a sign function and c is a margin threshold. Considering the non-smooth and non-differentiable properties of hinge function

$h(x) = \max(0, x)$, there is usually another form of the binary classification loss function used for person re-id,

$$\min_{L} f_{binary}(L) = \sum_{i=1}^{M} \sum_{j=1}^{N} l_{\beta}(y_{ij}(d_{q_i,g_j} - c)), \qquad (12)$$

where $l_{\beta}(x) = \frac{1}{\beta}\log(1 + e^{\beta x})$ is a smooth approximation of hinge function with $\lim_{\beta \to \infty} l_{\beta}(x) = \max(0, x)$.

(2) the triplet loss function,

$$\min_{L} f_{triplet}(L) = \sum_{i=1}^{M} \sum_{g_j^{i+} \in \mathcal{G}^{i+}} \sum_{g_j^{i-} \in \mathcal{G}^{i-}} \max(0, d_{q_i,g_j^{i+}} - d_{q_i,g_j^{i-}} + c),$$
$$(13)$$

where c is a margin threshold.

(3) the quadruplet loss function,

$$\min_{L} f_{quadruplet}(L) = \sum_{i=1}^{M} \sum_{g_j^{i+} \in \mathcal{G}^{i+}} \left(\sum_{g_j^{i-} \in \mathcal{G}^{i-}} \max(0, d_{q_i,g_j^{i+}} - d_{q_i,g_j^{i-}} + c_1) \right.$$

$$\left. + \sum_{v \neq i, g_n \in \mathcal{G}^{v-}, g_n \notin \mathcal{G}^{i+}} \max(0, d_{q_i,g_j^{i+}} - d_{q_v,g_n} + c_2) \right),$$
$$(14)$$

where c_1 and c_2 are the margin thresholds.

For the binary classification loss function, just the upper bound of positive pairs' distances and the lower bound of negative pairs' distances are constrained by the threshold value of c, and the margin between the positive pair and negative pair is not constrained. Instead, the value of p controls the margin in the proposed loss function and we can set the value of p resulting in a large margin between positive pair and negative pair in the new learnt space, which is profitable for performance in person re-id.

For the triplet loss function, the value of c directly determines the margin between positive pair and negative pair in the new learnt space. A small value of c results in the small margin between positive pair and negative pair and vice versa. However, in generally we don't know what the value of margin should be, so it is difficult to choose a certain value of margin (i.e. set the value of c). Instead, the value of p controls the degree of the margin in the proposed loss function, and we know that a large margin in the new learnt is advantage for performance, and based on this, we can set the value of p.

For the quadruplet loss function, a stricter constraint on margin is established. And similar to the triplet loss function, it is difficult to choose the appropriate values of margin for the quadruplet loss function. Even worse is that there are two parameters c_1 and c_2 which are need to be set.

Our proposed ranking loss function, as well as the three loss functions, all aim to drive the distance of positive pair to the minimum of the distances of all pairs for each query person. But for different loss functions, there are different ways to reach the goal. And it is the most direct way for the proposed ranking loss function, which is more accordant with person re-id problem. In addition, from Eqs. 11–14 we can see that all negative pairs involve in the computation for each positive pair, resulting in the high demand of computing. Therefore, researchers proposed to solve the model with one positive pair vs. a fraction of negative pairs for the binary classification loss function, one positive pair vs. a hardest negative pair (i.e. a negative pair with the smallest distance among all negative pairs) for the triplet loss function and quadruplet loss function. Even so, there is the problem of sample imbalance in the binary classification loss function, and the improved models for the triplet loss function and quadruplet loss function are intractable to solve due to the operation of finding the hardest negative pair. Instead, there does not exist the problem of sample imbalance in the proposed ranking loss function since we just impose constraints on the rank of positive pair, meanwhile, only two pairs for each positive pair are involved in the computation for our model, with almost the same performance and higher computational efficiency compared to using all pairs.

5   Experiments

In this section, we conduct experiments from three aspects: (1) evaluate the performance of the proposed method with different settings; (2) compare the proposed method with other loss function based methods; (3) compare the proposed method with state-of-the-art methods. Before starting, we make a detailed introduction for the settings relevant to the experiments.

5.1   Experimental Settings

Datasets. Two publicly available datasets are used in experiments: VIPeR [20] and CUHK01 [21]. The **VIPeR** dataset includes 632 pedestrian image pairs captured by two different cameras in an outdoor environment with only one image per person for each view. The **CUHK01** dataset has 971 identities taken from two camera views in a campus environment with 2 images of every person under each camera view.

Feature. There are three feature descriptors used in the experiments: Local Maximal Occurrence (LOMO) [9], Gaussian Of Gaussian (GOG) [22] and Histogram of Intensity Pattern & Histogram of Ordinal Pattern (HIPHOP) [23]. For the LOMO descriptor, the horizontal occurrence of local features described by the Scale Invariant Local Ternary Pattern (SILTP) and HSV histogram are maximized to make a stable representation against viewpoint changes. For the GOG descriptor, the person image is described by cascaded Gaussian distributions in which both means and covariances are considered. For HIPHOP descriptor, it describes the person image based on AlexNet [24] convolution neural network.

Evaluation Protocol. We evaluate the performance of person re-id methods by Cumulative Matching Characteristics (CMC) where Rank r represents the expectation of correct match at r-th in the ranking list. The reported results are the average results of 10 times of the partition of training set and test set. For each partition, similar to most publications, the identities are randomly divide into two equal parts used for training set and test set in VIPeR dataset respectively; 485 identities and 486 ones are used for training and testing with single-shot (M1) and multi-shot (M2) setting in CUHK01 dataset.

5.2   Analysis of the Proposed Method

p-norm vs. min. We aim to learn an optimal feature transformation L by which the distance of positive pair is the minimum value of distances of all sample pairs with the same query person in the new feature space. The p-norm is used as a smooth approximation of the minimum function in Eq. 3. The superiority of p-norm compared with the minimum function has been analyzed theoretically in Sect. 3.2. In this subsection, we validate the derived theoretical results by the experiment with GOG feature descriptor employed. The CMC curves of R-Loss(p-norm) and R-Loss(min) on VIPeR and CUHK01 datasets are reported in Fig. 2. We can observe that, R-Loss(p-norm) improves the performance of R-Loss(min) by a large margin on all datasets. By using p-norm as a smooth approximation of minimum function, the Rank 1 increases 24.55%, 17.53% and 20.02% on VIPeR, CUHK01(M1) and CUHK01(M2) datasets, respectively. It reveals that the optimization algorithm by using the gradient descent scheme in the R-Loss(p-norm) model can converge to a better solution than in the R-Loss(min) model.

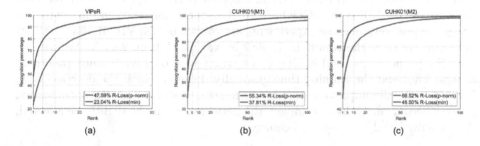

Fig. 2. Comparison of CMC curves for the proposed method by using p-norm function and minimum function.

On the Parameter p. In Sect. 3.2, we present a detailed analysis about the selection of parameter p and draw a conclusion that a larger value of p but not getting closer to the value of zero based on a basic constraint $p < 0$ is beneficial to the accuracy of person re-id. In this subsection, we compare the performance of the proposed R-Loss method with different values of p on VIPeR and CUHK01 datasets, and LOMO descriptor and GOG descriptor are used as the feature representation of person, respectively. As shown in Fig. 3, when $p \to -\infty$, the accuracy of Rank1 gradually degrades on all datasets. More specifically, when $p < -10$, the accuracy rapidly degrades on all datasets. It indicates that a lower value of p with $p \to -\infty$ is disadvantage to the performance. Besides, we can also see that the accuracy of Rank1 degrades rapidly with $p = -1$ on CUHK01(M1) and CUHK01(M2) datasets. Although the proposed method with $p = -1$ has well performance on VIPeR dataset, setting the value of p close to the value of zero is a riskier choice. Therefore, we set $p = -5$ in the experiments.

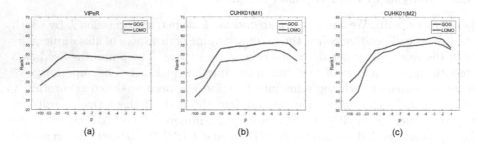

(a)   (b)   (c)

Fig. 3. The performances of Rank1 for the proposed method with different value of p.

On the Parameter k. In the process of optimizing the model in Eq. 4, we introduce a simplified algorithm to find the optimal solution. At each iteration of optimization algorithm, the first k sample pairs with smallest distances for each positive pair are used in the computation. In this subsection, we investigate the effects of k on the performance and running time of the proposed R-Loss method. Here, we use the LOMO and GOG feature descriptors for representing the person image, respectively, and the experiments are carried out on VIPeR and CUHK01 datasets. We show the results in Table 2 by varying k from 2 to N. We can see that the proposed method is kind of invariant to k on performance (fluctuate around 2%), and the running time gradually decreases with the decrease of k. When $k = N$, all samples are used for optimizing model so that the optimization process become much more complex, the performance might slightly be affected. As a result, $k = 2$ is an optimal choice.

5.3   Comparison with Other Loss Function Based Methods

In this paper, we propose a novel metric learning based person re-id method by optimizing a ranking loss function. Compared with the binary classification loss based [5,6], the triplet loss based [1,7] and the quadruplet loss based methods [2], there is no need to select the parameters carefully and no problem of sample imbalance in the proposed ranking loss based method. In the following, we will verify a more critical advantage of the proposed method compared with classical loss function based methods: a better generalization ability on the testing set (Table 1).

For a fair comparison, GOG feature descriptor is used in this comparison experiment. Similar to most of methods, we set $c = 1$ for both the binary classification loss function and the triplet loss function, and $c_1 = 1$, $c_2 = 0.5$ for the triplet loss function. The comparison results are shown in Table 3 the proposed

Table 1. Effects of k on the performance and running time of the proposed R-Loss method. Running time refers to one iteration time of optimization algorithm. $k = N$ represents the case for using all samples in optimization.

k	VIPeR				CUHK01(M1)				CUHK01(M2)			
	GOG		LOMO		GOG		LOMO		GOG		LOMO	
	$r=1$	T(s)	$r=1$	T(s)	$r=1$	T(s)	$r=1$	T(s)	$r=1$	T(s)	$r=1$	T(s)
2	47.59	0.39	39.49	0.36	55.34	9.07	51.55	9.35	67.90	9.34	64.81	9.29
5	47.82	0.77	39.49	0.37	55.98	9.28	51.86	9.44	69.14	9.50	65.84	9.49
10	48.82	0.81	39.75	0.38	56.19	9.57	51.65	9.58	68.52	9.64	66.26	9.65
N	46.61	1.48	38.32	1.42	54.33	32.84	50.41	32.70	65.84	32.39	64.20	32.63

Table 2. Comparison with methods based on other loss function on VIPeR and CUHK01 datasets. The best results (%) are respectively shown in red. Better viewed in colour.

Methods	VIPeR				CUHK01(M1)				CUHK01(M2)			
	$r=1$	$r=5$	$r=10$	$r=20$	$r=1$	$r=5$	$r=10$	$r=20$	$r=1$	$r=5$	$r=10$	$r=20$
Binary	46.23	77.34	87.78	93.64	32.33	51.32	60.91	71.71	37.02	59.63	69.84	80.12
Binary (smooth)	46.46	78.42	88.42	94.43	51.44	76.14	84.16	90.63	62.61	84.73	90.16	94.67
Triplet	30.09	62.41	76.93	87.09	45.54	69.25	78.05	85.93	54.69	78.07	86.13	91.91
Quadruplet	33.01	66.11	77.91	88.54	36.00	59.14	68.75	77.91	44.14	69.03	78.48	86.26
R-Loss	47.59	78.86	88.42	93.96	55.34	77.51	85.14	91.16	66.52	86.13	91.58	95.29

R-Loss method outperforms other loss function based methods on all datasets. Specifically, our method achieves about 3.9% gain at Rank 1 compared with the second result from the binary classification loss (smooth) based method on CUHK01 dataset with single-shot and multi-shot setting.

5.4   Comparison with State-of-the-Art Methods

In this section, we evaluate our method against the state-of-the-art person re-id methods. The experiment results of our method are presented by a simple fusion of scores obtained by the three types of features mentioned above.

Result on VIPeR Dataset. We compare the proposed method with 13 existing person re-id methods. From the results shown in Table 4, we can see that our method achieves the highest performance at Rank1, Rank5 and Rank20. More specifically, our method beats the closest competitor EBG [25] by 1.11% at Rank1. EBG [25] as a feature extraction based method where a deep neural network was proposed to solve the background bias problem, still yield the poorer results compared with our proposed method based on classical metric learning technology. It indicates that the deep learning based methods cannot currently work well on the small person re-id dataset.

Result on CUHK01 Dataset. The proposed R-Loss method is compared with traditional methods and deep learning based methods in CUHK01 dataset with

Table 3. Comparison with the state-of-the-art methods on VIPeR dataset. The best results for deep learning based and traditional methods (%) are respectively shown in boldface and red. Better viewed in colour.

	Method	Reference	r = 1	r = 5	r = 10	r = 20
Deep learning	IDLA	2015CVPR [26]	34.81	63.60	75.63	84.49
	Deep Ranking	2016TIP [27]	38.40	69.20	81.30	90.40
	TCP	2016CVPR [28]	47.80	74.70	84.80	91.10
	PDC	2017ICCV [29]	51.27	74.05	84.18	91.46
	DeepAlign	2017ICCV [30]	48.70	74.70	85.10	**93.00**
	EBG	2018CVPR [25]	**51.90**	74.40	84.80	90.20
	MLS	2018CVPR [31]	50.10	73.10	84.35	–
	MC-PPMN	2018AAAI [32]	50.13	**81.17**	**91.46**	–
Traditional	WARCA	2016ECCV [33]	40.22	68.16	80.70	91.14
	TMA	2016ECCV [34]	48.19	–	87.65	93.54
	PatchM&LocalM	2017PR [1]	46.50	69.30	80.70	–
	MVLDML+	2018TIP [35]	50.00	79.20	88.50	94.70
	GCT	2018AAAI [36]	49.40	77.60	87.20	94.00
	R-Loss	Our	53.01	83.07	90.82	96.27

Table 4. Comparison with the state-of-the-art methods on CUHK01 dataset. The best results for deep learning based and traditional methods (%) are respectively shown in boldface and red. Better viewed in colour.

	Method	Reference	r = 1	r = 5	r = 10	r = 20
Deep learning	IDLA	2015CVPR [26]	47.50	71.60	80.30	87.50
	TCP	2016CVPR [28]	53.70	84.30	91.00	96.30
	Deep Ranking	2016TIP [27]	50.40	70.00	84.80	92.00
	DeepAlign	2017ICCV [30]	75.00	93.50	95.70	**97.70**
	MC-PPMN	2018AAAI [32]	**78.95**	**94.67**	**97.64**	–
Traditional	WARCA	2016ECCV [33]	65.64	85.34	90.48	95.04
	PatchM&LocalM	2017PR [1]	53.50	82.50	91.20	96.10
	GCT	2018AAAI [36]	61.90	81.90	87.60	92.80
	MVLDML+	2018TIP [35]	61.40	82.70	88.90	93.90
	R-Loss	Our	73.66	90.64	94.14	96.87

multi-shot setting. Table 4 shows that the best results are from the deep learning based method MC-PPMN [32] where deep feature representations for semantic-components and color-texture distributions are learned based on pyramid person matching network. However, the proposed method is competitive among the traditional methods at all Rank.

6   Conclusions

In this paper, we propose a novel ranking loss function from a new perspective to solve the person re-id problem. The loss function is optimized aiming to make the distance of positive pair be the minimum value of distances of all pairs with the given query person, which is more accordant with person re-id problem. Moreover, we propose to use p-norm to approximate the minimum function to obtain a smooth and continuously differentiable loss function, which is favorable for model solution. In addition, just the first two sample pairs with smallest distances are used in the process of model optimization for improving the efficiency of model solution, with almost the same accuracies as the model using all pairs. Extensive experiments with thorough analysis demonstrate that the proposed R-Loss method achieves superior performance than state-of-the-art methods on VIPeR and CUHK01 datasets. In future research, we will explore to apply the ranking loss to deep learning scheme so that a competitive performance can be achieved on the large datasets.

Acknowledgment. This work is supported by the National Key R&D Program of China under Grant 2017YFC0803505. We appreciate Hao Dou's help on this paper.

References

1. Zhao, Z., Zhao, B., Su, F.: Person re-identification via integrating patch-based metric learning and local salience learning. Pattern Recogn. **75**, 90–98 (2017)
2. Chen, W., Chen, X., Zhang, J., Huang, K.: Beyond triplet loss: a deep quadruplet network for person re-identification. In: Computer Vision and Pattern Recognition, vol. 2 (2017)
3. Sun, C., Wang, D., Lu, H.: Person re-identification via distance metric learning with latent variables. IEEE Trans. Image Process. **26**(1), 23–34 (2016)
4. Zhou, S., Wang, J., Shi, R., Hou, Q., Gong, Y., Zheng, N.: Large margin learning in set to set similarity comparison for person re-identification. IEEE Trans. Multimed. **PP**(99), 1–1 (2017)
5. Jurie, F., Mignon, A.: PCCA: a new approach for distance learning from sparse pairwise constraints. In: Computer Vision and Pattern Recognition, pp. 2666–2672 (2012)
6. Li, Z., Chang, S., Liang, F., Huang, T.S., Cao, L., Smith, J.R.: Learning locally-adaptive decision functions for person verification. In: IEEE Conference on Computer Vision and Pattern Recognition, pp. 3610–3617 (2013)
7. Ding, S., Lin, L., Wang, G., Chao, H.: Deep feature learning with relative distance comparison for person re-identification. Pattern Recogn. **48**(10), 2993–3003 (2015)
8. Farenzena, M., Bazzani, L., Perina, A., Murino, V., Cristani, M.: Person re-identification by symmetry-driven accumulation of local features. In: Computer Vision and Pattern Recognition, pp. 2360–2367 (2010)
9. Liao, S., Hu, Y., Zhu, X., Li, S.Z.: Person re-identification by local maximal occurrence representation and metric learning. In: Computer Vision and Pattern Recognition, pp. 2197–2206 (2015)

10. Su, C., Li, J., Zhang, S., Xing, J., Gao, W., Tian, Q.: Pose-driven deep convolutional model for person re-identification. In: 2017 IEEE International Conference on Computer Vision (ICCV), pp. 3980–3989. IEEE (2017)
11. Pedagadi, S., Orwell, J., Velastin, S., Boghossian, B.: Local fisher discriminant analysis for pedestrian re-identification. In: Computer Vision and Pattern Recognition, pp. 3318–3325 (2013)
12. Cao, M., Chen, C., Hu, X., Peng, S.: From groups to co-traveler sets: pair matching based person re-identification framework. In: IEEE International Conference on Computer Vision Workshop, pp. 2573–2582 (2017)
13. Chen, C., Cao, M., Hu, X., Peng, S.: Key person aided re-identification in partially ordered pedestrian set. In: Conference the British Machine Vision Conference (2017)
14. Zhong, Z., Zheng, L., Cao, D., Li, S.: Re-ranking person re-identification with k-reciprocal encoding. In: 2017 IEEE Conference on Computer Vision and Pattern Recognition (CVPR), pp. 3652–3661. IEEE (2017)
15. Karanam, S., Gou, M., Wu, Z., Rates-Borras, A., Camps, O., Radke, R.J.: A systematic evaluation and benchmark for person re-identification: Features, metrics, and datasets. IEEE Trans. Pattern Anal. Mach. Intell., 1 (2016)
16. Zhang, L., Xiang, T., Gong, S.: Learning a discriminative null space for person re-identification. In: Computer Vision and Pattern Recognition, pp. 1239–1248 (2016)
17. Wang, F., Zuo, W., Lin, L., Zhang, D., Zhang, L.: Joint learning of single-image and cross-image representations for person re-identification. In: Computer Vision and Pattern Recognition, pp. 1288–1296 (2016)
18. Zhou, S., Wang, J., Wang, J., Gong, Y., Zheng, N.: Point to set similarity based deep feature learning for person re-identification. In: Computer Vision and Pattern Recognition, pp. 5028–5037 (2017)
19. Wen, Y., Zhang, K., Li, Z., Qiao, Y.: A discriminative feature learning approach for deep face recognition. In: Leibe, B., Matas, J., Sebe, N., Welling, M. (eds.) ECCV 2016. LNCS, vol. 9911, pp. 499–515. Springer, Cham (2016). https://doi. org/10.1007/978-3-319-46478-7_31
20. Gray, D., Brennan, S., Tao, H.: Evaluating appearance models for recognition, reacquisition, and tracking. In: IEEE International Workshop on Performance Evaluation for Tracking and Surveillance (PETS) (2007)
21. Li, W., Zhao, R., Wang, X.: Human reidentification with transferred metric learning. In: Lee, K.M., Matsushita, Y., Rehg, J.M., Hu, Z. (eds.) ACCV 2012. LNCS, vol. 7724, pp. 31–44. Springer, Heidelberg (2013). https://doi.org/10.1007/978-3-642-37331-2_3
22. Matsukawa, T., Okabe, T., Suzuki, E., Sato, Y.: Hierarchical Gaussian descriptor for person re-identification. In: IEEE Conference on Computer Vision and Pattern Recognition, pp. 1363–1372 (2016)
23. Chen, Y.-C., Zhu, X., Zheng, W.-S., Lai, J.-H.: Person re-identification by camera correlation aware feature augmentation. IEEE Trans. Pattern Anal. Mach. Intell. **40**(2), 392–408 (2018)
24. Krizhevsky, A., Sutskever, I., Hinton, G.E.: Imagenet classification with deep convolutional neural networks. In: International Conference on Neural Information Processing Systems, pp. 1097–1105 (2012)
25. Tian, M., et al.: Eliminating background-bias for robust person re-identification. In: The IEEE Conference on Computer Vision and Pattern Recognition (CVPR), June 2018

26. Ahmed, E., Jones, M., Marks, T.K.: An improved deep learning architecture for person re-identification. In: Computer Vision and Pattern Recognition, pp. 3908–3916 (2015)
27. Chen, S.Z., Guo, C.C., Lai, J.: Deep ranking for person re-identification via joint representation learning. IEEE Trans. Image Process. **25**(5), 2353–2367 (2016)
28. Cheng, D., Gong, Y., Zhou, S., Wang, J., Zheng, N.: Person re-identification by multi-channel parts-based CNN with improved triplet loss function. In: Computer Vision and Pattern Recognition, pp. 1335–1344 (2016)
29. Su, C., Li, J., Zhang, S., Xing, J., Gao, W., Tian, Q.: Pose-driven deep convolutional model for person re-identification. In: The IEEE International Conference on Computer Vision (ICCV), October 2017
30. Zhao, L., Li, X., Zhuang, Y., Wang, J.: Deeply-learned part-aligned representations for person re-identification. In: The IEEE International Conference on Computer Vision (ICCV), October 2017
31. Guo, Y., Cheung, N.-M.: Efficient and deep person re-identification using multi-level similarity. In: The IEEE Conference on Computer Vision and Pattern Recognition (CVPR), June 2018
32. Mao, C., Li, Y., Zhang, Y., Zhang, Z., Li, X.: Multi-channel pyramid person matching network for person re-identification (2018)
33. Jose, C., Fleuret, F.: Scalable metric learning via weighted approximate rank component analysis. In: Leibe, B., Matas, J., Sebe, N., Welling, M. (eds.) ECCV 2016. LNCS, vol. 9909, pp. 875–890. Springer, Cham (2016). https://doi.org/10.1007/978-3-319-46454-1_53
34. Martinel, N., Das, A., Micheloni, C., Roy-Chowdhury, A.K.: Temporal model adaptation for person re-identification. In: Leibe, B., Matas, J., Sebe, N., Welling, M. (eds.) ECCV 2016. LNCS, vol. 9908, pp. 858–877. Springer, Cham (2016). https://doi.org/10.1007/978-3-319-46493-0_52
35. Yang, X., Wang, M., Tao, D.: Person re-identification with metric learning using privileged information. IEEE Trans. Image Process. **PP**(99), 1 (2018)
36. Zhou, Q., et al.: Graph correspondence transfer for person re-identification (2018)

Unsupervised Transformation Network Based on GANs for Target-Domain Oriented Multi-domain Image Translation

Hongwei Ge[1(✉)] [iD], Yao Yao[1], Zheng Chen[2], and Liang Sun[1] [iD]

[1] College of Computer Science and Technology, Dalian University of Technology,
Dalian 116023, China
hwge@dlut.edu.cn
[2] Department of Computer Science and Engineering,
Washington University in St. Louis, St. Louis, MO 63130, USA

Abstract. Multi-domain image translation with unpaired data is a challenging problem. This paper proposes a generalized GAN-based unsupervised multi-domain transformation network (UMT-GAN) for image translation. The generation network of UMT-GAN consists of a universal encoder, a reconstructor and a series of translators corresponding to different target domains. The encoder is used to learn the universal information among different domains. The reconstructor is designed to extract the hierarchical representations of the images by minimizing the reconstruction loss. The translators are used to perform the multi-domain translation. Each translator and reconstructor are connected to a discriminator for adversarial training. Importantly, the high-level representations are shared between the source and multiple target domains, and all network structures are trained together by using a joint loss function. In particular, instead of using a random vector z as inputs to generate high-resolution images, UMT-GAN rather employs the source domain images as the inputs of the generator, hence help the model escape from collapsing to a certain extent. The experimental studies demonstrate the effectiveness and superiority of the proposed algorithm compared with several state-of-the-art algorithms.

Keywords: Image-to-image translation ·
Generative adversarial networks · Multi-domain

1 Introduction

The goal of image-to-image translation is to learn the mapping between an input image and an output image. The expected transformation by using the mapping is capable of gaining domain-oriented specificity under latent domain-invariant representation. Image-to-image translation has been widely applied in the fields of image processing, computer graphics and computer vision, such as colorization [2,36], image super-resolution [7,13,17,31], inpainting [25], and style transfer [9].

© Springer Nature Switzerland AG 2019
C. V. Jawahar et al. (Eds.): ACCV 2018, LNCS 11362, pp. 398–413, 2019.
https://doi.org/10.1007/978-3-030-20890-5_26

Some early works are devoted to adopt convolutional neural networks (CNNs) to solve the tasks of image-to-image translation. A variety of CNN models with different loss functions have been designed for specific tasks [2,7,23,36]. In recent years, generative adversarial networks (GANs), introduced by Goodfellow et al. in 2014 [10], have become a popular choice for image translation tasks [6,16,25,26,28,31]. The basic idea of GANs is to generate the samples through the competition of generative network and discriminative network in a zero-sum game framework. Typically, the generative network aims to learn a mapping from a latent feature space to a particular data distribution, while the discriminative network is used to discriminate the samples from the true data distribution and candidates produced by the generator. Some variants of GANs have been contributed to specific tasks [4,12,24]. Conditional GANs [24] (cGANs) have been demonstrated to be a simple and effective improvement by adding the condition information to the inputs of generator and discriminator. Based on cGAN, Pix2pix [12] is a representative framework designed for the kind of problems with available paired images, which aims to model the conditional distributions of the natural images conditioned on the input images [16,28,31]. However, it is difficult to provide a large number of paired images or ground truth in different domains for the complex practical tasks and the expensive cost of manual annotation.

To address these difficulties, some unsupervised GAN-based models without employing any paired data have been proposed for image-to-image translation between two different domains. DiscoGAN [14], DualGAN [35] and CycleGAN [37] couple two GANs together, and each GAN is responsible for generating and discriminating images in their respective domain. Further, to make the two generators strongly coupled, additional reconstruction losses are introduced for guiding the training process. The research shows that this mechanism can alleviate the problem of model collapse to a certain extent [8]. Besides, CoGAN [21] and UNIT [20] use a weight-sharing constraint to learn a joint distribution without any paired images in different domains. DCGANs [27] projects a uniform distribution to a small spatial extent convolutional representation with many feature maps and converts this obtained high level representation into a pixel image with specific size. WaterGAN [19] generates realistic underwater images from in-air image and depth pairings in an unsupervised way.

Notwithstanding the successful application of the unsupervised GAN-based methods, the aforementioned researches focus on the tasks of image-to-image translation between two domains. These methods are limited when extended to multi-domain image translation, since it is necessary to establish and train a model for each pair of image domains. To tackle this problem, some works are proposed to simultaneously generate multiple outputs in different target domains. Zhu et al. [38] propose a BicycleGAN that encourages the bijection mapping between the latent and output space. Recently, StarGAN [3] is proposed to perform diverse image-to-image translation using a single model conditioned on the target domain label. More recently, several concurrent works [18,34] employ the disentangled feature representation for learning multi-domain image translation from unpaired training data.

To address the multi-domain image-to-image translation without paired data, this paper proposes an unsupervised multi-domain transformation network (UMT-GAN) based on GANs with hierarchical representations learning and weight-sharing mechanism. The UMT-GAN takes full advantage of the hierarchical representation ability from deep neural models, the model restrain capacity from weight-sharing mechanism and the guidance ability from different target domains. The hierarchical representations of the input image are learned by an encoder and an reconstructor and the acquired universal information from encoder and high-level representations from reconstructor are shared with translators to realize the multi-domain image translation.

The following parts of this paper are structured as follows. Section 2 gives the background of the related works and also explains the motivations of the paper. Section 3 gives the details of the proposed unsupervised multi-domain transformation network UMT-GAN for image translation. Section 4 presents the experimental studies. Finally, in Sect. 5, the paper is concluded.

2   Related Work

Recent years have witnessed that the algorithms employing the idea of generative adversarial network [10] have achieved impressive results in image generation and representation learning. The generative adversarial networks generate realistic samples that are indistinguishable from natural images by constructing a generative network and a discriminative network to learn the underlying distribution of the images. The basic principle of GANs is not to memorize all the input data, but to learn specific semantic and structural properties. The images generated by GANs are sharper and more realistic as compared with restricted Boltzmann machines and variational auto-encoders, since GANs can effectively obtain the high-frequency information [12].

Afterwards, some developed GAN models have constantly improved the performance of specific tasks. For example, InfoGAN [1], LAPGAN [5] and cGANs [24] have been applied to image translation in recent years for their simple implementation and striking results. The cGANs [24] take class labels as conditional information of generator and discriminator to generate specific images. Isola et al. [12] propose the generic framework based on cGANs to learn a loss function to train the mapping from input image to output image for adapting different image translation problems. Further, Wang et al. [31] improve the cGANs by using a novel adversarial loss as well as a coarse-to-fine generator and a multi-scale discriminator architecture for synthesizing high resolution photo-realistic images from semantic label maps. Although these methods can generate impressive images by using paired data as supervision, it is still a challenging task to build a dataset with paired images for each image translation problem.

Some unsupervised learning methods based on GANs have been developed for image translation without paired data. CycleGAN [37] uses two groups of generators and discriminators, and two generators are used to learn the bidirectional mapping between two domains while two discriminators are used to distinguish the natural images from the generated images in the respective domain. Besides, the cycle consistency loss is presented to reduce the space of possible mappings and model collapse. The cycle consistency loss has been one of popular constraints. Similar works include DiscoGAN [14] and DualGAN [35]. DiscoGAN is an improved GAN architecture to discover the relations between two domains without any explicit pair labels. In DualGAN, one primal GAN and one dual GAN form a closed loop. The translators are trained from two unlabeled image dataset and allow images from either domain to be translated. Another effective technology to address the image translation is weight-sharing strategy presented in CoGAN [21] under the assumption that the images in different domains possess the identical underlying characteristic structure. The generators can learn a joint distribution in different domains by sharing the weights representing high-level semantic features. However, the errors from the discriminators in CoGAN will cause a direct effect on the accuracy of the shared high-level semantics and the random input vector z may lead to model collapse when generating high-resolution images.

A significant limitation of these methods mentioned above is the lack of diversity in the outputs. Different models need to be built and trained independently for every pair of image domains when dealing with multi-domain image translation. Simply injecting a random noise z to the generator to match any distribution in the target domains is also not an effective solution to achieve multi-domain image generation. Thus, these methods have limited scalability and robustness in handling more than two domains. Zhu et al. [38] propose a BicycleGAN that enforces the bijection mapping between the latent and target space to tackle the model collapse problem and produce more diverse results. However, this framework requires ground-truth paired supervision. As a recent scalable approach, StarGAN [3] adopts a single model containing one encoder, one decoder and one discriminator to translate multi-domain facial images. StarGAN is capable of learning mappings among multiple domains by a mask vector that makes StarGAN focus on the explicitly known label. MUNIT [34] decomposes image representation into a domain-invariable content code and a domain-specific style code respectively, and then recombines its content code with a random style code sampled from the target domain to guide image translation. The similar disentangled representation is employed in current work [18] for diverse image translation from unpaired training data.

This paper proposes a GAN-based unsupervised multi-domain transformation network (UMT-GAN). The motivation is mainly to address the problem of multi-domain image translation without paired data and improve the performance of multi-domain image translation. In UMT-GAN, a universal encoder is adopted to learn the common information among different domains. A reconstructor is designed to extract the hierarchical representations of the images and restrain the potential model space. Some translators with high-level representation sharing mechanism are designed to perform the translation across multiple domains simultaneously. All modules in the framework are trained together by using a joint loss function in an adversarial way. The strategy of using source images as inputs can also help the model escape from collapsing to a certain extent.

3   Unsupervised Multi-domain Transformation Network UMT-GAN

In this section, we describe the proposed unsupervised multi-domain transformation network UMT-GAN in detail. UMT-GAN is an integrated framework by specific modules with different functions. UMT-GAN can use unpaired data to translate across multiple domains simultaneously.

3.1   Network Structure of UMT-GAN

The goal of UMT-GAN is to learn an unsupervised transformation network that translates an image from the source domain X to multiple target domains $Y_i, i = 1, ..., n$ simultaneously, given the real images $\{x\} \in X$, $\{y_i\} \in Y_i$ without any paired information. In order to better build an effective model to perform the multi-domain translation tasks, the following factors are considered. Importantly, the basic principle of model establishment is based on a latent characteristic manifold assumption, which assumes that the images translated into different domains may have the same underlying representation [20], though they have different surface appearance. So we can train an encoder to learn the universal information among different domains. Moreover, some reasonable constraints based on prior knowledge or rules need to be exerted on the designed network structure to restrain the model capacity and alleviate the problems of vanishing gradient and model collapse. Thus, we design a reconstructor to acquire the hierarchical features and share the high-level semantics with different domain translators. Besides, target-domain oriented information facilitates the generation of the images for specific domain under latent domain-invariant representation. Therefore, we train an exclusive translator for each target domain in a generative adversarial way. The proposed structure of UMT-GAN is shown in Fig. 1. UMT-GAN consists of a generation network and a series of domain-specific discriminators. The generation network G is composed of a universal encoder E, a reconstructor R and a series of domain-specific translators $T_i, i = 1, ..., n$. The encoder is used to learn the universal information among different domains. The reconstructor can extract the hierarchical representations of the input images $x \in X$ by minimizing the reconstruction loss. The translators are used to perform the multi-domain translation. The reconstructor R and each translator T_i are connected to a discriminator $(D_r, or\ D_{ti})$ for adversarial training, and the discriminators are used to distinguish the real members from the generated images in each domain. Importantly, the high-level representations are shared between the reconstructor and the multiple translators through the weight-sharing strategy, and all network structures are trained together by using a joint loss function.

In the generator network, the reconstructor and the translators are decoders with identical structure. In the training phase, the encoder is firstly used to learn the universal information from the input images, and then the output vector from the encoder is sent to both the reconstructor and translators for generating

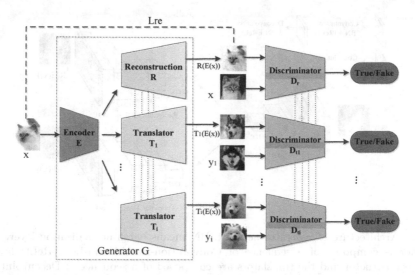

Fig. 1. Proposed unsupervised transformation network architecture for multi-domain image-to-image translation. R is used to reconstruct the input images while T_i is used to translate the input images to target domain. D_r and D_{ti} are used to distinguish the real members from the generated images of each domain. The discriminators are enforced the weight-sharing strategy.

samples to be discriminated. In the translating phase, the input image is fed to the encoder, and then the translators can output the target images for different domains. The architecture of the generation network is shown in Fig. 2. For the reconstructor and translators, they will gradually decode information from abstract concepts to material details. In this process, the weight-sharing strategy is firstly applied in the layers that decode the high-level representations to share the mutual representations for keeping the consistency of the underlying information. Then the layers that decode details map the shared information to individual domain. The discriminator is trained to distinguish the natural images from the generated images in the respective domain. In this paper, the architectures of discriminators for different domains are identical CNNs similar to the encoder. The first layers of discriminator extract detail features, while the last layers extract high-level semantic features. We employ the weight-sharing constraint in the latter layers of discriminators for different domains, since the input images have the similar high-level semantics in multiple domains. Moreover, the strategy of sharing the weights between the discriminators reduces the total numbers of network parameters.

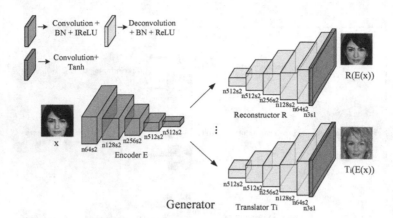

Fig. 2. Architecture of generator network. BN means batch-normalization layer. The encoder is composed of a sequence of Convolution-BatchNorm-LeakyReLU layers. The reconstructor and the translators are composed of a sequence of Deconvolution-BatchNorm-ReLU layers and a Convolution-Tanh layer. The number of channels in each layer is shown in figure.

3.2 Loss Function of UMT-GAN

In this section, we construct the loss function of UMT-GAN from different aspects.

Adversarial Loss. We apply adversarial losses to each pair of reconstructor/translator and its connected discriminator. For the reconstructor, the adversarial loss is expressed as:

$$L_{GAN}^R(E, R, D_r) = E_{x \sim p_{data}(x)}[log D_r(x)] + E_{x \sim p_{data}(x)}[log(1 - D_r(R(E(x))))] \quad (1)$$

where E tries to encode the input images and R tries to generate the reconstructed images $R(E(x))$ that is same as the input images, while D_r aims to distinguish between the generated samples $R(E(x))$ and real samples $x \sim p_{data}$.

For each translator T_i, the similar adversarial loss is written as:

$$L_{GAN}^{T_i}(E, T_i, D_{ti}) = E_{y_i \sim p_{data}(y_i)}[log D_{ti}(y_i)] + E_{x \sim p_{data}(x)}[log(1 - D_{ti}(T_i(E(x))))] \quad (2)$$

where T_i tries to translate the input image to $T_i(E(x))$ and make $T_i(E(x))$ look as similar as possible to the images from target domain Y_i, while D_{ti} aims to distinguish between the translated sample $T_i(E(x))$ and real sample y_i.

Reconstruction Loss. CycleGAN [37] shows that the integration of the adversarial losses with additional reconstruction losses can train generators more stably and generate better results, which further validates the advantage of restraining model capacity. And using a pixel loss function, e.g., L1 or L2 norm, to measure the output images is one of the most straightforward methods [2,23]. The experimental studies on cGAN shows that L1 distance often leads to less blurriness than L2 [12]. So, UMT-GAN uses the adversarial losses to model the high frequency information and the L1-norm of differences between pixels to force the low frequency structure. The reconstruction loss is written as follows.

$$L_{re}(E, R) = E_{x \sim p_{data}(x)} \left[\|x - R(E(x))\|_1\right] \tag{3}$$

Overall Loss. Finally, all network structures including encoder, reconstructor, translators and discriminators are trained together by using a joint loss function in a generative adversarial way. We define the translators as $T = \{T_i, i = 1, ..., n\}$ and their corresponding discriminators as $D_t = \{D_{ti}, i = 1, ..., n\}$.

The full loss function of the translators is written as:

$$L_{GAN}^T = \sum_{i=1}^{n} L_{GAN}^{T_i}(E, T_i, D_{ti}) \tag{4}$$

and the overall loss function is formulated as follows.

$$\min_{E,R,T} \max_{D_r,D_t} L(E, R, T, D_r, D_t) = L_{GAN}^R + L_{GAN}^T + \lambda L_{re} \tag{5}$$

4   Experimental Studies

To validate the effectiveness of the proposed unsupervised multi-domain transformation network for translating across multiple domains simultaneously, several sets of experiments are conducted. The obtained qualitative and quantitative results are analyzed and compared with other state-of-the-art methods.

4.1   Baselines Methods

For comparisons, the following state-of-the-art algorithms for image-to-image translation are selected as baselines.

CycleGAN [37] learns the mapping between two different domains X and Y without paired images via cycle-consistent losses $\|(F(G(x)) - x\|_1$ and $\|G(F(y)) - y)\|_1$. We train different CycleGAN models for each pair of domains.

CoGAN [21] learns a joint distribution of multi-domain images without paired data. One generator is for domain A and another is for domain B, with weight-sharing on the first few layers. The generators of CoGAN produce images from a shared latent representation, which is different from our network.

Pix2pix [12] is based on conditional GAN structure and minimizes the reconstruction loss and the adversarial loss to train the model with paired data.

StarGAN [3] adopts a single generator to translate an input image into multiple target domains conditioned on the target domain labels. By minimizing the classification loss and the adversarial loss, the input image can be mapped to the target domains.

MUNIT [34] disentangles the image into a domain-invariant content code and a domain-specific style code, and recomposes the content code with a random style code to realize multi-domain image translation.

4.2 Datasets

We evaluate our model on several datasets.

CelebA. The CelebA dataset [22] consists of 202599 celebrity images with 40 attribute annotations such as pale skin, male and black hair. We take three attributes for conducting the experiments: blond hair, male and smiling. All the images are center-cropped and resized to 64×64.

Animal Categories Translation. The dataset of animal categories translation in [18] is also adopted. We collect images from 3 domains including Siamese, Husky and Samoyed. The images are center-cropped to 178×178 and resized to 128×128.

Facade. The CMP Facade Database [29] contains 400 training images and 100 test images. All the images are scaled to 256×256 pixels.

4.3 Parameter Settings

The proposed UMT-GAN is trained using the Adam solver [15] with momentums $\beta_1 = 0.5$ and $\beta_2 = 0.999$. The learning rate is taken as 0.0002 as suggested in [27]. Leaky ReLU with a slope of 0.2 is used in the encoder, and ReLU is used in the decoder except the last layer where Tanh is used. For the final objective function, we empirically set $\lambda = 100$ for all experiments. The batch size is set to 64 for the face attributes translation, 4 for animal categories translation and 1 for photo generation from architectural labels tasks. The number of shared layers in the reconstructor and translators is 4 in CelebA, 4 in animals, and 3 in Facades respectively.

4.4 Evaluation Criteria

The translated images obtained by using different methods are assessed by qualitative observation and quantitative metric. We employ the following quantitative metrics to evaluate the performance as used in some generative networks [17,28,30]. Structural Similarity Index (SSIM) [33] measures the similarity between the generated image and the ground truth image based on their luminance, contrast and structural aspects. Higher SSIM means the generated image more similar with the ground truth. Peak Signal to Noise Ratio (PSNR) [11] measures the peak signal-to-noise ratio between the generated image and its original version. Universal Quality Index (UQI) [32] models image distortion from loss of correlation, luminance, and contrast. The higher the values, the better the quality of the generated image.

4.5 Experimental Results

Analysis of the Loss Function. To analyze the components of the overall objective formulated in Eq. 5, we conduct ablation studies for the loss function. We remove the reconstruction loss L_{re} (Eq. 3) and the adversarial loss L_{GAN}^R (Eq. 1) in turn. Figure 3 shows the qualitative results of these variations on the

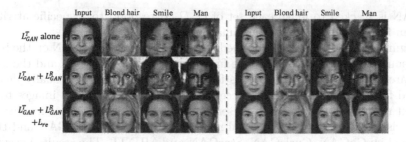

Fig. 3. Analysis of the objective function on the facial attribute translation. From left to right: input images, blond hair, smile, and man. From top to bottom: the encoder and translation networks alone (Eq. 4), translation networks with adversarial loss of the reconstruction network (Eq. 1 + Eq. 4), translation networks with adversarial loss and reconstruction loss of the reconstruction network (Eq. 1 + Eq. 3 + Eq. 4).

Fig. 4. Facial attribute translation on CelebA dataset. From top to bottom, the figure shows the results for blond hair, smile and man attributes.

translation task of face attributes with three attributes of blond hair, male and smiling. It can be seen that only using the translators leads to blurry results and slightly model collapse. While combining the adversarial loss L_{GAN}^R with L_{GAN}^T, the output can learn more information about the face attributes but the model collapse is still existing. Finally, when adding the reconstruction loss L_{re} into the overall objective, the better results are obtained and the model collapse also disappears. Thus, each loss item in the overall objective plays an important role and the joint loss integrating reconstruction loss and the generative adversarial losses can generate more realistic translated images.

Facial Attribute Translation. The proposed UMT-GAN is applied to face attributes translation task on the CelebA database, and the results are compared with different methods. UMT-GAN, StarGAN and MUNIT are the models for multiple domains and can be directly trained for multi-domain image translation. CycleGAN is trained multiple times by feeding images with different attributes, since CycleGAN can only transform images between two domains at a time.

CoGAN is stacked to make each set of G, D correspond to a specific attribute domain for realizing multi-domain image translation.

Figure 4 shows the results obtained by the proposed UMT-GAN on the blond hair, smile and man attributes. The first row is the input images and the latter rows are the corresponding outputs for different domains. As visually demonstrated from Fig. 4, UMT-GAN successfully translates the input images to the desired multiple domains while preserving structures in the input images. For comparisons, Fig. 5 shows the visual results obtained by UMT-GAN and those obtained by CoGAN, CycleGAN, StarGAN and MUNIT. The result shows that our proposed algorithm is efficient and competitive.

Animal Category Translation. In this section, we translate the input image to target domains and keep the consistent orientation. The model is trained with the dataset in [18]. The translation results are shown in Fig. 6 and the visual comparisons with CoGAN, CycleGAN, and MNUIT are shown in Fig. 7. The task is to translate the animal from the input image into Husky and Samoyed and keep the orientation of the animal. From the Figs. 6 and 7, it can be observed that the proposed UMT-GAN effectively completed the task.

Architecture. Figure 8 show some samples on architectural labels to photos compared with CycleGAN, CoGAN, Pix2pix and MUNIT. The dataset provides paired samples. Our model does not utilize paired information. Pix2pix is a representative framework designed for image translation with available paired images. Table 1 presents the quantitative evaluation results using the metrics of PSNR, SSIM, and UQI. Pix2pix obtains the best quantitative results because it uses the additional paired information. The results show that our algorithm

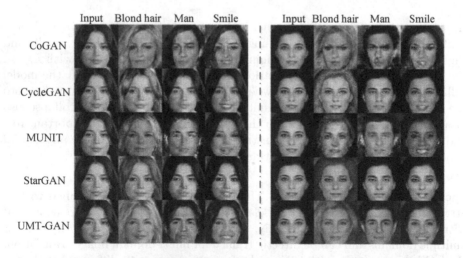

Fig. 5. Comparisons on facial attribute translation. The first column shows the input images, and the next three columns show the attribute translation results.

Fig. 6. Image translation results of animal category translation by UMT-GAN. UMT-GAN effectively keep the orientation of the animals.

Table 1. Comparisons with CoGAN, CycleGAN and Pix2pix on architectural labels to photos.

	PSNR (db)	SSIM	UQI
CoGAN	10.3329	0.0009	0.0010
CycleGAN	**13.2281**	0.0398	0.0250
Pix2pix	13.0053	**0.0475**	**0.0754**
MUNIT	11.7241	0.0437	0.0704
UMT-GAN	11.2128	0.0452	0.0648

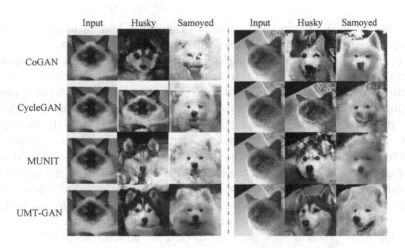

Fig. 7. Comparisons of animal translation. The first column shows the input images, and the next two columns show the translation results.

can preserve the structures in the label images well. The quality of our images is competitive with those produced by CycleGAN, CoGAN and MUNIT trained without pairwise supervised images and comparable with those produced by supervised Pix2pix.

Input	Ground truth	CoGAN	CycleGAN	Pix2pix	MUNIT	UMT-GAN

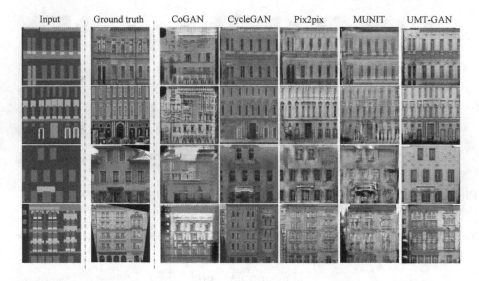

Fig. 8. Translation results from architectural labels to photos. From left to right: the input images, the ground truth, the outputs of CoGAN, CycleGAN, Pix2pix, MUNIT and the proposed UMT-GAN. Our method successfully preserves the structures in the label images.

5   Conclusions

This paper aims at solving the problem of the multi-domain image translation without paired data. So a GAN-based unsupervised multi-domain transformation network (UMT-GAN) for image translation is proposed. In UMT-GAN, a universal encoder is adopted to learn the common information among different domains. A reconstructor is designed to extract the hierarchical representations of the images and restrain the potential model space. Some translators with high-level representation sharing mechanism are designed to perform the translation across multiple domains simultaneously. Each translator and reconstructor are connected to a discriminator for adversarial training. The UMT-GAN takes full advantage of the hierarchical representation ability from deep neural models, the model restrain capacity from weight-sharing mechanism and the guidance ability from different target domains. The experimental studies demonstrate the effectiveness and superiority of the proposed algorithm. In future work, we aim to develop more powerful unsupervised models for domain adaptation or latent information transfer, and make extensive application.

Acknowledgment. The authors are grateful for the support of the National Natural Science Foundation of China (61572104, 61402076, 61502072), the Fundamental Research Funds for the Central Universities (DUT17JC04), and the Project of the Key Laboratory of Symbolic Computation and Knowledge Engineering of Ministry of Education, Jilin University (93K172017K03).

References

1. Chen, X., Duan, Y., Houthooft, R., Schulman, J., Sutskever, I., Abbeel, P.: Info-GAN: interpretable representation learning by information maximizing generative adversarial nets. In: Advances in Neural Information Processing Systems, Barcelona, pp. 2172–2180 (2016)
2. Cheng, Z., Yang, Q., Sheng, B.: Deep colorization. In: Proceedings of the IEEE International Conference on Computer Vision, Santiago, pp. 415–423 (2015)
3. Choi, Y., Choi, M., Kim, M., Ha, J.W., Kim, S., Choo, J.: StarGAN: unified generative adversarial networks for multi-domain image-to-image translation. In: The IEEE Conference on Computer Vision and Pattern Recognition, Salt Lake City (2018)
4. Creswell, A., White, T., Dumoulin, V., Arulkumaran, K., Sengupta, B., Bharath, A.A.: Generative adversarial networks: an overview. IEEE Signal Process. Mag. **35**(1), 53–65 (2018)
5. Denton, E.L., Chintala, S., Fergus, R., et al.: Deep generative image models using a Laplacian pyramid of adversarial networks. In: Advances in Neural Information Processing Systems, pp. 1486–1494 (2015)
6. Dolhansky, B., Canton Ferrer, C.: Eye in-painting with exemplar generative adversarial networks. In: Proceedings of the IEEE Conference on Computer Vision and Pattern Recognition, Salt Lake City, pp. 7902–7911 (2018)
7. Dong, C., Chen, C.L., He, K., Tang, X.: Image super-resolution using deep convolutional networks. IEEE Trans. Pattern Anal. Mach. Intell. **38**(2), 295–307 (2016)
8. Gan, Z., et al.: Triangle generative adversarial networks. In: Advances in Neural Information Processing Systems, Long Beach, pp. 5247–5256 (2017)
9. Gatys, L.A., Ecker, A.S., Bethge, M.: Image style transfer using convolutional neural networks. In: Proceedings of the IEEE Conference on Computer Vision and Pattern Recognition, Las Vegas, pp. 2414–2423 (2016)
10. Goodfellow, I.J., et al.: Generative adversarial nets. In: Advances in Neural Information Processing Systems, pp. 2672–2680 (2014)
11. Huynh-Thu, Q., Ghanbari, M.: Scope of validity of psnr in image/video quality assessment. Electron. Lett. **44**(13), 800–801 (2008)
12. Isola, P., Zhu, J.Y., Zhou, T., Efros, A.A.: Image-to-image translation with conditional adversarial networks. In: IEEE Conference on Computer Vision and Pattern Recognition, pp. 5967–5976. IEEE, Honolulu (2017)
13. Johnson, J., Alahi, A., Fei-Fei, L.: Perceptual losses for real-time style transfer and super-resolution. In: Leibe, B., Matas, J., Sebe, N., Welling, M. (eds.) ECCV 2016. LNCS, vol. 9906, pp. 694–711. Springer, Cham (2016). https://doi.org/10.1007/978-3-319-46475-6_43
14. Kim, T., Cha, M., Kim, H., Lee, J.K., Kim, J.: Learning to discover cross-domain relations with generative adversarial networks. In: Precup, D., Teh, Y.W. (eds.) International Conference on Machine Learning, vol. 70, pp. 1857–1865. PMLR, Sydney, Australia (2017)
15. Kingma, D., Ba, J.: Adam: a method for stochastic optimization. In: International Conference on Learning Representations, San Diego (2015)
16. Kupyn, O., Budzan, V., Mykhailych, M., Mishkin, D., Matas, J.: DeblurGAN: blind motion deblurring using conditional adversarial networks. In: Proceedings of the IEEE Conference on Computer Vision and Pattern Recognition, Salt Lake City, pp. 8183–8192 (2018)

17. Ledig, C., et al.: Photo-realistic single image super-resolution using a generative adversarial network. In: IEEE Conference on Computer Vision and Pattern Recognition, Honolulu, pp. 105–114 (2017)
18. Lee, H.Y., Tseng, H.Y., Huang, J.B., Singh, M., Yang, M.H.: Diverse image-to-image translation via disentangled representations. In: Proceedings of the European Conference on Computer Vision, Munich, Germany, pp. 35–51(2018)
19. Li, J., Skinner, K.A., Eustice, R.M., Johnson-Roberson, M.: WaterGAN: Unsupervised generative network to enable real-time color correction of monocular underwater images. IEEE Robot. Autom. Lett. **3**(1), 387–394 (2018)
20. Liu, M.Y., Breuel, T., Kautz, J.: Unsupervised image-to-image translation networks. In: Advances in Neural Information Processing Systems, Long Beach, pp. 700–708 (2017)
21. Liu, M.Y., Tuzel, O.: Coupled generative adversarial networks. In: Advances in Neural Information Processing Systems, Barcelona, pp. 469–477 (2016)
22. Liu, Z., Luo, P., Wang, X., Tang, X.: Deep learning face attributes in the wild. In: Proceedings of the IEEE International Conference on Computer Vision, Santiago, pp. 3730–3738 (2015)
23. Long, J., Shelhamer, E., Darrell, T.: Fully convolutional networks for semantic segmentation. In: Proceedings of the IEEE Conference on Computer Vision and Pattern Recognition, Boston, pp. 3431–3440 (2015)
24. Mirza, M., Osindero, S.: Conditional generative adversarial nets. arXiv preprint arXiv:1411.1784 (2014)
25. Pathak, D., Krahenbuhl, P., Donahue, J., Darrell, T., Efros, A.A.: Context encoders: feature learning by inpainting. In: Proceedings of the IEEE Conference on Computer Vision and Pattern Recognition, Las Vegas, pp. 2536–2544 (2016)
26. Qian, R., Tan, R.T., Yang, W., Su, J., Liu, J.: Attentive generative adversarial network for raindrop removal from a single image. In: Proceedings of the IEEE Conference on Computer Vision and Pattern Recognition, Salt Lake City, pp. 2482–2491 (2018)
27. Radford, A., Metz, L., Chintala, S.: Unsupervised representation learning with deep convolutional generative adversarial networks. In: International Conference on Learning Representations (2016)
28. Regmi, K., Borji, A.: Cross-view image synthesis using conditional GANs. In: Proceedings of the IEEE Conference on Computer Vision and Pattern Recognition, Salt Lake City, pp. 3501–3510 (2018)
29. Tyleček, R., Šára, R.: Spatial pattern templates for recognition of objects with regular structure. In: Weickert, J., Hein, M., Schiele, B. (eds.) GCPR 2013. LNCS, vol. 8142, pp. 364–374. Springer, Heidelberg (2013). https://doi.org/10.1007/978-3-642-40602-7_39
30. Wang, C., Xu, C., Wanga, C., Tao, D.: Perceptual adversarial networks for image-to-image transformation. IEEE Trans. Image Process. **27**(8), 4066–4079 (2018)
31. Wang, T.C., Liu, M.Y., Zhu, J.Y., Tao, A., Kautz, J., Catanzaro, B.: High-resolution image synthesis and semantic manipulation with conditional GANs. In: Proceedings of the IEEE Conference on Computer Vision and Pattern Recognition, Salt Lake City, pp. 8798–8807 (2018)
32. Wang, Z., Bovik, A.C.: A universal image quality index. IEEE Signal Process. Lett. **9**(3), 81–84 (2002)
33. Wang, Z., Bovik, A.C., Sheikh, H.R., Simoncelli, E.P.: Image quality assessment: from error visibility to structural similarity. IEEE Trans. Image Process. **13**(4), 600–612 (2004)

34. Huang, X., Liu, M.-Y., Belongie, S., Kautz, J.: Multimodal unsupervised image-to-image translation. In: Ferrari, V., Hebert, M., Sminchisescu, C., Weiss, Y. (eds.) ECCV 2018. LNCS, vol. 11207, pp. 179–196. Springer, Cham (2018). https://doi.org/10.1007/978-3-030-01219-9_11
35. Yi, Z., Zhang, H., Tan, P., Gong, M.: DualGAN: unsupervised dual learning for image-to-image translation. In: IEEE International Conference on Computer Vision, pp. 2868–2876. IEEE, Venice (2017)
36. Zhang, R., Isola, P., Efros, A.A.: Colorful image colorization. In: Leibe, B., Matas, J., Sebe, N., Welling, M. (eds.) ECCV 2016. LNCS, vol. 9907, pp. 649–666. Springer, Cham (2016). https://doi.org/10.1007/978-3-319-46487-9_40
37. Zhu, J.Y., Park, T., Isola, P., Efros, A.A.: Unpaired image-to-image translation using cycle-consistent adversarial networks. In: IEEE International Conference on Computer Vision, Venice, pp. 2242–2251 (2017)
38. Zhu, J.Y., et al.: Toward multimodal image-to-image translation. In: Advances in Neural Information Processing Systems, Long Beach, CA, pp. 465–476 (2017)

A Trainable Multiplication Layer for Auto-correlation and Co-occurrence Extraction

Hideaki Hayashi$^{(\boxtimes)}$ and Seiichi Uchida

Kyushu University, 744 Motooka Nishi-ku, Fukuoka, Japan
{hayashi,uchida}@ait.kyushu-u.ac.jp

Abstract. In this paper, we propose a trainable multiplication layer (TML) for a neural network that can be used to calculate the multiplication between the input features. Taking an image as an input, the TML raises each pixel value to the power of a weight and then multiplies them, thereby extracting the higher-order local auto-correlation from the input image. The TML can also be used to extract co-occurrence from the feature map of a convolutional network. The training of the TML is formulated based on backpropagation with constraints to the weights, enabling us to learn discriminative multiplication patterns in an end-to-end manner. In the experiments, the characteristics of the TML are investigated by visualizing learned kernels and the corresponding output features. The applicability of the TML for classification and neural network interpretation is also evaluated using public datasets.

Keywords: Neural network · Feature extraction · Auto-correlation · Co-occurrence

1 Introduction

Typified by the success of convolutional neural networks (CNNs) in recent computer vision research, studies using deep learning-based methods have demonstrated success in several fields [1,4,13,14,30]. Unlike the traditional machine learning techniques based on handcrafted features, these deep learning-based methods automatically extract features from raw input data via end-to-end network learning.

To exploit the end-to-end learning capability of the deep neural networks, numerous studies have investigated the development of a network layer that

Supported by Qdai-jump Research Program and JSPS KAKENHI Grant Number JP17K12752 and JP17K19402.

Electronic supplementary material The online version of this chapter (https://doi.org/10.1007/978-3-030-20890-5_27) contains supplementary material, which is available to authorized users.

© Springer Nature Switzerland AG 2019
C. V. Jawahar et al. (Eds.): ACCV 2018, LNCS 11362, pp. 414–430, 2019.
https://doi.org/10.1007/978-3-030-20890-5_27

represents a certain function by incorporating a model into a layer structure [5,20,27]. For example, Wang *et al.* [27] proposed a trainable structural layer called a global Gaussian distribution embedding network, which involves global Gaussian [17] as an image representation.

Despite such challenging efforts, the majority of layer structures are based on inner products of the input features and weight coefficients. There has been minimal research attempting to introduce multiplication of the input features. In classical pattern recognition techniques, however, multiplication of the input features is important because it represents auto-correlation or co-occurrence of the input features.

This paper proposes a trainable multiplication layer (TML) for a neural network that can be used to calculate the multiplication between the input features. Taking an image as an input, the TML raises each pixel value to the power of a weight and then multiplies them, thereby extracting the higher-order local auto-correlation from the input image. The TML can also be used to extract co-occurrence from the feature map of a CNN. The training of the TML is formulated based on backpropagation with constraints to the weights, enabling us to learn discriminative multiplication patterns in an end-to-end manner.

The contributions of this work are as follows:

- A trainable multiplication layer is proposed.
- The learning algorithm of the TML based on constrained optimization is formulated.
- Applicability to classification and network interpretation is demonstrated via experiments.

2   Related Work

2.1   Multiplication in a Neural Network Layer

The majority of the existing neural network layers focus on the multiplication of the input features and weight coefficients; there are limited studies that discuss a network layer that calculates the multiplication of the input features. Classically, Sigma-Pi Unit based on the summation of multiplication is applied to a self-organizing map [25,28]. Incorporation of probabilistic models such as a Gaussian mixture model into the neural network structure consequently leads to the development of a network layer based on multiplication [5,22,23]. In recent work, Shih *et al.* [20] proposed a network layer that detects co-occurrence by calculating multiplications between the feature maps of a CNN. Kobayashi [7] achieved a trainable co-occurrence activation by decomposing and approximating a multiplication operation.

Although such multiplication-based layers are not actively studied, they have the potential to create an efficient network structure because they can express auto-correlation and co-occurrence directly. This paper therefore focuses on the development of the multiplication-based neural network layer.

2.2   Higher-Order Local Auto-correlation

Higher-order local auto-correlation (HLAC) is a feature extraction method proposed by Otsu [19]. HLAC is frequently used in the field of image analysis [3,6,18,24]. For L displacements $a_1, \ldots, a_L$, the Lth-order autocorrelation function is defined as

$$R_L(a_1, \ldots, a_L) = \sum_{D'} f(r)f(r + a_1) \cdots f(r + a_L), \tag{1}$$

$$D' = \{r | r + a_l \in D, \forall l \in \{1, 2, \ldots, L\}\}, \tag{2}$$

where $f(r)$ is the pixel value of the input image at a coordinate r, D is a set of coordinates of the input image.

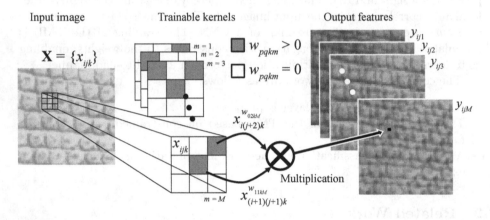

Fig. 1. Overview of forward calculation conducted in the TML. This figure shows a simple case where the number of input channels K is 1 and the kernel size is 3×3.

In HLAC, the patterns of the displacement must be prepared manually. The number of displacement patterns increases explosively based on the mask size and order; hence, they are limited practically.

3   Trainable Multiplication Layer

3.1   Layer Structure

Figure 1 presents an overview of the forward calculation in the TML. The main idea behind this layer is to achieve the multiplication of the input values chosen by the kernels, which is different from the well-known convolutional layer that conducts multiplication of the input values and kernels.

Given an input image or feature map of a convolutional layer $\mathbf{X} \in \mathbb{R}^{N_1 \times N_2 \times K}$, where N_1, N_2, and K are the number of rows, columns, and channels, respectively, the forward pass of the TML is defined as follows:

$$y_{ijm} = \prod_{k=0}^{K-1} \prod_{p=0}^{H-1} \prod_{q=0}^{W-1} x_{(i+p)(j+q)k}^{w_{pqkm}}, \tag{3}$$

where x_{ijk} $(i = 0, \ldots, N_1-1, j = 0, \ldots, N_2-1, k = 0, \ldots, K-1)$ is the (i, j, k)-th element of $\mathbf{X}$ and $w_{pqkm} \geq 0$ is the (p, q)-th weight of the m-th kernel for channel k $(p = 0, \ldots, H-1, q = 0, \ldots, W-1, m = 0, \ldots, M-1; M$ is the number of kernels). Since any number to the zero power is one (we define the value of zero to the power of zero to also be one), the forward pass of the proposed layer is regarded as the multiplication of the input values, where the value of the kernel at the corresponding coordinate is greater than zero.

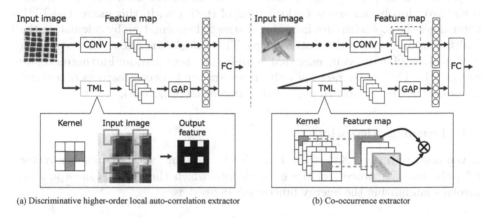

(a) Discriminative higher-order local auto-correlation extractor   (b) Co-occurrence extractor

Fig. 2. Two usages of the TML in a CNN: (a) used as discriminative higher-order local auto-correlation extractor and (b) used as co-occurrence extractor. The abbreviations GAP, CONV, and FC denote global average pooling, convolutional layer, and fully connected layer, respectively.

In practice, (3) is calculated in the logarithmic form to prevent under/overflow. Assuming that $x_{ijk} > 0$, since $\mathbf{X}$ is an image or a feature map passed through a ReLU function, (3) is rewritten as follows:

$$z_{ijmpqk} = \log\left(x_{(i+p)(j+q)k} + \epsilon\right), \tag{4}$$

$$y_{ijm} = \exp\left(\sum_{k=0}^{K-1} \sum_{p=0}^{H-1} \sum_{q=0}^{W-1} w_{pqkm} z_{ijmpqk}\right), \tag{5}$$

where ϵ is a small positive quantity to avoid $\log 0$.

3.2 Usage of the Layer in a Convolutional Neural Network

The TML is used as a part of a CNN-based deep neural network. Figure 2 shows two different usages of the TML in a CNN. Specifically, Fig. 2(a) shows the case that the TML is the use as a discriminative higher-order local auto-correlation (DHLAC) extractor; Fig. 2(b) shows the use as a co-occurrence extractor.

The former usage is proposed to achieve the discriminative learning of the displacement patterns in HLAC. In this usage, the TML is inserted immediately behind the input image. The output features calculated by the TML are then passed through a global average pooling (GAP) [12]. GAP calculates the average of each feature map and the resulting vector is input to the next layer. This GAP is placed to simulate the integral computation of HLAC. Because the displacement patterns are represented by the power functions to be differentiable, they are trainable as kernel patterns.

The latter usage is designed to calculate the co-occurrence between feature maps. In the deeper layer of a CNN, feature maps calculated by a convolutional layer involve abstracted information of the input. In this usage, the TML determines the co-occurrence from this abstracted information by calculating the multiplication between the feature maps. This calculation allows the extraction of non-Markovian co-occurrence that is useful for classification. Furthermore, we can use the TML to extract not only co-occurrence between features of a single network, but also co-occurrence between two or more networks.

3.3 Learning Algorithm

Given a set of images $\mathbf{X}^{(n)}$ $(n = 1, \ldots, N)$ for training with the teacher vector $\boldsymbol{t}^{(n)}$, the training process of the network into which the TML is incorporated involves minimizing the energy function E defined as

$$\text{minimize } E = \frac{1}{N} \sum_{n=1}^{N} \text{Loss}(\boldsymbol{O}^{(n)}, \boldsymbol{t}^{(n)}) + \lambda \|\boldsymbol{w}\|_1 \tag{6}$$

$$\text{subject to } \sum_{k=0}^{K-1} \sum_{p=0}^{H-1} \sum_{q=0}^{W-1} w_{pqkm} = C_1, \tag{7}$$

$$0 \le w_{pqkm} \le C_2, \tag{8}$$

where $\text{Loss}(\boldsymbol{O}^{(n)}, \boldsymbol{t}^{(n)})$ is the loss function defined by the final network output vector $\boldsymbol{O}^{(n)}$ corresponding to $\mathbf{X}^{(n)}$ and the teacher vector $\boldsymbol{t}^{(n)}$. The operator $\| \cdot \|_1$ indicates the L_1 norm, $\boldsymbol{w}$ is all of the kernels presented in a vectorized form, and λ is a constant. The constants C_1 and C_2 are hyperparameters that influence the training results, and the details are described in the next section. The L_1 regularization is recruited expecting to obtain sparse kernels based on the concept of the TML. The first constraint shown in (7) sets the total value of each kernel and prevents overflow. The second constraint shown in (8) prevents each kernel from being overly sparse because each kernel must have two or

---

Algorithm 1. Algorithm of weight updating

Require: Parameters C_1, C_2, and λ, training image set $\mathbf{X}^{(n)}$, teacher vector $\boldsymbol{t}^{(n)}$.
Ensure: Trained network.
1: Initialize the kernels $\boldsymbol{w}$ and other network weights $\boldsymbol{\theta}$.
2: **while** $\boldsymbol{w}$ and $\boldsymbol{\theta}$ have not converged **do**
3:     Calculate E.
4:     Calculate gradients of E with respect to $\boldsymbol{w}$ and $\boldsymbol{\theta}$.
5:     Update $\boldsymbol{w}$ and $\boldsymbol{\theta}$ using gradient-based updating.
6:     $\boldsymbol{w} \leftarrow \mathrm{clip}(\boldsymbol{w}, 0, C_2)$
7:     $\boldsymbol{w}_m \leftarrow C_1 \boldsymbol{w}_m / \mathrm{sum}(\boldsymbol{w}_m)$ for $m = 0, \ldots, M-1$
8: **end while**

---

more nonzero elements to be a meaningful kernel. It could appear that the L_1 regularization in (6) is redundant as the L_1 norm is fixed to a constant value by both constraints. However, the L_1 regularization influences the gradient vectors to obtain a sparse solution during the network learning.

Algorithm 1 shows the procedure to solve the above optimization, where $\boldsymbol{w}_m$ is the vectorized m-th kernel. In this algorithm, gradient-based weight updating to decrease the energy function E and weight modification to maintain the constraints are calculated alternately. Although this is an approximated approach different from the well-known Lagrange multiplier, we employ this approach to strictly satisfy the constraints during the network learning.

To calculate backpropagation, the partial derivative of E with respect to each kernel w_{pqkm} is required. Since the TML consists of multiplication and power functions, the partial derivative is calculated simply as follows:

$$
\begin{aligned}
\frac{\partial E}{\partial w_{pqkm}} &= \frac{\partial E}{\partial y_{ijm}} \frac{\partial y_{ijm}}{\partial w_{pqkm}} \\
&= \frac{\partial E}{\partial y_{ijm}} \prod_{k=0}^{K-1} \prod_{p=0}^{H-1} \prod_{q=0}^{W-1} x_{(i+p)(j+q)k}^{w_{pqkm}} \log x_{(i+p)(j+q)k} \\
&= \frac{\partial E}{\partial y_{ijm}} y_{ijm} \log x_{(i+p)(j+q)k},
\end{aligned}
\tag{9}
$$

where the form of $\frac{\partial E}{\partial y_{ijm}}$ depends on the layer connected between the TML and the output.

As outlined above, the TML incorporated in the deep network calculates DHLAC of the input image or co-occurrence between the feature maps. The kernels are trained in an end-to-end manner via backpropagation with constraints.

4   Investigation of the Layer Characteristics

Before beginning the classification experiments, we investigated the characteristics of the TML by training a relatively shallow network with the TML inserted, and visualizing the learned kernels and corresponding feature maps.

4.1   Relationships Between Hyperparameters and Learned Kernels

The TML has important hyperparameters including C_1, C_2 for the learning constraints, and the kernel size. We investigated the changes in the learned kernels and the corresponding features according to the parameter variation.

In this trial, LeNet-5 [11] was used as the basic structure. The TML was inserted immediately behind the input. The ReLU activation function [16] was used for the convolution layers and the sigmoid function was used for the fully connected layer.

For the training data, we used the MNIST dataset [11]. This dataset includes ten classes of handwritten binary digit images with a size of 28×28; it contains 60,000 training images and 10,000 testing images. The network was trained with all the training data for each hyperparameter.

Following the network training, we visualized the learned kernels and the responses for the testing images. First, we observed the changes in the learned kernels according to the parameters for the constraints. Because the ratio of C_1 to C_2 influences the training results, we varied the value of C_2 as $C_2 = 1.0, 0.5, 0.33, 0.25$ for fixed a C_1 of 1.0. The kernel size and λ were set as 3×3 and $\lambda = 0.01$, respectively.

(a) $C_2 = 1.0$ (b) $C_2 = 0.5$ (c) $C_2 = 0.33$ (d) $C_2 = 0.25$

Fig. 3. Changes in learned kernels according to C_2. The kernel size and other parameters are fixed as 3×3, $C_1 = 1.0$, and $\lambda = 0.01$.

Figure 3 shows the changes in the learned kernels according to C_2. In this figure, the values of the learned kernels normalized by C_2 are displayed in a grayscale heat map, and therefore black and white pixels show "0" and C_2, respectively. The number of nonzero elements in each kernel increases according to the decrease in the value of C_2. Since the total value of elements in each kernel is fixed to C_1 and the upper limit of each element is suppressed by C_2, the number of nonzero elements approximates to C_1/C_2 if the L_1 regularization functions appropriately. These results demonstrate that the number of nonzero elements, which is equivalent to the order in HLAC, can be controlled by changing the ratio of C_1 to C_2.

Secondly, the kernel size was varied as 3×3, 5×5, 7×7, and 9×9 for the fixed value of $C_1 = 1.0$, $C_2 = 0.5$, and $\lambda = 0.01$. Figure 4 shows the learned kernels and the corresponding output features according to the kernel size. The kernel pattern and output feature pattern placed at the same location correspond to each other. The learned kernel values displayed in the left panels are also

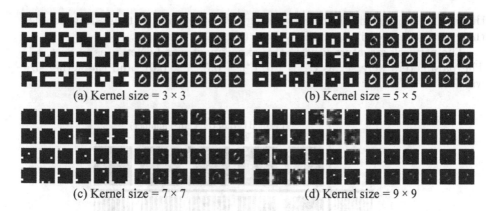

(a) Kernel size = 3 × 3   (b) Kernel size = 5 × 5

(c) Kernel size = 7 × 7   (d) Kernel size = 9 × 9

Fig. 4. Learned kernels (left panels) and corresponding output features (right panels) for each kernel size. Other parameters are fixed as $C_1 = 1.0$, $C_2 = 0.5$, and $\lambda = 0.01$.

normalized in the same manner as Fig. 3. The values of the output features shown in the right panels are rescaled from $[0, 1]$ to $[0, 255]$ before visualization.

In terms of kernel size variation, the characteristics of the learned kernels and output features changed depending on the kernel size. In Fig. 4(a), the number of nonzero elements is two in each kernel and these elements adjoin each other in the majority of the kernels. Kernels with neighboring nonzero elements extract rather local correlation, and the output features are virtually the same as the input images. However, kernels with nonzero elements apart from each other extract different output features according to the kernel pattern. In Fig. 4(b), the number of kernels with nonzero elements apart from each other increased and hence a richer variation of output features was obtained compared to Fig. 4(a). Figure 4(c) and (d) include kernels that have gray pixels. This means that three or more values are multiplied in a calculation and therefore high-order autocorrelation is extracted. These results indicate that the number of nonzero elements in each kernel can be controlled to a certain extent by the ratio of C_1 to C_2, and the variety of the output features changes according to the kernel size.

4.2   Characteristics as a DHLAC Extractor

We verified if the TML can make discriminative responses by observing the learned kernel patterns and the corresponding output features for the synthetic texture patterns.

The texture dataset used in this experiment contained six classes of 32×32 artificially generated images from the following procedure (examples are displayed in the leftmost panels in Fig. 5): First, six stripe patterns, different for each class, were drawn on a 1024×1024 black image. Then, uniform random noise in the range of $[0, 1]$ was added to the images. Finally, a set of randomly cropped 32×32-sized images were used as the dataset. We generated 100 training images for each class (600 training images in total). After training, we observed the learned kernels and the corresponding output features to the testing samples that were generated independently from the training images.

The network structure used in this experiment was LeNet-5, as in Sect. 4.1. The parameters were set as $C_1 = 1.0$, $C_2 = 0.5$, $\lambda = 0.01$, and the kernel size was 9×9.

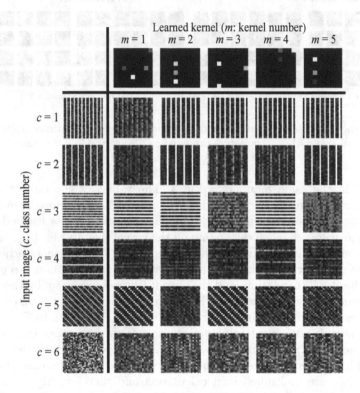

Fig. 5. Output features for each combination of the input image and learned kernel.

Figure 5 shows the output features for each combination of the input image and learned kernel. The row and column correspond to the class number and kernel number, respectively. As with Fig. 4, the features are rescaled $[0, 1]$ to $[0, 255]$.

Figure 5 indicates that different output features are obtained according to the combination of the class and the kernel. For example, for the input image of $c = 5$, the slanting white stripe remains only in the output features from $m = 1$ and $m = 3$. This is because the kernels $m = 1$ and $m = 3$ have nonzero elements apart diagonally from each other. For the other classes, the pattern remains in the output features if the direction or interval of the pattern corresponds to those of the kernel patterns. This means that the TML learned kernels that can extract discriminative features from the input image.

4.3   Characteristics as a Co-occurrence Extractor

To investigate the capability of the TML for extracting co-occurrence features, we visualized the co-occurring regions detected by the TML.

For the use as a co-occurrence extractor, the TML was connected to the fully connected layer as shown in Fig. 2(b). In this experiment, the TML was inserted between the second convolutional layer and the fully connected layer of the LeNet-5. Because this fully connected layer maps the input vector into the likelihood for each class, the weights of this layer represent the relevance between each dimension of the input vector and each class. Based on this fact, we extracted the most relevant kernel to the target category. We then defined the co-occurrence features as the input features to the TML that were activated by the kernel relevant to the target category.

Fig. 6. Visualization of the co-occurrence features. The top panels show examples of the original MNIST images. The bottom panels are the corresponding co-occurrence features highlighted over the original images.

Figure 6 shows the visualization results of the co-occurrence features. In this figure, it appears that the distinctive features for each category are highlighted. For example, the bilateral lines of "0" are highlighted. In "7" the upper left edge and vertical line are highlighted. These results demonstrate the capability of the TML for extracting co-occurrence features that are useful for classification from CNN feature maps.

5   Classification Experiments

To evaluate the applicability of the TML, we conducted a classification experiment using public datasets.

5.1   Dataset

We used the following datasets in this experiment.
MNIST: As described in the previous section, this dataset includes ten classes of handwritten binary digit images with a size of 28×28. We used 60,000 images as training data and 10,000 images as testing data.

Fashion-MNIST: Fashion-MNIST [29] includes ten classes of binary fashion images with a size of 28 × 28. It includes 60,000 images for training data and 10,000 images for testing data.

CIFAR10: CIFAR10 [9] is labeled subsets of the 80 million tiny images dataset. This dataset consists of 60,000 32 × 32 color images in 10 classes, with 6,000 images per class. There are 50,000 training images and 10,000 test images.

Kylberg: The Kylberg texture dataset [10] contains unique texture patches for each class. We used its small subset provided by the author which includes six classes with 40 samples each. We divided the original 576 × 576 patches into nine 64 × 64 nonoverlapping patches and considered each patch as one sample; thus 2,160 samples were available. We conducted 10-fold cross-validation and calculated the classification accuracy.

Brodatz: The Brodatz texture dataset [2] contains 112 texture classes with a size of 640 × 640. We divided each image into 100 64 × 64 nonoverlapping patches, and considered each patch as one sample; thus 11,200 samples were available. We conducted 10-fold cross-validation to calculate the accuracy.

Table 1. Comparison of recognition rates (%).

	MNIST	Fashion	CIFAR10	Kylberg	Brodatz
Baseline CNN	99.27	92.44	81.43	99.12	91.69
Baseline CNN + HLAC	99.31	92.09	**82.23**	99.31	91.33
Baseline CNN + TML (DHLAC)	**99.39**	92.45	81.50	99.02	**92.51**
Baseline CNN + TML (Co-occurrence)	99.27	**92.54**	81.49	**99.35**	91.56

5.2 Experimental Setup

As the baseline, we used a simple CNN (called "baseline CNN" hereinafter) to clarify the effect of the TML. The baseline CNN consisted of five convolutional layers with four maxpooling layers between them; it also included two fully connected layers (the structure is illustrated in the supplemental file). In the network, dropout was conducted after the first and second maxpooling and the first fully connected layer.

The effectiveness of the TML was then examined by connecting the TML to the baseline CNN, both as a DHLAC extractor and a co-occurrence extractor. The kernel size of the TML was set as 5 × 5. We also compared the results to the results using HLAC instead of the TML.

5.3 Results

Table 1 shows the recognition rates for each dataset. In all datasets, applying the TML to the CNN improved the classification performance. In particular, the use as DHLAC demonstrated remarkable performance for the Brodatz dataset. This is because texture is based on a repeated structure, and hence auto-correlation information is effective for the classification. Moreover, the discriminative training of the HLAC features conducted by the TML functioned efficiently. These results confirm the applicability of the TML for classification.

6 Applications

6.1 Interpretation of the Network

In this section, we demonstrate that the TML can be used to interpret on which part of an input image the CNN focuses. In the usage as a co-occurrence extractor, the TML is connected between the feature maps and the fully connected layer (Fig. 2(b)). By tracing this structure in the reverse direction in the trained network, it is possible to extract features having a strong influence for classification. It should be emphasized that the purpose of this experiment is not to improve classification accuracy, rather, it is to improve interpretability.

Fig. 7. Visualization of network interpretation results using the TML. The areas having a strong influence for classification extracted by the TML are highlighted.

Specifically, we interpret a trained network in the following procedure: 1. Perform a forward calculation for a certain input image; 2. Calculate the largest weight among the weights of the fully connected layer between the unit that outputs the posterior probability of the target class and the features calculated by the TML; 3. Extract the kernel of the TML connecting the largest weight calculated in the previous step; 4. Extract CNN feature maps connecting to nonzero elements of the kernel; and 5. Visualize the extracted feature maps by upsampling them to the size of the input image and overlapping them on the input image. The property of the TML that the learned kernel acquires sparsity allows this calculation.

We used the Caltech-UCSD Birds-200-2011 dataset (CUB-200-2011) [26]. Each species of birds has unique characteristics such as feather pattern and body shape. This fact makes the interpretation of visualization results easier. This dataset contains 200 species of bird images and consists of 5,994 images for training data and 5,794 images for test data. Although this dataset is frequently used for fine-grained classification and segmentation, we used this dataset for only visualization in this experiment.

The basic network structure used in this experiment was the LeNet-5. The TML was inserted between the second convolutional layer and the fully connected layer. The parameters were set as $C_1 = 1.0$, $C_2 = 0.5$, $\lambda = 0.01$, and 1×1 for the kernel size.

Figure 7 shows examples of the visualization results. In Fig. 7, images of the same species are arranged in each column. The feather patterns or body shapes unique for each species are highlighted. For example, in the far left panels, yellowish green patterns on the head and the wing are highlighted. These results indicate the applicability of the proposed TML for interpreting a neural network.

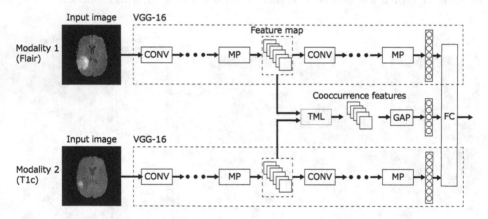

Fig. 8. Network architecture for MRI classification. The abbreviations MP, GAP, CONV, and FC denote max pooling, global average pooling, convolutional layer, and fully connected layer, respectively. Each VGG-16 model takes different modality images as input. The co-occurrence features between two networks are extracted by the TML.

6.2 Co-occurrence Extraction Between Two Networks for Multimodal Data

In this experiment, we applied the TML to multimodal data classification. As mentioned in Sect. 3.2, the TML can also be used to extract co-occurrence between two networks. By extracting the co-occurrence between the features of two CNNs that take input data from different modalities, it is expected that the two networks complement each other.

The problem we addressed in this experiment is tumor detection in magnetic resonance (MR) images. In MR imaging, there are different modalities depending on a setting of pulse sequences. Because each modality has a different response, extracting co-occurrence between multiple modalities could possibly improve tumor detection accuracy.

We prepared an MR image dataset containing two modalities (Flair and T1c) from the multimodal brain tumor image segmentation benchmark (BraTS) [15]. This dataset consisted of three-dimensional brain MR images with tumor annotation. We created two-dimensional axial (transverse) slice images and separated them into tumor and non-tumor classes based on the annotation. The dataset contained 220 subjects; we randomly divided these into 154, 22, and 44 for training, validation, and testing, respectively. Because approximately 60 images were extracted from each subject, we obtained 8,980, 1,448, and 2,458 images for training, validation, and testing, respectively. We resized the images from 240 × 240 pixels to 224 × 224 to fit the network input size.

Figure 8 illustrates the network architecture used in this experiment. The network was constructed based on VGG-16 [21]. VGG-16 has three fully connected layers following five blocks consisting of convolutional layers and a max pooling layer. We applied the TML to the CNN features after the b-th max pooling layer from the top. For comparison, we calculated the classification accuracy for a single VGG-16 with each modality and two VGG-16's concatenated at the first fully connected layer.

Table 2. Comparison of classification accuracies for the MRI dataset.

Method	Modality	Accuracy (%)
Single VGG	Flair	94.22
Single VGG	T1c	89.86
Concatenated two VGGs	Flair and T1c	94.47
Ours ($b = 1$)	Flair and T1c	95.16
Ours ($b = 2$)	Flair and T1c	95.57
Ours ($b = 3$)	Flair and T1c	**96.14**
Ours ($b = 4$)	Flair and T1c	95.85
Ours ($b = 5$)	Flair and T1c	95.77

Table 2 shows the results of the MR image classification. This confirms that the TML is effective for improving classification performance. In particular, the improvement is greatest for $b = 3$. One possible explanation for this is that the information necessary for classification is extracted to the extent that position information is not lost in the middle of the network, and extracting co-occurrence from such information is effective for multimodal data classification. This result demonstrates the effectiveness of co-occurrence extraction using the TML.

7   Conclusion

In this paper, we proposed a trainable multiplication layer (TML) for a neural network that can be used to calculate the multiplication between the input features. Taking an image as an input, the TML raises each pixel value to the power of a weight and then multiplies them, thereby extracting the higher-order local auto-correlation from the input image. The TML can also be used to extract co-occurrence from the feature map of a convolutional network. The training of the TML is formulated based on backpropagation with constraints to the weights, enabling us to learn discriminative multiplication patterns in an end-to-end manner. In the experiments, the characteristics of the TML were investigated by visualizing learned kernels and the corresponding output features. The applicability of the TML for classification was also evaluated using public datasets. Applications such as network interpretation and co-occurrence extraction between two neural networks were also demonstrated.

In future work, we plan to investigate the practical applications of the proposed TML. We will also expand the layer to the 3D structure in the same manner as cubic HLAC [8]. Application to time-series data analysis is also expected by constructing a one-dimensional structure.

References

1. Amodei, D., et al.: Deep speech 2: end-to-end speech recognition in English and Mandarin. In: International Conference on Machine Learning, pp. 173–182. IMLS, New York (2016)
2. Brodatz, P.: Textures: A Photographic Album for Artists and Designers. Dover Publications, New York (1966)
3. Fujino, K., Mitani, Y., Fujita, Y., Hamamoto, Y., Sakaida, I.: Liver cirrhosis classification on M-mode ultrasound images by higher-order local auto-correlation features. J. Med. Bioeng. **3**(1), 29–32 (2014)
4. Greenspan, H., van Ginneken, B., Summers, R.M.: Guest editorial deep learning in medical imaging: overview and future promise of an exciting new technique. IEEE Trans. Med. Imaging **35**(5), 1153–1159 (2016)
5. Hayashi, H., Shibanoki, T., Shima, K., Kurita, Y., Tsuji, T.: A recurrent probabilistic neural network with dimensionality reduction based on time-series discriminant component analysis. IEEE Trans. Neural Networks Learn. Syst. **26**(12), 3021–3033 (2015)
6. Hu, E., Nosato, H., Sakanashi, H., Murakawa, M.: A modified anomaly detection method for capsule endoscopy images using non-linear color conversion and Higher-order Local Auto-Correlation (HLAC). In: Proceedings of the 35th Annual International Conference of the IEEE Engineering in Medicine and Biology Society (EMBC), pp. 5477–5480. IEEE, Osaka (2013)
7. Kobayashi, T.: Trainable co-occurrence activation unit for improving ConvNet. In: Proceedings of the International Conference on Acoustics, Speech and Signal Processing (ICASSP), pp. 1273–1277. IEEE, Calgary (2018)
8. Kobayashi, T., Otsu, N.: Action and simultaneous multiple-person identification using cubic higher-order local auto-correlation. In: Proceedings of the 17th International Conference on Pattern Recognition (ICPR), vol. 4, pp. 741–744. IEEE, Cambridge (2004)

9. Krizhevsky, A., Hinton, G.: Learning multiple layers of features from tiny images. Technical report, University of Toronto (2009)

10. Kylberg, G.: The kylberg texture dataset v. 1.0. External report (Blue series) 35, Centre for Image Analysis, Swedish University of Agricultural Sciences and Uppsala University, Uppsala, Sweden (2011)

11. LeCun, Y., Bottou, L., Bengio, Y., Haffner, P.: Gradient-based learning applied to document recognition. Proc. IEEE **86**(11), 2278–2324 (1998)

12. Lin, M., Chen, Q., Yan, S.: Network in network. In: Proceedings of the International Conference on Learning Representations (ICLR), Banff, Canada (2014)

13. Ma, L., Lu, Z., Li, H.: Learning to answer questions from image using convolutional neural network. In: Proceedings of the Thirtieth AAAI Conference on Artificial Intelligence, Phoenix, Arizona, pp. 3567–3573 (2016)

14. Majumder, N., Poria, S., Gelbukh, A., Cambria, E.: Deep learning-based document modeling for personality detection from text. IEEE Intell. Syst. **32**(2), 74–79 (2017)

15. Menze, B.H., et al.: The multimodal brain tumor image segmentation benchmark (BRATS). IEEE Trans. Med. Imaging **34**(10), 1993–2024 (2015)

16. Nair, V., Hinton, G.E.: Rectified linear units improve restricted Boltzmann machines. In: Proceedings of the 27th International Conference on Machine Learning (ICML), Haifa, Israel, pp. 807–814 (2010)

17. Nakayama, H., Harada, T., Kuniyoshi, Y.: Global Gaussian approach for scene categorization using information geometry. In: Proceedings of the Conference on Computer Vision and Pattern Recognition (CVPR), pp. 2336–2343. IEEE, San Francisco (2010)

18. Nosato, H., Sakanashi, H., Takahashi, E., Murakawa, M.: An objective evaluation method of ulcerative colitis with optical colonoscopy images based on higher order local auto-correlation features. In: Proceedings of the 11th International Symposium on Biomedical Imaging (ISBI), pp. 89–92. IEEE, Beijing (2014)

19. Otsu, N., Kurita, T.: A new scheme for practical flexible and intelligent vision systems. In: Proceedings of the IAPR Workshop on Computer Vision, pp. 431–435. IAPR, Tokyo (1988)

20. Shih, Y.F., Yeh, Y.M., Lin, Y.Y., Weng, M.F., Lu, Y.C., Chuang, Y.Y.: Deep co-occurrence feature learning for visual object recognition. In: Proceedings of the Conference on Computer Vision and Pattern Recognition (CVPR). IEEE, Honolulu (2017)

21. Simonyan, K., Zisserman, A.: Very deep convolutional networks for large-scale image recognition. In: Proceedings of the International Conference on Learning Representations (ICLR), San Diego, CA (2015)

22. Tsuji, T., Bu, N., Fukuda, O., Kaneko, M.: A recurrent log-linearized Gaussian mixture network. IEEE Trans. Neural Networks **14**(2), 304–316 (2003)

23. Tsuji, T., Fukuda, O., Ichinobe, H., Kaneko, M.: A log-linearized Gaussian mixture network and its application to EEG pattern classification. IEEE Trans. Syst. Man Cybern. Part C (Appl. Rev.) **29**(1), 60–72 (1999)

24. Uehara, K., Sakanashi, H., Nosato, H., Murakawa, M., Miyamoto, H., Nakamura, R.: Object detection of satellite images using multi-channel higher-order local auto-correlation, pp. 1339–1344 (2017)

25. Valle-Lisboa, J.C., Reali, F., Anastasía, H., Mizraji, E.: Elman topology with sigma-pi units: an application to the modeling of verbal hallucinations in schizophrenia. Neural Networks **18**(7), 863–877 (2005)

26. Wah, C., Branson, S., Welinder, P., Perona, P., Belongie, S.: The Caltech-UCSD Birds-200-2011 Dataset. Technical report (2011)

27. Wang, Q., Li, P., Zhang, L.: G2DeNet: global Gaussian distribution embedding network and its application to visual recognition. In: Proceedings of the Conference on Computer Vision and Pattern Recognition (CVPR), pp. 2730–2739. IEEE, Honolulu (2017)
28. Weber, C., Wermter, S.: A self-organizing map of sigma-pi units. Neurocomputing **70**(13), 2552–2560 (2007)
29. Xiao, H., Rasul, K., Vollgraf, R.: Fashion-MNIST: a novel image dataset for benchmarking machine learning algorithms. arXiv preprint arXiv:1708.07747 (2017)
30. Zhang, T., Kahn, G., Levine, S., Abbeel, P.: Learning deep control policies for autonomous aerial vehicles with MPC-guided policy search. In: Proceedings of the International Conference on Robotics and Automation (ICRA), pp. 528–535. IEEE, Stockholm (2016)

Cross-View Action Recognition Using View-Invariant Pose Feature Learned from Synthetic Data with Domain Adaptation

Yu-Huan Yang[1], An-Sheng Liu[1], Yu-Hung Liu[1], Tso-Hsin Yeh[1], Zi-Jun Li[1], and Li-Chen Fu[1,2(✉)]

[1] National Taiwan University, Taipei 10617, Taiwan
{r05921001,d00921006,r06921066,r05921061,r05921097}@ntu.edu.tw
[2] NTU Research Center for AI and Advanced Robotics, Taipei 10617, Taiwan
lichen@ntu.edu.tw
http://www.ntueeacl.com, http://ai.robo.ntu.edu.tw

Abstract. Recognizing human activities from unknown views is a challenging problem since human shapes appear quite differently from different viewpoints. In this paper, we learn a View-Invariant Pose (VIP) feature for depth-based cross-view action recognition. The proposed VIP feature encoder is a deep convolutional neural network that transfers human poses from multiple viewpoints to a shared high-level feature space. Learning such a deep model requires a large corpus of multi-view paired data which is very expensive to collect. Therefore, we generate a synthetic dataset by fitting human physical models with real motion capture data in the simulators and rendering depth images from various viewpoints. The VIP feature is learned from the synthetic data in an unsupervised way. To ensure the transferability from synthetic data to real data, domain adaptation is employed to minimize the domain difference. Moreover, an action can be considered as a sequence of poses and the temporal progress is modeled by recurrent neural network. In the experiments, our method is applied on two benchmark datasets of multi-view 3D human action and has been shown to achieve promising results when compared with the state-of-the-arts.

Keywords: Action recognition · Domain adaptation · Cross-view · Deep learning

1 Introduction

Human action understanding [11] from videos has raised lots of attention in computer vision because of its wide applications, such as human-robot interaction (HRI), smart home, healthcare, and surveillance systems. Over the last

Supported by NTU Research Center for AI and Advanced Robotics and the Ministry of Science and Technology (MOST) under the Grants No. MOST 107-2634-F-002-018- and MOST 106-2218-E-002-043.

C. V. Jawahar et al. (Eds.): ACCV 2018, LNCS 11362, pp. 431–446, 2019.
https://doi.org/10.1007/978-3-030-20890-5_28

decade, action analysis evolved from hand-crafted schemes limited to the controlled environment to nowadays advanced algorithms learned from large-scale data and applied to complexed daily activities. Encouraged by the huge success of deep learning for image recognition, several works tried to employ deep neural networks to tackle the problem of RGB-based action recognition [6,14,28,29].

For the indoor surveillance applied to smart home and healthcare environments, there are other issues needed to be concerned. Among them, the privacy issue attracts more and more attention recently. Hsu *et al.* [13] proposed a privacy-free indoor action detection system using only depth videos which is less privacy sensitive. Besides, compared with color sensors, depth cameras offer several advantages including working under varying illumination conditions and being invariant to different colors and textures. Given such considerations, we only adopt depth sensors for our action analysis.

Despite the impressive results achieved by depth-based approaches [20,33], their performances drop sharply when the viewpoint changes. Because most existing methods learned information from a specific viewpoint and human shapes vary due to different human orientations or camera settings (including height and distance). Figure 1 illustrates some scenarios. Several works [9,22–25,34] tried to solve such issues by designing models for cross-view action recognition where the recognition is conducted from a different or unseen view. In this paper, we propose a View-Invariant Pose (VIP) feature which is robust to viewpoint variations.

Recently, we have noticed a coming trend, that instead of manually collecting large-scale datasets, training on synthetic data [4,24,31] could also bring competitive results while evaluating on real data. This brings lots of benefits in some cases. For instance, approaches for depth estimation based on color images require a large quantity of accurately labeled data which however is impractical to be annotated manually. Varol *et al.* [31] automatically synthesized training set with ground truth depth maps using simulators. In this paper, we synthesize a large-scale depth-based dataset containing various human poses from multiple viewpoints to help us subsequently learn the VIP feature, which significantly reduces the amount of efforts in collecting and annotating the real data.

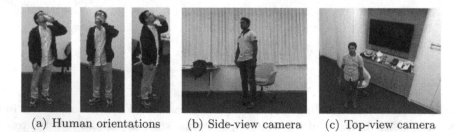

(a) Human orientations   (b) Side-view camera   (c) Top-view camera

Fig. 1. Difference of viewpoints in NTU RGB+D action recognition dataset [27]. Note that (b) and (c) show the difference between camera settings.

However, there is an inevitable visual gap between the synthetic data and real data. Thus, the learned features from two different datasets reside in different domains. The so-called domain adaptation [3] thus plays a crucial role to bridge the gap by mapping two domains into a common space. In this paper, we develop a strategy to learn a domain-invariant feature representation through adversarial training [8]. Besides, given that an action can be considered as a sequence of poses, we adopt Long Short-Term Memory (LSTM) [12] to describe the temporal dependencies in actions.

In summary, we propose a learning-based action recognition system which takes depth videos as input to identify human activities from different viewpoints. The cross-view knowledge is learned from synthetic data in an unsupervised way and also transferred to real data through adversarial domain adaptation. Our method has been evaluated on two open datasets, both with a variety of multi-view 3D human actions and it turns out that the results have demonstrated the effectiveness and robustness of the proposed VIP feature. To our best knowledge, the presented work should be the earliest one incorporating domain adaptation to address action recognition by learning from synthetic data.

2 Related Works

2.1 Action Recognition with Deep Neural Networks

Due to the impressive results achieved by deep learning on image classification, image segmentation, object detection, etc., so far there have been several works which adopted deep neural networks to learn spatial and temporal information for action recognition [6,14,28,29].

Ji et al. [14] extended the traditional 2D Convolutional Neural Networks (CNNs) to 3D CNNs where the temporal dimension is involved in the convolutions. Tran et al. [29] designed a Convolutional 3D (C3D) architecture and found $3 \times 3 \times 3$ the best kernel size to extract spatio-temporal features. On the other hand, instead of extracting features with a single CNN, Simonyan and Zisserman [28] trained two CNNs, one for RGB images and the other one for optical flow, and combined the learned information with late fusion. Donahue et al. [6] proposed an end-to-end recurrent convolutional network which processes the input video frame with a CNN and learns the temporal information with a Recurrent Neural Network (RNN) by feeding in the CNN features sequentially. However, these methods are not designed for cross-view action recognition as they cannot generalize to novel viewpoints.

2.2 Cross-View Action Recognition

Most existing action recognition methods have mainly focused on actions captured from a fixed viewpoint. However, the same human action may appear quite differently when observed from different viewpoints. A practical system should be capable of recognizing activities from different or unseen viewpoints. A simple solution is to collect data from all possible views and train a separate model for each view. This approach does not scale well as it needs a large amount of labeled data for each view and this is infeasible as the action types increase.

To address this issue, knowledge transfer based methods [9,22–25,34] become popular recently. They tried to find a view-invariant latent space where the learned feature could be compatible among all different views. Rahmani *et al.* [22] designed a hand-crafted feature called Histogram of Oriented Principal Components (HOPC), which is robust to viewpoint variations, to detect and describe spatio-temporal interest points. Zhang *et al.* [34] assumed that there exists a smooth virtual path between two viewpoints and they connected cross-view action descriptors by applying an infinite sequence of linear transformations on view-dependent features. Although this method can operate in the absence of paired features between the source and target views, they still require some samples from the target view for training.

Some methods relied on motion capture data to learn cross-view features. For example, Gupta *et al.* [9] used non-linear Circulant Temporal Encoding (nCTE) to find the best match for each training video in large mocap database and synthesized multi-view data for augmentation. Rahmani and Mian [23] proposed a Non-linear Knowledge Transfer Model (NKTM) where knowledge from multiple views is transferred to a single predefined canonical view by learning from synthetic data. Rahmani *et al.* [25] further extended NKTM to Robust Non-linear Knowledge Transfer Model (R-NKTM) that removes the need for pre-defining canonical view which is actually action-dependent. However, these methods cannot be applied to depth videos as they depend on dense trajectories which are not reliable in depth maps.

2.3 Domain Adaptation

Several works [4,23–25,31] synthesized data for training and applied the learned knowledge to real data. However, there may exist a domain shift as the synthetic data are generated within a different distribution from real data. As a result, domain adaptation [3] plays an essential role as it bridges the gap between two domains. Recently, there is a trend to combine feature learning and domain adaptation into a unified training process [30].

In addition to the main task, Ganin and Lempitsky [7] added a domain classifier to tell the domain from which the data came. They further proposed a gradient reversal layer to jointly learn the feature representation and align two domains by backpropagation. Chen *et al.* [4] synthesized training images for 3D human pose estimation based on 2D color images. They added a domain mixer along with a pose regressor and showed that such a domain adaptation technique could significantly improve the main task on target data.

3   Proposed Method

Overview. In this paper, we propose a learning-based action recognition system feeding on depth videos to identify human activities from novel viewpoints.

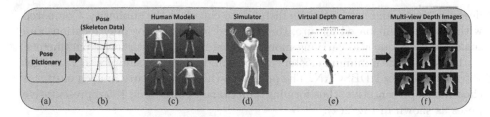

Fig. 2. The designed pipeline for synthesizing multi-view depth images of human poses.

This section consists of three parts: (1) generating a synthetic dataset, (2) learning View-Invariant Pose (VIP) feature, and (3) modeling temporal information.

3.1 Generate a Synthetic Dataset

Learning a deep View-Invariant Pose (VIP) feature representation requires a large corpus of multi-view paired data which is very hard and expensive to manually collect and label. Inspired by [24], we design a simple but efficient pipeline to synthesize depth images of possible combinations of human poses, human geometries, and viewpoints. Figure 2 gives an overview of the involved steps and we express the details in the following.

Build a Pose Dictionary. Given the fact that an action can be viewed as a sequence of poses, the possible pose space is much smaller than the possible action space. In addition, several bag-of-word based action recognition methods [26,32] have discriminated actions by the occurrence of each pose-related codeword in an action. Based on these observations, learning a pose-related feature could generalize well to action space with different kinds of sequence combinations.

As we need to fit 3D human models with a predefined pose in the simulator, we must rely on highly accurate skeleton data such as motion capture database. We choose CMU Motion Capture database [1] which contains more than 2500 motion sequences (over 4 million poses) covering a variety of actions. It is obtained with high-precision camera array and body markers, resulting in quite accurate 3D skeletal joint positions. This database is treated as the pose space from which we sample poses.

In order to efficiently learn pose-related features from the pose space, we firstly build a dictionary containing the most representative poses. Unsupervised clustering algorithm is applied on the skeletons sampled from this pose space. Different from [24] and k-means, which is hard to predefine "k" value, HDBSCAN [19] is used for finding the "k" value automatically by soft clustering.

Besides, we design an orientation-based skeletal feature rather than a displacement-based feature used in [24] to compare the similarity between two poses. We calculate rotation angles between body limbs. As a result, we use 19 DOFs in total (4 for each arm, 4 for each leg, 1 for head, and 2 for torso) to describe a pose and use Euclidean distance to calculate the similarity. Compared with displacement-based feature, the designed feature is not only location- and scale-invariant but also carrying more physical meaning with fewer parameters.

By setting the minimum cluster size to 20 and minimum samples to 25, we get 195 clusters from HDBSCAN. The pose with the highest score in each cluster is chosen as representative, thus forming a dictionary containing 195 representative poses as shown in Fig. 2(a).

Synthesize Images with Simulators. In order to cope with the variety of subjects, we utilize the open source MakeHuman software [2] to synthesize 3D human models covering different combinations of gender, body shape, hair style, and clothes as shown in Fig. 2(c).

Furthermore, we use another open source package, Blender software [35], to set up an animation simulator. Our goal is to synthesize depth images of human poses captured from various viewpoints. For each 3D human model, we re-target its rigs to fit all the poses in the pose dictionary as depicted in Fig. 2(d). Besides, 180 virtual cameras with distinct latitudes and longitudes are uniformly placed on a hemisphere surrounding the subject (see Fig. 2(e)) and the depth images are rendered with normalized pixel value in [0, 255]. Different from [24], our pipeline does not include hidden point removal and surface fitting. Thus, we collect a large-scale synthetic dataset containing paired depth images of human poses captured from multiple viewpoints as shown in Fig. 2(f).

3.2   Learn View-Invariant Pose Feature

In this section, we describe how to learn the View-Invariant Pose (VIP) feature representation that transfers human poses from any view to a shared high-level feature space. Moreover, the VIP knowledge is distilled from the synthetic data.

Unsupervised Learning. As depicted in the top row of Fig. 3 (e.g., the synthetic data domain), the proposed architecture for learning VIP feature consists of two parts, one being an encoder E and the other one being a pose classifier C_P. Here, an underlying assumption is that the same human pose observed from different viewpoints share the same high-level feature representation. We design the encoder E as a CNN-based structure to extract the pose-related feature from different views into a universal feature space and we refer the extracted feature of image x as VIP feature f_x^{VIP}. Then the pose classifier C_P aims to tell which pose appears in the image x based on f_x^{VIP}.

While training such a framework, the input images x come from the synthetic data. Besides, we do not use any action label from mocap data but only the dummy pose label, making the training process unsupervised. For each pose $k = 1, 2, \ldots, 195$ in the pose dictionary, the corresponding synthetic depth images rendered from all viewpoints are assigned the same dummy pose label k. The label contains no physical meaning but the dictionary index.

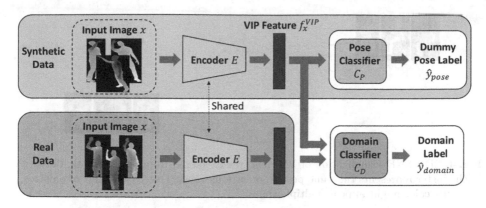

Fig. 3. The proposed architecture for learning View-Invariant Pose (VIP) feature with domain adaptation. The orange block represents the synthetic domain while the blue one denotes the real domain. Note that the encoder E is shared across two domains. (Color figure online)

For the encoder E, we use "Xception network" [5] which is comprised of depthwise separable convolutions. The last fully connected layer is replaced with a 256-neuron layer as a bottleneck layer, resulting VIP feature f_x^{VIP} as a 256-dimension vector. As for the pose classifier C_P, we design a simple one-layer neural network followed by a softmax activation, consisting of 195 neurons corresponding to each dummy pose label.

The inputs to our training architecture are depth images $x \in synthetic$ sampled from synthetic data with the corresponding ground truth dummy pose labels y_{pose}. We consider VIP loss L_{VIP} as the standard cross-entropy of pose classification as listed below. Here, syn is an abbreviation for $synthetic$.

$$L_{VIP} = - \sum_{x \in syn} \sum_{k=1}^{195} [y_{pose} = k] \log(p_{x,k}) \tag{1}$$

$$p_x = C_P(f_x^{VIP}) \tag{2}$$

$$f_x^{VIP} = E(x) \tag{3}$$

where $x \in \mathbb{R}^{128 \times 128 \times 3}$ is the warped input image, $f_x^{VIP} \in \mathbb{R}^{256}$ refers to the encoded VIP feature of image x, $p_x \in \mathbb{R}^{195}$ indicates the softmax activations of the pose classifier, and $p_{x,k} \in \mathbb{R}$ is the k-th element of p_x, meaning the possibility of image x being pose k. We use this architecture to find a high-level feature space shared by all possible views. To be more specific, regardless of the input view, we encourage the VIP features to be as similar as possible for all views of the same pose.

To qualitatively visualize the view-invariant property, we project the learned VIP features extracted from synthetic data to a 2D space by t-SNE [18]. As we can see in Fig. 4, each cluster represents VIP features of the same pose from

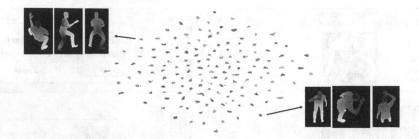

Fig. 4. 2D t-SNE visualization of VIP features extracted from the synthetic dataset. Each cluster represents the same pose from various views. Due to the limit of palettes, the same color might appear multiple times.

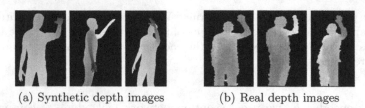

(a) Synthetic depth images   (b) Real depth images

Fig. 5. The visual difference between synthetic and real depth images. The real images come from UWA 3D multi-view activity II dataset [22]. Note that real images contain blurred contours caused by noise.

different views. That is to say, the VIP features of the same pose appear quite similar across different viewpoints in the high-dimension space, which demonstrates that the encoder does extract the pose information excluding viewpoints.

Adversarial Domain Adaptation. After we obtained the VIP feature encoder E from the synthetic data, here comes a concern about whether we could directly adopt it on the real data. In other words, do VIP features of a pose from synthetic data and those of a similar pose from real data appear similar? Ideally, training and testing data should live in the same domain, such that the model learned from training data can be applied to testing data with no degradations. However, there is a visual gap between the synthetic and real depth images (see Fig. 5) as well as their corresponding VIP features (see Fig. 6(a)), causing the phenomenon called "domain shift."

It has been shown that a trained CNN model can be adapted to a new domain through fine-tuning. However, in our case, there is no such a large multi-view real dataset with pose labels, it is not suitable to directly fine-tune the encoder E. As a result, we utilize domain adaptation technique where source data and target data come from similar but different distributions. Inspired by [7], we add a domain classifier C_D along with the existing encoder E and pose classifier C_P, combining domain adaptation and VIP feature learning into a unified training process (see Fig. 3). The encoded VIP feature f_x^{VIP} is sent to the pose classifier C_P for dummy pose prediction, as well as to domain classifier C_D for domain prediction.

The domain classifier C_P is designed as a 3-layer neural network. The first two layers are comprised of 64 neurons followed by a leaky ReLU and the last layer aims at binary classification using one neuron with sigmoid activation. We consider a VIP feature f_x^{VIP} to be domain-invariant if a strong domain classifier C_D cannot distinguish from two domains. In our case, we refer the source domain to synthetic data and target domain to real data. The adversarial training technique [8] is utilized to jointly align the distributions of VIP features across two domains and transfer the view-invariant property to the target domain.

Now the inputs to our training architecture are not only synthetic depth images $x \in syn$ with dummy pose labels y_{pose} but also real depth images $x \in real$ without pose labels. It is an unsupervised domain adaptation with the absence of target pose labels. We design two loss functions L_{domain} and L_{conf} for adversarial domain adaptation as follows:

$$L_{domain} = -\sum_{x \in real} \log(d_x) - \sum_{x \in syn} \log(1 - d_x) \tag{4}$$

$$L_{conf} = -\sum_{x} [0.5 \log(d_x) + 0.5 \log(1 - d_x)] \tag{5}$$

$$d_x = C_D(f_x^{VIP}) \tag{6}$$

where $d_x \in \mathbb{R}$ denotes the probability of image x coming from real domain, L_{domain} is the domain loss, and L_{conf} is the confusion loss. Note that during domain adaptation, all training data are unpaired, which means that there are no one-to-one corresponding images across domains.

Our proposed framework has two major differences from [7]. First, instead of using a gradient reverse layer, we confuse the domain classifier C_D by enforcing it to output a uniform distribution over domain labels with Eq. (5) for all synthetic and real images. Second, an adversarial scheme is used to update the networks. The process of learning VIP feature with domain adaptation is summarized in Algorithm 1. Such a three-stage training scheme is observed more stable and less sensitive to the optimization parameters [16]. The detailed training process will be presented in Sect. 4. Figure 6 shows the qualitative results observed from TensorBoard. Note that the two domains align with each other. Specifically, the domain shift is minimized during the domain adaptation.

3.3   Model Temporal Information

The VIP feature only contains static and spatial information and we need to further combine temporal information to describe actions. With the temporal variations in each action, Recurrent Neural Networks (RNNs) are appealing in that they can directly map varying-length inputs. However, traditional RNNs are limited to learning long-term temporal dependencies because of vanishing and exploding gradient problems. LSTM [12] overcomes these challenges by introducing the gating mechanism and demonstrates its power on a large variety of problems.

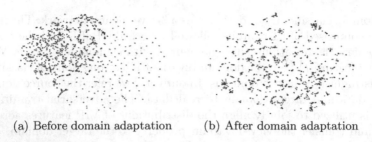

(a) Before domain adaptation   (b) After domain adaptation

Fig. 6. The qualitative visualization of the domain adaptation process. The blue points represent VIP features extracted from real data while the orange points denote the synthetic ones. Note that the domain shift is minimized after domain adaptation. (Color figure online)

Algorithm 1. Learning VIP feature with domain adaptation

    Data : Synthetic depth images $x \in syn$ and corresponding dummy pose labels
            y_{pose}; Real depth images $x \in real$
    Result: VIP feature encoder E for real domain
1 **for** *Iters. of VIP feature with domain adaptation* **do**
2   **for** *Iters. of VIP feature* **do**
3   Update encoder E and pose classifier C_P to minimize Eq. (1) on
            $x \in syn$ and y_{pose}
4   **end**
5   **for** *Iters. of domain* **do**
6   Update domain classifier C_D to minimize Eq. (4) on $x \in syn$ and
            $x \in real$
7   **end**
8   **for** *Iters. of encoder* **do**
9   Update encoder E to minimize Eq. (5) on $x \in syn$ and $x \in real$
10   **end**
11 **end**

Figure 7 illustrates the proposed pipeline for recognizing actions in videos. Given an input video of length T, $X = \{x_t | t = 1, 2, \ldots, T\}$, we consider an action as a sequence of poses and use the encoder E to extract the VIP feature from each input frame. Thus, we transform the input video X into a sequence of VIP features, $F_X^{VIP} = \{f_{x_t}^{VIP} | t = 1, 2, \ldots, T\}$ where $f_{x_t}^{VIP} = E(x_t)$. The LSTM module acts as an action classifier C_A trying to discriminate actions based on F_X^{VIP}.

We design a 2-layer stacked LSTM with 256 hidden units and aggregate the outputs from all layers with residual connection [10]. A fully-connected layer with 128 neurons followed by a ReLU activation and a fully-connected layer with C neurons followed by a softmax activation are further added on the top of the stacked LSTM, where C denotes the number of action types. The input to the LSTM module is a sequence of VIP features F_X^{VIP} and the output is a

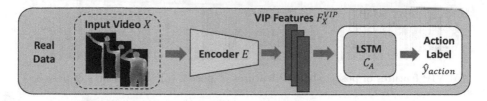

Fig. 7. Modeling temporal information in an input video using LSTM.

probability distribution $a_X \in \mathbb{R}^C$ over all action classes. The objective of the LSTM module is to minimize the action loss L_{action} as the following:

$$L_{action} = - \sum_{X} \sum_{c=1}^{C} \; [y_{action} = c] \log(a_{X,c}) \tag{7}$$

$$a_X = C_A(F_X^{VIP}) \tag{8}$$

where $a_{X,c} \in \mathbb{R}$ is the c-th element of a_X, which indicates the probability of video X belonging to c-th action class, C is the number of action types, and y_{action} denotes the ground truth action label.

As the LSTM module is learned based on view-invariant features, we can generalize to novel or unseen views with the same LSTM module even if the training data come from specific views. The detailed training process will be presented Sect. 4.

4   Experiments

To verify the proposed method, it is evaluated on two public benchmark datasets, including NTU RGB+D action recognition dataset [27] and UWA 3D multi-view activity II dataset [22]. Our proposed method is denoted as VIP+DA (View-Invariant Pose with Domain Adaptation). The performance is compared with state-of-the-arts and the quantitative results of these methods are reported from their original papers and [21,25]. According to the input modalities, they can be categorized into the following types:

- RGB-based methods: 3D convolution (3D Conv) [14], non-linear Circulant Temporal Encoding (nCTE) [9], Non-linear Knowledge Transfer Model (NKTM) [23], and Robust NKTM (R-NKTM) [25]
- Depth-based methods: Super Normal Vector (SNV) [33], 2D Histogram of Oriented Gradients (HOG^2) [20], Long-Term Motion Dynamics (LTMD) [17], Histogram of Oriented 3D Point Cloud (HOPC) [22], and Human Pose Model with Temporal Modeling (HPM+TM) [24]
- Skeleton-based methods: Part-Aware LSTM (PA-LSTM) [27] and Spatio-Temporal LSTM with Trust Gates (ST-LSTM+TG) [15]
- Multi-modality method: Depth+Skeleton with Rank Pool (D+S-RP) [21]

(a) VIP features of pose 1 (b) VIP features of pose 2 (c) VIP features of pose 3

Fig. 8. Qualitative visualization of view-invariant property.

As summarized in Algorithm 1, we set *Iters. of VIP feature with domain adaptation* to 4, *Iters. of VIP feature* to 1, *Iters. of domain classifier* to 2, and *Iters. of encoder* to 1. Stochastic gradient descent with mini-batch of 32 samples is utilized and the networks are updated by Adam optimizer with learning rate equal to 5×10^{-6}. The VIP knowledge is adapted to these two action datasets respectively. During modeling the temporal information, LSTM is updated by backpropagation through time. Besides, the encoder is jointly fine-tuned on NTU RGB+D action recognition dataset while fixed on UWA 3D multi-view activity II dataset. The learning process is monitored with early stopping.

In addition, Fig. 8 qualitatively visualize the view-invariant property by concatenating the extracted $f_x^{VIP} \in \mathbb{R}^{256}$ of the same pose observed from 180 views as an 180×256 image. Each element in f_x^{VIP} is normalized into $[0, 255]$. As expected, the VIP features appear very similarly across all 180 viewpoints for each pose.

4.1 NTU RGB+D Action Recognition Dataset

This dataset [27] is currently the largest publicly available dataset for 3D action recognition, which contains more than 56,000 samples. It is collected by Kinect v2 and labeled with 60 action classes including daily, health-related, and interactive actions performed by 40 subjects from several camera views. Figure 9(a) shows sample frames from different views. Moreover, 17 camera settings are adopted to get more viewpoint variations.

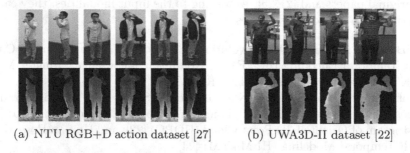

(a) NTU RGB+D action dataset [27]   (b) UWA3D-II dataset [22]

Fig. 9. Multi-view RGB and depth images from action datasets.

Table 1. Comparison of action recognition accuracy (%) on the NTU RGB+D dataset [27].

Methods	Data type	Cross-subject	Cross-view
SNV [33]	Depth	31.8	13.6
HOG^2 [20]	Depth	32.2	22.3
LTMD [17]	Depth	66.2	-
PA-LSTM [27]	Skeleton	62.9	70.3
ST-LSTM+TG [15]	Skeleton	69.2	77.7
D+S-RP [21]	Depth+Skeleton	75.2	83.1
VIP+DA (ours)	Depth	86.1	86.5

The viewpoint and large intra-class variations make this dataset very challenging. We follow the cross-subject and cross-view evaluations [27] and report the classification accuracy in percentage.

Table 1 shows the performances of several methods. Since there are few RGB-based methods implemented on this dataset, we choose some skeleton-based methods to compare with. Our method outperforms all existing methods on both cross-subject and cross-view evaluations. Although skeleton data are somewhat immune to viewpoint variations, they cannot include interactions with environmental objects. Our method achieves 3.4% better than the nearest competitor, D+S-RP [21] on the cross-view setting. It is worthy to note that our method only depends on depth information that is less privacy sensitive. Thus, the result shows the effectiveness and applicability of our proposed method.

4.2 UWA 3D Multi-view Activity II Dataset

The UWA3D-II dataset [22] is comprised of 30 human actions performed by 10 subjects and recorded from 4 viewpoints (front, left, right, and top) in a nonsynchronous way using the Kinect v1. Figure 9(b) shows sample frames from different views.

This dataset is challenging because the videos were recorded at different times from varying viewpoints and the data contains high similarity across action classes. For instance, action drinking and phone answering have very similar arm movements. Moreover, in the top view setting, the lower body part was not properly captured due to self-occlusion. We follow the cross-view evaluation suggested by [22] where videos from two views are used for training and the videos from remaining views are used for testing, leading to 12 different cross-view combinations in this evaluation protocol.

The results are summarized in Table 2. Our proposed method (VIP+DA) outperforms most state-of-the-arts and performs equally well compared with D+S-RP [21] by achieving 84.9% mean accuracy. D+S-RP depends on not only depth data but also skeleton data which may not always be accurately acquired in real applications due to self-occlusion. This result also shows the applicability and robustness of the proposed VIP feature to viewpoint variations.

Table 2. Comparison of action recognition accuracy (%) on the UWA3D-II dataset [22]. Each column represents a different cross-view setting. For example, V_{12}^3 means the model is trained on view 1 and view 2 while tested on view 3.

Methods	Data type	V_{12}^3	V_{12}^4	V_{13}^2	V_{13}^4	V_{14}^2	V_{14}^3	V_{23}^1	V_{23}^4	V_{24}^1	V_{24}^3	V_{34}^1	V_{34}^2	Mean
CVP [34]	Depth	36.0	34.7	35.0	43.5	33.9	35.2	40.4	36.3	36.3	38.0	40.6	37.7	37.3
HOPC [22]	Depth	52.7	51.8	59.0	57.5	42.8	44.2	58.1	38.4	63.2	43.8	66.3	48.0	52.2
3D Conv [14]	RGB	59.5	59.6	56.6	64.0	59.5	60.8	71.7	60.0	69.5	53.5	67.1	50.4	61.0
nCTE [9]	RGB	55.6	60.6	56.7	62.5	61.9	60.4	69.9	56.1	70.3	54.9	71.7	54.1	61.2
NKTM [23]	RGB	60.1	61.3	57.1	65.1	61.6	66.8	70.6	59.5	73.2	59.3	72.5	54.5	63.5
R-NKTM [25]	RGB	64.9	67.7	61.2	68.4	64.9	70.1	73.6	66.5	73.6	60.8	75.5	61.2	67.4
HPM+TM [24]	Depth	80.6	80.5	75.2	82.0	65.4	72.0	77.3	67.0	83.6	81.0	83.6	74.1	76.9
D+S-RP [21]	Depth+ Skeleton	86.8	87.0	80.7	89.1	78.1	80.9	86.5	79.3	85.1	86.9	89.4	80.0	84.2
VIP+DA (ours)	Depth	85.8	86.5	85.7	87.3	80.5	81.0	85.9	86.1	85.1	83.2	88.8	82.7	84.9

It is interesting to note that for several actions in this dataset such as holding back, holding head, coughing, and sneezing, there are no similar actions in the CMU mocap database [1]. However, we can still achieve high performance for these activities, which demonstrates the generalization ability of our VIP feature.

5   Conclusion and Future Works

We propose a cross-view action recognition system which takes depth video as input to recognize human activities from different viewpoints. We use a deep CNN to extract View-Invariant Pose (VIP) feature by mapping human poses observed from different views into a shared view-invariant feature space. In addition, we designed a pipeline to synthesize depth images containing human poses observed from multiple viewpoints. The VIP knowledge is subsequently learned from the synthetic data in an unsupervised way and further transferred to real data through adversarial domain adaptation. As for recognizing actions from input videos, we adopt LSTM to mine the temporal dependencies. Experimental results show that the proposed method achieves promising performance over state-of-the-arts on two benchmark multi-view 3D human action datasets.

Regarding future works, we note that action detection system is more practical in real applications where the input is an untrimmed video sequence and not only the action categories but also the temporal locations are analyzed. We expect that the VIP feature is also suitable for cross-view action detection.

References

1. CMU graphics lab motion capture database. http://mocap.cs.cmu.edu
2. MakeHuman: open source tool for making 3D characters. http://www.makehuman. org
3. Ben-David, S., Blitzer, J., Crammer, K., Kulesza, A., Pereira, F., Vaughan, J.W.: A theory of learning from different domains. Mach. Learn. **79**(1–2), 151–175 (2010)

4. Chen, W., et al.: Synthesizing training images for boosting human 3D pose estimation. In: IEEE Fourth International Conference on 3D Vision (3DV), pp. 479–488 (2016)
5. Chollet, F.: Xception: deep learning with depthwise separable convolutions. In: IEEE Conference on Computer Vision and Pattern Recognition (CVPR), July 2017
6. Donahue, J., et al.: Long-term recurrent convolutional networks for visual recognition and description. In: Proceedings of the IEEE Conference on Computer Vision and Pattern Recognition, pp. 2625–2634 (2015)
7. Ganin, Y., Lempitsky, V.: Unsupervised domain adaptation by backpropagation. In: Proceedings of the International Conference on Machine Learning (2014)
8. Goodfellow, I., et al.: Generative adversarial nets. In: Advances in Neural Information Processing Systems, pp. 2672–2680 (2014)
9. Gupta, A., Martinez, J., Little, J.J., Woodham, R.J.: 3D pose from motion for cross-view action recognition via non-linear circulant temporal encoding. In: Proceedings of the IEEE Conference on Computer Vision and Pattern Recognition, pp. 2601–2608 (2014)
10. He, K., Zhang, X., Ren, S., Sun, J.: Deep residual learning for image recognition. In: Proceedings of the IEEE Conference on Computer Vision and Pattern Recognition, pp. 770–778 (2016)
11. Herath, S., Harandi, M., Porikli, F.: Going deeper into action recognition: a survey. Image Vis. Comput. **60**, 4–21 (2017)
12. Hochreiter, S., Schmidhuber, J.: Long short-term memory. Neural Comput. **9**(8), 1735–1780 (1997)
13. Hsu, T.W., Yang, Y.H., Yeh, T.H., Liu, A.S., Fu, L.C., Zeng, Y.C.: Privacy free indoor action detection system using top-view depth camera based on key-poses. In: IEEE International Conference on Systems, Man, and Cybernetics (SMC), pp. 4058–4063 (2016)
14. Ji, S., Xu, W., Yang, M., Yu, K.: 3D convolutional neural networks for human action recognition. IEEE Trans. Pattern Anal. Mach. Intell. **35**(1), 221–231 (2013)
15. Liu, J., Shahroudy, A., Xu, D., Chichung, A.K., Wang, G.: Skeleton-based action recognition using spatio-temporal LSTM network with trust gates. IEEE Trans. Pattern Anal. Mach. Intell. **40**, 3007 (2017)
16. Liu, Y.C., Chiu, W.C., Wang, S.D., Wang, Y.C.F.: Domain-adaptive generative adversarial networks for sketch-to-photo inversion. In: IEEE 27th International Workshop on Machine Learning for Signal Processing (MLSP), pp. 1–6 (2017)
17. Luo, Z., Peng, B., Huang, D.A., Alahi, A., Fei-Fei, L.: Unsupervised learning of long-term motion dynamics for videos. In: IEEE Conference on Computer Vision and Pattern Recognition (CVPR) (2017)
18. van der Maaten, L., Hinton, G.: Visualizing data using t-SNE. J. Mach. Learn. Res. **9**, 2579–2605 (2008)
19. McInnes, L., Healy, J., Astels, S.: HDBSCAN: hierarchical density based clustering. J. Open Source Softw. **2**(11), 205 (2017)
20. Ohn-Bar, E., Trivedi, M.M.: Joint angles similarities and HOG2 for action recognition. In: IEEE Conference on Computer Vision and Pattern Recognition Workshops (CVPRW), June 2013
21. Rahmani, H., Bennamoun, M.: Learning action recognition model from depth and skeleton videos. In: Proceedings of the IEEE Conference on Computer Vision and Pattern Recognition, pp. 5832–5841 (2017)

22. Rahmani, H., Mahmood, A., Huynh, D., Mian, A.: Histogram of oriented principal components for cross-view action recognition. IEEE Trans. Pattern Anal. Mach. Intell. **38**(12), 2430–2443 (2016)
23. Rahmani, H., Mian, A.: Learning a non-linear knowledge transfer model for cross-view action recognition. In: Proceedings of the IEEE Conference on Computer Vision and Pattern Recognition, pp. 2458–2466 (2015)
24. Rahmani, H., Mian, A.: 3D action recognition from novel viewpoints. In: Proceedings of the IEEE Conference on Computer Vision and Pattern Recognition, pp. 1506–1515 (2016)
25. Rahmani, H., Mian, A., Shah, M.: Learning a deep model for human action recognition from novel viewpoints. IEEE Trans. Pattern Anal. Mach. Intell. **40**, 667 (2017)
26. Seidenari, L., Varano, V., Berretti, S., Del Bimbo, A., Pala, P.: Recognizing actions from depth cameras as weakly aligned multi-part bag-of-poses. In: IEEE Conference on Computer Vision and Pattern Recognition Workshops (CVPRW), pp. 479–485 (2013)
27. Shahroudy, A., Liu, J., Ng, T.T., Wang, G.: NTU RGB+D: a large scale dataset for 3D human activity analysis. In: IEEE Conference on Computer Vision and Pattern Recognition (CVPR), June 2016
28. Simonyan, K., Zisserman, A.: Two-stream convolutional networks for action recognition in videos. In: Advances in Neural Information Processing Systems, pp. 568–576 (2014)
29. Tran, D., Bourdev, L., Fergus, R., Torresani, L., Paluri, M.: Learning spatiotemporal features with 3D convolutional networks. In: IEEE International Conference on Computer Vision (ICCV), pp. 4489–4497 (2015)
30. Tzeng, E., Hoffman, J., Saenko, K., Darrell, T.: Adversarial discriminative domain adaptation. In: Proceedings of the IEEE Conference on Computer Vision and Pattern Recognition, p. 4 (2017)
31. Varol, G., et al.: Learning from synthetic humans. In: IEEE Conference on Computer Vision and Pattern Recognition (CVPR) (2017)
32. Wang, C., Wang, Y., Yuille, A.L.: An approach to pose-based action recognition. In: IEEE Conference on Computer Vision and Pattern Recognition (CVPR), pp. 915–922 (2013)
33. Yang, X., Tian, Y.: Super normal vector for activity recognition using depth sequences. In: Proceedings of the IEEE Conference on Computer Vision and Pattern Recognition, pp. 804–811 (2014)
34. Zhang, Z., Wang, C., Xiao, B., Zhou, W., Liu, S., Shi, C.: Cross-view action recognition via a continuous virtual path. In: Proceedings of the IEEE Conference on Computer Vision and Pattern Recognition, pp. 2690–2697 (2013)
35. Blender: a 3D modelling and rendering package. http://www.blender.org

ImaGAN: Unsupervised Training of Conditional Joint CycleGAN for Transferring Style with Core Structures in Content Preserved

Kang Min Bae$^{(\boxtimes)}$ ⓘ, Minuk Ma ⓘ, Hyunjun Jang ⓘ, Minjeong Ju ⓘ, Hyoungwoo Park ⓘ, and Chang D. Yoo

KAIST, Daejeon, South Korea
{kmbae94,akalsdnr,wiseholi,jujeong94,
hyoungwoo.park,cd_yoo}@kaist.ac.kr

Abstract. This paper considers conditional image generation that merges the structure of one object with the style of another. In short, the style of an image has been substituted or replaced by the style of another image. An architecture for extracting the structure of one image and another architecture for merging the extracted structure and the style of another image is considered. The proposed ImaGAN architecture consists of two networks: (1) style removal network R that removes style information and leaves only the edge information and (2) the generation network G that fills the extracted structure with the style of another image. This architecture allows various pairing of style and structure which would not have been possible with image-to-image translation method. This architecture incurs minimal classification error compared prior style transfer and domain transfer algorithms. Experimental result using edges2handbags and edges2shoes dataset reveal that ImaGAN can transfer the style of one image to another without distorting the target structure.

Keywords: Image-to-image translation · Style transfer · CycleGAN · Conditional generation · Deep learning

1 Introduction

We often wonder what it would look like to merge the structure of one object with the style of another. For instance, merging the structure of a yellow rain boot with the style of a leather bag will create leather rain boot which we can only imagine. Assume elements from two domains $x_{A_1} \in A_1$ and $x_{A_2} \in A_2$ as depicted in Fig. 1 where each element in the domains share structural similarities, but can have different styles. The main task is to transfer the style of x_{A_1} to x_{A_2} with the core structures of x_{A_2} preserved. In general, transferring the style while preserving the structure is a challenging problem owing to the difficulty in

© Springer Nature Switzerland AG 2019
C. V. Jawahar et al. (Eds.): ACCV 2018, LNCS 11362, pp. 447–462, 2019.
https://doi.org/10.1007/978-3-030-20890-5_29

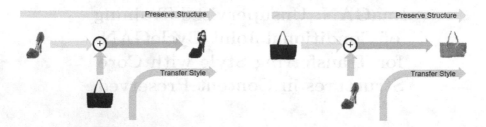

Fig. 1. Main task: For given two inputs, content and style image, the task is to transfer the style from style image and apply it to content image while preserving the structure.

defining the concept of structure and style. There are two related research areas: (1) style transfer and (2) image-to-image translation.

Style transfer considers transferring the source style to that of the target image. Gatys *et al.* [7] tried to apply convolutional neural networks (CNNs) for neural style transfer. Following this work, there have been numerous efforts [3,6,9,10,12,17,19,24] to make this transfer as fast as possible and seamless. Huang *et al.* [10] proposed a straightforward method for style transfer. These methods generally do not preserve fine-grained structural information and loose edge information.

Aside from style transfer, there have been considerable interest in image-to-image translation [1,2,11,13–15,29]. Isola *et al.* [11] adopted conditional adversarial networks for image-to-image translation. Zhu *et al.* [29] proposed cycle-consistent adversarial networks for unpaired image-to-image translation. Kim *et al.* [15] proposed DiscoGAN which jointly trains two generative adversarial networks (GAN) to learn cross-domain relations. The majority of the previous works requires two domains: domain of stylized image and domain of un-stylized image. However, gathering such dataset is often costly.

To overcome the aforementioned challenges, this paper proposes ImaGAN. The ImaGAN can be viewed as a conditional version of CycleGAN [29]. Similar to the CycleGAN [29], two GANs are jointly trained with cycle-consistency constraints. However, in contrast to the CycleGAN [29], the ImaGAN allows to user to select the structure and the style of the generated image. For this ImaGAN is composed of two parts: (1) style removal network R that removes the style of an image such that only the edge information is left, and (2) generation network G fills the style of the image whose style has been removed by style removal network. Experiments on edges2handbags and edges2shoes dataset revealed that ImaGAN can transfer the style of one image to another without distorting the target structure.

The contents of this paper is organized as follows. Section 2 introduces some related works. Section 3 describes the detailed formulation of the task, and the proposed architecture. Section 4 covers implementation and discusses the experimental results and compare it with other algorithms. In Sect. 5, summaries and suggestions for future work are given.

2 Related Works

2.1 Artistic Style Transfer

The seminal work of Gatys *et al.* [7] applied convolutional neural networks for artistic style transfer. Motivated by this work, various methods were suggested to improve the original neural style transfer algorithm in terms of speed, transfer effect, and controllability. Many initial methods were optimization-based [7,17,18,25]. Johnson *et al.* [12] introduced feed-forward neural network-based method which is more than three-orders of magnitude faster than optimization-based methods while achieving similar quality of transfer result. Huang *et al.* [10] proposed adaptive instance normalization (AdaIN) which directly transforms the statistics of the content feature maps by using the mean and standard deviation of the feature maps of the style image. Chen *et al.* [4] proposed a zero-shot style transfer method which swapped the patches of content feature maps with the nearest style features. Recently, Shen *et al.* [22] adopted to use meta networks that generate the filters of convolutional neural networks for arbitrary style transfer. Although the task that these algorithms attempt to solve is highly related to the task this paper explores, directly applying those methods is not appropriate due to structural distortion for artistic effect.

2.2 Image-to-Image Translation

Isola *et al.* [11] proposed the pix2pix architecture for translating image of one domain to the image of another domain. The model could convert an edge bag into real bag, and segmentation map into real photo. Zhu *et al.* [29] proposed CycleGAN which is GAN with cycle consistency that eliminated the need of paired image dataset. Kim *et al.* [15] proposed the DiscoGAN that learns cross domain relations using cycle consistency.

Numerous methods were proposed to tackle image-to-image translation with task-specific constraints. Kaur *et al.* [14] proposed FaceTex that transfers the texture of source face image to target face, and preserve the identity of the target. Chang *et al.* [2] proposed PairedCycleGAN, a method to makeup a face image with the makeup style of another face image, which assumed that make-up can be completely disentangled from face identity information. Recently, Joo et al. [13] proposed a GAN-based method that generates fusion image with one's identity and another's pose. Joo et al. devised identity loss for identity preservation and Min-Patch training method for better optimization. Wenqi *et al.* [26] proposed TextureGAN to apply given texture to raw edge images using local texture loss. These previous works assumes the existence of two domains; one with stylized images and the other with un-stylized images. However, gathering such dataset is often prohibitively expensive. The proposed method is not limited to such domain setting.

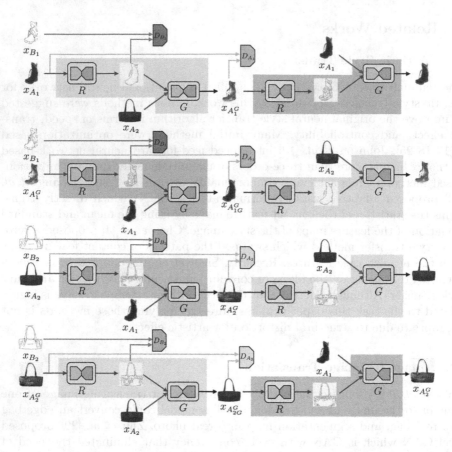

Fig. 2. Main architecture: style removal network R generates edge image using input x_{A_1}. Generation network G generates new style image x_{A_G} using reference style image x_{A_2}. Since cycle consistency has to be preserved, R network generates edge image using x_{A_G} and G network tries to generate original x_{A_1} using $R(x_{A_G})$ and x_{A_1}. There are four different discriminators that discriminates each domains. For third and fourth cycle, different discriminator compared to first and second cycle.

3 Proposed Method

3.1 Overview

Suppose there are two domains A_* and B_*. The elements from domain A_* share similar structures (all bags look alike, and all shoes look alike), while they may have very different color and texture. The domain B_*, is the set of edge images for A_*. For any element sampled from A_* is denoted as $x_{A_*} \in \mathbb{R}^{w \times h \times c}$ where w, h, c denotes width, height and channel, there exists corresponding edge image $x_{B_1} \in B_1 \subset \mathbb{R}^{w \times h \times c}$. Namely, the elements from domain B_1 contain only the structure information. Assume A_2 and B_2 are similarly defined and sampled elements from four domains are stated in Fig. 3. It is assumed that disentangling content and style information is possible.

Under this setting, the task is to generate image $x_{A_1^G}$ which has the same structure with x_{A_1} and style with x_{A_2}. To achieve this, two function R and G are defined which are implemented by encoder-decoder type deep neural networks. Given $x_{A_1} \in A_1$, network R removes all style information and gives $R(x_{A_1})$. With $R(x_{A_1})$ as structure information and x_{A_2} as style image, network G generates new stylized image $x_{A_1^G}$. The generated image $x_{A_1^G}$ is again processed by R so that the structural information is extracted, and is followed by G with x_{A_1} to recover the original image x_{A_1}. This stage is applied in similar ways to $x_{A_1^G}, x_{A_2}$, and, $x_{A_2^G}$ as depicted in Fig. 2. For the generated images in the intermediate stage, domain classifiers with GAN type losses are added for realistic image generation. To be specific, the images x_{A_1}, x_{B_1}, x_{A_2}, and x_{B_2} can denote a shoe image, the contour of x_{A_1}, a handbag image, and the contour of x_{A_2}, respectively.

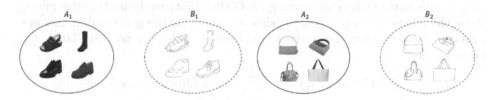

Fig. 3. Sampled images from set A_1, A_2, B_1 and B_2

3.2   Style Removal Network

To extract structure information, Style removal network R removes style of given input image and leaves structural information. Without removing the style of an input image, generation produces results which are unpredictable. In the experiment section, the ablation study for style removal network is provided. One straightforward method to overcome this would be to use the knowledge from neural style transfer algorithms such as AdaIN [10]. However, it was already mentioned that neural style transfer algorithms distort the target structure. To overcome this challenge, network R removes the style from the input so that the generator cannot refer to the style information for the content image. When x_{A_1} is processed by R, only structure information is left in the form of contour, and the result $R(x_{A_1})$ must be the same, ideally, as x_{B_1}. Network R is trained to minimize the loss, $\mathcal{L}_R = \mathcal{L}_{B_1} + \mathcal{L}_{B_2} + \mathcal{L}_{G_R}$, where $\mathcal{L}_{B_1}$, $\mathcal{L}_{B_2}$, and $\mathcal{L}_{G_R}$ are defined as:

$$\mathcal{L}_{B_1} = \mathbb{E}[||x_{B_1} - R(x_{A_1})||_2^2],$$
$$\mathcal{L}_{B_2} = \mathbb{E}[||x_{B_2} - R(x_{A_2})||_2^2],$$
$$\mathcal{L}_{G_R} = \mathbb{E}[\log(D_{B_1}(R(x_{A_1}))) + \log(D_{B_2}(R(x_{A_2})))]. \tag{1}$$

However, $\mathcal{L}_{B_1}$ and $\mathcal{L}_{B_2}$ losses are not sufficient for training style removal network. For realistic conditional image generation, GAN [8] type loss is also adopted. The function D_{B_1} and D_{B_2} try to discriminate whether $R(x_{A_1})$ and $R(x_{A_2})$ are in the domain B_1 and B_2, respectively, while R tries to fool the discriminators. Therefore the total loss of style removal Network $\mathcal{L}_R$ is represented as

$$\mathcal{L}_R = \mathcal{L}_{B_1} + \mathcal{L}_{B_2} + \mathcal{L}_{G_R}. \tag{2}$$

3.3   Generation Network

Generation network G generates new style of object using style-removed image and style-reference image. Unlike style removal network, generation network takes two inputs, $R(x_{A_1})$ and x_{A_2} (or $R(x_{A_2})$ and x_{A_1}). Generation network will detach styles from reference style image x_{A_2}, and apply it to $R(x_{A_1})$. Simple concatenation scheme is used to accept two inputs at the same time. Cycle consistency loss [29] was used to enforce the final image to match the original image. This part of the architecture gives G the ability to stylize the edge image using the reference image. Cycle consistency losses for the generated images are also calculated to compensate the non-existence of the ground truth labels for those images.

$$\mathcal{L}_{\text{cyc}} = \mathbb{E}[||G(R(x_{A_1^G}), x_{A_1}) - x_{A_1}||_2^2] + \mathbb{E}[||G(R(x_{A_{1G}^G}), x_{A_2}) - x_{A_1^G}||_2^2]$$
$$+ \mathbb{E}[||G(R(x_{A_2^G}), x_{A_2}) - x_{A_2}||_2^2] + \mathbb{E}[||G(R(x_{A_{2G}^G}), x_{A_1}) - x_{A_2^G}||_2^2], \tag{3}$$

where

$$x_{A_1^G} = G(R(x_{A_1}), x_{A_2}), \quad x_{A_2^G} = G(R(x_{A_2}), x_{A_1}),$$
$$x_{A_{1G}^G} = G(R(x_{A_1^G}), x_{A_2}), \quad x_{A_{2G}^G} = G(R(x_{A_2^G}), x_{A_1}).$$

To constrain the structure of input image, mean squared error (MSE) loss between edge images is used. This structure loss preserves the structure while reconstructing back to the original image by minimizing

$$\mathcal{L}_{\text{str}} = \mathbb{E}[||R(x_{A_1}) - R(x_{A_1^G})||_2^2 + ||R(x_{A_{1G}^G}) - R(x_{A_1^G})||_2^2]$$
$$+ \mathbb{E}[||R(x_{A_2}) - R(x_{A_2^G})||_2^2 + ||R(x_{A_{2G}^G}) - R(x_{A_2^G})||_2^2]. \tag{4}$$

To generate more realistic images, GAN type loss is used. Assume there are two discriminator that discriminates whether inputs are in domain A_1 and A_2. Therefore, the generation loss of generation network can be expressed as:

$$\mathcal{L}_{G_G} = \mathbb{E}[\log(D_{A_1}(x_{A_1^G})) + \log(D_{A_2}(x_{A_2^G}))]$$
$$+ \mathbb{E}[\log(D_{A_1}(x_{A_{1G}^G})) + \log(D_{A_2}(x_{A_{2G}^G}))]. \tag{5}$$

where generation network tries to generate images that look more similar to the elements in each domain A_1 and A_2. The reason why generation network takes output of style removal network $R(x_{A*})$ rather than directly takes content image x_{A_*}, is to avoid reconstructing the same input. When x_{A_1} and x_{A_2} are given to the generation network, generation network simply outputs x_{A_1} without changing any style. This is due to cycle consistency loss. Without style removal network R, $\mathcal{L}_{\text{cyc}}$ becomes 0 when $G(a, b) = b$ where $a, b \in \mathbb{R}^{w \times h \times c}$. To avoid this unintended result, style removal network was introduced. Therefore, the whole generation process cannot be satisfied without style removal network. Finally the total loss of generation network is the summation of cycle consistency loss, structure loss and generation loss which is represented as

$$\mathcal{L}_G = \mathcal{L}_{\text{cyc}} + \mathcal{L}_{\text{str}} + \mathcal{L}_{G_G}. \tag{6}$$

3.4 Discriminator Network

Adversarial loss for four different discriminator networks D_{B_1}, D_{B_2}, D_{A_1} and D_{A_2} was used. Let D_* to denote a discriminator that judges whether input is in domain $*$. For each discriminator loss is represented as:

$$\mathcal{L}_{D_{B_1}} = \mathbb{E}[\log(D_{B_1}(x_{B_1})) + \log(1 - D_{B_1}(R(x_{A_1})))], \tag{7}$$

$$\mathcal{L}_{D_{B_2}} = \mathbb{E}[\log(D_{B_2}(x_{B_2})) + \log(1 - D_{B_2}(R(x_{A_2})))], \tag{8}$$

$$\mathcal{L}_{D_{A_1}} = \mathbb{E}[\log(D_{A_1}(x_{A_1})) + \log(1 - D_{A_1}(x_{A_1^G})) + \log(1 - D_{A_1}(x_{A_{1G}^G}))], \tag{9}$$

$$\mathcal{L}_{D_{A_2}} = \mathbb{E}[\log(D_{A_2}(x_{B_2})) + \log(1 - D_{A_2}(x_{A_2^G})) + \log(1 - D_{A_1}(x_{A_{2G}^G}))]. \tag{10}$$

The discriminator D_{A_1} accepts real image x_{A_1} and fake image x_{A^G}, and tries to determine if they are elements of domain A_1. The other discriminators D_{A_2}, D_{B_1}, and D_{B_2} operate under by similar principles, but with appropriate real and fake images and for different domains A_2, B_1, and B_2, respectively. Since $x_{A_{*G}^G}$ is a function of $R(x_{A_*})$, training D_{B_1} and D_{B_2} comes ahead of training D_{A_1} and D_{A_2}. The total loss of Discriminator Network is given as summation of four different discriminator loss which is given as

$$\mathcal{L}_D = \mathcal{L}_{D_B} + \mathcal{L}_{D_A} \tag{11}$$

where

$$\mathcal{L}_{D_B} = \mathcal{L}_{D_{B_1}} + \mathcal{L}_{D_{B_2}} \tag{12}$$

$$\mathcal{L}_{D_A} = \mathcal{L}_{D_{A_1}} + \mathcal{L}_{D_{A_2}}. \tag{13}$$

3.5 Training Networks

The goal of whole network is to minimize total loss which is expressed as

$$\mathcal{L} = \mathcal{L}_D + \mathcal{L}_R + \mathcal{L}_G. \tag{14}$$

Minimizing the total loss $\mathcal{L}$ at the same time is very difficult task. Therefore, four step training was devised to orchestrate all sub-networks.

Algorithm 1. Training Algorithm for ImaGAN

Maximum number of iteration = N
Initialize whole network

1: **for** t in 1:N **do**
2:     Sample k images with edge images from $A_1 \times B_1$: $\{x^i_{A_1}, x^i_{B_1}\}^k_{i=1}$
3:     Sample k images with edge images from $A_2 \times B_2$: $\{x^i_{A_2}, x^i_{B_2}\}^k_{i=1}$
4:     Generate $R(x^i_{A_1})$ and $R(x^i_{A_2})$ for $i = 1, ..., k$
5:     Update D_{B_1} and D_{B_2} with respect to minimize $\mathcal{L}_{D_B}$

$$\mathcal{L}_{D_B} = \sum_{i=1}^{k} \sum_{j=1}^{2} \log(D_{B_j}(x^i_{B_j})) + \log(1 - D_{B_j}(R(x^i_{A_j})))$$

6:     Generate $x_{A^G_1}$, $x_{A^G_2}$, $x_{A^G_{1G}}$ and $x_{A^G_{2G}}$
7:     Update D_{A_1} and D_{A_2} with respect to minimize $\mathcal{L}_{D_A}$

$$\mathcal{L}_{D_A} = \sum_{i=1}^{k} \sum_{j=1}^{2} \log(D_{A_j}(x_{A_j})) + \log(1 - D_{A_j}(x^i_{A^G_j})) + \log(1 - D_{A_j}(x^i_{A^G_{jG}}))$$

8:     Update R network with respect to minimize $\mathcal{L}_R$

$$\mathcal{L}_R = \sum_{i=1}^{k} \sum_{j=1}^{2} \|x_{B_j} - R(x_{A_j})\|^2_2 + \log(D_{B_j}(R(x_{A_j})))$$

9:     Generate $G(R(x_{A^G_{1G}}), x_{A_2})$ and $G(R(x_{A^G_{2G}}), x_{A_1})$
10:     Update G network with respect to minimize $\mathcal{L}_G$

$$\mathcal{L}_G = \mathcal{L}_{\text{cyc}} + \mathcal{L}_{\text{str}} + \mathcal{L}_{G_G}$$

$$\mathcal{L}_{\text{cyc}} = \sum_{i=1}^{k} \|G(R(x^i_{A^G_1}), x^i_{A_1}) - x^i_{A_1}\|^2_2 + \|G(R(x^i_{A^G_2}), x^i_{A_2}) - x^i_{A_2}\|^2_2$$

$$+ \|G(R(x^i_{A^G_{1G}}), x^i_{A_2}) - x^i_{A^G_1}\|^2_2 + \|G(R(x^i_{A^G_{2G}}), x^i_{A_1}) - x^i_{A^G_2}\|^2_2$$

$$\mathcal{L}_{\text{str}} = \sum_{i=1}^{k} \sum_{j=1}^{2} \|R(x^i_{A_1}) - R(x^i_{A^G_1})\|^2_2 + \|R(x^i_{A^G_{1G}}) - R(x^i_{A^G_1})\|^2_2$$

$$\mathcal{L}_{G_G} = \sum_{i=1}^{k} \sum_{j=1}^{2} \log(D_{A_j}(x^i_{A^G_j})) + \log(D_{A_j}(x^i_{A^G_{jG}}))$$

The goal of the discriminators is to discriminate the results from style removal network and generation network while the goal of these generation functions is to fool all discriminators at once. Training D_{B_1} and D_{B_2} begins the training process. The goal of this step is to minimize $\mathcal{L}_{D_B}$ so that D_{B_1} and D_{B_2} are trained at the same time. One caution in the course of training is to block the gradient flow so as not to update irrelevant networks. For example, when calculating the cycle consistency loss for $x_{A^G_1}$ as depicted in the second row of Fig. 2, the network R

that was used to generate $x_{A_1^G}$ in the first row is not updated. Using the given losses, the whole training process is shown in Algorithm 1. Mini-batch setting was used for practical implementation where k denotes the size of mini-batch.

4 Experiments

4.1 Dataset

In this paper, edges2shoes [27] and edges2handbags [28] dataset were used. These dataset were originally established for colorization when only edge images are given. However, in this paper, colored images were used as input images, and edge images were used as the ground truth labels to train style removal network. edges2shoes dataset is a shoe dataset consisting of 50k catalog images collected from Zappos.com. The images are divided into 4 major categories: shoes, sandals, slippers, and boots. The shoes are centered on a white background and pictured in the same orientation for convenient analysis. edges2handbags dataset, consisting of 137k images collected from Amazon, is placed on white background with handbags looking in the same direction at the center like the edges2shoes dataset. Finally, at test time, a pair of shoe and handbag images are fed into the system to check if the style is transferred, and the structure is preserved (Fig. 4).

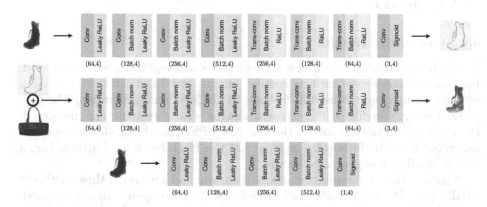

Fig. 4. For all: a tuple of integer (a, b) denotes output channel size is a and filter size is b. **Top:** architecture of Style removal network. **Middle:** generation network. The circle with cross inside denotes concatenation of two input along channel dimension. **Bottom:** discriminator networks for inputs in domain A and B.

4.2 Network Architecture

For style removal network and generation network, encoder-decoder architecture were used where the input size is down sized to $\frac{1}{16}$ of its input size. For generation network, naive deep CNN architecture cannot have multiple inputs. Therefore concatenating two inputs over channel dimension was used. To generate images where the pixels have bounded values, sigmoid function was used at the output layer. The strides were two for all convolution layers. For all generators and discriminators, leaky ReLU with $\alpha = 0.2$ were used as a activation function when performing the encoding process. In the decoding process, ReLU was used as the activation function.

4.3   Implementation Detail

Implementation was conducted by using PyTorch [21] framework. For optimizing each network, individual Adam optimizers [16] were used. For optimizing D_{B_1} and D_{B_2} networks, initial learning rate was set to 0.0001, $\beta_1 = 0.5$ and $\beta = 0.999$ with 0.0001 weight decay parameter. The same setting was used for D_{A_1} and D_{A_2} networks. For style removal network and generation network, Adam optimizer with initial learning rate 0.0001, $\beta_1 = 0.5$ and $\beta = 0.999$ with no weight decay parameter. To get reasonable output, at least 10k iteration was required. All input images from domain A and B were resized to 64×64 and batch size was set to 200. When the number of sampled data from each domain are different, simple resampling was performed. The edges2handbags and edges2shoes datasets contain 3 channel edge image rather than gray-scale image. Therefore 3 channel edge image was used instead of gray-scale image at training time. Titan X GPU was used to train the proposed network. Using this GPU, it took about 8–9 h to reach 10k iteration.

4.4   Qualitative Results

Using the proposed network, new style of shoes and handbags were generated. First shoe images were used as content images and handbag as style images to generate new style shoes. Fig. 6 shows the bidirectional generation. The proposed ImaGAN architecture generated images with core structures preserved. For example, on the left part of the first row of Fig. 2, a black slip-on shoe was generated from the brown slip-on shoe and the black handbag. Furthermore, a brown handbag was generated jointly.

Figure 5 shows the result of comparing our method with other three methods: AdaIN [10], DiscoGAN [15], and CycleGAN [29]. Compared to our method, AdaIN tends to generate images that look more artistic. Although AdaIN also sometimes generate reasonable images, the method is unstable compared to our method. For instance, in the second, seventh, and eighth rows, AdaIN colorizes the background with blurred shoe output image. DiscoGAN and CycleGAN also generates visually acceptable shoe images, but controlling the shape of the generated shoes is impossible. Therefore it is hard to obtain the desired shape of generated shoes.

4.5   Generating Bi-directionally

The proposed ImaGAN network can accept 2 different content domains using same network parameters. In Fig. 6 the bi-directional generation results for

Inputs		Results		Input	Results	
Content	Style	Ours	AdaIN[10]	Style	DiscoGAN[15]	CycleGAN[29]

Fig. 5. Ours column denotes Our proposed method's result. Our method can take both content and style image and generate new style shoe image. AdaIN [10] can also take content and style image. However, DiscoGAN and CycleGAN can only take one input. Therefore results from DiscoGAN and CycleGAN have arbitrary shape of shoes while our results have exact shape of shoes.

Content	Style	Ours Shoe	AdaIN[10] Shoe	Content	Style	Ours Handbag	AdaIN[10] Handbag

Fig. 6. Experimental results for the generating conditional shoes, handbags comparing with AdaIN. For the same two input images, first column and third column represents that input order is changed. For each inputs, second and fourth columns depicts the bi-directional results for our results and AdaIN [10].

domain A and B is shown. By using four different cycles, the proposed network generates results bi-directionally with identical network parameters.

4.6   Classification Score

It is difficult to quantitatively evaluate the performance of the proposed method. To obtain objectivity and reliability simultaneously, top-1 and top-5 classification accuracy was utilized as the quantitative measure. As shown in Table 1, the high classification accuracy on generated images verifies that the generated images by proposed method look more reasonable.

Table 1. Top-1 and top-5 classification accuracy by ILSVRC 2012 [5] pre-trained Inception V3 [23].

	Original dataset	Ours	AdaIN [10]	CycleGAN [29]	DiscoGAN [15]
Top-1	62.0%	**54.0%**	37.5%	49.0%	51.0%
Top-5	89.0%	**80.5%**	65.5%	79.5%	77.0%

4.7   Conditional Generating from One Content Image to Many

The proposed network can generate multiple stylized image for single content image by switching into various style images. Cycle-consistency loss fused with other losses allows to tackle new type of problems. Different from CycleGAN [29], the proposed model can generate multiple images by varying the style image as in Fig. 7. The conditional one-to-many generation ability of ImaGAN originated from the novel four-stream operation that shares parameters of R and G. This multi-tasking objective of R and G promotes stable learning.

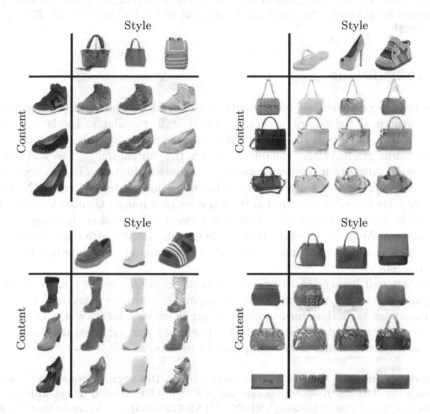

Fig. 7. With single content image, multiple images can be generated with different style images. The network not only applies handbag style to shoe content but also applies shoe style to handbag content with same parameters.

4.8   Ablation Study

One of the key novelties of our method is the use of edge image to preserve the structure information. Without the edge extraction network R, the generator network G prefers copying the input to creating a new, stylized content image as depicted in Fig. 2. The network R eliminates the memory about the style image and lets G have the input and output from different domains, prohibiting simple copying of input (Fig. 8).

Input		Results		Input		Results		Input		Results	
A_1	A_2	w/ R	w/o R	A_1	A_2	w/ R	w/o R	A_1	A_2	w/ R	w/o R

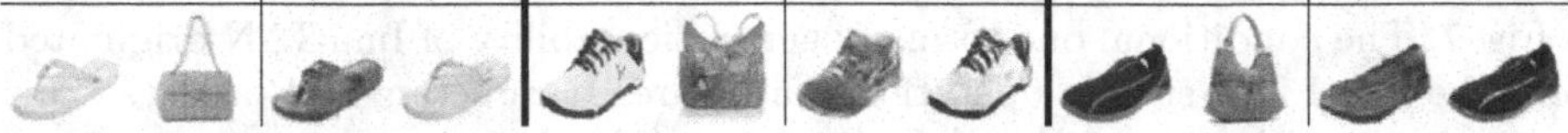

Fig. 8. The experimental result of ablation study. The results column presents the generated images under the condition of with and without R. (w/ R: with R, w/o R: without R)

5   Conclusions

This paper considered the problem of conditional image-to-image translation with structural constraints. Previous neural style transfer methods were not suitable for solving the task due to the inherent artistic rendering effect that destroys fine-grained structural information of the content image. Few and recent methods of image-to-image translation considered similar tasks. In this work, the ImaGAN, a novel architecture composed of two jointly trained CycleGANs that first extracts the edge information from the content image, then stylizes it. The system is end-to-end trainable and able o generate bi-directionally using shared parameters. We observed competitive style transfer results with edges2handbags and edges2shoes dataset, and demonstrated the stability of the method through experiments.

Using traditional edge detectors such as Sobel or Canny [20], can be utilized to generate elements in domain B. Applying the proposed method to other domains such as clothes, furnitures, faces, etc is left as a future work. We expect the proposed method to have practical applications that facilitate designing new style of objects ranging from shoes, bags to furnitures.

Acknowledgments. This research was supported by Basic Science Research Program through the National Research Foundation of Korea(NRF) funded by the Ministry of Science, ICT & Future Planning(NRF-2017R1A2B2006165) and Institute for Information & communications Technology Promotion (IITP) grant funded by the Korea government (MSIP) (No. 2018-0-00198), Object information extraction and real-to-virtual mapping based AR technology.

References

1. Azadi, S., Fisher, M., Kim, V.G., Wang, Z., Shechtman, E., Darrell, T.: Multi-content GAN for few-shot font style transfer. CoRR abs/1712.00516 (2017). http://arxiv.org/abs/1712.00516
2. Chang, H., Lu, J., Yu, F., Finkelstein, A.: PairedCycleGAN: asymmetric style transfer for applying and removing makeup. In: The IEEE Conference on Computer Vision and Pattern Recognition (CVPR), June 2018

3. Chen, D., Yuan, L., Liao, J., Yu, N., Hua, G.: StyleBank: an explicit representation for neural image style transfer. In: 2017 IEEE Conference on Computer Vision and Pattern Recognition, CVPR 2017, Honolulu, HI, USA, 21–26 July 2017, pp. 2770–2779 (2017)

4. Chen, T.Q., Schmidt, M.: Fast patch-based style transfer of arbitrary style. CoRR abs/1612.04337 (2016). http://arxiv.org/abs/1612.04337

5. Deng, J., Berg, A., Satheesh, S., Su, H., Khosla, A., Fei-Fei, L.: ILSVRC 2012 (2012). http://www.image-net.org/challenges/LSVRC

6. Dumoulin, V., Shlens, J., Kudlur, M.: A learned representation for artistic style. CoRR abs/1610.07629 (2016). http://arxiv.org/abs/1610.07629

7. Gatys, L.A., Ecker, A.S., Bethge, M.: Image style transfer using convolutional neural networks. In: 2016 IEEE Conference on Computer Vision and Pattern Recognition, CVPR 2016, Las Vegas, NV, USA, June 27–30, 2016, pp. 2414–2423 (2016)

8. Goodfellow, I., et al.: Generative adversarial nets. In: Ghahramani, Z., Welling, M., Cortes, C., Lawrence, N.D., Weinberger, K.Q. (eds.) Advances in Neural Information Processing Systems 27, pp. 2672–2680. Curran Associates, Inc. (2014). http://papers.nips.cc/paper/5423-generative-adversarial-nets.pdf

9. Gupta, A., Johnson, J., Alahi, A., Fei-Fei, L.: Characterizing and improving stability in neural style transfer. In: IEEE International Conference on Computer Vision, ICCV 2017, Venice, Italy, 22–29 October 2017, pp. 4087–4096 (2017)

10. Huang, X., Belongie, S.J.: Arbitrary style transfer in real-time with adaptive instance normalization. In: IEEE International Conference on Computer Vision, ICCV 2017, Venice, Italy, 22–29 October 2017, pp. 1510–1519 (2017)

11. Isola, P., Zhu, J., Zhou, T., Efros, A.A.: Image-to-image translation with conditional adversarial networks. In: 2017 IEEE Conference on Computer Vision and Pattern Recognition, CVPR 2017, Honolulu, HI, USA, 21–26 July 2017, pp. 5967–5976 (2017)

12. Johnson, J., Alahi, A., Fei-Fei, L.: Perceptual losses for real-time style transfer and super-resolution. In: Leibe, B., Matas, J., Sebe, N., Welling, M. (eds.) ECCV 2016, Part II. LNCS, vol. 9906, pp. 694–711. Springer, Cham (2016). https://doi.org/10.1007/978-3-319-46475-6_43

13. Joo, D., Kim, D., Kim, J.: Generating a fusion image: one's identity and another's shape. CoRR abs/1804.07455 (2018). http://arxiv.org/abs/1804.07455

14. Kaur, P., Zhang, H., Dana, K.J.: Photo-realistic facial texture transfer. CoRR abs/1706.04306 (2017). http://arxiv.org/abs/1706.04306

15. Kim, T., Cha, M., Kim, H., Lee, J.K., Kim, J.: Learning to discover cross-domain relations with generative adversarial networks. In: Precup, D., Teh, Y.W. (eds.) Proceedings of the 34th International Conference on Machine Learning, Sydney, Australia, 6–11 August 2017. Proceedings of Machine Learning Research, vol. 70, pp. 1857–1865. PMLR, International Convention Centre (2017). http://proceedings.mlr.press/v70/kim17a.html

16. Kingma, D.P., Ba, J.: Adam: a method for stochastic optimization. CoRR abs/1412.6980 (2014). http://arxiv.org/abs/1412.6980

17. Li, C., Wand, M.: Combining Markov random fields and convolutional neural networks for image synthesis. In: 2016 IEEE Conference on Computer Vision and Pattern Recognition, CVPR 2016, Las Vegas, NV, USA, 27–30 June 2016, pp. 2479–2486 (2016)

18. Li, Y., Wang, N., Liu, J., Hou, X.: Demystifying neural style transfer. In: Proceedings of the Twenty-Sixth International Joint Conference on Artificial Intelligence, IJCAI 2017, Melbourne, Australia, 19–25 August 2017, pp. 2230–2236 (2017)

19. Li, Y., Fang, C., Yang, J., Wang, Z., Lu, X., Yang, M.: Universal style transfer via feature transforms. In: Advances in Neural Information Processing Systems 30: Annual Conference on Neural Information Processing Systems 2017, Long Beach, CA, USA, 4–9 December 2017, pp. 385–395 (2017). http://papers.nips.cc/paper/6642-universal-style-transfer-via-feature-transforms
20. Maini, R., Aggarwal, H.: Study and comparison of various image edge detection techniques
21. Paszke, A., et al.: Automatic differentiation in PyTorch. In: NIPS-W (2017)
22. Shen, F., Yan, S., Zeng, G.: Meta networks for neural style transfer. CoRR abs/1709.04111 (2017). http://arxiv.org/abs/1709.04111
23. Szegedy, C., Vanhoucke, V., Ioffe, S., Shlens, J., Wojna, Z.: Rethinking the inception architecture for computer vision. In: Proceedings of the IEEE Conference on Computer Vision and Pattern Recognition, pp. 2818–2826 (2016)
24. Ulyanov, D., Lebedev, V., Vedaldi, A., Lempitsky, V.S.: Texture networks: feed-forward synthesis of textures and stylized images. In: Proceedings of the 33rd International Conference on Machine Learning, ICML 2016, New York City, NY, USA, 19–24 June 2016, pp. 1349–1357 (2016). http://jmlr.org/proceedings/papers/v48/ulyanov16.html
25. Wilmot, P., Risser, E., Barnes, C.: Stable and controllable neural texture synthesis and style transfer using histogram losses. CoRR abs/1701.08893 (2017). http://arxiv.org/abs/1701.08893
26. Xian, W., et al.: TextureGAN: controlling deep image synthesis with texture patches. In: The IEEE Conference on Computer Vision and Pattern Recognition (CVPR), June 2018
27. Yu, A., Grauman, K.: Fine-grained visual comparisons with local learning. In: Computer Vision and Pattern Recognition (CVPR), June 2014
28. Zhu, J.-Y., Krähenbühl, P., Shechtman, E., Efros, A.A.: Generative visual manipulation on the natural image manifold. In: Leibe, B., Matas, J., Sebe, N., Welling, M. (eds.) ECCV 2016, Part V. LNCS, vol. 9909, pp. 597–613. Springer, Cham (2016). https://doi.org/10.1007/978-3-319-46454-1_36
29. Zhu, J.-Y., Park, T., Isola, P., Efros, A.A.: Unpaired image-to-image translation using cycle-consistent adversarial networks. In: 2017 IEEE International Conference on Computer Vision (ICCV) (2017)

Stochastic Normalizations as Bayesian Learning

Alexander Shekhovtsov$^{(\boxtimes)}$ and Boris Flach

Department of Cybernetics, Czech Technical University in Prague,
Prague, Czech Republic
shekhovtsov@gmail.com

Abstract. In this work we investigate the reasons why Batch Normalization (BN) improves the generalization performance of deep networks. We argue that one major reason, distinguishing it from data-independent normalization methods, is randomness of batch statistics. This randomness appears in the parameters rather than in activations and admits an interpretation as a practical Bayesian learning. We apply this idea to other (deterministic) normalization techniques that are oblivious to the batch size. We show that their generalization performance can be improved significantly by Bayesian learning of the same form. We obtain test performance comparable to BN and, at the same time, better validation losses suitable for subsequent output uncertainty estimation through approximate Bayesian posterior.

1 Introduction

Recent advances in hardware and deep NNs make it possible to use large capacity networks, so that the training accuracy becomes close to 100% even for rather difficult tasks. At the same time, however, we would like to ensure small generalization gaps, *i.e.* a high validation accuracy and a reliable confidence prediction. For this reason, regularization methods become very important.

As the base model for this study we have chosen the All-CNN network of [23], a network with eight convolutional layers, and train it on the CIFAR-10 dataset. Recent work [7] compares different regularization techniques with this network and reports test accuracy of 91.87% with their probabilistic network and 90.88% with dropout but omits BN. Figure 1 shows how well BN generalizes for this problem when applied to exactly the *same* network. It easily achieves validation accuracy 93%, being significantly better than the dedicated regularization techniques proposed in [7]. It appears that BN is a very powerful regularization method. The goal of this work is to try to understand and exploit the respective mechanism. Towards this end we identify two components: one is a non-linear reparametrization of the model that preconditions gradient descent and the other is stochasticity.

Electronic supplementary material The online version of this chapter (https://doi.org/10.1007/978-3-030-20890-5_30) contains supplementary material, which is available to authorized users.

C. V. Jawahar et al. (Eds.): ACCV 2018, LNCS 11362, pp. 463–479, 2019.
https://doi.org/10.1007/978-3-030-20890-5_30

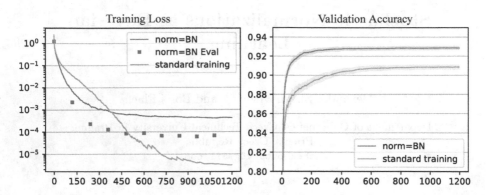

Fig. 1. The regularization effect of BN during the training epochs (x-axis). *Left:* Batch Normalization, designed for better and faster minimization of the training loss, converges to a small but non-zero value. Standard training reaches numerical accuracy. When BN is switched to the evaluation mode (BN Eval) the loss on the *same* training data is by an order of magnitude smaller, *i.e.*, it shows generalization when switching the mode. *Right:* BN clearly achieves a higher validation accuracy. The learning rate is chosen by numerically optimizing the training loss in 5 epochs for each method. Please refer to Appendix A (see supplementary material) for details regarding the experimental setup.

The reparametrization may be as well achieved by other normalization techniques such as *weight normalization* [19] and *analytic normalization* [22] amongst others [1,14]. The advantage of these methods is that they are deterministic and thus do not rely on batch statistics, often require less computation overhead, are continuously differentiable [22] and can be applied more flexibly, *e.g.* to cases with a small batch size or recurrent neural networks. Unfortunately, these methods, while improving on the training loss, do not generalize as good as BN, which was observed experimentally in [8,22]. We therefore look at further aspects of BN that could explain its regularization.

Ioffe and Szegedy [11] suggest that the regularization effect of BN is related to the randomness of batch-normalization statistics, which is due to random forming of the batches. However, how and why this kind of randomness works remained unclear. Recent works demonstrated that this randomness can be reproduced [25] or simulated [2] at test time to obtain useful uncertainty estimates. We investigate the effect of randomness of BN on training. For this purpose we first design an experiment in which the training procedure is kept exactly the same (including the learning rate) but the normalization statistics in BN layers are computed over a larger random subset of training data, the *normalization batch*. Note that the training batch size, for which the loss is computed is fixed to 32 throughout the paper. Changing this value significantly impacts the performance of SGD and would compromise the comparison of normalization techniques. The results shown in Fig. 2 confirm that using larger normalization batches (1024) decreases the stochasticity of BN (the expected training loss gets closer to the evaluation model training loss) but, at the same time, its validation loss and accuracy get worse. The effect is not very strong, possibly due to the fact that BN in convolutional networks performs spatial averaging, significantly reducing the variance in most layers. Yet modeling and explaining it statistically allows to understand the connection to Bayesian learning and to apply such regularization with deterministic normalization techniques. Decoupling this regularization from the batch size and the spatial sizes of the layers and learning the appropriate amount of randomness allows to significantly reduce overfitting and to predict a better calibrated uncertainty at test time.

1.1 Contribution

We begin with the observation that BN and the deterministic normalization techniques rely on the same reparametrization of the weights and biases. In BN the node statistics taken over batches are used for normalization and followed by new affine parameters (scale and bias). We measure how random BN is, depending on the batch size and spatial dimensions of the network. We propose the view that BN can be represented as a noise-free normalization followed by a stochastic scale and bias. Next, we verify the hypothesis that such noises are useful for the two considered deterministic normalization techniques: weight normalization [19] and analytic normalization [22]. Furthermore, the view of stochastic scale and bias allows to connect BN to variational Bayesian inference [9] over these parameters and to variational dropout [12]. We test the complete Bayesian learning approach that learns noise variances of scale parameters and show that combining it with deterministic normalizations allows to achieve significant improvements in validation accuracy and loss. The results on the test set, on which we did not perform any parameter or model selection, confirm the findings.

1.2 Related Work

There are several closely related works concurrent with this submission [2, 15, 20, 25]. Work [20] argues that BN improves generalization because it leads to a smoother objective function, the authors of [15] study the question why BN is often found incompatible with dropout, and works [2, 25] observe that randomness in batch normalization can be linked to optimizing a lower bound on the expected data likelihood [2] and to variational Bayesian learning [25]. However, these works focus on estimating the uncertainty of outputs in models that have been already trained using BN. They do not make any proposals concerning the learning methods. The derivation and approximations made in [25] to establish a link to Bayesian learning is different from ours and, as we argue below, in fact gives poor recommendations regarding such learning. Overall, we remark that a better understanding of the success of BN is a topic of high interest.

The improved methods that we propose are also closely related to *variational dropout* [12] as discussed below. We give a new interpretation to variational dropout and apply it in combination with normalization techniques.

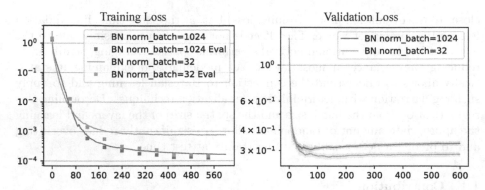

Fig. 2. The effect of randomness in BN. The training is performed with the same parameters. In the experiment with normalization batch 1024, BN layers use statistics of the data consisting of the training batch size 32 and 992 other samples chosen randomly at each step of SGD, all dependencies contribute to the total derivative. We observe that the gap between training and evaluation modes becomes smaller (as expected) but also that the validation loss increases. The validation accuracies are 93.0 ± 0.3 and 92.4 ± 0.3, respectively.

1.3   Background

Let $X = w^{\mathsf{T}}\hat{X} + a$ be an output of a single neuron in a linear layer. Batch normalization introduced by Ioffe and Szegedy [11] is applied after a linear layer before the non-linearity and has different training and test-time forms:

$$\text{training mode:} \quad X' = \frac{X - M}{S}, \qquad \text{evaluation mode:} \quad X'' = \frac{X - \mu}{\sigma}, \quad (1)$$

where (M, S^2) are the mean and variance statistics for a batch and μ and σ^2 are such statistics over the whole training distribution (in practice estimated with running averages during the training). The normalized output X' is invariant to the bias a and to the scaling of the weight vector w, *i.e.*, it projects out two degrees of freedom. They are then reintroduced after the normalization by an additional affine transformation $\tilde{X} = X's + b$ with free parameters s and b, so that the final class of modeled functions stays unchanged. BN has the following useful properties.

- Initialization. When a BN layer is introduced in a network, s and b are initialized as $s = 1$, $b = 0$. This resets the initial scale and bias degrees of freedom and provides a new initialization point such that the output of the BN layer will initially have zero mean and unit variance for the first training batch. The non-linearity that follows BN, will be not saturated for a significant portion of the batch data and the training may start efficiently.
- Reparametrization. BN combined with a subsequent affine layer can be viewed as a non-linear reparametrization of the network. It was noted in [19] that such reparametrizations change the relative scales of the coordinates, which is equivalent to a preconditioning of the gradient (applying an adaptive linear transform to the gradient before each step) [16, §8.7].

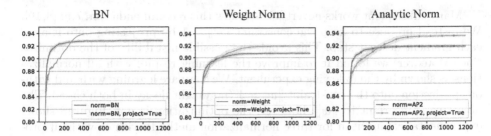

Fig. 3. Validation accuracies obtained by the normalization techniques with and without projection on constraints $\|w\| = 1$ for all scaling invariant weights. Validation losses at the final point are improved as well as follows: Batch Norm: $0.31 \rightarrow 0.22$, Weigh Norm: $0.9 \rightarrow 0.75$, Analytic Norm: $0.7 \rightarrow 0.45$.

Let us also note that a common explanation of BN as reducing the *internal covariate shift* [11] was recently studied and found to be not supported by experiments [20].

We will also consider *deterministic* normalization techniques, that do not depend on the selection of random batches: *weight normalization* (WN) [19] and *analytic normalization* [22]. We write all the discussed normalizations in the form

$$\tilde{X} = \frac{w^{\mathsf{T}}\hat{X} - \hat{\mu}(w)}{\hat{\sigma}(w)} s + b, \tag{2}$$

where $\hat{\mu}(w)$ and $\hat{\sigma}(w)$ are different per method. For BN, they are the batch mean and standard deviation and depend on the batch as well as parameters of all preceding layers. For WN, $\hat{\mu}(w) = 0$ and $\hat{\sigma}(w) = \|w\|$. It does the minimum to normalize the distribution, namely if $\hat{X}$ was a vector normalized to zero mean and unit variance then so is $w\hat{X}/\|w\|$. However, if the assumption does not hold (due to the preceding non-linearities and scale-bias transforms), weight normalization cannot account for this.

For analytic normalization $\hat{\mu}(w)$ and $\hat{\sigma}(w)$ are the approximate statistics of $w\hat{X}$, computed by propagating means and variances of the training set through all the network layers. Thus they depend on the network parameters and the statistics of the whole dataset. All three methods satisfy the following 1-homogeneity properties: $\hat{\mu}(\gamma w) = \gamma\hat{\mu}(w)$, $\hat{\sigma}(\gamma w) = |\gamma|\hat{\sigma}(w)$, which imply that (2) is invariant to the scale of w in all three methods.

2   Importance of Reparametrization

The original work [11] recommended to use additional regularization $\lambda\|w\|$ with *weight decay* λ. However, when used together with normalization, it leads to the learning problem of the form $\min_w f(w/\hat{\sigma}(w)) + \lambda\|w\|$ (for clarity, we restrict the optimized parameters to the weight vector w of a single neuron). This problem is ill-posed: it has no minimizer because decreasing the norm of w is always a descent direction and at $\|w\| = 0$ the function is undefined.

Many subsequent works nevertheless follow this recommendation, *e.g.* [8,19]. We instead propose to keep the constraint $\|w\| = 1$ by projecting onto it after each gradient descent step. This avoids the possible instability of the optimization. Moreover, we found it to improve the learning results with all normalizations as shown by the following experiment. We compare learning with and without projection onto the constraint $\|w\| = 1$ (no weight decay in both cases). The objective is invariant to $\|w\|$, however, the optimization is not. Figure 3 shows experimental comparison for three normalization methods with or without projecting on the constrain $\|w\| = 1$. It appears that projecting on the constraint has a significant impact on the validation performance. Notice that [19] propose quite the opposite with weight normalization: to allow $\|w\|$ vary freely. Their explanation is as follows. The gradient of the reparametrized objective f with respect to w is given by

$$\nabla_w f(w) = \frac{1}{\|w\|} g_\perp, \tag{3}$$

where g is the gradient w.r.t. normalized weight $v = w/\|w\|$ and $g_\perp$ denotes the components of g orthogonal to w. Thus, the gradient steps are always orthogonal to the weight vector w and would progressively increase its norm. In its turn, the magnitude of the gradient in w decreases with the increase of $\|w\|$ and therefore smaller steps are made for larger $\|w\|$. [19] argues (theoretically and experimentally) that this is useful for optimization, automatically tuning the learning rate for w. We observed that in small problems, the norm $\|w\|$ does not grow significantly, in which case there is no difference between projecting and not projecting. However, the experiments in Fig. 3 show that in larger problems optimized with SGD there is a difference: allowing $\|w\|$ to be free leads to smaller steps in $\|w\|$ and to a worse accuracy in a longer run.

3   Importance of Stochasticity

It has been noted in [11] that BN provides similar regularization benefits as dropout, since the activations observed for a particular training example are affected by the random selection of examples in the same mini-batch. In CNNs, statistics M and S^2 in (1) are the sample mean and sample variance over the *batch and spatial* dimensions:

$$M = \frac{1}{n} \sum_{i=1}^{k} \sum_{j=1}^{z} X_{i,j}, \qquad S = \frac{1}{n} \sum_{i=1}^{k} \sum_{j=1}^{z} (X_{i,j} - M)^2, \tag{4}$$

where k is the batch size, z is the spatial size (we represent the spatial dimensions by a 1D index), $X_{i,j}$ is a response for sample i at spatial location j and $n = kz$. Because M and S depend on a random sample, for a given input $X = x$ the training-time BN output X' can be considered as a random estimator of the test-time BN $x'' = (x - \mu)/\sigma$.

3.1   Model of BN Stochasticity

In this section we propose a simplified model of BN stochasticity replacing the randomness of batches by independent noises with known distributions. Despite the simplifying assumptions, this model allows to predict BN statistics and general dependencies such as the dependence on the batch size, which we then check experimentally.

For this theoretical derivation we will assume that the distribution of network activations X over the full dataset is approximately normal with statistics (μ, σ^2). This assumption seems appropriate because the sample is taken over the whole dataset and also over multiple spatial locations in a CNN. We will also assume that the activations $X_{i,j}$ for different training inputs i and different spatial coordinates j are i.i.d.. This assumption is a weaker one as we will see below. We can write the train-time BN as

$$\frac{x - M}{S} = \left(\frac{x - \mu}{\sigma} + \frac{\mu - M}{\sigma}\right)\frac{\sigma}{S}, \tag{5}$$

i.e. expressing the output of the batch normalization through the exact normalization $(x - \mu)/\sigma$ (cf. test-time BN) and some corrections on top of it. Using the above independence assumptions, M is a random variable distributed as $\mathcal{N}(\mu, \frac{1}{n}\sigma^2)$. It follows that

$$\frac{\mu - M}{\sigma} \sim \frac{1}{\sqrt{n}}\mathcal{N}(0, 1), \quad \frac{S^2}{\sigma^2} \sim \frac{1}{n}\chi_{n-1}^2 \quad \text{and} \quad \frac{\sigma}{S} \sim \sqrt{n}\chi_{n-1}^{-1}, \tag{6}$$

where χ^2 is chi-squared distribution and χ^{-1} is the inverse chi distribution[1]. The expression in (5) has therefore the same distribution as

$$\left(\frac{x - \mu}{\sigma} + V\right)U, \tag{7}$$

if $V \sim \frac{1}{\sqrt{n}}\mathcal{N}(0, 1)$ and $U \sim \sqrt{n}\chi_{n-1}^{-1}$ are independent r.v. with known distributions (i.e., not depending on the network parameters).

We verify this model experimentally as follows. In a given (trained) network we draw random batches as during learning, propagate them through the network with BN layers and collect samples of $(\mu - M)/\sigma$ and σ/S in each layer. We repeat this for several batch sizes. In Fig. 4 left we see that the model of S^2/σ^2 holds rather well: the real statistics is close to the theoretical prediction. Furthermore, the model predicts that the variance of BN (namely of the expression $(x - M/S)$) decreases as $1/(kz)$ with the batch size k and spatial size z of the current layer. Figure 4 middle clearly confirms the dependence on the batch size k in all layers. The dependence on the spatial size z (Fig. 4 right) is not so precise, as the inputs are de facto spatially correlated, which we have ignored.

---

[1] Using well known results for the distribution of the sample mean and variance of normally distributed variables. The inverse chi distribution is the distribution of $1/S$ when S^2 has a chi squared distribution [13].

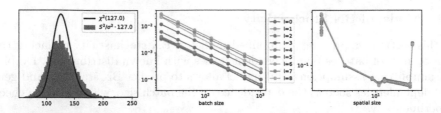

Fig. 4. Verification of BN statistics in a learned network. *Left:* Observed distribution of $(n-1)S^2/\sigma^2$ in a unit in layer 6 of size $z = 2 \times 2$, batch size $k = 32$, versus the model χ^2_{n-1}. *Middle:* measured variance of BN output versus batch size in different layers. The slope -1 in this log-log scale confirms $1/k$ dependence. *Right:* measured variance of BN output multiplied by k versus the spatial size of a layer. Here the slope is only approximately -1, due to spatial correlations, especially in the input layer (largest size).

Concurrently to this work, the authors of [2] have proposed a similar model for BN stochasticity and demonstrated that the distributions of U and V can be used at test time for improving the test data likelihoods and out-of-domain uncertainties. However, they did not explore using this model during the learning.

3.2   Regularizing Like BN

We now perform the following experiment. We measure the variances σ^2_V and σ^2_U of the random variables $V = (\mu - M)/\sigma$ and $U = \sigma/S$ in a network trained with BN. For example, the average standard deviation of the multiplicative noise, σ_U, in the consecutive layers was (0.05, 0.03, 0.026, 0.023, 0.02, 0.026, 0.041, 0.045, 0.071). We then retrain the network with stochastic normalization using the expression (7), in which $\frac{x-\mu}{\sigma}$ is replaced with a deterministic method (either weight or the analytic normalization) and noises V, U in (7) are distributed as $\mathcal{N}(0, \sigma^2_V)$ and $\mathcal{N}(1, \sigma^2_U)$. It is important to note that the noises V, U are *spatially correlated* as are the original quantities they approximate. This may seem unnecessary, however we will see in the next section that these correlated activation noises can be reinterpreted as parameter noises and are closely related to Bayesian learning. In Fig. 5 we compare training using noise-free normalizations and noisy ones. The results indicate that injecting noises to deterministic normalization techniques does regularize the training but the amount of noise can be still increased to make it more efficient. In the next section we consider learning the noise values instead of picking them by hand.

We argue that the combination of noise following the normalization is particularly meaningful. The base network, without normalizations is equivariant to the global scale of weights. To see this, note that linear layers and ReLU functions are 1-homogeneous: scaling the input by γ will scale the output by γ. Consider an additive noise ξ injected in front of non-linearities as was proposed *e.g.* in [7]:

$$\ldots W^{k+1}\text{ReLU}(W^k x + b^k + \xi) + b^{k+1} \ldots, \tag{8}$$

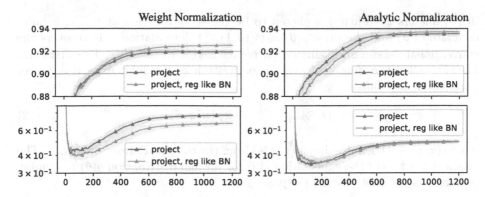

Fig. 5. Deterministic normalization techniques with noises like in BN. The noises appear to improve validation accuracy (*top*) and validation loss (*bottom*) noticeable for weight normalization and insignificantly for analytic normalization.

where ξ has a fixed distribution such as $\mathcal{N}(0, 0.01)$ [7]. Then, scaling W^k and b^k by $\gamma > 1$ and scaling W^{k+1} by $1/\gamma$ allows the model to increase the signal-to-noise ratio and to suppress the noise completely. In contrast, when noises are injected after a normalization layer, as in (5), the average signal to noise ratio is kept fixed.

3.3 BN as Bayesian Learning

Let $D = ((x^t, y^t) \,|\, t = 1, \dots |D|)$ be our training data. In Bayesian framework, given a prior distribution of parameters $p(\theta)$, first the posterior parameter distribution $p(\theta|D)$ given the data is found, then for prediction we marginalize over parameters:

$$p(y \,|\, x, D) = \int p(y \,|\, x, \theta) p(\theta \,|\, D) d\theta, \tag{9}$$

A practical Bayesian approach is possible by using a variational approximation to the parameter posterior, as was proposed for neural networks by [9]. It consists in approximating the posterior $p(\theta \,|\, D)$ by a simple distribution $q(\theta)$ from a parametric family with parameters ϕ, for example, a diagonal multivariate normal distribution $\mathcal{N}(\hat{\theta}, \sigma^2)$ with $\phi = (\hat{\theta}, \sigma)$. The approximate Bayesian posterior (9) becomes

$$p(y \,|\, x, D) \approx \int p(y \,|\, x, \theta) q(\theta) d\theta, \tag{10}$$

which allows at least for the Monte Carlo (MC) approximation. The distribution q is found by minimizing the KL-divergence between $q(\theta)$ and $p(\theta \,|\, D)$

$$\mathrm{KL}(q(\theta) \| p(\theta \,|\, D)) = \mathbb{E}_{\theta \sim q} \left[-\sum_t \log p(y^t | x^t, \theta) \right] + \mathrm{KL}(q(\theta) \| p(\theta)) + const \tag{11}$$

in parameters ϕ. When q is chosen to be the delta-function at $\hat{\theta}$ (*i.e.* a point estimate of θ) and the prior $p(\theta)$ as $\mathcal{N}(0, 1/\lambda I)$, formulation (11) recovers the conventional maximum likelihood [9] regularized with $\lambda \|\hat{\theta}\|^2/2$. The first term in (11), called the *data evidence* can be written as the joint expectation over parameters and data:

$$|D| \underset{\substack{\theta \sim q \\ (x,y) \sim D}}{\mathbb{E}} \left[-\log p(y \mid x, \theta) \right], \tag{12}$$

where $(x, y) \sim D$ denotes drawing (x, y) from the training dataset uniformly. The gradient w.r.t. ϕ of the expectation (12) for normal distribution $q(\theta)$ (assuming $p(y \mid x, \theta)$ is differentiable a.e.) expresses as

$$|D| \underset{\substack{\theta \sim q \\ (x,y) \sim D}}{\mathbb{E}} \left[-\nabla_\phi \log p(y \mid x, \theta) \right]. \tag{13}$$

Using the parametrization $\theta = \hat{\theta} + \sigma \xi$, $\xi \sim \mathcal{N}(0, 1)$, gradient (13) simplifies to

$$|D| \underset{\substack{\xi \sim \mathcal{N}(0,1) \\ (x,y) \sim D}}{\mathbb{E}} \left[-\nabla_\phi \log p(y \mid x, \hat{\theta} + \sigma \xi) \right]. \tag{14}$$

For a more general treatment of differentiating expectations see [21]. A stochastic gradient optimization method may use an unbiased estimate with mini-batches of size M:

$$\frac{|D|}{M} \sum_{m=1}^{M} -\nabla_\phi \log p(y^m \mid x^m, \hat{\theta} + \sigma \xi). \tag{15}$$

This means that during learning we randomly perturb parameters for every input sample. It becomes apparent that *any noises in the parameters during the standard maximum likelihood learning are closely related to the variational Bayesian learning.*

In order to connect BN to Bayesian learning, it remains to define the form of the approximating distribution q that would correspond to the noisy model of BN with an affine transform as given by

$$\left(\frac{w^{\mathsf{T}} x - \mu}{\sigma} + V \right) U s + b. \tag{16}$$

We reinterpret (16) as a model with a stochastic affine transform defined by a stochastic scale S and a stochastic bias B:

$$\left(\frac{w^{\mathsf{T}} x - \mu}{\sigma} + B \right) S. \tag{17}$$

We define the approximate posterior q over parameters w, S, B to be factorized as $q(w)q(S, B)$, where $q(w)$ is a delta distribution, *i.e.* a point estimate, and $q(S, B)$ is a coupled distribution over scale and bias defined as a distribution of a parametric mapping of independent random variables U and V:

$$S = Us, \quad B = V + b/(Us). \tag{18}$$

We let the prior $p(S, V)$ to be defined through the prior on U, V and the same mapping (18). The invariance of KL divergence under parameter transformations allows us to write

$$\mathrm{KL}(q(S, B) \| p(S, B)) = \mathrm{KL}(q(U) \| p(U)) + \mathrm{KL}(q(V) \| p(V)). \tag{19}$$

This completes the construction, which can now be summarized as the following proposition.

Proposition 1. *Assuming that BN can be well approximated with a noisy normalization modeled by (7), the BN learning is equivalent to variational Bayesian learning [9] with stochastic scale-bias parameter distribution with fixed $q(U)$, $q(V)$ and prior on w which is uniform on the sphere $\|w\| = 1$ (for all normalized units).*

Note, that the distribution of $q(S, B)$ still depends on two parameters and is optimized, but the KL divergence term vanishes. In other words, BN, optimizes only the data evidence term, but does not have the KL prior (it is considered constant). Note also that by choosing a suitable prior, a regularization such as $\|b\|^2$ can be derived as well.

Concurrently to this work, [25] proposed an explanation of BN as Bayesian learning with a different interpretation. They associate the stochasticity to noises in the linear transform parameters w and build a sequence of approximations to justify the weight norm regularization $\|w\|$ as the KL prior. While this matches the current practices of applying weight decay, it leads to the problem of regularizing the degrees of freedom to which the network is invariant, as we discussed in Sect. 2. It is therefore likely that some of the approximations made in [25] are too weak. Furthermore, the authors do not draw any applications of their model to experiments or learning methods.

Our interpretation is also only an approximation based on the simplified stochastic model of BN (7). However, one more argument in favor of the Bayesian learning view of BN is the following. It appears that from the initialization to convergence of BN learning, the standard deviations of U, V are in fact changing, especially in the final layer, growing by a factor of up to 5. So BN appears to increase the regularization towards convergence, which is also the case when we optimize these distributions with Bayesian learning.

3.4   Connection to Variational Dropout

Kingma et al. [12] proposed a related regularization method called *variational dropout*. More specifically, in the case of ReLU non-linearities and fully connected linear layers, the non-negative stochastic scaling S applied to the output of a linear layer (17), can be equivalently applied to the input of the subsequent linear layer, which then expresses as

$$\sum_j W_{ij}(x_j S_j) + b_i = \sum_j (W_{ij} S_j) x_j + b_i, \tag{20}$$

matching the *variational dropout with correlated white noise* [12, Sect. 3.2]. They consider approximate Gaussian posterior $q(S) \sim \mathcal{N}(1, \sigma^2)$, a log-uniform prior on S, given by $p(\log(|S|)) = const$ and no priors on w and b and apply the variational Bayesian learning to this model. This model is rather economical, in that an extra variance variable σ^2 is introduced per input channel and not per weight coefficient and performed better than the other studied variants of variational dropout [12]. Extending this model to the convolutional networks retains little similarity with the original dropout [24]. The main difference being that the noise is applied to parameters rather than activations. See also [6] discussing variational dropout and such correlations in the context of RNNs.

3.5 Normalization with Bayesian Learning

We propose now how the model (17) can be applied with other normalization techniques. For simplicity, we report results with bias b being deterministic, *i.e.* consider the model

$$\left(\frac{w^\mathsf{T} x - \mu}{\sigma} + b\right)S. \tag{21}$$

We expect that the normalized output $(w^\mathsf{T} x - \mu)/\sigma$ approximately has zero mean and unit variance over the dataset. This allows to set reasonable prior for S. In our experiments we used $p(S) \sim \mathcal{N}(1, 10^2)$ (we do not expect scaling by a factor more than 10 in a layer, a rather permissive assumption) and no prior on b. We then seek point estimates for w and b and a normal estimate of S parametrized as $q(S) \sim \mathcal{N}(s, \sigma_S^2)$. A separate value of variance σ_S^2 may be learned per-channel or just one value may be learned per layer. In the former case, the learning has a freedom to chose high variances for some channels and in this way to make an efficient selection of model complexity.

The KL divergence on the scale parameter $\mathrm{KL}(q(S)\|p(S))$ with these choices is, up to constants, $-\log \sigma^2 + \frac{\sigma^2}{\sigma_0^2} + \frac{(s-1)^2}{\sigma_0^2}$. We observe, that the most important term, the only one that pushes the variance σ up and prevents overfitting is $-\log \sigma^2$. The very same term occurs in the KL divergence to the scale-uniform prior [12]. The remaining terms balance how much of variance is large enough, *i.e.* may only decrease the regularization strength and penalize large value of s.

We identified one technical problem with such KL divergences when used in stochastic gradient optimization: when σ approaches zero, the derivative $-1/\sigma$ is unbounded. This may cause instability of SGD optimization with momentum. To address this issue we reparametrize σ as a piece-wise function $\sigma = e^u$ if $u < 0$ and $\sigma = u + 1$ if $u \geq 0$. This makes sure that derivatives of both $\log \sigma$ and σ are bounded. Note that a simpler parametrization $\sigma = e^u$ has quickly growing derivatives of the linear terms in σ and that the data evidence as composition of log softmax and piecewise-linear layers is approximately linear in each variance σ as seen from the parametrization (15). Note that using a sampling-based estimate of the KL divergence as in [3] does not circumvent the problem because it contains exactly the same problematic term $-\log \sigma$ in every sample.

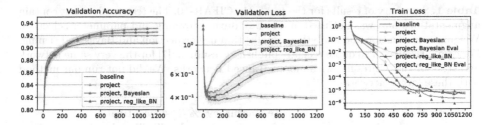

Fig. 6. All improvements to weight normalization. Bayesian Learning leads to significantly reduced validation loss and improved accuracy. For Bayesian learning, the *training loss* shows as solid line the expected data evidence estimated as running mean during training and triangles show the training loss with mean parameters. The *validation loss* plot uses mean parameters. The MC estimate of the validation loss of the final model with 10 samples is 0.25, significantly lower than the value 0.4 in the plot when using mean parameters.

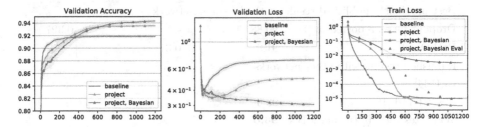

Fig. 7. Analytic Normalization with Bayesian learning in comparison with projection only and with the baseline version [22].

Figures 6 and 7 show the results for this Bayesian learning model with weight and analytic normalization. In the evaluation mode we substitute mean values of the scales, s. In Table 1 we also show results obtained by MC estimation of the posterior (9). It is seen that the validation accuracy of both normalizations is improved by the Bayesian learning. Its most significant impact is on the validation loss, which is particularly important for an accurate estimation of uncertainties for predictions made with the model. MC estimates of the validation losses, better approximating the Bayesian posterior (10), are yet significantly lower as seen in Table 1. It is interesting to inspect the learned noise values. For analytic normalization we obtained in the consecutive layers the average $\sigma_S/s = (0.39, 0.34, 0.18, 0.29, 0.27, 0.29, 0.31, 0.61, 0.024)$, corresponding to standard deviation of $U = S/s$. Compared the respective noises in BN Sect. 3.2, these values are by up to an order of magnitude larger except in the last layer. The learned noises put more randomness after the input and in the penultimate layer that has 192 channels. The final linear transform to 10 channels followed by spatial pooling can indeed be expected to tolerate more noise.

Table 1. Summary of results for the *test set* in CIFAR-10. The test set does not contain augmentations and was not used in any way during training and parameter selection. Weight normalization and analytic normalization use projection and Bayesian learning. For comparison we also quote recently published results in [7] for the very same network and state-of-the art results with more advanced networks. We did not run our method with these larger networks.

Method	Test accuracy, %	Test negative log likelihood		
		Single-pass	MC-10	MC-30
No normalization	90.7	1.45	-	-
Baseline BN	92.7	0.34	-	-
BN with projection	94.1	**0.29**	-	-
Weight normalization	93.5	0.48	0.27	0.24
Analytic normalization	**94.4**	0.38	**0.22**	**0.20**
Best previously published results with the same network				
Dropout [5] as reported in [7]	90.88	-	-	0.327
ProbOut [7]	91.9	0.37	-	-
Published results with other networks				
ELU [4]	93.5			
ResNet-110 [10]	93.6			
Wide ResNet [26] (includes BN)	**96.0**			

4   Other Datasets

To further verify applicability of our proposed improvements, we made an experiment with a quite different problem: segmentation of the dataset "DIC-HeLa" from the ISBI cell tracking challenge [17] illustrated in Fig. 8. A CNN model for this problem was proposed in [18]. The difficulty of this dataset is that it contains

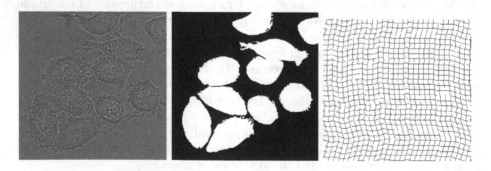

Fig. 8. *Left:* exemplar image from the dataset (512 × 512). *Middle:* exemplar training segmentation. *Right:* exemplar deformation applied to a grid image.

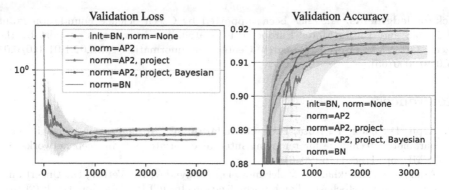

Fig. 9. Comparison of methods on the cell segmentation dataset DIC-HeLa [17] with a deep fully convolutional network (11 conv layers).

only 20 fully annotated training images, and the cells are hard to segment. Even when using significant data augmentation by non-rigid transforms as illustrated in Fig. 8 right, there is still a gap between training and validation accuracy. The Bayesian learning approach in combination with analytic normalization gives a noticeable improvement as shown in Fig. 9. Please refer to Appendix A.2 (see supplementary material) for details of this experiment. One of the open problems, is how to balance the prior KL divergence term, as in the case of a fully convolutional networks with data augmentation, we do not have a clear notion of a number of training examples. Results in Fig. 9 are obtained with KL factor 0.1 per classified pixel (meaning the augmentation is worth 10 examples).

5   Conclusion

We have studied two possible causes for a good regularization of BN. The effect achieved due to the interplay of the introduced reparametrization and SGD appears to play the major role. We have improved this effect empirically by showing that performing the optimization in the normalized space improves generalization for all three investigated normalization methods. We have analyzed the question of how the randomness of batches helps BN. The effect was quantified, the randomness measured and modeled as injected noises. The interpretation as Bayesian learning is a plausible explanation for why it helps to improve generalization. We further showed that such regularization helps other normalization techniques to achieve similar performance. This allows to improve performance in scenarios when BN is not suitable and to learn the model randomness instead of fixing it by batch size and the architecture of the network. We found that variational Bayesian learning may occasionally diverge due to a delicate balance of the KL divergence prior. This question and the utility of the learned uncertainty are left for future work.

Acknowledgments. A.S. has been supported by Czech Science Foundation grant 18-25383S and Toyota Motor Europe. B.F. gratefully acknowledges support by the Czech OP VVV project "Research Center for Informatics" (CZ.02.1.01/0.0/0.0/ 16_019/0000765).

References

1. Arpit, D., Zhou, Y., Kota, B.U., Govindaraju, V.: Normalization propagation: a parametric technique for removing internal covariate shift in deep networks. In: ICML, pp. 1168–1176 (2016)
2. Atanov, A., Ashukha, A., Molchanov, D., Neklyudov, K., Vetrov, D.: Uncertainty estimation via stochastic batch normalization. In: ICLR Workshop Track (2018)
3. Blundell, C., Cornebise, J., Kavukcuoglu, K., Wierstra, D.: Weight uncertainty in neural networks. In: ICML, pp. 1613–1622 (2015)
4. Clevert, D.A., Unterthiner, T., Hochreiter, S.: Fast and accurate deep network learning by exponential linear units (ELUs). In: ICLR (2016)
5. Gal, Y., Ghahramani, Z.: Dropout as a Bayesian approximation: representing model uncertainty in deep learning. In: ICML, pp. 1050–1059 (2016)
6. Gal, Y., Ghahramani, Z.: A theoretically grounded application of dropout in recurrent neural networks. In: NIPS, pp. 1027–1035 (2016)
7. Gast, J., Roth, S.: Lightweight probabilistic deep networks. In: CVPR, June 2018
8. Gitman, I., Ginsburg, B.: Comparison of batch normalization and weight normalization algorithms for the large-scale image classification. CoRR abs/1709.08145 (2017)
9. Graves, A.: Practical variational inference for neural networks. In: NIPS, pp. 2348–2356 (2011)
10. He, K., Zhang, X., Ren, S., Sun, J.: Deep residual learning for image recognition. In: CVPR, pp. 770–778 (2016)
11. Ioffe, S., Szegedy, C.: Batch normalization: accelerating deep network training by reducing internal covariate shift. In: ICML, vol. 37, pp. 448–456 (2015)
12. Kingma, D.P., Salimans, T., Welling, M.: Variational dropout and the local reparameterization trick. In: NIPS, pp. 2575–2583 (2015)
13. Lee, P.: Bayesian Statistics: An Introduction. Wiley, Hoboken (2012)
14. Lei Ba, J., Kiros, J.R., Hinton, G.E.: Layer normalization. ArXiv e-prints, July 2016
15. Li, X., Chen, S., Hu, X., Yang, J.: Understanding the disharmony between dropout and batch normalization by variance shift. CoRR abs/1801.05134 (2018)
16. Luenberger, D.G., Ye, Y.: Linear and Nonlinear Programming. Springer, New York (2015)
17. Maška, M., et al.: A benchmark for comparison of cell tracking algorithms. Bioinformatics **30**(11), 1609–1617 (2014)
18. Ronneberger, O., Fischer, P., Brox, T.: U-Net: convolutional networks for biomedical image segmentation. In: Navab, N., Hornegger, J., Wells, W.M., Frangi, A.F. (eds.) MICCAI 2015. LNCS, vol. 9351, pp. 234–241. Springer, Cham (2015). https://doi.org/10.1007/978-3-319-24574-4_28
19. Salimans, T., Kingma, D.P.: Weight normalization: a simple reparameterization to accelerate training of deep neural networks. In: NIPS (2016)
20. Santurkar, S., Tsipras, D., Ilyas, A., Madry, A.: How does batch normalization help optimization? (no, it is not about internal covariate shift). CoRR 1805.11604 (2018)

21. Schulman, J., Heess, N., Weber, T., Abbeel, P.: Gradient estimation using stochastic computation graphs. In: NIPS, pp. 3528–3536 (2015)
22. Shekhovtsov, A., Flach, B.: Normalization of neural networks using analytic variance propagation. In: Computer Vision Winter Workshop, pp. 45–53 (2018)
23. Springenberg, J., Dosovitskiy, A., Brox, T., Riedmiller, M.: Striving for simplicity: the all convolutional net. In: ICLR (Workshop Track) (2015)
24. Srivastava, N., Hinton, G., Krizhevsky, A., Sutskever, I., Salakhutdinov, R.: Dropout: a simple way to prevent neural networks from overfitting. JMLR **15**, 1929–1958 (2014)
25. Teye, M., Azizpour, H., Smith, K.: Bayesian uncertainty estimation for batch normalized deep networks. In: ICML (2018)
26. Zagoruyko, S., Komodakis, N.: Wide residual networks. In: BMVC, pp. 87.1–87.12, September 2016

Contextual Object Detection with a Few Relevant Neighbors

Ehud Barnea[✉] and Ohad Ben-Shahar

Department of Computer Science, Ben-Gurion University, Beer-Sheva, Israel
{barneaeh,ben-shahar}@cs.bgu.ac.il

Abstract. A natural way to improve the detection of objects is to consider the contextual constraints imposed by the detection of additional objects in a given scene. In this work, we exploit the spatial relations between objects in order to improve detection capacity, as well as analyze various properties of the contextual object detection problem. To precisely calculate context-based probabilities of objects, we developed a model that examines the interactions between objects in an exact probabilistic setting, in contrast to previous methods that typically utilize approximations based on pairwise interactions. Such a scheme is facilitated by the realistic assumption that the existence of an object in any given location is influenced by only few informative locations in space. Based on this assumption, we suggest a method for identifying these relevant locations and integrating them into a mostly exact calculation of probability based on their raw detector responses. This scheme is shown to improve detection results and provides unique insights about the process of contextual inference for object detection. We show that it is generally difficult to learn that a particular object *reduces* the probability of another, and that in cases when the context and detector strongly disagree this learning becomes *virtually impossible* for the purposes of improving the results of an object detector. Finally, we demonstrate improved detection results through use of our approach as applied to the PASCAL VOC and COCO datasets.

Keywords: Context · Object detection

1 Introduction

The task of object detection entails the analysis of an image for the identification of all instances of objects from predefined categories [7,11]. While most methods employ local information, in particular the appearance of individual objects [5], the contextual relations between objects were also shown to be a valuable source of information [23,26]. Thus, the challenge is to combine the local appearance at each image location with information regarding the other objects or detections.

Even when focusing on how context could influence the detection of a single object, one immediately realizes that the difficulty stems from the varying number of objects that can be used as predictors, their individual power of prediction, and more importantly, their *combined* effect as moderated by the complex

© Springer Nature Switzerland AG 2019
C. V. Jawahar et al. (Eds.): ACCV 2018, LNCS 11362, pp. 480–495, 2019.
https://doi.org/10.1007/978-3-030-20890-5_31

interactions between the predictors themselves. Unfortunately, however, most previous works that employ relations between objects and their context focused on pairwise approximations [1, 26, 30], assuming that the different objects that serve as sources of contextual information do not interact among themselves.

More current detectors based on convolutional neural networks are also able to reason about context since the receptive field of neurons grows with depth, eventually covering the entire image. However, the extent to which such a network is able to incorporate context is still not entirely understood [19]. To include more explicit contextual reasoning in the detection process, several approaches suggested to include additional layers such as bidirectional recurrent neural networks (RNNs) [2], or attention mechanisms [17]. These methods have shown to improve detection results, but the types of contextual information they can encode remains unclear. Additionally, such networks are not able to reason about object relations in a manner invariant to viewpoint, requiring training data in which all meaningful relations between all groups of objects are observed from all relevant viewpoints.

As mentioned above, some complications in addressing the full fledged contextual inference problem may emerge from attempting to model the relations between all (detected or predicted) objects to *all* other detections or image locations. But in reality, such comprehensive contextual relations are rarely observed or needed, as the existence of objects (or lack thereof) is correlated to just *few* other locations in space (and thus to the detected objects in those locations). This notion is exemplified in Fig. 1. In this paper we employ exactly this assumption to calculate a score for any given query detection. To do so, we first define the relevant context for that detection as the (few) other most informative detections, and then we use only these detections to calculate (in a closed form fashion) the probability that the query detection is indeed an object.

The suggested approach, facilitated by the decision to employ only few informative detections, provides several contributions. First, it is shown to improve the results of state-of-the-art object detectors. Second, unlike previous methods that require costly iterative training procedures, training our model is as quick and simple as just counting. Third, we represent object relations in a framework that allows to incorporate scale-invariant relations, reducing the number of needed examples, thus simplifying the training phase even further. Finally, using the derived calculation we observe various aspects and obtain novel insights related to the contextual inference of objects. In particular, we show that the effect of context is relative to the prior probability of the query object. As we show, this typically small quantity makes it difficult to infer when an object *reduces* the probability of another, and it practically prohibits the *improvement* of detection probability when the context *strongly disagrees* with the raw detector result. These and further observations and insights are analyzed in our results.

Fig. 1. An example scene with overlaid detections where thicker boxes represent higher confidence. Employing the green box detections as the context of a query red box detection can affirm (or reject) the presence of a keyboard. In this case, the contextual information supplied by the low confidence speakers and mouse detections may become redundant once the confidently detected chair and monitor have been accounted for. In this paper we propose a rigorous model that makes a decision for each query detection by identifying and using only its most informative detections for a more tractable decision. (Color figure online)

2   Relevant Work

Valuable information regarding image or scene elements may be obtained by examining their context. Indeed, different kinds of context were employed for various inference problems [12,13,20,27,31]. In this work we focus on employing long-range spatial interactions between objects. This problem has also gained attention, where the standard framework is that of employing fully-connected Markov random fields (MRF) and conditional random fields (CRF) with pairwise potentials [6,9,21,30]. This pairwise assumption is at the heart of the decision process, as it entails that a decision about an object is made by employing information supplied by its neighbors but without considering interactions *between* these neighbors. Other notable works make such assumption, where all detections affect each other in a voting scheme that is weighted by confidence [26], as a sum weighted by the probability of an object given by the detector [23], or a more complex voting mechanism that favors the most confident hypotheses and gives higher relevance to the object relations observed during training [24]. Yet another popular tool for reasoning with many elements is to employ linear classifiers [8,32] or more complicated set classifiers [4] in a pairwise interaction scheme.

Seeking more accurate representations, schemes that incorporate higher order models have been suggested for different kinds of problems in computer vision other than contextual object detection [14]. One such noteworthy model was suggested for objects that were not detected at all, where new detection hypotheses are generated by sampling pairwise and higher order relations using methods from topic modeling [22]. While this method was facilitated by context, it did not play a role in re-scoring existing or new detections. Other higher order models include neural networks that implicitly or explicitly reason about context as discussed in the Introduction.

A fundamental aspect of our work deals with finding the most relevant set of location variables for a prediction about another location. This problem can be abstracted as finding the structure of a graph (even if only locally) and algorithms for doing so can be grouped to roughly three types [15]. *Constraint-based methods* make local decisions to connect dependent variables, *score-based methods* penalize the entire graph according to an optimization criterion, and *model averaging methods* employ multiple graph structures. While our problem is better related to the constraint-based approach, most algorithms in this class seek to find the structure without considering current beliefs, a set of measures that change dramatically after observing the detections. To better support such cases, Chechetka and Guestrin [3] proposed to learn evidence-specific structures for CRFs, in which a new structure is chosen based on given evidence. This approach, however, is limited to trees. In a different approach, contextual information sources were dynamically separated to those that accept or reject each detection [33], but in a non-probabilistic framework. To facilitate structure learning in our extended graph configurations we therefore propose a different regime based on local structure exploration for each variable during the process of belief propagation. As will be discussed, our computational process is inspired by Komodakis and Tziritas [16] since it prioritizes variables for the message passing process according to their confidence regarding the labels they should be assigned.

3 Suggested Approach

The input to our algorithm is a set of detections $\mathcal{Y} = \{Y_1, Y_2, ..., Y_n\}$, such that each detection $Y_i = (t_i, l_i, s_i, c_i)$ comprises type t_i, location l_i, size s_i, and confidence c_i. A random variable X_i is created for each detection Y_i, denoting the probability of having an object of type t_i at location l_i with size s_i. For the sake of brevity, in the remainder of this text we refer to X_i as representing an empty location if it is indeed empty, or as a location containing an object of different type or size.

Our goal is to calculate a new confidence for each location variable X_i using detections $\mathcal{Y}$. To do so, we calculate the probability $P(X_i|\mathcal{Y})$ in a belief propagation process, where the context of X_i is dynamically selected as the most informative *small* set $\mathcal{N}_i$ of location variables $\mathcal{X}_{j \neq i}$, which is the set of all location variables except X_i. The initial beliefs are determined according to the detector, followed by iterations in which an updated belief is calculated for each X_i by identifying the best set $\mathcal{N}_i$ and employing the current belief of its variables for a decision about X_i. Alas, it turns out that this calculation can be very sensitive and produce problematic results when the detector and context strongly disagree. We therefore identify these cases first, then calculate $P(X_i|\mathcal{Y})$ accordingly.

3.1   Calculation of Object Probability

We assume that location and detection variables are connected according to the graph structure shown in Fig. 2. More formally, we assume that detection Y_i directly depends only on the existence of an object at X_i, so

$$P(Y_i, \mathcal{Y}_{j \neq i} | X_i) = P(Y_i | X_i) P(\mathcal{Y}_{j \neq i} | X_i) \ . \tag{1}$$

We further assume that X_i directly depends only on its detection Y_i and on a small set $\mathcal{N}_i$ of location variables. Therefore

$$P(\mathcal{Y}_{j \neq i} | X_i, \mathcal{N}_i) = P(\mathcal{Y}_{j \neq i} | \mathcal{N}_i) \ . \tag{2}$$

We note that variables in the set $\mathcal{N}_i$ may or may not directly depend on each other.

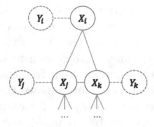

Fig. 2. Assumed graph structure when calculating $P(X_i | \mathcal{Y})$ in an iteration in which $\mathcal{N}_i = \{X_j, X_k\}$ is the set of most relevant neighbors for the location variable X_i. Each detection variable from $\mathcal{Y}$ is associated with a single location variable, the query X_i and the variables in $\mathcal{N}_i$ form a clique, and the rest of the variables are connected to X_i only via $\mathcal{N}_i$. We note that different graph structures are used for each X_i in each iteration according to current beliefs.

Employing these assumptions and the set $\mathcal{N}_i$ (identified as described in Sect. 3.4), we calculate $P(X_i | \mathcal{Y})$ in the following way:

$$P(X_i | \mathcal{Y}) = \sum_{\mathcal{N}_i} P(X_i, \mathcal{N}_i | \mathcal{Y})$$

Applying Bayes' rule we first obtain

$$P(X_i | \mathcal{Y}) = \sum_{\mathcal{N}_i} P(\mathcal{Y} | X_i, \mathcal{N}_i) P(X_i, \mathcal{N}_i) \frac{1}{P(\mathcal{Y})} \ .$$

Employing Eq. 1 entails

$$P(X_i | \mathcal{Y}) = \sum_{\mathcal{N}_i} P(Y_i | X_i, \mathcal{N}_i) P(\mathcal{Y}_{j \neq i} | X_i, \mathcal{N}_i) P(X_i, \mathcal{N}_i) \frac{1}{P(\mathcal{Y})}$$

$$P(X_i | \mathcal{Y}) = \sum_{\mathcal{N}_i} P(Y_i | X_i) P(\mathcal{Y}_{j \neq i} | X_i, \mathcal{N}_i) P(X_i, \mathcal{N}_i) \frac{1}{P(\mathcal{Y})} \ .$$

Employing Eq. 2 provides

$$P(X_i|\mathcal{Y}) = \frac{1}{P(\mathcal{Y})} P(Y_i|X_i) \sum_{\mathcal{N}_i} P(\mathcal{Y}_{j \neq i}|\mathcal{N}_i) P(X_i, \mathcal{N}_i) \ ,$$

and applying Bayes' rule again provides

$$P(X_i|\mathcal{Y}) = \frac{P(Y_i|X_i)}{P(\mathcal{Y})} \sum_{\mathcal{N}_i} P(\mathcal{N}_i|\mathcal{Y}_{j \neq i}) \frac{P(\mathcal{Y}_{j \neq i})}{P(\mathcal{N}_i)} P(X_i, \mathcal{N}_i) \ ,$$

which results in

$$P(X_i|\mathcal{Y}) = \frac{P(\mathcal{Y}_{j \neq i})}{P(\mathcal{Y})} P(Y_i|X_i) \sum_{\mathcal{N}_i} P(\mathcal{N}_i|\mathcal{Y}_{j \neq i}) P(X_i|\mathcal{N}_i) \ , \tag{3}$$

an expression reminiscent of the belief propagation process suggested by Pearl [25]. This is further developed by applying Bayes' rule once more:

$$P(X_i|\mathcal{Y}) = \frac{P(Y_i)P(\mathcal{Y}_{j \neq i})}{P(\mathcal{Y})} P(X_i|Y_i) \sum_{\mathcal{N}_i} P(\mathcal{N}_i|\mathcal{Y}_{j \neq i}) \frac{P(X_i|\mathcal{N}_i)}{P(X_i)} \ .$$

Finally, we denote the first term with ξ, which is a normalizing constant and need not be explicitly calculated. We thus obtain:

$$P(X_i|\mathcal{Y}) = \xi \cdot P(X_i|Y_i) \sum_{\mathcal{N}_i} P(\mathcal{N}_i|\mathcal{Y}_{j \neq i}) \frac{P(X_i|\mathcal{N}_i)}{P(X_i)} \tag{4}$$

an expression we assert is more informative than Eq. 3, as it is now apparent that the way in which the context $\mathcal{N}_i$ affects X_i is relative to its prior probability $P(X_i)$. We note that instead of calculating ξ, we normalize the values of $P(X_i|\mathcal{Y})$ calculated with $\xi = 1$, so that their sum equals to 1 as in a standard belief propagation process [25].

As can be seen, apart from $P(\mathcal{N}_i|\mathcal{Y}_{j \neq i})$ this expression contains only functions over a small number of variables (for small sizes of $\mathcal{N}_i$). We therefore restrict the size of $\mathcal{N}_i$ to the maximum that still enables to properly represent and learn these functions, as employing more neighbors would require more memory and more training examples.

We are left with the term $P(\mathcal{N}_i|\mathcal{Y}_{j \neq i})$, which is more complicated to calculate. This term is the (joint) belief of variables in $\mathcal{N}_i$ given all detections but Y_i, and can be seen as a weighting factor to the extent we are confident about assignments for $\mathcal{N}_i$. We therefore suggest to approximate it as the product of individual beliefs of variables in $\mathcal{N}_i$:

$$P(\mathcal{N}_i|\mathcal{Y}_{j \neq i}) = \Pi_{X_j \in \mathcal{N}_i} P(X_j|\mathcal{Y}_{j \neq i}) \ . \tag{5}$$

With this approximation, the representation of $P(X_i|\mathcal{Y})$ based on Eqs. 4 and 5 now consists of simple functions (that are easily measured from data), and terms of the form $P(X_j|\mathcal{Y}_{j \neq i})$, which can be seen as the messages in a standard belief propagation process.

Finally, given detections $\mathcal{Y}$ provided by a base detector applied to an image, a new confidence is calculated for each detection X_i. Its most informative neighbors $\mathcal{N}_i$ are identified as explained in Sect. 3.4, and used for the calculation of the probability $P(X_i|\mathcal{Y})$ in a belief propagation process. The confidence assigned to X_i is then $P(X_i = True|\mathcal{Y})$.

3.2   Scale Invariant Representation

The term $P(X_i|\mathcal{N}_i)$ in Eq. 4 represents relations between several locations. Such a term must be calculated for each set of locations, requiring to observe many examples of object groups in each location. To reduce this complexity we make the (very reasonable) assumption that relations between objects are independent of the viewer, and suggest a representation that is invariant to different object scales.

Similar to the spatial features employed by Cinbis and Sclaroff [4], we represent the spatial relation $P(X_i|\mathcal{N}_i)$ with respect to the size of a reference object $X_j \in \mathcal{N}_i$. The relative location of X_i (and any other non-reference object $X_k \in \mathcal{N}_i$) is represented as

$$\frac{l_i - l_j}{s_j f_j} \ , \tag{6}$$

where l_i, l_j are the locations of the center points of X_i and X_j, s_j is the height of X_j, and $f(t_j)$ is a scaling factor for s_j according to t_j, the type of X_j assigned by the base detector. Object scales are also represented relative to the reference X_j

$$log(\frac{s_i}{s_j}) \ . \tag{7}$$

Using this representation, the probability $P(X_i|\mathcal{N}_i \setminus X_j, X_j = True)$ is measured for any assignment to X_i and to the variables in $\mathcal{N}_i$ except X_j, which contains an object used as a reference frame. Specifically, we count the occurrences of objects of each type in each location and scale relative to reference objects of type t_j that appear in training data.

A non-parametric representation of $P(X_i|\mathcal{N}_i)$ requires a value for every possible assignment of the variables. The described method for measuring $P(X_i|\mathcal{N}_i)$ requires at least one variable $X_j \in \mathcal{N}_i$ that is not empty (i.e., contains an object) with which to construct a reference frame. However, in some assignments there may be no such X_j. Hence, for assignments in which all the variables in $\mathcal{N}_i$ are empty while X_i is not, we simply use X_i as reference:

$$P(X_i|\mathcal{N}_i) = P(X_k|X_i, \mathcal{N}_i \setminus X_k)\frac{P(X_i|\mathcal{N}_i \setminus X_k)}{P(X_k|\mathcal{N}_i \setminus X_k)} \ , \tag{8}$$

where X_k is arbitrarily picked from $\mathcal{N}_i$. Notice how the terms of the quotient operate on one less variable.

Finally, the probability for the assignment in which all the variables are empty is calculated by subtracting the probability of the complementary event from one.

3.3   The Implications of High Probability Derivative

To better understand the way contextual information is combined with the detector response we revisit Eq. 4 and examine its behavior when the context is known. Thus, for some assignment to the members of $\mathcal{N}_i$ we assume that $P(\mathcal{N}_i|\mathcal{Y}_{j\neq i}) = 1$, and so Eq. 4 reduces to:

$$P(X_i|\mathcal{Y}) = \xi \cdot P(X_i|Y_i)\frac{P(X_i|\mathcal{N}_i)}{P(X_i)} \ . \tag{9}$$

A graph of Eq. 9 for different detector responses is presented in Fig. 3. As can be seen, the addition of context strengthens a detection when the context-based probability is bigger than the prior, and weakens it when the opposite occurs. The red and blue curves, representing especially strong and weak detections respectively, *exhibit large derivative regions where the detector and context strongly disagree.* It may also be the case when the detector is confident and the context is independent, *i.e.*, $P(X_i|\mathcal{N}_i) = P(X_i) = 0.02$ in the case of Fig. 3. In these cases, the overall probability greatly changes with small perturbations of the context-based probability $P(X_i|\mathcal{N}_i)$. Because this quantity is measured from data, great errors are to be expected when the number of samples does not suffice.

Owing to this, many cases are indeed observed where detections are incorrectly assigned with low probabilities despite a confident detector and when the context is seemingly independent. Failing to address such cases leads to poor results, as we show in Sect. 4, and a specific case can be seen in Fig. 4. Hence, to handle such cases, for each assignment to the members of $\mathcal{N}_i$ we calculate the derivative of $P(X_i|\mathcal{Y})$ at $x = P(X_i|\mathcal{N}_i)$ and if it exceeds a threshold we ignore

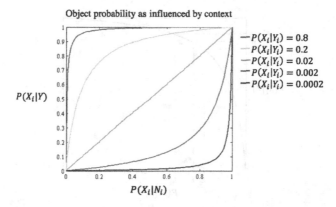

Fig. 3. The overall object probability $P(X_i|\mathcal{Y})$ as a function of the context-based probability $P(X_i|\mathcal{N}_i)$ for some variable assignment. Each curve represents a different value of local detector response $P(X_i|Y_i)$, for a relatively large prior probability of $P(X_i) = 0.02$. This visualizes the way in which both sources of information are combined for a final decision. See the text for further analysis. (Color figure online)

the context by setting $P(X_i|\mathcal{N}_i) = P(X_i)$, essentially assuming that X_i and $\mathcal{N}_i$ are independent, and thus, that the context has no effect.

Another way to identify these cases is to estimate the number of samples needed to ensure a low error. Let $p^* = P(X_i|\mathcal{Y})$ and $h^* = P(X_i|\mathcal{N}_i)$, as depicted in Fig. 5. If we allow a maximal error of ϵ, we require that:

$$|p - p^*| < \epsilon \ ,$$

where p is the value calculated using measured data. For h, the measured value of $P(X_i|\mathcal{N}_i)$, to provide an error that does not exceed ϵ, it is required to stay within the limits of h_1 and h_2, that are the values of $P(X_i|\mathcal{N}_i)$ that correspond to $P(X_i|\mathcal{Y}) = p^* - \epsilon$ and $P(X_i|\mathcal{Y}) = p^* + \epsilon$ respectively. Thus:

$$|h - h^*| < \min(|h^* - h_1|, |h^* - h_2|) = \epsilon_h \ ,$$

where ϵ_h is the allowed measurement error for h.

Fig. 4. A recurring case in which a confident detection (in the left) is assigned with a low probability. The probability of the left detection is calculated using the detector confidence and the detection in the right. While it is reasonable that the context affects the detection, it should not do so to the extent of nullifying a confident detection.

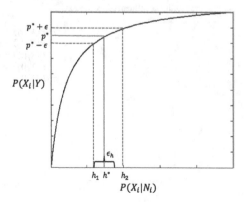

Fig. 5. The overall probability $P(X_i|\mathcal{Y})$ and its error in relation to h^*, the value of $P(X_i|\mathcal{N}_i)$ we measure from data. See the text for details.

We then employ Hoeffding's inequality [29] to estimate m, the number of samples Z_i required for h:

$$h = \frac{1}{m} \sum_{i=1}^{m} Z_i \ .$$

We assume that the indicator variables Z_i are sampled $i.i.d$ and note that their expectation is equal to h^*. Therefore, the probability of measuring h with large overall error can be expressed as:

$$P(|p - p^*| > \epsilon) < P(|h - h^*| > \epsilon_h) < 2e^{-2m\epsilon_h^2} = \delta \ .$$

Finally, to guarantee a maximal error of ϵ with probability δ, the number of required samples m is:

$$m > \frac{\ln(\frac{2}{\delta})}{2\epsilon_h^2} \ . \tag{10}$$

This expression enables to calculate the needed number of samples for $P(X_i|\mathcal{N}_i)$ in each case and then to employ it only when enough data is provided (even when the derivative is high). In our experiments the derivative was used to identify problematic cases, while m is used for discussion in Sect. 4.

3.4   Identification of Relevant Detections

The described algorithm requires to identify the most relevant set of locations $\mathcal{N}_i \in \mathcal{S}$ to use as context for X_i, where $\mathcal{S}$ is the set of subsets of $\mathcal{X}_{j \neq i}$. To limit the size of $\mathcal{N}_i$, we consider only subsets for which the cardinality is equal or smaller than a predefined number that is given as a parameter of the model.

The set $\mathcal{N}_i$ was used for the assumption that X_i does not depend on other locations (or their detections) given $\mathcal{N}_i$:

$$P(X_i|\mathcal{N}_i, \mathcal{Y}_{j \neq i}) = P(X_i|\mathcal{N}_i) \ . \tag{11}$$

Thus, the most suitable $\mathcal{N}_i$ would be

$$\arg\min_{\mathcal{N}_i \in \mathcal{S}} \sum_{X_i, \mathcal{N}_i} |P(X_i|\mathcal{N}_i, \mathcal{Y}_{j \neq i}) - P(X_i|\mathcal{N}_i)| \ . \tag{12}$$

However, this calculation requires a function over many variables $\mathcal{Y}_{j \neq i}$, which seems as complicated as calculating $P(X_i|\mathcal{Y})$. We hence suggest a different way to determine $\mathcal{N}_i$. Basically, we would like to employ the set $\mathcal{N}_i$ that would be the best predictor for X_i using our current beliefs for the different variables. For this reason, we pick $\mathcal{N}_i$ as those variables that are the least independent of X_i and weigh them according to the current beliefs

$$\arg\max_{\mathcal{N}_i \in \mathcal{S}} \sum_{X_i, \mathcal{N}_i} |P(X_i|\mathcal{N}_i) - P(X_i)| \cdot P(\mathcal{N}_i|\mathcal{Y}_{j \neq i}) \ , \tag{13}$$

where $P(\mathcal{N}_i|\mathcal{Y}_{j \neq i})$ is calculated as in Eq. 5.

4   Results and Discussion

We evaluate the proposed approach using the PASCAL VOC 2007 dataset where initial detections are provided by the Fast R-CNN detector [10]. Training and validation set objects are used to measure the probability of an object given its context $P(X_i|\mathcal{N}_i)$ as described in Sect. 3.2. For the probability of an object given its detection $P(X_i|Y_i)$ we simply use the confidence c_i provided by the base detector. To determine $P(X_i)$, we assume that the prior probability of an object is fixed regardless of image location and size, but depends on the object type. The value of $P(X_i)$ for each type is found by an exhaustive search to maximize the method's average precision (AP) on the training and validation set.

The results of our approach are summarized in Table 1, and specific examples including the detections identified as most informative can be seen in Fig. 6. Included in the table are the base Fast R-CNN detector, our proposed model with two most informative detections and *no* treatment for large derivatives (dFNM), our model with randomly selected context (rFNM), and finally, our contextual inference model *with* treatment for large derivatives and two most informative detections (FNM). We note that it is also possible for a single detection to be identified as the most informative, and that employing two detections to reason about a third constitutes a triple-wise model. In all variants of our computational

(a)   (b)   (c)

Fig. 6. Example detections (red) with their most informative neighbors (green). The confidence of correct chair/sheep detections in (a) increased following the use of our context model, and the confidence of the incorrect bottle (top) and tv/monitor (bottom) detections in (b) decreased. The hard to detect chair/sheep in (a) gain a boost in confidence due to the favorable context in which they appear. Similarly, The false detections in (b) are weakened due to their unusual location and size in relation to the other objects that serve as their context. Detections in (c) represent recurring mistakes due to localization errors, in which an increased confidence was provided for a false person detection (top) and a false cat detection (bottom). In both cases, object parts that were mistaken for full fledged objects are strengthened due to the use of context. (Color figure online)

model the results are reported after a single iteration of belief propagation, as usually just two or three iterations were needed for convergence.

As can be seen, our suggested approach (FNM) improves detection results and greater improvement is observed for the detection of chairs, sheep, televisions and bottles. The model in which large derivative regions are not handled (dFNM) is worse than the detector alone, which fits the analysis performed in Sect. 3.3.

For additional comparison, we test the ability of our model to improve detection results of the Faster R-CNN detector [28] over the COCO dataset [18]. In this case the suggested model (FNM) improved the mAP from 66.5 to 66.9 where the largest improvement of 2.6 was observed for sheep. We also compare our results to the ION contextual detector [2] that employs the same base detector and dataset (PASCAL 2007) and reports the results provided by the added context layers (but without additional components that are unrelated to context). In a nutshell, both ION and our approach provide a comparable improvement, where the mAP of the base detector was increased by 0.98 and 0.52, respectively, and our model provided a larger improvement than ION on 8 out of 20 object categories using a *significantly simpler and quicker* model. Moreover, please recall that our computational approach can also be applied to the results provided by networks with context such as ION for an additional boost.

4.1   Impracticality of Learning Certain Properties

The graph of Eq. 9 in Fig. 3 sheds light on the way information supplied by the local detector is combined with the context. As can be seen, the contextual information can either increase or decrease the probability of an object, where different probabilities of the local detector response affect the rate of change.

Using Eq. 10, we examine the difficulty of learning different properties with regard to the number of samples needed to stay within the limits of an allowed error. In this section we show the impracticality of learning certain properties even under modest error requirements. We first examine the requirements for learning relations that decrease the probability of objects without necessarily seeking to improve detections. As a test case, we set $P(X_i) = 0.02$, which is a relatively high prior probability for location X_i to contain an object. So, to

Table 1. Detection results in average precision (AP) of the base detector Fast R-CNN (FRCNN) and different variants of our model on all objects in the PASCAL VOC 2007 test set. Employing our model without treatment for large derivatives (dFNM) hurts detection results, and when large derivatives are treated (FNM) our model provides improved detection results. This improvement is not observed with randomly selected context (rFNM). The most significant increase is obtained for object categories such as chairs, sheep, televisions, and bottles, which benefit more from the use of context.

Method	aero	bike	bird	boat	bottle	bus	car	cat	chair	cow	table	dog	horse	mbike	persn	plant	sheep	sofa	train	tv	mAP
FRCNN	72.15	72.51	61.19	42.98	28.67	**69.89**	70.67	81.14	36.15	69.61	55.90	77.31	76.69	**69.01**	64.55	28.24	57.35	59.97	75.58	62.58	61.61
dFNM	72.08	69.82	**61.93**	41.79	25.12	67.73	69.73	80.84	39.00	69.22	54.30	74.91	76.38	66.41	62.83	28.20	59.33	57.46	74.94	59.30	60.57
rFNM	72.11	72.57	61.21	**43.20**	28.56	69.69	70.73	**81.38**	33.74	69.63	55.47	77.29	76.77	68.86	64.56	28.46	57.44	**60.13**	76.10	62.71	61.53
FNM	**72.29**	**72.63**	61.68	43.15	**29.64**	69.81	**70.76**	81.36	**39.00**	69.73	**56.01**	**77.63**	76.78	68.93	64.85	28.90	59.46	60.09	**76.26**	**63.58**	**62.13**

decide with high certainty ($\delta = 0.1$) whether an assignment to the members of $\mathcal{N}_i$ reduces the probability of X_i, that is $P(X_i|\mathcal{N}_i) < P(X_i)$, an ϵ_h error of at most 0.02 is required. According to Eq. 10, this requires at least 3745 samples of that relation (or even more for the average prior probability).

Seeking to improve detection results, let us examine one test case in which the context-based probability $P(X_i|\mathcal{N}_i)$ is half of the prior probability $P(X_i)$:

$$P(X_i|\mathcal{N}_i) = \frac{P(X_i)}{2} = 0.01 \ .$$

For confident detections $P(X_i|Y_i) = 0.8$, the overall probability of X_i to contain an object in this case is $P(X_i|\mathcal{Y}) = 0.6644$. If we require a modest overall error of at most $\epsilon = 0.1$, then according to the construction in Sect. 3.3, a measurement error less than $\epsilon_h = 0.0034$ is required. In this case, for a high certainty ($\delta = 0.1$) the number of required samples is 127,095. Similarly, for more accurate results ($\epsilon = 0.05$), as much as 400,048 samples are required. Of course, in more extreme cases many more samples would be required. The need to collect datasets that large renders such relations impractical to learn by observing object occurrences.

The suggestion here was to handle the cases when the detector and context strongly disagree by assuming independence from context $P(X_i|\mathcal{N}_i) = P(X_i)$ according to the derivative. This decision to ignore the context (instead of the detector) corresponds to similar processes we observe in the human visual system, as exemplified in Fig. 7. And yet, it is important to note that there are indeed cases in which our contextual computation successfully reduces the probability of an object. Two such cases can be seen in Fig. 6b.

Also important is the rate of change of the graph in Fig. 3 for different detector responses $P(X_i|Y_i)$ depicted by the differently colored curves. The central curve, calculated for $P(X_i|Y_i) = 0.02$, behaves as a straight line. The red and

(a)   (b)

Fig. 7. Examples of disagreement between the context and the detector (based on local appearance) where in both cases the human visual system seems to resolve this conflict by ignoring the context. The insets show the corresponding situation of the conditional probability as discussed in Fig. 3. **(a)** Most observers do not have a problem to immediately spot the rider despite its improbable configuration relative to the motorbike. **(b)** When looking directly at the expected position of the front wheel, most observers report its absence even though motorbikes are mostly observed to have two wheels.

yellow curves behave similarly to the blue and magenta ones. However, the scale of the latter curves is significantly smaller, reducing the high derivative cases to those in which the detector is extremely confident that an object is not present. From this we conclude that it is generally simpler to learn relations that increase the probability of an object in comparison to those that decrease its probability.

5 Conclusions

The problem of including context in object detection is important but difficult, as decision over many locations is needed. We have suggested to employ only a small number of locations for a more accurate decision, and presented a method for the identification of the most informative set of locations, and a formulation that employs it to infer the probability of objects at different locations in a probabilistic fashion. Key benefits of our computational approach is how it facilitates better understanding of certain aspects of the problem, and in particular it allowed to conclude that it is impractical to infer relations that decrease or increase the probability of detections when the detector and the context strongly disagree, or that in general it is more difficult to infer conditions that reduce the probability of an object rather than relations that increase it. Finally, we have demonstrated how our approach improves detection results using a model that is quick and simple to train and to employ for context-based inference.

Acknowledgments. This research was supported in part by Israel Ministry of Science, Technology and Space (MOST Grant 54178). We also thank the Frankel Fund and the Helmsley Charitable Trust through the ABC Robotics Initiative, both at Ben-Gurion University of the Negev, for their generous support.

References

1. Arbel, N., Avraham, T., Lindenbaum, M.: Inner-scene similarities as a contextual cue for object detection (2017). arXiv preprint
2. Bell, S., Lawrence Zitnick, C., Bala, K., Girshick, R.: Inside-outside net: detecting objects in context with skip pooling and recurrent neural networks. In: CVPR, pp. 2874–2883 (2016)
3. Chechetka, A., Guestrin, C.: Evidence-specific structures for rich tractable CRFs. In: Advances in Neural Information Processing Systems, pp. 352–360 (2010)
4. Cinbis, R.G., Sclaroff, S.: Contextual object detection using set-based classification. In: Fitzgibbon, A., Lazebnik, S., Perona, P., Sato, Y., Schmid, C. (eds.) ECCV 2012, Part VI. LNCS, vol. 7577, pp. 43–57. Springer, Heidelberg (2012). https://doi.org/10.1007/978-3-642-33783-3_4
5. Dalal, N., Triggs, B.: Histograms of oriented gradients for human detection. In: CVPR, pp. 886–893 (2005)
6. Desai, C., Ramanan, D., Fowlkes, C.C.: Discriminative models for multi-class object layout. Int. J. Comput. Vis. **95**(1), 1–12 (2011)
7. Felzenszwalb, P., McAllester, D., Ramanan, D.: A discriminatively trained, multi-scale, deformable part model. In: CVPR, pp. 1–8 (2008)

8. Felzenszwalb, P.F., Girshick, R.B., McAllester, D., Ramanan, D.: Object detection with discriminatively trained part-based models. IEEE Trans. Pattern Anal. Mach. Intell. **32**(9), 1627–1645 (2010)
9. Galleguillos, C., Rabinovich, A., Belongie, S.: Object categorization using co-occurrence, location and appearance. In: CVPR, pp. 1–8 (2008)
10. Girshick, R.: Fast R-CNN. In: ICCV, pp. 1440–1448 (2015)
11. Girshick, R., Donahue, J., Darrell, T., Malik, J.: Rich feature hierarchies for accurate object detection and semantic segmentation. In: CVPR (2014)
12. Heitz, G., Koller, D.: Learning spatial context: using stuff to find things. In: Forsyth, D., Torr, P., Zisserman, A. (eds.) ECCV 2008, Part I. LNCS, vol. 5302, pp. 30–43. Springer, Heidelberg (2008). https://doi.org/10.1007/978-3-540-88682-2_4
13. Hoiem, D., Efros, A.A., Hebert, M.: Putting objects in perspective. Int. J. Comput. Vis. **80**(1), 3–15 (2008)
14. Kohli, P., Rother, C.: Higher-order models in computer vision. In: Image Processing and Analysing with Graphs: Theory and Practice, Chap. 3, pp. 65–92. CRC Press (2012)
15. Koller, D., Friedman, N.: Probabilistic Graphical Models: Principles and Techniques. MIT Press, Cambridge (2009)
16. Komodakis, N., Tziritas, G.: Image completion using efficient belief propagation via priority scheduling and dynamic pruning. IEEE Trans. Pattern Anal. Mach. Intell. **16**(11), 2649–2661 (2007)
17. Li, J., Wei, Y., Liang, X., Dong, J., Xu, T., Feng, J., Yan, S.: Attentive contexts for object detection. IEEE Trans. Multimed. **19**(5), 944–954 (2017)
18. Lin, T.-Y., et al.: Microsoft COCO: common objects in context. In: Fleet, D., Pajdla, T., Schiele, B., Tuytelaars, T. (eds.) ECCV 2014, Part V. LNCS, vol. 8693, pp. 740–755. Springer, Cham (2014). https://doi.org/10.1007/978-3-319-10602-1_48
19. Luo, W., Li, Y., Urtasun, R., Zemel, R.: Understanding the effective receptive field in deep convolutional neural networks. In: NIPS, pp. 4898–4906 (2016)
20. Mairon, R., Ben-Shahar, O.: A closer look at context: from coxels to the contextual emergence of object saliency. In: Fleet, D., Pajdla, T., Schiele, B., Tuytelaars, T. (eds.) ECCV 2014, Part V. LNCS, vol. 8693, pp. 708–724. Springer, Cham (2014). https://doi.org/10.1007/978-3-319-10602-1_46
21. Mottaghi, R., et al.: The role of context for object detection and semantic segmentation in the wild. In: CVPR, pp. 891–898 (2014)
22. Oramas, J., Tuytelaars, T.: Recovering hard-to-find object instances by sampling context-based object proposals. CVIU **152**, 118–130 (2016)
23. José Oramas, M., De Raedt, L., Tuytelaars, T.: Allocentric pose estimation. In: ICCV (2013)
24. José Oramas, M., De Raedt, L., Tuytelaars, T.: Towards cautious collective inference for object verification. In: WACV (2014)
25. Pearl, J.: Probabilistic Reasoning in Intelligent Systems: Networks of Plausible Inference. Morgan Kaufmann, San Francisco (1988)
26. Perko, R., Leonardis, A.: A framework for visual-context-aware object detection in still images. CVIU **114**(6), 700–711 (2010)
27. Rabinovich, A., Vedaldi, A., Galleguillos, C., Wiewiora, E., Belongie, S.: Objects in context. In: ICCV, pp. 1–8. IEEE (2007)
28. Ren, S., He, K., Girshick, R., Sun, J.: Fast R-CNN: towards real-time object detection with region proposal networks. In: NIPS, pp. 91–99 (2015)

29. Shalev-Shwartz, S., Ben-David, S.: Understanding Machine Learning: From Theory to Algorithms. Cambridge University Press, Cambridge (2014)
30. Torralba, A., Murphy, K.P., Freeman, W.T.: Contextual models for object detection using boosted random fields. In: NIPS, pp. 1401–1408 (2004)
31. Torralba, A., Sinha, P.: Statistical context priming for object detection. In: ICCV, vol. 1, pp. 763–770. IEEE (2001)
32. Wolf, L., Bileschi, S.: A critical view of context. Int. J. Comput. Vis. **69**(2), 251–261 (2006)
33. Yu, R., Chen, X., Morariu, V.I., Davis, L.S.: The role of context selection in object detection. British Machine Vision Conference abs/1609.02948 (2016)

Album to Family Tree: A Graph Based Method for Family Relationship Recognition

Chao Xia[1], Siyu Xia[2(✉)], Ming Shao[3], and Yun Fu[4]

[1] School of Biomedical Engineering, Shanghai Jiao Tong University, Shanghai, China
[2] School of Automation, Southeast University, Nanjing 210096, China
xia081@gmail.com
[3] CIS, College of Engineering, University of Massachusetts Dartmouth,
Dartmouth, MA, USA
mshao@umassd.edu
[4] ECE, College of Engineering, Northeastern University,
Boston, MA, USA
yunfu@ece.neu.edu

Abstract. Image-based kinship recognition is an important research area in the social network. Beyond kinship verification, family relationship recognition is a challenging task with little existing literature. In this paper, we propose a pictorial structure based method for automatic family tree construction. Unlike traditional work based on a single image, an album-oriented method can leverage the cooperation of multiple instances associated with the same identity. In this way, the reliability of kinship similarity can be improved. Besides, the family tree structure is used to describe kinship relations among each pair of members. The experimental result shows that the proposed method can construct a family tree effectively and improve the overall accuracy of kinship identification.

Keywords: Kinship recognition · Family relationship recognition · Pictorial structure

1 Introduction

It becomes increasingly popular to share photos on social media websites such as Youtube, WeChat and Facebook, which host billions of images. A large proportion of them are taken within family, friends and colleagues. Usually, people shown in the same album or photo are tied to each other and bear certain social relationship. Therefore, recognizing the identity of people in these photos could help social network understand the relationships of user.

Supported by the National Natural Science Foundation of China under Grant 61671151 and 61728103.

Facial images carry many important features, such as eye shape, skin color, nose position and so on. In addition to the widely discussed single person face detection [11] and face recognition [16,20,23] problem, mining the relationships among multiple people in the image is a meaningful research area. Besides the visual features of human faces, some researchers also paid close attention to social context of the photos, including face location information, scene information, text information and so on. These context information can provide critical clues for the visually indistinguishable identification tasks. As a result, researchers proposed some methods to combine visual features with context information, such as probabilistic graphical model, Apriori algorithm [2]. These methods aim to find out the intrinsic relevance of the characters in the photos and improve identification accuracy.

As a common social relationship, kinship is established by blood relation and has the following two characteristics. First, people who have kinship render facial similarity so called "familiar features". Second, kinship has specific types. We can infer the specific kinship type between two people by jointly taking their age, sex and facial similarity information into consideration. Most importantly, kinship recognition has many potential applications, such as finding missing children, analyzing family photos and assisting criminal investigations [18].

Fang et al. contributed the pioneer work [7] to kinship verification in 2010. Since then, as a new research direction of face analysis, kinship verification has attracted more and more researchers [19,22,27]. They aimed to identify whether the kinship exists between a given pair of people or not. For a family, there are specific types of kinship among family members. Through identifying kinship between each pair of individuals in the family, we can construct the relationship of entire family members and get the description of family structure. In this paper, we call this family structure "family tree". However, there is little research in this area, possibly due to the limitation of publicly available family photo databases and great challenges of this problem.

Motivated by the aforementioned problems of prior works, in this paper, we introduce a graph based method for family tree construction using family album set. Our work can be divided into three parts: face clustering, parents-child kinship identification and family tree construction. Through face clustering, the facial images of each person and the node number of family tree are obtained. Then, we identify parents-child core relationship and construct the skeleton of family tree. After that, a graph model is used to construct and adjust family tree. Finally, pinpoint the position of each family member in the family tree. The general framework of our method is illustrated in Fig. 1.

There are three main contributions in our work. First, we collect a family album dataset from real-world social network. Our dataset contains 60 families, including more than 5000 images, and each family album has nearly 100 images. Second, an album based face clustering method is introduced, which can overcome environmental disturbances and provide contextual information. Lastly, for family relationship recognition, we jointly verify parents-child together with family tree construction through a graph model. In this way, the shared information between different pairs can build a reliable family relationship network.

In the rest of the paper, we discuss some related works in Sect. 2, and describe the proposed method in Sect. 3. Experimental results are provided in Sect. 4. Section 5 is conclusion.

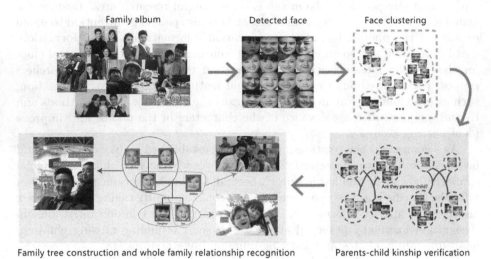

Fig. 1. Framework of our album based family tree construction method. There are three key steps: face clustering, arent-child kinship verification and family tree construction.

2   Related Work

Kinship recognition aims to determine whether a pair of people have kinship or not. If exists, analyzing the specific type they have. In recent years, kinship recognition has received more and more attention in machine learning and computer vision fields. There are three major tasks in kinship recognition area:

1. Kinship verification. Kinship verification is a binary classification task, which judge whether a given pair of people have kinship or not.
2. Kinship recognition. Different from kinship verification, kinship recognition is a multi-class classification task, which aims to identify the specific kinship type for a given pair of people with unknown kinship.
3. Family classification. Family classification treats a whole family as a class. It will retrieve the families for the test face from the training data.

In general, kinship verification method can be divided into three categories: subspace learning, matric learning and deep learning. Due to internal differences between children and parents, and external factors such as lighting, expression and poses, general image feature descriptors, such as local binary patterns (LBP) [1] and histogram of oriented gradient (HOG) [4] are incapable of solving this task alone.

Subspace learning attempts to map the original high-dimensional feature to a low-dimensional subspace. Where the feature similarity increases for facial images with kinship and those without kinship decreases. Yan et al. [29] mentioned a middle-level feature learning based method, which used a large scale unsupervised dataset LFW [10] and a small scale kinship dataset to learn middle-level feature. They wanted to get more semantic information from original images to improve recognition results. Xia et al. [26,28] introduced a transfer subspace learning method to bridge the gap between source and target distributions by finding an intermediate distribution.

Metric learning is the most widely used method for kinship verification. Lu et al. [14] proposed a Neighborhood Repulsed Metric Learning (NRML) method to learn a distance metric, in which facial images with kinship are projected as close as possible while the irrelevant ones as far as possible. They also proposed Multiview NRML (MNRML) method to find an universal distance metric for feature fusion.

Compared with low level feature, deep learning can provide more discriminative features. Kohli et al. [13] mentioned a Filtered Contractive Deep Belief Networks (fcDBN), which is a stack of multiple Restricted Boltzmann Machines. Experimental result on the CornellKin [7], UBKinFace [21], [26], KFW-I [14], KFW-II [14] datasets indicates that the proposed method has a remarkable promotion.

Kinship recognition aims to find the specific kinship type among all family members, which is the most related work to our family tree construction. Guo et al. [9] predicted family kinship graph by using a fully connected graph model and pairwise kinship relation. In comparison to pairwise classification results, graph model can share structure information and coordinate all pairwise kinship in the family. However, the number of candidate graphs increase dramatically when family people number larger than 4.

While there have been a few methods proposed recently to approach kinship recognition, they are still far from practical needs. On the one hand, the community lacks large-scale and complete family image dataset. Currently, the largest dataset is FIW [18], but in this dataset, images of a family may be taken a few years apart, and thus bring in age errors. On the other hand, the facial appearance difference between parents and children poses great challenges for the kinship algorithms. We may refer to some extra information beyond facial images for help.

3   Method

Visual facial images are easily affected by different factors, such as lighting condition, facial expressions and poses, and thus it is very difficult to obtain a satisfactory result by using a single family photo to analyze kinship relation. In the era of "Big Data", we tend to collect multiple family photos of the same event or family (e.g., users uploaded several family photos for the same holiday event in an album). We start from family album and build family tree through: (1) face clustering, (2) kinship verification and (3) graph model building. For a family album, people show up in different groups, but their union formulate the whole family album (with everyone in there). We treat family relationship structure as a family tree, and each photo in the family album as a branch of family tree. Ultimately, our goal is to achieve a complete family tree and the position of each family member in the tree by combining deformable part model method with the coordination between different branches. We will detail these methods in the following sections.

3.1 Context Based Face Clustering Algorithm

The first step for family tree construction is to go through the album and clustering whole facial images into different classes by characters. A good clustering result can help us to determine the number of family members, which has a great impact on the following results. To that end, we propose a novel clustering algorithm that considers both cluster number and the co-occurrence context within family album for a better face clustering task. Our method is built on a clustering algorithm "Chinese Whisper" (CW) [3] which was introduced by Biemann to solve natural language processing problem at first. It can automatically determine cluster numbers. In addition, since there are numbers of images in the album and each image contains multiple faces, we can use co-occurrence information [30] to adjust clustering results along with CW model. There are two main constraints. Firstly, faces appearing in the same photo should belong to different classes. This is based on the fact that a person can only appear once in a photo, which is a strict restriction. We call this "Dis-Connect constrains". Then, if the co-occurrence information of two classes are highly similar, we may consider these two classes as the same class. This is based on the phenomenon that people tend to take photos with the same group, which is a non-strict proposal. We call this "Connect proposal". We add these two constraint information to CW clustering method, the improved algorithm is listed in Algorithm 1.

We may also refer to other popular clustering methods and follow the same pipeline to design face clustering algorithm. For example, Density-Based Spatial Clustering of Applications with Noise (DBSCAN) clustering algorithm [5] and Affinity Propagation (AP) clustering algorithm [8] are also suitable for our problem. DBSCAN is a density-based clustering algorithm, which finds out all the core objects according to the given neighborhood parameters, and then uses any core object as a starting point to gather the samples whose density is reachable into a cluster. AP clustering algorithm treats all nodes in the graph as potential cluster centers at the beginning and classify data points according to the similarity between them. Specially, the cluster centers of AP are existing data point. For face image clustering in family albums, we can also add the context constraints discussed before to these two clustering methods. For each face, we use FaceNet [20] to extract a 128 dimensional whole face feature. Experiments result in Sect. 4.2 shows the improvements of context information to origin clustering methods.

3.2   Parents-Child Kinship Verification

After collecting the number of family members and facial images of each of them from face clustering, we are allowed to get access to multiple images of each person from different photos, which can help us overcome the random disturbance. Then, we start kinship verification from the most discriminative type: parent-child relation. In this step, we only identify whether a given pair of people are parent-child or not. After we verify this kin relation, other kinship categories such as grandparent-grandchildren and sibling-sibling can be inferred through the built family tree.

Algorithm 1. Constrained Chinese Whisper algorithm for album face clustering

---

1: **Input:** Face image set $F = \{f_1, f_2, \ldots, f_n\}$, Constraint information set $\mathbf{D}$, Number of iterations N, Similarity threshold *threshold*
2: **Output:** Class division $\{C_1, C_2, \ldots, C_k\}$
3: Construct undirected graph $G = (V, E), V = \{v_i, \ldots, v_n\}, v_i \leftarrow f_i$
4: **for all** nodes in the graph **do**
5:     **if** $sim(f_i, f_j) > threshold$ **and** $\{f_i, f_j\} \notin D$ **then**
6:         $e(i, j)$ exist, add v_j to $Neibor(v_i)$
7:     **end if**
8: **end for**
9: Take each sample as a class $v_i \leftarrow C_i$
10: **for** $iter = 1, \ldots, N$ **do**
11:     **for all** nodes in the graph **do**
12:         **if** ite=1 **then**
13:             $C_i \leftarrow \arg\max_{C_j} \|Neibor(v_j)\| \{v_j | \forall v_j \in Neibor(v_i)\}$
14:         **else**
15:             $\forall v_j \in Neibor(v_i)$, if $\{v_k | \forall v_k \in Neibor(v_i), j \neq k, C_j = C_k\}$
16:             Then $\|Neibor(v_j)\| + = \|Neibor(v_k)\|$
17:             $C_i \leftarrow \arg\max_{C_j} \|Neibor(v_j)\| \{v_j | \forall v_j \in Neibor(v_i)\}$
18:         **end if**
19:     **end for**
20: **end for**
21: **Combine classes according to Connect proposal**

We first estimate age and sex information for each cluster. The age and sex estimation results for the person with plenty of images usually have a high degree of confidence. For the cluster with small samples, we can further use existing information in the family and kinship constraint rules to adjust the estimation results. Then, we utilize these information to generate all the possible couple pairs and the corresponding candidate children.

There have been some researches for album based face recognition [12, 25, 31] and most of them use feature learning or dictionary learning. However, these two methods are separated because some discriminative information used in dictionary learning may be destroyed by feature learning and vice versa. To solve this problem, Lu et al. [15] mentioned Simultaneous Feature and Dictionary Learning (SFDL) method, which jointly learned feature and dictionary from primitive face image pixels. In this paper, we use features of the couples to construct dictionary and regard a child as a sample to be searched for. In this way, we can find the best matched parents for a child and build parents-child relationship.

Motivated by the biological process of inheritance. Fang et al. [6] divided a face image into 12 facial parts and built kinship recognition model using facial parts rather than whole face image. Taking the differences between multiple face images in the album into consideration, we choose eyebrows, eyes, face, nose, mouth and chin 6 facial parts. Figure 2 is an illustration of facial parts.

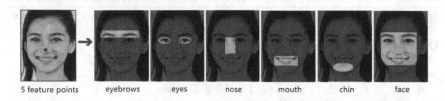

Fig. 2. Facial parts segmentation, including eyebrows, eyes, face, nose, mouth and chin 6 parts.

We treat a couple as a whole and use their images to build facial part library, we do this for every possible couple in the family. Then we try to find a closest couple for a child by regarding his(her) image as a sample to be searched for. More specifically, we extract 6 facial parts from all the image set and use the method in [6] to extract feature, then, construct a corresponding dictionary D(p) for each facial part p. For children image, we can search each facial part feature in the corresponding dictionary to obtain a best reconstruction, because each part of his(her) face is a dynamic combination of their parents. We use Sparse Group Lasso algorithm [6] to solve this problem, which can be described as follows:

$$\arg\min_{\alpha} \|y - D\alpha\|_2^2 + \lambda_1 \sum_{j=1}^{M} \|\alpha_{G_j}\|_2 + \lambda_2 \|\alpha\|_1 \tag{1}$$

where y is face feature vector to be sreached, D is all the features in the dictionary, M is the number of couples in the dictionary, $\alpha = [\alpha_{G_1}, \alpha_{G_2}, \ldots, \alpha_{G_M}]$ is the reconstruction weights in M pairs of couples. $\lambda_1 \sum_{j=1}^{M} \|_2$ is the combination of ℓ_1 and ℓ_2 norms. For all of the α_{G_j} in the α, we choose the couple with the highest reconstruction weights as the parents of the child being searched.

So far, we can find the best matching parents for a given child. If both husband and wife have their own parents, we can find their parents in the same way. Once the grandparent-parent-child relationship established, the skeleton of a family tree are also formed.

3.3   Graph Based Family Tree Construction

We use a directed graph $G = (V, E)$ to describe a family tree, where nodes $V = \{v_1, ..., v_n\}$ represent family member set, edge $e_{ij} = (v_i, v_j) \in E$ represent the directional link between node v_i and node v_j. The link e_{ij} means there are parents-child relation between v_i and v_j, v_i corresponding to parents and v_j corresponding to child. Location information of nodes can be described as $L = \{l_1, ..., l_n\}$, where $l_i (i = 1, ..., n)$ corresponding to node v_i. In this way, we can construct a family tree by maximizing the following energy function:

$$E(v_1, ..., v_n) = \sum_{i=1}^{n} P_i(l_i) + \sum_{ij}^{n} C_{ij}(l_i, l_j) \tag{2}$$

where $P_i(l_i)$ represent the possibility of putting v_i in position l_i, $C_{ij}(l_i, l_j)$ represent the compatibility of arranging v_i, v_j in l_i, l_j respectively.

$P_i(l_i)$ describe the confidence of arranging face v_i in position l_i, where we use face feature as measures. Suppose n is the number of family member, the face feature sets of all family member is $F = [f_1, f_2, ..., f_n]$, the face feature of the input face v_i is f_i, the corresponding class of position l_i is C_i. $P_i(l_i)$ is the confidence of arranging feature l_i in the class C_i, which is equivalent to the conditional probability $P(f_i|C_i)$. We can use Mahalanobis distance to measure the distance between f_i to the class center μ_{C_i} as follows

$$D = \log(det|V_{C_i}|) + (f_i - \mu_{C_i})^T \cdot V_{C_i}^{-1} \cdot (f_i - \mu_{C_i}) \tag{3}$$

$$\mu_{C_i} = \frac{1}{|C_i|} \sum_{1 \le j \le |C_i|} f_j \tag{4}$$

where μ_{C_i} is the center point of class C_i, V_{C_i} is its covariances matrix.

We use range transform to map the distance D to probability P as follows:

$$P = 1 - \frac{D - min(D)}{max(D) - min(D)} \tag{5}$$

Then, let us consider $C_{ij}(l_i, l_j)$. $C_{ij}(l_i, l_j)$ is the compatibility of arranging v_i, v_j in l_i, l_j, respectively, which lies in (1) kinship constraint rules, (2) age and gender information, (3) co-occurrence information three factors. The kinship constraint rules are listed in Table 1. The age difference between two adjacent generations should be between 18 and 40 years old, while in the same generation should less than 20 years old.

As defined above, the best position for the whole family people can be described as:

$$L^* = \arg\max_{L} (\sum_{i=1}^{n} P_i(l_i) + \sum_{ij}^{n} C_{ij}(l_i, l_j)) \tag{6}$$

Solving Eq. (6) is a NP-hard problem. But we can get some efficient solution by defining G as a tree. To meet this requirement, we take a pair of parents as a whole and regard parents-child relation as the only connection between nodes.

Table 1. Kinship constraint rules

• A child has only one pair of parents	(A-B: Parents-Child) $\Rightarrow \neg$ (C-B: Parents-Child)
• Parents of husband and wife are differ	[(A-B: Parents-Son) $\wedge$ (A-C: Parents-Daughter)] $\Rightarrow \neg$(B-C: Husband-Wife)
• Siblings of husband and wife are differ	[(A-B: Siblings) $\wedge$ (A-C: Siblings)] $\Rightarrow \neg$(B-C: Husband-Wife)
• Siblings have the same parents	[(A-B: Parents-Child) $\wedge$ (A-C: Parents-Child)] $\Rightarrow$ (B-C: Siblings)
• Siblings have the same sibling	[(A-B: Siblings) $\wedge$ (A-C: Siblings)] $\Rightarrow$ (B-C: Siblings)

Now, we consider energy function. For leaf node v_j, its only connection is parent node v_i. To calculate its energy function, we only need to take parent node v_i and edge (v_i, v_j) into consideration. The energy function of leaf node at position l_j can be defined as:

$$E_j(l_j) = \max_{l_j} P_i(l_i) + C_{ij}(l_i, l_j) \tag{7}$$

We further consider the nodes except for root node. We define the node we are paying attention to as v_j, its parent node as v_i and its child nodes as $v_c \in Ch_j$. Suppose the energy of its child node v_c is $E_c(l_j)$. We can get the energy of v_j as:

$$E_j(l_j) = \max_{l_j} P_i(l_i) + C_{ij}(l_i, l_j) + \sum_{v_c \in Ch_j} E_c(l_j) \tag{8}$$

For node v_j, the best position l_j can be calculated by:

$$l_j{}^\star = \arg \max_{l_j}(P_j(l_j) + C_{ij}(l_i, l_j) + \sum_{v_c \in Ch_j} E_c(l_j)), v_j \in (V \setminus \{v_r\}) \tag{9}$$

Finally, we consider root node v_r. There are no parent node for root node. Similarity, the best position l_r can be calculated by:

$$l_r{}^\star = \arg \max_{l_r}(P_j(l_j) + \sum_{v_c \in Ch_r} E_c(l_r)) \tag{10}$$

Above all, we can solve this problem by recursive function and dynamic programming method. By maximizing the energy function, we can get the best position of each node, the family tree are also formed. From family tree, we can get the relationship between each pair of people on the tree. For example, we know A→B is father→son, A→C is father→son, we can infer B↔C is sibling↔sibling. Other types of kinship can also be inferred like this.

4   Experiment

In this section, the effects of our context based face clustering method are tested on Gallagher dataset and our own dataset respectively. Then, the performance of family tree construction method is evaluated.

4.1   Datasets

So far, public available datasets related to kinship include UBKinFace [21,26], Family101 [6] and Family in the Wild (FIW) [18]. These datasets can be classified into family structure datasets and non-family structure datasets according to whether there is a family relationship or not. For non-family structure datasets, KinFaceW [14] (including KFW-I and KFW-II) is the largest, which were widely used in kinship verification. For family structure datasets, FIW is the largest labeled dataset, which contains 1000 families including more than 30000 images and 11 types of kinship. The detail information of these databases are listed in Table 2.

Table 2. A review of kinship datasets

Dataset	Family number[a]	People number	Face number
CornellKin [7]	×	300	300
UBKinFace-I [21]	×	180	270
UBKinFace-II [26]	×	400	600
KFW-I [14]	×	1066	1066
KFW-II [14]	×	2000	2000
Family101 [6]	101	607	14816
Siblings [24]	×	184	1158
Group-Face [9]	106	-	395
TSKinFace [17]	×	2589	-
FIW [18]	1000	10676	30725

[a] × means non-family structure datasets, ignore family number item

The family structure datasets containing more than 4 family members are Family101 and FIW. Nevertheless, in FIW, images of a family may be taken a few years apart, and thus bring in age errors. We take the photo contributor as the representative of the family album. These photos may include his(her) father, mother, couple, sibling and children. We carefully collected photos to ensure a appropriate family scale and album size for learning tasks. Finally, we choose 30 families from FIW and search their origin images on the internet again, besides we collect another 30 families to construct our dataset. Our dataset contains 60 families including 5896 images and each family have at least 50 images. More than 90 percent families contain three generations. Classical family tree structure

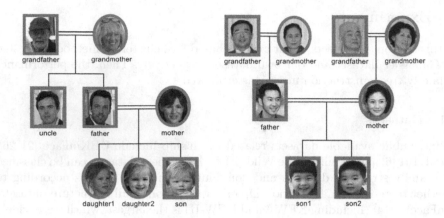

Fig. 3. Two examples of classical family tree structure.

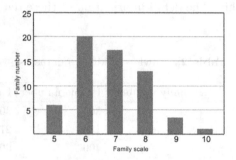

Fig. 4. Family size distribution in our dataset.

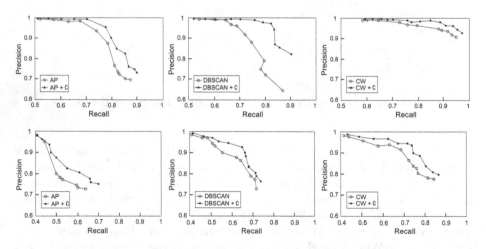

Fig. 5. A comparison of three different clustering methods on Gallagher dataset and our own dataset. 'C' means constraint information. Compared with original algorithm, constraint information can improve clustering performance.

Fig. 6. An example of the improvement of constraint information to face clustering result. The left part shows the adjustment of multi-person clustered into single class, while the right part shows the adjustment of single person clustered into multi-class.

and family size distribution of our dataset are shown in Figs. 3 and 4 respectively. Different from FIW, we keep the original image and provide human face position information to facilitate following research work.

4.2   Context Based Face Clustering Results

We take precision(P) and recall(R) as measurements of clustering method. A good algorithm should have both high precision rate and high recall rate. We test CW, DBSCAN and AP three different clustering method on Gallagher dataset and our own dataset and verify the effects of constraint information. Figure 5 is a comparison of different clustering methods. Experimental result shows that the constraint information can improve clustering effects. Specifically, Chinese

Table 3. The accuracy of 11 kinds of kinship

Kinship type	Before fixing %	After fixing %
Father-Son(F-S)	70.28	73.84
Father-Daughter(F-D)	63.56	71.30
Mother-Son(M-S)	65.84	76.21
Mother-Daughter(M-D)	60.17	75.96
Brother-Brother(B-B)	58.62	69.54
Sister-Sister(S-S)	54.28	68.97
Brother-Sister(B-S)	60.25	71.02
Grandfather-Grandson(GF-GS)	58.36	67.59
Grandfather-Granddaughter(GF-GD)	59.60	69.34
Grandmother-Grandson(GM-GS)	53.68	70.23
Grandmother-Granddaughter(GM-GD)	54.97	71.62
All types	59.96	71.42

Whisper clustering algorithm get the best performance on both datasets. Figure 6 shows an example of the adjustment of constraint information to face clustering result. The left part of the figure shows the situation of multi-person clustered into single class, while the right part is the situation of a single person clustered into multi-class.

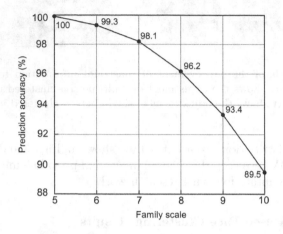

Fig. 7. Family member role prediction accuracy.

4.3   Kinship Recognition Results by Family Tree

Due to computational limitation, the method in [9] is unfit for the family in our dataset, the maximum number of people they can dealwith is four. So in this part, we test the effect of the graph model to family tree construction and kinship recognition results. Table 3 shows kinship classification results before and after the adjustment of graph model. The classification accuracy of all types of kinship rise from 59.96% to 71.42%. We further statistic the accuracy of family member role prediction among the family with different scales. The statistical results in Fig. 7 shows that our family tree structure get a excellent performance on the family with no more than 10 people.

5   Conclusions

In this paper, we proposed an effective method for family tree construction using a family album. Including face clustering, parents-child kinship verification and family relationship network construction three main steps. A family album dataset for family kinship recognition is introduced. Experiment results on the Gallagher dataset and our own dataset shows the effectiveness of our context based face clustering algorithm. Finally, our family tree based method gets an excellent performance on family network construction task, kinship classification results are also improved. In the future, we will combine our family tree structure model with transfer learning and generative adversarial network method to improve the performances of family kinship recognition.

References

1. Ahonen, T., Hadid, A., Pietikainen, M.: Face description with local binary patterns: application to face recognition. IEEE Trans. Pattern Anal. Mach. Intell. **28**(12), 2037–2041 (2006)
2. Bharadwaj, S., Vatsa, M., Singh, R.: Aiding face recognition with social context association rule based re-ranking. In: IEEE International Joint Conference on Biometrics, pp. 1–8 (2014)
3. Biemann, C.: Chinese whispers: an efficient graph clustering algorithm and its application to natural language processing problems. In: The Workshop on Graph Based Methods for Natural Language Processing, pp. 73–80 (2006)
4. Dalal, N., Triggs, B.: Histograms of oriented gradients for human detection. In: IEEE Computer Society Conference on Computer Vision & Pattern Recognition, pp. 886–893 (2005)
5. Ester, M.: A density-based algorithm for discovering clusters in large spatial databases with noise, pp. 226–231 (1996)
6. Fang, R., Gallagher, A., Chen, T., Loui, A.: Kinship classification by modeling facial feature heredity (2013)
7. Fang, R., Tang, K.D., Snavely, N., Chen, T.: Towards computational models of kinship verification. In: IEEE International Conference on Image Processing, pp. 1577–1580 (2010)
8. Frey, B.J., Dueck, D.: Clustering by passing messages between data points. Science **315**(5814), 972–976 (2007). https://doi.org/10.1126/science.1136800. http://science.sciencemag.org/content/315/5814/972
9. Guo, Y., Dibeklioglu, H., Maaten, L.V.D.: Graph-based kinship recognition. In: International Conference on Pattern Recognition, pp. 4287–4292 (2014)
10. Huang, G.B., Mattar, M., Berg, T., Learned-Miller, E.: Labeled faces in the wild: a database for studying face recognition in unconstrained environments. Month (2007)
11. Jain, V., Learned-Miller, E.: FDDB: A Benchmark for Face Detection in Unconstrained Settings (2010)
12. Kim, T.K., Kittler, J., Cipolla, R.: Discriminative learning and recognition of image set classes using canonical correlations. IEEE Trans. Pattern Anal. Mach. Intell. **29**(6), 1005 (2007)
13. Kohli, N., Vatsa, M., Singh, R., Noore, A., Majumdar, A.: Hierarchical representation learning for kinship verification. IEEE Trans. Image Process. **26**(1), 289–302 (2016)
14. Lu, J., Zhou, X., Tan, Y.P., Shang, Y., Zhou, J.: Neighborhood repulsed metric learning for kinship verification. In: Visual Communications and Image Processing, pp. 331–45 (2016)
15. Lu, J., Wang, G., Deng, W., Moulin, P.: Simultaneous feature and dictionary learning for image set based face recognition. In: Fleet, D., Pajdla, T., Schiele, B., Tuytelaars, T. (eds.) ECCV 2014. LNCS, vol. 8689, pp. 265–280. Springer, Cham (2014). https://doi.org/10.1007/978-3-319-10590-1_18

16. Parkhi, O.M., Vedaldi, A., Zisserman, A.: Deep face recognition. In: British Machine Vision Conference, pp. 41.1–41.12 (2015)
17. Qin, X., Tan, X., Chen, S.: Tri-subject kinship verification: understanding the core of a family. IEEE Trans. Multimed. **17**(10), 1855–1867 (2015)
18. Robinson, J.P., Shao, M., Wu, Y., Fu, Y.: Family in the wild (FIW): a large-scale kinship recognition database (2016)
19. Robinson, J.P., Shao, M., Zhao, H., Wu, Y., Gillis, T., Fu, Y.: Recognizing families in the wild (RFIW): data challenge workshop in conjunction with ACM MM 2017. In: Proceedings of the 2017 Workshop on Recognizing Families in the Wild, pp. 5–12. ACM (2017)
20. Schroff, F., Kalenichenko, D., Philbin, J.: FaceNet: a unified embedding for face recognition and clustering. In: IEEE Conference on Computer Vision and Pattern Recognition, pp. 815–823 (2015)
21. Shao, M., Xia, S., Fu, Y.: Genealogical face recognition based on UB kinface database, pp. 60–65 (2011)
22. Shao, M., Xia, S., Fu, Y.: Identity and kinship relations in group pictures. In: Fu, Y. (ed.) Human-Centered Social Media Analytics, pp. 175–190. Springer, Cham (2014). https://doi.org/10.1007/978-3-319-05491-9_9
23. Taigman, Y., Yang, M., Marc, Wolf, L.: DeepFace: closing the gap to human-level performance in face verification. In: IEEE Conference on Computer Vision and Pattern Recognition, pp. 1701–1708 (2014)
24. Vieira, T.F., Bottino, A., Laurentini, A., Simone, M.D.: Detecting siblings in image pairs. Vis. Comput. **30**(12), 1333–1345 (2014)
25. Wang, R., Shan, S., Chen, X., Gao, W.: Manifold-manifold distance with application to face recognition based on image set. In: IEEE Computer Society Conference on Computer Vision and Pattern Recognition, pp. 1–8 (2008)
26. Xia, S., Shao, M., Fu, Y.: Kinship verification through transfer learning. In: International Joint Conference on Artificial Intelligence, pp. 2539–2544 (2011)
27. Xia, S., Shao, M., Fu, Y.: Toward kinship verification using visual attributes. In: 2012 21st International Conference on Pattern Recognition (ICPR), pp. 549–552. IEEE (2012)
28. Xia, S., Shao, M., Luo, J., Fu, Y.: Understanding kin relationships in a photo. IEEE Trans. Multimed. **14**(4), 1046–1056 (2012)
29. Yan, H., Lu, J., Zhou, X.: Prototype-based discriminative feature learning for kinship verification. IEEE Trans. Cybern. **45**(11), 2535 (2015)
30. Zhang, L., Kalashnikov, D.V., Mehrotra, S.: A unified framework for context assisted face clustering. In: ACM Conference on International Conference on Multimedia Retrieval, pp. 9–16 (2013)
31. Zhu, P., Zuo, W., Zhang, L., Shiu, C.K., Zhang, D.: Image set-based collaborative representation for face recognition. IEEE Trans. Inform. Forensics Secur. **9**(7), 1120–1132 (2014)

Robust Multimodal Image Registration Using Deep Recurrent Reinforcement Learning

Shanhui Sun[1], Jing Hu[2], Mingqing Yao[2], Jinrong Hu[2],
Xiaodong Yang[2], Qi Song[1], and Xi Wu[2]

[1] CuraCloud Corporation, Seattle, USA
[2] Department of Computer Science, Chengdu University of Information Technology,
Chengdu 610225, People's Republic of China
xi.wu@cuit.edu.cn

Abstract. The crucial components of a conventional image registration method are the choice of the right feature representations and similarity measures. These two components, although elaborately designed, are somewhat handcrafted using human knowledge. To this end, these two components are tackled in an end-to-end manner via reinforcement learning in this work. Specifically, an artificial agent, which is composed of a combined policy and value network, is trained to adjust the moving image toward the right direction. We train this network using an asynchronous reinforcement learning algorithm, where a customized reward function is also leveraged to encourage robust image registration. This trained network is further incorporated with a lookahead inference to improve the registration capability. The advantage of this algorithm is fully demonstrated by our superior performance on clinical MR and CT image pairs to other state-of-the-art medical image registration methods.

Keywords: Multimodal image registration · Reinforcement learning · Reward function · Lookahead inference

Supported in part by the National Natural Science Foundation of China under Grant 61602065, Sichuan province Key Technology Research and Development project under Grant 2017RZ0013, Scientific Research Foundation of the Education Department of Sichuan Province under Grant No. 17ZA0062; J201608 supported by Chengdu University of Information and Technology (CUIT) Foundation for Leaders of Disciplines in Science, project KYTZ201610 supported by the Scientific Research Foundation of CUIT.
S. Sun and J. Hu—Contributed equally to this paper.

Electronic supplementary material The online version of this chapter (https://doi.org/10.1007/978-3-030-20890-5_33) contains supplementary material, which is available to authorized users.

© Springer Nature Switzerland AG 2019
C. V. Jawahar et al. (Eds.): ACCV 2018, LNCS 11362, pp. 511–526, 2019.
https://doi.org/10.1007/978-3-030-20890-5_33

1   Introduction

Image registration is a basic yet important pre-process in many applications such as remote sensing, computer-assisted surgery and medical image analysis and processing. In the context of brain registration, for instance, accurate alignment of the brain boundary and corresponding structures inside the brain such as hippocampus are crucial for monitoring brain cancer development [1]. Although extensive efforts have been made over three decades, image registration remains an open problem given the complexity clinical situations faced by the algorithms.

The core of image registration is to seek a spatial transformation that establishes pixel/voxel correspondence between a pair of fixed and moving images under rotation, scaling and translation transformation condition. Conventionally, the mapping between two images is obtained by minimizing an objective function with regard to some similarity criterion [1]. Therefore, two factors are fundamental: image feature representations and similarity measure [2]. Common image features include gradient, edge, geometric shape and contour, image skeleton, landmark, response of Gabor filter, or the intensity histogram. Recently, local invariant features have been widely applied to image registration [3]. As for similarity measure, sum-of-squared-differences, correlation coefficient, correlation ratio and mutual information are commonly used [4]. Three-dimensional extensions of these similarity measures have also been proposed to facilitate medical image registration.

Regarding the complexity of visual appearance of an image in presence of noise, outliers, bias field distortion, and spatially varying intensity distortion, defining the above-mentioned two factors appropriately is a challenging task. Although extensive studies have been carried out on the design of these two factors, they are somewhat designed manually and cannot be quite adaptable in the wide range of image modalities [1,4,5]. To this end, inspired by the success of neural architectures and deep learning for their strong semantic understanding, several works have generated image feature or similarity metric from scratch by using a deep convolutional neural network, without attempting to use any hand-crafted formations [6–10].

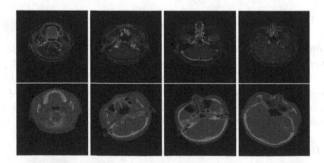

Fig. 1. Varying human anatomy in 2D multimodal image registration. Top: MR images (fixed image). Bottom: CT images (moving image). The goal of image registration is to align the moving image to the fixed image.

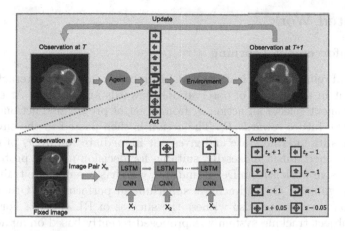

Fig. 2. Overview of our proposed framework. The upper part illustrates a sequential decision making driven by the agent who interacts with environment. The environment produces next observation image. The left bottom part depicts registration agent using CNN-LSTM network. The right bottom shows action types.

Recently, another type of approaches has also been proposed with focus on predicting registration parameters directly [5]. High parameter dimensionality and the non-linearity between image appearance and registration parameters render predictions non-trivial. More specifically, high dimensionality of data and parameter space (e.g. nine degree-of-freedom) challenge 3D medical image registration; while the challenges of 2D medical image registration are huge variability in appearances and shapes as indicated in Fig. 1.

Within the notion of the third type, we cast image registration as a sequential decision-making framework, in which both feature representations and similarity metric are implicitly learned from deep neural networks. An overview of our framework is shown in Fig. 2. An artificial agent explores the space of spatial transformation and determines the next best transformation parameter at each time step. Unlike other similar image registration methods that either use pre-trained neural network or learn the greedy exploration process in a supervised manner [11,12], our method explores the searching space freely by using a multithread actor-critic scheme (A3C). Our major contributions are:

- We present a novel reinforcement learning (RL) framework for image registration utilizing a combined policy and value network. This actor-critic network can explore transformation parameter spaces freely, thereby avoiding the local minima when a pose is far from initial displacement.
- To the best of our knowledge, this is the first RL-based image registration method that handle similarity transformation. To cope with the transformation parameter unit discrepancy, we introduce a new reward function driven by landmark error. Experiments also suggest that using such reward function helps convergence.
- A Monte Carlo rollout strategy is performed as a look-ahead guidance in the test phase, whose "terminating" prediction is not trivial due to unknown terminal states.

2   Related Work

2.1   Reinforcement Learning

In a classical reinforcement learning (RL) framework, an agent interacts with an environment in a sequence of observations, rewards and actions. At each time-step t, the agent selects an action a_t from a set of pre-defined actions, so as to maximize the future rewards R_t. The action is then passed to the environment and modifies its internal state and gives out immediate reward r_t of this input action. This mechanism makes RL suitable for decision-making problems. The most impressive work is from DeepMind [13], who has been able to train an agent to play the game of Go and achieve superhuman performance. Other research fields in computer vision also witness the success of RL [14–18]. For instance, an active object tracking system was proposed recently based on an actor-critic reinforcement learning model [16], and this kind of actor-critic model was also validated to be effective in an image captioning scenario [17].

In general, there are two types of RL methods: on-policy and off-policy. The former includes Sarsa, n-step method and actor-critic method and the latter includes Q-learning. In this paper, the framework of actor-critic is adopted. More specifically, the policy function is called an actor, which takes actions based on the current policy $\pi(a_t|s_t; \theta)$; the value function is called a critic, which serves as a baseline to evaluate the quality of the action by returning the state value $V(s_t; \theta_v)$ for the current state under policy π. To reduce the variance in policy gradient, an advantage function $A(a_t; s_t) = R_t - V(s_t; \theta_v)$ is used for action a_t at state s_t, where the expected future return R_t is calculated as a discounted sum of future rewards up to T time steps with discount factor $\gamma \in (0, 1]$: $R_t = \sum_{t'=t}^{t+T-1} \gamma^{t'-t} r_{t'}$. Parameters θ of policy network and parameters θ_v of value network are updated as follows:

$$\theta \leftarrow \theta + \tau \nabla_\theta \log \pi(a_t|s_t; \theta)(R_t - V(s_t; \theta_v)) + \beta \nabla_\theta H(\pi(s_t; \theta)) \tag{1}$$

$$\theta_v \leftarrow \theta_v - \frac{1}{2}\tau \nabla_{\theta_v}(R_t - V(s_t; \theta_v))^2 \tag{2}$$

where τ is the learning rate, $H(\cdot)$ is the entropy and β is a regularization factor.

Among the actor-critic frameworks, A3C [19] is the one that employs asynchronous parallel threads. Multiple threads run at the same time with unrelated copies of the environment, each generating its own sequences of training samples and maintaining an independent environment-agent interaction. The network parameters are shared across the threads and updated every T time steps asynchronously using Eqs. (1) and (2) in each thread. A3C is reported to be fast yet stable [16].

2.2   Image Registration

Early image registration processes can be roughly classified into two types: intensity-based methods and feature-based methods. The former, focusing on the image's gray spaces, maximizes the similarity between pixel intensities to determine the alignment between two images. Cross correlation and mutual information are considered to be gold standard similarity measures for this kind of methods. The latter extracts salient invariant image features and uses the correlation between those features to determine the optimal alignment. The main difficulty of early registration methods comes from the great variability of image when captured by different physical principles and environments, which translates in the lack of a general rule for images to be represented and compared. Motivated by the great advancement in computer vision triggered by deep learning technologies like convolutional neural networks (CNNs), several researchers have proposed to apply such techniques to the field of image registration. For example, Wu *et al.* [8] combined CNN with independent subspace analysis, the learned image features were then used to replace the handcrafted features in HAMMER registration model. Simonovsky *et al.* [7] employed CNNs to estimate a similarity cost between two patches from differing modalities.

Recently, another way to formulate image registration problem is to directly predict transformation parameters [5]. Based on large deformation diffeomorphic metric mapping (LDDMM) registration framework, Yang *et al.* [20] designed a deep encoder-decoder network to initialize the momentum value for each pixel and then evolved over time to obtain the final transformation. Miao *et al.* [21] proposed a CNN-based regression approach or 2D/3D images, in which the CNNs are trained with artificial examples generated by manually adapting the transformation parameters for the input training data. However, this method requires a good initialization in proximity to the true poses. Liao *et al.* [11] formulated image registration as a sequential action learning problem and leveraged supervised learning to greedily choose alignment action at each exploration step for the sake of huge parameter searching space and the comparatively limited training data. However, the greedy searching may not be global optimal. Ma *et al.* [22], the most relevant work to ours, extended work [11] via Q-learning framework trained using reinforcement learning. Although this work manages to search the transformation parameter space freely, a huge amount of state-action histories have to be saved during training. This becomes challenging when extended to 3D medical image registration.

3   Method

3.1   Problem Formulation

Let $\mathbf{I}_f$ be a fixed image and $\mathbf{I}_m$ be a moving image. The task of image registration is to estimate the best spatial similarity transformation T_t from $\mathbf{I}_m$ to $\mathbf{I}_f$. T_t is parameterized by 4 parameters with 2 translations $[t_x, t_y]$, one rotation α and one scaling s:

$$T_t\left(t_x, t_y, s, \alpha\right) = \begin{bmatrix} s\cos\alpha & -s\sin\alpha & t_x \\ s\sin\alpha & s\cos\alpha & t_y \end{bmatrix} \tag{3}$$

As illustrated in Fig. 2, we formulate this image registration problem as a sequential decision making process that at each time step, the agent decides

Table 1. Details of the combined policy and value network structure. C16-8-S4 represents 16 feature maps of convolution 8 × 8 kernel with stride 4. FC256 indicates fully connected layer with 256 output dimensions. LSTM256 indicates that the dimension of all the elements (hidden state and input node) in the LSTM unit is 256.

Layer	1	2	3	4	5	6
Parameter	C16-8-S4	C16-4-S2	C32-4-MS-2	FC256	LSTM256	Policy (8)/Value (1)

which variable in T_t should be altered so that the moving image can be sequentially aligned to the fixed image. This process is modeled as a Markov Decision Process (MDP) with (S, A, r_t, γ), where S is a set of states and A is a set of actions, r_t is the reward function the agent receives when taking a specific action at a specific state, γ is the discount factor that controls the importance of future rewards. In contrast to previous work [11] and [22], we solved MDP in the framework of actor-critic using a new state approximation network, a novel reward function and a novel inference procedure. We focus on learning the policy function π via deep reinforcement learning. More specifically, a new deep neural network is devised as a non-linear function approximator for π, where action a_t at time t can be drawn by $a_t \sim \pi(s_t; \theta)$, where s_t is composed of $\mathbf{I}_m$ and $\mathbf{I}_f$ at time t.

3.2   State Space Approximation and Action Definition

In work [11] and [22], state space is approximated using CNN and thereby neighbouring frames are not considered in the process of decision making. In our work, we utilize CNN to encode image states and a long short-term memory (LSTM) recurrent neural network to encode hidden states between neighbouring frames. Figure 3 illustrates overview of the proposed network architecture. The input of the network is a concatenation of $\mathbf{I}_m$ and $\mathbf{I}_f$. The LSTM layer has two output (FC) layers: policy function, $\pi(s_t; \theta)$ and state value function, $v(s_t; \theta_v)$. Table 1 illustrates the details of our neural network. Each convolutional layer as well as the fully connected layer are followed by a eLU activation function. The action space consists of 8 candidate transformations that lead to the change of ±1 pixel in translations, ±1° for rotation, and ±0.05 for scaling. At time t, after the selection of action a_t by the agent, the transformation matrix T_{t+1} becomes $a_t \circ T_t$.

3.3   Reward Definition

Given a certain state, a reward is generated to reflect the value of current selected action. The definition of reward is somehow a tricky concept, as it mimics human learning. A wrong definition of reward will lead, with a high probability, to unsatisfactory learning results [23]. It is a natural intuition for most deep learning-based image registration methods that the reward function should encourage the transformation matrix, generated from the sequential actions made by the

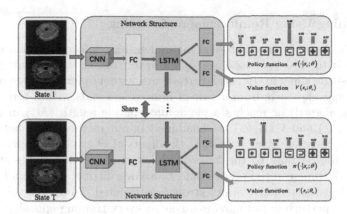

Fig. 3. The architecture of the proposed neural network. The network weights are shared for each LSTM unroll step and LSTM unroll T times in our work.

agent, to be closed to the ground truth. Therefore, the reward function in work [11] and [22] is inversely proportional to Euclidean distance between these two matrices.

However, considering scaling effect causes parameter unit discrepancy in our framework, since the scaling is in a comparatively small unit, and its parameter change is only ± 0.05 whereas the parameter change for translation and rotation is ± 1. This implies that the Euclidean distance for scaling in two transformation matrices can be small, despite the rotation and translation being large. There-fore, a large reward is still obtained even scaling is not well registered. Although using a scalar to weight the contribution between scaling and other two parameters can mitigate this effect, the value of scalar should be carefully tuned. Instead of fine-tuning a specific weight function, we alternatively using landmark error to define the reward function. In our method, the key-points selected by scale invariant feature transform (SIFT) features [24] are viewed as landmarks. These landmark reference set $\mathbf{p}_G$ are computed from the ground truth of moving image. Afterwards, they are warped ($\tilde{\mathbf{p}}_G$) using the perturbation transformation matrix. Then, for each action a_t, the warped landmarks are transformed back using T_{t+1}. The Euclidean distance D between the transformed landmarks and the corre-sponding ground truth is used to define the reward for action a_t:

$$r_t = -D = -\frac{1}{\#\{\mathbf{p}_G\}} \sum_i \|p_i - \tilde{p}_i \circ T_{t+1}\|_2, p_i \in \mathbf{p}_G, \tilde{p}_i \in \tilde{\mathbf{p}}_G \qquad (4)$$

where p_i and $\tilde{p}_i$ are the landmark points, $\circ$ denotes the align operator, $\#\{\}$ calculates the number of points. In addition, if D is smaller than a threshold, we assume that the terminal is triggered, and a terminal reward is set in this situation.

3.4   Training Using Reinforcement Learning

We train the agent in an end-to-end manner using reinforcement learning algorithm similar to A3C proposed in [19]. However, rather than running different copies of a single game in [19], each thread runs with a different image pair in our work. The episode starts from a pair of images and ends with a terminal state (image pair aligned) or reaches a maximum episode length (M_e) in our work. Since $\pi\left(\cdot\left|s_t;\theta\right)\right.$ and $V\left(s_t;\theta_v\right)$ are combined in our method, parameters of the agent are represented by $\Theta = \{\theta,\theta_v\}$. Gradients of Θ are backpropagated from the actor-critic outputs to the lower-level layers. Note that different training episodes with similar initial poses would cause over-fitting, since small change of actions make two successive states strongly correlated. To handle this problem, we randomly perturb initial moving image at every training episode.

3.5   Training Using Supervised Learning

For better comparison, we also train the neural network (to more specific, the policy network) via supervised learning. Under this strategy, the agent at each time step selects the "optimal" action a_t that has the minimal distance for the new transformation $a_t \circ T_t$ to the ground truth transformation T_g among all the legal actions. Recall that in reinforcement learning, the action a_t is selected according to the output probability distribution over all legal actions. Therefore, in supervised learning strategy, only the shortest path for action space is explored.

To train the neural network, the policy network $\pi\left(\cdot\left|s_t;\theta\right)\right.$ is trained by minimizing cross entropy loss: $-\sum_{t=1}^{T}\log\pi\left(a_t\left|s_t;\theta\right)\right.$ and the value network $V\left(s_t;\theta_v\right)$ is trained by minimizing the mean squared loss $\left(R_t - V\left(s_t;\theta_v\right)\right)^2$.

3.6   Inference with Monte Carlo Rollout

For training, the agent learns a registration policy that maps the current state to the optimal action. For inference in test, the agent applies the learned policy to approach the correct alignment. The stopping criteria in test phase is based on value network prediction $v_t \geq trs$, where v_t is a predict value at time t and trs is a value threshold close to the terminal reward. However, it is not trivial to find a good trs from the critic network as a termination since terminal state is unknown in the test phase, so this value can only be determined empirically on training data with new random perturbations. But, we often observe that either transformation parameters jitter around specific values or the terminal is not reachable in the test phase. To handle this challenge, a Monte Carlo (MC) method is proposed in the test phase to simulate multiple searching paths, so as to predict a better action. Note that we only perform MC rollout when v_t reaches trs; otherwise the action is the one that with a highest policy probability.

To perform MC rollout, a number N_{mc} of trajectories are simulated from the state s_t, whose $v_t \geq trs$, with a fixed searching depth D_{mc}. For each trajectory i, the agent at first randomly selects an action, then subsequent actions $a_{t'}$ are chosen following $a_{t'} \sim \pi(s_{t'}; \theta)$ and at the same time obtained the corresponding values by value network. Suppose that the trajectory i finally gets a transformation matrix with parameters $[t_{xi}, t_{yi}, s_i, \alpha_i]$. Moreover, accumulating the values along trajectory i obtains the total path value $V_i = \sum_{ri=t}^{t+D_{mc}} v_{ri}$, where ri is an explored node at trajectory i. We computed the final parameters each based on weighted average:

$$[t_x, t_y, s, \cos\alpha, \sin\alpha] = \frac{1}{\sum_{i=1}^{N_{mc}} V_i} \sum_{i=1}^{N_{mc}} V_i \times [t_{xi}, t_{yi}, s_i, \cos\alpha_i, \sin\alpha_i], \quad (5)$$

where α can be computed from $\cos\alpha$ and $\sin\alpha$. The idea behind this formula is that it forms a Monte Carlo importance sampling along different trajectories [26], and the empirical mean results an approximation to the expected value.

4   Experiment and Results

Dataset. In this paper, we apply our proposed framework to multi-modality image registration problem. The dataset used in our experiment contains 100 paired axis view MR images and CT images each from 99 patients diagnosed as nasopharyngeal carcinoma. The original CT and MR images have different resolutions, i.e. CT has the resolution of $0.84 \times 0.84 \times 3$ mm and MR has the resolution of $1 \times 1 \times 1$ mm. In term of image preprocessing, these CT images were resampled to an isotropic resolution of 1 mm. In addition, since the ground truth alignment of these two data modalities is unfortunately not easily obtainable, the standard of alignment is estimated using an off-the-shelf toolbox Elastix [27] for the sake of efficiency. More specifically, the MR image is treated as a fixed image while the CT image is treated as a moving image. Pre-registration for all MR and CT pairs for the same patient was carried out in 3D by Elastix with standard parameters. Taking into consideration that adjacent slices are strongly correlated, only six slices out of 100 are selected for each modality to exhibit considerable variation between images, which ends up with 594 MR-CT pairs for our experiments.

We randomly selected 79 patients as the training data resulting 474 image pairs, and 20 patients as testing data resulting 120 image pairs. In training stage, at each episode, the moving images are randomly perturbed with translation $[-25, 25]$ pixels with a step 1 pixel for x and y axes respectively, a rotation $[-30°, 30°]$ with a step $1°$, and a scaling factor $[0.75, 1.25]$ with a step 0.05. The training procedure thus sees 160000 initial image pairs (20000 training episodes $\times$ 8 threads). For testing, two data sets were generated using different moving image perturbation distribution. Each moving image has 64 perturbations. As a result, we have 7680 image pairs in each data set. "E_1" is a data set consisting of moving images that are perturbed using the same perturbation priors as those used for generating training data. "E_2" is a data set consisting of moving images that are perturbed using a larger range: translation $[-30, 30]$ pixels for x and y axes respectively, a rotation $[-45°, 45°]$, and a scaling factor $[0.75, 1.25]$. All the training images and testing images are resized to 168×168 in our experiments.

Methods Used for Comparison. To evaluate the effectiveness of our method, we compare it with a SIFT-based image registration method [24], a pure SL method (named as "pure SL") which contains a feedforward network with CT and MRI as inputs and transformation matrix as output (used a same CNN network architecture as in our RL model), as well as several variations of the proposed framework so as to demonstrate our contributions in agent training, reward function and lookahead inference. Recall that in our method the policy and value networks are trained by RL (named as "RL"), a landmark error based method is proposed for reward function (named as "LME"), and Monte Carlo rollout strategy is used for prediction in the last step (named as "MC"). Three corresponding substitutes are also used in later experiments, including agent trained with SL (named as "SL"), reward function calculated by the transformation matrix distance (named as "matrix"), and no lookahead inference. In general, the methods used in our experiments are: [SIFT, pure SL, RL-matrix, SL-matrix, RL-matrix-MC, SL-matrix-MC, RL-LME, SL-LME, RL-LME-MC (the proposed method), SL-LME-MC]. Note that in all experiments, target registration error (TRE) is used as a quantitative measure, which is the distance after registration between corresponding points not used in transformation matrix calculation [25].

Training and Testing Details. We trained the agent with 8 asynchronous threads, and with the Adam optimizer at an initial learning rate of 0.0001, $\gamma = 0.99$ and $\beta = 0.1$. Training episodes had the maximum length of 20000 cycles, and the maximum length (M_e) of each episode is 500 steps. Each episode is terminated whenever the agent reaches a distance terminal (in terms of landmark error or transformation matrix error) or the maximum episode length. The distance threshold for terminal is 1 for both kinds of errors, and the terminal reward in RL training is 10. The boostrapping length (the network weights updating frequency) in training procedure is 30. Each thread randomly selects a new training image pair at every two episodes. Stopping thresholds trs are RL-LME: 10, RL-LME-MC: 9, SL-LME: -0.05 and SL-LME-MC: -0.1. We also applied these thresholds to their "matrix" counterparts. For MC rollout methods, simulation number $N_{mc} = 20$ and searching depth $D_{mc} = 10$.

Evaluation and Results. We evaluated the models and inference variants (w/o MC) on datasets E_1 and E_2, respectively. Table 2 summarizes the quantitative results. It is clear that all the deep-learning based image registration methods significantly outperform the method using SIFT. It is important to note that our method is far better than pure SL, which makes sense because the distance between the moving image and fixed image is so large that a direct regression learned by the latter is not feasible. The improved performance by SL-matrix, SL-matrix-MC and SL-LME suggests that using discrete action step by step is beneficial for the "bad" registration scenario. Table 2 also proves that these three components, including model "RL", LME-based reward function and predication strategy, all contribute to the good performance of the proposed method. Furthermore, the proposed method is also compared with Elastix, which is used

Table 2. Evaluation of methods on different datasets (E_1 and E_2) in terms of TRE. The statistics mean (μ), standard deviation (std), median (50th) and 90% percentile (90th) are performed. The bold numbers indicate the best performer in that column. Note that 2D Elastix results may exist bias due to it was performed using the same cost function as ground truth generation algorithm.

	E_1			E_2		
	$\mu \pm std$	50th	90th	$\mu \pm std$	50th	90th
SIFT	11.79 ± 9.81	9.04	19.99	12.15 ± 9.89	9.13	20.06
Elastix	$\mathbf{1.31 \pm 1.06}$	**0.91**	**2.46**	2.33 ± 1.86	**1.07**	5.33
Pure SL	4.59 ± 3.00	3.72	8.28	6.62 ± 5.11	5.11	13.12
SL-matrix	2.29 ± 2.92	1.81	3.77	2.99 ± 4.72	2.04	4.83
SL-matrix-MC	2.88 ± 4.52	2.12	4.39	3.58 ± 13.20	2.20	5.17
SL-LME	2.60 ± 6.62	1.34	3.15	3.06 ± 7.12	1.41	4.35
SL-LME-MC	3.10 ± 41.67	1.09	3.03	3.16 ± 20.69	1.19	4.20
RL-matrix	1.59 ± 1.61	1.32	2.96	1.95 ± 3.55	1.40	3.41
RL-matrix-MC	1.31 ± 1.64	1.00	2.38	1.81 ± 8.00	**1.07**	3.21
RL-LME	1.66 ± 1.56	1.30	3.12	1.91 ± 2.39	1.41	3.61
RL-LME-MC (Ours)	1.39 ± 1.45	0.98	2.59	$\mathbf{1.66 \pm 2.30}$	1.08	**3.17**

as a gold standard to pre-align the original MR-CT pairs for our experiments. Although we have found that this software can obtain a very accurate alignment for each image pair, the deformation between original MR-CT is in fact not severe. Is Elastix still a gold standard for our method when it applies to a more challenging data, i.e. the testing dataset used in our experiment, is worth looking into. Therefore, we performed a 2D version Elastix registration on E_1 and E_2. Note that 2D Elastix may yield registration results closer to ground truth, since the same cost function is used as the one used for ground truth generation. Such a comparison is made and summarized in Table 2. A visual comparison is also presented in Fig. 4. We can see that Elastix fails to register images with large deformation whereas our method is more robust to the challenging cases.

5   Discussion

From the above experiments, it is clear that the proposed RL-LME-MC image registration framework is more powerful and robust than the other methods, which validates the effectiveness of the advocated three components. But, besides these three factors, the network architecture (CNN+LSTM) is also worth looking into. In this section, the importance of LSTM is firstly discussed. After that, the above-mentioned three components of our proposed are respectively analyzed. Last, we also talk about the difference between our method and Elastix.

5.1   Network Architecture Analysis

Although there are several image registration methods that have been proposed
so far, to the best of our knowledge, only one work that handles registration
problem using RL solely. A Dueling Network framework was used in their work,
focusing on learning the action value for the agent. Our method, however, alternatively uses A3C to learn both action probability and state value for the agent.
In this way, there is no need for our method to use a replay-memory that hinders
the future application of RL to 3D image registration in case of high dimensionality. But, lacking replay-memory requires our neural network should be elegant
enough to obtain a good feature representation that facilitates neural network
training.

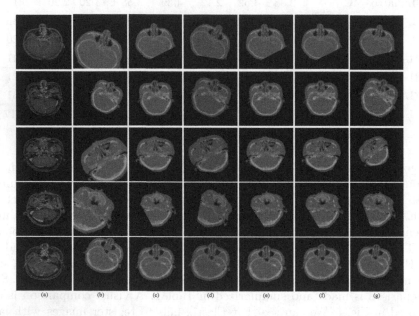

Fig. 4. Examples of registration results. (a) Fixed image, (b) Initial moving image, (c)
Ground truth poses, results of (d) Elastix (e) SL-matrix, (f) RL-LME-MC (Ours), (g)
Pure SL.

A CNN-LSTM network is proposed in this paper, where the LSTM is leveraged to learn the information (hidden state) among consecutive frames that
are correlated in fact. A natural question is "how important is LSTM for our
method". To answer it, we trained a new neural network that substitutes LSTM
with FC128 (named as "CNN-LME"). Figure 5(a) and (b) compares this new
network with our proposed one in terms of agent's speed reaching terminals
and cumulative reward per episode. Clearly, incorporating LSTM into CNN
facilitates a more efficient and stable convergence. We believe such efficiency
attributes to the capability of LSTM unit that takes into account historical

states when producing output. In addition, CNN-LME-MC results 2.61 ± 3.19 pixels on E_1 and 3.52 ± 5.70 pixels on E_2 in terms of TRE (mean±standard deviation). This result is worsen than our approach.

5.2 Impacts of Three Components in Our Method

Model RL. To assess the merits of RL, it is compared with a SL-based network using the same architecture. Although there are several reasonable doubts about the assert that RL surpasses SL, we have found in our study that using RL achieved higher registration accuracy than all the cases using SL, as reflected in Table 2. It should be noted that the advantage for RL is more obvious when handling E_2, the perturbation of which is larger than the training data. This implies that by exploring more path enables RL a very strong learning ability and generalization ability.

Reward Function. Reward function is a fundamental factor in RL. Although in Table 2, no significant improvement of quantitative score is observed by using LME over matrix. It is even worse, in certain cases, that using LME obtained lower scores (see the third and fourth rows in Table 2 for details). However, we have found in our pilot study that for the model CNN-LME, if its reward function is changed into matrix, this new model (CNN-matrix) fails to converge and in fact very unstable within the same number of training steps, as shown in Fig. 5(c) and (d). Although so far the mechanism behind this phenomenon is uncertain, it, on the hand, proves that defining a proper reward function can somewhat compensate for a weak network architecture.

Lookahead. According to Table 2, it is slightly better for a RL neural network than its SL counterpart to be embedded with a prediction step. This is possibly due to the reason that the action selected at each time step in RL is towards the goal of maximizing the future return. Incorporating a prediction step to RL would reinforce such intendancy. On the contrary, SL follows a greedy strategy that only considers the local optimal action. Hence, using a lookahead strategy implies averaging actions from future time steps, which would be highly likely to worsen the "optimal" situation compared with using the action at one time step. In addition, for "MC", we made an early stopping (smaller ths) for compensating Monte Carlo computation expense. However, if the agent is stopped "too" early, using MC rollout may not reach an optimal solution. Due to this, an increased standard deviation can be observed at method RL-matrix-MC on E_2 data set. But, relaxing the threshold will address this problem.

5.3 Comparison with Elastix

Elastix [27] is a state-of-the-art medical image registration software that has been widely used in several research projects and it is still under active development. Both 2D and 3D image registration frameworks are provided, only dissimilar at

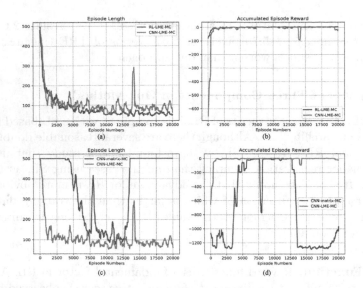

Fig. 5. Learning curves for different models. Steps per episode when agents reach terminals for (a) RL-LME vs CNN-LME and (c) CNN-matrix vs CNN-LME. Cumulative rewards per episode for (b) RL-LME vs CNN-LME and (d) CNN-matrix vs CNN-LME.

image processing part. Based on the observation that Elastix performs well when the pose of moving image is in proximity to the fixed image's, its 3D version is used to generate the ground truth for our experiment. In comparison, the 2D Elastix could provide us a good reference to understand our method, although its results would be biased since it has a similar framework to the 3D algorithm. On data set E_1, 2D Elastix outweighs others. However, on data set E_2, where we observed the pose of moving image is far from fixed image's, i.e. a large part of image missed, or in other words, a large portion is out of field of view, Elastix algorithm fails to fulfill the alignment task, as reflected in experiment results (Fig. 4 and Table 2). Quantitatively, Elastix performs much worse than our approach in terms of 90% percentile on this large range testing data set. This is because Elastix is basically a least square optimization, and thereby is not robust to outliers and lack of high-level semantics understanding (e.g. parts, shapes and temporal context) which is crucial for robust alignment. In contrast, our proposed method performed similar on E_1 in terms of mean, standard deviation, median and 90% percentile statistics of TRE, but much better on E_2. This implies that our method is able to perform semantic understanding as well as extrapolation although perturbation range is not included in the training prior.

6   Conclusion

In this paper, we present a new learning paradigm in the context of image registration based on reinforcement learning. Different from previous work that also build upon reinforcement learning, our method devised a combined policy network and value network to respectively generate the action probability and state value, without the need of extra storage on exploration history. To learn this network, we use a state-of-the-art reinforcement learning approach A3C with a novel landmark error based reward function. A Monte Carlo rollout prediction step is also proposed to further improvement. We evaluate our method with image slices from MR and CT scans, and find that our method achieves state-of-the-art performance on standard benchmark. Detailed analyses on our method are also conducted to understand its merits and properties. Our future work includes the sub-pixel image registration, extension to 3D registration, as well as the generalization to other computer vision problems.

References

1. de Vos, B.D., Berendsen, F.F., Viergever, M.A., Staring, M., Išgum, I.: End-to-end unsupervised deformable image registration with a convolutional neural network. In: Cardoso, M.J., et al. (eds.) DLMIA/ML-CDS -2017. LNCS, vol. 10553, pp. 204–212. Springer, Cham (2017). https://doi.org/10.1007/978-3-319-67558-9_24
2. Zhao, C., Zhao, H., Lv, J., Sun, S., Li, B.: Multimodal image matching based on multimodality robust line segment descriptor. Neurocomputing **177**, 290–303 (2016)
3. Liao, S., Chung, A.C.S.: Feature based nonrigid brain MR image registration with symmetric alpha stable filters. IEEE Trans. Med. Imaging **29**, 106–119 (2010)
4. Razlighi, Q.R., Kehtarnavaz, N., Yousefi, S.: Evaluating similarity measures for brain image registration. J. Vis. Commun. Image Represent. **27**, 977–987 (2013)
5. Litjens, G., et al.: A survey on deep learning in medical image analysis. Med. Image Anal. **42**, 60–88 (2017)
6. Uzunova, H., Wilms, M., Handels, H., Ehrhardt, J.: Training CNNs for image registration from few samples with model-based data augmentation. In: Descoteaux, M., Maier-Hein, L., Franz, A., Jannin, P., Collins, D.L., Duchesne, S. (eds.) MICCAI 2017. LNCS, vol. 10433, pp. 223–231. Springer, Cham (2017). https://doi.org/10.1007/978-3-319-66182-7_26
7. Simonovsky, M., Gutiérrez-Becker, B., Mateus, D., Navab, N., Komodakis, N.: A deep metric for multimodal registration. In: Ourselin, S., Joskowicz, L., Sabuncu, M.R., Unal, G., Wells, W. (eds.) MICCAI 2016. LNCS, vol. 9902, pp. 10–18. Springer, Cham (2016). https://doi.org/10.1007/978-3-319-46726-9_2
8. Wu, G., Kim, M., Wang, Q., Gao, Y., Liao, S., Shen, D.: Unsupervised deep feature learning for deformable registration of MR brain images. In: Mori, K., Sakuma, I., Sato, Y., Barillot, C., Navab, N. (eds.) MICCAI 2013. LNCS, vol. 8150, pp. 649–656. Springer, Heidelberg (2013). https://doi.org/10.1007/978-3-642-40763-5_80
9. Sokooti, H., de Vos, B., Berendsen, F., Lelieveldt, B.P.F., Išgum, I., Staring, M.: Nonrigid image registration using multi-scale 3D convolutional neural networks. In: Descoteaux, M., Maier-Hein, L., Franz, A., Jannin, P., Collins, D.L., Duchesne, S. (eds.) MICCAI 2017. LNCS, vol. 10433, pp. 232–239. Springer, Cham (2017). https://doi.org/10.1007/978-3-319-66182-7_27

10. Cao, X., et al.: Deformable image registration based on similarity-steered CNN regression. In: Descoteaux, M., Maier-Hein, L., Franz, A., Jannin, P., Collins, D.L., Duchesne, S. (eds.) MICCAI 2017. LNCS, vol. 10433, pp. 300–308. Springer, Cham (2017). https://doi.org/10.1007/978-3-319-66182-7_35

11. Liao, R., et al.: An artificial agent for robust image registration. In: AAAI, pp. 4168–4175 (2017)

12. Krebs, J., et al.: Robust non-rigid registration through agent-based action learning. In: Descoteaux, M., Maier-Hein, L., Franz, A., Jannin, P., Collins, D.L., Duchesne, S. (eds.) MICCAI 2017. LNCS, vol. 10433, pp. 344–352. Springer, Cham (2017). https://doi.org/10.1007/978-3-319-66182-7_40

13. Silver, D., et al.: Mastering the game of go with deep neural networks and tree search. Nature **529**, 484–489 (2016)

14. Bellver, M., Giró-i Nieto, X., Marqués, F., Torres, J.: Hierarchical object detection with deep reinforcement learning. arXiv preprint arXiv:1611.03718 (2016)

15. Caicedo, J.C., Lazebnik, S.: Active object localization with deep reinforcement learning. In: 2015 IEEE International Conference on Computer Vision (ICCV), pp. 2488–2496. IEEE (2015)

16. Luo, W., Sun, P., Mu, Y., Liu, W.: End-to-end active object tracking via reinforcement learning. arXiv preprint arXiv:1705.10561 (2017)

17. Ren, Z., Wang, X., Zhang, N., Lv, X., Li, L.J.: Deep reinforcement learning-based image captioning with embedding reward. arXiv preprint arXiv:1704.03899 (2017)

18. Tan, B., Xu, N., Kong, B.: Autonomous driving in reality with reinforcement learning and image translation. arXiv preprint arXiv:1801.05299 (2018)

19. Mnih, V., et al.: Asynchronous methods for deep reinforcement learning. In: International Conference on Machine Learning, pp. 1928–1937 (2016)

20. Yang, X., Kwitt, R., Niethammer, M.: Fast predictive image registration. In: Carneiro, G., et al. (eds.) LABELS/DLMIA-2016. LNCS, vol. 10008, pp. 48–57. Springer, Cham (2016). https://doi.org/10.1007/978-3-319-46976-8_6

21. Miao, S., Wang, Z.J., Liao, R.: A CNN regression approach for real-time 2D/3D registration. IEEE Trans. Med. Imaging **35**, 1352–1363 (2016)

22. Ma, K., et al.: Multimodal image registration with deep context reinforcement learning. In: Descoteaux, M., Maier-Hein, L., Franz, A., Jannin, P., Collins, D.L., Duchesne, S. (eds.) MICCAI 2017. LNCS, vol. 10433, pp. 240–248. Springer, Cham (2017). https://doi.org/10.1007/978-3-319-66182-7_28

23. Zhao, D., Hu, Z., Xia, Z., Alippi, C., Zhu, Y., Wang, D.: Full-range adaptive cruise control based on supervised adaptive dynamic programming. Neurocomputing **125**, 57–67 (2014)

24. Lowe, D.G.: Distinctive image features from scale-invariant keypoints. Int. J. Comput. Vis. **60**, 91–110 (2004)

25. Fitzpatrick, J.M., West, J.B.: The distribution of target registration error in rigid-body point-based registration. IEEE Trans. Med. Imaging **20**, 917–927 (2001)

26. Kocsis, L., Szepesvári, C.: Bandit based Monte-Carlo planning. In: Fürnkranz, J., Scheffer, T., Spiliopoulou, M. (eds.) ECML 2006. LNCS (LNAI), vol. 4212, pp. 282–293. Springer, Heidelberg (2006). https://doi.org/10.1007/11871842_29

27. Klein, S., Staring, M., Murphy, K., Viergever, M.A., Pluim, J.P.W.: Elastix: a toolbox for intensity-based medical image registration. IEEE Trans. Med. Imaging **29**, 196–205 (2010)

Image Super-Resolution Using Knowledge Distillation

Qinquan Gao[1], Yan Zhao[1], Gen Li[2], and Tong Tong[2(✉)]

[1] Fuzhou University, Fuzhou 350116, Fujian, China
{gqinquan,N161127032}@fzu.edu.cn
[2] Imperial Vision Technology, Fuzhou 350000, Fujian, China
{ligen,ttraveltong}@imperial-vision.com
http://www.fzu.edu.cn

Abstract. The significant improvements in image super-resolution (SR) in recent years is majorly resulted from the use of deeper and deeper convolutional neural networks (CNN). However, both computational time and memory consumption simultaneously increase with the utilization of very deep CNN models, posing challenges to deploy SR models in realtime on computationally limited devices. In this work, we propose a novel strategy that uses a teacher-student network to improve the image SR performance. The training of a small but efficient student network is guided by a deep and powerful teacher network. We have evaluated the performance using different ways of knowledge distillation. Through the validations on four datasets, the proposed method significantly improves the SR performance of a student network without changing its structure. This means that the computational time and the memory consumption do not increase during the testing stage while the SR performance is significantly improved.

Keywords: Super-resolution · Convolutional neural networks · Teacher-student network · Knowledge distillation

1 Introduction

Super-resolution (SR) is a classical problem in computer vision. It has important application value in monitoring equipment, satellite images, medical imaging and many other fields. Single image super-resolution (SISR) aims to recover a corresponding high-resolution (HR) image from a low-resolution (LR) image. SR is an ill-posed inverse problem since multiple HR images can be obtained from a given LR image. In traditional interpolation approaches such as bilinear interpolation, bicubic interpolation and so on, a fixed formulation is used to perform weighted averaging using the information of neighborhood pixels within the input LR images to calculate the losing information in the upscaled HR

This work has been supported by the Fujian Provincial Natural Science Foundation of China (2016J05157).

© Springer Nature Switzerland AG 2019
C. V. Jawahar et al. (Eds.): ACCV 2018, LNCS 11362, pp. 527–541, 2019.
https://doi.org/10.1007/978-3-030-20890-5_34

images. However, such interpolation approaches do not produce enough high-frequency details to generate sharp HR images.

In recent years, due to the rapid development of GPU and deep learning (DL) techniques, convolutional neural networks (CNN) are widely used to address the SR problem, and provide significantly improved performance in the reconstruction of HR images. As the pioneering work for SR using CNN, Dong et al. [2] proposed SRCNN which directly learns an end-to-end mapping between the input LR images and their corresponding HR images. SRCNN has successfully demonstrated that CNN-based approaches provide an effective way to solve the SR problem, and can reconstruct a large amount of high-frequency details for the HR images. Inspired by VGG-net [16], Kim et al. [8] proposed a Very Deep convolutional network for image Super-Resolution (VDSR). The network structure of VDSR is composed of 20 convolutional layers. Since a large number of convolutional layers are stacked in VDSR, a large amount of neighboring information within a large receptive field of LR images is used to predict the high-frequency information of HR images, resulting in more accurate reconstruction results than a shallow network. VDSR demonstrates that "the deeper the better" is also true in SR. Furthermore, much deeper SR networks were proposed in SRResNet [11] and SRDenseNet [19] respectively to obtain further improvement in SR.

Previous studies show that SR reconstruction performance can be significantly improved by increasing the depth of CNNs. However, the computational time and the memory consumption increase at the same time. In many practical scenarios using low-power devices such as mobile phones and some embedded terminals, the power consumption is a critical constrain in deploying deep CNN models. In addition, it is difficult to run very deep SR convolutional neural networks in realtime on these low-power devices. Deploying these state-of-the-art SR models in real-time applications remains a big challenge. This has stimulated research on the acceleration and compression of neural networks to develop energy-efficient CNN models. Knowledge distillation (KD) proposed by Hinton et al. [5] as a model compression framework that simplifies the training of deep networks by following teacher-student paradigm. The framework transfers knowledge from a deep network (refer to as teacher network) to a smaller network (refer to as student network). The student network is trained to predict the output of a teacher network. In a recent work [15], a strong teacher model was used to train a thin and deep model so that the process of network training can be improved. Not only the output of the teacher network but also the middle feature maps of the teacher network were used in [15] as learning targets in the loss function during the training.

In this paper, we propose to use knowledge distillation to improve the reconstruction performance of a student SR model under the constraint that it does not change the model structure of the student network and does not increase the computational time. Characteristics calculated from middle feature maps of a teacher network were propagated to the student SR network. As a result, the SR reconstruction of the student network is expected to be improved so that low-power devices such as mobile phones and some embedded terminals can efficiently run image SR model. Overall, the main contributions of this work are:

- First, this is the first work that utilizes the strategy of teacher-student network to transfer the knowledge from a teacher SR network to a student SR network, thereby greatly enhancing the SR reconstruction performance of the student network without changing its structure.
- Second, in order to determine the effective knowledge propagation from a teacher network to a student network, we have evaluated and compared multiple different ways of statistical map extraction. In the end, an optimal way is selected to propagate the teacher network's knowledge to the student network.
- Third, MobileNet is used for a student SR model. Compared to a teacher SR network, the student SR model requires less amount of computational resources, and can efficiently run on low-power mobile phones and embedded devices, thus providing a promising way to deploy SR models in a timely fashion on a computationally limited device.

Related studies are introduced in Sect. 2 and the proposed method is introduced in Sect. 3, followed by the experimental results and visual comparisons in Sect. 4. Finally, the paper concludes in Sect. 5.

2 Related Works

2.1 Image Super Resolution via Deep Learning

In SR problem, given a LR image, our goal is to reconstruct a SR image that is as similar as possible to its corresponding HR image. Recent studies using CNN have shown significantly improvement on SR. Dong et al. [2] first proposed to apply CNN in SR and referred to as SRCNN. Although the structure of SRCNN is very simple by using only three convolutional layers, it has demonstrate the successful application of CNN in SR. In [2], a bicubic interpolation was used to upscale the input LR images to the target spatial resolution. After that, an end-to-end mapping between the upscaled LR images and the corresponding HR images were learnt using CNN, which includes three steps: (a) patch extraction and representation: a convolutional layer was used to extract patches and to reshape them as high-dimensional vectors; (b) non-linear mapping: the high-dimensional vectors from the first step were nonlinearly mapped to another set of high-dimensional vectors; (c) in the end, these patches were used to generate the SR output.

FSRCNN was proposed in [3] to optimize and speed up SRCNN [2]. Instead of using bicubic interpolation as a preprocessing step in SRCNN [2], a deconvolutional layer was used at the end of the network to enlarge the image resolution. In this way, the interpolation preprocessing step was removed and an end-to-end mapping was directly learnt from the original low-resolution images to the high-resolution images. A compact hourglass-shape CNN structure was adopted in [3] to speedup the process of SRCNN. The input feature dimension was shrinked at the beginning of the network and was expanded back afterwards. In the end, the FSRCNN [3] has achieves a speed up of more than 40 times compared to SRCNN [2].

Kim et al. [8] proposed a very deep CNN structure that used 20 convolutional layers. The residual between the upscaled LR images and the HR images were calculated and used as training target in [8]. The LR images were upscaled using bicubic interpolation. Since LR images and HR images share a large amount of low-frequency details, the residual learning pushes the network to learn the high-frequency difference. The method of learning residual image between LR images and HR images is referred to as global residual learning by Tai et al. [17]. The global residual learning has been demonstrated to speed up the training process in [8]. In addition, the images and feature maps were zero padded in [8] before each convolutional operation, which ensures that all feature maps and the final output image have consistent same size. This can solve the problem that the image gets smaller and smaller after gradually convolutional operation.

SRResNet [11] was proposed to further improve SR reconstruction performance by adding more convolutional layers. The gradient vanishing problem in very deep super-resolution CNNs was effectively solved using the ResNet [4] structure. Lim et al. [12] proposed EDSR to optimize SRResNet [11] by removing the batch normalization layers, which are unnecessary modules for SR reconstruction. The original ResNet [4] was first proposed to address high-level computer vision tasks such as image classification and object detection. It may be not appropriate to directly apply the ResNet structure to low-level tasks such as super-resolution and other image restoration problems. After the batch normalization layers were removed, the EDSR stacked more convolutional layers than SRResNet and achieved superior restoration quality.

2.2 Knowledge Distillation

As we can see from the above section, the SR networks become deeper and deeper with the development of DL. In order to deploy SR on a computationally limited device, it is critical to compress the SR model and make it small but still effective. The teacher-student network, which is a type of transfer learning, provides one possible solution. The teacher network is generally a very deep CNN and has many convolutional layers, while the student network has a lightweight structure. The teacher network has much better performance than the student network. As a result, decisions or features calculated from the teacher network can be used to guide the training of the student network in order to improve the performance of the student network. Hinton et al. [5] first proposed this structure which they referred to as "knowledge distillation". In their method [5], "soft target" is first calculated from the teacher network. After that, the "soft target" added to replace traditional ground truth label as the training target during training the student network. It has been demonstrated that the image classification performance can be significantly improved in the MNIST dataset using this training strategy. Zagoruyko et al. [20] use the attention maps for knowledge distillation instead of soft targets. It has been demonstrated that the performance of a student CNN network can be significantly improved by forcing it to mimic the attention maps of a powerful teacher network [20]. However, the above studies focus on the high-level computer vision tasks, while the application of knowledge distillation on low-level tasks such as SR has been less studied and may have some problems. For example, the propagation of soft targets from a teacher network to a student network may not work in SR. In this work, we have investigated several way for the knowledge distillation process. As far as we know, this is the first work to apply knowledge distillation on image super-resolution task.

For SR, models with very deep CNNs such as SRResNet [11] or SRDenseNet [19] have shown good restoration performance, and can be a good choice for a teacher SR network. In order to make it possible to deploy SR models for mobile and embedded vision applications, MobileNet [6] was chosen in our work as the student SR network. MobileNet uses depthwise separable convolution to build a lightweight deep neural network and requires low computational resources. Its effectiveness has been shown on across a wide range of applications including object detection and image classification. It significantly reduces the size of the network, but maintains similar classification accuracies [6]. In our work, we have shown the successful application of MobileNet in image SR and used it as our student SR network. In addition, we also demonstrates that the student SR network based on MobileNet can be further improved by using the knowledge distillation strategy.

3   Method

In this section, we describe our method to show how we apply the teacher-student network in SR task. The structures of the teacher network for SR (TNSR) and the student network for SR (SNSR) are introduced in Sects. 3.1 and 3.2 respectively. After that, different feature maps are extracted from both networks and treated as the propagated knowledge. The propagation of knowledge from TNSR to SNSR is described in Sect. 3.3.

3.1   Structure of Teacher Network

The structure of our TNSR is shown in Fig. 1. It consists of three parts in the TNSR structure. The first part of TNSR is feature extraction and representation, which consists of a convolutional layer and a non-linear activation layer. The first part's operation $F_1(X)$ is formulated as:

$$F_1(X) = max(0, W_1 * X + B_1) \tag{1}$$

where W_1 and B_1 represent the weights and biases respectively in the first convolutional layer. W_1 consists of m filters with a spatial size of $f \times f$. '$*$' denotes the convolutional operation. X is the input LR image.

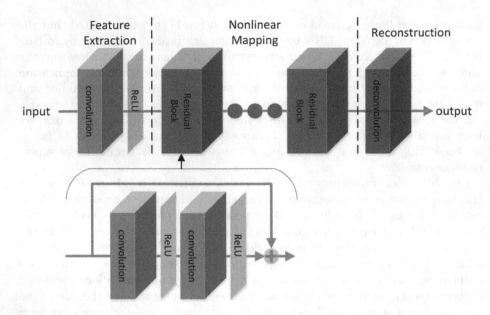

Fig. 1. The structure of the proposed teacher super-resolution network

The second part of TNSR is a non-linear mapping step, which consists of 10 residual blocks [4]. There are two convolutional layers in each residual block as shown in Fig. 1. Each convolutional layer is followed by a non-linear activation layer. A skip connection is used to sum up the input and the output feature maps of each residual block. In this way, only the residual information between the input and output of each residual block is learnt. By using the skip connections in TNSR, it can address the gradient vanishing problem in training a very deep network [4]. Each residual block can be formulated as:

$$F_{2n+1}(X) = max(0, W_{2n+1} * F_{2n}(X) + B_{2n+1}) + F_{2n-1}(X) \qquad (2)$$

where n represents the number of residual block. $F_{2n+1}(X)$ represents the output of each residual block. W_{2n+1} and B_{2n+1} are the weights and the biases respectively of the second layer in the residual block. $F_{2n}(X)$ denotes the output of the first convolutional layer and the non-linear activation layer in the residual block. $F_{2n-1}(X)$ are the input feature maps of the residual block.

The final part of TNSR uses a deconvolution layer to reconstruct the high-resolution output. In previous studies such as SRCNN [2] and VDSR [8], bicubic interpolation was used to upscale LR images into the high-resolution space, and then treated as the input of CNNs. Since all convolutional operations were performed in the high-resolution space, the computational complexity is very high. In addition, the interpolation preprocessing step may affect the SR reconstruction performance. As a result, a deconvolution layer was proposed in [3] to replace the interpolation operation and to learn the upscaling mapping between the LR images and the HR images. Recent works including LapSRN [10] and SRDenseNet [19] have also employed deconvolution layer to reconstruct the HR images. A deconvolution layer can be considered as an inverse operation of a convolution layer, and was generally stacked at the end of SR networks [3]. There are two advantages to use deconvolution layers for upscaling. First, it can accelerate the reconstruction process of SR. Since the upscaling operation is carried out at the end of the network, all convolutional operations are performed in the LR space. If the upscaling factor is r, it will approximately reduce the computational cost by r^2. In addition, a large amount of contextual information from LR images can be used to infer the high-frequency details since a large reception field is covered by adding the deconvolution layer at the end of SR networks.

3.2   Structure of Student Network

The structure of SNSR is shown in Fig. 2. SNSR includes three parts: the first part is a feature extraction layer and the final part consists of a deconvolution layer for reconstruction, which are the same as the TNSR. Inspired by the MobileNet work [6], three depthwise separable convolution blocks were used in the second part. Each block consists of a depthwise convolutional layer and a 1×1 convolutional layer called pointwise convolution. The depthwise convolutional layer applies a single filter to each input channel, while the pointwise convolution applies a 1×1 convolution to combine the outputs of the depthwise convolution. We removed the batch normalization layers from MobileNet [6] as this has been demonstrated not helpful for SR in previous studies [19]. Both depthwise convolution and pointwise convolution are followed by a nonlinear activation layer.

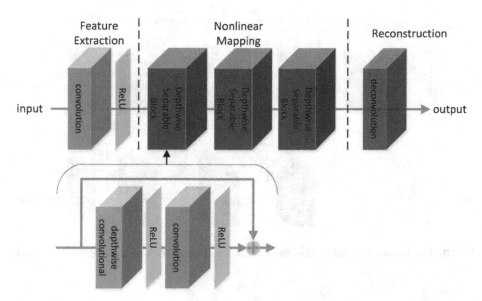

Fig. 2. The structure of the proposed student super-resolution network

If a 3×3 filter is used, the depthwise separable convolution block uses between 8 to 9 times less computation than a standard convolution according to the [6]. This can significantly save a large amount of computational resources with only a small reduction in accuracies on image classification and object detection [6].

3.3   Knowledge Distillation and Propagation

In order to propagate useful knowledge from a teacher network to a student network, statistical maps are extracted from TNSR and SNSR respectively. As shown in Fig. 3, statistical maps are calculated using the outputs of the 4th, 7th and 10th residual blocks of TNSR, and denoted as t_1, t_2 and t_3 respectively that described low-level, mid-level, high-level visual information. These maps represent characteristics in TNSR from low-level features to high-level features. In SNSR, we extract corresponding levels of statistical maps using the outputs of the first, second and third depthwise separable convolution blocks, denoting as s_1, s_2 and s_3 respectively. After that, we use the information in t_1, t_2, t_3 to guide the information s_1, s_2, s_3 during training SNSR. Statistical features are calculated from the middle outputs of networks rather than the direct use of the middle outputs. This has been shown more effectively in image classification [20] than a direct propagation of the middle outputs. The middle outputs of networks can be represented as a tensor $T \in R^{C \times H \times W}$ which consists of C feature channels with a spatial dimension of $H \times W$. A statistical map is then calculated from the tensor T:

$$G : T \in R^{C \times H \times W} \rightarrow S \in R^{H \times W} \tag{3}$$

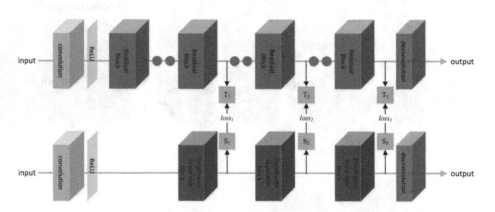

Fig. 3. The knowledge distillation from a teacher SR network to a student SR network

where G is a function to map the tensor outputs T to a statistical map $S \in R^{H \times W}$. In this work, four types of mapping functions are used for calculating the statistical map. The first mapping function is formulated as:

$$(G_{mean})^p(T) = (\frac{1}{i} \sum_{i=1}^{C} T_i)^p \tag{4}$$

where the average map of T is first calculated and raised to a power of $p \geqslant 1$. The second mapping function is formulated as:

$$(G^p)_{mean}(T) = \frac{1}{i} \sum_{i=1}^{C} (T_i^p) \tag{5}$$

where a power of $p \geqslant 1$ over T is first calculated. After that, the average is calculated as the statistical map for knowledge propagation. The maximum value across C channels of feature maps in T is calculated as another type of statistical map:

$$G_{max}(T) = max_{i=1,C} T_i \tag{6}$$

In addition, the minimum value across feature maps in T is also calculated as a statistical map:

$$G_{min}(T) = min_{i=1,C} T_i \tag{7}$$

During training the student network, the statistical maps s_1, s_2, s_3 extracted from SNSR are forced to be as similar as the statistical maps t_1, t_2, t_3 extracted from TNSR. In addition, the SR reconstructed image is forced to be similar as the original HR image. Therefore, the total loss for training SNSR can be formulated as:

$$loss = loss_0(\widetilde{Y}, Y) + \lambda_1 loss_1(s_1, t_1) + \lambda_2 loss_2(s_2, t_2) + \lambda_3 loss_3(s_3, t_3) \tag{8}$$

where λ_i is the weight of $loss_i$. $loss_0$ calculates the loss between the reconstructed image $\widetilde{Y}$ and the the original HR image Y. $loss_1$, $loss_2$ and $loss_3$ represent the losses between the statistical maps of SNSR and TNSR. Instead of using mean square errors as the loss function, a robust loss called the Charbonnier penalty function is adopted to handle outliers [10] and defined as:

$$\mathcal{L}_{cha}(Y, \widetilde{Y}) = \sqrt{(Y - \widetilde{Y})^2 + \epsilon^2} \tag{9}$$

where ϵ is set to 0.001 empirically. The Charbonnier loss function is applied to calculate all losses in Eq. 8.

4   Experiments and Results

4.1   Datasets and Metrics

We used publicly available benchmark datasets for training and testing. Both the DIV2K [18] dataset and the Flickr2K dataset [18] were used for training. The DIV2K dataset consists of 800 images and the Flickr2K dataset consists of 2650 images. During testing, the Set5 dataset [1] and the Set14 dataset [21] are often used for SR benchmarks. In addition, the BSD100 dataset [13] from Berkeley segmentation dataset and the Urban100 dataset [7] dataset were also included for testing. The peak signal-to noise (PSNR) was used to evaluate the SR reconstruction result. Since the SR model was trained using the luminance channel in YCbCr space, the PSNR was calculated on the Y-channel only in our work.

4.2   Implementation Details

Non-overlapping patches were cropped from LR images with a size of 40×40 for training. LR images were obtained by downsampling the HR images using bicubic interpolation. Each image has been transformed into YCbCr space and only the Y-channel was used for training. In TNSR, the filter size of convolutional layers was set to 3×3, and the number of feature maps was set to 64. In SNSR, the filter size of depthwise convolution layer was set to 3×3, and the number of output channels were set to 64. All experiments used Adam [9] for optimization during training. The learning rate was set to a fixed value 0.0001, and the batch-size was set to 32. The training process stopped after no improvements of the loss was observed after 500000 iterations. A NVIDIA Titan X GPU was used for training and testing.

4.3   Important of Different Level of Feature Maps

We have analyzed the importance of different feature maps in the process of knowledge distillation. Different weights in Eq. 8 were set for comparison study. The results are show in Table 1. As shown in the results, the propagation of information from first and second feature maps have significantly improve the SR reconstruction performance, while the third feature maps have negative effect on the results. This indicates that the high level features (third part) may not be useful in a low-level computer vision task (super-resolution in our case). Therefore, we used the first part and the second part as feature maps for knowledge distillation in the following experiments.

4.4   Comparison of Different Ways for Knowledge Distillation

We have compared the performance using different statistical maps for knowledge distillation. Four statistical maps were generated using Eq. 4 where the power coefficient was set to 1, 2, 3 and 4 respectively. These statistical maps

Table 1. The results of SNSR is guided by TNSR with different weights

Operation	scale	Set5	Set14	BSDS100	Urban100
bicubic	×3	30.49	27.55	27.21	24.46
TNSR	×3	34.13	30.10	28.95	27.62
SNSR	×3	32.07	28.90	28.08	25.49
$\lambda_0 = 1, \lambda_1 = 1, \lambda_2 = 0, \lambda_3 = 0$	×3	32.39	29.13	28.22	25.79
$\lambda_0 = 1, \lambda_1 = 0, \lambda_2 = 1, \lambda_3 = 0$	×3	32.39	29.13	28.22	25.79
$\lambda_0 = 1, \lambda_1 = 1, \lambda_2 = 0, \lambda_3 = 1$	×3	32.17	28.98	28.12	25.62
$\lambda_0 = 1, \lambda_1 = 1, \lambda_2 = 1, \lambda_3 = 0$	×3	32.38	29.12	28.23	25.79
$\lambda_0 = 1, \lambda_1 = 1, \lambda_2 = 0, \lambda_3 = 1$	×3	32.22	29.03	28.18	25.69
$\lambda_0 = 1, \lambda_1 = 0, \lambda_2 = 1, \lambda_3 = 1$	×3	32.29	29.07	28.19	25.72
$\lambda_0 = 2, \lambda_1 = 1, \lambda_2 = 1, \lambda_3 = 0$	×3	**32.43**	29.14	**28.25**	**25.82**
$\lambda_0 = 2, \lambda_1 = 1, \lambda_2 = 0, \lambda_3 = 1$	×3	32.27	29.03	28.17	25.68
$\lambda_0 = 2, \lambda_1 = 0, \lambda_2 = 1, \lambda_3 = 1$	×3	32.32	29.08	28.21	25.74
$\lambda_0 = 1, \lambda_1 = 1, \lambda_2 = 1, \lambda_3 = 1$	×3	32.30	29.05	28.19	25.73
$\lambda_0 = 3, \lambda_1 = 1, \lambda_2 = 1, \lambda_3 = 1$	×3	32.38	**29.16**	**28.25**	25.81

were represented as (G_{mean}), $(G_{mean})^2$, $(G_{mean})^3$ and $(G_{mean})^4$ in our work. Another three statistical maps were generated using Eqs. 5, 6 and 7, and were denoted as $(G^2)_{mean}$, G_{max} and G_{min} respectively. The same statistical maps were extracted from both the teacher network and the student network. During training SNSR, the statistical maps of SNSR were forced to be as similar as those of TNSR using the loss function as described in Eq. 8. In addition, the propagation of original feature maps were also carried out for comparison. Figure 4 shows the performance of SNSR in terms of PSNR using different maps

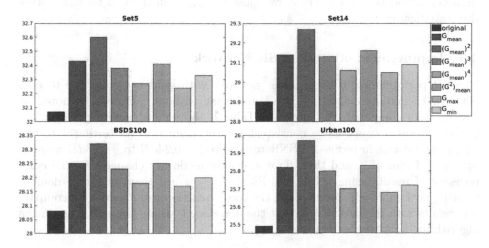

Fig. 4. Comparison of the performance of SNSR using 7 different ways for knowledge distillation

Table 2. Comparison of different methods. TNSR is teacher network for SR, SNSR is student network unguided by TNSR, $SNSR_{(G_{mean})^2}$ is student network guided by TNSR

Method	Scale	PSNR				Flops(G)	Params
		Set5	Set14	BSDS100	Urban100		
bicubic	×2	33.68	30.33	29.56	26.88	–	–
RAISR	×2	36.15	32.13	–	–	–	–
TNSR	×2	37.84	33.40	32.08	31.45	2.373	740.23K
SNSR	×2	36.29	32.27	31.11	28.83	0.051	16.07K
$SNSR_{(G_{mean})^2}$	×2	**36.74**	**32.53**	**31.35**	**29.37**	0.051	16.07K
bicubic	×3	30.49	27.55	27.21	24.46	–	–
RAISR	×3	32.21	28.86	–	–	–	–
TNSR	×3	34.13	30.10	28.95	27.62	2.488	776.13K
SNSR	×3	32.07	28.90	28.08	25.49	0.049	15.62K
$SNSR_{(G_{mean})^2}$	×3	**32.60**	**29.27**	**28.32**	**25.97**	0.049	15.62K
bicubic	×4	28.43	26.10	25.96	23.14	–	–
RAISR	×4	29.84	27.00	–	–	–	–
TNSR	×4	31.85	28.43	27.43	25.64	2.593	805.83K
SNSR	×4	30.32	27.43	26.83	24.25	0.271	81.67K
$SNSR_{(G_{mean})^2}$	×4	**30.57**	**27.63**	**26.95**	**24.48**	0.271	81.67K

for knowledge distillation. As shown in the figure, the proposed method achieved the highest PSNR using $(G_{mean})^2$ as the statistical maps. It also demonstrates that $(G_{mean})^p$ and $(G^p)_{mean}$ are better choices for knowledge distillation in SR than G_{max} and G_{min}. Therefore, we chose $(G_{mean})^2$ in the end for calculating the statistical maps.

4.5 Improvement of Student SR Network

The SR performance of the student network with guidance from the teacher network (denoted as $SNSR_{(G_{mean})^2}$) and that without guidance (denoted as SNSR) were compared. As shown in Table 2, the reconstruction performance of the student network has a consistent improvement over all testing datasets. The improvement in terms of PSNR ranges from $+0.24dB$ to $+0.53dB$ with an upscaling factor of 3, and their flops and params do not changed. Visual comparisons of results using SNSR and $SNSR_{(G_{mean})^2}$ are given in Fig. 5, demonstrating noticeable improvements in the reconstruction results. And we compare our results with the RAISR [14] that the non-deep learning fast super resolution algorithms in mobile devices.

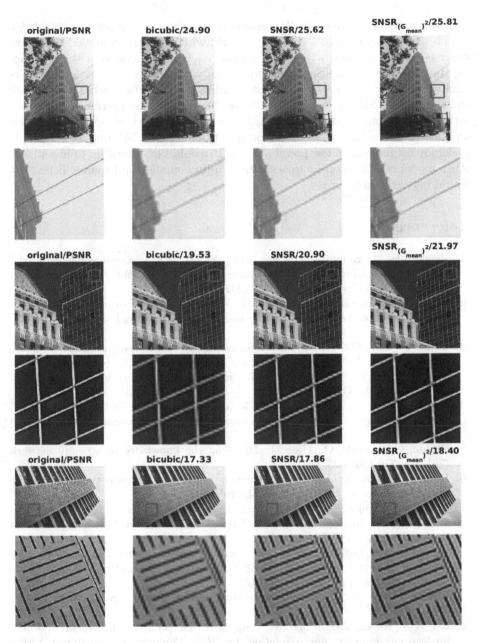

Fig. 5. Visual comparisons of results using SNSR and SNSR$_{(G_{mean})^2}$ with an upscaling factor of 3, SNSR is student network unguided by TNSR, SNSR$_{(G_{mean})^2}$ is student network guided by TNSR. PSNR is shown on the top of each sub-figure

5   Conclusions

In this paper, knowledge distillation has been used to transfer the knowledge from a teacher network to a student network, which greatly improved the image super-resolution reconstruction performance of a student network without changing its structure or requiring additional computational cost. In order to determine an effective way to propagate information between the teacher SR network and the student SR network, different statistical maps were extracted from both networks and compared. In addition, the student network utilized a depthwise separable convolution to reduce the computational cost for SR, making it possible to deploy SR models on low power devices. It would be interesting to investigate other model compression approaches in building smaller and more efficient SR neural networks in future.

References

1. Bevilacqua, M., Roumy, A., Guillemot, C., Morel, M.L.A.: Low-complexity single-image super-resolution based on nonnegative neighbor embedding. In: British Machine Vision Conference (BMVC) (2012)
2. Dong, C., Change Loy, C., Kaiming, H., Xiaoou, T.: Image super-resolution using deep convolutional networks. IEEE Trans. Pattern Anal. Mach. Intell. **38**(2), 295–307 (2016)
3. Dong, C., Loy, C.C., Tang, X.: Accelerating the super-resolution convolutional neural network. In: Leibe, B., Matas, J., Sebe, N., Welling, M. (eds.) ECCV 2016, Part II. LNCS, vol. 9906, pp. 391–407. Springer, Cham (2016). https://doi.org/10.1007/978-3-319-46475-6_25
4. He, K., Zhang, X., Ren, S., Sun, J.: Deep residual learning for image recognition. In: IEEE Conference on Computer Vision and Pattern Recognition, pp. 770–778 (2016)
5. Hinton, G., Vinyals, O., Dean, J.: Distilling the knowledge in a neural network (2015). arXiv:1503.02531
6. Howard, A.G., et al.: MobileNets: efficient convolutional neural networks for mobile vision applications (2017). arXiv:1704.04861
7. Huang, J.B., Singh, A., Ahuja, N.: Single image super-resolution from transformed self-exemplars. In: International Conference on Computer Vision and Pattern Recognition, pp. 5197–5206 (2015)
8. Kim, J., Kwon Lee, J., Mu Lee, K.: Accurate image super-resolution using very deep convolutional networks. In: IEEE Conference on Computer Vision and Pattern Recognition, pp. 1646–1654 (2016)
9. Kingma, D.P., Ba, J.: Adam: a method for stochastic optimization (2014). arXiv:1412.6980
10. Lai, W.S., Huang, J.B., Ahuja, N., Yang, M.H.: Deep Laplacian pyramid networks for fast and accurate super-resolution. In: IEEE Conference on Computer Vision and Pattern Recognition, pp. 624–632 (2017)
11. Ledig, C., et al.: Photo-realistic single image super-resolution using a generative adversarial network. In: IEEE Conference on Computer Vision and Pattern Recognition, pp. 105–114 (2016)

12. Lim, B., Son, S., Kim, H., Nah, S., Lee, K.M.: Enhanced deep residual networks for single image super-resolution. In: IEEE Conference on Computer Vision and Pattern Recognition (CVPR) Workshops, pp. 1132–1140 (2017)

13. Martin, D., Fowlkes, C., Tal, D., Malik, J.: A database of human segmented natural images and its application to evaluating segmentation algorithms and measuring ecological statistics. In: International Conference on Computer Vision, vol. 2, pp. 416–423. IEEE (2001)

14. Romano, Y., Isidoro, J., Milanfar, P.: RAISR: rapid and accurate image super resolution. IEEE Trans. Comput. Imaging **3**(1), 110–125 (2016)

15. Romero, A., Ballas, N., Kahou, S.E., Chassang, A., Gatta, C., Bengio, Y.: FitNets: hints for thin deep nets (2014). arXiv:1412.6550

16. Simonyan, K., Zisserman, A.: Very deep convolutional networks for large-scale image recognition (2014). arXiv:1409.1556

17. Tai, Y., Yang, J., Liu, X.: Image super-resolution via deep recursive residual network. In: IEEE Conference on Computer Vision and Pattern Recognition, pp. 2790–2798 (2017)

18. Timofte, R., et al.: NTIRE 2017 challenge on single image super-resolution: methods and results. In: Computer Vision and Pattern Recognition Workshops, pp. 1110–1121 (2017)

19. Tong, T., Li, G., Liu, X., Gao, Q.: Image super-resolution using dense skip connections. In: IEEE International Conference on Computer Vision, pp. 4809–4817 (2017)

20. Zagoruyko, S., Komodakis, N.: Paying more attention to attention: improving the performance of convolutional neural networks via attention transfer (2016). arXiv:1612.03928

21. Zeyde, R., Elad, M., Protter, M.: On single image scale-up using sparse-representations. In: Boissonnat, J.-D., et al. (eds.) Curves and Surfaces 2010. LNCS, vol. 6920, pp. 711–730. Springer, Heidelberg (2012). https://doi.org/10.1007/978-3-642-27413-8_47

Visual-Linguistic Methods for Receipt Field Recognition

Rinon Gal[1]([✉]), Nimrod Morag[1], and Roy Shilkrot[1,2]

[1] WAY2VAT, Habarzel 34A, 6971051 Tel-Aviv, Israel
{rinong,nimrodm}@way2vat.com
[2] Stony Brook University, 100 Nicolls Road, Stony Brook, NY 11794, USA
roy.shilkrot@stonybrook.edu

Abstract. Receipts are crucial for many businesses' operation, where expenses are tracked meticulously. Receipt documents are often scanned into images, digitized and analyzed before the information is streamed into institutional financial applications. The precise extraction of expense data from receipt images is a difficult task owed to the high variance in fonts and layouts, the frailty of the print paper, unstructured scanning environments and an immeasurable amount of domains. We propose a method that combines visual and linguistic features for automatic information retrieval from receipt images using deep network architectures, which outperforms existing approaches. Our *Skip-Rect Embedding* (SRE) descriptor is demonstrated in two canonical applications for receipt information retrieval: field extraction and Optical Character Recognition (OCR) error enhancement.

1 Introduction

Tracking business expenses using scanned receipt images is a widespread practice in the organizational finance world. As a result, extracting accounting data from receipt images has been a central pursuit in automatic document analysis over the past three decades [10]. Understanding the relationship between text *format* and text *layout* is a crucial step in accurate information retrieval. For example the sum "$10.99" in a US receipt will likely appear next to the word "Total:" or "Amount due:" and follow the canonical format "$NN.NN" (Fig. 1).

While such geometric relationships have been used in the past for information retrieval from receipts [18], the problem still stands as challenging for reasons such as OCR errors, non-axis-aligned imaging, non-horizontal language or the high variance of receipt document layouts and word vocabulary. As noted, a strong indicator of semantic meaning for words and data in a receipt document are the immediate neighbors. However, the compounding error in geometry (e.g. warping, sparsity) and format (e.g. OCR mis-reading) break simple assumptive rule-based models [5] or extraction using layout templates or graphs [18].

Electronic supplementary material The online version of this chapter (https://doi.org/10.1007/978-3-030-20890-5_35) contains supplementary material, which is available to authorized users.

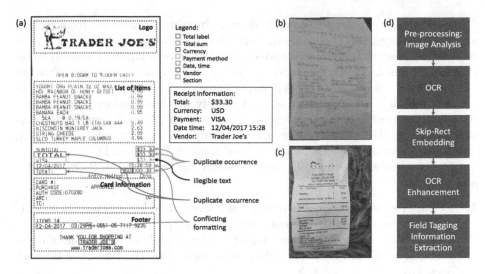

Fig. 1. Example receipt and relative location of key information within it. Difficulty of extracting information from receipts stems from multiple sources: duplicate information, conflicting formatting, OCR-impossible text, warping from paper creasing (b), difficult backgrounds (c), and other reasons. (d) Rough sketch of a processing pipeline for analyzing a receipt image using the SRE

We propose that linguistic models for semantic analysis can be adapted geometrically to overcome problems arising in sparse structured documents. For example in the absence of complete sentences in a receipt, the Skip-Gram method, which models semantic meaning using the company of the word [12], can be used geometrically to learn the relationship between sums (e.g "$NN.NN") and their neighboring labels (e.g. "Total:"). To this end we propose **"Skip-Rect Embedding"** (SRE): a descriptor that jointly learns the relationship between textual format and spatial proximity in the OCR-enhanced image. We show that this descriptor is useful for several applications in document analysis and improves prediction over naïve approaches.

An expected advantage of using a SRE descriptor enhancement, is that a deep network used to analyze the embedded document is relieved of the task of learning the meanings and relationships of visual glyphs and characters (in essence, performing OCR). The higher level learning can be dedicated for solving the task at hand, e.g. finding the total sum in the receipt. This flexibility allows for the use of more powerful commercial or open source OCR software during the tagging pipeline, even if provided in 'black-box' format. However this comes at a cost, since the low-level embedding is suspect to noise from the external OCR operation (e.g. letters mis-read or words completely missing). For that purpose we propose a **character-level embedding (Char2Vec)** for the words in the document, which is able to look past OCR mistakes. Such an embedding can be learned in an unsupervised fashion, leveraging considerably larger amounts of data. These data can be automatically generated from OCR results for invoice images, rather than the manual annotation required by networks responsible for higher level reasoning.

In this paper, we propose a method for extracting information from receipt and invoice images by (1) creating a robust character-level embedding from OCR results, (2) creating an image overlayed with the embedding data and (3) using this embedding image to jointly learn spatial and linguistic features. We train our model using a mix of supervised and unsupervised techniques. Since datasets for receipt image analysis are in a short supply, we built our own proprietary dataset that consists of 5,094 images of invoices with 23,013 human-tagged bits of information. We demonstrate our method's superiority using several baselines, and achieve almost 88% accuracy on a hard dataset (see Table 1).

The components of the full tagging system are presented in Sects. 3 and 4 and include:

1. A Char2Vec network for generating word level embeddings from their character level content and geometric context (Sect. 3).
2. A network for generating a heat-map of label probabilities using a base image overlayed with word-embedding data as generated by the Char2Vec network (Sect. 4).
3. An 'inverted softmax' linear classifier for determining the best candidate word to match for each label, based on the heat-map generated by the network and a set of hand-crafted features (Sect. 4.1).

2   Related Work

Analyzing an image of a receipt or invoice requires reading the text as well as the document layout, and understanding the relationship between them. Several works for **receipt image analysis systems** have proposed methods utilizing spatial connections [3,5,7], such as 4-way proximity, to extract information from receipt images. Some textual formatting considerations were suggested as well [5] in form of regular expressions, however machine learning based methods, while in existence [14], are not yet prolific. Unlike these methods we learn the spatial and linguistic features jointly in a unified context.

Methods for invoice document image analysis, focusing on e.g. classification [20] or segmentation [1], avoid using outputs of an OCR operation due to the high level of errors [9], while our method overcomes this hurdle. Another key interest in document image understanding is **layout analysis**, with several recent methods using convolutional approaches to study relationship between text and location [4]. Unlike our proposed method, these prior works focus on visual representations alone and do not incorporate a language model.

Insofar as understanding a receipt image can be aided by finding the semantic meaning of words, we employ a word embedding method. Embedding the meaning of words is a common pursuit in language processing. Some prolific methods for word embedding are GLOVE [15], Skip-gram and continuous bag-of-words [12], however recently methods were proposed to perform Character-to-Vector (Char2Vec, C2V) embeddings using convolutional [6] and recurrent approaches [2]. Character-level embedding is especially useful when inter-character relationships are important, for example in language identification

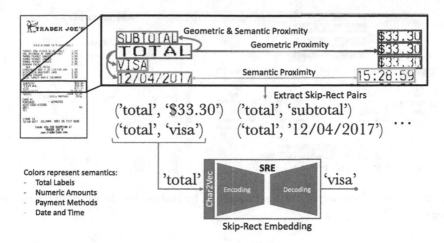

Fig. 2. Our Skip-Rect Embedding method. Proxemic words in the image are paired, and a deep convolutional model seeks to find an optimal embedding that encodes both geometric and semantic consistency

and part-of-speech tagging [17]. Using an embedding for a language model is also making strides in visual analysis, in applications such as visual relationship detection [11] and image captioning [8].

3 Spatial Character-to-Vector (Char2Vec) Skip-Rect Embedding

Linguistic embedding methods are concerned with finding a representation for the context in which a word resides, using neighboring words in the sentence, morphological clues or encyclopedic and dictionary-term proximity. The fundamental Word-to-Vector (Word2Vec) embeddings turn words encoded in arrays of characters to vectors of numbers. These embeddings have been shown to maintain semantic relations and meaningful distance metrics [13].

Our goal is to find an embedding which encapsulates similar semantic relations in an invoice image, where structured sentences are a rarity. A further complication, arising from dealing with OCR-generated text, is that a large portion ($\sim$35%[1]) of the text is misread or split. This in turn leads to both a dilution in individual words occurrences, as well as a high probability of previously unseen words appearing in every new document. The standard practice of dealing with such unknowns in a Word2Vec model, is the addition of an 'unknown' word token, to which all unknown words are assigned. Given the high percentage of unknown words in our OCR results, this is no longer a viable option. A similar situation can be found in the literature in works relating to the analysis of

---

[1] Based on experiments we performed using the prolific Tesseract OCR engine on preprocessed, phone-captured images [19].

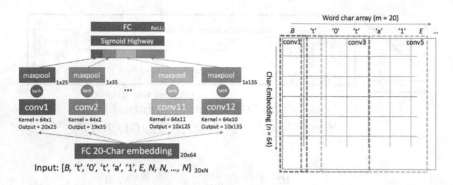

Fig. 3. A character-to-vector architecture we use for embedding the words in the receipt image

Tweets, where Char2Vec models are instead employed to learn word embeddings from the character-level content of words [22].

Embedding Model. Taking inspiration from Skip-gram [13], we pose the input word vs. a neighboring target word in a pair, and seek to find an embedding that encodes this pair-wise relationship. For a neighbor we use a 'word' (used hereafter to refer to any one string generated by the OCR) that is in an immediate geometric proximity to the input word in the receipt image. For example, words that *mean* "Total" (e.g. "Amount", "Bedrag", "Due") often appear in a pair next to actual amounts. See Fig. 2 for an illustration of this process.

Each neighbor word is normalized: capitalization and punctuation removed, and then replaced with a dictionary index in a 1-hot encoding vector. The dictionary is composed of the 10,000 most common words in the corpus. Following [6], we take a fixed 20-entry vector for the character array in the input word using the ordinal number (UTF-8 code point) for each character. We designate a maximal code point value (the UTF-8 encoding for the Euro sign), and replace any character with higher encoding by a special token *ABOVE_MAX*. We also add special tokens (*BEGIN, END*) to denote the beginning and end of a word respectively, and a *NULL* token as padding (see Fig. 3). In total we have 8368 possible values for each entry. This vector is put through an initial embedding layer. Each character's ordinal is treated as an entry in a 1-hot vector, which is multiplied by a matrix of weights of size $[8368 \times 64]$, resulting in a numeric vector of 64 values for each letter. Afterwards we apply a Time-Delayed Convolutional Network [6] with 12 convolutions of increasing lengths with **tanh** activation followed by max-pooling, and concatenate all these to a single vector. The convolutions encode the sequential relationship between characters (essentially learning to recognize indicative n-grams). To get a compact representation we pass these vectors through a sigmoid highway layer [21] and a fully-connected layer with ReLU activation (Fig. 3), with a total of 256 output nodes. The result is the 256-dimensional embedding vector of the input word.

Training. In order to train the network, this embedding vector is passed through another fully-connected layer with 10,000 outputs (the same length as our 'neighbor' 1-hot vector) and a softmax activation. The loss function is categorical cross-entropy, where the result of this final layer is compared to the 1-hot encoding of the neighbor word. See Fig. 6 for an illustration.

Creating the Data Set. The 5,094 receipt images dataset is taken and subjected to augmentation using synthetic image transformations and simulated noise to receive an order of 22,670 receipt images. The OCR software is then used on each image. In order to create a list of word pairs, a 2-dimensional KD-Tree is built from the center coordinates of all words' bounding rectangles, as found by the OCR. For each such word the tree is queried to find its 4 nearest neighbors, creating 4 pairs of 'input' (the original word) and 'target' words (the neighbors). For the purpose of determining proximity, we use simple L^2 distances. Brief experiments with adjusted distance metrics (such that words with horizontal vicinity are considered 'closer' than words with vertical vicinity) did not lead to noticeable changes in the embedding. The word pairs are filtered to remove any instance where the 'target' has a low occurrence rate (less than 10 appearances throughout our corpus), or words with less than 4 characters that are not on a hand-picked whitelist. This is done to filter out very short OCR-noise, which occurs in all contexts and thus provides no real information. The whitelist contains short words which are both common and hold special semantic meaning, such as 'VAT', 'tax' or 'due'. In total our Char2Vec training dataset contains roughly 7,000,000 word pairs.

3.1 OCR Robustness with Unsupervised Learning

Using a large dataset with raw OCR results for unsupervised learning is useful from a number of perspectives. First, more data allows for training a richer model while keeping overfitting at bay. Second, obtaining a human-tagged dataset of character-level annotation is prohibitively expensive. Lastly, using raw OCR results allows our model to be robust to mistakes commonly occurring in our OCR. OCR results containing misreadings are treated as regular words in our model, and their semantic meaning is also learned. Any new words encountered by the model can similarly be embedded based on their n-gram content.

In order to evaluate our Char2Vec model's robustness to OCR reading errors, we conducted the following experiment: First, the Char2Vec model was used to find an embedding for each word found in our top 10,000 words dictionary. A set of 47 invoices were transcribed by hand and then passed through basic data augmentation steps (rotations, blurring, adding salt-and-pepper and shot noise) in order to generate a total of 121 images. Each of these images was preprocessed and binarized, and passed through the Tesseract OCR engine. Each word longer than 3 characters that was detected by the OCR was embedded using the same Char2Vec model. For each of these embeddings, the dictionary words were queried to find the one which is closest in embedding to the OCR-read word, and the OCR-read word was replaced by this 'closest embedding' word. We then calculated the overlap between the transcribed words and those found

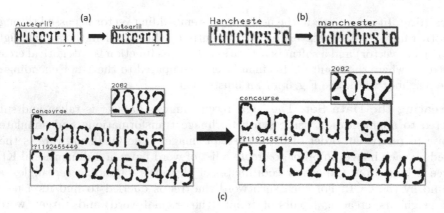

Fig. 4. Example OCR result words (green) and their corrected versions (blue). The corrections are: (a) 'autegril?' → 'autogrill', (b) 'hancheste' → 'manchester' and (c) 'congoyrge' → 'concourse' (Color figure online)

by the OCR, and the overlap between the transcribed words and those output by the Char2Vec nearest-embedding step. Any words not treated or normalized by our Char2Vec model were ignored, that is - any word whose *transcribing* contained numbers, punctuation, or words shorter than 4 characters.

In total, the OCR managed to correctly read 80.35% of the words that met our filtering criteria. After the Char2Vec correction step, the overlap increased to 91.78%. Some examples of corrected words are displayed in Fig. 4. These results indicate that our Char2Vec embedding can indeed provide some measure of robustness to OCR errors, as the embeddings of misread words are shown to be close to those of their correct spelling versions.

In addition to the above, a standard auto-encoder network was implemented in order to provide dimensionality reduction for our embeddings where smaller representations are desired. This auto-encoder network has 2 fully connected hidden layers of sizes 64 and 32. The output of the encoding step is taken as the lower-dimensional representation. We found that this dimensionality reduction step does not have a negative impact on the quality of our tagging results further down the pipeline, while significantly reducing the memory footprint and run-times of the next stages of our network.

3.2 The Embedding Image

In order to utilize the semantic information contained in our embedding model for image processing, a 32-channel **embedding image** was created. For each word read by the OCR, the 256-dimensional embedding vector is extracted, the auto-encoder is used to reduce it to 32 dimensions, and then every pixel within that word's bounding rectangle is 'colored' by the values of the embedding. The embedding image (see an example in Fig. 5) is thus given by:

$$I(x, y, 0...32) = \begin{cases} Encoder\,(Char2Vec\,(word_j)) & \text{if } (x, y) \in Rect\,(word_j) \\ 0 & \text{otherwise} \end{cases} \quad (1)$$

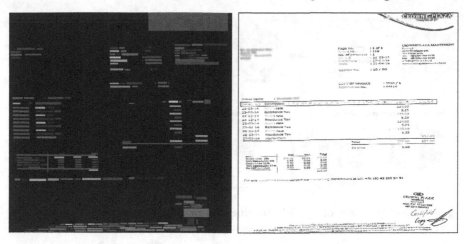

Fig. 5. Left: Embedding results for a receipt image. **Right:** The embeddings overlayed on the original invoice image. The RGB colors represent the first 3 features of the embedding vector. Numbers with one non-decimal digit are marked in blue, those with two are in light blue, while words resembling 'total' are in dark purple. Note that some words were not read by the OCR, and thus have no embedding (black). Parts of the invoice have been blurred to preserve privacy (Color figure online)

4   Field Extraction with SRE

Having created a model to encode semantic and geometric relations between invoice words, we turn to the task of using this information to extract specific invoice 'fields'. These fields include such examples as DATETIME, VAT.AMT. (VAT amount), or VEND.NAME (vendor name). We chose to first focus on the TOT.AMT. (total amount) field, as it is one of the most basic needs in understanding the content of the receipt, as well as one of the most difficult fields to correctly identify.

We previously noted that some fields are more likely to appear with specific spatial relations to each other. In addition, the signals (words) we are looking for are relatively thin, and comprise a very small part of the image. This in turn clues that convolutional methods are suitable for finding fields in the image, especially in the prolific pyramidal encoder-decoder architecture. We therefore utilize an encoder-decoder patterned convolutional network (U-Net [16]). This architecture consists of a set of repeated convolutional and max pooling steps, followed by a set of upscaling steps with transpose convolutions that share weights and skip-connections with their convolution counterparts. The U-Net's output (a set of 35 features per pixel) is passed through a 1×1 fully convolutional layer that outputs a set of n_{out} predictions per pixel, one per possible field label, plus a background label. These predictions are passed through a softmax layer and provide the per-class segmentation probabilities for each pixel. See Fig. 6 for an illustration. Each channel of the network's output is thus a heat-map of a different output class likelihood per pixel, where high values represent higher

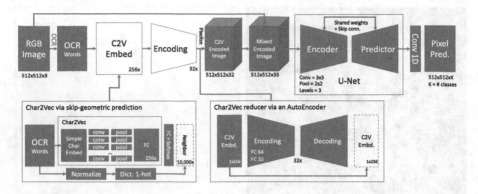

Fig. 6. The architecture of our field-tagging network, and two externally trained networks for the Char2Vec and its compression

confidence for that area of the image to contain that field. This architecture also allows the network to learn relational information between the different output classes (e.g. left-of relations) in order to improve the tagging accuracy for all of them. The network is trained using a softmax cross-entropy loss over the per-pixel field-class prediction, where the contribution of each pixel to the loss function is further weighted according to its correct class. These weights were fine-tuned using a grid search, and help account for the scarcity of positive label pixels in the image.

The input image fed into the U-Net architecture is a 35-layer 'RGB-Embedding' image, created by appending the channels of the **embedding image** of Sect. 3.2 to the RGB-layers of the invoice image.

4.1   Reversed Field-Tagging Decision

Given the prediction heatmap images, we must still select the words that represent each field. Receipt images can often contain multiple instances of each field, e.g. TOT.AMT. (see example in Fig. 1). We chose to contend ourselves with finding for each field (e.g. TOT.AMT., VAT.AMT.) the single best candidate from all OCR results. This task is approached by learning to provide a score for each field (e.g. the TOT.AMT.), for each detected word in the OCR'ed receipt image. The word that received the highest score for each field is then chosen. Our insight is that this can be formulated as a 'reversed' softmax problem: instead of looking at each OCR output and giving it a field designation ("the most likely field for the OCR word 'T0t41' is the TOT.AMT.") we pick a field and label it with OCR candidates ("the most likely word for the TOT.AMT. field is 'T0t41' ").

For each OCR'ed word j we compose a descriptor vector x_j, which consists of some hand-crafted features such as: "is numeric?", "number of decimal dots", "length in characters", "y coordinate in the image" etc., along with features derived from the field-tagger heat maps, such as the total, mean and standard deviation of field confidences within each word's bounding rectangle. The tag score of such a word is defined as:

$$S_j\left(x_j\right) = \sum_{i=1}^{m} \theta_i x_j^i, \tag{2}$$

where the θ_i are parameters to be determined by the learning process, and are fixed for all words j. We are interested in finding the parameters θ such that the score given to the word representing the invoice TOT.AMT. is greater than the score given to all other words. The problem is mapped to a softmax regression problem by converting these scores to probabilities of a word being the TOT.AMT., using:

$$p\left(\text{word}_j = \text{TOT.AMT.} \mid x^{(l)}\right) = \frac{e^{S_j\left(x_j^{(l)}\right)}}{\sum_{k=1}^{n} e^{S_k\left(x_k^{(l)}\right)}} = \frac{e^{\sum_{i=1}^{m} \theta_i x_j^{i,(l)}}}{\sum_{k=1}^{n} e^{\sum_{i=1}^{m} \theta_i x_k^{i,(l)}}}, \tag{3}$$

where (l) denotes the set of features belonging to example l (e.g. the l-th invoice).

Hypothesis. Given the above, the hypothesis for the probability that a word in example l is the total amount will be given by:

$$h_\theta\left(x^{(l)}\right) = \begin{bmatrix} p\left(\text{word}_1 = \text{TOT.AMT.} \mid x^{(l)}\right) \\ \cdots \\ p\left(\text{word}_n = \text{TOT.AMT.} \mid x^{(l)}\right) \end{bmatrix} = \frac{1}{\sum_{k=1}^{n} e^{S_k\left(x_k^{(l)}\right)}} \begin{bmatrix} e^{S_1\left(x_1^{(l)}\right)} \\ \cdots \\ e^{S_n\left(x_n^{(l)}\right)} \end{bmatrix}, \tag{4}$$

and the choice for the total amount will be the word for which the probability is maximal.

Cost Function. Similarly to softmax regression, the cost function (with q training examples, where each training example l has n_l words) is defined by:

$$J(\theta) = -\frac{1}{q} \sum_{l=1}^{q} \sum_{j=1}^{n_l} \mathbb{I}\left(\text{word}_j^{(l)} = \text{TOT.AMT.}^{(l)}\right) \times \log\left(\frac{e^{S_j\left(x_j^{(l)}\right)}}{\sum_{k=1}^{n_l} e^{S_k\left(x_k^{(l)}\right)}}\right) + \frac{\lambda}{2} \sum_{i=1}^{m} \theta_i^2, \tag{5}$$

where $\mathbb{I}(x)$ (an indicator function) is 1 if $x = $ true and 0 otherwise.

The gradient of the cost function with respect to the $\{\theta\}$ is given by:

$$\frac{\partial J(\theta)}{\partial \theta_i} = -\frac{1}{q} \sum_{l=1}^{q} \left[x_j^{i,(l)} - \frac{\sum_{r=1}^{n_l} x_r^{i,(l)} e^{S_r\left(x_r^{(l)}\right)}}{\sum_{k=1}^{n_l} e^{S_k\left(x_k^{(l)}\right)}} \right] + \lambda \theta_i, \tag{6}$$

where j is the index for which $\text{word}^{(l)} = \text{TOT.AMT.}^{(l)}$. Note that contrary to the standard softmax, the $\{\theta\}$ are shared between the 'output classes' (the candidate words). We optimize for θ with a standard gradient descent algorithm over all of the samples in the dataset. The result of the inference process using this field is the final requested information: which amount in the OCR'ed receipt is the TOT.AMT., which is the VAT.AMT., etc.

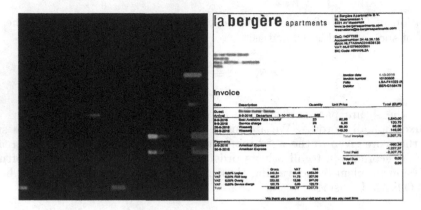

Fig. 7. Results of the automatic field tagging process. **Left:** Field confidences per pixel. Red indicates a date, blue a total amount and green a total label. **Right** The same field confidences, overlayed on the invoice image itself. Note not all occurrences of the word 'Total' peak the detector, rather only ones linked to a total amount. Parts of the invoice have been blurred to preserve privacy (Color figure online)

5   Experimental Results and Evaluation

Several experiments were conducted in order to study the effects of the embedding step on prediction quality and test the assumption that the network can leverage geometric relationships between different field types to improve their tagging accuracy. While experimenting, we divided our dataset as follows: Of the 5,094 tagged images, 5% were held out as a constant test set. All accuracy metrics shown are against this same set. Of the remaining 4,840 invoices, for each experiment 90% were used for training and the remaining 10% used for validation and hyperparameter tuning. A different split was randomly generated for each experiment. Whenever we used data augmentation, we ensured all augmented variations of an invoice remain within the same set.

In Figs. 7 and 8 we show the heat-maps generated by the different experimental models for the TOT.AMT. field. In Table 1 we show the accuracy metrics for total amount detection at the end of our pipeline, as well as the validation dice scores for the U-Net part of the model. The provided accuracy metrics are the percentage of invoices where the tagging framework managed to pinpoint one of the correct instances of the TOT.AMT., and takes into consideration only those invoices for which the OCR engine managed to correctly read the amount in at least one location.

We also provide comparisons to several baseline models, including an LSTM model based on the work of Palm et al. [14]. As they do not provide code, data or a benchmark method, we implemented their algorithm from scratch as closely as possible to their description, trained and evaluated it on our own dataset. Key differences between our implementation and theirs are as follows:

1. We make use of our own Char2Vec embedding and word features (the same ones used for our own models) in place of those presented in the paper.

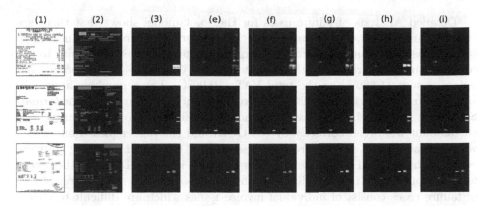

Fig. 8. Tagging results for a set of invoices using our different models. For each of the three invoices we show: (1) - The preprocessed invoice image, (2) - the first three embedding image channels, (3) - the human labeler tags for total amounts, (e)–(i) - total amount heatmaps for our different models, using the same identities as Table 1

2. Our dataset being significantly smaller, we are unable to utilize the same layer sizes as the cited paper without over-fitting the training data. After some experimentation, we elected to shrink the dense layers to 100 hidden units, and the bi-directional LSTM to 75 hidden units.
3. We do not separate our predictions to inside-outside-beginning (IOB) labels, instead using only one 'outside' class and one class for each of our predicted fields. This should minimally impact TOT.AMT. predictions that largely appear as a single word.

The accuracy metrics can be seen to improve with addition of more fields to the deep network step. We expect this trend to continue as even more fields are added and the network is able to exploit both the additional spatial relationships and the increase in bits of tagged data.

A surprising result was that the network performs better when supplied with only the base invoice image, rather than with an embedding image that includes semantic OCR information. We speculate that this is in large due to instances where the OCR was unable to read the total text in the regions labeled as a total amount (see Fig. 8 for one such example). In such an instance, the embedding layers contain no information, while the base image still contains information that can be leveraged. Having to provide a positive label where there is a distinct lack of signal is a likely cause of confusion for the network. As a result, we investigated a joint model, where we use a combination of features extracted from the two network types - both one which includes the embedding image and one which includes the original invoice image alone. We found that this combined model provides the best downstream results. This shows that the embedding layers contain information that can help improve accuracy, and suggests that the two network configurations each hold an advantage for a different class of invoice. A more refined analysis of the instances where they outperform each-other is left for future work.

Detailed Analysis of failure cases for the joint model shows that there are three primary points of confusion for the network. The most common issue (53.32%) is confusion with total numbers that appear in close proximity to the total amount, primarily the total amount before VAT (26.66%), the amount paid before change (16.66%) or the total VAT (10.00%). These numbers appear in similar proximity to total labels as the true amount, and share the same format. Second on the list (16.66%) were instances in which only some appearances of the amount were read correctly by the OCR, and the tagger picked one which was misread. Lastly, there were instances (13.33%) where the tagging software selected the price of a line item, rather than their total. Together these core issues amount to 76.66% of all misclassifications on our test set. The remainder of failure cases consist of individual invoice issues which are difficult to collectively classify. We propose a possible solution to each of the core issues that we will further investigate in later work.

The frequency of confusion with numbers in the vicinity of the true amount may be reduced by the addition of more amount-like fields to the U-Net's segmentation output, specifically those different amounts which are being erroneously selected (such as the CHANGE.AMT, the CHANGE.LBL, the VAT.AMT. and the VAT.LBL). The misread amount issue may be tackled by weighting the

Table 1. Downstream total-amount-tagging accuracy (*Amt. Acc.*) and U-Net validation-set dice scores (where applicable) for each experiment performed. A = *Amount*, T.L. = *Total Label*, D = *Date*. (a) Naïve tagger: always picks largest number with 2 decimal digits. (b) Same as (a) but attempts to rescue amounts with common OCR mistakes, such as 9 ↔ g or 0 ↔ o. (c) LSTM method described by Palm et al. [14]. (d) Inverse softmax step alone, no U-Net features. (e) Using U-Net features, trained only to provide a 'total amount' heatmap using the full embedding image (RGB layers + embedding layers). (f) Same as (e) but trained to provide a 'total label' heatmap as well. (g) Same as (f), but trained to provide a 'date' heatmap as well. (h) Same as (g), but using only the RGB channels of the image as input. (i) Same as (g), but using only the 32 embedding layers of the image as input. (j) Combined model feeding features from both (i) and (h) into the 'inverse softmax' step

Experiment	Amt. Acc.	Dice score
(a) Naïve	45.72%	-
(b) Naïve + Basic Rescue	73.67%	-
(c) LSTM Baseline	80.48%	-
(d) Softmax Only	81.86%	-
(e) Softmax + U-Net, A Only, Full Embedding	84.66%	0.5825
(f) Softmax + U-Net, A + T.L., Full Embedding	85.72%	0.5299
(g) Softmax + U-Net, A + T.L. + D, Full Embedding	86.36%	0.5966
(h) Softmax + U-Net, A + T.L. + D, Only Image	87.21%	**0.6367**
(i) Softmax + U-Net, A + T.L. + D, Only Embedding	84.28%	0.5910
(j) Two Part Model: Joint (h) + (i)	**87.86%**	-

scores (for example, by the addition of another hand-crafted feature), such that words with high appearance counts are more likely to be chosen. An instance of the amount that was misread is less likely to be identical in value to the other instances. Lastly, the line item issue may see improvement through investigation of top-down approaches, where a segmentation of the invoice into broad parts (e.g. the itemized table, the supplier information...) may be fed into the network as a feature that will help further differentiate the total-amount area from other tabulated amount areas.

6 Conclusions

Format and geometric position are imperative signals for tabular document image analysis, and invoice images in particular. These features convey relationship, context and content, which are useful for information extraction and correction.

In this work, we proposed using a character-level embedding to support high-level information extraction from receipt and invoice images. We introduced a joint model, based on convolutional neural networks for both image and text analysis, that is able to locate particular pieces of information in the image based on their semantic information. We then experimentally showed that the resulting language embeddings are meaningful and our detector is able to find the information with high accuracy on difficult examples.

We proposed a language model based on character-level embedding joined with visual representation, which sums up to a bottom-up approach of analyzing a document image - from the low-level features to a high-level understanding. A different approach suggests marrying this bottom-up outlook with a top-down one, such as document layout analysis or document type classification, which may bring about an overall improvement. A further improvement which pends investigation is the addition of coordinate dependent weights or features to the network. We speculate such a change may allow our network to better leverage knowledge about the absolute coordinates of a word (total amounts being more likely to appear in the right parts of the image, for example).

We would like to further explore this visual-linguistic space of document analysis, to inch closer to human-level recognition rates.

References

1. Aslan, E., Karakaya, T., Unver, E., Akgül, Y.S.: A part based modeling approach for invoice parsing. In: VISIGRAPP (3: VISAPP), pp. 392–399 (2016)
2. Cao, K., Rei, M.: A joint model for word embedding and word morphology. arXiv preprint arXiv:1606.02601 (2016)
3. Cesarini, F., Francesconi, E., Gori, M., Soda, G.: Analysis and understanding of multi-class invoices. Doc. Anal. Recogn. 6(2), 102–114 (2003)

4. Chen, K., Seuret, M., Liwicki, M., Hennebert, J., Ingold, R.: Page segmentation of historical document images with convolutional autoencoders. In: 2015 13th International Conference on Document Analysis and Recognition (ICDAR), pp. 1011–1015. IEEE (2015)
5. Hamza, H., Belaïd, Y., Belaïd, A.: Case-based reasoning for invoice analysis and recognition. In: Weber, R.O., Richter, M.M. (eds.) ICCBR 2007. LNCS (LNAI), vol. 4626, pp. 404–418. Springer, Heidelberg (2007). https://doi.org/10.1007/978-3-540-74141-1_28
6. Jaech, A., Mulcaire, G., Ostendorf, M., Smith, N.A.: A neural model for language identification in code-switched tweets. In: Proceedings of the Second Workshop on Computational Approaches to Code Switching, pp. 60–64 (2016)
7. Janssen, B., Saund, E., Bier, E., Wall, P., Sprague, M.A.: Receipts2Go: the big world of small documents. In: Proceedings of the 2012 ACM symposium on Document Engineering, pp. 121–124. ACM (2012)
8. Johnson, J., Karpathy, A., Fei-Fei, L.: DenseCap: fully convolutional localization networks for dense captioning. In: Proceedings of the IEEE Conference on Computer Vision and Pattern Recognition, pp. 4565–4574 (2016)
9. Kang, L., Kumar, J., Ye, P., Li, Y., Doermann, D.: Convolutional neural networks for document image classification. In: 2014 22nd International Conference on Pattern Recognition (ICPR), pp. 3168–3172. IEEE (2014)
10. Klein, B., Agne, S., Dengel, A.: Results of a study on invoice-reading systems in Germany. In: Marinai, S., Dengel, A.R. (eds.) DAS 2004. LNCS, vol. 3163, pp. 451–462. Springer, Heidelberg (2004). https://doi.org/10.1007/978-3-540-28640-0_43
11. Lu, C., Krishna, R., Bernstein, M., Fei-Fei, L.: Visual relationship detection with language priors. arXiv:1608.00187 [cs], July 2016
12. Mikolov, T., Chen, K., Corrado, G., Dean, J.: Efficient estimation of word representations in vector space. arXiv:1301.3781 [cs, stat], January 2013
13. Mikolov, T., Sutskever, I., Chen, K., Corrado, G., Dean, J.: Distributed representations of words and phrases and their compositionality. arXiv:1310.4546 [cs, stat], October 2013
14. Palm, R.B., Winther, O., Laws, F.: CloudScan-a configuration-free invoice analysis system using recurrent neural networks. arXiv preprint arXiv:1708.07403 (2017)
15. Pennington, J., Socher, R., D. Manning, C.: GloVe: global vectors for word representation. (2014). https://nlp.stanford.edu/pubs/glove.pdf
16. Ronneberger, O., Fischer, P., Brox, T.: U-Net: convolutional networks for biomedical image segmentation. In: Navab, N., Hornegger, J., Wells, W.M., Frangi, A.F. (eds.) MICCAI 2015. LNCS, vol. 9351, pp. 234–241. Springer, Cham (2015). https://doi.org/10.1007/978-3-319-24574-4_28
17. Santos, C.D., Zadrozny, B.: Learning character-level representations for part-of-speech tagging. In: Proceedings of the 31st International Conference on Machine Learning (ICML 2014), pp. 1818–1826 (2014)
18. Schulz, F., Ebbecke, M., Gillmann, M., Adrian, B., Agne, S., Dengel, A.: Seizing the treasure: transferring layout knowledge in invoice analysis. In: 10 International Conference on Document Analysis and Recognition (ICDAR), Barcelona, Spain (2009)
19. Smith, R.: An overview of the Tesseract OCR engine. In: Proceedings of the Ninth International Conference on Document Analysis and Recognition, ICDAR 2007, vol. 02, pp. 629–633. IEEE Computer Society, Washington, DC, USA (2007). http://dl.acm.org/citation.cfm?id=1304596.1304846

20. Sorio, E., Bartoli, A., Davanzo, G., Medvet, E.: Open world classification of printed invoices. In: Proceedings of the 10th ACM symposium on Document engineering, pp. 187–190. ACM (2010)
21. Srivastava, R.K., Greff, K., Schmidhuber, J.: Highway Networks. arXiv:1505.00387, May 2015
22. Vosoughi, S., Vijayaraghavan, P., Roy, D.: Tweet2vec: learning Tweet embeddings using character-level CNN-LSTM encoder-decoder. In: Proceedings of the 39th International ACM SIGIR Conference on Research and Development in Information Retrieval, SIGIR 2016, pp. 1041–1044. ACM, New York, NY, USA (2016). https://doi.org/10.1145/2911451.2914762, http://doi.acm.org/10.1145/2911451.2914762

Cascaded Pyramid Mining Network for Weakly Supervised Temporal Action Localization

Haisheng Su[iD], Xu Zhao[✉][iD], and Tianwei Lin[iD]

Department of Automation, Shanghai Jiao Tong University, Shanghai, China
{suhaisheng,zhaoxu,wzmsltw}@sjtu.edu.cn

Abstract. Weakly supervised temporal action localization, which aims at temporally locating action instances in untrimmed videos using only video-level class labels during training, is an important yet challenging problem in video analysis. Many current methods adopt the *"localization by classification"* framework: first do video classification, then locate temporal area contributing to the results most. However, this framework fails to locate the entire action instances and gives little consideration to the local context. In this paper, we present a novel architecture called **Cascaded Pyramid Mining Network (CPMN)** to address these issues using two effective modules. First, to discover the entire temporal interval of specific action, we design a two-stage cascaded module with proposed **Online Adversarial Erasing (OAE)** mechanism, where new and complementary regions are mined through feeding the erased feature maps of discovered regions back to the system. Second, to exploit hierarchical contextual information in videos and reduce missing detections, we design a pyramid module which produces a scale-invariant attention map through combining the feature maps from different levels. Final, we aggregate the results of two modules to perform action localization via locating high score areas in temporal **Class Activation Sequence (CAS)**. Extensive experiments conducted on THUMOS14 and ActivityNet-1.3 datasets demonstrate the effectiveness of our method.

Keywords: Temporal action localization · Weak supervision · Online Adversarial Erasing · Scale invariance · Class Activation Sequence

1 Introduction

Due to the rapid development of computer vision along with the increasing amount of videos, many breakthroughs have been observed on video content analysis in recent years. Videos from realistic scenarios are often complex, which may contain multiple action instances of different categories with varied lengths.

This research is supported by the funding from NSFC programs (61673269, 61273285, U1764264).

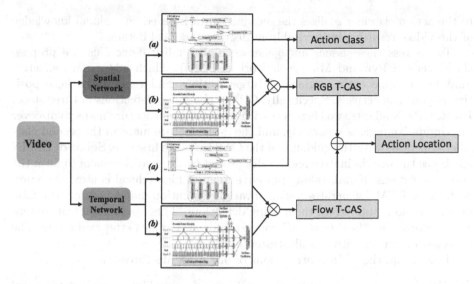

Fig. 1. Overview of our approach. Two-stream network is used to encode visual features for our algorithm to perform action classification and temporal action localization concurrently. The (a) Cascaded Classification Module (CCM) with Online Adversarial Erasing (OAE) method and the (b) Pyramid Attention Module (PAM) are proposed to compute attention-based cascaded Temporal Class Activation Sequence (T-CAS) from the two streams separately, which can be employed to locate the entire regions of specific actions in temporal domain with high accuracy.

This problem leads to a challenging task: temporal action localization, which requires to not only handle the category classification of untrimmed videos but also determine the temporal boundaries of action instances. Nevertheless, it implies the huge amounts of temporal annotations for training an action localization model, which are more labor-intensive to obtain than video-level class labels.

Contrary to the fully supervised counterparts, Weakly Supervised Temporal Action Localization (WSTAL) task learns TAL using only video-level class labels, which can be regarded as a temporal version of Weakly Supervised Object Detection (WSOD) in image. A popular series of models in WSOD generate Class Activation Maps (CAMs) [42] to highlight the discriminative object regions contributing to the classification results most. Inspired by [42], recently many WSTAL works generate the Class Activation Sequence (CAS) to locate the action instances in temporal domain. However, many drawbacks have been observed in this *"localization by classification"* mechanism: (1) the CAS fails to generate dense detections of target actions, causing many missing detections; (2) the classification network usually leverages features of discriminative rather than entire regions for recognition, failing to handle the action instances with varied lengths; (3) some true negative regions are falsely activated, which is mainly due to the action classifier realizes the recognition task based on a global knowledge of the video, resulting in inevitably neglecting the local details.

To address these issues and generate high quality detections, we propose the Cascaded Pyramid Mining Network (CPMN), which adopts two effective modules to mine entire regions of target actions and remove the false positive regions respectively. Specifically, CPMN generates detections in three steps. **First**, CPMN adapts two classifiers with different input feature maps to discover discriminative regions separately, and the input feature maps of the second classifier are erased with the guidance of the CAS from the first one. **Second**, CPMN combines the discriminative regions discovered by the two classifiers to form the entire detections. **Final**, taking full advantage of hierarchical contextual representations, CPMN generates a scale-invariant attention map to correct the false positive regions and reduce the missing detections. These pyramidal feature representations offer *"local to global"* context information for better evaluation. The overview of our algorithm is illustrated in Fig. 1.

To sum up, the main contributions of our work are three-fold:

(1) We propose a new architecture (CPMN) for weakly supervised temporal action localization in untrimmed videos, where entire temporal regions of action instances are located with less missing detections.
(2) We introduce an Online Adversarial Erasing (OAE) method to discover entire regions of target actions using two cascaded classifiers with different input feature representations, and explicitly handle the action instances with varied lengths by exploiting hierarchical contextual information.
(3) Extensive experiments demonstrate that our method achieves the state-of-the-art performance on both THUMOS14 and ActivityNet-1.3 datasets.

2   Related Work

Action Recognition. Action recognition has been widely studied in recent years, which aims to identify one or multiple action categories of a video. Earlier works mainly focus on hand-crafted feature engineering, such as improved Dense Trajectory (iDT) [31,32]. With the development of convolutional neural networks, many deep learning based methods [6,25,29,34] have been applied to action recognition task and achieve convincing performance. Two-stream network [6,25,34] typically consists of two branches which learn the appearance and motion information using RGB image and optical flow respectively. C3D network [29] simultaneously captures appearance and motion features using a series of 3D convolutional layers. These action recognition models are usually adopted to extract frame or unit level visual representation in long and untrimmed videos.

Weakly Supervised Object Detection. Weakly supervised object detection aims to locate the objects using only image-level labels. Current works mainly include bottom-up [2,3] and top-down [27,36,40,42] mechanisms. Proposals are first generated in [2,3] using selective search [30] or edge boxes [43], which are further classified and the classification results are merged to match the image labels. Zhou et al. [42] and Zhang et al. [40] aim to find out the relationship between the neural responses of image regions and classification results, and then locate top activations area as detections. Singh et al. [27] propose to improve the localization map by randomly hiding some regions during training, so as to force the network to look for other discriminative parts. However, without effective guidance, this attempt is blind and inefficient. Recently, Wei et al. [36] employ Adversarial Erasing (AE) approach to discover more object regions in images by training classification network repeatedly, with discriminative regions erasing of different degrees, which is somewhat impractical and time-consuming. Our work differs from these methods in designing an Online Adversarial Erasing (OAE) approach which only needs to train a network for entire regions mining.

Weakly Supervised Temporal Action Localization. Action localization in temporal domain [5,15,17,38] is similar to object detection in spatial domain [8,9,18,20,21], as well as the case under weak supervision. WSTAL aims to locate action instances in untrimmed videos including both temporal boundaries and action categories while relying on video-level class label only. Based on the idea proposed in [3], Wang et al. [33] formulate this task as a proposal-based classification problem, where temporal proposals are extracted with the priors of action shot. However, the use of softmax function across proposals blocks it from distinguishing multiple action instances. Singh et al. [27] hide temporal regions to force attention learning. However, it's not applicable owing to the complexity and varied lengths of videos. In our work, the Pyramid Attention Module (PAM) is proposed to hierarchically classify the videos from local to global, thus the pyramidal attention map is generated by combining feature maps from different levels, which can be scale-invariant to the action instances.

3 Our Approach

3.1 Problem Definition

We denote an untrimmed video as $X_v = \{x_t\}_{t=1}^{l_v}$, where l_v is the number of frames and x_t is the t-th frame in X_v. Each video X_v is annotated with a set of temporal action instances $\Phi_v = \{\phi_n = (t_n^s, t_n^e, \varphi_n)\}_{n=1}^{N_v}$, where N_v is the number of temporal action instances in X_v, and t_n^s, t_n^e, φ_n are starting time, ending time and category of instance ϕ_n respectively, where $\varphi_n \in \{1, ..., C\}$ and C is the number of action categories. During training phase, only the video-level action label set $\psi_v = \{\varphi_n\}_{n=1}^{N_v}$ is given, and during test phase, Φ_v need to be predicted.

3.2 Video Features Encoding

To apply CPMN, first feature representations need to be extracted to describe visual content of the input video in our work. UntrimmedNet [33] is employed as visual encoder, since this kind of architecture using multiple two-stream networks has shown great performance and becomes a prevalent practice adopted in action recognition and temporal action localization tasks.

Given a video containing l_v frames, we use video unit as the basic processing unit in our framework for computational efficiency. Hence the video is divided into l_v/n_u consecutive video units without overlap, where n_u is the frame number of a unit. Then we compose a unit sequence $U = \{u_j\}_{j=1}^{l_u}$ from the video X_v, where l_u is the number of units. A video unit can be represented as $u_j = \{x_t\}_{t=f_s}^{f_s+n_u}$, where f_s is the starting frame and $f_s + n_u$ is the ending frame. Each unit is fed to the pre-trained visual encoder to extract representation. Concretely, the center RGB frame inside a unit is processed by spatial network and stacked optical flow derived around the center frame is processed by temporal network, then we concatenate output scores of UntrimmedNet [33] in fc-action layer to form the feature vector $f_{u_j} = \{f_{S,u_j}, f_{T,u_j}\}$, where f_{S,u_j} and f_{T,u_j} are output score vector of spatial and temporal network respectively with length G. Final, the unit-level feature sequence $F = \{f_{u_j}\}_{j=1}^{l_u}$ is used as input of CPMN.

3.3 Cascaded Pyramid Mining Network

To generate high quality detections with accurate temporal regions under weak supervision, we propose a multi-stage framework to achieve this goal. In CPMN, we first design a module to discover the entire action regions in a cascaded way. Then we introduce another module to combine the temporal feature maps from pyramidal feature hierarchy for prediction, making it possible to handle action instances with varied lengths. Final, we fuse the results from these two modules for action localization in temporal domain.

Network Architecture. The architecture consists of three sub-modules: cascaded classification module, pyramid attention module and temporal action localization module. *Cascaded classification module* is a two-stage model which includes two classifiers as shown in Fig. 2, aiming to mine different but complementary regions of target action in the video through a cascaded manner. *Pyramid attention module* is proposed to generate the class probability of each input unit feature, through classifying the input feature sequence with hierarchical resolutions separately. The architecture of this module is illustrated in Fig. 3. Final, *temporal action localization module* fuses the cascaded localization sequence and the pyramidal attention map to make it more accurate.

Cascaded Classification Module. The goal of this module is to locate the entire regions of target actions in the video, where two cascaded classifiers are needed. As shown in Fig. 2, the Cascaded Classification Module (CCM) contains two separate classifiers with the same structure. In each stage (i.e. the localization stage and the mining stage), the classifier handles the input unit-level features and adopts two 1-D temporal convolutional layers followed by a global average pooling layer to get the video-level representation, which is then passed through a fully connected (FC) layer and a Sigmoid layer for video classification. The two convolutional layers have the same configurations: kernel size 3, stride 1 and 512 filters with ReLU activation. Denote the last convolutional features and the averaged feature representation as $Z \in \mathbb{R}^{T \times K}$ and $\overline{Z} = \{\frac{\sum_t Z_t(k)}{T}\}_{k=1}^{K}$ respectively, where T is the length of input feature sequence, K is the channel

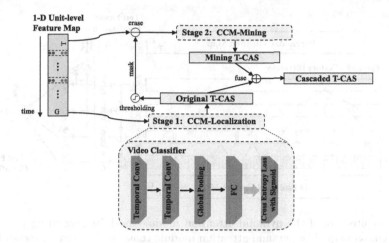

Fig. 2. Architecture of the cascaded classification module. The extracted unit-level feature representations are fed to two cascaded video classifiers for localization sequence inference individually. The two classifiers of the same structure share the input feature maps, and we erase the input features of discriminative regions highlighted by the first classifier, to drive the second classifier to discover more relevant regions of target actions in the video. Final, the two T-CASs are integrated for a better localization.

number and $Z_t(k)$ is the k-th feature map at time t. Then based on the idea in [42], we derive the 1-D Temporal Class Activation Sequence (T-CAS). We denote $w^c(k)$ as the k-th element of the weight matrix $\boldsymbol{W} \in \mathbb{R}^{K \times C}$ in the classification layer corresponding to class c. The input to the Sigmoid layer for class c is

$$s^c = \sum_{k=1}^{K} w^c(k)\overline{Z}(k) = \sum_{k=1}^{K} w^c(k) \sum_{t=1}^{T} Z_t(k) = \sum_{t=1}^{T} \sum_{k=1}^{K} w^c(k)Z_t(k), \quad (1)$$

$$M_t^c = \sum_{k=1}^{K} w^c(k)Z_t(k), \quad (2)$$

where M_t^c is denoted as T-CAS of class c, which indicates the activations of each unit feature contributing to a specific class of the video.

Then we conduct a threshold on the T-CAS obtained in the first stage to generate a mask which represents the discriminative regions discovered by the first classifier, and the mask is used to erase the input features of the second stage for classification. Such an online adversarial erasing operation allows the second classifier to leverage features from other regions for supporting the video-level labels. Final, we integrate the two T-CASs, $M^c(A)$ and $M^c(B)$, which are generated in the two stages separately, to form the cascaded localization sequence $M^c(Cas)$. Concretely, $M_t^c(Cas) = max\{M_t^c(A), M_t^c(B)\}$, where $M_t^c(Cas)$ is the t-th element in the cascaded action localization sequence of class c.

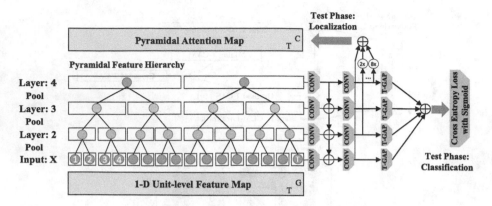

Fig. 3. Architecture of the pyramid attention module used for generating the multi-scale attention map. The pyramid attention module consists of several branches based on feature representations of hierarchical resolutions, for the purpose of classifying the video from local to global. And a global average pooling layer is employed to encode the video-level prediction of each branch and then we aggregate the multiple prediction results from different levels. Final, the pyramidal attention map is constructed through combining the multi-scale feature maps in the prediction layers during test phase.

Pyramid Attention Module. This module is designed to handle action instances with varied lengths. We achieve this goal in two steps. First, we semantically classify the feature representations with hierarchical temporal resolutions individually, aiming at processing the input unit-level feature sequence from local to global. Then we combine temporal feature maps in prediction layers from different levels to form the pyramidal attention map.

As shown in Fig. 3, we stack three 1-D max pooling layers on the input feature sequence, thus obtain the pyramidal feature hierarchy. After subsampling with a scaling step of 2 layer by layer, the feature sequence length of the l-th layer is $T_l = \frac{T}{2^{l-1}}$. Then for each level, we first conduct a temporal convolutional layer with kernel size 1, stride 1 and 512 filters to handle the feature sequence. Among these levels, we use lateral connections to exploit hierarchical context. Then we employ another convolutional layer to predict the classification scores of units associated with each feature map respectively. Each prediction layer consists of C filters with kernel size 1 and stride 1. And we continue to append a global average pooling layer on the label maps $\mathbf{K}_l \in \mathbb{R}^{T_l \times C}$ of each level separately to aggregate the video-level predictions. Final, we average among these prediction results to match the video-level class labels.

During test phase, we form the class heatmaps $\mathbf{H} = \{H^c\}_{c=1}^C$ by combining the output label maps in prediction layers from different levels. For example, with the coarser-resolution label map generated in l-th layer, we upsample the temporal resolution by a factor of 2^{l-1} through repeating the score vector in temporal dimension. Then every class heatmap is normalized to $[0, 1]$ as follows,

$$H^c = (H^c - min(H^c))/(max(H^c) - min(H^c)), \tag{3}$$

where H^c is the heatmap for class c, which indicates the class probability of each unit feature semantically.

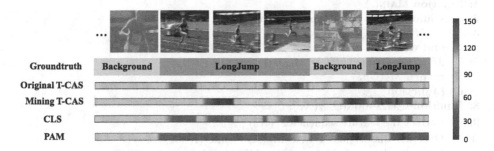

Fig. 4. Illustration of the comparison of ground-truth temporal intervals, original T-CAS, mining T-CAS, cascaded localization sequence (CLS) and pyramidal attention map (PAM) for the *LongJump* action class on THUMOS14.

Temporal Action Localization Module. The goal of this module is to fuse the cascaded action localization sequence and the pyramidal attention map obtained above for temporal action localization. As shown in Fig. 4, the CLS can identify more regions of target actions but some false positive regions are also activated by mistake. Since the class heatmap is generated using element-wise addition of label maps at multiple scales, the results are too smooth to indicate the accurate action boundaries. But they can provide important temporal priors to constrain the CLS. We let the class heatmap play the role of an attention map, which is used to correct the false positive regions and reduce missing detections. Then we fuse CLS and PAM to generate the attention-based cascaded T-CASs respectively as follows,

$$\Phi_{t,RGB}^c = sigmoid(M_{t,RGB}^c(Cas)) \cdot H_{t,RGB}^c, \tag{4}$$

$$\Phi_{t,Flow}^c = sigmoid(M_{t,Flow}^c(Cas)) \cdot H_{t,Flow}^c. \tag{5}$$

Then for each action class, we conduct a threshold on the $\Phi_{t,RGB}^c$ and $\Phi_{t,Flow}^c$ separately, and different from the method [42] which only retains the bounding box that covers the largest connected components, we keep all connected units that pass the predefined threshold θ_{TCAS} from each class and modality.

3.4 Training of CPMN

The training details of the cascaded classification module and the pyramid attention module in CPMN are introduced in this section.

Algorithm 1. Training procedure of cascaded classification module.

Input: Training data, $\Theta_{cas} = \{\Theta_{cas}(X_v)\}_{v=1}^{D}$; threshold, ζ;
Output: Cascaded T-CAS, $M^c(Cas)$;
1: **function** MAIN( )
2:     **while** training is not convergent **do**
3:         $M^c(A), M^c(B) \leftarrow$ CAS_TRAIN$(\Theta_{cas}(X_v), \zeta)$
4:     **end while**
5:     $M^c(Cas) \leftarrow \max(M_t^c(A), M_t^c(B))$
6:     **return** $M^c(Cas)$
7: **end function**
8: **function** CAS_TRAIN$(\Theta_{cas}(X_v), \zeta)$
9:     Extract the feature sequence $F'(X_v)$
10:     Generate the original T-CAS $M^c(A) \leftarrow \text{infer}(F'(X_v), \psi_v)$
11:     Generate the mask $M^c(mask) \leftarrow M^c(A) > \zeta$
12:     Obtain the erased feature sequence $F'_{erase}(X_v) \leftarrow \text{erase}(F'(X_v), M^c(mask))$
13:     Generate the mining T-CAS $M^c(B) \leftarrow \text{infer}(F'_{erase}(X_v), \psi_v)$
14:     **return** $M^c(A), M^c(B)$
15: **end function**

Cascaded Classification Module. Given an input video X_v, we form unit sequence U and extract corresponding feature sequence F with length l_u. Since an untrimmed video usually comes up with extremely irrelevant frames with action instances only occupying small parts, we totally test three sampling methods to simplify the feature sequence for computational cost reduction: (1) uniform sampling: units are extracted with a regular interval σ from U, thus the final unit sequence and feature sequence are $U' = \{u_j'\}_{j=1}^{l_u'}$ and F' separately, where $l_u' = \frac{l_u}{\sigma}$; (2) sparse sampling: we first divide the video into P segments $\{S_1, S_2, ..., S_P\}$ with equal length, then during each training epoch, we randomly sample one unit from each segment to form the unit sequence of length P; (3) shot-based sampling: considering the action structure, we sample the unit sequence U based on action shots, which are generated by shot boundary detector [28]. Evaluation results of these sampling methods are shown in Sect. 4.3.

After sampling, we construct the training data of each video as $\Theta_{cas}(X_v) = \{U'(X_v), F'(X_v), \psi_v\}$ and taking it as input, the first classifier leverages the most discriminative regions for classification while the second classifier handles the erased feature sequence for entire regions mining. We test different erasing thresholds ζ from 0.3 to 0.7 and the evaluation results are shown in Sect. 4.3. And we employ cross-entropy loss and l_2 regularization loss as final loss function to train the two multi-label classifiers separately:

$$L_{cas} = \sum_{v=1}^{D} \psi_v \cdot log(y_v^{predict}) + \lambda \cdot L_2(\Xi_{cas}), \qquad (6)$$

where $y_v^{predict}$ is the predicted class scores of the video and D is the number of training videos. λ balances the cross-entropy loss and l_2 loss, and Ξ_{cas} is the cascaded classification model. Algorithm 1 illustrates the training procedure.

Pyramid Attention Module. The pyramid attention module is trained to handle the action instances with arbitrary intervals. Considering the maximum length d_{max} of ground-truth action instances in dataset, we slide windows with length T_ω which can cover the d_{max}. The training data of video X_v is constructed as $\Theta_{mul}(X_v) = \{\Omega = \{U_\omega, F_\omega\}_{\omega=1}^{N_\omega}, \psi_v\}$, where N_ω is number of windows. Taking a sliding window with corresponding feature sequence F_ω as input, the pyramid attention module generates label maps with different lengths, then combine these maps in a bottom-up way and concatenate all windows results to form the video pyramidal attention maps. The multi-label cross-entropy loss function is also adopted to train the pyramid attention module.

3.5   Prediction and Post-processing

During prediction, we follow the same data preparation procedures of training phase to prepare the testing data, except for the following two changes: (1) in the cascaded classification module, we use uniform sampling method to sample the input feature sequence in order to increase the prediction speed and guarantee the stable results; (2) in the pyramid attention module, if the length of input video is shorter than T_ω, we will pad the input feature sequence to T_ω so that there is at least one window for the multi-tower network to predict. Then given a video X_v, we use CPMN to generate proposal set $\Gamma = \{\tau_n\}_{n=1}^{N_p}$ based on the thresholding attention-based cascaded T-CAS of top-2 predicted classes [33], where N_p is the number of candidate proposals and we set the threshold θ_{TCAS} as 20% of the max value of the derived T-CAS. For each proposal denoted by $[t_{start}, t_{end}]$, we first calculate the mean attention-based cascaded T-CAS among the temporal range of the proposal as p_{act}:

$$p_{act} = \sum_{t=t_{start}}^{t_{end}} \frac{M_{t,RGB}^c(Cas) \cdot H_{t,RGB}^c + M_{t,Flow}^c(Cas) \cdot H_{t,Flow}^c}{2 \cdot (t_{end} - t_{start} + 1)}, \qquad (7)$$

then we fuse p_{act} and the class scores p_{class} with multiplication to get the confidence score p_{conf}:

$$p_{conf} = p_{act} \cdot p_{class}. \qquad (8)$$

Since we keep all connected units that pass the predefined threshold θ_{TCAS} from each class and each modality as proposals, we may generate multiple predictions with different overlap. Then we conduct non-maximum suppression with predefined threshold θ_{NMS} in these prediction results to remove the redundant predictions of confidence score p_{conf}. Finally we get the prediction instances set $\Gamma' = \{\tau_n'\}_{n=1}^{N_p'}$, where N_p' is the number of final prediction instances.

4   Experiments

4.1   Dataset and Setup

Dataset. ActivityNet-1.3 [4] is a large-scale video dataset for action recognition and temporal action localization tasks used in the ActivityNet Challenge 2017 and 2018, which consists of 10,024 videos for training, 4,926 for validation and 5,044 for testing, with 200 action classes annotated. Each video is annotated with average 1.5 temporal action instances. **THUMOS14** [14] dataset contains 1010 videos for validation and 1574 videos for testing with video-level labels of 101 action classes, while only a subset of 200 and 213 videos separately are temporally annotated among 20 classes. We train our model with the validation subset without using the temporal annotations. In this section, we compare our method with state-of-the-art methods on both ActivityNet-1.3 and THUMOS14.

Evaluation Metrics. Following the conventions, we use mean Average Precision (mAP) as evaluation metric, where Average Precision (AP) is calculated on each class separately. We report mAP values at different Intersection over Union (IoU) thresholds. On ActivityNet-1.3, mAP with IoU thresholds $\{0.5, 0.75, 0.95\}$ and average mAP with IoU thresholds set $\{0.5 : 0.05 : 0.95\}$ are used. On THUMOS14, mAP with IoU thresholds $\{0.1, 0.2, 0.3, 0.4, 0.5\}$ are used.

Implementation Details. We use the UntrimmedNet [33] and TSN [34] for visual feature encoding of THUMOS14 and ActivityNet-1.3 separately, where ResNet network [10] is used as spatial network and BN-Inception network [12] is adopted as temporal network. The two visual encoders are both implemented using Caffe [13] and the TSN is pre-trained on ActivityNet-1.3. During feature extraction, the frame number of a unit n_u is set to 5 on THUMO14 and is set to 16 on ActivityNet-1.3. In CPMN, the cascaded classification module and the pyramid attention module are both implemented using TensorFlow [1]. On both datasets, the two modules are both trained with batch size 16 and learning rate 0.001 for 30 epochs, then 0.0001 for another 120 epochs. The erasing threshold ζ used in CCM is 0.4 and the window size T_ω used in the PAM is 64. Besides, the regularization term λ is 0.0025. For NMS, we set the threshold θ_{NMS} to 0.3 on THUMO14 and 0.5 on ActivityNet-1.3 by empirical validation.

4.2   Comparison with State-of-the-Art Methods

We first evaluate the overall results of our proposed framework for action localization and compare our method with several state-of-the-art approaches including both fully and weakly supervised methods. Table 1 illustrates the localization performance on the THUMOS14 dataset. We can observe that our proposed algorithm achieves better performance than the two existing weakly supervised methods, and is even competitive to some fully supervised approaches. For example, when the IoU threshold α is 0.5, the mAP of our method is more than twice higher as the one of [27], which significantly convinces that our proposed online adversarial erasing strategy is more reasonable than randomly hiding. And the substantial performance gaining over the previous works under different IoU thresholds confirms the effectiveness of our CPMN.

We also present our results on the validation set of the ActivityNet-1.3 dataset to further validate our localization performance. In ActivityNet-1.3, since the length of videos is not too long like THUMOS14, we directly resize the extracted feature sequence to length $l_\omega = 64$ by linear interpolation. And we choose attention-based cascaded T-CAS of top-1 class [35] as our detections. The evaluation results on ActivityNet-1.3 are shown in Table 2, from which we can see that our algorithm is generalized enough to this dataset, and significantly outperforms most fully supervised approaches with convincing performance. Meanwhile, we are the first to evaluate weakly supervised method on this dataset.

Table 1. Comparison of our method with other state-of-the-arts on THUMOS14 dataset for action localization, including both full supervision and weak supervision.

Supervision	Method	mAP@$tIoU$ (α)						
		0.1	0.2	0.3	0.4	0.5	0.6	0.7
Fully supervised	Oneata et al. [19]	36.6	33.6	27.0	20.8	14.4	-	-
	Richard et al. [22]	39.7	35.7	30.0	23.2	15.2	-	-
	Shou et al. [24]	47.7	43.5	36.3	28.7	19.0	10.3	5.3
	Yuan et al. [39]	51.0	45.2	36.5	27.8	17.8	-	-
	Lin et al. [15]	50.1	47.8	43.0	35.0	24.6	15.3	7.7
	Zhao et al. [41]	60.3	56.2	50.6	40.8	29.1	-	-
	Gao et al. [7]	60.1	56.7	50.1	41.3	**31.0**	19.1	9.9
Weakly supervised	Singh et al. [27]	36.4	27.8	19.5	12.7	6.8	-	-
	Wang et al. [33]	44.4	37.7	28.2	21.1	13.7	-	-
	CPMN	**47.1**	**41.6**	**32.8**	**24.7**	**16.1**	10.1	5.5

Table 2. Results on validation set of ActivityNet-1.3 in terms of mAP@$tIoU$ and average mAP. Note that all compared methods are fully supervised.

Supervision	Method	0.5	0.75	0.95	Average
Fully supervised	Singh et al. [26]	34.5	-	-	-
	Heilbron et al. [11]	40.00	17.90	4.70	21.70
	Wang et al. [35]	42.28	3.76	0.05	14.85
	Shou et al. [23]	43.83	25.88	0.21	22.77
	Xiong et al. [37]	39.12	23.48	5.49	23.98
	Lin et al. [16]	48.99	32.91	7.87	32.26
Weakly supervised	CPMN	39.29	24.09	6.71	24.42

Figure 6 visualizes the localization performance of our proposed method on THUMOS14 dataset. As shown in Fig. 6(a), the video includes two different action classes, and our Attention-based Cascaded (AC) T-CAS of corresponding class can localize the entire regions of target actions individually. It confirms that the two cascaded classifiers are successful in mining different but complementary target regions. And in Fig. 6(b), there are many action instances densely distributed in the video, however, our method can effectively highlight the regions which may contain actions, which demonstrates that our modified T-CAS is able to generate dense detections. Besides, the Fig. 6(c) presents a video with similar appearance and little dynamic motions along the temporal dimension, which is a difficult scene even for humans to distinguish between adjacent frames, resulting in inevitably missing detections. Nevertheless, our algorithm is still robust enough to discover some discriminative regions even with some false positives. To conclude, the proposed cascaded action localization sequence together with the pyramidal attention map is intuitive to promote the overall localization performance.

4.3   Ablation Study

In this section, we evaluate CPMN with different implementation variations to study their effects and investigate the contribution of several components proposed in our network. All the experiments for our ablation study are conducted on THUMOS14 dataset.

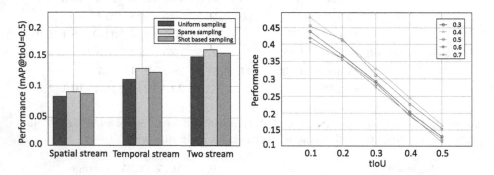

Fig. 5. Evaluation of the CPMN with different sampling methods (**left**) and erasing thresholds (**right**) used in the CCM on THUMOS14.

Sampling Strategy. The input untrimmed video usually exists substantial redundant frames which are useless for the cascaded model to leverage discriminative regions for recognition. In order to reduce computational cost, we sample the input feature sequence instead of using all units for video categorization. We first evaluate the Cascaded Classification Module (CCM) with different sampling methods, including uniform sampling, sparse sampling and shot-based sampling. The evaluation results are illustrated in Fig. 5 (left). We can observe that the shot-based sampling method which takes action structure into consideration shows better performance than uniform sampling and sparse sampling which serves as a data augmentation step leads to the best performance. Therefore we finally adopt sparse sampling to sample the input feature sequence of the CCM during training phase.

Erasing Threshold. We continue to study the influence of different erasing thresholds ζ which we use to identify the discriminative regions highlighted by the first classifier of the CCM and create a mask for online adversarial erasing step. As shown in Fig. 5 (right), we test the thresholds from 0.3 to 0.7 and report the performance over different IoU. We observe that when the threshold $\zeta = 0.4$, the localization performance of the two-stage model is boosted and the

Table 3. Performance with respect to architecture choices. In first column, only original T-CAS without adversarial mining and attention map is used for action localization.

Original T-CAS	✓	✓	✓
Mining T-CAS		✓	✓
Pyramidal Attention Map (PAM)			✓
mAP ($\alpha = 0.5$)	11.4	14.5	16.1

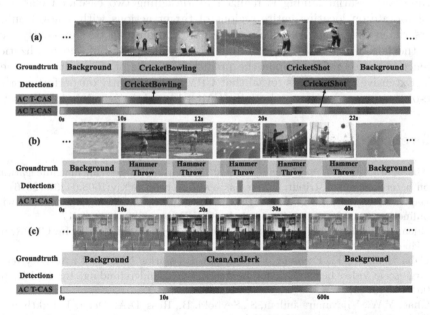

Fig. 6. Visualization of the action instances located by CPMN on THUMOS14. Figure (a) shows that entire regions of two actions are separately located in corresponding T-CAS. Figure (b) shows that dense predictions can be generated by our approach with less missing detections. Figure (c) shows that even the instances with small length and similar appearance, our model still can locate it with less false positives.

value larger or smaller than 0.4 would fail to encourage the second classifier to mine entire regions of target actions and may bring background noise.

Architecture of CPMN. As shown in Table 3, we investigate the contribution of each module proposed in our method. We choose the architecture sharing the same idea with CAM [42] for discriminative localization as our baseline model without online erasing step to mine entire regions and the pyramidal attention map. The comparison results reveal that the original T-CAS together with the mining T-CAS can promote the performance and with the help of pyramidal attention map, the localization performance can be further boosted. These observations suggest that these modules are all effective and indispensable in CPMN. Note that we also test the CCM with more classifiers. Specifically, we add the third classifier to handle the erased feature maps guided by the first two classifiers. However, we don't find any significant improvement.

5   Conclusion

In this paper, we propose the Cascaded Pyramid Mining Network (CPMN) for weakly supervised temporal action localization. Our method includes two main steps: cascaded adversarial mining and pyramidal attention map inference. Cascaded adversarial mining is realized by designing two cascaded classifiers to collaborate on locating entire regions of target actions with a novel online adversarial erasing step. And the pyramidal attention map tries explicitly handling the falsely activated regions and missing detections in the localization sequence, which is inferred upon the prediction results of the multi-tower network. Extensive experiments reveal that CPMN significantly outperforms other state-of-the-art approaches on both THUMOS14 and ActivityNet-1.3 datasets.

References

1. Abadi, M., Agarwal, A., Barham, P., et al.: Tensorflow: large-scale machine learning on heterogeneous distributed systems. arXiv preprint arXiv:1603.04467 (2016)
2. Bai, P., Tang, X., Wang, X., Liu, W.: Multiple instance detection network with online instance classifier refinement. In: CVPR, pp. 4322–4328 (2017)
3. Bilen, H., Vedaldi, A.: Weakly supervised deep detection networks. In: CVPR, pp. 2846–2854 (2016)
4. Caba Heilbron, F., Escorcia, V., Ghanem, B., Carlos Niebles, J.: ActivityNet: a large-scale video benchmark for human activity understanding. In: CVPR, pp. 961–970 (2015)
5. Chao, Y.W., Vijayanarasimhan, S., Seybold, B., Ross, D.A., Deng, J., Sukthankar, R.: Rethinking the faster R-CNN architecture for temporal action localization. In: CVPR, pp. 1130–1139 (2018)
6. Feichtenhofer, C., Pinz, A., Zisserman, A.: Convolutional two-stream network fusion for video action recognition. In: CVPR, pp. 1933–1941 (2016)
7. Gao, J., Yang, Z., Nevatia, R.: Cascaded boundary regression for temporal action detection. arXiv preprint arXiv:1705.01180 (2017)

8. Girshick, R., Donahue, J., Darrell, T., Malik, J.: Rich feature hierarchies for accurate object detection and semantic segmentation. In: CVPR, pp. 580–587 (2014)

9. He, K., Gkioxari, G., Dollar, P., Girshick, R.: Mask-RCNN. arXiv:1703.06870v2 (2017)

10. He, K., Zhang, X., Ren, S., Sun, J.: Deep residual learning for image recognition. In: CVPR, pp. 770–778 (2016)

11. Heilbron, F.C., Barrios, W., Escorcia, V., Ghanem, B.: SCC: semantic context cascade for efficient action detection. In: CVPR, pp. 3175–3184 (2017)

12. Ioffe, S., Szegedy, C.: Batch normalization: accelerating deep network training by reducing internal covariate shift. arXiv preprint arXiv:1502.03167 (2015)

13. Jia, Y., et al.: Caffe: convolutional architecture for fast feature embedding. In: Proceedings of the 22nd ACM International Conference on Multimedia, pp. 675–678. ACM (2014)

14. Jiang, Y., et al.: THUMOS challenge: action recognition with a large number of classes. In: Computer Vision-ECCV Workshop 2014 (2014)

15. Lin, T., Zhao, X., Shou, Z.: Single shot temporal action detection. In: Proceedings of the 2017 ACM on Multimedia Conference, pp. 988–996. ACM (2017)

16. Lin, T., Zhao, X., Shou, Z.: Temporal convolution based action proposal: submission to activitynet 2017. arXiv preprint arXiv:1707.06750 (2017)

17. Lin, T., Zhao, X., Su, H., Wang, C., Yang, M.: BSN: boundary sensitive network for temporal action proposal generation. arXiv preprint arXiv:1806.02964 (2018)

18. Lin, T.Y., Dollár, P., Girshick, R.B., He, K., Hariharan, B., Belongie, S.J.: Feature pyramid networks for object detection. In: CVPR, vol. 1, p. 4 (2017)

19. Oneata, D., Verbeek, J., Schmid, C.: The LEAR submission at THUMOS2014. THUMOS Action Recognition challenge (2014)

20. Redmon, J., Divvala, S., Girshick, R., Farhadi, A.: You only look once: unified, real-time object detection. In: CVPR, pp. 779–788 (2016)

21. Redmon, J., Farhadi, A.: Yolo9000: better, faster, stronger. arXiv preprint arXiv:1612.08242 (2016)

22. Richard, A., Gall, J.: Temporal action detection using a statistical language model. In: CVPR, pp. 3131–3140 (2016)

23. Shou, Z., Chan, J., Zareian, A., Miyazawa, K., Chang, S.F.: CDC: convolutional-de-convolutional networks for precise temporal action localization in untrimmed videos. In: CVPR, pp. 1417–1426. IEEE (2017)

24. Shou, Z., Wang, D., Chang, S.F.: Temporal action localization in untrimmed videos via multi-stage CNNs. In: CVPR, pp. 1049–1058 (2016)

25. Simonyan, K., Zisserman, A.: Two-stream convolutional networks for action recognition in videos. In: Advances in Neural Information Processing Systems, pp. 568–576 (2014)

26. Singh, G., Cuzzolin, F.: Untrimmed video classification for activity detection: submission to activitynet challenge. arXiv preprint arXiv:1607.01979 (2016)

27. Singh, K.K., Lee, Y.J.: Hide-and-seek: forcing a network to be meticulous for weakly-supervised object and action localization. In: ICCV (2017)

28. Su, H., Zhao, X., Lin, T., Fei, H.: Weakly supervised temporal action detection with shot-based temporal pooling network. In: Cheng, L., Leung, A.C.S., Ozawa, S. (eds.) ICONIP 2018. LNCS, vol. 11304, pp. 426–436. Springer, Cham (2018). https://doi.org/10.1007/978-3-030-04212-7_37

29. Tran, D., Bourdev, L., Fergus, R., Torresani, L., Paluri, M.: Learning spatiotemporal features with 3D convolutional networks. In: ICCV, pp. 4489–4497 (2015)

30. Uijlings, J.R., Van De Sande, K.E., Gevers, T., Smeulders, A.W.: Selective search for object recognition. IJCV **104**, 154–171 (2013)

31. Wang, H., Kläser, A., Schmid, C., Liu, C.L.: Action recognition by dense trajectories. In: CVPR, pp. 3169–3176. IEEE (2011)
32. Wang, H., Schmid, C.: Action recognition with improved trajectories. In: ICCV, pp. 3551–3558 (2013)
33. Wang, L., Xiong, Y., Lin, D., Van Gool, L.: UntrimmedNets for weakly supervised action recognition and detection. In: CVPR, vol. 2 (2017)
34. Wang, L., et al.: Temporal segment networks: towards good practices for deep action recognition. In: Leibe, B., Matas, J., Sebe, N., Welling, M. (eds.) ECCV 2016. LNCS, vol. 9912, pp. 20–36. Springer, Cham (2016). https://doi.org/10.1007/978-3-319-46484-8_2
35. Wang, R., Tao, D.: UTS at activitynet 2016. ActivityNet large scale activity recognition challenge 2016, 8 (2016)
36. Wei, Y., Feng, J., Liang, X., Cheng, M.M., Zhao, Y., Yan, S.: Object region mining with adversarial erasing: a simple classification to semantic segmentation approach. In: CVPR, vol. 1, p. 3 (2017)
37. Xiong, Y., Zhao, Y., Wang, L., Lin, D., Tang, X.: A pursuit of temporal accuracy in general activity detection. arXiv preprint arXiv:1703.02716 (2017)
38. Xu, H., Das, A., Saenko, K.: R-C3D: region convolutional 3D network for temporal activity detection. In: ICCV, pp. 5794–5803 (2017)
39. Yuan, Z.H., Stroud, J.C., Lu, T., Deng, J.: Temporal action localization by structured maximal sums. In: CVPR, vol. 2, p. 7 (2017)
40. Zhang, J., Bargal, S.A., Lin, Z., Brandt, J., Shen, X., Sclaroff, S.: Top-down neural attention by excitation backprop. IJCV **126**, 1084–1102 (2018)
41. Zhao, Y., Xiong, Y., Wang, L., Wu, Z., Tang, X., Lin, D.: Temporal action detection with structured segment networks. In: ICCV, vol. 2 (2017)
42. Zhou, B., Khosla, A., Lapedriza, A., Oliva, A., Torralba, A.: Learning deep features for discriminative localization. In: CVPR, pp. 2921–2929 (2016)
43. Zitnick, C.L., Dollár, P.: Edge boxes: locating object proposals from edges. In: Fleet, D., Pajdla, T., Schiele, B., Tuytelaars, T. (eds.) ECCV 2014. LNCS, vol. 8693, pp. 391–405. Springer, Cham (2014). https://doi.org/10.1007/978-3-319-10602-1_26

Coarse-to-Fine: A RNN-Based Hierarchical Attention Model for Vehicle Re-identification

Xiu-Shen Wei[1](✉)[iD], Chen-Lin Zhang[2][iD], Lingqiao Liu[3][iD], Chunhua Shen[3][iD], and Jianxin Wu[2][iD]

[1] Megvii Research Nanjing, Megvii Technology, Nanjing, China
weixs.gm@gmail.com
[2] National Key Laboratory for Novel Software Technology,
Nanjing University, Nanjing, China
{zhangcl,wujx}@lamda.nju.edu.cn
[3] School of Computer Science, The University of Adelaide, Adelaide, Australia
{lingqiao.liu,chunhua.shen}@adelaide.edu.au

Abstract. Vehicle re-identification is an important problem and becomes desirable with the rapid expansion of applications in video surveillance and intelligent transportation. By recalling the identification process of human vision, we are aware that there exists a native hierarchical dependency when humans identify different vehicles. Specifically, humans always firstly determine one vehicle's coarse-grained category, *i.e.*, the car model/type. Then, under the branch of the predicted car model/type, they are going to identify specific vehicles by relying on subtle visual cues, *e.g.*, customized paintings and windshield stickers, at the fine-grained level. Inspired by the coarse-to-fine hierarchical process, we propose an end-to-end RNN-based Hierarchical Attention (RNN-HA) classification model for vehicle re-identification. RNN-HA consists of three mutually coupled modules: the first module generates image representations for vehicle images, the second hierarchical module models the aforementioned hierarchical dependent relationship, and the last attention module focuses on capturing the subtle visual information distinguishing specific vehicles from each other. By conducting comprehensive experiments on two vehicle re-identification benchmark datasets VeRi and VehicleID, we demonstrate that the proposed model achieves superior performance over state-of-the-art methods.

Keywords: Vehicle re-identification · Hierarchical dependency · Attention mechanism · Deep learning

The first two authors contributed equally to this work. This research was supported by NSFC (National Natural Science Foundation of China) under 61772256 and the program A for Outstanding Ph.D. candidate of Nanjing University (201702A010). Liu's participation was in part supported by ARC DECRA Fellowship (DE170101259).

© Springer Nature Switzerland AG 2019
C. V. Jawahar et al. (Eds.): ACCV 2018, LNCS 11362, pp. 575–591, 2019.
https://doi.org/10.1007/978-3-030-20890-5_37

1   Introduction

Vehicle re-identification is an important yet frontier problem, which aims at determining whether two images are taken from the same specific vehicle. It has diverse applications in video surveillance [30], intelligent transportation [37] and urban computing [40]. Moreover, vehicle re-identification has recently drawn increasing attentions in the computer vision community [19,20,23].

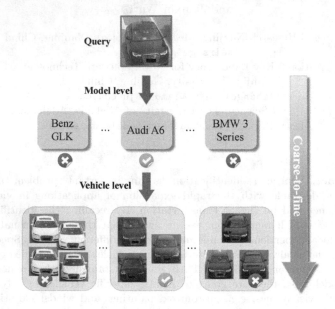

Fig. 1. Illustration of coarse-to-fine hierarchical information as a latent but crucial cue for vehicle re-identification. (Best viewed in color and zoomed in.) (Color figure online)

Compared with the classic person re-identification problem, vehicle re-identification could be more challenging as different specific vehicles can only be distinguished by slight and subtle differences, such as some customized paintings, windshield stickers, favorite decorations, etc. Nevertheless, there still conceals some latent but crucial information for handling this problem. As shown in Fig. 1, when humans identify different vehicles, they always follow a *coarse-to-fine* identification process. Specifically, we tend to firstly determine this specific vehicle belongs to which car model/type. The first step can eliminate many distractors, *i.e.*, vehicles with similar subtle visual appearances but belonging to the other different car models/types. In the following, within the candidate vehicle set of the same car model/type, humans will carefully distinguish different vehicles from each other by using these subtle visual cues. Apparently, there is a hierarchical dependency in this coarse-to-fine process, which is yet neglected by previous studies [16,19,20,23].

Motivated by such human's identification process, we propose a unified RNN-based Hierarchical Attention (RNN-HA) classification model for vehicle re-identification. Specifically, as shown in Fig. 2, our RNN-HA consists of three main modules: *(1)* the representation learning module, *(2)* the RNN-based hierarchical module and *(3)* the attention module. The first module encodes the discriminative information of vehicle images into the corresponding deep convolutional descriptors. Then, the second RNN-based hierarchical module will mimic the coarse-to-fine identification process. Concretely, at the coarse-grained level classification (for car models), we first aggregate these deep descriptors by global average pooling (named as "image embedding vector x_1" in Fig. 2), which is expected to retain global information contributing to the coarse-grained level. We then feed the image embedding vector x_1 as the input at time step 1 into the RNN-based hierarchical module. The output at time step 1 is used for the coarse-grained level classification. More importantly, the same output is also treated as the source for generating an attention guidance signal which is crucial for the subsequent fine-grained level classification. At the fine-grained level classification (for specific vehicles), to capture subtle appearance cues, we leverage an attention module where the aforementioned attention guidance signal will evaluate which deep descriptors should be attended or overlooked. Based on the attention module, the original deep descriptors are transformed into the attended descriptors which reflect those image regions containing subtle discriminative information. After that, the attended descriptors are aggregated by global average pooling into the attention embedding vector x_2 (cf. Fig. 2). Then, the attention embedding vector x_2 is fed into RNN at time step 2 for the fine-grained level classification. In the evaluation, we employ the trained RNN-HA model as a feature extractor on test vehicle images (whose vehicle categories are disjoint with the training categories) to extract the outputs at time step 2 as the feature representations. For re-identification, these representations are first ℓ_2-normalized, and then the cosine acts as the similarity function for computing relative distances among different vehicles.

In experiments, we perform the proposed RNN-HA model on two vehicle re-identification benchmark datasets, *i.e.*, *VeRi* [19] and *VehicleID* [16]. Empirical results show that our RNN-HA model significantly outperforms state-of-the-art methods on both datasets. Furthermore, we also conduct ablation studies for separately investigating the effectiveness of the proposed RNN-based hierarchical and attention modules in RNN-HA.

In summary, our major contributions are three-fold:

– For vehicle re-identification, we propose a novel end-to-end trainable RNN-HA model consisting of three mutually coupled modules, especially two crucial modules (*i.e.*, the RNN-based hierarchical module and the attention module) which are tailored for this problem.
– Specifically, by leveraging powerful RNNs, the RNN-based hierarchical module models the coarse-to-fine category hierarchical dependency (*i.e.*, from car model to specific vehicle) beneath vehicle re-identification. Furthermore, the attention module is proposed for effectively capturing subtle visual appearance cues, which is crucial for distinguishing different specific vehicles (*e.g.*, two cars of the same car model).

– We conduct comprehensive experiments on two challenging vehicle re-identification datasets, and our proposed model achieves superior performance over competing previous studies on both datasets. Moreover, by comparing with our baseline methods, we validate the effectiveness of two proposed key modules.

2   Related Work

We briefly review two lines of related work: vehicle re-identification and developments of deep neural networks.

2.1   Vehicle Re-identification

Vehicle re-identification is an important application in video surveillance, intelligent transportation and public security [5,16,19,20,36]. It is a frontier research area in recent years with limited related studies in the literature.

Feris *et al.* [5] proposed an attribute-based approach for vehicle search in surveillance scenes. By classifying with different attributes, *e.g.*, colors and sizes, retrieval was performed on searching vehicles with such similar attributes in the database. In 2015, Yang *et al.* [36] proposed the large-scale car dataset *CompCar* for multiple car-related tasks, such as car model classification, car model verification and attribute prediction. However, the category granularity of the studying tasks in [25,36] just stayed in the car model level, which was not fine enough for the specific vehicle level. Very recently, Liu *et al.* [19] and Liu *et al.* [16] proposed their vehicle re-identification dataset *VeRi* and *VehicleID*, respectively. After that, vehicle re-identification started to gain attentions in the computer vision community.

Specifically, the *VeRi* dataset [19] contains over 50, 000 images of 776 vehicles captured by twenty cameras in a road network. On this dataset, [19] proposed an appearance-based method named FACT combining both low-level features (*e.g.*, color and texture) and high-level semantic information extracted by deep neural networks. Later, [20] and [23] tried to deal with vehicle re-identification by using not only appearance information but also complex and hard-acquired spatio-temporal information. On the other hand, the *VehicleID* dataset [16] is a large-scale vehicle dataset containing about 26, 000 different vehicles with 222, 000 images. Liu *et al.* [16] proposed a mixed structured deep network with their coupled cluster loss to learn the relative distances of different vehicles on that dataset, which only depended on appearance cues.

In this paper, we attempt to use our RNN-HA model to deal with vehicle re-identification by depending on purely visual appearance cues. The reason is that appearance information is directly beneath vehicle images, and the images are easy to collect. Compared with that, complex and expensive spatio-temporal information is much harder to gather. For example, the two existing *large-scale* car/vehicle datasets, *e.g.*, *CompCar* [36] and *VehicleID* [16], only provide the appearance-based labels such as car types, models and identified annotations.

Whilst, they do not provide any spatio-temporal information. Moreover, our experimental results prove that it is practical to use only appearance information for accurate vehicle re-identification, cf. Table 2.

2.2 Deep Neural Networks

Deep convolutional neural networks (DCNNs) try to model the high-level abstractions of the visual data by using architectures composed of multiple non-linear transformations. Recent progresses in diverse computer vision applications, e.g., large-scale image classification [14], object detection [2,18] and semantic segmentation [21], are made based on the developments of the powerful DCNNs.

On the other hand, the family of Recurrent Neural Networks (RNNs) including Gated Recurrent Neural Networks (GRUs) [3] and Long-Short Term Memory Networks (LSTMs) [8] have recently achieved great success in several tasks including image captioning [11,28,33,35], visual question answering [6,34], machine translation [26], etc. These works prove that RNNs are able to model the temporal dependency in sequential data and learn effective temporal feature representations, which inspires us to rely on RNNs for modeling the hierarchical coarse-to-fine characteristic (i.e., from car model to specific vehicle) beneath the vehicle re-identification problem.

3   Model

We propose a novel RNN-based hierarchical attention (RNN-HA) classification model to solve the vehicle re-identification problem. In this section, we present our RNN-HA model by introducing its key constituent modules, i.e., the representation learning module, the RNN-based hierarchical module and the attention module, respectively. The framework of our model is illustrated in Fig. 2.

3.1   Representation Learning Module

As shown in Fig. 2, the first module of RNN-HA is to learn a holistic image representation from an input vehicle image via traditional convolutional neural networks. The obtained deep image representations will be processed by the following modules. This representation learning module consists of multiple traditional convolutional layers (equipped with ReLU and pooling). However, different from previous vehicle re-identification methods (e.g., [16,23]), we discard fully connected layers, and utilize convolutional activations for subsequent processing.

Concretely, the activations of a convolution layer can be formulated as an order-3 tensor T with $h \times w \times d$ elements, which includes a set of 2-D feature maps. These feature maps are embedded with rich spatial information, and are also known to obtain mid- and high-level information, e.g., object parts [17,24]. From another point of view, these activations can alternatively be viewed as an

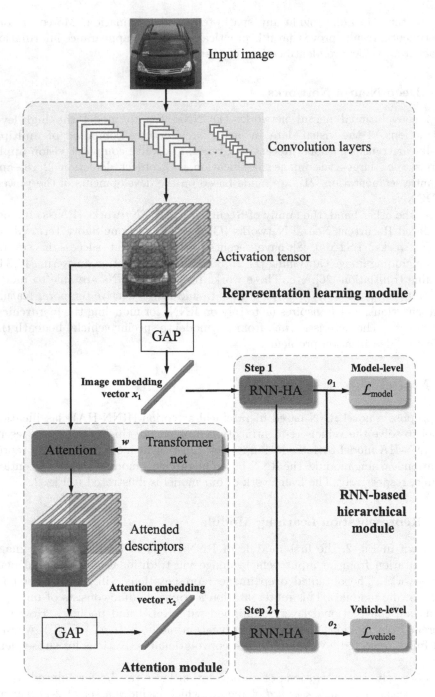

Fig. 2. Framework of the proposed RNN-HA model. Our model consists of three mutually coupled modules, *i.e.*, representation learning module, RNN-based hierarchical module and attention module. (Best viewed in color.) (Color figure online)

array of d-dimensional deep descriptors extracted at $h \times w$ locations. Apparently, these deep convolutional descriptors have more local/subtle visual information and more spatial information than those of the fully connected layer features.

After obtaining the activation tensor, at the coarse-grained classification level (*i.e.*, model-level), we directly apply global average pooling (GAP) upon these deep descriptors and regard the pooled representation as the "image embedding vector" x_1. Then, x_1 will be fed as the input at time step 1 into the RNN-based hierarchical module. Whilst, at the fine-grained classification level (*i.e.*, vehicle-level), these deep descriptors plus the intermediate output of the RNN-based hierarchical module will be used for generating the attended descriptors with the following attention embedding vector x_2, cf. Fig. 2.

3.2   Crucial Modules in RNN-HA

In the following sections, we elaborate the RNN-based hierarchical module and the attention module which are two crucial modules of our RNN-HA model.

RNN-based Hierarchical Module. Recurrent Neural Network (RNN) [8] is a class of neural network that maintains internal hidden states to model the dynamic temporal behavior of sequences with arbitrary lengths through directed cyclic connections between its units. It can be considered as a hidden Markov model extension that employs non-linear transition function and is capable of modeling long/short term temporal dependencies.

We hereby employ RNN to capture the latent hierarchical label dependencies existing in vehicle re-identification. Concretely, we choose Gated Recurrent Units (GRUs) [3] as the gating mechanism to implement RNN. GRUs have fewer parameters than another popular gating mechanism, *i.e.*, LSTM [8], which makes GRU much easier to optimize. Moreover, evaluations by Chung *et al.* [4] found that when LSTM and GRU have the same amount of parameters, GRU slightly outperforms LSTM. Similar observations were also corroborated in [12].

GRU contains two gates: an update gate z and a reset gate r. We follow the model used in [3]. Let σ be the sigmoid non-linear activation function. The GRU updates for time step t given inputs x_t, h_{t-1} are:

$$z_t = \sigma(W_{xz}x_t + W_{hz}h_{t-1} + b_z), \tag{1}$$

$$r_t = \sigma(W_{xr}x_t + W_{hr}h_{t-1} + b_r), \tag{2}$$

$$n_t = \tanh(W_{xg}x_t + r_t \odot W_{hg}h_{t-1} + b_g), \tag{3}$$

$$h_t = (1 - z_t) \odot n_t + z_t \odot h_{t-1}. \tag{4}$$

Here, $\odot$ represents the product with a gate value, and various W matrices are learned parameters.

As shown in Fig. 2, we decompose the coarse-to-fine hierarchical classification problem into an ordered prediction path, *i.e.*, from car model to specific vehicle. The prediction path can reveal the hierarchical characteristic beneath this two-stage classification problem. Meanwhile, the probability of a path can be computed by the RNN model.

As aforementioned, since we aim to solve coarse-grained classification at the first step, global image features which represent global visual information are required. Thus, the image embedding vector x_1 produced by simply global average pooling is used as the input at the first time step ($t = 1$) in the hierarchical module. Then, the output vector o_1 at $t = 1$ is employed for computing the coarse-grained (model-level) classification loss, $i.e.$, $\mathcal{L}_{\text{model}}$. At the same time, o_1 will be transformed via a transformer network (cf. the green sub-module in Fig. 2) into an attention guidance signal w. The attention signal can guide the subsequent attention network to learn which deep descriptors should be attended when identifying different specific vehicles. The details of the attention network are presented in the next sub-section.

Now suppose we obtain a well-trained attention network, it could focus on these descriptors corresponding to subtle discriminative image regions ($e.g.$, customized paintings, favorite decorations, etc.), and neglect these descriptors corresponding to common patterns ($e.g.$, the similar headlights, car roofs, etc.). Based on the attentions on descriptors, we can obtain the attention embedding vector x_2 which is also the input of the RNN-based hierarchical module at $t = 2$. The rest procedure at time step 2 is computing the loss in fine-grained classification ($i.e.$, vehicle-level classification) based on the output vector o_2.

At last, the final loss of our RNN-HA is formed by the summation of both the coarse-grained ($i.e.$, model-level) and fine-grained ($i.e.$, vehicle-level) classification loss as:

$$\mathcal{L} = \mathcal{L}_{\text{model}} + \mathcal{L}_{\text{vehicle}} . \tag{5}$$

In our implementation, the traditional cross entropy loss function is employed in each loss branch. Note that, there is no tuning parameter in this equation, which reveals RNN-HA is generalized and not tricky.

Attention Module. After performing the coarse-grained classification, it is required to identify different specific vehicles at this fine-grained level. What distinguishes different vehicles from each other is the subtle visual information, such as customized paintings, windshield stickers, favorite decorations, etc. To capture these subtle but important cues, we propose to use an attention model to focus processing only on the attended deep descriptors reflecting those cues. Meanwhile, discarding those descriptors corresponding to common patterns, $e.g.$, the same car roofs of the same one car model, is also crucial for identifying specific vehicles.

To achieve these goals, we rely on the output o_1 of the RNN-based hierarchical module at $t = 1$ by regarding it as the guidance signal for the subsequent attention learning. Specifically, we design a transformer network to transform o_1 into a new space where it could play a role as the attention guidance signal w. The transformer network contains two fully connected layers with a ReLU layer between them. After this transforming, w is utilized for evaluating which deep descriptors should be attended or overlooked.

Given an input image, $\boldsymbol{f}_{(i,j)} \in \mathbb{R}^d$ is the deep descriptor in the (i,j) spatial location in the activation tensor of the last convolutional layer, where $i \in \{1, 2, \ldots, h\}$ and $j \in \{1, 2, \ldots, w\}$. Based on the attention guidance signal $\boldsymbol{w}$, we can get the corresponding unnormalized attention scores $s_{(i,j)} \in \mathbb{R}^1$ of $\boldsymbol{f}_{(i,j)}$ by:

$$s_{(i,j)} = g(\boldsymbol{w}^\top \boldsymbol{f}_{(i,j)}), \tag{6}$$

where $g(\cdot)$ is the softplus function, i.e., $g(x) = \ln(1 + \exp(x))$. Since we only aim to concern with the relative importance of the deep descriptors within an image, we further normalize the attention scores into the $[0, 1]$ interval for aggregating the descriptors:

$$a_{(i,j)} = \frac{s_{(i,j)} + \epsilon}{\sum_i \sum_j (s_{(i,j)} + \epsilon)}, \tag{7}$$

where $a_{(i,j)}$ is the normalized attention score, and ϵ is a small constant set to 0.1 in our experiments.

Thus, different deep descriptors will receive the corresponding (normalized) attention scores depending on how much attention paid to itself. Finally, we can get the attended feature representation $\hat{\boldsymbol{f}}_{(i,j)} \in \mathbb{R}^d$ by applying $a_{(i,j)}$ to $\boldsymbol{f}_{(i,j)}$ as follows:

$$\hat{\boldsymbol{f}}_{(i,j)} = a_{(i,j)} \odot \boldsymbol{f}_{(i,j)}, \tag{8}$$

where $\odot$ is the element-wise multiplication. Then, after global average pooling employed in $\hat{\boldsymbol{f}}_{(i,j)}$, we can obtain the attention embedding vector:

$$\boldsymbol{x}_2 = \frac{1}{h \times w} \sum_i \sum_j \hat{\boldsymbol{f}}_{(i,j)}. \tag{9}$$

Then, $\boldsymbol{x}_2 \in \mathbb{R}^d$ will be fed as the input into the RNN-based hierarchical module at $t = 2$. At last, by treating different vehicles as classification categories, the output o_2 at $t = 2$ is used for recognizing vehicles at the fine-grained level. As each module is differentiable, the whole RNN-HA model is end-to-end trainable.

Additionally, in theory, the proposed RNN-based hierarchical module can be composed of more time steps, i.e., $t > 2$. Since the vehicle datasets used in experiments have two-level hierarchical labels, we use our RNN-HA with $t = 2$ for the vehicle re-identification problem. Beyond that, the proposed RNN-HA model can also deal with the hierarchical fine-grained recognition problem, e.g., [9], which reveals the generalization usage of our model.

4   Experiments

In this section, we first describe the datasets and evaluation metric used in experiments, and present the implementation details. Then, we report vehicle re-identification results on two challenging benchmark datasets.

4.1   Datasets and Evaluation Metric

To evaluate the effectiveness of our proposed RNN-HA model, we conduct experiments on two benchmark vehicle re-identification datasets, *i.e.*, *VeRi* [19] and *VehicleID* [16].

The *VeRi* dataset contains more than $50,000$ images of 776 vehicles with identity annotations and car types. The car types in *VeRi* include the following ten kinds: "sedan", "SUV", "van", "hatchback", "MPV", "pickup", "bus", "truck" and "estate". The *VeRi* dataset is split into a training set consisting of $37,778$ images of 576 vehicles and a test set of $11,579$ images belonging to 200 vehicles. In the evaluation, a subset of $1,678$ images in the test set are used as the query images. The test protocol in [19,20] recommends that evaluation should be conducted in an image-to-track fashion, in which the image is used as the query, while the gallery consists of tracks of the same vehicle captured by other cameras. The mean average precision (mAP), top-1 and top-5 accuracy (CMC) are chosen as the evaluation metric for the *VeRi* dataset.

Compared with *VeRi*, *VehicleID* is a large-scale vehicle re-identification dataset, which has a total of $26,267$ vehicles with $221,763$ images, and $10,319$ vehicles are labeled with models such as "Audi A6", "Ford Focus", "Benz GLK" and so on. There are 228 car models in total. *VehicleID* is split into a training set with $110,178$ images of $13,134$ vehicles and a testing set with $111,585$ images of $13,133$ vehicles. For *VehicleID*, the image-to-image search is conducted because each vehicle is captured in one image by one camera. For each test dataset (size $= 800, 1,600$ and $2,400$), one image of each vehicle is randomly selected into the gallery set, and all the other images are query images. We repeat the above processing for ten times, and report the average results. Following the previous work [16], the evaluation metric for *VehicleID* is top-1, top-5 accuracy (CMC).

4.2   Implementation Details

In our experiments, vehicles' identity annotations of both datasets are treated as the vehicle-level classification categories, while the car types of *VeRi* and the car models of *VehicleID* are regarded as the model-level classification categories for these two datasets, respectively. Note that, for both datasets, the vehicle-level classification categories of training and testing are disjoint. All images are of 224×224 image resolution. After training RNN-HA, we employ our model as a feature extractor for extracting test image features. Specifically, the output o_2 at time step 2 of our RNN-HA is the acquired image representation. In the evaluation, o_2 of test images are firstly ℓ_2-normalized, and then the cosine distance acts as the similarity function in re-identification.

For fair comparisons, following [16], we adopt *VGG_CNN_M_1024* [1] as the base model of our representation learning module. For the RNN-based module, the number of hidden units in GRU is $1,024$, and the zero vector is the hidden state input at time step 0. During training, we train our unified RNN-HA in an end-to-end manner by employing the RMSprop [29] optimization method with its default parameter settings to update model parameters. The learning rate is set to 0.001 at the beginning, and five epochs later, it is reset to 0.0001. The batch size is 64. We implement our model by the open-source library PyTorch.

4.3   Main Results

We present the main vehicle re-identification results by firstly introducing state-of-the-arts and our baseline methods, then following the comparison results on two datasets.[1]

Comparison Methods. We compare nine vehicle re-identification approaches which are evaluated on *VehicleID* and *VeRi*. The details of these approaches are introduced as follows. Among them, many state-of-the-art methods, *e.g.*, [13,16, 42], also employ both vehicle-level and model-level supervision, which has the same formation as ours.

- *Local Maximal Occurrence Representation (LOMO)* [15] is the state-of-the-art text features for person re-identification. We follow the optimal parameter settings given in [15] when adopting LOMO on these two vehicle re-identification datasets.
- *Color based feature (BOW-CN)* [38] is a benchmark method in person re-identification, which applies the Bag-of-Words (BOW) model [10,22] with Color Name (CN) features [31]. By following [38], a $5,600$-d BOW-CN feature is obtained as the color based feature.
- *Semantic feature learned by CNN (GoogLeNet)* adopts the GoogLeNet model [27] which is fine-tuned on the CompCars dataset [36] as a powerful feature extractor for high-level semantic attributes of the vehicle appearance. The image feature of this method is $1,024$-d extracted from the last pooling layer of GoogLeNet.
- *Fusion of Attributes and Color features (FACT)* [19] is proposed for vehicle re-identification by combining deeply learned visual feature from GoogLeNet [27], BOW-CN and BOW-SIFT feature to measure only the visual similarity between pairs of query images.
- *Siamese-Visual* [23] relys on a siamese-based neural network which has a symmetric structure to learn the similarity between a query image pair with appearance information.
- *Triplet Loss* [32] is adopted in vehicle re-identification by learning a harmonic embedding of each input image in the Euclidean space that tends to maximize the relative distance between the matched pair and the mismatched pair.
- *Coupled Cluster Loss (CCL)* [16] is proposed for improving triplet loss by replacing the single positive/negative input sample by positive/negative images sets, which can make the training phase more stable and accelerate the convergence speed.

---

[1] Note that, in Tables 1 and 2, we only compare with the appearance-based methods for fair comparisons.

Table 1. Comparison of different methods on *VeRi* [19].

Methods	mAP	Top-1	Top-5
LOMO [15]	9.64	25.33	46.48
BOW-CN [38]	12.20	33.91	53.69
GoogLeNet [36]	17.89	52.32	72.17
FACT [19]	18.75	52.21	72.88
Siamese-Visual [23]	29.48	41.12	60.31
VAMI [42]	50.13	77.03	90.82
FC-HA (w/o RNN)	47.19	61.56	76.88
RNN-H w/o attention	48.92	63.28	78.82
Our RNN-HA	52.88	66.03	80.51
Our RNN-HA (ResNet)	**56.80**	**74.79**	**87.31**

- *Mixed Diff+CCL* [16] adopts a mixed network structure with a coupled cluster loss to learn the relative distances of different vehicles. Note that, the most different point between it and our model is that it used these two level categories in a simple parallel fashion, while we formulate them into a hierarchical fashion. Experimental results could validate the effectiveness of our proposed hierarchical model, and justify the hierarchical fashion should be the optimal option.
- *CLVR* [13] consists of two branches in the cross-modality paradigm, where one branch is for the vehicle model level and the other is for the vehicle ID level. Again, the two level categories in their model are not formulated into a hierarchical fashion like ours.
- *VAMI* [42] proposes a viewpoint-aware attentive multi-view inference model by leveraging the cues of multiple views to deal with vehicle re-identification.

Additionally, to investigate the impacts of the various modules in our end-to-end framework, we analyze the effects of the RNN-based hierarchical module and the attention module by conducting experiments on two baselines:

- *FC-HA (w/o RNN)* replaces the RNN hierarchical module by simply employing traditional fully-connected layers as direct transformation, but keeps the attention mechanism.
- *RNN-H w/o attention* keeps the hierarchical module, but removes the attention module from our proposed RNN-HA model. Specifically, the inputs x_1 and x_2 at $t = 1$ and $t = 2$ are both the representations global average pooled by these deep convolutional descriptors.

Comparison Results on *VeRi*. Table 1 presents the comparison results on the *VeRi* dataset. Our proposed RNN-HA model achieves 52.88% mAP, 77.03% top-1 accuracy and 90.91% top-5 accuracy on *VeRi*, which significantly outperforms the other state-of-the-art methods. These results validate the effectiveness of

Table 2. Comparison of different methods on the *VehicleID* dataset [16].

Methods	Test size = 800		Test size = 1,600		Test size = 2,400	
	Top-1	Top-5	Top-1	Top-5	Top-1	Top-5
LOMO [15]	19.7	32.1	18.9	29.5	15.3	25.6
BOW-CN [38]	13.1	22.7	12.9	21.1	10.2	17.9
GoogLeNet [36]	47.9	67.4	43.5	63.5	38.2	59.5
FACT [19]	49.5	67.9	44.6	64.2	39.9	60.5
Triplet Loss [32]	40.4	61.7	35.4	54.6	31.9	50.3
CCL [16]	43.6	64.2	37.0	57.1	32.9	53.3
Mixed Diff+CCL [16]	49.0	73.5	42.8	66.8	38.2	61.6
CLVR [13]	62.0	76.0	56.1	71.8	50.6	68.0
VAMI [42]	63.1	83.3	52.8	75.1	47.3	70.3
FC-HA (w/o RNN)	56.7	74.5	53.6	70.6	48.6	66.3
RNN-H w/o attention	64.5	78.8	62.4	75.9	59.0	74.2
Our RNN-HA	68.8	81.9	66.2	79.6	62.6	77.0
Our RNN-HA (672)	74.9	85.3	71.1	82.3	68.0	81.4
Our RNN-HA (ResNet+672)	**83.8**	**88.1**	**81.9**	**87.0**	**81.1**	**87.4**

the proposed model. Moreover, RNN-HA has a gain of 5.69% mAP and 15.47% top-1 accuracy comparing with the FC-HA baseline method, which proves the effectiveness of the RNN-based hierarchical design. Also, compared with "RNN-H w/o attention", RNN-HA achieves a gain of 3.96% mAP and 11.75% top-1 accuracy. It justifies our proposed attention module when identifying different specific vehicles at the fine-grained classification level.

In addition, to further improve the re-identification accuracy, we simply replace the *VGG_CNN_M_1024* model of the representation learning module with *ResNet-50* [7]. Our modified model is denoted as "RNN-HA (ResNet)", which obtains 56.80% mAP, 80.79% top-1 accuracy and 92.31% top-5 accuracy on *VeRi*.

Comparison Results on *VehicleID*. For the large-scale dataset, *VehicleID*, we report the comparison results in Table 2. On different test settings (*i.e.*, test size = 800, 1,600 and 2,400), our proposed RNN-HA achieves the best re-identification performance on this large-scale dataset. An interesting observation in both tables is that the FC-HA baseline method outperforms all the Siamese or triplet training methods on both *VeRi* and *VehicleID*. It is consistent with the observations in recently most successful person re-identification approaches, *e.g.*, [39,41]. These approaches argue that a classification loss is superior for the re-identification task, while the triplet loss or siamese-based nets perform unsatisfactorily due to its tricky training example sampling strategy.

Fig. 3. Examples of the attention maps on *VehicleID*. The brighter the region, the higher the attention scores. (Best viewed in color and zoomed in.)

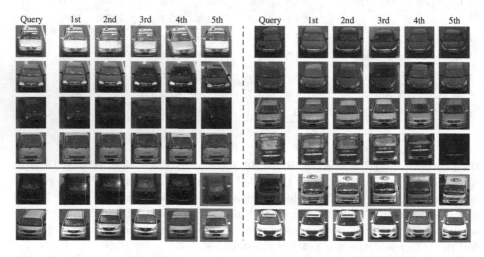

Fig. 4. The top-5 re-identification results on the large-scale *VehicleID* dataset. The upper eight examples are successful, while the lower four examples are failure cases. Red boxes denote false positives. (Best viewed in color and zoomed in.) (Color figure online)

From the qualitative perspective, Fig. 3 shows the learned attention maps (*i.e.*, $a_{(i,j)}$ in Eq. 7) of several random sampled test vehicle images. We can find that the attended regions accurately correspond to these subtle and discriminative image regions, such as windshield stickers, stuffs placed behind windshield or rear windshield, and customized paintings. In addition, Fig. 4 presents several re-identification results returned by our RNN-HA on *VehicleID*.

Furthermore, on this large-scale dataset, we also use input images with a high image resolution, *i.e.*, 672×672, since higher resolution could benefit to learn a more accurate attention map. The RNN-HA model with the 672×672 resolution is denoted by "RNN-HA (672)". Apparently, it improves the re-identification top-1 accuracy by 5–6%. Besides, based on the high resolution, we also modify RNN-HA by equipping it with *ResNet-50*, and report its results as "RNN-HA (ResNet+672)" in Table 2. On such challenging large-scale dataset, even though we only depend on appearance information, our model could achieve 83.8% top-1 accuracy, which reveals its effectiveness in real-life applications.

5   Conclusion

In this paper, we noticed there is a coarse-to-fine hierarchical dependency natively beneath the vehicle re-identification problem, *i.e.*, from coarse-grained (car models/types) to fine-grained (specific vehicles). To model this important hierarchical dependent relationship, we proposed a unified RNN-based hierarchical attention (RNN-HA) model consisting of three mutually coupled modules. In RNN-HA, after obtaining the deep convolutional descriptors generated by the first representation learning module, we leveraged the powerful RNNs and further designed a RNN-based hierarchical module to mimic such hierarchical classification process. Moreover, at the fine-grained level, the attention module was developed to capture subtle appearance cues for effectively distinguish different specific vehicles.

On two benchmark datasets, *VeRi* and *VehicleID*, the proposed RNN-HA model achieved the best re-identification performance. Besides, extensive ablation studies demonstrated the effectiveness of individual modules of RNN-HA. In the future, it is promising to further improve the re-identification performance by incorporating more attributes information into our proposed RNN-HA framework.

References

1. Chatfield, K., Simonyan, K., Vedaldi, A.: Return of the devil in the details: delving deep into convolutional nets. arXiv preprint arXiv:1405.3531 (2014)
2. Chen, C., Liu, M.-Y., Tuzel, O., Xiao, J.: R-CNN for small object detection. In: Lai, S.-H., Lepetit, V., Nishino, K., Sato, Y. (eds.) ACCV 2016. LNCS, vol. 10115, pp. 214–230. Springer, Cham (2017). https://doi.org/10.1007/978-3-319-54193-8_14
3. Cho, K., et al.: Learning phrase representations using RNN encoder-decoder for statistical machine translation. In: EMNLP, pp. 1724–1735, October 2014
4. Chung, J., Gulcehre, C., Cho, K., Bengio, Y.: Empirical evaluation of gated recurrent neural networks on sequence modeling. arXiv preprint arXiv:1412.3555 (2014)
5. Feris, R.S., Siddiquie, B., Zhai, Y., Datta, A., Brown, L.M., Pankanti, S.: Large-scale vehicle detection, indexing, and search in urban surveillance videos. IEEE TMM **14**(1), 28–42 (2015)
6. Gao, H., Mao, J., Zhou, J., Huang, Z., Wang, L., Xu, W.: Are you talking to a machine? Dataset and methods for multilingual image question answering. In: NIPS, pp. 2296–2304, December 2015
7. He, K., Zhang, X., Ren, S., Sun, J.: Deep residual learning for image recognition. In: CVPR, pp. 770–778, June 2016
8. Hochreiter, S., Schmidhuber, J.: Long shot-term memory. Neural Comput. **9**(8), 1735–1780 (1997)

9. Hou, S., Feng, Y., Wang, Z.: VegFru: a domain-specific dataset for fine-grained visual categorization. In: ICCV, pp. 541–549, October 2017

10. Jégou, H., Douze, M., Schmid, C., Pérez, P.: Aggregating local descriptors into a compact image representation. In: CVPR, pp. 3304–3311, June 2010

11. Johnson, J., Karpathy, A., Fei-Fei, L.: DenseCap: fully convolutional localization networks for dense captioning. In: CVPR, pp. 4565–4574, June 2016

12. Jozefowicz, R., Zaremba, W., Sutskever, I.: An empirical exploration of recurrent network architectures. In: ICML, pp. 2342–2350, July 2015

13. Kanac, A., Zhu, X., Gong, S.: Vehicle re-identification by fine-grained cross-level deep learning. In: BMVC, pp. 770–781, September 2017

14. Krizhevsky, A., Sutskever, I., Hinton, G.E.: ImageNet classification with deep convolutional neural networks. In: NIPS, pp. 1097–1105, December 2012

15. Liao, S., Hu, Y., Zhu, X., Li, S.Z.: Person re-identification by local maximal occurrence representation and metric learning. In: CVPR, pp. 2197–2206, June 2015

16. Liu, H., Tian, Y., Wang, Y., Pang, L., Huang, T.: Deep relative distance learning: tell the difference between similar vehicles. In: CVPR, pp. 2167–2175, June 2016

17. Liu, L., Shen, C., van den Hengel, A.: Cross-convolutional-layer pooling for image recognition. IEEE TPAMI **39**(11), 2305–2313 (2016)

18. Liu, W., et al.: SSD: single shot MultiBox detector. In: Leibe, B., Matas, J., Sebe, N., Welling, M. (eds.) ECCV 2016. LNCS, vol. 9905, pp. 21–37. Springer, Cham (2016). https://doi.org/10.1007/978-3-319-46448-0_2

19. Liu, X., Lin, W., Ma, H., Fu, H.: Large-scale vehicle re-identification in urban suveillance videos. In: ICME, pp. 1–6, July 2016

20. Liu, X., Liu, W., Mei, T., Ma, H.: A deep learning-based approach to progressive vehicle re-identification for urban surveillance. In: Leibe, B., Matas, J., Sebe, N., Welling, M. (eds.) ECCV 2016. LNCS, vol. 9906, pp. 869–884. Springer, Cham (2016). https://doi.org/10.1007/978-3-319-46475-6_53

21. Long, J., Shelhamer, E., Darrell, T.: Fully convolutional networks for semantic segmentation. In: CVPR, pp. 3431–3440, June 2015

22. Sánchez, J., Perronnin, F., Mensink, T., Verbeek, J.: Image classification with the fisher vector: theory and practice. IJCV **105**(3), 222–245 (2013)

23. Shen, Y., Xiao, T., Li, H., Yi, S., Wang, X.: Learning deep neural networks for vehicle Re-ID with visual-spatio-temporal path proposals. In: ICCV, pp. 1900–1909, October 2017

24. Singh, B., Han, X., Wu, Z., Davis, L.S.: PSPGC: part-based seeds for parametric graph-cuts. In: Cremers, D., Reid, I., Saito, H., Yang, M.-H. (eds.) ACCV 2014. LNCS, vol. 9005, pp. 360–375. Springer, Cham (2015). https://doi.org/10.1007/978-3-319-16811-1_24

25. Sochor, J., Herout, A., Havel, J.: BoxCars: 3D boxes as CNN input for improved fine-grained vehicle recognition. In: CVPR, pp. 3006–3015, June 2016

26. Sutskever, I., Vinyals, O., Le, Q.V.: Sequence to sequence learning with neural networks. In: NIPS, pp. 3104–3112, December 2014

27. Szegedy, C., et al.: Going deeper with convolutions. In: CVPR, pp. 1–9, June 2015

28. Tan, Y.H., Chan, C.S.: phi-LSTM: a phrase-based hierarchical LSTM model for image captioning. In: Lai, S.-H., Lepetit, V., Nishino, K., Sato, Y. (eds.) ACCV 2016. LNCS, vol. 10115, pp. 101–117. Springer, Cham (2017). https://doi.org/10.1007/978-3-319-54193-8_7

29. Tieleman, T., Hinton, G.E.: Neural networks for machine learning. Coursera (Lecture 65 - RMSprop)

30. Varela, M., Velastin, S.A.: Intelligent distributed surveillance systems: a review. IEEE Trans. Vis. Image Signal Process. **152**(2), 192–204 (2005)

31. Weijier, J.V.D., Schmid, C., Verbeek, J., Larlus, D.: Learning color names for real-world applications. IEEE TIP **18**(7), 1512–1523 (2009)
32. Weijier, J.V.D., Schmid, C., Verbeek, J., Larlus, D.: Deep feature learning with relative distance comparison for person re-identification. Pattern Recogn. **48**(10), 2993–3003 (2015)
33. Wu, Q., Shen, C., Liu, L., Dick, A., van den Hengel, A.: What value to explicit high level concepts have in vision to language problems? In: CVPR, pp. 203–212, June 2016
34. Wu, Q., Wang, P., Shen, C., Dick, A., van den Hengel, A.: Ask me anything: free-form visual question answering based on knowledge from external sources. In: CVPR, pp. 4622–4630, June 2016
35. Xu, K., et al.: Show, attend and tell: neural image caption generation with visual attention. In: ICML, pp. 2048–2057, July 2015
36. Yang, L., Luo, P., Loy, C.C., Tang, X.: A large-scale car dataset fro fine-grained categorization and verification. In: CVPR, pp. 3973–3981, June 2015
37. Zhang, J., Wang, F.Y., Lin, W.H., Xu, X., Chen, C.: Data-driven intelligent transportation systems: a survey. IEEE Trans. Intell. Transp. Syst. **12**(4), 1624–1639 (2011)
38. Zheng, L., Shen, L., Tian, L., Wang, S., Wang, J., Tian, Q.: Scalable person re-identification: a benchmark. In: ICCV, pp. 1116–1124, December 2015
39. Zheng, L., Yang, Y., Hauptmann, A.G.: Person re-identification: Past, present and future. arXiv preprint arXiv:1610.02984 (2016)
40. Zheng, Y., Capra, L., Wolfson, O., Yang, H.: Urban computing: concepts, methodologies, and applications. ACM Trans. Intell. Syst. Technol. **5**(38), 1–55 (2014)
41. Zheng, Z., Zheng, L., Yang, Y.: A discriminatively learned CNN embedding for person re-identification. arXiv preprint arXiv:1611.05666 (2016)
42. Zhou, Y., Shao, L.: Viewpoint-aware attentive multi-view inference for vehicle re-identification. In: CVPR, pp. 6489–6498, June 2018

Oral Session O2: Object Tracking and Segmentation

FuCoLoT – A Fully-Correlational Long-Term Tracker

Alan Lukežič[1]($\boxtimes$), Luka Čehovin Zajc[1], Tomáš Vojíř[2], Jiří Matas[2], and Matej Kristan[1]

[1] Faculty of Computer and Information Science, University of Ljubljana,
Ljubljana, Slovenia
`alan.lukezic@fri.uni-lj.si`
[2] Faculty of Electrical Engineering, Czech Technical University in Prague,
Prague, Czech Republic

Abstract. We propose FuCoLoT – a <u>Fu</u>lly <u>Co</u>rrelational <u>Lo</u>ng-term <u>T</u>racker. It exploits the novel DCF constrained filter learning method to design a detector that is able to re-detect the target in the whole image efficiently. FuCoLoT maintains several correlation filters trained on different time scales that act as the detector components. A novel mechanism based on the correlation response is used for tracking failure estimation. FuCoLoT achieves state-of-the-art results on standard short-term benchmarks and it outperforms the current best-performing tracker on the long-term UAV20L benchmark by over 19%. It has an order of magnitude smaller memory footprint than its best-performing competitors and runs at 15 fps in a single CPU thread.

1 Introduction

The computer vision community has recently witnessed significant activity and advances of model-free short-term trackers [22,40] which localize a target in a video sequence given a single training example in the first frame. Current short-term trackers [1,12,14,28,37] localize the target moderately well even in the presence of significant appearance and motion changes and they are robust to short-term occlusions. Nevertheless, any adaptation at an inaccurate target position leads to gradual corruption of the visual model, drift and irreversible failure. Another major source of failures of short-term trackers are significant occlusion and target disappearance from the field of view. These problems are addressed by long-term trackers which combine a short-term tracker with a detector that is capable of reinitializing the tracker.

A long-term tracker development is complex as it entails: (i) the design of the two core components - the short term tracker and the detector, (ii) an algorithm for their interaction including the estimation of tracking and detection uncertainty, and (iii) the model adaptation strategy. Initially, memory-less displacement estimators like the flock-of-trackers [20] and the flow calculated at keypoints [34] were considered. Later, methods applied keypoint detectors [19,31,34,35], but these require large and sufficiently well textured targets.

© Springer Nature Switzerland AG 2019
C. V. Jawahar et al. (Eds.): ACCV 2018, LNCS 11362, pp. 595–611, 2019.
https://doi.org/10.1007/978-3-030-20890-5_38

Cascades of classifiers [20, 30] and more recently deep feature object detection systems [15] have been proposed to deal with diverse targets. The drawback is in the significant increase of computational complexity and the subsequent reduction in the range of possible applications. Recent long-term trackers either train the detector on the first frame only [15, 34], thus losing the opportunity to learn target appearance variability or adapt the detector [19, 30] and becoming prone to failure due to learning from incorrect training examples.

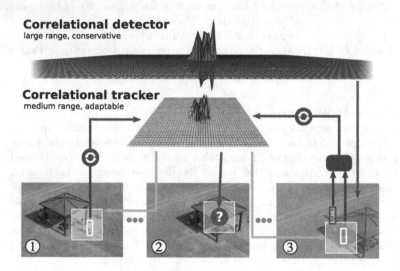

Fig. 1. The FuCoLoT tracker framework: a short-term component of FuCoLoT tracks a visible target (1). At occlusion onset (2), the localization uncertainty is detected and the detection correlation filter is activated in parallel to short-term component to account for the two possible hypotheses of uncertain localization. Once the target becomes visible (3), the detector and short-term tracker interact to recover its position. Detector is deactivated once the localization uncertainty drops.

The paper introduces FuCoLoT - a novel <u>Fu</u>lly <u>Co</u>rrelational <u>Lo</u>ng-term <u>T</u>racker. FuCoLoT is the first long-term tracker that exploits the novel discriminative correlation filter (DCF) learning method based on the ADMM optimization that allows to control the support of the discriminative filter. The method was first used in CSRDCF [28] to limit the DCF filter support to the object segmentation and to avoid problems with shapes not well approximated by a rectangle.

The first contribution of the paper is the observation, and its use, that the ADMM optimization allows DCF to search in an area with size unrelated to the object, e.g. in the whole image. The decoupling of the target and the search region sizes allows implementing the detector as a DCF. Both the short-term tracker and the detector of FuCoLoT are DCFs operating efficiently on the same representation, making FuCoLoT "fully correlational". For some time,

DCFs have been the state-of-the-art in short-term tracking, topping a number of recent benchmarks [22,23,23,24,40]. However, with the standard learning algorithm [18], a correlation filter cannot be used for detection because of two reasons: (i) the dominance of the background in the search regions which necessarily has the same size as the target model and (ii) the effects of the periodic extension on the borders. Only recently theoretical breakthroughs [10,21,28] allowed constraining the non-zero filter response to the area covered by the target.

As a second contribution, FuCoLoT uses correlation filters trained on *different time scales* as a detector to achieve resistance to occlusions, disappearance, or short-term tracking problems of different duration. Both the detectors and its short-term tracker is implemented by a CSRDCF core [28], see Fig. 1.

The estimation of the relative confidence of the detectors and the short-term tracker, as well as of the localization uncertainty, is facilitated by the fact that both the detector and the short-term tracker output the same representation - the correlation response. We show that this leads to a simple and effective method that controls their interaction. As another contribution, a stabilizing mechanism is introduced that enables the detector to recover from model contamination.

Extensive experiments show that the proposed FuCoLoT tracker by far outperforms all trackers on a long-term benchmark and achieves excellent performance even on short-term benchmarks. FuCoLoT has a small memory footprint, does not require GPUs and runs at 15 fps on a CPU since both the detectors and the short-term tracker enjoy efficient implementation through FFT.

2   Related Work

We briefly overview the most related short-term DCFs and long-term trackers.

Short-Term DCFs. Since their inception as the MOSSE tracker [3], several advances have made discriminative correlation filters the most widely used methodology in short-term tracking [22]. Major boosts in performance followed introduction of kernels [18], multi-channel formulations [11,16] and scale estimation [8,27]. Hand-crafted features have been recently replaced with deep features trained for classification [9,12] as well as features trained for localization [37]. Another line of research lead to constrained filter learning approaches [10,28] that allow learning a filter with the effective size smaller than the training patch.

Long-Term Trackers. The long-term trackers combine a short-term tracker with a detector – an architecture first proposed by Kalal et al. [20] and now commonly used in long-term trackers. The seminal work of Kalal et al. [20] proposes a memory-less flock of flows as a short-term tracker and a template-based detector run in parallel. They propose a P-N learning approach in which the short-term tracker provides training examples for the detector and pruning events are used to reduce contamination of the detector model. The detector is implemented as a cascade to reduce the computational complexity.

Another paradigm was pioneered by Pernici et al. [35]. Their approach casts localization as local keypoint descriptors matching with a weak geometrical model. They propose an approach to reduce contamination of the keypoints model that occurs at adaptation during occlusion. Nebehay et al. [34] have shown that a keypoint tracker can be utilized even without updating and using pairs of correspondences in a GHT framework to track deformable models. Maresca and Petrosino [31] have extend the GHT approach by integrating various descriptors and introducing a conservative updating mechanism. The keypoint methods require a large and well textured target, which limits their application scenarios.

Several methods achieve long-term capabilities by careful model updates and detection of detrimental events like occlusion. Grabner et al. [17] proposed an online semi-supervised boosting method that combines a prior and online-adapted classifiers to reduce drifting. Chang et al. [5] apply log-polar transform for tracking failure detection. Kwak et al. [26] proposed occlusion detection by decomposing the target model into a grid of cells and learning an occlusion classifier for each cell. Beyer et al. [2] proposed a Bayes filter for target loss detection and re-detection for multi-target tracking.

Recent long-term trackers have shifted back to the tracker-detector paradigm of Kalal et al. [20], mainly due to availability of DCF trackers [18] which provide a robust and fast short-term tracking component. Ma et al. [29,30] proposed a combination of KCF tracker [18] and a random ferns classifier as a detector. Similarly, Hong et al. [19] combine a KCF tracker with a SIFT-based detector which is also used to detect occlusions.

The most extreme example of using a fast tracker and a slow detector is the recent work of Fan and Ling [15]. They combine a DSST [8] tracker with a CNN detector [36] which verifies and potentially corrects proposals of the short-term tracker. The tracker achieved excellent results on the challenging long-term benchmark [32], but requires a GPU, has a huge memory footprint and requires parallel implementation with backtracking to achieve a reasonable runtime.

3   Fully Correlational Long-Term Tracker

In the following we describe the proposed long-term tracking approach based on constrained discriminative correlation filters. The constrained DCF is overviewed in Sect. 3.1, Sect. 3.2 overviews the short-term component, Sect. 3.3 describes detection of tracking uncertainty, Sect. 3.4 describes the detector and the long-term tracker is described in Sect. 3.5.

3.1   Constrained Discriminative Filter Formulation

FuCoLoT is based on discriminative correlation filters. Given a search region of size $W \times H$ a set of N_d feature channels $\mathbf{f} = \{\mathbf{f}_d\}_{d=1}^{N_d}$, where $\mathbf{f}_d \in \mathcal{R}^{W \times H}$, are extracted. A set of N_d correlation filters $\mathbf{h} = \{\mathbf{h}_d\}_{d=1}^{N_d}$, where $\mathbf{h}_d \in \mathcal{R}^{W \times H}$, are correlated with the extracted features and the object position is estimated as the location of the maximum of the weighted correlation responses

$$\mathbf{r} = \sum\nolimits_{d=1}^{N_d} w_d(\mathbf{f}_d \star \mathbf{h}_d),$$

(1)

where $\star$ represents circular correlation, which is efficiently implemented by a Fast Fourier Transform and $\{w_d\}_{d=1}^{N_d}$ are channel weights. The target scale can be efficiently estimated by another correlation filter trained over the scale-space [8].

We apply the recently proposed filter learning technique (CSRDCF [28]), which uses the alternating direction method of multipliers (ADMM [4]) to constrain the learned filter support by a binary segmentation mask. In the following we provide a brief overview of the learning framework and refer the reader to the original paper [28] for details.

Constrained Learning. Since feature channels are treated independently, we will assume a single feature channel (i.e., $N_d = 1$) in the following. A channel feature $\mathbf{f}$ is extracted from a learning region and a fast segmentation method [25] is applied to produce a binary mask $\mathbf{m} \in \{0, 1\}^{W \times H}$ that approximately separates the target from the background. Next a filter of the same size as the training region is learned, with support constrained by the mask $\mathbf{m}$. The discriminative filter $\mathbf{h}$ is learned by introducing a dual variable $\mathbf{h}_c$ and minimizing the following augmented Lagrangian

$$\mathcal{L}(\hat{\mathbf{h}}_c, \mathbf{h}, \hat{\mathbf{l}}|\mathbf{m}) = \|\mathrm{diag}(\hat{\mathbf{f}})\overline{\hat{\mathbf{h}}}_c - \hat{\mathbf{g}}\|^2 + \frac{\lambda}{2}\|\mathbf{m} \odot \mathbf{h}\|^2 + \tag{2}$$
$$2[\hat{\mathbf{l}}^H \mathcal{F}(\mathbf{h}_c - \mathbf{m} \odot \mathbf{h})]_{\mathrm{Re}} + \mu\|\mathcal{F}(\mathbf{h}_c - \mathbf{m} \odot \mathbf{h})\|^2,$$

where $\mathbf{g}$ is a desired output, $\hat{\mathbf{l}}$ is a complex Lagrange multiplier, $(\hat{\cdot}) = \mathcal{F}(\cdot)$ denotes Fourier transformed variable, $[\cdot]_{\mathrm{Re}}$ is an operator that removes the imaginary part and μ is a non-negative real number. The solution is obtained via ADMM [4] iterations of two closed-form solutions:

$$\hat{\mathbf{h}}_c^{i+1} = \left(\hat{\mathbf{f}} \odot \overline{\hat{\mathbf{g}}} + (\mu\mathcal{F}(\mathbf{m} \odot \mathbf{h}^i) - \hat{\mathbf{l}}^i)\right) \odot^{-1} \left(\overline{\hat{\mathbf{f}}} \odot \hat{\mathbf{f}} + \mu^i\right), \tag{3}$$

$$\mathbf{h}^{i+1} = \mathbf{m} \odot \mathcal{F}^{-1}[\hat{\mathbf{l}}^i + \mu^i\hat{\mathbf{h}}_c^{i+1}]/(\frac{\lambda}{2D} + \mu^i), \tag{4}$$

where $\mathcal{F}^{-1}(\cdot)$ denotes the inverse Fourier transform. In the case of multiple channels, the approach independently learns a single filter per channel. Since the support of the learned filter is constrained to be smaller than the learning region, the maximum response on the training region reflects the reliability of the learned filter [28]. These values are used as per-channel weights w_d in (1) for improved target localization.

Note that the constrained learning [28] estimates a filter implicitly padded with zeros to match the learning region size. In contrast to the standard approach to filter learning like e.g., [18] and multiplying with a mask post-hoc, the padding is explicitly enforced during learning, resulting in an increased filter robustness. We make an observation that adding or removing the zeros at filter borders keeps the filter unchanged, thus correlation on an arbitrary large region via FFT is possible by zero padding the filter to match the size. These properties make the constrained learning an excellent candidate to train the short-term component (Sect. 3.4) as well as the detector (Sect. 3.4) in a long-term tracker.

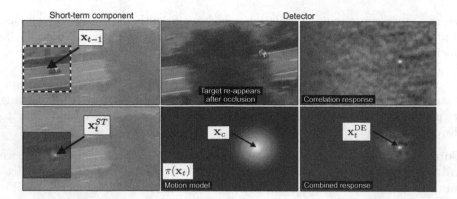

Fig. 2. The short-term component (left) estimates the target location at the maximum response of its DCF within a search region centered at the estimate in the previous frame. The detector (right) estimates the target location as the maximum in the whole image of the response of its DCF multiplied by the motion model $\pi(\mathbf{x}_t)$. If tracking fails, the prior $\pi(\mathbf{x}_t)$ spreads.

3.2 The Short-Term Component

The CSRDCF [28] tracker is used as the short-term component in FuCoLoT. The short-term component is run within a search region centered on the target position predicted from the previous frame. The new target position hypothesis $\mathbf{x}_t^{ST}$ is estimated as the location of the maximum of the correlation response between the short-term filter $\mathbf{h}_t^{ST}$ and the features extracted from the search region (see Fig. 2, left).

The visual model of the short-term component $\mathbf{h}^{ST}$ is updated by a weighted running average

$$\mathbf{h}_{t+1}^{ST} = (1 - \eta)\mathbf{h}_t^{ST} + \eta\tilde{\mathbf{h}}_t^{ST}, \tag{5}$$

where $\mathbf{h}_t^{ST}$ is the correlation filter used to localize the target, $\tilde{\mathbf{h}}_t^{ST}$ the filter estimated by constrained filter learning (Sect. 3.1) in the current frame, and η is the update factor.

3.3 Tracking Uncertainty Estimation

Tracking uncertainty estimation is crucial for minimizing short-term visual model contamination as well as for activating target re-detection after events like occlusion. We propose a self-adaptive approach for tracking uncertainty based on the maximum correlation response.

Confident localization produces a well expressed local maximum in the correlation response $\mathbf{r}_t$, which can be measured by the peak-to-sidelobe ratio $\mathrm{PSR}(\mathbf{r}_t)$ [3] and by the peak absolute value $\max(\mathbf{r}_t)$. Empirically, we observed that multiplying the two measures leads to improved performance, therefore the localization quality is defined as the product

$$q_t = \mathrm{PSR}(\mathbf{r}_t) \cdot \max(\mathbf{r}_t). \tag{6}$$

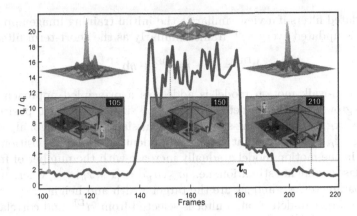

Fig. 3. Localization uncertainty measure (7), reflects the correlation response peak strength relative to its past values. The measure rises fast during occlusion and drops immediately afterwards.

The following observations were used in design of tracking uncertainty (or failure) detection: (i) relative value of the localization quality q_t depends on target appearance changes and is only a weak indicator of tracking uncertainty, and (ii) events like occlusion occur on a relatively short time-scale and are reflected in a significant reduction of the localization quality. Let $\bar{q}_t$ be the average localization quality computed over the recent N_q confidently tracked frames. Tracking is considered uncertain if the ratio between $\bar{q}_t$ and q_t exceeds a predefined threshold τ_q, i.e.,

$$\bar{q}_t/q_t > \tau_q. \tag{7}$$

In practice, the ratio between the average and current localization quality significantly increases during occlusion, indicating a highly uncertain tracking, and does not require threshold fine-tuning (an example is shown in Fig. 3).

3.4 Target Loss Recovery

A visual model not contaminated by false training examples is desirable for reliable re-detection after a long period of target loss. The only known certainly uncontaminated filter is the one learned at initialization. However, for a short-term occlusions, the most recent uncontaminated model would likely yield a better detection. While contamination of the short-term visual model (Sect. 3.2) is reduced by the long-term system (Sect. 3.5), it cannot be prevented. We thus maintain as set of several filters $\mathcal{H}^{\mathrm{DE}} = \{\mathbf{h}_i^{\mathrm{DE}}\}_{i \in 1,...N_{\mathrm{DE}}}$ updated at different *temporal scales* to deal with potential model contamination.

The filters updated frequently learn recent appearance changes, while the less frequently updated filters increase robustness to learning during potentially undetected tracking failure. In our approach, one of the filters is never updated (the initial filter), which guarantees full recovery from potential contamination of the updated filters if a view similar to the initial training image appears. The i-th filter is updated every n_i^{DE} frames similarly as the short-term filter:

$$\mathbf{h}_i^{\mathrm{DE}} = (1 - \eta)\mathbf{h}_i^{\mathrm{DE}} + \eta\tilde{\mathbf{h}}_t^{\mathrm{ST}}. \tag{8}$$

A random-walk motion model is added as a principled approach to modeling the growth of the target search region size. The target position prior $\pi(\mathbf{x}_t) = \mathcal{N}(\mathbf{x}_t; \mathbf{x}_c, \Sigma_t)$ at time-step t is a Gaussian with a diagonal covariance $\Sigma_t = \mathrm{diag}(\sigma_{xt}^2, \sigma_{yt}^2)$ centered at the last confidently estimated position $\mathbf{x}_c$. The variances in the motion model gradually increase with the number of frames Δ_t since the last confident estimation, i.e., $[\sigma_{xt}, \sigma_{yt}] = [x_w, x_h]\alpha_s^{\Delta_t}$, where α_s is scale increase parameter, x_w and x_h are the target width and height, respectively.

During target re-detection, a filter is selected from $\mathcal{H}^{\mathrm{DE}}$ and correlated with features extracted from the entire image. The detected position $\mathbf{x}_t^{\mathrm{DE}}$ is estimated as the location maximum of the correlation response multiplied with the motion prior $\pi(\mathbf{x}_t)$ as shown in Fig. 2 (right). For implementation efficiency only a single filter is evaluated on each image. The algorithm cycles through all filters in $\mathcal{H}^{\mathrm{DE}}$ and all target size scales $\mathcal{S}^{\mathrm{DE}}$ in subsequent images until the target is detected. In practice this means that all filters are evaluated approximately within a second of the sequence (Sect. 4.1).

3.5   Tracking with FuCoLoT

The FuCoLoT integrates the short-term component (Sect. 3.2), the uncertainty estimator (Sect. 3.3) and target recovery (Sect. 3.4) as follows.

Initialization. The long-term tracker is initialized in the first frame and the learned initialization model $\mathbf{h}_1^{\mathrm{ST}}$ is stored. In the remaining frames, N_{DE} visual models are maintained at different time-scales for target localization and detection $\{\mathbf{h}_i^{\mathrm{DE}}\}_{i \in 1, \ldots N_{\mathrm{DE}}}$, where the model updated at every frame is the short-term visual model, i.e., $\mathbf{h}_t^{\mathrm{ST}} = \mathbf{h}_{N_{\mathrm{DE}}}^{\mathrm{DE}}$, and the model that is never updated is equal to the initialization model, i.e., $\mathbf{h}_1^{\mathrm{DE}} = \mathbf{h}_1^{\mathrm{ST}}$.

Localization. A tracking iteration at frame t starts with the target position $\mathbf{x}_{t-1}$ from the previous frame, a tracking quality score q_{t-1} and the mean $\bar{q}_{t-1}$ over the recent N_q confidently tracked frames. A region is extracted around $\mathbf{x}_{t-1}$ in the current image and the correlation response is computed using the short-term component model $\mathbf{h}_{t-1}^{\mathrm{ST}}$ (Sect. 3.2). Position $\mathbf{x}_t^{\mathrm{ST}}$ and localization quality q_t^{ST} (6) are estimated from the correlation response $\mathbf{r}_t^{\mathrm{ST}}$. When tracking is confident at $t - 1$, i.e., the uncertainty (7) $\bar{q}_t/q_t$ was smaller than τ_q, only the short-term component is run. Otherwise the detector (Sect. 3.4) is activated as well to address potential target loss. The detector filter $\mathbf{h}_i^{\mathrm{DE}}$ is chosen from the sequence of stored detectors $\mathcal{H}^{\mathrm{DE}}$ and correlated with the features extracted from the entire image. The detection hypothesis $\mathbf{x}_t^{\mathrm{DE}}$ is obtained as the location of the maximum of the correlation multiplied by the motion model $\pi(\mathbf{x}_t)$, while the localization quality q_t^{DE} (6) is computed only on the correlation response.

Update. In case the detector has not been activated, the short-term position is taken as the final target position estimate. Alternatively, both position hypotheses, i.e., the position estimated by the short-term component as well as the position estimated by the detector, are considered. The final target position is estimated as the one with higher quality score, i.e.,

$$(\mathbf{x}_t, q_t) = \left\{ \begin{array}{ll} (\mathbf{x}_t^{ST}, q_t^{ST}) \; ; \; q_t^{ST} \geq q_t^{DE} \\ (\mathbf{x}_t^{DE}, q_t^{DE}) \; ; \; \text{otherwise} \end{array} \right. . \tag{9}$$

If the estimated position is reliable (7), a constrained filter $\tilde{\mathbf{h}}_t^{ST}$ is estimated according to [28] and the short-term component (5) and detector (8) are updated. Otherwise the models are not updated, i.e., $\eta = 0$ in (5) and (8).

4   Experiments

4.1   Implementation Details

We use the same standard HOG [7] and colornames [11,39] features in the short-term component and in the detector. All the parameters of the CSRDCF filter learning are the same as in [28], including filter learning rate $\eta = 0.02$ and regularization $\lambda = 0.01$. We use 5 filters in the detector, updated with the following frequencies $\{0, 1/250, 1/50, 1/10, 1\}$ and size scale factors $\{0.5, 0.7, 1, 1.2, 1.5, 2\}$.

The random-walk motion model region growth parameter was set to $\alpha_s = 1.05$. The uncertainty threshold was set to $\tau_q = 2.7$ and the parameter "recent frames" was $N_q = 100$. The parameters did not require fine tuning and were kept constant throughout all experiments. Our Matlab implementation runs at 15 fps on OTB100 [40], 8 fps on VOT16 [23] and 6 fps on UAV20L [32] dataset. The experiments were conducted on an Intel Core i7 3.4 GHz standard desktop.

4.2   Evaluation on a Long-Term Benchmark

The long-term performance of the FuCoLoT is analyzed on the recent long-term benchmark UAV20L [32] that contains results of 11 trackers on 20 long term sequences with average sequence length 2934 frames. To reduce clutter in the plots we include top-performing tracker SRDCF [10] and all long-term trackers in the benchmark, i.e., MUSTER [19] and TLD [20]. We add the most recent state-of-the-art long-term trackers CMT [34], LCT [30], and PTAV [15] in the analysis, as well as the recent state-of-the-art short-term DCF trackers CSRDCF [28], CCOT [12] and CNN-based MDNet [33] and SiamFC [1].

Results in Fig. 4 show that on benchmark, FuCoLoT by far outperforms all top baseline trackers as well as all the recent long-term state-of-the-art. In particular FuCoLoT outperforms the recent long-term correlation filter LCT [30] by 102% in precision and 106% in success measures. The FuCoLoT also outperforms the currently best-performing published long-term tracker PTAV [15] by over 22% and 26% in precision and success measures, respectively. This is an excellent result especially considering that FuCoLoT does not apply deep

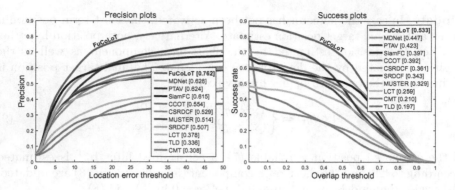

Fig. 4. UAV20L [32] benchmark results. The precision plot (left) and the success plot (right).

Table 1. Tracking performance (AUC measure) for fourteen tracking attributes and eleven trackers on the UAV20L [32].

Tracker	Scale Var.	Aspect Change	Low Res.	Fast Motion	Full Occ.	Partial Occ.	Out-of-View	Back. Clutter	Illum. Var.	Viewp. Change	Camera Motion	Similar Object
FuCoLoT	① 0.526	① 0.500	① 0.472	① 0.400	① 0.460	① 0.526	① 0.488	① 0.538	① 0.513	① 0.499	① 0.528	① 0.573
MDNet	② 0.438	③ 0.385	① 0.357	② 0.383	0.188	② 0.419	② 0.439	0.149	③ 0.403	② 0.444	② 0.432	② 0.525
PTAV	③ 0.416	② 0.410	② 0.390	③ 0.349	② 0.357	③ 0.415	③ 0.389	② 0.435	② 0.430	③ 0.418	③ 0.420	0.426
SiamFC	0.383	0.328	0.242	0.264	③ 0.237	0.364	0.386	③ 0.239	0.371	0.356	0.383	0.436
CCOT	0.378	0.322	0.277	0.275	0.183	0.368	0.352	0.188	0.382	0.330	0.380	③ 0.463
CSRDCF	0.346	0.293	0.232	0.194	0.210	0.339	0.326	0.227	0.359	0.308	0.348	0.403
SRDCF	0.332	0.270	0.228	0.197	0.170	0.320	0.329	0.156	0.295	0.303	0.327	0.397
MUSTER	0.314	0.275	0.278	0.206	0.200	0.305	0.309	0.230	0.242	0.318	0.307	0.342
LCT	0.244	0.201	0.183	0.112	0.151	0.244	0.249	0.156	0.232	0.225	0.245	0.283
CMT	0.208	0.169	0.139	0.199	0.134	0.173	0.184	0.104	0.146	0.212	0.187	0.203
TLD	0.193	0.196	0.159	0.235	0.154	0.201	0.212	0.111	0.167	0.188	0.202	0.225

features and backtracking like PTAV [15] and that it runs in near-realtime on a single thread CPU. The FuCoLoT outperforms the second-best tracker on UAV20L, MDNet [33] which uses pre-trained network and runs at cca. 1fps, by 21% in precision and 19% in success measure.

Table 1 shows tracking performance in terms of the AUC measure for the twelve attributes annotated in the UAV20L benchmark. The FuCoLoT is the top performing tracker across all attributes, including full occlusion and out-of-view, where it outperforms the second-best PTAV and MDNet by 29% and 11%, respectively. These attributes focus on the long-term tracker capabilities since they require target re-detection.

Figure 5 shows qualitative tracking examples for the FuCoLoT and four state-of-the-art trackers: PTAV [15], CSRDCF [28], MUSTER [19] and TLD [20]. In all these sequences the target becomes fully occluded at least once. FuCoLot is the only tracker that is able to successfully track the target throughout Group2, Group3 and Person19 sequences, which shows the strength of the proposed correlation filter based detector. In Person 17 sequence, the occlusion is shorter, thus the short-term CSRDCF [28] and long-term PTAV [15] are able to track as well.

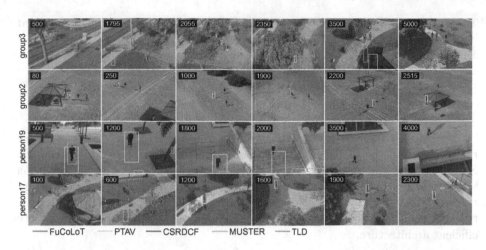

─── FuCoLoT   ─── PTAV   ─── CSRDCF   ─── MUSTER   ─── TLD

Fig. 5. Qualitative results of the FuCoLoT and four state-of-the-art trackers on four sequences from [32]. The selected sequences contain full occlusions which highlight the re-detection ability of a tracker.

4.3 Re-detection Capability Experiment

In the original UAV20L [32] dataset, the target disappears and reappears only 39 times, resulting in only 4% of frames with the target absent. This setup does not significantly expose the target re-detection capability of the tested trackers. To address this, we have cropped the images in all sequences to 40% of their size around the center at target initial position. An example of the dataset modification is shown in Fig. 6. This modification increased the target disappearance/reappearance to 114 cases, and the target is absent in 34% of the frames.

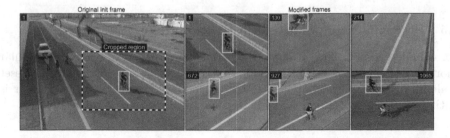

Fig. 6. Re-detection experiment - an example of the modification of a sequence. Yellow bounding-boxes denote the ground-truth position of the target. The target leaves the field-of-view more frequently in the dataset with cropped images. (Color figure online)

Table 2. Re-detection experiment on the UAV20L [32] dataset with images cropped to increase the number of times the target leaves and re-enters the field of view.

Tracker	FuCoLoT	MDNet	CCOT	PTAV	SiamFC	TLD	CSRDCF
AUC	**0.314**	0.240	0.220	0.213	0.205	0.160	0.158

The top six trackers from Sect. 4.2 and a long-term baseline TLD [20] were re-evaluated on the modified dataset (results in Table 2). The gap between the FuCoLoT and the other trackers is further increased. FuCoLoT outperforms the second-best MDNet [33] by 30% and the recent long-term state-of-the-art tracker PTAV [15] by 47%. Note that FuCoLoT outperforms all CNN-based trackers using only hand-crafted features, which speaks in favor of the highly efficient architecture.

4.4 Ablation Study

Several modifications of the FuCoLoT detector were tested to expose the contributions of different parts in our architecture. Two variants used the filter extracted at initialization in the detector with a single scale detection (FuCoLoT$_{D^0S1}$) and multiple scale detection (FuCoLoT$_{D^0SM}$) and one variant used the most recent filter from the short-term tracker in the detector with multiple scale detection (FuCoLoT$_{DSTSM}$). The results are summarized in Table 3.

In single-scale detection, the most recent short-term filter (FuCoLoT$_{DSTS1}$) marginally improves the performance of the (FuCoLoT$_{D^0S1}$) and achieves 0.499 AUC. The performance improves to 0.505 AUC by adding multiple scales search in the detector (FuCoLoT$_{DSTSM}$) and further improves to 0.533 AUC when considering filters with variable temporal updating in the detector (FuCoLoT). For reference, all FuCoLoT variants significantly outperform the FuCoLOT short-term tracker without our detector, i.e. the CSRDCF [28] tracker.

4.5 Performance on Short-Term Benchmarks

For completeness, we first evaluate the performance of FuCoLoT on the popular short-term benchmarks: OTB100 [40], and VOT2016 [23]. A standard no-reset evaluation (OPE [40]) is applied to focus on long-term behavior: a tracker is initialized in the first frame and left to track until the end of the sequence.

Table 3. Ablation study of the FuCoLoT tracker on UAV20L [32].

Tracker	FuCoLoT$_{D^0S1}$	FuCoLoT$_{DSTS1}$	FuCoLoT$_{DSTSM}$	FuCoLoT	CSRDCF [28]
AUC	0.489	0.499	0.505	**0.533**	0.361

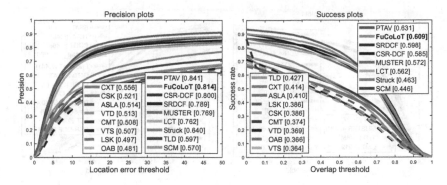

Fig. 7. OTB100 [40] benchmark results. The precision plot (left) and the success plot (right).

Tracking quality is measured by precision and success plots. The success plot shows all threshold values, the proportion of frames with the overlap between the predicted and ground truth bounding boxes as greater than a threshold. The results are summarized by areas under these plots which are shown in the legend. The precision plots in Figs. 7 and 8 show a similar statistics computed from the center error. The results in the legends are summarized by percentage of frames tracked with an center error less than 20 pixels.

The benchmarks results have some long-term trackers and the most recent PTAV [15] – the currently best-performing published long-term tracker. Note that PTAV applies preemptive tracking with backtracking and requires future frames to predict position of the tracked object which limits its applicability.

OTB100 [40] contains results of 29 trackers evaluated on 100 sequences with average sequence length of 589 frames. We show only the results for top-performing recent baselines, and recent top-performing state-of-the-art trackers SRDCF [10], MUSTER [19], LCT [30] PTAV [15] and CSRDCF [28].

The FuCoLoT ranks among the top on this benchmark (Fig. 7) outperforming all baselines as well as state-of-the-art SRDCF, CSRDCF and MUSTER. Using only handcrafted features, the FuCoLoT achieves comparable performance to the PTAV [15] which uses deep features for re-detection and backtracking.

VOT2016 [23] is a challenging recent short-term tracking benchmark which evaluates 70 trackers on 60 sequences with the average sequence length of 358 frames. The dataset was created using a methodology that selected sequences which are difficult to track, thus the target appearance varies much more than in other benchmarks. In the interest of visibility, we show only top-performing trackers on no-reset evaluation, i.e., SSAT [23,33], TCNN [23,33], CCOT [12], MDNetN [23,33], GGTv2 [13], MLDF [38], DNT [6], Deep-SRDCF [10], SiamRN [1] and FCF [23]. We add CSRDCF [28] and the long-term trackers TLD [20], LCT [30], MUSTER [19], CMT [34] and PTAV [15].

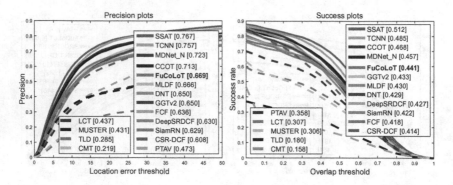

Fig. 8. VOT2016 [23] benchmark results. The precision plot (left) and the success plot (right).

The FuCoLoT is ranked fifth (Fig. 8) according to the tracking success measure, outperforming 65 trackers, including trackers with deep features, CSR-DCF and PTAV. Note that four trackers with better performance than FuCoLoT (SSAT, TCNN, CCOT and MDNetN) are computationally very expensive CNN-based trackers. They are optimized for accurate tracking on short sequences, without an ability for re-detection. The FuCoLoT outperforms all long-term trackers on this benchmark (TLD, CMT, LCT, MUSTER and PTAV).

5   Conclusion

A fully-correlational long-term tracker – FuCoLot – was proposed. FuCoLoT is the first long-term tracker that exploits the novel DCF constrained filter learning method [28]. The constrained filter learning based detector is able to re-detect the target in the whole image efficiently. FuCoLoT maintains several correlation filters trained on different time scales that act as the detector components. A novel mechanism based on the correlation response quality is used for tracking uncertainty estimation which drives interaction between the short-term component and the detector.

On the UAV20L long-term benchmark [32] FuCoLoT outperforms the best method by over 19%. Experimental evaluation on short-term benchmarks [23,40] showed state-of-the-art performance. The Matlab implementation running at 15 fps will be made publicly available.

Acknowledgement. This work was partly supported by the following research programs and projects: Slovenian research agency research programs and projects P2-0214 and J2-8175. Jiří Matas and Tomáš Vojíř were supported by The Czech Science Foundation Project GACR P103/12/G084 and Toyota Motor Europe.

References

1. Bertinetto, L., Valmadre, J., Henriques, J.F., Vedaldi, A., Torr, P.H.S.: Fully-convolutional siamese networks for object tracking. In: Hua, G., Jégou, H. (eds.) ECCV 2016. LNCS, vol. 9914, pp. 850–865. Springer, Cham (2016). https://doi.org/10.1007/978-3-319-48881-3_56

2. Beyer, L., Breuers, S., Kurin, V., Leibe, B.: Towards a principled integration of multi-camera re-identification and tracking through optimal Bayes filters. CoRR abs/1705.04608 (2017)

3. Bolme, D.S., Beveridge, J.R., Draper, B.A., Lui, Y.M.: Visual object tracking using adaptive correlation filters. In: Computer Vision and Pattern Recognition, pp. 2544–2550 (2010)

4. Boyd, S., Parikh, N., Chu, E., Peleato, B., Eckstein, J.: Distributed optimization and statistical learning via the alternating direction method of multipliers. Found. Trends Mach. Learn. **3**(1), 1–122 (2011)

5. Chang, H.J., Park, M.S., Jeong, H., Choi, J.Y.: Tracking failure detection by imitating human visual perception. In: Proceedings of the International Conference on Image Processing, pp. 3293–3296 (2011)

6. Chi, Z., Li, H., Lu, H., Yang, M.H.: Dual deep network for visual tracking. IEEE Trans. Image Process. **26**(4), 2005–2015 (2017)

7. Dalal, N., Triggs, B.: Histograms of oriented gradients for human detection. In: Computer Vision and Pattern Recognition, vol. 1, pp. 886–893 (2005)

8. Danelljan, M., Häger, G., Khan, F.S., Felsberg, M.: Discriminative scale space tracking. IEEE Trans. Pattern Anal. Mach. Intell. **39**(8), 1561–1575 (2017)

9. Danelljan, M., Bhat, G., Shahbaz Khan, F., Felsberg, M.: Eco: efficient convolution operators for tracking. In: Computer Vision and Pattern Recognition, pp. 6638–6646 (2017)

10. Danelljan, M., Hager, G., Shahbaz Khan, F., Felsberg, M.: Learning spatially regularized correlation filters for visual tracking. In: International Conference on Computer Vision, pp. 4310–4318 (2015)

11. Danelljan, M., Khan, F.S., Felsberg, M., van de Weijer, J.: Adaptive color attributes for real-time visual tracking, pp. 1090–1097 (2014)

12. Danelljan, M., Robinson, A., Shahbaz Khan, F., Felsberg, M.: Beyond correlation filters: learning continuous convolution operators for visual tracking. In: Leibe, B., Matas, J., Sebe, N., Welling, M. (eds.) ECCV 2016. LNCS, vol. 9909, pp. 472–488. Springer, Cham (2016). https://doi.org/10.1007/978-3-319-46454-1_29

13. Du, D., Qi, H., Wen, L., Tian, Q., Huang, Q., Lyu, S.: Geometric hypergraph learning for visual tracking. IEEE Trans. Cyber. **47**(12), 4182–4195 (2017)

14. Du, D., Wen, L., Qi, H., Huang, Q., Tian, Q., Lyu, S.: Iterative graph seeking for object tracking. IEEE Trans. Image Process. **27**(4), 1809–1821 (2018)

15. Fan, H., Ling, H.: Parallel tracking and verifying: a framework for real-time and high accuracy visual tracking. In: International Conference on Computer Vision, pp. 5486–5494 (2017)

16. Galoogahi, H.K., Sim, T., Lucey, S.: Multi-channel correlation filters. In: International Conference on Computer Vision, pp. 3072–3079 (2013)

17. Grabner, H., Leistner, C., Bischof, H.: Semi-supervised on-line boosting for robust tracking. In: Forsyth, D., Torr, P., Zisserman, A. (eds.) ECCV 2008. LNCS, vol. 5302, pp. 234–247. Springer, Heidelberg (2008). https://doi.org/10.1007/978-3-540-88682-2_19

18. Henriques, J.F., Caseiro, R., Martins, P., Batista, J.: High-speed tracking with kernelized correlation filters. IEEE Trans. Pattern Anal. Mach. Intell. **37**(3), 583–596 (2015)
19. Hong, Z., Chen, Z., Wang, C., Mei, X., Prokhorov, D., Tao, D.: Multi-store tracker (muster): a cognitive psychology inspired approach to object tracking. In: Computer Vision and Pattern Recognition, pp. 749–758, June 2015
20. Kalal, Z., Mikolajczyk, K., Matas, J.: Tracking-learning-detection. IEEE Trans. Pattern Anal. Mach. Intell. **34**(7), 1409–1422 (2012)
21. Kiani Galoogahi, H., Sim, T., Lucey, S.: Correlation filters with limited boundaries. In: Computer Vision and Pattern Recognition, pp. 4630–4638 (2015)
22. Kristan, M., et al.: A novel performance evaluation methodology for single-target trackers. IEEE Trans. Pattern Anal. Mach. Intell. **38**, 2137 (2016)
23. Kristan, M., et al.: A novel performance evaluation methodology for single-target trackers. In: Proceedings of the European Conference on Computer Vision (2016)
24. Kristan, M., et al.: The visual object tracking vot2015 challenge results. In: International Conference on Computer Vision (2015)
25. Kristan, M., Perš, J., Sulič, V., Kovačič, S.: A graphical model for rapid obstacle image-map estimation from unmanned surface vehicles. In: Cremers, D., Reid, I., Saito, H., Yang, M.-H. (eds.) ACCV 2014. LNCS, vol. 9004, pp. 391–406. Springer, Cham (2015). https://doi.org/10.1007/978-3-319-16808-1_27
26. Kwak, S., Nam, W., Han, B., Han, J.H.: Learning occlusion with likelihoods for visual tracking. In: International Conference on Computer Vision, pp. 1551–1558 (2011)
27. Li, Y., Zhu, J.: A scale adaptive kernel correlation filter tracker with feature integration. In: Agapito, L., Bronstein, M.M., Rother, C. (eds.) ECCV 2014. LNCS, vol. 8926, pp. 254–265. Springer, Cham (2015). https://doi.org/10.1007/978-3-319-16181-5_18
28. Lukežič., Vojíř, T., Čehovin Zajc, L., Matas, J., Kristan, M.: Discriminative correlation filter with channel and spatial reliability. In: Computer Vision and Pattern Recognition, pp. 6309–6318 (2017)
29. Ma, C., Huang, J.B., Yang, X., Yang, M.H.: Adaptive correlation filters with long-term and short-term memory for object tracking. Int. J. Comput. Vis. **126**(8), 771–796 (2018)
30. Ma, C., Yang, X., Zhang, C., Yang, M.H.: Long-term correlation tracking. In: Computer Vision and Pattern Recognition, pp. 5388–5396 (2015)
31. Maresca, M.E., Petrosino, A.: MATRIOSKA: a multi-level approach to fast tracking by learning. In: Petrosino, A. (ed.) ICIAP 2013. LNCS, vol. 8157, pp. 419–428. Springer, Heidelberg (2013). https://doi.org/10.1007/978-3-642-41184-7_43
32. Mueller, M., Smith, N., Ghanem, B.: A benchmark and simulator for UAV tracking. In: Leibe, B., Matas, J., Sebe, N., Welling, M. (eds.) ECCV 2016. LNCS, vol. 9905, pp. 445–461. Springer, Cham (2016). https://doi.org/10.1007/978-3-319-46448-0_27
33. Nam, H., Han, B.: Learning multi-domain convolutional neural networks for visual tracking. In: Computer Vision and Pattern Recognition, pp. 4293–4302, June 2016
34. Nebehay, G., Pflugfelder, R.: Clustering of static-adaptive correspondences for deformable object tracking. In: Computer Vision and Pattern Recognition, pp. 2784–2791 (2015)
35. Pernici, F., Del Bimbo, A.: Object tracking by oversampling local features. IEEE Trans. Pattern Anal. Mach. Intell. **36**(12), 2538–2551 (2013)
36. Tao, R., Gavves, E., Smeulders, A.W.M.: Siamese instance search for tracking. In: Computer Vision and Pattern Recognition, pp. 1420–1429 (2016)

37. Valmadre, J., Bertinetto, L., Henriques, J., Vedaldi, A., Torr, P.H.S.: End-to-end representation learning for correlation filter based tracking. In: Computer Vision and Pattern Recognition, pp. 2805–2813 (2017)

38. Wang, L., Ouyang, W., Wang, X., Lu, H.: Visual tracking with fully convolutional networks. In: International Conference on Computer Vision, pp. 3119–3127, December 2015

39. van de Weijer, J., Schmid, C., Verbeek, J., Larlus, D.: Learning color names for real-world applications. IEEE Trans. Image Process. **18**(7), 1512–1523 (2009)

40. Wu, Y., Lim, J., Yang, M.H.: Object tracking benchmark. IEEE Trans. Pattern Anal. Mach. Intell. **37**(9), 1834–1848 (2015)

Customized Multi-person Tracker

Liqian Ma[1(✉)], Siyu Tang[2,3], Michael J. Black[2], and Luc Van Gool[1,4]

[1] KU-Leuven/PSI, TRACE (Toyota Res in Europe), Leuven, Belgium
{liqian.ma,luc.vangool}@esat.kuleuven.be
[2] Max Planck Institute for Intelligent Systems, Tübingen, Germany
black@tuebingen.mpg.de
[3] University of Tübingen, Tübingen, Germany
stang@tuebingen.mpg.de
[4] ETH Zurich, Zürich, Switzerland

Abstract. This work addresses the task of multi-person tracking in crowded street scenes, where long-term occlusions pose a major challenge. One popular way to address this challenge is to re-identify people before and after occlusions using Convolutional Neural Networks (CNNs). To achieve good performance, CNNs require a large amount of training data, which is not available for multi-person tracking scenarios. Instead of annotating large training sequences, we introduce a *customized multi-person tracker* that automatically adapts its person re-identification CNNs to capture the discriminative appearance patterns in a *test sequence*. We show that a few high-quality training examples that are *automatically* mined from the test sequence can be used to fine-tune pre-trained CNNs, thereby teaching them to recognize the uniqueness of people's appearance in the test sequence. To that end, we introduce a hierarchical correlation clustering (HCC) framework, in which we utilize an existing robust correlation clustering tracking model, but with different graph structures to generate local, reliable tracklets as well as globally associated tracks. We deploy intuitive physical constraints on the local tracklets to generate the high-quality training examples for customizing the person re-identification CNNs. Our customized multi-person tracker achieves state-of-the-art performance on the challenging MOT16 tracking benchmark.

Keywords: Tracking · Person re-identification · Adaptation

1 Introduction

Tracking multiple people in unconstrained videos is crucial for many vision applications, e.g. autonomous driving, visual surveillance, crowd analytics, etc. Recent

---

L. Ma and S. Tang—Equal contributions.

Electronic supplementary material The online version of this chapter (https://doi.org/10.1007/978-3-030-20890-5_39) contains supplementary material, which is available to authorized users.

© Springer Nature Switzerland AG 2019
C. V. Jawahar et al. (Eds.): ACCV 2018, LNCS 11362, pp. 612–628, 2019.
https://doi.org/10.1007/978-3-030-20890-5_39

approaches for multiple-person tracking tend to use some form of tracking-by-detection [2,21,23,33,34], whereby a state-of-the-art person detector localizes the targets in each frame. Then the task of the tracker is to associate those detections over time. While achieving state-of-the-art tracking results, most approaches still struggle with challenges such as long-term occlusions, appearance changes, detection failures, etc.

One closely related task is person re-identification (re-ID), which associates people across non-overlapping camera views. Major progress in re-ID has been made recently through the use of Convolutional Neural Networks (CNNs), also in the context of tracking [13,17]. We argue that the full potential of CNNs for re-ID has not yet been explored, due to the lack of proper training data for the target sequences. The illumination conditions, resolution, frame-rate, camera motion and angle can all significantly differ between training and target sequences. Consequently, we would like to leverage the power of CNNs without labeling huge amounts training data for multi-person tracking. Rather than train networks in the traditional way, the key idea is to adapt them to each sequence.

Specifically, we propose an adaptation scheme to automatically customize a sequence-specific multi-person tracker. As with any adaptative tracking scheme, it is critical not to introduce tracking errors into the model, which lead to drift. The key observation is that, once we obtain reliable local tracklets on a test sequence, we can use an intuitive physical constraint that non-overlapping tracklets in the same frame are very likely to contain different people. This allows us to harvest high-quality training examples for adapting a generic re-ID CNN, with a low risk of drift. Our experiments show that this customization approach produces a significant improvement in associating people as well as in the final tracking performance.

Generating reliable local tracklets in crowded sequences is not trivial. Since person detection in such scenes can be quite noisy, resulting in false positive detections and inaccurate localizations. In this work, we build on the recent tracking formulations based on correlation clustering [26,30,31], otherwise known as the minimum cost multicut problem. This leads us to a hierarchical data association approach. At the lower level, we use the similarity measure from robust patch matching [31] to produce reliable local tracks. This allows us to automatically mine high-quality training samples for the re-ID CNNs from the test sequence. At the higher level, the similarity measures generated by the adapted re-ID CNNs provide a robust clustering of local tracks. We call this two-pass tracking scheme *Hierarchical Correlation Clustering (HCC)*. The HCC framework, and the adaptation of the re-ID net, operationalize the customization: The HCC produces local tracks, from which the training examples for adapting the re-ID net are mined. The adapted re-ID net then generates much more accurate similarity measures, which help the robust association of local tracks and result in long-lived, persistent final tracks.

Contributions. We make the following contributions: *(i)* we propose an effective adaptation approach to automatically customize a multi-person tracker to previously unseen crowded scenes. The customized tracker adapts itself to the uniqueness of people's appearance in a test sequence; *(ii)* we revisit the idea of formulating tracking as a correlation clustering problem [30,31]. To facilitate the reliable adaptation, we use a hierarchical tracking approach. We use different graph construction schemes at different levels, yet the optimization problem remains the same; *(iii)* we perform extensive experiments on the adaptation scheme and improve the state-of-the-art for the challenging MOT16 benchmark [22]. HCC is the top-performing method at the time of submission.

1.1 Related Work

Tracking-by-Detection. Many multi-person tracking methods build on top of tracking-by-detection [3,27,31,34,38]. Zhang et al. [38] formulate the data association problem of multi-target tracking as a min-cost flow problem, where the optimal solution is obtained in polynomial time. Pirsiavash et al. [23] also proposes a network flow formulation, which can be solved by a successive shortest path algorithm. Wang et al. [34] extend the network flow formulation to simultaneously track interacting objects. Conceptually different from the network flow based formulation, the tracking task is modeled as a correlation clustering problem in [26,30,31] and in this work, where the detections are jointly associated within and across frames.

Hierarchical Data Association. Modeling tracking as a hierarchical data association problem has been proposed in many works [6,26,30,35]. In general, detections are associated from neighboring frames to build a tracklet representation and then longer tracks are merged from the tracklets. In [35], the authors propose a two-stage tracking method. For the first stage, they use bipartite-graph matching to aggregate the local information to obtain local tracklets. For the second stage, the association of the tracklets is formulated as a set cover problem. Hierarchical data association has also been employed in [6], whereby the tracklets are generated by greedy searching using an aggregated local flow descriptor as the pairwise affinity measure. Our work differs in the way the local and the global associations are formulated, namely as one and the same optimization problem, thus substantially simplifying the overall tracking framework.

Learning the Appearance Model. Dehghan et al. [8] track multiple objects via online learning, solving the detection and data association tasks simultaneously. Several works explicitly model the appearance of targets. Kim et al. [13] introduce an appearance model that combines long-term information and employs the features generated by a generic DNN. Xian et al. [36] formulate multiple people tracking as a Markov decision process, the policies of which are estimated from the training data. Their appearance models follow the temporal evolution of the targets. Leal-Taixé et al. [17] introduce several CNNs to model the similarity between detection pairs.

One closely related work [15] learns discriminative appearance models using simple physical constraints. They use hand-crafted features to model appearance and measure the similarity with the χ_2 distance. Our work differs in two respects:

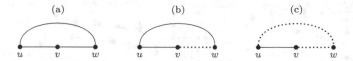

Fig. 1. Examples of feasible/infeasible solutions. The original graph is depicted in (a), where $V = u, v, w$ and $E = uv, vw, uw$. In (b) and (c), a solid line means joining the nodes, a dotted line indicates that the edge is a cut. The decomposition in (b) is infeasible, whereas that in (c) is valid, belonging to the feasible set.

first, we focus on adapting a generic ConvNet to test sequences, which is challenging since ConvNets can easily diverge given a few noisy training examples; second, [15] utilizes the tracking framework proposed by [11], where the low-level, middle-level and high-level data association are solved by a two-threshold strategy, a Hungarian algorithm and an EM algorithm respectively, whereas our local and global associations employ the same optimization method, again substantially simplifying the overall tracking framework. A similar approach is proposed in [5] for human pose estimation in a video sequence, where a generic ConvNet pose estimator is adapted to a person-specific pose estimator by propagating labels using dense optical flow and image-based matching. Unlike us, they focus on single-person tracking.

Correlation Clustering for Tracking. Correlation clustering [9] based tracking formulations have been proposed in [26, 30–32]. Their main advantage is that the detections within and across frames can be jointly clustered, resulting in a robust handling of noisy detections. The use of attractive and repulsive pairwise edge potentials enables a uniform prior distribution for the number of persons, which is determined by the solution of the problem. We extend this idea by using different graph connectivities. Our hierarchical correlation clustering approach, combined with the adaptation scheme, yields better tracking performance.

2   Tracking by Correlation Clustering

Here we introduce the general correlation clustering based tracking formulation that follows [30] and [31]. We describe the model parameters, feasible set and objective function to provide a basic understanding of the formulation and we do not claim novelty with respect to the formulation.

For a target video, let $G = (V, E)$ be an undirected graph whose nodes V are the human detections in a batch of frames or even an entire video. The edges E connect pairs of detections that hypothetically indicate the same target. With respect to the graph, the output of our tracking algorithm is a partition of G, where the node set V is partitioned into different connected components, and each connected component corresponds to one target. The edges $E' \subseteq E$ that straddle distinct components are the cuts of the graph. We define a binary variable x_e for each edge in the graph, where $x_e = 1$ indicates that the edge e is

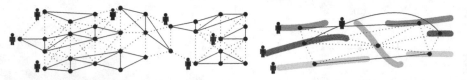

(a) From detections to local tracks by local correlation clustering

(b) From local tracks to global tracks by global correlation clustering

Fig. 2. Illustration of the local and global graph. A dotted line indicates that the edge is a cut. For simplicity, not all the edges are drawn. In (a), the detection graph is partitioned into 7 components, indicating 7 people. In (b), the tracks generated by (a) are associated, resulting in 4 persons. The tracks belonging to the same person are depicted in the same color. (Best viewed in color) (Color figure online)

a cut and 0 otherwise. Obtaining the partition of G is equivalent to finding the 01-vector $x \in \{0,1\}^E$ on the edge set.

Feasible Solution. Not all the 01 labelings of the edges lead to valid graph decompositions. As shown in Fig. 1(b), x_{uv} and x_{uw} join the nodes u, v, w, indicating that all three are in the same cluster. Yet, x_{vw} is a cut, implying v and w should be in different clusters. To avoid such inconsistent edge labeling, we introduce the cycle constraints defined in Eq. 1: for any cycles in the graph G, if one of its edges is labeled as a cut ($x_e = 1$), then there must be at least one more cut in the cycle.

$$\forall C \in \text{cycles}(G)\, \forall e \in C :$$
$$x_e \leq \sum_{e' \in C \setminus \{e\}} x_{e'}. \tag{1}$$

Objective Function. Based on image observations, we compute pairwise features for every edge in the graph. The edge features are denoted as f. We assume independence of the feature vectors. Given the features f and the feasible set Z, the conditional probability of the labeling vector x of the edges is given by

$$p(x|f, Z) \propto p(Z|x) \prod_{e \in E} p(x_e|f^e) \tag{2}$$

where $p(Z|x)$ gives positive and constant probability to every feasible solution ($x \in Z$) and 0 to all infeasible solutions. Minimizing the negative log-likelihood of Eq. 2, we obtain our objective function:

$$\min_{x \in \{0,1\}^E} \sum_{e \in E} c_e x_e \tag{3}$$

with the costs c_e defined as $\log \frac{1-p_e}{p_e}$ and p_e defined as $\frac{1}{1+\exp(-\langle \theta, f^e \rangle)}$.

Given the features f^e extracted from a training sequence, the model parameter θ is obtained by maximum likelihood estimation. To solve the instances of Eq. 3, we apply a heuristic approach proposed in [12].

3   Customized Multi-person Tracker

Here we present how to customize a multi-person tracker. Operationalizing the customization requires two main components: a hierarchical tracking framework, where we obtain reliable tracklets as well as the final tracks (Sect. 3.1) and an adaptation scheme where we fine-tune a general re-ID net to a sequence-specific model (Sect. 3.2).

3.1   Hierarchical Correlation Clustering

The tracking framework introduced in Sect. 2 is general and allows different kinds of graph connectivity. One case is to only connect the detections that are in the neighboring frames. As the detections are close in time, the similarity measures that are based on the local image patch matching are robust [31]. One can therefore obtain high-quality reliable tracks by the tracking formulation introduced in Sect. 2. The downside is that the tracks break when there are occlusions and/or missing detections.

Another way of constructing the graph is to build a fully-connected graph over the entire sequence. Then the detections before and after occlusions can be clustered for the same person, or separated otherwise. By introducing recent, advanced techniques for re-ID, it becomes possible to compute reasonable similarity measures between the detections that are far apart in time, despite large changes in appearance. However, as shown in our experiments, the domain gap between the training sequences and the test sequence is substantial, meanwhile training data for multi-person tracking is hard to obtain, therefore the direct application of a state-of-the-art person re-ID model does not yield satisfactory results. Moreover, since the feasible set of such a graph is huge, a few mistakes in the similarity measures could lead to a bad decomposition, resulting in dramatic tracking errors. For example, similar looking, but temporally distant, people could be clustered together.

To utilize the advantages of different graph connectivity strategies and operationalize the tracker customization, we decouple the tracking problem into two sub-problems: local data association and global data association. For detections that are temporally close, we employ the robust similarity measure of [31]. We construct the graph in a way that there are edges between detections that are sufficiently close in time, as shown in Fig. 2(a). By constraining the feasible set of the optimization problem, we obtain reliable tracks of people before and after occlusions. In the experiments, we show that our local tracks already achieve reasonable tracking performance.

Furthermore, given reliable tracklets, we employ intuitive physical constraints to mine positive and negative examples to adapt a generic re-ID net to the test sequence. Without any ground truth information, the adapted re-ID net produces significantly better similarity measures for the test sequence. Such similarity measures facilitate a globally connected graph based on the local tracks (Fig. 2(b)), which enables the re-ID even between long-term occlusions.

Local Clustering. We introduce a graph $G^{local} = (V, E^{local})$, where the edges E^{local} connect detections that are in the same image or that are close in time. We apply the image patch matching based edge potential proposed in [31]. More specifically, for a pair of images and every detection therein, we employ Deep Matching [24] to generate a set of locally matched keypoints, denoted as M_i, where i is the detection index. Then for pairs of detections, we compute the intersection of the matched points as $M_{ij}^I = |M_i \cap M_j|$ and the union as $M_{ij}^U = |M_i \cup M_j|$. Based on M_{ij}^I, M_{ij}^U, and the detection confidences C_i and C_j, we define the pairwise feature f as $(IOU_{M_{ij}}, \min_C, IOU_{M_{ij}} \cdot \min_C, IOU_{M_{ij}}^2, \min_C^2)^\top$, where $\min_C$ is the minimum detection confidence between C_i and C_j, and $IOU_{M_{ij}}$ is the intersection over union of the matched keypoints, denoted as $IOU_{M_{ij}} = \frac{M_{ij}^I}{M_{ij}^U}$.

Given the pairwise features f for the training sequences, we estimate the model parameter θ via maximum likelihood estimation. On the test sequences, we compute the cost c_e on the edges (E^{local}) using the corresponding features and the learned parameter θ. By optimizing the objective function (Eq. 3) which is defined on the graph G^{local}, we obtain a decomposition of G^{local}, in other words, the clusters of detections. We obtain our local tracks by estimating a smooth trajectory using the corresponding detections. Implementation details are presented in the experiments.

Global Clustering. We return to the global clustering step. In order to bridge local tracks split by long-term occlusions, we construct a fully connected graph $G^{global} = (V, E^{global})$. Its node set contains all the local tracks generated from the previous step. Computing reliable pairwise probabilities p_e is key to global clustering. To that end, we employ the person re-ID net to decide whether two local tracks show the same person or not. Furthermore, we propose an adaptation scheme to fine-tune the generic re-ID net to the test sequence without any ground truth labels. We present the details of our re-ID net and the adaptation scheme in the next section. Extensive experiments on learning to re-identify persons in a test sequence are given in Sect. 4

3.2 Adapting a Generic Re-ID Net

We begin by describing the architecture of the re-ID net and then introduce the approach to adapt a generic Re-ID net on a test sequence. The adaptation pipeline is actually divided into three stages: The re-ID net is first trained on the large re-ID dataset Market-1501 [39] with the initial weights that are trained on ImageNet. Then the model is fine tuned on the training sequences of the MOT15 [16] and MOT16 benchmarks [22], which are arguably the two largest tracking datasets exhibiting diverse scenes. The last stage is the re-ID net adaptation, which happens during testing time by finetuning the model parameters with the mined pairwise examples from the test sequence.

Such adaptation could help the re-ID net in two ways: First, it helps to adapt the model parameters to the test scene, which might be captured under significantly different imaging conditions compared to the training sequences. Second, the re-ID net has the opportunity to "see" the people in the test sequence and learn about what makes people look the same or different. The adapted re-ID net shows a significant improvement both for re-ID and tracking, cf. Sect. 4.

Network Architecture. For the person re-ID module, we adopt a Siamese CNN architecture [4], which has been widely used for person/face verification [7,37]. Figure 3 shows the architecture of our re-ID net. The convolutional neural network (CNN) is used to extract a 1024-D feature vector x of the person image in each branch. Then, the feature vector pair (x_1, x_2) is passed into an element-wise subtraction layer $f(x_1, x_2)$ to obtain the difference vector d. We test 3 different types of non-linearities in the subtraction layer: rectified linear unit (ReLU) $f(x_1, x_2) = \max(x_1 - x_2, 0)$, absolute value non-linearity $f(x_1, x_2) = |x_1 - x_2|$ and square value non-linearity $f(x_1, x_2) = (x_1 - x_2)^2$. The ReLU operation performs the best during the offline finetuning stage, and also costs less computation than square value non-linearity. Then, the difference vector d is passed to a 1024-D fully-connected layer followed by a 2-D output layer with a softmax operation. Inspired by the joint face verification-classification in [28], we add a 1024-D fully-connected layer followed by a N-D classification layer with a softmax operation to classify the identity of each training image. In our experiments, we validate that incorporating the identification information can significantly improve the verification performance.

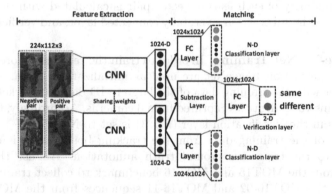

Fig. 3. Re-ID network architecture. The image pairs are passed into two weights sharing CNN branches to extract the 1024-D feature vectors followed by the matching part consisting of a subtraction layer, a 1024-D fully connected layer and a 2-D verification layer. During offline training, the classification layers are added to the re-ID net to use the identification info for network optimization.

We use a weight-sharing GoogLeNet [29] in each CNN branch because of its good performance and fewer parameters than other CNN models. In order to make the CNNs more suitable for the pedestrian images, we modify the input layer size from $224 \times 224 \times 3$ to $224 \times 112 \times 3$ and change the kernel size of the last max-pooling layer from 7×7 to 7×4. Since there are two N-D auxiliary

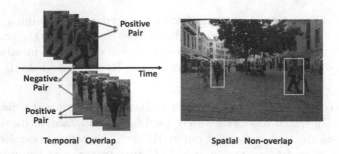

Fig. 4. Training examples mined from test sequence. The two tracklets overlap temporally but not spatially, hence show two identities.

classification subnets in each GoogLeNet, we minimize 7 cross entropy losses including. the losses of 6 classification layers and 1 verification layer.

The classification layers are only used in the network training phase. In the testing phase, the verification layer is used to calculate the similarities between the image pairs. This also applies to the adaptation step, as we only optimize the network with the verification loss, since tracklets without temporal overlap may contain the same identities and we can not obtain identification information about the test sequence. Furthermore, to reduce the computational burden, we divide the network into two parts: feature extraction and matching (Fig. 3). First, we feed-forward each image through one CNN branch and store its feature vector. Then, the similarity of each feature vector pair is calculated with the matching part, including the subtraction layer, fully connected layer, and verification layer.

Generic Re-ID Net Training. In order to train the re-ID net more efficiently, the weights trained on ImageNet are used as initialization. Then, we finetune the re-ID net with the training data of the large re-ID dataset Market-1501 [39], which contains 1501 identities captured from 6 cameras. Accordingly, the number of the nodes in the classification layer (Fig. 3) is set to $N = 1501$.

The size of the training data from the tracking benchmarks is often quite small, due to the expensive ground truth annotation. We use the training sequences from the MOT15 and MOT16 benchmark to collect training images, except that the MOT16-02 and MOT16-11 sequences from the MOT16 training set are left for collecting test examples. We have in total 478 identities for finetuning our re-ID model which is pre-trained on the Market-1501 dataset.

Adaptation on Test Sequences. Now we turn to the adaptation step, where we mine training examples from the target video to finetune our re-ID net. As mentioned in Sect. 3, the local clustering step of the tracking approach produces local tracks of people when they are likely to be fully visible. These local tracks are like spatio-temporal "curves" that can start and stop at any frame, depending on the detections and the scene. An illustration of the local tracks is shown in Fig. 2(b). The spatio-temporal locations of the local tracks enforce intuitive constraints: if two tracks pass through the same frame but do not overlap spatially, they then most probably correspond to different people in the video. An example is shown in Fig. 4. The positive pairs are the detection images that come from the same track, and the negative pairs are from the two tracks that have temporal overlap but no spatial overlap.

To avoid including too many noisy training examples during the finetuning, we discard 20% of the head and tail images of local tracks, as the starting and/or the ending part of the tracks sometimes have inaccurate detection bounding boxes. Furthermore, we compute the average detection score of the detections within a local track. Based on the average score, we learn the probability of the local track to be a true positive on the MOT16 training sequences. During the training example mining, we exclude the local tracks that are more likely to be on the background of the scene by only considering the tracks whose probabilities of being true positives are larger than 0.5. Two tracks without temporal overlap may contain the same identity. We have no information about the identity of the people in the video. Therefore, during the finetuning stage, we only use the verification information, in other words, the classification subnet is not used.

The adapted re-ID net produces the cut/join probabilities between each pair of local tracks. Then we use the probabilities to compute the costs of the objective function (Eq. 3). Similar to the local clustering step, we solve the instances of the optimization problem by the heuristic approach proposed in [12].

4   Experiments

In this section, we present our experiments with the proposed re-ID net (Sect. 4.1), the adaptation approach (Sect. 4.2) and multi-person tracking (Sect. 4.3).

4.1   Re-ID Net Architecture Evaluation

Training/Test Data Collection. On the Market-1501 dataset, we train the re-ID model using its standard training set. In order to evaluate the performance of the re-ID net on the tracking data, we collect training and test examples from the MOT15 and MOT16 training set, which contain 576 identities in total. We randomly select 80% identities (460) from each sequence as the training set and the rest 20% (116) as the test set. The MOT benchmark also provides person detections on every frame. The detections are considered as true positives for a certain identity if their intersection-over-union (IOU) with the ground truth of the identity are larger than 0.5. Then the positive (negative) examples are pairs of detections that are assigned to the same (different) identities.

Metric. The metric used in the following person re-identification experiments is the verification accuracy.

Re-ID Net Implementation Details. On Market-1501, we train the re-ID net for 80k iterations using the initial weights trained on ImageNet. Adam [14] is used as the optimizer with $\beta_1 = 0.9$ and $\beta_2 = 0.999$. The initial learning rate is set to 1e-4 and the minibatch size is 128. We use random left-right flips for data augmentation.

Verification-Net and Classification-Net. In order to evaluate the effectiveness of the proposed classification subnet of our re-ID net, we compare two network architectures: using only the verification layer (V-Net) and using both verification and classification layers (V+C-Net). In Table 1, the first two rows show the verification accuracy of the two re-ID nets trained on Market-1501. The mean accuracy of V+C-Net is 80.7% which is significantly higher than the result (68.8%) for V-Net. We further finetune both re-ID networks on the MOT training data. In this case, the training and test data are quite similar as they are both from the MOT benchmark. Nevertheless, the V+C-net still outperforms V-net by 3.1%. These experiments suggest that training the classification task and the verification task jointly improves the verification accuracy. Therefore we use the V+C-Net in the following experiments.

Table 1. MOT16 Re-ID accuracy (%)

Model	Training	PosAcc.	NegAcc.	Mean
V-Net	Market-1501	65.5	72.0	68.8
V+C-Net	Market-1501	90.4	70.9	80.7
V-Net	Market-1501/MOT	100.0	90.2	95.1
V+C-Net	Market-1501/MOT	98.0	98.4	**98.2**

4.2 Adaptation Evaluation

Setup. To evaluate the adaptation scheme of the re-ID net in the context of multi-person tracking, we need to finetune the network on proper tracking test sequences. Here, we choose the MOT16-02 and MOT16-11 sequences as the test set. For the offline trained generic re-ID nets, we provide three different versions: ImageNet model, the one fine tuned on Market-1501, the one further fine tuned on the MOT training set (excluding MOT16-02 and MOT16-11).

For adapting the re-ID net on the test sequence, we employ two kinds of training strategis: only finetuning the fully-connected layer (AdaptationFC), and finetuning the whole network end-to-end (AdaptationE2E). The training examples are mined using the tracks generated by the local correlation clustering (HCC^l). All the adapted models are obtained with 3 epochs to avoid overfitting.

Results. As shown in Table 2, of the two generic re-ID models, the one further fine tuned on the MOT data improves the mean accuracy on MOT16-02 from 78.5% to 84.8%. For the adaptation schemes, the end-to-end model (AdaptationE2E) significantly improves the performance on MOT16-02 from 84.8% to 88.3%, where the AdaptationFC decreases the accuracy to 82.9%. These results

Table 2. Analysis on the adaptation approach

Model	OfflineTraining	MOT16-02			MOT16-11		
		PosAcc.	NegAcc.	Mean	PosAcc.	NegAcc.	Mean
Generic Net	Market-1501	82.6	73.4	78.0	82.7	81.3	82.0
Generic Net	Market-1501/MOT	83.7	85.9	84.8	85.8	90.6	88.2
AdaptationFC	Market-1501/MOT	76.4	89.4	82.9	88.2	88.0	88.1
AdaptationE2E	Market-1501/MOT	83.1	93.4	**88.3**	91.8	95.4	**93.6**
AdaptationE2E	Market-1501	82.6	93.4	88.0	91.7	94.9	93.3
AdaptationE2E	ImageNet	78.4	87.3	82.9	78.9	85.7	82.3

suggest that it is important to adapt the CNN features to the test scene. We further perform the adaptation on the models that are trained on the Market-1501 and ImageNet. The results are significant: without finetuning the model on the tracking sequence (MOT training set), the adaptation method already produces 88.0% accuracy; even the model trained on ImageNet, which has never seen person re-ID data before, already produces reasonable accuracy.

The same tendency is observed on the MOT16-11 sequence. Adapting the model that is further trained on the MOT set performs the best (93.6%), and is slightly better than the generic model that is trained on Market-1501 (93.3%). These results clearly validate the effectiveness of the proposed adaptation approach. Even without the annotated tracking data, the re-ID net that is adapted on the test sequence produces a good verification accuracy.

4.3   Tracking Experiments

We perform comparisons with recent tracking work on the challenging MOT16 Benchmark [22]. The benchmark contains a training and a test set, each with 7 sequences that are captured with different camera motion, and different imaging and scene conditions. For the test sequences, the training sequences that are captured under the same framerate and camera motion (moving/static) are provided. The model parameter θ for local clustering are learned from the training sequences that have the same framerate and camera motion (moving/static) via maximum likelihood estimation. To validate the effectiveness of different components of the proposed method, we select MOT16-02 and MOT16-11 as validation set to perform our analysis, in line with the previous section.

Tracking Implementation Details. As the detections provided by the benchmark are very noisy, we could also obtain small clusters on the background. In all the tracking experiments presented below, we remove the clusters whose sizes are smaller than 5. Given the detection cluster of a target, we estimate its tracks by using the code from [21] which estimates a spline curve for each target. We also fill in the missing detections when there are gaps in time due to occlusion or detection failures. However, when the gaps are too big, estimating the position and scale of missing detections of the tracks becomes difficult. Therefore, we fill in the missing detections within a certain temporal distance. In our experiments, for the sequences captured by a moving camera, the missing detections are filled in when the temporal gap is less than fps, where fps is the frame-rate of the sequence. For the sequences captured by a static camera, the missing detections are filled when the temporal gap is less than $2 \times fps$. These hyper-parameters are set according to the performance on the validation set.

Evaluation Metric. Following the MOT16 Benchmark, we apply the standard CLEAR MOT metrics [1]. The most informative metric is the multiple object tracking accuracy (MOTA) which is a combination of false positives (FP), false negatives (FN), and identity switches (IDs). Other important metrics are ID F1 Score (IDF1) [25], mostly tracked (MT) tracks, mostly lost (ML) tracks, fragmentation (FM), recall (Rcll) and precision (Prcn).

Comparison of Tracking Performance with Local and Global Clustering Setup. In this section, we compare the tracking performance of local (HCC^l) and global (HCC^g) correlation clustering. The HCC^l should generate reliable tracks that are robust to detection noise and abrupt camera motion. Once the target is fully occluded or missed by the detector within a short temporal window, the tracks will be terminated and a new track will start when the target is visible again. Given the local tracks, the global graph is constructed in such a way that all the local tracks are connected to each other, to enable the re-ID of the target within a much longer temporal window, even the whole sequence.

Results. It can be seen from Table 3 that on the MOT16-02 sequence, HCC^l achieves a MOTA of 19.5%. With the global clustering step, the MOTA is increased to 20.3% with generic re-ID model, and is further improved to 21.3% with the adapted re-ID model. Intuitively, the HCC^l could produce more ID switches and false negatives, because the underlying graph is constructed in the way that only the detections close in time are connected. With a well trained re-ID net and a reasonable filling in strategy, the HCC^g should reduce the number of ID switches and false negatives. Analyzing the data corroborates our hypotheses: the number of ID switches goes from 62 (HCC^l) to 33 (HCC^g), suggesting the effectiveness of the global correlation clustering step. Similar observation can be made on the MOT16-11 sequence. The overall MOTA increases from 53.3% to 55.1%. The number of ID switches decreases from 24 to 8, indicating that the majority of previously interrupted tracks are re-linked by the global clustering.

Comparison of Tracking Performance with the Generic and Adapted re-ID Net Setup. In this section, we compare the tracking performance of the generic re-ID model ($HCC^g_{generic}$) and the adapted re-ID model ($HCC^g_{adaptation}$). For both of them, the local tracks are identical. For $HCC^g_{generic}$, the similarities between the local tracks are computed with the generic re-ID net; for $HCC^g_{adaptation}$, the similarities between the local tracks are computed with the adapted one. As shown in Table 2, the accuracy of the similarity measure indicates the superior performance of the adapted model. It stands to reason that such superiority should be translated into a better performance of the tracking task.

Results. It can be seen from Table 3 that for both the MOT16-02 and MOT16-11 sequences, the adapted model produces a better MOTA (20.3% to 21.3%, 54.2% to 55.1% respectively). Besides, with the adapted model, we obtain better MOTP and Prcn, which suggests that the overall tracking performance is superior.

Results on the MOT16 Benchmark. To compare with the state-of-the-art multi-target tracking models, we evaluate our tracking model on the MOT16 test set. The evaluation is performed according to the benchmark and the results are publicly available[1]. In Table 4, we compare with all the published works. Generally speaking, for the 9 metrics that are considered by the benchmark, our model achieves the best performance on MOTA, IDs, Frag, and the second best performance on FP. Such results suggest the advantages and effectiveness of the proposed tracking approach.

Table 3. Comparison of tracking performance: 1. local clustering vs global clustering; 2. generic vs. adapted re-ID net

Method	MOT16-02				MOT16-11			
	FP	FN	IDs	MOTA	FP	FN	IDs	MOTA
HCC^l	507	13784	62	19.5	408	3861	24	53.2
$HCC^g_{generic}$	1045	13120	43	20.3	429	3763	7	54.2
$HCC^g_{adaptation}$	867	13131	33	21.3	352	3762	8	55.1

Table 4. Comparison on the MOT16 test set. Best in bold, second best in blue

Method	MOTA	IDF1	MT	ML	FP	FN	IDs	Frag	Hz	Detector
MOTDT [19]	47.6	50.9	15.2%	38.3%	9253	**85431**	792	1858	**20.6**	Public
NLLMPa [18]	47.6	47.3	17.0%	40.4%	5844	89093	629	768	8.3	Public
FWT [10]	47.8	44.3	**19.1%**	**38.2%**	8886	85487	852	1534	0.6	Public
GCRA [20]	48.2	48.6	12.9%	41.1%	5104	88586	821	1117	2.8	Public
LMP [32]	48.8	**51.3**	18.2%	40.1%	6654	86245	481	595	0.5	Public
HCC	**49.3**	50.7	17.8%	39.9%	5333	86795	**391**	**535**	0.8	Public

---

[1] https://motchallenge.net/results/MOT16/.

5   Conclusion

In this paper, we address the challenging problem of tracking multiple people in crowded scenes, where long-term occlusion is arguably the major challenge. To that end, we propose an adaptation scheme that explores the modeling capability of deep neural networks, by mining training examples from the target sequence. The adapted neural network produces reliable similarity measures, which facilitate person re-ID after long-term occlusion. Furthermore, we utilize an overall rigorous formulation [30,31] to hierarchically link and associate people. The combination of the tracking formulation and the adaptation scheme results in an effective multi-person tracking approach that demonstrates a new state-of-the-art.

Acknowledgments. This research was supported in part by Toyota Motors Europe and the German Research Foundation (DFG CRC 1233). **Disclosure** MJB has received research gift funds from Intel, Nvidia, Adobe, Facebook, and Amazon. While MJB is a part-time employee of Amazon, his research was performed solely at, and funded solely by, MPI.

References

1. Bernardin, K., Stiefelhagen, R.: Evaluating multiple object tracking performance: the CLEAR MOT metrics. Image Video Process. **2008**(1), 1–10 (2008)
2. Breitenstein, M.D., Reichlin, F., Leibe, B., Koller-Meier, E., Van Gool, L.: Online multiperson tracking-by-detection from a single, uncalibrated camera. TPAMI **33**(9), 1820–1833 (2011)
3. Brendel, W., Amer, M., Todorovic, S.: Multiobject tracking as maximum weight independent set. In: CVPR, pp. 1273–1280. IEEE (2011)
4. Bromley, J., et al.: Signature verification using a "siamese" time delay neural network. IJPRAI **7**(4), 669–688 (1993)
5. Charles, J., Pfister, T., Magee, D., Hogg, D., Zisserman, A.: Personalizing human video pose estimation. In: CVPR, pp. 3063–3072. IEEE, Las Vegas (2016)
6. Choi, W.: Near-online multi-target tracking with aggregated local flow descriptor. In: ICCV, pp. 3029–3037. IEEE, Santiago (2015)
7. Chopra, S., Hadsell, R., LeCun, Y.: Learning a similarity metric discriminatively, with application to face verification. In: CVPR, pp. 539–546. IEEE, San Diego (2005)
8. Dehghan, A., Tian, Y., Torr, P.H.S., Shah, M.: Target identity-aware network flow for online multiple target tracking. In: CVPR, pp. 1146–1154. IEEE, Boston (2015)
9. Grötschel, M., Wakabayashi, Y.: A cutting plane algorithm for a clustering problem. Math. Program. **45**(1), 59–96 (1989)
10. Henschel, R., Leal-Taixé, L., Cremers, D., Rosenhahn, B.: Fusion of head and full-body detectors for multi-object tracking. In: CVPRW, pp. 1541–1550. IEEE, Salt Lake City (2018)
11. Huang, C., Wu, B., Nevatia, R.: Robust object tracking by hierarchical association of detection responses. In: Forsyth, D., Torr, P., Zisserman, A. (eds.) ECCV 2008, Part II. LNCS, vol. 5303, pp. 788–801. Springer, Heidelberg (2008). https://doi.org/10.1007/978-3-540-88688-4_58

12. Keuper, M., Levinkov, E., Bonneel, N., Lavoue, G., Brox, T., Andres, B.: Efficient decomposition of image and mesh graphs by lifted multicuts. In: ICCV, Santiago, pp. 1751–1759 (2015)
13. Kim, C., Li, F., Ciptadi, A., Rehg, J.M.: Multiple hypothesis tracking revisited. In: ICCV, pp. 4696–4704. IEEE, Santiago (2015)
14. Kingma, D., Ba, J.: Adam: a method for stochastic optimization. In: ICLR, San Diego, pp. 13–23 (2015)
15. Kuo, C.H., Huang, C., Nevatia, R.: Multi-target tracking by on-line learned discriminative appearance models. In: CVPR, pp. 685–692. IEEE, San Francisco (2010)
16. Leal-Taixé, L., Milan, A., Reid, I., Roth, S., Schindler, K.: MOTChallenge 2015: towards a benchmark for multi-target tracking. arXiv:1504.01942
17. Leal-Taixé, L., Canton-Ferrer, C., Schindler, K.: Learning by tracking: Siamese CNN for robust target association. In: CVPRW, pp. 418–425. IEEE, Las Vegas (2016)
18. Levinkov, E., et al.: Joint graph decomposition & node labeling: problem, algorithms, applications. In: CVPR, pp. 1904–1912. IEEE, Honolulu (2017)
19. Long, C., Haizhou, A., Zijie, Z., Chong, S.: Real-time multiple people tracking with deeply learned candidate selection and person re-identification. In: ICME, pp. 1–6. IEEE, San Diego (2018)
20. Ma, C., et al.: Trajectory factory: tracklet cleaving and re-connection by deep Siamese Bi-GRU for multiple object tracking. In: ICME, pp. 1–6. IEEE, San Diego (2018)
21. Milan, A., Roth, S., Schindler, K.: Continuous energy minimization for multitarget tracking. TPAMI **36**(1), 58–72 (2014)
22. Milan, A., Leal-Taixé, L., Reid, I.D., Roth, S., Schindler, K.: MOT16: a benchmark for multi-object tracking (2016). arXiv:1603.00831
23. Pirsiavash, H., Ramanan, D., Fowlkes, C.C.: Globally-optimal greedy algorithms for tracking a variable number of objects. In: CVPR, pp. 1201–1208. IEEE, Colorado Springs (2011)
24. Revaud, J., Weinzaepfel, P., Harchaoui, Z., Schmid, C.: Deepmatching: hierarchical deformable dense matching. IJCV **120**(3), 300–323 (2016)
25. Ristani, E., Solera, F., Zou, R., Cucchiara, R., Tomasi, C.: Performance measures and a data set for multi-target, multi-camera tracking. In: Hua, G., Jégou, H. (eds.) ECCV 2016, Part II. LNCS, vol. 9914, pp. 17–35. Springer, Cham (2016). https://doi.org/10.1007/978-3-319-48881-3_2
26. Ristani, E., Tomasi, C.: Tracking multiple people online and in real time. In: Cremers, D., Reid, I., Saito, H., Yang, M.-H. (eds.) ACCV 2014, Part V. LNCS, vol. 9007, pp. 444–459. Springer, Cham (2015). https://doi.org/10.1007/978-3-319-16814-2_29
27. Shitrit, H.B., Berclaz, J., Fleuret, F., Fua, P.: Tracking multiple people under global appearance constraints. In: ICCV, pp. 137–144. IEEE, Spain (2011)
28. Sun, Y., Chen, Y., Wang, X., Tang, X.: Deep learning face representation by joint identification-verification. In: NIPS, Montreal, pp. 1988–1996 (2014)
29. Szegedy, C., et al.: Going deeper with convolutions. In: CVPR, pp. 1–9. IEEE, Boston (2015)
30. Tang, S., Andres, B., Andriluka, M., Schiele, B.: Subgraph decomposition for multi-target tracking. In: CVPR, pp. 5033–5041. IEEE, Boston (2015)
31. Tang, S., Andres, B., Andriluka, M., Schiele, B.: Multi-person tracking by multicut and deep matching. In: Hua, G., Jégou, H. (eds.) ECCV 2016, Part II. LNCS,

vol. 9914, pp. 100–111. Springer, Cham (2016). https://doi.org/10.1007/978-3-319-48881-3_8

32. Tang, S., Andriluka, M., Andres, B., Schiele, B.: Multiple people tracking by lifted multicut and person re-identification. In: CVPR, pp. 3701–3710. IEEE, Honolulu (2017)

33. Tang, S., Andriluka, M., Schiele, B.: Detection and tracking of occluded people. IJCV **110**(1), 58–69 (2014)

34. Wang, X., Turetken, E., Fleuret, F., Fua, P.: Tracking interacting objects using intertwined flows. TPAMI **38**(11), 2312–2326 (2016)

35. Wu, B., Nevatia, R.: Detection and tracking of multiple, partially occluded humans by Bayesian combination of edgelet based part detectors. IJCV **75**(2), 247–266 (2007)

36. Xiang, Y., Alahi, A., Savarese, S.: Learning to track: online multi-object tracking by decision making. In: ICCV, pp. 4705–4713. IEEE, Santiago (2015)

37. Yi, D., Lei, Z., Liao, S., Li, S.Z.: Deep metric learning for person re-identification. In: ICPR, pp. 34–39. IEEE, Stockholm (2014)

38. Zhang, L., Li, Y., Nevatia, R.: Global data association for multi-object tracking using network flows. In: CVPR. IEEE (2008)

39. Zheng, L., Shen, L., Tian, L., Wang, S., Wang, J., Tian, Q.: Scalable person re-identification: a benchmark. In: ICCV, pp. 1116–1124. IEEE, Santiago (2015)

Long-Term Visual Object Tracking Benchmark

Abhinav Moudgil[(✉)] and Vineet Gandhi

Center for Visual Information Technology, Kohli Center on Intelligent Systems,
International Institute of Information Technology, Hyderabad, India
abhinav.moudgil@research.iiit.ac.in, vgandhi@iiit.ac.in

Abstract. We propose a new long video dataset (called Track Long and Prosper - TLP) and benchmark for single object tracking. The dataset consists of 50 HD videos from real world scenarios, encompassing a duration of over 400 min (676K frames), making it more than 20 folds larger in average duration per sequence and more than 8 folds larger in terms of total covered duration, as compared to existing generic datasets for visual tracking. The proposed dataset paves a way to suitably assess long term tracking performance and train better deep learning architectures (avoiding/reducing augmentation, which may not reflect real world behaviour). We benchmark the dataset on 17 state of the art trackers and rank them according to tracking accuracy and run time speeds. We further present thorough qualitative and quantitative evaluation highlighting the importance of long term aspect of tracking. Our most interesting observations are (a) existing short sequence benchmarks fail to bring out the inherent differences in tracking algorithms which widen up while tracking on long sequences and (b) the accuracy of trackers abruptly drops on challenging long sequences, suggesting the potential need of research efforts in the direction of long-term tracking. Dataset and tracking results are available at https://amoudgl.github.io/tlp/.

1 Introduction

Visual tracking is a fundamental task in computer vision and is a key component in wide range of applications like surveillance, autonomous navigation, video analysis and editing, augmented reality etc. Many of these applications rely on long-term tracking, however, only few tracking algorithms have focused on the challenges specific to long duration aspect [18,19,31,36]. Although they conceptually attack the long term aspect, the evaluation is limited to shorter sequences or couple of selected longer videos. The recent correlation filter [2,6,9,45] and deep learning [3,14,33,43] based approaches have significantly advanced the field, however, their long term applicability is also unapparent as the evaluation is limited to datasets with typical average video duration of about 20–40 s. Not just the

Electronic supplementary material The online version of this chapter (https://doi.org/10.1007/978-3-030-20890-5_40) contains supplementary material, which is available to authorized users.

© Springer Nature Switzerland AG 2019
C. V. Jawahar et al. (Eds.): ACCV 2018, LNCS 11362, pp. 629–645, 2019.
https://doi.org/10.1007/978-3-030-20890-5_40

evaluation aspect, the lack of long term tracking datasets has been a hindrance for training in several recent state of the art approaches. These methods either limit themselves to available small sequence data [33, 43] or use augmentation on datasets designed for other tasks like object detection [14].

Motivated by the above observation, we propose a new long duration dataset called Track Long and Prosper (TLP), consisting of 50 long sequences. The dataset covers a wide variety of target subjects and is arguably one of the most challenging datasets in terms of occlusions, fast motion, viewpoint change, scale variations etc. However, compared to existing generic datasets, the most prominent aspect of TLP dataset is that it is larger by more than 20 folds in terms of average duration per sequence, which makes it ideal to study challenges specific to long duration aspect. For example, drift is a common problem in several tracking algorithms and it is not always abrupt and may occur due to accumulation of error over time (which may be a slow procedure and can be difficult to gauge in short sequences). Similarly, long sequences allow us to study the consistency of a tracker to recover from momentary failures.

We select 17 recent state of the art trackers which are scalable to be evaluated on TLP dataset and provide a thorough evaluation in terms of tracking accuracy and real time performance. Testing on such a large dataset significantly reduces the overfitting problem, if any, and reflects if the tracker is actually designed to consistently recover from challenging scenarios. To present a further perspective, we provide a comprehensive attribute wise comparison of different tracking algorithms by selecting various sets of short sequences (derived from original TLP sequences), in which each set only contains sequences where a particular type of challenge is dominant (like illumination variation, occlusions, out of view etc.).

We observe that the rankings from previous short sequence datasets like OTB50 [41] significantly vary from the rankings obtained on the proposed TLP dataset. Several top ranked trackers on recent benchmarks fail to adapt to long-term tracking scenario and their performance drops significantly. Additionally, the performance margin notably widens among several trackers, whose performances are imperceptibly close in existing benchmarks. More specifically, apart from MDNet [33], performance of all other evaluated tracker drops below 25% on commonly used metric of area under the curve of success plots. Our investigation hence strongly highlights the need for more research efforts in long term tracking and to our knowledge the proposed dataset and benchmark is the first systematic exploration in this direction.

2   Related Work

2.1   Tracking Datasets

There are several existing datasets which are widely used for evaluating the tracking algorithms and are summarized in Table 1. The OTB50 [41], OTB100 [42] are the most commonly used ones. They include 50 and 100 sequences respectively and capture a generic real world scenario (where some videos are taken from platforms like YouTube and some are specifically recorded for tracking application).

Table 1. Comparing TLP with other object tracking datasets.

	Frame rate (FPS)	# videos	Min duration (sec)	Mean duration (sec)	Max duration (sec)	Total duration (sec)
UAV123 [32]	30	123	3.6	30.5	102.8	3752
OTB50 [41]	30	51	2.3	19.3	129	983
OTB100 [42]	30	100	2.3	19.6	129	1968
TC128 [27]	30	129	2.3	14.3	129	1844
VOT14 [23]	30	25	5.7	13.8	40.5	346
VOT15 [22]	30	60	1.6	12.2	50.2	729
ALOV300 [34]	30	314	0.6	9.2	35	2978
NFS [11]	240	100	0.7	16	86.1	1595
TLP	24/30	50	**144**	**484.8**	**953**	**24240**

They provide per frame bounding box annotation and per sequence annotation of attributes like illumination variation, occlusion, deformation etc.

The ALOV300++ dataset [34] focuses on diversity and includes more than 300 short sequences (average length of only about 9 s). The annotations in ALOV300++ dataset are made every fifth frame. A small set of challenging sequences (partially derived from OTB50, OTB100 and ALOV300++ datasets) has been used in VOT14 [23] and VOT15 [22] datasets. They extend the rectangular annotations to rotated ones and provide per frame attribute annotations, for more accurate evaluation. Both of these datasets have been instrumental in yearly visual object tracking (VOT) challenge.

Some datasets have focused on particular type of applications/aspects. TC128 [27] was proposed to study the role of color information in tracking. It consists of 128 sequences (some of them are common to OTB100 dataset) and provides per frame annotations and sequence wise attributes. Similarly, UAV [32] targets the tracking application, when the videos are captured from low-altitude unmanned aerial vehicles. The focus of their work is to highlight challenges incurred while tracking in video taken from an aerial viewpoint. They provide both real and synthetically generated UAV videos with per frame annotations.

More recently, two datasets were proposed to incorporate the benefits of advances in capture technology. The NFS [11] dataset was proposed to study the fine grained variations in tracking by capturing high frame rate videos (240 FPS). Their analysis shows that since high frame video reduces appearance variation per frame, it is possible to achieve state of the art performance using substantially simpler tracking algorithms. Another recent dataset called AMP [46], explores the utility of 360° videos to generate and study tracking with typical motion patterns (which can be achieved by varying the camera re-parametrization in omni-directional videos). Contemporary to our work, [29] and [37] also review recent trackers for long-term tracking. However, they limit the long-term tracking definition to the ability of a tracker to re-detect after object goes out of view and the quality of their long term datasets is lower than our proposed TLP dataset, in terms of resolution and per sequence length. We evaluate the trackers from a holistic perspective and show that even if there is no apparent major challenge or target disappearance, tracking consistently for a long period of time is an extremely challenging task.

Although recent advances pave the way to explore several novel and specific fine grained aspects, the crucial long term tracking aspect is still missing from most of the current datasets. The typical average length per sequence is still only about 10–30 s. The proposed TLP dataset takes it to about 8–9 min per sequence, making it the largest densely annotated high-resolution dataset for the application of visual object tracking.

2.2   Tracking Methods

Most of the earlier approaches trained a model/classifier considering the initial bounding box marked by the user as "foreground" and areas farther away from the annotated box as "background". The major challenge in most of these approaches is to properly update the model or the classifier over time to reduce drift. This problem has been tackled in several innovative ways, such as Multiple Instance Learning [1], Online Boosting [12], P-N Learning [19], or by using ensemble of classifiers trained/initiated at difference instances of time [44]. Most of the recent advances, however, have focused only in two major directions i.e Correlation Filter (CF) based tracking [2,6,9,45] and deep learning based tracking [3,14,33,43]. The CF based trackers have gained huge attention due to their computational efficiency derived by operating in Fourier domain and the capability of efficient online adaptation. The interest in CF based approaches was kindled by the MOSSE [4] tracker proposed by Bolme et al., which demonstrated an impressive speed of about 700 FPS. Thereafter, several works have built upon this idea and have significantly improved tracking accuracy. The list includes ideas of using kernelized correlation filters [15]; exploiting multi-dimensional features [10,16]; combining template based features with pixel wise information for robustness to deformation and scale variations [2,26]; employing kernel ridge regression to reduce drift [31] etc. The work by Kiani et al. [21] identified the boundary effects in Fourier domain as one of the reasons for sub-optimal performance of CF based approaches. Solutions such as Spatially regularized CF [8] and Background aware CF [20] were later proposed to mitigate the boundary effects.

More recent efforts in CF based trackers utilize deep convolutional features instead of hand crafted ones like HOG [5]. Multiple convolutional layers in a hierarchical ensemble of independent DCF trackers was employed by Ma et al. [30]. Danelljan et al. [9] extended it by fusing multiple convolutional layers with different spatial resolutions in a joint learning framework. This combination of deep CNN features has led CF based trackers to the top of several benchmarks like OTB50; however, they come with an additional computational cost. Some recent efforts have been made to enhance running speeds by using ideas like factorized convolutions [6]; however, the speeds are still much slower than the traditional CF trackers.

Fig. 1. First frames of all the 50 sequences of TLP dataset. The sequences are sorted in ascending order on the basis of mean success rate (defined in Sect. 4) of all trackers at IoU threshold of 0.5. The sequences at the bottom right are more difficult to track than the ones at the top left.

Deep learning based trackers present another paradigm in visual object tracking. Data deficiency appeared to be the major limitation in early attempts [25, 40]. Later approaches [17,39] learnt offline tasks like objectness or saliency offline from object detection datasets and benefited from it during online tracking. However, the gap between the two tasks turned out to be a limitation in these works. The work by Nam *et al.* [33] proposed a novel direction by posing the tracking problem as evaluating the positive and negative candidate windows randomly sampled around the previous target state. They proposed a two phase training, first domain dependent and offline to fix initial layers and second online phase to update the last fully connected layer.

Siamese frameworks [3,14] have been proposed to regress the location of the target, given the previous frame location. They either employ data augmentation using affine transformations on individual images [14] or use video detection datasets for large scale offline training [3]. In both these approaches, the network is evaluated without any fine tuning at the test time, which significantly increases their computational efficiency. However, this comes at the cost of losing ability to update appearance models or learn target specific information, which may be crucial for visual tracking. More recently, Yun *et al.* [43] proposed a tracker controlled by action-decision network (ADNet), which pursues the target object by sequential actions iteratively, utilizing reinforcement learning for visual tracking.

3   TLP Dataset

The TLP dataset consists of 50 videos collected from YouTube. The dataset was carefully curated with 25 indoor and 25 outdoor sequences covering a large variety of scene types like sky, sea/water, road/ground, ice, theatre stage, sports arena, cage etc. Tracking targets include both rigid and deformable/articulated objects like vehicle (motorcycle, car, bicycle), person, face, animal (fish, lion, puppies, birds, elephants, polar bear), aircraft (helicopter, jet), boat and other generic objects (e.g sports ball). The application aspect was also kept into account while selecting the sequences, for example we include long sequences from theatre performances, music videos and movies, which are rich in content, and tracking in them may be useful in context of several recent applications like virtual camera simulation or video stabilization [13,24]. Similarly, long term tracking in sports videos can be quite helpful for automated analytics [28]. The large variation in scene type and tracking targets can be observed in Fig. 1. We further compare the TLP dataset with OTB in Fig. 2, to highlight that the variation in bounding box size and aspect ratio with respect to the initial frame is significantly larger in TLP and the variations are also well balanced. The significant differences in duration of sequences in OTB and TLP are also apparent.

The per sequence average length in TLP dataset is over 8 min. Each sequence is annotated with rectangular bounding boxes per frame, which were done using the VATIC [38] toolbox. The annotation format is similar to OTB50 and OTB100 benchmarks to allow for easy integration with existing toolboxes. We have 33/50 sequences (amounting to 4% frames in total) in TLP dataset where the target goes completely out of view and thus, we provide absent label for each frame in addition to the bounding box annotation. All the selected sequences are single shot (do not contain any cut) and have a resolution of 1280×720. Similar to VOT [22], we choose the sequences without any cuts, to be empirically fair in evaluation, as most trackers do not explicitly model a re-detection policy. However, the recovery aspect of trackers still gets thoroughly evaluated on the TLP dataset, due to presence of full occlusions and out of view scenarios in several sequences.

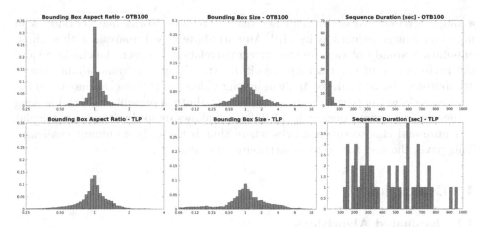

Fig. 2. Column 1 and 2: Proportional change of the targets aspect ratio and bounding box size (area in pixels) with respect to the first frame in OTB100 and TLP. Results are compiled over all sequences in each dataset as a histogram with log scale on the x-axis. Column 3: Histogram of sequence duration (in seconds) across the two datasets.

TinyTLP and TLPattr: We further derive two short sequence datasets from TLP dataset. The TinyTLP dataset consists of first 600 frames (20 s) in each sequence of the TLP dataset to compare and highlight the challenges incurred due to long-term tracking aspect. The length of 20 s was chosen to align the average per sequence length with OTB100 benchmark. The TLPattr dataset consists of total 90 short sequences focusing on different attributes. Six different attributes were considered in our work i.e (a) fast motion of target object or camera, (b) illumination variation around target object between consecutive frames, (c) large scale variation of the target object, (d) partial occlusions of the target object by other objects or background, (e) out of view or full occlusions, where object leaves the camera view or it is not visible at all and (f) background clutter. The TLPattr dataset includes 15 short sequences corresponding to each of the attribute.

Each sequence in TLPattr is carefully selected in such a way that the only dominant challenge present in it is a particular attribute, it is assigned to. For example, for fast motion, we first select all instances in entire TLP dataset where the motion of the center of the ground truth bounding box between consecutive frames is more than 20 pixels. We temporally locate every such fast motion event and curate a short sequence around it by selecting 100 frames before and after the fast motion event. We then sort the short sequences based on the amount of motion (with the instance with most movement between two frames as the top sequence) and manually shortlist 15 sequences (starting from the top), where fast motion is the only dominant challenge present and simultaneously avoiding selection of multiple short sequences from the same long video. For attributes like illumination variation and background clutter the selection was fully manual. The rationale behind curating the TLPattr dataset was the following: (a) Giving a single attribute to entire sequence (as in previous works like OTB50) is ill posed on long sequences as in TLP. Any attribute based analysis with such an annotation would not capture the correct correlation between the challenge and the performance of the tracking algorithm. (b) Using per frame annotation of attributes is also difficult for analysis in long videos, as the tracker may often fail before reaching the particular frame where attribute is present and (c) The long sequences and variety present in TLP dataset allows us to single out a particular attribute and choose subsequences where that is the only dominant challenge. This paves the way for accurate attribute wise analysis.

4   Evaluation

4.1   Evaluated Algorithms

We evaluated 17 recent trackers on the TLP and TinyTLP datasets. The trackers were selected based on three broad guidelines i.e.: (a) they are computationally efficient for large scale experiments; (b) their source codes are publicly available and (c) they are among the top performing trackers in existing benchmarks. Our list includes CF trackers with hand crafted features, namely SRDCF [8], MOSSE [4], DCF [16], DSST [7], KCF [16], SAMF [26], Staple [2], BACF [20] and LCT [31]; CF trackers with deep features: ECO [6] and CREST [35] and deep trackers i.e. GOTURN [14], MDNet [33], ADNet [43] and SiamFC [3]. We also included TLD [19] and MEEM [44] as two older trackers based on PN learning and SVM ensemble, as they specifically target the drift problem for long-term applications. We use default parameters on the publicly available version of the code when evaluating all the tracking algorithms.

4.2   Evaluation Methodology

We use precision plot, success plot and longest subsequence measure for evaluating the algorithms. The precision plot [1, 41] shows the percentage of frames whose estimated location is within the given threshold distance of the ground truth. A representative score per tracker is computed, by fixing a threshold over the distance (we use the threshold as 20 pixels). The success metric [41] computes the intersection over union (IoU) of predicted and ground truth bounding boxes and counts the number of successful frames whose IoU is larger than a given threshold. In out of view scenarios, if the tracking algorithm explicitly predicts the absence, we give it an overlap of 1 otherwise 0. The success plot shows the ratio of successful frames as the IoU threshold is varied from 0 to 1. A representative score for ranking the trackers is computed as the area under curve (AUC) of its success plot. We also employ the conventional success rate measure, counting frames above the threshold of 0.50 (IoU > 0.50).

LSM Metric: We further propose a new metric called Longest Subsequence Measure (LSM) to quantify the long term tracking behaviour. The LSM metric computes the ratio of the length of the longest successfully tracked continuous

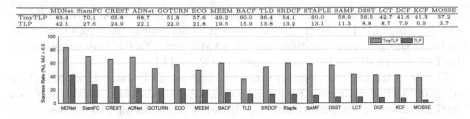

	MDNet	SiamFC	CREST	ADNet	GOTURN	ECO	MEEM	BACF	TLD	SRDCF	STAPLE	SAMF	DSST	LCT	DCF	KCF	MOSSE
TinyTLP	83.4	70.1	65.8	68.7	51.8	57.6	49.2	60.0	36.4	54.1	60.0	58.9	56.5	42.7	41.6	41.3	37.2
TLP	42.1	27.6	24.9	22.1	22.0	21.8	19.5	15.9	13.8	13.2	13.1	11.3	8.8	8.7	7.9	6.9	3.7

Fig. 3. Success rate of individual trackers on TinyTLP and TLP datasets. The algorithms are sorted based on their performance on TLP.

subsequence to the total length of the sequence. A subsequence is marked as successfully tracked, if $x\%$ of frames within it have IoU > 0.5, where x is a parameter. LSM plot shows the variation in the normalized length of longest tracked subsequence per sequence, as x is varied. A representative score per tracker can be computed by fixing the parameter x (we use the threshold as 0.95).

The LSM metric captures the ability of a tracker to track continuously in a sequence within a certain bound on failure tolerance (parameter x) and bridges the gap over existing metrics which fail to address the issue of frequent momentary failures. For example, it often happens in long sequences that tracker loses the target at some location and freezes there. If coincidentally the target passes the same location (after a while), the tracker starts tracking it again. LSM penalizes such scenarios by considering only the longest continuous tracked subsequences.

4.3 Per Tracker Evaluation

Figure 3 presents the success rate of each individual tracker on TinyTLP and TLP datasets. The MDNet tracker is the best performing tracker on both the datasets. TLD is the worst performing tracker on TinyTLP and MOSSE performs worst on TLP dataset. The performance significantly drops for each tracker on TLP dataset, when compared to TinyTLP dataset, which clearly brings out the challenges incurred in long-term tracking. The relative performance drop is minimum in MDNet where the success rate reduces from 83.4% to 42.1% (roughly by a factor of 2) and is most in MOSSE tracker, which reduces from 37.2% in TinyTLP to 3.7% in TLP (reduction by more than a factor of 10).

In general, the relative performance decrease is more in CF trackers with hand crafted features as compared to CF+deep trackers. For instance, trackers like BACF, SAMF, Staple give competitive or even better performance than CREST and ECO over TinyTLP dataset, however, their performance steeply decreases on TLP dataset. Although all the CF based trackers (hand crafted or CNN based) are quite susceptible to challenges such as long term occlusions or fast appearance changes, our experiments suggest that using learnt deep features reduces accumulation of error over time and reduces drift. Such accumulation of error is difficult to quantify in short sequences and the performance comparison may not reflect the true ability of the tracker. For example, BACF outperforms ECO on TinyTLP by about 2%, however it is 6% worse than ECO on TLP. Similarly, the performance difference of SAMF and ECO is imperceptible on TinyTLP, which differs by almost a factor of 2 on TLP.

The deep trackers outperform other trackers on TLP dataset, with MDNet and SiamFC being the top performing ones. ADNet is third best tracker on TinyTLP, however, its performance significantly degrades on TLP dataset. It is interesting to observe that both MDNet and ADNet refine last fully connected layer during online tracking phase, however, MDNet appears to be more consistent and considerably outperforms ADNet on TLP. The offline trained and freezed SiamFC and GOTURN perform relatively well (both appearing in top five trackers on TLP), however SiamFC outperforms GOTURN, possibly because it is trained on larger amount of video data. Another important observation is that the performance of MEEM surpasses all state of the art CF trackers with hand crafted features on TLP dataset. The ability to recover from failures also allows TLD tracker (giving lowest accuracy on TinyTLP) to outperform several recent CF trackers on TLP.

4.4 Overall Performance

The overall comparison of all trackers on TinyTLP and TLP using Success plot, Precision plot and LSM plot are demonstrated in Fig. 4. In success plots, MDNet clearly outperforms all the other trackers on both TinyTLP and TLP datasets with AUC measure of 68.1% and 36.9% respectively. It is also interesting to observe that the performance gap significantly widens up on TLP and MDNet clearly stands out from all other algorithms. This suggests that the idea of separating domain specific information during training and online fine tuning of background and foreground specific information, turns out to be an extremely important one for long term tracking. Furthermore, analyzing MDNet and ADNet both of which employ the strategy of online updates on last FC layers during tracking, it appears that learning to detect instead of learning to track gives a more robust performance in long sequences. The performance drop of SiamFC and GOTURN on TLP also suggests a similar hypothesis.

The steeper success plots in TLP as compared to TinyTLP dataset, suggest that accurate tracking gets more and more difficult in longer sequences, possibly due to accumulation of error. The lower beginning point on TLP (around 40–50% for most trackers compared to 80–90% on TinyTLP), indicates that most trackers entirely drift away before reaching halfway through the sequence. The rankings in success plot on TLP are also quite contrasting to previous benchmarks. For instance, ECO is the best performing tracker on OTB100 closely followed by MDNet (with almost imperceptible difference), and its performance significantly slides on TLP. Interestingly, MEEM breaks into top five trackers in AUC measure of success plot on TLP (ahead of ECO). In general there is striking drop of performance between TinyTLP and TLP for most CF based trackers (more so for hand crafted ones). CREST is most consistent among them and ranks in top 5 trackers for both TinyTLP and TLP.

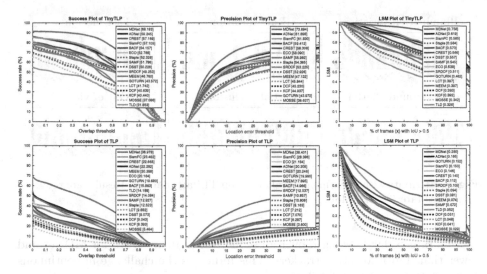

Fig. 4. Overall Performance of evaluated trackers on TinyTLP and TLP with success plot, precision plot and LSM plot respectively (each column). For each plot, ranked trackers are shown with corresponding representative measure i.e. AUC in success plots; 20 pixel threshold in precision plots and 0.95 as length ratio in LSM plots.

The precision plots also demonstrate similar trends as success plots, however they bring couple of additional subtle and interesting perspectives. The first observation is that SiamFC's performance moves closer to performance of MDNet on TLP dataset. Since SiamFC is fully trained offline and does not make any online updates, it is not accurate in scaling the bounding box to the target in long term, which brings down its performance in IoU measure. However, it still hangs on to the target due to the large scale training to handle challenges in predicting the consecutive bounding boxes, hence the numbers improve in the precision plot (again precision plot on TinyTLP does not capture this observation). The ADNet tracker is ranked two on TinyTLP using precision measure, however, it drops to 4th position on TLP. The GOTURN tracker also brings minor relative improvement in precision measure and moves ahead of MEEM on TLP.

The LSM plots show the ratio of longest successfully tracked continuous subsequence to the total length of the sequence. The ratios are finally averaged over all the sequences for each tracker. A sequence is successfully tracked if $x\%$ of frames in it have IoU > 0.5. We vary the value x to draw the plots and the representative number is computed by keeping $x = 95\%$. This measure explicitly quantifies the ability to continuously track without failure. MDNet performs the best on this measure as well. The relative performance of CREST drops in LSM measure, as it partially drifts away quite often, however is able to recover from it as well. So its overall success rate is higher, however, the average length of longest continuous set of frames it can track in a video is relatively low. In general, the ratio of largest continuously tracked subsequence to sequence length (with

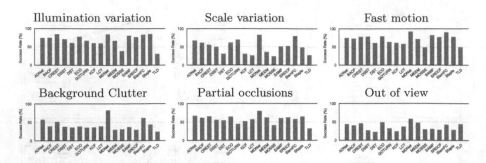

Fig. 5. Attribute wise performance evaluation on TLPattr dataset. Results are reported as success rate (%) with IoU > 0.5.

success rate > 0.95) averaged over all sequences is about 1/4th for MDNet and lower than 1/6th for other trackers. This indicates the challenge in continuous accurate tracking without failures.

4.5   Attribute Wise Performance Evaluation

The average attribute wise success rates of all the trackers on TLPattr dataset are shown in Fig. 5. Each attribute in TLPattr dataset includes 15 short sequences corresponding to it (dominantly representing the particular challenge). Out of view appears to be the most difficult challenge hindering the performance of the trackers followed by background clutter, scale variation and partial occlusions. Most of the trackers seem to perform relatively better on sequences with illumination variation and fast motion. On individual tracker wise comparison, MDNet gives best performance across all the attributes, clearly indicating the tracker's reliable performance across different challenges.

Another important perspective to draw from this experiment is that the analysis on short sequences (even if extremely challenging) is still not a clear indicator of their performance on long videos. For example, Staple and CREST are competitive in performance across all the attributes, however their performance on full TLP dataset differs by almost a factor of two in success rate measure (CREST giving a value 24.9 and Staple is only 13.1). Similarly comparison can be drawn between DSST and GOTURN, which are competitive in per attribute evaluation (with DSST performing better than GOTURN on fast motion, partial occlusions, background clutter and illumination variation). However, in long terms setting, their performance varies by a large margin (GOTURN giving success rate of 22.0, while DSST is much inferior with a value of 8.8).

4.6   Evaluation on Repeated TinyTLP Sequences

The essence of our paper is the need to think "long term" in object tracking, which is crucial for most practical applications of tracking. However, it remains unclear if there exists a "long term challenge in itself" and one can always argue

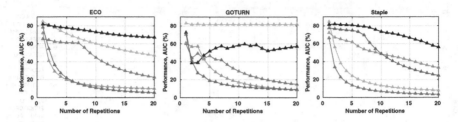

Fig. 6. Results of three different trackers on 20 times elongated TinyTLP sequences (by reversing and concatenating the sequence in iterative way). Each color represents a different sequence and each triangle represents a repetition.

that the performance drop in long videos is just because of "more challenges" or "frequent challenges". To investigate this further, we conduct a small experiment where we take a short sequence and repeat it 20 times to make a longer video out of it, by iteratively reversing and attaching it at the end to maintain the continuity. This increases the length of the sequence without introducing any new difficulty or challenges. In Fig. 6, we present such an experiment with three different trackers ECO (deep+CF, best performing tracker on OTB), GOTURN (pure deep) and Staple (pure CF) on 5 TinyTLP sequences for each tracker, where the tracker performs extremely well in the first iteration. We can observe that the tracking performance degrades for all three algorithms (either gradually or steeply) as the sequences get longer, which occurs possibly due to error accumulated over time. This again highlights the fact the tracking performance not just depends on the challenges present in the sequence but also gets affected by the length of the video. Hence, a dataset like TLP, interleaving the challenges and the long term aspect, is necessary for comprehensive evaluation of tracking algorithms.

4.7 Run Time Comparisons

The run time speeds of all the evaluated algorithms are presented in Fig. 7. For fair evaluation, we tested all the CPU algorithms on a 2.4 GHz Intel Xeon CPU with 32 GB RAM and we use a NVIDIA GeForce GTX 1080 Ti GPU for testing GPU algorithms. The CF based trackers clearly are most computationally efficient and even CPU algorithms run several folds faster than real time. The deep CF and deep trackers are computationally more expensive. MDNet gives lowest tracking speeds and runs at 1 FPS even on GPU. Among deep trackers GOTURN is the fastest tracker, however SiamFC and ADNet bring a good trade off in terms of overall success rate and run time speeds on GPU.

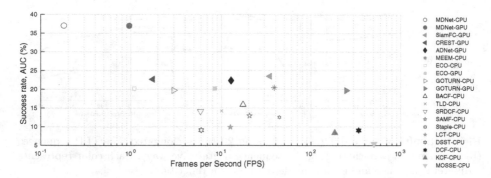

Fig. 7. Runtime comparison of different tracking algorithms.

5   Conclusion

This work aims to emphasize the fact that tracking on large number of tiny sequences, does not clearly bring out the competence or potential of a tracking algorithm. Moreover, even if a tracking algorithm works well on extremely challenging small sequences and fails on moderately difficult long sequences, it will be of limited practical importance. To this end, we propose the TLP dataset, focusing on the long term tracking application, with notably larger average duration per sequence, a factor which is of extreme importance and has been neglected in the existing benchmarks. We evaluate 17 state of the art algorithms on the TLP dataset, and the results clearly demonstrate that almost all state of the art tracking algorithms do not generalize well on long sequence tracking, MDNet being the only algorithm achieving more than 25% on the AUC measure of success plots. However, MDNet is also the slowest among the evaluated 17 trackers in terms of run time speeds.

Interestingly, if we only select the first 20 s of each sequence for evaluation (calling it TinyTLP dataset), the performance of all the trackers increases by multiple folds across different metrics. Another important observation is that the evaluations on small datasets fail to efficiently discriminate the performances of different tracking algorithms, and closely competing algorithms on TinyTLP result in quite different performance on TLP. The dominant performance of MDNet suggests that the ideas of online updating the domain specific knowledge and learning a classifier cum detector instead of a tracker (which regresses the shift), are possibly some cues to improve the performance in long term setting. Our evaluation on repeated TinyTLP sequences shows that temporal depth indeed plays an important role in the performance of evaluated trackers and appropriately brings out their strengths and weaknesses. To the best of our knowledge, TLP benchmark is the first large-scale evaluation of the state of the art trackers, focusing on long duration aspect and makes a strong case for much needed research efforts in this direction, in order to track long and prosper.

References

1. Babenko, B., Yang, M.H., Belongie, S.: Robust object tracking with online multiple instance learning. IEEE Trans. Pattern Anal. Mach. Intell. **33**(8), 1619–1632 (2011)
2. Bertinetto, L., Valmadre, J., Golodetz, S., Miksik, O., Torr, P.H.S.: Staple: complementary learners for real-time tracking. In: CVPR, June 2016
3. Bertinetto, L., Valmadre, J., Henriques, J.F., Vedaldi, A., Torr, P.H.: Fully-convolutional Siamese networks for object tracking. arXiv preprint arXiv:1606.09549 (2016)
4. Bolme, D.S., Beveridge, J.R., Draper, B.A., Lui, Y.M.: Visual object tracking using adaptive correlation filters. In: CVPR (2010)
5. Dalal, N., Triggs, B.: Histograms of oriented gradients for human detection. In: CVPR (2005)
6. Danelljan, M., Bhat, G., Shahbaz Khan, F., Felsberg, M.: Eco: efficient convolution operators for tracking. In: CVPR (2017)
7. Danelljan, M., Häger, G., Khan, F., Felsberg, M.: Accurate scale estimation for robust visual tracking. In: BMVC (2014)
8. Danelljan, M., Hager, G., Shahbaz Khan, F., Felsberg, M.: Learning spatially regularized correlation filters for visual tracking. In: ICCV (2015)
9. Danelljan, M., Robinson, A., Shahbaz Khan, F., Felsberg, M.: Beyond correlation filters: learning continuous convolution operators for visual tracking. In: Leibe, B., Matas, J., Sebe, N., Welling, M. (eds.) ECCV 2016. LNCS, vol. 9909, pp. 472–488. Springer, Cham (2016). https://doi.org/10.1007/978-3-319-46454-1_29
10. Danelljan, M., Shahbaz Khan, F., Felsberg, M., Van de Weijer, J.: Adaptive color attributes for real-time visual tracking. In: CVPR (2014)
11. Galoogahi, H.K., Fagg, A., Huang, C., Ramanan, D., Lucey, S.: Need for speed: a benchmark for higher frame rate object tracking. arXiv:1703.05884 (2017)
12. Grabner, H., Leistner, C., Bischof, H.: Semi-supervised on-line boosting for robust tracking. In: Forsyth, D., Torr, P., Zisserman, A. (eds.) ECCV 2008. LNCS, vol. 5302, pp. 234–247. Springer, Heidelberg (2008). https://doi.org/10.1007/978-3-540-88682-2_19
13. Grundmann, M., Kwatra, V., Essa, I.: Auto-directed video stabilization with robust l1 optimal camera paths. In: CVPR (2011)
14. Held, D., Thrun, S., Savarese, S.: Learning to track at 100 FPS with deep regression networks. In: Leibe, B., Matas, J., Sebe, N., Welling, M. (eds.) ECCV 2016. LNCS, vol. 9905, pp. 749–765. Springer, Cham (2016). https://doi.org/10.1007/978-3-319-46448-0_45
15. Henriques, J.F., Caseiro, R., Martins, P., Batista, J.: Exploiting the circulant structure of tracking-by-detection with kernels. In: Fitzgibbon, A., Lazebnik, S., Perona, P., Sato, Y., Schmid, C. (eds.) ECCV 2012. LNCS, vol. 7575, pp. 702–715. Springer, Heidelberg (2012). https://doi.org/10.1007/978-3-642-33765-9_50
16. Henriques, J.F., Caseiro, R., Martins, P., Batista, J.: High-speed tracking with kernelized correlation filters. TPAMI **37**(3), 583–596 (2015)
17. Hong, S., You, T., Kwak, S., Han, B.: Online tracking by learning discriminative saliency map with convolutional neural network. In: ICML (2015)
18. Hua, Y., Alahari, K., Schmid, C.: Occlusion and motion reasoning for long-term tracking. In: Fleet, D., Pajdla, T., Schiele, B., Tuytelaars, T. (eds.) ECCV 2014. LNCS, vol. 8694, pp. 172–187. Springer, Cham (2014). https://doi.org/10.1007/978-3-319-10599-4_12

19. Kalal, Z., Mikolajczyk, K., Matas, J.: Tracking-learning-detection. IEEE Trans. Pattern Anal. Mach. Intell. **34**(7), 1409–1422 (2012)
20. Kiani Galoogahi, H., Fagg, A., Lucey, S.: Learning background-aware correlation filters for visual tracking. In: CVPR (2017)
21. Kiani Galoogahi, H., Sim, T., Lucey, S.: Correlation filters with limited boundaries. In: CVPR (2015)
22. Kristan, M., et al.: The visual object tracking VOT2015 challenge results. In: ICCV Workshops, pp. 1–23 (2015)
23. Kristan, M., et al.: The visual object tracking VOT2014 challenge results. In: Agapito, L., Bronstein, M.M., Rother, C. (eds.) ECCV 2014. LNCS, vol. 8926, pp. 191–217. Springer, Cham (2015). https://doi.org/10.1007/978-3-319-16181-5_14
24. Kumar, M., Gandhi, V., Ronfard, R., Gleicher, M.: Zooming on all actors: automatic focus+ context split screen video generation. In: Ben, B., Chen, M. (eds.) Computer Graphics Forum, vol. 36, pp. 455–465. Wiley Online Library, Chichester (2017)
25. Li, H., Li, Y., Porikli, F.: Robust online visual tracking with a single convolutional neural network. In: Cremers, D., Reid, I., Saito, H., Yang, M.-H. (eds.) ACCV 2014. LNCS, vol. 9007, pp. 194–209. Springer, Cham (2015). https://doi.org/10.1007/978-3-319-16814-2_13
26. Li, Y., Zhu, J.: A scale adaptive kernel correlation filter tracker with feature integration. In: Agapito, L., Bronstein, M.M., Rother, C. (eds.) ECCV 2014. LNCS, vol. 8926, pp. 254–265. Springer, Cham (2015). https://doi.org/10.1007/978-3-319-16181-5_18
27. Liang, P., Blasch, E., Ling, H.: Encoding color information for visual tracking: algorithms and benchmark. IEEE Trans. Image Process. **24**, 5630–5644 (2015)
28. Lu, W.L., Ting, J.A., Little, J.J., Murphy, K.P.: Learning to track and identify players from broadcast sports videos. IEEE Trans. Pattern Anal. Mach. Intell. **35**(7), 1704–1716 (2013)
29. Lukežič, A., Zajc, L.Č., Vojíř, T., Matas, J., Kristan, M.: Now you see me: evaluating performance in long-term visual tracking. arXiv:1804.07056 (2018)
30. Ma, C., Huang, J.B., Yang, X., Yang, M.H.: Hierarchical convolutional features for visual tracking. In: ICCV (2015)
31. Ma, C., Yang, X., Zhang, C., Yang, M.H.: Long-term correlation tracking. In: CVPR (2015)
32. Mueller, M., Smith, N., Ghanem, B.: A benchmark and simulator for UAV tracking. In: Leibe, B., Matas, J., Sebe, N., Welling, M. (eds.) ECCV 2016. LNCS, vol. 9905, pp. 445–461. Springer, Cham (2016). https://doi.org/10.1007/978-3-319-46448-0_27
33. Nam, H., Han, B.: Learning multi-domain convolutional neural networks for visual tracking. In: CVPR (2016)
34. Smeulders, A.W., Chu, D.M., Cucchiara, R., Calderara, S., Dehghan, A., Shah, M.: Visual tracking: an experimental survey. TPAMI **36**(7), 1442–1468 (2014)
35. Song, Y., Ma, C., Gong, L., Zhang, J., Lau, R., Yang, M.H.: CREST: convolutional residual learning for visual tracking. In: ICCV (2017)
36. Supancic, J.S., Ramanan, D.: Self-paced learning for long-term tracking. In: CVPR (2013)
37. Valmadre, J., et al.: Long-term tracking in the wild: a benchmark. arXiv:1803.09502 (2018)
38. Vondrick, C., Patterson, D., Ramanan, D.: Efficiently scaling up crowdsourced video annotation. IJCV **101**(1), 184–204 (2013). Springer

39. Wang, N., Li, S., Gupta, A., Yeung, D.Y.: Transferring rich feature hierarchies for robust visual tracking. arXiv preprint arXiv:1501.04587 (2015)
40. Wang, N., Yeung, D.Y.: Learning a deep compact image representation for visual tracking. In: NIPS, pp. 809–817 (2013)
41. Wu, Y., Lim, J., Yang, M.H.: Online object tracking: a benchmark. In: CVPR (2013)
42. Wu, Y., Lim, J., Yang, M.H.: Object tracking benchmark. IEEE Trans. Pattern Anal. Mach. Intell. 37(9), 1834–1848 (2015)
43. Yun, S., Choi, J., Yoo, Y., Yun, K., Young Choi, J.: Action-decision networks for visual tracking with deep reinforcement learning. In: CVPR (2017)
44. Zhang, J., Ma, S., Sclaroff, S.: MEEM: robust tracking via multiple experts using entropy minimization. In: Fleet, D., Pajdla, T., Schiele, B., Tuytelaars, T. (eds.) ECCV 2014. LNCS, vol. 8694, pp. 188–203. Springer, Cham (2014). https://doi.org/10.1007/978-3-319-10599-4_13
45. Zhang, T., Xu, C., Yang, M.H.: Multi-task correlation particle filter for robust object tracking. In: CVPR (2017)
46. Cehovin Zajc, L., Lukezic, A., Leonardis, A., Kristan, M.: Beyond standard benchmarks: Parameterizing performance evaluation in visual object tracking (2017)

Learning Rotation Adaptive Correlation Filters in Robust Visual Object Tracking

Litu Rout[1]([✉]), Priya Mariam Raju[1], Deepak Mishra[1],
and Rama Krishna Sai Subrahmanyam Gorthi[2]

[1] Department of Avionics, Indian Institute of Space Science and Technology,
Thiruvananthapuram 695 547, Kerala, India
liturout1997@gmail.com, priyamariyam123@gmail.com, deepak.mishra@iist.ac.in
[2] Department of Electrical Engineering, Indian Institute of Technology Tirupati,
Tirupati 517 506, Andhra Pradesh, India
rkg@iittp.ac.in

Abstract. Visual object tracking is one of the major challenges in the field of computer vision. Correlation Filter (CF) trackers are one of the most widely used categories in tracking. Though numerous tracking algorithms based on CFs are available today, most of them fail to efficiently detect the object in an unconstrained environment with dynamically changing object appearance. In order to tackle such challenges, the existing strategies often rely on a particular set of algorithms. Here, we propose a robust framework that offers the provision to incorporate illumination and rotation invariance in the standard Discriminative Correlation Filter (DCF) formulation. We also supervise the detection stage of DCF trackers by eliminating false positives in the convolution response map. Further, we demonstrate the impact of displacement consistency on CF trackers. The generality and efficiency of the proposed framework is illustrated by integrating our contributions into two state-of-the-art CF trackers: SRDCF and ECO. As per the comprehensive experiments on the VOT2016 dataset, our top trackers show substantial improvement of 14.7% and 6.41% in robustness, 11.4% and 1.71% in Average Expected Overlap (AEO) over the baseline SRDCF and ECO, respectively.

Keywords: Rotation adaptiveness · False Positive Elimination · Displacement consistency

1 Introduction

Visual object tracking finds applications in diverse fields like traffic monitoring, surveillance systems, human computer interaction etc. Though the same object is being tracked throughout a given video sequence, the conditions under which the

---

Electronic supplementary material The online version of this chapter (https://doi.org/10.1007/978-3-030-20890-5_41) contains supplementary material, which is available to authorized users.

C. V. Jawahar et al. (Eds.): ACCV 2018, LNCS 11362, pp. 646–661, 2019.
https://doi.org/10.1007/978-3-030-20890-5_41

video is captured may vary due to changes in the environment, object, or camera. Illumination variations, object deformations, object rotations etc. are various challenges that occur due to changes in the aforementioned factors. A good tracking algorithm should continue tracking a desired object and its performance should remain unaffected under all these conditions.

Most of the existing trackers can be classified as either generative or discriminative. The generative trackers [1,4,15,17,31] use the object information alone to search for the most probable region in an image that matches the initially specified target object. On the other hand, the discriminative trackers [2,7,11,13,14,18,28] use both the object and background information to learn a classifier that discriminates the object from its background. The discriminative trackers, to a large extent, make use of CFs as classifiers. The main advantage of CFs is that correlation can be efficiently performed in the Fourier domain as simple multiplication, as proven by Parseval's theorem. For this reason, CF trackers are learned and all computations are performed efficiently in the Fourier domain that leads to drastic reduction in computational complexity [13]. Thus, the CF trackers have gained popularity in the community because of their strong discriminative power, which emerges due to implicit inclusion of large number of negative samples in training.

Despite all the advancements in CF tracking, most of these algorithms are not robust enough to object deformations, rotations, and illumination changes. These limitations are due to the inherent scarcity of robust training features that can be derived from the preceding frames. This restricts the ability of the learned appearance model to adapt the changes in target object. Therefore, we propose rotation adaptiveness and illumination correction schemes in order to extract sophisticated features from previous frames that helps in learning robust appearance model. The rotation adaptiveness, up to some extent, tackles the issues of object deformation due to the robustness in representation.

The main contributions of this paper are as follows. (a) An Illumination Correction filter (IC) (Sect. 3) is introduced in the tracking framework that eliminates the adverse effects of variable illuminations on feature extraction. (b) We propose an approach to incorporate rotation adaptiveness (Sect. 4) in standard DCF by optimizing across the orientations (Sect. 4.4) of the target object in the detector stage. The orientation optimization helps in extracting robust features from properly oriented bounding boxes unlike most state-of-the-art trackers that rely on axis aligned bounding boxes. (c) Building on it, we supervise the sub-grid localization cost function (Sect. 4.4) in the detector stage of DCF trackers. This cost function is intended to eliminate the false positives during detection. (d) Further, we show the impact of enhancing smoothness through displacement correction (Sect. 5), and demonstrate all these contributions on two popular CF trackers: Spatially Regularized Discriminative Correlation Filters (SRDCF) [7], and Efficient Convolution Operators (ECO) [5].

Though we have demonstrated the importance of our contributions by integrating with SRDCF and ECO, the proposed framework is generic, and can be well integrated with other state-of-the-art correlation filter trackers. The rest of the paper is structured as following. At first we discuss the previous works

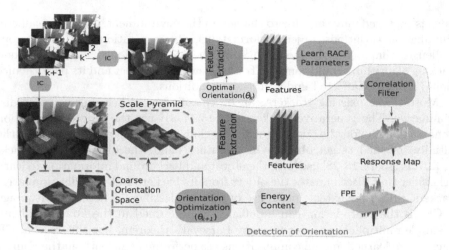

Fig. 1. As the pipeline indicates, both train (k^{th}) and test $(k + 1^{th})$ frames undergo illumination correction (IC) prior to feature extraction. The training features are then used to learn the parameters of Rotation Adaptive Correlation Filter (RACF). During detection stage, each candidate patch passes through a coarse orientation space from which the orientation optimizer picks a seed orientation. The seed orientation is usually the object's immediate previous orientation which is then used by Newton's iterative optimization scheme as initial point to determine optimal orientation for $k + 1^{th}$ frame. The optimizer maximizes the total energy content in the False Positive Eliminated (FPE) convolutional response map. The response map corresponds to the winning scale in the scale pyramid. Note that the optimal orientation in the first frame (θ_1) is assumed to be $0°$ without loss of generality. Thereafter, the optimal orientations in the subsequent frames are determined through a deterministic optimization strategy.

related to ours (Sect. 2), followed by the illumination correction filter (Sect. 3), the detailed description of rotation adaptive correlation filters (Sect. 4), and displacement consistency (Sect. 5). Thereafter, we provide experimental evidence (Sect. 6) to validate our contributions. In Fig. 1, we show the pipeline of our overall architecture.

2   Related Works

Numerous variants of the CF tracker have been proposed by adding constraints to the basic filter design, and by utilizing different feature representations of the target object. Initial extensions start with the KCF tracker [13] which uses a kernel trick to perform efficient computations in the Fourier domain. The Structural CF tracker [18] uses a part based technique in which each part of the object is independently tracked using separate CFs. Danelljan *et al.* [7] proposed the SRDCF tracker which uses a spatial regularizer to weigh the CF coefficients in order to emphasize the target locations and suppress the background information. Thus, the SRDCF tracker includes a larger set of negative patches in training, leading to a much better discriminative model.

The earlier trackers directly used the image intensities to represent the target object. Later on, feature representations such as color transformations [3,13,23,24], Colornames [9] etc. were used in CF trackers. Due to significant advancement of deep neural networks in object detection, features from these networks have also found applications in tracking, giving rise to substantial gain in performance. The deep trackers, such as DeepSRDCF [6], MDNet [22], and TCNN [21], clearly indicate the distinctive feature extraction ability of deep networks. The HCF tracker [19] exploits both semantic and fine-grained details learned from a pre-trained Convolutional Neural Network (CNN). It uses a multi-level correlation map to locate the target object. The CCOT tracker [8] uses DeepSRDCF [6] as the baseline and incorporates an interpolation technique to learn the filter in continuous domain with multi-resolution feature maps. The ECO tracker [5] reduces the computational cost of CCOT by using a factorized convolution operator that acts as a dimensionality reduction operator. ECO also updates the features and filters after a predefined number of frames, instead of updating after each frame. This eliminates redundancy and over-fitting to recently observed samples. As a result, the deep feature based ECO tracker does reasonably well on diverse datasets outperforming other CF trackers by a large margin.

Among rotation adaptive tracking, Zhang et al. propose an exhaustive template search in joint scale and spatial space to determine the target location, and learn a rotation template by transforming the training samples to Log-Polar domain, as explained in RAJSSC [30]. We learn rotation adaptive filter in the cartesian domain by incorporating orientation in the standard DCF, unlike exhaustive search. In contrast to a recent rotation adaptive scheme SiameseFC-DSR, as proposed by Rout et al. [26], we incorporate rotation adaptiveness directly in the standard DCF formulation, by performing a pseudo optimization on a coarse grid in the orientation space, leading to robust training of CF. Qianyun et al. [10] use a multi-oriented Circulant Structure with Kernel (CSK) tracker to get multiple translation models each dominating one orientation. Each translation model is built upon the KCF tracker. The model with highest response is picked to estimate the object's location. The main difference is that we do not learn multiple translation models at various orientations, as proposed in multi-oriented CSK, in order to reduce computational cost. In contrast, we optimize the total energy content in convolution responses at the detector stage with respect to object's orientation. The multi-channel correlation filter is then learned from a set of training samples which are properly oriented through a deterministic approach. Note that our training process requires a single model.

3   Illumination Correction (IC) Filter

Illumination changes occur in a video due to dynamically changing environmental conditions, such as waving tree branches, low contrast regions, shadows of other objects etc. This variable illumination gives rise to low frequency interference, which is one of the prominent causes of disturbing the object's appearance.

As the appearance of an object changes dramatically under different lighting conditions, the learned model fails to detect the object, leading to reduction in accuracy and robustness. Also, we may sometimes be interested in high frequency variations, such as edges, which are part of the dominant features in representing an object. Though these issues are investigated extensively in image processing community, to our knowledge, necessary attention for the same is not paid explicitly, even in the state-of-the-art trackers. Though deep features have shown to be fairly invariant to random fluctuations in input image, such as blur, white noise, illumination variation etc. the experimental results in Sect. 6 shows that trackers with deep features also fail to track the object under these challenges. Therefore, we intend to introduce Illumination Correction filter (IC) in the tracking paradigm in order to tackle the aforementioned issues up to some degree without affecting the usual tracked scenarios. At first, we employ a standard contrast stretching mechanism [25] to adjust the intensities of each frame. The contrast stretched image is then subjected to unsharp masking [25], a popular image enhancement technique in order to suppress the low frequency interference, and enhance high variations. To our surprise, the performance of the baseline trackers improves by a considerable amount just by enhancing the input images, as given in Sect. 6. This validates the fact that the robust feature extractors still lack high quality visual inputs, which otherwise can lead to substantial gain in performance.

4   Rotation Adaptive Correlation Filters (RACF)

Here, we elaborate the training and detection phase of rotation adaptive correlation filters in light of standard SRDCF. For the ease of understanding and clearly distinguishing our contributions, we have used identical notations as in SRDCF [7]. First, we explain standard SRDCF training and detection process, and then, we integrate rotation adaptiveness with false positive elimination into the optimization framework of CF, unlike heuristic template search [26,30].

4.1   SRDCF Training and Detection

In the standard DCF formulation, a multi-channel correlation filter f is learned from a set of training samples $\{(x_k, y_k)\}_{k=1}^{t}$. Each training sample x_k has a d-dimensional feature map, which is extracted from an image region. All the samples are assumed to be of identical spatial resolution $M \times N$. Thus, we have a d-dimensional feature vector $x_k(m, n) \in \mathbb{R}^d$ at each spatial location $(m, n) \in \Omega := \{0, \ldots, M-1\} \times \{0, \ldots, N-1\}$. We also denote feature layer $l \in \{1, \ldots, d\}$ of x_k by x_k^l. The target of each training sample x_k is denoted as y_k, which is a scalar valued function over the domain Ω. The correlation filter f has a stack of d layers, each of which is a $M \times N$ convolution filter f^l. The response of the convolution filter f on a $M \times N$ sample x is computed by,

$$S_f(x) = \sum_{l=1}^{d} x^l * f^l. \tag{1}$$

Here, $*$ represents circular convolution. The desired filter f is obtained by minimizing the L^2-error between convolution response $S_f(x_k)$ of training sample x_k and the corresponding label y_k with a more general Tikhonov regularizer $w : \Omega \to \mathbb{R}$,

$$\varepsilon(f) = \sum_{k=1}^{t} \alpha_k \left\| S_f(x_k) - y_k \right\|^2 + \sum_{l=1}^{d} \left\| \frac{w}{MN} \cdot f^l \right\|^2. \tag{2}$$

Here, $\cdot$ denotes point-wise multiplication. With the help of Parseval's theorem, the filter f can be equivalently computed by minimizing the Eq. (2) in the Fourier domain with respect to Discrete Forurier Transform (DFT) coefficients $\hat{f}$,

$$\hat{\varepsilon}(\hat{f}) = \sum_{k=1}^{t} \alpha_k \left\| \sum_{l=1}^{d} \hat{x}_k^l \cdot \hat{f}^l - \hat{y}_k \right\|^2 + \sum_{l=1}^{d} \left\| \frac{\hat{w}}{MN} * \hat{f}^l \right\|^2. \tag{3}$$

Here, $\hat{\ }$ denotes the DFT of a function. After learning the DFT coefficients $\hat{f}$ of filter f, it is typically applied in a sliding-window-like manner on all cyclic shifts of a test sample z. Let $\hat{s} := \mathcal{F}\{S_f(z)\} = \sum_{l=1}^{d} \hat{z}^l \cdot \hat{f}^l$ denote DFT ($\mathcal{F}$) of the convolution response $S_f(z)$ evaluated at test sample z. The convolution response $s(u,v)$ at continuous location $(u,v) \in [0,M) \times [0,N)$ are interpolated by,

$$s(u,v) = \frac{1}{MN} \sum_{m=0}^{M-1} \sum_{n=0}^{N-1} \hat{s}(m,n) \, e^{i2\pi\left(\frac{m}{M}u + \frac{n}{N}v\right)}. \tag{4}$$

Here, i denotes the imaginary unit. The maximal sub-grid location (u^*, v^*) is then computed by optimizing $\arg\max_{(u,v)\in[0,M)\times[0,N)} s(u,v)$ using Newton's method, starting at maximal grid-level score $(u^{(0)}, v^{(0)}) \in \Omega$. In a nutshell, the standard SRDCF adapts translation invariance efficiently by exploiting the periodic assumption with spatial regularization, but this does not learn rotation adaptiveness inherently. Therefore, we propose to extend the discriminative power of SRDCF by learning rotation adaptive filters through a deterministic optimization procedure.

4.2 RACF Training and Detection

First, we incorporate rotation adaptiveness in spatially regularized correlation filters by learning from appropriately oriented training samples. Similar to SRDCF, we solve the resulting optimization problem in the Fourier domain, by employing a deterministic orientation in each training sample. Let θ_k denotes the orientation corresponding to x_k. Without loss of generality, it can be assumed that $\theta_k = 0, \forall k \le 1$. The training sample x_k undergoes rotation θ_k by,

$$x_k^\theta(m,n)_{(m,n)\in\Omega} = \begin{cases} x_k(m',n') , & (m',n') \in \Omega \\ 0 , & elsewhere \end{cases} \tag{5}$$

where (m, n) and (m', n') are related by,

$$\begin{bmatrix} n \\ m \end{bmatrix} = \begin{bmatrix} \cos(\theta_k) & -\sin(\theta_k) \\ \sin(\theta_k) & \cos(\theta_k) \end{bmatrix} \begin{bmatrix} n' \\ m' \end{bmatrix}. \tag{6}$$

In other words, x_k^θ is obtained by rotating x_k anti-clockwise with an angle θ_k in the Euclidean space and cropping same size $M \times N$ as x_k. In order to avoid wrong gradient estimation due to zero paddings, we use a common solution that bands the rotated image patch with cosine window. This does not disturb the structure of the object assuming that the patch size is larger than the target object. This is different from standard SRDCF, in a sense that we learn the multi-channel correlation filter f from properly oriented training samples $\{(x_k^\theta, y_k)\}_{k=1}^t$. The training stage of rotation adaptive filters is explained in the following Sect. 4.3.

4.3   Training: Learning RACF Parameters

The convolution response $S_f(x_k^\theta)$ of the rotated training sample $x_k^\theta \in \mathbb{R}^d$ is computed by,

$$S_f(x_k^\theta) = \sum_{l=1}^d x_k^{\theta l} * f^l. \tag{7}$$

After incorporating rotation into the DCF formulation, the resulting cost function is expressed as,

$$\varepsilon_\theta(f) = \sum_{k=1}^t \alpha_k \left\| S_f(x_k^\theta) - y_k \right\|^2 + \sum_{l=1}^d \left\| \frac{w}{MN} \cdot f^l \right\|^2. \tag{8}$$

Similar to SRDCF, we perform the Gauss-Seidel iterative optimization in Fourier domain by computing DFT of Eq. (8) as,

$$\hat{\varepsilon}_\theta(\hat{f}) = \sum_{k=1}^t \alpha_k \left\| \sum_{l=1}^d \hat{x}_k^{\theta l} \cdot \hat{f}^l - \hat{y}_k \right\|^2 + \sum_{l=1}^d \left\| \frac{\hat{w}}{MN} * \hat{f}^l \right\|^2. \tag{9}$$

The Eq. (9) is vectorized and simplified further by using fully vectorized real-valued filter, as implemented in the standard SRDCF [7]. The aforementioned training procedure is feasible, provided we obtain the object's orientation corresponding to all the training samples beforehand. In the following Sect. 4.4, we propose an approach to localize the target object and detect its orientation by optimizing a newly formulated objective function.

4.4   Detection: Localization of the Target Object

At the detection stage, the correlation filter f learned from t training samples are utilized to compute the convolution response of a test sample z obtained from $(t+1)^{th}$ frame, which is then optimized to locate the object in that $(t+1)^{th}$

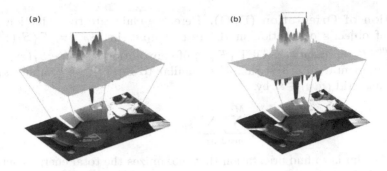

Fig. 2. Sample frames from the sequence glove of VOT2016 [16]. The blue, green, and red rectangle shows the output of groundtruth, ECO, and F-ECO (with FPE), respectively. Convolution response of shaded (red) region obtained directly (a) without, and (b) with optimization through false positive elimination. (Color figure online)

frame. For example, at $t = 1$, we learn the coefficients of f from $(x_{k=1}^{\theta=0°}, y_{k=1})$ and detect the object location, (u_{k+1}^*, v_{k+1}^*), and orientation, θ_{k+1} in the $(t+1)^{th}$, i.e., 2nd frame. For efficient detection of scale, we construct multiple resolution test samples $\{z_r\}_{r \in \{\lfloor \frac{1-S}{2} \rfloor, ..., \lfloor \frac{S-1}{2} \rfloor\}}$ by resizing the image at various scales a^r, as implemented in SRDCF [7]. Here, S and a denote the number of scales and scale increment factor, respectively. Next, we discuss the false positive elimination scheme, which offers notable gain in the overall performance.

False Positive Elimination (FPE). As per our extensive experiments, we report that the convolution response map of test sample may sometimes contain multiple peaks with equal detection scores. This situation usually arises when the test sample is constructed from an image region that consists of multiple objects with similar representations as target object. In fact, this issue can occur in many real world scenarios, such as glove, leaves, rabbit etc. sequences from VOT2016 dataset [16]. Therefore, we propose to maximize $\frac{s(u,v)}{\|(u-u_k^*, v-v_k^*)\|}$ unlike SRDCF, which focuses on maximizing $s(u, v)$ alone. Here, (u_k^*, v_k^*) denote the sub-grid level target location in the kth frame. Thereby, we intend to detect the object that has high response score as well as minimum deviation from previous location. Arguably, this hypothesis is justified by the fact that it is less likely for an object to undergo drastic deviation from immediate past location. Due to identical representation in feature space, both the gloves have equal response score as shown in Fig. 2(a). However, the FPE scheme mitigates this issue, as shown in Fig. 2(b), by maximizing the response score subject to minimum deviation from previous centroid which in turn creates a very distinct decision boundary. Note that the Gauss-Seidel optimization of total energy content through FPE directly yields this scalar valued response (Fig. 2(b)) without any post-processing.

Detection of Orientation (DoO). Here, we elaborate the detection mechanism of object's orientation in the test sample. Let $\hat{s}_\theta := \mathcal{F}\{S_f(z^\theta)\} = \sum_{l=1}^{d} \hat{z}^{\theta l} \cdot \hat{f}^l$ represents the DFT ($\mathcal{F}\{.\}$) of convolution response $S_f(z^\theta)$, evaluated at θ orientation of test sample z. Similar to Eq. (4), we compute $s_\theta(u,v)$ on a coarse grid $(u,v) \in \Omega$ by,

$$s_\theta(u,v) = \frac{1}{MN} \sum_{m=0}^{M-1} \sum_{n=0}^{N-1} \hat{s}_\theta(m,n) e^{i2\pi\left(\frac{m}{M}u + \frac{n}{N}v\right)}. \tag{10}$$

Then, the aim is to find orientation that maximizes the total energy content in the convolution response map by,

$$\theta_{k+1} = \arg\max_{\theta \in \Phi} \left\{ \sum_{u=0}^{M-1} \sum_{v=0}^{N-1} \left(\frac{S_\theta(u,v)}{\|(u - u_k^*, v - v_k^*)\|} \right)^2 \right\}. \tag{11}$$

Here, $\Phi := \{\theta_k \pm a\delta\}$, where $a = 0,1,2,\ldots,A$. Thus, the orientation space Φ consists of $(2A+1)$ number of rotations with step size δ. In our experiments, we have used $\delta = 5°$, and $A = 2$ based on the fact that an object's orientation is less likely to change drastically between consecutive frames. Nevertheless, the orientation can be further optimized by Newton's approach, or any suitable optimization algorithm, starting at optimal coarse orientation θ_{k+1}. Also, a suitable combination of A and δ can be chosen for searching exhaustively in Φ, but at the expense of time complexity. Next, we incorporate the FPE and DoO techniques in Fast Sub-grid Detection method of standard SRDCF (Sect. 4.4) formulation.

Fast Sub-Grid Detection. We apply the Newton's optimization strategy, as in SRDCF, for finding the sub-grid location that maximizes the detection score. However, we incorporate the false positive elimination and optimal orientation in the standard SRDCF sub-grid detection. Thus, we compute the sub-grid location that corresponds to maximum detection score by,

$$\left(u_{k+1}^*, v_{k+1}^*\right) = \arg\max_{(u,v) \in [0,M) \times [0,N)} \left\{ \frac{S_{\theta_{k+1}}(u,v)}{\|(u - u_k^*, v - v_k^*)\|} \right\}, \tag{12}$$

starting at $(u^{(0)}, v^{(0)}) \in \Omega$, such that $\left\{ \frac{S_{\theta_{k+1}}(u^{(0)},v^{(0)})}{\|(u^{(0)} - u_k^*, v^{(0)} - v_k^*)\|} \right\}$ is maximal.

5   Displacement Consistency

Motivated by the displacement consistency techniques, as proposed in [26], we enhance the degree of smoothness imposed on the movement variables, such as speed and angular displacement. We update the sub-grid location, (u_{k+1}^*, v_{k+1}^*) obtained from Eq. (12) by,

$$\begin{aligned} \left(u_{k+1}^*, v_{k+1}^*\right) &= (u_k^*, v_k^*) + d_{1n} \angle \varphi_{1n}, \\ d_{1n} &= \omega_d \times d_1 + (1 - \omega_d) \times d_0, \\ \varphi_{1n} &= \omega_a \times \varphi_1 + (1 - \omega_a) \times \varphi_0, \end{aligned} \tag{13}$$

where, $d_0 = \left\|(u_k^* - u_{k-1}^*, v_k^* - v_{k-1}^*)\right\|$, $d_1 = \left\|(u_{k+1}^* - u_k^*, v_{k+1}^* - v_k^*)\right\|$, $\varphi_0 = \arctan(u_k^* - u_{k-1}^*, v_k^* - v_{k-1}^*)$, $\varphi_1 = \arctan(u_{k+1}^* - u_k^*, v_{k+1}^* - v_k^*)$, $\omega_d = 0.9, \omega_a = 0.9$. The abrupt transition from (u_k^*, v_k^*) to (u_{k+1}^*, v_{k+1}^*) is restricted by reducing the contribution of d_1 and φ_1 slightly to 0.9. Note that for $\omega_d = \varphi = 1$, the updated (u_{k+1}^*, v_{k+1}^*) of Eq. (13) remains unaltered from the optimal solution of Eq. (12). In the following Sect. 6, we briefly describe our experimental setup, and critically analyze the results.

6 Experiments

First, we detail the experimental setup, and then carry out the ablation studies to analyze the effect of each individual component towards overall tracking performance. Then we conduct extensive experiments to compare with various state-of-the-art trackers both qualitatively and quantitatively on VOT2016 [16] and OTB100 [29] benchmark. In all our experiments, we use VOT toolkit and OTB toolkit for evaluation on VOT2016 and OTB100 benchmark, respectively.

6.1 Implementation Details

In order to perform an unbiased analysis that may arise due to varying numerical precision of different systems, we evaluate all the models, including baseline SRDCF and ECO on the same system under identical experimental setup. All the experiments are conducted on a single machine: Intel(R) Xeon(R) CPU E3-1225 v2 @ 3.20 GHz, 4 Core(s), 4 Logical Processor(s) and 16 GB RAM. The proposed tracker has been implemented on MATLAB with Matconvnet. We use the similar parameter settings as baseline, apart from the additional parameters $\delta = 5°$, and $A = 2$ in rotation adaptive filters. These settings are selected because the orientation does not change drastically between consecutive frames. In IC, we use output intensity range $[0, 255]$ for contrast stretching, and a threshold 0.5 for unsharp masking. This intensity range is selected so as to match with the conventional representation (uint8) of most images. On the other hand, this threshold is selected manually by observing qualitative results on VOT2016.

6.2 Estimation of Computational Complexity

The Fast Fourier Transform (FFT) of a 2-dimensional signal of size $M \times N$ can be computed in $\mathcal{O}(MN \log MN)$. Since there are d feature layers, S scales, and $(2A + 1)$ orientations, the training and detection stage of our algorithm requires $\mathcal{O}(ASdMN \log MN)$ FFT computations. To compute the convolution response, the computed FFTs require $\mathcal{O}(ASdMN)$ multiplication operations, and $\mathcal{O}(ASMN)$ division operations. The division operations are used in False Positive Elimination (FPE) strategy. Assuming that the Newton's optimization converges in N_{Ne} iterations, the total time complexity of matrix multiplication and FPE sums up to $\mathcal{O}((ASdMN + ASMN)N_{Ne})$. In contrast to standard

SRDCF [7], we learn the multi-resolution filter coefficients from properly oriented training samples. After detection of orientation through optimization of total energy content on a coarse grid, the training samples are oriented appropriately in $\mathcal{O}\left(MN\right)$ time complexity. The fraction of non-zero elements in A_t of size $dMN \times dMN$, as given in standard SRDCF, is bounded by the upper limit $\frac{2d+k^2}{dMN}$. Thus, the total time complexity of standard SRDCF training, assuming that the Gauss-Seidel optimization converges in N_{GS} iterations, sums up to $\mathcal{O}\left(\left(d+k^2\right)dMNN_{GS}\right)$. In addition to the standard SRDCF training, our approach requires $\mathcal{O}\left(MN\right)$ operations to orient the samples, leading to a total complexity of $\mathcal{O}\left(MN + \left(d+k^2\right)dMNN_{GS}\right)$. Therefore, the overall time complexity of our RIDF-SRDCF is given by,

$$\mathcal{O}\left(ASdMN \log MN + \left(ASdMN + ASMN\right)N_{Ne} + MN + \left(d+k^2\right)dMNN_{GS}\right) \tag{14}$$

and that of SRDCF is given by,

$$\mathcal{O}\left(dSMN \log MN + SMNN_{Ne} + \left(d+k^2\right)dMNN_{GS}\right) \tag{15}$$

Note that the overall complexity of both of these are largely dominated by $\mathcal{O}\left(\left(d+k^2\right)dMNN_{GS}\right)$, leading to only slight increment in computational cost due to the additional terms, but resulting in significant improvement in overall performance of RIDF-SRDCF relative to standard SRDCF. In fact, the RIDF-SRDCF runs at 5fps and SRDCF runs at 7fps on our machine.

6.3   Ablation Studies

We progressively integrate Displacement consistency (D), False positive elimination (F), Rotation adaptiveness (R), Illumination correction (I), and their combinations into ECO framework for faster experimentation, and assimilate the impact of each individual component on AEO, which is the standard metric on VOT2016 benchmark. We evaluate each Ablative tracker on a set of 16 videos (Table 1) during the development phase. The set is constructed from the pool of 60 videos from VOT2016 dataset. A video is selected if its frames are labelled as either severe deformation, rotation, or illumination change. Note that the FPE scheme improves the performance in every integration, and illumination correction alone provides a gain of 7.7% over base RDF-ECO. As per the results in Table 1, the proposed ideas independently and together provide a good improvement relative to base model.

6.4   Comparison with the State of the Arts

Here, we demonstrate detailed evaluation results to experimentally validate the efficacy of our contributions in hotistic visual object tracking challenge. We use VOT2016 benchmark during development stage and hyper parameter tuning. To analyze the generalization ability of proposed contributions, we benchmark our trackers with same parameter settings on both VOT2016 and OTB100.

Table 1. Quantitative evaluation of Ablative trackers on a set of 16 challenging videos from VOT2016 benchmark.

Tracker	ECO	D-ECO	DF-ECO	R-ECO	RF-ECO	RD-ECO	RDF-ECO	RIDF-ECO
AEO	0.357	0.360	0.362	0.383	0.386	0.395	0.402	0.433
%Gain	Baseline	0.8	1.4	7.3	8.1	10.6	12.6	21.3

Evaluation on VOT2016. We evaluate the top performing models from Table 1, including Ablative trackers of SRDCF, on VOT2016 dataset. As per the results in Table 2, the I-SRDCF, RDF-SRDCF, and RIDF-SRDCF provide a considerable improvement of 3.53%, 10.60%, and 11.41% in AEO, 4.83%, 17.87%, and 13.04% in robustness, respectively. The RIDF-ECO performs favourably against the state-of-the-art trackers including MDNet (won VOT2015) and CCOT (won VOT2016) with a slight improvement of 1.71% in AEO, and as high as 6.41% in robustness. The percentage gain is computed relative to baseline.

Table 2. State-of-the-art comparison on whole VOT2016 dataset.

Trackers	SRDCF	I-SRDCF	RDF-SRDCF	**RIDF-SRDCF**	TCNN	CCOT	ECO	MDNet	**RIDF-ECO**
AEO	0.1981	0.2051	0.2191	0.2207	0.3249	0.3310	0.3563	0.3584	0.3624
Failure rate (Robustness)	2.07	1.97	1.70	1.80	0.96	0.83	0.78	0.76	0.73

Evaluation on OTB100. As per the evaluation on OTB100 (Table 3), the proposed RIDF-ECO performs favourably against baseline and also the state-of-the-art trackers in most of the existing categories. As per the quantitative study in Table 3, our method finds difficulties in dealing with Background Clutter, Deformation and Out-of-plane rotation. Though our contributions strengthen the performance of ECO in these failure cases, it is definitely not better than MDNet. Of particular interest, the SRDCF tracker with deep features, i.e. DeepSRDCF lags behind SRDCF with RIDF, i.e. RIDF-SRDCF in success rate as well as precision which are the standard metrics in OTB100 benchmark. Note that exactly same hyper parameters are used in the evaluation on OTB100 as on VOT2016. This verifies the fact that rotation adaptive filters along with other contributions generalizes well across OTB100 and VOT2016 benchmark datasets.

Evaluation of CF Trackers. To qualitatively assess the overall performance of RIDF-SRDCF, we compare our results with baseline approach and few other CF trackers on challenging sequences from VOT2016, as shown in Fig. 3. Further, we quantitatively assess the performance by comparing the Average Expected Overlap (AEO) of few correlation filter based trackers, as shown in Fig. 4. The proposed RIDF-SRDCF outperforms the standard SRDCF in most of the individual categories that leads to 11.4% and 13.04% overall improvement in AEO and robustness, respectively. The categorical comparison, as can be inferred from Fig. 4, shows 56.25%, 23.53%, 38.46%, 5.26%, and 16.66% gain in Illumination change, Size change, Motion Change, Camera motion, and Empty categories, respectively. Note that the percentage improvement is computed relative to base SRDCF. In Table 4, we compare our rotation adaptive scheme with two recent approaches that aims at addressing this issue heuristically. As per our experiments, we report that the proposed rotation adaptive scheme outperforms these counterparts on VOT2016 benchmark. Since base CF trackers are used as core components in most trackers, we believe that the proposed performance gain will be reflected positively in all their derivatives.

Table 3. State-of-the-art comparison on OTB100 dataset.

Trackers	RIDF-ECO	ECO	MDNet	CCOT	RIDF-SRDCF	DeepSRDCF	SRDCF	CFNet	Staple	KCF
Out-of-view	0.767	0.726	0.708	0.725	0.712	0.619	0.555	0.423	0.518	0.550
Occlusion	0.721	0.710	0.702	0.692	0.652	0.625	0.641	0.573	0.610	0.535
Illumination variation	0.702	0.662	0.688	0.676	0.649	0.631	0.620	0.561	0.601	0.530
Low resolution	0.734	0.652	0.663	0.642	0.588	0.438	0.537	0.545	0.494	0.384
Background clutter	0.648	0.638	0.697	0.620	0.634	0.616	0.612	0.592	0.580	0.557
Deformation	0.687	0.687	0.722	0.657	0.652	0.645	0.641	0.618	0.690	0.608
In-plane rotation	0.696	0.645	0.656	0.653	0.635	0.625	0.615	0.606	0.596	0.510
Out-of-plane rotation	0.682	0.665	0.707	0.663	0.646	0.637	0.618	0.593	0.594	0.514
Fast motion	0.716	0.698	0.671	0.694	0.693	0.640	0.599	0.547	0.526	0.482
Overall success rate	0.702	0.691	0.678	0.671	0.641	0.635	0.598	0.589	0.581	0.477
Overall precision	0.937	0.910	0.909	0.898	0.870	0.851	0.789	0.777	0.784	0.696

Fig. 3. Qualitative analysis of RIDF-SRDCF. The proposed tracker successfully tracks the target under severe rotation, unlike SRDCF and KCF. The rotation adaptive filters assist in determining the orientation of the target object effectively that leads to substantial gain in overall performance. To avoid clumsiness only few bounding boxes are plotted and other variants are quantified in Fig. 4.

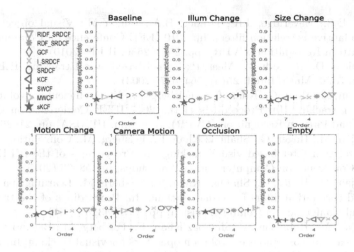

Fig. 4. Average Expected Overlap analysis of correlation filter based trackers.

Table 4. Comparison with two recent rotation adaptive trackers on VOT2016.

Trackers	RAJSSC	SRDCF	SiameseFC-DSR	**RIDF-SRDCF**	ECO	**RIDF-ECO**
AEO	0.1664	0.1981	0.2084	0.2207	0.3563	0.3624

7   Concluding Remarks

In this study, we demonstrated that employing a simple, yet effective image enhancement technique prior to feature extraction, can yield considerable gain in tracking paradigm. We analyzed the effectiveness of proposed rotation adaptive correlation filter in standard DCF formulation, and showed compelling results on popular tracking benchmarks. We renovated the sub-grid detection approach by optimizing object's orientation through false positive elimination, which was reflected favourably in the overall performance. Also, the supervision of displacement consistency on CF trackers showed promising results in various scenarios. Moreover, since the DCF formulation is used as backbone of most state-of-the-art trackers, we believe that the proposed rotation adaptive scheme in correlation filters can be suitably integrated into many frameworks and will be useful in boosting the tracking research forward. In future, we will assimilate the performance of proposed tracker on other publicly available datasets [12,20,27].

References

1. Adam, A., Rivlin, E., Shimshoni, I.: Robust fragments-based tracking using the integral histogram. In: 2006 IEEE Computer Society Conference on Computer Vision and Pattern Recognition, vol. 1, pp. 798–805. IEEE (2006)
2. Babenko, B., Yang, M.H., Belongie, S.: Robust object tracking with online multiple instance learning. IEEE Trans. Pattern Anal. Mach. Intell. **33**(8), 1619–1632 (2011)

3. Bolme, D.S., Beveridge, J.R., Draper, B.A., Lui, Y.M.: Visual object tracking using adaptive correlation filters. In: 2010 IEEE Conference on Computer Vision and Pattern Recognition (CVPR), pp. 2544–2550. IEEE (2010)

4. Comaniciu, D., Ramesh, V., Meer, P.: Kernel-based object tracking. IEEE Trans. Pattern Anal. Mach. Intell. 25(5), 564–577 (2003)

5. Danelljan, M., Bhat, G., Khan, F.S., Felsberg, M.: ECO: efficient convolution operators for tracking. In: Proceedings of the 2017 IEEE Conference on Computer Vision and Pattern Recognition (CVPR), Honolulu, HI, USA, pp. 21–26 (2017)

6. Danelljan, M., Hager, G., Shahbaz Khan, F., Felsberg, M.: Convolutional features for correlation filter based visual tracking. In: Proceedings of the IEEE International Conference on Computer Vision Workshops, pp. 58–66 (2015)

7. Danelljan, M., Hager, G., Shahbaz Khan, F., Felsberg, M.: Learning spatially regularized correlation filters for visual tracking. In: Proceedings of the IEEE International Conference on Computer Vision, pp. 4310–4318 (2015)

8. Danelljan, M., Robinson, A., Shahbaz Khan, F., Felsberg, M.: Beyond correlation filters: learning continuous convolution operators for visual tracking. In: Leibe, B., Matas, J., Sebe, N., Welling, M. (eds.) ECCV 2016. LNCS, vol. 9909, pp. 472–488. Springer, Cham (2016). https://doi.org/10.1007/978-3-319-46454-1_29

9. Danelljan, M., Shahbaz Khan, F., Felsberg, M., Van de Weijer, J.: Adaptive color attributes for real-time visual tracking. In: IEEE Conference on Computer Vision and Pattern Recognition (CVPR), Columbus, Ohio, USA, 24–27 June 2014, pp. 1090–1097. IEEE Computer Society (2014)

10. Du, Q., Cai, Z.Q., Liu, H., Yu, Z.L.: A rotation adaptive correlation filter for robust tracking. In: 2015 IEEE International Conference on Digital Signal Processing (DSP), pp. 1035–1038. IEEE (2015)

11. Fan, H., Ling, H.: Parallel tracking and verifying: a framework for real-time and high accuracy visual tracking. In: Proceedings IEEE International Conference Computer Vision, Venice, Italy (2017)

12. Galoogahi, H.K., Fagg, A., Huang, C., Ramanan, D., Lucey, S.: Need for speed: a benchmark for higher frame rate object tracking. arXiv preprint arXiv:1703.05884 (2017)

13. Henriques, J.F., Caseiro, R., Martins, P., Batista, J.: High-speed tracking with kernelized correlation filters. IEEE Trans. Pattern Anal. Mach. Intell. 37(3), 583–596 (2015)

14. Huang, C., Lucey, S., Ramanan, D.: Learning policies for adaptive tracking with deep feature cascades. In: IEEE International Conference on Computer Vision (ICCV), pp. 105–114 (2017)

15. Kalal, Z., Mikolajczyk, K., Matas, J.: Tracking-learning-detection. IEEE Trans. Pattern Anal. Mach. Intell. 34(7), 1409–1422 (2012)

16. Kristan, M., et al.: A novel performance evaluation methodology for single-target trackers. IEEE Trans. Pattern Anal. Mach. Intell. 38(11), 2137–2155 (2016). https://doi.org/10.1109/TPAMI.2016.2516982

17. Kwon, J., Lee, K.M.: Visual tracking decomposition. In: 2010 IEEE Conference on Computer Vision and Pattern Recognition (CVPR), pp. 1269–1276. IEEE (2010)

18. Liu, S., Zhang, T., Cao, X., Xu, C.: Structural correlation filter for robust visual tracking. In: Proceedings of the IEEE Conference on Computer Vision and Pattern Recognition, pp. 4312–4320 (2016)

19. Ma, C., Huang, J.B., Yang, X., Yang, M.H.: Hierarchical convolutional features for visual tracking. In: Proceedings of the IEEE International Conference on Computer Vision, pp. 3074–3082 (2015)

20. Mueller, M., Smith, N., Ghanem, B.: A benchmark and simulator for UAV tracking. In: Leibe, B., Matas, J., Sebe, N., Welling, M. (eds.) ECCV 2016. LNCS, vol. 9905, pp. 445–461. Springer, Cham (2016). https://doi.org/10.1007/978-3-319-46448-0_27

21. Nam, H., Baek, M., Han, B.: Modeling and propagating CNNs in a tree structure for visual tracking. arXiv preprint arXiv:1608.07242 (2016)

22. Nam, H., Han, B.: Learning multi-domain convolutional neural networks for visual tracking. In: 2016 IEEE Conference on Computer Vision and Pattern Recognition (CVPR), pp. 4293–4302. IEEE (2016)

23. Nummiaro, K., Koller-Meier, E., Van Gool, L.: An adaptive color-based particle filter. Image Vis. Comput. 21(1), 99–110 (2003)

24. Oron, S., Bar-Hillel, A., Levi, D., Avidan, S.: Locally orderless tracking. Int. J. Comput. Vis. 111(2), 213–228 (2015)

25. Petrou, M., Petrou, C.: Image enhancement. In: Image Processing: The Fundamentals, pp. 293–394 (2010). Chapter 4

26. Rout, L., Sidhartha, Manyam, G.R., Mishra, D.: Rotation adaptive visual object tracking with motion consistency. In: 2018 IEEE Winter Conference on Applications of Computer Vision (WACV), pp. 1047–1055, March 2018

27. Smeulders, A.W., Chu, D.M., Cucchiara, R., Calderara, S., Dehghan, A., Shah, M.: Visual tracking: an experimental survey. IEEE Trans. Pattern Anal. Mach. Intell. (1) (2013)

28. Wang, S., Lu, H., Yang, F., Yang, M.H.: Superpixel tracking. In: 2011 IEEE International Conference on Computer Vision (ICCV), pp. 1323–1330. IEEE (2011)

29. Wu, Y., Lim, J., Yang, M.H.: Online object tracking: a benchmark. In: IEEE Conference on Computer Vision and Pattern Recognition (CVPR) (2013)

30. Zhang, M., Xing, J., Gao, J., Shi, X., Wang, Q., Hu, W.: Joint scale-spatial correlation tracking with adaptive rotation estimation. In: Proceedings of the IEEE International Conference on Computer Vision Workshops, pp. 32–40 (2015)

31. Zhang, T., Liu, S., Ahuja, N., Yang, M.H., Ghanem, B.: Robust visual tracking via consistent low-rank sparse learning. Int. J. Comput. Vis. 111(2), 171–190 (2015)

Let's Take a Walk on Superpixels Graphs: Deformable Linear Objects Segmentation and Model Estimation

Daniele De Gregorio[1]([⊠])(iD), Gianluca Palli[2](iD), and Luigi Di Stefano[1](iD)

[1] DISI, University of Bologna, 40136 Bologna, Italy
d.degregorio@unibo.it
[2] DEI, University of Bologna, 40136 Bologna, Italy

Abstract. While robotic manipulation of rigid objects is quite straight-forward, coping with deformable objects is an open issue. More specifically, tasks like tying a knot, wiring a connector or even surgical suturing deal with the domain of Deformable Linear Objects (DLOs). In particular the detection of a DLO is a non-trivial problem especially under clutter and occlusions (as well as self-occlusions). The pose estimation of a DLO results into the identification of its parameters related to a designed model, e.g. a basis spline. It follows that the stand-alone segmentation of a DLO might not be sufficient to conduct a full manipulation task. This is why we propose a novel framework able to perform both a semantic segmentation and b-spline modeling of multiple deformable linear objects simultaneously without strict requirements about environment (i.e. the background). The core algorithm is based on biased random walks over the Region Adiacency Graph built on a superpixel oversegmentation of the source image. The algorithm is initialized by a Convolutional Neural Networks that detects the DLO's endcaps. An open source implementation of the proposed approach is also provided to easy the reproduction of the whole detection pipeline along with a novel cables dataset in order to encourage further experiments.

1 Introduction

Plenty of manipulation tasks deal with objects that can be modeled as non-rigid *linear* – or more generally *tubular* – structures. In case the task has to be executed by a robot in an unstructured environment, particular effort must be devoted to effectiveness, reliability and efficiency of the automated perception sub-system. Tying knots, for example, is a common though hard to automate

This work was supported by the European Commissions Seventh Framework Programme (FP7/2007-2013) under grant agreement no. 601116.

Electronic supplementary material The online version of this chapter (https://doi.org/10.1007/978-3-030-20890-5_42) contains supplementary material, which is available to authorized users.

C. V. Jawahar et al. (Eds.): ACCV 2018, LNCS 11362, pp. 662–677, 2019.
https://doi.org/10.1007/978-3-030-20890-5_42

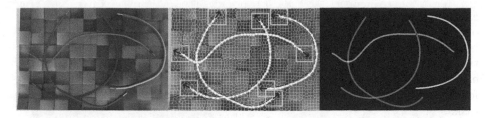

Fig. 1. Application of our algorithm to an image featuring a complex background (left). The first kind of output (center) is a *Walk* (white dots) over the Region Adjacency Graph (RAG) of the superpixel segmentation which allows for computing a b-spline model of each object. Yellow boxes highlight detection of cables terminals. The second output (right) consists in a segmentation of the whole image. (Color figure online)

activity. In particular, in surgical operations like suturing, *grasp and knot-tying* is a very important and repetitive sub-task [1–3]. Similar knot-tying and path planning procedures, like e.g. knots untangling, are also relevant to contexts like service, collaborative and rescue robotics [4–7]. As for industrial scenarios, one of the hardest tasks involving flexible linear objects is wire routing in assembly processes [8–11]. This paper focuses primarily on the industrial field and extends the original concepts introduced in the WIRES project described in [12]. As the project aims at automatizing the switchgear wiring procedure, cable modeling by perception is key to address sub-tasks like cable grasp, terminal insertion, wireways routing and, not least in importance, simulation and validation.

In this paper we propose a novel computer vision algorithm for generic Deformable Linear Object (DLO) detection. As highlighted in Fig. 1, the proposed algorithm yields a twofold representation of detected objects, namely a b-spline model for each target alongside with segmentation of the whole image. This twofold representation helps addressing both relatively simpler application settings dealing with cable detection as well as more complex endeavours calling for estimation of cable bend. The proposed algorithm consists of two distinct modules: the first, which may be considered as a pre-processing stage, detects the end-caps regions of DLOs by exploiting off-the-shelf Convolutional Neural Networks [13,14]; the second module, instead, is the core of this work and allows for identifying DLOs based on the *coarse* position of their endpoints in images featuring complex backgrounds as well as occlusions (e.g. cables crossing other cables) and self-occlusions (e.g. a cable crossing itself, also several times).

The algorithm exploits an over-segmentation of the source image into superpixels to build a Region Adjacency Graph (*RAG* [15]). This representation enables to detect the area enclosing each target object by efficiently analyzing meaningful regions (i.e. superpixels) only rather than the whole pixels set. The task is accomplished by an iterative procedure capable to find the best path (or *walk*) through the RAG between two seed points by analyzing several local and global features (e.g. visual similarity, overall curvature etc.). This iterative procedure yields a directed graph of superpixels conducive to vectorization and b-spline approximation. As better explained in the remainder of the paper, our approach is mostly unsupervised (i.e. only the endpoints detection CNN is trained supervisedly) and relies on just a few parameters that can be easily tuned manually (or estimated based on the characteristics of object's material, e.g. elasticity or the plasticity). As we shall see in Sect. 2, our algorithm outperforms other known approaches that one may apply to try solving the addressed task.

2 Related Work

Although the literature concerning DLOs is more focused on manipulation than on perception (see e.g. [3]), we may refer to the broader topic of *Curvilinear Objects Segmentation* to highlight related works as well as suitable alternatives to evaluate our proposal comparatively. As described in [16], the aforementioned topic pertains several kinds of objects, as summarized in Table 1. Our target objects are *Cables*, which, however, share similar properties in terms of *Intersections* and *Bifurcations* with the other categories highlighted in bold in Table 1,

Table 1. Curvilinear objects alongside with their key features. *Curvature* expresses the high-level shape representation for that object. *Intersections* indicates whether a crossing between two objects is allowed or not ($A = Allowed$, $N = Not$); *Bifurcations* denotes whether an object may bifurcate into multiple parts (A) or not (N).

Object Type	Curvature	Intersections	Bifurcations
Cables	**Spline Model**	**A**	**N**
Fingerprints	Low and Bounded	N	A
Guidewires	**Spline Model**	**N**	**N**
Pavement Cracks	Random	A	A
Power Lines	**Spline Model**	**A**	**N**
Roads	Model Based	A	A
Ropes	**Spline Model**	**A**	**N**
Surgery Threads	**Spline Model**	**A**	**N**
Vessels	Low and Bounded	N	A

As far as *Cables* are concerned, visual perception is typically addressed in fairly simple settings. In [17] *Augmented Reality* markers are deployed to track end-points. In other works, like [8] and [18], detection relies on background removal[1].

Moving to the domain of knot-tying with *Ropes*, the basic approach still turns out to be background removal, like in [7], or its 3D counterpart – plane

---

[1] In [18] the authors deal with a thin flexible manipulator which may be described as a cable due to the high number of degrees of freedom.

removal– like in [4] and [19]. All these methods produce a raw set of points on which a region growing algorithm is run to attain a vectorization of the target object. A different approach is used in [6], with the model of the object registered to the 3D point cloud in real-time in order to avoid the segmentation step. As described in [5], deep learning can also be used to track a deformable object: deep features are associated with rope configurations so to establish a direct mapping toward energy configurations without any explicit modeling step. This approach, however, may hardly work effectively in presence of complex and/or unknown backgrounds.

In the medical field, *Surgery Threads* detection is just the same kind of problem, albeit at a smaller scale. Also the literature dealing with this domain is more focused on manipulation than on detection issues, either assuming the latter as solved [20] or addressing it by hand-labeled markers [1]. A more scalable approach is proposed in [21] and [2], where the authors borrow the popular Frangi Filter [22] from the field of *vessels segmentation* in order to enhance the curvilinear structure of suture threads and produce a binary segmentation amenable to estimate a spline model.

Despite Table 1 would suggest *Ropes*, *Guidewires*, *Powelines* and *Surgery Threads* to exhibit more commonalities with *Cables*, applications domains like *Vessels Segmentation* or *Road detection* can provide interesting insights and solutions for curvilinear object detection. Akin to most object detection problems, the most successful approaches to *Vessels Segmentation* leverage on deep learning. In [23] the authors trained a Convolutional Neural Network (CNN) with hundreds of thousands labeled images in order to obtain a very effective detector. This supervised approach, however, mandates availability of a huge training set and lots of man-hours, a combination quite unlikely amenable to real-world industrial settings. Similar considerations apply to other remarkably effective *vessels segmentation* approaches based on supervised learning like [24] and [25]. Yet, in this realm several methods exploiting 2D filtering procedures are very popular and may be applied within a *cable* detection pipeline for industrial applications. The first interesting approach was developed by Frangi *et al.* [22] (hereinafter *Frangi* algorithm[2]) and consists in a multi-scale filtering procedure capable of enhancing tubular structures. Another methods, described in [26], deploys a pre-processing stage based on *ridge* detection (hereinafter *Ridge* algorithm[3]) to detect vessels. Although the authors use the outcome of this stage to feed a pixel-wise classifier, we found that the stage itself is very useful to highlight generic tubular structures and hence choose to compare this algorithm with ours in the experiments. Given that both the *Frangi* and *Ridge* algorithms deal with detection/enhancement of 2D curvilinear structure, we decided to include in the evaluation also *ELSD* [27], which is a popular parameter-less algorithm aimed at detection of line segments and elliptical arcs.

---

[2] https://github.com/ntnu-bioopt/libfrangi.
[3] https://github.com/kapcom01/Curviliniar_Detector.

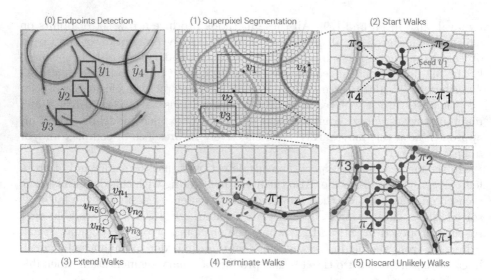

Fig. 2. A graphical representation of the whole pipeline described in detail in Sect. 3

3   Algorithm Description

The basic idea underlying our algorithm is to detect DLOs as suitable *walks* within an adjacency graph built on superpixels. We provide first an overview of the approach with the help of Fig. 2, which illustrates the following main steps of the whole pipeline.

0. **Endpoints Detection:** The first step consists in detecting endpoints. This is numbered as zero because it may be thought of as an external process not tightly linked to the rest of the algorithm. Indeed, any external algorithm capable to produce detections around targets $(y_1...y_k)$ may be deployed in this step.

1. **Superpixel Segmentation:** The source image $\mathcal{I}$ is segmented into adjacent sub-regions (superpixels) in order to build a set of segments exhibiting a far smaller cardinality than the whole pixel set. Moreover, an adjacency graph is created on top of this segmentation in order to keep track of the neighborhood of each superpixel. Eventually, those superpixels containing the 2D detections obtained in the previous step are marked as *seeds* $(v_1...v_k)$.

2. **Start Walks:** From each *seed* we can start an arbitrary number of *walks* $(\pi_1...\pi_P)$ by moving into adjacent superpixels as defined by the adjacency graph.

3. **Extend Walks:** For each *walk* we move forward along the adjacency graph by choosing iteratively the best next superpixel (e.g. v_{n_3} in Fig. 2-(3)) between the neighbourhood $\{v_{n_1}, ..., v_{n_c}\}$ of the current one.

4. **Terminate Walks:** When a *walk* reaches another *seed* (or lies in its neighborhood) it is marked as closed. Due to the iterative nature of the computation, a maximum number of extending steps is allowed for each search to ensure a bounded time complexity.
5. **Discard Unlikely Walks:** As a set of random walks are started in *Step 2*, we keep only the most likely ones and mark others as outliers.

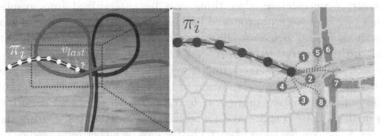

(1) Example of crossing and self-crossing wires

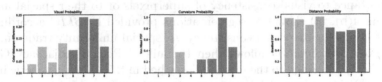

(2) Visual likelihood (3) Curvature likelihood (4) Distance likelihood

Fig. 3. (1) shows a complex configuration dealing with crossing and self-crossing wires. The zoom highlights the last node (v_{last}) alongside with the candidates to select the next node, *i.e.* first and second order neighbours (green and blue dots, respectively). (2), (3) and (4) plot the Visual, Curvature and Distance likelihoods, respectively. Based on the contribution of all the three likelihood terms, node 7 is selected to extend the current *walk*. (Color figure online)

In the remainder of this Section we will describe in detail the different concepts, methods and computations needed to realize the whole pipeline. In particular, in Sect. 3.1 we address Superpixels together with the Region Adjacency Graph; in Sect. 3.2 we define *walks* and how they can be built iteratively by analyzing local and global features; in Sect. 3.3 we propose a method to start the random walks by exploiting an external Object Detector based on a CNN and, to conclude, in Sect. 3.4 we describe how to deploy walks to attain a semantic segmentation of the image as depicted in Fig. 1.

3.1   Superpixel Segmentation and Adjacency Graph

The main aim of *Superpixel Segmentation* is to replace the rigid structure of the pixel grid with an higher-level subdivision into more meaningful primitives called *superpixels.* These primitives group regions of perceptually similar raw pixels, thereby potentially reducing the computational complexity of further processing steps. As regards the Cable Detection and Segmentation problem (i.e. DLOs with a thickness higher than a single pixel, in the majority of applications), our assumptions are that the target wire can be represented as a subset of *similar* adjacent superpixels. Thus, the overall problem can be seen as a simple iterative search through the superpixels set subject to model-driven constraints (e.g. avoiding solutions with implausible curvature or non-uniform visual appearance).

Superpixel Segmentation algorithms can be categorized into graph-based approaches (e.g. the method proposed by Felzenszwalb *et al.* [28]) and gradient-ascent methods (e.g. *Quick Shift* [29]). In our experiments we found the state-of-the-art algorithm referred to as *SLIC* [30] to perform particularly well in terms of both speed and accuracy. Accordingly, we deploy *SLIC* in our *Superpixel Segmentation* stage. *SLIC* is an adaptation of the k-means clustering algorithm to pixels represented as 5D vectors $(l_i, a_i, b_i, x_i, y_i)$, with (l_i, a_i, b_i) denoting color channels in the CIELAB space and (x_i, y_i) image coordinates. During the clustering process the compactness of each cluster can be either increased or reduced to the detriment of visual similarity. In other words we can choose easily to assign more importance to visual consistency of superpixels or to their spatial uniformity. Figure 4(b), (c) show two segmentations provided by *SLIC* according to different settings for the visual consistency vs. spatial uniformity trade-off.

Superpixel Segmentation allows then to build a Region Adjacency Graph (RAG in short) according to the method described in [15]. Thus, a generic image I can be partitioned into disjoint non-empty regions $R_0, ..., R_i$ (i.e. the superpixels) such as $I = \bigcup R_i$. Accordingly, an undirected weighted graph is given by $G = (V, E)$, where V is the set of nodes v_i, corresponding to each region R_i, and E is the set of edges $e_{j,k}$ such as that $e_{j,k} \in E$ if R_i and R_j are adjacent. A graphical representation of this kind of graph is shown in Fig. 4-(d), where black dots represents nodes v_i and black lines represent edges $e_{j,k}$. In this quite straightforward to observe that in Fig. 4-(d) there exists a *walk* trough the graph G, highlighted by white dots, which covers a target DLO (i.e. the red cable in the middle).

It is worth pointing out that our approach is similar to a Region Growing algorithm, with a seed point corresponding to the cable's tip and the search space bounded by the RAG. The main difference with a classical Region Growing approach is that we restrict the search along a *walk* applying several model-base constraints rather than relying only on visual similarity only. In particular, the shape of the *walk* is considered by assigning geometric primitives to the elements of the adjacency graph, i.e. 2D points for our nodes v_i and 2D segments for our edges $e_{j,k}$, as further described in Sect. 3.2. In simple terms, the geometric consistency of the curve superimposed on a *walk* is analyzed to choose the next node during the iterative search, and all unlikely configurations are discarded.

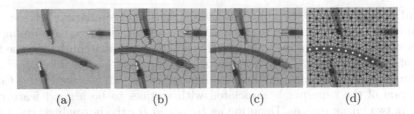

(a)   (b)   (c)   (d)

Fig. 4. (a) Original input image. (b) SLIC superpixels segmentation with low compactness. (c) Segmentation with high compactness. (d) The Region Adjacency Graph (RAG) built on the (c) segmentation.

3.2   Walking on the Adjacency Graph

Formally, a walk over a graph $G = (V, E)$ is a sequence of alternating vertices and edges $(v_{i_1}, e_{i_1, i_2}, v_{i_2}, ..., v_{i_{l-1}}, e_{i_{l-1}, i_l}, v_{i_l})$, where an edge e_{i_j, i_k} connects nodes v_{i_j} and v_{i_k}, and l is the length of the walk. The definition of *walk* is more general with respect to the *path* or *trail* over the graph because it admits repeated vertices, a common situation when dealing with self-crossing cables. It is important to notice that the Region Adjacency Graph shown in Fig. 4(d) is a *simple-connectivity relationship* graph, or, equivalently, connectivity is of order $d = 1$, with this meaning that only directly connected regions are mapped into the graph. We can build also RAGs with order $d > 1$, thereby allowing, for example, second or third order connectivity. All this translates into the possibility to *jump* during the walk also to the vertex not directly connected to the current region. This turns out very useful, for example, to deal with intersections like that depicted in Fig. 3, where vertices v_1, v_2, v_3, v_4 are of order $d = 1$ and vertices v_5, v_6, v_7, v_8 of order $d = 2$.

For the sake of simplicity, we can define a generic *walk* as $\pi_i = (v_{i_1}, ..., v_{i_l})$, i.e. an ordered subset of vertices, without considering edges. Under the hypothesis that the target walk π_i is superimposed to a portion of the object, the problem is to *extend* the walk in such a way that the next node $v_{i_{l+1}}$ does belong to the sought DLO. An exemplar situation is illustrated in Fig. 3, where we have a current path π_i which ends with v_{last} and we wish to choose between the 8 vertices the best one to extend the *walk*. Considering the new path $\hat{\pi}_{i, v_n}$, i.e. the path π_i with the addition of vertex v_n, we cast the problem as the estimation of the likelihood of the new path given the current one, which we denote as $p(\hat{\pi}_{i, v_n} | \pi_i)$. Moreover, we estimate this likelihood based on visual similarity, curvature smoothness and spatial distance features and assume these features to be independent:

$$p(\hat{\pi}_{i, v_n} | \pi_i) = p_V(\hat{\pi}_{i, v_n} | \pi_i) \cdot p_C(\hat{\pi}_{i, v_n} | \pi_i) \cdot p_D(\hat{\pi}_{i, v_n} | \pi_i) \tag{1}$$

The three terms $p_V(\cdot)$, $p_C(\cdot)$ and $p_D(\cdot)$ are referred to as *Visual, Curvature* and *Distance* likelihood, respectively, and computed as follows.

Visual Likelihood. $p_V(\hat{\pi}_{i,v_n}|\pi_i)$ measures the visual similarity between the previous path π_i and the path achievable by adding node v_n. Assuming an evenly coloured DLO, we can compute this similarity by matching only the last node of π_i, v_{last}, with v_n. Although, in principle, it may be possible to use any arbitrary visual matching function, as highlighted in [31] we found the Color Histogram of the superpixels associated with vertices to be a good feature to compare two image regions. Denoting as H_{last} and H_n the normalized color histograms (in the HSV color space) of the two regions associated with v_{last} and v_n, respectively, we can compute their distance with the intersection equation: $d(H_{last}, H_n) = \sum_I min(H_{last}(I), H_n(I))$. Then we normalize this distance in the range $[0, 1]$ using the *Bradford* normal distribution:

$$p_V(\hat{\pi}_{i,v_n}|\pi_i) = \frac{c_V}{log(1 + c_V)(1 + c_V(1 - d(H_{last}, H_n)))} \tag{2}$$

where c_V is a parameter that enables to control the shape of the distribution and, hence, the weight assigned to the visual similarity information in the overall computation of the likelihood (Eq. 1). Figure 3(2) plots the visual likelihoods computed for the different neighbours of v_{last}, which suggests nodes 6 and 7 to represent the most likely superpixels to extend the *walk*.

Curvature Likelihood. $p_C(\hat{\pi}_{i,v_n}|\pi_i)$ is concerned with estimating the most likely configuration of a DLO's curvature. Following the intuitions of Predoehl *et al.* [32], for each new node v_n we can assume that the object's curvature changes smoothly along the *walk*. To quantify this smoothness criterion we exploit the product of the von Mises distributions of the angles between two successive vertices. As introduced in Sect. 3.1, by extending the model of our adjacency graph with geometric primitives we can assign a 2D point $\mathbf{p}_{i_j}$ corresponding to the centroid of the associated superpixel to each vertex v_{i_j}, as well as a unit vector $\mathbf{u}_{i_{j,k}}$ to each edge $e_{i_{j,k}}$ by considering the segment joining two consecutive centroids $\mathbf{p}_{i_j}, \mathbf{p}_{i_k}$. As shown in Fig. 5, this allows for measuring the angle difference between two consecutive edges. By denoting as $\phi_a = \phi_{j,k,m}$ the angle difference between two consecutive edges $\mathbf{u}_{i_{j,k}}, \mathbf{u}_{i_{k,m}}$, the overall von Mises distribution allowing to establish upon the smoothness of the curvature of a target DLO is given by:

$$p_C(\hat{\pi}_{i,v_n}|\pi_i) = \prod_a \mathcal{M}(\frac{\phi_a - \phi_{a+1}}{2}, m) \tag{3}$$

where $\mathcal{M}(\cdot)$ is the von Mises distribution at each vertex. An exemplar estimation is shown in Fig. 3(3): vertices 2 and 7 appear to be the most likely candidates to extend the *walk* as they minimize the curvature changes of the target π_i.

Distance Likelihood. $p_D(\hat{\pi}_{i,v_n}|\pi_i)$ is the term concerned with the spatial distance of the next vertex in the *walk*. This term is mainly introduced to force the iterative procedure to choose the nearest available vertex without undermining

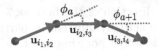

Fig. 5. A generic unit vector **u** can be assigned to each edge in the adjacency graph so as to compute the angle difference ϕ_a, between consecutive edges.

the chance to pick a far vertex instead, for example when we want to deal with an intersection (see Fig. 3(1)). Thus, similarly to Eq. 2 we normalize the distance in pixel between two nodes, $d_{pixel}(\mathbf{P}_{i_{last}}, \mathbf{P}_{i_n})$, according to the Bradford normal distribution:

$$p_D(\hat{\pi}_{i,v_n}|\pi_i) = \frac{c_D}{log(1 + c_D)(1 + c_D(1 - d_{pixel}(\mathbf{P}_{i_{last}}, \mathbf{P}_{i_n}))} \quad (4)$$

with c_D tuned such that the decay of the distribution is slow to prefer nearest vertex but not enough to discard the furthest points. Figure 3(4) highlights how, thanks to the normalization in Eq. 4, second order neighbours $(5, ..., 8)$ are not excessively penalized with respect to first order ones $(1, ..., 4)$ and hence have the chance to be picked in case they exhibit a high visual similarity and/or yield a particularly smooth *walk*.

Estimation of the Most Likely Walk. $p(\hat{\pi}_{i,v_n}|\pi_i)$ can therefore be computed for all considered neighbours in order to pick the most likely vertex, v_n, to extend the *walk*, with:

$$n = \arg \max_n p(\hat{\pi}_{i,v_n}|\pi_i) \quad (5)$$

Considering again the example in Fig. 3, although the farthest from v_{last}, vertex 7 is selected to extend the *walk* as it shows a high visual likelihood as well as a high curvature likelihood.

3.3   Starting and Terminating Walks

As described Sect. 3, *walks* need to be initialized with *seed* superpixels located at DLOs' endpoints. Purposely, we deployed a Convolutional Neural Network to detect endpoints. In particular, we fine-tuned the publicly available YOLO v2 model [13] pre-trained on ImageNet based on the images from our *Electrical Cable* Dataset (see Sect. 4.1) and by performing several data augmentations. As already mentioned, the endpoint detection module may be seen as an external process with respect to our core algorithm and, as such, in the comparative experimental evaluation we will use the same set of endpoints obtained by YOLO v2 to initialize all considered methods.

As illustrated in Fig. 2(1), the endpoint detection step predicts a set of bounding boxes $\hat{y}_i$ around the actual endpoints. For each such prediction we find the superpixel containing the central point of the box. The graph vertex v_i corresponding to this superpixel is marked as a *seed* to start a new *walk*. As no prior information concerning the direction of the best *walk* across the target DLO is available, multiple *walks* are actually started, in particular along each possible direction (see Fig. 2(3)). It is worth pointing out that the considered directions are those defined by the *seed* vertex and all its neighbours in the graph, which, as discussed in Sect. 3.2, can be both first order ($d = 1$) as well as higher order ($d > 1$) neighbours. Each started *walk*, then, is iteratively extended according to the procedure described in Sect. 3.2.

As for the criteria to terminate *walks*, first of all we set a maximum number of iterations to extend a *walk*. We also terminate a *walk* if it reaches another *seed* vertex in the adjacency graph. More precisely, as depicted in Fig. 2(5), we terminate a *walk* if the distance from the current vertex and a *seed* is smaller than a radius threshold r. Thus, given a *seed*, all *walks* started from that *seed* will terminate and we will have to pick only the optimal one. Purposely, we exploit again the *Curvature* analysis described in Sect. 3.2 and use a formulation similar to Eq. 3 to pick the smoothest path (i.e. the *walk* with the highest value of $P_C(\cdot)$).

3.4   Segmentation and Model Estimation

The simplest technique to segment the image is to assign different labels to the superpixels belonging to the different *walks* alongside with a background label to those superpixels not included into any *walk*. Besides, we estimate a B-Spline approssimation (with the algorithm described in [33]) for each walk based on the centroids of the its superpixels $\mathbf{p}_0, ..., \mathbf{p}_l$. Then, given the B-Spline model we can refine the segmentation by building a pixel mask. In particular, by evaluating the smoothing polynomial we can sample densely the points belonging to each parametrised curve and then adjust the thickness of the segmented output based on the mean size of the superpixels belonging to the *walk*. The accurate segmentation provided by this procedure is shown in Fig. 1, where the right image contains the colored B-Splines built over the walks represented in the middle image (the color is estimated by averaging the color of the corresponding superpixels).

4   Experimental Results

4.1   Software and Dataset

We provide an open source software framework called *Ariadne* available online[4]. The name *Ariadne* is inspired by the name of Minos's daughter, who, in Greek mythology, used a thread to lead Theseus outside the Minotaur's maze. The software is written in Python and implements the described approach. We created also a novel dataset which, to the best of our knowledge, is the first *Electrical Cable* dataset for detection and segmentation. We used this dataset to perform

---

[4] https://github.com/m4nh/ariadne.

quantitative and qualitative evaluations of our approach with respect to others curvilinear structure detector.

The Dataset is made up of two separated parts: the first consists of 60 cable images with homogeneous backgrounds (white, wood, colored papers, etc.); the second includes 10 cable images with complex backgrounds. In Fig. 7, the first 3 rows deal with homogenous backgrounds whilst the other with complex one.

For each image in the dataset we provide an hand-labeled binary mask superimposed over each target cable separately and an overall mask that is the union of them. Furthermore, we provide a discretization of the B-Spline for each cable in every image which consists in a set of 2D points in pixel coordinates useful to have a lighter model of the cable and track easily its endings. Further details can be found on the dataset website[5].

4.2 Segmentation Results

To test our approach we compared it to the popular Curvilenar Object Detector discussed in Sect. 2: the Frangi 2D Filter [22], the Ridge Algorithm [26] and the more generic one ELSD [27]. For each algorithm we produce a mask $M_{prediction}$ associated with the detected curvilinear structures and compare it, by means of the Intersection Over Union, $IoU = \frac{M_{gt} \cap M_{prediction}}{M_{gt} \cup M_{prediction}}$, to the ground truth M_{gt} provided by our dataset. Table 1 reports the weighted IoU on N images, where the weight is proportional to the number of cables C present in the image: $IoU_{weighted} = \frac{1}{C \cdot N} \sum_i C \cdot IoU_i$. The first row refers to images featuring a homogeneous background (60 images with a total of 395 cables), the second to those having a complex background (10 images and a total of 40 cables). As for our algorithm, we used: a 3D Color Histogram with 8 bins for each channel as Visual similarity feature; a Von Mises distribution with $m = 4$ to compute the Curvature likelihood and a degree $d = 3$ for the adjacency graph (i.e. it means that we search in a neighborhood of level 3 during our walk construction, as described in Sect. 3.2). For both our approach and the competitors we exploit the information about the endpoints provided by the initialization step: for *Ariadne* we use this information to start random walks, for the competitors to discard many outliers. The results reported in Table 1 show how our approach outperforms the other methods by a large margin, although it is fair to point out that the competitors are generic curvilinear detectors and not specific DLO detectors. It is also worth highlighting that our method is remarkably robust with respect to complex backgrounds and that this is achieved without any training or fitting procedure. Hence, our approach could be used in any real industrial application without

Fig. 6. Segmentation timings (complex background).

5 https://github.com/m4nh/cables_dataset.

requiring prior knowledge of the environment. Finally, Fig. 7, present some qualitative results obtained by our approach. Moreover, an additional qualitative evaluation is present in the supplementary material, where we tested Ariadne, as a naive proof-of-concept, also in similar challenging contexts like *Roads* and *Rivers* segmentation (Table 2).

Table 2. The Intersection Over Union of the cable segmentations obtained with our approach compared with the three major curvilinear structure detectors.

	Ariadne	Frangi [22]	Ridge [26]	ELSD [27]
Homogeneous background	**0.754**	0.406	0.293	0.225
Complex background	**0.583**	0.063	0.023	0.147

4.3 Timings and Failure Cases

Ariadne is an iterative approach, with the number of iterations depending on the length of the DLO. Thus, as depicted in Fig. 6, we can estimate an average iteration time of about 21 ms and an average segmentation time of about 670 ms

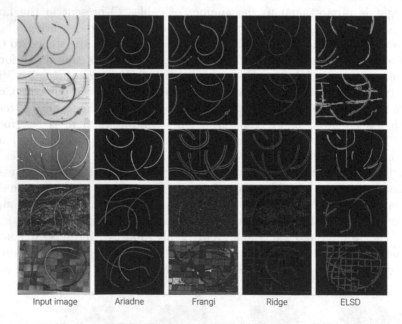

Input image   Ariadne   Frangi   Ridge   ELSD

Fig. 7. Qualitative evaluation of the different algorithms. The first column represent the input image, whereas the other columns, in order: the result yielded by *Ariadne*, *Frangi* [22], *Ridge* [26] and *ELSD* [27]. The difficultly increases from a row to the following: indeed the first row represent a very simple example with white background while the last example, instead, can be considered very hard.

(a) Failure due to adjacent cables.   (b) Failure due to perspective.

Fig. 8. Failure cases.

(Python implementation). Moreover, Fig. 8(a), (b) shows the two main failure cases that we found for *Ariadne*. In (a), as two DLOs (blue and green) are adjacent and exhibit very similar colour and curvature, the walk may jump on the wrong cable. In (b), as the distance between the DLO and the camera varies greatly, the density of Superpixels is not constant and the walk can cover only a portion of the sought object or even completely fail.

5   Concluding Remarks

We presented an effective unsupervised approach to segment DLOs in images. This segmentation method may be deployed in industrial applications involving wire detection and manipulation. Our approach requires an external detector to localize cable terminals, as otherwise we should start *walks* at every superpixel, which would be almost unworkable, although not impossible. So far we deploy an external detector which provides only the approximate position of the endpoints. We are currently working to develop a smarter endpoint detector capable to infer also the orientation of the cable terminal in order to dramatically shrink the number of initial *walks*. Another future development concerns building a much larger Electrical Cable dataset equipped with ground truth information suitable to train a specific CNN aimed at cable segmentation and compare this supervised approach to *Ariadne*. It is worth pointing out that, in specific and known in advance settings, a supervised approach may turn out peculiarly effective: in such circumstances *Ariadne* could be used to vastly ease and speed up the manual labeling procedure.

References

1. Javdani, S., Tandon, S., Tang, J., O'Brien, J.F., Abbeel, P.: Modeling and perception of deformable one-dimensional objects. In: 2011 IEEE International Conference on Robotics and Automation (ICRA), pp. 1607–1614. IEEE (2011)
2. Jackson, R.C., Yuan, R., Chow, D.L., Newman, W., Çavuşoğlu, M.C.: Automatic initialization and dynamic tracking of surgical suture threads. In: 2015 IEEE International Conference on Robotics and Automation (ICRA), pp. 4710–4716. IEEE (2015)
3. Saha, M., Isto, P.: Manipulation planning for deformable linear objects. IEEE Trans. Robot. **23**, 1141–1150 (2007)

4. Lui, W.H., Saxena, A.: Tangled: learning to untangle ropes with RGB-D perception. In: 2013 IEEE/RSJ International Conference on Intelligent Robots and Systems (IROS), pp. 837–844. IEEE (2013)
5. Nair, A., et al.: Combining self-supervised learning and imitation for vision-based rope manipulation. In: 2017 IEEE International Conference on Robotics and Automation (ICRA), pp. 2146–2153 (2017)
6. Schulman, J., Lee, A., Ho, J., Abbeel, P.: Tracking deformable objects with point clouds. In: 2013 IEEE International Conference on Robotics and Automation (ICRA), pp. 1130–1137. IEEE (2013)
7. Hopcroft, J.E., Kearney, J.K., Krafft, D.B.: A case study of flexible object manipulation. Int. J. Robot. Res. **10**, 41–50 (1991)
8. Remde, A., Henrich, D., Wörn, H.: Picking-up deformable linear objects with industrial robots (1999)
9. Yue, S., Henrich, D.: Manipulating deformable linear objects: sensor-based fast manipulation during vibration. In: Proceedings of the IEEE International Conference on Robotics and Automation, ICRA 2002, vol. 3, pp. 2467–2472. IEEE (2002)
10. Alvarez, N., Yamazaki, K., Matsubara, T.: An approach to realistic physical simulation of digitally captured deformable linear objects. In: IEEE International Conference on Simulation, Modeling, and Programming for Autonomous Robots (SIMPAR), pp. 135–140. IEEE (2016)
11. Koo, K.m., Jiang, X., Kikuchi, K., Konno, A., Uchiyama, M.: Development of a robot car wiring system. In: IEEE/ASME International Conference on Advanced Intelligent Mechatronics, AIM 2008, pp. 862–867. IEEE (2008)
12. Gregorio, D.D., Zanella, R., Palli, G., Pirozzi, S., Melchiorri, C.: Integration of robotic vision and tactile sensing for wire-terminal insertion tasks. IEEE Trans. Autom. Sci. Eng., 1–14 (2018)
13. Redmon, J., Farhadi, A.: Yolo9000: better, faster, stronger. In: 2017 IEEE Conference on Computer Vision and Pattern Recognition (CVPR), pp. 6517–6525. IEEE (2017)
14. Huang, J., et al.: Speed/accuracy trade-offs for modern convolutional object detectors (2017)
15. Trémeau, A., Colantoni, P.: Regions adjacency graph applied to color image segmentation. IEEE Trans. Image Process. **9**, 735–744 (2000)
16. Bibiloni, P., González-Hidalgo, M., Massanet, S.: A survey on curvilinear object segmentation in multiple applications. Pattern Recogn. **60**, 949–970 (2016)
17. Jiang, X., Koo, K.M., Kikuchi, K., Konno, A., Uchiyama, M.: Robotized assembly of a wire harness in a Car production line. Adv. Robot. **25**, 473–489 (2011)
18. Camarillo, D.B., Loewke, K.E., Carlson, C.R., Salisbury, J.K.: Vision based 3-D shape sensing of flexible manipulators. In: IEEE International Conference on Robotics and Automation, ICRA 2008, pp. 2940–2947. IEEE (2008)
19. Schulman, J., Ho, J., Lee, C., Abbeel, P.: Learning from demonstrations through the use of non-rigid registration. In: Inaba, M., Corke, P. (eds.) Robotics Research. STAR, vol. 114, pp. 339–354. Springer, Cham (2016). https://doi.org/10.1007/978-3-319-28872-7_20
20. Moll, M., Kavraki, L.E.: Path planning for deformable linear objects. IEEE Trans. Robot. **22**, 625–636 (2006)
21. Padoy, N., Hager, G.D.: 3D thread tracking for robotic assistance in tele-surgery. In: 2011 IEEE/RSJ International Conference on Intelligent Robots and Systems (IROS), pp. 2102–2107. IEEE (2011)

22. Frangi, A.F., Niessen, W.J., Vincken, K.L., Viergever, M.A.: Multiscale vessel enhancement filtering. In: Wells, W.M., Colchester, A., Delp, S. (eds.) MICCAI 1998. LNCS, vol. 1496, pp. 130–137. Springer, Heidelberg (1998). https://doi.org/10.1007/BFb0056195

23. Liskowski, P., Krawiec, K.: Segmenting retinal blood vessels with deep neural networks. IEEE Trans. Med. Imaging **35**, 2369–2380 (2016)

24. Melinščak, M., Prentašić, P., Lončarić, S.: Retinal vessel segmentation using deep neural networks. In: VISAPP 2015 (10th International Conference on Computer Vision Theory and Applications) (2015)

25. Li, Q., Feng, B., Xie, L., Liang, P., Zhang, H., Wang, T.: A cross-modality learning approach for vessel segmentation in retinal images. IEEE Trans. Med. Imaging **35**, 109–118 (2016)

26. Staal, J., Abràmoff, M.D., Niemeijer, M., Viergever, M.A., Van Ginneken, B.: Ridge-based vessel segmentation in color images of the retina. IEEE Trans. Med. Imaging **23**, 501–509 (2004)

27. Pătrăucean, V., Gurdjos, P., von Gioi, R.G.: A parameterless line segment and elliptical arc detector with enhanced ellipse fitting. In: Fitzgibbon, A., Lazebnik, S., Perona, P., Sato, Y., Schmid, C. (eds.) ECCV 2012. LNCS, pp. 572–585. Springer, Heidelberg (2012). https://doi.org/10.1007/978-3-642-33709-3_41

28. Felzenszwalb, P.F., Huttenlocher, D.P.: Efficient graph-based image segmentation. Int. J. Comput. Vis. **59**, 167–181 (2004)

29. Vedaldi, A., Soatto, S.: Quick shift and kernel methods for mode seeking. In: Forsyth, D., Torr, P., Zisserman, A. (eds.) ECCV 2008. LNCS, vol. 5305, pp. 705–718. Springer, Heidelberg (2008). https://doi.org/10.1007/978-3-540-88693-8_52

30. Achanta, R., Shaji, A., Smith, K., Lucchi, A., Fua, P., Süsstrunk, S.: SLIC superpixels compared to state-of-the-art superpixel methods. IEEE Trans. Pattern Anal. Mach. Intell. **34**, 2274–2282 (2012)

31. Ning, J., Zhang, L., Zhang, D., Wu, C.: Interactive image segmentation by maximal similarity based region merging. Pattern Recogn. **43**, 445–456 (2010)

32. Predoehl, A., Morris, S., Barnard, K.: A statistical model for recreational trails in aerial images. In: 2013 IEEE Conference on Computer Vision and Pattern Recognition (CVPR), pp. 337–344. IEEE (2013)

33. Dierckx, P.: Curve and Surface Fitting with Splines. Oxford University Press, New York (1995)

AttentionMask: Attentive, Efficient Object Proposal Generation Focusing on Small Objects

Christian Wilms[✉] and Simone Frintrop

University of Hamburg, Hamburg, Germany
{wilms,frintrop}@informatik.uni-hamburg.de

Abstract. We propose a novel approach for class-agnostic object proposal generation, which is efficient and especially well-suited to detect small objects. Efficiency is achieved by scale-specific objectness attention maps which focus the processing on promising parts of the image and reduce the amount of sampled windows strongly. This leads to a system, which is 33% faster than the state-of-the-art and clearly outperforming state-of-the-art in terms of average recall. Secondly, we add a module for detecting small objects, which are often missed by recent models. We show that this module improves the average recall for small objects by about 53%. Our implementation is available at: https://www.inf.uni-hamburg.de/en/inst/ab/cv/people/wilms/attentionmask.

1 Introduction

Generating class-agnostic object proposals is an important part of many state-of-the-art object detectors [9,10,13,33,34] as well as instance segmentation systems [2,12,25], since it reduces the number of object candidates to a few hundreds or thousands. The results of object proposal systems are either bounding boxes or pixel-precise segmentation masks. Both streams have received a massive boost recently due to the rise of deep learning [19,24,29,30,32,34]. The task of generating class-agnostic object proposals is different from object detection or instance segmentation as those systems predict a class label and use this information when generating boxes or masks [2,12,25,34]. Thus, they generate class-specific and not class-agnostic results.

Despite the impressive performance gain since the arrival of deep learning based class-agnostic object proposal systems, some major problems still persist. For example, most systems perform well on medium or large sized objects, but exhibit a dramatic drop in performance on small objects [19,29,30]. See Fig. 1 for an example. However, in our daily lives we are surrounded by many small

---

Electronic supplementary material The online version of this chapter (https://doi.org/10.1007/978-3-030-20890-5_43) contains supplementary material, which is available to authorized users.

C. V. Jawahar et al. (Eds.): ACCV 2018, LNCS 11362, pp. 678–694, 2019.
https://doi.org/10.1007/978-3-030-20890-5_43

Fig. 1. Result of FastMask [19] (left) and the proposed AttentionMask (right) on small objects, highlighting one strength of AttentionMask. The filled colored contours denote found objects, while the red contours denote missed objects. (Color figure online)

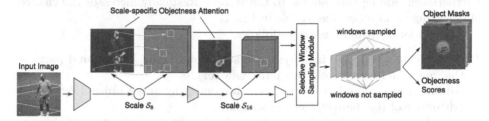

Fig. 2. Overview of the proposed AttentionMask system: An image is fed through the base net (yellow) and further downscaled to different scales ($\mathcal{S}_8, \mathcal{S}_{16}, \ldots$). At each scale a scale-specific objectness attention is calculated and windows (green) are sampled in the feature maps (blue boxes) at the most promising locations only to make calculations more efficient. Windows pruned due to low attention are marked in red. Each window is scored and an object mask is created. Due to the more efficient usage of the resources by introducing scale-specific objectness attention, we are able to split the base net and add a module ($\mathcal{S}_8$) to better detect small objects like the tennis balls in this example. (Color figure online)

objects, e.g., pens, a computer mouse, or coins. The significant loss when trying to detect small objects originates mainly from subsampling the original image in order to reduce the computational complexity.

A second problem of most recent class-agnostic object proposal systems is an inefficient use of the resources. Most systems use an image pyramid and sample many windows that have to be processed individually [29,30,32]. Although [32] optimize the scale selection, there is a lot of redundancy with overlapping windows and multiple scales. Hu et al. [19] took a first step by transferring the sampling of windows to the feature space and thus feeding the input image only once through the base net. However, still many unnecessary windows are sampled in background regions that can be easily omitted. Humans, for instance, have no problem to quickly ignore background regions as they developed the mechanism of visual attention to focus processing on promising regions [28].

In this paper, we propose AttentionMask, a new deep learning system to generate class-agnostic object proposals in a more efficient way, which opens the chance to process more scales and thus enables us to better detect smaller objects. AttentionMask is based on the FastMask architecture [19], which is extended in two essential ways: first, to increase the efficiency, we use the biologically-inspired approach of visual attention [28] and include *scale-specific objectness attention maps*. This attention focuses the sampling of windows on promising parts of the image, i.e., containing objects of a specific scale, (green windows in Fig. 2) while omitting sampling of windows in background regions (red windows in Fig. 2). Second, taking advantage of the lower consumption of resources in terms of both memory and processing time, we are able to add an additional module (S_8 in Fig. 2). This new module extracts features earlier in the network, which suffer less from the subsampling (cf. Fig. 2). Our results show that the scale-specific objectness attention significantly increases the efficiency in runtime and memory consumption as well as improving results considerably. Furthermore, adding this module to the system drastically increases the chance of detecting small objects as visible in Fig. 1.

Our major contributions are as follows:

1. Introducing a scale-specific objectness attention to omit background parts of the image and increase efficiency (33% faster).
2. Adding a new module to the system for detecting small objects by taking advantage of the more efficient processing.
3. Introducing an efficient system that clearly outperforms state-of-the-art-methods (+8% to +11%), especially on detecting small objects (+53%).

The rest of the paper is organized as follows. Sect. 2 gives an overview over related work in class-agnostic object proposal generation and visual attention. In Sect. 3, we introduce the baseline network and in Sect. 4 our key methodological contributions. Sect. 5 gives an overview over technical details of our approach, while in Sect. 6 results and an evaluation against state-of-the-art methods are presented. The paper closes with concluding remarks in Sect. 7.

2   Related Work

This section gives an overview over the most relevant work in the field of class-agnostic object proposal generation and visual attention.

Object Proposal Generation. Since the seminal work of Alexe et al. [1] on class-agnostic object proposal generation, many systems, both hand-crafted [16, 31, 37, 38] and deep learning based [19, 29, 30, 32], have been proposed to generate bounding boxes or pixel-precise segmentation masks of the object proposals. Hosang et al. [17] give a good overview over early hand-crafted work.

Bounding box proposal systems score many sliding windows to select the most promising ones using hand-crafted features [1, 6, 44] or deep learning [24, 34]. Closest to the presented system are [6, 24, 44]. [6, 44] use hand-crafted features to generate proposals with low runtime. [24] combine features from early and final layers of a network to better detect small objects. In contrast to those works, we generate pixel-precise proposals, which is more challenging.

A slightly different objective than regressing boxes is the generation of pixel-precise segmentation masks. The systems either group segments together using a variety of strategies to from a diverse set of proposals [37, 38] or use CNN-based methods [7, 19, 29, 30, 32], which achieve better results. DeepMask [29] and

SharpMask [30] rely on a patch-based processing of the image. For each patch, a segmentation mask as well as an objectness score is computed. SharpMask, in contrast to DeepMask, uses refinement modules for more precise masks. Still, an image has to be fed through the system in multiple scales and multiple patches. To estimate the scales that are relevant for the content, [32] developed ScaleNet. To not feed the same image parts multiple times through the base net, Hu et al. [19] propose FastMask. FastMask feeds the image only once through the base net at one scale and derives a feature pyramid. On the resulting feature maps of different scales, windows are sampled to find objects of different sizes. FastMask, explained in more detail in Sect. 3, serves as the base for our AttentionMask. AttentionMask differs from the aforementioned using a notion of visual attention to sample windows only in the most promising locations of the feature maps and as a result freeing up resource to be able to focus more on finding small objects.

Visual Attention. Visual attention is a mechanism of human perception that focuses the processing in the brain on the most promising parts of the visual data [28]. The concept of visual attention has been studied in psychology and neuroscience for decades and early computational models of visual attention [21, 36] have been inspired by psychological models [35, 39]. Later, many different computational models of visual attention have been proposed [8, 11, 18, 20, 22].

In addition to these approaches which explicitly model visual attention, a recent trend uses the term "attention" in a more general sense, indicating that the processing in a deep network is concentrated on specific image regions for very different tasks such as visual question answering [41] or image captioning [5, 40, 42]. Most related to our approach are the works of [4, 23]. [4] learn to weight features of different scales for semantic segmentation computing attention for each scale. [23] use attention of different scales to determine promising bounding boxes for object detection. Both approaches address different problems than we do: [4] addresses semantic segmentation while [23] works on object detection.

3 Baseline Network: FastMask

Since the core structure of AttentionMask is based on FastMask [19], we briefly explain the model here for completeness. FastMask is a CNN-based system that generates pixel-precise class-agnostic proposal masks. The main idea behind FastMask is to increase the efficiency by feeding the image only once through the base net and do both, constructing a scale pyramid and sampling windows in feature space. This approach is called one-shot paradigm. In contrast, most CNN-based proposal systems follow the multi-shot paradigm, constructing an image pyramid and sample windows in image space, which are individually passed through the network [29, 30, 32]. This leads to redundancy as the windows partially overlap or contain the same image area in different scales. The one-shot paradigm removes this redundancy in the base net to speed up the process.

Following this one-shot paradigm, FastMask uses a ResNet [14] as base net with four strided convolutions (factor 2) to compute an initial feature map of the input image that is downscaled by a factor of 16 compared to the input. This feature map is further downscaled multiple times by the factor 2 using *residual neck modules* introduced by [19] yielding a feature pyramid. From those feature maps, all possible windows of a fixed size are sampled. Using the same fixed size on feature maps of different scales leads to windows of different size in the original image, i.e., objects of different size can be found. Working with 4 scales, i.e., downscaling the image through the base net and having three neck modules, results in the scales 16, 32, 64 and 128 denoted as S_{16}, S_{32}, S_{64}, and S_{128} respectively. Thus, each window is a feature representation of a patch of the image with four different patch sizes. To be more robust to object sizes, FastMask has a second optional stream with S_{24}, S_{48}, S_{96}, and S_{192}, obtained by a new branch using stride 3 in the last strided convolution of the base net.

The windows of the different scales form a batch of feature maps. Each of the windows is fed into a sub-network that calculates the likelihood of an object being centered and fully contained in the window. The most promising k windows are further processed to derive a segmentation mask of that object. Since the aspect ratio of the windows is always the same and the objects are not necessarily centered, an *attentional head* is introduced to prune features in irrelevant parts of the windows before segmentation. The final result are k pixel-precise masks with according objectness scores.

4   Methods

In this section, we introduce AttentionMask, visualized in Fig. 3, a novel deep learning system generating pixel-precise class-agnostic object proposals. While the core structure is based on FastMask (cf. Sect. 3), our approach is essentially different in two aspects: first, it adds attentional modules at every scale that generate scale-specific objectness attention maps and enables a strong reduction of the sampled windows and thus a more efficient processing. Second, we add a module to the early stage of the base net to improve the detection of smaller objects. Sampling more windows from the new module is only feasible, since we reduce the number of windows sampled per scale using the scale-specific objectness attention maps. The following sections first describe the general architecture of our system and then focus on the two major novel components in more detail.

4.1   General Overview

Similarly to FastMask and in contrast to DeepMask [29] and SharpMask [30], AttentionMask follows the one-shot paradigm, thus feeding the image only once through the base net. The base net is a ResNet, which we split into two parts before the last strided convolution. This leads to an additional scale S_8 that we use for better detection of small objects (see Sect. 4.3). The resulting feature

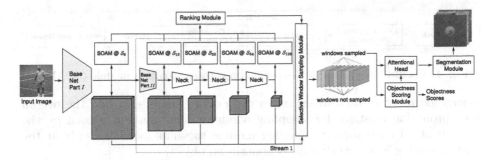

Fig. 3. Overview of the proposed AttentionMask. The base net (yellow) is split to allow $\mathcal{S}_8$. At each scale $(\mathcal{S}_n)$, features are extracted (blue boxes) and a scale-specific objectness attention module (SOAM) computes an attention map. Based on the joint ranking of the attention values, windows are only sampled in the most promising areas. Those windows are fed through the objectness scoring module, to generate objectness scores as well as the attentional head and the segmentation module to generate pixel-precise class-agnostic segmentations. (Color figure online)

map of the second part of the base net is further downscaled from $\mathcal{S}_{16}$ to $\mathcal{S}_{32}, \mathcal{S}_{64}$, and $\mathcal{S}_{128}$ using residual neck components [19]. Before sampling the windows, we introduce the new scale-specific objectness attention modules at each scale, which compute an attention value for each position of the feature maps, determining whether the location is part of an object of the scale (Sect. 4.2). According to the joint ranking of those attention values across the scales, windows are sampled only at the most promising locations in the feature maps with a new selective window sampling module. The resulting batch of windows is fed into an objectness scoring sub-network [19] to generate objectness scores. Based on this score, the most promising k windows are processed by the attentional head [19] to prune background features and a segmentation module. Finally, all segmentation masks are scaled back to the size of the according windows in the original image to get pixel-precise class-agnostic segmentation masks.

4.2 Scale-Specific Objectness Attention

The first major novel component of AttentionMask that we propose is a scale-specific objectness attention module (SOAM) to focus the sampling of sliding windows at the most promising locations. These are regions that are likeliest to fully contain an object. In contrast to salient object detection systems, where attention is used to focus on the most salient object, here we use a specialized scale-specific objectness attention to focus on all objects of a certain scale. Different from the attentional head of FastMask, this module enables the system to significantly reduce the amount of sampled windows by focusing computation on the promising windows early in the network, which makes processing more efficient. As visible in Fig. 3, the SOAMs are integrated between the features of the different scales and the ranking module. Thus, the SOAMs take the output of the base net or a further downscaled version and produce a scale-specific objectness attention map for each scale. Since now an attention value is assigned to every location in the feature maps, the locations across all scales can be ranked

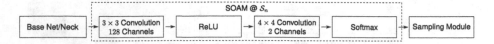

Fig. 4. Detailed view of our scale-specific objectness attention module (SOAM).

jointly according to their attention in the ranking module to find the overall most promising locations for sampling windows. This ranking is used by the subsequent selective window sampling module to sample windows only at the most promising locations that likely contain an object.

We view the problem of calculating the scale-specific objectness attention maps as a semantic segmentation problem with only two classes, *object* and *non-object*. For the design of the SOAMs we follow the approaches of [3,27] on semantic segmentation using a fully-convolutional solution. Our approach, visualized in Fig. 4, is to calculate the scale-specific objectness attention from the features of a scale using a 3×3 convolutional layer with 128 channels and ReLU activation and a 4×4 convolutional layer with 2 channels, i.e., one for each of the classes (the size of 4×4 is needed as the windows are sampled with an evenly sized 10×10 mask). This configuration has the best trade-off between efficiency and effectiveness, as the results in Table 1 indicate. Finally, softmax is applied to get the probabilities and as a result the scale-specific objectness attention map, which is the probability of the class *object*. As a result of the SOAMs, we are now able to prioritize the potential windows as well as only sample and process the most promising candidates, which saves time and memory as all sampled windows form one batch for the subsequent computation. Figure 5 shows an example of the calculated scale-specific objectness attention maps. For details about the training procedure, see Sect. 5.2.

How Are the SOAMs Different to the Attentional Head of FastMask? The attentional head selects within a sampled window the most relevant location for the central object, while our SOAMs select the most promising locations to sample windows in the feature maps of different scales. The aim of the attentional head is to remove background clutter that might prevent a proper segmentation of the object, while the SOAMs aim to reduce the number of sampled windows for increased efficiency. Therefore, the modules operate in very different stages of the network and follow different objectives.

Why Not Compute One Attention Map for All Scales? Calculating one objectness attention map for all scales, though, would lead to many windows sampled on large scales like S_8, which only show parts of larger objects. Therefore, using a distinct objectness attention map for each scale is key to remove obvious false positives and reduce the number of windows. For results using only one objectness attention map see Table 1 row 2.

4.3   Generating Proposals for Small Objects

As a second novelty of AttentionMask, we introduce a module for an additional larger scale (S_8) to improve detection of small objects. Small objects are regularly

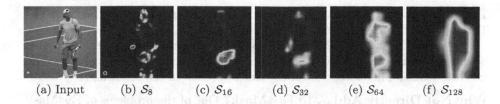

(a) Input   (b) $\mathcal{S}_8$ (c) $\mathcal{S}_{16}$ (d) $\mathcal{S}_{32}$ (e) $\mathcal{S}_{64}$ (f) $\mathcal{S}_{128}$

Fig. 5. Scale-specific objectness attention maps for an image. The different scales high-light objects or object parts of different size. Only due to the new scale $\mathcal{S}_8$ we are able to detect the two tennis balls. The maps are rescaled to image size for better visibility.

Table 1. Approaches for calculating scale-specific objectness attention.

	AR@100	Time
4 × 4, 2 channels	0.258	0.20 s
4 × 4, 2 ch., only one scale	0.216	0.25 s
3 × 3, 128 ch. + 4 × 4, 2 ch.	**0.261**	**0.21 s**
3 × 3, 256 ch. + 4 × 4, 2 ch.	0.261	0.23 s

Table 2. Approaches for adding $\mathcal{S}_8$ to AttentionMask.

	AR@100	Time
Dilated convolution (i)	0.292	0.30 s
Direct connection (ii)	**0.287**	**0.21 s**
Reverse connection (iii)	0.285	0.26 s

missed when only using $\mathcal{S}_{16}$ and subsequent scales as small objects do not cover enough area inside the sampled windows. Adding $\mathcal{S}_8$ however, leads to a large amount of new windows. For an input image of size 800×600, about 7500 windows are additionally sampled, more than in all subsequent scales together. To keep the efficiency of the system, scale-specific objectness attention is essential to reduce the amount of sampled windows and keep the problem feasible. There-fore, we propose to use the scale-specific objectness attention and utilize the freed resources to add another scale to the top of the feature scale space, i.e., $\mathcal{S}_8$, to foster detection of small objects. Without the scale-specific objectness attention this would not be possible, due to memory limitations on modern GPUs.

Since the output of the base net of FastMask is a feature map of $\mathcal{S}_{16}$, there is no natural $\mathcal{S}_8$ yet. We investigated three ways of calculating a $\mathcal{S}_8$ feature map in AttentionMask, inspired by different approaches. (i) One way of preventing the resolution of the feature maps of a CNN from decreasing with increasing depth is the use of dilated convolution as in [3,43]. Inspired by the success of those systems in semantic segmentation, we replaced the last strided convolution by a dilated convolution with factor 2 in this and all subsequent layers to keep the resulting feature map at $\mathcal{S}_8$. Despite a good performance, see Table 2, the dilated convolutions slow down the network significantly (+36%). (ii) Inspired by [23], we directly extract features before the last strided convolution. Despite not having the full depth of the base net, those features are still relevant for small objects, as those are usually less complex due to their small size in the image. (iii) We also evaluated the reverse connection approach presented in [23].

The reverse connection here is a deconvolutional layer connecting $\mathcal{S}_{16}$ with $\mathcal{S}_8$. Through this reverse connection, information from $\mathcal{S}_{16}$ can flow back to $\mathcal{S}_8$.

As shown in Table 2, the second approach of directly extracting features before the last strided convolution performs well, while leading to the fastest execution time. Therefore, we will use this approach in the following.

Why Not Directly Add $\mathcal{S}_8$ to FastMask? One of the problems of FastMask is the memory consumption, especially in training. Adding $\mathcal{S}_{192}$, e.g., for the above mentioned input image of size 800×600 results in only 20 more windows. As described above, adding $\mathcal{S}_8$ leads to around 7500 additional windows. Memory usage would prevent the system from being trained on modern GPUs. Using a further neck is also not possible as they can only downscale but not upscale.

5   Implementation Details

In this section, we present technical details of AttentionMask splitting the base net, connecting the SOAMs with the new selective window sampling module and variations of AttentionMask. Furthermore, details about training are given.

5.1   Architecture Details

Adding $\mathcal{S}_8$ to better detect small objects (Sect. 4.3) leads to splitting up the base net. We use as our base net a ResNet-50 without the *conv5*-module. Given the inherent structure of the stripped ResNet, we split the network between the *conv3*- and *conv4*-modules, thus moving the final strided convolution to the second part of the base net. This enables us to extract features of the *conv3d*-layer, the final layer of the *conv3*-module, for $\mathcal{S}_8$.

To use the scale-specific objectness attention introduced in Sect. 4.2 for selecting windows, all attention maps have to be ranked jointly. This is done by the new ranking module that jointly ranks the locations in the maps across the different scales. This ranking is used in the new selective window sampling module to only sample windows at the most promising locations in the feature maps.

Similar to [19], we add a second stream to AttentionMask, increasing the number of scales from 5 to 9. This is done by duplicating the *conv4*-module of the ResNet and use strided convolutions with stride 2 and 3, which leads to scales $\mathcal{S}_{16}$ (stream 1) and $\mathcal{S}_{24}$ (stream 2). However, [19] are not able to train this model entirely and have to transfer weights between the necks. In contrast to that, we are also able to train the full model with two streams and 9 scales, due to our efficient attention modules. In total, we run 3 versions of the model distinguished by the scales used: (i) AttentionMask$_{192}^{16}$ uses the scales $\mathcal{S}_{16}$ to $\mathcal{S}_{192}$, which corresponds to the model of [19] just adding attention. (ii) AttentionMask$_{192}^8$ adds $\mathcal{S}_8$ to the previous model resulting in 9 scales. (iii) To compare AttentionMask with other models having eight scales [19,29,30] we use a third version with $\mathcal{S}_8$ to $\mathcal{S}_{128}$ (AttentionMask$_{128}^8$). Furthermore, [19] proposed to use PVANet [15] as base net to make inference faster. However, as the model from [19] is not publicly available, we did not include a version using PVANet in the paper.

5.2   Joint Training

Training AttentionMask consists of multiple different tasks and thus multiple losses. Training the baseline network follows [19] and uses three losses for the objectness score $\mathcal{L}_{objn}$, the attentional head output $\mathcal{L}_{ah}$ and the segmentation mask $\mathcal{L}_{seg}$ respectively. See the supplementary material for further details. For training the SOAMs, we calculate the softmax over the output and compute the loss $\mathcal{L}_{att_n}$ at $\mathcal{S}_n$. The ground truth is created based on the ground truth masks for all objects that fit to the scale $\mathcal{S}_n$ of a scale-specific objectness attention map. An object fits to $\mathcal{S}_n$, if both side lengths of the object are within 40% to 80% of the sampled window side length of $\mathcal{S}_n$ in the original image. For handling the significant imbalance in the ground truth at different scales, we follow [23] by sampling for each positive pixel in a ground truth map 3 negative pixels. A comparison with other strategies is presented in the supplementary material.

Thus, the overall loss is

$$\mathcal{L} = w_{objn}\mathcal{L}_{objn} + w_{ah}\mathcal{L}_{ah} + w_{seg}\mathcal{L}_{seg} + w_{att}\sum_n \mathcal{L}_{att_n}, \tag{1}$$

with $w_{objn}, w_{ah}, w_{seg}$, and w_{att} being weights to balance the influence of the tasks. In our experiments we set $w_{objn} = 0.5, w_{ah} = 1.25, w_{seg} = 1.25$ and, $w_{att} = 0.25$, as it gave the best results. Note that during training, there is no connection between the SOAMs and the selective window sampling module. Instead, the ground truth data is used to sample windows, as it leads to a better performance (evaluation in supplementary material). Details regarding the hyperparameters and solver can be found in the supplementary material.

6   Experiments

This section presents results and the evaluation of AttentionMask compared to several state-of-the-art methods in terms of performance and efficiency as well as ablation experiments analyzing AttentionMask in more detail. The evaluation is carried out on the MS COCO dataset [26]. The MS COCO dataset has more than 80.000 training images with pixel-precise annotations of objects. As done by [7,19,29,30], we use the first 5.000 images of the validation set for testing. Training was conducted on the training set of MS COCO.

Following [7,17,19,29,30], we report average recall (AR) at 10, 100 and 1000 proposals, which correlates well with the performance of object detectors using these proposals [17]. Additionally, we separate our evaluation with respect to the performance for different object sizes. We follow the MS COCO classification into small objects (area $< 32^2$), medium objects ($32^2 <$ area $< 96^2$), and large objects ($96^2 <$ area) and report the AR with respect to those classes at 100 proposals. We further report the inference runtime when generating 1000 proposals. All experiments, except for InstanceFCN (numbers taken from [19]), were carried out in a controlled environment with a NVIDIA GeForce GTX TITAN X.

The state-of-the-art methods we compare to are FastMask [19], DeepMask-Zoom [29,30], SharpMask as well as SharpMaskZoom [30] and InstanceFCN [7].

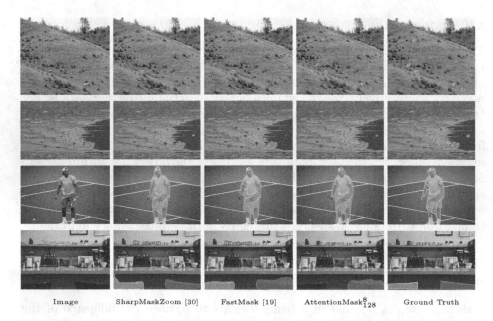

Image   SharpMaskZoom [30]   FastMask [19]   AttentionMask$^8_{128}$ Ground Truth

Fig. 6. Qualitative results of SharpMaskZoom [30], FastMask [19] and AttentionMask$^8_{128}$ on the MS COCO dataset. The filled colored contours denote found objects, while not filled red contours denote missed objects. (Color figure online)

We also compare to the hand-crafted system MCG [31]. Despite a comparison to bounding box methods does not seem fair, as explained in Sect. 2, we also compare to the very fast bounding box systems BING and EdgeBoxes. A comparison to instance segmentation methods is not fair as well due to their class-specific nature as explained in the introduction. As described in Sect. 5.1, we will compare three versions of AttentionMask (AttentionMask$^8_{128}$, AttentionMask$^8_{192}$, and AttentionMask$^{16}_{192}$) that differ in the scales used. We did not include the results of FastMask with PVANet as base net, as the model is not publicly available.

6.1   Qualitative Results

The qualitative results visualized in Fig. 6 show the superior ability of Attention-Mask to detect small objects compared to other state-of-the-art class-agnostic object proposal systems. For instance, the sheep (1st row) as well as the birds (2nd row) are all detected by AttentionMask. SharpMaskZoom and FastMask are not able to detect most of those small objects. Both images also show significant textures in some areas, which do not hamper the performance of the scale-specific objectness attention as the windows are still sampled at the correct locations. Returning to the earlier tennis example, the results in the third row show the ability of AttentionMask to detect both balls (bottom left and in his right hand). This emphasizes the effectiveness of the additional scale S_8 and the attention focusing on the spots of the tennis balls in S_8 as visualized in

Table 3. Results on MS COCO with pixel-precise proposals. S, M, L denote small, medium, large objects. (Bounding box results in supplementary material)

Method	AR@10	AR@100	AR@1k	AR^S@100	AR^M@100	AR^L@100	Time
MCG [31]	0.077	0.186	0.299	-	-	-	45 s
DeepMaskZoom [30]	0.151	0.286	0.371	0.093	0.389	0.466	1.35 s
SharpMask [30]	0.154	0.278	0.360	0.035	0.399	0.513	1.03 s
SharpMaskZoom [30]	0.156	0.304	0.401	0.099	0.412	0.495	2.02 s
InstanceFCN [7]	0.166	0.317	0.392	-	-	-	1.50 s
FastMask [19]	0.169	0.313	0.406	0.106	0.406	0.517	0.33 s
AttentionMask$^8_{128}$	0.182	0.349	0.444	**0.162**	0.421	0.560	0.22 s
AttentionMask$^8_{192}$	**0.183**	**0.355**	**0.450**	0.157	0.426	0.590	0.22 s
AttentionMask$^{16}_{192}$	0.176	0.336	0.412	0.097	**0.438**	**0.594**	**0.21 s**

Fig. 5. Finally, the last row shows an example of a cluttered household environment with many small objects like the glasses on the shelf. AttentionMask is the only one of the three systems to detect almost all of them, although it is even hard for humans to detect the glasses in the input image given the low contrast. A more detailed version of this image highlighting the glasses can be seen in Fig. 1. More qualitative results can be found in the supplementary material.

6.2 Quantitative Results

The findings of the qualitative results, which showed that AttentionMask is significantly better in detecting small objects, can be confirmed by the quantitative results. In addition, AttentionMask outperforms all state-of-the-art methods in all 7 categories, including inference runtime. Table 3 shows the results of the different state-of-the-art methods and the three versions of Attention-Mask. It is clearly visible that the two versions of AttentionMask that use S_8 perform much better on small objects than any other method. The gain of AttentionMask$^8_{128}$, e.g., in AR^S@100 compared to FastMask is 53% and compared to SharpMaskZoom even 59% (all using 8 scales). A more detailed evaluation on small objects across different numbers of proposals is given in Table 4 and Fig. 7a. Both show that AttentionMask$^8_{128}$ significantly outperforms state-of-the-art methods on small objects across different numbers of proposals. As Fig. 7b and Table 3 show, across all scales the results of the three AttentionMask versions significantly outperform state-of-the-art as well. Compared to FastMask, SharpMaskZoom and InstanceFCN, the increase in AR@100 for AttentionMask$^8_{128}$, e.g., is between 10% and 15%. Similar observation can be made for AR@10 and AR@1000.

In addition to outperforming state-of-the-art in terms of AR, the runtime for AttentionMask$^8_{128}$ is reduced compared to FastMask (-33%), SharpMaskZoom (-89%) and others without using a specialized base net as proposed in [19]. Compared to the efficient bounding box systems BING and EdgeBoxes (detailed numbers in supplementary material), our approach shows significantly better results

Table 4. Detailed results on small objects of the MS COCO dataset.

Method	AR^S@10	AR^S@100	AR^S@1k
DeepMaskZoom [29,30]	0.034	0.093	0.158
SharpMask [30]	0.010	0.035	0.093
SharpMaskZoom [30]	**0.036**	0.099	0.176
FastMask [19]	**0.036**	0.109	0.176
AttentionMask$^8_{128}$	0.029	**0.162**	**0.293**

Table 5. Analysis of the scale-specific objectness attention at different scales.

Scale	Recall	Pruned
S_8	0.781	0.939
S_{16}	0.831	0.924
S_{32}	0.982	0.640
S_{64}	0.969	0.594
S_{128}	0.918	0.704

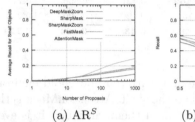
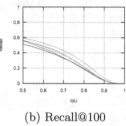
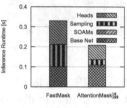

(a) AR^S (b) Recall@100   (c) Inference Runtime

Fig. 7. Detailed analysis of (a) AR^S over different number of proposals, (b) recall at 100 proposals for different IoU values and (c) detailed runtime for inference.

(0.508 AR@100) compared to BING (0.084 AR@100) and EdgeBoxes (0.174 AR@100) on bounding boxes. Thus, despite BING and EdgeBoxes being fast as well (0.20 s for BING and 0.31 s for EdgeBoxes), AttentionMask shows a more favorable trade-off between state-of-the-art performance and fast execution.

Adding S_{192} to AttentionMask does not improve the results significantly (AR@100 from 0.349 to 0.355). As expected, mostly large sized objects are added due to the addition of S_{192} (AR^L@100 from 0.560 to 0.590). The runtime for inference stays about the same compared to AttentionMask$^8_{128}$. Thus, adding a smaller scale like S_8 as introduced here is significantly more favorable.

6.3   Ablation Experiments

To analyze AttentionMask in more detail, we run multiple ablation experiments. For comparison between different structures of the SOAMs, we already provided results in Sect. 4.2 and Table 1, showing that more complex structures do not improve the results significantly. Similarly, we provided in Sect. 4.3 and Table 2 an analysis of different ways of integrating S_8 to the system. Ablative experiments regarding different training strategies and the use of ground truth attention during training can be found in the supplementary material.

Influence of S_8. The results for AttentionMask$^{16}_{192}$ in Table 3 show the influence of the scale-specific objectness attention without adding S_8. Compared to FastMask the results are better across all scales (0.336 vs. 0.313 for AR@100), emphasizing the positive effect of the introduced scale-specific objectness attention. Compared to AttentionMask$_{128}^8$, it is clearly visible that the numbers for small objects dropped as well as the overall result (0.336 vs.0.349 for AR@100). Thus, the addition of $\mathcal{S}_8$, only possible due to the time and memory efficiency gained by the introduced SOAMs, is crucial for the success of the system. Running FastMask with $\mathcal{S}_8$ is not possible due to the memory consumption.

Runtime Evaluation. Evaluating the results of the scale-specific objectness attention shows that in AttentionMask$_{192}^{16}$, 86.7% of the needed windows are sampled while reducing the overall amount of windows by 85.0%. This reduces the runtime for inference by 33% compared to FastMask. Figure 7c gives a more detailed overview of the time consumed by the different stages: base net, SOAMs, window sampling and heads (segmentation + objectness). It is clearly visible that the time required for computing the attention maps is minimal (0.007s). However, the time required for window sampling and the heads is significantly reduced (−0.131s). This demonstrates the time efficiency due to the introduced scale-specific objectness attention and the new sampling scheme.

Influence of Scale-Specific Objectness Attention. Further analyzing the scale-specific objectness attention at different scales (cf. Table 5) shows the intended effect of pruning many unnecessary windows early in the process. For instance, at $\mathcal{S}_{16}$, 92.4% of the windows are pruned, leading to a reduction of 1791 windows for an image of size 800×600. However, the recall, necessary windows that are found, is still at 83.1%. Thus, only few objects are lost through the scale-specific objectness attention. A similar behavior can be observed at other scales. Across $\mathcal{S}_8$ to $\mathcal{S}_{128}$ 91.7% of the windows are pruned, leading to 9420 pruned windows in the example above. Still, the recall is at 80.3%.

7 Conclusions

State-of-the-art class-agnostic object proposal systems are usually based on an inefficient window sampling. In this paper, we have introduced scale-specific objectness attention to distinguish very early between promising windows containing an object and background windows. We have shown that this reduces the number of analyzed windows drastically (−91.7%), freeing up resources for other system parts. Here, we have exploited these resources for addressing a second problem of current class-agnostic object proposal systems: the meager performance for small objects. This is especially important in real-world applications, since we are surrounded by many small objects. We added an additional module to our system, which significantly improves the detection of small objects, while across all scales outperforming state-of-the-art methods as well. Note that adding this module was only possible due to the resources freed by using scale-specific objectness attention. Our results clearly show the improvement in runtime (33% faster) and recall for small objects (+53%) as well as across all scales (+8% to +11%), which makes the approach especially suitable for extensions to video object proposal generation and the processing of real-world data.

References

1. Alexe, B., Deselaers, T., Ferrari, V.: Measuring the objectness of image windows. TPAMI **34**(11), 2189–2202 (2012)
2. Chen, L.C., Hermans, A., Papandreou, G., Schroff, F., Wang, P., Adam, H.: MaskLab: instance segmentation by refining object detection with semantic and direction features. In: CVPR, pp. 4013–4022. IEEE (2018)
3. Chen, L.C., Papandreou, G., Kokkinos, I., Murphy, K., Yuille, A.L.: DeepLab: semantic image segmentation with deep convolutional nets, atrous convolution, and fully connected CRFs. TPAMI **40**(4), 834–848 (2017)
4. Chen, L.C., Yang, Y., Wang, J., Xu, W., Yuille, A.L.: Attention to scale: Scale-aware semantic image segmentation. In: CVPR, pp. 3640–3649. IEEE (2016)
5. Chen, L., et al.: SCA-CNN: spatial and channel-wise attention in convolutional networks for image captioning. In: CVPR, pp. 6298–6306. IEEE (2017)
6. Cheng, M.M., Zhang, Z., Lin, W.Y., Torr, P.H.S.: BING: binarized normed gradients for objectness estimation at 300fps. In: CVPR, pp. 3286–3293. IEEE (2014)
7. Dai, J., He, K., Li, Y., Ren, S., Sun, J.: Instance-sensitive fully convolutional networks. In: Leibe, B., Matas, J., Sebe, N., Welling, M. (eds.) ECCV 2016. LNCS, vol. 9910, pp. 534–549. Springer, Cham (2016). https://doi.org/10.1007/978-3-319-46466-4_32
8. Frintrop, S., Werner, T., Martín García, G.: Traditional saliency reloaded: a good old model in new shape. In: CVPR, pp. 82–90. IEEE (2015)
9. Girshick, R.: Fast R-CNN. In: ICCV, pp. 1440–1448. IEEE (2015)
10. Girshick, R., Donahue, J., Darrell, T., Malik, J.: Rich feature hierarchies for accurate object detection and semantic segmentation. In: CVPR, pp. 580–587. IEEE (2014)
11. Harel, J., Koch, C., Perona, P.: Graph-based visual saliency. In: NIPS, pp. 545–552. MIT Press (2007)
12. He, K., Gkioxari, G., Dollár, P., Girshick, R.: Mask R-CNN. In: ICCV, pp. 2980–2988. IEEE (2017)
13. He, K., Zhang, X., Ren, S., Sun, J.: Spatial pyramid pooling in deep convolutional networks for visual recognition. In: Fleet, D., Pajdla, T., Schiele, B., Tuytelaars, T. (eds.) ECCV 2014. LNCS, vol. 8691, pp. 346–361. Springer, Cham (2014). https://doi.org/10.1007/978-3-319-10578-9_23
14. He, K., Zhang, X., Ren, S., Sun, J.: Deep residual learning for image recognition. In: CVPR, pp. 770–778. IEEE (2016)
15. Hong, S., Roh, B., Kim, K.H., Cheon, Y., Park, M.: PVANet: lightweight deep neural networks for real-time object detection. arXiv preprint arXiv:1611.08588 (2016)
16. Horbert, E., Martín García, G., Frintrop, S., Leibe, B.: Sequence-level object candidates based on saliency for generic object recognition on mobile systems. In: ICRA, pp. 127–134. IEEE (2015)
17. Hosang, J., Benenson, R., Dollár, P., Schiele, B.: What makes for effective detection proposals? TPAMI **38**(4), 814–830 (2015)
18. Hou, Q., Cheng, M.M., Hu, X., Borji, A., Tu, Z., Torr, P.: Deeply supervised salient object detection with short connections. In: CVPR, pp. 5300–5309. IEEE (2017)
19. Hu, H., Lan, S., Jiang, Y., Cao, Z., Sha, F.: FastMask: segment multi-scale object candidates in one shot. In: CVPR, pp. 2280–2288. IEEE (2017)
20. Huang, X., Shen, C., Boix, X., Zhao, Q.: SALICON: reducing the semantic gap in saliency prediction by adapting deep neural networks. In: ICCV, pp. 262–270. IEEE (2015)

21. Itti, L., Koch, C., Niebur, E.: A model of saliency-based visual attention for rapid scene analysis. TPAMI **20**(11), 1254–1259 (1998)
22. Klein, D.A., Frintrop, S.: Center-surround divergence of feature statistics for salient object detection. In: ICCV, pp. 2214–2219. IEEE (2011)
23. Kong, T., Sun, F., Yao, A., Liu, H., Lu, M., Chen, Y.: RON: reverse connection with objectness prior networks for object detection. In: CVPR, pp. 5244–5252. IEEE (2017)
24. Li, H., Liu, Y., Ouyang, W., Wang, X.: Zoom out-and-in network with recursive training for object proposal. arXiv preprint arXiv:1702.05711 (2017)
25. Li, Y., Qi, H., Dai, J., Ji, X., Wei, Y.: Fully convolutional instance-aware semantic segmentation. In: CVPR, pp. 4438–4446. IEEE (2017)
26. Lin, T.-Y., et al.: Microsoft COCO: common objects in context. In: Fleet, D., Pajdla, T., Schiele, B., Tuytelaars, T. (eds.) ECCV 2014. LNCS, vol. 8693, pp. 740–755. Springer, Cham (2014). https://doi.org/10.1007/978-3-319-10602-1_48
27. Long, J., Shelhamer, E., Darrell, T.: Fully convolutional networks for semantic segmentation. In: CVPR, pp. 3431–3440. IEEE (2015)
28. Pashler, H.: The Psychology of Attention. MIT Press, Cambridge (1997)
29. Pinheiro, P.O., Collobert, R., Dollár, P.: Learning to segment object candidates. In: NIPS, pp. 1990–1998. MIT Press (2015)
30. Pinheiro, P.O., Lin, T.-Y., Collobert, R., Dollár, P.: Learning to refine object segments. In: Leibe, B., Matas, J., Sebe, N., Welling, M. (eds.) ECCV 2016. LNCS, vol. 9905, pp. 75–91. Springer, Cham (2016). https://doi.org/10.1007/978-3-319-46448-0_5
31. Pont-Tuset, J., Arbelaez, P., Barron, J.T., Marques, F., Malik, J.: Multiscale combinatorial grouping for image segmentation and object proposal generation. TPAMI **39**(1), 128–140 (2017)
32. Qiao, S., Shen, W., Qiu, W., Liu, C., Yuille, A.: ScaleNet: guiding object proposal generation in supermarkets and beyond. In: ICCV, pp. 1809–1818. IEEE (2017)
33. Redmon, J., Divvala, S., Girshick, R., Farhadi, A.: You only look once: unified, real-time object detection. In: CVPR, pp. 779–788. IEEE (2016)
34. Ren, S., He, K., Girshick, R., Sun, J.: Faster R-CNN: towards real-time object detection with region proposal networks. In: NIPS, pp. 91–99. MIT Press (2015)
35. Treisman, A.M., Gelade, G.: Cogn. Psychol. **12** (1980)
36. Tsotsos, J.K.: An inhibitory beam for attentional selection. In: Harris, L.R., Jenkin, M. (eds.) Spatial Vision in Humans and Robots. Cambridge University Press (1993)
37. Uijlings, J.R., Van De Sande, K.E., Gevers, T., Smeulders, A.W.: Selective search for object recognition. IJCV **104**(2), 154–171 (2013)
38. Werner, T., Martín-García, G., Frintrop, S.: Saliency-guided object candidates based on gestalt principles. In: Nalpantidis, L., Krüger, V., Eklundh, J.-O., Gasteratos, A. (eds.) ICVS 2015. LNCS, vol. 9163, pp. 34–44. Springer, Cham (2015). https://doi.org/10.1007/978-3-319-20904-3_4
39. Wolfe, J.M., Cave, K., Franzel, S.: Guided search: an alternative to the feature integration model for visual search. J. Exp. Psychol. Hum. Percept. Perform. **15**, 97–136 (1989)
40. Xu, K., et al.: Show, attend and tell: neural image caption generation with visual attention. In: ICML, pp. 2048–2057. PMLR (2015)
41. Yang, Z., He, X., Gao, J., Deng, L., Smola, A.: Stacked attention networks for image question answering. In: CVPR, pp. 21–29. IEEE (2016)
42. You, Q., Jin, H., Wang, Z., Fang, C., Luo, J.: Image captioning with semantic attention. In: CVPR, pp. 4651–4659. IEEE (2016)

43. Yu, F., Koltun, V.: Multi-scale context aggregation by dilated convolutions. arXiv preprint arXiv:1511.07122 (2015)
44. Zitnick, C.L., Dollár, P.: Edge boxes: locating object proposals from edges. In: Fleet, D., Pajdla, T., Schiele, B., Tuytelaars, T. (eds.) ECCV 2014. LNCS, vol. 8693, pp. 391–405. Springer, Cham (2014). https://doi.org/10.1007/978-3-319-10602-1_26

Semantic Bottleneck for Computer Vision Tasks

Maxime Bucher[1,2](✉), Stéphane Herbin[1], and Frédéric Jurie[2]

[1] ONERA, Université Paris-Saclay, 91123 Palaiseau, France
bucher.maxime@gmail.com
[2] Normandie Univ, UNICAEN, ENSICAEN, CNRS, Mont-Saint-Aignan, France

Abstract. This paper introduces a novel method for the representation of images that is semantic by nature, addressing the question of computation intelligibility in computer vision tasks. More specifically, our proposition is to introduce what we call a *semantic bottleneck* in the processing pipeline, which is a crossing point in which the representation of the image is entirely expressed with natural language, while retaining the efficiency of numerical representations. We show that our approach is able to generate semantic representations that give state-of-the-art results on semantic content-based image retrieval and also perform very well on image classification tasks. Intelligibility is evaluated through user centered experiments for failure detection.

1 Introduction

Image-to-text tasks have made tremendous progress since the advent of deep learning approaches (see *e.g.*, [1]). The work presented in this paper builds on these new types of image-to-text functions to evaluate the capacity of textual representations to semantically and fully encode the visual content of images for demanding applications, in order to allow the prediction function to host a *semantic bottleneck* somewhere in its processing pipeline (Fig. 1). The main objective of a semantic bottleneck is to play the role of an *explanation* of the prediction process since it offers the opportunity to examine meaningfully on what ground will further predictions be made, and potentially decide to reject them either using human common sense knowledge and experience, or automatically through dedicated algorithms. Such an explainable semantic bottleneck instantiates a good tradeoff between prediction accuracy and interpretability [2].

Reliably evaluating the quality of an explanation is not straightforward [2–5]. In this work, we propose to evaluate the explainability power of the semantic bottleneck by measuring its capacity to detect failure of the prediction function, either through an automated detector as [6], or through human judgment. Our proposal to generate the surrogate semantic representation is to associate a global and generic textual image description (caption) and a visual quiz in the

© Springer Nature Switzerland AG 2019
C. V. Jawahar et al. (Eds.): ACCV 2018, LNCS 11362, pp. 695–712, 2019.
https://doi.org/10.1007/978-3-030-20890-5_44

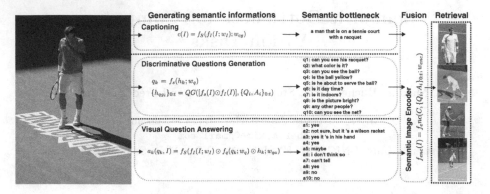

Fig. 1. Semantic bottleneck approach: images are replaced by purely but rich textual representations, for tasks such as multi-label classification or image retrieval.

form of a small list of questions and answers that are expected to refine contextually the generic caption. The production of this representation is adapted to the vision task and learned from annotated data.

The main contributions of this paper are: *(i)* The design of two processing chains for content-based image retrieval and multi-label classification hosting a semantic bottleneck; *(ii)* An original scheme to select sequentially a list of questions and answers to form a semantic visual quiz; *(iii)* A global fusion approach jointly exploiting the various components of the semantic representation for image retrieval or multi-label classification; *(iv)* A complete evaluation on the MS-COCO database exploiting Visual Dialog annotations [1] showing that it is possible to enforce a semantic bottleneck with only 5% of performance loss on multi-label classification, but a 10% performance gain for image retrieval, when compared to image feature-based approaches; *(v)* An evaluation of the semantic bottleneck explanation capacity as a way to detect failure in the prediction process and improve its accuracy by rejection.

2   Related Works

Extracting Semantic Information From Images. The representation of images with semantic attributes has received a lot of attention in the recent literature. However, with the exception of the DAP model [7], which is not performing very well, such models produce vector representations that are not intelligible at all. In contrast, image captioning [8,9] is by nature producing intelligible representations and can be used to index images. As an illustration, Gordo *et al.* [10] addressed the task of retrieving images that share the same semantics as the query image using captions. Despite the success of such recent methods, it has been observed [11] that such approaches produce captions that are similar when they contain one common object, despite their differences in other aspects. Addressing this issue, [12] proposed a contrastive learning method for image captioning encouraging distinctiveness, while maintaining the overall quality of the generated captions. Another way to enrich the caption is to generate a set of questions/answers such as proposed in the Visual Dialog framework [1,13,14]. This is what we propose to do by learning how to build dialogs complementary to image captions.

Transferring Information From Other Domains. Producing semantic description of images in natural languages is barely possible without transferring semantic information – expressed as semantic attributes, natural language expressions, dictionaries, *etc.*– from auxiliary datasets containing such information to novel images. This is exactly what Visual Question Answering models can do, the VQA challenge offering important resources, in the form of semantic images, questions, or possible answers. Research on VQA has been very active during the last two years. [15] proposed an approach relying on Recurrent Neural Network using Long Short Term Memory (LSTM). In their approach, both the image (CNN features) and the question are fed into the LSTM to answer a question about an image. Once the question is encoded, the answers can be generated by the LSTM. [16] study the problem of using VQA knowledge to improve image-caption ranking. [17], motivated by the goal of developing a model based on grounded regions, introduces a novel dataset that extends previous approaches and proposes an attention-based model to perform this task. On their side, [18] proposed a model receiving the answers as input and predicts whether or not an image-question-answer triplet is correct. Finally, [19] proposes another VQA method combining an internal representation of the image content with the information extracted from general knowledge bases, trying to make the answering of more complex questions possible.

Producing Intelligible Representations. The ubiquitousness of deep neural networks in modern processing chains, their structural complexity and their opacity have motivated the need of bringing some kind of intelligibility in the prediction process to better understand and control its behavior. The vocabulary and concepts connected to intelligibility issues are not clearly settled. (explanation, justification, transparency, *etc.*) Several recent papers have tried to clarify those expressions [2–5,20–23] and separate the various approaches in two goals: build interpretable models and/or provide justification of the prediction. [24] for instance, described an interpretable proxy (a decision tree) able to explain the logic of each prediction of a pretrained convolutional neural networks. The generation of explanations as an auxiliary justification has been addressed in the form of a visual representation of informative features in the input space, usually heat maps or saliency maps [25–27], as textual descriptions [28], or both [29]. A large body of studies [30–33] have been interested in visually revealing the role of deep network layers or units. Our semantic bottleneck approach fuses those two trends: it provides a directly interpretable representation, which can be used as a justification of the prediction, and it forces the prediction process itself to be interpretable in some way, since it causally relies on an intermediate semantic representation.

Evaluating Explanations. The question of clearly evaluating the quality or usability of explanations remains an active problem. [25] described a human-centered experimental evaluation assessing the predictive capacity of the visual explanation. [27] proposed to quantify explanation quality by measuring two desirable features: continuity and selectivity of the input dimensions involved in the explanation representation. [34,35] described geometric metrics to assess the quality of the visual explanation with respect to landmarks or objects in the image. [36] questioned the stability of saliency based visual explanations by showing that a simple constant shift may lead to uninterpretable representations. In our work, we take a dual approach: rather than evaluating the capacity of the explanation to be used as a surrogate or a justification of an ideal predictive process, we evaluate its quality as an ability of detecting bad behavior, *i.e.* detect potential wrong predictions.

Generating Distinctive Questions. If the generation of questions about text corpora has been extensively studied (see *e.g.*, [37]), the generation of questions about images has driven less attention. We can, however, mention the interesting work of [38] where discriminative questions are produced to disambiguate pairs of images, or [39] which introduced the novel task (and dataset) of visual question generation. We can also mention the recent work of Das *et al.* [40] which bears similarity with our approach but differs in the separation between the question generator and semantic representation encoder, and is not applied to the same tasks. Our work builds on the observation made by [41,42] – questions that are asked about an image provide information regarding the image and can help to acquire relevant information about an image – and proposes to use automatically generated discriminative questions as cues for representing images.

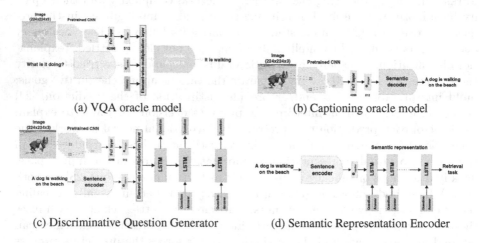

(a) VQA oracle model   (b) Captioning oracle model

(c) Discriminative Question Generator   (d) Semantic Representation Encoder

Fig. 2. Functional diagrams of the various components of the global algorithm.

3   Approach

This paper proposes a method allowing to turn raw images into rich semantic representations—a semantic bottleneck—which can be used alone (without using the image itself) to compare images or classify them. At the heart of this image encoder is a process for generating an ordered set of questions related to the image content, which are used, jointly with the answers to these questions, as an image substitute. Questions are generated sequentially, each question (as well as its answer) inducing the next questions to be asked. Such a set of questions/answers should semantically represent the visual information of images and be useful for disambiguating image representations in retrieval and classification task. Answering the question is done with a VQA model, used as an oracle, playing the role of a fine-grained information extractor. Furthermore, this sequence of Q/A is designed to be complementary to an image caption which is also automatically generated. We can use the analogy of human reasoning, starting with the image caption as a starting point and asking question to an oracle to get iteratively more information on the image. The proposed visual dialog allows to enrich image caption representations and leads to a stronger semantic representation. Finally, captions and visual dialogs are combined and turned into a compact representation that can be used easily to compare images (for retrieval task) or to infer class labels (classification tasks).

Consequently, our model is composed of two main components: (i) a discriminative visual question generator (ii) an encoding block taking Q/A and captions as inputs and producing an image representation. These two blocks, trained end-to-end, rely on two oracles: (i) an image caption generator which visually describes images with natural language sentences. (ii) a visual question answering model capable of answering free-from questions related to images. We call these last 2 parts of the model *oracles* as they are trained independently of the main tasks and used as external knowledge base.

3.1   Vector Space Embedding, Encoders, Decoders

The core objective of our approach is to generate semantic expressions in natural language (questions, answers or captions) that could represent images compactly and informatively. We define the various natural language elements as sequences of words from a fixed vocabulary of words and punctuation $\{w_0, \ldots, w_{n_w}\}$, where w_0 has the special meaning of marking the end of all phrases as a "full stop". The space of all possible sequences in natural language is denoted by $\mathcal{P}$. Any caption (c), question (q) or answer (a) belongs to the same set $\mathcal{P}$.

Most of learning based algorithms exploit vector space representations as inner states, or in the optimized criterion. A first issue is therefore to make possible the embedding of natural language expressions, and also images, into a vector space. For simplicity of design, we made all the necessary embeddings belong to a S-dimensional real valued vector space. Typically, to give an order of magnitude, we took $S = 512$ in our experiments. We therefore define semantic *encoders* as mappings from $\mathcal{P}$ to $\mathbb{R}^S$, and semantic *decoders* or *generators* as mappings from the vector space $\mathbb{R}^S$ to $\mathcal{P}$.

Image Encoder. The first element to be encoded is the source image $I \in \mathcal{I}$. The encoder (denoted as f_I) is a mapping $f_I : \mathcal{I} \to \mathbb{R}^S$, provided by last FC layer (fc7) of a VGG-VeryDeep-19 network [43] (pre-trained on Imagenet [44]) followed by a non-linear projection (fully connected layer + tanh non-linearity unit) reducing the dimensionality of the fc7 features (4096-d) to S. The parameters of the non-linear projection, denoted as w_I, are the only parameters of this embedding that have to be learned, the parameters of the VGG-VeryDeep-19 being considered as fixed. We write $f_I(I; w_I)$ to make apparent the dependency on the parameters w_I, when needed.

Natural Language Encoder. This encoder maps any set of words and punctuation $s \in \mathcal{P}$ (captions, questions, answers) to the embedding space $\mathbb{R}^S$. We will use 3 different natural language encoders in the global algorithm, for captions, questions and answers, all sharing the same structure and the same weights. We hence refer to them using the same notation (f_p). The encoder uses a standard Long Short Term Memory network (LSTM) [45]. Used as an encoder, the LSTM is simply a first order dynamic model: $y_t = \text{LSTM}_p(y_{t-1}, p_t)$ where y_t is the concatenation of the long-term cell state and the short-term memory, and p_t is the current input at time t. Given a natural language sequence of words $p = \{p_t\}_{t=1:T_p}$, its encoding $f_p(p)$ is equal to the memory state y_t after iterating on the LSTM T_p times and receiving the word p_t at each iteration. Denoting w_p the set of weights of the LSTM model, the natural language embedding is therefore defined as: $y_{T_p} = f_p(p; w_p)$ with the initial memory cell $y_0 = 0$.

In practice, instead of using words by their index in a large dictionary, we encode the words in a compact vector space, as in the word2vec framework [46]. We found it better since synonyms can have similar encodings. More precisely, this local encoding is realized as a linear mapping w_{w2vec}, where w_{w2vec} is a matrix of size $n_{w2vec} \times n_w$ and each original word is encoded as a one-hot vector of size n_w, the size of the vocabulary. The size of the word embedding n_{w2vec} was 200 in our experiments. This local word embedding simply substitutes $w_{w2vec}.p_t$ to p_t in the LSTM input.

Semantic Decoder. The semantic decoder is responsible for taking an embedded vector $s \in \mathbb{R}^S$ and producing a sequence of words in natural language belonging to $\mathcal{P}$. It is denoted by f_s. All the semantic decoders we exploit have the structure of an LSTM network. Several semantic decoders will be used for questions, answers and captions in the overall algorithm, but with distinct weights and different inputs. These LSTMs have an output predicting word indexes according to a softmax classification network: $p_{t+1} = \text{Softmax}(y_t)$ which is re-injected as input of the LSTM at each iteration.

Formally, we can write the semantic decoder as a sequence of words generated by an underlying LSTM first order dynamic process with observations p_t as $y_t = \text{LSTM}_s(y_{t-1}, p_t)$. At time t the input receives the word generated at the previous state p_t, and predicts the next word of the sentence p_{t+1}. When the word w_0 meaning "full stop" is generated at time T_s, it ends the generation. The global decoding is therefore a sequence of words of length $T_s - 1$: $f_s(s; w) = \{p_t\}_{t=1:T_s-1}$

with the initial state of the LSTM being the embedded vector to decode ($y_0 = s$) and the first input being null ($p_0 = 0$). The symbol w refers to the learned weights of the LSTM and the softmax weights, and is different for each type of textual data that will be generated (captions, questions and answers).

3.2 Captioning Model

The visual captioning part of the model is used as an external source of knowledge, and is learned in a separate phase. It takes an image (I) and produces a sentence in natural language describing the image. We used an approach inspired by the winner of the COCO-2015 Image Captioning challenge [8]. This approach, trainable end-to-end, combines a CNN image embedder with a LSTM-based Sentence Generator (Fig. 2(b)). More formally, it combines an image encoder and a semantic decoder, such are described previously, which can be written as: $c(I) = f_s(f_I(I; w_I); w_{cg})$ where w_{cg} is the specific set of learned weights of the decoder. This caption model acts as an oracle, providing semantic information for the Visual Discriminative Question Selection component, and to the Semantic Representation Encoder.

3.3 Visual Question Answering Model

The VQA model is the second of the two components of our model used as oracles to provide additional information on images. Its role is to answer independent free-form questions about an image. It receives questions (Q) in natural language and an image (I) and provides answers in natural language ($a(Q, I)$). Our problem is slightly different from standard VQA because the VQA model now has to answer questions sequentially from a dialog. It means that the question Q_k can be based on the answer of the previous questions Q_{k-1} and answers $a(Q_{k-1}, I)$. We first present the formulation of a standard VQA and then show how to extend it so it can answer questions from a dialog.

Inspired by [47], our VQA model combines two encoders and one decoder of those described previously (Fig. 2-a):

$$a(Q, I) = f_s(f_I(I; w_{Iqa}) \odot f_p(Q; w_{pqa}); w_{qa}) \qquad (1)$$

The fusion between image and question embeddings is done by an element wise product ($\odot$) between the two embeddings, as proposed by [47].

We now consider the case where questions are extracted from a dialog by extending Eq. (1), where k represents the k-th step of the dialog. We introduce another term h_k in the element-wise product to encode the history of the dialog as:

$$a_k(Q_k, I) = f_s(f_I(I; w_{Iqa}) \odot f_p(Q_k; w_{pqa}) \odot h_k; w_{qa}) \qquad (2)$$

The history h_k is simply computed as the mean of the previously asked questions/answers, and encoded using f_p. This state integrates past questions and is expected to help the answering process. We tried other schemes to summarize history (concatenation, LSTM) without clear performance increase.

We prefer the VQA model to the Visual Dialog model [1], as this latter is optimized for the task of image guessing, while we want to fine-tune the question/answer sequence for different tasks (multi-label prediction and image retrieval).

3.4   Discriminative Question Generation

This part of the model is responsible for taking an image and a caption – which is considered as the basic semantic representation of the image – and produces a sequence of questions/answers that are complementary to the caption for a specific task (multi-label classification or retrieval).

The caption describing the image is generated using the captioning model presented in Sect. 3.2, and denoted $c(I) \in \mathcal{P}$. This caption is encoded with $f_p(c(I); w_p) \in \mathbb{R}^S$. Image and caption embeddings are then combined by an element-wise product $f_p(c(I)) \odot f_I(I)$ used as an initial encoded representation of the image.

This representation is then updated iteratively by asking and answering question, one by one, hence iteratively proposing a list of discriminative questions. Again, we use a LSTM network (Fig. 2-c), but instead of providing a word at each iteration as for $f_s(s; w)$ we inject a question/answer $[\tilde{q}_k, \tilde{a}_k]$ pair encoded in a vector space from the natural language question/answer $[Q_k, A_k]$ using f_p, with initial memory $y_0 = f_I(I) \odot f_p(c(I))$ and initial input $\tilde{q}_0 = \tilde{a}_0 = 0$: $y_k = \text{LSTM}_q(y_{k-1}, [\tilde{q}_k, \tilde{a}_k])$ The actual questions are then decoded from the inner LSTM memory y_k and fed to the VQA model to obtain the answer using Eq. (2): $Q_{k+1} = f_s(y_k; w_{sq})$, and, $A_{k+1} = a_{k+1}(Q_{k+1}, I)$

Using this iterative process, we generate, for each image, a sequence of questions-answers refining the initial caption: $f_q(I; w_q) = \{Q_k, A_k\}_{k=1:K}$ where w_q is the set of weights of the underlying LSTM network of the previous equation, and K is an arbitrary number of questions.

3.5   Semantic Representation Encoder

Our objective is to evaluate the feasibility of substituting a rich semantic representation to an image and achieve comparable performance than an image feature based approach, for several computer vision tasks. This representation has to be specifically generated to the target task, to be efficient.

Once again, many modern computer vision approaches relying on a learning phase require that data are given as fixed dimension vectors. The role of the module described here is to encode the rich semantic representation in $\mathbb{R}^S$ to feed the retrieval or the multi-label classification task.

The encoder makes use of a LSTM network where the question/answer sequence $\{Q_k, A_k\}_{k=1:K}$ is used as input, $y_k = \text{LSTM}_e(y_{k-1}, [\tilde{q}_k, \tilde{a}_k])$ and the initial memory state y_0 is equal to the encoded caption $f_p(c(I); w_p)$ (Fig. 2(d)).

If w_e is the set of weights from the underlying LSTM, the rich semantic representation y_K is encoded as: $y_K = f_{enc}\left(\left[\{Q_k, A_k\}_{k=1:K}, c(I)\right]; w_e\right)$.

3.6   Training the Model

The global training is divided in two phases. The first phase learns the two so-called oracles independently: image captioning and VQA. The second phase learns to generate the visual quiz, the image encoder and the semantic encoder jointly for a specific task, based on information provided by the two oracles.

The parameters of the VQA, namely w_{Iqa} and w_{pqa} for the encoders, and w_{qa} (Eq. 2) are learned in a supervised way on the Visual Dialog dataset [1]. The learning criterion consists in comparing the answer words generated by the model with those of the ground truth for each element of the sequence of questions, and is measured by a cross entropy.

The captioning is also learned by comparing each word sequentially generated by the algorithm to a ground truth caption, and is also measured by a cross entropy loss.

The question/answer generator $f_q(I; w_q)$ and the semantic representation encoder f_{enc} are learned jointly end to end. Each of the modules manages its own loss: for the question generator, the sequence of questions is compared to the ground truth of questions associated with each image using a cross entropy at each iteration. The semantic encoding, however, is specifically evaluated by a task-dependent loss: a cross entropy loss for each potential label for the multi-label classification task, a ranking loss for the image retrieval task. When the question generation model converges, only the task-dependent loss is kept in order to fine-tune the question selection part.

The retrieval loss is a bit more complex than the others (cross entropy). Basically, it is based on the assumption that ground truth captions are the most informative image representations and that any other representation should follow the same similarity ranking as captions provide. We follow the approach proposed in [10] to define the retrieval loss as a function of triplet data q, d^+ (positive pair) and d^- (negative pair) to be $L(q, d_+, d_-) = \max(0, m - \phi(q)^T \phi(d^+) + \phi(q)^T \phi(d^-))$ where q and d^+ are expected to be more similar than q and d^-, and ϕ is the representation function to be learned, i.e. the output of f_{enc}, and m is a free coefficient playing the role of a margin. The reference similarity comparison is computed from ground truth captions using $tf\text{-}idf$ representations, as suggested by [10].

4   Experiments

We validated the proposed method on 2 tasks: (i) content based image retrieval (CBIR) based on semantics, where queries are related to the semantic content of the images – which is more general and harder than searching for visually similar images. We adopted the evaluation protocol proposed by Gordo et al. [10]. It uses captions as a proxy for semantic similarity and compares $tf\text{-}idf$ representations of captions, and measures the performance as the normalized discounted cumulative gain (NDCG), which can be seen as a weighted mean average precision, the relevance of one item with respect to the query being the dot product between their tf-idf representations. (ii) Multi-label image classification: each image can be assigned to different classes (labels), generally indicating the presence of the object type represented by the label. Per-class average precision and mAP are the performance metrics for this task.

Both series of experiments are done on the Visual Dialog dataset [1], relying on images of MS COCO [48]. Each image is annotated with 1 caption and 1 dialog (10 questions and answers), for a total of 1.2M questions-answers. Ground truth Dialog has been made in order to retrieve a query image from a pool of candidate images. A dialog should visually describe a query image and be suitable for retrieval and classification tasks. We use the standard train split for learning and validation split for testing, as the test set is not publicly available.

Our approach has several hyper-parameters: the word embedding size, $LSTM$ state size, learning rate, m. They are obtained through cross-validation. In this procedure, 20% of training data is considered as validation set, allowing to choose the hyper-parameters maximizing the NDCG/mean average precision on this so-obtained validation set. In practice, typical value for $LSTM$ state size (resp. embedding size) is 512 (resp. 200). The margin m is in the range [1.0–2.0]. Model parameters are initialized according to a centered Gaussian distribution ($\sigma = 0.02$). They are optimized with the Adam solver [49] with a cross-validated learning rate (typically of 10^{-4}), using mini-batches of size 128. In order to avoid over-fitting, we use dropout [50] for each layer (probability of a drop of 0.2 for the input layers and of 0.5 for the hidden layers). Both oracles (captioning and VQA) are fine-tuned on the tasks. Finally, while it would be interesting to average the performance on several runs, in order to evaluate the stability of the approach, this would be prohibitive in terms of computational time. In practice, we have observed that the performance is very stable and does not depend on initialization.

4.1   Experiments on Semantic Image Retrieval

We now evaluate our approach on semantic content-based retrieval, where the images sharing similar semantic content with an image query have to be returned by the system. As described before, the retrieval loss is optimized with triplets: an image query and two similar/dissimilar images. For triplet selection, we applied hard negative mining by sampling images according to the loss value (larger loss meaning higher probability to be selected). We found hard negative mining to be useful in our experiments.

Table 1 reports the NDCG performance for 3 values of R (R = k means that the top k images are considered for computing the NDCG), and the area under the curve (for R between 1 and 128) on 4 different models. The visual baseline exploits a similarity metric between image features extracted from the FC7 layer of a VGG19 network, which is learned on the train set using the same triplet approach as described in Sect. 3.6. I + [10] corresponds to the visual embedding

Table 1. NDCG on semantic retrieval. Performance/Area Under the Curve for different values of R.

Method/R	8	32	128	AUC
$f_i(I)$ + ML (baseline)	45.8	51.7	59.3	69.7
I + [10]	47.6	55.9	62.3	72.7
$\{I, c(I)\}$ + [10]	57.0	58.5	63.3	75.1
Our approach $f_{enc}(I)$	**59.3**	**61.7**	**67.1**	**79.9**

Table 2. Semantic retrieval. NDCG/AUC after removing some components of the model.

Modality/R	8	32	128	AUC
$c(I)$	55.1	56.3	62.4	73.6
$\{Q_k, A_k\}_{1:10}$ generic	41.8	50.4	57.7	65.7
$\{Q_k, A_k\}_{1:10}$ task adapted	45.8	55.7	60.0	71.9
$tf - idf\{c(I), \{Q_k, A_k\}_{1:10}\}$	54.9	57.2	63.4	75.1
Our approach $f_{enc}(I)$	**59.3**	**61.7**	**67.1**	**79.9**

Table 3. Multi-label classification performance.

Modality	mAP
$f_i(I)$ (baseline)	61.1
$c(I)$	51.6
$\{Q_k, A_k\}_{1:10}$	49.9
$f_{enc}(I)$	56.0
$\{I, f_{enc}(I)\}$	**64.2**

noted (V, V) in [10]. $\{I, c(I)\}$ + [10] is the joint visual and textual embedding (V+T, V+T) with the difference that we don't feed the ground truth captions but the generated one, for fair comparison.

We observed that the area under the curve improves by +4.8% with our semantic bottleneck approach compared to the image feature similarity approach. We stress here that, unlike [10], we only exploit a semantic representation and not image features.

Empirical results of Table 2 show the usefulness of our semantic encoder. Indeed, with the same modalities (caption, questions and answers), $tf - idf\{c(I), \{Q_k, A_k\}_{1:10}\}$ performs 4.8% lower. Table 2 also shows the importance of adapting the VQA oracle to the task with +6.2% gain compared to a generic oracle not fine-tuned to the task.

4.2 Experiments on Multi-label Classification

With the MS COCO [48] dataset, each image is labeled with multi-object labels (80 object categories), representing the presence of broad concepts such as animal, vehicle, person, *etc.* in the image. For the baseline approach, we used image features provided by a VGG-VeryDeep-19 network [43] pre-trained on ImageNet [44] with weights kept frozen up to the 4,096-dim top-layer hidden unit activations (fc7), and fed to a final softmax layer learned on the common training set.

Table 3 (bottom) reports the per-class mean average precision for the visual baseline and the various components of our model. Our fully semantic approach $f_{enc}(I)$ underperforms only by 5% the baseline. This is quite encouraging as in our setting the image is only encoded by a caption and 10 questions/answers. The main advantage of our model is that one can have access to the intermediate semantic representation for inspection, and may provide an explanation of the good or bad result (see Sect. 4.3). Figure 3 also reports the performance given by (i) generated caption $c(I)$ only, (ii) questions/answers $\{Q_k, A_k\}_{1:10}$ only. These experiments shows that captions are more discriminative than questions/answers (+1,7%), at least given the way they are generated. We also report the performance obtained by combining our image representation with image features (denoted as $\{I, f_{enc}(I)\}$). This configuration gives the best performance (+8,2%) and outperforms the baseline (+3.1%). As a sanity check, we also computed the mAP when using ground truth annotations for both the captions and the VQA. We obtained a performance of 72.2%, meaning that with good oracles it's possible for our semantic bottleneck to obtain a performance better than with images (61.1%).

Fig. 3. Combining captions and dialogs: query (top-left images), generated captions, task-specific dialogs, images retrieved using the caption (first rows) and those given by our model (second rows). Dialogs allowed to detect important complementary

Fig. 4. Adapting dialogs to tasks: query (top-left images), generated captions, generic and task-specific dialogs, images retrieved using the caption and generic dialog (first rows), and those given by our model (second rows).

4.3   Semantic Bottleneck Analysis

This section aims at giving some insights on (i) why the performance is improved by combining captions and dialogs and (ii) why making the semantic bottleneck adapted to the task improves the performance.

Regarding the first point, we did a qualitative analysis of the outputs of the semantic retrieval task, by comparing the relevance of the first ranked images when adding the dialogs to the captions (see Fig. 3). The Figure gives both the caption and the dialog automatically generated, as well as the images ranked first accordingly to the caption (first rows) and accordingly to our model combining the caption and the dialog. We marked in green the important complementary information added by the dialog. The dialog was able to detect drinks as an important feature of the image.

Table 4. Statistics of generated words after fine tuning the generators to the tasks

task/words	classes	playing	eating	wearing	doing	color	how many	in/outdoor	day/night
classification	88%	19%	39%	29%	14%	42%	39%	42%	53%
retrieval	78%	14%	28%	21%	16%	85%	81%	54%	79%

Regarding the second point, we compared the quality of the retrieval with and without adapting the dialogs to the task. Figure 4 illustrates our observations by giving both captions and dialogs automatically generated, as well as the images ranked first accordingly to captions combined with generic dialogs (first rows) and with task adapted dialogs (second rows). We marked in red the questions/answers that we found not relevant to the query in the generic dialog and in green those that have been given by the task adapted dialog to emphasize the complementary information they bring. The dialog was able to identify vehicles as an important feature of the image. Figure 5 illustrates the same type of caption correction by the dialog for the multi-label classification task.

Generated captions are, in general, brief and consistent with the images (see examples of Figs. 4, 5 and 7). Because we chose a simple sampling strategy (in order to have a trade-off between computation and interpretation) a few captions are syntactically incorrect. We argue that this should not impact the performance, as the generated captions reflect the image content. We also observed that several questions are repeated. While question repetition is not as critical as it is for the actual dialog generation, it can be overcome if needed by encoding the question history (h_k in Eq. (6)), for instance by explicitly penalizing repetitions in the LSTM criterion, or, by exploiting a reinforcement learning approach such as in [40].

Table 4 illustrates the effect of fine-tuning question generation by showing the percentage of time each word in the first row occurs in a dialog, across the two tasks ('classes' means any of the object class names). We observed that the generated dialogs of the classification task contain more verbs that can be associated to the presence of object classes (eating $\Rightarrow$ food classes, playing $\Rightarrow$ sport classes, wearing $\Rightarrow$ clothes classes). Generated dialogs for the retrieval task contain more words characterizing the scene (in/outdoor, day/night) or referencing specific object features (color, how many).

We also made experiments showing how the semantic bottleneck can be modified manually to make image search more interactive. Figure 6 shows an example where we changed 2 oracle answers (zebras becomes cows and their number is increased by one). The 2nd row depicts the impact of this modification.

Semantic representation:
caption:
people are snowboarding down a mountain
dialog:
how many people are there? two
is there snow? no
where are they snowboarding? a lake
do you see any mountain? no
is it sunny? no cloudy
where are they snowboarding? a lake
is it day time? yes
is there snow? no
do you see any mountain? no
is it day time? yes

Predicted labels: person, skis, boat

Semantic representation:
caption:
a group of men talking
dialog:
how many people are there? can't count
is it sunny? no
is it day time? yes
what are they wearing? a suit
what color? dark blue
is it raining now? yes
is it day time? yes
how many people are there? can't count
is it sunny? no
where are they? on a beach

Predicted labels: person, tie, umbrella

Fig. 5. Left-hand side: incorrect caption corrected by the dialog. Right-hand side: objects missing from the captions discovered by asking relevant questions.

Semantic representation:
a group of animals grazing on grass next to each other.
what are the animals? zebras
how many? 2
are there other animals ? : no
is this a zoo ? : probably
is the grass long ? : no
are they all grazing ? : yes all
can you see any trees ? : yes
any rocks ? : no
is it sunny ? yes
do you see any people ? no people

- what are the animals? zebras
- how many? 2

+ what are the animals? there are horses and cows
+ how many? 3

Fig. 6. Incrementally updating the representation.

4.4   Evaluating Failure Predictions

The potential capacity of the semantic bottleneck to detect failure in the prediction process is illustrated by Fig. 7. Failure is detected when the representation contains incorrect semantic information—the caption or dialog are wrong—or insufficient information for further inference. We focus our evaluation on multi-label image classification, since a clear definition of failure in the case of content based image retrieval is complex, can be subjective (how decide if images are completely dissimilar from the request?) and task oriented (what are retrieved images used for?). We developed two evaluation protocols: one with humans in the loop, judging the semantic bottleneck capacity to predict consistent labels, and an automatic model optimized to predict success or failure for each class. We compare our approaches to a baseline based on score prediction thresholding. In order to evaluate the semantic bottleneck capacity, we first train our model for a multi-label classification task and extract the generated semantic representation (caption and dialog) and class prediction.

Fig. 7. Predicting failure cases from the proposed semantic representation. Left-hand side: caption and Q/A are consistent but not rich enough to predict the 'giraffe' label. Right-hand side: the semantic representation is incorrect leading to the inference of erroneous labels. In such cases, the bottleneck representation can be used for debugging.

Table 5. Failure prediction statistics.

	False negative		False positive	
	#true	#predicted	#true	#predicted
GT.	614	-	588	-
Users	308	379	213	485
Classifier	250	490	180	530

Table 6. Multi-label classification.

	Label		Image	
	mAP %		mAP %	
No selection	54.3	100	54.3	100
Users	84.2	96	86.1	53
Classifier	79.8	93	81.7	49
conf. thresh	66.1	93	73.5	49

Human Based Failure Prediction Study. For 1000 randomly chosen test images, users were instructed to evaluate the capacity of the semantic bottleneck to contain enough information to predict the correct classes. The image and the generated semantic representation are shown to the users, which can select for each of the 80 labels of MS-COCO 1 among 3 cases: (i) *false negative*. The semantic representation missed the label (*e.g.* caption and dialog do not mention about the horse in the picture). (ii) *false positive*. The semantic representation hallucinates the object (*e.g.* seeing a car in a kitchen scene). (iii) *correct*. The algorithm has succeeded to predict the label, either its absence or its presence. Table 5 shows failure cases of the multi-label classification (614 false negative and 588 false positive). Human subjects were able to identify half of the failures (308/614 FN and 213/588 FP) with a precision of $\approx 60\%$ (308/379 and 213/485).

Failure detection can also be evaluated through two other sets of experiments: *Label rejection*: suspicious labels are rejected, others are kept. *Image rejection*: when there is a suspicious label, the image is rejected. Table 6 shows both experiments, and reads as follows: classification performance is of 54.3% when evaluating on 100% of the test set. When user rejects 4% of the labels, the performance goes to 84.2%. When our rejection algorithm keeps 93% of the data, the performance improves to 79.8%, which is close to human performance. We see a strong improvement for both our methods. Failure prediction improves the average precision of 30% percent with 4% of deleted image in average for each class.

We also proposed two automatic algorithms for failure prediction. The first one, referenced as 'classifier' in Tables 5 and 6, is based on an independent ternary linear classifier for each class with 3 possible outputs: `correct`, `FN`, `FP`. The input is the image I concatenated with the last hidden state of the semantic representation encoder $[\{Q_k, A_k\}_{k=1:K}, c(I)]$. The ground truth is built by comparing the output from the multi-label classification and the true classes. The model is optimized using a cross entropy loss. It is less accurate (can detect $\approx 41\%$ of false positive with $\approx 51\%$ of precision) but has the advantage of reducing human effort. We also show in the last row of Table 6 the performance of a second algorithm consisting in thresholding the confidence score outputted by the multi-label classifier for each label, and tuned to reach the same rejection rate as the other failure detection algorithm. This confidence thresholding algorithm gives a smaller performance increase after rejection.

5   Conclusions

In this paper we have introduced a novel method for representing images with semantic information expressed in natural language. Our primary motivation was to question the possibility of introducing an intelligible bottleneck in the processing pipeline. We showed that by combining and adapting several state-of-the-art techniques, our approach is able to generate rich textual descriptions that can be substituted for images in two vision tasks: semantic content based image retrieval, and multi-label classification. We quantitatively evaluated the usage of this semantic bottleneck as a diagnosis tool to detect failure in the prediction process, which we think contributes to a clearer metric of explainability, a key concern to mature artificial intelligence.

References

1. Das, A., et al.: Visual dialog. In: CVPR (2016)
2. Gilpin, L.H., Bau, D., Yuan, B.Z., Bajwa, A., Specter, M., Kagal, L.: Explaining explanations: an approach to evaluating interpretability of ML. arXiv:1806.00069 (2018)
3. Doshi-Velez, F., Kim, B.: A roadmap for a rigorous science of interpretability. arXiv:1702.08608 (2017)
4. Biran, O., Cotton, C.: Explanation and justification in ML: a survey. In: IJCAI (2017)
5. Ras, G., Haselager, P., van Gerven, M.: Explanation methods in deep learning: users, values, concerns and challenges. arXiv:1803.07517 (2018)
6. Zhang, P., Wang, J., Farhadi, A., Hebert, M., Parikh, D.: Predicting failures of vision systems. In: CVPR (2014)
7. Lampert, C.H., Nickisch, H., Harmeling, S.: Attribute-based classification for zero-shot visual object categorization. TPAMI (2014)
8. Vinyals, O., Toshev, A., Bengio, S., Erhan, D.: Show and tell: lessons learned from the 2015 MSCOCO image captioning challenge. TPAMI (2017)

9. Lu, J., Xiong, C., Parikh, D., Socher, R.: Knowing when to look: adaptive attention via a visual sentinel for image captioning. In: CVPR (2017)
10. Gordo, A., Larlus, D.: Beyond instance-level image retrieval: leveraging captions to learn a global visual representation for semantic retrieval. In: CVPR (2017)
11. Dai, B., Lin, D., Urtasun, R., Fidler, S.: Towards diverse and natural image descriptions via a conditional GAN. In: CVPR (2017)
12. Dai, B., Lin, D.: Contrastive learning for image captioning. In: NIPS (2017)
13. Seo, P.H., Lehrmann, A., Han, B., Sigal, L.: Visual reference resolution using attention memory for visual dialog. In: NIPS (2017)
14. Lu, J., Kannan, A., Yang, J., Parikh, D., Batra, D.: Best of both worlds: transferring knowledge from discriminative learning to a generative visual dialog model. In: NIPS (2017)
15. Malinowski, M., Rohrbach, M., Fritz, M.: Ask your neurons: a neural-based approach to answering questions about images. In: ICCV (2015)
16. Lin, X., Parikh, D.: Leveraging visual question answering for image-caption ranking. In: Leibe, B., Matas, J., Sebe, N., Welling, M. (eds.) ECCV 2016. LNCS, vol. 9906, pp. 261–277. Springer, Cham (2016). https://doi.org/10.1007/978-3-319-46475-6_17
17. Zhu, Y., Groth, O., Bernstein, M., Fei-Fei, L.: Visual7w: grounded question answering in images. In: CVPR (2016)
18. Jabri, A., Joulin, A., van der Maaten, L.: Revisiting VQA baselines. In: ECCV (2016)
19. Wu, Q., Wang, P., Shen, C., Dick, A., van den Hengel, A.: Ask me anything: free-form visual question answering based on knowledge from external sources. In: CVPR (2016)
20. Lipton, Z.C.: The mythos of model interpretability. In: ICML (2016)
21. Doran, D., Schulz, S., Besold, T.R.: What does explainable AI really mean? A new conceptualization of perspectives. arXiv:1710.00794 (2017)
22. Hohman, F.M., Kahng, M., Pienta, R., Chau, D.H.: Visual analytics in deep learning: an interrogative survey for the next frontiers. In: TVCG (2018)
23. Guidotti, R., Monreale, A., Turini, F., Pedreschi, D., Giannotti, F.: A survey of methods for explaining black box models. arXiv:1802.01933 (2018)
24. Zhang, Q., Yang, Y., Wu, Y.N., Zhu, S.C.: Interpreting CNNs via decision trees. arXiv:1802.00121 (2018)
25. Selvaraju, R.R., Cogswell, M., Das, A., Vedantam, R., Parikh, D., Batra, D.: Grad-CAM: visual explanations from deep networks via gradient-based localization. In: ICCV (2017)
26. Rajani, N.F., Mooney, R.J.: Using explanations to improve ensembling of visual question answering systems. In: IJCAI (2017)
27. Montavon, G., Samek, W., Müller, K.R.: Methods for interpreting and understanding deep neural networks. Digit. Sign. Process. Rev. J. (2018)
28. Hendricks, L.A., Akata, Z., Rohrbach, M., Donahue, J., Schiele, B., Darrell, T.: Generating visual explanations. In: Leibe, B., Matas, J., Sebe, N., Welling, M. (eds.) ECCV 2016. LNCS, vol. 9908, pp. 3–19. Springer, Cham (2016). https://doi.org/10.1007/978-3-319-46493-0_1
29. Park, D.H., et al.: Multimodal explanations: justifying decisions and pointing to the evidence. In: CVPR (2018)
30. Mahendran, A., Vedaldi, A.: Understanding deep image representations by inverting them. In: CVPR (2015)

31. Zeiler, M.D., Fergus, R.: Visualizing and understanding convolutional networks. In: Fleet, D., Pajdla, T., Schiele, B., Tuytelaars, T. (eds.) ECCV 2014. LNCS, vol. 8689, pp. 818–833. Springer, Cham (2014). https://doi.org/10.1007/978-3-319-10590-1_53

32. Dosovitskiy, A., Brox, T.: Inverting visual representations with convolutional networks. In: CVPR (2016)

33. Olah, C., et al.: The building blocks of interpretability. Distill (2018)

34. Zhang, Q., Cao, R., Shi, F., Wu, Y.N., Zhu, S.C.: Interpreting CNN knowledge via an explanatory graph. arXiv:1708.01785 (2017)

35. Bau, D., Zhou, B., Khosla, A., Oliva, A., Torralba, A.: Network dissection: quantifying interpretability of deep visual representations. In: CVPR (2017)

36. Kindermans, P.J., et al.: The (un)reliability of saliency methods. arXiv:1711.00867 (2017)

37. Serban, I.V., et al.: Generating factoid questions with recurrent neural networks: the 30M factoid question-answer corpus. In: ACL (2016)

38. Li, Y., Huang, C., Tang, X., Change Loy, C.: Learning to disambiguate by asking discriminative questions. In: CVPR (2017)

39. Mostafazadeh, N., Misra, I., Devlin, J., Mitchell, M., He, X., Vanderwende, L.: Generating natural questions about an image. In: ACL (2016)

40. Das, A., Kottur, S., Moura, J.M.F., Lee, S., Batra, D.: Learning cooperative visual dialog agents with deep reinforcement learning. In: ICCV 2017 (2017)

41. Ganju, S., Russakovsky, O., Gupta, A.: What's in a question: using visual questions as a form of supervision. In: CVPR (2017)

42. Zhu, Y., Lim, J.J., Fei-Fei, L.: Knowledge acquisition for visual question answering via iterative querying. In: CVPR (2017)

43. Simonyan, K., Zisserman, A.: Very deep convolutional networks for large-scale image recognition. In: ICLR (2014)

44. Russakovsky, O., et al.: Imagenet large scale visual recognition challenge. IJCV (2015)

45. Hochreiter, S., Schmidhuber, J.: Long short-term memory. Neural Comput. (1997)

46. Mikolov, T., Chen, K., Corrado, G., Dean, J.: Efficient estimation of word representations in vector space. In: ICLR (2013)

47. Antol, S., et al.: VQA: visual question answering. In: ICCV (2015)

48. Lin, T.-Y., et al.: Microsoft COCO: common objects in context. In: Fleet, D., Pajdla, T., Schiele, B., Tuytelaars, T. (eds.) ECCV 2014. LNCS, vol. 8693, pp. 740–755. Springer, Cham (2014). https://doi.org/10.1007/978-3-319-10602-1_48

49. Kingma, D., Ba, J.: Adam: a method for stochastic optimization. In: ICLR (2015)

50. Srivastava, N., Hinton, G.E., Krizhevsky, A., Sutskever, I., Salakhutdinov, R.: Dropout: a simple way to prevent neural networks from overfitting. JMLR (2014)

Author Index

Printed in the United States
By Bookmasters